Managing in a
Global Economy

Demystifying International Macroeconomics

Second Edition

John E. Marthinsen
Babson College

CENGAGE
Learning®

Australia • Brazil • Mexico • Singapore • United Kingdom • United States

Managing in a Global Economy: Demystifying International Macroeconomics, Second Edition

John E. Marthinsen

Vice President, General Manager, Social Science & Qualitative Business: Erin Joyner

Product Director: Michael Worls

Content Developer: Ted Knight

Product Manager: Steven Scoble

Product Assistant: Vicki Ross

Marketing Coordinator: Christopher Walz

Media Developer: Anita Verma

Manufacturing Planner: Kevin Kluck

Marketing Manager: Katie Jergens

Art and Cover Direction, Production Management, and Composition: PreMediaGlobal

Cover Image: © Zoonar/Thinkstock

Intellectual Property Project Manager: Amber Hosea

Library of Congress Control Number: 2013953087

ISBN-13: 978-1-285-05542-8

ISBN-10: 1-285-05542-X

Cengage Learning
200 First Stamford Place, 4th Floor
Stamford, CT 06902
USA

Cengage Learning is a leading provider of customized learning solutions with office locations around the globe, including Singapore, the United Kingdom, Australia, Mexico, Brazil, and Japan. Locate your local office at: **www.cengage.com/global**

Cengage Learning products are represented in Canada by Nelson Education, Ltd.

To learn more about Cengage Learning Solutions, visit **www.cengage.com**

Purchase any of our products at your local college store or at our preferred online store **www.cengagebrain.com**

Printed in the United States of America
1 2 3 4 5 6 7 18 17 16 15 14

Brief Contents

Table of Contents

PART 2 REAL LOANABLE FUNDS MARKET

CHAPTER 6
MONETARY AGGREGATES: MEASURING MONEY   143

CHAPTER 7
FINANCIAL INTERMEDIATION, MARKETS, AND INTERMEDIARIES   161

CHAPTER 8
THE POWER OF FINANCIAL INSTITUTIONS TO CREATE MONEY   183

PART 6 LONG-TERM ECONOMIC CHANGES

CHAPTER 21
CAUSES OF LONG-TERM GROWTH AND INFLATION 717

CHAPTER 22
LONG-TERM EXCHANGE RATE MOVEMENTS AND COMPARATIVE ADVANTAGE 751

INDEX 775

ABBREVIATIONS 789

Preface

INTRODUCTION

Macroeconomics is often taught as if there were high theoretical and mathematical hurdles to clear before one could possibly understand the broad forces that move economies in different directions. The problem with this approach is that it disconnects the discipline from the set of decision-making tools used by most businesses, thereby putting economics out of reach of those who stand to gain the most from understanding it, such as entrepreneurs and business executives, but also politicians, journalists, and others, who are simply trying to make sense of an increasingly complex world.

Managing in a Global Economy: Demystifying International Macroeconomics (MGE) takes a commonsense approach to macroeconomics. It was written with the intention of illustrating that most macroeconomic relationships are logical, reasonable, and intuitive; and when it seems that they are not, the source of the problem is usually with the explanation.

The goal of this book is to provide readers with a framework for understanding how national and international macroeconomic markets interact, how they impact business performance, and, therefore, how they affect commercial, financial, and political decisions. To accomplish this goal, it is important for economic causes and effects to be logical and consistent with readers' common sense and intuition because only then will macroeconomic concepts be internalized and used. The chances of this happening are far less when these powerful concepts, tools, and relationships are perceived as nothing more than a collection of whimsical theories dreamed up by nonpractitioners.

Economic theory has a rich history, but the economics presented in this text is not ancient and will not lose its application with time. Macro-level supply and demand forces are alive and kicking and impacting our lives on a daily basis. Their presence and importance should be evident in the current-day applications, case studies, and examples that are peppered throughout this text.

International macroeconomics brings structure and organization to commercial, financial, political, and social insights, experiences, and training. Its logic and circuitry are useful for analyzing current, past, and possible future economic events, and this usefulness is not tied to any geographic location. For business managers, what could be more important than macroeconomic variables, such as economic growth, inflation, interest, and exchange rates? The problem is these variables are determined by market forces and not managers, which is why good managers do not try to control them. Rather, they strive to anticipate, react to, and cope with the shifting tides of economic fortune and misfortune, just as good sailors try to anticipate, react to, and cope with changing weather conditions over which they have no control.

Possessing a solid macroeconomic framework empowers managers with the ability to:

- create, critically evaluate, and effectively use country analyses to improve financial statement projections (e.g., income statements, balance sheets, and cash flow statements);
- integrate anticipated economic changes and government policies into corporate strategies that increase competitiveness and performance;
- formulate reasoned opinions about the causes of and cures for chronic economic illnesses in countries; and
- understand the economic impact and sustainability of proposed political legislation.

Some aspects of macroeconomics are very controversial, but at the same time, there is a common body of basic economic facts, definitions, and relationships that is universally accepted. Therefore, considerable care is taken in each chapter to explain these noncontroversial fundamentals. In Lego™-like fashion, Parts 1 to 5 of *MGE* build, brick-by-brick, a structure for understanding more complex economic relationships. These chapters focus on interpreting the measures, interactions, and theories that are most helpful for short-term planning periods, such as one-year to two-year budgets and three-year to five-year business plans.

Clearly, the shorter the period, the less flexibility a firm has to change course by making adjustments in its production, employment, financing, and/or investment policies. Nevertheless, even during short periods, businesses need realistic expectations of future cash flows. Otherwise, they could not plan for lines of credit when cash flows will be short or to develop investment strategies when excess funds will be earned. Macroeconomics can help sharpen cash flow projections and improve the planning process.

Long-term business planning is usually more strategic than short-term planning because it offers a greater degree of business flexibility and maneuverability. Therefore, the last two chapters of this book focus on understanding economic relationships that cause long-term changes in macroeconomic variables, such as inflation, output, and exchange rates. This knowledge is essential for 10-year to 20-year scenario-planning analyses.

WHAT'S NEW IN THE SECOND EDITION?

My colleagues at Babson and I have been using *MGE* since (and even before) its first publication in 2008. I owe an enormous debt of gratitude to my former students for their thoughtful feedback before the first edition was published, and I owe the same debt of gratitude to students since then, who have provided insights on ways to better communicate international macroeconomics.

Feedback comes in many forms—sometimes it's sugar-coated and sometimes blunt and unfiltered. One clear message has been that the text is too long for the six intensive weeks we spend at Babson studying international macroeconomics. This is especially true for my international students, who claim English as their second (or third, fourth, or more) language. In reaction to this feedback, I have separated each chapter into "The Basics" and "The Rest of the Story." "The Basics" section contains material that is essential to build a solid macroeconomic foundation. "The Rest of the Story" provides readers, in general, and professors, in particular, with flexibility to pick and choose topics of interest that support their time constraints, interests, and, also, breaking economic events.

Chapter 3, "Understanding and Monitoring Labor Market Conditions," has a significantly expanded section on the forces behind outsourcing, off-shoring, and (now) reshoring. This chapter dives into the debate about whether or not offshoring takes jobs from domestic workers and/or reduces production and income (i.e., gross domestic product). The results may be different from what you expect.

Chapter 5, "Inflation: Who Wins, and Who Loses," adds a new topic to "The Rest of the Story" section, entitled "How to Discover 'The Market's' Expectation about Future Inflation." It addresses how one can tell if his/her personal expectations about future inflation rates are different from market perceptions. This topic complements the following section entitled "What Determines Inflationary Expectations?"

Part 2 ("Real Loanable Funds Market") of *MGE* covers Chapters 6 to 11 and focuses on U.S. and global financial markets. These chapters have been updated to reflect new economic realities caused by the Great Recession (2007–2009) and events since it ended. Among the fresh topics discussed are the:

- Federal Reserve's decision to pay interest on bank reserve deposits,
- considerable relaxation in quality of financial assets the Federal Reserve is willing to purchase (e.g., mortgage-backed securities) under conditions of extreme economic hardship,
- ten major causes of bank failures,
- precipitous drop in the U.S. money multiplier due to the increase in banks' voluntarily held excess reserves,
- Swiss National Bank's trials and tribulations in 2012 to stem the franc's rapid appreciation relative to the euro, and
- possibility of a central bank becoming insolvent and the implications when a central bank's balance sheet looks less healthy than many of the banks it regulates.

Chapter 10, "The Economics of Virtual Currencies," of Part 2 is new to this edition. It explores the fascinating and rapidly growing sector of our financial markets dealing with virtual currencies, such as Bitcoins, Q-coins, and Facebook credits. Already, two of these once-prominent virtual currencies have appeared on the scene, grown to considerable size, and then vanished. Others have survived, new ones have been introduced, and more are sure to come with time. While individual virtual currencies may come and go, they are now part of an ongoing evolutionary process of creative destruction. Stateless and unregulated, virtual currencies are noteworthy because, if they grow to significant size, these currencies hold the power to thwart central banks' abilities to control their nations' (or currency areas') money supplies and inflation rates. They also hold the potential to disrupt fiscal policies by making economic transactions stealth-like, which means untraceable and, therefore, nontaxable.

Missing from Part 3 (i.e., "The Real Goods Sector) of *MGE's* first edition was a full discussion of the spending and fiscal multipliers. This omission has been rectified in this edition with the addition of spending multipliers to Chapter 12, "Price and Output Fluctuations" and fiscal multipliers to Chapter 13, "Fiscal Policy and Automatic Stabilizers: What Managers Need to Know."

Part 4 (Chapters 14 to 16) covers the "Foreign Exchange Market." Luck of timing allowed me to update these chapters with the most recent information (2013) from the Bank for International Settlement's *Triennial Survey*. With the book's length in mind, I removed from Chapter 12 the appendices that discussed futures and options markets.

Chapter 16, "Balance of Payments Fundamentals," has been substantially revised in this edition—and for good reason. From the beginning, I have tried to ensure that the economics in this text is not too tightly bound to the United States. To this end, I have used the International Monetary Fund's (IMF's) methodology for reporting and analyzing nations' balance of payments statistics. Since the publication of *MGE's* first edition, the IMF has changed its balance-of-payments reporting methodology. Therefore, Chapter 16 fully incorporates these important changes, and the subsequent four chapters (i.e., Chapters 17–20), which are in Part 5, "Short-Term Economic Changes: Putting It All Together," have been edited to be consistent with the balance of payments revisions in Chapter 16.

The last significant addition to *MGE* is Chapter 20, "Causes, Cures, and Consequences of the Great Recession." The Great Recession lasted from December 2007 to June 2009 and will go down in history as a punctuating event in the twenty-first century—a once in (nearly) a hundred-year event, with its equivalent occurring during the Great Depression of the 1920s and 1930s. This chapter focuses on the economic and political incentives that created this economic and financial crisis. It goes on to clarify how the problems were diagnosed and what fiscal and monetary policies were implemented to stop the bleeding, cauterize the wounds, and start the healing process.

Set into context are the roles played by subprime loans, leverage, moral hazard, financial opaqueness, regulatory changes, monetary policies, political pressures, securitization, and government sponsored entities (GSEs). The fiscal and monetary cures chosen by the U.S. government and central bank (i.e., the Federal Reserve) are also covered and put into context. This discussion is followed by an evaluation of these cures' effectiveness.

OVERVIEW OF THE TEXT

MGE is divided into six parts. Each chapter in Parts 1–5 adds an important building block to an integrated macroeconomic framework called the *Three-Sector Model*, which will be used to explain how economic, political, and social shocks can cause multiple and interrelated short-term economic changes. At each step of the way, readers are urged to ask themselves whether or not the economic concepts introduced and reasoning used meet *their* tests of common sense. Part 6 deals with long-term economic relationships.

Part 1 focuses on how to monitor and anticipate changes in a nation's economic conditions. One full chapter is devoted to explaining measures of labor market performance. Part 1 also explains the difference between inflation-adjusted (i.e., real) and nominal macroeconomic variables, such as gross domestic product (GDP), gross national product (GNP), interest rates, and wages. Inflation is also a central focus, as are the beneficiaries and victims of inflation. This section addresses, in considerable detail, whether inflation hurts a nation's overall standard of living or merely redistributes income and wealth among competing groups within the nation. Finally, Part 1 ends with a discussion of business cycles, what causes them, how they are transmitted internationally, and the impact they have on a company's performance and projected financial statements.

Part 2 focuses on the *real loanable funds market* (also called the *real credit market*), where interest rates are determined by the forces of supply and demand. This part explains money, banking, and financial intermediation in both a national and international context. Part 2 also focuses on how the real risk-free interest rate and the quantity of real loanable funds (i.e., real credit) per period are determined in the one-year to five-year time frame, which are periods normally associated with budgets and business plans. As previously mentioned, a new chapter on virtual currencies has been added to this part, which explains how these monetary instruments are created and their potential powers to disrupt fiscal and monetary policies.

Part 3 uses aggregate supply and aggregate demand analysis in the *real goods sector* to determine a nation's equilibrium real GDP and price level (i.e., GDP Price Index). More importantly, it explains what causes these macroeconomic variables to change within a one-year to five-year time frame. As previously mentioned, new sections have been added to these chapters, which focus on spending and fiscal multipliers. Part 3 ends with a discussion of fiscal policy and what governments can do, if anything, in the short run to create healthier national balance sheets and economic conditions.

Part 4 focuses on the foreign exchange market, with special attention to its structure, key market participants, effect on a nation's monetary base, and the causes of exchange rate movements. Care is also taken to explain how to read and understand spot and forward currency quotations. Part 4 addresses not only why exchange rates change but also how these changes affect companies' performance and competitive positions. Stress is put on the important distinction between real and nominal exchange rates.

Part 4 also covers balance of payments concepts. It uses the IMF approach to reporting balance of payments figures (rather than the approach of any one nation) because country analyses are often comparative, and IMF data can be used for cross-country evaluations. This chapter explains the most important balance of payments measures, how they can help interpret current economic events, and how managers can use them to improve decision-making skills.

Part 5 puts together Parts 1–4 by synthesizing the real loanable funds, real goods, and foreign exchange markets. The goal of this section is to provide an integrated framework for explaining, interpreting, and understanding how key macroeconomic variables are determined and why they change during a one-year to five-year time period. A central feature of this section is its explanation of how changes in one market cause predictable changes in the other markets. Understanding these interrelationships enables managers to avoid inconsistencies in their financial analyses and company planning models, such as assuming inflation rates will rise significantly over the coming five years while assuming at the same time that interest rates and exchange rates will remain unchanged.

The Three-Sector Model empowers readers to conduct country analyses of their own, understand the analyses of others, critically evaluate articles and editorials in the business media (e.g., *The Wall Street Journal*, the *Financial Times*, and the *Economist*), better formulate financial statement projections, and contribute meaningfully to corporate strategy and planning discussions. One entire chapter in Part 5 is devoted to analyzing the short-term effects of shocks to countries with flexible exchange rates. Another chapter is devoted exclusively to analyzing the short-term effects of shocks to countries with fixed exchange rates. Prominent in Part 5 is the role of international capital mobility[1] and how variations in this mobility affect economic outcomes. Part 5 ends with a case study of the Great Recession, which lasted from 2007 to 2009 and will be remembered by many as a low point in U.S. monetary, fiscal, and regulatory control.

Part 6 opens macroeconomic analysis to long-term business planning issues, which are particularly important to companies that are considering strategic maneuvers, such as mergers, acquisitions, divestitures, as well as changes in sourcing, production, or market positioning. This part begins by discussing scenario planning, how to measure economic growth, and the major causes of long-term development. Then, it uses monetarism, which is based on the quantity theory of money, to explore the causes of long-term inflation. Part 6 goes on to discuss the long-run Phillips curve controversy, which centers on whether nations face a long-term trade-off between unemployment and inflation. The natural-rate hypothesis is used to facilitate this discussion.

Planning for exchange rate movements and anticipating changes in international patterns of trade and production are crucial to any company's long-term financial health. Purchasing power parity theory is used in Part 6 as the springboard for our discussion of long-term exchange rate movements. The concept of comparative advantage, which is clearly one of the most important and powerful of all economic concepts, is used to explain global movements in trade and production.

Part 6 ends with a brief discussion entitled "Countries Are Not Companies," which explains why the economic reasoning behind good firm-level decisions is often different from the reasoning used at the macroeconomic level. For this reason, successful chief executive officers and chief financial officers may not be the best treasury officials and central bankers, and top-notch public policymakers may not be the best business leaders.

Understanding Part 6 is a must for anyone formulating long-term scenario plans for their companies. It is also a must for politicians and others who are interested in the kind of world we will leave to our children and grandchildren.

---

[1] In general, international capital mobility is the responsiveness of global investment flows to relative international interest rate changes.

ACKNOWLEDGMENTS

I mentioned in the first edition of *MGE* that "[w]riting a book is a lesson in humility," and this time around has made me realize, even more, the truth in this statement. There are many people who have contributed to the thoughts expressed here and supported their development. My first and most heartfelt thanks go to my family—Laraine, Eric, and Nils and now, also, Effie and my beloved John and Alec—for their constant and unwavering encouragement and patience. My friends continue to be an enormous source of support and strength.

I am especially grateful for the goodwill and helpful feedback of many students at Babson College who, at first, used various pre-publication drafts of this book. They helped me improve its content and assisted greatly in weeding out many of the typos and unplanned redundancies.

The list of students who provided insightful feedback has hundreds of names on it, but a few students' comments were so helpful and went so far beyond the norm that I gratefully acknowledge their contributions. Among the students who were especially helpful were Brian Bothwell, Paul Heimlicher, Andrew Light, Bryan Matthews, Anushree Nekkanti, Henry Osborn, Enio Pinto, Adrian Studer, and David Wilusz.

In the middle of writing the second edition, I had the good sense to hire a recent Babson graduate to read and provide feedback on every chapter and revision I made. I count among my luckiest decisions the one to hire Stacey Sicard, who provided me with a continuous stream of thoughtful, helpful, and reliable feedback, while attending to a young and growing family, as well as starting a career.

My colleagues at Babson were, as usual, generous with their time, patient, and forthcoming with useful suggestions. For the first edition, I owe special thanks to Professors Hsiang-Ling Han and Robert McAuliffe. For the second edition, I extend the same special thanks to Professors Nestor Azcona, Frederic Chartier, and Santiago Umaschi, as wells as George Urban, for their helpful and timely feedback.

Outside Babson College, professors from colleges and universities around the world reviewed various chapters and shared their thoughts with me. I am grateful for the time they spent reviewing this text and extend my special thanks to the following:

Anthony Paul Andrews,
  Governor's State University

Len Anyanwu,
  Union College

Ilgaz Arikan,
  Georgia State University

Harjit K. Arora,
  LeMoyne College

Mina Baliamoune-Lutz,
  University of North Florida

Anoop Bhargava,
  Medaille College, Finger Lakes Community College

Michael W. Brandl,
  University of Texas, Austin

Richard Guy Cox,
  University of Arkansas, Little Rock

Bogdan Daraban,
  Shenandoah University

Yoshi Fukasawa,
  Midwestern State University

Satyajit Ghosh,
  University of Scranton

J. Robert Gillette,
  University of Kentucky

David Golub,
Rutgers University

Carl Gwin,
Baylor University

Ryan W. Herzog,
Gonzaga University

Fadhel Kaboub,
Denison University

Brian T. Kench,
The University of Tampa

John M. Krieg,
Western Washington University

F. Langdana,
Rutgers University

Gary F. Langer,
Roosevelt University

Catherine Langlois,
Georgetown University

Carlos F. Liard-Muriente,
Central Connecticut University

Ida A. Mirzaie,
Ohio State University

Shariar Mostashari,
Campbell University

John J. Nader,
Grand Valley State University

ABM Nasir,
North Carolina Central University

Norman P. Obst,
Michigan State University

J. Brian O'Roark,
James Madison University

Kwang Woo (Ken) Park,
Minnesota State University

John Pharr,
Cedar Valley College

Tony Pizur,
Capella University

Abe Qastin,
Lakeland College

James Richard,
Regis University

Duane J. Rosa,
West Texas A&M University

William Seyfried,
Winthrop University

Edward F. Stuart,
Northeastern Illinois University

Della Lee Sue,
Marist College

Abdulhamid Sukar,
Cameron University

Philipp Szmedra,
Georgia Southwestern University

Dr. Joe Ueng,
University of St. Thomas, Houston

Kelly Whealan,
George Embry Riddle Aeronautical University

Jaejoon Woo,
DePaul University

Chunming Yuan,
University of Maryland, Baltimore County

Alexander Zampieron,
Bentley University

It has been a pleasure to work with the team at Cengage Learning. In particular, I thank Michael Worls, senior content manager; Ted Knight, developmental editor; Jennifer Ziegler, project manager and site lead; and Kristina Mose-Libon, designer. Creating a book of this scope was much easier with this competent and talented crew.

DEDICATION

I dedicate this book to Dr. Henri B. Meier, a trusted friend, mentor, and colleague, whose insights have been invaluable to me for many years. Henri Meier has had a profound positive influence on my life, and I wish to thank him for helping me draw the important link between theory and practice.

About the Author

John E. Marthinsen is Professor of Economics and International Business at Babson College in Babson Park, MA, where he holds The Distinguished Chair in Swiss Economics. His primary research interests are in the areas of corporate finance and international financial markets. An award-winning teacher, he is also the author of many articles and books. Among his related books are *Swiss Finance: Capital Markets, Banking, and the Swiss Value Chain* (co-authored with Henri B. Meier and Pascal B. Gantenbein, 2013), *Risk Takers: Uses and Abuses of Financial Derivatives* (Addison-Wesley, 2005 and 2009), *Wealth by Association: Global Prosperity through Market Unification* (co-authored with John C. Edmunds, Praeger, 2003), and *Switzerland: A Guide to the Capital and Money Market* (co-authored with Henri B. Meier, Euromoney, 1996).

John Marthinsen received his B.A. in 1970 from Lycoming College. Both his M.A. (1972) and Ph.D. (1974) degrees were earned at the University of Connecticut.

John Marthinsen has extensive consulting experience, working for both domestic and international companies and banks, as well as for the U.S. government. He has also lectured at the University of Bern and University of Basel in Switzerland and the University of Nuremberg in Germany. From 1992 to 1998, he served as Chairman of Babson College's Economics Division, and from 2000 to 2009, he was a member of the Board of Directors for Givaudan SA, a Swiss-based flavors and fragrances company.

Chapter 1

Introduction to International Macroeconomics

INTRODUCTION

Important business decisions have one thing in common. They are rarely based on the skills and insights of one discipline, alone. Rather, good judgments require a blend of diverse fields, such as economics, accounting, entrepreneurship, ethics, finance, information systems, law, marketing, operations, organizational behavior, and strategy. Ignoring an essential discipline could render a decision misguided and its results ineffective. This is especially important to managers because companies are held accountable for their financial performance and ethical behavior, with scores kept in dollars, euros, pesos, yen, and yuan, and results tallied on scorecards called income statements, balance sheets, and cash flow statements. Successful companies earn above-average returns, which delight their principal stakeholders (i.e., shareholders, employees, customers, and suppliers), and unsuccessful ones are obvious take-over candidates or destined to fail.

> Important business decisions are multidisciplinary.

To achieve their business goals and objectives, effective managers adjust their strategies to different competitive environments. For example, vitamin companies and other bulk chemical manufacturers sell relatively homogeneous products in very competitive international markets. The prices of these products are set by the global forces of supply and demand. Therefore, a company's success in these industries depends on factors such as high efficiency, low-cost production, effective global distribution networks, and top-quality customer service. By contrast, pharmaceutical businesses operate in differentiated international markets, where research, development, speed to market, and meeting regional health and safety standards are the key success factors.

> Different competitive environments require different competitive behaviors.

A major take-away from industry analysis is the more competitive an industry, the less control a firm has over its prices and the more it must rely on cost minimization tactics to increase profits and stakeholder value. Firms strive to gain special competitive advantages over industry rivals via product differentiation, patents, copyrights, strategic marketing, and control of vital inputs. But over time and in the absence of government protection, these special advantages are eroded by imitation and competition, as the industry moves gradually from imperfect competition toward a more competitive market structure.

> Companies can gain competitive advantages via product differentiation, patents, copyrights, strategic marketing, and control of vital inputs, but these advantages are eroded by imitation and competition.

A considerable amount of time and effort is often devoted to understanding the relationship between a firm and its industry, and for good reason. Sustainable profitability requires efficiency and a thorough grasp of shifting industry trends. But focusing exclusively on these two levels of management ignores important broader issues. Exhibit 1-1 shows that firms and industries

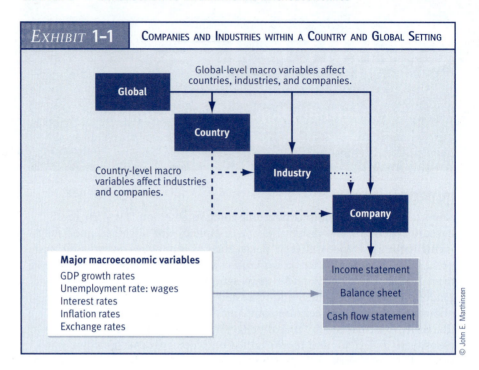

EXHIBIT **1-1** — **COMPANIES AND INDUSTRIES WITHIN A COUNTRY AND GLOBAL SETTING**

© John E. Marthinsen

operate within wide national and global markets. The macroeconomic variables determined in these markets and the cultural norms that evolve from broad socioeconomic settings are crucial factors influencing company and industry performance. An old aphorism says that "a rising tide lifts all boats," and this is clearly true for company performance. Surging markets can hide a collection of corporate sins and mask a multitude of managerial ineptitudes.

International macroeconomics focuses on how firms and industries are affected by broad-sweeping variables that are determined in national and international arenas. For instance, company sales are influenced by the rate of national and international income growth. Competitiveness is affected by changes in nations' relative wages, as well as inflation and exchange rates. Borrowing costs, the availability of credit, and returns on nonoperating assets (e.g., earnings from financial investments) are all determined in expansive national and international markets. Firms and industries have little or no influence over these variables; nevertheless, good decisions must clearly identify, measure, and address them. In the twenty-first century, there is a variety of financial tools that can hedge unwanted risks, just as there is a throng of strategic business plans that aim to turn specific risks into competitive advantages.

> **International macro-economics focuses on variables over which firms have no control, but the risks associated with changes in these variables can be managed.**

Once the firm and industry are put into the context of the national and international marketplaces, decision making becomes more interesting and complex, requiring more nuanced strategies. To highlight the role of macroeconomic assumptions, business propositions are usually couched in alternative scenarios (e.g., realistic, optimistic, and pessimistic) and crucial decision variables are identified. Credible financial and strategic plans rely on assumptions that are within realistic bounds and have logical interrelationships.

This is where a competent understanding of macroeconomics can play an important role. For example, suppose a financial analysis presented to you was based on the assumptions of falling interest rates, rapidly rising inflation, and an appreciating domestic currency? How would you react? How should you react? Would you consider the relationship among these three assumptions to be logical, or would you suspect a lack of rigor and attention to detail? If you are unsure how you would (or should) respond, then read on because answering such questions is the focus of this textbook.

BUSINESS USES OF MACROECONOMIC ANALYSES

Well-founded macroeconomic analyses can act like beacons of light when significant business decisions must be made. The structure and rigor that these analyses bring to the decision-making process are as important as the projections and conclusions they generate.

Meaningful projections and scenario analyses of cash flows, income statements, balance sheets, and risk measures need reasonable and internally consistent assumptions about economic variables, such as prices, economic growth, interest rates, and exchange rates. Usually, these assumptions are placed prominently at the top of spreadsheets so they can be changed to perform sensitivity analyses.

Those responsible for developing these analyses often present, explain, and defend them in front of groups of seasoned (often highly critical) individuals, among whom may be the company's chief executive officer, chief operating officer, chief financial officer, treasurer, directors, division heads, and department chiefs. Closely examining the assumptions and conclusions of such analyses is important because mergers, acquisitions, capital budgeting projects, and marketing plans can involve millions (in some cases, billions) of dollars of expenditures and can have significant effects on a company's strategy and profitability.

We might go even further and say that, unless some overriding strategic goal takes precedence, financial projections are the primary basis on which business decisions are usually made. Therefore, the integrity and reliability of a study's conclusions depend on the choice of assumptions and analytical methodology used. If they cannot be defended, are thought to be unreasonable, or are interpreted as being illogical, the entire analysis might be dismissed.

Even if country analyses and financial projections are based on the most up-to-date, realistic, and internally consistent macroeconomic assumptions, they are not crystal balls into the future. The value of a macroeconomic analysis is measured by the extent to which it reduces the odds of making bad decisions, which means increasing the odds of making good ones. The future is not predictable, so anyone conducting a macroeconomic analysis should expect inaccuracies in his or her assumptions and predictions. At the same time, the future is imaginable, and using reasoned macroeconomic analysis with sensible assumptions can increase the chances of making the right choices.

Macroeconomic analyses provide insight and structure to business decisions.

The future is not predictable, but how it might look is imaginable. International macroeconomics helps clear the vision and interpret the implications of alternative scenarios.

In the context of a firm, there are important differences between short-term and long-term macroeconomic analyses. In this text, *short term* refers to a time horizon that is consistent with a company's budget or business plan, which is approximately one to five years. Technically, the *long term* is any period longer than five years, but most businesses that perform long-term "scenario" analyses do so for 10- to 20-year periods (see Macro Memo 1-1: Business Planning Documents).

MACROECONOMIC ANALYSIS FOR ECONOMISTS AND POLICYMAKERS

Economists and policymakers are also interested in macroeconomic analyses for the insights they provide on how to keep nations on sustainable expansionary paths. To do so, they must keep in mind the short-term and long-term implications of their policies.

SHORT-TERM MACROECONOMIC ANALYSES

In the short-run, economists and policymakers tend to focus on changing the demand for goods and services so that nations realize their production, employment, and consumption potentials. They are generally less concerned with expanding this capacity, which tends to change slowly over time. During this short-term period, absolute and relative prices vary, but they are significantly less flexible than in the long run. The particular components of demand that are at the center of policymakers' attention are personal consumption expenditures, business investments,[1] government spending, and net exports. The extent to which policymakers' actions are actually capable of improving economic conditions is an ongoing debate in the economics profession.

> Short-term macroeconomic analyses tend to focus on factors that enable countries to produce up to their potential—a potential that changes slowly over time.

LONG-TERM MACROECONOMIC ANALYSES

In contrast to their short-run counterparts, long-run macroeconomic analyses allow much more time for absolute and relative prices to adjust. For this reason, they tend to emphasize factors that improve a country's production potential, rather than focusing on achieving current capabilities.

> Long-run macroeconomic analyses focus considerable attention on factors that increase countries' output potential.

Exhibit 1-2 summarizes the factors that are most important for short-term and long-term macroeconomic analyses.

The reason economic theory shifts from demand-oriented factors in short-term analyses to supply-oriented factors in the long term is clear. If growth and prosperity could be secured simply by implementing expansionary fiscal policies (i.e., increasing government spending and/or lowering taxes) and/or monetary policies (i.e., increasing the money supply), then all countries would be prosperous and its residents rich. This is obviously not the case. To consume more, nations have to produce more, and to increase production, they need well-educated workforces, incentives to invent and invest, access to technological improvements, constructive labor-management relations,

---

[1] In the context of a nation's demand and output, business investment (i.e., gross private domestic investment) includes new machinery, tools, equipment, factories, other construction projects, and changes in inventories. It does not include financial investments, such as stocks and bonds.

MACRO MEMO   1-1

Business Planning Documents

Business planning for operational and strategic purposes usually relies on four major reporting documents: budgets, business plans, capital budgets, and scenario plans. Because they contain proprietary (confidential) information, these documents are meant for internal audiences only. Strategic plans are presented formally to upper-level management and boards of directors. Planning documents that have little strategic value and are more operational in nature are used almost exclusively by management teams. This Macro Memo explains these planning documents and the differences among them.

Budget: Very Short-Term Planning Document

Budgets are very short-term planning documents that itemize a company's estimated revenues and expenses for time periods of one to three years. Because of their short time horizons budgets have very little operational flexibility. Therefore, they are rarely used as strategic plans and often reported only to division and department heads, as well as the executive committee, rather than a company's board of directors.

Business Plan: Short-Term Planning Document

Business plans are short-term planning documents that lay out a company's operational and financial goals for three- to five-year periods. These plans typically focus on projected cash flows and operational profits. Therefore, they provide important feedback to chief financial officers (CFOs) and treasurers, whose job is to finance anticipated cash deficiencies and invest cash surpluses.

For most (nonfinancial) companies, business plans tend to concentrate on projected cash flows from operations, but there is no compelling reason why they could not include nonoperating cash flows, as well. Because of their relatively long-term time horizons, as compared with budgets, business plans are strategic documents that are presented formally to boards of directors.

Business plans focus on strategic initiatives, anticipated competitor actions and reactions, customer trends, pricing and marketing initiatives, new-product development, old-product retirement, changes in factory utilization, input sourcing, outsourcing, and potential mergers and acquisitions. They are intended to be forward-looking documents. Due to changing conditions, business plans rarely turn out as expected and, therefore, are seldom used retrospectively to evaluate actual company performance. At the same time, they are valuable learning exercises that can give direction to the company and uncover (occasionally) interesting opportunities and synergies.

Capital Budget: Short-Term and Long-Term Planning Document

Capital budgets forecast the anticipated revenues and expenditures for particular projects (e.g., building a new factory or acquiring a new machine). Based on capital budgets, companies can compare their costs of capital with forecasted returns (e.g., internal rates of return) to decide whether the investments make economic and/or strategic sense. Because they focus on specific projects, rather than the company's broader goals, capital budgets are generally not strategic documents.

Scenario Plan: Long-Term Planning Document

Scenario plans have time horizons lasting from 10 to 20 years. Because they are the longest business planning document and have the widest panoramic view of the future, scenario plans are often delivered in the form of thought-provoking presentations made in front of executive committees and boards of directors. Typically, these plans do not forecast cash flows or profits. Rather, they focus on structural issues, such as possible long-term changes in a company's product portfolio and shifts in business interests, as well as industry and global trends. Therefore, scenario plans tend to concentrate on broad-based demographic changes, as well as technological, business, government, and other macroenvironmental trends.

EXHIBIT 1-2	SHORT-TERM VERSUS LONG-TERM MACROECONOMIC ANALYSES

Short-Term Macroeconomics 1–5 years	Long-Term Macroeconomics 10–20 years
Focus mainly on factors that increase demand ◆ Sensible monetary and fiscal policies ◆ Prudent international trade and investment policies ◆ Strong focus on the major components of demand • Personal consumption • Business investment • Government spending • Net exports ◆ Reactions to supply-side changes due to: • Major commodity price fluctuations (e.g., oil) • Exchange rate movements • Changes in government rules	**Focus mainly on factors that increase supply** ◆ Private sector's role • Investments in physical and human capital • Advancements in technology and innovation • Constructive labor-management relations • Effective corporate governance policies ◆ Government's role • Promote institutions and policies to improve economic efficiency • Define individual property rights • Create a stable, fair, and predictable political environment—low business risks • Encourage competitive markets • Implement reasonable marginal tax rates • Promote the free movement of goods, services, capital, and labor • Enact wise monetary and fiscal policies

© 2015 John E. Marthinsen

well-grounded corporate governance practices, fair and reasonable governments and tax rates, as well as the freedom to invest, trade, and pursue economic opportunities.

THREE-SECTOR MODEL

The short-term economic analyses in this text are all based on the simultaneous interaction of three key macroeconomic markets (see Exhibit 1-3). For now, we will call them (generically) the financial market, goods and services market, and foreign exchange market. The *financial market* (also called the *credit market*) is where the interest rates and the equilibrium quantity of credit each period are determined by the supply and demand forces of lenders and borrowers.[2] Oftentimes, the financial press calls this market "Wall Street," which is why Wall Street disasters are termed "financial crises." Keys to unlocking the intricacies of this market are understanding the incentives behind borrower behavior, money and how it is created, other sources of credit (loanable funds), as well as the role of central banks, financial institutions, and international capital flows.

The *goods and services market* is where a nation's average price level (i.e., price index) and real output per period are determined by businesses that supply products and consumers, businesses, governments, and foreigners that demand them.[3] The media often refer to this market as "Main Street," and

---

[2] In later chapters, we will refine our description of the financial market by focusing on the *real loanable funds market*.

[3] In later chapters, we will refine our description of the goods and services market by calling it the *real goods and services market* (also, known as the *real goods market*).

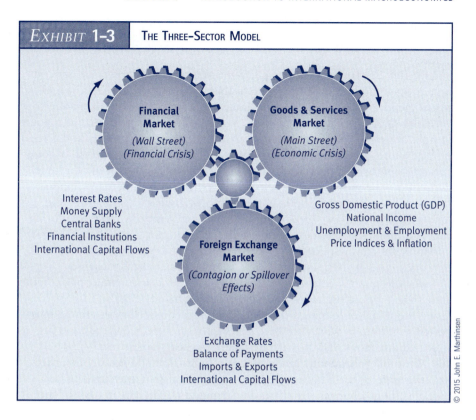

EXHIBIT 1-3   THE THREE-SECTOR MODEL

Financial Market
(Wall Street)
(Financial Crisis)

Goods & Services Market
(Main Street)
(Economic Crisis)

Foreign Exchange Market
(Contagion or Spillover Effects)

Interest Rates
Money Supply
Central Banks
Financial Institutions
International Capital Flows

Gross Domestic Product (GDP)
National Income
Unemployment & Employment
Price Indices & Inflation

Exchange Rates
Balance of Payments
Imports & Exports
International Capital Flows

© 2015 John E. Marthinsen

Main-Street catastrophes are called "economic crises." Keys to unlocking the workings of this market are understanding gross domestic product (GDP), unemployment and employment rates, as well as inflation and price indices, such as the GDP price index and consumer price index.

Finally, the *foreign exchange market* is where exchange rates and the equilibrium quantities of foreign exchange each period are determined by the suppliers and demanders of international currencies. If the financial and/or economic conditions in the domestic market are exported to foreign nations, then they are said to have "contagion or spill-over effects." Essential to understanding foreign exchange markets is fluency with exchange rates and a rich array of balance of payments[4] concepts, such as imports, exports, international capital flows, and the effects of central bank intervention.

Much can be learned from understanding how each of these three markets functions in isolation, but the greatest rewards from international macroeconomics are harvested by knowing how all three interact simultaneously (i.e., understanding how shocks to one or more of them affect the others).

> The Three-Sector Model considers simultaneous changes in variables determined in the financial, goods and services, and foreign exchange markets.

---

[4] The balance of payments shows the net transactions between the residents of one nation and the residents of the rest of the world during a given period of time.

It is only then that sound business judgments, reasoned political decisions, and insightful conclusions about past, present, and expected future events can be made.

Exhibit 1-3 portrays the three key macroeconomic markets as interconnected, spinning gears. The purpose of this visual is twofold. First, it reinforces the idea that macroeconomic analyses are concerned mostly with flow variables rather than stock variables. A *stock variable* is measured at a point in time. Examples of stock variables are a nation's money supply and capital infrastructure, as well as company assets and liabilities. By contrast, a *flow variable* is measured over a time period because only by knowing the time period does the measure make sense. An example will show why. Suppose a friend said she earned $2,000. Without knowing whether she earned the amount per hour, day, week, month, quarter, or year, this piece of information is meaningless. Besides income, other examples of macroeconomic flow variables are consumption, investment, government spending, imports, exports, taxes, deficits, and a nation's balance of payments measures.

Macroeconomic equilibrium should be viewed as a dynamic, harmonious state, where opposing forces (i.e., supply and demand) meet and balance. Using the visual in Exhibit 1-3, macroeconomic equilibrium should be interpreted as a state in which all three gears move at expected speeds and in expected directions. It is *not* a state where the gears are at rest.[5]

Most macroeconomic analyses begin by assuming a nation's markets are in a state of dynamic equilibrium and remain that way until some external shock changes supply and/or demand conditions in one (or more) market(s). Then, macroeconomic tools are used to explain the likely economic impacts of this shock. Assuming that a nation's markets are initially in equilibrium is mainly for convenience and ease of analysis; it is not a necessity. Under normal conditions, results would be the same (even if the nation did not start in equilibrium) because macromarkets should be constantly moving an economy toward equilibrium. When external shocks occur, they simply change the equilibrium endpoints to which markets are moving.

This brings us to the second important reason for visualizing a macroeconomic system as three, interdependent, turning gears. Changes in the speed and direction of any gear cause predictable fluctuations in the speed and direction of the other gears. In short, no gear should move without causing logical and predictable changes in the others.

WHEN REALITY DIFFERS FROM EXPECTATIONS

There will be instances when real-world events differ from the conclusions of our Three-Sector Model. In such cases, there are two basic courses of action: abandon the Three-Sector Model in favor of another paradigm or treat the

> Stock variables are measured at a point in time, and flow variables are measured over a time period.

> Macroeconomic equilibrium can be viewed as three interdependent, spinning gears that are moving simultaneously at a harmonious rate.

---

[5] Using another analogy, macroeconomic equilibrium is like the water level in a bathtub, where the water flowing in through the faucet equals the water flowing out through the drain. Despite the flows, the water level stays the same. Equilibrium should not be viewed as the water level in a bathtub with no running water, faucet, or drain.

discrepancies as aberrations. In many cases, market events that appear to be inconsistent with economic logic are just signals that additional information is needed. We are all familiar with optical illusions and magic tricks that seem to defy both physical laws of nature and common sense, but relatively few people believe that supernatural or magical forces in the universe actually cause these effects. In a similar sense, when real-world results seem to differ from economic logic, the difference can usually be explained by a missing detail or the need to take a more refined look at the issue.

> When macroeconomic conclusions seem inconsistent with real-world events, it is often a sign that additional information is needed.

READING THE ECONOMIC TEA LEAVES

Picture yourself as a newly appointed general manager or finance manager working in an unfamiliar country for a multinational company. During the coming weeks and months, you will be expected to learn and understand your new business environment like no one else in the organization. You will become the go-to person when strategic and operational questions about this country or region arise. Succeed at your new tasks, and you will be rewarded—oftentimes financially, but equally often with more responsibilities. If you fail to live up to expectations, you will be moved sideways or out.

> Country analysis is the systematic investigation of a nation's economic, political, and social strengths, weaknesses, opportunities, and threats.

How can you systematically evaluate the short-term economic health of a nation and/or region? Where do you begin your analysis? Answering these questions is the purpose of *country analysis*, which is the systematic investigation of a nation's economic, political, and social strengths, weaknesses, opportunities, and threats.

This textbook provides the framework and tools needed to perform systematic macroeconomic analyses, which can be used to improve and reinforce broad country analyses. The framework and tools described herein are valuable, but equally important are the credibility and trust that upper management places on you, the analyst. Such credibility and trust are usually the byproducts of many years of experience.

Regardless of whether you live in Africa, Antarctica, Australia, Eurasia, North America, or South America, your company's health and well-being are likely to be affected in substantial ways by the ebbs and flows of national and international economic conditions. For developed nations, economic growth is important due to the noticeable difference it can make in domestic residents' quality of life. For develop*ing* nations, economic growth is essential because it can make the difference between life and death.

LET'S BEGIN!

With these preliminaries in mind, let's begin our study of international macroeconomics. How are the economic conditions in your nation? Are people working hard or hardly working? Is the economy functioning or malfunctioning? What countries in the world interest you the most? Is any country of particular interest for your job? This text constructs an integrated economic framework that will be helpful regardless of when and where it is used. It is intended to be both a means to better understand the world around us and a way to add breadth and depth to important business decisions.

CONCLUSION

Having a solid understanding of international macroeconomics opens a new world of intellectual discovery to anyone who can master its basic logic—and virtually anyone can. Macroeconomics provides insights into political and economic debates, offers a solid base for making many business decisions, and opens the daily news to a higher level of understanding and critical review. Among the many issues addressed by macroeconomics are the:

- likelihood and causes of recessions (or depressions);
- impact of business cycles on companies' health and vitality;
- economic forces that cause short-term and long-term changes in inflation and exchange rates;
- effects that exchange rate changes have on a nation's output, inflation, employment, and interest rates, as well as their effects on company sales, prices, and expenses;
- short-term and long-term effects of monetary and fiscal policies;
- destructive or constructive effects of large government budget deficits or surpluses;
- costs and benefits of a balanced budget amendment;
- destructive or constructive effects of large balance of payments deficits or surpluses;
- causes of currency crises, such as those that occurred in Mexico in 1994, the Asian Tiger Countries in 1997, Russia in 1998, and Argentina in 2001, and forces that could create similar crises in the future;
- economic implications for countries that abandon their domestic currencies and adopt a foreign or common currency, such as the dollar or euro;
- economic effects and wisdom of imposing international capital controls; and
- fundamental causes of long-term economic growth and the role (if any) the government should play in stimulating this growth.

All of these issues can be analyzed with macroeconomic tools and reasoning. For this reason, the aim of this book is to provide readers with the skills, framework, and macroeconomic intuition to do so.

REVIEW QUESTIONS

1. What three financial statements form the basis for most company decisions? What major macroeconomic variables influence these financial statements?

2. What are the three markets considered by the Three-Sector Model? Briefly explain each market and what macroeconomic variables are determined in them.

3. What is the difference between stock and flow variables? Name three macroeconomic stock variables and three macroeconomic flow variables.

4. Is macroeconomic equilibrium a stock concept or a flow concept? Explain.

5. Explain the differences among budgets, business plans, capital budgets, and scenarios. For what purposes is one more important than the others?

DISCUSSION QUESTIONS

6. "Even though companies cannot control macroeconomic variables, anticipating the effects of changes in these variables and understanding macroeconomic interrelationships can be very useful to businesses." Explain whether this statement is true or false.

7. What business decisions can be improved with the help of short-term macroeconomic analysis? What business decisions can be improved with the help of long-term macroeconomic analysis?

8. How important are monetary and fiscal policies to long-term economic growth? What are the most important economic variables determining a nation's long-term economic growth rate?

PART 1

UNDERSTANDING A NATION'S ECONOMIC CONDITIONS

Chapter 2

Taking an Economic Pulse: Measuring National Output and Income

INTRODUCTION

Starting or growing a business in a healthy economy is easier than in a weak or struggling one, but how does one tell if a nation's economy is sick, well, recovering, or deteriorating? Two of the most widely used measures of economic health are gross domestic product (GDP) and gross national product (GNP), due to their close connection to key macroeconomic indicators of economic fitness and well-being, such as unemployment rates, business profitability, wage rates, and stock prices. This chapter distinguishes between GDP and GNP and explains their strengths and weaknesses as economic thermometers. It goes on to link them to the circular flow diagram and important related concepts, such as macroeconomic equilibrium, expenditure and income components of GDP, and leakages and injections from the circular flow of spending and earnings.

THE BASICS

GROSS DOMESTIC PRODUCT AND GROSS NATIONAL PRODUCT

Output and income are two sides of the same coin because when output is produced, income must be earned. If the costs of production are less than the revenues that businesses earn, then the residual accrues to company owners in the form of profits. The point is that, in the end, the value of a nation's output must be equal to the value of incomes earned. Broadly speaking, gross domestic product (GDP) and gross national product (GNP) are similar in the sense that both measure a nation's output and income, but beyond that, it is important to know exactly what is being measured, what is not, and how these measures differ.

GROSS DOMESTIC PRODUCT (GDP)

GDP measures the market value of all final goods and services produced for the market by resources (i.e., land, labor, capital, and entrepreneurs), regardless of whether they are domestically or foreign owned, within a nation's geographic borders over a given period of time. There is much to keep in mind with this definition; so let's review the key parts.

> GDP measures the market value of final goods and services produced for the market within a nation's geographic borders during a period of time.

Market Value: GDP combines a wide and diverse assortment of goods and services. Without market values, a nation would have no way to sum these products into a single aggregate number. Instead, it would have to report output in terms of physical units and measures, such as tons of steel, liters of milk, miles of transportation services, number of cars, and hours of consulting services. By contrast, multiplying the quantities of goods and services produced by their prices allows dissimilar products to be combined. The currencies (e.g., dollar, euro, peso, or yen) of nations serve as units of account for combining unlike goods and services into one aggregate figure, and exchange rates (i.e., the price of one currency in terms of another currency) allow us to compare the GDP of one nation to the GDPs of other nations.

Final: Many goods are produced in stages. For instance, bread requires grain to be harvested, milled into flour, combined with other ingredients, baked, and, finally, distributed to consumers through retail outlets. When a consumer buys bread in the grocery store, the final price includes all of these intermediate steps. Therefore, if GDP included both the value of each production stage *and* the final price, it would be double counting. Focusing attention only on final goods and services avoids this problem and correctly measures GDP.[1]

Produced: GDP includes all goods and services produced, regardless of whether they are sold. Goods that are produced but not purchased go into business inventories and are included as part of a nation's *gross private domestic investment*, which is discussed later in this chapter.

For the Market: Normally, GDP includes only production and incomes earned in open and legal markets. Open markets usually do not exist for the use of public goods, such as clean air and clean water. Because companies and individuals utilize them without charge, they are excluded from GDP.[2]

Similarly, black market activities and underground transactions are also excluded from GDP because these nonmarket transactions are not reported and, therefore, evade detection. The volume of black market activity is considerable. A 2007 report by the United Nations Office on Drugs and Crime (UNODC) estimated that opium trade accounts for more than half of Afghanistan's illicit GDP.[3] In a 2011 report, UNODC found that money laundering by drug and human traffickers, counterfeiters, and small arms smugglers amounted to $1.6 trillion, which was 2.5% of global GDP in 2009. An International Monetary Fund (IMF) study provided a reality check by estimating these transactions at 2% to 5% of global GDP.[4]

---

[1] Another way to solve the double-counting problem is to sum only the value added at each stage of the production process and, therefore, to exclude the final price. The sum of these added values equals the final purchase price.

[2] Pollution can result when businesses exploit natural resources, such as clean air and clean water. In the absence of any market solution to this problem (with a market price to match), government regulations may be required.

[3] United Nations Office on Drugs and Crime, Opium Amounts to Half of Afghanistan's GDP in 2007, Reports UNODC, https://www.unodc.org/india/afghanistan_gdp_report.html (accessed October 13, 2012).

[4] United Nations Office on Drugs and Crime (UNODC), Estimating Illicit Financial Flows Resulting from Drug Trafficking and Other Transnational Organized Crimes: Research Report, October 2011, http://www.unodc .org/documents/data-and-analysis/Studies/Illicit_financial_flows_2011_web.pdf. UNODC, Illicit Money: How Much is Out There?, http://www.unodc.org/unodc/en/frontpage/2011/October/illicit-money_-how-much-is-out-there.html (accessed October 13, 2012).

The larger a nation's underground economy, the more distorted its reported GDP. Consider Colombia. What would happen to the size of Colombia's GDP if that nation decided one day to include the value of domestically produced illicit drugs (e.g., coca, heroin, poppies, and marijuana)? During the 1990s, Colombia produced about 80% of the world's cocaine, and the estimated wholesale value of all its illicitly produced products was equal to about 1% of the nation's GDP, which was nearly $100 billion.[5] Because these products were part of the underground economy, they were not included in Colombia's GDP, but if the nation decided to include an imputed value for them, its GDP would have increased automatically by about 1%.

Imagine the international surprise in 1999, when Colombia decided to include in its GDP figures an imputed wholesale value for all the illicit drugs produced domestically.[6] Immediately following the announcement, Colombia's ranking on the worldwide GDP tables improved.

By Resources, Regardless of Whether They Are Domestically or Foreign Owned, Within a Nation's Borders: GDP measures production that takes place within a nation's geographic borders, regardless of whether the goods and services are produced by domestic citizens or foreign citizens. For example, the goods or services produced by a Japanese citizen who works in the United States are included in U.S. GDP.

By analogy, GDP treats a nation like a huge machine and asks, "How much did the machine produce?" It does not consider whether the machine was operated by a domestic citizen or a foreign citizen. It is concerned only with the amount produced by the machine itself.

Over a Given Period of Time: GDP is a flow measure that has significance only over a period of time. For example, a statement such as "This nation's GDP equals $1 trillion" is meaningless until you know whether the time period over which it is measured is a week, month, quarter, year, or decade.

GROSS NATIONAL PRODUCT (GNP)

GNP measures the market value of all final goods and services produced for the market *by domestically owned resources, regardless of where they are in the world*, over a given period of time. Except for the italicized phrase in the previous sentence, GNP and GDP have the same definitions. Both GNP and GDP measure the *market values* of all *final goods and services produced* in *open markets over a given period of time*. The single major difference is that GDP includes only production within a nation's borders, and GNP includes production anywhere in the world, as long as it is created by domestically owned resources.

> GNP measures the market value of final goods and services produced for the market by a nation's resources (regardless of location) over a period of time.

[5] See Charles Penty, "Drug Crops Will Be in Colombia GDP," Bloomberg News, June 10, 1999, p. 1; Editorial, "A Sadly Accurate GDP," *Journal of Commerce*, June 10, 1999, p. 7.
[6] In fact, Colombia revised its GDP figures back to 1994 by adding imputed values for illicit drug transactions.

WHICH MEASURE, GDP OR GNP, IS MORE IMPORTANT?

For most countries, GDP and GNP are so close in value that it makes little difference which one is used to measure production or income. Nevertheless, GDP receives relatively more attention than GNP because of what it is trying to measure, which is the value of production on domestic soil. One of the main reasons for this emphasis is because nations seek low unemployment rates, and unemployment is a measure of joblessness within a nation's geographic boundaries.[7]

CIRCULAR FLOW DIAGRAM

> The circular flow diagram separates the economy into the business sector and household sector.

The circular flow diagram is a valuable tool for conceptualizing macroeconomic information and the macroeconomy. An economy may be categorized in many alternative ways. For example, it can be divided into its capital goods and consumer goods sectors, agricultural and nonagricultural sectors, or domestic and foreign sectors. The circular flow diagram divides the economy into the business sector (also called the *producer* sector) and the household sector (also called the *consumer* sector).

> The business sector supplies products and demands resources used in the production process. The household sector demands products and supplies resources used in the production process.

The business sector produces goods and services and also demands resources that are used in the production process. The household sector consumes the goods and services produced by the business sector and supplies resources used in the production process.

THE BOTTOM PORTION OF THE CIRCULAR FLOW DIAGRAM

> The bottom portion of the circular flow diagram shows the relationship between the household supply of resources and the business demand for these resources.

The bottom portion of the circular flow diagram shows how the business sector and the household sector interact through the resource market. The resource market is where the household sector supplies resources (also called *factors of production*) and the business sector demands them. From this interaction, the prices of resources and the quantities of resources hired per period are determined (see Exhibit 2-1).

Resources that are owned by the household sector and sold to the business sector are divided into four different economic categories: labor, capital, natural resources, and the entrepreneur (see Exhibit 2-1). *Labor* includes both

---

MACRO MEMO   2-1

What Sector Are You In?

What sector are you in? People who are gainfully employed are in both the household *and* business sectors; so, it is not the case that an individual has to be in one sector or the other. Of course, some individuals, like students and young children, are in only the household (consumer) sector because they are not employed (i.e., not a part of the producer sector), but they do consume. The important take-away from this section is that the circular flow diagram divides an economy by functions (i.e., consumption and production) rather than by characteristics, such as gender.

---

[7]See Robert Reich, "Who Is Us?" *Harvard Business Review*, January 1, 1990, p. 11, product number 90111.

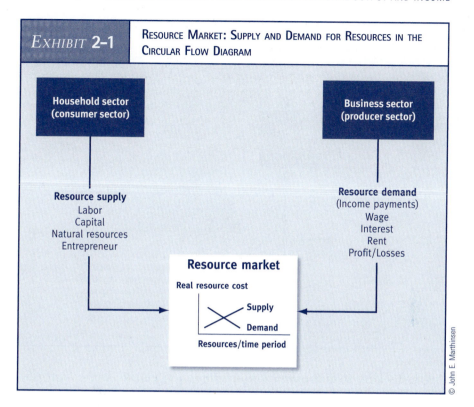

EXHIBIT 2-1   RESOURCE MARKET: SUPPLY AND DEMAND FOR RESOURCES IN THE CIRCULAR FLOW DIAGRAM

© John E. Marthinsen

the physical and mental capabilities of individuals. The return to labor is called the *wage*. *Capital* includes all human-made aids to production, and the return to capital is called *interest*.

The return to *natural resources* is called *rent*. We know the word *rent* as the monthly payment made for an apartment or a house—a payment that is usually associated in some way with land—but in economics, rent is the return to *any* natural resource (e.g., the return to coal, forestry, or land).

The last resource is the *entrepreneur*, and the return to the entrepreneur is called *profit or loss*. Entrepreneurs are different from laborers because they are the founders of companies or the initiators of new lines of business within existing companies. As a result, they willingly take on risks that are not associated with normal employment. Because of their risk-taking activities, entrepreneurs are compensated with a profit, which distinguishes their contribution to economic activity from the contributions of labor.

> The return to labor is called the wage. Interest is the return to capital, rent is the return to natural resources, and profit is the return to the entrepreneur.

A Helpful Way to View the Resource Market

A useful way to conceptualize the interconnections between the amount of resources supplied by the household sector and the amount demanded by the business sector is to picture a mountain of goods and services produced and made available for sale each period (see Exhibit 2-2). A significant portion of macroeconomic analysis is concerned with making sure the mountain of goods and services produced each period (e.g., each year) is purchased. Macroeconomic analysis also seeks to ensure that the amount produced is

> A helpful way to capture circular flow activity is to picture a mountain of goods and services produced each period as resources are used in the production process.

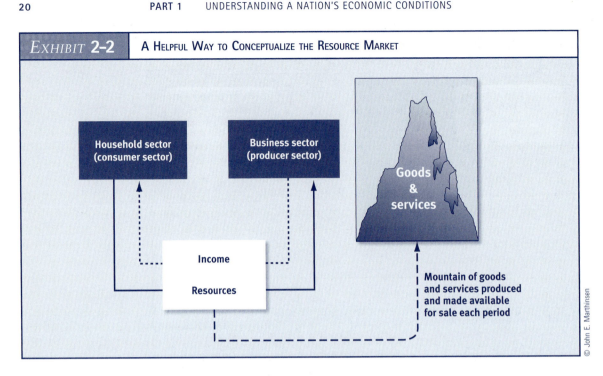

EXHIBIT 2-2   A HELPFUL WAY TO CONCEPTUALIZE THE RESOURCE MARKET

sufficiently large so that everyone who wants a job has one. In the next section, we will discuss who purchases this mountain of goods and services and how much they buy.

THE TOP PORTION OF THE CIRCULAR FLOW DIAGRAM

Until now, our focus has been on the bottom portion of the circular flow diagram, so let's turn our attention to the upper portion. In the last section, we visualized the resource market (the bottom portion of the circular flow) as one in which a mountain of goods and services was produced and made available for sale each period (see Exhibit 2-2).

The top portion of the circular flow diagram shows the linkages between the household sector and the business sector in the *real goods and services market*.[8] As Exhibit 2-3 shows, the goods and services market connects the amount of goods and services supplied by the business sector with the amount demanded by the household sector.

Stepping back, we can see that the flows in both the top and bottom portions of the circular flow are related to supply and demand. In the top portion, the household sector demands goods and services, which the business sector supplies. By contrast, in the lower portion of the circular flow diagram, the roles of supplier and demander are reversed. The business sector demands resources, which the household sector supplies (see Exhibit 2-4).

> The top portion of the circular flow diagram shows the linkages between the household sector and the business sector in the market for goods and services.

---

[8] Throughout the text, the term "real goods and services market" is used interchangeably with "real goods market."

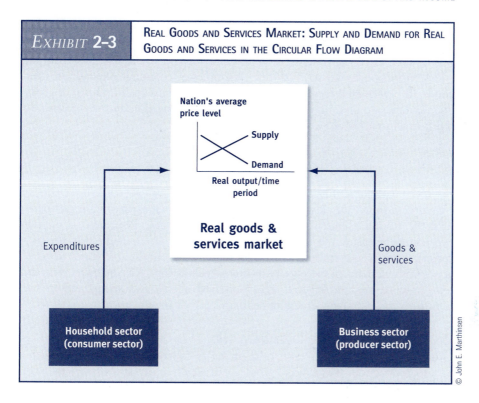

EXHIBIT 2-3   REAL GOODS AND SERVICES MARKET: SUPPLY AND DEMAND FOR REAL GOODS AND SERVICES IN THE CIRCULAR FLOW DIAGRAM

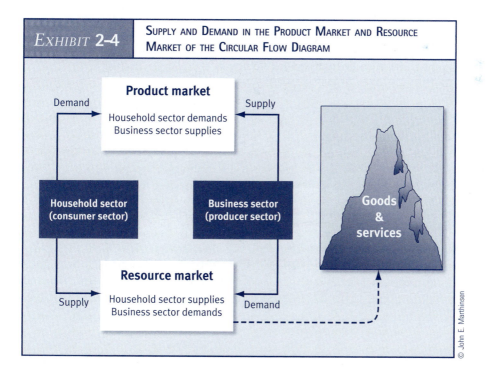

EXHIBIT 2-4   SUPPLY AND DEMAND IN THE PRODUCT MARKET AND RESOURCE MARKET OF THE CIRCULAR FLOW DIAGRAM

FOCUS ON MACROECONOMIC EXPENDITURES

What are the principal sources of demand? This question will be answered as we continue to concentrate on the upper portion of the circular flow diagram.

A nation's demand (D) includes all sources of economic expenditures for goods and services, which are: personal consumption expenditures (C), gross private domestic investment (I), government spending (G), and net exports (NE). In short:

$$D = C + I + G + NE.$$

PERSONAL CONSUMPTION EXPENDITURES (C)

Exhibit 2-5 shows the flow of spending, called *personal consumption expenditures* (C), from the household sector to the business sector. Personal consumption expenditures measure the amount spent *per period* by the household sector on consumer goods and services. It includes the purchase of durable goods (e.g., goods with lifespans of three years or more, such as cars, washing machines, and refrigerators), nondurable goods (e.g., food, beverages, and clothing), and services (e.g., banking, plumbing, entertainment, and dry cleaning).

> Personal consumption expenditures include the purchase of durable goods, nondurable goods, and services.

GROSS PRIVATE DOMESTIC INVESTMENT (I)

Gross private domestic investment (I) includes expenditures on human-made aids to production. It is called "gross" because these investments are for both new investments and for the replacement of depreciated capital.[9] It is called "private" because these investments are not part of government spending, and it is called "domestic" because the expenditures are invested in the domestic economy and not abroad.

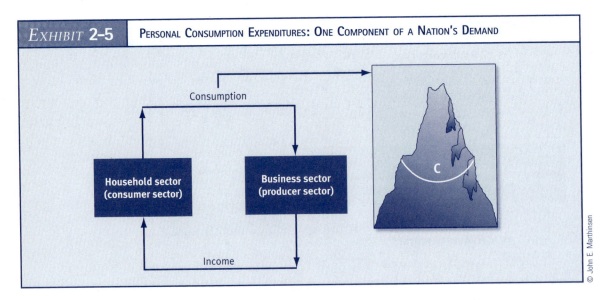

| EXHIBIT **2-5** | PERSONAL CONSUMPTION EXPENDITURES: ONE COMPONENT OF A NATION'S DEMAND |

© John E. Marthinsen

---

[9] New investment is also called net investment. Therefore, Net investment $\equiv$ Gross investment $-$ Depreciation.

In discussions where GDP is concerned, it is important to remember that investment expenditures are for tangible (real) assets and not for financial assets, such as stocks, bonds, notes, and collateralized obligations. Included in gross private domestic investment are purchases of newly produced machinery, tools, equipment, construction (both residential and business), and changes in business inventories.

For most people, the spending that is included in gross private domestic investment is straightforward, uncomplicated and, therefore, generally consistent with their common sense. Nevertheless, changes in business inventories deserve special attention, while residential construction deserves clarification.

Business inventories can fall or rise for planned and unplanned reasons. If producers expect consumer demand to increase in the future, they often invest now in larger inventories to meet the surge in anticipated sales.

> Gross private domestic investment includes expenditures for purchases of newly produced machinery, tools, equipment, construction, and changes in business inventories.

MACRO MEMO 2-2

Why Stocks and Bonds Are *Not* Part of Gross Private Domestic Investment

Investments can be separated into two major categories: real investments and financial investments. Real investments are included in GDP because they are newly produced goods. By contrast, financial investments, such as stocks and bonds, are excluded from GDP because their nominal values do not reflect the production of equivalent-valued goods or services.* In short, a $1 billion bond issue does not imply the creation of a billion dollars of new goods or services.

The same point can be made in a different way by remembering the distinction between a company's assets and liabilities. One of the most basic and important accounting tautologies (truisms) is that *a company's assets* must equal the sum of *its liabilities*† *plus shareholders' equity*.‡ Similarly, changes in a company's assets must equal the sum of changes in its liabilities and shareholders' equity. The take-away is that assets must be owned by someone. If they are owned by the company, they are called equity (or net worth), and ownership rights by outsiders are called liabilities. Capital goods, such as machinery, equipment, tools, construction, and inventories, are assets on a company's balance sheet, but someone has to own them.

Suppose XYZ Corporation purchased a new machine costing $10 million and financed the purchase by issuing $10 million of new stocks and bonds. Including in gross private domestic investment both the new machine and its financing would overstate the true level of investment in the economy. In effect, it would be double counting by including the asset and ownership (i.e., liability and equity) values.

Finally, newly issued financial securities are not included in gross private domestic investment for a third reason. New debt and equity instruments are claims on *all* company assets and not just the newly purchased ones. In other words, they are claims on current and past investments.

*Of course, financial services are needed to create, market, and resell financial investments. These services are included in GDP, but their values are quite different and separate from the values of the nominal financial investments themselves.

†Liabilities earn fixed or variable interest returns, which companies are *obligated to pay*, regardless of whether they earn profits.

‡Stock owners (shareholders) earn their returns from periodic company dividends and/or capital gains (or losses), when they sell their shares. Companies are *not required to pay* dividends or to repurchase their shares. Therefore, shareholders are not guaranteed a return on their investments.

If they expect demand to fall, they do the opposite. By contrast, inventories can fall or rise due to unforeseen reasons, such as changes in consumer demand. When demand falls unexpectedly, inventories rise, leaving businesses holding unwanted stores of goods. They often react to the increase by laying off workers and/or reducing their hours. When demand rises unexpectedly, just the opposite happens. Inventories fall and businesses hire new workers. Regardless of whether the changes in inventories are planned or unplanned, any increase is included as part of gross private domestic investment. What makes these changes even more important is they are among the most volatile components of gross private domestic investment.

If any component of gross private domestic investment defies common sense, it is residential construction. Many people ask, "Why is residential construction counted as investment, when it so clearly has nothing to do with business productivity or profitability?"

The reason for including residential construction as a type of investment is because individuals *could have* rented their homes and thereby derived a source of business income. Most individuals choose not to do so, but they could if they desired. As a result, residential construction represents a sort of shadow market for commercial construction or the opportunity cost for living in your own home.

GOVERNMENT SPENDING (G)

Government spending
includes expenditures for
goods and services at all
levels of government.
Transfer payments by the
government are not
included.

Government spending is a major component of a nation's demand, and it is larger than you might first expect because this source of demand includes spending at all levels: federal, state (or provincial or cantonal), and local. At the same time, only payments by the government for newly produced goods and services are included in this spending category, which means transfer payments by the government are excluded.

In this book, we will focus primarily on government spending at the federal level because it is the federal government that normally enacts discretionary fiscal policies. Nevertheless, in some countries (e.g., Switzerland and Brazil), spending at lower levels of government (e.g., cantons and states) can be an important portion of overall public spending and therefore exert a major influence on overall economic activity.

NET EXPORTS (NE)

The final component of total expenditures is *net exports*. Net exports include a nation's exports of goods and services to foreign nations *minus* its imports of goods and services from foreign nations. Imports are subtracted from exports because imports are expenditures on foreign-produced goods and services, and GDP reflects domestic production only.[10] Another way to

---

[10] A more technical explanation for why imports are subtracted from exports can be found in Appendix 2–1: *Shouldn't a Nation's Demand Include Only Exports? Why Do We Net Out Imports?*

understand this point is in terms of the circular flow diagram. Net exports (rather than just exports) are used as the final component of demand because purchases of foreign products do nothing to eliminate the mountain of goods and services produced domestically each period. Therefore, imports must be netted from spending to determine how many *domestically produced* goods and services are purchased.

> Net exports include a nation's exports of goods and services minus its imports of goods and services.

The value of imports can be greater than exports; therefore, net exports can be (and often is) a negative number. Nevertheless, it is still called "net exports." Exhibit 2-6 shows net exports for the United States from January 1960 to October 2012. Notice how dramatically the U.S. net export position turned negative since the 1960s.

TOTAL EXPENDITURES

Exhibit 2-7 summarizes what we have learned so far. The demand (D) for a nation's goods and services is composed of personal consumption expenditures (C), plus gross private domestic investment (I), plus government spending (G), plus net exports (NE), and these sources of demand purchase different portions of the mountain of goods and services produced each period. With this in mind, we will now move on to explain the first of two ways to view macroeconomic equilibrium.

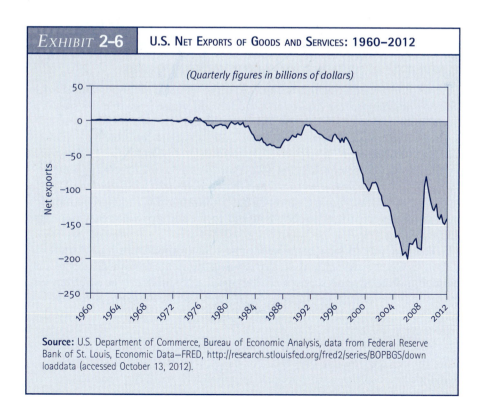

| EXHIBIT 2-6 | U.S. NET EXPORTS OF GOODS AND SERVICES: 1960–2012 |

(Quarterly figures in billions of dollars)

Source: U.S. Department of Commerce, Bureau of Economic Analysis, data from Federal Reserve Bank of St. Louis, Economic Data—FRED, http://research.stlouisfed.org/fred2/series/BOPBGS/down loaddata (accessed October 13, 2012).

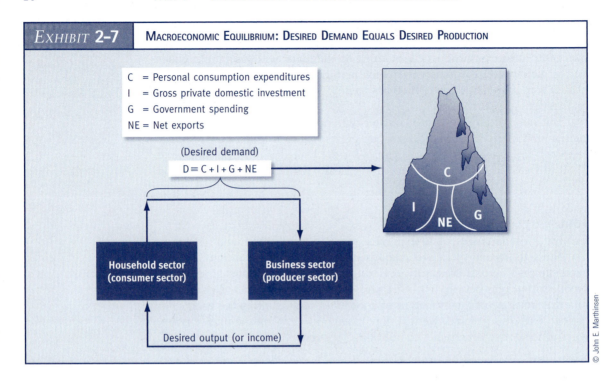

EXHIBIT 2-7   MACROECONOMIC EQUILIBRIUM: DESIRED DEMAND EQUALS DESIRED PRODUCTION

C = Personal consumption expenditures
I   = Gross private domestic investment
G = Government spending
NE = Net exports

(Desired demand)

$$D \equiv C + I + G + NE$$

Household sector
(consumer sector)

Business sector
(producer sector)

Desired output (or income)

© John E. Marthinsen

MACROECONOMIC EQUILIBRIUM I: DESIRED QUANTITY SUPPLIED = DESIRED QUANTITY DEMANDED

Macroeconomic equilibrium occurs when the value of all goods and services that the business sector *desires* to produce and make available for sale is equal to the value of the goods and services that the household sector *desires* to purchase. Alternatively, one could say that equilibrium occurs when the *anticipated (or expected) amount of goods and services demanded* by the household sector is equal to the *anticipated (or expected) amount supplied* by the business sector. The adjectives *desired, anticipated, expected, and intended* are synonymous and important in macroeconomics because they refer to what people intend to do and not what they actually end up doing.

The first way to view macroeconomic equilibrium is in terms of the *desired amount supplied* and *desired amount demanded*. With respect to the mountain of goods and services analogy used in Exhibit 2-7, equilibrium means that the mountain produced each period by the business sector is completely and willingly swept off the market, with no surplus or shortage remaining at the end.

Disequilibrium occurs when the desired amount demanded is different from the desired amount supplied. For example, if the desired amount demanded is insufficient to purchase all the newly produced products,

> Macroeconomic equilibrium occurs when the desired amount supplied equals the desired amount demanded.

business inventories rise. As a result, companies have an incentive to lay off workers, reduce hours, and/or cut prices. By contrast, if the desired amount demand exceeds the desired amount supplied, business inventories fall, causing companies to hire, increase workers' hours, and/or raise prices.

Is Equilibrium Good or Bad for a Nation?

Is equilibrium good or bad for a nation? Before answering this question, remember that macroeconomic equilibrium occurs when the goods and services that businesses desire to produce are equal to the amount domestic and foreign buyers desire to purchase. With this definition of equilibrium in mind, it may be clear that macroeconomic equilibrium is neither good nor bad. It depends. The amount produced could be far below a nation's capacity, thereby leading to severe unemployment, or far above it, leading to inflation and strains on domestic resources. Macroeconomic equilibrium means only that there is no tendency for businesses to change the amount of resources they demand, alter the quantity goods and services they supply, or vary their prices. When the products that businesses desire to produce are purchased in full, inventories remain steady, and there is no need to increase or decrease production.

THE REST OF THE STORY

SHORTCOMINGS OF GDP AND GNP AS MEASURES OF ECONOMIC HEALTH

GDP and GNP are two of the most frequently used measures of output and income, but they have shortcomings that limit their value as measures of economic health and well-being.

Exclude Nonmarket Transactions

GDP and GNP measure the market values of final goods and services, which means products and services that are not traded and priced in open markets are excluded. As a result, the services of homemakers (e.g., child care, cooking, chauffeuring, and cleaning) and the numerous jobs we all do around the house (e.g., painting, performing home and auto repairs, landscaping, and calculating tax returns) are excluded. The problem is that all of these activities would be included if households had to hire someone to do them. As a result of these exclusions, the output of a nation can suffer some bizarre and outlandish distortions. For example, a nation's GDP falls whenever a resident marries his or her fitness trainer, golf instructor, accountant, or therapist.

> GDP and GNP exclude nonmarket transactions.

Exclude Black Market and Underground Transactions

Meaningful statistics on output and income are difficult to collect when a significant portion of a nation's population operates in the underground economy. The underground economy is made up of individuals who are employed but appear not to be because they report only part or none of their incomes. In many cases, the jobs these individuals take are legal, but their incomes are not reported to avoid paying taxes.[11] Jobs that lend themselves to such activities allow workers to be paid in cash (e.g., house cleaners, painters, plumbers, lawyers, and electricians) or involve goods or services that can be bartered (e.g., "I'll fix your car if you'll install my kitchen cabinets").

The underground economy is also populated by individuals who practice illegal occupations. Drug trafficking, prostitution, pimping, robbery, extortion, money laundering, and forgery are just a few examples of such occupations. Two common threads connect legal and illegal underground economy jobs. In both circumstances, a fair representation of income earned is not reported; also, people who are fully employed appear not to be. Therefore, the underground economy may give the illusion that a macroeconomic problem is more severe than it really is, causing the government or central bank to intervene when there is no need.

What is and is not counted in GDP can vary from country to country. For instance in September 2006, Greece changed its national income accounts to better measure the nation's rapidly growing service sector. As a result, segments of the underground economy, such as prostitution and money laundering, were suddenly included in Greece's GDP. In part, the change in national accounting practices was because Greece wanted to avoid violating the European Union's (EU) Stability and Growth Pact, which limited the budget deficits of member nations to 3% of GDP. Previously, Greece had been found guilty by Eurostat, the EU's statistical agency, of underestimating its budget deficits. Due to these changes, Greece's GDP increased by about 25%. If allowed, they enabled the nation to meet the EU deficit requirement (and avoid fines) without cutting government spending or increasing taxes.[12]

Do Not Properly Account for Quality Improvements

The quality of goods and services changes as time passes—usually for the better. In fact, quality improvements have been so dramatic (and price reductions so persistent) in some industries, such as electronics, communications, and pharmaceuticals, that many consumers intentionally postpone purchases to get better deals. For goods, such as computers, and services, such as surgical vision correction, a year can make a significant difference in terms of quality and cost. Unfortunately, quality improvements that neither raise a product's price nor increase the quantity sold are unmeasured and, therefore, excluded from GDP and GNP.

> **GDP and GNP exclude black market and underground transactions.**

> **GDP and GNP ignore quality improvements that do not result in price or quantity increases.**

---

[11] Even though these jobs are legal, falsifying income taxes is illegal.

[12] See Kerin Hope and George Parker, "Oldest Profession Helps Boost Greek National Output by 25%," *The Financial Times*, September 29, 2006, p. 1 http://www.ft.com/intl/cms/s/0/9c380e34-4f99-11db-9d85-0000779e2340.html (accessed October 29, 2012).

Do Not Account for Increased Leisure and Other Factors that Improve the Quality of Life

GDP and GNP measure output and income; they do not measure human well-being. If they did, they would account for the value of increased leisure time that most individuals have enjoyed over the past century. What is the value of having a few extra hours to read, exercise, meet with friends, practice a musical instrument, ski, or just sleep? In general, the average workweek has been declining for the past century. Leisure is something that people gladly purchase as their incomes rise.

In addition, GDP and GNP do not account for vast improvements that companies have made in workplace safety, air quality, sanitation, and noise levels. What would you pay to work in an environment where physical injury was not a worry and capricious, undisciplined behavior by managers was not a threat?

GDP and GNP do not account for improvements in the quality of life due to increased leisure.

Count Harmful and Dangerous Output the Same as Useful Output

Anything that has a price tag and is traded in an open market is included in GDP and GNP. This means that the costs associated with traffic accidents, natural disasters, terrorist attacks, wars, and environmental disasters increase GDP and GNP as much as the discovery and production of lifesaving medicines, safer automobiles, more efficient airplanes, and better health care services.

GDP and GNP count equally the monetary value of economic goods and economic bads.

LEAKAGES AND INJECTIONS APPROACH TO MACROECONOMIC EQUILIBRIUM

What is a macroeconomic leakage or injection? What are the various categories of leakages or injections? How are they related to macroeconomic equilibrium?

An Easy Way to Understand This Section

One of the easiest ways to understand macroeconomic leakages and injections is to visualize a nation's economy as a large inner tube with air circulating from top to bottom and bottom to top. This is no ordinary inner tube because the air in it represents the income earned by the household sector when it sells resources to the business sector (bottom flow) and revenues earned by the business sector when it sells products to the household sector (top flow). The more air, the greater the inner tube's pressure, just as more production and income circulating in a nation's circular flow mean greater GDP.

Macroeconomic leakages are like air escaping through valves in the top of the inner tube, and injections are like air being pumped right back into the tube through separate taps. If leakages of air exceed injections, pressure falls and the inner tube deflates. Similarly, if economic leakages exceed injections, production, incomes, and GDP fall. Let's take a more in-depth look at these relationships and explain why macroeconomic equilibrium is linked to the *desired* leakages and *desired* injections of a nation rather than the actual leakages and actual injections.

Macroeconomic Leakages

Any income that is not spent on domestically produced goods and services is called a *leakage* from the circular flow. These leakages are categorized into three areas: saving, taxes, and imports.

Income earned by the household sector that is not spent on domestically produced goods and services is a leakage from the circular flow.

Saving (S)

Saving (S) is what is left over after you deduct consumption expenditures and taxes from your income. Normally, consumption and taxes take only a portion of our incomes, so a nation's saving is positive. Saving is important for many reasons, but for now it is important because saving is a leakage or reduction from the potential demand for an economy's goods and services (see Exhibit 2-8).

Saving poses an interesting dilemma. The household sector earns only enough income each period to purchase the goods and services produced in that period. Therefore, if consumption were a nation's sole form of expenditure, then equilibrium could occur only if net saving was equal to zero. We know this because equilibrium requires the desired amount supplied (i.e., the goods and services willingly produced by the business sector) to equal desired amount demanded (i.e., the products willingly purchased by the household sector).

Most nations in the world have positive saving rates, so how is it possible for them ever to be in equilibrium? The answer to this question is easier to understand when we remember that consumption is not the only form of expenditure for domestically produced goods and services. There are three others: gross private domestic investment (I), government spending (G), and exports (EX).

TAXES (T)

Taxes (T) are leakages from the circular flow of expenditures because they are a portion of household income that is not spent on domestically produced goods and services. These funds go to the government, and the government may decide to spend more or less than the amount received. Remember that

EXHIBIT 2-8	LEAKAGES OF SAVING FROM THE CIRCULAR FLOW

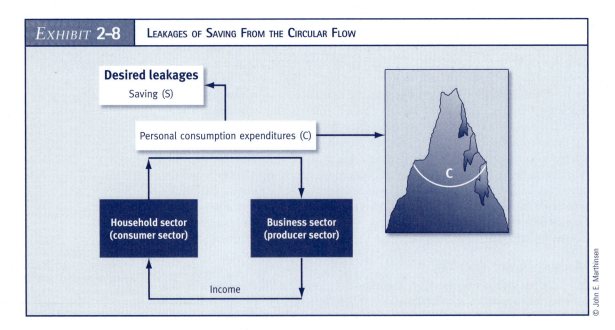

© John E. Marthinsen

MACRO MEMO   2-3

Saving versus Savings

Saving (no s at the end) is an economic *flow* concept because it *occurs over a period of time*. Savings (with an s at the end) is a *stock* concept because it is the value of all accumulated saving at *a given point in time*. An easy way to remember the difference is the s at the end of savings stands for "stock" concept.

there is no short-run need for governments to spend exactly what they earn in tax revenues. When governments spend more than they earn in taxes, they normally finance the deficit by borrowing—just like any business or individual would. When governments spend less than they earn in tax revenues, the surplus can be used to retire old debt.

IMPORTS (IM)

Imports (IM) are a leakage from the circular flow of expenditures because they involve spending on foreign-produced goods and services, rather than domestically produced products. In terms of our mountain of goods and services analogy, import expenditures do nothing to remove the goods and services produced domestically each period. Rather, they remove parts of foreign mountains of goods and services.

Exhibit 2-9 summarizes the three major types of macroeconomic leakages.

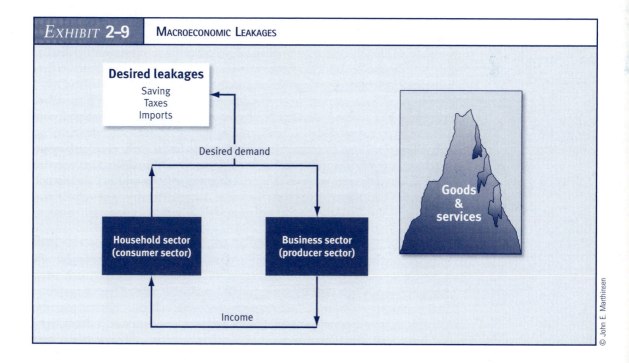

EXHIBIT 2-9   MACROECONOMIC LEAKAGES

Macroeconomic Injections

Macroeconomic leakages from the circular flow of national expenditures reduce the demand for the mountain of domestically produced goods and services, but that does not pose any major problems as long as there are ways for these leakages to be redirected back into the economy in the form of spending injections.

Fortunately, such demand has three major sources; in fact, we have already discussed them. The macroeconomic injections are gross private domestic investment (I), government spending (G), and exports (EX) (see Exhibit 2-10).

Macroeconomic Equilibrium II:

Desired Leakages = Desired Injections

There are two equally valid ways of defining macroeconomic equilibrium. The first one was already discussed: Equilibrium occurs when the desired amount demanded equals the desired amount supplied, which means that desired C, I, G, and NE are equal to the desired amount supplied.

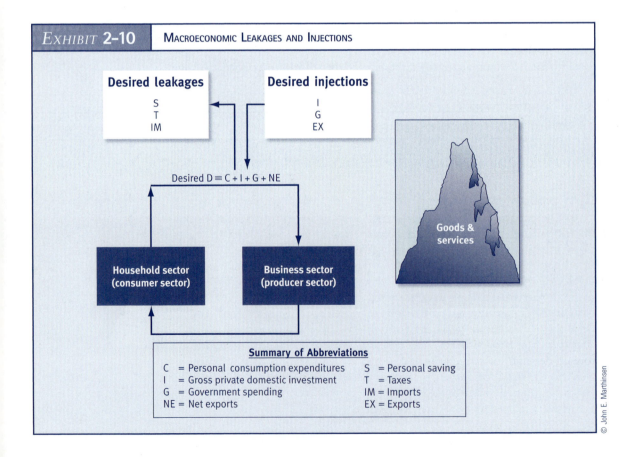

| Exhibit 2-10 | Macroeconomic Leakages and Injections |

Desired leakages

S
T
IM

Desired injections

I
G
EX

Desired D $\equiv$ C + I + G + NE

Household sector (consumer sector)

Business sector (producer sector)

Goods & services

Summary of Abbreviations

C = Personal consumption expenditures
I = Gross private domestic investment
G = Government spending
NE = Net exports

S = Personal saving
T = Taxes
IM = Imports
EX = Exports

© John E. Marthinsen

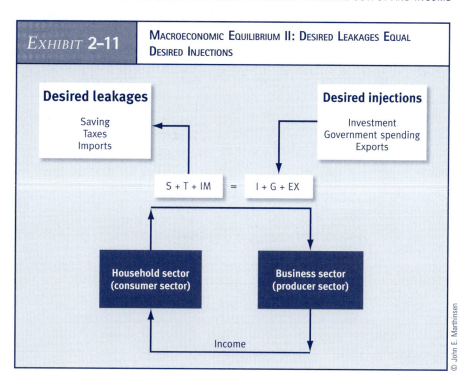

| EXHIBIT 2-11 | MACROECONOMIC EQUILIBRIUM II: DESIRED LEAKAGES EQUAL DESIRED INJECTIONS |

Desired leakages

Saving
Taxes
Imports

Desired injections

Investment
Government spending
Exports

$$S + T + IM \ = \ I + G + EX$$

**Household sector
(consumer sector)**

**Business sector
(producer sector)**

Income

© John E. Marthinsen

Macroeconomic equilibrium also occurs when *desired* leakages equal *desired* injections, which means that desired saving plus taxes plus imports are equal to desired investment plus government spending plus exports. In short, equilibrium occurs when desired:

$$S + T + IM = I + G + EX.$$

Notice how this second way of looking at equilibrium does not require desired saving to equal investment, taxes to equal government spending, or imports to equal exports. It requires only that the sum of the three leakages equal the sum of the three injections (see Exhibit 2-11).

> Macroeconomic equilibrium occurs when desired leakages equal desired injections.

USING DISEQUILIBRIUM IN THE CIRCULAR FLOW TO EXPLAIN RECESSIONS

Let's use the circular flow diagram to explain the economic implications of a recession. Suppose the business sector produced more than the economy demanded. This could occur for a variety of reasons, such as unexpected cuts in business investments, fluctuations in government spending, shifting foreign demand, or reductions in consumer spending due to the expectation (real or perceived) of declining economic activity. As a result, a cascading chain of economic actions and reactions would occur.

If national production exceeded the amount demanded, business inventories would rise (see Exhibit 2-12). Rising inventories would provide businesses with an incentive to lay off workers and/or to cut their hours of employment. As a result, unemployment and layoffs would rise.

EXHIBIT 2-12	USING THE CIRCULAR FLOW TO EXPLAIN A RECESSION (PART 1)

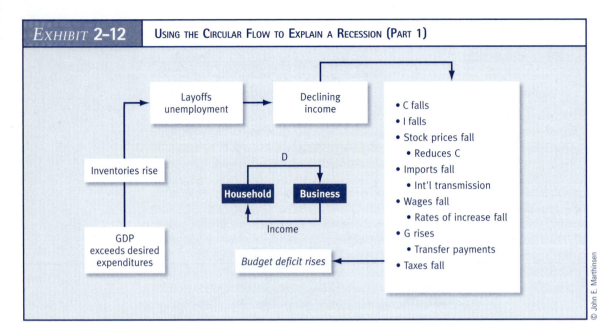

© John E. Marthinsen

If fewer resources were hired, then the household sector would earn less income, which would further erode the demand for goods and services. As consumption expenditures fell, business incentives to invest would diminish. The declining demand for goods and services and the added costs of carrying large inventories would hurt business profitability, causing businesses' stock prices to fall. Because stocks are a substantial part of the household sector's wealth, declining stock prices would provide consumers with yet another incentive to reduce their demands for goods and services.

The downward spiral in economic activity would not stop at the nation's borders. Declining income would cause the demand for foreign goods and services to fall, which would reduce foreign nations' exports and incomes. In this way, the domestic recession could be transmitted (exported) to foreign lands.

A falling economy would also affect wages. As workers lost their jobs, there would be downward pressure on wages. Even though absolute wage rates may not actually fall, they would be unlikely to rise quickly. If wages rose by less than the rate of inflation, then labor's real (i.e., inflation-adjusted) salary would fall, thereby cutting product demand even more.

At this point, it might seem that, when an economy turns sour, all the follow-on effects reinforce the downturn, but that is not true. Most nations have automatic stabilizers, which are passive changes in government transfers and taxes activated by expanding or contracting economic activity.

They are called "automatic" because the government does not have to pass special legislation for them to take effect, and they are called "stabilizers" because these changes in government transfers and taxation cushion economies from excessive expansions and plunging contractions. Automatic stabilizers function in much the same way shock absorbers cushion drivers from otherwise-bumpy rides.

For example, when economic activity declines, a nation's GDP falls and unemployment rate rises, thereby causing automatic increases in government transfer payments for unemployment compensation and social welfare programs. In a similar sense, when economic activity declines, the taxes collected by governments at all levels fall.[13]

Because transfer payments rise automatically and government taxes fall automatically during a recession, governments usually experience rising budget deficits when economic activity declines. These deficits do not actually push the economy forward. Rather, they prevent it from falling deeper into a recession. When government deficits are caused by the automatic stabilizers, they are called *passive deficits*.[14]

Other important economic actions and reactions occur during a recession. Exhibit 2-13 shows that when GDP exceeds expenditures and inventories rise, businesses often try to reduce their brim-filled warehouses by reducing prices or, at a minimum, by lowering their markups. As a result, a nation's inflation rate usually falls during a recession.

Not only are the prices of newly produced goods and services reduced, but also the prices of important assets, such as real estate (e.g., homes), apartment buildings, artworks, antiques, and precious metals, fall. As a

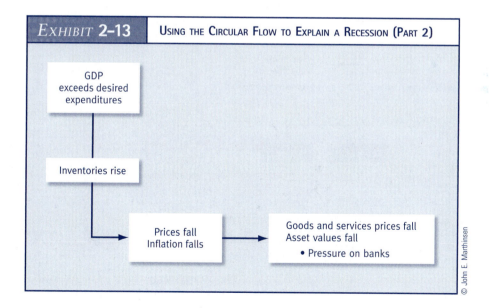

| EXHIBIT 2-13 | USING THE CIRCULAR FLOW TO EXPLAIN A RECESSION (PART 2) |

GDP exceeds desired expenditures

Inventories rise

Prices fall
Inflation falls

Goods and services prices fall
Asset values fall
• Pressure on banks

© John E. Marthinsen

---

[13] Imagine how harsh the world would be if wage earners were required to pay the same level of taxes regardless of how low their incomes fell and how inequitable it would be if their taxes remained the same regardless of how high their incomes rose.

[14] Chapter 13, "Fiscal Policy and Automatic Stabilizers: What Managers Need to Know," explains passive deficits and automatic stabilizers in greater detail.

result, household wealth declines, causing consumer spending to fall and the recession to worsen.

If the recession causes individuals to default on their mortgages—either because they cannot afford to make the payments or because their property values fall below the mortgage values—banks would be forced to take possession of these properties. Declining property values, as occurred in Japan and Thailand in the 1990s and the United States between 2007 and 2009, could put intense pressure on these banks because the foreclosed properties would have to be sold at substantially reduced prices. The losses associated with these sales could threaten banks' profitability, liquidity, and solvency.

Banks' equity is often small in relation to their total assets (e.g., 8% or less). Therefore, financial institutions might react to massive defaults by restricting credit to businesses at precisely the time when economic activity was souring. Credit could also be curtailed if the recession caused bank failures or inflicted serious losses on banks' interest-earning portfolios.

Exhibit 2-14 provides an overview of all the economic effects explained in this section.

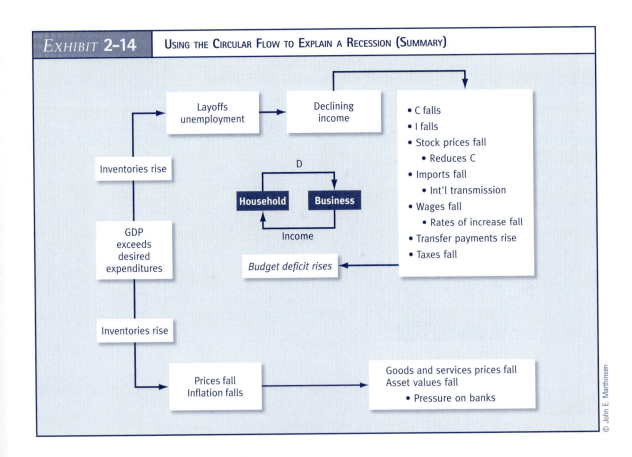

EXHIBIT 2-14   **USING THE CIRCULAR FLOW TO EXPLAIN A RECESSION (SUMMARY)**

© John E. Marthinsen

ANOTHER WAY TO DIFFERENTIATE GDP AND GNP

Earlier in this chapter, GDP and GNP were both defined as "output" and then differentiated by the resources used to create that output. This section shows that GDP and GNP can also be defined as "income" and then differentiated by who earns that income. This distinction is made easier by remembering a major lesson from our circular flow discussion, namely *what goes around the top portion of the circular flow diagram must come around the bottom portion.* In short, the value of output produced must equal the value of incomes earned.

Exhibit 2-15 helps clarify the difference between GDP and GNP by using Switzerland as an example. Notice on the left side of the exhibit that final output produced within Switzerland's national borders causes income payments to both Swiss-owned resources (Box A) and resources owned by the rest of the world (Box B). Together, the incomes earned from all newly produced (final) goods and services in Switzerland (i.e., Boxes A plus B) are equal to the nation's GDP:

$$GDP \equiv A + B.$$

Similarly, the incomes earned from newly produced (final) goods and services in the rest of the world are equal to the amounts earned by Swiss-owned resources that reside outside Switzerland (Box C) plus the incomes earned by resources owned by the rest of the world, which are outside Switzerland (Box D). Therefore, Switzerland's GNP is the sum of Box A (i.e., incomes

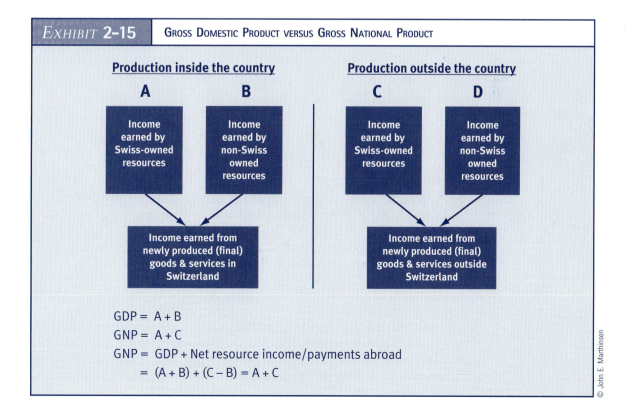

EXHIBIT 2-15   GROSS DOMESTIC PRODUCT VERSUS GROSS NATIONAL PRODUCT

Production inside the country

A   B

Income earned by Swiss-owned resources

Income earned by non-Swiss owned resources

Income earned from newly produced (final) goods & services in Switzerland

Production outside the country

C   D

Income earned by Swiss-owned resources

Income earned by non-Swiss owned resources

Income earned from newly produced (final) goods & services outside Switzerland

GDP = A + B
GNP = A + C
GNP = GDP + Net resource income/payments abroad
    = (A + B) + (C − B) = A + C

© John E. Marthinsen

earned from newly produced (final) output by Swiss-owned resources in Switzerland) plus Box C (i.e., incomes earned by newly produced (final) output produced by Swiss-owned resources that reside outside Switzerland):

$$GNP = A + C.$$

The net income that Switzerland earns from (or pays to) the rest of the world is equal to $C - B$. Box C is what Swiss-owned resources earn from the rest of the world, and Box B is what the Swiss pay to foreign-owned resources that reside in Switzerland. If Switzerland earns net income from the rest of the world, then $C - B$ is positive. If it pays net income to the rest of the world, then $C - B$ is negative.

$$NI_f = C - B, \text{ where } NI_f \text{ is net income earned from } (+)/$$
$$\text{paid to } (-) \text{ the rest of the world.}$$

Let's consolidate what we have learned. We know now that:

$$GDP \equiv A + B,$$

$$GNP \equiv A + C, \text{ and}$$

$$NI_f \equiv C - B.$$

Therefore,

$$GNP \equiv GDP + NI_f.$$

Because

$$(A + C) \equiv (A + B) + (C - B).$$

GNP equals GDP plus net income earned from (paid to) foreigners.

In short, GNP equals GDP plus the net income a nation earns from $(+)$ or pays to $(-)$ foreign nations.

CONCLUSION

GDP and GNP are important measures of economic activity. Both of them measure a nation's output and income, but they differ in one important way. GDP measures production (and the income associated with it) within a nation's borders. GNP measures the output (and the income associated with it) of a nation's resources, regardless of where they are in the world.

The circular flow diagram is a valuable tool for conceptualizing real and financial flows in an economy. It separates the economy into two parts: the business sector, which supplies goods and services and demands resources, and the household sector, which demands goods and services and supplies resources. Macroeconomic equilibrium requires that desired quantity supplied equals desired quantity demanded or, equivalently, that desired leakages from the circular flow of expenditures equal the desired injections.

REVIEW QUESTIONS

1. Distinguish between GNP and GDP. What is included, and what is excluded?

2. Klaus Trafobia owns East Street Garage and Car Sales. In 2013, he acquired a rundown 1998 Volvo station wagon for $1,500, which he intended to fix up and resell. What was the impact on the nation's GDP if Klaus refurbished the Volvo in 2013 and resold it for $5,000?

3. If Paula Ticks marries her gardener, will the nation's GDP rise, fall, or stay the same? Explain.

4. Is it accurate to say that, if there are more stages of production (i.e., more steps between the production of raw materials and the production of a final product), then GDP will be higher?

5. Many Turkish citizens work in the EU and send a portion of their paychecks back home each month. Assuming that Turkey is a net exporter of such labor, should Turkey's GNP be less than, equal to, or greater than its GDP?

6. Is it true that GDP is equal to GNP plus income from foreign sources minus income paid to foreigners? Explain.

7. If GDP is the market value of all final goods and services, then why are wages included in GDP? Is it double counting to include both wages and product prices?

8. Is it true that a nation's principal sources of demand/expenditures *must be* closely related to the components of income, or can they diverge substantially? Explain.

9. After each of the following items, indicate whether it is included in U.S. GDP as personal consumption (C), gross private domestic investment (I), government spending (G), net exports (NE), or not included (X). After each entry, give a brief explanation why you chose your answer.

   a. Foreign aid   _____

   b. Government welfare payments   _____

   c. Razors produced this year but unsold   _____

   d. The construction of a new home   _____

   e. IBM shares issued this year   _____

   f. Colgate shares issued last year and bought this year _____

   g. Stealth bomber research by the government   _____

   h. Apples used in Mrs. Smith's Apple Pies   _____

   i. Vitamins sold this year but produced last year   _____

   j. GM trucks sold to Mexico   _____

10. Which of the following economic variables are stock variables, and which are flow variables?

    GDP, GNP, saving, savings, wealth, investment, capital, money supply, exports, imports, government spending, consumption, income, earnings, assets, and liabilities

11. Is macroeconomic equilibrium good or bad for a nation, or does it depend?

12. Between 2000 and 2012, foreign direct investments in China were far greater than the direct investments that China made in other countries. Explain whether these flows caused China's GDP to be greater than, less than, or equal to its GNP.

13. Explain two ways to define macroeconomic equilibrium.

14. Suppose gross private domestic investment equals $100 billion, government spending equals $250 billion, *net* exports equal −$60 billion, saving equals $70 billion, and government taxes equal $230 billion. Is it true that there is macroeconomic disequilibrium, and the forces of supply and demand are causing business inventories to fall, inflation to rise, the government's budget deficit to fall, and net exports to rise?

15. Explain whether you agree or disagree with each italicized part of the following statement: If South Africa's gross private domestic investment plus government spending plus *net* exports is less than saving plus government taxes, then *GDP must be rising*, and *planned business inventories must be falling*.

16. What are the problems with GNP and GDP as measures of economic health?

DISCUSSION QUESTIONS

17. When a country has a net export surplus, what is it gaining, and what is it giving up? Explain.

18. How do improvements in product quality affect GDP? Explain.

19. "Macroeconomics tells us that, if the government does not balance its budget, and simultaneously the nation does not balance its exports and imports, then that nation cannot be in short-term macroeconomic equilibrium." Comment on the validity of this statement.

20. What are "net exports"? In macroeconomics, why does a nation's demand include net exports and not just "exports"?

Appendix 2-1
Shouldn't a Nation's Demand Include Only Exports? Why Do We Net Out Imports?

Why does demand include *net exports* (i.e., exports minus imports) and not *exports*, alone? After all, when we incorporate gross private domestic investment into demand, we don't net out saving. What follows is a rather technical answer to this beguiling question. Therefore, to make things simple, the short answer is this: Imports are subtracted from demand because they are already included in consumption, gross private domestic investment, and government spending. Subtracting imports from demand just removes spending that should not be included in GDP.

A second way to understand this relationship is to consider a country that imports components, increases their value (e.g., by processing, assembling, or adding value to them in some other way), and then exports the finished or semi-finished products. It would be a gross exaggeration to represent the entire value of these exported goods as the demand for this nation's domestically produced goods and services because only the value added was produced domestically.

Suppose this country imported $100 million worth of ingredients, processed them, and then exported $120 million of finished goods. The net demand for that country's goods and services would be only $20 million (i.e., $120 million worth of exports minus $100 million worth of imports), and the net earnings of the country from this activity would only be $20 million. Counting the entire $120 million as part of this nation's demand would inaccurately reflect the extent to which domestically produced goods and services were being purchased.

Let's start with a basic, but important fact. A nation's output can be purchased by domestic consumers, businesses, and governments, and it can also be purchased by foreigners. Let's abbreviate the domestic demand for a nation's goods and services as follows:

C_D = domestic consumers' purchases of domestically produced output;
I_D = domestic businesses' purchases of domestically produced output; and
G_D = domestic governments' purchases of domestically produced output.

Foreign purchases of a nation's output are not separated into consumer, business, and government categories. Rather, they are simply called "exports." Therefore, the foreign demand for a nation's goods and services is abbreviated as follows:

EX = exports of domestically produced output.

We can summarize what we have learned until now by the following relationship for demand:

$$D = C_D + I_D + G_D + EX.$$ **Equation 1**

Now that the components of demand have been identified, let's see how Equation 1 is equivalent to the equation we used in this chapter for demand—namely,

$$D = C + I + G + (EX - IM) = C + I + G + NE,$$

where IM is the abbreviation for imports.[15]

Until now, we have been concerned with how domestically produced output is purchased, so C, I, and G have had D subscripts to represent domestic consumers', businesses', and governments' purchases of a nation's goods and services. At the same time, we know that consumers purchase domestically produced goods and services as well as foreign-produced products. Therefore, we can abbreviate total consumption in the following way:

$$C = C_D + C_{IM},$$

where C is total consumption and C_{IM} is the import component of domestic consumption.

Similarly, domestic businesses and governments can purchase both domestically produced and foreign-produced goods and services; therefore, we can abbreviate these relationships as follows:

$$I = I_D + I_{IM},$$ where I is total investment and I_{IM} is the import component of gross private domestic investment;

$$G = G_D + G_{IM},$$ where G is total government spending and G_{IM} is the import component of government spending.

We can summarize these relationships as follows:

$$C + I + G = (C_D + C_{IM}) + (I_D + I_{IM}) + (G_D + G_{IM}).$$ **Equation 2**

But $C_{IM} + I_{IM} + G_{IM}$ is just another name for a nation's total imports (IM), so we can rearrange Equation 2 as follows:

$$C + I + G = (C_D + I_D + G_D) + (C_{IM} + I_{IM} + G_{IM}).$$

---

[15] *IM* is used as the abbreviation for imports because *I* is used to represent gross private domestic investment, and *M* will be used later in this book to represent money supply. To make the abbreviations for imports and exports somewhat consistent, *EX* is used to abbreviate exports rather than *E* or *X*.

Therefore,

$$C + I + G = (C_D + I_D + G_D) + IM,$$

which means that

$$(C_D + I_D + G_D) = C + I + G - IM. \qquad \textbf{Equation 3}$$

From Equation 1, we know that $D = (C_D + I_D + G_D) + EX$. Combining Equation 1 with Equation 3 gives us exactly the result we want—namely,

$$D = C + I + G + (EX - IM). \qquad \textbf{Equation 4}$$

Now that we have derived the economic relationship we wanted (i.e., Equation 4), let's prove that it is correct. From Equation 3, we know that

$$(C_D + I_D + G_D) = (C + I + G) - IM,$$

which can be rewritten as

$$(C + I + G) = (C_D + I_D + G_D) + IM.$$

Therefore, Equation 4 can be stated as

$$D = (C + I + G) + (EX - IM) = (C_D + I_D + G_D + IM) + (EX - IM). \quad \textbf{Equation 5}$$

Canceling imports from Equation 5 gives

$$D = (C_D + I_D + G_D + \cancel{IM}) + (EX - \cancel{IM}) = (C_D + I_D + G_D + EX),$$

which is identical to Equation 1.

Chapter 3

Understanding and Monitoring Labor Market Conditions

INTRODUCTION

Labor market conditions are important to a broad cross section of every nation. To policymakers, central bankers, and politicians, they provide critical feedback on the successes or failures of macroeconomic and social policies. To businesses, they offer valuable insights on labor cost projections, how difficult it will be to fill vacant positions, the chances that valued employees will leave in search of better opportunities elsewhere, and prospects that fiscal and monetary policies will be changed, thereby impacting key macroeconomic variables, such as interest, inflation, and exchange rates.

As important as labor market conditions are to governments and businesses, they are even more important to individuals. Policymakers and businesses can afford to treat unemployment rates as statistics, reflecting averages over large populations, but individuals cannot be so cavalier. Either they have jobs or they do not. A low or declining national unemployment rate may offer some peace of mind that employment prospects are just around the corner, but it is cold solace to those without jobs and experiencing depression-like conditions in their homes.

> Labor market conditions are important to governments, central banks, businesses, and individuals.

Labor market conditions are also important to individuals on an emotional level because jobs are so intimately tied to a person's identity and perception of belonging. Losing a job results in sacrificed income, but it can also reduce self-esteem, lower self-confidence, and cause considerable mental distress. For these reasons, numerous studies have shown high, positive correlations between a nation's unemployment rate and incidences of suicides, criminal offenses (e.g., homicides and robberies), alcoholism, drug addiction, heart attacks, and admissions to psychiatric hospitals.[1] This collateral damage reduces a nation's productivity and diminishes overall economic well-being to the same extent as the loss of output caused by fewer people working.

> Joblessness can reduce self-esteem, lower self-confidence, and cause mental distress.

A nation's labor market conditions are reflected in a variety of closely monitored economic statistics. Among the most visible are the employment and unemployment rates, but also closely watched are participation rates, wages and benefits earned, as well as labor force mobility and size. More granular

---

[1] To appreciate the breadth, depth, and number of these studies, readers are invited to conduct a brief Internet search using a search phrase such as "relationship between unemployment and suicides" or "relationship between unemployment and criminal offenses/alcoholism/drug addiction/heart attacks/admissions to psychiatric hospitals." The list is impressive even if the search is restricted only to those studies published during the past two years.

measures add body and meaning to overall labor market statistics, such as the average duration (i.e., length) of unemployment, number of discouraged workers, and the age, gender, and ethnic composition of the unemployed population. Large differences in unemployment based on gender or race are signals for concern, just as much as increases in the overall unemployment rate, but the policy solutions to these demographic problems can be quite different.

This chapter focuses on how to interpret a nation's labor market conditions through monthly economic statistics. Deciphering these indicators to make informed decisions requires an appreciation of how they are calculated, what they reveal, and what they mask. For instance, we will find that there are four different types of unemployment that are caused by and respond to different stimuli. Trying to cure them all with the same economic medicine might be a mistaken use of time and scarce resources.

THE BASICS

WHO USES UNEMPLOYMENT RATE INFORMATION?

Let's explore more deeply the business, government, and central bank uses of labor market statistics.

BUSINESS USES OF UNEMPLOYMENT STATISTICS

Unemployment rates have direct and significant effects on companies' profits and cash flows. On the cost side, falling unemployment rates put upward pressures on wages due to the reduced availability of skilled and unskilled workers. On the revenue side, falling unemployment rates usually go hand-in-hand with rising gross domestic product (GDP), increased demand, and greater sales growth.

> Labor market conditions are helpful for predicting costs of production and top-line sales growth.

For many companies, wages and salaries are among the most important (if not the most important) costs of production, and the compensation needed to attract and retain good talent is moored firmly to a nation's labor market conditions. Useful financial projections (e.g., for capital budgeting projects, annual budgets, business plans, new-product initiatives, and/or product line expansions) require thoughtful and realistic estimates of how rapidly labor costs will change over planning horizons. Credible unemployment forecasts can help to establish a basis for these business projections.

If the current unemployment rate was high and expected to rise, then companies might assume, for the purposes of planning, that there will be rather gentle and diffused upward pressures on wages. By contrast, if the current unemployment rate was low and expected to fall, then companies would be prudent to assume that labor costs will rise. Under these conditions, not only will it cost more to hire new talent, but the expense to retain existing employees will rise. In tight markets, service-oriented and technology-oriented businesses that require distinctive skills often find it especially difficult to match the availability of skilled employees with salaries that can attract them.

Expected changes in labor market conditions also have significant implications for companies' human resource policies. They influence decisions about whether and when to terminate or temporarily lay off employees, as well as recruitment choices concerning whether to hire permanent (with full benefits) or temporary help. Companies that need workers with relatively specialized skills must be especially sensitive to labor market conditions. To lose a key worker (especially to a competitor) can be like losing a patent, trade secret, or other valuable asset. Human resource directors must be especially cognizant of labor market fluctuations because they affect employee turnover, productivity, and loyalty. Accurate labor market information provides human resource directors with a clearer view of the pay scales and fringe benefits required to remain competitive.[2]

Labor market fluctuations affect employee turnover, productivity, and loyalty.

Chief financial officers and treasurers also use labor market conditions to make informed decisions about the current and expected financial needs of their companies. They determine how and when to fund expected liquidity deficiencies. Insufficient cash flows need to be covered by lines of credit, new debt and/or stock issues, or the sale of assets. Tapping these funding sources may take time, so early warning signals are needed for company operations to run smoothly. Similarly, labor market conditions affect decisions about how best to handle projected cash surpluses. Should these funds be retained and invested in the growing company, used to repurchase outstanding shares, or returned to shareholders in the form of dividends? Judicious planning takes time, and the more time a company has, the easier it is to make well-considered decisions.

Changing labor market conditions also have indirect effects on economic activity via their influence on government and central bank policies and the effect these policies (actual and anticipated) have on business expectations. For instance, as a nation's unemployment rate rises, governments and central banks often respond with expansionary fiscal policies (i.e., increasing government spending and/or reducing taxes) and expansionary monetary policies (i.e., increasing the money supply). These actions have direct and indirect effects on key macroeconomic variables, such as inflation, interest rates, and exchange rates, which can, in turn, affect a nation's GDP growth rate, living standards, and human well-being. Each of these macroeconomic variables enters directly into investment planning decisions because of its effect on business income and cash flows.

Changing labor market conditions have direct and indirect effects on economic activity via their influence on government decisions, central bank policies, and business expectations.

GOVERNMENT AND CENTRAL BANK USES OF UNEMPLOYMENT STATISTICS

Do changing unemployment rates affect state, local, and national elections? A common belief is that low and falling unemployment levels improve the odds that incumbents (both individuals and parties) will stay in office. As a result, providing an economic climate for job creation and employment is normally high on candidates' lists of reelection priorities.

---

[2] Many companies pay more for new recruits than they are willing to pay for current talent. This is most visible when workers leave their jobs, requiring their former companies to hire new employees. Being forced into the job market confronts these firms with workplace realities. Higher rates of worker turnover can increase costs, reduce productivity, diminish employee goodwill, and weaken loyalty. In effect, employee skills that companies pay to develop are lost when these employees exercise their right to find jobs with better pay, wider options, greater mobility, and/or more attractive benefits.

The unemployment rate and employment rate are among a nation's principal labor market measures. They are used frequently by the media and play important roles in economic, political, and social discussions. To react to these monthly statistics and their trends in constructive ways that meet the employment challenges of current and expected economic situations, politicians, central bankers, and businesses need to understand both the strengths and weaknesses of these economic indicators. It is also essential for this information to be accurate and timely because acting too quickly or slowly on faulty signals could be costly and destabilizing to a nation.

MEASURING EMPLOYMENT AND UNEMPLOYMENT

Measures of *employment* and *unemployment* are based on arbitrary definitions that navigate around some thorny, practical issues. Ultimately, they are used to separate individuals into one of three categories: Employed, Unemployed, or Not in the Labor Force. For most of us, a rising unemployment rate and falling employment rate signal worsening economic conditions, but how should we interpret these statistics when the unemployment rate and employment rate simultaneously rise? Correctly deciphering economic statistics requires an understanding of how they are constructed, which is the goal of this section.

WHO ARE THE EMPLOYED?

What does it mean to be officially categorized as *employed*? Is someone employed if she works only 20 hours a week but would like to work full-time? Could she work as little as an hour each week and still be considered employed? How does someone who works 80 hours each week figure into labor market statistics? Is he counted as having one or two jobs? How about those with multiple jobs? Do they count more than once? A useful guiding principle to answering these questions is to ask, "Do the individuals under consideration have *any* visible source of employment income?" If the answer is yes, then they are considered to be employed.

A surveyed individual is classified as employed if he or she has worked for *any number* of hours during the relevant survey period.[3] It makes no difference whether the work is for 1 hour or 80 hours, if the individual had one job or two, and no provision is made for those who work part-time but want full-time employment. Classifying individuals in this way could create the false impression that whoever works for at least one hour is no longer an economic problem, but keep in mind that policymakers have other statistics that attempt to unveil the degree of national underemployment. For example, statistics are collected on workers who are *marginally attached to the labor force*. Included in this category are *involuntary part-time workers* and *discouraged workers* (i.e., those who tried but have given up looking for jobs)—more about this later.

> The employed are those individuals who have worked for any number of hours during the relevant survey period.

---

[3] Individuals are also counted as *employed* if they were on paid leave, worked in their own businesses, professions, or farms, or worked without pay at least 15 hours in family businesses or farms.

WHO ARE THE UNEMPLOYED?

What does it mean to be unemployed? If the answer seems easy and trivial, then consider this: Does it make a difference to the unemployment statistics whether someone quits his job, is fired, or is laid off? How about when someone is out of work due to a strike, vacation, or when she is forced to remain home due to bad weather? To answer these questions, a helpful guiding principle is to ask, "In which circumstances is there a nationwide labor market problem?" In other words, what type of joblessness is a reflection of some broad-based economic malfunction and/or insufficient demand? What type of unemployment should be brought to the attention of macroeconomic policymakers, and, when it is, can the government make a positive difference?

Most countries have adopted the International Labor Organization's (ILO) recommendations for reporting unemployment statistics, or they have created internal rules that closely parallel the ILO standards. According to these standards, individuals are unemployed if they are (1) without a job, (2) available to work (e.g., not in a hospital, asylum, or prison), *and* (3) actively seeking employment.[4] Therefore, if someone loses her job and stops looking (or fails to look) for a new one, she is not counted in the official statistics as "unemployed"; rather, she is considered *Not in the Labor Force*.

> The unemployed are those individuals without a job, available to work, and actively seeking employment.

How about people who are taking vacations or out of work due to strikes or labor-management disputes? Vacationers are treated as employed because they are not considered to be a fundamental macroeconomic problem that policymakers can or should address. The same is true for individuals who are absent from work due to illness, bad weather, or personal reasons. They all are classified as employed.

As for strikers, they must be out of work for a considerable amount of time to be classified as *unemployed*. For instance, the U.S. unemployment survey is centered on the 12th day of each month, and most U.S. workers are paid on a weekly, biweekly, or monthly basis. A striker would be considered to be unemployed only if he/she worked no hours during the pay interval covering the 12th day of the month. For some workers, this interval could be as short as a week and, for others, as long as a month.

How about people who involuntarily lose their jobs as opposed to those who quit? Individuals become unemployed for a variety of reasons. Some are laid off due to falling demand, and many of them expect to be rehired as soon as conditions improve. Others have no such expectations. There are also workers who are dismissed for cause, usually with no expectation of being rehired by the same company, and still others who voluntarily terminate their employment by resigning or retiring. Finally, many unemployed individuals are new to the labor force or reentrants. In all of these cases, individuals are classified as unemployed only if they are without jobs, available, and actively seeking work.

---

[4] In the United States, unemployed individuals must have searched for jobs within the four weeks prior to and including the 12th day of the survey month. Laid off individuals who expect to be rehired need not search for new jobs to be counted as unemployed.

WHO IS IN THE LABOR FORCE, AND WHO IS NOT?

A nation's *labor force* is made up of two groups: individuals who are classified as employed and those who are classified as unemployed, available to work, and actively seeking employment. Anyone who is not in these two categories is classified as *Not in the Labor Force*. Students, homemakers, retirees, and discouraged workers are not in the labor force unless they are seeking employment.

> The labor force includes individuals who are employed and unemployed. All others are not in the labor force.

CALCULATING THE UNEMPLOYMENT AND EMPLOYMENT RATES

Monthly labor market surveys separate respondents in the civilian,[5] non-institutional[6] population into three major categories: (1) employed; (2) unemployed, available, and actively seeking work; or (3) not in the labor force (see Exhibit 3-1).[7] Suppose the number of people in these three categories is equal to 95 million, 5 million, and 50 million, respectively, which means the noninstitutional population 16 years of age and older is equal to 150 million (see Exhibit 3-1).

Calculating the Unemployment Rate

The unemployment rate is calculated by dividing the number of individuals who are unemployed, available, and actively seeking work by the total labor force.

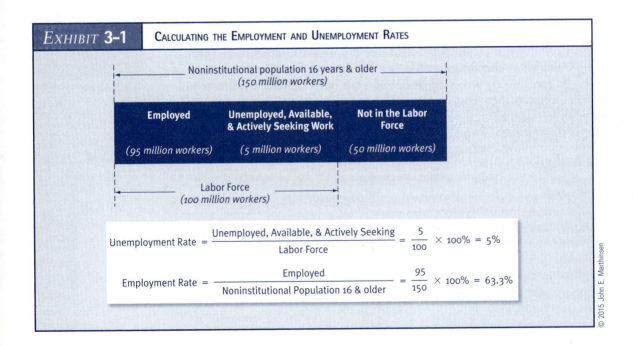

| EXHIBIT 3-1 | CALCULATING THE EMPLOYMENT AND UNEMPLOYMENT RATES |

Noninstitutional population 16 years & older
(150 million workers)

Employed	Unemployed, Available, & Actively Seeking Work	Not in the Labor Force
(95 million workers)	(5 million workers)	(50 million workers)

Labor Force
(100 million workers)

$$\text{Unemployment Rate} = \frac{\text{Unemployed, Available, \& Actively Seeking}}{\text{Labor Force}} = \frac{5}{100} \times 100\% = 5\%$$

$$\text{Employment Rate} = \frac{\text{Employed}}{\text{Noninstitutional Population 16 \& older}} = \frac{95}{150} \times 100\% = 63.3\%$$

© 2015 John E. Marthinsen

[5] *Civilian* means individuals who are not in the armed forces.
[6] *Noninstitutional* means individuals are outside institutions, such as hospitals, asylums, and prisons.
[7] Notice that U.S. unemployment statistics are *not* extracted from lists of individuals who qualify for unemployment insurance.

$$\text{Unemployment rate} = \frac{\text{Unemployed, Available, \& Actively Seeking Work}}{\text{Labor Force}}$$

If 5 million people meet these three criteria and the labor force equals 100 million, then the unemployment rate equals 5% (see Exhibit 3-1).

Calculating the Employment-to-Population Ratio (Employment Rate)

The employment-to-population ratio or *employment rate*, as it is also called, is calculated to broaden economic perspectives and avoid some of the problems (discussed later in the chapter) with the unemployment rate measure. This would be a nonsensical exercise if the employment rate were merely the complement of the unemployment rate (i.e., an unemployment rate of 5% meant an employment rate of 95%); fortunately, this is not the case.

The employment rate measures the number of people *employed* relative to the entire civilian noninstitutional population 16 years of age and older.

$$\text{Employment rate} = \frac{\text{Employed}}{\text{Noninstitutional Population 16 \& Older}}$$

Using the data from Exhibit 3-1, if the number of individuals employed is 95 million and the noninstitutional population 16 years of age and older is 150 million, then the employment rate equals 63.3% (see Exhibit 3-1).

Can the Unemployment and Employment Rates Rise and Fall Together?

More frequently than you might expect, the unemployment rate and the employment rate move in the same direction, thereby giving conflicting signals. For example, a rising unemployment rate indicates declining economic activity, but a rising employment rate indicates just the opposite. How is it possible for these two measures to move in the same direction? The answer is easier to understand if we use the information from Exhibit 3-1, which is replicated in Exhibit 3-2. Notice that the initial unemployment rate and employment rate are 5% and 63.3%, respectively.

Suppose two million people left the *Not in the Labor Force* category and entered the labor force. Suppose further that one million of them found jobs, and one million were unemployed, available, and actively seeking work. As Exhibit 3-2 shows, these shifts in composition of the noninstitutional population would raise the unemployment rate from 5% to 5.9% and raise the employment rate from 63.3% to 64%.

FOUR TYPES OF UNEMPLOYMENT

"If we can put a man on the moon, land a spaceship on Mars, and drive robotic vehicles over its surface, then why can't the government create 100% full employment?" Let's use this question as the basis for identifying four commonly cited types of unemployment: frictional, structural, seasonal, and cyclical unemployment. They will be useful for understanding why a 0% unemployment rate is not a national goal and why there is no single solution to the unemployment problem.

The unemployment rate equals the number of people unemployed, available, and actively seeking work divided by the labor force.

The employment rate equals the number of people employed divided by the civilian noninstitutional population 16 years of age and older.

The unemployment rate and the employment rate can (and occasionally do) move in the same direction.

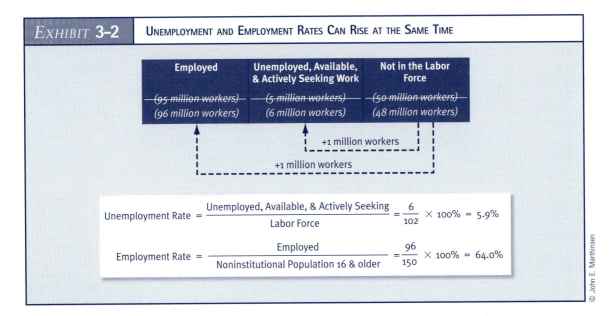

EXHIBIT 3-2 | **UNEMPLOYMENT AND EMPLOYMENT RATES CAN RISE AT THE SAME TIME**

Employed	Unemployed, Available, & Actively Seeking Work	Not in the Labor Force
~~(95 million workers)~~	~~(5 million workers)~~	~~(50 million workers)~~
(96 million workers)	(6 million workers)	(48 million workers)

+1 million workers

+1 million workers

$$\text{Unemployment Rate} = \frac{\text{Unemployed, Available, \& Actively Seeking}}{\text{Labor Force}} = \frac{6}{102} \times 100\% = 5.9\%$$

$$\text{Employment Rate} = \frac{\text{Employed}}{\text{Noninstitutional Population 16 \& older}} = \frac{96}{150} \times 100\% = 64.0\%$$

© John E. Marthinsen

FRICTIONAL UNEMPLOYMENT

In every nation, jobs are constantly being created and destroyed. As a result, people are continually moving from one job to another, seeking their first employment opportunities, and waiting for the best offer. While in transit and during their job searches, these individuals are classified as *unemployed*. This type of joblessness is called *frictional unemployment*.

Frictional unemployment is usually short term, and it is a natural byproduct of any dynamic economy where opportunities are persistently opening and closing. The wholesome churning of economic activity is a sort of silver lining to this type of joblessness. On the negative side, frictional unemployment is partly the consequence of imperfect information flows between job demanders (the unemployed) and job suppliers (businesses). Even if enough jobs were available, and even if these jobs matched exactly with the skills of the unemployed, it would take time for the companies to discover and interview potential job applicants and for unemployed workers to decide which offer they wished to take. Therefore, the size and duration of frictional unemployment are largely functions of the frequency of labor turnover and the speed of finding the best matches.

The frictional unemployment rate varies over time and from country to country because it depends on economic incentives, such as the level of unemployment compensation, as well as demographic and legal factors, such as labor market mobility, male and female participation rates, labor market entry and exit rates, labor union strength, real wage flexibility, the minimum wage, and lawful barriers to hiring and firing. For this reason, when nations estimate their normal levels of frictional unemployment or when international comparisons are made, calculations and comparisons should consider these differences.

> **Frictional unemployment is due to the normal creation and destruction of jobs in a healthy economy. It is not considered a macroeconomic problem.**

Unemployment compensation is a good example of a financial incentive that affects frictional unemployment. When an unemployed person is supported financially by unemployment compensation, the sacrifice (opportunity cost) associated with joblessness is blunted. Many analysts feel that generous unemployment compensation has a powerful effect on the length of time it takes such an individual to find a new job. They argue that the intensity with which an individual seeks a new job changes with both the financial and emotional costs of being jobless.

Because frictional unemployment is usually short term and its effects are beneficial, policymakers do not target a 0% rate. No economy, especially a growing one, would want the government to set a goal of having 100% of its labor force employed because such a policy would not allow for healthy job creation and destruction. Nevertheless, public policies, such as reforming unemployment insurance compensation, changing maternity leave policies, and reducing search costs by establishing job clearing houses, can affect people who are frictionally unemployed—especially in the long run. For these reasons, the frictional unemployment rate should not be viewed as an unchanging and unchangeable constant.

STRUCTURAL UNEMPLOYMENT

Structural unemployment is caused by a mismatch between the skills demanded by businesses and the talents supplied by unemployed workers. This mismatch could be due to factors such as technological advancements that leave workers with skills that are no longer demanded (e.g., film developers and travel agents), significant changes in resource prices (e.g., oil), swings in the composition of domestic demand, the shifting sands of international competition, lack of experience, educational mismatches, and geographic imbalances (e.g., high-growth versus low-growth regions). For instance, unemployed schoolteachers, who have been laid off because of local budget cuts or individuals who have lost their jobs due to low-cost foreign labor, may need months or years to acquire new skills (e.g., computer programming) and move to areas with growing businesses.

> Structural unemployment is due to the mismatch between job skills and job opportunities.

In 2008, factories producing automobile parts in Michigan were closing due to declining demand from the Great Recession. At the same time, the demand for workers with oil and gas skills was booming in North Dakota. One way to reduce the structural element of these mismatched local job markets would have been to publicize the availability of jobs in North Dakota, encourage the unemployed to move there, and help train these workers so they developed the skills needed to succeed.

Possible solutions to the structural unemployment problem should not be overestimated or underestimated. Clearly, significant increases in aggregate demand would sweep many structurally unemployed individuals into growing job markets as companies reach further into the applicant pool to fund training and internship programs.[8] In the absence of such demand, the solution to

[8] Paul Krugman, "Structure of Excuses," *The New York Times*, September 26, 2010, www.nytimes.com/2010/09/27/opinion/27krugman.html (accessed September 24, 2013).

structural unemployment lies in concerted efforts to reduce barriers to labor mobility through better educational opportunities, training, innovative ways of matching individuals' skills to jobs, informational job clearinghouses, and employment guidance.

Oftentimes, the possibility of finding a new job with equally attractive compensation, benefits, and advancement opportunities is almost nonexistent. Quite naturally, people are reluctant to accept reductions in their living standards. This reluctance reduces a nation's labor mobility, thereby raising its level of structural unemployment.

An unemployed nuclear engineer might not be interested in working at a fast-food restaurant. Not only would the wage be out of line with her skills, but also the opportunity for advancement and personal job gratification would be missing. The issue here is not whether an alternative job exists but whether the unemployed person's pay and job satisfaction criteria are met. One way in which governments have tried to address the structural unemployment problem is by creating job corps programs that teach new skills and by providing relocation expenses to unemployed workers who are willing to move from depressed areas.

In many nations, teenage unemployment tends to be much higher than the average of the overall labor force. This type of unemployment is structural in a demographic sense because many teens are just beginning to develop the skills and work habits that will make them valued and desired employees.

Seasonal Unemployment

Seasonal unemployment is caused by predictable, yearly changes in labor supply and demand due to factors such as weather, holidays, and school schedules. For instance, during the winter, construction workers lose their jobs because of inclement weather conditions, and each spring and summer the unemployment rate rises as college, university, and high school students leave school and seek summer jobs. Predictably, in spring, construction workers are reemployed, and during the fall, the mismatch between the supply and demand for school-age labor changes, as students return to their classrooms. Seasonal unemployment is not a serious macroeconomic problem, but it can account for significant portions of month-to-month changes in the unemployment rate, thereby wreaking havoc on a nation's unemployment statistics. For this reason, unemployment rates are often *seasonally adjusted* to take out the impact of these predictable changes and allow policymakers to identify and focus on the fundamental sources of unemployment.

> Seasonal unemployment is due to predictable, periodic changes in the supply and demand for labor.

Cyclical Unemployment

Cyclical unemployment is caused by recessions or slow economic growth. It is called *cyclical* because of the strong inverse relationship this type of unemployment has to changes in the business cycle. Robust economic growth reduces cyclical unemployment; recessions increase it. Even weak growth can raise the cyclical unemployment rate, if the number of individuals entering the labor force exceeds the number of new jobs created.

Cyclical unemployment is related directly to a deficiency in national demand; therefore, it is the type of joblessness that is of fundamental

EXHIBIT 3-3	SUMMARY OF UNEMPLOYMENT TYPES

Type of Unemployment	Source
Frictional	Caused by natural adjustments that occur in an economy as jobs are created and destroyed and as the labor force expands and contracts
Structural	Caused by a mismatch between job skills needed and those possessed by the unemployed
Seasonal	Caused by predictable changes in yearly unemployment conditions, such as weather conditions, harvest cycles, vacations, and holidays
Cyclical	Caused by slow or negative economic growth

© John E. Marthinsen

concern to macroeconomic policymakers (e.g., central bankers, elected leaders, and treasury ministers/secretaries). Governments and central banks can influence aggregate spending by changing fiscal and monetary policies, so their actions may have significant effects on this type of unemployment. When cyclical unemployment is zero, a nation is said to be at *full employment*.

It may seem as if full employment is a rather elusive goal that no country ever achieves, but that is a misconception. During the 1990s, when U.S. unemployment was below 5%, the nation was considered to be at full employment. Furthermore, even though other countries may define their full employment levels differently from the United States, during the past 30 years, some have reached full employment. Japan and Switzerland are just two examples of countries with unemployment rates (on occasion) low enough to be classified as fully employed.

Exhibit 3-3 summarizes the four types of unemployment discussed in this chapter.

Cyclical unemployment is due to insufficient demand, and it is considered to be a macroeconomic problem.

EMPLOYMENT RATE OR UNEMPLOYMENT RATE: WHICH IS A MORE ACCURATE MEASURE OF ECONOMIC HEALTH?

The employment and unemployment rates each have strengths and weaknesses. Careful analyses usually consider both of them when determining a nation's economic condition. In a very real sense, they complement each other. By simile, one can think of the employment rate as measuring the size of a donut, and the unemployment rate as measuring the size of the hole. This section reviews the major advantages, disadvantages, and common misperceptions about unemployment and employment rates.

COMMON MISPERCEPTIONS ABOUT THE UNEMPLOYMENT RATE

The unemployment rate is useful for interpreting economic performance, but it can be a deceiving statistic if misunderstood.

The Unemployment Rate Can Overstate Economic Hardship

Consider two households, the Wolfs and the Conaways, both of which have three family members. The Wolf household has only one income earner. By contrast, the Conaway household has three income earners: both spouses and a 20-year-old son, who lives at home. If the Conaways' son were fired, the unemployment rate would rise by the same amount as when the sole income earner in the Wolf family lost his job. Despite the fact that the level of economic hardship would be greater for the Wolfs than for the Conaways, the unemployment figures would not reflect this difference.

When there are multiple family income earners, the unemployment rate may overstate a nation's true level of economic hardship.

Understanding the contrasting economic situations of the Wolfs and the Conaways helps to explain one of the reasons caution should be taken when making direct comparisons between unemployment rates over time. For example, a majority of U.S. households today have multiple income earners, but the same could not be said for the 1950s, when relatively few U.S. households had more than one income earner.

Individuals who falsely report that they are *actively seeking work* cause the unemployment rate to overstate the true level of economic hardship.

A nation's unemployment rate could also be a poor measure of labor market conditions if a significant number of the unemployed falsely reported that they were actively seeking work, which would result in unemployment rates higher than they ought to be.[9] Overstating the true level of economic hardship could lead economic policymakers to conclude that expansionary policies were needed, when, in truth, the economy was not in any serious danger from recession.

The Unemployment Rate Can Understate Economic Hardship

The unemployment rate does not include individuals who have searched for work, been unsuccessful, and then, in frustration, stopped looking. *Discouraged workers* are individuals who would like jobs but have given up actively searching for them due to the lack of realistic prospects.[10] These individuals are not included in a nation's workforce and, therefore, not counted as *unemployed*.

Discouraged workers are not considered unemployed, causing the unemployment rate to underestimate the level of economic hardship.

Anyone estimating future labor market trends should consider discouraged workers as a potential source of labor market supply. When an economy recovers and/or the possibility of securing employment improves, discouraged workers often reenter the workforce, thereby putting downward pressure on labor costs (or moderating their rate of increase). To the extent that the group of discouraged individuals is a significant portion of the jobless population, the unemployment rate will *underestimate* a nation's true level of macroeconomic hardship.

---

[9] Some unemployed individuals may falsely indicate that they are actively seeking work to qualify for unemployment benefits or because they are embarrassed to admit that they are neither working nor looking.

[10] In the United States, *discouraged workers* are individuals who are unemployed, are available for work, and have searched for a job during the past 12 months but have given up looking because they believe either no jobs exist or jobs are not available for individuals with their skills. See U.S. Department of Labor, Bureau of Labor Statistics, *BLS Glossary*, www.bls.gov/bls/glossary.htm#D (accessed September 24, 2013).

The Unemployment Rate Lags Economic Activity

The unemployment rate tends to lag significant turning points in economic activity. When a nation slides into a recession, company managers often cut employees' hours before they release, lay off, or fire them. Therefore, the unemployment rate does not rise immediately after a recession begins. Managers are reluctant to let employees go because recessions can last for very short periods, and losing talented workers is expensive. When demand recovers, hiring and training inexperienced workers can cause costs per unit to rise and productivity to fall. On the plus side, downturns provide opportunities for managers to prune low-productivity workers from their workforces and not rehire them when the economy recovers.

At the onset of an expansion, businesses often increase the hours of their existing workforces before they hire new talent. As a result, the unemployment rate does not fall when economic recoveries begin. By avoiding additional expenses, such as health care and other benefits for new workers, managers can keep down their operating and nonoperating costs, thereby increasing productivity as output rises.

The unemployment rate is usually a better measure of past economic performance than it is of current or future conditions. Moreover, the unemployment rate is not as useful as other indicators (e.g., the employment rate) for measuring business cycle movements. Nevertheless, by following unemployment trends over time, we can get a better understanding of a nation's overall level of economic performance.

> The unemployment rate is a lagging economic indicator.

COMMON MISPERCEPTIONS ABOUT THE EMPLOYMENT RATE

Like the unemployment rate, the employment rate is often misinterpreted.

Involuntary part-time workers

The employment rate overstates the health of a nation because it counts part-time workers as *employed*, regardless of whether they are seeking full-time jobs or more hours. It is worthwhile remembering that individuals are counted as *employed* if they work for only one hour during the relevant survey period.

> Counting part-time workers as *employed* causes the unemployment rate to understate the true level of economic hardship.

Underemployment The employment rate does not account for individuals who are working below their physical or mental capabilities. Possession of an income-paying job is all that is needed to qualify as employed. Without any consideration for underemployed individuals, nations have no measure of lost opportunities—opportunities to improve economic well-being and to develop human resource skills.

> The employment rate masks underemployment and, therefore, the underutilization of a nation's labor resources.

Underemployed workers have jobs that require skills and/or experiences that do not make full use of their talents. For instance, part-time workers who would like full-time jobs are underemployed, as are waiters with Ph.D.s and doctors who drive taxicabs for a living.

Because they receive paychecks, underemployed workers are considered by labor market statistics to be *employed*. Consequently, nations that seem to be benefiting from strong employment rates could actually be suffering considerable losses due to *underemployment*. As a nation's underemployment rate rises, economic growth slows and living standards fall progressively behind where they should be.

For businesses that are interested in projecting labor market conditions, such as future wages and/or the availability of workers, underemployment masks a potential source of supply. Because they earn less than their skills are worth (or less than these workers feel their skills are worth), underemployed workers continue to search for more suitable jobs. Due to their willingness to change employment quickly when opportunities arise, underemployed workers put downward pressure on wages, particularly in certain areas.

Strengths of the Employment Rate

Despite its problems, the employment rate is considered one of the best indicators of a nation's current macroeconomic conditions. In the United States, it is one of the four main indicators used to date business cycle expansions and contractions.[11] Not only does the employment rate provide direct, contemporaneous information on overall labor conditions, it has been shown to be one of the most timely, significant, reliable, and consistent macroeconomic variables available.

For purposes of taking the pulse of a nation's labor market, the employment rate has some significant advantages over the unemployment rate. For instance, the number of people employed is more stable and easier to determine than the number of people unemployed, available, and actively seeking work. This is especially true in nations where an individual's employment status can be cross-checked by his/her income tax returns. Therefore, the employment rate tends to have fewer sampling errors, which improves its quality relative to the unemployment rate.

Another reason why unemployment may be relatively difficult to accurately measure is because it is based on whether someone is *actively seeking work*. Due to the relatively broad definition of *actively seeking work*, the unemployment rate can be affected by shifts in the status of individuals between *unemployed and actively seeking work* and *not in the labor force*.

What exactly does *actively seeking work* mean? In the United States, to be actively seeking work, an individual must fulfill any one of the following criteria: (1) placing or answering employment advertisements, having job interviews, or contacting prospective employers; (2) checking union or professional registers; (3) contacting employment agencies (private or public); (4) asking friends or relatives about job opportunities; (5) inquiring with school or university job centers; or (6) writing letters of application. One wonders how reliable a statistic can be if all one has to do to qualify as *actively seeking work* is check occasionally with friends and relatives.[12] At the same time,

> The *employed* are easier to identify than the group of individuals who are *unemployed, available, and actively seeking work.*

---

[11] U.S. business cycles are dated by the National Bureau of Economic Research (NBER). Besides the employment rate, the NBER uses three other monthly indicators: real (i.e., inflation-adjusted) personal income less transfer payments, volume of real sales of the manufacturing and trade sectors, and industrial production. Of the four measures, the employment rate is considered to be the broadest and best.

[12] Bureau of Labor Statistics, *Frequently Asked Questions*, http://www.bls.gov/dolfaq/blsfaqtoc.htm (accessed September 24, 2013).

strong and weak social networking linkages can have powerful positive results.

Final Comments on Interpreting Unemployment and Employment Rates

It is relatively easy to find flaws in any macroeconomic measure. Clearly, all the criticisms mentioned in this chapter are well known by labor economists around the world, but often they are not well understood by politicians and the general public. The challenge is not to find fault but rather to fully understand the limitations of our economic indicators and develop better measures that reveal critical labor market information at a reasonable cost. Many nations have already developed useful supplementary labor market measures, such as the number of discouraged and part-time workers, families with multiple income earners, as well as unemployment rates differentiated by age, gender, geographic location, and duration. Voters, politicians, and business managers all make decisions based on their perceptions, and unless they understand the nuances of labor market measures, such as the employment and unemployment rates, they could easily make poorly considered choices.

THE REST OF THE STORY

FULL EMPLOYMENT AND THE NATURAL RATE OF UNEMPLOYMENT

It may be disconcerting to learn that countries around the world define *full employment* differently, but it is also heartening to know that these differences are usually reasonable and logical. Each country has its own socioeconomic and institutional idiosyncrasies, and these differences influence its unemployment rate. As a result, reaching a 3% unemployment rate may be far easier (i.e., with far less sacrifice) for one nation than it is for another country.

What is given up when a nation strives for full employment? Often, the cost of lower unemployment is higher inflation. Therefore, the *natural rate of unemployment* is defined as the unemployment rate that allows a nation to sustain its current level of inflation. In other words, at this rate of unemployment, inflation has no inherent tendency to rise or fall. For this reason, the natural rate of unemployment is often called the *nonaccelerating inflation rate of unemployment* (NAIRU), but it may, more accurately, be called the *nonincreasing inflation rate of unemployment* (NIIRU) because the rate of acceleration is not really the point.[13] These names buttress the strong link that exists among the unemployment rate, stable inflation, and the full-employment goals.

> Another name for the natural rate of unemployment is the nonaccelerating inflation rate of unemployment (NAIRU) or nonincreasing inflation rate of unemployment (NIIRU).

---

[13] Joseph Stiglitz, Reflections on the Natural Rate Hypothesis, *Journal of Economic Perspectives*, Volume 11, Number 1, Winter 1997, pp. 3–10. In Chapter 21, "Causes of Long-Term Growth and Inflation," we will find NAIRU/NIIRU occurs where a nation's actual inflation rate equals its expected inflation rate. In a sense, the natural rate of unemployment is like a huge economic magnet that has the long-term effect of pulling a nation back in the direction of NAIRU/NIIRU.

In general, the natural rate of unemployment tends to be lower in countries that have less generous social welfare payments, greater degrees of labor mobility, higher worker participation rates, lower minimum wages, weaker unions, and more flexible real wage rates. Because these factors vary from country to country, each nation can have a different natural rate of unemployment. Similarly, because these factors change over time, natural rates of unemployment change with them. Therefore, the full employment goals of nations fluctuate over time.

The natural rate of unemployment varies among nations and over time because of social, economic, and institutional differences and changes.

OTHER LABOR MARKET MEASURES

Even though the unemployment rate and the employment rate are the most popular measures of labor market conditions, they are not the only ones used by policymakers, businesses, and individuals. Other key gauges are the level of labor market participation, length of time it takes unemployed workers to find new jobs, and unemployment composition.

LABOR FORCE PARTICIPATION RATE

The labor force participation rate is equal to a nation's labor force as a percent of its noninstitutional population 16 years of age and older (see Exhibit 3-4). This indicator provides information on the portion of a nation's working-age population that is willing, available, and able to work.

In general, labor participation rates in the United States experienced dramatic increases between 1960 and 2000, rising from about 59% to 67% (see Exhibit 3-5). Thereafter to 2013, it fell. The increase was heavily influenced by demographic changes, such as increases in female participation rates

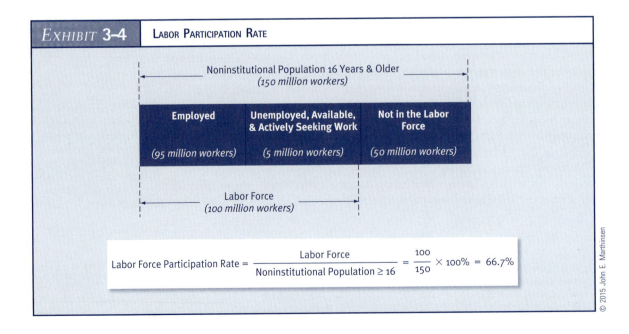

EXHIBIT 3-4   LABOR PARTICIPATION RATE

Noninstitutional Population 16 Years & Older (150 million workers)

Employed	Unemployed, Available, & Actively Seeking Work	Not in the Labor Force
(95 million workers)	(5 million workers)	(50 million workers)

Labor Force (100 million workers)

$$\text{Labor Force Participation Rate} = \frac{\text{Labor Force}}{\text{Noninstitutional Population} \geq 16} = \frac{100}{150} \times 100\% = 66.7\%$$

© 2015 John E. Marthinsen

| EXHIBIT 3-5 | U.S. LABOR FORCE PARTICIPATION RATE: OVERALL, MEN, AND WOMEN: JANUARY 1961 TO APRIL 2013 |

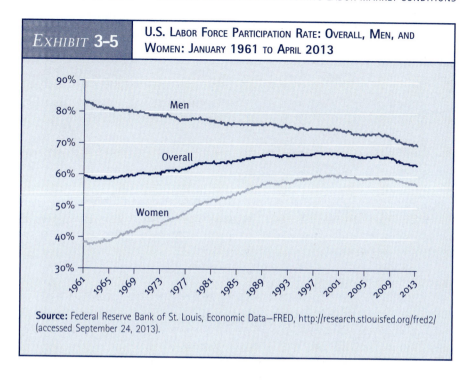

Source: Federal Reserve Bank of St. Louis, Economic Data—FRED, http://research.stlouisfed.org/fred2/ (accessed September 24, 2013).

(i.e., the proliferation of families with multiple income earners) and strong economic growth. Between the early 1960s and 2000, female participation rates rose from about 38% to 60%, while participation rates among men declined from 83% in 1960 to about 75% in 2000. After 2007, the fall in labor participation was heavily influenced by the financial crisis and its effects on the labor market.

UNEMPLOYMENT DURATION

A lengthening time lag between when individuals lose their jobs and find new ones is a prominent signal of deteriorating labor market conditions.[14] Exhibit 3-6 shows that, between 1970 and 2013, the average (mean) unemployment duration for the United States varied between about 9 weeks and 41 weeks, which is a sizeable difference. Clearly, the longer it takes to find a job, the more precarious and weak labor market conditions are.

> Unemployment duration (i.e., the length of time needed to find a new job) is another prominent measure of labor market conditions.

UNEMPLOYMENT COMPOSITION

Focusing on average unemployment rates is useful for anyone interested in monitoring a nation's macroeconomic problems, but this statistic hides important differences in the composition of the unemployed. For example, Exhibit 3-7 shows how widely the April 2013 U.S. unemployment rate varied among

---

[14]This point was addressed in our discussion of frictional unemployment.

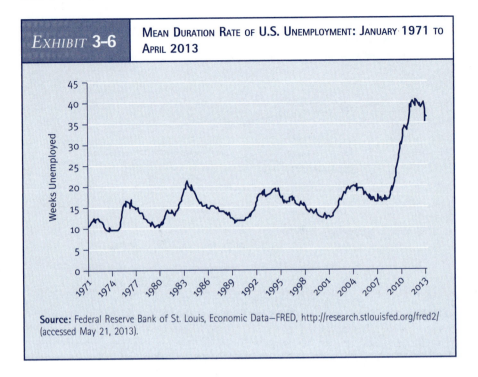

EXHIBIT **3-6**   MEAN DURATION RATE OF U.S. UNEMPLOYMENT: JANUARY 1971 TO APRIL 2013

Source: Federal Reserve Bank of St. Louis, Economic Data—FRED, http://research.stlouisfed.org/fred2/ (accessed May 21, 2013).

EXHIBIT **3-7**	UNEMPLOYMENT BY DEMOGRAPHIC CHARACTERISTIC: APRIL 2013
Category	**Rate**
White	
Overall	6.7%
Men 20 & older	6.4%
Women 20 & older	5.7%
Teenagers (16 to 19)	21.8%
Black or African American	
Overall	13.2%
Men 20 & older	12.6%
Women 20 & older	11.6%
Teenagers (16 to 19)	40.5%

Source: Bureau of Labor Statistics, http://www.bls.gov/webapps/legacy/cpsatab2.htm (accessed May 21, 2013).

different demographic groups. The unemployment rate among white men, 20 years of age and older (6.4%), was 6.2% lower than the rate for comparably aged black or African American men (12.6%). Similarly, white women, 20 years of age and older (5.7%), had an unemployment rate 5.9% lower than the rate for black or African American women of a similar age (11.6%). Finally, the unemployment rate for white teenagers (21.8%)[15] was more than three times the rate of white individuals 20 years of age and older (6.7%), but 18.7% below the rate for black or African American teens (40.5%).

> Many differences in the composition of a nation's unemployment rate can be traced to factors related to race, ethnicity, and gender.

GLOBAL LABOR CONDITIONS

Labor market conditions vary considerably around the world. This section briefly explores some of these differences.

GLOBAL UNEMPLOYMENT RATES

Exhibit 3-8 shows the unemployment rates for selected nations in 2011. Particularly striking was the more than twofold difference between Switzerland's unemployment rate (3.8%) and those of its relatively close neighbors Italy (8.5%), France (9.7%), and Poland (9.7%), as well as the nearly sixfold difference between the unemployment rates in Switzerland and Spain (21.7%).

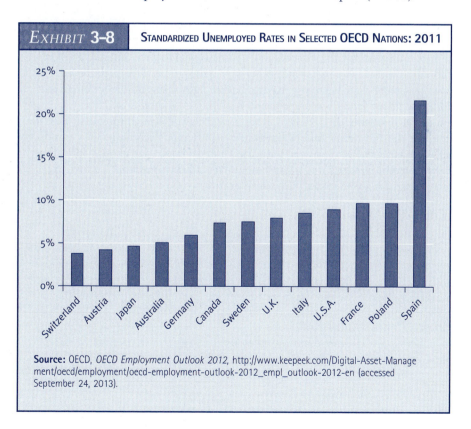

EXHIBIT 3-8 | STANDARDIZED UNEMPLOYED RATES IN SELECTED OECD NATIONS: 2011

Source: OECD, *OECD Employment Outlook 2012*, http://www.keepeek.com/Digital-Asset-Management/oecd/employment/oecd-employment-outlook-2012_empl_outlook-2012-en (accessed September 24, 2013).

---

[15] Teens in this context are 16 to 19 years old.

Why are there such large differences in unemployment rates from nation to nation or from region to region (e.g., the European Union versus North America)? There is no single cause. Rather, the sources of these dissimilarities can be traced to demographic, structural, and macroeconomic factors, such as differences in the degree of labor market mobility, wage flexibility, and economic growth rates.

The national unemployment figures reported by one nation are not always equivalent to those reported elsewhere; thus, one must be very careful not to draw hasty and improper conclusions when comparing one country's labor market conditions to another's. Oftentimes, it is like comparing apples and oranges. Japan is a good example. From 1990 to 2012, Japan's real GDP grew, on average, at a tepid rate, but its unemployment rate remained substantially lower than many other developed nations. How could that be?

Part of the answer can be traced to culture. Many Japanese women work in temporary jobs, and when economic activity slows or declines, they voluntarily leave the workforce. These jobless women are not considered to be "unemployed" because they are not actively seeking work. This cultural trait offers Japanese employers greater operational flexibility, and it provides men with more employment opportunities and better job security.

Another reason for Japan's relatively low unemployment rate is the social stigma tied to being unemployed. Consequently, many Japanese companies cut the hours of their employees rather than fire them.[16] Because part-time workers are classified as "employed" and because Japan's workforce employs large numbers of part-time workers, the nation's low unemployment rate is actually an illusion. Economic reality is not what it appears to be when viewed through the lens of the unemployment rate. Therefore, to draw meaningful international comparisons, adjustments for Japan's strong cultural idiosyncrasies should be made.

India is another good example of how a nation's unemployment rate may not give the full dimension of economic well-being. Because India's standard of living is significantly lower than the United States, one cannot infer that equal unemployment rates mean equal levels hardship. Other demographic factors must also be taken into consideration.

GLOBAL EMPLOYMENT RATES

Employment rates can also vary considerably from country to country. Exhibit 3-9 shows the employment rates in 2011 for 14 major countries, ranging from Turkey, with the lowest employment rate of 48.4% to Switzerland with a 79.3% employment rate. The average of all 14 countries (66.1%) was marginally below the employment rate in the United States (66.6%).

GLOBAL PARTICIPATION RATES

In general, global participation rates tend to mirror variations in the employment rates of nations (compare Exhibit 3-9 with Exhibit 3-10).

---

[16]See U.S. Department of Labor, Bureau of Labor Statistics, Foreign Labor Statistics, *Frequently Asked Questions,* http://www.bls.gov/fls/flsfaqs.htm#japaneseunemployment (accessed September 24, 2013). Also see Constance Sorrentino, "International Unemployment Rates: How Comparable Are They?" *Monthly Labor Review,* June 2000, 3–20.

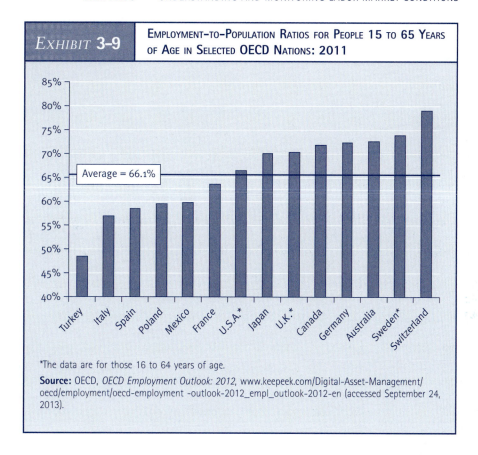

| EXHIBIT 3-9 | EMPLOYMENT-TO-POPULATION RATIOS FOR PEOPLE 15 TO 65 YEARS OF AGE IN SELECTED OECD NATIONS: 2011 |

Average = 66.1%

*The data are for those 16 to 64 years of age.

Source: OECD, *OECD Employment Outlook: 2012*, www.keepeek.com/Digital-Asset-Management/oecd/employment/oecd-employment -outlook-2012_empl_outlook-2012-en (accessed September 24, 2013).

The higher a nation's labor force participation rate, the greater is its potential output. Exhibit 3-10 shows that the U.S. labor force participation rate in 2011 (73%) was significantly lower than countries such as Switzerland (83%), Sweden (80%), and Canada (78%), but at the same time it was considerably higher than rates in Italy (62%), Turkey (64%), Poland (66%), and Mexico (68%). The leading causes of differences in labor force participation rates among nations are variations in economic incentives, cultural norms, expectations, and religious beliefs—especially regarding the role that women should play in the workforce. Not only do labor force participation rates differ by nation, they vary over time and by demographic characteristics, too, such as ethnicity, age, education, gender, and financial background.

THE UNDERGROUND ECONOMY AND UNEMPLOYMENT

The underground economy can be divided into a shadow economy and black market economy. The difference is that the activities included in one are legal, and the activities included in the other are illegal. Their commonalities are that both are hidden, neither pays its fair share of taxes, and both distort a nation's true unemployment statistics. The shadow economy includes people doing

> The underground economy can be divided into shadow (legal) and black market (illegal) economies.

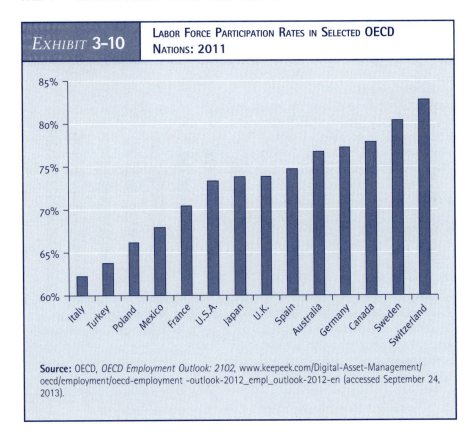

Exhibit **3-10**	**Labor Force Participation Rates in Selected OECD Nations: 2011**

Source: OECD, *OECD Employment Outlook: 2102*, www.keepeek.com/Digital-Asset-Management/oecd/employment/oecd-employment -outlook-2012_empl_outlook-2012-en (accessed September 24, 2013).

perfectly legal jobs (e.g., carpenters, painters, taxi drivers, tutors, cleaners, and bar owners) who either underreport or fail to report their incomes. In some professions, payments in cash can be quickly pocketed and not reported to the government for tax purposes, or goods and services can be bartered to avoid paying taxes. Small- and medium-sized companies, especially in the construction, hospitality, restaurant, retail, transportation, and wholesale industries, are particularly active in the shadow economy.[17] By contrast, the black market is composed of individuals engaged in illegal activities (e.g., drug trade, extortion, smuggling, fraud, and prostitution), who do not report their true incomes and employment status for fear of imprisonment or fines.

Black market and shadow economy transactions prevent accurate calculations of employment statistics because individuals, who have jobs, claim to

---

[17] Friedrich Schneider and A.T. Kearney, "The Shadow Economy, 2013," VISA Europe, Johannes Kepler University Linz, http://www.visaeurope.com/en/about_us/corporate_responsibility/idoc.ashx?docid=c982eb5e -2e26-49ad-acc9-5c01145f2064&version=-1 (accessed June 3, 2013). Friedrich Schneider, "Size and Development of the Shadow Economy of 31 European Countries and 5 Other Countries from 2003 to 2011," September 2011; "The Shadow Economy, 2011: Using Electronic Payment Systems to Combat the Shadow Economy," VISA Europe, Johannes Kepler University Linz, http://media.hotnews.ro/media_server1 /document-2011-05-8-8602539-0-shadeceurope31-sept2010-revisedversion.pdf (accessed June 3, 2013).

be unemployed and actively seeking work. As a result, there is the illusion of greater macroeconomic problems than actually exist—or the problems lie elsewhere.

The underground economy blurs and obfuscates meaningful labor statistics because its workers are relatively cheap, accounting for them is off-the-books, and labor laws regarding employment conditions and workers' rights are frequently violated. Therefore, companies participating in the underground economy (e.g., sweatshops, construction sites, and farms) have unfair cost advantages over those companies that do not use it. Not only do underground-based companies offer lower-than-market wages, but they also avoid paying benefit expenses, such as retirement, health insurance, and Social Security contributions. As a result, legal, open-economy jobs may be lost to the underground economy, causing the nation's reported unemployment rate to rise.

> The underground economy obscures meaningful labor statistics.

The underground economy is not included in GDP, but estimates show that it would account for at least 10% of the U.S. economy and, possibly, as much as 25% or more. Of these jobs, about 25% are estimated to be illegal.[18] As flagrant and widespread as the underground economy is in the United States, it is likely to be even larger in other countries. For example, Europe's (legal) shadow market has been estimated between 8% of GDP in Switzerland and 30% or more of GDP in Bulgaria, Croatia, Estonia, and Lithuania. While France, Germany, and Italy have small shadow economies compared to many neighbors, they accounted for 40% of Europe's €2.2 trillion shadow economy in 2011 due to their relative size.[19]

In general, the more efficient a nation is at identifying individuals who earn incomes and collecting taxes from them, the smaller its underground economy. Underground transactions most often occur when cash is used and the risk of detection is low. Therefore, one way to reduce this market's size and growth is to make transactions easier to trace by encouraging electronic (noncash) payments. Mexico, Poland, and South Korea have subsidized the use of electronic payment terminals, which significantly increased their use.

> Efficient income identification and tax collection can reduce the underground economy.

More forceful measures are also available, such as conducting tax audits and onsite inspections to verify workers' employment status, requiring identification cards for certain occupations, and imposing penalties on companies violating employment laws. Countries such as Italy, Poland, Portugal, and Spain have enacted laws that heavily penalize companies engaged in underground activities. These penalties range from outright fines to the loss of government subsidies to forced repayment of past subsidies to business closures

---

[18] Bruce Wiegand, *Off the Books: A Theory and Critique of the Underground Economy, Reynolds Series in Sociology* (Lanham, MD: Rowman & Littlefield, 1992); Owen Lippert and Michael Walker, *The Underground Economy: Global Evidence of Its Size and Impact* (Vancouver: Fraser Institute, 1997).

[19] Ibid., p. 3., Renzo Oris, Davide Raggi, and Francesco Turino, "Estimating the Size of the Underground Economy: A DSGE Approach," *Quaderni DSE Working Paper No. 818,* March 12, 2012, SSRN, http://papers.ssrn.com/sol3/papers.cfm?abstract_id=2021261 (accessed September 24, 2013). Michael Pickardt and Jordi Sardà, Size and Causes of the Underground Economy in Spain: A Correction of the Record and New Evidence from the MCDR Approach, Econstor, January 2012, www.econstor.eu/dspace/handle/10419/55038 (accessed September 24, 2013).

(permanent or temporary). Italy's punitive measures in this area raised an estimated €9.1 billion in extra tax revenues during 2009.[20]

Finally, an alternative approach to solving the underground economy problem is to induce these activities out of darkness and into sunlight. This might be done by simplifying and lowering taxes (e.g., value added and income taxes), providing benefits and cutting red tape for small businesses, and providing incentives to shadow market participants who fess up to their proper tax obligations. If successful, these measures would broaden the tax bases of nations and improve the accuracy of their unemployment statistics.

OFFSHORING AND ITS EFFECT ON GDP, UNEMPLOYMENT, AND INCOME DISTRIBUTION

Rising unemployment rates often turn the eyes of politicians and disgruntled workers to foreign countries, whose imports are believed to be taking jobs from domestic residents. Similar concerns are raised about outsourcing jobs to foreign nations. Do cheap foreign labor rates cause significant job losses in nations such as the United States? Opinions vary widely, but evidence and logic seem to indicate that outsourcing to foreign nations has done more to redistribute income than it has to increase unemployment rates and/or reduce GDP.[21] In large part, this is because, today, many jobs are in service sectors and, therefore, require direct customer-to-business contact.[22] The delivery of most medical treatments, day care, and hospitality services are just a few examples of jobs that must be close to the consumer for them to be supplied effectively.

OUTSOURCING VERSUS OFFSHORING

A good place to begin this discussion is to distinguish between outsourcing and offshoring. *Outsourcing* is a generic term, which refers to the act of delegating company responsibilities to external vendors. These responsibilities might be operational (e.g., component production and procurement) or nonoperational (e.g., back-office administration, programming, call center operations, and portfolio management). The external vendors can be domestic-owned or foreign-owned companies.

> "Outsourcing" means delegating company responsibilities to external vendors.

---

[20] Friedrich Schneider and A.T. Kearney, Ibid., p. 6.

[21] A U.S. Labor Department study found that only 2.5% of the lost jobs were caused by outsourcing to foreign countries. During the first quarter of 2004, only 4,633 jobs were lost to foreign outsourcing, which was small in comparison with the 147 million workers in the U.S. labor force. By contrast, domestic outsourcing and firm relocation accounted for double the number of job losses as foreign outsourcing. See Christopher Swann, "Offshoring Fails to Make Its Mark on Jobless Total," *Financial Times*, June 11, 2004, 1. Also see Christopher Swann, "Offshoring Linked to 2.5% of Lost Jobs—U.S. Employment Data," *Financial Times*, June 11, 2004, 8. Sharon P. Brown and Lewis B. Siegel, "Mass Layoff Data Indicate Outsourcing and Offshoring Work," *Monthly Labor Review*, August 2005, 3–10.

[22] In 2012, just 14% of all *private* (nongovernment) U.S. jobs were in the goods-producing sector; 86% were in the service-providing sector. See Bureau of Labor Statistics, Table B-6. Employment of production and nonsupervisory employees on private nonfarm payrolls by industry sector, seasonally adjusted(1), http://www.bls.gov/news.release/empsit.t22.htm (accessed September 24, 2013).

When these operational or nonoperational responsibilities are handled by companies located in foreign nations, the activity is called *offshoring*, which is the focus of this section. The foreign companies hired to do outsourced activities may be domestically owned or foreign-owned. They may even be affiliates or subsidiaries of the domestic companies purchasing the offshored products or services. As a result, offshoring is not necessarily transacted with "external" firms. The common denominator is that companies doing the offshored work are located in foreign countries.[23]

Companies have been outsourcing for decades. It never seemed to be a particularly contentious or sensitive issue when jobs from one part of the country were outsourced to other parts of the same country because job losses were perceived as an "us versus us" issue. This perception changed with offshoring because jobs were thought to be lost to foreign nations. That made it an "us versus them" issue, raising concerns about unfair trade practices, artificially low foreign wages, managed exchange rates, and uneven rules with regard to environmental standards, labor conditions, and human rights. Strong opinions exist in countries, such as the United States, that offshoring has exported jobs to countries such as China, India, and the Philippines.

Economic Forces Driving Outsourcing and Offshoring

Outsourcing and offshoring provide obvious benefits to consumers who can purchase higher-quality products at lower prices. Businesses also benefit from lower costs and higher profits, many of which flow to shareholders via more attractive dividends and capital gains.

Companies that engage in outsourcing and offshoring activities do so for a variety of good reasons. Not only do they increase operating and pricing flexibility by transforming fixed into variable costs, but outsourcing and offshoring also help businesses improve quality, speed process cycles, and permit access to wider and deeper pools of resources, talents, and skills.

Offshoring has been encouraged by global deregulation, reductions in international trade barriers, greater world-wide competition, and risk mitigation strategies based on diversification. During the 1980s and 1990s, reductions in transportation costs and international trade barriers led to the growth of offshoring in manufacturing, which caused the loss or displacement of many blue-collar jobs. The more recent wave of offshoring has been prompted by advances in information and communication technologies (e.g., fiber optics, computers, and the Internet) and has caused the loss or displacement of many white-collar jobs.

The aforementioned improvements in transportation and communication technologies have enabled companies to fragment their production processes and outsource/offshore activities that were once thought to be untradeable. They have allowed businesses to focus on areas of core competence and

> Outsourcing to foreign nations is called "offshoring."

> Outsourcing and off-shoring are popular because they improve business profits.

> Global deregulation, lower trade barriers, greater competition, and better diversification are forces behind offshoring.

[23] For example in the IT services area, firms such as Accenture offshore certain aspects of their solutions portfolio and managed services to take advantage of lower labor costs in foreign countries, such as the Philippines. The work is done offshore, but the human resources are still Accenture employees.

offload the rest. Jobs that previously could not have been done conveniently or profitably abroad, such as call centers and diagnostic labs, have found their way to foreign shores.

Offshoring Is a Revolving Door

The same forces that have spawned offshoring have also made it a revolving door, as companies in developing nations now find it increasingly advantageous to locate certain activities (e.g., corporate headquarters) in developed nations with better infrastructures. More generally, countries that complain about offshoring's negative effect on domestic employment often forget that they are also the recipients of the offshoring activities of foreign nations. For instance, many Japanese companies have constructed automobile and electronics manufacturing sites across the United States. Therefore, it is the *net* loss (or gain) of jobs that matters most.

Does Offshoring Reduce a Nation's GDP?

Is offshoring bad for a nation? A 2010 survey conducted by NBC News and the *Wall Street Journal* found that 86% of Americans believed that offshoring was the main cause of the nation's economic problems.[24] Let's take a closer look at the net effect offshoring has on a nation's GDP, unemployment rate, and income distribution. We will find that the answers are not as obvious as they might first appear.

An example will help to show why. Suppose that offshoring resulted in loss of 100,000 U.S. jobs to China, and suppose further the losses were traced to a large wage differential; the displaced U.S. workers were earning annual salaries equal to $60,000, and the employed Chinese workers earned only $5,000 per year.

By losing 100,000 jobs, U.S. GDP would fall by $6 billion.[25] Some of the unemployed (unfortunately, relatively few) would soon find new jobs at higher salaries. Others (again, relatively few) would never find new jobs. The most likely scenario is for the vast majority to find new jobs but at substantially lower salaries. Let's trace the consequences.

If the national unemployment rate were 7%, then we might expect 93% of the unemployed workers to find new jobs. To make our example more conservative, let's err on the negative side and assume that only 90% of them find new jobs, and the jobs they find earn only half their previous wages (i.e., $30,000). Firing 100,000 workers earning $60,000 per year would reduce U.S. GDP by $6 billion, but rehiring 90% of them at annual wages equal to $30,000 would partially offset the loss by $2.7 billion, resulting in a net decrease in U.S. GDP by $3.3 billion.

At this point, it may seem as if the case against offshoring was opened and closed, but we must also consider the effects offshoring has on business

---

[24] The Story So Far: Offshoring Has Brought Huge Benefits, But at a Heavy Political Price, *The Economist Magazine*, January 19, 2013, http://www.economist.com/news/special-report/21569574-offshoring-has -brought-huge-economic-benefits-heavy-political-price-story-so (accessed May 24, 2013).

[25] Remember that the income approach to calculating GDP sums wages, interest, rent, and profits.

profits. Offshoring reduced U.S. business costs substantially. Instead of paying 100,000 workers $60,000 per year, businesses were able to import these goods or services, paying foreign workers only $5,000 per year, which amounts to $0.5 million for the 100,000 workers. As a result, business costs fell from $6 billion to $0.5 million—a net saving of $5.5 billion. Combining offshoring's effects on workers and businesses produces an interesting result: U.S. wages fell by $3.3 billion, but profits rose by $5.5 billion, resulting in a net increase in GDP by $2.2 billion.

It is clear from this exercise that its conclusion rests on the assumptions made. Could offshoring have caused GDP to fall? What would it have taken to turn the tables? If we concentrate only on the percent of unemployed workers who found jobs paying (on average) $30,000 a year, then 83% of those who lost their jobs would have to remain unemployed to offset the gains to businesses. This result is highly unlikely on two grounds. First, there is no reason to believe that offshore-displaced workers should have an unemployment rate disproportionately higher than the national average. Second, countries such as the United States have central banks and governments that use expansionary monetary and fiscal policies to reduce swelling unemployment rates. If offshoring caused the unemployment rate to rise, actions would be taken.

DOES OFFSHORING REDISTRIBUTE NATIONAL INCOME?

Even if offshoring does not reduce a nation's GDP, it has the potential to significantly redistribute incomes from labor to business. A progressive tax system could help to smooth potential problems, but it is also important to keep in mind that higher business profits flow to individuals from all walks of life because of the many pension fund and household investments made in company shares.

> Offshoring seems to have its greatest effect on income redistribution.

TRANSITION COSTS OF OFFSHORING

It is easy to be analytical and objective when discussing the loss of someone else's job and reduction in someone else's quality of life. While offshoring may provide significant long-term benefits, it is disruptive in the short run and can negatively affect the lives of many families. Short-term transition costs must also be considered. Along with the loss of wages and benefits (e.g., health insurance and pensions), there can be an erosion of skills and, for many, a loss of self-worth. For those young enough to change careers, there are retraining and relocation costs. For governments, there are additional transfer payments to finance social welfare programs, such as food stamps and unemployment compensation. For communities, tax bases erode, thereby limiting the services they can provide, such as the teachers they can hire.

> Offshoring can have high transactions costs.

OFFSHORING IS A TWO-WAY STREET

If outsourcing is an inevitable part of the cost reduction process, then offshoring is an inevitable part of globalization. Outsourcing and offshoring enable companies to produce cheaper and better products and to penetrate and exploit their market potential, which is why they do it—most of them with the blessings of their shareholders. Offshoring is not an irrevocable decision. If foreign suppliers fail to deliver on their side of the bargain (e.g., to produce at lower costs and/or higher quality), then companies can and will respond by changing course. This could involve moving production and/or services to new foreign locations or bringing them back home, which is called *reshoring*.[26]

"Reshoring" means bringing offshored jobs back home.

Indeed, many companies have decided to reshore their production and service activities. Culture clashes are often cited as major causes, but perhaps more important are the ways companies have reacted to communication and coordination problems, apprehensions about reduced flexibility, the loss of cost controls and predictability, quality concerns, weak contract enforceability, and perceived disrespect for basic property rights, especially intellectual property, such as patents, copyrights, and trade secrets. Some companies have noticed and regretted the erosion of in-house knowledge, and others have felt the heat of negative backlashes from domestic governments, shareholders, and unions for the effects offshoring had (or was felt to have had) on domestic employment, community services, and worker conditions.

THE FUTURE OF OFFSHORING

In the future, offshoring will be transformed by economic and political forces in developed and developing nations. As it grows, relative international incomes, prices, and exchange rates will adjust to choke off some or all of the incentives to offshore. In fact, this has been happening for some years now in countries, such as China and India, where wage increases have far outpaced those in the United States and Western Europe. Social issues must also be considered. As nations develop, residents will expect better living conditions, including those that extend beyond their salaries. They will want reasonable social lives and time to spend with friends and family. Time zone differences (e.g., between New York and Mumbai) force many outsource workers (especially in customer service centers and call centers) to work late evening shifts. Such hours can put considerable stress on their family lives. As a result, companies providing outsourced services often suffer from high attrition rates, low morale, and disappointing productivity. Increasing demand and strong competition are also reducing the margins of companies that offer offshore services.

One alternative to outsourcing is protectionism (e.g., tariffs, quotas, and exchange controls), but protectionism is contrary to more than 200 years of economic logic and experience. Protectionism can definitely postpone job losses in the short run, but it is unlikely to prevent them indefinitely. Only by producing affordable, quality products can a country ensure that jobs will remain at home.

CONCLUSION

In the outsourcing/offshoring debate, it is important to remember that international trade is not a zero-sum game; there does not have to be a loser for

---

[26] Special Report: Outsourcing and Offshoring, *The Economist Magazine*, January 19, 2013.

every winner. It is equally important to remember that outsourcing/offshoring is disruptive, which means winners and losers are inevitable. Consumers are clear winners, but some businesses lose while others gain. As a result, decisions should be based on net gains or net losses and not on the existence or possibility of any losses. At the same time, these net gains and losses should be weighted by the ethical standards each nation sets for itself.

U.S. LABOR MARKET ISSUES

CASE STUDY: CALCULATING U.S. LABOR MARKET CONDITIONS

The Bureau of Labor Statistics (BLS) calculates the U.S. unemployment rate from monthly data in the Current Population Survey (CPS), which is conducted by the U.S. Bureau of the Census and covers 60,000 members of the civilian, noninstitutional population aged 16 years and older. The method used by the BLS is similar to the one used in many other nations (e.g., Canada, Mexico, Australia, Japan, and members of the European Union).[27]

Exhibit 3-11 summarizes the historical data for the United States in April 2013. Of a total population equal to 316.8 million people, 245.2 million were in the civilian labor force, which meant 71.6 million were children, soldiers, and institutionalized individuals (e.g., prison inmates). Of the civilian noninstitutional population, 155.3 million individuals were in the labor force and 89.9 million were not in the labor force. Finally, of the 155.3 million individuals in the U.S. labor force, 143.6 million were employed and 11.7 million were unemployed, available, and actively seeking work. As a result, the U.S. unemployment rate and employment rates in April 2013 were 7.5% and 58.6%, respectively (see Exhibit 3-11).

Exhibits 3-12 and 3-13 show the unemployment and employment rates, respectively, for the United States between 1960 and 2013. It is clear from Exhibit 3-12 that the U.S. unemployment in October 2009 (10%), which was just after the Great Recession, was very high but not the worst since 1960. In 1982, it reached 10.8%. Even though the unemployment rate was above the desired level in April 2013, it was trending downward, which was a positive factor for the Obama administration. As for the U.S. employment rate, Exhibit 3-13 shows that it had fallen precipitously from 2008 and was significantly below rates that once exceeded 64%. Nevertheless, this rate seemed to be leveling, which was a positive factor for the incumbent president.

HOW HEALTHY ARE U.S. LABOR CONDITIONS? THE ANSWER MAY DEPEND ON WHO YOU ASK[28]

Are labor conditions improving or worsening? The answer to this question may depend on who you ask. The U.S. Census Bureau conducts two monthly labor surveys for the BLS. One is the *Current Population Survey* (CPS), which

---

[27] For statistics and descriptions of U.S. labor market conditions, visit www.bls.gov. For international comparisons, the most popular BLS web page is http://data.bls.gov/cgi-bin/surveymost?ln.

[28] Bureau of Labor Statistics, Employment Situation Technical Note, www.bls.gov/news.release/empsit.tn.htm (accessed September 24, 2013).

EXHIBIT 3-11	U.S. UNEMPLOYMENT AND EMPLOYMENT CONDITIONS: APRIL 2013

Total Population 316.8			
Civilian Noninstitutional Population (≥16) 245.2			Children, Soldiers, & Inmates 71.6
Labor Force 155.3		Not in the Labor Force 89.9	
Employed Part-time Full time 143.6	Unemployed 11.7	Not actively seeking work (87.6) Marginally attached to the labor force (2.3) • Discouraged (0.8) • Other (looked w/i last 12 months) (1.5)	

$$\text{Unemployment Rate} = \frac{\text{Unemployed, Available, \& Actively Seeking}}{\text{Labor Force}} = \frac{11.7}{143.6 + 11.7} \times 100\% = 7.5\%$$

$$\text{Employment Rate} = \frac{\text{Employed}}{\text{Noninstitutional Population} \geq 16} = \frac{143.6}{245.2} \times 100\% = 58.6\%$$

Source: Bureau of Labor Statistics, Employment Situation Summary, http://www.bls.gov/cps/ (accessed May 21, 2013).

EXHIBIT 3-12	U.S. CIVILIAN UNEMPLOYMENT RATE: JANUARY 1961 TO APRIL 2013

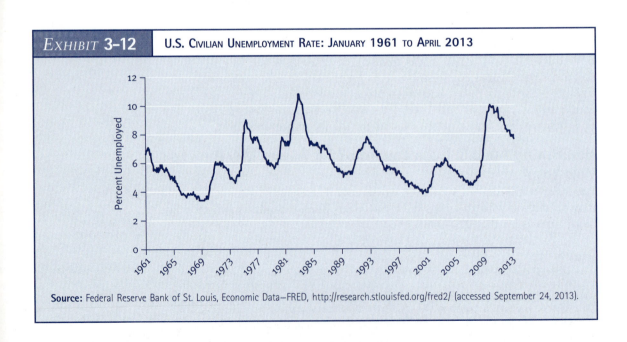

Source: Federal Reserve Bank of St. Louis, Economic Data—FRED, http://research.stlouisfed.org/fred2/ (accessed September 24, 2013).

EXHIBIT 3-13	U.S. EMPLOYMENT RATE: JANUARY 1961 TO APRIL 2013

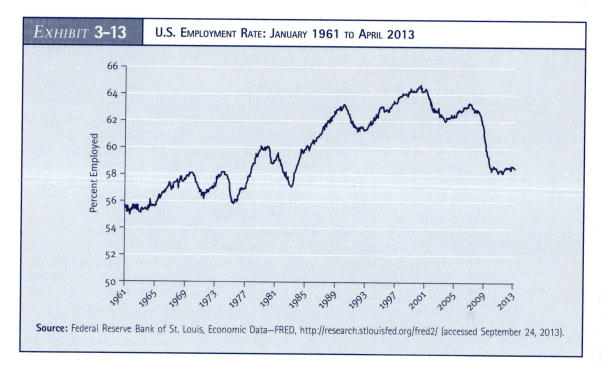

Source: Federal Reserve Bank of St. Louis, Economic Data—FRED, http://research.stlouisfed.org/fred2/ (accessed September 24, 2013).

is also called the *Household Survey*, and the other is the *Current Employment Statistics Survey* (CES), which is also called the *Establishment Survey*. The *Household Survey* (CPS) interviews about 60,000 eligible households, which are selected to reflect the entire civilian noninstitutional population in the United States. From these interviews, BLS determines the U.S. labor force, employment, and unemployment statistics.

The *Establishment Survey* (CES) interviews approximately 141,000 businesses and government agencies from a database of about 486,000 different worksites. From its interviews, CES determines U.S. employment, hours worked, and (nonfarm) earnings. Basically, the difference between the two surveys is that the *Household Survey (CPS) asks people* whether they have jobs, and the *Establishment Survey (CES) asks companies* (manufacturing and service) and government entities how many workers they employ.

Some technical and conceptual differences between CPS and CES can cause their results to differ. Among them are the sample periods (i.e., the reference week within the month surveyed), seasonal adjustments, people on unpaid leave (CPS counts them as employed and CES does not), and individuals under 16 years of age (CES counts them, while CPS includes only workers 16 years of age and older), but the major reason for differences between CPS and CES is who the surveys interview.

CPS counts as employed self-employed individuals, unpaid workers in family businesses or private households, and workers in the agricultural sector. These people are not counted in the *Establishment Survey*. By contrast, CES interviews private nonfarm businesses (factories, offices, and stores), as

> The major reason for differences between CPS and CES is who the surveys interview.

well as federal, state, and local government entities. Therefore, individuals who have two jobs and work in two different places can be counted twice by CES. Because CPS randomly samples individuals, it eliminates this double-counting problem.

A potentially serious (nonsampling) problem with the *Establishment Survey* is its limited ability to make timely and accurate determinations of job growth in new businesses. CES's database includes only *established* entities. Because this database does not include newly opened (seedling) companies, the beneficial employment effects from entrepreneurial start-ups may not be captured by CES. To remedy this systematic underestimation of employment, BLS adjusts the *Establishment Survey* results with a statistical estimation procedure constructed to account for company deaths and births. By contrast, the *Household Survey* samples individuals (not businesses), making it more likely to identify the beneficial employment effects of embryonic companies.

Domestic outsourcing is another area that might cause CPS and CES survey results to diverge. In an effort to cut costs, industrial companies are increasingly outsourcing support services, such as maintenance, food service, information technology, and accounting. When they do, they often use small, independent service companies. As a result, jobs that were previously classified as "manufacturing" become classified as "services," even though these new jobs are exactly the same as the old ones. Established companies that are losing jobs (either due to outsourcing or failure) are likely to be part of the CES database; therefore, CES picks up these lost jobs quickly. But the jobs gained by independent, start-up enterprises are not included in the CES sample set until sometime later or until remedied by estimation procedures. Therefore, CES may give the impression that the U.S. manufacturing sector is being gutted of jobs, when it is not, and it may give the impression that U.S. unemployment is rising, when it is not. CPS interviews individuals and not companies; therefore, the chances of this error occurring are less. People with outsourced jobs respond to interviewers by saying that they are actively employed.

Exhibit 3-14 shows that, normally, the CPS and CES track each other closely, but there have been times when they differed significantly. The period from November 2001 to about January 2004 has been called the *U.S. Jobless Recovery*.[29] From August 2002 to November 2003, CES showed significant yearly reductions in employment, but CPS recorded significant yearly increases, which reinforces the fact that measures of labor market conditions can depend on whether individuals or businesses are interviewed. Strikingly, in January and November 2003, the difference between the two surveys was more than 2 million jobs! In January, CPS reported year-on-year increases of 1,716,000 jobs, while CES reported losses of 300,000 jobs. In November, CPS

[29] See Allan. H. Meltzer, "A Jobless Recovery?" *The Wall Street Journal* (Eastern Edition), September 26, 2003, p. A8; Ben S. Bernanke, "The Jobless Recovery: Remarks by Governor Ben S. Bernanke at the Global Economic and Investment Outlook Conference," Carnegie Mellon University, Pittsburgh, Pennsylvania, November 6, 2003, www.federalreserve.gov/boarddocs/speeches/2003/200311062/default.htm (accessed September 24, 2013).

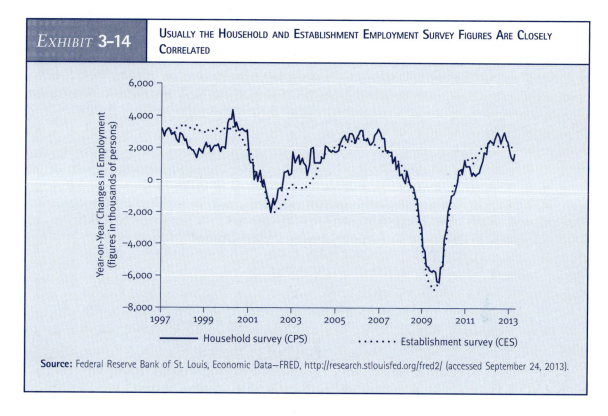

| EXHIBIT 3-14 | USUALLY THE HOUSEHOLD AND ESTABLISHMENT EMPLOYMENT SURVEY FIGURES ARE CLOSELY CORRELATED |

Source: Federal Reserve Bank of St. Louis, Economic Data—FRED, http://research.stlouisfed.org/fred2/ (accessed September 24, 2013).

and CES reported year-on-year changes of positive 1,903,000 jobs and minus 219,000 jobs, respectively. Only after December 2003 did both indices begin, again, to move in closer tandem.

In the United States, the Great Recession started in December 2007 and ended in June 2009. During the first four months of this recession, CPS and CES diverged, on average, by 667,000 jobs, and during the last four months, they diverged by 753,000 jobs. Beguilingly, during the first four months, CES exceeded CPS, but afterwards, their roles were reversed. With only a few exceptions during the intervening years, CPS and CES came closer together as the recession unfolded, with the average difference between the two surveys for the entire 19-month recession equaling 227,000 jobs.

UNDOCUMENTED IMMIGRANTS AND THE U.S. UNEMPLOYMENT RATE

Do undocumented (illegal) aliens affect unemployment statistics? The U.S. unemployment rate is calculated from surveys, and the interview questions do not inquire about the legal status of those being interviewed. The *Household Survey* asks only if an individual is domestic or foreign born. There are no questions about legal status. The *Establishment Survey* interviews companies; so the issue of legal status is not addressed. Therefore, it is highly likely that undocumented aliens enter into the U.S. employment statistics, but the chances of them having a significant impact are relatively small.

IF ONLY I COULD BE A FLY ON THE WALL

At 8:30 A.M. on the first Friday of every month, the U.S. BLS reports the nation's unemployment rate—along with a rich assortment of other labor market information. Of all the economic statistics reported by the U.S. government each month, the information contained in this report is arguably the most influential of all. Investors anticipate it and, if the data is different from that expected, they act immediately.

Suppose you could be a fly on the wall at the BLS, able to learn the news before it hit the market. Your money worries would be solved for life because you could profitably trade stocks, bonds, commodities, and/or currencies and earn massive profits. Your wealth would materialize like a submarine surfacing next to a rowboat. Any car, house, vacation, or adventure your heart desired would be affordable, and not just that, you would have the time to enjoy them all because you would never again have to work—ever. Sound good? If it does, you're not alone, which is why BLS takes every effort to protect its sensitive information.

The Lock-Up[30]

BLS solves the confidentiality problem by (literally) locking-up those who have prior access to this information and forcing them to release it simultaneously. The only exceptions are the president of the United States, chairman of the Council of Economic Advisors, and Federal Reserve chairman, who get the labor market report a day before its official public release. Who are the others who get prior knowledge of these sensitive figures?

About two dozen news reporters are allowed to inspect the labor-market data before their official release. They arrive at BLS's offices on 3rd Avenue and C Street in Washington D.C. well before 8:00 A.M. Upon entering the building, they are given ID badges and ushered by armed guard to the BLS's windowless secure pressroom, called the "lock-up room." At 7:55 A.M., a BLS official places a call to the U.S. Naval Observatory to confirm and adjust, if needed, the time so that it exactly matches Observatory's super-accurate atomic clock. At 8:00 A.M., the press room door is closed and locked. Armed guards make sure that no one leaves or enters for the next 30 minutes, and everyone inside is asked to turn off all communication devices. The lock-up has begun. Those under "house arrest" have just 30 minutes to read the report, distill the information, and compose their stories.

At 8:28 A.M., television reporters are allowed to leave so they have time to make their daily 8:30 A.M. broadcasts. At 8:30 A.M., the news hits the market, and within seconds this information is communicated worldwide with blitzing speed. Newspapers, business media, and online services publish the news, interpret the figures, and spread the information through highly efficient global information networks.

European markets, which have been open for hours, react immediately, as do electronically traded derivative markets that operate continuously

---

[30] Bernard Baumohl, *The Secrets of Economic Indicators: Hidden Clues to Future Economic Trends and Investment Opportunities* (Wharton School Publishing, Pearson Education Inc., 2012).

throughout the 24-hour trading day. Those who have accurately predicted the statistics can sit back as their profits soar. Those who guessed wrong scramble to hedge or otherwise unwind their positions. The stakes are high, and the lingering question is how, if at all, the central bank and/or government will react to the news. Expectations and the prices of stocks, bonds, commodities, and currencies all snap to attention as the news filters through the international community.

In September 2012, BLS improved its lock-up procedures to better protect sensitive labor-market information from premature public disclosure.[31] Under the improved rules, news reporters who are given prior access to sensitive information are permitted either to use their own computers and other communication equipment in the lock-up facility or to use equipment provided by the BLS. A combination is also possible. External equipment must meet certain BLS specifications, be shipped directly from the manufacturer to the BLS, and be open to inspection upon arrival. When news reporters enter BLS's secure press room, they are required to sign a new Embargo Agreement, which spells out sanctions for reporters and news organizations that violate the confidentiality terms of the agreement. Temporary suspension or permanent expulsion is possible.

Let's return to the fly on the wall simile. Suppose you were able to get prior access to confidential unemployment data and knew the reported figures would be dramatically different from prevailing expectations. What would you do? What trades would you make? For instance, suppose you knew the unemployment rate would be much lower than the market anticipated. Would you buy or sell stocks? How about bonds, commodities, and currencies? Which ones would you buy or sell? Would it make a difference? These questions will be answered as you learn more about macroeconomics. A clear understanding of how these markets act and interact is a major goal of this book.

CONCLUSION

Measures of labor market conditions—such as the unemployment rate, employment rate, labor force participation rate, and unemployment duration—are neither arcane concepts nor mere academic statistics. Rather, they are practical barometers that gauge a nation's level of economic hardship or prosperity. For businesses and individuals, it is important to understand a nation's vital labor statistics in order to make prudent decisions. For policymakers, it is also important to understand these measures so that proper diagnoses can be made of existing or impending economic problems and credible solutions can be enacted.

Unemployment rates vary over time and internationally due to differences in economic, social, and demographic factors. For this reason, care should be

---

[31] Bureau of Labor Statistics, Update to the April 10, 2012, Policy Statement on DOL Lock-Ups, July 5, 2012, www.dol.gov/dol/media/lockup-summary.pdf; U.S. Department of Labor Press Lock-Ups Policy Statement and News Organization Agreement Overview, July 19, 2012, www.dol.gov/dol/media/lockup-organization-agreement.pdf; *Frequently Asked Questions*, July 10, 2012, www.dol.gov/dol/media/lockup-questions.pdf (accessed September 24, 2013).

taken when drawing conclusions from comparative data. Because there are different types of unemployment (e.g., frictional, structural, seasonal, and cyclical), there is no single solution to reducing it—but increased demand certainly helps. Moreover, because measures of labor market conditions might overstate or understate the true level of economic hardship in a nation, government policies and business decisions should be based on a broad selection of key labor market measures.

REVIEW QUESTIONS

1. Choose among the alternative answers in italics and fill in the blank lines: "If workers, who are currently unemployed and actively seeking jobs, leave the labor force, the employment rate *rises/falls/stays the same* _____ because _____, and the unemployment rate *rises/falls/stays the same* _____ because _____."

2. Suppose the noninstitutional population over 16 remains the same. Is it possible for a nation's unemployment rate to fall at the same time its employment rate falls?

3. Explain what happens to a nation's unemployment rate, employment rate, and labor force participation rate if unemployed individuals become so discouraged that they stop looking for jobs.

4. In the following cases, what happens, if anything, to the nation's unemployment rate?
   a. Individuals have their weekly hours cut from 40 to 30 hours.
   b. Massive layoffs occur due to a decline in economic activity.
   c. A sharp reduction in college and university applications occurs because high school students decide to work rather than get advanced degrees. It takes six months for them to find employment.
   d. Due to a sluggish economy, many of the high school graduates in Question 4c get jobs that are substantially below their abilities.
   e. There is a significant increase in the number of homemakers looking for work to pay for their children's university educations.
   f. Due to a rapidly growing economy, executives with well-paying jobs send their résumés and letters of application to potential employers offering more interesting positions.

5. Is it accurate to say that as a nation's economy falls into recession, its structural and frictional unemployment rates should rise?

6. Explain the natural rate of unemployment and why this economic measure is important to economists, businesses, and policymakers. What is the relationship, if any, between the natural rate of unemployment and a nation's potential output?

7. Explain how the unemployment rate both understates and simultaneously overstates the true level of economic hardship in a nation.

8. Are the unemployment rate and employment rate leading, lagging, or coincident economic indicators?

9.   Explain the four different types of unemployment. Briefly provide ways in which each type of unemployment might be reduced.

10. Why don't governments try to achieve 0% unemployment?

11. Is the unemployment rate or employment rate a better measure of economic health? Take a position, and be able to defend it against someone else in class with a different opinion.

12. Is the Household Survey (aka Current Population Survey) or Establishment Survey a better measure of economic health? Take a position, and be able to defend it against someone else in class with a different opinion.

13. What is *outsourcing*? How, if at all, is it different from *offshoring*? Why is offshoring so controversial? What are the advantages and disadvantages of out-sourcing/offshoring? Explain how you feel about the net effects of outsourcing.

14. Explain how factors such as ethnicity, age, education, gender, and financial background affect a nation's labor force participation rate.

15. There are many measures of labor market conditions besides the unemployment rate and employment rate. List the measures that you feel are most important, and of these measures, explain which of them you feel best reflects economic conditions.

DISCUSSION QUESTION

16. Explain how a forecasted increase in unemployment and reduction in GDP might affect a company's cash flow projections over a capital budgeting period (e.g., five years).

Appendix 3-1

A Quick Historic Look at U.S. Unemployment

Exhibit A3-1 shows the unemployment rate for the United States between 1960 and 2013. During this period, it varied within a range of 3.4% (at the end of 1968 and beginning of 1969) to 10.8% (at the end of 1982). In a close and hotly contested presidential race, the brief recession from April 1960 to February 1961 was instrumental in Richard M. Nixon's loss to Democratic challenger John F. Kennedy.

From 1961 to December 1969, the U.S. unemployment rate fell as the economy expanded. Part of the stimulus came from Presidents Kennedy and Johnson's expansionary fiscal policies, such as the 1964 income tax cuts, defense spending associated with the Vietnam War, and expenditures related to the U.S. space program.

Between December 1969 and November 1970, the United States suffered an 11-month recession that raised the nation's unemployment rate from 3.5% to 5.9%. The U.S. recovery from this recession during the early years of the 1970s was interrupted in 1973 when the OPEC nations quadrupled the price of oil, which raised business costs of production, increased inflation, reduced consumer spending, and resulted in numerous layoffs.

As a result, between November 1973 and March 1975, the United States entered into its most prolonged recession of the post–World War II period. Lasting 16 months, U.S. unemployment rose from 4.8% to 8.6%. Increased unemployment during the 1970s was due not only to the oil price shocks unleashed by the OPEC cartel but also to the increase in female labor force participation rates, which marked the beginning of a strong U.S. women's liberation movement and changing attitudes toward work.

From 1975 to 1979, the United States adjusted to oil shocks and demographic changes in the workforce, but beginning in 1980, the nation entered into a two-year period where it experienced a double-dip recession. One recession lasted from January 1980 to July 1980 (6 months) and the other lasted from July 1981 to November 1982 (16 months). U.S. unemployment rose from 6.3% to 10.8%. Then, from 1982 to 1990, the United States entered a protracted period of expansion, which reduced the unemployment rate in June 1990 to almost 5.2%.

From July 1990 to March 1991, U.S. growth was again interrupted as the United States slipped into a recession just prior to the presidential election. The slide raised the U.S. unemployment rate to 6.8% and was a critical factor causing George H. W. Bush to lose the 1992 presidential race to Bill Clinton.

Between March 1991 and March 2001, the United States enjoyed its longest continuous expansion of the post–World War II period. From July 1997

| EXHIBIT A3-1 | A QUICK HISTORIC LOOK AT THE U.S. UNEMPLOYMENT RATE: JANUARY 1961 TO APRIL 2013 |

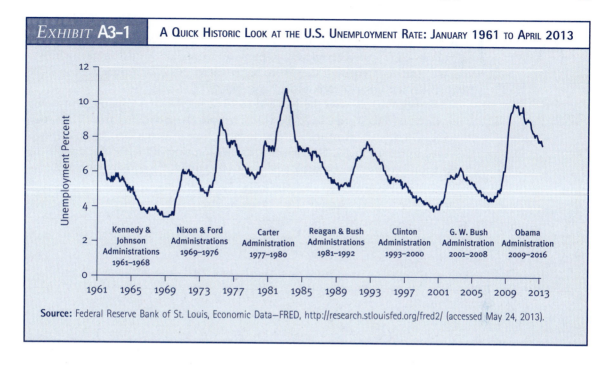

Kennedy &
Johnson
Administrations
1961–1968

Nixon & Ford
Administrations
1969–1976

Carter
Administration
1977–1980

Reagan & Bush
Administrations
1981–1992

Clinton
Administration
1993–2000

G. W. Bush
Administration
2001–2008

Obama
Administration
2009–2016

Source: Federal Reserve Bank of St. Louis, Economic Data–FRED, http://research.stlouisfed.org/fred2/ (accessed May 24, 2013).

to March 2001, the U.S. unemployment rate was below 5%. Just a few years earlier, few economic analysts would have predicted that such a low rate was achievable and sustainable in the United States.

Starting in March 2001 and lasting until November 2001, the United States entered another economic recession. The unemployment rate rose from 4.3% to 5.5%. After November 2001, the United States recovered with relatively robust growth in spending and production, but the unemployment rate was slow to respond. Exhibit A3-1 shows that, despite expansion, the U.S. unemployment rate continued to rise between November 2001 and June 2003. Only after June 2003 did it begin to fall, albeit at a relatively slow rate.

As the 2004 presidential election neared, George W. Bush was criticized by Democratic challenger John F. Kerry for the lack of job creation. After more than two years of recovery, the U.S. unemployment was stuck at around 5.7%. President George W. Bush was concerned that his reelection chances might be torpedoed by a sluggish domestic economy in the same way the reelection of his father George H. W. Bush was thwarted in 1991 by a relatively high unemployment rate. Nevertheless, George W. Bush won the 2004 election, and from December 2004 to August 2006, the U.S. unemployment rate fell from 5.4% to 4.7%.

In 2008, Barack Obama won the presidential election and inherited one of the worst economic recessions since the Great Depression of the 1930s. Between January 2009, when he first took office, and October 2009, the U.S. unemployment rate rose steadily from 7.8% to 10%. From there it began a slow descent, making this recovery one of the slowest in recorded U.S. history.

By early fall 2012, just two months before the presidential election, the U.S. unemployment rate stood at 8.3%, and the Obama administration was reacting daily to repeated attacks by Republican candidate Mitt Romney, who asked American voters if they were better off in 2012 than they were in 2008 when Barack Obama took office.

Barack Obama won the November 2012 presidential election, and from January 2013 to April 2013, the U.S. unemployment rate fell from 7.9% to 7.5%. Green sprouts of recovery seemed to appear as the U.S. stock market surged to record highs. Nevertheless, the nation was still leery of a double-dip recession because the unemployment rate remained abnormally high and resistant to expansionary monetary and fiscal policies.

Chapter 4

Inflation, Real GDP, and Business Cycles

INTRODUCTION

"Where's the beef?" This is the question that business managers should be asking themselves as they prepare their short-term budgets and business plans. The "beef" for any business comes from increasing the quantity of *real* goods and services sold to customers, reducing *real* costs of production, and earning *real* profits from judicious investment decisions.

Like the distorted reflections we see of ourselves in carnival mirrors, inflation disfigures the image of both business performance and the economic world around us. For this reason, managers should understand what inflation is and how to remove its contorting effects from their analyses. Only in this way can they get a clear view of economic reality.

This chapter explains inflation, what it measures, and, equally important, what it does not measure. The chapter goes on to describe hyperinflation and provides insights into some of the challenges confronting people and businesses operating in high-inflation countries. Most important, the chapter explains how to remove the effects of inflation from nominal production and income statistics, such as gross domestic product (GDP) so that a nation's past, current, and expected future economic growth rates come into clearer view. The chapter ends with a brief discussion of business cycles and how they are measured.

THE BASICS

WHAT IS INFLATION?

In 1917, before the hazards of smoking were so clear, Vice President Thomas R. Marshall said on the floor of the U.S. Senate, "What this country needs is a good five-cent cigar." About a decade and a half later, Marshall's quip was revised by New York journalist Franklin P. Adams, who said, "There are plenty of good five-cent cigars in the country. The trouble is they cost a quarter. What this country needs is a good five-cent nickel."

Inflation is like an acid that erodes the purchasing power of a nation's currency. The greater the inflation, the greater the erosion. Consider the U.S. dollar's loss of purchasing power during the century between 1913 and 2013. What do you think it cost in 2013 for a basket of goods and services worth $100 in 1913? You might be surprised to learn that, due to inflation, products with a $100 price tag in 1913 cost about $2,363 in 2013! In other words, one 1913 dollar was worth about 23.63 dollars with a 2013 vintage.[1]

Inflation is a sustained increase in the average price level. If the price of every good and service in a nation rose by the same percentage—say, 3%—then the inflation rate would be easy to calculate, but such homogeneous changes in prices never occur. The prices of goods and services change at different rates. Some product prices rise rapidly, others rise slowly, some stay the same, and others even fall, depending on market factors, such as the level of demand and competitive structure of the industry. It is for this reason that the inflation rate is calculated as a weighted average of percentage price changes, with the weights reflecting the relative importance of each product being considered. As long as the weighted average of products with increasing prices exceeds the weighted average of those with decreasing prices, inflation occurs.

Inflation is a sustained increase in the average price level.

To better understand how the inflation rate is calculated, consider the following example. Suppose the residents of a country spent, on average, 20% of their income on food, 50% on housing, and 30% on clothing and other expenditures (see Exhibit 4-1, Columns 1 and 2). If food prices increased by 4%, housing prices rose by 10%, and clothing/other prices fell by 6%, the average rate of inflation would be 4.0%. This result can be calculated in just two steps.

Inflation occurs when the percent weighted average of prices increases.

First, multiply the inflation rate for each product group (Rows 1 to 3 in Column 3) by its relative importance (Column 2). The result (which is shown in Column 4) is the contribution that each expenditure group makes to the inflation rate. Second, determine the average inflation rate for the nation by

EXHIBIT 4-1	INFLATION RATE: WEIGHTED AVERAGE OF PERCENTAGE PRICE CHANGES		
	COLUMN 1	COLUMN 2	COLUMN 3	COLUMN 4
	Product Group	Weight of Each Product Group (Sum = 100%)	Inflation Rate of Each Product Group	Weighted Average (Col. 2 × Col. 3)
Row 1	Food	20%	4%	+0.8%
Row 2	Housing	50%	10%	+5.0%
Row 3	Clothing and other	30%	−6%	−1.8%
Row 4	Average inflation rate	(Sum of Rows 1, 2, and 3)		+4.0%

[1] A helpful place to find information on the value of the U.S. dollar between any two dates is the Federal Reserve Bank of Minneapolis's Web site, www.minneapolisfed.org/research/data/us/calc/ (accessed May 26, 2013).

summing the weighted inflation rates of the three expenditure groups (Rows 1 to 3 in Column 4).

INFLATION MEASURES

Three major price indices are normally used to measure a nation's inflation rate. These indices are the *GDP Price Index*, *Consumer Price Index*, and *Producer Price Index*. The price index that should be used depends on the question(s) in need of an answer.

> There are three major price indices: the GDP Price Index, Consumer Price Index, and Producer Price Index.

GDP Price Index

The *GDP Price Index* (also called the *GDP Price Deflator* or *Implicit Price Index*) is the broadest measure of a nation's inflation rate because it includes price changes of all final goods and services included in GDP (see Exhibit 4-2). For business managers, economists, and policymakers interested in country analyses or comparative economic studies, the GDP Price Index is likely to be the index of choice.

> The GDP Price Index is the broadest measure of inflation because it covers all final goods and services (except imports) produced over a period of time.

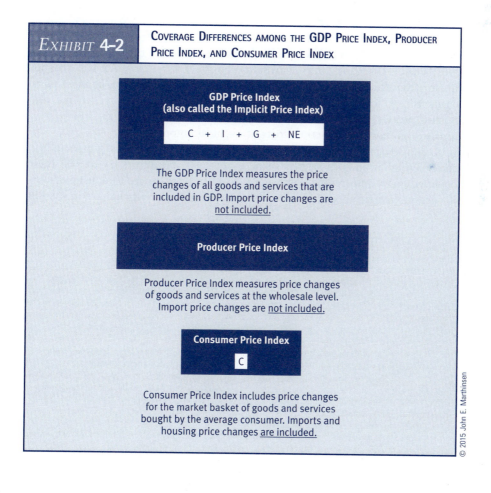

| EXHIBIT 4-2 | COVERAGE DIFFERENCES AMONG THE GDP PRICE INDEX, PRODUCER PRICE INDEX, AND CONSUMER PRICE INDEX |

GDP Price Index
(also called the Implicit Price Index)

C + I + G + NE

The GDP Price Index measures the price changes of all goods and services that are included in GDP. Import price changes are not included.

Producer Price Index

Producer Price Index measures price changes of goods and services at the wholesale level. Import price changes are not included.

Consumer Price Index

C

Consumer Price Index includes price changes for the market basket of goods and services bought by the average consumer. Imports and housing price changes are included.

© 2015 John E. Marthinsen

Consumer Price Index (CPI)

The *Consumer Price Index* (CPI) measures the weighted-average change in prices for a *market basket* of goods and services purchased by the *typical* domestic consumer.[2] Because it reflects only consumer-related products, the CPI is a much narrower measure of inflation than the GDP Price Index, which includes price changes for consumers, businesses (e.g., new plants and equipment), governments, and exporters[3] (see Exhibit 4-2).

The CPI tries to capture consumers' actual out-of-pocket expenses. Therefore, it includes retail markups, taxes on goods and services (e.g., sales and excise taxes), distribution costs, and the prices of imported consumer goods.

Government surveys, which are updated approximately every decade, determine domestic consumers' spending patterns, and from them, the CPI's "typical" market basket of goods and services is defined.[4] Once defined, the government calculates each month how much it would cost to purchase the CPI's market basket, and the weighted-average percentage change in its price is the nation's inflation rate.[5]

Producer Price Index (PPI)

The *Producer Price Index* (PPI) measures price changes from the seller's perspective, which means at the wholesale level (i.e., before the retail markups, sales taxes, excise taxes, and distribution costs). This price index is a broader measure than the CPI because it includes, for example, the price changes of all inputs that go into the production process, as well as capital investments, and finished products that are ready to sell to consumers. Because the PPI measures *domestic* production costs, it excludes imports.[6]

Often, changes in the PPI precede changes in the CPI. This is especially true when inflation is caused by rising input costs. Producers try to pass these increased costs onto retailers, who in turn raise retail prices to consumers. Business managers should beware if they try to use current changes in the PPI

---

[2] In the United States, the Department of Labor reports two CPI numbers. *CPI-U* covers almost all consumers in urban (U) or metropolitan areas and accounts for about 87% of the U.S. population. *CPI-W*, which stands for "urban wage earners and clerical workers," covers a subset of the population in CPI-U and accounts for only 32% of the U.S. population. Taxes associated with the purchase of goods or services (e.g., sales, property, and excise taxes, tolls, and parking fees) are included in the CPI, but taxes unrelated to the purchase of a good or service (e.g., income and Social Security taxes) are excluded. See U.S. Department of Labor, Bureau of Labor Statistics, *Consumer Price Indexes: Frequently Asked Questions*, www.bls.gov/cpi/cpifaq.htm (accessed May 26, 2013).

[3] The CPI focuses almost exclusively on price changes of consumer products, but there are some minor exceptions, such as residential housing, which is included in gross private domestic investment.

[4] The most recent survey in the United States was over the two-year period from 2007 to 2008, and it was based on quarterly interviews and on diary listings of interviewees' purchases. In all, the survey included 28,000 weekly diaries and 60,000 quarterly interviews on more than 200 product categories. See U.S. Department of Labor, Bureau of Labor Statistics. *Consumer Price Indexes: Frequently Asked Questions*, www.bls.gov/cpi/cpifaq.htm (accessed May 26, 2013).

[5] In the United States, economic assistants place thousands of phone calls each month to collect data on the approximately 80,000 items in the market basket. See U.S. Department of Labor, Bureau of Labor Statistics, *Consumer Price Indexes: Frequently Asked Questions*, www.bls.gov/cpi/cpifaq.htm (accessed May 26, 2013).

[6] Each commodity is assigned to one specific part of the overall production process (i.e., crude materials, intermediate products, or final products) so that the same product is not counted twice.

to predict future movements in the CPI because the causal link is rather weak. Even though the CPI and the PPI often move in the same direction, they do not always change by the same degree, at the same time, or in logical sequence. One reason for this weak link is because the goods and services included in the CPI are only a fraction of the products included in the PPI. Similarly, the PPI excludes items that play very important roles in the CPI (e.g., housing). Finally, even if input costs increase, producers' ability to pass them to retailers, as well as retailers' ability to pass them to consumers, depends on the industry's competitive condition.

WHAT IS PRICE STABILITY?

For most nations, *price stability* usually means low, nonvolatile rates of inflation. For the clear majority of developed nations during the twentieth and, now, twenty-first centuries, the goal has been a low-variance, average rate between 1% and 3%. Many people wonder, "If price stability is the goal, then why don't governments and central bankers try to achieve 0% inflation? Shouldn't a 0% inflation rate be the ideal?" One major reason for the more modest 1% to 3% goal is because price indices may misrepresent the actual inflation rate. For instance, price indices may not account properly for quality changes, new-product introductions, and the substitution of lower-priced products for relatively higher-priced ones.[7] If these three factors cause the reported CPI to overstate the true, underlying inflation rate by 1%, then targeting 0% annual inflation, when adjusted for these factors, would actually be a goal of 1% deflation. Another reason for concern is the possibility that tying the inflation too closely to zero risks having a sudden economic shock cause deflation, which is an economic condition that may have substantially worse consequences than mild inflation.[8]

> Price stability normally means a low, nonvolatile inflation rate.

There are other, perhaps less grounded, reasons why a 0% inflation goal may be misguided. For instance, some people feel that a small amount of inflation is needed to stimulate economic growth. They argue that rising prices promote business profitability and therefore promote employment by increasing production and investments in plant and equipment. According to this line of reasoning, business profitability increases with inflation because business costs, such as wages and other resource prices, are less flexible than the prices of final goods and services. As a result, inflation allows producers to pass along price increases to consumers faster than their resources costs rise, resulting in increased profits.

The problem with the reasoning behind this argument is that it ignores the likelihood that current increases in resource costs are based on past expectations

---

[7] See **The Rest of the Story**: *Inflation Related Topics: Shortcomings of the CPI* for a brief explanation of these factors.

[8] See, for example, the remarks by Governor Ben S. Bernanke before the National Economists Club, "Deflation: Making Sure 'It' Doesn't Happen Here," Washington, D.C., November 21, 2002, www.federalreserve.gov /boarddocs/speeches/2002/20021121/default.htm (accessed May 25, 2013); also see the remarks by Governor Ben S. Bernanke before the Economics Roundtable, "An Unwelcome Fall in Inflation?" University of California, San Diego, La Jolla, California, July 23, 2003, www.federalreserve.gov/boarddocs/speeches/2003 /20030723/ (accessed May 26, 2013).

EXHIBIT 4-3	REAL VERSUS NOMINAL GDP		
COLUMN 1	COLUMN 2	COLUMN 3	COLUMN 4
Year	Nominal GDP	Price Index	Real GDP
1990	$P_{1990} \times Q_{1990}$		
2009	$P_{2009} \times Q_{2009}$		
2014	$P_{2014} \times Q_{2014}$		
	GDP rises if P or Q rises		

© 2015 John E. Marthinsen

of inflation. We will look more deeply at this issue in Chapter 5, "Inflation: Who Wins, and Who Loses?" where we will find that it is only when inflation rises above what was expected that business profitability should benefit from rising inflation.

REAL VERSUS NOMINAL GDP

How do rising prices affect GDP? Can the influence of inflation be removed from GDP figures so that the real production behind them can be revealed? To answer these questions, we must distinguish between real GDP and nominal GDP.

Column 2 of Exhibit 4-3 shows that nominal GDP for 1990, 2009, and 2014 is calculated by multiplying the price of all final goods and services produced in a given period by the quantity produced in that same period. For example, in 1990 the nominal GDP was the average price level in 1990 times the quantity of final goods and services produced in 1990 (i.e., $P_{1990} \times Q_{1990}$).

Exhibit 4-3 shows that nominal GDP can increase if either prices or outputs rise, but for a nation's standard of living to improve, increases in output, and not prices, are important. The problem is that rising prices also cause nominal GDP to increase, which can give a false sense that the economy is doing better than it really is. Because of this, economists adjust nominal GDP by taking out the effects of inflation. This inflation-adjusted figure is called *real GDP*.

Exhibit 4-4 (Column 4) shows that real GDP is calculated by multiplying the quantities produced in a given year by the average price level of a

Nominal GDP is equal to the sum of all final goods and services produced during a period times their market prices. Nominal GDP $\equiv \Sigma\ (P_i \times Q_i)$

Real GDP is equal to nominal GDP after adjusting for the effects of price changes (i.e., inflation or deflation).

EXHIBIT 4-4	REAL VERSUS NOMINAL GDP		
COLUMN 1	COLUMN 2	COLUMN 3	COLUMN 4
Year	Nominal GDP	Price Index	Real GDP
1990	$P_{1990} \times Q_{1990}$		$P_{2009} \times Q_{1990}$
2009	$P_{2009} \times Q_{2009}$		$P_{2009} \times Q_{2009}$
2014	$P_{2014} \times Q_{2014}$		$P_{2009} \times Q_{2014}$

© 2015 John E. Marthinsen

specified base year. If 2009 were the base year, then real GDP in 1990 would be the average price level in 2009 times the quantity produced in 1990. Real GDP in 2014 would be the average price level in 2009 times the quantity produced in 2014.

With real GDP, the average price level does not vary, so the only way real GDP can change is if output changes. Therefore, real GDP is a better measure of a nation's economic health than nominal GDP. For this reason, real GDP plays a prominent role in most serious macroeconomic analyses.

CALCULATING THE GDP PRICE INDEX

Once a nation's nominal GDP and real GDP are known, its GDP price index can be calculated by dividing yearly nominal GDP by real GDP. It is clear from Exhibit 4-5 that, after like terms are eliminated, the nation's GDP price index is simply its average price level for any given year divided by the average price level in the base year.

Exhibit 4-5 shows the results when 2009 is used as the base year. Dividing nominal GDP by real GDP creates price indices equal to the average price level for final goods and services in 1990, 2009, and 2014 divided by the average price level for final goods and services in 2009. On average, if prices rose from 1990 to 2009, then the price index for 1990 would be less than 1.0. If prices rose, on average, from 2009 to 2014, then the price index in 2014 would be greater than 1.0. The price index in the base year is always equal to 1.0.

For many analyses, information might be available for a nation's nominal GDP and price index but not for its real GDP. Exhibit 4-6 shows that calculating real GDP is as easy as dividing nominal GDP in any given year by the price index for that year. This has the effect of removing the influence of price changes from the nominal GDP measure and replacing it with a common (base year) price. Notice in Exhibit 4-6, Column 4, price levels in all but the base year cancel out and are replaced with the price level in the base year.

On average, if prices rose from 1990 to 2009, then, the price index for 1990 would be less than one. Therefore, when nominal GDP in 1990 is divided

> The GDP price index is used to convert nominal GDP to real GDP.

EXHIBIT 4-5	DERIVING THE PRICE INDEX: BASE YEAR = 2009		
Year	Nominal GDP / Real GDP	≡ Cancelling Terms	Price Index
1990	$\dfrac{P_{1990} \times Q_{1990}}{P_{2009} \times Q_{1990}}$	$\equiv \dfrac{P_{1990} \times Q_{1990}}{P_{2009} \times Q_{1990}}$	$\equiv \dfrac{P_{1990}}{P_{2009}}$
2009	$\dfrac{P_{2009} \times Q_{2009}}{P_{2009} \times Q_{2009}}$	$\equiv \dfrac{P_{2009} \times Q_{2009}}{P_{2009} \times Q_{2009}}$	$\equiv \dfrac{P_{2009}}{P_{2009}} = 1$
2014	$\dfrac{P_{2014} \times Q_{2014}}{P_{2009} \times Q_{2014}}$	$\equiv \dfrac{P_{2014} \times Q_{2014}}{P_{2009} \times Q_{2014}}$	$\equiv \dfrac{P_{2014}}{P_{2009}}$

EXHIBIT 4-6	CALCULATING REAL GDP USING NOMINAL GDP AND PRICE INDEX		
COLUMN 1	COLUMN 2	COLUMN 3	COLUMN 4
Year	Nominal GDP $\div$	GDP Price Index $\equiv$	Real GDP
1990	$P_{1990} \times Q_{1990}$ $\div$	$\dfrac{P_{1990}}{P_{2009}}$ $\equiv$	$P_{2009} \times Q_{1990}$
2009	$P_{2009} \times Q_{2009}$ $\div$	$\dfrac{P_{2009}}{P_{2009}}$ $\equiv$	$P_{2009} \times Q_{2009}$
2014	$P_{2014} \times Q_{2014}$ $\div$	$\dfrac{P_{2014}}{P_{2009}}$ $\equiv$	$P_{2009} \times Q_{2014}$

by this price index, it has the effect of inflating the 1990 GDP to 2009 price levels. This might be clearer by comparing Columns 2 and 4 in Exhibit 4-6. Because the prices in 2009 are greater than the prices in 1990, $P_{2009} \times Q_{1990}$ is greater than $P_{1990} \times Q_{1990}$.

By contrast, consider the nominal and real GDPs in 2014. If prices rose, on average, from 2009 to 2014, then the price index for 2014 would be greater than one. When nominal GDP in 2014 is divided by this price index, it has the effect of deflating the 2014 GDP to 2009 price levels. Because the prices in 2009 are less than the prices in 2014, $P_{2009} \times Q_{2014}$ is less than $P_{2014} \times Q_{2014}$.

Exhibit 4-7 shows the nominal GDP, real GDP, and GDP Price Index for the United States from 2000 to 2012. Notice that 2009 is the base year. We know this because the price index is 1.00. Also notice how the real GDP figures for each year prior to 2009 are greater than the nominal GDP figures. This occurs because prices rose each year (albeit slightly), and real GDP figures are stated in terms of 2009 prices. For similar reasons, real GDP is less than nominal GDP in all years after 2009.

BUSINESS CYCLES

What are business cycles, and why are they important to business managers? What causes them, and who determines when recessions or expansions start and end? After centuries of fluctuating economic activity, have nations gotten better at controlling or predicting business cycles, or are these cycles as frequent, extreme, and fickle as ever?

WHAT ARE BUSINESS CYCLES?

Business cycles are *recurring*, *irregular*, and *unsystematic* movements in *real economic activity* around a long-term trend. They are recurring because, even though nations have put their best efforts into preventing recessions, downturns in economic activity (followed by recoveries) have occurred for as far back as history is written, and these cycles will surely continue in the future.

Unlike the smooth and symmetric patterns of sound or light waves, business cycles are irregular and appear as jagged, uneven movements around the

Business cycles are recurring, irregular, and unsystematic movements in real economic activity around a long-term trend.

Exhibit 4-7	U.S. Nominal GDP, GDP Price Index, and Real GDP, 2000–2012		
Year	**Nominal GDP**	**GDP Price Index***	**Real GDP**
2000	10,289.7	0.8189	12,565.2
2001	10,625.3	0.8377	12,684.4
2002	10,980.2	0.8505	12,909.7
2003	11,512.2	0.8675	13,270.0
2004	12,277.0	0.8913	13,774.0
2005	13,095.4	0.9199	14,235.6
2006	13,857.9	0.9482	14,615.2
2007	14,480.3	0.9733	14,876.8
2008	14,720.3	0.9924	14,833.6
2009 – base year	**14,417.9**	**1.0000**	**14,417.9**
2010	14,958.3	1.0121	14,779.4
2011	15,533.8	1.0320	15,052.4
2012	16,244.6	1.0500	15,470.7

*Chain index using 2009 as the base year.

Source: Bureau of Economic Analysis, National Economic Accounts, www.bea.gov/national/index. htm#gdp (accessed October 19, 2013).

long-term trend. Business cycles are also unsystematic, which means they are random and difficult (some believe impossible) to predict. A considerable amount of time and effort has been devoted to predicting business cycles. Unfortunately, most of these predictions have been highly inaccurate.

How Are Business Cycles Measured?

Exhibit 4-8 shows a hypothetical business cycle. A recession occurs when there is a significant contraction in economic activity that is spread broadly across the economy and lasts for more than a few months. The duration of a recession is from the peak of the business cycle to the trough (i.e., low point).

An expansion is exactly the opposite. It occurs when broad-based economic activity improves significantly and is sustained for more than a few months. The duration of an expansion is from the cycle's trough to its peak.

The entire business cycle can be measured from one peak to the next peak, or it can be measured from one trough to the next. In Exhibit 4-8, the business cycle is measured from peak to peak.

To identify the phases of a business cycle, a nation needs to measure its *real economic activity*, but how is this done? Often, real GDP is used as a proxy. An increase in real GDP means that production is rising, which usually causes increased employment and improved economic conditions. Declining real GDP implies that the opposite is happening.

A recession is a significant and sustained contraction in economic activity. An expansion is just the opposite.

Business cycles are measured from peak to peak or from trough to trough.

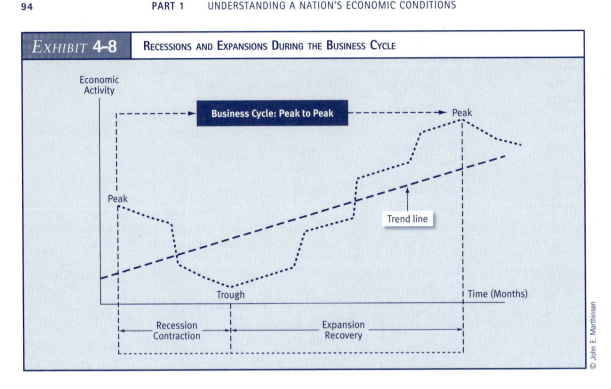

EXHIBIT 4-8 | **RECESSIONS AND EXPANSIONS DURING THE BUSINESS CYCLE**

© John E. Marthinsen

The association between real GDP and business cycles is so strong that the media and many analysts often define a recession as a decline in real GDP for at least two consecutive quarters. Even though this definition appeals to common sense, it is only a rule of thumb (i.e., unofficial shortcut) and not the way recessions and expansions are *officially* measured or dated.[9]

Rule of thumb: A recession occurs when real GDP declines for two consecutive quarters.

Real GDP is just one of many macroeconomic variables that could be used to describe the level of and changes in real economic activity. The problem with real GDP is that it is reported only quarterly, and when it is, initial estimates are often inaccurate due to incomplete information and revisions of submitted information. In fact, the differences between initial GDP estimates and the final reported statistics can be quite large. For these reasons, other economic variables are used to measure and date business cycles—variables that not only provide a clear reflection of real economic activity but also are

[9] To prove that the two-consecutive-quarters rule is a shortcut or approximation (and not an official rule) for defining recessions, we only need to look at historical records. From 1947 to 2012, the United States suffered 12 recessions. In 10 of them, real GDP fell for at least two consecutive quarters, but two *official* recessions (i.e., from April 1960 to February 1961 and from March 2001 to November 2001) occurred without having real GDP fall for two consecutive quarters. In fact, there was one downturn in economic activity (from January to July 1947) when real GDP fell for two consecutive quarters without triggering an *official* recession. To understand who officially dates U.S. recessions, see **The Rest of the Story**: *Topics Related to U.S. Business Cycles: Who Measures U.S. Business Cycles?*

timelier and have initial estimates that are more accurate than real GDP—
more about this later.

WHAT CAUSES BUSINESS CYCLES?

There is no single cause of business cycles. The stimulus could come from the
demand or supply side. Furthermore, random shocks that set a nation's economy into a tailspin or that ignite a recovery could be domestic-based or
foreign-based, and they could originate in the real, financial, political, and/or
social sectors. Examples of real sector stimuli are natural disasters, drastic
increases in the prices of essential resources (e.g., oil), and the worsening of
business and/or consumer expectations. On the financial side, a downward
spiral could be set off by the collapse of a banking system, a burst housing
bubble, speculative international capital flows, or hyperinflation. The political
and social causes of recessions could be escalating social unrest (e.g., riots,
terrorism, worker strikes, civil wars, as well as ethnic, cultural, or religious
turmoil), political instability, corruption, massive bureaucratic failures, and
deterioration in the perceived fairness of the political process.

> Business cycles can be caused by supply-side or demand-side factors that originate in domestic-based or foreign-based real, financial, political, and/or social sectors.

If these shocks were anticipated and could be planned for, then dramatic
changes in economic activity might not occur. Problems occur when they
come as complete surprises, catching businesses, governments, and consumers
unaware. Production and spending patterns adjust as the economy reacts to
the unexpected movements, and these adjustments work their way through the
economy, causing cumulative changes in economic activity that are larger than
the initial shock.

WHY ARE BUSINESS CYCLES IMPORTANT TO MANAGERS?

The cash flows of companies whose sales and/or costs are tied closely to the
business cycle are typically more volatile than those that are not. The more
volatile a company's cash flows, the higher is its credit risk (i.e., default risk),
and as credit risk rises, so do borrowing costs (i.e., cost of capital).

Cash flows are tied directly to companies' top-line growth (i.e., revenues)
and costs. The more sensitive these cash flows are to economic fluctuations, the
more important it is to have awareness and ability to react quickly to business
cycle activity. The durable goods industry (e.g., cars, furniture, phones, and
major appliances) is a good example of a relatively high-risk industry because
its sales are tied directly and strongly to the business cycle. During economic
downturns, customers often postpone expenditures on durable goods. As a
result, sales in the durable goods industry can decline substantially during a
recession, causing cash flows of the manufacturers to plummet.

PROCYCLICAL, COUNTERCYCLICAL, AND ACYCLICAL VARIABLES

Virtually any capital budgeting analysis depends on macroeconomic assumptions about future changes in GDP growth, interest rates, production costs, and
exchange rates. Exhibit 4-9 shows the relationship between many important
macroeconomic variables and the business cycle. These relationships are as
important to someone analyzing a capital budgeting project as they are to
someone required to evaluate and make reasoned public policy decisions based
on them.

EXHIBIT 4-9	PROCYCLICAL, COUNTERCYCLICAL, AND ACYCLICAL MACROECONOMIC VARIABLES		
Market Affected	**Procyclical**	**Countercyclical**	**Acyclical**

Real Goods Market	Demand
	• Consumption
	• Investments in:
	  - Plant and equipment
	  - Machinery and tools
	  - Construction
	  - Planned inventories
	• Government tax revenues
	• Imports
		Demand
		• Investments in unplanned inventories
		• Government transfer payments
			Demand
			• Exports

	Price Indices • Consumer Price Index • GDP Price Index • Producer Price Index	Other • Bankruptcies	Supply • Weather conditions
	Labor Market Conditions • Employment rate • Labor productivity • Real wages	Labor Market Conditions • Unemployment rate	
Real Loanable Funds Market	Monetary Aggregates • Money multiplier • Money supply • Credit		
	Interest Rates • Short-term nominal interest • Long-term nominal interest		Interest Rates • Real interest

Procyclical variables, such as consumption, planned investment, prices, wages, and nominal interest rates, move in the same direction as the business cycle. Therefore, if an economy is expanding, these variables rise; if it is receding, they fall. Countercyclical variables move in the opposite direction from the business cycle. For instance, rising economic activity causes unemployment, bankruptcies, and government transfer payments (e.g., for social welfare programs) to fall.[10] Finally, acyclical macroeconomic variables, such

---

[10] Automatic changes in government transfer payments due to movements in macroeconomic activity are examples of *automatic stabilizers*. For example, as an economy expands, social welfare needs (e.g., due to a lower unemployment rate) decline, causing government transfer payments to fall. During an economic downturn, just the opposite happens. Unemployment rises, causing government transfer payments for social welfare benefits to increase automatically.

as exports and real interest rates, vary independently from the business cycle. These variables are market-determined, but the forces of supply and demand change in ways unrelated to the business cycle.

> Procyclical economic variables move in the same direction as economic activity. Countercyclical variables move in the opposite direction. Acyclical variables move independently from the business cycle.

CAN BUSINESSES PREDICT BUSINESS CYCLES?

How wonderful it would be if there was an accurate and reliable way to forecast major turning points in economic activity. Unfortunately, business cycles are very hard to predict because changes in economic activity can be caused by a very broad range and combination of economic variables. For instance, a recession might be set off by a single shock (e.g., a dramatic increase in oil prices), multiple independent shocks (e.g., crop failures and political upheaval), or a string of interconnected and self-perpetuating shocks (e.g., exchange rate problems that lead to protectionist legislation). Determining exactly where the next bolt of positive or negative economic energy will come from is not an easy task; the possibility of economic activity changing due to multiple combinations of factors greatly increases the chances of being wrong.

Predicting future economic activity, especially turning points,[11] is also difficult because forecasts are usually extrapolations of historic trends, or they are based on historic interrelationships. For the past to predict the future, these historic trends and/or interrelationships must repeat themselves in pattern and intensity, and this is not always the case.

Many companies and individuals earn healthy livings selling business cycle forecasts. It is easy to see why great sums would be paid for these forecasts, if they were accurate. Companies would be willing to pay dearly to know when a nation will slide into its next recession, how long it will stay there, and when it will recover. Often, hundreds of millions of dollars, euros, or yen are on the line when companies plan to build, borrow, and/or hire. Accurate business cycle information could make a huge difference in the profitability of any capital budgeting project.

Predicting Business Cycles Using Leading Economic Indicators (LEI)

One way to forecast business cycles movements is by using a nation's index of leading economic indicators (LEI). The economic variables included in this index are chosen on the basis of their proven economic significance, reliability, consistency, timeliness, and conformity to past business cycles. In other words, they are chosen not because economic theory indicates that they should be important predictors of business cycles but rather because of their past effectiveness at predicting cycles.[12]

> Leading economic indicators help predict changes in business cycles and are chosen based on their economic significance, reliability, consistency, timeliness, and conformity to past business cycles.

The LEI index is considered, by many, to be an economic crystal ball that allows us to see into the future. It is closely watched, published monthly, and reported in many nations.

[11] A *turning point* is the date at which expanding economic activity changes to a downturn or when a downturn changes to an expansion.
[12] See **The Rest of the Story**: *Topics Related to U.S. Business Cycles: Predicting Business Cycles: U.S. Index of Leading Economic Indicators* for a review of the leading indicators that best predict U.S. business cycles.

THE REST OF THE STORY

INFLATION-RELATED TOPICS

SHORTCOMINGS OF THE CPI

The CPI has shortcomings that should be kept in mind because they affect the interpretation of inflation figures. Among the most important are the use of nonrepresentative market baskets and the inaccurate treatment of quality changes, new products, and substitution effects.

Nonrepresentative Market Basket for Consumers: The CPI measures price changes of a *typical* market basket consumed by the *average* consumer, but many individuals and groups do not have similar spending patterns. Exhibit 4-10 shows the categories and weights of the goods and services included in the U.S. CPI. If these weights do not reflect the spending patterns of particular groups, then the CPI will not be a good measure of how inflation affects their costs of living. Judge for yourself. Do the weights in Exhibit 4-10 closely mirror the way you spend your income?

Because the CPI measures price changes only for the goods and services included in the typical market basket, it is not a true cost-of-living index, which would include a much wider range of factors that affect living standards, such as water quality, access to public goods, education, noise levels, leisure, and safety.[13] At the same time, the CPI is timely, well-known, and considered by many to be a fair measure of how changing prices affect household living costs. Therefore, it is often used in salary negotiations by unions and individuals. Because the CPI is linked directly to operating costs, business managers are well advised to understand it.

Does the CPI represent the cost of living in your region? Many nations, like the United States, publish city and regional CPI statistics to supplement their national CPI figures. They do this because the cost of living in any particular city or region may be quite different from the national average. Therefore, the best price index to use is the one that most closely represents the particular living costs of a company's workers. If the firm is located in Boston, then the Boston-area CPI should be used.

One of the problems with having wages and salaries tied to the CPI is that profits can be squeezed between stagnant or declining product prices and rising operating costs. A rising CPI causes labor costs to rise in tandem. But just because consumer prices are rising, on average, does not mean that the product prices for any particular company or industry must rise at the same rate. Prices in highly competitive, sluggish, and fading industries usually increase at rates that are slower than the CPI. They may even fall. Therefore, managers in these industries, who grant CPI-based salary increases, should have a clear

---

[13] See U.S. Department of Labor, Bureau of Labor Statistics, *Consumer Price Indexes: Frequently Asked Questions*, www.bls.gov/cpi/cpifaq.htm (accessed May 26, 2013). The BLS distinguishes between the CPI, which is often called a "cost-of-living index," and a more broadly defined "cost-of-living measure," which evaluates price changes in consumers' overall well-being or quality of life.

Categories	Category Weight	Component Weight
Food	14.2%	
- Food at home		8.5%
- Food away from home		5.7%
Energy	10.0%	
- Energy commodities (fuel oil, motor oil)		6.3%
- Energy services (electricity and gas)		3.7%
Commodities less food and energy	19.5%	
- Apparel		3.6%
- New and used vehicles		5.1%
- Medical care commodities		1.7%
- Alcoholic beverages		0.9%
- Tobacco and smoking products		0.8%
- Other		7.4%
Services less energy services	56.3%	
- Shelter		31.5%
- Medical care services		5.5%
- Transportation services		5.8%
- Other		13.5%
All Items	100.0%	100.0%

Exhibit 4-10 | **U.S. Consumer Price Index Categories, March 2013**

Source: U.S. Department of Labor, Table 1, "Consumer Price Index for All Urban Consumers (CPI-U): U.S. City Average, by Expenditure Category and Commodity and Service Group," www.bls.gov/news.release/pdf/cpi.pdf, table 1 (accessed May 27, 2013).

idea of how to reduce per unit costs in other areas. If they do not, company profits will decline, which could lead to the managers' dismissal, cause unwelcome takeover bids, or seal the company's demise.

It is important for managers to keep in mind that, if they do not compensate their employees, at least, for the rate of inflation, they are at risk to lose their most qualified workers. One of the keys to business success is for managers to surround themselves with people who are better than they are. Therefore, any business strategy that is based on earning profits at the expense of the workforce is bound to fail.

Inaccurate Treatment of Quality Changes, New Products, and the Substitution Effect: An accurate measure of inflation must correctly account for quality changes and the introduction of new products because price increases caused by quality improvements are not inflationary. To do this, the CPI's market basket of goods and services should be (but is not) constantly updated to include new inventions (e.g., the Internet, magnetic resonance imaging (MRI), global positioning systems (GPS), pacemakers, and digital music), novel discoveries (e.g., polymerase chain reaction, coronary bypass surgery, and HIV protease inhibitors), and improvements in product speed and functionality (e.g., computers, televisions, and mobile phones).[14]

Similarly, the CPI will be biased upward if it does not account for substitution effects. When the relative prices of goods and services change, consumers make substitutions. For example, rising prices cause consumers to purchase relatively low-priced, private-label products instead of national brands (e.g., Safeway yogurt instead of Dannon or Yoplait), shop more frequently at factory outlets, and visit discount stores. To the extent the CPI measures price changes of a fixed market basket, these substitution effects will not be reflected accurately in the inflation rate.

> The CPI often ignores quality changes, new products, and the substitution of low-priced products for high-priced ones.

Given the strong and meaningful linkages CPI has to domestic economies, even small biases can be significant. For example, U.S. tax brackets and social welfare expenditures are automatically indexed to the CPI. Over the course of a decade, a difference of just 1% between the actual and reported CPI could change the federal government's debt by as much as $1 trillion.[15]

OTHER MEASURES OF INFLATION

The GDP Price Index, CPI, and PPI are not the only measures of inflation. Among the most important others are:

- Personal consumption expenditure price index (PCEPI), which measures changes in the prices of domestic consumer goods and services purchased by the household sector. In contrast to the CPI, PCEPI does not use a fixed market basket to determine consumer price changes. As a result, many analysts prefer this measure to the CPI because PCEPI accounts for changes in consumption patterns due to changing relative prices.
- Core inflation, which measures price changes for consumer goods and services but without the influence of relatively volatile sectors, such as food and energy. Short-term changes in food and energy prices often are uncontrollable and can become unhinged from a nation's long-run inflation trend. As a result, many analysts feel that the core inflation rate, rather than the CPI or PCEPI, should be used to determine a government's or central bank's long-term inflation policy.

---

[14] BLS makes hedonic (i.e., pleasure) quality adjustments to the CPI for changes in product quality and the introduction of new products. These adjustments are estimates of improved consumer pleasure and are based on regression models. See BLS, Frequently Asked Questions about Hedonic Quality Adjustment in the CPI, www.bls.gov/cpi/cpihqaqanda.htm (accessed May 26, 2013).

[15] A 1997 study found that the CPI overestimates U.S. inflation by about 1.1% per year, but a more recent study indicated that the CPI underestimates overall inflation (excluding shelter and apparel) only by about 0.005% per year. See David S. Johnson, Stephen B. Reed, and Kenneth J. Steward, "Price Measurement in the United States: A Decade after the Boskin Report," www.bls.gov/opub/mlr/2006/05/art2full.pdf (accessed May 26, 2013). Also see "BLS, Common Misconceptions about the Consumer Price Index: Questions and Answers," www.bls.gov/cpi/cpiqa.htm#Question_4 (accessed May 26, 2013). The 1997 report is: Michael J. Boskin et al., "Adjusting the Consumer Price Index to Better Measure Cost of Living: Implications for Entitlements, Taxes, and Economic Growth," January 22, 1997, www.thenewatlantis.com/docLib/20120213_AdjustingtheCPI.pdf (accessed May 26, 2013).

- Employment Cost Index (ECI), which measures the weighted-average cost of an hour of labor. It includes wage and salary payments, employee benefits, and contributions to social insurance programs.
- International indices that measure only changes in import and export prices, as well as regional price indices that are more finely tuned to the differences in geographic locations.

CALCULATING THE COMPOUND ANNUAL INFLATION RATE

Every price index has a base year, which is chosen on the basis of its stability relative to other years in the decade. Years of significant economic, political, or climatic disruptions, such as oil embargos, wars, or natural disasters, would not normally be chosen. From decade to decade, the base year is changed to keep the index and frame of reference current.

The base year is anchored at 1.00 regardless of the actual prices in that year. Price levels in subsequent and previous years are measured by how much they vary from that base-year value. For example, Exhibit 4-11 presents rounded CPI figures for England between 1998 and 2012.[16] We know that the base year for England's CPI is 2005 because the price index in 2005 is 1.00. At the end of 2012, the index was equal to 1.23, which means for the seven-year period between the end of 2005 and 2012, English prices rose cumulatively by 23%. On average, goods priced at £100 in 2005 cost £123 in 2012. Similarly, a price index equal to 0.91 in 1998 means that English prices in 1998 were 9% less than in 2005. In other words, goods and services priced at £100 in 2005 cost, on average, only £91 in 1998.

Usually, inflation rates are measured on a yearly basis. If we always started from the base year and there was only one year's change to consider, then calculating the inflation rate would be an easy matter. We could simply compute the difference between the base year's index of 1.00 and the next year's index and read off the inflation rate. For example, in Exhibit 4-11, the index changed between 2005 and 2006 by 0.02 (i.e., from 1.00 to 1.02), which is a 2% increase.

EXHIBIT 4-11	ENGLAND: CONSUMER PRICE INDEX, 1998–2012

Year	Price Index
1998	0.91
2004	0.98
2005	1.00
2006	1.02
2012	1.23

© 2015 John E. Marthinsen

---

[16] Office for National Statistics, Consumer Price Indices, April 2013, www.ons.gov.uk/ons/rel/cpi/consumer
-price-indices/april-2013/index.html (accessed May 26, 2013).

Unfortunately, it is usually not so simple. For example, we may wish to calculate the inflation between two sequential years but not have the luxury of starting in the base year. Even more complicated, we may start sometime other than the base year and wish to calculate the compound annual inflation rate between two dates that are many years apart. Let's take each of these challenges in order. We will find that the solution is easier than might be expected.

Calculating the total percentage change in prices (not the compound annual change) between two years when the starting point is not the base year is accomplished by dividing the change in the price index (PI) by the index in the starting year. For instance, the inflation rate between 2004 and 2005 is 2.04% because the change in the PI is 0.02 and the starting index is 0.98.[17] Similarly, the total percentage change in prices between 1998 and 2012 is 35.16% because the change in PI is 0.32 and the starting index is 0.91.[18]

Calculating the compound annual change in prices is a bit more complicated but not much. Fortunately, there is an intuitive mathematical formula, and, once understood, this formula can be used to calculate all rates of inflation regardless of the starting year, number of years (or days or months) considered, and the index (i.e., the GDP Price Index, CPI, or PPI) used. In calculating the annual inflation rate over any period of time, we have to consider the effects of compounding because each year's inflation rate is built on the previous year's price change. Over a long period of time, the cumulative effects of compounding can be significant.

Let's derive the formula for calculating a nation's compound yearly inflation rate by using the figures in Exhibit 4-11. Suppose we wanted to calculate this rate for the eight-year period between 2004 and 2012. The 2012 PI of 1.23 was the result of prices rising during the eight-year period by some unknown (average) compound annual rate. So, we can say

$$1.23 = 0.98 \times (1 + \text{Compound Annual Inflation from 2004 to 2012})^8$$

This can be abbreviated as follows:

$$1.23 = 0.98 \times (1 + \text{CAIR}_{2004 \text{ to } 2012})^8$$

where CAIR is an abbreviation for "compound annual inflation rate." A more general statement of the equation above is:

$$\text{PI}_{\text{Year X}} = \text{PI}_{\text{Year 0}} \times (1 + \text{CAIR}_{\text{Year 0 to X}})^{\text{Number of years between Year 0 and Year X}}$$

The only unknown in this equation is the compound yearly inflation rate, CAIR. Rearranging terms, Exhibit 4-12 shows the formula that solves for the compound annual inflation rate (CAIR).

---

[17] $(\text{PI}_{\text{Year X}} - \text{PI}_{\text{Year 0}})/\text{PI}_{\text{Year 0}} \times 100\% = (\text{PI}_{2005} - \text{PI}_{2004})/\text{PI}_{2004} = (1.00 - 0.98)/98 \times 100\% = (0.02/0.98) \times 100\% = 0.0204 \times 100\% = 2.04\%$

[18] $(0.32/0.91) = 0.3516 = 35.16\%$

EXHIBIT **4-12**	**MEASURING COMPOUND ANNUAL INFLATION RATES**

$$\text{CAIR}_{\text{Year 0 to Year X}} = \left[\left(\text{PI}_{\text{Year X}} / \text{PI}_{\text{Year 0}} \right)^{(1/\text{Number of years between Year 0 \& Year X})} - 1 \right] \times 100\%$$

© John E. Marthinsen

Therefore, using the equation in Exhibit 4-12, we find that the compound (average) annual inflation rate from 2004 to 2012 was 2.88%.

$$\text{CAIR}_{\text{2004 to 2012}} = \left[(1.23/0.98)^{(1/8)} - 1 \right] \times 100\% = 2.88\%$$

HYPERINFLATION

Hyperinflation is like *pornography* in the sense that neither word has an official definition, but people know it when they see it. Because hyperinflation has no official definition, care should be taken to clarify what is meant when the term is used.

One of the most common unofficial definitions is that *hyperinflation occurs when a nation's prices increase above 50% per month for a sustained period.*[19] Consider the implications. If prices rose by 50% per month, the annual level of inflation would be almost 13,000% per year![20]

The story-line for nations with hyperinflation almost always has a two-part ending. Near the end, the old and valueless currency continues to circulate, but a dominant foreign currency replaces it (de facto) for purposes of valuing goods and services. Individuals and businesses still try to pay with the worthless domestic currency, but an unwillingness to accept it causes the dominant foreign currency to be used for this purpose, as well. Eventually, the old currency is abolished and a new one is created to replace it.

There are many examples of hyperinflation dating back centuries. For instance, during the U.S. Revolutionary War, the Continental Congress issued bills of credit to pay for the war, but the bills were overissued. Between 1775, when they were first issued, and 1781 (only six years later), the value of these bills fell to one five-hundredths of their original value. The expression "Not worth a Continental" came from this experience.[21] In the same way, during the U.S. Civil War in the 1860s, the United States had another bout with inflation as greenbacks were printed excessively by the North to finance the war.

So far, our examples have focused on the United States, but if we stopped there, we would be ignoring some of the world's most catastrophic examples of inflation. For instance, in Germany between 1918 and 1923, the price level rose 1.4 trillion times. At one point, a candy bar in Germany cost about 200 billion marks, and residents were using paper currency notes with denominations as

> The unofficial definition of hyperinflation is when a nation's monthly inflation rate exceeds 50% for a sustained period.

[19] Phillip Cagan, "The Monetary Dynamics of Hyperinflation," in *Studies in the Quantity Theory of Money*, ed. Milton Friedman (Chicago: University of Chicago Press, 1956).

[20] $(1 + 0.50)^{12} - 1 = 128.75 = 12,875\%$

[21] It is because of the hyperinflation during the Revolutionary War that the U.S. Constitution prohibits states from coining money and emitting bills of credit.

high as one billion marks. The old currency (i.e., the Reichsmark) stopped serving its intended, useful purpose and was replaced in 1923 by a new currency (i.e., the Rentenmark) at an exchange rate of one trillion-to-one.

Here is a taste of what everyday life was like in Germany during the 1920s, when hyperinflation ravaged the nation. People who dined at restaurants would pay for their meals before they ate them because afterward the price might be double. They would cover their walls with currency because it was cheaper than wallpaper. Given the choice, pickpockets would steal tissues from pedestrians' pockets and leave the worthless marks where they were. People could be seen walking to the store with wheelbarrows full of money just to purchase a loaf of bread. The prices of many goods and services, as well as the currency denomination of long-term contracts, were quoted in foreign currencies rather than marks.

Workers were paid twice a day (e.g., once at noon and at the end of the day), and trusted relatives or friends would meet them at the gate to spend the earnings as fast as possible. The problem was, at the same time people were trying to get rid of their earnings as soon as possible, store shelves were bare because merchants were bartering their wares for objects of real value.

Germany's hyperinflation undermined all the valuable functions that money performs. Because the German mark lost significant value by the minute, it was not used as a store of value or suited for contracts of any length. Because fewer merchants accepted it and began pricing their goods and services in terms of other currencies, the mark no longer served as Germany's medium of exchange or unit of account.

As high and outrageous as Germany's inflation rate was from 1918 to 1923, it pales in comparison to Hungary's at the end of World War II. In a two-year period between 1944 and 1946, the Hungarian PI rose by about 800 octillion percent![22] As is the case with all examples of hyperinflation, the cause of Hungary's inflation was the overissuance of money by the central bank. At that time, the Bank of Hungary printed money so fast that it had time to print just one side of the bills. It was not unusual to see pengös (i.e., the Hungarian currency) in denominations of 100 quintillion (100 million trillion).[23]

Many think that superhigh levels of inflation are relics of the past—events that happened years ago and, even then, only during or immediately after major wars or as a result of shocks of massive dimensions. Exhibit 4-13 shows some recent examples of superhigh inflation rates. For example, during the 1980s, countries such as Bolivia, Nicaragua, and Peru also had inflation rates that averaged in excess of 1,000%. In 1989 and 1990, Argentina experienced inflation rates of 4,900% and 1,350%, respectively. In 1995, Yugoslavia's inflation, just for the month of January, was 313,000,000%, placing it in second place, behind Hungary, for the highest inflation rate in the twentieth century. During the twenty-first century, Zimbabwe wins first prize for the

---

[22] An octillion is a one followed by 27 zeroes. The highest-denomination Hungarian bill was worth 10,000,000,000,000,000,000,000 (10 billion trillion) pengös.

[23] The pengö was replaced by a new currency, called the *forint*, at a rate of 400 octillion pengös per forint.

EXHIBIT 4-13	EXAMPLES OF COUNTRIES WITH VERY HIGH INFLATION RATES, 1973–2008		
Country	**Years**	**Number of Years**	**Compound Annual Inflation Rate**
Albania	1991–1992	1	226%
Angola	**1992–1996**	**4**	**1,388%**
Argentina	1976	1	444%
Argentina	1977–1988	12	217%
Argentina	**1989–1990**	**2**	**2,671%**
Armenia	**1992–1994**	**2**	**4,381%**
Azerbaijan	1992–1995	3	986%
Belarus	**1992–1995**	**3**	**1,247%**
Bolivia	1983–1984	2	620%
Bolivia	**1985**	**1**	**11,750%**
Brazil	1980–1987	8	154%
Brazil	1988–1989	2	956%
Brazil	**1990–1994**	**4**	**1,200%**
Bulgaria	1991	1	334%
Bulgaria	**1997**	**1**	**1,061%**
Chile	1973–1976	4	329%
Democratic Republic of Congo	**1990–1996**	**6**	**2,354%**
Croatia	**1993**	**1**	**1,516%**
Israel	1984–1985	2	338%
Kazakhstan	**1992–1994**	**2**	**1,527%**
Kyrgyz Republic	**1993**	**1**	**1,086%**
Macedonia	1993	1	339%
Mexico	1986–1988	3	110%
Moldova	1992–1994	2	518%
Mongolia	1991–1993		234%
Nicaragua	1985–1987	3	532%
Nicaragua	**1988–1991**	**4**	**6,375%**
Peru	**1988–1990**	**3**	**2,631%**
Poland	1989–1990	2	391%
Romania	1990–1994	4	188%
Russia	1992–1995	3	391%
Sierra Leone	1985–1987	3	107%
Suriname	1993–1995	2	296%
Tajikistan	1992–1995	3	849%

(Continued)

EXHIBIT 4-13	CONTINUED		
Country	Years	Number of Years	Compound Annual Inflation Rate
Turkmenistan	**1992–1996**	**4**	**1,427%**
Uganda	1979–1983	5	108%
Uganda	1985–1989	5	148%
Ukraine	**1992–1995**	**3**	**1,217%**
Uzbekistan	1992–1995	3	653%
Vietnam	1986–1988	3	394%
Yugoslavia	**1993–1994**	**1**	**5% × 10^{15}**
Zimbabwe	**November 2008**	**0.08**	**853% × 10^{21}**

Source: International Monetary Fund, *The World Economic Outlook Database*, www.imf.org/external/pubs/ft/weo/2000/02/data/pcpi_a.csv (accessed May 27, 2013). For Zimbabwe, see Steve H. Hanke, R.I.P. Zimbabwe Dollar, CATO Institute, www.cato.org/zimbabwe (accessed May 27, 2013). Thayer Watkins, "The Danger of Printing Too Much Money," http://usdcrisis.com/history/the-danger-of-printing-too-much-money/ (accessed May 27, 2013).

Bolded figures are annual inflation rates over 1,000% per year.

nation with highest inflation, when its inflation rate rose to 853% × 10^{21} during November 2008.[24] The Zimbabwe dollar still circulated but was largely replaced by foreign currencies, mainly the U.S. dollar.

DEFLATION

People are usually happy when the prices of individual goods and services they like to purchase (e.g., cell phones, computers, clothing, and/or vacations) fall. But if this is true, why does deflation, which is a decline in the average price of all goods and services, raise dark clouds of concern for monetary and fiscal policymakers?

The simple answer is that declining prices can lower incomes or reduce economic growth, which decreases purchasing power. This issue will be addressed more fully in Chapter 5, "Inflation: Who Wins, and Who Loses?", where we will find that a large part of the answer lies in expectations. In short, we will discover that if the deflation is expected, the victims (and beneficiaries) of inflation are substantially reduced. Another part of the answer lies in why prices, on average, fall. There are two fundamental reasons for declining national price levels. The first is an increase in the supply of all goods and services (called *aggregate supply*), and the second is a reduction in demand (called *aggregate demand*). Increases in supply are caused by beneficial changes, such as improved productivity and declining resource prices, which lead to rising output and employment. One would expect these price

[24] 853% × 10^{21} ≡ 853,000,000,000,000,000,000,000%

reductions to be met with public glee as the nation's living conditions improved.[25] Therefore, the problem with falling prices is when demand is falling because the decline in prices occurs simultaneously with declining output and rising unemployment. The effect of changing aggregate demand is a primary focus of this book and will be considered from Chapter 5, "Inflation: Who Wins, and Who Loses?" through the end of the book.

In a nation of declining prices, there are clear beneficiaries and victims. Among the beneficiaries are those with substantial cash holdings, fixed incomes, and investments in high dividend earning stocks. These individuals have cash, and in an economic atmosphere of declining prices, "cash is king."

Among the victims are individuals and businesses that accumulated substantial amounts of debt prior to the onset of deflation and now watch as their incomes and/or jobs are threatened or as their top-line revenue growth slows or declines.[26] Homeowners also are victims if they need to sell their homes at a capital gain. Other examples of inflationary victims are local, state, and national governments whose tax bases erode as incomes and assets values fall.

> Declining national price levels are caused by increases in the supply of all goods and services and/or reductions in demand.

TOPICS RELATED TO U.S. BUSINESS CYCLES

WHO MEASURES U.S. BUSINESS CYCLES?

In the United States, the National Bureau of Economic Research (NBER), a private organization, is responsible for measuring and dating U.S. business cycles.[27] The most important macroeconomic measure used by the NBER to date these cycles is the employment rate (i.e., the employment-to-population ratio), but three other variables (i.e., real personal income, volume of sales of the manufacturing and trade sectors, and industrial production) are also used. The NBER chose these four economic indicators over many others because they are reported monthly and have been shown to be economically significant, reliable, consistent, and accurate.

> The four most important variables used to measure U.S. business cycles are (1) the employment rate, (2) real personal income, (3) volume of sales of the manufacturing and trades sectors, and (4) industrial production.

PREDICTING BUSINESS CYCLES: U.S. INDEX OF LEADING ECONOMIC INDICATORS

What are the leading economic indicators (LEI) in the United States? Who chooses them, and how accurate have they been in predicting turning points in economic activity? The U.S. LEI index is published monthly by the U.S. Conference Board.[28] Exhibit 4-14 shows the 10 indicators included in this index and provides a brief explanation for why they are included. You should find, as you read these descriptions, that the relationship between the indicators included in the index and real economic activity is logical and has a strong link to common sense.

[25] There are very few examples of deflation caused by persistent increases in aggregate supply. China is sometimes offered as a recent example.

[26] Consider this. If you borrow at a 0% interest rate but prices (and your salary) fall by 5%, then the actual burden of your debt is 5%.

[27] For further information, visit the NBER Web site at www.nber.org/ (accessed May 26, 2013).

[28] The Conference Board is a nonprofit institution that creates and disseminates knowledge about management and the marketplace. The U.S. Commerce Department compiled the leading indicators index until 1995.

EXHIBIT **4-14**	U.S. LEADING ECONOMIC INDICATORS
1. Average weekly hours, manufacturing	Employers usually adjust work hours before hiring or firing employees.
2. Average weekly initial claims of unemployment insurance	Unemployment claims are usually very sensitive to economic activity. This index is inverted, which means an increase in claims implies a worsening of the economy.
3. Manufacturers' new orders, consumer goods and materials	An increase in current new orders implies increased production later. This inflation-adjusted series focuses on goods purchased mainly by consumers.
4. ISM Index of New Orders	The Institute of Supply Management tracks new order volume for more than 300 U.S. manufacturers. An increase in this index implies rising real GDP and, often, an escalating inflation rate.
5. Manufacturers' new orders, nondefense capital goods	An increase in current orders implies greater production later. This inflation-adjusted index focuses on goods purchased by producers.
6. Building permits, new private housing	An increase in current building permits implies more construction and construction jobs in the future.
7. Stock prices, Standard & Poor's 500 stock index	A rise in stock prices implies that investors are bullish (i.e., optimistic) about future business prospects.
8. Leading Credit Index	This non-price-oriented composite index replaced the money supply (M2) component of LEI in 2012. The Leading Credit Index (LCI) was introduced by the Conference Board to measure financial market forces that most reliably point to economic turning points. It has six components: two of them measure credit quality and risk (i.e., two-year swap rate and three-month LIBOR vs. Treasury bill yield); another two measure the degree of financial market speculation (i.e., margin account balances at brokers/dealers and AAII Investor Sentiment Survey), and the final two components measure credit availability (i.e., Fed Senior Loan Office Survey and security repurchase agreements).*
9. Interest spread between a 10-year U.S. Treasury bond and the overnight federal funds rate	The difference between long-term and short-term interest rates is a reflection of a yield curve's steepness. The yield curve provides information about expected future interest rate changes.
10. Consumer expectations	This survey index is the only economic indicator that is based totally on expectations.

*The Conference Board, Changes to the Conference Board Leading Economic Index® for the U.S. "Aim for More Accurate Business Cycle Predictor," January 5, 2012, www.prnewswire.com/news-releases/changes-to-the-conference-board-leading-economic-index-for-the-us-aim-for-more-accurate -business-cycle-predictor-136734748.html (accessed May 26, 2013). Gad Levanon, Jean-Claude Manini, Ataman Ozyildrim, Brian Schaitkin, and Jennelyn Tanchua, "Using the *Leading Credit Index™* to Predict Turning Points in the U.S. Business Cycle," The Conference Board Working Papers, December 2011 (released August 17, 2012), www.conference-board.org/publications/publicationdetail.cfm?publicationid=2065 (accessed May 26, 2013).

Source: The Conference Board, "Leading Economic Indicators and Related Composite Indexes," www.conference-board.org/ (accessed May 27, 2013).

Despite the care that has gone into choosing the LEI index, its track record of predicting future economic activity is mixed. There have been many times when the index provided valuable, early warnings of impending economic changes. But lead times have averaged between six and nine months, and these lead times have fluctuated rather widely. Moreover, this index has provided plenty of false signals. Like the boy in Aesop's fable who cried wolf too often, the index has warned of recessions that never occurred.[29]

The U.S. leading economic indicators have not always been accurate at predicting changes in economic activity.

Companies with new product, marketing, or investment strategies should keep these variable lead times and false signals firmly in mind—especially if a project's success depends heavily on an early rush of positive cash flows. In general, significant investment decisions should not be based solely on the index of LEI. If they are, as much flexibility as possible should be built into their design and implementation.

U.S. BUSINESS CYCLES FROM 1947 TO 2012

Introduction

Exhibit 4-15 shows movements in U.S. real GDP between 1947 and 2012. It provides visual confirmation that recessions in the United States have been recurring and irregular. During this 65-year period, output grew at an average rate of about 3.2%, while the population grew by only 1.4% per year. It was a period of rising living standards, but the road to prosperity for the United States had some bumpy stretches because the United States experienced 12 recessions.[30]

Are U.S. Business Cycles Short Term?

Business cycles are often characterized as short-term movements around a long-term trend, but this raises a definitional issue. From Exhibit 4-15, it is clear that business cycles wrap themselves around the long-term trend, but from peak to peak (or from trough to trough), a business cycle can last a decade or more. For instance, since World War II, U.S. recessions have lasted, on average, less than a year, but the average expansion has lasted about five years.[31] As a result, the average U.S. business cycle has lasted almost six years.

U.S. Business Cycles Before and After 1982

Exhibit 4-16 shows the peak and trough dates for U.S. business cycles since 1945. Notice that nine of the 12 recessions occurred during the 37-year period between 1945 and 1982, and three occurred during the 30 years from 1982 to 2012. Compared to the recessions occurring between 1982 and 2007, the recessions between 1947 and 1982 were more numerous and also more than 30% longer.

---

[29] Analysts use different rules of thumb, such as three consecutive quarters' decline in the leading economic indicators forewarns of a recession that is six to nine months away. Others use the rule of thumb that a 1% decline in the index and reductions in at least half the indicators portends a recession.

[30] Since 1857, the United States has experienced 33 recessions. National Bureau of Economic Research, "Business Cycle Expansions and Contractions," www.nber.org/cycles/cyclesmain.html (accessed May 26, 2013).

[31] On average, U.S. recessions have lasted 11.1 months, and expansions have lasted 58.4 months. NBER, "Business Cycle Expansions and Contractions."www.nber.org/cycles/ (accessed May 27, 2013).

Exhibit 4-15	U.S. Recessions and Movements in U.S. Real GDP: 1947 (I) to 2013 (I)

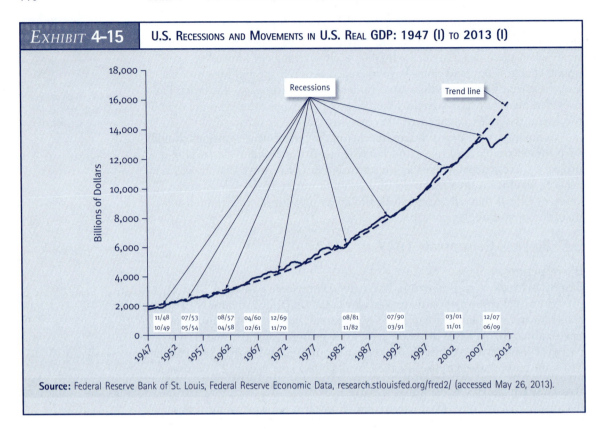

Source: Federal Reserve Bank of St. Louis, Federal Reserve Economic Data, research.stlouisfed.org/fred2/ (accessed May 26, 2013).

HAS THE UNITED STATES LEARNED TO TAME THE U.S. BUSINESS CYCLE?

Until the Great Recession, which lasted from December 2007 to June 2009, some economists wondered if fundamental changes in the U.S. economy had reduced the frequency and amplitude of U.S. business cycles.[32] Throughout the twentieth century, many U.S. companies had increased their operational flexibility by converting fixed into variable costs. The implementation and use of *just-in-time* (JIT) inventory management was only one example of how companies were able to trim costs, increase flexibility, and gain efficiencies by reducing their inventory-to-sales ratios. Rather than keeping large stocks of inputs on hand, businesses relied more heavily on their suppliers to provide inventories on an "as-needed" basis.

Implementation of JIT inventory management requires high levels of communication and responsiveness between customers and their suppliers, as well as technological advances in the areas of data warehousing and analysis.

---

[32] See, for instance, William C. Dudley and Edward F. McKelvey, *The Brave New Business Cycle: No Recession in Sight* (New York: U.S. Economic Research, Goldman Sachs, January 1997).

EXHIBIT 4-16	U.S. BUSINESS CYCLE EXPANSIONS AND CONTRACTIONS: 1945–2012

BUSINESS CYCLE REFERENCE DATES		DURATION IN MONTHS			
PEAK	TROUGH	CONTRACTION	EXPANSION	CYCLE	
(Quarterly dates are in parentheses)		Peak to Trough	Previous Trough to Peak	Trough from Previous Trough	Peak from Previous Peak
February 1945 (I)	October 1945 (IV)	8	80	88	93
November 1948 (IV)	October 1949 (IV)	11	37	48	45
July 1953 (II)	May 1954 (II)	10	45	55	56
August 1957 (III)	April 1958 (II)	8	39	47	49
April 1960 (II)	February 1961 (I)	10	24	34	32
December 1969 (IV)	November 1970 (IV)	11	106	117	116
November 1973 (IV)	March 1975 (I)	16	36	52	47
January 1980 (I)	July 1980 (III)	6	58	64	74
July 1981 (III)	November 1982 (IV)	16	12	28	18
Average		11	49	59	59
July 1990 (III)	March 1991 (I)	8	92	100	108
March 2001 (I)	November 2001 (IV)	8	120	128	128
December 2007 (V)	June 2009 (II)	18	73	91	81
Average		11	95	106	106

Source: National Bureau of Economic Research, "Business Cycle Expansions and Contractions," www.nber.org/cycles/ (accessed May 27, 2013).

With fewer inventories to finance, nonoperating business costs fell and profits increased. In contrast to the pre-1982 period, when most recessions were led by significant changes in businesses' inventories, the recessions in the 1982 to 2006 period were not inventory-led. Similarly, companies made increasing use of a *JIT-time labor pool*, which is the term used to describe extended work-weeks and the hiring of temporary and part-time workers rather than full-time employees, who earn a full menu of benefits (e.g., health insurance, vacation and sick days, as well as dental insurance).[33]

JIT inventory management caused a marked improvement in the stability of U.S. inventory management. As a result, it helped to stabilize investment demand and, thereby, dampen business cycle activity. But investment spending was not the only component of U.S. demand that was thought to have become more stable. The volatility of government spending and residential housing investment had also fallen. In addition, management of U.S. monetary aggregates and U.S. interest yields by the Federal Reserve (i.e., the U.S. central bank) had contributed to more steady demand.[34]

Concurrent with the trend toward greater stability in each of the major components of U.S. demand was a shift in U.S. demand away from goods and toward services. In general, the demand for services tends to be more stable than the demand for manufactured products. Therefore, the booming services industry may have been part of the reason for reduced business cycle fluctuations in the United States.

Another factor cited was the extensive use that companies made of risk management tools, such as financial derivatives and real derivatives (e.g., forwards, futures, options, and swaps), as well as risk mitigation measures, such as as value-at-risk analysis. The global explosion of derivatives markets allowed companies to partition their risks, hedge those they were unwilling and/or unable to bear, and keep those they wished to accept. Companies were empowered with the ability to transform their risk-return alternatives from what they had into something closer to what they wanted.[35] As a result, they became less sensitive to changes in many economic variables, such as commodity prices, interest rates, credit risk, and exchange rates.

Businesses may have also been disciplined by the increasingly aggressive merger and acquisition environment around the world. Poorly run companies became takeover targets, thereby threatening the jobs of ineffective managers. In addition, U.S. companies seemed to be in a continual process of restructuring, which meant they no longer waited for recessions to prune dead wood. As a result, when recessions occurred, there was less need to lay off workers.

Finally, trends toward globalization and financial deregulation were cited as possible factors that dampened U.S. business cycle movements. Financial

---

[33] Of course, the social costs of this business trend toward using temporary workers have fallen on the backs of workers.

[34] Robert J. Gordon, *What Caused the Decline in U.S. Business Cycle Volatility?* NBER Working Paper No. 11777, November 2005, http://www.nber.org/papers/w11777 (accessed September 24, 2013).

[35] For example by purchasing and/or selling financial derivatives, a company can hedge an unwanted accounts receivable (i.e., a long exposure), or it can transform this exposure into a more desired payoff profile.

EXHIBIT 4-17	POSSIBLE WAYS TO TAME THE BUSINESS CYCLE

- Improve business flexibility
  - Change fixed costs to variable costs
    - JIT inventories
    - JIT labor (e.g., temporary workers)
  - Continual restructuring
  - Globalization: Supply diversification
  - Use of risk mitigation techniques (e.g., derivative instruments & value-at-risk measures)
- Stabilize macroeconomic demand
  - Reduce the volatility of consumption, investment, and net exports
  - More stable monetary and fiscal policies
  - Shift to demand toward services
- Financial deregulation

© 2015 John E. Marthinsen

deregulation was viewed as a means of opening international financial flows between nations and promoting competition among financial intermediaries. It has also allowed interest rates and exchange rates to move with the forces of supply and demand, rather than by central bank or government decree. As a result, the U.S. and world financial systems were viewed as more efficient.

Changes in international trade flows were also important. Companies sourced internationally, and increasingly faced international competitors. The diversification of international suppliers reduced U.S. companies' operational vulnerability to single-source vendors, and increased competition provided strong incentives for suppliers to improve product quality and service.

Exhibit 4-17 summarizes the major forces that many thought had tamed U.S. business cycles.

The Great Recession of 2007 to 2009 is important, in this regard, mainly because it shattered beliefs that the business-cycle dragon had been slain. The economic downturn was so deep, lasted so long, affected so many people, and wiped out so much wealth that serious reconsideration has had to be given to the shocks that cause recessions and how these shocks can trump any and all of the mitigating factors suggested in this section.

CONCLUSION

The GDP Price Index, Consumer Price Index, and Producer Price Index are the three most commonly used measures of inflation. The GDP Price Index is the broadest inflation index. Therefore, it is the one used most frequently in country analyses and comparative economic studies. By contrast, the CPI provides the best information on how inflation influences household living costs. Therefore, the CPI is used most often in salary negotiations. Finally, the PPI shows price changes at the wholesale level, before retail markups, taxes, and distribution costs are added. This index is used largely in connection with analyses of business production costs.

Nominal GDP fluctuates with prices, but higher prices do not mean better living standards. To make GDP a more effective measure of human well-being, the effects of inflation must be removed. In effect, real GDP multiplies the amount produced in a nation each period by the price level in a base period. Because base-year prices are common to all periods, the only way real GDP can change is if output changes.

This chapter represents an important first step toward understanding and measuring inflation. It is also a valuable starting point for distinguishing between real and nominal economic variables, as well as opening the discussion about the causes and cures of business cycles. In Chapter 5, "Inflation: Who Wins, and Who Loses", we will broaden our analysis of real and nominal economic variables to determine how inflation hurts or helps individuals, businesses, governments, and the nation as a whole.

REVIEW QUESTIONS

1. What is inflation? What is hyperinflation?

2. If real GDP was $400 billion and the GDP Price Index was 0.9, what would nominal GDP be?

3. "If Japanese prices decreased each year from 1990 to 2013, and 2009 was the base year, then Japan's nominal GDP should have been less than real GDP in each year." Is this statement true or false? Explain.

4. Does an increase in inflation always cause an increase in nominal GDP? Explain.

5. What does *The Wall Street Journal* mean when it says that a nation's (e.g., South Korea's) economy grew "at a *real rate* of 9.2%"? Explain.

6. What is a business cycle? How are business cycles measured?

7. Why are business cycles difficult to predict?

8. Is it accurate to say that business cycles are "very short-term fluctuations" in real economic activity around a long-term trend?

9. What is a recession?

10. Indicate whether the following variables are procyclical, countercyclical, or acyclical.
    a. Imports
    b. Microsoft sales
    c. Layoffs
    d. Passive government spending (e.g., transfer payments)

11. What are the shortcomings of price indices?

12. The following data are for Argentina from 1985 to 2005:

Year	GDP Price Index
1985	0.003
1986	0.005
1991	86.129
2000	100.000
2005	169.609

a. Calculate the compound average annual inflation rate from 1985 to 1986, 1985 to 1991, 1991 to 2000, and 2000 to 2005.
b. Write a brief report that compares Argentina's inflation rate from 1985 to 1991, 1991 to 2000, and 2000 to 2005.

DISCUSSION QUESTIONS

13. Is it accurate to say that no one knows what causes business cycles (even after they occur)?

14. Is the GDP price index the best price index for all macroeconomic analyses? If it is, explain why. If it is not, explain the analyses for which the other measures (i.e., consumer price index or producer price index) should be used.

15. What is the index of LEI, and how are the indicators in the index chosen? Is the index a good predictor of future economic activity?

16. Explain why a company's ability to change its fixed costs to variable costs might be very important for maintaining business profitability during the course of a complete business cycle.

17. In 2013, the Bank of Japan (BoJ) set a goal to raise the nation's annual inflation rate to 2%. Explain why a targeted increase in the nation's CPI may not reflect the true, underlying inflation rate. In short, why might BoJ's 2% inflation goal have an impact on consumers and businesses that is less than 2%?

Chapter 5

Inflation: Who Wins, and Who Loses?

INTRODUCTION

Inflation has the power to give and to take—especially when it is unexpected. For any business, high and variable inflation can create uncertainty that leads to lower investment levels, falling profits, and reduced demands for labor. Inflation can also damage a business' international competitive position,[1] thereby eroding earnings and further dimming expansion hopes. At the same time, businesses that correctly anticipate inflation can make considerable profits. The key is in knowing how.

For individuals and governments, inflation also has the power to give and to take. Rising inflation can make paupers of those with few debts and a portfolio full of fixed income securities (e.g., bonds). At the same time, it can give a king's ransom to those with investment assets that rise with inflation, like real estate, antiques, and precious metals. As for governments, the taxes they collect and the real burden of the debts they pay are affected by inflation. Therefore, rising prices can play a significant role in what governments can and cannot afford to do.

This chapter discusses the purchasing power of money, which is measured in terms of the goods and services money can buy. It also examines inflation, which reduces this purchasing power and has the ability to redistribute income—hurting some groups and helping others. Which sectors of the economy benefit from inflation? Which sectors are hurt? How do businesses fare when inflation increases? Can they always raise prices fast enough to hit their profit targets? How about the average taxpayer, debtor, creditor, or the nation as a whole? Does inflation reduce a nation's overall well-being, or does it merely redistribute purchasing power among competing groups? We will use these questions as springboards for our discussion of the victims and beneficiaries of inflation.

> Inflation can increase business risks, erode international competitiveness, and threaten household wealth.

---

[1] These higher prices could be (and in the long run, should be) offset by changes in the country's exchange rate, but exchange rates are influenced by many factors other than inflation. Therefore, they may not adjust immediately to offset the effects of relative international price changes. Temporary imbalances caused by sluggish-moving exchange rates could, therefore, result in reduced exports and increased imports. We will discuss exchange rates in Chapter 14, "Basics of Foreign Exchange Markets," and Chapter 15, "Exchange Rates: Why Do They Change?"

THE BASICS

INFLATION DIMINISHES PURCHASING POWER

Purchasing power is measured in terms of how many goods and services it buys. Therefore, inflation is like a silent thief that steals purchasing power from our paychecks. To understand why, think of how well off you would be if you earned the same income as your grandfather, when he was your age.

Exhibit 5-1 shows the corrosive effects that inflation would have on a family earning $100,000 per year in 2014 and receiving no salary increases for the next 10 years. If the annual inflation were 1%, the family's purchasing power after 10 years will have fallen from $100,000 to $90,438. In other words, $100,000 will purchase only 90.4% of what it could purchase 10 years earlier. At 10%, the purchasing power will have fallen in 10 years to $34,868, and at 50%, the purchasing power of $100,000 will have fallen to a mere $98!

One of the problems with inflation is that it gives the illusion of prosperity without the substance. Exhibit 5-2 shows that between January 1961 and January 2013, U.S. prices rose by about 673%.[2] During these years, the average American's standard of living improved, but, nevertheless, a family earning a yearly salary of $10,000 in 1960 needed about $69,500 in 2012 to break even with inflation.[3] That is a substantial salary increase just to stay in the same place.

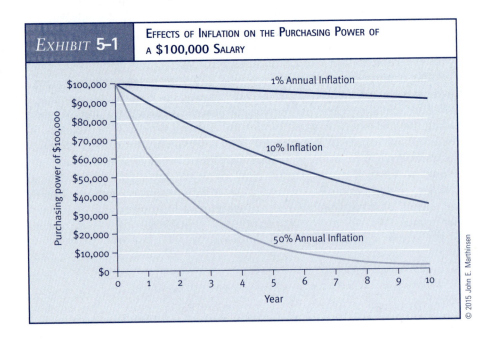

EXHIBIT **5-1**   EFFECTS OF INFLATION ON THE PURCHASING POWER OF A **$100,000** SALARY

© 2015 John E. Marthinsen

---

[2] The Consumer Price Index for all urban workers rose between January 1961 and January 2013 from 15.26 to 118.66, which is a 673% change.

[3] The family would have to earn even more if taxes took an increasing share of its income.

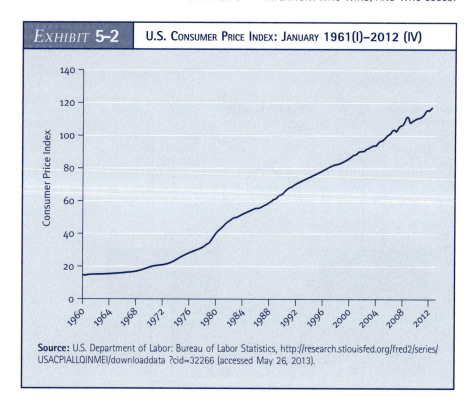

| EXHIBIT 5-2 | U.S. CONSUMER PRICE INDEX: JANUARY 1961(I)–2012 (IV) |

Source: U.S. Department of Labor: Bureau of Labor Statistics, http://research.stlouisfed.org/fred2/series/ USACPIALLQINMEI/downloaddata ?cid=32266 (accessed May 26, 2013).

FRAMING THE INFLATION ISSUE

Though it may seem from the previous examples that inflation harms a nation, the case is hard to prove. The circular flow diagram helps explain why more careful scrutiny is needed (see Exhibit 5-3).

In Chapter 2, "Taking an Economic Pulse: Measuring National Output and Income," we learned that the circular flow diagram shows how businesses and consumers interact via the real goods market and the resource market. The real goods market (i.e., the top portion of the circular flow) is where consumers in the household sector demand goods and services, and producers in the business sector supply them. From this interaction between supply and demand, the prices and annual rate of a nation's output (i.e., real GDP) are determined.

Inflation is the percentage change in the average price of goods and services; therefore, it is a measure that relates to the top portion of the circular flow diagram—but what about the bottom portion? We know from the circular flow diagram that any financial flows that are channeled through the real goods market (i.e., the top portion of the diagram) also must flow through the resource market (i.e., the bottom portion). In other words, what goes around must come around. If consumers are paying higher prices for goods and services, then someone has to be earning the

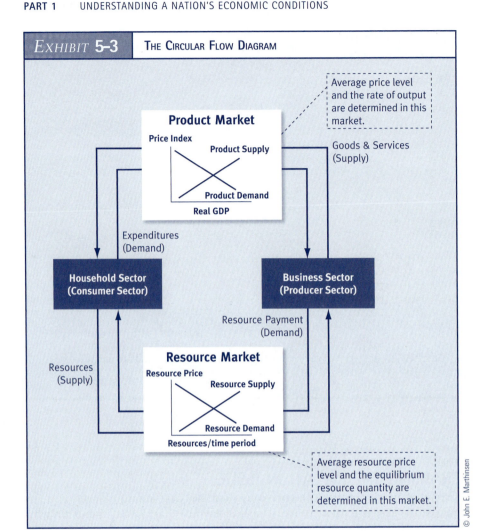

Exhibit **5-3**   THE CIRCULAR FLOW DIAGRAM

higher revenues. Alternatively, one could say that if inflation is raising business sales revenues, then someone has to be earning them. These funds might be going to labor in the form of higher wages and salaries, to natural resource owners (e.g., owners of land, oil, and forests) in higher rents, to capital owners in higher interest, or to entrepreneurs (i.e., businesses) in higher profits.

The point is that higher prices mean higher resource earnings, but if some individuals' incomes are increasing at rates slower than inflation, then other individuals' incomes must be rising at rates faster than inflation. For this reason, proving that a nation's *overall* well-being is harmed by inflation is more complex than it might first seem. At the end of this chapter, we will address how inflation affects a nation's overall standard of living, but before we do, let's investigate more closely the redistributive effects of inflation.

From the circular flow diagram we know that what is paid for goods and services must also be earned by someone. Therefore, the negative effects of inflation are largely due to the redistribution of income.

IN TIMES OF INFLATION, IS IT BETTER TO BE A DEBTOR OR CREDITOR?

Suppose you were the chief financial officer (CFO) of a public company, and at a quarterly investor analysts meeting, you were asked the following question: "In times of inflation, is your strategy to increase or decrease the company's debt level?" There may be many ways to explain your approach to handling high or low inflation, but in the end, the answer to this particular question will probably be "It depends." And this answer would be the same regardless of whether the question was asked to a CFO, professor of economics, or head of an ordinary household. Let's see why.

If you borrowed funds at 8% during a year when inflation was relatively high—for example 7%—then the effective annual cost of borrowing would be 1% because, even though you would be paying back 8% more dollars, each dollar's purchasing power would be worth 7% less. As a result, the *real* (inflation-adjusted) interest rate would be only 1%. Therefore, inflation seems to benefit borrowers and hurt lenders.

The problem with this conclusion is that it assumes lenders are always victims of inflation (and borrowers are always beneficiaries), with no ability to change their circumstances. What is often forgotten is that lenders have alternatives, one of which is to invest their funds in assets that will rise with the rate of inflation.

Nominal interest rates are the rates we see daily in the news. They are the rates that borrowers pay and the ones that lenders/savers receive. When expected inflation increases, lenders tend to restrict the supply of loanable funds to the credit markets, which raises nominal interest rates and thereby compensates them for the effects of expected inflation.

> Nominal interest rates are the ones we see in the news and pay or earn when we borrow or lend.

Lenders do not determine interest rates. Rather, interest rates are determined by the forces of supply *and* demand. Nevertheless, expected inflation

---

MACRO MEMO   5-1

"... And I'm Not Going to Take It Any More": Chinese Households Fight Back*

Chinese households have begun to take active measures against government controls that limit the interest they earn on savings deposits at state-run banks. During the past decade, rates on one-year deposits (about 3%) have been below the nation's prevailing inflation rate, resulting in handsome profits for banks, artificially low borrowing rates for state owned enterprises (SOEs), and a dissatisfied public. Household impatience from persistently earning negative real rates of interest has germinated the development of wealth-management products that offer attractive combinations of (relatively) low risk and (relatively) high returns (about 4.2%). From close to nothing just a few years ago, wealth-management products in China reached ¥7.1 trillion (about $1.2 trillion) by the end of 2012—about 8% of China's banking system deposits. The risks on wealth-management products are higher than on deposits in state banks, and investment transparency still needs to be improved, but Chinese households have clearly voted with their yuan in an attempt to earn positive real rates of return.

*Tom Orlik and Paul Mozur, "China's Consumers Fight Back, Explore Options," *The Wall Street Journal*, May 24, 2013, http://online.wsj.com/article/SB10001424127887323582904578484890981557734.html?mod=rss_mobile_uber_feed (accessed May 27, 2013).

EXHIBIT 5-4	RELATIONSHIP AMONG NOMINAL INTEREST RATE, REAL INTEREST RATE, AND EXPECTED INFLATION

> Real Interest Rate
> + Expected Inflation Rate over Relevant Future Time Period
> $\cong$ Nominal Interest Rate

© John E. Marthinsen

affects nominal interest rates in a very predictable way. At low levels of expected inflation, the nominal interest is (approximately) equal to the real interest rate plus the expected rate of inflation (see Exhibit 5-4). The real interest rate reflects a nation's *time value of money*. This means that it mirrors the extent to which lenders are willing and able to give up goods, which they could have purchased today, for goods and services that they will be able to purchase in the future. Expected inflation is the anticipated percent by which a debt's real burden or an investment's real return will be reduced.

If the annual desired real interest rate were 3%, then lenders would expect to be 3% better off next year, and borrowers would expect to pay this 3% charge for the opportunity of getting funds today that otherwise might not be available. At a real interest rate equal to 3%, if expected inflation were 0%, then the nominal interest rate should be 3% because lenders would not have to be compensated for any reduction next year in the purchasing power of their loans.

By contrast, if expected inflation were 5%, then borrowers and lenders would expect prices to strip 5% of the purchasing power from any funds received next year. As a result, the nominal interest rate should rise to 8% (i.e., 3% real interest plus 5% expected inflation) to compensate lenders for the expected loss of the currency's purchasing power.

It is important to note that nominal interest rates are influenced by the *expected* inflation rate, rather than the current or past inflation rate. This should make sense because funds are lent and borrowed over a future period. Therefore, the inflation rate that is expected over this future period should influence the nominal rate.

To show how unexpected changes in inflation redistribute income, suppose you lent me $100,000 for one year, figuring that if the future were anything like the past, you would be happy at the end of the year being 3% better off in real terms (i.e., you could purchase 3% more goods and services at the end of the year than you could at the beginning of the year). If the expected inflation rate for the coming year were 5%, then charging me an 8% interest rate would compensate you for the expected loss in purchasing power due to inflation.

If the actual inflation rate turned out to be 5%, your real return would be exactly what you expected to receive, and my real payment would be exactly what I expected to pay. Under these circumstances, inflation would not have benefited or harmed either one of us (see Exhibit 5-5).

By contrast, if the actual inflation rate turned out to be only 2%, I (the borrower) would be harmed and you (the lender) would be helped by the *unexpectedly low* inflation because you would have earned a real rate of

The expected real interest rate is the rate that market participants anticipate paying and earning after taking out the influence of expected inflation.

Nominal interest rates are influenced by the *expected* inflation rate, rather than the current or past inflation rate.

EXHIBIT **5-5**	EFFECTS OF INFLATION WHEN EXPECTED INFLATION = ACTUAL INFLATION	
1	Expected real interest rate *(beginning of the period)*	3%
2	+ Expected inflation rate *(beginning of the period)*	5%
3	= **Actual nominal interest rate** *(beginning of the period)*	8%
4	– Actual inflation rate during the period	5%
5	= **Actual real interest rate** *(end of period) (Rows 3–4)*	3%

© 2015 John E. Marthinsen

EXHIBIT **5-6**	EFFECTS OF INFLATION WHEN EXPECTED INFLATION > ACTUAL INFLATION	
1	Expected real interest rate *(beginning of the period)*	3%
2	+ Expected inflation rate *(beginning of the period)*	5%
3	= **Actual nominal interest rate** *(beginning of the period)*	8%
4	– Actual inflation rate during the period	2%
5	= **Actual real interest rate** *(end of period) (Rows 3–4)*	6%

© 2015 John E. Marthinsen

return equal to 6% (i.e., 8% nominal rate minus the 2% loss of purchasing power due to inflation) rather than 3% (i.e., 8% nominal rate minus 5% expected inflation). Similarly, I would be harmed because I paid a real rate of 6% rather than 3% (see Exhibit 5-6).

Suppose the actual inflation rate were 7%, rather than the expected 5%. Under these circumstances, your real return (and my real payment) would be only 1%. The unexpectedly high inflation would have reduced your purchasing power and reduced the real burden of my payments. I would have gained, and you would have lost as a result of the actual inflation exceeding the expected inflation (see Exhibit 5-7). Indeed, if the inflation rate were greater than 8%, you could actually earn a negative real rate of interest, which means you would be worse off at the end of the year (i.e., in terms of your purchasing power) than you were before the loan was made.

Governments are usually large borrowers; therefore, inflation affects them in the same way it affects the private debtors. When inflationary expectations rise (fall), the nominal cost of issuing new debt increases (falls). Also, when the actual inflation rate increases above the expected rate, governments (as debtors) are helped and lenders are hurt.

Let's return to the original question: Is it better to be a borrower or a lender in times of inflation? We can conclude from our analysis, so far, that the answer depends on whether the actual inflation is greater than, less than, or

> Because most governments are large debtors, they are influenced by inflation in the same way private debtors are influenced.

Exhibit **5-7**	Effects of Inflation When Expected Inflation < Actual Inflation	
1	Expected real interest rate *(beginning of the period)*	3%
2	+ Expected inflation rate *(beginning of the period)*	5%
3	= **Actual nominal interest rate *(beginning of the period)***	8%
4	− Actual inflation rate during the period	7%
5	= **Actual real interest rate *(end of period)* (Rows 3–4)**	1%

© John E. Marthinsen

Exhibit **5-8**	When Are Lenders and Borrowers Hurt and Helped by Inflation?		
Event		**Hurt**	**Helped**
Actual Inflation > Expected Inflation		Lenders	Borrowers
Actual Inflation = Expected Inflation		No one	No one
Actual Inflation < Expected Inflation		Borrowers	Lenders

© John E. Marthinsen

equal to expected inflation. If actual inflation is equal to expected inflation, then neither lenders nor borrowers would be hurt or helped by inflation. If the actual inflation is greater than expected inflation, then lenders would be hurt and borrowers would be helped. If the actual inflation is less than the expected inflation, then lenders would be helped and borrowers would be hurt.

Note that this result does not depend on whether actual inflation rises or falls, but but rather on whether it rises or falls more than expected. Exhibit 5-8 summarizes our results and leads us to the conclusion that, in terms of borrowers and lenders, for every beneficiary, there appears to be a victim. As a result, inflation (so far) does not appear to have a *net* negative effect on the entire nation.

DOES INFLATION BENEFIT BUSINESSES AT THE EXPENSE OF WORKERS?

Relative to their employees, are businesses helped or harmed by inflation? Clearly, businesses are not always helped. If they were, companies and industry associations would hire lobby groups and find other means to sway public opinion and policymakers toward raising the inflation rate. In the struggle between business owners (e.g., shareholders) and workers for their share of company sales revenues, we will find that inflation is not the steak knife that divides these earnings. Rather, the blade that distributes business earnings is the difference between actual and expected inflation.

The blade that distributes business earnings is the difference between actual and expected inflation.

Profiting from a Misaligned Real Interest Rate

Even though nominal interest rates are the ones we see most often, they are not the ones that most influence our behavior. Rather, real interest rates affect borrowing and lending decisions. An example might show why this is true.

Suppose the historic real interest rate was 3% and the nominal interest rate was 10%, but you expected the inflation rate over the coming year to be 15%. According to your expectations, the nominal interest rate should be 18% (i.e., the 3% real rate plus the 15% expected inflation). But if the nominal interest rate quoted in the market was only 10%, then this would be quite a bargain. But how could you profit from this misaligned nominal interest rate? The answer is to borrow up to your limits at the 10% nominal rate, invest the funds in goods that will rise in value with the expected inflation rate, store the goods in inventory, and, after one year, sell them at a 15% higher price.

Suppose you borrowed $100,000 at the 10% nominal interest rate, purchased inventories (i.e., any goods that would rise in value at or above the inflation rate), and stored them for one year. After a year, the principal and interest repayment on your loan would amount to $110,000 (i.e., $100,000 principal plus 10% interest), but the inventories could be sold for $115,000 ($100,000 plus 15% due to inflation), thereby leaving you with a $5,000 (i.e., 5%) gain.*

Let's go back and look at this example through another lens. If you expected inflation during the coming year to be 15% and the nominal interest rate was 10%, then your (expected) real interest rate would be −5% because

Real interest = Nominal interest − Expected inflation
$$-5\% \quad = \quad 10\% \quad - \quad 15\%$$

An expected real interest equal to −5% means that instead of interest being a charge you must pay, it becomes a reimbursement from borrowing.

To reinforce the point that real interest rates (and not nominal interest rates) affect borrowers' and lenders' behavior, suppose you expected inflation to be 2% during the next year, which means you expected the one-year nominal interest rate to be 5% (i.e., the 3% real rate plus the 2% expected inflation). If the actual nominal interest rate was 10%, you could profit by lending as much as possible. If your expectations were correct, inflation would strip away 2% of the purchasing power, leaving you with an 8% real return (i.e., 10% nominal rate minus the 2% inflation). Had the markets been properly aligned, you would have earned only the 3% historic real rate of return.

The take-away from this Macro Memo is the real burden of a 10% nominal interest rate can be high or low depending on expected inflation. Therefore, what determines whether individuals will be borrowers or lenders is not the nominal interest rate but rather the real interest rate.

*If there were any storage costs, they would be deducted from your earnings.

Suppose you are the executive responsible for negotiating annual salary increases with the company's labor union. Both sides agreed to an average wage increase of 9%, based on the expectation that labor productivity will rise by 3% and inflation will rise by 6%. Once this raise is negotiated, how could the company or union members be harmed (or helped) by inflation? As was the case with lenders and borrowers, workers could be harmed or helped only if the actual rate of inflation turns out to be different from the rate expected by the union. If the expected inflation next year is 6% and the

Exhibit 5-9	WHEN ARE LABORERS AND BUSINESSES HURT AND HELPED BY INFLATION?		
Event		**Hurt**	**Helped**
Actual inflation > Expected inflation		Labor	Business
Actual inflation = Expected inflation		No one	No one
Actual inflation < Expected inflation		Business	Labor

© John E. Marthinsen

negotiated wage increase is 9%, then workers will be harmed if the actual inflation rate is higher than 6%.[4]

> If actual inflation is greater than expected inflation, then the real cost of resources falls for businesses and increases profits. Businesses gain at the expense of resource owners.

For example, if the actual inflation turns out to be 8%, workers will earn only a 1% increase in their real incomes instead of the 3% they expected (and desired). At the same time, businesses will be helped because they expect to pay 3% more in real wages but end up paying only 1% more. As a result of this unexpected inflation, the prices of newly produced goods and services and the value of business inventories will rise at an average annual rate of 8%, causing profits to rise in tandem.

If actual inflation is less than expected inflation, just the opposite will occur (i.e., in terms of which group will be harmed by inflation and which group will be helped). Exhibit 5-9 summarizes how labor and business groups are hurt or helped when a nation's expected inflation is different from its actual inflation.

In general, the stronger a resource's bargaining position, the better chances it has to benefit at the expense of business and other resource groups. For instance, in an industry where demand is increasing, resources with specialized skills are needed, and talent is scarce, individuals and unions have considerable power. As a result, they can command an increasing share of the inflated national revenues at the expense of other resources (e.g., other labor groups, landowners, capital owners, and businesses/entrepreneurs).

As was the case with borrowers and lenders, when analyzing the beneficiaries and victims of inflation, it appears as if labor wins whenever business loses, and vice versa. But if the winners and losers offset each other, then can we go so far to say that the nation as a whole is not harmed by inflation? Again, let's wait until the end of the chapter to voice an opinion on this issue.

DOES INFLATION BENEFIT GOVERNMENTS AT THE EXPENSE OF TAXPAYERS?

When governments are net borrowers, they are affected by unexpected inflation in the same way any private borrower is affected. In particular, if actual inflation is higher than expected, then the real value of a government's debt and the real value of its interest payments fall (and vice versa).

---

[4]This discussion glosses over an important timing issue. When prices rise, businesses benefit immediately, but inflation helps labor only *after* inflation occurs. Therefore, the longer the period between when inflation occurs and when labor compensation is adjusted, the greater the burden put on workers.

Let's look at how inflation also affects government tax receipts. As inflation rises, a nation's tax base increases. If a progressive, nonindexed income tax system were in place, higher nominal incomes would force taxpayers into elevated income tax brackets and act as a hidden source of tax revenue for the governments. As a result, governments would gain by inflation at the expense of taxpayers, regardless of whether the inflation was expected or not.

In some countries, this is exactly what happens. In fact, it was not until 1985 that the U.S. federal income tax system was reformed so that tax brackets were adjusted each year to keep them inflation-neutral. With the passage of this legislation, the U.S. government eliminated the benefits of this particular source of passive income. At the same time, it remained the silent beneficiary where taxes were not indexed, such as the alternative minimum tax and capital gains tax.

> Governments could be the beneficiaries of inflation if tax brackets are not indexed and inflation pushes business and household incomes into higher tax brackets.

DOES INFLATION HURT RETIREES?

Most people are quick to point out that the obvious victims of inflation are people on pensions and collecting Social Security benefits. Inflation robs purchasing power from their fixed incomes and turns the job of making ends meet into a much more difficult chore. It is almost sacrilege to dispute the claim that these individuals are victims of inflation. In fact, some of them do suffer from rising prices, but others do not.

One reason the effects of inflation are nebulous is because not all pensions are fixed. Many of them rise automatically with the inflation rate, or they are adjusted periodically by companies to account for the effects of inflation and/or to reflect changing norms in pension compensation.

Furthermore, even though inflation erodes the purchasing power of fixed incomes, it also increases the value of assets owned by retirees (e.g., houses, jewelry, clocks, watches, paintings, precious metals, and stamps). Plainly, many retirees would be reluctant to sell assets, like their homes or heirlooms, just to earn the capital gains, but many that downsize their homes reap capital gains by moving into condos and senior living communities. As well, novel financial vehicles have been developed that permit the elderly to liquidate assets and cash in their equity. Borrowing on the basis of collateral and home equity loans are two examples. Reverse mortgages are another example because they pay retirees fixed monthly amounts based on the equity values of their homes. The main point is that inflation may actually help some members of the fixed income group.

The impact that inflation has on retirees also depends greatly on their spending patterns. The Consumer Price Index (CPI) reflects the expenditures of an average consumer, but most retired individuals do not spend like this average consumer. Therefore, they could be affected more or less than the average by rising prices. For instance, retirees are likely to be more affected than the average consumer by rising medical costs. At the same time, they are probably less affected by rising borrowing rates. Retirees often own homes. Therefore, they are not in the market for real estate loans. They may even benefit from rising interest rates if they are net lenders with floating-rate investments.

Finally, many retired individuals receive Social Security benefits from the government, which may increase over time due to newly passed legislation and/or cost-of-living adjustments. The U.S. Social Security System is a good case in point. Legislated changes in these benefits since 1950 and automatic cost-of-living adjustments since 1975 have significantly elevated benefits above increases in the cost of living.[5]

This is not to say that fixed income earners are usually helped by inflation. The point is simply that not all of them are harmed. Those who are harmed (e.g., those with fixed incomes, no supplementary benefits, and few assets) are the true victims of inflation. But if this is the case, how large is the total loss, and should the government implement economic policies solely to alleviate the burdens on this group? Might a better alternative be to implement policies (e.g., government aid and lower taxes) that address the problems of this particular group rather than enacting policies that affect everyone?

Not all fixed income earners are harmed by inflation. It depends on factors such as their spending patterns and wealth composition.

DOES INFLATION HURT THE NATION AS A WHOLE?

We know from the circular flow diagram that "what goes around must come around." As a result, it may appear as if inflation has no net effect on a nation's overall well-being because it only redistributes income from one group to another. In short, it *may appear* as if the inflation issue is really a question of who will earn more or less, rather than a question of whether the nation as a whole will suffer. Clearly, this is not the case.

It is true that, as long as inflation does not destroy work incentives or reduce productivity, real GDP *can* continue to grow in nations with rapidly rising prices. Germany is a good example. For most of the hyperinflation years of the early 1920s, Germany's real GDP increased. It was only near the end, when individuals found it more profitable to speculate than to work, that the economic system collapsed.

Inflation hurts the nation as a whole if it reduces work incentives and productivity.

Even though economic growth and high inflation *can* coexist, there are many reasons why they will not. For one, relatively high inflation can hurt a nation's international competitiveness. Whenever exchange rates do not adjust quickly and accurately to relieve international inflation rate differences, competitive gaps open. For instance, a 15% rise in a nation's average price level combined with a 4% decline in its currency value translates into an approximate 11% increase in the price of domestic goods and services relative to foreign prices. Therefore, changes in relative international inflation rates that are not offset by equal and opposite nominal exchange rate changes can cause a nation's exports to fall and imports to rise.[6]

Inflation can reduce a nation's international competitiveness.

In an environment of rapidly rising prices, the ability to decipher whether absolute prices or relative prices are changing becomes much more difficult. As a result, the potential for strategic errors and misallocations of resources increases. Inflation (especially rapid and unpredictable inflation) can cause

---

[5] These benefits were also extended to the retired workers' wives, widows, surviving parents, and children under age 18. Security Online, *Historical Background and Development of Social Security*, www.ssa.gov /history/briefhistory3.html (accessed May 27, 2013).

[6] We will discuss exchange rates in Chapter 14, "Basics of Foreign Exchange Markets," and Chapter 15, "Exchange Rates: Why Do They Change?"

dramatic shifts in relative prices, which can translate into large and unexpected changes in real earnings and real returns. Because nominal contracts are negotiated with expected inflation rates in mind, variations between expected and actual inflation rates can cause serious harm, and the groups that are harmed can change from year to year. Inflation uncertainty is a risk that is sure to add a premium to the cost of doing business.

Inflation can distort relative price signals and increase business risk.

Inflation also affects "menu costs," which are the added expenses that companies pay for bookkeeping, accounting, and marketing. How can companies advertise or establish fixed prices for customers when prices are rising rapidly, day by day or hour by hour? The whole notion of distributing printed catalogues evaporates when fixed prices cannot be maintained for any substantial period of time. If the prices quoted today must be changed tomorrow, then how are these new prices communicated to the consuming public?

Inflation increases menu costs.

In the age of the Internet, the electronic transmission of changing price information could help in this regard. Price changes can be communicated quicker and cheaper than in former years. Nevertheless, it takes time and effort to make these changes, and the added costs (costs that would not be present at lower inflation rates) reduce productivity and profitability.

Inflation can also affect buying and selling patterns. For example, to protect themselves against rapidly rising prices, companies tend to negotiate purchase-and-sales agreements with ever-shorter time horizons. The constant need to renegotiate contracts can raise the costs of doing business. For companies fighting for survival in high-inflation environments, the need to correctly forecast price changes also increases along with the financial penalties of forecast errors.

Inflation can shorten contract periods.

Inflation can seriously complicate valuation estimates, producing problematic results. When inflation rates rise (e.g., in excess of 100% per year), how can companies accurately value their assets, liabilities, expenses, and revenues? What is the cost of performing these valuation exercises, and how accurate can they be when historic benchmarks are no longer valid?

Inflation can complicate valuation estimates.

One of the biggest potential threats of excessive inflation is on the political side. When inflation rises beyond acceptable levels, politicians often pass price control legislation. These laws artificially restrict prices and only serve to mask the true sources of the inflation. The controls create an array of new problems—often bigger than inflation itself. For instance, even though they reduce or eliminate the open manifestation of inflation, they create shortages, reduce quality and size, as well as increase administrative overhead due to the number of added government employees needed to oversee the controls.

Inflation may prompt governments to impose wage and price controls.

Finally, because inflation premiums are built into price schedules, a nation could end up chasing its own inflationary tail for a short time (i.e., have self-perpetuating inflation). With ever-rising inflation, markets come to expect that next year's inflation rate will be greater than this year's inflation. When this happens, inflation can take on a life of its own for a short time because people have to estimate the future inflation rate in order to conduct normal business (e.g., borrow, as well as sign labor, supplier, and sales contracts). The expectation that prices will be higher next year than this year could result in high inflation without any fundamental causes. Like a speeding, runaway car, the inertia of higher prices would be enough to propel them forward.

To put this issue into better perspective, there are no historic examples of sustained inflation caused purely by inflationary expectations. People form their expectations based on the world around them. For instance, a rapid increase in the money supply or a natural disaster could spark inflationary expectations. But when they are ignited, the job of public policymakers (e.g., presidents, prime ministers, central bankers, congressmen, and parliaments) becomes even more difficult. Not only must they address the underlying causes of inflation; they must also address the public's perceptions about inflation.

THE REST OF THE STORY

NOMINAL INTEREST RATE AND EXPECTED INFLATION: THE PRECISE FORMULA

Adding expected inflation to the real interest rate provides a good approximation of the nominal interest rate when expected inflation is low. But as expected inflation rises, this approximation becomes increasingly less reliable because it does not account for the lost purchasing power of the interest earned. In other words, an interaction term between the real interest rate and expected inflation is missing.

To understand the interaction term, suppose you lent me $1,000, expecting to receive back the principal, real rate of return, and expected inflation. Therefore, you expect to receive $1,000 \times (1 + R) \times (1 + P^e)$, where R is the real rate of interest and P^e is the expected inflation. Cross-multiplying, we find that you expect to receive $1,000 \times [1 + R + P^e + (R \times P^e)]$. The ($1,000 \times 1$) is your principal, ($1000 \times R$) is the real return you want to earn, ($1,000 \times P^e$) is the return to compensate you for the expected inflation, and [$1,000 \times (R \times P^e)$] is the interaction term that compensates you for the decline in purchasing power of your real interest. At low inflation rates, this interaction term is close to zero and is normally dropped. At high inflation rates, the interaction term can be significant, and thus it must be included. Exhibit 5-10 summarizes these relationships.

Therefore, a more precise relationship between the nominal interest rate and expected inflation for high-inflation countries is shown in Exhibit 5-10.

EXHIBIT **5-10**	PRECISE FORMULA: RELATING THE REAL INTEREST, NOMINAL INTEREST, AND EXPECTED INFLATION RATES

Real interest rate
+ Expected inflation rate
+ (Real interest rate × Expected inflation rate)
= Nominal Interest Rate

HOW TO DISCOVER "THE MARKET'S" EXPECTATION ABOUT FUTURE INFLATION

We now understand that the nominal interest rate incorporates the real interest rate and the market's expectation about future inflation, but how can the average person determine what "the market" is expecting? This question is especially important for those entering into contracts and looking to make good deals or speculators who feel they can outsmart the market and earn above-average returns. Good deals are made and above-average profits earned when an individual's inflationary expectations turn out to be more accurate than the market's expectations.

This section explains three different methods that can help uncover the market's inflationary expectations. As you might expect, none is perfect, but they, at least, provide a credible way to start the process of calculating the market's inflationary expectations so the estimates can be compared to your own.[7]

METHOD #1: CONDUCTING SURVEYS

One of the best ways to uncover market sentiment about future inflation is to conduct surveys and simply ask people their opinions. Surveys on expected inflation are conducted around the world by private organizations, governments, and central banks. Some of them randomly choose and interview individuals/households; others interview financial professionals (e.g., economists and bankers) who work on a daily basis with issues such as these and are likely to provide more objective answers than the average household member.

In the United States, the most prominent survey is the Thomson Reuters/ University of Michigan Survey of Consumers,[8] which interviews approximately 500 households each month. Two others, the Livingston Survey (LS)[9] and Survey of Professional Forecasters (SPF), are managed by the Philadelphia Federal Reserve.[10] The semi-annual LS interviews 30 to 40 economists, representing the business, government, financial, and academic communities. SPF is a quarterly survey that interviews 30 to 50 private economists representing the business community. Finally, the twice-monthly American Life Panel is an internet survey conducted by RAND.

The United States is not alone in its use of surveys to uncover the market's expected inflation. Central banks and private financial institutions in many European Union nations (e.g., England, Holland, and Italy), and other

---

[7] To learn more about determining a nation's expected inflation rate, see Bharat Trehan, "Survey Measures of Expected Inflation and the Inflation Process," Federal Reserve Bank of San Francisco Working Papers, February 2010, http://www.frbsf.org/publications/economics/papers/2009/wp09-10bk.pdf; Wilbert van der Klaauw, Wändi Bruine de Bruin, Giorgio Topa, Simon Potter, "Rethinking the Measurement of Household Inflation Expectations: Preliminary Findings," Federal Reserve Bank of New York Staff Reports, no. 359, December 2008, http://www.newyorkfed.org/research/staff_reports/sr359.html (accessed May 27, 2013).

[8] Thomson Reuters, Thomson Reuters/University of Michigan Surveys of Consumers, http://thomsonreuters .com/products_services/financial/financial_products/a-z/umichigan_surveys_of_consumers/ (accessed May 27, 2013).

[9] Federal Reserve Bank of Philadelphia, Livingston Survey, http://www.phil.frb.org/research-and-data/real -time-center/livingston-survey/ (accessed May 27, 2013).

[10] Federal Reserve Bank of Philadelphia, Survey of Professional Forecasters, http://www.phil.frb.org/research -and-data/real-time-center/survey-of-professional-forecasters/ (accessed May 27, 2013).

countries, such as Australia and South Africa, conduct regular inflation surveys. Many of these non-U.S. surveys are qualitative (i.e., they ask only if inflation will rise, fall, or stay the same) rather than quantitative (i.e., asking for a specific expected inflation rate). When they are qualitative, statistical methods are often used to derive reportable, quantitative inflation estimates.

METHOD #2: USING TREASURY INFLATION PROTECTED SECURITIES (TIPS)[11]

The U.S. Treasury offers Treasury Inflation Protected Securities (TIPS), which provide investors with a source of shelter against unexpected inflation.[12] TIPS are offered with a fixed *real* rate of interest and, then, semiannually, both the coupon and principal are adjusted for the actual inflation that occurs. Inflation increases the periodic coupon payments on TIPS and also increases the principal that will be received at maturity. Deflation reduces them. TIPS are issued in 5-year, 10-year, and 30-year maturities, and they come in denominations as low as $100.

Let's see how TIPS can be used to help determine the expected U.S. inflation rate. Suppose the return on a 5-year TIPS, which incorporates no expected inflation premium, was 3%, and the return on a 5-year conventional Treasury security, which incorporates an expected inflation premium, was 7%. The difference (i.e., 4%) can be viewed as an estimate of expected annual inflation rate for the coming five years.[13]

METHOD #3: MAKING ECONOMETRIC FORECASTS USING TIME SERIES MODELS

Sophisticated econometric methods are also used by economists, financial analysts, central banks, and think tanks to forecast inflation rates and uncover market expectations about inflation.[14] Forecasts are usually based on past movements and historic causes of inflation. These models can be highly accurate, but their accuracy depends on the past causes and patterns of inflation repeating themselves in the future.

A few relatively recent studies[15] have indicated that survey forecasts outperform econometric forecasting methods, but the verdict is still out on which

---

[11] Charles T. Carlstrom and Timothy S. Fuerst, "Expected Inflation and TIPS," Federal Reserve Bank of Cleveland Commentary, November 2004, http://www.clevelandfed.org/research/commentary/2004/nov.pdf (accessed May 27, 2013).

[12] TreasuryDirect, "Treasury Inflation-Protected Securities (TIPS)," www.treasurydirect.gov/indiv/products/prod _tips_glance.htm (accessed May 27, 2013).

[13] Caution is advised when using this method because Treasury securities and TIPS are not homogeneous. Therefore, their interest differential might misestimate expected inflation. One difference is the liquidity in their respective markets. The TIPS market is less liquid than the Treasury securities market; so this liquidity premium should also be part of the interest differential. Another reason these securities are not homogeneous is because the coupon payments and principal (at maturity) for conventional treasury securities are fixed (i.e., they do not vary from issuance to maturity). By contrast, the coupon and principal on TIPS fluctuate with the actual inflation rate.

[14] Two frequently used statistical methods are ARIMA, which is an abbreviation for autoregressive integrated moving average models (sometimes called Box-Jenkins models), and ARMAX, which is an abbreviation for an ARIMA model with exogenous independent variables.

[15] Andrew Ang, Geert Bekaert, and Min Wei, "Do Macro Variables, Asset Markets, or Surveys Forecast Inflation Better?" National Bureau of Economic Research, Working Paper 11538, August 2005, http://www.nber.org /papers/w11538.pdf; R. W. Hafer and S. E. Hein, "On the Accuracy of Time-Series, Interest Rate, and Survey Forecasts of Inflation," *Journal of Business*, University of Chicago Press, vol. 58(4), 1985, pp. 377–98.

of the three methods is best. In the future, new forecasting methods are bound to appear. Already, a relatively recent one suggests there is a link between the slope of the yield curve[16] and expected inflation.[17]

WHAT DETERMINES INFLATIONARY EXPECTATIONS?

How do people form their expectations about inflation rates? The answer to this question is important because whenever inflationary expectations change, behavior changes. For example, higher expected inflation should lead to greater wage demands, anticipatory increases in prices, and speculative asset buying. There are two major theories on how inflationary expectations are formed: *adaptive expectations* and *rational expectations*.

ADAPTIVE EXPECTATIONS THEORY

According to the adaptive expectations theory (AE), people form their opinions about future inflation by considering two major factors: (1) past rates of inflation and (2) the difference between what they thought inflation would be and what it actually was. As for the first factor, if inflation rates in the past were high, AE posits that people would expect these high rates to continue in the future. Therefore, AE views this first factor as a sort of weighted average of current and past inflation rates, with the most recent rates having greatest importance.

> AE considers past inflation rates and the difference between the expected and actual inflation rates.

As for the second factor that determines inflationary expectations, AE suggests that people build premiums or discounts into their inflationary expectations that reflect the extent to which they were fooled in the past. For example, if they expected inflation this year to equal 3%, but it turned out to be 8%, then the positive 5% differential would be reflected wholly or partially in their expectations for next year's inflation rate.[18] This second factor can be viewed as a weighted average of current and past inflation prediction errors, with the most recent errors having the greatest weight. Exhibit 5-11 shows a simple way to view AE.

RATIONAL EXPECTATIONS THEORY

The rational expectations theory (RE) is based on two major assumptions. First, it assumes that people form their expectations based on *all available information* and not just on past rates of inflation and past prediction

EXHIBIT **5-11**	ADAPTIVE EXPECTATIONS THEORY

Weighted average of past inflation rates
+ Weighted average of past inflation prediction errors
———————————————————————————
= Current inflationary expectations

© John E. Marthinsen

---

[16] The yield curve shows the relationship between nominal interest rates and maturity.

[17] Arthuro Estrella, "Why Does the Yield Curve Predict Output and Inflation?" *The Economic Journal*, Vol. 115, Iss. 505, pp: 722–744.

[18] Statistical analyses of historic inflation and nominal interest data would be needed to find out whether people incorporate the entire 5% or only a portion of it into their inflationary expectations.

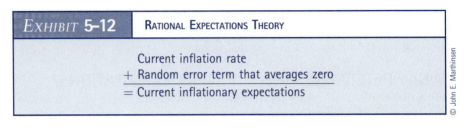

mistakes. For example, if the Bank of Japan announced today a credible change in its monetary policy or inflation targeting, RE would anticipate this new information to be incorporated immediately into people's expectations of future Japanese inflation, even if the announcement had no connection to past inflation rates or past prediction errors.[19]

The second RE assumption is that markets are efficient; therefore, they incorporate new information quickly and efficiently into their inflationary expectations. Of course, we all know that people make mistakes and can act incorrectly on new information. Fortunately, these mistakes do not detract from RE as long as new information is incorporated in an unbiased manner. In other words, it does not matter as long as people do not systematically overreact or underreact to the new information.

If we combine the two RE assumptions, we get an interesting (and, for many, unexpected) result. If people take all information into account when forming their inflationary expectations and if they do it in an unbiased manner, then the current inflation rate is the best measure of inflationary expectations. Any variations between current inflation and actual future inflation would be due to an unpredictable error term that, on average, should equal zero. According to RE, using the current inflation rate as a proxy for expected future inflation is about as good as anyone can do. Exhibit 5-12 shows a simple way to view RE.

> **RE considers all relevant information and assumes that markets are efficient.**

> **The rational expectations theory states that inflationary expectations are based on all currently available information.**

A Final Word on AE and RE

AE and RE are not mutually exclusive. If new information is built slowly into people's inflation forecasts, then AE may be the best way to determine expectations about future inflation. Clearly, if new information is important and becomes known, why would anyone exclude it from their inflation predictions? Perhaps it is best to view the formation of inflationary expectations as a process that efficiently and effectively incorporates the best of both the AE and RE approaches.

INDEXATION

Indexation is a way to help protect the interests of society from the arbitrary, redistributive effects of unexpected inflation. Think of what it would be like to live in a country with nationwide indexation. Borrowers, lenders, labor,

---

[19] In 2013, the Bank of Japan (BOJ) announced its intention to raise the domestic inflation rate to 2% within two years. Given its past efforts and lack of success, many analysts questioned BOJ's ability to hit this inflation target, which diminished the credibility of the bank's new monetary goal.

management, businesses, and customers would no longer need to incorporate the expected rate of inflation into their contracts. Rather, they would negotiate a real interest rate, real wage rate, or real price and then adjust it afterward for the actual amount of inflation.

For example, suppose borrowers and lenders negotiated a real interest rate equal to 3% per year. If the actual inflation rate during the year were 0%, then borrowers would pay back at the end of the year the principal plus 3% interest. If the actual inflation were 5%, they would pay 8% interest, and if inflation fell by 2%, they would pay 1%.

Similarly, suppose labor and management negotiated a real wage rate increase of 3% per year (i.e., 0.25% per month). When salaries and wages were paid each month, compensation would be increased or decreased by the actual amount of inflation during that month. Finally, businesses and their customers would negotiate real prices and, at payment, adjust these prices to reflect the actual amount of inflation or deflation.

Suppose a family earned $80,000 a year, had $10,000 in a bank deposit, and held a 30-year mortgage. With full indexation and an actual inflation rate of 10%, the following adjustments would occur at year's end: (1) the $80,000 salary would automatically rise to $88,000 (i.e., $80,000 + [10% of $80,000] = $88,000), and any further increase in salary beyond 10% (e.g., due to productivity improvements or exceptional performance) would be negotiated separately; (2) interest on the $10,000 bank account would rise automatically to reflect the actual inflation rate. If the real interest earned on the account were 3%, the depositor would receive 13%, which means the bank account at the end of the year would be $11,300; (3) the base value of the mortgaged house would rise by 10%, so that later, when the house was sold, this 10% increase would not be taxed as a capital gain; (4) the mortgage rate would rise by the rate of inflation; and (5) the homeowner's insurance premium would rise to reflect the newly inflated value of the house.

One of the major benefits of indexation is that it substantially neutralizes the redistributive effects of unexpected inflation. The type of inflation it deals with best is inflation caused by increases in demand (i.e., demand-pull inflation).[20] For example, if the central bank were to increase the money supply, thereby giving the nation more spending power, this increased demand would put upward pressure on the prices of goods, services, and resources. Assuming the increased money supply did not change real GDP, higher inflation would mainly redistribute income among various income groups. Indexing would prevent (or at least reduce) the income redistribution effects of any unexpected inflation.

By contrast, indexation is not as effective in dealing with inflation originating from the supply side of the market. Consider the following example. Suppose Japan suffered an earthquake and tsunami similar to the ones in March 2011. Prices in Japan would rise due to the shortages that would

---

[20] In Chapter 12, "Price and Output Fluctuations," demand-pull inflation will be explained fully, along with cost-push inflation and spiral inflation.

occur. No amount of indexation could make the resulting change in prices neutral or restore the economy to the standard of living it enjoyed before the catastrophe. The nation would no longer be trying to equitably distribute an existing or larger pie. Rather, it would be trying to divide a smaller pie, and this is a process that always claims more victims than beneficiaries.

Indexation is also criticized because it may build inflation into the system, causing last year's inflation to influence this year's supply and demand conditions. To the extent that expectations alone could be a cause of persistent inflation, this criticism has merit because these expectations could impede the success of monetary policy.

Indexation is not a newly discovered means of neutralizing the redistributive effects of inflation. It is centuries old,[21] and over its many years of use, indexation has been used in numerous ways, such as alimony payments, bank deposit rates, labor contracts, interest rates on government securities, long-term delivery contracts, leases, food stamp payments, Social Security benefits, insurance premiums, and mortgage rates.

In general, the popularity of indexation varies directly with the prevailing rate of inflation. When the inflation rate is relatively low, scarcely a word is heard about it, but when inflation rises (especially to high levels), grassroots sentiment in favor of indexation surges.

One of the major benefits of indexation is political because indexation neutralizes the effects of unexpected inflation and thereby eliminates (or substantially reduces) the victims and beneficiaries of inflation. As a result, it makes the jobs easier for policymakers (e.g., central banker and elected leaders) because indexation reduces the need for political action committees and lobbyists.

THE GIBSON PARADOX

Understanding that the credit markets incorporate an inflationary premium into the nominal interest rate helps explain a paradox that was posed early in the twentieth century by A. H. Gibson, a British statistician. Gibson noticed that interest rates were relatively high when a nation's money supply growth rate rose, and they were relatively low when it slowed. This result was counter to his intuition. If there was more money available, he reasoned that interest costs should be low and not high. After all, if the supply of money rose, shouldn't the cost of renting it fall?

This paradox can be reconciled by distinguishing between nominal and real interest rates. What Gibson was witnessing was the relationship among the nominal interest rate, money supply, and expected inflation. Nominal interest rates include both the real interest rate and expected inflation. Increasing the availability of money may reduce the real interest rate, which would reduce the nominal interest, but it is also likely to increase expected inflation, which would increase the nominal interest rate. As a result, the net

---

[21] There is evidence of indexation as far back as 1567. The first modern-day usage of indexation in the United States occurred in the 1940s when the United Auto Workers won this provision as part of its negotiated settlement.

effect on the nominal interest rate depends on whether the real interest effect is stronger or weaker than the expected inflation effect.

The relationship between expected inflation and nominal interest rates is fundamental in economics, and one that gives considerable insight into how borrowers respond to changes in credit conditions. For instance, many people wondered why U.S. borrowers during the 1970s did not reduce their demand for credit when interest costs rose rapidly. Many possible explanations can be suggested,[22] but one of the major reasons was because *real* interest rates during the 1970s were not high. Nominal interest rates were high due to rapidly rising expected inflation rates.

Similarly, at the turn of the twenty-first century, nominal interest rates in the United States were at 40-year lows, but so was the U.S. inflation rate. As a result, demand for loans was not explosive because it responded to real interest rates (i.e., the nominal interest rate after deducting expected inflation), which were not at their historic lows.

> The Gibson paradox is resolved by understanding that nominal interest rates rise with expected inflation, and expected inflation rises with the excess creation of money.

INFLATION AND THE COST OF HIGHER EDUCATION

Let's consider a disquieting example of inflation and its effect on educational costs (see Exhibit 5-13). During the 2012–2013 academic year, the average cost of a year's worth of university-level education in the United States was about $35,000.[23] Suppose your child was born in 2014, and the annual inflation rate was expected to be 12% for the next 18 years (i.e., until your child was old enough to attend a university). At 12%, it takes about six years

EXHIBIT 5-13	COST OF A U.S. UNIVERSITY EDUCATION FOR ONE YEAR AT VARIOUS INFLATION RATES			
Annual Inflation	2014 Your child is born this year	2020 Your child is 6 years old	2026 Your child is 12 years old	2032 Your child is 18 years old
3%	$35,000	41,792	49,902	59,585
4%	$35,000	44,286	56,036	70,904
6%	$35,000	49,648	70,427	99,902
8%	$35,000	55,541	88,136	139,861
12%	$35,000	69,084	136,359	269,149
16%	$35,000	85,274	207,761	506,188

© 2015 John E. Marthinsen

[22] For example, the increase in credit demand could have been due to expectations of changing capital gains taxes or due to rising incomes as many families switched from one income earner to two income earners.

[23] During the 2012–2013 academic year, the average cost of an in-state college/university was $22,261, and the average cost of a private college/university was $43,289. COLLEGEdata, "What's the Price Tag for a College Education?" https://www.collegedata.com/cs/content/content_payarticle_tmpl.jhtml?articleId=10064 (accessed May 27, 2013).

for prices to double; so, when your child was six years old, the cost of just one year at a university would be about $70,000, but your child would still be too young to attend. If inflation continued at the same 12% annual rate, by the time your child was 12 years old, a year's worth of university-level education would cost almost $140,000, but again, your child would still be too young to attend. Finally, by the time your child was 18 years old and ready to attend a university, the annual price tag would be about $270,000—and that is just at a 12% inflation rate over an 18-year period (see Exhibit 5-13)!

CONCLUSION

One of the important lessons from this chapter is that it is hard to identify the victims (and beneficiaries) of inflation until after inflation occurs. Markets (e.g., credit and labor markets) incorporate inflationary expectations into interest rates, prices, and resource costs. Therefore, it is only when expected inflation is different from actual inflation that income redistribution occurs.

For the nation as a whole, inflation mainly redistributes income from people in weak negotiating positions (e.g., individuals in declining industries and fixed income earners) to people in strong negotiating positions (e.g., individuals in expanding industries and possessing marketable skills). At the same time, if inflation and price volatilities curtail business investments, change work incentives, or diminish productivity in any way, they can reduce a nation's overall well-being.

REVIEW QUESTIONS

1. Suppose that after 20 years, you decide to attend your high-school reunion and, by chance, run into an old friend who reminds you of a wager that you lost to her. Expecting immediate payment, she agrees to charge you no interest but asks that you compensate her for the loss of purchasing power caused by inflation. During the past 20 years, the average inflation rate was 5%. If the original wager was $150, what would you owe today? If you successfully argued that the average annual inflation was only 3.5% and not 5%, how much would you save?

2. "Lenders are always hurt by an increase in the inflation rate." Comment on the validity of this statement.

3. Are wage earners usually hurt by unexpectedly high inflation? Explain.

4. How might retirees be hurt by unexpectedly high inflation? How might they be helped by unexpectedly high inflation?

5. Comment on the validity of this statement: "Governments always benefit from inflation."

6. Is the approximation formula for calculating nominal interest rates most useful in times of relatively high inflation or relatively low inflation? Explain.

7. Based on what you believe the inflation rate will be during the coming year, suppose you estimate that the current real interest rate equals −15%. What can you do to profit from this expectation? How much do you expect to gain? Are you arbitraging (i.e., earning a risk-free return) or speculating? If you are speculating, what might cause you to lose on your bet?

8. If the real interest rate was 3%, the past year's inflation rate was 30%, and the expected inflation rate for the coming year was 40%, use the approximation formula to determine the nominal rate of interest. What would the nominal interest rate equal using the more precise formula?

9. Explain the costs and benefits of indexation.

DISCUSSION QUESTIONS

10. Suppose a business analyst argued that Argentina should reduce inflation drastically because nominal interest rates would fall with lower expected inflation and thereby stimulate economic activity. Do you agree with this opinion?

11. "If a nation has indexation, then all the redistributive gains and losses from unexpected inflation will be eliminated." Comment on the validity of this statement.

12. "Inflation (either high or low) reduces the entire nation's standard of living." Comment on the validity of this statement.

13. You have been asked by your boss to create a five-year financial forecast. Your company will not be borrowing any new funds over the next five years, and it has fixed interest rates on the existing debt. How important is it to consider the potential effects of inflation in your five-year forecast?

14. Chile's interest rates have long been indexed to inflation. What does that mean? Is indexation a positive or negative characteristic for foreign companies that are considering direct investments (e.g., plant and equipment expenditures) in Chile?

PART 2

REAL LOANABLE FUNDS MARKET

Chapter 6

Monetary Aggregates: Measuring Money

INTRODUCTION

What is money? As individuals, we never seem to have enough of it because the more we have, the more we can buy. But things are different for nations. Unless a nation's production increases in tandem with its money supply, only inflation and income redistribution occur. The problem with money is that it can give the illusion of greater wealth, higher purchasing power, and increased well-being, when in fact nothing has changed—or things have gotten worse.

Money is a lubricant that makes economic transactions more efficient. For that reason, we are all better off with money than without it. At the same time, an ever-increasing money supply does not imply ever-increasing efficiency. Once a nation has reached a threshold level of money, where normal transactions can be managed efficiently, the impact of newly created money on economic activity is mainly through its effects on prices, expectations, and speculation. Nevertheless, the effects that money has on an economy can be powerful, which is why central banks and their monetary policies are of intense interest to a broad cross section of national and international communities.

> Money is an economic lubricant that makes economic transactions more efficient.

This chapter explains money, its functions, and why nations measure it. Understanding the basics of money is important because in the next chapter, we will discuss how private financial intermediaries (e.g., banks) create money. Then in Chapter 8, "Who Controls the Money Supply and How?" we will go on to discuss how central banks control financial institutions' ability to lend and therefore how they control money supplies of their nations. See Exhibit 6-1.

THE BASICS

COMMODITY MONEY VERSUS FIAT MONEY

Why do people and businesses accept coins and paper currency in exchange for valuable goods and services, when they realize that the intrinsic value of a currency, like the dollar or euro, is far less than its purchasing power? For example, in the United States, it costs slightly more than five cents to produce a one-dollar bill, but its purchasing power is still one dollar.[1]

---

[1] Due to the extra colors and/or security, the 2013 cost of $5, $20, and $50 notes was 9.8 cents each; $1 and $2 notes cost 5.4 cents each; $10 notes cost 9.0 cents each, and $100 notes cost 7.8 cents each. Board of Governors of the Federal Reserve System, *Current FAQs: How Much Does It Cost to Produce Currency and Coin?* www.federalreserve.gov/faqs/currency_12771.htm (accessed May 27, 2013).

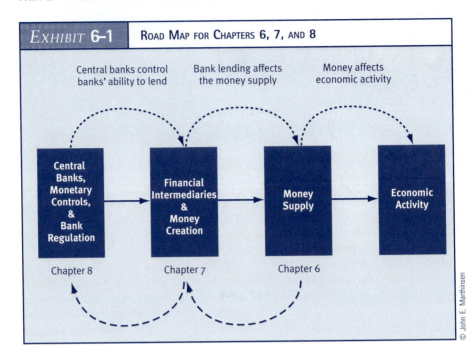

EXHIBIT 6-1   ROAD MAP FOR CHAPTERS 6, 7, AND 8

Central banks control banks' ability to lend

Bank lending affects the money supply

Money affects economic activity

Central Banks, Monetary Controls, & Bank Regulation

Financial Intermediaries & Money Creation

Money Supply

Economic Activity

Chapter 8

Chapter 7

Chapter 6

© John E. Marthinsen

Trust is the key to money's acceptability.

Few of us spend much time thinking about questions such as these, but the answer is *trust*. People and businesses accept money because they trust that others will accept it from them. Because of this, central banks play a pivotal role as gatekeepers of nations, whose job is to ensure that the trust people have in their currencies is maintained.

Societies used money (in one form or another) for hundreds of years before governments or central banks existed; thus, the use and creation of money has never depended on governments or monetary authorities. Money exists to make life easier. It is usually durable, easy to carry or access, and divisible into smaller units. For these reasons, gold, silver, copper, gems, beads, shells, and cigarettes have all been used, at one time, as money.

One significant benefit from using currencies with practical uses is, if worse comes to worst, the commodity can always be used (e.g., gold jewelry) or consumed (e.g., wheat) instead of being spent. Another advantage of commodity money is that it is more difficult to produce than paper money, and, therefore, it cannot be as easily manipulated for political advantage. For this reason, there are strong advocates in many countries who would like their currencies to be backed by precious metals.

Currencies that are not backed by precious metals of equal value are called *fiat money* (which means "money by decree") because they are given their value by the government. In almost all countries, monopoly institutions, such as central banks, have the power to issue fiat money. Governments enhance the acceptability of this money by giving it *legal tender* status, which means it must be accepted for certain transactions, such as the payment of debts. At the same

Fiat money is not backed fully by a commodity, such as gold or silver.

Susan B. Anthony Dollar: Issued but Rarely Used

Just because governments define particular financial assets as "money" does not mean that they will be accepted and used. For instance, the Susan B. Anthony* dollar was introduced in 1979 by the U.S. government as a durable substitute for the one-dollar bill, but these dollar coins were not widely accepted. Some felt that they too closely resembled quarters and preferred using dollar bills. Retailers did not welcome them because counting out change in dollar coins and bills was considered burdensome. In 2000, a new dollar coin with the picture of Native American Sacagawea was minted, but in 2012 production of the Sacagawea dollar was reduced by more than 90% from 2011 due to a government surplus from lack of adoption.†

*Susan B. Anthony (1820–1906) was a pioneer in the fight for abolitionism and temperance, but she is probably best remembered for her fight for women's suffrage.

†From 1805 to 1806, Sacagawea (1788–1812) and her French Canadian husband, Toussaint Charbonneau, helped guide the Lewis and Clark expedition across the United States from St. Louis, Missouri, to Fort Clatsop, Oregon. United States Mint, Coin Production Figures, www.usmint.gov/about_the_mint/coin_production/index.cfm?action=production_figures&allCoinsYear=2011#starthere (accessed October 10, 2012).

time, just because the government issues currency does not mean it will be used (see Macro Memo 6-1: Susan B. Anthony Dollar: Issued but Rarely Used.)

FUNCTIONS OF MONEY

In general, money serves four major functions. It is a unit of account, medium of exchange, store of value, and standard of deferred payment. These functions are easier to understand if one thinks of "the dollar," "the euro," "the peso," or "the yen," every time the word "money" is used.

> Money functions as a unit of account, medium of exchange, store of value, and standard of deferred payment.

The unit-of-account function means that money is the unit in terms of which everything is valued and the basis for establishing relative prices between goods and services. The medium-of-exchange function means that individuals exchange goods and services for money and then reexchange the money for other goods and services. Money is not held for its own sake but rather for the things it can buy, which means holding money is just a temporary respite between selling one thing and buying or investing in something else.

Money's store-of-value and standard-of-deferred-payment functions relate to its use over a period of time. Money is a store of value because it is one way to accumulate wealth. It is a standard of deferred payment because people write contracts denominated in money, and the contracts are settled in the future.

INFLATION ERODES THE FUNCTIONS OF MONEY

Nothing erodes the usefulness, effectiveness, and convenience of money more than inflation. If high enough, inflation can completely erase the trust that people have in their currencies and force them to transact business in other ways, such as bartering goods and services or accepting only foreign currencies.

> Inflation undermines the usefulness, effectiveness, and convenience of money.

To see why, imagine yourself in a country where the daily inflation rate is 100%. If the price of a loaf of bread on Monday were $1, it would be $2 on Tuesday, $32 by Saturday, and $536,870,912 by the end of the month. Under these circumstances, who would be willing to accept such a rapidly depreciating asset in exchange for intrinsically valuable goods? The answer is "almost no one" because inflation would have destroyed virtually all of the major benefits from having money.

With such high inflation, money would no longer be a *store of value* that linked present saving to future buying power. Only if the interest rate compensated for the inflationary loss in expected purchasing power would one be willing to hold money.

High inflation would also destroy money's role as a *medium of exchange* because few would be willing to accept it. Remember that fiat money has value only if it is accepted by others. Once it loses acceptability in exchange, money loses its value as a medium of exchange.

Finally, hyperinflation would destroy money's uses as a *unit of account* and *standard of deferred payment*. If the currency were no longer used as either a medium of exchange or as a store of value, there would be little reason to value goods, services, or contracts in terms of it. Hyperinflation would force merchants to bear the cost of constantly having to raise their prices or the cost of quoting the prices of their products in foreign currencies.

WHY DO NATIONS MEASURE THEIR MONEY SUPPLIES?

Because of the strong link between changes in the money supply and changes in a nation's spending patterns, there is widespread interest in knowing both how fast the money supply is growing and how fast it should grow. Central bankers have an interest in measuring money supply changes so that they can prevent both excessive spending, which could cause inflation and protect against insufficient liquidity that might trigger a recession. For planning purposes, business executives are equally interested in knowing the rate of change in the money supply. An increased money supply implies greater nominal purchasing power, as well as logical follow-on changes in important economic variables, such as nominal interest rates, exchange rates, prices, and wages. This knowledge lends itself to rational decisions concerning pricing, borrowing, hiring, and production.

Changes in the money supply affect nominal purchasing power.

There is virtually no controversy in financial circles about the potential impact changes in a nation's money supply should have on nominal expenditures, but there is considerable disagreement about the transmission mechanism and lag. Two mainstream schools of thought on this issue (namely, Keynesian theory and monetarist theory) capture the debate.

Keynesians believe there is an indirect link between changes in a nation's money supply and changes in its expenditures (see Exhibit 6-2). Their reasoning is as follows: if a nation's real money supply increases, the added liquidity should cause real interest rates to fall; and if real interest rates fall, businesses and consumers should borrow and spend more, which increase expenditures for goods and services.[2] This indirect link between money and

---

[2] The important distinction between real interest rates and nominal interest rates should be kept in mind. Real borrowing increases only if real interest rates fall.

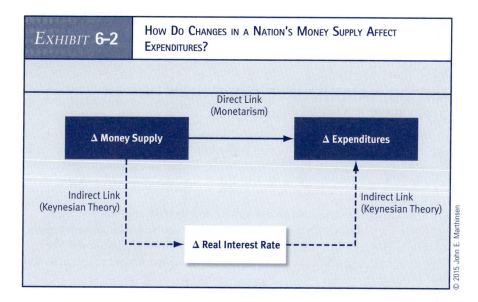

| EXHIBIT 6-2 | HOW DO CHANGES IN A NATION'S MONEY SUPPLY AFFECT EXPENDITURES? |

© 2015 John E. Marthinsen

economic activity seems logical, and it is well used in economics—especially in short-run analyses. In Parts 2 to 5 of this book, we will use the Keynesian perspective for our analyses of the short-term effects of monetary policy.

The monetarists believe there is a direct link between changes in a nation's money supply and changes in expenditures. Therefore, regardless of whether a nation's real interest rate fluctuates, expenditures should eventually change when its money supply changes. Their reasoning is as follows: If a central bank increases the money supply above the public's demand to hold it, the resulting disequilibrium (i.e., surplus) increases the desire to get rid of the extra cash people are holding. As a result, they spend and invest the funds, thereby stimulating economic activity.

This direct link between money and economic activity also is logical, and it is well used in economics—especially in long-run analyses. Therefore, in the final portion of this book (Part 6), we will will use the monetarist perspective for our analyses of the long-term effects of monetary policy.[3]

Keynesians and monetarists focus on different pages of the financial press. For Keynesians, fluctuations in the money supply are important mainly if they change real and nominal interest rates; so, Keynesians focus their reading on the financial pages dealing with money market interest rates, bond yields, and expected inflation. By contrast, monetarists focus on central bank releases showing changes in the money supply and monetary aggregates. Money supply statistics are published once a week in the United States. By contrast, nominal interest rates are reported second by second throughout each working day and published daily in the news.

One might ask why there is a need to choose. Why not consider both measures? As a practical matter, most analysts do consider changes in the

> Keynesian theory focuses on the indirect link between money supply changes and fluctuations in spending.

> Monetarism focuses on the direct link between money supply changes and fluctuations in spending.

> Interest rate information is timelier than money supply information.

[3] Monetarism will be the focus of our discussion in Chapter 21, "Causes of Long-Term Growth and Inflation."

money supply *and* changes in interest rates, but if these measures give conflicting signals (e.g., an expanding money supply and rising real interest rates), then a choice must be made.

WHY DO NATIONS HAVE MORE THAN ONE MONEY SUPPLY MEASURE?

The financial assets that are included in a nation's money supply are measurable, and central banks have a great deal of influence over them. Therefore, it is crucial that the money supply be correctly defined. Otherwise, the central bank would be targeting the wrong measure, and the economic consequences could be unfortunate.

What assets are included in the money supply? What assets should be included? Do nations include the same financial assets in their money supply measures? Are gold and silver parts of the money supply? Should they be? How about savings accounts, time deposits, money market mutual funds, and food stamps?

Two major criteria help us determine whether a financial asset should be included in a nation's money supply. To be included, it should be linked closely to spending and reported in a timely manner. Over time, new financial assets are introduced and spending patterns change. Therefore, money supply measures that once captured these two major criteria might fail to do so in the future. This is why money supply definitions of nations change over time and why many nations have more than one money supply measure.

> The financial assets included in a nation's money supply should be reported frequently and linked closely to spending.

M1, M2, AND THE MONETARY BASE

The names given to major money supply measures of nations are, to say the least, uninspired. Most nations have M1 and M2 money supply measures, but it does not stop there. Some nations monitor and target M3, and, the U.S. central bank reports the MZM[4] money supply.

Because central banks decide on the specific financial assets that enter into their money measures, the money supply definitions among nations may differ slightly. International organizations, such as the International Monetary Fund, try to overcome these small discrepancies by compiling global statistics and reporting them in standardized form. As a result, the job of comparing country statistics is made easier.

It is far less important to memorize the specific financial assets included in a nation's money supply than it is to understand the critical factor (i.e., liquidity) that distinguishes one from the other. Money supply definitions are organic in the sense that they change over time and may be different from country to country. Finding the most recent definition is as simple as visiting the central bank's home page.[5]

---

[4] MZM is an abbreviation for *money with zero maturity.* See Federal Reserve Bank of St. Louis, "MZM Money Stock," FRED Economic Data, http://research.stlouisfed.org/fred2/series/MZM (accessed May 28, 2013).

[5] A list of 31 major central banks and their home page URLs is included at the end of Chapter 9, "Who Controls the Money Supply and How?"

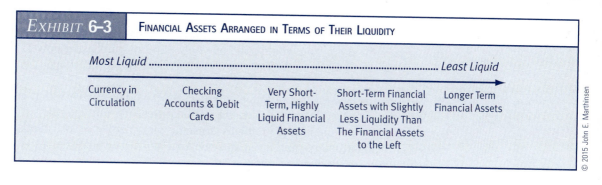

EXHIBIT 6-3   **FINANCIAL ASSETS ARRANGED IN TERMS OF THEIR LIQUIDITY**

Most Liquid .... Least Liquid

| Currency in Circulation | Checking Accounts & Debit Cards | Very Short-Term, Highly Liquid Financial Assets | Short-Term Financial Assets with Slightly Less Liquidity Than The Financial Assets to the Left | Longer Term Financial Assets |

© 2015 John E. Marthinsen

Liquidity Is the Key

The key factor differentiating one money supply measure from another is *liquidity*, which is the ability to convert an asset into cash quickly and without substantial loss of value. Therefore, cash is the most liquid asset, and durable assets, such as houses, airplanes, and heavy machinery, are the least liquid.[6]

Exhibit 6-3 shows a continuum of financial assets that vary in liquidity (real or perceived). The most liquid assets are on the left, and as we move to the right, they become progressively less liquid. When people have no cash, what do they use? Most of them turn to (and often prefer) checking accounts and debit cards to tap their bank accounts and credit cards to tap their available lines of credit. If they have no cash, no funds in their checking or debit accounts, and no credit cards, they turn to other liquid financial assets, like savings accounts, money market mutual funds, money market deposit accounts, or time deposits.

> Liquidity is the ability to convert an asset into cash quickly and without substantial loss of value.

M1 Money Supply

The M1 money supply includes only financial assets that fulfill all four functions of money: unit of value, medium of exchange, store of value, and standard of deferred payment. Therefore, M1 includes currency in circulation and checking accounts because these financial assets are used to pay for most goods and services.[7]

"Currency *in circulation*" includes only the currency (notes and coins) outside banks, the national treasury, central bank, and other financial institutions. To understand why, suppose you had $100 in your wallet. Those funds would represent $100 worth of purchasing power to you and would be part of the money supply. If you deposited these funds into a checking account,

> M1 includes currency in circulation and checking deposits.

---

[6] A $300,000 house might be sold quickly if the homeowner is willing to settle for a very low price (e.g., $100,000), which is why an asset's market value must be maintained to be called "liquid."

[7] How about credit cards? Many people use credit cards if they have no cash, but care must be taken with credit cards because they are not part of a nation's money supply until they are used. Here's why. Suppose Ann Talope has a credit card with a $5,000 line of credit. Until the card is used, the credit line is not recorded as part of the nation's money supply because it is neither currency in circulation nor a checking account. That changes when Ann uses her credit card to purchase, say, a $50 sweater. As a result of this transaction, Ann's credit card company transfers $50 to the merchant's (sweater seller's) checking account, and Ann ends up with the equivalent of a zero-interest loan until her credit card bill comes due.

what would happen to your purchasing power? The answer is "nothing" because the currency you held would fall by the same amount your checking account rose. In short, you would still have only $100 of purchasing power. All you did was to replace currency with an equivalent-valued checking account.

The same is true for the nation as a whole. By excluding currency that is inside private financial intermediaries, the national treasury, and the central bank, a country's money supply remains constant when people deposit funds in their checking accounts, and it remains constant when they withdraw funds in cash from their checking accounts.

Consider what would happen if the money supply included both currency inside and outside financial intermediaries. The money supply would rise every time someone made a cash deposit into a checking account, and it would fall whenever someone withdrew funds from a checking account.

In Exhibit 6-4, a vertical line is drawn just after "checking accounts." All financial assets to the left are included in M1, and all financial assets to the right are excluded.

M2 Money Supply

M2 includes everything in M1 as well as a few short-term financial assets, which have a large impact on spending because they are highly liquid. Let's take a closer look at the difference between M1 and M2.

M1 includes only those assets that can be readily used as a medium of exchange. Therefore, they are strongly connected to the spending activities of individuals and businesses. As a result, when public holdings of M1 rise, so should spending. But if the purpose of measuring the money supply is to establish a link between private spending and a collection of financial assets called "money," then perhaps the M1 definition of money is too narrow. How much people spend is influenced not only by the amount of currency

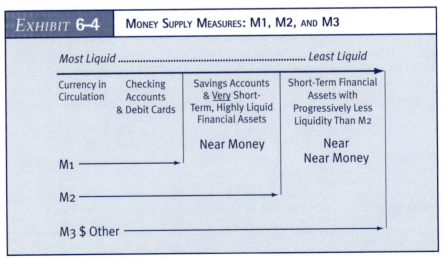

EXHIBIT 6-4   MONEY SUPPLY MEASURES: M1, M2, AND M3

Most Liquid .... *Least Liquid*

Currency in Circulation	Checking Accounts & Debit Cards	Savings Accounts & Very Short-Term, Highly Liquid Financial Assets	Short-Term Financial Assets with Progressively Less Liquidity Than M2
		Near Money	Near Near Money

M1 ⟶

M2 ⟶

M3 $ Other ⟶

they have in their wallets and size of their checking accounts but also by other highly liquid assets (i.e., assets that can be turned quickly into cash and without substantial loss of value), such as savings accounts, small time deposits, and money market mutual funds.[8]

For this reason, broader measures of money are reported that include these less liquid financial assets. In most cases, these assets cannot be spent directly, or they have restrictions on their use. Nevertheless, if they have a significant influence on spending, then there is a strong argument for measuring them and including them in the money supply definition.

After currency in circulation and checking accounts, the financial assets with the highest levels of liquidity are called *near money*. Therefore, the M2 definition in Exhibit 6-4 has a vertical line after the categories of financial assets including M1 and near money.

> M2 includes all the financial assets in M1 plus near money.

M3 and Other Money Supply Measures

M3 and other money supply measures include financial assets with increasingly less liquidity than M2. We will refer to the financial assets that are included in M3 but not in M2 as *near, near money* because they are more closely related to wholesale investments by institutional investors and large corporations than they are to the expenditure patterns of individuals and businesses (see Exhibit 6-4).

> M3 includes all the financial assets in M2 plus near, near money.

Money Supply Definitions Are Not Fixed and Unchanging

As new financial instruments are invented and work their way into popular use, central banks redefine their money supply measures to include them. Similarly, as old financial instruments fall into disuse or as money supply measures fail to provide central banks with useful information, monetary aggregates are redefined or dropped. Therefore, the broad conceptual differences between money supply definitions, such as M1 and M2, should be kept in mind, but the specific financial assets included in any money supply measure should always be double-checked.

The United States provides a good example of how mercurial money supply measures can be. In November 2005, the Board of Governors of the U.S. Federal Reserve announced that it would cease publication of M3 starting in March 2006.[9] One of the main reasons for its decision was the board felt that M3 provided no more information about economic activity than M2. It also dropped the measure because the estimated annual reporting costs for the Federal Reserve and its reporting banks outweighed the benefits from having timely access to the M3 figure.[10] Discontinuing M3 in the United States stood in stark contrast to other nations and currency areas, such as the European Monetary Union, where M3 was (and is) the primary indicator and target for monetary authorities.

---

[8] See **The Rest of the Story:** *Financial Assets Included in the U.S. M1 and M2 Money Supply Measures* for an explanation of these financial assets.

[9] Federal Reserve, *Discontinuance of M3*, Federal Reserve Release H. 6. Money Stock Measures, November 10, 2005, www.federalreserve.gov/releases/h6/discm3.htm (accessed May 28, 2013). The Federal Reserve also announced that it would stop reporting repurchase agreements and eurodollar deposits.

[10] Interested parties can still obtain this information, albeit much more infrequently, by using the U.S. Flow of Funds Accounts, which are reported quarterly by the Federal Reserve.

Total Reserves and the Monetary Base

In addition to the major money supply measures (e.g., M1 and M2), nations have other monetary aggregates, which are important for conducting monetary policy and attract a great deal of media attention. Two of them are reserves and the monetary base.

Reserves are the assets that private financial intermediaries hold in relatively strict proportion to their deposit liabilities. Failure to hold the proper amount can result in sanctions and penalties by monetary regulators. Any reserves held above the required level are excess, and banks can lend or invest them as they please.

Reserves are an important monetary aggregate for two major reasons. First, they are the basis for a banking system's ability to lend. Increased reserves means increased lending potential. Second, they are controlled by central banks—controlled in the sense that it is safe to say that the banking system's aggregate reserves change only if and when the central bank wants them to change.

In the United States, two assets qualify as reserves: cash in the vaults of financial intermediaries and the deposits of these financial institutions at the central bank (i.e., the Fed). Cash earns no interest; so banks have a clear incentive to minimize the amounts they hold. By contrast, the Fed pays interest (albeit a low one relative to other market rates) on the deposits that financial intermediaries hold there.[11] With this portion of their reserves, banks must consider the tradeoff between having reserves that are safely tucked away in the Fed versus having them earn higher (but riskier) returns if invested or lent elsewhere.

Assets that qualify as reserves can vary by country. Some central banks have expanded asset lists, permitting safe, interest-earning assets, such as government securities, to be counted as reserves.

The monetary base (sometimes called *high-powered money*) is composed of reserves held by financial institutions and currency in circulation. It is one of the most important of all monetary aggregates because the monetary base is the raw material from which a nation's money supplies are made. The monetary base is also important because (with only a few minor exceptions) changes in it are caused solely by central banks. In contrast, central banks do not have as much control over M1 and M2 because these monetary aggregates are affected by the behavior of the nonbank public (e.g., businesses and individuals) as well as by banks and other financial intermediaries.

In Chapter 7, "Financial Intermediation, Markets, and Intermediaries", we will discuss the effects that financial intermediaries and the nonbank public have on M1 and M2. We will also investigate how changes in a nation's monetary base cause amplified changes in a nation's money supply. In general, we will find that, as a central bank changes the monetary base, the nation's money supply rises or falls by a multiplier effect (see Exhibit 6-5).

Banks hold reserves to back deposit liabilities.

In the United States, reserves include cash in the vault plus financial institutions' deposits at the Fed.

The monetary base includes currency in circulation plus the reserves of financial intermediaries.

[11] The Financial Services Regulatory Act of 2006 authorized the Federal Reserve to pay interest on the reserve balances that banks held at the Fed. See U.S. Congress, S. 2856 (109th): Financial Services Regulatory Relief Act of 2006, http://www.govtrack.us/congress/bills/109/s2856 (accessed May 27, 2013).

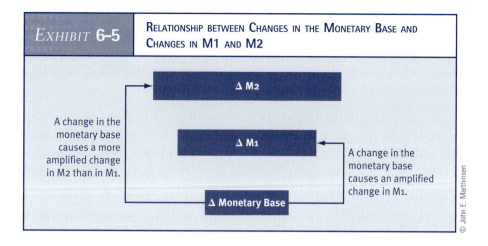

EXHIBIT 6-5   RELATIONSHIP BETWEEN CHANGES IN THE MONETARY BASE AND CHANGES IN M1 AND M2

Δ M2

Δ M1

A change in the monetary base causes a more amplified change in M2 than in M1.

A change in the monetary base causes an amplified change in M1.

Δ Monetary Base

© John E. Marthinsen

THE REST OF THE STORY

DISADVANTAGES OF BARTERING

Economies can function without money, but money makes them run more smoothly and efficiently. Resorting to barter is like moving from a world of jet planes, mobile phones, advanced diagnostics, and biotech treatments to a world of oxen-drawn carriages, smoke signals, superstition, and witchcraft. What specific problems do societies encounter when they barter goods and services? Why does bartering cause a nation's living standards to plummet?

Multiplicity of Trading Ratios (No Unit of Account)

The first problem is determining and remembering the prices of everything people want to buy in terms of the goods and services they want to sell. Without a unit of account, such as the dollar, euro, or yen, imagine how difficult this would be. For example, bakers would have to know how many loaves of bread it took to purchase a car, pencil, shirt, and hundreds of other products that they bought each year.

> Bartering is inefficient because it requires a multiplicity of trading ratios.

Indivisibility Problems

Bartering makes the production of complicated goods and services problematic because people making such products would not want to be paid with them. For example, assembly line workers producing cars and airplanes would not want to be paid in auto and airplane parts because few others would want to trade their goods and services for them. By contrast, bakers, tailors, and farmers would have a far easier time trading because they produce and sell products that are more easily divisible.

> Bartering is inefficient for products that cannot easily be divided.

Time Wasted Due to the Need for a Mutual Coincidence of Wants and Surpluses

Another problem with bartering is the considerable amount of time and extra effort required to make even the simplest transactions. Not only do we have to locate individuals who want our goods and/or services, but we have to make sure they have surpluses of goods or services that we want to buy.

No Standardized Way to Store Wealth

Finally, how would wealth be stored in a barter economy? If you were thinking that the answer might be the purchase of gold or silver, just remember that precious metal prices can vary considerably and may not be the best way to store wealth. For example, in January 1980 the price of gold reached $850 per ounce, but by June 1982 it had fallen to $297 per ounce. Similarly, in September 2011, an ounce of gold sold for $1,895, but by mid-May 2013, it had fallen under $1,400.[12] Commodity prices are a function of relatively unstable and unpredictable supply and demand forces. Retrospectively, it seems as if gold would have been a good way to store wealth during the past 40+ years, but the owner's wealth would have depended on exactly when the gold was bought and sold and whether or not the owner had the financial courage to stay in this precious metal as it was hemorrhaging gains.

U.S. MONETARY AGGREGATES[13]

Until this point, we have been very general about what financial assets are included in the M1 and M2 money supply definitions because there can be slight variations among nations. Therefore, let's get specific and see what the United States includes in its major monetary aggregates.

M1—THE NARROWEST DEFINITION OF MONEY IN THE UNITED STATES

M1 is the narrowest U.S. money supply measure. It includes currency in circulation (paper bills and coins) and checking deposits (sometimes called *transactions accounts* or *checkable deposits*).

As we can see in Exhibit 6-6, an assortment of financial assets qualifies as "checking deposits"—namely, demand deposits, NOW accounts, ATS accounts, and credit union share drafts—but all of these accounts have one common characteristic: checks can be written on them.

The U.S. central bank ("the Fed") makes a preliminary announcement of the nation's M1 supply on Thursday of each week, which is then reported in the financial press (e.g., *The Wall Street Journal* and *Financial Times*) on the following Friday or Monday. Changes in these monetary aggregates are closely monitored because they signal potential shifts in future spending and possible central bank reaction to the changing economic climate.

Exhibit 6-7 shows the week-average money supply figures released by the Fed for April 22 and April 29, 2013. Notice that Columns 1 and 2 report the money supply figures for M1 and M2. The abbreviation *sa* after M1, M2, and M3 indicates that the figures are "seasonally adjusted" by the Federal Reserve. This adjustment is made when there are predictable, recurring, and

---

[12] Federal Reserve Bank of St. Louis, *Gold Fixing Price 3:00 p.m. (London Time) in London Bullion Market, based in U.S. Dollars,* http://research.stlouisfed.org/fred2/tags/series/?t=gold (accessed May 27, 2013).

[13] All the definitions for the U.S. money supply measures together with historical information on them can be found at Board of Governors of the Federal Reserve System, Data Download Program, www.federalreserve.gov/datadownload/Choose.aspx?rel=h6 (accessed May 28, 2013).

EXHIBIT 6-6	U.S. M1 MONEY SUPPLY DEFINITION

M1 = CURRENCY IN CIRCULATION + CHECKING DEPOSITS

Currency in Circulation includes:

Notes and coins outside the U.S. Treasury
Notes and coins outside Federal Reserve Banks
Notes and coins outside the vaults of depository institutions
Traveler's checks issued by nonbank financial intermediaries

Checking deposits include:

Demand deposits at commercial banks
Other checkable deposits, such as
- Negotiable orders of withdrawal (NOW) accounts at depository institutions
- Automatic Transfer Service (ATS) accounts at depository institutions
- Credit union share draft accounts
- Demand deposits at thrift institutions

Source: Federal Reserve, Federal Reserve Statistical Release: H.6. Money Stock Measures, www.federalreserve.gov/releases/h6/current/h6.htm (accessed May 28, 2013).

EXHIBIT 6-7	U.S MONETARY AGGREGATES ON APRIL 29 AND 22, 2013

FEDERAL RESERVE DATA
MONETARY AGGREGATES
(Figures in billions of dollars)

		Week Average	
		April 29	April 22
Money supply (M1)	sa	2,573.6	2,549.7
Money supply (M1)	nsa	2,645.9	2,565.4
Money supply (M2)	sa	10,534.9	10,501.3
Money supply (M2)	nsa	10,475.4	10,571.8

Note: nsa, not seasonally adjusted; sa, seasonally adjusted.

Source: Federal Reserve, Federal Reserve Statistical Release, Money Stock Measures, May 28, 2013, www.federalreserve.gov/releases/H6/ (accessed May 28, 2013).

periodic changes in the money supply that have nothing to do with central bank policy (e.g., cash withdrawals due to holiday shopping). Seasonal adjustments smooth out these predictable movements and highlight any changes in monetary policy. By contrast, the abbreviation *nsa* indicates that the reported figures are "not seasonally adjusted."

Columns 3 and 4 under Week Average report the money supply data for the weeks ending April 29, 2013, and April 22, 2013, respectively. For example, the first line shows that on April 29, 2013, M1 was equal to $2,573.6 billion, and at the end of the previous week, it was $2,549.7 billion, which is a weekly increase of slightly under 1%.

The M1 figures that are reported each week are based on sample data from approximately 15 large U.S. banks, and they provide only a rough initial estimate of the actual U.S. money supply. Over the course of the following few weeks, as more information becomes available, these preliminary figures are revised (often substantially) by the central bank.

Despite any initial measurement inaccuracies, weekly money supply figures have considerable influence on the financial markets. Many bond brokers, financial analysts, politicians, and business executives closely follow these weekly fluctuations. Numerous transactions and decisions are based on expected changes in these money supply figures, and many careers have been spawned or destroyed by correctly or incorrectly estimating them.

M2—THE SECOND BROADEST MONEY SUPPLY MEASURE

Exhibit 6-8 shows the financial assets included in M2. Notice that it includes all the financial assets in M1 plus a select group of other (slightly) less liquid assets. Currently, the U.S. Federal Reserve uses M2 as its major policy target. Like the M1 money supply, M2 figures are released weekly by the Federal Reserve.

TOTAL RESERVES AND MONETARY BASE

Exhibit 6-9 shows data for total reserves and the monetary base as reported by the Federal Reserve for the two weeks ending on Wednesday, May 1, 2013. Total reserves[14] were $1,878,249 million, and the U.S. monetary base was $3,004,539 million. We will have much more to say in Chapter 7, "Financial Intermediation, Markets, and Intermediaries" about these (and other) monetary aggregates, but for now it is most important to understand

EXHIBIT 6–8	U.S. M2 MONEY SUPPLY DEFINITION

M2 = M1 + NEAR MONEY
"Near money" includes:

      Savings deposits (including money market deposit accounts)
      Small time deposits (i.e., less than $100,000)*
      Retail money market mutual funds*

*Excludes individual retirement accounts (IRAs) and Keogh balances at depository institutions.

Source: Federal Reserve Statistical Release, H.6 Money Stock Measures, Release Date: May 23, 2013, www.federalreserve.gov/releases/H6/Current/ (accessed May 28, 2013).

---

[14] Total reserves equal cash in financial intermediaries' vaults and the deposits of these financial institutions at the Fed.

| EXHIBIT 6-9 | U.S MONETARY AGGREGATES ON MAY 1, 2013 |

MEMBER BANK RESERVE CHANGES

	Two Weeks Ending May 1, 2013 *(Figures in millions of dollars)*
Total Reserves (nsa)	1,878,249
Nonborrowed reserves (nsa)	1,877,842
Borrowing from the Fed (nsa)	407
Required reserves (nsa)	126,266
Excess reserves (nsa)	1,751,983
Monetary base (nsa)	3,004,539

Note: Averages of daily figures, not adjusted for changes in reserve requirements. Figures are in millions of dollars and exclude extended credit.

Note: nsa, not seasonally adjusted

Source: Federal Reserve Statistical Release, Aggregate Reserves of Depository Institutions, and the Monetary Base - H.3, www.federalreserve.gov/releases/h3/current/ (accessed May 28, 2013)

the basic differences and where the most recent information on them can be found.

Before leaving this section, notice that the Fed reports important components of total reserves. Total reserves can be separated into nonborrowed reserves ($1,877,842 million) and borrowed (from the Fed) reserves ($407 million). It can also be separated into required reserves ($126,266 million) and excess reserves ($1,751,983 million). These components will gain importance as we move to Chapter 7, "Financial Intermediation, Markets, and Intermediaries" and discuss money creation.

FINANCIAL ASSETS INCLUDED IN THE U.S. M1 AND M2 MONEY SUPPLY MEASURES

CURRENCY IN CIRCULATION (PART OF M1)

Currency in circulation includes all coins and bills issued by the U.S. Treasury and Federal Reserve, which are held outside private financial intermediaries (e.g., banks), the Federal Reserve District banks, and the U.S. Treasury. Currency in circulation also includes traveler's checks of nonbank issuers (e.g., American Express). Traveler's checks issued by depository institutions are already part of demand deposits.

DEMAND DEPOSITS (PART OF M1)

Demand deposits are non-interest-earning checking accounts offered by commercial banks (as opposed to other thrift institutions, such as savings and loan associations, credit unions, or mutual savings banks). Checks must be honored by the bank "on demand" (i.e., with no waiting period).

NONBANK-ISSUED TRAVELER'S CHECKS (PART OF M1)

Traveler's checks are purchased by individuals for cash from nonbank financial institutions. They can be used to purchase goods and services throughout the world. If the traveler's checks are lost or stolen, the issuer reimburses the owners at no cost.

NOW ACCOUNTS (PART OF M1)

NOW accounts are interest-earning savings accounts on which depositors can write "negotiable orders of withdrawal." Negotiable orders of withdrawal are identical to demand deposits, except that they earn interest, and the bank can require a depositor to wait a short period (e.g., 30 days) before honoring them.

ATS ACCOUNTS (PART OF M1)

ATS accounts give depositors "automatic transfer service" from their savings accounts to their checking accounts. They enabled banks during the 1970s to evade a federal rule prohibiting depositors from earning interest on their checking accounts.

With ATS accounts, depositors open two accounts at their banks, namely, interest-earning savings accounts and non-interest-earning demand deposits. All their deposited funds are placed into the interest-earning savings accounts, with the non-interest-earning checking accounts carrying zero balances. Customers are then allowed to write checks on the accounts with zero balances. To prevent these checks from bouncing, depositors authorize their banks to transfer funds, as needed, from their savings accounts to their demand deposits. In this way, depositors have the convenience of checking accounts and the interest earnings of savings accounts.

CREDIT UNION SHARE DRAFTS (PART OF M1)

Credit union share drafts are interest-earning checking accounts (like NOW accounts) offered by credit unions.

SAVINGS DEPOSITS (NEAR MONEY)

Savings deposits are interest-earning deposits on which checks cannot be written. They are generally open-ended, which means depositors can withdraw or deposit any amount they wish, but banks do have the ability to require a short waiting period before honoring withdrawals (even though they seldom do). Savings deposits are less active than checking accounts. This is one reason why banks are generally able to offer a higher interest rate on savings accounts than they can on checking deposits.

SMALL TIME DEPOSITS (NEAR MONEY)

Small time deposits are interest-earning accounts with fixed maturities and values less than $100,000. Because early withdrawals carry interest penalties, these deposits are less volatile sources of funds for financial intermediaries than checking accounts and savings accounts. Therefore, they usually earn a higher rate of interest.

Money Market Mutual Funds (Near Money)

Money market mutual funds permit investors to pool their funds for the purpose of buying large-denomination, high-interest-earning securities that a single investor might not be able to afford, such as $1 million eurodollar deposits or large repurchase agreements. Because these funds purchase many securities, they give small investors the ability to diversify their portfolios far beyond what they could do individually. Technically, depositors are buying shares of money market mutual funds and receiving dividends (rather than interest) as a return. Depositors/investors can write checks on these accounts, but such privileges are typically limited in some ways (e.g., a minimum amount per check or a maximum number of checks per month).

Money Market Deposit Accounts (Near Money)

Money market deposit accounts were created to help banks compete with money market mutual funds. Previously, banks were required to bear greater regulatory burdens than nonbank financial intermediaries offering money market funds. Under the Garn–St. Germain Act of 1982, banks were given the right to offer deposits equivalent to money market mutual funds. Unlike money market mutual funds, money market deposit accounts are federally insured.

CONCLUSION

Money is useful because it serves as a unit of account, medium of exchange, store of value, and standard of deferred payment, but the usefulness of money does not increase simply by creating more of it. Once a nation has enough money to meet its needs, more is useful only if it increases production. Money is not something that is ordained by government. Rather, the public will use whatever financial instruments it finds most convenient. Most financial instruments were created by the private sector. In some cases, they were created to circumvent federal banking regulations.

Because of the strong link between changes in a nation's money supply and changes in spending, there is widespread interest in knowing how best to define the money supply, how fast it is growing, and how fast it should grow. Central bankers have an interest in measuring money supply changes so they can prevent both excessive growth that could lead to inflation and insufficient liquidity that might trigger recessions. For planning purposes, business executives are equally interested in knowing the rate of change in the money supply. An increased money supply implies greater nominal purchasing power and greater credit availability, both of which cause predictable changes in important economic variables, such as nominal interest rates, exchange rates, prices, and wages. This knowledge lends itself to better business decisions concerning pricing, borrowing, hiring, and production.

Central banks define their nations' money supplies, but the definitions they use are not static. Rather, they change as new financial instruments are introduced and old ones are abandoned. If the goal is to define money in ways that reflect purchasing power, then the invention and use of new financial assets will constantly stimulate the need for new money supply measures.

REVIEW QUESTIONS

1. What effect will each of the following transactions/events have on the monetary base and M2 money supply? Briefly explain.
   a. You take a $20,000 loan (in the form of a check) from the Bank of America and use it to buy a new car.
   b. The car dealer in Question 1a places the $20,000 in his checking account.

2. In Hungary after World War II, goods and services were purchased with pengös (the domestic currency), but inflation was so high that prices were quoted in dollars. What functions of money were pengös fulfilling in Hungary? What functions were dollars fulfilling? Briefly explain.

3. Suppose Skip Tumalu deposits $400 cash in his checking account at a bank in Atlanta, Georgia. As a result of this transaction, what happens to the size of M1 and M2?

4. If U.S. residents take funds out of their checking accounts and put them into time deposits, explain what happens, if anything, to the size of M1, M2, and the monetary base?

5. Why do many nations have more than one money supply measure (e.g., M1 and M2)?

6. Which of the following statements (there could be more than one) is correct? If a statement is incorrect, provide a corrected version.
   a. To calculate the monetary base, one must add currency held both inside financial intermediaries and outside financial intermediaries to deposits that financial intermediaries hold at the central bank.
   b. To calculate the monetary base, you do not have to know the level of customer deposits in the banking system.
   c. To calculate the monetary base, one must determine only the amount that financial intermediaries hold in reserves, as the two terms (i.e., monetary base and reserves) mean the same thing.

7. Should a nation's money supply be backed by a commodity, such as gold? What are the advantages, and what are the disadvantages?

DISCUSSION QUESTIONS

8. Why do nations measure their money supplies?

9. In terms of the functions of money, is there really any functional difference between M1 and M2?

10. Is it accurate to say that M2 is a more important monetary aggregate than the monetary base because people can spend M2 but cannot spend all the financial assets in the monetary base? Explain.

Chapter 7

Financial Intermediation, Markets, and Intermediaries

INTRODUCTION

For most businesses, having sufficient access to lines of credit at financial institutions, such as banks, is as essential to their health and economic vitality as having sufficient access to water supplies is for families. In the course of providing liquidity to businesses and individuals, financial intermediaries create money for the nation as a whole. The speed at which a nation's money supply changes is important because it affects the rate and sustainability of economic growth and development. For this reason, central banks must ensure that their nations' money supplies are not growing too slowly or too rapidly because the former could lead to recession and the latter to unwanted inflation. Controlling the money supply means controlling financial intermediaries.

This chapter discusses the value that financial intermediaries bring to national (and international) financial markets and the major risks (i.e., credit, liquidity, and market risks) they face in their day-to-day activities. It goes on to examine financial markets and makes an important distinction between money and capital markets, as well as between primary and secondary markets. Central banks control financial intermediaries by regulating and supervising their balance sheet activities. Therefore, this chapter highlights the assets and liabilities that are important to the money creation process, as well as the important role that a nation's check-clearing process plays. It ends by delving into the causes and effects of financial disintermediation, companies' uses of check clearing in their cash management systems, and the ten major causes of bank failures.

THE BASICS

FINANCIAL INTERMEDIARIES

What role do financial intermediaries play in an economy? Why do people place funds in financial intermediaries, such as banks and thrift institutions, when they could lend directly to borrowers and earn higher returns?

DIRECT VERSUS INDIRECT FINANCING

To frame our discussion, let's divide the economy into two segments, with ultimate lenders and savers (lenders/savers) on one side and ultimate

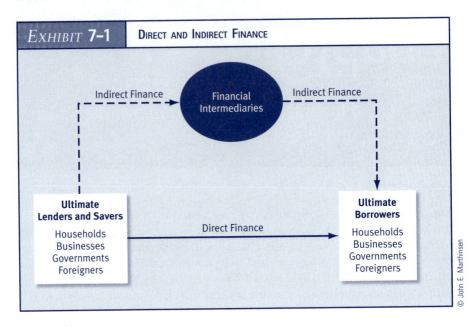

EXHIBIT 7-1   **DIRECT AND INDIRECT FINANCE**

Indirect Finance → Financial Intermediaries → Indirect Finance

Ultimate Lenders and Savers

Households
Businesses
Governments
Foreigners

Direct Finance →

Ultimate Borrowers

Households
Businesses
Governments
Foreigners

© John E. Marthinsen

borrowers on the other side (see Exhibit 7-1). When borrowers raise funds directly from lenders/savers, they engage in *direct financing*. For example, when companies make new stock or bond issues, they engage in direct financing. Rather than borrow deposited funds, which are pooled in financial intermediaries, these companies draw on national and international financial markets (i.e., stock markets and bond markets) to acquire the needed capital.

When borrowers tap financial markets directly, they use the services of financial institutions, such as investment banks, and pay fees for these services. Nevertheless, the source of the borrowed funds is from the market and not from the investment banks. By contrast, financial intermediaries pool funds and lend to customers, which adds a layer of costs that are not incurred with direct finance. A major goal of this section is to explain the benefits that lenders/savers and borrowers derive from using financial intermediaries and why the net benefits of doing so are likely to be greater than the costs financial intermediaries charge.

RISKS, RETURNS, AND VALUE OF FINANCIAL INTERMEDIARIES

Why do lenders/savers and borrowers use financial intermediaries, when doing so means paying fees and expenses that would not be paid if they engaged in direct financing? They do so because financial intermediaries provide a combination of risk and return characteristics that are difficult to duplicate at a reasonable cost.

Benefits of Financial Intermediaries to Lenders/Savers

Lenders/savers could earn higher returns by purchasing financial instruments, such as commercial paper,[1] notes, and bonds, directly in the market. Instead, they deposit their funds in financial intermediaries because these investments are convenient, have negligible transaction and information costs, and carry relatively low risks.[2] Among the major risks that every lender/saver must consider are credit risks, liquidity risks, and market risks. In all three areas, financial intermediaries offer attractive instruments.

Credit risk is the chance that borrowers will be unable or unwilling to repay their debts, thereby leaving lenders/savers with financial assets that are worthless or devalued. Therefore, credit risks are based on the solvency, performance, and continued access of borrowers to liquidity.

For this reason, governments typically have the lowest borrowing costs in a nation because they also have the best credit ratings. Their stellar credit ratings are because most borrow in their own currencies and have the power to tax and/or to print money. Therefore, governments have relatively secure funding sources for the repayment of debts, which means their chances of defaulting are slim.[3]

Financial intermediaries also have relatively low credit risks because they have widely diversified portfolios. In addition, their risks are limited by legislation, regulation, and the market itself because poorly managed financial institutions tend to lose their depositors. In particular, large depositors, whose balances exceed insurance limits, tend to pay closer attention than fully insured depositors to a bank's performance and exposures.

Liquidity risk is the chance that lenders/savers will own financial assets that cannot be sold quickly unless their prices are cut substantially. Liquid securities are ones that are traded in large volumes each day. Owners of these securities have an easy time selling them because their transactions are an insignificant part of the overall volume. By contrast, lightly traded securities present liquidity risks because investors cannot be sure these assets will sell quickly and at firm prices. Deposits of financial intermediaries are highly liquid because depositors have almost instant access to cash.

> Deposits at financial institutions are generally convenient, low-cost, and safe investments. They have relatively low credit, liquidity, and market risks.

> Diversification, regulation, and market forces jointly help to reduce the credit risks of financial intermediaries.

> For lenders/savers, liquidity risk is the chance that the investment assets they financed and now own cannot be sold quickly and without substantial loss of value.

[1] Commercial paper is an unsecured debt instrument that is issued by corporations, usually, to finance working capital needs, such as accounts receivable, inventories, and other net short-term assets. Normally, these short-term securities have maturities up to 270 days. This market is an important source of liquidity for companies with name recognition (i.e., companies that can engage in direct financing).

[2] For example, the cost and risks associated with making bank deposits (both large and small) are much lower than the costs and risks associated with buying a bond or a share or lending directly to a borrower. In the United States and in many other countries, bank deposits are insured either in full or up to a maximum level. Therefore, most small savers do not even check the current credit ratings or past financial performances of the banks they use.

[3] By adopting the euro as their common currency, member countries of the European Monetary Union (EMU) have given up their individual rights to create and control money and handed this power to the European Central Bank. As a result, there are EMU countries that have the power to tax but still carry lower credit ratings than some large multinational companies. More than just printing *and* taxing powers are needed for high credit ratings, and the United States provides a good example. In August 2011, Standard & Poor's downgraded the U.S. government's credit rating from AAA to AA+ as a result of the federal debt's growing size in relation to GDP, weakness of the U.S. economy, and political gridlock connected to addressing its underlying debt problems.

The difference between solvency and liquidity is crucial because solvent companies can (and do) fail from a lack of liquidity. For example, a company that has purchased a considerable amount of highly rated, long-term bonds may be solvent because total asset values exceed total liabilities. Nevertheless, if this company had an urgent need for cash and borrowing from banks was not an option, the absence of a liquid market for the company's long-term securities might force it to default on crucial payments. Short of default, illiquidity might prevent the company from making important strategic moves and/or threaten its profitability due to the losses suffered by selling these long-term, illiquid assets at severely discounted prices.

Market risk is the threat that a financial asset's value will fall due to unfavorable movements in macroeconomic variables, such as interest rates, prices, and exchange rates. Even government securities that have almost no default or liquidity risk could face considerable market risks.

For deposits at financial intermediaries with short-term maturities, customers face very limited market risks. These accounts mature rather quickly. Therefore, if interest rates rise, depositors can roll over (i.e., redeposit) their maturing funds and earn the higher returns. As a result, interest rate fluctuations do not affect the value of financial intermediary deposits as significantly as they affect the value of long-term, fixed rate financial instruments, such as bonds.

To see why, suppose you paid $10,000 for a 10-year government bond earning 10% interest, but at the end of the first year you decide to purchase a car. Needing funds for the down payment, you decide to sell the government bond. The U.S. government has little chance of defaulting on its debts during the next nine years, so you face almost no credit risk. In addition, the market for U.S. government bonds is very deep, so your securities face virtually no liquidity risk. Nevertheless, your bond does face market risk because an increase in interest rates would reduce its nominal value. Let's see why and by how much.

There would be no reason for the government to buy back your bond before maturity; so to sell your security, you would have to use the secondary market. Because your bond would still have nine years remaining until maturity, the return you offer to potential buyers in the secondary market would have to be competitive with the return on a newly issued, nine-year security of equal risk.

Suppose the yield on financial instruments with nine-year maturities (like yours) rose to 15%. Printed on the face of your security is the government's promise to pay only a 10% annual return and to repay $10,000 at maturity. The only way you could make your bond attractive to potential buyers would be to lower its price. How far would the price have to fall to make it attractive to a buyer? The answer is you would have to lower the price to $7,614 (by almost 24%). Only then would a buyer earn the additional yearly equivalent of 5% that is needed to compensate for the relatively low annual interest earned on your security.[4] In this example, your bond lost about 24% of its value in one year due to a 5% increase in yield (i.e., from 10% to 15%).

Solvent companies can fail due to a lack of liquidity.

Market risk is due to the movements in macroeconomic variables, such as interest rates and exchange rates, which play important roles in determining a company's revenues and costs.

Individuals who deposit funds at financial intermediaries face low-to-moderate market risk.

[4] A bond that costs $7,614, earns $1,000 for each of the next nine years, and returns $10,000 at the end of the ninth year has a return (i.e., internal rate of return) of 15%. The annualized value of the bond's $2,386 capital gain (i.e., the difference between the $7,614 purchase price and $10,000 terminal value) adds the extra 5% needed.

Risk is a double-edged sword because if the interest yield fell, you would earn capital gains on the sale of your bonds. For example, suppose a year after you purchased the 10-year government bond, the yield on new bonds fell to 5%. Now, your 10% security would be competing against newly issued, nine-year instruments earning only 5%. If you sold your bond, its market price would rise to $13,554, and this premium price would reduce the buyer's return by exactly 5% (i.e., the difference between the $13,554 purchase price and $10,000 received at maturity would be capital loss to the buyer).

If you were thinking that market risk affects only those individuals who have to sell their financial assets early, remember that there would be a significant opportunity cost from holding securities earning only 10% when market interest rates were 15%. Whenever interest rates rise unexpectedly, investors realize afterward that they would have been better off purchasing securities with 1-year maturities for each of the 10 years rather than purchase one security with a 10-year maturity and fixed yearly coupon (i.e., interest return).

Benefits of Financial Intermediaries to Borrowers

Borrowers also benefit from using financial intermediaries but in different ways from lenders/savers. For instance, financial intermediaries offer borrowers access to funds at very low transaction costs and information costs. Without financial intermediaries, borrowers would have to search for counterparties willing and able to lend the amounts and maturities needed.

Companies normally arrange lines of credit with banks and use these lines to finance temporary cash flow imbalances, such as working capital needs and initiating short-term marketing or strategic initiatives. If they wanted, these companies could borrow directly in the financial markets by issuing their own securities, such as bonds, notes, or commercial paper. But they choose to borrow from financial intermediaries because this type of financing gives companies a large degree of flexibility and control over their cash management practices and at a relatively low cost.

> Financial intermediaries provide borrowers with low-cost financial flexibility and added control over their cash flows.

FINANCIAL MARKETS

Before moving into specific discussions of banks and banking activities, let's begin by reviewing some basics about financial markets. In particular, we will focus on the differences between money markets and capital markets and the functions of primary and secondary markets.

Money Market versus Capital Market

One way to segment financial markets is to separate them into the money market and capital market. The money market is where financial instruments (or deposits) with maturities less than or equal to one year are bought and sold.[5] Examples of money market instruments are checking accounts, savings

---

[5] Money market securities also include financial assets that were issued originally with maturities longer than one year but have only a year or less remaining until they mature. The market for buying and selling foreign currencies is called the *foreign exchange market* (i.e., not the money market).

accounts, Treasury bills, repurchase agreements, certificates of deposit, short-term time deposits, and eurodollar deposits.[6]

The capital market is where financial instruments with maturities greater than one year are bought and sold. Examples of capital market instruments are stocks (equities) and interest-earning securities, such as bonds and notes issued by companies and governments (i.e., federal, state, and local).

PRIMARY VERSUS SECONDARY MARKETS

When borrowers first issue securities, there is a net flow of funds from lenders/savers to borrowers, and this flow is a source of financing for the original issuers. The market for securities when they are first issued is called the *primary market*.

Once issued, these same securities can be bought and sold numerous times before they mature.[7] The secondary market is where the titles to these already-issued securities are bought and sold. Secondary market transactions usually do not involve the original issuers of the securities, and this market is not a source of funds for the original security issuers.

The money creation process, which is the topic of the next chapter (i.e., Chapter 8, "The Power of Financial Institutions to Create Money"), is much easier to understand when it is set in the context of a bank's balance sheet; so we will begin by taking a brief look at the major assets and liabilities of a typical bank.

OVERVIEW OF A TYPICAL BANK'S BALANCE SHEET

A balance sheet lists the type and value of a company's assets, as well as the claims on these assets. Claims on a company's assets by nonowners are *liabilities*, and the claims on these assets by the owners of the company are *stockholders' equity*. Banks are financial companies; so all the accounting relationships that apply to companies also apply to banks.

SOME ACCOUNTING TAUTOLOGIES

Assets must be owned by someone, so an important accounting tautology (i.e., truism) is that the assets of a bank must equal the sum of its liabilities (outsiders' claims) plus stockholders' equity (insiders' claims) (see Exhibit 7-2).

This accounting tautology is true for all banks, in all countries, at all times. For example, if a bank had assets worth €100 million and liabilities equal to €80 million, its stockholders' equity must equal €20 million. In other

EXHIBIT 7-2	ACCOUNTING TAUTOLOGY 1
Assets ≡ Liabilities + Stockholders' Equity *The symbol ≡ means that the relationship is definitional (i.e., a tautology).*	

© John E. Marthinsen

---

[6]Eurodollar deposits are U.S. dollar deposits in banks located outside the United States.
[7]In the case of shares, they never mature.

EXHIBIT 7-3	ACCOUNTING TAUTOLOGY 2

$$\Delta \text{ Assets} \equiv \Delta \text{ Liabilities} + \Delta \text{ Stockholders' Equity}$$

The symbol Δ, which is the Greek letter delta, means "a change in:"

words, 80% of the assets belong to individuals outside the bank, and 20% belong to the bank's owners.

Ordinarily, the values attached to a bank's assets and liabilities are *book values*, which means they reflect the cost of these assets and liabilities at the time they were acquired. Valuing assets and liabilities at their historic prices is problematic because the older an asset (e.g., real estate or machinery), the more distorted its book value can be from its current market value. This difference could be important because in the event of liquidation, creditors and shareholders divide the resale value of the company at current market prices and not the book value.

> Book values reflect what assets and liabilities were worth when they were acquired. Market values reflect what they are currently worth.

Because a bank's assets must equal its liabilities plus stockholders' equity, changes in its assets must equal changes in the sum of liabilities plus stockholders' equity (see Exhibit 7-3).

The tautological relationship between changes in assets and changes in the sum of liabilities plus stockholders' equity is worth remembering because it highlights the fact that a bank is able to acquire new assets only by increasing its liabilities and/or stockholders' equity. In other words, the *sources of funds* for a bank come from increasing liabilities and stockholders' equity, and the *uses of funds* go toward acquiring assets. A bank makes profits only if there is a positive difference (i.e., spread) between the average cost of its sources of funds and the average return on its uses of funds (see Exhibit 7-4).

> Banks earn profits when the average return on their uses of funds exceeds the average cost of their sources of funds.

Exhibit 7-5 shows the major assets of a typical bank, along with its liabilities and stockholders' equity. To more fully understand the business of banking, let's describe each one of these assets and liabilities and then discuss check clearing.

MAJOR BANK ASSETS

Reserves

Reserves are highly liquid assets that must be held by banks in strict proportion to their deposit liabilities. Of course, banks can hold more reserves than required, but in doing so they are usually trading off profitability for safety because central banks pay either no interest or little interest on these deposits. Central banks determine not only the proportion of deposit liabilities that banks must hold as reserves but also the particular assets that qualify as reserves.[8] For example, in the United States, only cash in bank vaults and

[8] In some countries, the required reserve ratio is determined by legislation. Countries also differ with respect to the financial assets that qualify as reserves. Some permit banks to count highly liquid, safe assets, such as government securities. In this book, we will assume that only cash in the vault and deposits at the central bank count as reserves.

EXHIBIT **7-4**   SOURCES AND USES OF BANK FUNDS

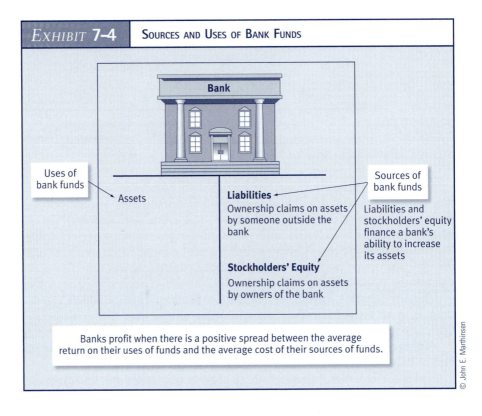

Uses of bank funds

Assets

Liabilities ←

Ownership claims on assets by someone outside the bank

Sources of bank funds

Liabilities and stockholders' equity finance a bank's ability to increase its assets

Stockholders' Equity

Ownership claims on assets by owners of the bank

Banks profit when there is a positive spread between the average return on their uses of funds and the average cost of their sources of funds.

© John E. Marthinsen

EXHIBIT **7-5**   TYPICAL BANK'S BALANCE SHEET

ASSETS	= LIABILITIES + STOCKHOLDERS' EQUITY
Reserves • Cash in the vault • Deposits at the central bank	**Deposits** • Checking deposits • Savings deposits • Time deposits, etc.
Loans • Principal & interest due	**Borrowing from the central bank** • Interest charged is called discount rate
Securities • Bonds, T-bills, etc.	**Borrowing from other banks** • Called the "interbank market" • In U.S. called "federal funds market"
Deposits at other banks • Called the "interbank market" • In U.S. called "federal funds market"	**Stockholders' equity** • Also called "Shareholders' equity" • Also called "Owners' equity"
Other assets • Buildings, computers, etc.	• Also called "Capital account"

© John E. Marthinsen

banks' deposits at the central bank (the Federal Reserve) qualify as reserves. Cash earns no interest yield, and deposits at the Federal Reserve earn a low rate compared to other asset alternatives. As a result, banks have an incentive to optimize their reserve assets to maintain desired risk-return ratios.

Before ending our discussion of bank reserves, it is useful to highlight two key points. First, the cash that is held in banks' vaults is not part of a nation's money supply. When cash is deposited in a bank, the funds move from "currency *in* circulation," which is a part of the money supply, to "currency *out of* circulation," which is not.

> The cash in bank vaults is not part of a nation's money supply.

A second key point is that reserves are needed not only to meet banks' reserve requirements and to satisfy depositors' demand for cash but also for the check-clearing process. An efficient check-clearing system is crucial to the health and well-being of any nation's financial system. Understanding check clearing is also essential for conceptualizing how banks and the banking system create money.

> Reserves are held to meet reserve requirements, satisfy customer demands for cash, and facilitate check clearing.

Loans

Banks make short-, medium-, and long-term loans to businesses and individuals. Businesses of all sizes borrow from banks for a variety of reasons. For instance, many small- and medium-sized companies lack the credit rating and name recognition needed to tap the financial markets directly; so they use banks as their primary source of funding.

Large companies also use banks even though they have direct access to the financial markets through their ability to issue financial instruments, such as commercial paper, notes, and bonds. Large companies use banks for financing short-term, operational cash flow imbalances (e.g., working capital to finance inventories and accounts receivable). Usually, this borrowing and lending process is simplified by companies arranging lines of credit with their banks. When funds are needed, these companies simply use the existing credit lines that are available.

> Bank loans and lines of credit are important sources of funds for businesses of all sizes.

MACRO MEMO   7-1

Since When Have Deposits at the Fed Earned an Interest Return?

For most of its history, the U.S. Federal Reserve paid no interest on the required or excess reserves that U.S. banks held at the central bank. To eliminate the implicit tax that noninterest-earning (required) reserves put on banks' profitability, the Fed began paying interest on these deposits in 2008. At the same time, the Fed also began paying interest on excess reserve balances that banks held at the central bank. The reason for making this latter policy change was to provide the Fed with an additional monetary tool.* The new yield gave banks an incentive to keep excess reserves with the Fed, but, to date, this incentive has not been large. In 2013, the interest return offered by the Fed on these reserve deposits was only 0.25%.

*The Financial Services Regulatory Relief Act of 2006 gave the Federal Reserve Banks authority to pay interest on deposit balances held by depository financial institutions at any of the 12 Reserve Banks. This authority was made contingent on Board of Governors regulations, effective October 1, 2011, but the Emergency Economic Stabilization Act of 2008 changed the effective date to October 1, 2008.

Source: Board of Governors of the Federal Reserve System, Interest on Required Balances and Excess Balances, http://www.federalreserve.gov/monetarypolicy/reqresbalances.htm (accessed June 3, 2013).

To protect themselves, banks must keep a careful watch on customers' financial health and changes in their business conditions. If a company fails to uphold its borrowing agreement with the bank, its credit lines are likely to be reduced. Big customers with large, safe capitalization levels and healthy credit ratings get the largest credit lines, but banks protect themselves by putting maximum limits on the lines they extend to any individual customer. Normally, these limits are set relative to the stockholders' equity of banks. For example, the maximum line extended to any one customer may be limited to 15% of a bank's stockholders' equity. Therefore, if the bank had $100 million in stockholders' equity, the maximum credit line it would extend to any individual customer would be $15 million.

Maximum limits on credit lines are imposed so that the failure of a large customer does not bankrupt the financial institution. They are also imposed to ensure that large customers do not have an undue influence on banks. Consider the old saying: "If you owe a bank $100, the bank owns you, but if you owe a bank $100 million, you own the bank."

Banks also make short-term and long-term loans to individuals. Short-term loans finance purchases of goods and services, such as cars, appliances, and vacations. Long-term loans are for expenditures, such as mortgage financing for houses and condominiums.

> Bank loans to any one customer are usually limited to a percent of the bank's stockholders' equity.

Securities

Securities are classified into two categories: debt instruments and equities. Debt instruments earn interest returns and offer no ownership rights in the companies that issue them. These interest-earning securities have priority when companies fail, and the proceeds of a liquidated company are distributed to inside and outside owners.

Equities have two potential sources of income, namely dividends, if the company earns profits and chooses to distribute them, and capital gains. They provide their holders with ownership rights in the companies that issue them. At the same time, equity holders have the lowest order of priority when a company is liquidated.

In some countries, like the United States, banks' ability to own stocks is restricted. One reason for this restriction is to ensure that financial institutions do not play disproportionate roles in the management and governance of nonfinancial companies. Restrictions are also imposed to avoid possible conflicts of interest. For example, if a large customer performed poorly and needed additional funding, a shareholder bank might feel compelled to extend a loan to the ailing company, just to keep it alive. These loans may not be in the best interests of depositors and other shareholders.

Deposits at Other Banks

Interbank borrowing and lending is vital to banks' liquidity management. Every bank employs at least one money trader whose job is to borrow when the bank has temporary shortages of funds and to lend when it has surpluses. Banks borrow and lend in the interbank market throughout the working day. Most of these transactions have overnight maturities, but longer-term deposits/loans are also possible.

Picture yourself as a money trader in a bank. It is 10:00 A.M., and a large deposit has just been made. Having no immediate loans to finance and no need to fund the purchase of securities for the bank's portfolio (also known as the *nostro account*), it would be your job to invest these funds as soon as possible so that the bank could start earning a return on them. The interbank market provides money traders with a large-volume, low-margin market on which funds can be transferred almost instantaneously.[9] This market is also significant for bank regulators because changes in the interbank interest rate are often a good reflection of the relative availability of funds in the banking system.

The interbank deposit market provides a convenient and safe way for banks to invest short-term funds.

Other Assets

Banks have hundreds of other assets, such as buildings, land, furniture, supplies, and computer equipment. Because these assets are not closely related to the money creation process, we will not discuss them and, instead, turn our attention to the major bank liabilities.

MAJOR BANK LIABILITIES

Banks have many potential sources of funds, and one of the main ones is from deposits (both domestic and foreign), such as checking-, savings-, and time-deposits/accounts. Banks also borrow from other banks and from the central bank.

Deposits

Checking Accounts: Checking accounts, checking deposits, checkable deposits, and *transaction accounts* are just different names for the same financial liabilities of banks. From a bank's perspective, checking accounts are vulnerable sources of funds because they can be withdrawn without notice. In fact, *demand deposits*, which are checking accounts owned mostly by companies, got their name because they can be withdrawn "on demand."

Checking accounts are the most liquid and potentially most volatile bank liabilities.

Because checking accounts are highly liquid and vulnerable sources of bank funds, they earn relatively little interest. The longer a bank can be assured that funds will remain in place, the greater the interest it is willing and able to pay for these funds. As mentioned in the previous chapter, checking accounts are included in the M1 and M2 money supply definitions.

Savings Deposits: Savings deposits are more stable sources of funds for banks than checking accounts because they are usually kept on deposit for longer periods of time. In contrast to checking accounts, savings accounts are not available to depositors on demand. Even though most of us have never been denied access to our savings accounts when we wanted to withdraw funds, banks have the right to deny this access for short periods of time. Moreover, depositors cannot spend savings deposits; rather they must first withdraw the

---

[9] In the United States, the interbank market for lending (and borrowing) is called the *federal funds market*. The adjective *federal* is used because the funds are transferred on a daily basis in the accounts of the Federal Reserve System (i.e., the U.S. central bank). This market is not related to the U.S. federal government or to U.S. federal government transactions.

funds in cash or transfer them to checking accounts. As a result, savings deposits are not as liquid as checking accounts and therefore earn higher rates of interest than checking accounts. In the United States, savings accounts are included in the M2 definition of money but not in M1.

Time Deposits: Time deposits are interest-earning accounts with fixed maturities. Early withdrawals usually trigger interest penalties, which makes them even less liquid than savings deposits. Because they are less volatile than either checking deposits or savings deposits, time deposits usually earn higher interest returns than savings accounts. In the United States, small time deposits (i.e., $100,000 or less) are included in the M2 definition of money but not in M1.

> Savings deposits are less liquid and potentially less volatile sources of funds for banks than checking deposits.

> Time deposits are less liquid and potentially less volatile sources of funds for banks than savings deposits.

Borrowings from Other Banks

We have already discussed how money traders at banks deposit surplus funds in other banks. Borrowing from other banks is the flip side of the coin, and banks borrow on the interbank market when they are short of funds. For example, if the credit department of a bank extended a large loan to a corporate customer, the money trader would be contacted to secure the needed funding. If the funds were not available internally, the money trader could finance the loan temporarily by borrowing in the interbank market.

> The interbank market is an important source of short-term funds for banks.

Borrowings from the Central Bank

Banks do not have to rely solely on deposits from customers or the interbank market as sources of financing. They can also borrow from the central bank, and the interest rate charged on these loans is called the *discount rate*.

Discount loans are for short time periods and collateralized with acceptable ("eligible") securities. This rate is set by a nation's central bank rather than by market forces of supply and demand. We will discuss the discount rate more thoroughly in Chapter 9, "Who Controls the Money Supply and How?"

> Banks can also borrow from central banks.

STOCKHOLDERS' EQUITY

Stockholders' equity (also called *shareholders' equity*, *owners' equity*, or the *capital account*) includes funds contributed to a bank by its owners (i.e., shareholders) in the form of paid-in equity and accumulations of undistributed profits earned by the bank. A bank is solvent only as long as its assets are greater than its liabilities, which means a solvent bank has a positive stockholders' equity.

With a bank's balance sheet in mind, let's turn our attention to check clearing. Every advanced nation has a highly sophisticated network of financial communication and transportation systems, which ensures that checks are cleared quickly, accurately, reliably, and efficiently.

> Stockholders' equity is the owners' claim on a bank's assets.

CHECK CLEARING

Check clearing is done through clearing houses, which are central depositories in which banks deposit funds and through which checks are routed as they wind their way back home. As checks reach the clearing houses, a bank's clearing account is increased or decreased depending on whether the checks are deposited by or written on that bank.

In most countries, the central bank is an integral part of the clearing system. One of the most important clearing houses in the United States is the Federal Reserve (the Fed), but U.S. banks also have the option of using private financial intermediaries, if doing so is cheaper and/or more convenient.

Let's use an example to help explain the check clearing process. We will assume the Federal Reserve is the clearing house for the two banks involved in the transaction. Suppose John Johnson purchases a small sailboat from Maria Martin by writing a check for $1,000 on his account at Colonial Bank in Providence, Rhode Island. Suppose further that Martin deposits the check in Sovereign Bank, Boston.

At the end of the day, Sovereign would send Johnson's check (along with all the other checks deposited that day) to the Fed.[10] When the Fed received Johnson's check, it would increase Sovereign's account by $1,000 and reduce Colonial's account by the same amount (see Exhibit 7-6).

Sovereign would now have a new liability in the $1,000 it owes to Martin, and it would have a new asset in the $1,000 deposit at the central

> Check clearing is done through clearing houses, and central banks are usually major clearing houses.

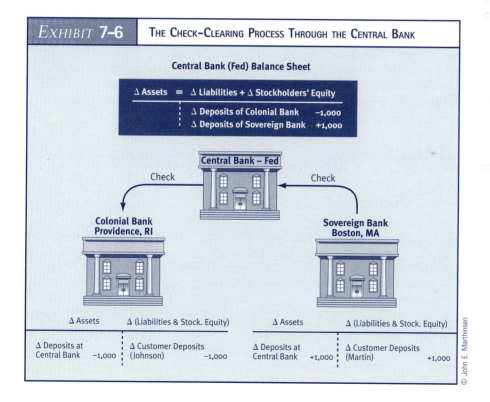

EXHIBIT 7-6   THE CHECK-CLEARING PROCESS THROUGH THE CENTRAL BANK

Central Bank (Fed) Balance Sheet

$$\Delta \text{ Assets } \equiv \Delta \text{ Liabilities } + \Delta \text{ Stockholders' Equity}$$

Δ Deposits of Colonial Bank	–1,000
Δ Deposits of Sovereign Bank	+1,000

Central Bank – Fed

Check   Check

Colonial Bank
Providence, RI

Sovereign Bank
Boston, MA

Δ Assets	Δ (Liabilities & Stock. Equity)		Δ Assets	Δ (Liabilities & Stock. Equity)
Δ Deposits at Central Bank –1,000	Δ Customer Deposits (Johnson) –1,000		Δ Deposits at Central Bank +1,000	Δ Customer Deposits (Martin) +1,000

© John E. Marthinsen

---

[10] Actually, the check would be sent to the Boston branch of the Federal Reserve System. The Boston Fed is one of 12 Federal Reserve banks in the Federal Reserve System. For more information on the U.S. Federal Reserve System, see Appendix 9-5, "Regulation of U.S. Banks and the Structure of the Federal Reserve System," in Chapter 9, "Who Controls the Money Supply and How?"

ΔM2 $\equiv$	ΔC_c +		ΔD	+ ΔN

EXHIBIT 7-7   **EFFECT OF THE CLEARED CHECK ON THE M2 MONEY SUPPLY**

ΔM2 $\equiv$	ΔC_c +	ΔD	+ ΔN
$0 =	$0 +	Δ Martin's Checking Account + $1,000 Δ Johnson's Checking Account − $1,000	+ $0
		Net = $0	

ΔM2 means a change in the M2 money supply.
ΔC_c means a change in currency in circulation.
ΔD means a change in checking deposits.
ΔN means a change in near money deposits.

© John E. Marthinsen

bank. Because deposits at the central bank count as reserves, Sovereign would have $1,000 of additional reserves.

Upon receiving the cleared check (or upon receiving notification that the check was written), Colonial would reduce Johnson's account by $1,000 and reduce (by the same amount) its deposits at the central bank. Because Colonial's reserves fell by the same amount Sovereign's reserves rose, the banking system's total reserves and the U.S. monetary base would remain the same.

Notice that check clearing has no effect on the nation's money supply. Johnson's checking account fell at Colonial Bank by the same amount Martin's checking account rose at Sovereign (see Exhibit 7-7).

THE REST OF THE STORY

INTERNATIONAL CHECK CLEARING

To clear checks internationally, banks follow almost an identical process as clearing them domestically; the only difference is the first step. Foreign banks plug into the domestic check-clearing system through correspondent banks. To see how, let's modify our last example by assuming that John Johnson bought the $1,000 sailboat from Heidi Meier, a Swiss resident who banked at Credit Suisse (CS) in Zurich.

International check clearing is done through correspondent bank relationships.

At the end of the day, CS would send Johnson's check (along with all the other U.S. checks deposited that day) to its correspondent banks in the United States. Suppose that Sovereign Bank was one of CS's correspondent banks. When Sovereign received Johnson's check, it would increase CS's deposits by $1,000 and send the check to the Fed for clearing. Once the check was cleared, Sovereign's account at the Fed would increase by $1,000. Therefore, Sovereign would have a new liability to CS for $1,000 and an equal amount of new assets in its deposits at the Fed (see Exhibit 7-8).

Upon receiving the cleared check (or upon receiving notification that the check was written), Colonial would reduce both Johnson's account by $1,000 and its deposits at the Federal Reserve. Finally, CS would have a new deposit

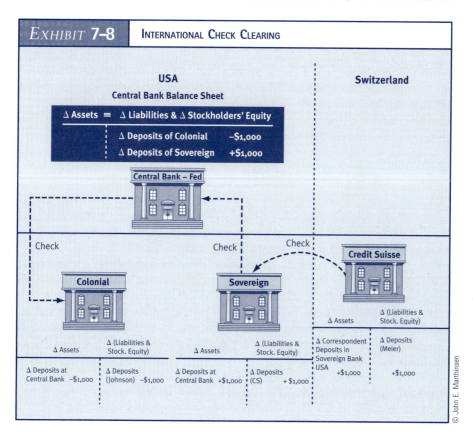

EXHIBIT 7-8 | INTERNATIONAL CHECK CLEARING

© John E. Marthinsen

liability to Heidi Meier equal to $1,000, and it would have a new $1,000 asset in its correspondent bank deposits at Sovereign Bank, Boston.

FINANCIAL DISINTERMEDIATION

Financial disintermediation occurs when customers attempt to withdraw funds from the banking system and invest them directly in the market, such as in government securities or mutual funds. For banks, the loss of funds can be like having the wind knocked out of them by a swift punch to the stomach. In the past, financial disintermediation has been caused mainly by well-meaning but misguided regulations and also by runs, which were stimulated by the loss of customer confidence in the banking/financial system or a loss of confidence in the domestic currency.[11] More recently, the Internet has presented disintermediation challenges to banks (and also to

> Financial disintermediation occurs when customers attempt to withdraw funds from financial intermediaries.

---

[11] A "run" occurs when there are massive customer withdrawals (institutional and/or retail) from a bank or other financial institution due to concerns about the bank's solvency and/or liquidity. Most financial institutions have long-term assets and short-term liabilities; so runs increase the chances of default because these financial institutions do not have sufficient sources of short-term funding. This lack of liquidity serves to supercharge customer withdrawals.

bank regulators) by the way it has altered the flow of funds. This topic is discussed below in greater detail.

Let's consider each of these three sources of financial disintermediation, but before discussing what financial disintermediation is, a helpful detour is understanding what it is not. To survive, banks pay competitive yields and provide services that attract customers and add value to their daily lives. Financial intermediaries carry on a healthy competition for funds as they alter their interest rates and benefits, but in such cases, the funds lost to one intermediary are gained by another; so this flow of funds is not lost to the system of financial intermediaries and, therefore, not an example of financial disintermediation.

Financial Disintermediation Caused by Regulations: Government or central bank regulations can cause (and have caused) financial disintermediation. For example in the United States, Regulation Q was passed during the 1930s to restrict the yields that domestic banks could offer on deposits. This regulation was not a problem in most years because market interest rates remained below the ceilings, but during the 1970s, they rose above the ceiling. As a result, depositors withdrew funds, en masse, from banks and invested them in higher-earning, unregulated assets, such as mutual funds, Treasury bills, and eurodollar deposits. As a result, the ability of many banks to finance commercial and mortgage loans was curtailed.

Financial Disintermediation Due to Bank Runs: The second type of financial disintermediation is due to bank runs, which are usually caused by fear and misinformation. Any hint that a bank or other financial intermediary will fail or delay making payments often spirits an immediate reaction by customers to withdraw funds as quickly as possible and invest them in safer assets, such as foreign-currency denominated bank deposits, money market mutual funds, unregulated offshore accounts in the same currency (e.g., eurodollar accounts), and commodities.

To meet these immediate customer demands, banks have only the cash held in their vaults, deposits at the central banks, and other highly liquid assets. Usually, these assets are just a small fraction of total deposit liabilities and insufficient to meet demand. Adding to the problem are fear and panic, which reinforce each other, provoking systemic shortages of funds in the financial system.

During the Great Depression of the 1930s, before U.S. bank accounts were insured, runs were rampant throughout the United States; thousands of banks failed. During the Great Recession from 2007 to 2009, despite having deposit insurance that covered most customers, runs caused the demise and/or acquisition of prominent banks and securities firms, such as Countrywide Financial (August, 2007), Bear Stearns (March, 2008), IndyMac (July, 2008), and Wachovia (September, 2008). In foreign nations, runs also occurred at well-known banks, such as Northern Rock in England (September, 2007), Landsbanki in Iceland (October, 2008), and Laiki Bank in Cyprus (March, 2013).

Financial Disintermediation Caused by the Internet: Recently, the Internet has challenged "traditional" banking in new and interesting ways. The Internet offers pricing and convenience benefits that have allowed web-based companies to compete in niche markets and forced banks to reconsider the fees they charge for connecting ultimate lenders and ultimate borrowers. These companies (e.g., Square) are able to connect iPhones, iPads, and Androids to readers that can scan credit cards at a cost of fewer than three cents per transaction. Other companies (e.g., Dwolla) allow users to transfer cash via phone, Twitter, or Facebook. Still others (e.g., Simple) offer handy and cost-effective digital banking services. Internet competition, as it exists today, is just the tip of an ever-growing iceberg. Banks have reacted and will be sure to react in the future to these challenges, but one point is clear. Evolving technological capabilities are transforming our financial systems, which means the future is likely to be very much different from the past.

CHECK CLEARING AND COMPANY CASH MANAGEMENT

How does check clearing fit into companies' cash management systems? Are there opportunities to profit from the check-clearing process? Check clearing affects the time period between when a check is written and when it is settled. As a result, lengthening or shortening this time period can influence profitability and the timing of cash flows. Therefore, it should be considered by companies when they establish domestic and international cash management systems.

> Optimizing check-clearing times is an important consideration in any company's cash management system.

Companies have an incentive to shorten the time it takes to collect receivables and to lengthen the time it takes to settle payables. By doing so, they can earn additional days of interest on bank accounts and marketable securities, and/or they can postpone using lines of credit, which reduces borrowing costs. In businesses where transactions are often for millions of dollars, euros, yen, or pesos, shortening receivables or lengthening payables by only a day or two can significantly affect a company's cash flows and bottom line.

MACRO MEMO   7-2

Facing the Music: Is Disintermediation in the Banking Sector Like Disintermediation in the Music Industry?

A parallel can be drawn between the way technology has caused disintermediation in the financial markets and the way it has caused disintermediation in the music industry. In the music industry, digital innovations, such as iTunes and Rhapsody, have caused a steep drop in recording studio sales. Albums that once sold for $15.99 now have their hit songs selected and sold individually for $0.99.

The price and convenience of using the new technologies to purchase individual songs has reduced music industry profits considerably. The stakes are high. In 2010, recording companies sold an impressive 83 million digital albums but an even more impressive 1.2 billion digital songs.*

*See Aaron Shapiro, "Time to Face the Music on Disintermediation," *American Banker*, March 27, 2013, http://www.american banker.com/magazine/122_2/time-to-face-the-music-on -disintermediation-1045671-1.html (accessed March 27, 2013).

Using Lockboxes to Shorten Receivable Collection Periods

One way to shorten the time it takes to collect receivables is by setting up lockboxes. A *lockbox* is simply a checking account at a bank near its customers.

Suppose your company is headquartered in New York City, but many of your customers are located in California. When customers pay their invoices, the checks they write may take two to three days before they arrive at your headquarters in New York City, and it may take another day or two before your accounting staff processes the checks internally and deposits them in a bank.

Every day that a customer's check is in transit or being processed is a day of lost interest earnings. Lockboxes help to speed the collection process. Instead of having customers mail their checks to New York City, they would be asked to mail them to mailbox addresses in nearby towns, perhaps in the same city as the customers are located. For a fee, banks will clear out these lockboxes each day (or a few times each day) and credit your account with the receipts.

Lockboxes can be used for national and international check-clearing purposes. Typically, companies with good cash management systems have both lockboxes and standing orders for their banks to sweep any surplus funds at the end of each working day into interest-earning deposits.

Using the Extended Disbursements Float to Lengthen Payables

The *extended disbursements float* is the time it takes between when a check is written and when it is cleared through the banking system. One way companies can lengthen this period is by writing checks on banks that are as remote as possible from their suppliers' headquarters, core banks, or lockboxes. For example, to pay suppliers located in San Francisco, a company might originate payments from a New York City bank. To pay suppliers in Tampa, Florida, it might originate payments from a bank in Nome, Alaska.

Of course, cash management practices such as these could result in the loss of supplier goodwill because the days gained by the payer are lost by the payee. For this reason, many business payments are done electronically so that physical checks do not have to be processed and settlement is instantaneous.

CAUSES OF BANK FAILURES

Most banks have failed for a relatively small number of identifiable reasons.[12] Exhibit 7-9 lists these major causes.

---

[12] Sal Bommarito, "Financial Meltdown 101: 10 Reasons Why Banks Fail," *policymic*, http://www.policymic .com/articles/10304/financial-meltdown-101-10-reasons-why-banks-fail (accessed June 1, 2013).

EXHIBIT 7-9	MAJOR CAUSES OF BANK FAILURES

	Cause	Explanation
1	Nonperforming (i.e., "bad") loans	Bad loans reduce future cash flows and profits of banks because borrowers stop paying annual interest charges, and, at maturity, they do not repay the principal. The full impact of such losses falls on banks' thin equity bases, causing some to fail.
2	Lack of liquidity (Excessive cash flow risks)	Because they fund long-term assets with short-term liabilities, even solvent banks can fail if there is a run or an extraordinary need for cash.
3	Excessive balance sheet risks	Major balance sheet risks can be created when banks mismatch the maturities, currency denominations, and/or interest rate resetting dates of their assets and liabilities. If fluctuations in market rates and prices are large enough, they can trigger bank failures.
4	Disproportionate proprietary trading	Banks that wager their own funds may also be putting at risk the deposits of customers. Threats to these financial institutions' health and solvency are intensified by their relatively slender equity levels. Recently, governments and central bank regulators have focused attention on financial institutions that make large wagers with proprietary funds. The U.S. Congress addressed this issue when it included the "Volcker Rule" in its 2010 Dodd-Frank Act.
5	Pursuing unprofitable nonbank activities	The wave of financial deregulation between 1980 and 2010 expanded bank activities into relatively unfamiliar areas, such as investment banking, finance companies, and leasing. The profitability and solvency of some banks were challenged by their poor performances in these new territories. Many of these activities were managed through bank holding companies or subsidiaries.
6	Risk management mistakes	Banks measure market risks with sophisticated financial measures, such as value-at-risk analysis and contingent value-at-risk analysis. These measures have three major problems. They assume: (1) the future will be like the past, (2) returns are normally distributed, and (3) people reading/interpreting them understand what these measures mean.
7	Excessive speculative use of derivatives	Derivatives are like fire in the sense that they can be be highly useful and reduce risks, if properly used, but they can be equally dangerous, if not. Due to their high leverage levels, changes in market prices can cause considerable and quick changes in derivative values.
8	Rogue employees	Giving employees both back-office and front-office responsibilities is a recipe for problems because it invites undetectable fraud and deception. Banks have to be aware of employees who know the back alleyways between financial accounts.
9	Regulatory costs	Changes in regulations can burden banks with huge compliance costs that make the continuation of operating activities impossible.*

*Of course, regulations can also help to save banks from themselves, which seems to have been the case in India during the U.S. financial crisis of 2007 to 2009. Relatively strict government regulations forced Indian banks to take a more circumspect and paced approach to profitability and balance sheet growth. As a result, they did not suffer the same hardships as their U.S. counterparts. See "Indian Banks Starred in Downturn," *The National*, December 12, 2012, www.thenational.ae/business/industry-insights/finance/indian-banks-starred-in-downturn (accessed June 1, 2013).

Source: Based on Sal Bommarito, "Financial Meltdown 101: 10 Reasons Why Banks Fail," policymic, http://www.policymic.com /articles/10304/financial-meltdown-101-10-reasons-why-banks-fail (accessed June 1, 2013).

CONCLUSION

Financial intermediaries are able to compete with direct methods of financing because they offer a combination of risk and return benefits that would be hard to duplicate at a reasonable cost. For lenders/savers, the major risks to consider are credit risk, liquidity risk, and market risk. Individuals, as well as small- and medium-sized companies, use financial intermediaries because they have few other alternatives. Large companies can tap the financial markets directly, but they use financial intermediaries because of their convenience and the low cost of this short-term-funding source. With the knowledge we have of financial institutions' assets and liabilities, the check-clearing process, and financial markets, we can now explore the money creation powers of banks and the banking system, which is the topic of Chapter 8, "The Power of Financial Institutions to Create Money."

REVIEW QUESTIONS

1. Why don't borrowers and lenders interact directly? What are the advantages of using financial intermediaries?

2. When Bank A clears a check written on Bank B:
   a. What happens to Bank B's reserves and excess reserves?
   b. What happens to Bank A's reserves and excess reserves?
   c. What happens to the banking system's excess reserves and the total level of banking system reserves?

3. Which of the following is an example of direct financing, and which is an example of indirect financing?
   a. Fred Fornow borrows $20,000 to purchase a new car.
   b. Gloria Gregory deposits $10,000 in a money market mutual fund.
   c. DuPont Inc. makes a $100 million 10-year bond issue to finance the building of a plant in China.
   d. Henrietta Hernandez purchases $15,000 worth of Bank of America shares in a new stock issue.
   e. IBM issues $400 million in five-year notes yielding 6.5%. The notes are purchased mainly by foreign residents.

4. Explain credit-, market-, and liquidity risks.

5. Explain the type(s) of risk Lafayette Bank takes in the following examples.
   a. Lafayette Bank extends a one-year loan to Joe Johnson to purchase a new washer and dryer for his home.
   b. Lafayette Bank extends a 30-year, fixed-interest-rate loan to Joe Johnson for the purchase of a new home.
   c. Lafayette Bank extends a 30-year, floating-interest-rate loan to Joe Johnson for the purchase of a new home.
   d. Lafayette Bank purchases $100,000 in 10-year government bonds.
   e. Lafayette Bank purchases $200,000 in 10-year municipal bonds.

6. Explain the difference between insolvency and illiquidity.

7. Suppose XYZ Inc.'s equity was 100% of its assets (i.e., the company had no liabilities). Explain if it is possible for this company to default due to liquidity risk.

8. What is the difference between the money market and capital market? Which market is more important for financing the day-to-day transactions of a company?

9. Explain the difference between the primary and secondary markets.

10. In what way, if any, is the secondary market related to liquidity risk?

11. Under what circumstances, if any, is it possible for a bank's assets not to equal the sum of its liabilities plus stockholders' equity?

12. Is it true that the sources of a bank's funds must equal its uses? Explain.

13. Why does every bank have a vested interest in optimizing its reserve assets? What does a bank lose by keeping too many reserves? What does it risk by keeping too few reserves?

14. Why would a bank impose limits on the amount it lends to any single customer? What risk is it trying to mitigate?

15. What is financial disintermediation?

16. Explain how government or central bank restrictions on the interest rate banks can pay on deposits could cause financial disintermediation.

17. What is a bank run?

18. Explain how the Internet has caused financial disintermediation.

19. What are lockboxes? How do they relate to a nation's check-clearing system? Why are they important to many companies' cash management systems?

20. Explain the extended disbursements float. How is it related to a nation's check-clearing system? How can companies use it for cash management purposes?

DISCUSSION QUESTIONS

21. Is it accurate to say that indirect finance exists mainly because of the encouragement of governments and central banks?

22. How does diversification reduce risk?

Chapter 8

The Power of Financial Institutions to Create Money

INTRODUCTION

Using money is such a routine part of our daily lives that it is easy to overlook the fact that the creation of money is a business, which is carried on by financial institutions for the purpose of making profits. Therefore, when central banks regulate their nations' money supplies, they also regulate financial intermediaries' profits.

This chapter discusses the money creation powers of financial intermediaries. Because most nations have a wide variety of them (e.g., commercial banks, savings banks, credit unions, and other thrift institutions), we will focus on those financial intermediaries that *take deposits and make loans*. As a group, we will call them "banks."

One of the best ways to understand the money creation process is by analyzing the changes that take place in a bank's balance sheet when it lends to customers. This discussion then dovetails into an analysis of the *banking system's*[1] money creation powers and how it is able to amplify the powers of a single bank. In Chapter 9, "Who Controls the Money Supply and How?" this foundation will be vital to understanding how a central bank regulates financial intermediaries and, thereby, controls its nation's money supply.

THE BASICS

CREATION OF MONEY BY A SINGLE BANK

Banks have the power to change a nation's money supply. They do so mainly by making loans and purchasing securities because these bank assets are paid for with newly created checking accounts or with cash from banks' vaults. Let's trace the effects that loans and security purchases have on a bank's balance sheet and then show the impact these changes have on a nation's money supply.

> Banks create money mainly by lending and purchasing securities.

Exhibit 8-1 shows the balance sheet of First National Bank prior to its making a loan. Notice that total assets equal $10,000 million, and the sum of the bank's liabilities plus stockholders' equity also equals $10,000 million.

First National Bank has total reserves (i.e., cash in the vault and deposits at the central bank) equal to $900 million, but what is the minimum amount

---

[1] The network of financial intermediaries that takes deposits and makes loans will be referred to as the "banking system."

EXHIBIT 8-1	FIRST NATIONAL BANK'S INITIAL BALANCE SHEET: HOW MUCH CAN IT LEND?

(Figures in millions of dollars)

ASSETS		LIABILITIES AND STOCKHOLDERS' EQUITY	
Cash in the vault	400	Deposit liabilities	6,000
Deposits at the Fed	500	Borrowing from the central bank	400
Loans	5,000	Borrowing from other banks	2,500
Securities	2,000	Other liabilities	300
Other assets	2,100	Stockholders' equity	800
Total assets	**10,000**	**Total liabilities and stockholders' equity**	**10,000**

© John E. Marthinsen

it is required to hold? To answer this question, we must know the banking system's required reserve ratio, which is set by the central bank.

The *required reserve ratio* (or the *reserve requirement*, for short) is the portion of a bank's deposit liabilities that must be held as reserve assets (see Exhibit 8-2). For example, if the central bank imposed a 10% reserve requirement, then for every dollar of deposit liability, a bank would be required to hold $0.10 in reserve assets.

The reserves that financial institutions must hold are regulated in two important ways by central banks. First, central banks set and determine the required reserve ratio for each type of deposit liability. The reserve ratio usually varies from one deposit liability to another, depending on its perceived volatility (i.e., riskiness). For example, the required reserve ratio for checking accounts is usually the highest because these deposits are considered to be the most volatile sources of bank funds. Time deposits and other low-volatility deposits carry lower (sometimes zero) reserve requirements.

The second way central banks control the reserves that banks must hold is by defining which particular assets qualify as reserves. For instance, in the United States, only cash in the vault and deposits at the Federal Reserve qualify as reserves. U.S. banks are not required to hold reserves against stockholders' equity or nondeposit liabilities, such as borrowings from other banks or borrowings from the central bank. The Federal Reserve could change these rules at any time by allowing a wider range of assets to qualify as reserves and by requiring a wider range of liabilities to be backed by reserves.

> Central banks determine the reserve ratio and the particular bank assets that qualify as reserves.

Let's return to our example. Suppose the central bank imposed a 10% reserve requirement on all deposit liabilities. Because First National Bank's

EXHIBIT 8-2	REQUIRED RESERVE RATIO

Required reserve ratio ≡ Required reserves per dollar of deposit liability

© John E. Marthinsen

Exhibit 8-3	Total Reserves, Required Reserves, and Excess Reserves		
	(Figures in millions)		
Total Reserves	=	Cash in the vault + Deposits at the Fed $400 + $500	= $900
− Required Reserves	=	Reserve ratio × Deposit Liabilities 10% × $6,000	= −$600
Excess Reserves	=	**Total Reserves − Required Reserves** **$900 − $600**	= **$300**

© John E. Marthinsen

deposit liabilities equal $6,000 million, it would be required to hold reserve assets equal to $600 million. First National is actually holding reserves equal to $900 million; therefore, the extra $300 million are *excess reserves*, and a single bank can always lend its excess reserves without worrying about violating central bank regulations (see Exhibit 8-3). Let's see why.

A bank can always safely lend its excess reserves.

Suppose First National lent all its excess reserves (i.e., $300 million) to Alice Atwood for the purchase of Texas real estate owned by Bart Brewster (see Exhibit 8-4). What effect would this loan have on First National Bank's

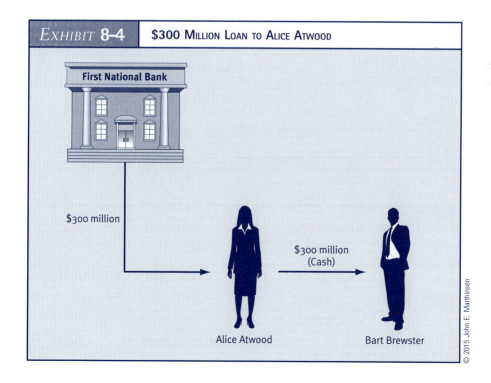

Exhibit 8-4 $300 Million Loan to Alice Atwood

First National Bank

$300 million

$300 million (Cash)

Alice Atwood   Bart Brewster

© 2015 John E. Marthinsen

balance sheet and the nation's money supply? Let's examine two possible ways the loan could be made, namely, by lending cash or by creating a new checking account for the borrower.

EFFECTS IF THE LOAN IS MADE IN CASH

Lending Atwood $300 million would cause First National's loans to increase by $300 million, and if the loan were made in cash, then First National's "cash in the vault" would fall by $300 million. Lending $300 million in cash to Atwood would increase the M1 and M2 money supplies because the nation's "currency in circulation" would rise by that amount (see Exhibit 8-5).

Exhibit 8-6 shows that this loan would change the composition of First National's assets from noninterest-earning cash reserves to an interest-earning loan.

Exhibit 8-7 shows First National's revised balance sheet after the cash loan. Because the bank lent all its excess reserves, First National's lending power should be exhausted. Let's see if this is true.

First National's total reserves are now equal to $600 million, and the bank's deposit liabilities have not changed; thus, its required reserves equal 10% of the $6,000 million deposit liabilities, or $600 million. Because First National's total reserves equal its required reserves, excess reserves are equal to zero (see Exhibit 8-8).

EFFECTS OF A LOAN IF THE BORROWER RECEIVES A CHECKING ACCOUNT

Let's do the same exercise as in the last section, but this time we will consider what happens if First National lends Alice Atwood $300 million by crediting her checking account (rather than paying her cash). Let's trace the effects on

> Cash loans increase a nation's money supply.

EXHIBIT 8-5	EFFECT ON M2 OF A $300 MILLION CASH LOAN

(Figures in millions)

ΔM2	=	ΔC_c	+	ΔD	+	ΔN
$300	=	$300	+	$0	+	0

© John E. Marthinsen

EXHIBIT 8-6	CHANGES IN FIRST NATIONAL'S BALANCE SHEET DUE TO A CASH LOAN

(Figures in millions)

Δ ASSETS		Δ (LIABILITIES AND STOCKHOLDERS' EQUITY)	
Δ Cash in the vault	−$300		
Δ Loans	+$300		
Δ Total assets	0	Δ Total liabilities and stockholders' equity	0

© John E. Marthinsen

| EXHIBIT **8-7** | FIRST NATIONAL BANK'S BALANCE SHEET AFTER THE CASH LOAN |

(Figures in millions of dollars)

	ASSETS		LIABILITIES AND STOCKHOLDERS' EQUITY	
Cash in the vault	400 − 300 = 100	Deposits liabilities	6,000
Deposits at the Fed	500	Borrowing from the central bank	400
Loans	5000 + 300 = **5,300**	Borrowing from other banks	2,500
Securities	2,000	Other liabilities	300
Other assets	2,100	Stockholders' equity	800
Total assets	10,000	**Total liabilities and stockholders' equity**	**10,000**

© John E. Marthinsen

| EXHIBIT **8-8** | FIRST NATIONAL'S EXCESS RESERVES AFTER THE CASH LOAN |

(Figures in millions)

Total Reserves	Cash in the vault + Deposits at the Fed $100 + $500	= $600
− Required reserves	Reserve ratio × Deposit Liabilities 10% × $6,000	= −$600
Excess reserves	Total reserves − Required reserves $600 − $600	= $0

© John E. Marthinsen

First National's balance sheet as the loan is made, spent, and cleared. Afterward, we will calculate First National's excess reserves. They should equal zero.

A loan to Atwood increases *loans* in First National's balance sheet by $300 million and, simultaneously, increases First National's checking account liabilities to Atwood by $300 million (see Exhibit 8-9).

Atwood then pays Bart Brewster for the Texas land, and Brewster deposits the check in his bank, which we will assume is the Second National Bank (see Exhibit 8-10).

At the end of the day, Second National sends the check to the Fed for clearing. The Fed increases Second National's account by $300 million and reduces First National's account by an equal amount. Then, the Fed sends the check to First National Bank (see Exhibit 8-11).

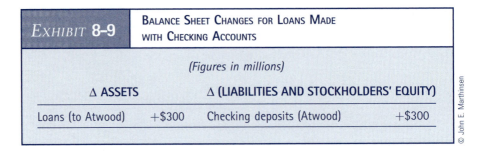

EXHIBIT 8-9	BALANCE SHEET CHANGES FOR LOANS MADE WITH CHECKING ACCOUNTS

(Figures in millions)

Δ ASSETS		Δ (LIABILITIES AND STOCKHOLDERS' EQUITY)	
Loans (to Atwood)	+$300	Checking deposits (Atwood)	+$300

© John E. Marthinsen

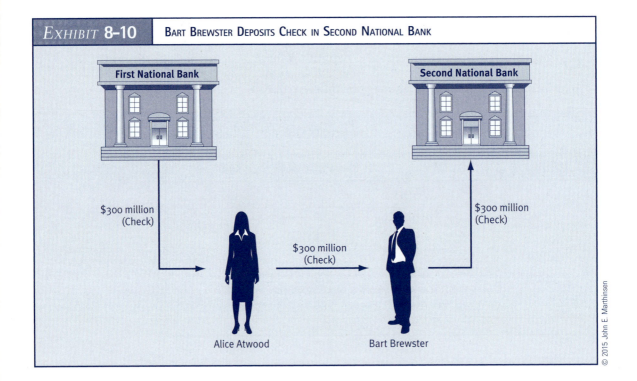

EXHIBIT 8-10   BART BREWSTER DEPOSITS CHECK IN SECOND NATIONAL BANK

First National Bank

Second National Bank

$300 million (Check)

$300 million (Check)

$300 million (Check)

Alice Atwood

Bart Brewster

© 2015 John E. Marthinsen

As Exhibit 8-11 shows, when First National receives the check, it reduces Atwood's checking account by $300 million and reduces its deposits at the Fed by $300 million.

Exhibit 8-12 summarizes all the changes in First National's balance sheet as a result of the loan. When the loan is made, First National's loans to Atwood rise by $300 million, and Atwood's checking account rises by $300 million. After the loan is spent and cleared, Atwood's checking account falls by $300 million, and First National's deposits at the Fed fall by $300 million. Therefore, the net effect is for First National's (low interest-earning) deposits at the Fed to fall by $300 million and its loans to rise by $300 million.

We can now calculate First National Bank's excess reserves to see if it has any additional lending power. Exhibit 8-12 shows that, after the loan has cleared, First National's total reserves equal $600 million, and the bank's

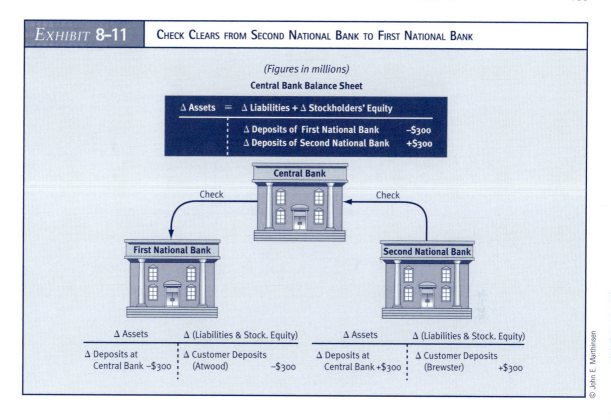

EXHIBIT 8-11   CHECK CLEARS FROM SECOND NATIONAL BANK TO FIRST NATIONAL BANK

(Figures in millions)

Central Bank Balance Sheet

Δ Assets	≡	Δ Liabilities + Δ Stockholders' Equity
		Δ Deposits of First National Bank −$300
		Δ Deposits of Second National Bank +$300

Central Bank

Check

Check

First National Bank

Second National Bank

Δ Assets	Δ (Liabilities & Stock. Equity)	Δ Assets	Δ (Liabilities & Stock. Equity)
Δ Deposits at Central Bank −$300	Δ Customer Deposits (Atwood) −$300	Δ Deposits at Central Bank +$300	Δ Customer Deposits (Brewster) +$300

© John E. Marthinsen

EXHIBIT 8-12   SUMMARY OF CHANGES IN FIRST NATIONAL BANK'S BALANCE SHEET

(Figures in millions)

ASSETS		LIABILITIES AND STOCKHOLDERS' EQUITY	
Cash in the vault	400	Old deposit liabilities	6,000
Old deposits at the Fed	500	*Increase in Atwood's account*	+300
Effect of cleared check	−300	*Atwood spends the funds*	−300
New deposits at the Fed	200	New deposit liabilities	6,000
Old loans	5,000	Borrowing from the central bank	400
Loan to Atwood	+300		
New loans	5,300	Borrowing from other banks	2,500
Securities	2,000	Other liabilities	300
Other assets	2,100	Stockholders' equity	800
Total assets	10,000	Total liabilities and stockholders' equity	10,000

© John E. Marthinsen

EXHIBIT 8-13	CALCULATION OF FIRST NATIONAL BANK'S EXCESS RESERVES AFTER THE LOAN IS MADE, FUNDS ARE SPENT, AND CHECK IS CLEARED

(Figures in millions)

Total reserves	Cash in the vault + Deposits at the Fed $400 + $200	= $600
− Required reserves	Reserve ratio × Deposit liabilities 10% × $6,000	= −$600
Excess reserves	Total reserves − Required reserves $600 − $600	= $0

© John E. Marthinsen

EXHIBIT 8-14	EFFECT ON M2 OF A $300 LOAN PAID IN CHECKING ACCOUNT FORM

(Figures in millions)

ΔM2	$\equiv$	ΔC_c	+	ΔD	+	ΔN
$300	=	$0	+	$300	+	0

© John E. Marthinsen

deposit liabilities equal $6,000 million. Therefore, the First National's required reserves also equal $600 million because it must hold 10% of the $6,000 million in deposit liabilities. As a result, First National's excess reserves equal zero (see Exhibit 8-13).

Exhibit 8-14 shows that when banks make loans using checking accounts, the *initial* effect on a nation's money supply is the same as when a cash loan is made. Atwood's loan causes the nation's checking accounts to rise by $300 million, and therefore the nation's M1 and M2 money supplies rise by $300 million.

Loans in the form of checking accounts increase a nation's money supply.

Once a loan is made, the nation's money supply rises and stays elevated until the loan is repaid. When Atwood pays Brewster for the Texas real estate, Atwood's checking account at First National falls by $300 million, but Brewster's checking account at Second National rises by $300 million. Therefore, the net effect on M1 and M2 from using already-borrowed funds to purchase the real estate is zero. Settlement merely transfers the $300 million checking account from Atwood to Brewster (see Exhibit 8-11).

Loans increase M1 and M2, and they remain elevated until the loans are repaid.

MONEY CREATION BY PURCHASING SECURITIES

Banks with excess reserves can lend them, but they also have the option of purchasing securities with these funds. Securities can be acquired either with cash or checking accounts, and their purchase has the same effect on a nation's money supply as loans. In fact, they have virtually the same effect on a bank's balance sheet. The only difference is an asset called "securities" increases instead of "loans."

Purchases of securities by a bank increase a nation's money supply in the same way as bank loans.

Understanding that banks have the alternative to lend or to purchase securities provides a useful insight into bank management. Suppose you were a bank manager with excess reserves to lend, but the economy was in a deep recession and loan demand was sluggish, despite low interest rates. What could you do with the excess reserves? One alternative would be to invest the noninterest-earning or low-interest-earning excess reserves in interest-earning securities. Another alternative is to keep them in the central bank. Even if loan demand were strong, bank managers might decide to purchase securities to diversify their risks and/or provide needed liquidity due to deep secondary markets for securities compared to loans.

MONEY CREATION IN THE BANKING SYSTEM AND THE MONEY MULTIPLIER

After First National Bank lent $300 million to Alice Atwood, it exhausted the bank's ability to create new loans, but the loan did not exhaust the banking system's ability to lend. Let's trace the lending potential of the banking system that was unlocked by First National Bank's loan.

Recall that Atwood's loan increased the M1 and M2 money supplies by $300 million. When Atwood paid Bart Brewster, the newly created funds were transferred from First National to Second National Bank. Brewster's deposit had the effect of increasing Second National Bank's reserves (i.e., deposits at the central bank) by $300 million, and increasing its deposit liabilities to Bart Brewster by $300 million (see Exhibit 8-15).

Of the $300 million in new deposit liabilities, Second National Bank must hold 10% (i.e., $30 million) as required reserves. Because Second National Bank's total reserves rose by a full $300 million, its excess reserves increased by $270 million (see Exhibit 8-16), and these funds could be safely lent without violating central bank reserve requirements.

Suppose Second National Bank lent the entire $270 million to Carol Carter for the purchase of a steel mill owned by Douglas Durrant. After payment was made, suppose Durrant deposited the check in the Third National Bank, and Third National Bank cleared the check with the Fed. Exhibit 8-17 shows the changes in Third National Bank's balance sheet after the check cleared. Third National would have $270 million in new deposit liabilities and $270 million in new reserves.

Of these new reserves, Third National would be required to hold 10% (i.e., $27 million). As a result, Third National's excess reserves would rise by $243 million (see Exhibit 8-18).

Exhibit **8-15**	EFFECT OF BREWSTER'S DEPOSIT ON SECOND NATIONAL BANK	
(Figures in millions)		
Δ ASSETS	Δ (LIABILITIES AND STOCKHOLDERS' EQUITY)	
Δ Deposits at the Fed +$300	Δ Deposit liabilities (Brewster)	+$300

© John E. Marthinsen

EXHIBIT 8-16	SECOND NATIONAL'S EXCESS RESERVES AFTER BREWSTER'S DEPOSIT

(Figures in millions)

Δ Total reserves	$\dfrac{\Delta \text{Cash in the vault} + \Delta \text{Deposits at the Fed}}{\$0 \qquad + \qquad \$300}$ = \$300
$- \Delta$ Required reserves	$\dfrac{- \text{Reserve ratio} \times \Delta \text{Deposit liabilities}}{10\% \qquad \times \qquad \$300}$ = $-\$30$
Δ Excess reserves	$\dfrac{\textbf{Total reserves} - \textbf{Required reserves}}{\$300 \qquad - \qquad \$30}$ = \$270

© John E. Marthinsen

EXHIBIT 8-17	CHANGES IN THIRD NATIONAL'S BALANCE SHEET AFTER DURRANT'S DEPOSIT

(Figures in millions)

Δ ASSETS		Δ (LIABILITIES AND STOCKHOLDERS' EQUITY)	
Δ Deposits at the Fed	+ \$270	Δ Deposit liabilities (Durrant)	+\$270

© John E. Marthinsen

EXHIBIT 8-18	THIRD NATIONAL'S EXCESS RESERVES AFTER DURRANT'S DEPOSIT

(Figures in millions)

Δ Total reserves	$\dfrac{\Delta \text{Cash in the vault} + \Delta \text{Deposits at the Fed}}{\$0 \qquad + \qquad \$270}$ = \$270
$- \Delta$ Required reserves	$\dfrac{\text{Reserve ratio} \times \Delta \text{Deposit liabilities}}{10\% \qquad \times \qquad \$270}$ = $-\$27$
Δ Excess reserves	$\dfrac{\textbf{Total reserves} - \textbf{Required reserves}}{\$270 \qquad - \qquad \$27}$ = \$243

© John E. Marthinsen

The initial \$300 million of excess reserves at First National Bank would work their way through the economy and banking system in repeated *lend-spend-deposit* cycles. With each iteration of the cycle, the nation's money supply would increase by 90% of the change in reserves, and excess reserves would be whittled away by 10% of the change in total reserves. The process would continue until there were no excess reserves left. At that point, the *banking system's* total reserves would be exactly equal to 10% of its total deposit liabilities.

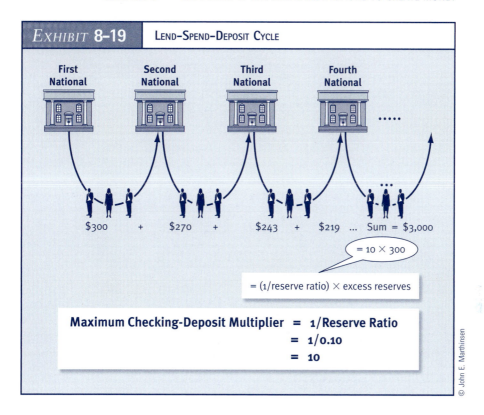

EXHIBIT **8-19**   LEND-SPEND-DEPOSIT CYCLE

First National   Second National   Third National   Fourth National

$300   + $270   + $243   + $219   ...   Sum = $3,000

= 10 × 300

= (1/reserve ratio) × excess reserves

Maximum Checking-Deposit Multiplier = 1/Reserve Ratio
= 1/0.10
= 10

© John E. Marthinsen

In our example, when the banking system's lend-spend-deposit cycle finally exhausted all the excess reserves, the nation's checking-deposit liabilities would have increased by $3,000 million, which is exactly 10 times the initial excess reserves at First National Bank (see Exhibits 8-19 and 8-20).

It is not by chance that the increase in the banking system's deposit liabilities is exactly 10 times First National's excess reserves. Notice that this amplification effect (i.e., *checking-deposit multiplier*) is exactly equal to one divided by the reserve ratio (i.e., 1/reserve ratio = 1/0.10 = 10).

In general, it is best to think of a checking-deposit multiplier equal to one divided by the reserve ratio as the *maximum possible* increase in checking accounts the banking system is capable of creating with a dollar of excess reserves. We will see shortly that, when real world constraints are considered, the checking-deposit multiplier is reduced considerably.

A MORE REALISTIC CHECKING-DEPOSIT MULTIPLIER

Despite the fact that the U.S. reserve ratio on checking accounts is less than 10%, Exhibit 8-21 shows that, from 1990 to 2013, the nation's checking-deposit multiplier was far below 10. In fact, for most of this period, it was below one. The reason the actual multiplier size was so small is because a few of the assumptions in our previous example were unrealistic. Let's highlight the unrealistic assumptions used in our example and then explain the effect

The simple checking-deposit multiplier is equal to one divided by the reserve ratio on checking accounts, but it is not the multiplier you should internalize. Rather, focus on the M2 money multiplier, which is explained in the next section.

EXHIBIT 8-20 CHECKING–DEPOSIT MULTIPLIER: POWER OF THE BANKING SYSTEM TO CREATE MONEY

(Figures in millions)

COLUMN 1 BANK	COLUMN 2 DEPOSITOR	COLUMN 3 Δ DEPOSITS = Δ RESERVES	COLUMN 4 Δ REQUIRED RESERVES (10% × Δ DEPOSITS)	COLUMN 5 Δ EXCESS RESERVES = Δ LOANS	COLUMN 6 BORROWER
First National				Original excess reserves = $300	Adam Atwood
Second National	Bart Brewster	$300	$30	$270	Carl Carter
Third National	Douglas Durrant	$270	$27	$243	Evelyn Eaton
Fourth National	Fred Farnside	$243	$24.3	$218.7	Greta Giro
Fifth National	Howard Huston	$218.70	$21.87	$196.83	Irene Inman
·	·	·	·	·	·
·	·	·	·	·	·
·	·	Declines to $0	Declines to $0	Declines to $0	

Total loans = $3,000

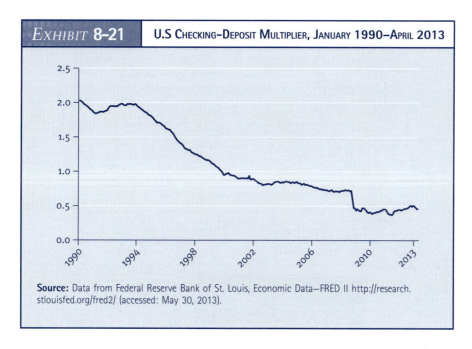

| EXHIBIT 8-21 | U.S CHECKING-DEPOSIT MULTIPLIER, JANUARY 1990–APRIL 2013 |

Source: Data from Federal Reserve Bank of St. Louis, Economic Data—FRED II http://research. stlouisfed.org/fred2/ (accessed: May 30, 2013).

that relaxing each one has on the checking-deposit multiplier, as well as the M1 and M2 money multipliers.

In our example, we assumed that:

- After each loan was spent, all the funds were redeposited in another bank. No funds leaked into currency in circulation.
- Banks lent all their excess reserves, keeping nothing as a safety net or as liquidity buffer for any other reasons.
- After each loan was spent, redeposits were always placed into checking accounts. None of the redeposited funds was placed in near-money accounts (e.g., savings deposits or time deposits).

Relaxing these assumptions breathes life into our example and helps us explain why the actual checking-deposit multiplier (as well as the M2 and M2 money multipliers) is smaller than one divided by the reserve ratio.

Before exploring these effects, let's reflect on the primary goal of this chapter and why a small bit of pivoting is needed at this point. Central banks are charged with controlling a nation's money supply and not just checking accounts. M1 consists of currency in circulation plus checking deposits, and M2 consists of all the financial assets in M1 plus near money. Because checking accounts are only a portion of M1 and M2, let's expand our analysis and focus on the M1 and M2 money multipliers.

M1 Money Multiplier

There are two equally valid ways to define the M1 money supply. M1 is equal to currency in circulation (C_c) plus checking deposits (D). It also equals a nation's monetary base (B) times the M1 money multiplier (mm_1) (see Exhibit 8-22).

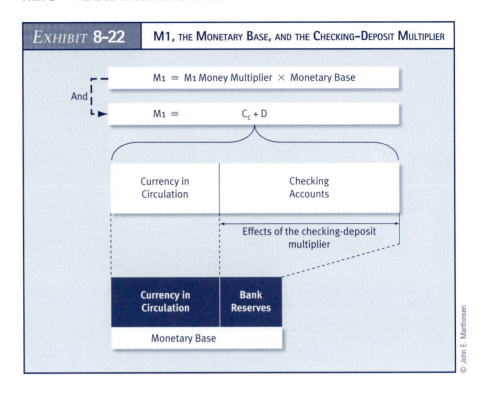

EXHIBIT 8-22   **M1, THE MONETARY BASE, AND THE CHECKING–DEPOSIT MULTIPLIER**

And

$$M1 \equiv M1 \text{ Money Multiplier} \times \text{Monetary Base}$$

$$M1 \equiv C_c + D$$

Currency in Circulation	Checking Accounts

Effects of the checking-deposit multiplier

Currency in Circulation	**Bank Reserves**

Monetary Base

© John E. Marthinsen

The monetary base is composed of currency in circulation and reserves of financial institutions, such as banks and thrift institutions. It can be thought of as the raw material from which a nation's money supply is created. As Exhibit 8-22 shows, a nation's monetary base and M1 differ only because of the amplification effects of the checking-deposit multiplier.

M2 Money Multiplier

As is the case with M1, there are two equally valid ways to define the M2 money supply. M2 is equal to currency in circulation (C_c) plus checking deposits (D) plus near money (N). It also equals the nation's monetary base (B) times the M2 money multiplier (mm_2) (see Exhibit 8-23).

EXHIBIT 8-23   **TWO WAYS TO DEFINE THE M2 MONEY SUPPLY**

$$M2 \equiv C_c + D + N \equiv mm_2 \times B$$

where	M2	$\equiv$	M2 money supply
	C_c	$\equiv$	currency in circulation
	D	$\equiv$	checking deposits
	N	$\equiv$	near money
	mm_2	$\equiv$	M2 money multiplier
	B	$\equiv$	monetary base

© John E. Marthinsen

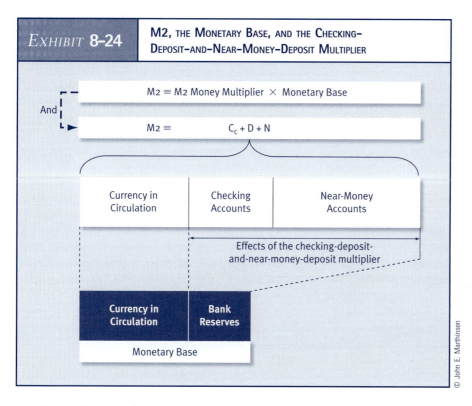

EXHIBIT 8-24 — M2, THE MONETARY BASE, AND THE CHECKING-DEPOSIT-AND-NEAR-MONEY-DEPOSIT MULTIPLIER

And

$$M2 \equiv M2 \text{ Money Multiplier} \times \text{Monetary Base}$$

$$M2 \equiv C_c + D + N$$

Currency in Circulation | Checking Accounts | Near-Money Accounts

Effects of the checking-deposit-and-near-money-deposit multiplier

Currency in Circulation | Bank Reserves

Monetary Base

© John E. Marthinsen

As Exhibit 8-24 shows, a nation's monetary base and M2 differ only by the amplification effects of the checking-deposit-and-near-money-deposit multiplier.

Breathing Life into the M1 and M2 Money Multipliers

Determining how each of the three assumptions in our checking-deposit-multiplier example affects the M1 and M2 money multipliers is relatively easy. All we have to do is answer one simple question, which is: By relaxing the assumption, does the banking system's lending ability rise or fall? If it rises, these money multipliers rise. If it falls, they fall.

Currency in circulation: If people withdraw cash from banks during the lend-spend-deposit cycle, then the banking system has less to lend, which decreases the M1 and M2 money multipliers.

Customary reserves: Voluntarily held excess reserves are called *customary reserves*. When bank managers hold more reserves than required, the M1 and M2 money multipliers fall because these holdings reduce the ability of the banking system to lend.

Bank managers hold excess reserves for a number of reasons—some planned and some not. For example, they hold them as a buffer or safety net against unforeseen changes in cash flows that might deplete reserves below their required levels. Excess reserves may also be held due to back-office inefficiencies and timing problems, leaving a bank with unwanted excess reserves. For example, a large deposit made at the end of the day may not be processed in time for the bank's money manager to lend the funds in the interbank market. Finally, an increase in customary reserves may reflect lending officers' reluctance to extend loans in turbulent economic conditions due to the perceived increases in credit risk.

Near-money deposits: If individuals in the lend-spend-deposit cycle place funds in near-money accounts instead of checking accounts, the M1 money multiplier falls and the M2 money multiplier rises. The easiest way to understand this conclusion is to remember that near money is not included in M1, and increases in these accounts typically come from checking accounts. The reason the M2 money multiplier rises is because near money is included in M2, and the reserve ratio for near money is lower than the reserve requirement for checking accounts, thereby increasing the banking system's ability to lend.[2]

Preferred asset ratio is the term used throughout this text to describe the public's and banking system's preferences to hold currency in circulation (C_c), near money (N), and customary reserves (U). They are called "ratios" because these asset demands are measured relative to checking deposits. Therefore, C_c/D and N/D are the public's preferred asset ratios for currency in circulation and near money, respectively, and U/D is the banking system's preferred asset ratio for customary reserves. Increases in C_c/D and U/D lower the M2 money multiplier, and increases in N/D raise it.

THE REST OF THE STORY

Let's take a closer look to see how relaxing the aforementioned assumptions in our checking-deposit-multiplier example changes the M1 and M2 money multipliers. We will find that our basic conclusions remain unchanged, but digging a bit deeper will allow us to consider more deeply the concept of preferred asset ratios and also some unexplored nuances of the M1 and M2 money multipliers.

EFFECTS OF CURRENCY IN CIRCULATION ON THE M1 AND M2 MONEY MULTIPLIERS

It is unrealistic to assume that, during the lend-spend-deposit cycle, no one will withdraw cash from banks. If they do, it becomes currency in circulation. Cash withdrawals reduce the M1 and M2 money multipliers because there are fewer reserves for the banking system to lend.

> When currency leaks into circulation after loans are made, the M1 and M2 money multipliers fall.

The ratio of the public's desired holdings of currency in circulation (C_c) relative to its checking accounts (D) is called the *preferred asset ratio for currency in circulation*. Therefore, the larger a nation's preferred asset ratio for currency in circulation (i.e., C_c/D), the smaller its checking-deposit multiplier.

In the extreme case, if Alice Atwood's entire $300 million loan were paid to Brad Brewster, and Brewster kept all the funds in currency in circulation, the checking-deposit multiplier would fall to one. In short, $300 million would be lent by First National, but none of it would reach Second National Bank; so the recurring rounds of lending would never occur. Exhibits 8-25 and 8-26 summarize the effects when 100% of a loan is held as currency in circulation.

---

[2] If the reserve ratio for near money were equal to the reserve ratio for checking accounts, then near money deposits would have no effect on the M2 money multiplier. In the United States, the reserve requirement on near money is zero.

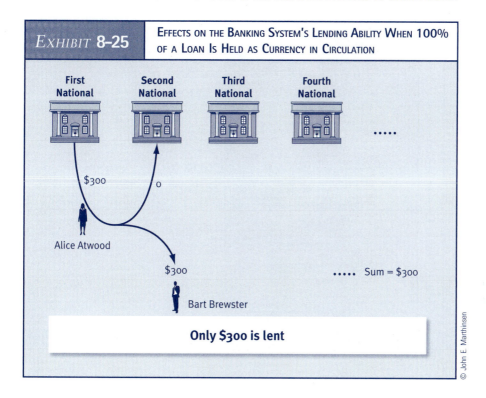

EXHIBIT 8-25   EFFECTS ON THE BANKING SYSTEM'S LENDING ABILITY WHEN 100% OF A LOAN IS HELD AS CURRENCY IN CIRCULATION

First National   Second National   Third National   Fourth National

$300   0

Alice Atwood

$300   ••••• Sum = $300

Bart Brewster

Only $300 is lent

© John E. Marthinsen

EFFECTS OF CUSTOMARY RESERVES ON M1 AND M2 MONEY MULTIPLIERS

Voluntarily held excess reserves are called *customary reserves*. Because they are held and not lent, customary reserves reduce the M1 and M2 money multipliers, regardless of the reason they are held. To illustrate, Exhibit 8-27 assumes that banks keep an extra 5% of their total reserves as customary reserves. Notice that this small fractional withholding causes our original checking-deposit multiplier to fall from 10 to 6.33.[3]

The ratio of the banks' desired customary reserves (U) to checking accounts (D) is called the *preferred asset ratio for customary reserves*. The larger a banking system's preferred asset ratio for customary reserves (i.e., U/D), the smaller the M1 and M2 money multipliers.

> An increase in the customary reserves preferred asset ratio causes the M1 and M2 money multipliers to fall.

EFFECTS OF NEAR–MONEY DEPOSITS ON THE M1 AND M2 MONEY MULTIPLIERS

Our initial example assumed that all the funds borrowed from one bank were eventually redeposited in checking accounts at other banks. But we know that people make deposits in other accounts, such as savings deposits and time deposits, which are a part of near money. The ratio of the public's desired holdings of near money (N) relative to its checking accounts (D) is called the *preferred asset ratio for near money*.

[3] $1,900 million ÷ $300 million = 6.33

EXHIBIT 8-26   EFFECTS ON THE BANKING SYSTEM'S LENDING ABILITY WHEN 100% OF A LOAN IS HELD AS CURRENCY IN CIRCULATION

(Figures in millions)

COLUMN 1 BANK	COLUMN 2 DEPOSITOR	COLUMN 3 Δ DEPOSITS = Δ RESERVES	COLUMN 4 Δ REQUIRED RESERVES (10% × Δ DEPOSITS)	COLUMN 5 Δ EXCESS RESERVES = Δ LOANS	COLUMN 6 BORROWER
First National				Original excess reserves = $300	Adam Atwood
The $300 is not deposited by Bart Brewster. Rather, he holds it in cash.					
Second National		$0	$0	$0	
Third National		$0	$0	$0	
Fourth National		$0	$0	$0	
Fifth National		$0	$0	$0	
	· · ·	· · ·	· · ·	· · ·	· · ·
		$0	$0	$0	

Total loans = $300

EXHIBIT 8-27 | EFFECTS OF CUSTOMARY RESERVES ON THE BANKING SYSTEM'S LENDING ABILITY

(Figures in millions)

COLUMN 1 BANK	COLUMN 2 DEPOSITOR	COLUMN 3 Δ DEPOSITS = Δ RESERVES	COLUMN 4 Δ REQUIRED RESERVES (10% × Δ DEPOSITS)	COLUMN 5 Δ EXCESS RESERVES	COLUMN 6 Δ CUSTOMARY RESERVES (5% × Δ DEPOSIT LIABILITIES)	COLUMN 7 Δ LOANS	COLUMN 8 BORROWER
First National				Original excess reserves = $300	$15	$285	Adam Atwood
Second National	Bart Brewster	$285.00	$28.50	$256.50	$14.25	$242.25	Carl Carter
Third National	Douglas Durrant	$242.25	$24.23	$218.03	$12.11	$205.91	Evelyn Eaton
Fourth National	Fred Farnside	$205.91	$20.59	$185.32	$10.30	$175.03	Greta Giro
· · ·	· · ·	· · ·	· · ·	· · ·	· · ·	· · ·	· · ·
		Declines to $0	Declines to $0	Declines to $0	Declines to $0	Declines to $0	

Δ Total loans = $1,900

2008: Federal Reserve Begins Paying Interest on U.S. Bank Reserves

In 2006, Congress authorized the Federal Reserve to pay interest on reserve balances held by depository financial institutions at the Fed, and in 2008, the Fed enacted this policy. Exhibit 8-28 shows the powerful stimulus this authorization and subsequent change in policy had on excess reserve holdings. Between January 2008 and May 2013, excess reserves grew from a relatively paltry level (i.e., $1.6 billion) to a mountainous size ($1,863.3 billion). As a result, the U.S. M1 and M2 money multipliers fell.

EXHIBIT 8-28	EXCESS RESERVES OF U.S. DEPOSITORY INSTITUTIONS: JANUARY 1981–MAY 2013

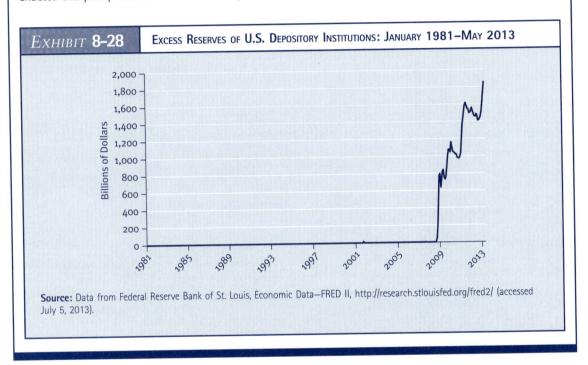

Source: Data from Federal Reserve Bank of St. Louis, Economic Data—FRED II, http://research.stlouisfed.org/fred2/ (accessed July 5, 2013).

Effect of Near-Money Deposits on the M1 Money Multiplier

An increase in the preferred asset ratio for near-money deposits (N/D) reduces the banking system's ability to create *checking accounts*. As checking accounts fall relative to the amount that could have been created (i.e., without near-money deposits), the M1 money multiplier falls.

Let's assume that only half of each loan is redeposited in checking accounts, and the remaining half is redeposited in near-money accounts. Assume further that the reserve ratio on near-money deposits is equal to 5%, and the reserve ratio on checking accounts remains at 10%. Exhibits 8-29 and 8-30 analyze the effects that these changes have on the checking-deposit multiplier, focusing on just the first round and potential second round of the lend-spend-deposit cycle.

Of the $300 million received by Brewster from Atwood, $150 million would be placed in a checking account, and $150 million is put into a

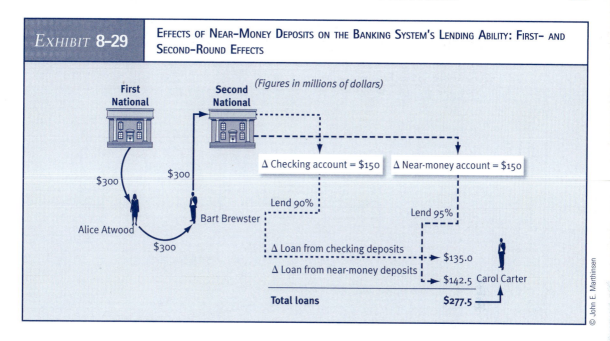

EXHIBIT 8-29   EFFECTS OF NEAR-MONEY DEPOSITS ON THE BANKING SYSTEM'S LENDING ABILITY: FIRST- AND SECOND-ROUND EFFECTS

near-money account. As a result, checking accounts would increase by half the amount compared to when all redeposits are in checking accounts.

The dampening effect that near-money deposits have on the M1 money multiplier is partially offset if near-money accounts have lower reserve requirements than checking accounts, which is normally the case. Because the reserve ratio on near-money deposits is only 5% and the reserve ratio on checking accounts is 10%, banks are able to lend more than they could if all deposits were placed in checking accounts.

Notice in Exhibits 8-29 and 8-30 how Second National Bank can lend $277.5 million when redeposits are split evenly between checking accounts and near-money accounts. This is because the bank must hold as required reserves only $7.5 million on its $150 million of near-money deposits[4] and $15 million on its $150 million of checking accounts.[5] Had all the funds been deposited fully into checking accounts, Second National could have lent only $270 million.

Despite the positive effects that a lower reserve ratio has on the M1 money multiplier, it is not enough to offset the dampening effects of funds flowing into near-money deposits (rather than into checking accounts).[6] Therefore, near-money deposits reduce the M1 money multiplier, but they increase the total amount of loans (i.e., checking accounts plus near-money accounts) that banks can make.

> An increase in the preferred asset ratio for near money has conflicting effects on the M1 money multiplier, but the net relationship is inverse.

---

[4] 5% × $150 million savings deposit = $7.5 million
[5] 10% × $150 million checking account = $15 million
[6] Only under very extreme and unrealistic conditions could the checking-deposit multiplier rise as (N/D) increases.

EXHIBIT 8-30　Effect of Near-Money Deposits on the Banking System's Lending Ability: Multiple Rounds of the Lend-Spend-Deposit Cycle

(Figures in millions)

COLUMN 1	COLUMN 2	COLUMN 3	COLUMN 4	COLUMN 5	COLUMN 6
			Δ REQUIRED RESERVES (10% × Δ CHECKING ACCOUNT) & (5% × Δ SAVINGS ACCOUNT)	Δ EXCESS RESERVES = Δ LOANS	
BANK	DEPOSITOR	Δ DEPOSITS			BORROWER
First National				Original excess reserves = $300	Adam Atwood
Second National	Bart Brewster	Checking account = $150.00 Savings account = $150.00 Total　$300.00	On checking account = $15.00 On savings account　= $7.50 Total　　　　= $22.50	300.00 −22.50 277.50	Carl Carter
Third National	Douglas Durrant	Checking account = $138.75 Savings account = $138.75 Total　$277.50	On checking account = $13.88 On savings account　= $6.94 Total　　　　= $20.81	$277.50 −$20.81 $256.69	Evelyn Eaton
Fourth National	Fred Farnside	Checking account = $128.34 Savings account = $128.34 Total　$256.69	On checking account = $12.83 On savings account　= $6.42 Total　　　　= $19.25	$256.69 −$19.25 $237.44	Greta Giro
Fifth National	Howard Huston	Checking account = $118.72 Savings account = $118.72 Total　$237.44	On checking account = $11.87 On savings account　= $5.94 Total............ = $17.81	$237.44 −$17.81 $219.63	Irene Inman
		· ·	· ·	·	·
		Declines to $0	Declines to $0	Declines to $0	

Δ Checking accounts = $2,000
Δ Saving accounts　 = $2,000
Δ Total　　　　　　 = $4,000

Total loans = $4,000

Exhibit 8-31	Major Factors Affecting the M1 And M2 Money Multipliers And Their Qualitative Relationships	
Δ RESERVE RATIO AND PREFERRED ASSET RATIOS	Δ M1 MONEY MULTIPLIER	Δ M2 MONEY MULTIPLIER (OUR FOCUS)
Reserve ratio rises	mm_1 falls	mm_2 falls
C_c/D rises	mm_1 falls	mm_2 falls
N/D rises	**mm_1 falls**	**mm_2 rises**
U/D rises	mm_1 falls	mm_2 falls

© John E. Marthinsen

Effect of Near-Money Deposits on the M2 Money Multiplier

The effect that the preferred asset ratio for near-money deposits (N/D) has on the M2 money multiplier is different from the effect it has on the M1 money multiplier. An increase in the public's relative holdings of near-money deposits, like savings deposits and time deposits, reduces the M1 money multiplier, but at the same time gives banks more to lend. Therefore, even though the M1 money multiplier falls when N/D rises, the M2 money multiplier rises. Funds that are not flowing into checking accounts are flowing into near-money accounts, which are included in M2.

Therefore, the M2 money multiplier has an inverse relationship to C_c/D and U/D, but it has a direct relationship to N/D. Exhibit 8-31 summarizes these relationships for both the M1 and M2 money multipliers.

To simplify our conclusions, we can restate the relationship among the M2 money supply, M2 money multiplier, and monetary base as follows:

$$M2 = mm_2(\overset{-}{rr_D}, \overset{-}{rr_N}, \overset{-}{C_c/D}, \overset{+}{N/D}, \overset{-}{U/D}) \times B$$

The negative signs above the abbreviations for the reserve ratio for checking accounts (i.e., rr_D), reserve ratio for near money (i.e., rr_N), and the preferred asset ratios for currency in circulation and customary reserves indicate that each of these factors is inversely related to the M2 money multiplier. When they rise (fall), the M2 money multiplier falls (rises). The positive sign over the near-money preferred asset ratio indicates a positive relationship. When N/D rises (falls), the M2 money multiplier rises (falls).

Exhibit 8-32 shows the actual M2 money multiplier in the United States between 1990 and 2013. Notice that it varied between (approximately) 12.0 in 1990 and 4.0 from 2009 to 2013, and it dropped sharply in 2008 during the Great Recession (2007–2009).

In Chapter 11, "Interest Rates and Why They Change," we will focus our discussion on how short-term interest rates are determined. In that discussion, changes in the *total* sources of real loanable funds will be critical. For this reason, our emphasis throughout this book will be put on changes in the M2 money supply and, therefore, changes in the M2 money multiplier.

Our emphasis throughout this book will be put on changes in the monetary base, the M2 money multiplier, and M2 money supply.

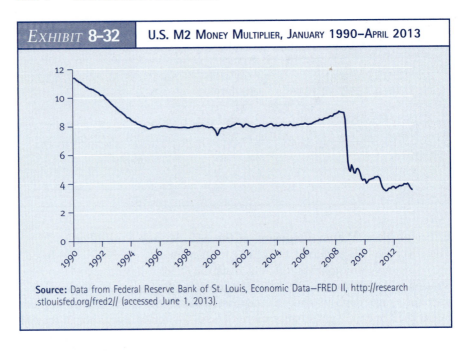

EXHIBIT **8-32** | U.S. M2 MONEY MULTIPLIER, JANUARY 1990–APRIL 2013

Source: Data from Federal Reserve Bank of St. Louis, Economic Data—FRED II, http://research .stlouisfed.org/fred2// (accessed June 1, 2013).

CONCLUSION

Among all the financial intermediaries, those that take deposits and make loans (i.e., banks) have special importance because they can create money by granting loans and/or purchasing securities. A nation's money supply increases regardless of whether a bank lends its excess reserves or purchases securities, and the money supply rises regardless of whether the loan is made in cash or checking account form. To be safe, banks should lend only their excess reserves.

The banking system can lend a multiple of the amount lent by a single bank. An increase in the reserve ratio on bank deposits reduces the M2 money multiplier. Similarly, an increase in a nation's preferred asset ratios for currency in circulation and customary reserves reduces the M2 money multiplier. But an increase in the preferred asset ratio for near money increases the M2 money multiplier.

Now that we have discussed money (Chapter 6), banking (Chapter 7), and the creation of money (this chapter), let's move on to the next chapter (Chapter 9, "Who Controls the Money Supply and How?"), where we will consider how central banks regulate banks and their nations' money supplies. An important take-away from this chapter is that movements in a nation's monetary base cause amplified changes in the domestic money supply. These money supply changes then go on to affect important macroeconomic variables, which can (and do) feed back to cause predictable changes in the M2 money multiplier. In the next chapter, we will find that changes in the money multiplier do not automatically feed back to cause changes in the monetary base because central banks have virtually complete control over when and if the monetary base changes.

REVIEW QUESTIONS

1. Is it accurate to say that, as banks lend money in the form of checking accounts, the M1 and M2 money supplies rise when the loan is made and then fall when the loan is spent? Explain.

2. Is it accurate to say that, as banks lend money in the form of checking accounts, that the M1 and M2 money supplies rise when the loan is made and then fall when the loan is paid back? Explain.

3. Suppose the required reserve ratio is 15%, and a Japanese bank has the following assets, liabilities, and stockholders' equity: reserves = ¥85 million, checking accounts = ¥500 million, loans = ¥400 million, borrowings from the Bank of Japan = ¥80 million, stockholders' equity = ¥75 million, securities = ¥150 million, and other assets = ¥20 million. Given this information, calculate the amount of excess reserves or the reserve deficiency for this bank.

4. If $1,000 is deposited in a bank with reserve requirements equal to 100%, explain how much the bank can lend. In general, how would banks with 100% reserve requirements increase their loans? Explain.

5. Suppose a bank has $2 million in excess reserves and $8 million in required reserves. A required reserve ratio of 10% is applicable to all deposits at the bank. What is the total amount of deposits at the bank? Explain.

6. Can a *banking system's* excess reserves be negative? Explain. If they can be and are negative, explain three ways the banking system can eliminate the deficiency. If they cannot be negative, explain why.

7. If the reserve requirement is 10%, and a depositor withdraws $500 from her checking account, by how much will the bank's excess reserves change? Explain.

8. Determine whether the following statements are true, false, or uncertain. Please correct the false statements.

    a. Having a high level of excess reserves is important to a banker because excess reserves reflect good bank management.
    b. Excess reserves are important to a banker because they indicate the profits that can be divided among the bank's owners.
    c. Excess reserves are important to a banker because, if they are not maintained, banking regulators may fine or shut down the bank.

9. Assume the required reserve ratio on all deposit liabilities is 15%. Calculate the level of excess reserves for Sovereign Bank. How much can Sovereign Bank safely lend?

SOVEREIGN BANK			
ASSETS		**LIABILITIES & EQUITY**	
Reserves	40,000	Deposits	200,000
Federal funds loans	20,000	Borrowing from the central bank	80,000
Loans	200,000	Federal funds borrowing	100,000
Securities	300,000	Other liabilities	150,000
Other	40,000	Stockholders' equity	70,000

10. Suppose the required reserve ratio for the banking system is 25%. Answer the following questions based on the balance sheet of Lafayette Bank:

LAFAYETTE BANK			
ASSETS		**LIABILITIES & EQUITY**	
Cash in the vault	60,000	Deposits	500,000
Deposits at the central bank	100,000	Borrowing from the central bank	70,000
Loans	800,000	Borrowing from other banks	400,000
Securities	100,000	Other liabilities	100,000
Other	30,000	Stockholders' equity	20,000

a. Calculate the level of excess reserves for Lafayette Bank.
b. How much can Lafayette Bank safely lend?
c. Show the *changes* in Lafayette Bank's balance sheet after the loan (in checking account form) has been made.
d. Show the *entire* balance sheet after the loan has been spent and cleared.

11. Suppose the banking system's only deposit liabilities are checking accounts, and the reserve requirement on them is 10%. If the banking system has excess reserves of $30 million and checking deposits of $500 million, calculate the banking system's total reserves.

12. If interest rates fall, what, if anything, should happen to the M2 multiplier? Briefly explain.

13. What happens to the M2 money multiplier, if anything, after holidays, when people withdraw less cash from banks to pay for presents?

14. Is it possible for a country's money supply to grow rapidly at the same time as its monetary base is falling? If not, explain why not. If it is possible, explain how it is possible, and mention factors that might cause the growth.

15. Is it accurate to say that the public decides what portion of the money supply will be held as currency in circulation? Explain.

16. In 2001, Domingo Cavallo, Argentina's economy minister, wanted Banco Central de la República Argentina (the central bank of Argentina) to reduce the reserve requirement applied to private banks. Suppose Argentina's total bank deposits equaled Ps 100 billion (100 billion pesos), the banking system had zero excess reserves, and the reserve ratio was 10%. Calculate the effect, if any, that Cavallo's policy would have on Argentina's monetary base, as well as the banking system's total reserves and excess reserves, if the reserve ratio was reduced to 8%. What would be the qualitative change in Argentina's M2 money multiplier?

17. Suppose Argentine deposits at private banks (i.e., checking accounts) fell by $3 billion as people rushed to convert deposits into cash. Explain the effect this withdrawal of deposits from private banks by the public had on Argentina's monetary base, M2 money multiplier, and excess reserves. Assume the reserve ratio is 10%.

DISCUSSION QUESTIONS

18. Japan suffered throughout the 1990s and into the 2000s from the after-effects of an asset price bubble that burst in 1990. The asset price bubble was caused by excessive money growth in the late 1980s that drove up the price of real estate. Explain how plummeting real estate prices could put severe pressure on Japan's domestic banking system.

19. It is the end of the banking day. You are the money trader at a bank that has $50 million of excess reserves, but there are no customers walking through the doors to borrow. What do you do?

Chapter 9

Who Controls the Money Supply and How?

INTRODUCTION

Changes in a nation's money supply can have significant effects on domestic inflation, interest rates, production, and employment, and often these effects spill over to other nations. Due to the potential impact monetary policies have on macroeconomic variables and company performance, understanding and anticipating the effects they might have on credit markets can pay huge dividends. For this reason, business managers and analysts throughout the world monitor the decisions of central bankers, placing special attention on the U.S. Federal Reserve System, European Central Bank (ECB), People's Bank of China, and Bank of Japan (BoJ) due to the size of the financial systems they regulate.

This chapter starts by discussing the difference between financial regulation and monetary policy. It then introduces a very helpful rule of thumb that answers virtually any question concerning when and if a nation's monetary base has changed. The chapter moves on to provide a more thorough explanation of the tools that central banks use to regulate their domestic money supplies. This task is made easier by the generic nature of the most important monetary tools, which means the same basic set is used (or can be used) by any central bank. Our discussion of these major monetary tools explains how central banks regulate their domestic money supplies, the influence they have over financial intermediaries and financial markets, and how changes in one country's monetary policies can affect other nations.

In Chapter 8, "The Power of Financial Institutions to Create Money," we learned that M2 equals the monetary base times the M2 money multiplier, which implies a nation's money supply varies only if one or both of these variables changes. This chapter focuses on the direct powers that central banks have over these two monetary variables and, therefore, the indirect ways in which they affect financial markets. The chapter ends with a brief discussion of how timing issues can complicate a central banker's job of effectively managing the money supply.

> Central banks around the world use the same basic set of monetary tools.

THE BASICS

REGULATION VERSUS MONETARY POLICY

When considering the monetary powers and role of central banks, it is important to distinguish between *financial regulation* and *monetary policy*. Financial regulation is concerned with controlling and monitoring the conduct, performance,

Bank regulation focuses on controlling and monitoring the conduct, performance, and condition of financial institutions.

and condition of financial institutions to ensure they are solvent, liquid, and carrying manageable risks. Central banks exert these powers, but they do so in conjunction with national treasuries/ministries and other regulatory authorities, such as state, provincial, or cantonal banking commissions.

To evaluate a financial intermediary's condition and performance, regulators often use the CAMELS rating system. CAMELS is an acronym for an intermediary's *C*apital adequacy, *A*sset quality, *M*anagement quality, *E*arnings, *L*iquidity, and *S*ensitivity to market risks (e.g., changing interest rates and exchange rates). In addition, regulators seek to ensure that financial intermediaries have sound corporate governance practices.

Effective regulation requires the implementation of proper rules and regulations, but it is equally important for regulators to construct efficient and effective ways of ensuring that these rules are followed. Well-timed audits and reviews of intermediaries' financial statements and corporate governance practices are essential. In cases where rules and regulations are not obeyed, there must be a strict, but fair, system of sanctions and/or penalties in place to deal with violators.

In contrast to financial regulation, monetary policy focuses on providing a nation (or a currency area, such as the European Monetary Union [EMU]) with the optimal amount of liquidity, which is a tricky job that central bankers do not always get right. When they err on the high side, inflation can occur; when they err on the low side, the threats are deflation and/or recession.

Monetary policy focuses on providing a nation with the optimal amount of liquidity.

RULE OF THUMB: "ABOVE THE LINE/BELOW THE LINE"

It is not always obvious what causes a nation's monetary base to change because appearances and first impressions can be deceptive. To get a sense for the confusion that might arise, what effect, if any, do *you* think the following transactions have on the U.S. monetary base?

1. Massive capital outflows from the United States, in amounts estimated at $500 billion per week, occur as foreign speculators sell U.S. stocks for dollars and then sell their dollars for Japanese yen.
2. The U.S. government raises personal income taxes by $40 billion, increases its spending by $100 billion, and borrows $60 billion to cover the deficiency.
3. Novartis, a Swiss company with headquarters in Basel, Switzerland, sells $100 million in the foreign exchange market and receives SFr 93 million (i.e., 93 million Swiss francs).
4. Mary Jones borrows $30,000 for a new car.
5. Heinz Meier, a German resident living in Berlin, borrows $200,000 from Bank of America in San Francisco.
6. The ECB and the U.S. Federal Reserve swap €18 million for $20 million.[1]

---

[1] *Central bank swaps* are short-term (usually 90-day) transactions between central banks that call for the immediate exchange of currencies and their reexchange in the future at a fixed exchange rate (i.e., price). For example, if the ECB wanted to temporarily increase its U.S. dollar reserves (perhaps to provide liquidity for intervening in the foreign exchange market to support the euro), one way to get the needed dollars would be to swap euros for dollars with the U.S. Federal Reserve. Under a normal swap agreement, the funds would be exchanged now and then swapped back after 90 days, usually at the same exchange rate as the original (spot) transaction was made.

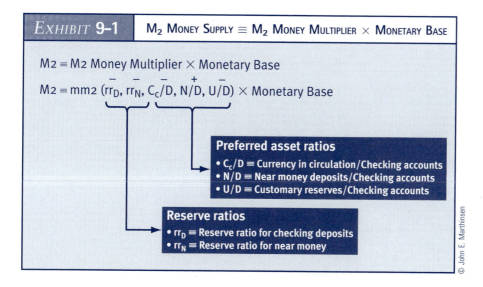

EXHIBIT 9-1   M₂ MONEY SUPPLY ≡ M₂ MONEY MULTIPLIER × MONETARY BASE

M2 ≡ M2 Money Multiplier × Monetary Base

$$M_2 \equiv mm_2 \left(\overset{-}{rr_D}, \overset{-}{rr_N}, \overset{-}{C_c/D}, \overset{+}{N/D}, \overset{-}{U/D} \right) \times \text{Monetary Base}$$

Preferred asset ratios
- C_c/D ≡ Currency in circulation/Checking accounts
- N/D ≡ Near money deposits/Checking accounts
- U/D ≡ Customary reserves/Checking accounts

Reserve ratios
- rr_D ≡ Reserve ratio for checking deposits
- rr_N ≡ Reserve ratio for near money

© John E. Marthinsen

SOME MONEY SUPPLY BASICS

Before we build a framework to answer these questions, let's begin by reviewing some important money supply basics. In Chapter 8, "The Power of Financial Institutions to Create Money," we learned that changes in a nation's money supply depend on two major factors: the M2 money multiplier and the monetary base (see Exhibit 9-1).

Central banks have a great deal of influence over the money multiplier because they determine the reserve ratios on financial intermediaries' deposit liabilities. At the same time, they do not have complete control over it because variations in the preferred asset ratios of households and banks can also affect the money multiplier. For example, increases in the amount of cash the public wishes to hold in circulation, increases in the amount of customary reserves that financial intermediaries wish to hold, and/or decreases in the amount of near money deposits (e.g., time deposits and savings deposits) that the public wishes to hold relative to checking accounts cause the M2 money multiplier to fall.

> The central bank does not have complete control of a nation's money supply because it does not fully control the money multiplier.

By contrast, central banks have almost complete control over their monetary bases. Therefore, virtually all questions regarding the causes of monetary base fluctuations can be answered by remembering that central banks have this near-monopoly power.

> The central bank has virtually complete control over a nation's monetary base.

In Exhibit 9-2, a horizontal line is drawn across the page with *all* central banks (e.g., U.S. Federal Reserve, ECB, Bank of England, BoJ, and Bank of Mexico) above the line. All the other stakeholders are below the line. For example, below the line are individuals, businesses, banks, other financial institutions, and governments (national, state, provincial, cantonal, and local).[2]

---

[2] In nations where the government and the central bank are not independent, the government should be placed above the line.

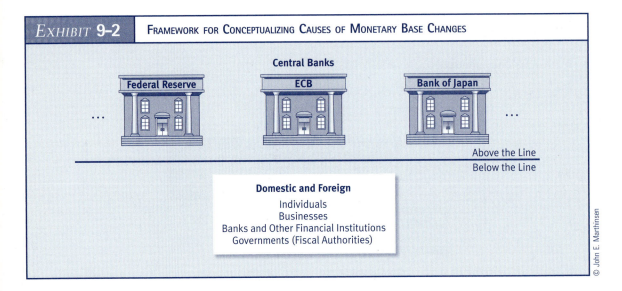

EXHIBIT 9-2   FRAMEWORK FOR CONCEPTUALIZING CAUSES OF MONETARY BASE CHANGES

Central Banks

Federal Reserve   ECB   Bank of Japan

...   ...

Above the Line
Below the Line

Domestic and Foreign
Individuals
Businesses
Banks and Other Financial Institutions
Governments (Fiscal Authorities)

© John E. Marthinsen

Rule of thumb for monetary base changes: *Above the Line/Below the Line*

Funds that are above our imaginary horizontal line are *not* a part of a nation's monetary base because the monetary base includes only currency *in circulation* and the reserves of financial intermediaries; both of these components are below the line. Keeping in mind that a central bank is the ultimate source of a nation's monetary base makes it easier to see that a large part of central bankers' jobs is finding ways to move funds below or above our imaginary line. They can move funds below the line by either purchasing items of value from individuals, businesses, or others (below the line), or by lending to them. Similarly, to reduce a nation's monetary base, the central bank must move funds above the horizontal line either by selling assets of value to someone below the line or by reducing loans to them. For this reason, a useful macroeconomic rule of thumb is: *A nation's monetary base changes only when funds cross our imaginary horizontal line due to a change in size of the central bank's balance sheet*[3] (see Exhibit 9-3).

A nation's monetary base changes only when funds cross our imaginary horizontal line, due to a change in size of the central bank's balance sheet.

Any time a central bank purchases something of value or makes a loan, it acquires an asset that increases the size of its balance sheet. Therefore, an easy way to determine whether a nation's monetary base has increased is to see if the central bank's balance sheet has increased. If the nation's monetary base has decreased, then the size of the central bank's balance sheet should have fallen (see Exhibit 9-4).

We know from Chapter 8, "The Power of Financial Institutions to Create Money," that the assets of a bank (or any company) must equal the sum of its liabilities plus stockholders' equity. Therefore, the assets side of a central bank's balance sheet cannot rise without the other side (i.e., its liabilities plus stockholders' equity) rising, as well. Central banks pay for their newly acquired assets simply by

---

[3] This rule of thumb covers about 99% of the changes in monetary base. There are a few minor exceptions to our rule of thumb, but they are relatively unimportant and will be discussed in Chapter 13, "Fiscal Policy & Automatic Stabilizers: What Managers Need to Know."

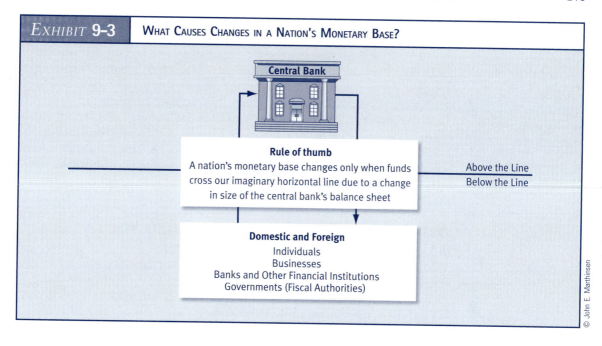

EXHIBIT 9-3 | **WHAT CAUSES CHANGES IN A NATION'S MONETARY BASE?**

Central Bank

Rule of thumb
A nation's monetary base changes only when funds cross our imaginary horizontal line due to a change in size of the central bank's balance sheet

Above the Line
Below the Line

Domestic and Foreign
Individuals
Businesses
Banks and Other Financial Institutions
Governments (Fiscal Authorities)

© John E. Marthinsen

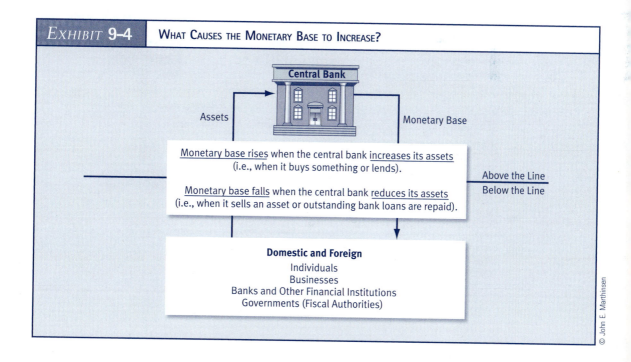

EXHIBIT 9-4 | **WHAT CAUSES THE MONETARY BASE TO INCREASE?**

Central Bank

Assets

Monetary Base

Monetary base rises when the central bank increases its assets (i.e., when it buys something or lends).

Monetary base falls when the central bank reduces its assets (i.e., when it sells an asset or outstanding bank loans are repaid).

Above the Line
Below the Line

Domestic and Foreign
Individuals
Businesses
Banks and Other Financial Institutions
Governments (Fiscal Authorities)

© John E. Marthinsen

writing checks on themselves, which increases their liabilities. Doing so requires nothing more than a few taps on their computer keyboards. These newly created central bank liabilities flow into the financial markets and become *deposits that banks hold at the central bank*, which are part of the nation's monetary base. Once increased, the monetary base enters into the nation's lend-spend-deposit cycles, which increases the nation's money supply by a multiplied amount.

Using just our rule of thumb, let's go back and examine why, for all six examples on page 212, the U.S. monetary base did not change. For Transactions 1–5, there was no change in the monetary base because these transactions were between counterparties that were entirely below our imaginary horizontal line. In Transaction 6, there was also no change because the transaction was entirely above the line.[4]

> Central banks create monetary base either by purchasing assets that are below the line or by lending to banks that are below the line. They pay for these assets and fund these loans by writing checks on themselves, which increases the nation's monetary base.

What Assets Do Central Banks Buy and Sell, to Whom Do They Lend, and with Whom Do They Deal?

A nation's monetary base changes by the same amount regardless of what is purchased or sold by the central bank and regardless of the counterparty (i.e., the financial intermediary or other individual with whom the central bank deals). In Exhibit 9-5, the monetary base increases by the same amount regardless of

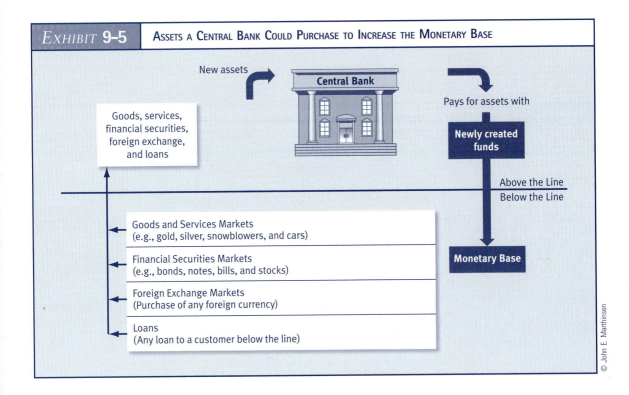

| EXHIBIT 9-5 | ASSETS A CENTRAL BANK COULD PURCHASE TO INCREASE THE MONETARY BASE |

New assets

Central Bank

Pays for assets with

Goods, services, financial securities, foreign exchange, and loans

Newly created funds

Above the Line
Below the Line

Monetary Base

Goods and Services Markets
(e.g., gold, silver, snowblowers, and cars)

Financial Securities Markets
(e.g., bonds, notes, bills, and stocks)

Foreign Exchange Markets
(Purchase of any foreign currency)

Loans
(Any loan to a customer below the line)

© John E. Marthinsen

[4] In "**The Rest of the Story**" section of this chapter, conclusions derived from this rule of thumb are discussed in much greater detail. See the subsections entitled "Monetary Effects of Open Market Operations," "Monetary Effects of Central Bank Foreign Exchange Market Intervention," and "Monetary Effects of Discount Rate and Discount Loan Changes."

whether the central bank purchases goods (e.g., gold, silver, oil, snow blowers, or cars), securities (e.g., government bonds, company shares, corporate bonds, municipal bonds, or mortgage-backed securities), or foreign exchange (e.g., euros, pesos, Swiss francs, yen, or Yuan). It also increases by the same amount regardless of whether it lends to a financial institution or other counterparty below the line. Moreover, the increase is the same regardless of whether the central bank deals with a domestic or foreign business, bank, government, church, or individual.

As long as the central bank transacts business with a counterpart below the line, the monetary base rises with each purchase or loan it makes. We know this because settlement always causes goods, services, securities, and/or loans to move northward above our imaginary horizontal line and the newly created monetary base to move southward below the line. Once it is below the line, the new monetary base enters into the familiar lend-spend-deposit cycle, causing a multiplied increase in the money supply.

Central banks try to be selective about what assets they acquire. For instance, they avoid transactions involving the purchase of goods, services, and private-sector securities and also avoid making loans to individuals or businesses. One reason for their caution is because these transactions could unfairly favor or penalize (or they could *appear* to unfairly favor or penalize) one company, individual, or asset over another.

Central banks prefer to purchase and sell government securities and convertible foreign currencies, and they prefer to lend only to financial intermediaries (see Exhibit 9-6), but in times of crisis, exceptions can be (and

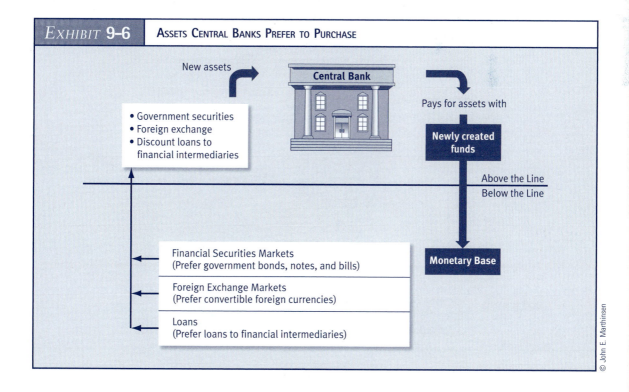

EXHIBIT 9-6   ASSETS CENTRAL BANKS PREFER TO PURCHASE

New assets

Central Bank

Pays for assets with

• Government securities
• Foreign exchange
• Discount loans to financial intermediaries

Newly created funds

Above the Line
Below the Line

Financial Securities Markets
(Prefer government bonds, notes, and bills)

Foreign Exchange Markets
(Prefer convertible foreign currencies)

Loans
(Prefer loans to financial intermediaries)

Monetary Base

© John E. Marthinsen

are) made. For example, during the Great Recession of 2007–2009, when the financial world went helter skelter, central banks retreated from their preferences and best practices by purchasing more risky assets, such as private mortgage-backed securities.

Purchases and sales of government securities by a central bank are called *open market operations*. The purchases or sales of foreign currencies are called *foreign exchange market intervention*, and central bank loans to financial institutions (below the line) are called *discount loans*.

MONETARY TOOLS OF CENTRAL BANKS

A central bank can change the nation's money supply by influencing the money multiplier and/or the monetary base. Four major monetary tools are available to accomplish this task: (1) the required reserve ratio (i.e., rr_D and rr_N), (2) open market operations, (3) foreign exchange market intervention, and (4) the discount rate. Changes in the reserve ratio influence the money multiplier, and changes in open market operations, foreign exchange market intervention, and discount rate affect the monetary base (see Exhibit 9-7).

REQUIRED RESERVE RATIO

The lending power of a financial institution is limited by the percent of its deposits liabilities that must be held as reserve assets, which earn little or no interest. For example, if $1,000 were deposited in a bank and the required

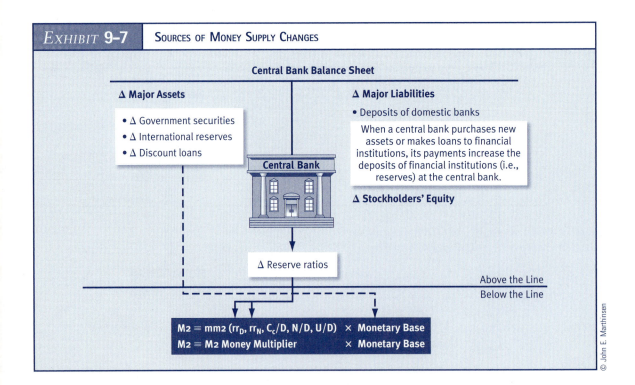

| EXHIBIT 9-7 | SOURCES OF MONEY SUPPLY CHANGES |

Central Bank Balance Sheet

Δ Major Assets

- Δ Government securities
- Δ International reserves
- Δ Discount loans

Central Bank

Δ Major Liabilities

- Deposits of domestic banks

When a central bank purchases new assets or makes loans to financial institutions, its payments increase the deposits of financial institutions (i.e., reserves) at the central bank.

Δ Stockholders' Equity

Δ Reserve ratios

Above the Line
Below the Line

$$M2 \equiv mm2\ (rr_D, rr_N, C_c/D, N/D, U/D)\ \times\ \text{Monetary Base}$$
$$M2 \equiv M2\ \text{Money Multiplier} \qquad\qquad \times\ \text{Monetary Base}$$

© John E. Marthinsen

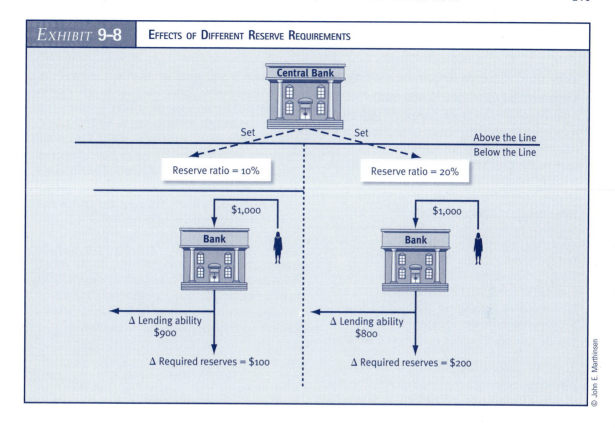

EXHIBIT **9-8**   EFFECTS OF DIFFERENT RESERVE REQUIREMENTS

reserve ratio were 10%, then the bank would need to hold $100 as required reserves (i.e., which are assets in the balance sheet) and could lend the rest. Raising the reserve ratio to 20% would reduce the bank's ability to lend because it would need to hold $200 of the $1,000 deposit as reserves and could lend only $800 (see Exhibit 9-8). The same would be true for other banks in the financial system.

Central banks determine not only the size of the reserve ratio but also the particular assets that qualify as reserves and whether these reserves earn a rate of return. For instance in the United States, only the cash in the vaults of financial institutions and deposits they hold at the Federal Reserve qualify as reserves. Historically, both were noninterest-earning assets, but in 2008, the Fed changed its policy and began paying banks interest on their deposits at the Fed.[5]

Reserve requirements are imposed to control the ability of financial intermediaries to create money. They do not protect banks or depositors from heavy withdrawals (i.e., runs) or ensure that funds will be available when exceptionally large customer withdrawals occur.

> **Reserve requirements are imposed to control bank lending and not to ensure liquidity or solvency.**

[5] See Board of Governors of the Federal Reserve System, Press Release, Release Date: October 6, 2008, www
.federalreserve.gov/monetarypolicy/20081006a.htm (accessed June 7, 2013).

MACRO MEMO   9-1

Why Don't Reserve Requirements Ensure Cash Will Be Available When Banks Need It or Protect Banks from Large Withdrawals?

A common belief is that central banks impose reserve requirements to ensure that banks will have sufficient cash to meet unexpectedly large withdrawals. Let's consider whether this belief is true. Suppose the reserve ratio was 10%, and a bank held exactly $100 million in reserves to back its $1,000 million of deposit liabilities. The bank would be just meeting its reserve requirements with nothing to spare. Do these reserves protect depositors? Clearly, they would not be sufficient if customers tried to withdraw (all at once) $150 million of the $1,000 million they deposited because the bank would have only $100 million on hand in reserves. The rest would already have been invested in loans and securities.

Suppose depositors' demands were much smaller; say they were only $10 million of the $1,000 million deposits. Would the bank have enough funds on hand to cover

even this relatively small demand and still meet its reserve requirements? Exhibit 9-9 shows that a withdrawal of $10 million would cause both the bank's cash reserves and deposit liabilities to fall by $10 million. A $10 million cash withdrawal would reduce the bank's reserves by $10 million, but its required reserves would fall only by $1 million. As a result, the bank would hold reserves of $90 million, but its required reserves would equal $99 million.* Therefore, the bank would be $9 million below the reserves required.

The take-away from this Macro Memo is that the reserve ratio is a monetary tool that allows central banks to control the ability of financial intermediaries to create money. It does not protect banks and depositors from bank runs or provide banks with spare funds to meet extraordinary customer withdrawals.

*Before the withdrawal, the reserve requirement was 10% of deposits worth $1,000 million, which equaled $100 million. Afterwards, they are 10% of deposits worth $990 million, which equals $99 million. Therefore, required reserves fall by only $1 million.

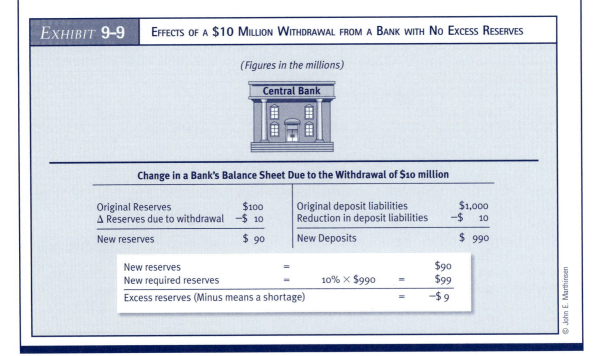

EXHIBIT 9-9   EFFECTS OF A $10 MILLION WITHDRAWAL FROM A BANK WITH NO EXCESS RESERVES

(Figures in the millions)

Central Bank

Change in a Bank's Balance Sheet Due to the Withdrawal of $10 million

Original Reserves	$100	Original deposit liabilities		$1,000
Δ Reserves due to withdrawal	−$ 10	Reduction in deposit liabilities		−$ 10
New reserves	$ 90	New Deposits		$ 990

New reserves	=			$90
New required reserves	=	10% × $990	=	$99
Excess reserves (Minus means a shortage)			=	−$ 9

Changing the reserve ratio is one of the strongest instruments in a central bank's monetary toolbox. Unfortunately, its great strength is often a weakness in disguise because central bankers are reluctant to use it. Changes in the reserve ratio indiscriminately affect all banks regardless of their reserve positions. Banks that have excess reserves or very liquid positions feel little impact when the reserve ratio is raised, but those with deficiencies or impending deficiencies could be significantly affected. Because of its broad and sweeping effects, the required reserve ratio is changed relatively infrequently, and when it is, the change is usually by a small amount and with considerable warning to the banking system.

> The reserve ratio is a rather blunt monetary tool because changes indiscriminately affect all banks regardless of their reserve positions.

Reserve Ratios for Banks Around the World

Many nations have voluntarily abandoned the reserve ratio as a monetary tool because they feel their other monetary tools are sufficient for the task. Among the industrialized nations that impose no reserve requirements on banks are Australia, Canada, Denmark, Mexico, New Zealand, Norway, and Sweden. Others, like the United Kingdom, have voluntary systems with no minimum required balance.[6]

OPEN MARKET OPERATIONS

Open market operations are the buying and selling of securities (normally government securities) by the central bank. They are called "open market" operations because central banks purchase and sell securities that have already been issued, which means central banks deal only in the (open) secondary markets. To place a buy or sell order, central banks contact security dealers (below our imaginary horizontal line), and the security dealers find willing and able counterparties, such as domestic or foreign individuals, financial institutions, businesses, and governments.

> Open market operations are the buying and selling of financial securities (usually, government-issued securities) by a central bank.

Exhibit 9-10 shows an example of open market purchases of government bonds by the central bank. The central bank purchases government securities and pays for these interest-earning assets with newly created monetary base. Therefore, with a few taps on their computer keyboards, a central bank can create monetary base out of nothing. Because the amounts are so large, this newly created monetary base is not printed but rather injected by changing checking accounts below the imaginary horizontal line.

In the end, the central bank ends up with new assets in the form of interest-earning government securities and pays for them by writing checks on itself. These new liabilities are *bank reserves*, which are part of the nation's

---

[6] An International Monetary Fund study in 2010 identified nine of 121 countries that had no minimal reserve requirements. In some countries, like Sweden, central banks have the power to determine reserve requirements but have set them at 0%. There is a significant difference between a reserve ratio equaling 0% because the central bank sets it there and a reserve ratio equaling 0% because the central bank has no power to change it. In the former case, the central bank can raise the reserve ratio without government permission. In the latter case, significant time and effort might be needed to get legislative permission. Simon Gray, "Central Bank Balances and Reserve Requirements," *IMF Working Paper: Monetary and Capital Markets Department*, February 2011, http://www.imf.org/external/pubs/ft/wp/2011/wp1136.pdf (accessed June 8, 1203). Yueh-Yun C. O'Brien, "Reserve Requirement Systems in OECD Countries," *Finance and Economics Series: Division of Research & Statistics and Monetary Affairs, Federal Reserve Board*, Washington D.C., 2007, http://www.federalreserve.gov/pubs/feds/2007/200754/200754pap.pdf (accessed June 8, 2013).

| EXHIBIT 9-10 | MONETARY EFFECTS OF OPEN MARKET OPERATIONS |

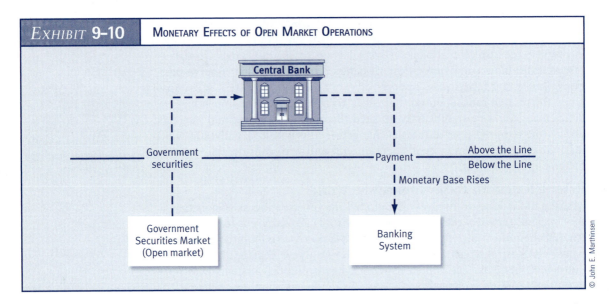

© John E. Marthinsen

monetary base. As for the counterparties below the line, they lose assets in the form of government securities, but they gain newly created monetary base, which the banking system can use to increase the nation's money supply by a multiplier effect.[7]

When discussing open market operations, it is important to keep in mind that the national government treasury (or finance ministry) is different from the central bank. The treasury is responsible for collecting taxes and making government-authorized expenditures. When taxes are not sufficient to cover government expenses, the treasury is responsible for borrowing to make up the difference. The government borrows directly from the public by issuing securities such as treasury bills, notes, and bonds. Once in the public domain, these securities are in the "open market," and central banks may purchase them.

The reason central banks do not purchase securities directly from the government is to separate the government, which can be considered the ultimate national spender, from the central bank, which can be considered the ultimate source of national liquidity. There is a strong belief (supported by evidence) that a nation's chances of suffering from severe inflation are reduced substantially if the central bank is independent from the treasury.

If a national government had substantial influence, it could coerce the central bank into purchasing excessive amounts of government debt, thereby increasing the nation's monetary base, money supply, and, ultimately, the

[7]For a more complete explanation of why the monetary base rises when a central bank purchases securities, please read in "The Rest of the Story" section of this chapter the subsection entitled "Monetary Effects of Open Market Operations." It provides greater detail on why the monetary effects of open market operations are the same regardless of the central bank's counterparty.

MACRO MEMO   9-2

The Relationship Between Central Bank Independence and Inflation

It is a fair generalization to say that all cases of hyperinflation experienced over the past 2,000 years have been caused by excessive money growth. For this reason, most nations (including the United States) have had strong interests in protecting their central banks from external pressures (e.g., political, media, and vested interests), while at the same time, ensuring that there are checks and balances on their central banks' powers. Academic research has provided strong evidence that independent central banks are best able to control their nations' inflation rates.* Exhibits 9-11 and 9-12 provide historical overviews of the correlation between central bank independence and inflation rates. For 15 developed countries, Exhibit 9-11 shows the inverse

relationship between the average inflation rate (1955 to 1988) and index of (central bank) independence. Exhibit 9-12 reinforces this relationship by plotting these same two variables and tracking their relationship for four overlapping periods.

*Among the studies are: Jeroen Klomp and Jakob de Haan, "Inflation and Central Bank Independence: A Meta-Regression Analysis," *Journal of Economic Surveys*, Volume 24, Number 4, 2010, pp. 593–621; Philip Keefer and David Stasavage, "The Limits of Delegation: Veto Players, Central Bank Independence, and the Credibility of Monetary Policy," *American Political Science Review*, Volume 97, Number 3, 2003, pp. 407–423; Charles T. Carlstrom and Timothy S. Fuerst, "Central Bank Independence and Inflation: A Note," *Economic Inquiry*, Volume 47, Number 1, 2009, pp. 182–186); Alberto Alesina and Lawrence H. Summers, "Central Bank Independence and Macroeconomic Performance: Some Comparative Evidence," *Journal of Money, Credit and Banking*, Volume 25, Number 2, 1993, pp. 151–162), and Federal Reserve Bank of St. Louis, "Central Bank Independence and Inflation," *Annual Report 2009*, http://www.stlouisfed.org/publications/ar/2009/pages/ar09_3b.cfm (accessed June 8, 2013).

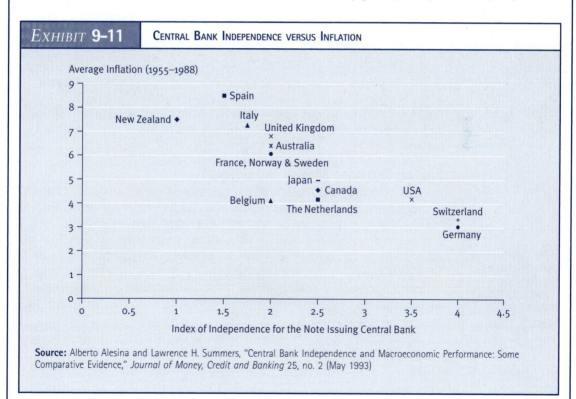

EXHIBIT 9-11 | CENTRAL BANK INDEPENDENCE VERSUS INFLATION

Source: Alberto Alesina and Lawrence H. Summers, "Central Bank Independence and Macroeconomic Performance: Some Comparative Evidence," *Journal of Money, Credit and Banking* 25, no. 2 (May 1993)

(CONTINUED)

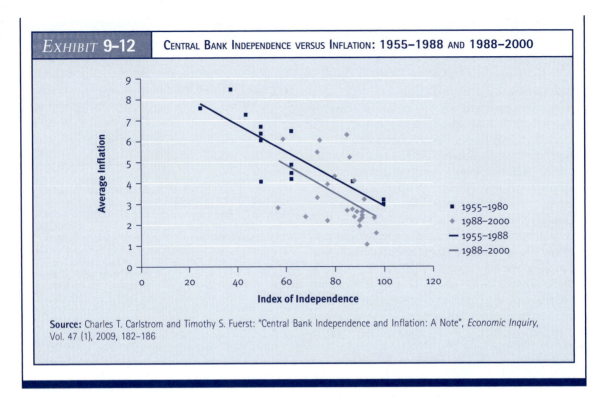

EXHIBIT 9-12 CENTRAL BANK INDEPENDENCE VERSUS INFLATION: **1955–1988** AND **1988–2000**

Source: Charles T. Carlstrom and Timothy S. Fuerst: "Central Bank Independence and Inflation: A Note", *Economic Inquiry*, Vol. 47 (1), 2009, 182–186

inflation rate.[8] By separating the spenders from the money creators, fiscal and monetary authorities can act as checks and balances on each other's actions.

FOREIGN EXCHANGE MARKET INTERVENTION

Foreign exchange market intervention has the same influence on a nation's monetary base as open market operations. As Exhibit 9-13 shows, the only major difference is foreign currencies, rather than government securities, are purchased or sold. To increase a nation's monetary base and therefore its money supply, the central bank purchases foreign currencies, and, in doing so, injects newly created reserves (i.e., monetary base) into the banking system. Once in the banking system, these funds can be lent and re-lent by financial intermediaries throughout the nation (i.e., they enter the lend-spend-deposit cycle).

Foreign exchange market intervention affects a nation's monetary base in the same way purchases and sales of government securities do.

---

[8] Japan's election of Shinzo Abe as president in December 2012 provides insight into the pressure a national government can put on a central bank to raise the domestic money supply. See Brian Bremner, "Japan's Central Bank Pressed to Boost Money Supply," *Bloomberg Businesss week: Global Economics*, July 9, 2013, http://www.businessweek.com/articles/2013-01-02/japans-central-bank-is-pressed-to-boost-money-supply.

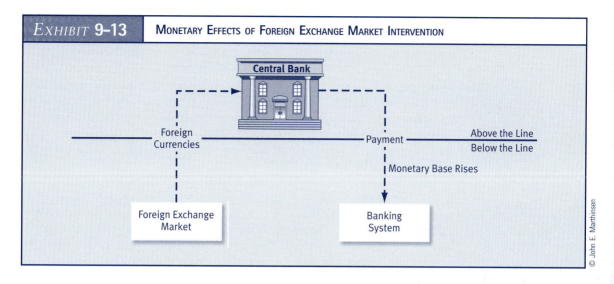

EXHIBIT 9-13 | **MONETARY EFFECTS OF FOREIGN EXCHANGE MARKET INTERVENTION**

Central Bank

Foreign Currencies — Payment — Above the Line / Below the Line

Monetary Base Rises

Foreign Exchange Market

Banking System

© John E. Marthinsen

To decrease these monetary aggregates, the central bank sells foreign currencies, thus taking bank reserves (i.e., monetary base) out of the system and forcing financial intermediaries to curtail their loans. Using foreign exchange market intervention to change a nation's monetary base is an especially important tool for countries with underdeveloped government security markets because they cannot buy or sell government securities easily and in large quantities.[9]

CHANGING THE DISCOUNT RATE

Financial institutions in need of reserves can borrow from two major sources: other banks and the central bank. When they borrow from other banks, they pay the interbank interest rate, which is determined by the forces of supply and demand.[10] A central bank has significant influence over this market-determined rate, but it does not set or determine it. To change the interbank rate, a central bank usually varies the availability of excess reserves in the banking system.

By contrast, the interest rate charged to banks that borrow from the central bank is called the *discount rate*, which is set and changed at the discretion of the central bank. Because the discount rate is not market-determined, the central bank can choose any level it wants and keep it there as long as it wants.

---

[9] For a more complete explanation of why the monetary base rises when a central bank purchases foreign currencies, please read in "**The Rest of the Story**" section of this chapter the subsection entitled "Monetary Effects of Foreign Exchange Market Intervention." It provides greater detail on why the monetary effects of foreign exchange transactions are the same regardless of a central bank's counterparty.

[10] In the United States, the interbank market is called the *federal* funds market. It got this name because borrowed and lent funds are transferred by means of debit and credit entries at the *Federal* Reserve Banks. By transacting their business through the Fed, banks can borrow and lend quickly and with minimum transaction costs.

One big difference between borrowing in the interbank market and borrowing from the central bank is that discount loans increase the monetary base and, therefore, are a source of new liquidity to the banking system. For this reason, central banks are often called *lenders of last resort* because, if the banking system should run short of liquidity, financial institutions could turn, as a *last resort*, to the central bank for relief. By contrast, the interbank market redistributes an existing supply of monetary base; for every financial intermediary that borrows, there must be a financial intermediary with surplus funds that lends. In other words, it is impossible for all banks to be net borrowers in the interbank market.

> Discount loans increase a nation's monetary base. The interbank market merely redistributes the existing monetary base.

Central banks lower or raise the discount rate to stimulate or dampen banks' demand for loans. Reducing the discount rate encourages banks to borrow from the central bank. These borrowed funds increase the nation's monetary base; they increase the money supply by an even greater amount because the new monetary base enters the lend-spend-deposit cycle, which increases the money supply by a multiplier effect. By contrast, increasing the discount rate makes loans from the central bank more expensive, which dampens borrowing incentives, thereby reducing the money supply or its growth rate.

> Reducing the discount rate encourages banks to borrow from the central bank, which increases the monetary base. Increasing the discount rate discourages bank borrowing from the central bank.

Exhibit 9-14 shows how a central bank can use the discount rate tool to affect the monetary base. By making loans to financial institutions, a central bank increases its assets by the amount lent. It then pays the borrower institutions by creating new monetary base. Discount loans increase central bank profitability because they are interest-earning assets. In effect, the central bank makes the loan simply (and virtually without cost) by increasing banks' deposits at the central bank. Because these loans can be created (and financed) with the stroke of pen or a few taps of a computer keyboard, it is easy to see

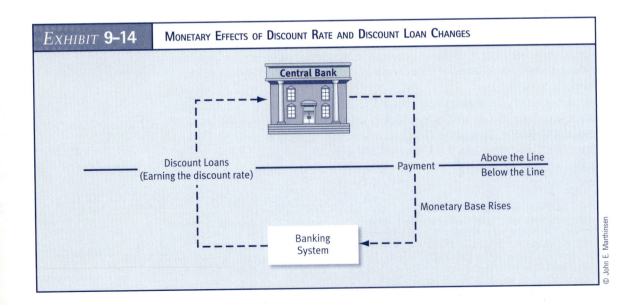

| EXHIBIT 9-14 | MONETARY EFFECTS OF DISCOUNT RATE AND DISCOUNT LOAN CHANGES |

© John E. Marthinsen

Discount Rate: The Weakest Instrument in the Fed's Monetary Toolkit

In the United States, the discount rate is considered by many to be the weakest of all monetary tools. To understand why, suppose the Fed wanted to stimulate economic activity by lowering the discount rate. If customers were not borrowing from banks, then banks would have little reason to borrow from the Fed. Therefore, the lower discount rate would not be as effective at increasing the monetary base as open market operations or foreign exchange market intervention.

In effect, the difference is similar to that of pushing on a string versus pulling on a string. If a central bank increases the monetary base by expansionary changes in open market operations or foreign exchange market intervention, bank managers have little choice but to invest (either by lending or purchasing securities) the excess reserves in their possession. Similarly, if the central bank increases the money multiplier by lowering the reserve ratio, bank managers must adjust to the new requirement. Otherwise, the new excess reserves would earn little or no interest on their new excess reserves. In short, investing funds that they are stuck with is different from voluntarily borrowing them from the central bank to lend or invest.

The Great Depression provides an excellent example of how ineffective the discount rate can be in times of severe economic hardship. Due to the shattering drop in economic activity, which started in 1929 and continued into the 1930s, demand for U.S. bank loans fell. The Federal Reserve responded by lowering the discount rate, but the private sector was not borrowing from banks; so banks had little need to borrow from the Federal Reserve. In short, a lower discount rate offered little incentive to banks that were already awash in liquidity.

how central banks could get carried away and lend too much to financial intermediaries, thereby over-inflating their money supplies.[11]

Most central banks change their discount rates rather infrequently; so when changes are made, they often receive featured coverage in the news due to the special meaning that financial markets attach to them—as if they signaled a shift in central bank policy or mindset. These "announcement effects" may cause market participants to change their behavior in anticipation of future central bank policies.

If there were unrestricted access to the discount window at rates below the interbank-market level, money dealers at banks could come to work each morning, borrow hundreds of millions of dollars from the central bank, invest the funds immediately in safe government securities or in the relatively safe interbank market, and be on the golf course before 10:00 A.M. Their business lives would be easy, and their profits would be secure. The problem is these loans would also expand the nation's money supply substantially and increase the inflation rate.

Since 2003, the U.S. Federal Reserve has set the discount rate above the federal funds (interbank) rate, thereby penalizing banks that access this

---

[11] For a more complete explanation of how the monetary base varies with changes in central bank discount loans, please read "Monetary Effects of Discount Rate and Discount Loan Changes", which is in "**The Rest of the Story**" section of this chapter.

borrowing facility.[12] In this light, the Fed can be viewed a *lender of last resort* in the sense that it became one of the last (most costly) places banks would go for loans. Prior to 2003, the discount rate was kept below the interbank interest rate, and excessive borrowing from the Fed was controlled by making access a *privilege* and not a *right*. The Fed monitored banks to make sure they were not using discount loans to increase their portfolios and arbitrage financial markets. Banks caught or suspected of such behavior could have been refused discount loans, fined, have their charters revoked, or lose membership in the Federal Reserve System.

MONETARY TOOLS IN ACTION

Let's see how the monetary tools of central banks are used. Suppose a nation had a low level of unemployment, but its inflation rate was beginning to rise at an unacceptable rate. To remove the inflationary pressures from the economy, the central bank could contract the money supply or reduce its rate of growth by increasing the reserve ratio, raising the discount rate, selling government securities in the open market, and/or selling foreign currencies in the foreign exchange market.

All of these monetary actions have one thing in common: they decrease the banking system's ability to lend. A higher reserve ratio directly reduces banks' excess reserves by forcing them to hold a larger percent of their deposits as idle required reserves, earning little or no interest. As a result, the nation's M2 money multiplier falls. A higher discount rate increases the cost that financial intermediaries must pay for reserves borrowed from the central bank, which reduces the monetary base. Finally, sales of government securities and sales of foreign exchange by the central bank reduce the banking system's reserves and force financial intermediaries to cut back loans. Both of these transactions also reduce the nation's monetary base.

Financial intermediaries react to the curtailed availability of liquidity and higher reserve requirements by raising real interest rates in order to ration their reserves. Higher real interest rates discourage borrowers from taking new loans. For example, higher real rates would be enough to dissuade some consumers from financing new cars, televisions, appliances, vacations, and furniture. Similarly, higher real rates would discourage businesses from financing marginal investment projects (e.g., new machinery, renovations, or plant expansions).

If the nation's loan demand falls, so will its demand for goods and services, causing business inventories to rise. To reduce their rising and unwanted inventories, businesses might decelerate production by running their factories for fewer hours, cutting back labor hours, and/or laying off workers.

By slowing production lines, the demand for factory inputs (i.e., labor and materials) would fall, putting pressure on suppliers to cut back employment, production, and prices. A chain reaction of cause-and-effect events would follow and cascade their way through the economy, resulting (usually) in lower

> **Contractionary monetary policy reduces a nation's monetary base and/or money multiplier, which reduces the money supply.**

> **By reducing the money supply or its growth rate, a central bank hopes to increase the nation's real interest rate, which reduces real consumer spending and business investments.**

---

[12] Federal Reserve Bank of San Francisco, *Educational Resources*, http://www.frbsf.org/education/activities/drecon/2004/0409.html (accessed July 9, 2013).

price levels (or lower inflation), a higher unemployment rate, and a lower employment rate.

As workers' incomes fell, they would respond by reducing their demand for goods and services, which would feed back, once again, to businesses that now face even weaker demand. Ultimately, these effects would be repeated in ever-widening circles of reduced spending, causing the nation's prices (or inflation rate) to fall and, perhaps, causing real output to fall, as well.

The cycle is reinforcing. A pattern of declining incomes that causes lower spending and leads to reduced incomes is a characteristic feature of economic downturns. When the economic slump is small or moderate, it is called a *recession*. When it is severe, it is called a *depression*. For this reason, the Great Depression, which lasted from 1929 through most of the 1930s and increased U.S. unemployment to historic heights, is generally considered the worst of the twentieth century's economic contractions.

LAGS IN MONETARY POLICY

Monetary policies lose their effectiveness if there are significant delays caused by (1) a failure to recognize fundamental economic changes, (2) sluggishness in implementing new monetary policies, and/or (3) having to wait extended periods until these policies take effect. At best, these lags are irritants that cause impatience and frustration. At worst, they are destabilizing and harmful to domestic and international markets. The longer the delay, the less likely it is that a pressing economic problem will be matched with the best monetary cure. The three major lags associated with monetary policy are called the recognition lag, implementation lag, and impact lag (see Exhibit 9-15).[13]

The *recognition lag* is the time between when a fundamental economic change occurs (e.g., pessimistic expectations causing business investments

> Three important lags can distort the effectiveness of monetary policies. They are the recognition lag, implementation lag, and impact lag.

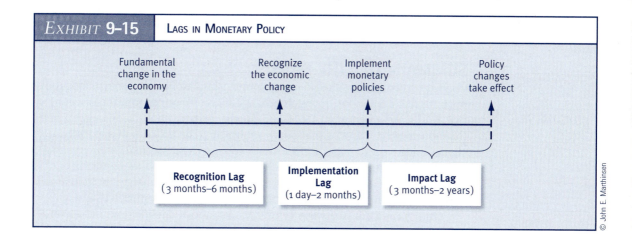

| EXHIBIT 9-15 | LAGS IN MONETARY POLICY |

Fundamental change in the economy — Recognize the economic change — Implement monetary policies — Policy changes take effect

Recognition Lag (3 months–6 months)
Implementation Lag (1 day–2 months)
Impact Lag (3 months–2 years)

© John E. Marthinsen

[13] Milton Friedman, "The Lag Effect of Monetary Policy," *Journal of Political Economy*, 1961, pp. 447–466, http://www.jstor.org/stable/1828534 (accessed June 8, 2013).

to fall) and policymakers recognize its implications (or potential implications). On average, it lasts between three and six months and is difficult to reduce because virtually all of the economic variables that track business cycles are reported either monthly or quarterly. When these statistics are reported, monetary authorities may not react to them immediately because initial estimates are frequently inaccurate or incomplete. Therefore, time is needed to correct, refine, and interpret this information. Furthermore, upward or downward fluctuations in these figures are often temporary and reversed when next reported.

The *implementation lag* is the time it takes a central bank to react to the new economic information. Fortunately, central banks can change their policies almost instantaneously because they meet regularly (e.g., every four to six weeks). In emergencies, they could meet immediately—even if the meetings were nothing more than telephone conference calls.

Finally, the *impact lag* is the period between when a policy is changed and when it takes full effect. For monetary policy, this lag is potentially the longest and most variable of all. It could be as short as three months or as long as two years for the monetary policies to take effect.

As a result of the lags in monetary policy, the interval between a change in economic activity and when monetary policy takes effect could be anywhere from six months to almost three years. By that time, the nation could be in a completely different economic condition. Such long lags could cause policies meant to dampen a hyperactive economy (e.g., unsustainable growth and rising inflation) to take effect when nation is entering a recession. Similarly, policies meant to stimulate a sluggish economy might take effect after it has already recovered on its own and is facing rising inflationary pressures.

One way economists and government officials have tried to shorten the recognition lag is by improving their economic forecasts. Sophisticated econometric models have been designed for this purpose, and nations also report leading economic indicators to signal future changes in economic activity. The problem with both of these forecasting methods is unevenness in their effectiveness. Nevertheless, many policymakers have found some to be useful.

SUMMARY OF "THE BASICS"

Central banks regulate their nations' money supplies by using four major tools: open market operations, foreign exchange market intervention, the discount rate, and reserve requirements. To adjust the money supply, they must change the monetary base and/or the money multiplier. The nation's monetary base changes due to open market operations, foreign exchange market intervention, and discount loans. Its money multiplier changes with reserve requirement adjustments, but the money multiplier is also affected by changes in individuals' and financial intermediaries' preferred asset ratios (see Exhibit 9-16).

Only transactions between central banks (above the line) and non–central bank counterparties (below the line) change a nation's monetary base. For that reason, fiscal policies of taxing, spending, and borrowing (entirely below the line), foreign exchange transactions among individuals (entirely below the line), and central bank swaps (entirely above the line) have no effect on a nation's monetary base.

The recognition lag is how long it takes the central bank to recognize that a fundamental economic change has occurred.

The implementation lag is how long it takes the central bank to change policies.

The impact lag is how long it takes the new central bank policies to work.

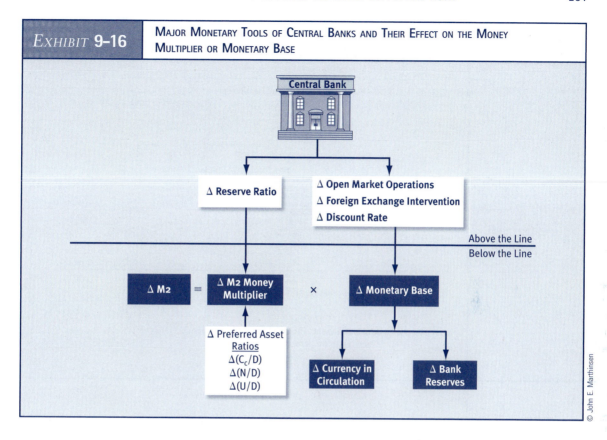

EXHIBIT 9-16   MAJOR MONETARY TOOLS OF CENTRAL BANKS AND THEIR EFFECT ON THE MONEY MULTIPLIER OR MONETARY BASE

© John E. Marthinsen

What is the current state of your home country's economy? Is the central bank pursuing expansionary or contractionary monetary policies? Are your central bank's policies in line with those of the president, prime minister, congress, or parliament? Are they openly criticized or complimented? Reading the financial pages of newspapers and magazines with these questions in mind and incorporating the information in this chapter should provide significant insights about the effects monetary policy has on economic activity.

THE REST OF THE STORY

CENTRAL BANKING: A BALANCE SHEET VIEW

INTRODUCTION

Variations in a nation's monetary base are dependent on changes in its central bank's balance sheet. In short, a nation's monetary base can rise or fall only if the central bank's balance sheet increases or decreases. Exhibit 9-17 shows the generic assets and liabilities that most central banks use to influence their nations' monetary bases. The composition of these assets can vary considerably from nation to nation. Let's briefly review these assets and liabilities.

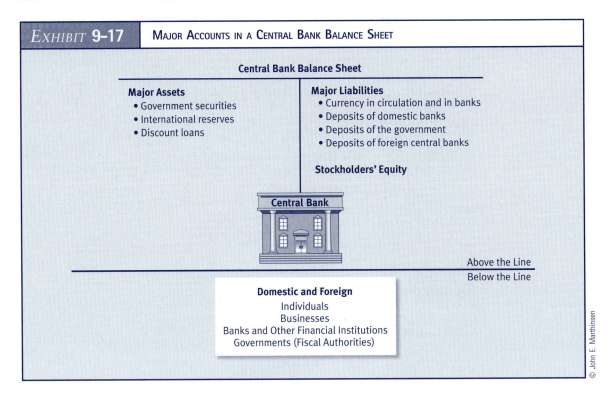

EXHIBIT 9-17   MAJOR ACCOUNTS IN A CENTRAL BANK BALANCE SHEET

Central Bank Balance Sheet

Major Assets
- Government securities
- International reserves
- Discount loans

Major Liabilities
- Currency in circulation and in banks
- Deposits of domestic banks
- Deposits of the government
- Deposits of foreign central banks

Stockholders' Equity

Central Bank

Above the Line
Below the Line

Domestic and Foreign
Individuals
Businesses
Banks and Other Financial Institutions
Governments (Fiscal Authorities)

© John E. Marthinsen

MAJOR CENTRAL BANK ASSETS RELATED TO CHANGES IN THE MONETARY BASE

Central banks have many assets, such as buildings, land, computers, cars, trucks, and planes, but the assets that are most important for conducting monetary policy are government securities, international reserves (mainly, convertible foreign currencies), and discount loans (see Exhibit 9-17).

Government Securities and Other Eligible Financial Instruments

Central banks purchase government securities and other eligible financial instruments from individuals, financial institutions, businesses, and institutions below our imaginary horizontal line. While it might be legal or, otherwise, permitted for them to purchase these securities directly from their national governments, few central banks do because of inflationary fears that arise when central banks are viewed as the ultimate financiers of big government spending programs. Rather, they purchase them in the *open market*, which means that they purchase from those who have already bought the securities in the primary market from the government and are now reselling them in the secondary market. For this reason, the term *open market operations* is used to describe central bank purchases and sales of government securities (i.e., they are purchased and sold in the "open market").

Due to the economic and financial downturn during the Great Recession (2007–2009), many central banks broadened the list of financial assets they were willing to purchase in the open market. For instance, the U.S. Federal Reserve purchased mortgage-backed securities, thereby exposing itself to

Purchases and sales of government securities by a central bank are called "open market operations."

higher credit risk. It also lengthened the maturity of the government securities it would purchase, thereby exposing itself to greater market risk.

International (Foreign Exchange) Reserves

A central bank acquires foreign currencies by purchasing them in private foreign exchange markets, which are below our imaginary horizontal line. But to purchase a foreign currency, the central bank must simultaneously sell its own. When the supply of a nation's currency increases in the foreign exchange market, its international value falls (i.e., depreciates) relative to the currency bought. An alternative way of saying the same thing is by increasing the demand for a foreign currency, the central bank raises (appreciates) the value of a foreign currency relative to the domestic currency.

Central banks intervene in the foreign exchange markets (below the line) to influence their exchange rates.

For example, suppose the Federal Reserve wanted to stimulate exports by lowering the dollar's value from €0.80/$ to €0.70/$. To lower the dollar's value, the Fed would sell sufficient quantities of dollars (i.e., purchase sufficient quantities of euros) to reduce the dollar's value from €0.80/$ to €0.70/$. These euros would end up as assets on the Federal Reserve's balance sheet. In particular, the Fed's asset would be a new deposit at the ECB (i.e., above our imaginary horizontal line).[14]

Discount Loans

When central banks lend to domestic banks and other financial intermediaries, the interest rate they charge is called the *discount rate*. These loans are collateralized, which means that the borrower must back them with securities that are acceptable to the central bank. Among the securities that typically qualify as "eligible paper" are government bonds, bills and notes, government-guaranteed securities, and other high-quality assets. Usually, discount loans have short-term maturities (e.g., one day to two weeks) and are not meant to be a continuing source of liquidity for any particular bank.

Central bank rules are modified or changed in times of crisis. For example, recent economic turmoil surrounding the debts of some countries in the EMU has caused the ECB (and other central banks) to expand the list of assets that qualify as eligible paper.

Central banks make collateralized loans to financial intermediaries and charge the discount rate.

MAJOR CENTRAL BANK LIABILITIES

A company's liabilities and stockholders' equity are the sources of financing for its assets, and the same is true for central banks. One difference between central banks and ordinary companies is central bank liabilities to financial intermediaries (below the line) are counted as bank reserves, which are part of the nation's monetary base. Fluctuations in other central bank liabilities are tied directly to the services a central bank performs for the banking system, government, and foreign central banks. Let's take a look at the most important central bank liabilities.

Currency in Circulation and Cash in the Vaults of Banks

If you open your wallet and take a close look at the paper currency (i.e., cash) inside, you will find that the currency (regardless of whether it is dollars,

---

[14] These funds could also be held by the Fed in financial institutions or invested below the line.

pounds, euros, ringgits, pesos, or yen) is a liability of the central bank that issued it. In the United States, these bills have "FEDERAL RESERVE NOTE" printed across the top, which indicates that they are liabilities of the U.S. Federal Reserve System.[15]

Have you ever wondered how a central bank gets paper currency into or out of circulation (i.e., below or above the line)? Spending it would be impractical because open market operations and discount loans are too large for cash transactions, and the settlement process would be too slow. Rather, central banks stand by passively and wait for banks to demand cash. The process goes something like this.

> A central bank increases the nation's currency in circulation by responding to banks' requests for cash. And banks' requests for currency are stimulated by customers' demands.

Suppose it was the December holiday season, when people tend to use more cash than normal for shopping and gift giving. If a bank found the cash in its vault was running low by $50,000, the bank manager would contact the central bank and ask for cash to be transferred as soon as possible. The central bank would respond to this request by reducing the bank's deposit account at the central bank by $50,000 and increasing by the same amount its liability called *currency in circulation and in banks*. The $50,000 of cash would then be delivered immediately to the bank by armored car.

Exhibit 9-18 shows the balance sheet changes that would result from the central bank sending $50,000 cash (i.e., dollar bills with various denominations, such as $1, $5, $10, $20, and $100) to the bank. For the central bank, the transaction merely exchanges one liability (deposits of banks) for another

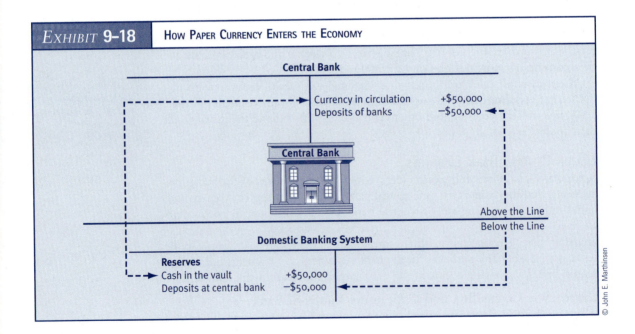

EXHIBIT 9-18   HOW PAPER CURRENCY ENTERS THE ECONOMY

Central Bank

Currency in circulation   +$50,000
Deposits of banks   −$50,000

Central Bank

Above the Line
Below the Line

Domestic Banking System

Reserves
Cash in the vault   +$50,000
Deposits at central bank   −$50,000

© John E. Marthinsen

---

[15] See Appendix 9-6: "U.S. Dollar Facts and Figures" for some interesting and amusing information about the U.S. dollar.

EXHIBIT 9-19	CASH INJECTIONS INTO THE ECONOMY DO NOT CHANGE THE MONETARY BASE

Δ Monetary Base = Δ Currency in Circulation   +   Δ Bank Reserves

Δ Monetary base	=	Δ Currency in circulation	+	Δ Cash in the vault	+	Δ Bank deposits at the central bank
0	=	0	+	$50,000	−	$50,000

© John E. Marthinsen

(currency in circulation), and for the bank, it simply exchanges one asset (deposits at the central bank) for another (cash in the vault).

Injecting paper currency into the economy has no effect on a nation's monetary base because the sum of currency in circulation and reserves of financial intermediaries remains unchanged. Due to the injection of cash, financial intermediaries' vault cash increases by the same amount as their deposits at the central bank fall (see Exhibit 9-19).

Central banks remove currency from circulation by using exactly the opposite steps. For example, during the course of the business day, paper currency is deposited in and withdrawn from banks. At the end of the day, banks take their excess cash, along with any bills that are worn or damaged, and send the currency back to the central bank. When the central bank receives the bills, it increases the deposit accounts of these banks by the amount sent back and reduces its currency in circulation liability. If the bills are still in good shape, the central bank just temporarily takes them out of circulation. If they are worn or damaged, it destroys them (usually by shredding the bills).

Deposits of Domestic Banks

It is important to remember that the deposits financial intermediaries hold at the central bank are part of a nation's monetary base. These deposits in a central bank are the liabilities of the central bank, but they are assets of the financial intermediaries that deposited them.

Financial intermediaries deposit funds in the central bank for two major reasons. First, they qualify as reserves for meeting their reserve requirements; second, they facilitate check clearing. Because an efficient check-clearing system is important to any economy, central banks usually play prominent roles as major clearing houses.[16]

In its role as a clearing house, a central bank sorts checks, routes them to and from banks, and increases or decreases members' accounts by the net amount of deposits or withdrawals. Clearing houses do not exist because

> Bank deposits at the central bank are part of a nation's monetary base. They are liabilities of the central bank and assets of banks.

---

[16] Many banks also clear their checks through private financial intermediaries, such as large commercial banks, rather than through the central bank. They do this mainly when the private financial intermediaries are more convenient and/or less costly than the central bank.

central banks created them. Rather, they existed long before central banks arrived on the scene and survived because they performed needed financial services efficiently and relatively inexpensively.

Deposits of the Government

A central bank is the financial (i.e., fiscal) agent of the national government, which means it helps the national treasury (or finance ministry) administer a number of important financial services for the central government. Among these services are the collection of taxes, issuance and redemption of debt, and payment of interest on outstanding debt. National governments also write checks on their balances at central banks. In other words, when the government wishes to purchase something, it writes a check on its account at the central bank.

> Central banks are the fiscal agents of national governments.

Normally, governments hold most of their deposits in commercial banks (below the line), but they write their checks on their central bank accounts (above the line). This system may seem a bit convoluted, but it is done to minimize the impact government taxes and expenditures might have on a nation's monetary base.

> Governments hold most of their deposits in financial intermediaries that are below the line.

For example, suppose a government held all its deposits in the central bank, and residents paid taxes equal to $100 billion. If the funds flowed above our imaginary horizontal line, they would reduce the nation's monetary base by $100 billion. Then, these same funds would come flowing back into the economy and inflate the monetary base when the government spent them.

It is for this reason that a government holds most of its funds in *tax and loan accounts* at financial institutions (below the line) and transfers funds to the central bank only when it is going to make payments. The funds are then spent quickly, so any change in the monetary base is very short. Moreover, such transfers are communicated to the central bank, so that any temporary changes in the monetary base can be offset. For our purposes, we will treat all government deposits as if they remained in financial intermediaries below the line. Therefore, payments and receipts have no effect on the monetary base.

Deposits of Foreign Central Banks

On the asset side of a central bank's balance sheet is an account called *international reserves*, which represents the foreign currency deposits this central bank holds in foreign central banks.[17] Therefore, it stands to reason that every central bank should have a counterpart liability that reflects the deposits it owes to foreign central banks. This account is called *deposits of foreign central banks*.

> Central banks hold deposits in foreign central banks. To the foreign central banks receiving these deposits, they are liabilities, but for the central banks depositing them, they are assets.

Perhaps, an example is the easiest way to understand changes in this account. Suppose the ECB wanted to lower the euro's value relative to the dollar (i.e., raise the value of the dollar relative to the euro). Because the exchange rate was $1.20/€, it purchased $120 million dollars from and sold €100 million to individuals and institutions below the line. As a result, the ECB would own $120 million in new reserves, which would be deposited with the Federal Reserve. Therefore, the Fed's deposit liabilities to the ECB would rise by $120 million.

---

[17] These funds could also be held by the central bank in bank accounts with financial intermediaries below the line.

Stockholders' Equity

Stockholders' equity represents the ownership claims of shareholders on the assets of a central bank. Like any entity, a central bank is solvent only if it has positive equity (i.e., the value of its assets exceed the value of its liabilities). But this is almost always the case because central banks earn profits on the assets they purchase, and they purchase interest-earning assets with money *they* create. Nevertheless, sharp reductions in the value of these assets can cause a significant deterioration in asset and equity values and raise disturbing questions about solvency and sustainability.

MACRO MEMO   9-4

Can a Central Bank Become Insolvent: Case Study of the Swiss National Bank (SNB)?

The SNB provides an excellent example of the possible dilemmas and concerns a central bank can face if its assets fall significantly in value.* Due to the Swiss franc's relative strength throughout the twentieth and twenty-first centuries, it has become a "safe-haven currency" that is highly demanded in times of financial turmoil. The Swiss franc strengthened between 2007 and 2012 due to a mixture of financial, economic, natural, and human-made disasters, such as the Great Recession (2007–2009), European debt crisis (2009–2013), as well as the earthquake, tsunami, and (Fukushima) nuclear accident in Japan (2011). As a result, strong and rapid short-term capital flowed to Switzerland in search of safety. The SNB faced a cruel dilemma: let the appreciating Swiss franc price domestic exports from the international markets and risk deflation or intervene in the foreign currency (mainly euro) markets and risk over-expanding the nation's monetary base.

SNB decided to intervene, causing the nation's monetary base to soar. Between 2007 and the third quarter of 2011, SNB's foreign currency assets more than quintupled, rising from SFr 51 billion to SFr 262 billion.[†] As these foreign currencies continued to depreciate, SNB's losses rose, amounting to SFr 26 billion in 2011 alone. The central bank's equity fell from 52% of assets in 2007 to 16% in 2010[‡] to 15% by the end of the third quarter 2011.[§]

Nevertheless, SNB announced in September 2011 its intention to cap the Swiss franc's value of €0.83/SFr, which resulted in further accumulations of international currency reserves.

Questions and concerns arose immediately about the consequences of SNB's declining equity. Would the central bank be able to freely conduct monetary policy? Was recapitalization necessary? Was it possible for a central bank to become insolvent?

In a speech responding to these concerns, Thomas Jordan, SNB's Vice Chairman, at that time, stated: "[t]he short answer to these questions is 'No', because the SNB cannot be compared with commercial banks or other private enterprises. For one thing, a central bank cannot become illiquid. This means that a central bank's capacity to act is not

---

*See Henri B. Meier, John E. Marthinsen, and Pascal A. Gantenbein, *Swiss Finance: Capital Markets, Banking, and the Swiss Value Chain* (Hoboken, NJ, John Wiley & Sons, 2013).

[†]Swiss National Bank, *SNB Balance Sheet Items*, http://www.snb .ch/en/iabout/stat/statpub/balsnb/stats/balsnb (accessed on July 9, 2013).

[‡]Provisions and equity capital amounted to SFr 42.59 billion, but SNB's 2010 (annual) loss reduced the Bank's equity (i.e., provisions, share capital, and distribution reserve) to 16% of assets.

[§]Swiss National Bank, *SNB Balance Sheet Items end of November 2011*, http://www.snb.ch/en/iabout/stat/statpub/balsnb/stats/balsnb /snbbil_A1 (accessed 31 July 9, 2013). Net losses amounted to only SFr 19.2 billion, due to SNB gains on other assets, such as gold.

(CONTINUED)

constrained if its equity turns negative."* Thomas focused on the immunity central banks gain from their income-generating powers connected to money creation. At the same time, he confirmed that persistent negative equity could "undermine the bank's credibility and its independence."[†] If for no other reason, a pintsized equity-to-asset ratio would put the central bank in the tenuous position of trying to regulate private financial institutions with standards that are significantly different from the ones it used internally. This was also an important issue for Switzerland because a diminutive central bank equity base could threaten the confidence global financial markets had in the Swiss franc and the SNB.

Stakes Are High for Other Nations

Exhibit 9-20 shows how high the stakes are for many countries that have accumulated trillions, billions, and hundreds of millions in foreign currency reserves. At the end of 2012, for every 1% depreciation of their foreign currency reserves, China, Japan, and Saudi Arabia stood to lose $33.5 billion, $13.5 billion, and $6.3 billion, respectively.

*Thomas Jordan, Vice Chairman of the SNB, Does the Swiss National Bank Need Equity? http://www.snb.ch/en/mmr/speeches /id/ref_20110928_tjn (accessed July 9, 2013).
[†]Ibid.

EXHIBIT 9-20	TOP 10 COUNTRIES IN FOREIGN CURRENCY AND GOLD RESERVES: DECEMBER 31, 2012

RANK	COUNTRY	FOREIGN EXCHANGE AND GOLD RESERVES (Figures in U.S. dollars)
1	China	3,312,000 million
2	Japan	1,351,000 million
3	Saudi Arabia	626,800 million
4	Russia	537,600 million
5	Taiwan	408,500 million
6	Brazil	371,100 million
7	Switzerland	331,900 million
8	South Korea	326,900 million
9	Hong Kong	317,300 million
10	India	287,200 million

Source: Central Intelligence Agency, *The World Factbook*, https://www.cia.gov/library/publications/the-world-factbook/rankorder /2188rank.html (accessed June 8, 2013)

MONETARY EFFECTS OF OPEN MARKET OPERATIONS

INTRODUCTION

Let's investigate how open market operations influence a nation's monetary base and money supply. To increase a nation's monetary base, the central bank purchases government securities, thereby injecting newly created reserves into the banking system. Once in the banking system, these funds can be lent and re-lent by financial intermediaries throughout the nation. By contrast, central banks decrease these monetary aggregates by doing the opposite. They sell government securities, thus taking reserves out of the system and forcing financial intermediaries to curtail their loans.

Open market operations have become the preferred monetary tool of many central banks around the world, especially in the industrialized nations. Most outright central bank purchases are for securities that have been issued by the national government, guaranteed by the national government, or issued by local governments.

> Open market operations are the preferred monetary tool of many central banks around the world.

REPURCHASE AGREEMENTS

Since the early 1990s, there has been a strong trend among central banks to conduct open market operations by using repurchase agreements and reverse repurchase agreements instead of outright security purchases or sales.[18] A *repurchase agreement (repo)* is a transaction between two parties in which Individual A sells a security to Individual B at a specific price and then simultaneously agrees to buy it back at a later date for a higher price. The difference between the sale and repurchase prices in a repo deal is, effectively, the interest earned or paid. Therefore, repos are like secured loans, whose credit risk is based on the quality of the securities collateralizing the deal and not on the counterparty.[19]

The assets sold and repurchased in these deals are usually fixed-interest-earning securities (i.e., fixed-income securities). The term "repurchase agreement" or "repo" is normally defined from the security dealer's perspective. Therefore, a repurchase agreement is when a security dealer is the borrower (i.e., the security sellers) and its customer is the lender.

> When a central bank enters into a "repurchase agreement," it *buys* securities from a dealer with a simultaneous agreement to sell them back at a higher price in the future. Central bank repos increase a nation's monetary base.

Central banks transact repo business only with eligible counterparties (dealers), which are mainly commercial banks, security houses, and money market dealers. Therefore, when a central bank (above the line) enters into a repo transaction with a security dealer (below the line), the central bank is lending and using the repurchase agreement securities as collateral. These transactions increase the nation's monetary base for the interval between when the securities are bought by the central bank and sold back to the dealer.

A *reverse repo* is just the opposite of the repo. In a reverse repo, a central bank (above the line) sells fixed-income securities to dealers (below the line) with a simultaneous agreement to repurchase them at a higher price in the future. Therefore, reverse repos reduce a nation's monetary base for the interval between when the securities are sold and repurchased.

> When a central bank enters into a "reverse repurchase agreement," it *sells* securities to a dealer with a simultaneous agreement to buy them back at a higher price in the future. Central bank reverse repos decrease a nation's monetary base.

The securities used for repo deals are usually domestic government securities or domestic, government-backed securities, but many central banks allow a broader range of financial assets to qualify for these deals than they would accept for outright purchases. *Eligible* securities can be denominated in the domestic currency or foreign currencies. Central banks try to be cautious

---

[18] Richard W. Kopcke, "The Practice of Banking in Other Industrialized Countries," *New England Economic Review*, Second Quarter 2002, p. 6. Also available online at http://www.bos.frb.org/economic/neer /neer2002/neer202a.pdf (accessed June 8, 2013).

[19] Technically, the securities in a repo transaction remain the assets of the borrowers (i.e., sellers). Therefore, all the returns (e.g., dividends and partial redemptions) paid by the original issuer of these securities accrue to the owners, who have borrowed using these securities as the collateral.

in their repo transactions by requiring that these securities have very low market, liquidity, and credit risks. As a result, most central bank repos have very short-term maturities (e.g., usually they mature within one or two weeks).[20] As the repo markets have become more liquid, their use by central banks has expanded. By using these markets, central banks have been better able to manage their liquidity and balance sheet risks.

OPEN MARKET OPERATIONS AND CENTRAL BANK COUNTERPARTIES

When a central bank buys or sells government securities, who are its counterparties, and does it make a difference to the ultimate effect on the monetary base? For example, if a central bank purchased government securities from banks, would the effect on the monetary base be different from when it purchased them from individuals or companies? Would it make a difference if these counterparties were domestic or foreign? Let's see why the counterparty makes no difference.

Open Market Operations: When a Central Bank Trades with Banks

Exhibit 9-21 shows the effects when a central bank purchases of $10 million of government securities from banks. The banks might be selling these

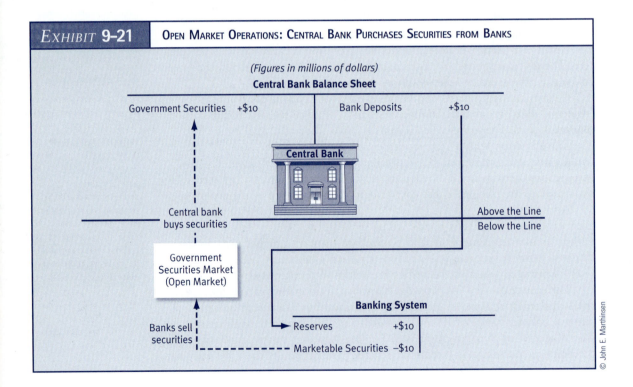

| EXHIBIT 9-21 | OPEN MARKET OPERATIONS: CENTRAL BANK PURCHASES SECURITIES FROM BANKS |

(Figures in millions of dollars)
Central Bank Balance Sheet

Government Securities +$10   Bank Deposits   +$10

Central Bank

Central bank buys securities   Above the Line
                                                            Below the Line

Government Securities Market (Open Market)

Banking System

Banks sell securities   Reserves   +$10
                               Marketable Securities   −$10

© John E. Marthinsen

---

[20] When repo transactions have maturities longer than one day, they are called *term repos*. Some central banks (e.g., the ECB) transact deals with maturities as long as three months, but they are the minority of repo transactions.

securities in order to gain liquidity needed to meet their reserve requirements, to make new loans, or as part of their normal portfolio adjustments. When a sale is made, the banks' marketable securities fall by $10 million, and the central bank's holdings of government securities rise by the same amount. The central bank pays for these securities by increasing the banks' deposits at the central bank, which causes bank reserves to increase by $10 million. Therefore, the nation's monetary base rises by $10 million.

Open Market Operations: When a Central Bank Trades with the Nonbank Public

What happens to the monetary base if the central bank purchases $10 million worth of government securities from an individual (like you or me) or from a company? We will find that it makes no difference. The monetary base increases, again, by $10 million.

Exhibit 9-22 shows the case where Thomas Smith (or the Tom Smith Company) sells $10 million of the government securities in his portfolio. The Fed pays for them by writing Smith a check. Smith's portfolio (not shown in the exhibit) falls by $10 million worth of securities and the Fed's holdings of government securities (top of the exhibit) rises by the same amount.

Smith deposits the central bank's check for $10 million in his bank, and the bank clears the check with the central bank. After the check clears, Smith's

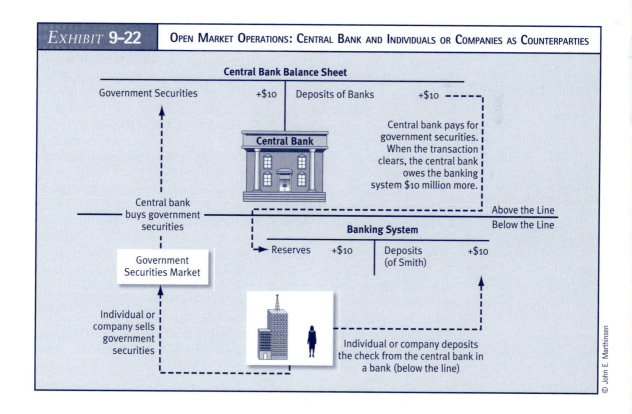

EXHIBIT 9-22   OPEN MARKET OPERATIONS: CENTRAL BANK AND INDIVIDUALS OR COMPANIES AS COUNTERPARTIES

Central Bank Balance Sheet

Government Securities   +$10 | Deposits of Banks   +$10

Central bank pays for government securities. When the transaction clears, the central bank owes the banking system $10 million more.

Central Bank

Central bank buys government securities

Above the Line
Below the Line

Banking System

Government Securities Market

Reserves   +$10 | Deposits (of Smith)   +$10

Individual or company sells government securities

Individual or company deposits the check from the central bank in a bank (below the line)

© John E. Marthinsen

bank has a $10 million deposit liability to Smith, and the deposits of Smith's bank at the central bank (a reserve asset) rise by $10 million. In addition, the Fed's assets rise by $10 million because it now owns the government securities sold by Smith. The central bank's liabilities also rise by $10 million because it now owes Smith's bank $10 million. As a result of this transaction, bank reserves rise by $10 million, and therefore, the U.S. monetary base rises by $10 million—just as they rose when the central bank purchased the securities from banks.

MONETARY EFFECTS OF CENTRAL BANK FOREIGN EXCHANGE MARKET INTERVENTION

Just as a central bank can have different domestic and foreign counterparties when it purchases or sells government securities, it may also have different counterparties when it purchases or sells foreign exchange. Let's determine whether the counterparty has any effect on the ultimate change in the monetary base. In other words, does it make a difference whether the central bank's counterparty is a domestic or foreign financial institution, individual, company, or government? We will find that it does not matter.

Foreign Exchange Intervention: When a Central Bank Trades with Domestic Banks

When a central bank intervenes in the foreign exchange market, it contacts the foreign exchange desk of a financial institution (below the line). Suppose the ECB sells €1 billion and purchases ¥100 billion in order to lower the value of the euro in terms of the yen from ¥110/€ to ¥100/€.[21] Suppose further that the ECB's counterparties are euro-area banks.

To pay for the yen, the ECB simply creates the euros needed, and it can do this by electronically making accounting entries in its balance sheet. The accounting entries reflect the fact that the ECB owes the euro-area banks connected to this foreign exchange deal an additional €1 billion. The ECB then transfers its newly purchased ¥100 billion from Japanese banks (below the line), where they were previously held by the euro-area banks, to the BoJ, which is above the line. Let's look more carefully at the transactions behind this deal.

Exhibit 9-23 shows that, as a result of these transactions, the ECB has a new €1 billion liability to euro-area banks. It also has a new asset, in the form of a ¥100 billion deposit at the BoJ. These transactions are labeled #1 in Exhibit 9-23.

After the funds are cleared and the transactions settled, the euro-area banks (below the line) lose the ¥100 billion they previously owned. The lost ¥100 billion were previously on deposit at their Japanese correspondent banks. Therefore, the deposits of euro-area banks at their Japanese correspondent banks fall by ¥100 billion. At the same time, the euro-area banks gain €1 billion, which the central bank created to purchase the yen. Therefore, the euro-area banks gain a €1 billion deposit at the ECB, which increases their

---

[21] This is equivalent to raising the value of the yen in terms of the euro from €0.0091/¥ to €0.0100/¥.

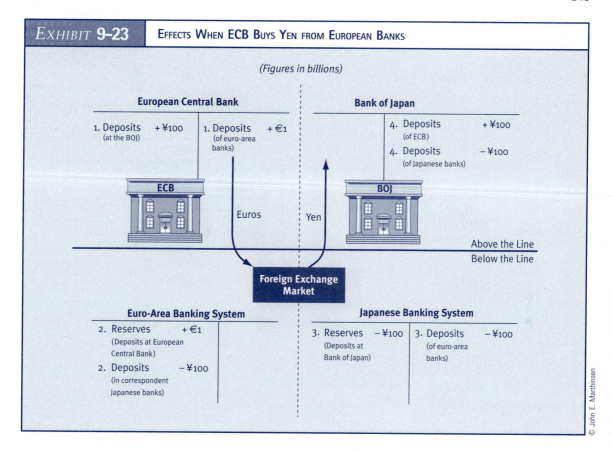

EXHIBIT 9-23 | EFFECTS WHEN ECB BUYS YEN FROM EUROPEAN BANKS

reserves and the euro area's monetary base. These transactions are labeled #2 in Exhibit 9-23.

Japanese banks (below the line) lose ¥100 billion of their liabilities to the euro-area banks. After the ECB transfers its newly purchased ¥100 billion to the BoJ, the Japanese banks also lose ¥100 billion of their deposits at the BoJ. As their deposits at the BoJ fall by ¥100 billion, Japanese banks' reserves and Japan's monetary base fall by ¥100 billion. These transactions are labeled #3 in Exhibit 9-23.

Finally, the BoJ gains a new ¥100 billion liability to the ECB, and it loses a ¥100 billion liability to the Japanese banks. These transactions are labeled #4 in Exhibit 9-23.

Foreign Exchange Intervention: When a Central Bank Trades with Foreign Banks

How, if at all, would things change if a central bank's counterparties were foreign banks, instead of domestic banks? In terms of the effect on the monetary base, the answer is "not at all." Exhibit 9-24 shows the effects when Japanese banks (rather than euro-area banks) are counterparties to the ECB's foreign exchange intervention. As in the previous example, suppose the ECB intervenes in the foreign exchange market to lower the value of the euro in

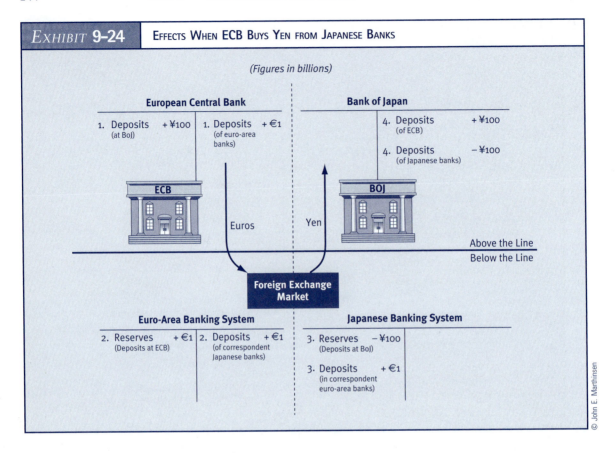

EXHIBIT 9-24　　EFFECTS WHEN ECB BUYS YEN FROM JAPANESE BANKS

(Figures in billions)

European Central Bank

1. Deposits　+¥100
(at BoJ)

1. Deposits　+€1
(of euro-area banks)

ECB

Euros

Bank of Japan

4. Deposits　+¥100
(of ECB)

4. Deposits　−¥100
(of Japanese banks)

BoJ

Yen

Above the Line
Below the Line

Foreign Exchange Market

Euro-Area Banking System

2. Reserves　+€1
(Deposits at ECB)

2. Deposits　+€1
(of correspondent Japanese banks)

Japanese Banking System

3. Reserves　−¥100
(Deposits at BoJ)

3. Deposits　+€1
(in correspondent euro-area banks)

© John E. Marthinsen

terms of the yen from ¥110/€ to ¥100/€, but this time its counterparties are Japanese banks.

The ECB pays for the yen simply by creating the euros it needs. The ECB then transfers its newly purchased ¥100 billion from Japanese banks (below the line) to the BoJ (above the line).

This example is a bit more complicated than the previous one, when euro-area banks were the counterparties. Therefore, to ease the discussion, picture the ECB sending the Japanese banks checks for €1 billion. The Japanese banks collect the funds by sending the ECB checks to their euro-area correspondent banks and then clearing them through the euro-area banking system. After the checks clear, the Japanese banks have €1 billion more on deposit in their euro-area correspondent banks. Therefore, the ECB owes the euro-area banks €1 billion more, but the ultimate owners of the funds are Japanese banks. Let's look more carefully at the transactions behind this deal.

Exhibit 9-24 shows that, as a result of these transactions, the ECB has a new, €1 billion liability to euro-area banks. It also has a new asset, in the form of a ¥100 billion deposit at the BoJ. These transactions are labeled #1 in Exhibit 9-24. So far, these transactions are identical to when euro-area banks were counterparties to this foreign exchange transaction.

After the deal is settled, the euro-area banks gain a new €1 billion liability to their Japanese correspondent banks. At the same time, they gain a €1 billion deposit at the ECB. This deposit is created when the ECB purchases the yen. The increase in the euro-area banks' deposits in the ECB causes both the euro area's bank reserves and monetary base to rise by €1 billion. These transactions are labeled #2 in Exhibit 9-24.

Japanese banks (below the line) gain €1 billion of assets, by means of their new deposits in euro-area banks. After the ECB transfers its newly purchased ¥100 billion to the BoJ, these Japanese banks lose ¥100 billion of their deposits at the BoJ. As their deposits at the Japanese central bank fall by ¥100 billion, Japanese banks' reserves and Japan's monetary base fall by ¥100 billion. These transactions are labeled #3 in Exhibit 9-24.

Finally, the BoJ gains a new ¥100 billion liability to the ECB, and it loses a ¥100 billion liability to the Japanese banks. These transactions are labeled #4 in Exhibit 9-24.

Foreign Exchange Intervention: When a Central Bank Trades with the Nonbank Public or Government

How would our results change if a central bank's counterparties were individuals, financial institutions, businesses, or governments, instead of domestic or foreign banks? As was the case in the previous example, the effect on the monetary base is the same.

Exhibit 9-25 shows the effects when nonbank counterparties deal with the ECB in the foreign exchange market. As in the previous two examples, suppose the ECB intervenes to lower the value of the euro in terms of the yen from ¥110/€ to ¥100/€, and it pays €1 billion to get ¥100 billion.

The ECB creates the euros needed to pay for the yen, and then it transfers the newly purchased yen from Japanese banks to the BoJ. Picture the ECB sending checks for €1 billion to these nonbank counterparties. The individuals who receive the checks collect the funds owed to them by clearing the checks through euro-area banking system. After the checks clear, these individuals have €1 billion more on deposit at their euro-area banks, and the ECB owes the euro-area banks €1 billion more. As in the previous examples, let's break down this example into smaller parts to see what the effect would be.

Exhibit 9-25 shows that the ECB has a new, €1 billion liability to euro-area banks and a new asset, in the form of a ¥100 billion deposit at the BoJ. These transactions are labeled #1 in Exhibit 9-25.

After the deal is settled, the euro-area banks gain a new €1 billion liability to their nonbank customers and a €1 billion deposit at the ECB. The increase in the euro-area banks' deposits in the ECB causes euro area's bank reserves and monetary base to rise by €1 billion. These transactions are labeled #2 in Exhibit 9-25.

Japanese banks lose ¥100 billion worth of liabilities they previously owed to nonbank customers. After the ECB transfers its newly purchased ¥100 billion to the BoJ, these Japanese banks also lose ¥100 billion of their deposits at the BoJ. As a result, Japanese banks' reserves and Japan's monetary base falls by ¥100 billion. These transactions are labeled #3 in Exhibit 9-25.

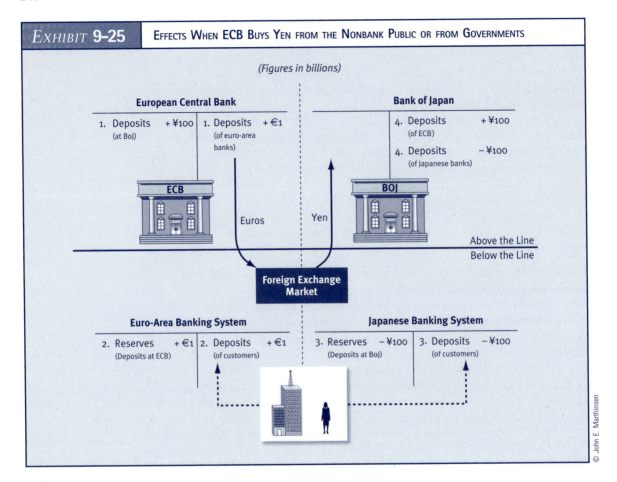

EXHIBIT 9-25 | EFFECTS WHEN ECB BUYS YEN FROM THE NONBANK PUBLIC OR FROM GOVERNMENTS

(Figures in billions)

European Central Bank

1. Deposits   + ¥100 | 1. Deposits   + €1
   (at BoJ)   (of euro-area banks)

ECB

Euros

Bank of Japan

4. Deposits   + ¥100
   (of ECB)

4. Deposits   − ¥100
   (of Japanese banks)

BOJ

Yen

Above the Line
Below the Line

Foreign Exchange Market

Euro-Area Banking System

2. Reserves   + €1 | 2. Deposits   + €1
   (Deposits at ECB)   (of customers)

Japanese Banking System

3. Reserves   − ¥100 | 3. Deposits   − ¥100
   (Deposits at BoJ)   (of customers)

© John E. Marthinsen

Finally, the BoJ gains a new ¥100 billion liability to the ECB, and it loses a ¥100 billion liability to the Japanese banks. These transactions are labeled #4 in Exhibit 9-25.

MONETARY EFFECTS OF DISCOUNT RATE AND DISCOUNT LOAN CHANGES

What happens when a central bank (above the line) lends funds to banks (below the line)? Exhibit 9-26 shows an example where the Bank of England lends £10 billion to domestic banks. As a result, English banks' assets and liabilities rise by £10 billion. Their new liability is "borrowings from the central bank," which the banks would be required to repay with interest (i.e., the discount rate). The Bank of England finances the loan simply by increasing the English banks' deposits at the Bank of England. As a result of this discount loan, the English banking system has £10 billion in additional reserves, causing the nation's monetary base to rise by the same amount.

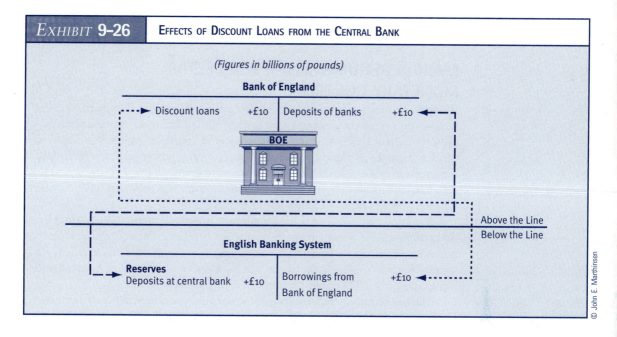

EXHIBIT **9-26**   **EFFECTS OF DISCOUNT LOANS FROM THE CENTRAL BANK**

(Figures in billions of pounds)

Bank of England

Discount loans   +£10   Deposits of banks   +£10

BOE

Above the Line
Below the Line

English Banking System

Reserves
Deposits at central bank   +£10

Borrowings from   +£10
Bank of England

© John E. Marthinsen

COLLARED DISCOUNT RATES

Some central banks control their domestic money supplies by setting two
discount rates, one for deposits and one for loans. When they do, these
rates form a collar around the short-term interest rates facing financial
institutions.

The higher rate sets ceiling for the interbank market because if short-term
market interest rates rise above this level, financial intermediaries borrow
from the central bank rather than from each other. The lower rate establishes
a floor because, if interbank deposit rates fall below this level, banks will
deposit their funds with the central bank rather than with each other. In
nations with collared rates, discount rate policy involves managing the spread
between the central bank's deposit rate and lending rate.

USE OF THE DISCOUNT RATE AROUND THE WORLD

In many countries, discount lending is called a *standing facility*. The active use
of standing facilities as monetary tools has been eclipsed by central banks'
increasing use of open market operations. Partly, this trend is due to the rapid
development of money markets, which have given central banks the flexibility
and liquidity needed to conduct monetary policy. In short, central banks
would rather buy and sell securities in the broad and deep government securities markets than rely on the discount rate tool, which requires banks to
initiate the borrowing transaction.

Buying securities in the open market provides central banks with a guarantee that the monetary base will increase when they transact their business,
and selling government securities guarantees them it will fall. By contrast,

lowering the discount rate increases the monetary base only if the financial intermediaries desire to borrow from the central bank.

MARGIN REQUIREMENTS: A SELECTIVE MONETARY CONTROL

Reserve requirements, open market operations, foreign exchange market intervention, and the discount rate are the most important monetary tools used by central banks to control their nations' money supplies, but some central banks, such as the U.S. Fed, are also given the power to determine margin requirements. We will see that margin requirements do not have a direct effect on a nation's monetary base or money multiplier, but they can have a powerful effect on the types of loans banks make.

A *margin requirement* is the percentage down payment an individual must make to purchase a security, such as a stock or bond. The rest of the security's purchase price can be borrowed. For example, if the margin requirement for a share were 90%, then 90% of the stocks' value would have to be paid outright, and only 10% could be borrowed to purchase the share.

> Margin requirements are the good-faith deposits that investors are required to make when they purchase a security. The remainder of the security's purchase price can be borrowed.

Margin requirements are like *good-faith performance deposits* because they protect brokers from customers whose stocks fall in value and then are unable to repay their loans. If the value of a security fell and an investor were unable to maintain the required margin amount, the broker could sell the security and use the proceeds to pay off the loan.

Margin requirements also regulate the level of risk that individuals can take when they purchase stocks and bonds. An example helps to explain why. If the margin requirement were 100%, then to purchase stocks worth $100,000, one would have to pay the full $100,000. If these stocks rose in value by 20%, they could be sold for $120,000 and earn a 20% return. In other words, if the margin requirement were 100%, the percentage return on invested capital would be equal to the percentage return on the shares purchased.

By contrast, suppose stocks worth $100,000 were purchased with 50% margin. To buy the shares, one would have to ante up $50,000 and could borrow the remaining $50,000 from a bank or broker. If share prices rose by 20%, the investment would be worth $120,000. With the $120,000, one could pay off the $50,000 loan and have $70,000 remaining. Earning a $20,000 return on the original $50,000 of personal funds invested translates into a return equal to 40%.[22]

> Margin requirements regulate the risks investors can take when they purchase securities.

In contrast to a margin requirement of 100%, when the investment return was 20%, reducing the margin requirement to 50% doubled the investment return to 40%.[23] This amplification effect is caused by leverage, which means

---

[22] ($20,000 ÷ $50,000) = 0.40 × 100% = 40%

[23] Of course, buying shares on margin would also mean paying interest costs on the borrowed funds, and these interest expenses would reduce the return. For instance, in the previous example, suppose the annual interest cost was 5%, the investor held the shares for one year, and at the end of the year, share prices rose by 20%. The investment return would fall from 40% to 35% because borrowing costs of $2,500 (i.e., 5% × $50,000 of borrowed funds) would reduce the annual return to $17,500 (i.e., $20,000 − $2,500 = $17,500).

utilizing borrowed money to increase the size of an investment. With a 50% margin requirement, for every $2 of investment assets, one needs to use only $1 of his/her own funds. Therefore, the leverage factor is equal to two.[24] When leverage equals two, any gain (or loss) made on personally invested funds is doubled.

If leverage sounds almost too good to be true, it is because we have only considered the rewards from leverage and not the possible losses. Stock prices can fall, and, when they do, the unpleasant side effects of leverage become immediately clear because leverage magnifies both gains and losses. To see why, suppose stocks worth $100,000 were purchased with a 100% margin requirement, and their prices fell by 20%. When they were sold, the shares would be worth only $80,000, which would be a 20% loss on the original position.

By contrast, suppose the stocks were purchased with 50% margin and their prices fell 20%. Selling them for $80,000 would allow the investor to repay his/her $50,000 margin loan, but he/she would be left with only $30,000. Because the investor started with $50,000 and ended with only $30,000, the percentage loss would be 40%.[25]

These examples show how margin requirements can influence the level of stock market speculation. Low margin requirements give investors the opportunity to leverage their investments with borrowed funds, which raises financial risk levels in the nation. High margin requirements reduce investors' and speculators' ability to leverage their returns.

A real-world example may help cement the role and effects of margin requirements. During most of the 1920s, stock prices in the United States rose almost continuously. As a result, many Americans expected prices to continue their ascent and invested heavily in the stock market. After all, why be left behind when everyone else is getting rich! With this in mind, consider the financial devastation that occurred when stock prices fell during the Great Depression. Margin requirements during the 1920s were as low as 10%, which added fuel to the stock-buying craze. Investors/speculators, who leveraged their positions to the maximum, faced potential gains and losses of 100% for every 10% change in the average stock price.

The U.S. stock market crashed in 1929 and continued to plummet in the following years. Individuals who had borrowed on 10% margin and got out of the market when stock prices fell by 10% were lucky. They only lost 100% of their invested funds, but they didn't lose more than they had invested. Investors who borrowed on 10% margin and got out when prices fell by 20% were less fortunate because they lost everything they invested and 100% more. In retrospect, they also could have considered themselves lucky.

When the market finally hit bottom, many families had lost their entire life's savings and were so hopelessly in debt that they needed more than a

---

[24] Leverage = Total amount of invested funds ÷ Own funds invested
[25] −$20,000 ÷ $50,000 = −0.40 × 100% = −40%

EXHIBIT 9-27	STOCK MARKET PRICES OF SEVEN BLUE CHIP U.S. COMPANIES, 1929 AND 1932		
STOCK NAME	PRICE ON SEPTEMBER 3, 1929	LOWEST PRICE DURING 1932	PERCENTAGE CHANGE
American Telephone & Telegraph	$304.00	$70.25	−76.9%
Bethlehem Steel	$138.75	$7.25	−94.8%
General Electric	$396.25	$8.50	−97.9%
General Motors	$71.75	$7.38	−89.7%
Gillette	$138.00	$10.38	−92.5%
Procter & Gamble	$92.13	$19.50	−78.8%
Radio Corporation of America	$99.88	$2.50	−97.5%

Sources: AT&T Historic Stock Data, http://www.att.com/ir/ (accessed June 5, 2006); *The Wall Street Journal*, "New York Stock Exchange Transactions," September 4, 1929, 32 (accessed through ProQuest, June 5, 2006); *The Wall Street Journal*, "New York Stock Exchange Transactions," December 31, 1932, 32 (accessed through ProQuest, June 5, 2006)

lifetime to repay their losses. For virtually anyone who invested during these years, the decline in prices left deep scars. To give a sense for their despair, Exhibit 9-27 shows the change in U.S. stock prices from 1929 to 1933 for seven of the highest-quality (i.e., "blue chip") U.S. stocks. Prices of these shares fell between 77% and 98%.

CONCLUSION

A nation's monetary base changes only if our imaginary horizontal line is crossed and the size of the central bank's balance sheet changes. This chapter deepened our understanding of the tools that central banks use to control their nations' (or currency areas') money supplies and credit conditions. This understanding empowers one with an appreciation for how a central bank can influence a nation's money supply via changes in the monetary base and/or money multiplier. Knowledge is power. Without it, discussions of monetary policies and their potential effects on financial and real markets are far less rich and productive.

In addition to the arsenal of monetary tools central banks have to influence their nations' money supplies are levers that affect other important aspects of the financial markets, such as the composition of bank loans and level of stock and bond market speculation. One of the most important powers is setting margin requirements, which are the good-faith down payments one must make upfront when purchasing a security. Even though this tool has no direct effect on a nation's monetary base or money multiplier, central banks use it to moderate the flow of borrowed funds into the stock markets. The higher the margin requirement, the lower the potential degree of stock and bond market speculation.

REVIEW QUESTIONS

1. To combat inflation in 2011, China's central bank raised the reserve requirement on private deposits held at banks. Explain how this reserve requirement change affected China's monetary base, money multiplier, and M2 money supply.

2. Fill in the following table. If the factors in the first column change as indicated, in which direction will the variables in the remaining columns change? Consider only the immediate and direct effects of these changes.

Impact	Monetary Base	Excess Reserves	Total Reserves
An increase in bank borrowing from the central bank			
Increased borrowing in the interbank (i.e., federal funds) market			
A decline in the required reserve ratio			
The president uses a budget surplus to reduce taxes			
Open market sales of government securities by the central bank			

3. How does each of the following transactions (by itself) affect Japan's M2 money supply, monetary base, and M2 money multiplier?
   a. BoJ, which is Japan's central bank, sells U.S. dollars (i.e., buys yen) to increase the value of the yen.
   b. Japan's Finance Ministry borrows ¥10 billion by issuing bonds.
   c. Lower interest rates cause the public to keep more of their deposits in checking accounts and less in savings accounts and time deposits.
   d. Japanese residents increase their holdings of currency relative to checking accounts.
   e. BoJ engages in open market sales of Japanese government securities.
   f. BoJ increases the required reserve ratio on checking accounts.
   g. BoJ lowers the discount rate, and banks respond enthusiastically by borrowing more.
   h. Japanese banks increase their borrowing in the interbank market.

4. Explain the lags in monetary policy. Is there a way to reduce any of these lags?

DISCUSSION QUESTIONS

5. In 2012, Cristina Fernández de Kirchner, President of Argentina, sent a bill to Congress that would allow the government to extract central bank reserves to help pay the nation's foreign debts. Suppose you were a CEO of a multinational company thinking of building a manufacturing presence in Argentina. What are the financial risks (if any) for your potential investments in Argentina if the central bank loses its independence from the government?

6. In 2002, the BoJ began the unprecedented policy of buying stocks on the Tokyo stock exchange. Explain the effect, if any, this policy had on Japan's excess reserves, monetary base, and money multiplier. Then discuss the potential problems a central bank could encounter by conducting open market operations in this manner.

7. In 2008, the U.S. Federal Reserve broke with tradition and began purchasing mortgage-backed securities (MBS) from faltering banks and investment banks. Explain the effects purchases of MBS had on the U.S. monetary base, money supply, and M2 money multiplier.

8. Is it possible for a central bank to become insolvent (i.e., the value of its assets less than the value of its liabilities)?

9. Is it correct to say that central banks have absolute control over their nations' money supplies? If so, how do central banks control the money supply? If not, explain why not.

Appendix 9-1

Who Regulates U.S. Banks?

INTRODUCTION

Exhibit A9-1 shows the composition and asset size of the U.S. banking system at the end of 2012. Holding assets of approximately $17.6 trillion, these 14,189 financial institutions are categorized as commercial banks, branches and agencies of foreign banks, savings institutions, and credit unions. Their regulation is managed by a patchwork of national and state regulatory authorities. In total, five federal regulatory agencies exert principal jurisdiction

EXHIBIT A9-1	STRUCTURE OF U.S. BANKS AND THEIR ASSETS, DECEMBER 31, 2012				
	NUMBER	PERCENT OF TOTAL	ASSETS (Billions of Dollars)	PERCENT OF TOTAL	
U.S. commercial banks	6,155	43.4	13,398	76.1	
- Federal Reserve members	2,137	15.1	11,276	64.1	
- National banks	1,294	9.1	9,271		52.7
- State member banks	843	6.09	2,005		11.4
- State nonmember banks	4,018	28.3	2,122	12.0	
U.S. branches and agencies of foreign banks	228	1.6	2,134	12.1	
Savings Institutions	987	7.0	1,059	6.0	
- OCC Regulated Federal charter	547	3.9	719	4.1	
- FDIC Regulated State charter	440	3.1	340	1.9	
Credit unions	6,819	48.1	1,022	5.8	
- Federal charter	4,272	30.1	557	3.2	
- State charter	2,547	18.0	465	2.6	
Total	14,189	100.0	17,613	100.0	

Source: Federal Financial Institutions Examination Council, "Assets, Liabilities, and Net Worth of U.S. Commercial Banks, Thrift Institutions, and Credit Unions as of December 31, 2012," *Annual Report 2012*, http://www.ffiec.gov/PDF/annrpt12.pdf (accessed June 8, 2013).

over these domestically chartered financial intermediaries: the Federal Reserve System, Federal Deposit Insurance Corporation (FDIC), National Credit Union Administration (NCUA), Office of the Comptroller of the Currency (OCC), and Office of Thrift Supervision (OTS). Of these regulators, the Federal Reserve System is the most important. Let's take a closer look at how the U.S. financial system is regulated and who regulates it.

REGULATION OF THE U.S. BANKING SYSTEM

Sunlight is said to be one of the best antiseptics; therefore, shedding light on the financial information flowing from banks to the public is a major goal of U.S. bank regulators. In this way, investors, depositors, and regulators have a transparent, useful, and timely means of assessing banks' financial condition and performance. Regulators try to ensure that individual banks are solvent, liquid, well managed, and carry only reasonable risks. They also seek to control systemic risks in the banking system, so that the failure of one financial institution does not spill over and affect the entire U.S. banking system or the international financial community.

Before a U.S. bank can begin operations, it must obtain a charter. The United States has a *dual banking system*, which means banks have the option of choosing either national or state charters. The OCC, a part of the U.S. Treasury, grants national charters. State charters are granted by state banking commissioners in each state. Similarly, U.S. thrift institutions and credit unions can apply for national or state charters. Federal thrift institutions are chartered by the OTS, and federal credit unions are chartered by the NCUA.

One problem with a dual banking system is that banks often choose the path of least resistance, basing their decisions on the regulator that imposes the fewest restrictions, rather than on the one that best serves the public interest. At one time, this conflict between bank profitability and public interest was a problem in the United States because relatively severe federal restrictions motivated banks to leave (or not enter) the national system and obtain state charters. This migration reduced the Fed's ability to control the money supply and to fulfill its federal mandate.

The Banking Act of 1980 helped resolve this problem by imposing a more uniform set of restrictions (and benefits) on state and national banks. For instance, all banks in the United States are now subject to Fed-imposed reserve requirements, but at the same time, they have been given equal access to loans from the Federal Reserve's discount window and to the Fed's check-clearing operations.

Even though the Banking Act of 1980 helped reduce the exodus of banks from the national system to the state systems, it did not reverse it. Today, only about 35%[26] of all U.S. commercial banks belong to the Federal Reserve System. Nevertheless, Fed members control slightly more than 84%[27] of all

---

[26] $(2{,}137 \div 6{,}155) = 0.347 \times 100\% = 34.7\%$
[27] $(\$11{,}276 \div 13{,}398) = 0.842 \times 100\% = 84.2\%$

commercial banking assets and 64%[28] of the assets of all U.S. banks and thrift institutions (see Exhibit A9-1).

REGULATION OF NATIONAL BANKS

Banks with national charters must join both the Federal Reserve System and the FDIC. Therefore, these banks are automatically subject to three layers of federal supervision: the OCC, the Federal Reserve System, and the FDIC.

The OCC grants charters, and also regulates, supervises, and examines federally chartered banks to ensure both their soundness and conformance to national regulations. It also licenses federal branches and agencies of foreign banks.[29]

The Federal Reserve System examines and supervises national banks. It also sets the reserve requirements for all banks. Finally, the FDIC is responsible for examining member banks and insuring their deposits up to $250,000 per depositor per insured financial intermediary.[30] This federal insurer pays claims from the two deposit insurance funds it administers (i.e., the Bank Insurance Fund and the Savings Association Insurance Fund, formerly the Federal Savings and Loan Insurance Corporation).

Since its inception in 1933, the FDIC has been one of the most stabilizing financial institutions in the United States. Its soothing influence has been as much psychological as financial. By insuring deposits, bank customers are less likely to overreact to unwelcome financial news concerning any particular bank or the banking system. Therefore, the chances of bank runs are reduced. Without this assurance, rumors that a bank might fail could set off panics as depositors rush to withdraw their savings. No bank in the United States or anywhere (not even the safest one) has enough cash and liquid assets (e.g., short-term securities) on hand to repay customers if they demand their deposits back, all at once.

Even though the FDIC has brought stability to the U.S. financial system, it may have come at a substantial cost. By relieving bank customers from the responsibility of scrutinizing the soundness of their banks' assets and the quality of their earnings, the FDIC may have inadvertently taken away a useful and effective financial watchdog. Serious questions have been raised as to whether the Great Recession of 2007–2009, which was sparked by the subprime crisis and excesses in the U.S. financial markets, would have been as severe if customers had been forced to evaluate the safety of their banks.

There appears to be considerable duplication of effort in the United States among the authorities that regulate federal banks; in fact, redundancies do exist, but much of the duplication is illusory. These regulators share

---

[28] ($11,276 ÷ 17,613) = 0.64 × 100% = 64.0%

[29] Regulation of U.S. offices of foreign banks is addressed by the International Banking Act of 1978, which subjects these banks to many of the provisions of the Federal Reserve Act and Bank Holding Company Act.

[30] Under the *Dodd-Frank Wall Street Reform and Consumer Protection Act of 2010*, Congress gave U.S. depositors unlimited insurance coverage for noninterest-bearing transaction accounts, but this provision expired on December 31, 2012. Since the beginning of 2013, the combined total of noninterest-bearing transaction accounts and interest-bearing deposits are now insured up to at least $250,000. FDIC, "Changes in FDIC Insurance Coverage," http://www.fdic.gov/deposit/deposits/changes.html (accessed June 8, 2013).

information, divide tasks, and cooperate in many other ways. For instance, the three federal regulatory institutions divide the responsibility of auditing banks and then share the results of these audits with the other two regulators.[31] Nevertheless, there is still considerable room for streamlining, and such reform is sure to come. In the past, bills to merge the three federal regulatory institutions have been submitted to Congress, and they are sure to be introduced in the future.

REGULATION OF STATE BANKS, FEDERAL CREDIT UNIONS, AND FEDERAL SAVINGS AND LOAN ASSOCIATIONS

State banks are examined and supervised by state banking commissions and by their deposit insurers (i.e., either the FDIC or a state deposit insurance company). State banks are under no obligation to join the Fed, and relatively few of them do. Exhibit A9-1 shows that only about 17% of the state banks have chosen to become Fed members.[32] As might be expected, state banking regulations vary widely.

The OTS charters, regulates, supervises, and examines federal thrift institutions, many state-chartered thrift institutions, and savings-and-loan holding companies. Finally, federally chartered credit unions are supervised by the NCUA, which charters, supervises and examines the federal credit union system. It also manages the Central Liquidity Facility for credit unions and administers the National Credit Union Share Insurance Fund.

---

[31] National banks are regulated and supervised by the OCC. State-chartered banks that become members of the Federal Reserve System are regulated and supervised by the Federal Reserve, and state-chartered banks that join the FDIC are regulated and supervised by the FDIC. The Federal Reserve regulates foreign banking operations, which includes U.S. banks operating abroad and foreign branch banks operating in the United States.

[32] $843 \div (843 + 4{,}018) = 0.173 \times 100\% = 17.3\%$

Appendix 9-2
Structure of the Federal Reserve System

This appendix focuses on the structure and functions of the Federal Reserve System (also called the Federal Reserve or simply "the Fed"). The Fed was chosen as the focus of this section because it is currently one of the most closely watched and widely scrutinized central banks in the world. In large part, its importance is due to the significant role the United States plays in the world economy. In the future, continued growth of the EMU and China could change the U.S. dollar's role relative to the euro and Yuan.

The Fed is primarily a banker's bank, with little or no day-to-day contact with private individuals and businesses. Its major responsibility is to control U.S. monetary aggregates (e.g., the money supply and monetary base) and national credit conditions in order to achieve broad macroeconomic goals, such as price stability, full employment, and a sustainable balance of payments[33] position. It also participates in the regulation and supervision of banks to ensure the health of the U.S. financial system.

The Federal Reserve System has three major tiers: the Board of Governors, 12 Federal Reserve District Banks, and approximately 2,100 member banks. Exhibit A9-2 shows the power structure of the Federal Reserve System, with the most powerful tier at the top of the pyramid and the least powerful tier at the bottom.

The Federal Reserve is called a "quasi-public" institution because the Board of Governors is a federal (government) agency, whose expenses are paid from U.S. taxes, but the 12 Federal Reserve Banks are private institutions run by boards of directors and owned (in a very weak sense) by member bank shareholders. Individuals working for the Federal Reserve Banks are private employees, whose salaries are paid from the operating revenues of the Federal Reserve System.[34]

The Fed earns significant profits, but it is not a profit-making entity. Rather, it is run for the public's welfare. Shareholder dividends are limited by law, and most of the Fed's profits are returned to the U.S. government.

---

[33] The balance of payments is a summary of all transactions between the residents of one nation and the residents of the rest of the world during a given time period. We will discuss this concept fully in Chapter 16, "Balance of Payments Fundamentals."

[34] Presidents of the 12 Federal Reserve Banks can (and often do) earn more than the members of the Board of Governors.

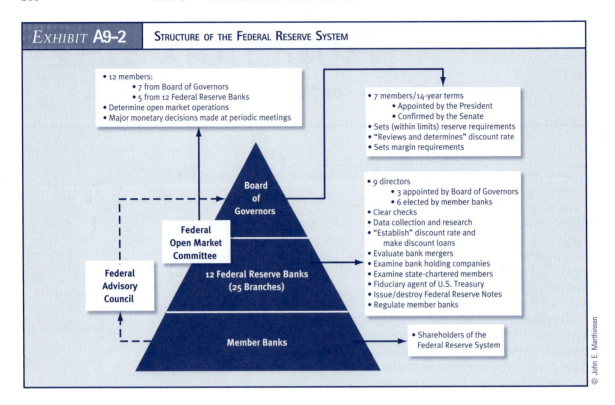

EXHIBIT **A9-2**   STRUCTURE OF THE FEDERAL RESERVE SYSTEM

- 12 members:
  - 7 from Board of Governors
  - 5 from 12 Federal Reserve Banks
- Determine open market operations
- Major monetary decisions made at periodic meetings

- 7 members/14-year terms
  - Appointed by the President
  - Confirmed by the Senate
- Sets (within limits) reserve requirements
- "Reviews and determines" discount rate
- Sets margin requirements

Board of Governors

Federal Open Market Committee

- 9 directors
  - 3 appointed by Board of Governors
  - 6 elected by member banks
- Clear checks
- Data collection and research
- "Establish" discount rate and make discount loans
- Evaluate bank mergers
- Examine bank holding companies
- Examine state-chartered members
- Fiduciary agent of U.S. Treasury
- Issue/destroy Federal Reserve Notes
- Regulate member banks

Federal Advisory Council

12 Federal Reserve Banks (25 Branches)

Member Banks

- Shareholders of the Federal Reserve System

© John E. Marthinsen

BOARD OF GOVERNORS

The Fed's major powers are concentrated in the hands of its seven-member Board of Governors. Board members are nominated by the president of the United States and confirmed by the Senate. They serve 14-year, nonrenewable terms and are supposed to represent a healthy cross section of the agricultural, commercial, financial, and industrial interests of the United States, as well as its geographic regions.[35] To promote these goals, no two governors may come from the same Federal Reserve district.

The governors' terms are staggered; so, in the absence of early retirement or death, a president can appoint only one governor every two years (terms expire on January 31). The chair and vice chair of the board are chosen by the president from the seven board members and, thereafter, confirmed by the Senate. They hold these positions for four years, and their terms may be renewed.

Among the most important board powers is its authority to set (within limits determined by Congress) the reserve requirements of all banks in the United States. The board also "reviews and determines" the discount rate,

---

[35] Even though each Board of Governors member is allowed only one, nonrenewable, 14-year term, he or she can serve out the remainder of someone else's unexpired term and thereby remain on the board for more than 14 years.

which is a power that is superior to the 12 Federal Reserve Banks' power to "establish" the discount rate. The Board of Governors also has the power to set margin requirements on the purchase of securities, approve bank mergers and applications for new bank-related business, as well as supervise foreign banks operating in the United States.

The chair of the Fed has special powers because he or she is the spokesperson for the system as a whole and is responsible for advising the president of the United States on monetary policy matters.

12 FEDERAL RESERVE BANKS

The 12 Federal Reserve Banks and their 25 branches are the operating arms of the Federal Reserve System. As a group, they are the second most powerful tier of the system. Each Federal Reserve Bank is managed by nine directors, three of whom are appointed by the Board of Governors, and six of whom are elected by the member banks. Of the six elected directors, three must be bankers, and the other three must be leaders in the agricultural, business, consumer, or labor sectors.

The major function of the Federal Reserve Banks is to administer the monetary policies of the Board of Governors and/or Federal Open Market Committee (discussed shortly). Among their other responsibilities are:

- acting as the fiscal agent of the U.S. Treasury[36];
- allowing or disallowing bank mergers, acquisitions, and control changes by state member banks, bank holding companies, and foreign banks;
- clearing checks and promoting the efficient handling of checks;
- collecting economic data and conducting research that is related to monetary policy and business conditions;
- evaluating bank applications for new lines of business;
- evaluating bank merger proposals;
- examining bank holding companies;
- holding reserves of depository institutions;
- implementing and monitoring statutes that protect consumers in credit and deposit transactions, as well as enforcing rules to protect bank secrecy and to guard against money laundering;
- moving cash (Federal Reserve Notes and coins) into and out of the U.S. banking system; and
- supervising, examining, and regulating members of the Federal Reserve System, Edge Act[37] and agreement corporations, as well as U.S. offices of foreign banks.[38]

Exhibit A9-3 shows a map of the United States with the boundaries of the 12 Federal Reserve Banks. Notice that these districts are not the same

---

[36] The Fed issues and redeems government securities, administers interest payments on government debt, manages debt repayments, and administers tax collections and redemptions.

[37] Edge Act corporations are federally chartered U.S. corporations, which are set up to stimulate international trade. The activities of these corporations are focused on international business transactions.

[38] Regulation of U.S. operations of foreign banks is done in conjunction with the OCC.

| EXHIBIT A9-3 | MAP OF THE FEDERAL RESERVE DISTRICTS |

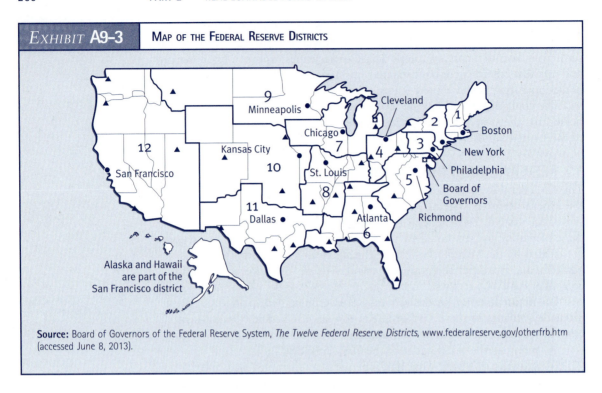

Source: Board of Governors of the Federal Reserve System, *The Twelve Federal Reserve Districts*, www.federalreserve.gov/otherfrb.htm (accessed June 8, 2013).

geographic size. The reason for this apparent gerrymandering is because, in 1913, Congress wanted 12 districts of approximately equal *financial* strength. Conditions have changed since 1913, but the geographic boundaries have not (except for the addition of Alaska and Hawaii to the San Francisco Fed's region). Today, despite its relatively small geographic size, the Federal Reserve Bank of New York is by far the most powerful district bank in the United States. This financial strength is a result of its proximity to New York City, one of the main financial centers of the world.

FEDERAL OPEN MARKET COMMITTEE

To understand U.S. monetary policy, one must understand the Federal Open Market Committee (FOMC), which is the group that makes virtually all the important monetary decisions in the U.S. monetary system. The FOMC meets eight times a year (about once every six weeks). Its voting members are composed of the seven Board of Governors members and five presidents of the 12 Federal Reserve Banks. As there are 12 Federal Reserve Bank presidents and only five voting positions for the Federal Reserve Banks, these presidents serve on a rotating basis. Only the president of the New York Federal Reserve Bank serves as a permanent member of the FOMC. This permanent-member status is justified not only because the New York Fed is the largest and most powerful Federal Reserve Bank, but also because open market operations and foreign exchange market intervention are normally conducted from the New York Fed.

Meetings of the FOMC are closed to the public, but an announcement is made immediately after each one (around 2:15 P.M.) regarding policy changes (e.g., the federal funds rate target or discount rate) and regarding the Fed's views on the risks associated with achieving its long-term monetary goals. This announcement also divulges the votes of each FOMC member. The minutes of each FOMC meeting are made public about six weeks after it is held.[39]

FOMC meetings have become so important in formulating U.S. monetary policy that all 12 presidents of the Federal Reserve Banks attend, even though only five have voting power. From this meeting, a "directive" is issued, which outlines the Federal Reserve's monetary policy goals. This directive is sent to the New York Federal Reserve Bank where open market operations and foreign exchange market intervention policies are implemented.

MEMBER BANKS

The final major tier of the Federal Reserve System is made up of approximately 2,100 member banks (see Exhibit A9-4). These financial institutions are the stockholders of their district Federal Reserve Banks. When a bank (national or state) joins the Federal Reserve System, it is required to buy stock of the Federal Reserve district in which it is located. This stock has no voting rights, and it earns a legislated annual dividend of 6%.

FEDERAL ADVISORY COUNCIL

The Federal Advisory Council (FAC) is a rather weak group within the Federal Reserve System. Each of the 12 Federal Reserve District Banks can choose one banker for the FAC. The council's responsibility is to meet with the Board of Governors at least four times each year and provide advice on any matter within the board's jurisdiction.

[39] Federal Reserve Bank of Richmond, *FAQs*, http://www.richmondfed.org/faqs/fomc/ (accessed June 8, 2013).

Appendix 9-3

Who Controls the Fed?

When Congress created the Federal Reserve System in 1913, it wanted a central bank whose daily activities would be largely independent from the President and Congress, but at the same time, it wanted a monetary authority that could be held accountable for its actions. Now, in the twenty-first century, about 100 years after the Fed was created, who controls the Fed?

CONGRESSIONAL AUTHORITY OVER THE FED

Fed decisions do not have to be ratified by Congress, and members of the Board of Governors cannot be removed for reasons connected to their monetary decisions. As a result, Congress has little daily control over the Fed. Of course, the Fed must operate within the laws and objectives of the Federal Reserve Act that created it.

On a grander scale, Congress created the Fed; so Congress has the ultimate power to abolish it, change its mandate, or alter the rules governing its behavior. But such changes would require acts of Congress, and on a practical level, they would be very hard to pass.

Aside from its ultimate authority to abolish the Fed or to change its mandate, Congress has a small degree of influence over the Fed by means of its confirmation hearings for new Board of Governors members. Congress also has oversight authority, as the Fed must report annually to the Speaker of the House of Representatives and twice annually to the banking committees of Congress. In these meetings, the chair of the Fed explains future plans for monetary policy in the context of evolving economic conditions and fiscal policy goals.

Congress has no financial power (i.e., often called "power of the purse") over the Fed. In fact, the Fed earns billions of dollars annually in profits, most of which is returned to the U.S. Treasury. These earnings are the net proceeds from fees earned by the Fed from the services it offers to banks (e.g., check clearing and funds transfers), seigniorage (i.e., profits from the difference between the face value of money and its printing costs), and the interest earned on the Fed's assets, such as U.S. government securities, discount loans, and foreign currency investments. Currently, the only significant financial power that Congress has over the Fed is the ability to set the salaries of Board of Governors members.[40]

---

[40] In 2012, the salary of the chairman was $199,700, and the salary of the other Board members (including the vice chairman) was $179,700. See Federal Reserve Bank of Richmond, *FAQs*, http://www.richmondfed .org/faqs/bog/ (accessed June 8, 2013).

PRESIDENTIAL AUTHORITY OVER THE FED

Decisions of the Fed do not have to be approved or ratified by the president of the United States, and members of the Board of Governors cannot be removed by the president for their monetary decisions. The president nominates members of the Board of Governors, and he or she appoints the chair and vice chair, but beyond these powers, the executive branch of the government exerts little influence over the Fed's policies. Barring early departures, a new member of the Board of Governors is chosen every two years, which means a president is empowered to choose two members during a four-year term. As a result, the president is prevented from packing the Fed with governors who will be sympathetic to his or her fiscal policies and who will implement accommodative monetary changes that may not be in the best interest of the nation. Moreover, the 14-year terms of Board of Governors members permit tenure of office that is well beyond the president's occupancy and therefore reduces any feelings of political loyalty or obligation.

MEMBER BANK AUTHORITY OVER THE FED

Member banks have the least control over the Fed. Even though they are shareholders of their district Federal Reserve Banks, stock ownership is more a condition of membership in the Federal Reserve System than it is a property right. Fed shares have no voting rights; they cannot be sold, traded, or pledged as collateral, and their annual dividend return is limited by law.

AUDITING THE FED

The financial accounts of the Federal Reserve Banks and Board of Governors are audited regularly by the Fed's permanent internal audit staff. To ensure the process is impartial and reliable, outside audits are also conducted by independent auditors and the General Accounting Office.[41] The Office of Inspector General of the Board of Governors can also audit the Fed's accounts. Recent legislation amended the United States Code to make these audits more transparent, comprehensive, timely, and accessible. The goal was (and is) to make the Fed more open and accountable to Congress.[42] These bills were years in the brewing, but the issues surrounding them came to a boil relatively recently as a result of the massive Fed assistance given to undisclosed U.S. and foreign financial intermediaries during the Great Recession (2007–2009). To ensure independence from political influence, Fed audits (to date) have covered operations, such as the discount window, funding sources, open market operations, and foreign bank agreements. They have not included audits of monetary policy and transactions the Fed performs for foreign central banks.

---

[41] Federal Reserve Bank of New York, How the Federal Reserve Is Audited, http://www.newyorkfed.org/about thefed/fedpoint/fed35.html (accessed July 9, 2013).

[42] Legislation was initiated and passed between 2009 and 2012 (e.g., *The Federal Reserve Transparency Act of 2009*, *Federal Reserve Sunshine Act of 2009*, and *Federal Reserve Transparency Act of 2012*).

POWERS OF THE MEDIA OVER THE FED

Even though the Fed enjoys statutory independence from outside influences, pressure and persuasion from the media and vested interest groups can (and does) influence its actions and should not be underestimated. Clear evidence of such pressure occurs when the nation is suffering from severe recessions, such as the ones experienced by the United States in 1981, 1982, and from 2007 to 2009 (e.g., the Great Recession). It also occurs when a nation's currency value rises substantially, as it did in the United States between 1980 and 1985.

Appendix 9-4
A Brief History of the Federal Reserve System

The Fed was created in 1913, just two days before Christmas, and it began operations in 1914. From an international perspective, the Fed was a relative newcomer to the central banking scene, having been created more than a century and a quarter after the U.S. Constitution was signed.

U.S. CONSTITUTION (1787)

Why did the United States wait so long to create a central bank? It is frequently forgotten that the U.S. Constitution did not create a central bank, just as it did not create a common currency, treasury, or federal banking system. What it created in 1787 was a common market and political union among the 13 original U.S. colonies. The Constitution's main purpose was to ensure the free flow of goods and resources (e.g., labor) across state borders, as well as to define and limit the powers of the federal government. It was not until the 1860s that the United States had anything close to a common currency and not until 1913 that the nation had a real central bank.

Because the U.S. Constitution did not explicitly empower the federal government with the ability to charter banks and regulate the issuance of paper money, it was assumed that states had permission to do so.[43] As a result, early U.S. banking history is mainly a story about state banks competing vigorously against each other, with no central bank or national government interference.

At that time, each bank printed its own money (i.e., banknotes), the value of which varied with factors such as a bank's reputation and the distance a banknote traveled from the bank that issued it.

FIRST AND SECOND BANKS OF THE UNITED STATES (1791 AND 1816)

Two attempts were made to create a federal bank, but each of them ended in disappointment. In 1791, the Federalists (led by Alexander Hamilton) convinced Congress to create the Bank of the United States. It was given a 20-year charter and a mandate to manage the nation's war debt, help finance federal budget deficits, and take the first steps toward creating a common currency. The bank was also created to provide the government with a fiscal agent (i.e., a taxing and paying agent).

---

[43] See John C. Edmunds and John E. Marthinsen, *Wealth by Association: Global Prosperity through Currency Unification* (Westport, CT: Praeger, 2003), chap. 5.

In contrast to the U.S. Federal Reserve, which is a banker's bank, the Bank of the United States competed directly with state banks by issuing its own banknotes, lending, purchasing securities, and taking deposits. It was relatively well managed, efficient, and government supported. As a result, the Bank of the United States grew rapidly and enjoyed a wide geographic reach relative to state banks.

With growth in size came ascension to power, and the Bank of the United States used this power to enforce monetary discipline on the relatively smaller and unevenly regulated state banks. The restrictive monetary forces that the Bank of the United States exerted on state banks were not authorized by Congress, but they were effective. One method used by the bank was accepting state banknotes only if they were backed by specie (e.g., gold). The bank also set up accounts in numerous state banks and then tested the soundness of these banks by massively withdrawing deposits and demanding to be paid in specie. The threat of such large redemptions put substantial pressure on state banks to act prudently.

A community of vested interest groups converged on Congress to oppose renewing the bank's charter in 1811. State bank owners were decidedly against renewal because the bank's enforcement powers reduced state bank profits. But there were other opposition groups as well. About 80% of the Bank of the United States' original funding came from foreign sources; therefore, a group of vocal opponents saw in the bank a loss of national autonomy. In addition, there were constructionists, who felt the U.S. Constitution did not give Congress the power to charter federal banks. The strength of these opposition groups was enough to defeat (by one vote) the Bank of the United States' charter renewal.

From 1811 to 1816, the United States relied solely on state banks, but in 1816, a federal charter for the Second Bank of the United States was passed. The bank was created (in large part) to regain some of the financial discipline that had been lost since the (First) Bank of the United States' charter was revoked. Like the (First) Bank of the United States, the Second Bank of the United States had a 20-year charter. It lent to the public, purchased securities, took deposits, issued its own banknotes, and became the fiscal agent of the U.S. government.

The Second Bank of the United States grew rapidly and soon had considerable financial clout. As a result, it began to discipline state banks in ways reminiscent of the (First) Bank of the United States. Due to the power it wielded, the Second Bank of the United States created a coalition of enemies that, in 1836, had enough power to block the renewal of its charter.

NATIONAL BANKING ACTS (1863–1865)

It was not until the 1860s that a national banking system was established in the United States. The Banking Acts of 1863–1865 were passed to create a banking system that would help finance the needs of the Northern states during the Civil War. To this end, they created national banks, which would serve as a marketplace for the federal government's newly issued bonds.

The acts also addressed some of the financial shortcomings of the rapidly growing state banks.

One goal of the National Banking Acts was to keep bank risks within tolerable limits and to ensure that these financial intermediaries were liquid and solvent. Therefore, the Acts more carefully controlled the quality of bank capital and assets (e.g., loans), and they subjected banks to stricter supervision, examination, reporting, and reserve requirements. For the first time in U.S. history, a regulator (the OCC) was established with a mandate to administer the national banking laws and to charter national banks, using transparent criteria rather than the often nebulous acts of state legislatures.

Even though the National Banking Acts alleviated many of the problems associated with unevenly regulated state banking systems, they created some of their own. One of the main difficulties related to the inflexibility of the U.S. money supply during times of economic expansion and contraction. Because banks could not pool their reserves, they were incapable of helping other financial institutions (or regions) in need of short-term liquidity or assisting the entire banking system in times of overall liquidity shortages.

At that time, the U.S. money supply was backed either by precious metals (e.g., gold and silver) or by federal government securities. The problem was there was no assurance that the quantities of these metals and government securities would fluctuate with the economy's needs. The supply of specie to the United States fluctuated with international production rates and balance of payments conditions, and the supply of government securities fluctuated with U.S. federal deficits.

After 1865, economic panics in the United States became regular occurrences. An especially severe economic recession in 1893 exposed some of the major flaws in the U.S. banking system and the need for financial reform. But it was not until the Panic of 1907 that bank reform in the United States moved forward. In 1907, bank-financed speculation in the stock market led to banking failures and runs on numerous other banks. About a dozen New York City banks were forced to put a temporary freeze on payments. As a result, Congress requested a comprehensive review of the U.S. monetary system. The review was conducted by the National Monetary Commission, and from its recommendations, the Federal Reserve System was born.

FEDERAL RESERVE SYSTEM (1913)

In 1913, the Fed was created mainly to (1) speed national check clearing, (2) serve as a "lender of last resort" for banks in need of short-term liquidity and to function as a "lender of last resort" for the banking system as a whole, (3) improve supervision of the banking system, and (4) become the fiscal agent of the U.S. Treasury.

In the beginning, the Federal Reserve System did not have significant discretionary powers over the domestic money supply. In fact, the Fed's mandate did not include macroeconomic goals, such as full employment, balance of payments equilibrium, or exchange rate stability. Rather, the central bank was supposed to act like a passive reservoir that automatically increased or decreased the nation's money supply as the economy expanded or contracted.

It is for this reason the word *bank* is not found in the Federal Reserve's name. In fact, someone unfamiliar with the United States and its central bank might think, by its name, that the Federal Reserve was a place to hunt rather than the center of U.S. monetary power.

To guard against the creation of a strong, centralized monetary authority, Congress created 12 Federal Reserve Banks of relatively equal financial strength. In the beginning, the locus of power in the Federal Reserve System was with the 12 Federal Reserve Banks. It was not in Washington, D.C. and clearly not with the moneyed interests on the East Coast.

Having 12 Federal Reserve districts was supposed to ensure that bank regulators and bank regulations would be sensitive to differing regional needs. The fear was that a single central bank located somewhere on the East Coast (e.g., in New York City or Washington, D.C.) would dictate monetary policies appropriate only for a portion of the country, with little regard for the needs of the nation as a whole. Of course, today the idea of having 12 separate Federal Reserve Banks with differing monetary policies is whimsical because any differences in dollar interest rates quickly would be arbitraged away. Nevertheless, that was the intention of Congress when it created the Federal Reserve System.

Today's Fed is very different from the one Congress envisioned in 1913, and the change can be attributed largely to the Great Depression. A string of banking acts was passed in the early 1930s that changed the Fed from a decentralized and passive monetary authority to a centralized and active one with preemptive monetary authority to offset unwelcome events. In addition, the banking acts of the 1930s empowered the seven-person Board of Governors with control over all the key monetary tools of the Federal Reserve System.

THE FED SINCE WORLD WAR II

Since World War II, legislation has percolated through the U.S. Congress, on a number of occasions, attempting to make the Fed more transparent and accountable. Perceived regulatory mistakes and financial excesses that caused the Great Recession of 2007–2009 put the Fed under intense scrutiny. Many criticized the Fed for its lack of regulatory foresight and control. During and after the Great Recession, the Fed came under another round of scrutiny due to its massive increase of the U.S. monetary base and the perceived cloak of financial secrecy that some felt surrounded the Fed's assistance to U.S. and foreign banks.

In the future, tension between political representatives and the Federal Reserve will continue the tug-of-war contest between accountability and independence. Due to the Great Recession, the pendulum clearly swung toward accountability. New legislation was passed and more is sure to come, but the lasting effect of this (or any) new legislation will be in the specific regulations that govern central bank behavior, and these are still being determined and promulgated.

Appendix 9-5
Central Banks Around the World

There has been a clear global trend toward increasing central banks' independence from governments and ensuring that their operations and decisions are as transparent as possible.[44] The Federal Reserve is one of the most independent central banks in the world.[45] In some countries, such as England,[46] Japan,[47] and the United States, this independence is due to government legislation, but in other countries, such as Canada,[48] the movement toward greater central bank independence has been more informal and evolutionary in nature.

In Appendix 9-3, "Who Controls the Fed?," we discussed the ways in which the U.S. Federal Reserve System is independent from politicians, media, and vested interests. The same is true for many other developed nations. For instance, the ECB, which began operations (along with the European System of Central Banks) in January 1999, is among the most independent central banks in the world. In fact, the ECB is considered by many to be more independent than the Fed because its monetary authority cannot be abolished or its mandate changed by legislation. For changes of this nature to take place in the EMU, all member nations must agree to amend the 1992 Maastricht Treaty.

The SNB is another example of a highly independent central bank. Established in 1907, the Swiss National Banking Act mandates SNB attention to price stability, while taking into consideration the condition and development of the Swiss economy.[49] Despite this legislation, then SNB has felt strong external pressures from media and political arenas. For example, from 2010 to 2012 substantial exchange rate movements and strong Swiss franc appreciation forced SNB to intervene in the foreign exchange markets in response to complaints from exporters and politicians, as well as a rising tide of unemployed. External pressures are also evident in the selection and appointment

---

[44] Events in Japan during 2012 and 2013 ran counter to this trend.

[45] Of the major central banks, only the ECB and SNB have higher levels of independence than the U.S. Federal Reserve System.

[46] In 1997, the Chancellor of the Exchequer gave the Bank of England the power to change domestic interest rates. The government retained the authority to overrule the Bank of England's actions in extreme economic circumstances, but for all practical purposes exerting such authority is unlikely to occur.

[47] In 1998, the BoJ was granted more independence from the Ministry of Finance.

[48] In Canada, the government still has ultimate authority over monetary policy, but in practice, this responsibility has been given to the Bank of Canada.

[49] See Swiss National Bank, National Bank Act, http://www.snb.ch/en/iabout/snb/legal/id/snb_legal_law/3 (accessed June 8, 2013).

process of central bank members; it can also play an important role in their resignation.[50]

Exhibit A9-4 lists the Web sites of 31 central banks around the world. Accessing them opens the door to a wealth of information about the history and structure of these central banks, their goals and functions, and their methods of implementing monetary policies.

EXHIBIT A9-4	CENTRAL BANKS AROUND THE WORLD	
COUNTRY	**CENTRAL BANK**	**WEB SITE**
1 Algeria	Bank of Algeria	http://www.bank-of-algeria.dz/
2 Argentina	Central Bank of the Republic of Argentina	http://www.bcra.gov.ar/index_i.htm
3 Australia	Reserve Bank of Australia	http://www.rba.gov.au/
4 Brazil	Central Bank of Brazil	http://www.bcb.gov.br/?english
5 Canada	Bank of Canada	http://www.bankofcanada.ca
6 China	People's Bank of China	http://www.pbc.gov.cn/english
7 Colombia	Bank of the Republic of Colombia	http://www.banrep.gov.co/index_eng.html
8 European Monetary Union	European Central Bank	http://www.ecb.int/home/
9 India	Reserve Bank of India	http://www.rbi.org.in/
10 Indonesia	Bank of Indonesia	http://www.bi.go.id/web/en/
11 Iraq	Central Bank of the Islamic Republic of Iran	http://www.cbi.ir/default_en.aspx
12 Iraq	Central Bank of Iraq	http://www.cbi.iq/index.php?pid=TheCbi
13 Israel	Bank of Israel	www.boi.org.il/en/
14 Japan	Bank of Japan	http://www.boj.or.jp/en/
15 Malaysia	Bank Negara Malaysia	http://www.bnm.gov.my/
16 Mexico	Bank of Mexico	http://www.banxico.org.mx/
17 New Zealand	Reserve Bank of New Zealand	http://www.rbnz.govt.nz/
18 Nigeria	Central Bank of Nigeria	http://www.cenbank.org/
19 Norway	Norges Bank	http://www.norges-bank.no/en/
20 Pakistan	State Bank of Pakistan	http://www.sbp.org.pk/
21 Peru	Central Reserve Bank of Peru	http://www.bcrp.gob.pe/home.html

(Continued)

[50] Henri B. Meier, John E. Marthinsen, and Pascal A. Gantenbein, *Swiss Finance: Capital Markets, Banking, and the Swiss Value Chain* (Hoboken, NJ: John Wiley & Sons, 2013).

EXHIBIT **A9–4**	**CONTINUED**		
	COUNTRY	**CENTRAL BANK**	**WEB SITE**
22	Russia	Central Bank of the Russian Federation	http://www.cbr.ru/eng/
23	Saudi Arabia	Saudi Arabian Monetary Agency	http://www.sama.gov.sa/sites/SAMAEN/Pages/Home.aspx
24	South Africa	South African Reserve bank	http://www.reservebank.co.za/
25	Switzerland	Swiss National Bank	http://www.snb.ch/en
26	Taiwan	Central Bank of China: Republic of China (Taiwan)	http://www.cbc.gov.tw/mp2.html
27	Thailand	Bank of Thailand	http://www.bot.or.th/english/Pages/BOTDefault.aspx
28	Turkey	Central Bank of the Republic of Turkey	http://www.tcmb.gov.tr/yeni/eng/
29	United Kingdom	Bank of England	http://www.bankofengland.co.uk
30	United States	Federal Reserve System	http://www.federalreserve.gov
31	Venezuela	Central Bank of Venezuela	http://www.bcv.org.ve/

Appendix 9-6

U.S. Dollar Facts and Figures[51]

More than 90% of all physical U.S. currency (i.e., cash) is in the form of Federal Reserve Notes. The rest is mainly coins, which are minted by the U.S. Treasury. If you read across the top of a U.S. dollar bill, you will see the words FEDERAL RESERVE NOTE, which means that it was issued by one of the 12 U.S. Federal Reserve Banks (see Exhibit A9-5). Today, the largest denomination dollar bill printed by the Federal Reserve is the $100 dollar bill, but in the past, gold-backed dollar bills as large as $100,000 were issued.

Even though Americans call their money "paper," it is actually made of cloth, with 25% linen, 75% cotton content, and tiny blue and red strands of synthetic fibers spread evenly throughout the bills. You might be surprised to learn that only about one-third of all dollar bills are held by U.S. residents; the rest is in foreign countries.

A one dollar bill (see Exhibit A9-5) has a rosette on the left side that shows the particular Federal Reserve Bank from which the bill was issued. In the center of the rosette is an assigned letter (A through L) for each of the 12 Federal Reserve Banks, and around the inside border of the rosette is the name of the Federal Reserve Bank that issued the bill. For example, the dollar bill

EXHIBIT A9–5	FEDERAL RESERVE NOTE (FRONT)

[51] "Fun Facts About Money," http://www.federalreserveeducation.org/about-the-fed/structure-and-functions/financial-services/fun_facts.cfm (accessed July 9, 2013).

EXHIBIT A9-6	FEDERAL RESERVE NOTE (BACK)

Source: "Fun Facts About Money," http://www.federalreserveeducation.org/about-the-fed/structure-and-functions/financial-services /fun_facts.cfm (accessed December 6, 2013).

shown in Exhibit A9-5 has B in the rosette, which means it was issued by the New York Fed.

The U.S. Bureau of Printing and Engraving prints about 26 million Federal Reserve notes each day. These notes have a nominal value of about $907 million, and producing them requires about 9.7 tons of ink. Each bill costs about 6.4 cents to manufacture, but it is still worth the denomination printed on the bill (e.g., $1, $5, $10, $20, or $100).

Even though dollar bills are printed in Washington, D.C. and Fort Worth, Texas, by the U.S. Bureau of Printing and Engraving, the Federal Reserve Banks act as conduits through which they are funneled into and out of the economy. A tour of the Federal Reserve Bank nearest your home will convince you that new dollar bills are issued by the Fed, and the old and used ones are destroyed by the Fed as well. In fact, Federal Reserve Banks give visitors a small, plastic bag of shredded money before they leave the tour.

The average life of a Federal Reserve Note depends upon its denomination, which determines the frequency of use.[52] About 45% of the notes printed each year are $1 bills. Of those newly printed one dollar bills, 95% are used to replace worn-out old notes.

The United States has become an increasingly litigious country, especially in matters involving the separation of church and state; so it is an interesting curiosity to many that the $1 bill continues to have "In God We Trust" on the back, and "ANNUIT COEPTIS" ("God favored our undertaking") appears just above the pyramid (see Exhibit A9-6). The motto "In God We Trust" appeared first on the dollar bill in 1963.

---

[52] A $1 bill lasts 21 months; $5 bill last 16 months; $10 bill lasts 18 months; $20 bill lasts for 2 years; $50 bill lasts 4.5 years, and $100 bill lasts 7.5 years.

Chapter 10

The Economics of Virtual Currencies

INTRODUCTION

What is virtual money, and how is it different from real money? The answer
to this question is one of the keys to unraveling the potential impact this rapidly growing type of currency has on the price and financial stability of many
nations around the world. Real money includes the physical notes and coins
that countries designate as legal tender,[1] such as dollar bills and quarters in
the United States. It also includes certain types of electronic money, such as
checking accounts, which are denominated in the same currency units as the
physical notes and have a fixed and formal connection to the legal tender. For
example, dollar checking accounts have the same denomination and value as
dollar bills. Virtual currencies are a type of electronic money, like checking
accounts, but are (so far) unregulated, internationally distributed, generally
disconnected from familiar financial intermediaries, and lacking any formal
connection to a nation's legal tender.

> Virtual currencies are a
> type of electronic money
> that is unregulated (so
> far), internationally dis-
> tributed, generally dis-
> connected from familiar
> financial intermediaries,
> and lacking any formal
> connection to a nation's
> legal tender.

   When virtual currencies were in their infancy, they were used almost
exclusively to purchase digital items in online worlds. Participation was limited to a handful of users with large mainframe computers and connections to
a fledgling communications network called the Internet. A fascination developed around virtual worlds due, in large part, to their limitless disregard for
familiar laws of physics, chemistry, and biology.[2] Users could create personal
avatars and live vicariously in worlds where life did not depend on food,
drink, or sleep, and natural laws of gravity, motion, and relativity did not
apply.[3] In rapid order, the breadth and depth of these online markets grew to
levels that few anticipated. Industry sources report that the sale of virtual
items, worldwide, generated revenues of $2 billion in 2007, $7 billion in
2010, and was forecasted to reach $15 billion by 2014.[4]

---

[1] "Legal tender" status means that *creditors* must accept the currency in payment for debts. It does not
require merchants (or the government) to do so.

[2] These environments are often called massively multiplayer online role-playing games (MMORPGs), multiple-
user domains (MUDs), and multiple online environments (MOEs).

[3] Virtual games are usually played using personal avatars, which are electronic images of individuals that can
be manipulated by a computer user. By contrast, social networks, typically, require no avatars. In Sanskrit,
"avatar" means "a form of self."

[4] Facebook, Inc., *United States Securities and Exchange Commission, Form S-1: Registration Statement*,
p. 4, http://www.sec.gov/Archives/edgar/data/1326801/000119312512034517/d287954ds1.htm (accessed
June 19, 2013).

This chapter distinguishes among four types of virtual currency systems (VCSs), each having a different level of connection to and impact on a nation's money supply and macroeconomic markets (i.e., real goods and services, real loanable funds, and foreign exchange markets).[5] The most detached and benign of them is virtual currency system #1 (VCS#1), and the most integrated and potentially disruptive or beneficial is VCS#4.

VCS#1 is a self-contained cyber-community whose virtual currency unit (VCU1) has no direct link to the real world. VCU1 cannot be bought or sold, and its supply increases only if users earn it by means of online performance or if issuers transfer VCU1 as gifts or promotions.

VCS#2 permits a one-way flow of funds from real to virtual currencies but not a reverse flow. Users can purchase VCU2 with real-world money using credit cards and other payment systems[6] as well as cash, but they cannot reverse the flow and repurchase a real-world currency. Zynga's currency, Gold, is an example of VCU2.

VCS#3 allows for the two-way flow of funds between virtual and real currencies. The limitation of VCU3 is that it can be spent only in its particular virtual world because merchants in the real world do not accept it. An example of a VCU3 currency is the Linden dollar, which is used in *Second Life*, a three-dimensional virtual world developed by Linden Lab.

Finally, the virtual currencies in VCS#4 can be freely bought, sold, and used for both virtual and real-world transactions.[7] They may float freely relative to other currencies, such as the Bitcoin, or have a fixed exchange rate, such as the Chinese Q-Coin once had relative to the Chinese yuan.[8]

Which of these four VCU currencies, if any, should be included in a nation's money supply? Do they affect real-world economic activity? Could their excessive creation cause unwanted inflation, encourage speculation, and/or spur online criminal activities (e.g., gambling, black markets, and tax evasion)? Should they be regulated? And if they should be regulated, are current central bank and government controls capable of doing so?

Many governments around the world have begun to pay closer attention to virtual currency transactions because their growth is rapid and, in some cases, almost impossible to trace. Bringing daylight and transparency to virtual transactions is viewed as a path toward reducing criminality and tax evasion.

Private businesses have also begun to integrate themselves into virtual communities by using them to market real-world wares. In doing so, they have tapped into potential goldmines of marketing alternatives that integrate

---

[5] Because there is no standard nomenclature to classify different virtual currency systems and their currencies, VCS#1, VCS#2, VCS#3, and VCS#4 are used in this text to refer to alternative virtual currency systems, and VCU1, VCU2, VCU3, and VCU4 are used to refer to the respective currencies of those systems.

[6] Among them are PayPal, mobile phones, Western Union's QuickPay, TravelersExpress' MoneyGram, and SafetyPay.

[7] Loyalty programs, such as OpenTable has for restaurants, allow users to earn points that are redeemable at businesses. Loyalty programs are not classified here as virtual currencies, although there is no bright line that separates one from the other.

[8] Because of the impact Q-coins were thought to have on the Chinese economy, they were banned by the Chinese government in 2009.

virtual currencies with social media, sentiment and social mobility analysis, as well as gamification. Like a rollercoaster ride, the prospects are as potentially exciting and rewarding as they are dangerous and threatening—especially in the area of personal privacy.

THE BASICS

VIRTUAL CURRENCY SYSTEMS

Let's take a closer look at the four alternative VCSs to determine if any (or all) pose credible threats to a nation's price and financial stability, payment systems, and/or real-world end users.[9] Price stability is measured by a nation's or currency area's inflation rate and volatility relative to national policy targets. Financial stability is measured by a financial system's ability to endure and recover from external shocks. Payment systems should operate by providing the efficient and uninterrupted flow of funds between counterparties. Any threat to this reliability strikes at the heart of a currency's use as a medium of exchange. Finally, end-user risks are measured by the extent to which virtual currencies might increase defaults, delay payments, create illiquidity problems, incur market-based losses in value, and/or present legal hazards to those who use them.

> Alternative virtual currency systems have the potential to threaten a nation's price and financial stability, payment systems, and/or real-world end users.

Virtual Currency System #1 (VCS#1)

The VCU1s in VCS#1 have no functional links to real-world currencies, transactions, and/or their financial and economic systems. Users often pay a monthly subscription fee, which allows them to play online games or interact in online communities. These currencies cannot be purchased or sold and are acquired mainly by demonstrating online playing skills and/or accomplishing certain online tasks. Because VCU1 is used exclusively in a virtual world, it has no significant macroeconomic effects, and therefore, no material impact on a nation's price and financial stability, payment systems, and/or end users.

> VCU1 has no functional links to real-world currencies.

If VCU1 has any negative economic effects, they are likely to be in the excessive amount of time users spend in their virtual worlds (e.g., playing games instead of doing something more productive), but this is a criticism that might apply to any recreation or entertainment service. VCU1 might also hurt a nation by altering relative prices between the virtual and real worlds, thereby affecting consumer behavior, but this impact is likely to be very small.

Virtual Currency System #2 (VCS#2)

VCS#2 allows users to purchase a virtual currency (VCU2) with real-world money, but it does not permit reverse flows from VCU2 back into the real world. There are two major sources of VCU2 supply. First, users can earn it by demonstrating online skills or fulfilling certain online tasks. Second, issuers

> VCU2 permits the one-way flow of transactions from real to virtual currencies.

[9] See European Central Bank, *Virtual Currency Schemes: October 2012*, p. 37, http://www.ecb.europa.eu/pub/pdf/other/virtualcurrencyschemes201210en.pdf (accessed June 19, 2013).

can make periodic gifts, sales, or transfers to customers. Gold Coins used in Zynga's Farmville II[10] and Gils in Final Fantasy XI[11] are types of VCS#2 currency.

The purchase of a VCU2 currency is like the purchase of any entertainment service because it increases the online company's sales and raises the online company's checking account by the same amount it reduces customers' bank accounts. Therefore, these transactions have no net effect on a nation's money supply, monetary base, or demand for real goods and services. As a result, even though online companies have the ability to create as many (or few) VCU1s as they like, their money-creation powers are confined to the virtual world with little or no spillover to the real economy.

VIRTUAL CURRENCY SYSTEM #3 (VCS#3)

VCU3 permits the two-way flow of transactions between real and virtual currencies, but it is not accepted by real-world merchants.

The virtual currencies in VCS#3 allow free, two-way convertibility between virtual and real currencies at exchange rates that can be fixed or flexible. For the flexible exchange rate systems, users can benefit or suffer from fluctuations in virtual currency values, which may invite currency speculation.[12]

The major sources of VCU3 supply are the same as for VCU2, namely from users demonstrating online skills and/or task-fulfillment abilities and also from periodic gifts, sales, or transfers from the issuer companies. Another growing source of supply is from companies that use VCU3 to market their wares through online promotions

A Linden dollar (sometimes called a Linden), which is currency used in the online virtual world called *Second Life*, is good example of a VCU3 currency. Residents (16 years or older) interact with each other through personal avatars in this three-dimensional virtual world. Lindens are used to buy, sell, rent, and trade virtual items (e.g., artwork, buildings, entertainment, jewelry, and vehicles) with other *Second Life* residents. Linden dollars can be purchased with dollars (or other currencies) on the LindeX exchange, which was created by Linden Lab, and also on independent exchanges. Linden dollars can also be converted into U.S. dollars (or other currencies) at market-based rates on independent currency exchanges. *Second Life* also distributes Linden dollars (L\$300 each month) to premium subscribers, and private companies distribute them through marketing promotions that offer Lindens as rewards.

The Linden's value is not freely fluctuating but rather managed by an implicit *Second Life* currency board. This conversion ability offers opportunities for users to profit from their online activities. In particular, they can buy, sell, deal, develop, and speculate in their online worlds. For example, users can earn capital gains on virtual real estate purchases, cash out by selling their appreciated properties for Lindens, and then sell their Lindens for a real-world currency. The stakes can be high, with some virtual items created on *Second Life* selling for

---

[10] Homepage, Farmville II, www.zynga.com (accessed June 22, 2013).

[11] Homepage, Final Fantasy XI, http://www.ige.com/ffxi/gil/finalfantasyxius_en.html (accessed June 21, 2013).

[12] In January 2010, the Supreme Court of South Korea upheld a lower court ruling that allowed the sale of online virtual assets for real-world currencies. The ruling acquitted two gamers and opened the door to a freer flow between the virtual and real worlds. Yoen ChoulWoong, "The Sale of Online-Game Virtual Assets is Legal?" *Korea IT Times*, January 12, 2010, http://www.koreaittimes.com/story/6661/sale-online-game-virtual-assets-legal (accessed June 21, 2013).

thousands of dollars. A German resident, who operates under the avatar, Anshe Chung, became a millionaire selling virtual items on *Second Life*.[13]

Even though issuers have the power to create unlimited amounts of VCU3, they appear to pose little or no threat to a nation's price and financial stability. To see why, let's continue with our example of *Second Life*. When users try to cash out their capital gains by selling Linden dollars for real currencies (e.g., dollars, euros, or yen), their real-world checking accounts increase by the same amount as their counterparties' (i.e., the buyers of Lindens and sellers of real-world currencies') checking accounts fall. As a result, the net effect on the nation's money supply, monetary base, and demand for real goods and services is zero.

The implications of these conclusions are important. The total value of transactions has increased to the point where the *Second Life* environment would rank among the top 20 GDPs in the world. Nevertheless, it has no strong feedback effects on a nation's price and financial stability, payment systems, and/or risks to real-world users. This result is the same regardless of whether VCU3 has a fixed or floating exchange rate relative to real currencies. It is also indifferent to the level of financial sophistication, such as the type, number, and quality of interconnections among online financial intermediaries, their ability to borrow and lend the virtual currency, and the interest paid or earned (if any) on loans and deposits. Excessive creation of VCU3 may inflate the prices of virtual goods and services, but their effects appear to have no significant spillover effects on the real world.

The introduction of formal clearing systems among virtual currencies is only a matter of time. In fact, social media companies (e.g., Currency Connect[14]) are already being created to promote site registrations and link users of different virtual currencies. If successful, they will allow users to transfer and convert (all or a portion of) their virtual currencies from one site to another. Their hope is to increase site traffic and optimize the value of users' virtual currency holdings, but this service should have no impact on real-world currencies.

VIRTUAL CURRENCY SYSTEM #4 (VCS#4)

VCS#4 has an independent currency that can be freely bought, sold, and used for money transfers and outright purchases of goods and services in both the virtual and real worlds. The primary difference between VCU3 and VCU4 is acceptability. VCU4 is accepted by real-world merchants; VCU3 is not.

Acceptability gives VCU4 owners an ability to affect real-world demand without changing any real-world monetary aggregate measures (e.g., money supply or monetary base). The stealth nature of these virtual currencies is disconcerting because it can blunt or render ineffective a nation's monetary policies or confuse and distort the signals on which related policy decisions are made.

If virtual currencies grow swiftly and with reckless abandon, they might threaten a nation's inflation targets and redistribute income in undesired ways.

> VCU4 is an independent currency that can be freely bought, sold, and used for virtual and real-world transactions.

---

[13] Anonymous, *What Is Second Life?* http://secondlife.com/whatis/ (accessed June 22, 2013). Also see Samuel Greengard, "Social Games, Virtual Goods," *Communication of the ACM*, Volume 54, Number 4, April 2011, p. 21.

[14] Homepage, Currency Connect, http://www.currencyconnect.com/ (accessed June 13, 2013).

Online issuers of these currencies have the power to create and distribute them with no central bank restraints, reserve requirements, or system leakages that would weaken the deposit expansion multiplier (e.g., leakages into currency in circulation, savings deposits, and time deposits).[15] Theoretically, the money multiplier facing online suppliers of VCU4 is infinite, which probably exaggerates reality because it ignores both market and regulatory reactions.

Two other ways VCU4 currencies might affect economic activity are through their *substitution effects* and the impact they have on the velocity of money.[16] These effects relate to the uses to which virtual currencies are put and the extent to which they reduce the demand for legal tender.[17] If virtual currencies circulate side-by-side with their real-world counterparts, they might erode the real currencies' function as units of account. Similarly, if virtual currencies substitute for real-world currencies, a decline in real currency usage may cause the velocity of real money to fall and, with it, reduce measured GDP. The cause-and-effect implications are discomforting because a nation's measured GDP might fall even though its actual GDP (virtual-currency value plus real-world value) stays the same or rises.

Of the four VCSs, VCS#4 poses the greatest threat to a nation's price and financial stability, payment systems, and real-world users because:

- It is an unregulated currency that is not supervised by any central bank, banking commission, or deposit insurance company.
- If there is no central bank or other lender of last resort, the virtual currency may not withstand a severe liquidity crisis caused, for example, by massive virtual currency sales.
- VCU4 operates largely outside normal financial intermediaries and payment systems. In fact, VCS#4 has its own payment systems, much like retail ones that exist in the real world. Therefore, operational efficiency, security, and confidentiality are at the discretion of the issuer.[18]
- For many nations, the legality of VCU4 currencies is still uncertain.[19]

> Virtual currencies may have substitution effects that reduce the velocity of real money and diminish the use of real currencies as units of account.

---

[15] In April 2013, OpenCoin announced its intention to gain a foothold in the burgeoning virtual currency market by giving away 100 billion newly created "Ripples" in the hope that the currency would catch on as a medium of exchange and developers would create applications using it. Stephen Foley, "Virtual Currencies Threaten to Go Viral," *Financial Times*, April 26, 2013, http://www.ft.com/intl/cms/s/0/55733b80-addf-11e2-a2c7-00144feabdc0.html#axzz2X9aVsgqo (accessed June 24, 2013).

[16] The velocity of money is the average number of times money changes hands per year to purchase newly produced goods and services.

[17] Virtual currency transactions are also untraceable and unreported, but the substitution effects and velocity do not refer to these attributes.

[18] Bitcoin crossed into the real-world financial sector in 2013 by partnering its main currency exchange, Mt. Gox, with CoinLab, which "is dedicated to making any Bitcoins accessible and easy for use by everyone." See CoinLab, http://coinlab.com/ (accessed June 19, 2013). Also see Michael Burshteynm, "Bitcoin: FBI and FinCEN Weigh In," *Berkley Technology Law Journal*, May 2, 2013, http://btlj.org/2013/05/02/Bitcoin-fbi-and-fincen-weigh-in/ (accessed June 19, 2013).

[19] In June 2013, California's Department of Financial Institutions issued a cease and desist order against Bitcoin Foundation for allegedly engaging in a money transmission business without a state license or authorization. Substantial fines and imprisonment could follow. What made this court order particularly bewildering was that Bitcoin *Foundation* operated (presumably) as a nonprofit, Washington D.C.–based corporation without money transmission abilities. Jon Matonis, "Forbes, Bitcoin Foundation Receives Cease and Desist Order from California," http://www.forbes.com/sites/jonmatonis/2013/06/23/bitcoin-foundation-receives-cease-and-desist-order-from-california/ (accessed June 24, 2013).

- VCU4 is not legal tender, has no formal link to any nation's (or currency areas) official currency, has no intrinsic value, and is not backed by any precious metal, such as gold.
- VCU4 currencies are likely to come under increasing scrutiny for two reasons. First they appear to be a preferred medium of exchange for illegal users, such as criminals, fraudsters, money launderers, human traffickers, terrorists, and drug dealers. Second, they are capable of tarnishing the reputation of central banks and weakening their monetary powers.
- Users of VCU4 are vulnerable to rule changes by the issuing company and, ultimately, are exposed to the credit risk of the issuer.
- For flexible-rate VCU4 currencies, users are subject to market risks.

Currently, the risk of virtual currencies destabilizing any major nation's financial system or causing rampant inflation (or deflation) is quite small due to their diminutive size and the ability of governments and central banks to impose controls that harness their impact. At the end of 2011, the value of virtual currencies in the United States was estimated between $1.32 billion[20] and $7.0 billion.[21] By comparison, the narrowest U.S. money supply, M1, stood at $2.2 trillion, and M2 equaled $9.6 trillion, which meant virtual currencies were a relatively small fraction of M1 (i.e., 0.060% to 0.32%) and M2 (0.014% to 0.073%).

> Due to their small relative size, virtual currencies do not currently appear to threaten any nation's financial or economic system.

MACRO MEMO 10-1

Virtual Currencies and Anti–Money Laundering Rules

As for government powers over virtual currencies, many nations already have, in place, anti–money laundering rules that can be used to harness their effects. In March 2013, the Financial Crimes Enforcement Network (FinCEN) of the U.S. Treasury Department issued an interpretive *guidance* to clarify the rules regarding money service businesses that create, obtain, distribute, exchange, accept, and/or transmit virtual currencies.* This guidance covers both centralized and decentralized VCSs and focuses on (1) administrators, who issue and redeem virtual currencies; (2) money transmitters, who transfer them; and (3) exchangers, who convert virtual

currencies into real currencies or into other virtual currencies. Individuals who use virtual currencies to purchase goods or services (i.e., users) are not subject to FinCEN's registration, reporting, and record-keeping regulations. In short, FinCEN's guidance requires administrators, money transmitters, and exchangers to record and report any virtual currency transaction that exceeds $10,000—just as it requires other financial companies, such as Western Union.

*Financial Crimes Enforcement Network (FinCEN), "Application of FinCEN's Regulations to Persons Administering, Exchanging, or Using Virtual Currencies," *FIN-2013-G001*, March 19, 2013, http://fincen.gov/statutes_regs/guidance/html/FIN-2013-G001.html (accessed June 19, 2013).

---

[20] Helen Leggatt, "2011 Social Gaming Revenues to Exceed $1 Billion," *BizReport: Social Marketing*, July 8, 2011, http://www.bizreport.com/2011/07/2011-social-gaming-revenues-to-exceed-1billion.html (accessed June 22, 2013).

[21] Facebook, Inc., *United States Securities and Exchange Commission, Form S-1: Registration Statement*, p. 4, http://www.sec.gov/Archives/edgar/data/1326801/000119312512034517/d287954ds1.htm (accessed June 22, 2013). Also see, Justin Smith and Charles Hudson, *Inside Virtual Goods: The U.S. Virtual Goods Market 2011–2012*, http://www.insidenetwork.com/index.php?which=reports (accessed June 22, 2013).

ARE VIRTUAL CURRENCIES "MONEY"?

The level and growth rate of a nation's money supply are important economic indicators for central bankers, managers, politicians, and individuals who understand that the faster a money supply grows the greater the chances that inflation will follow. Before a nation's money supply can be controlled, it must be accurately defined, and this task is not as easy as it may first appear. A nation's money supply should include financial instruments that most directly affect residents' spending, but there are many different means of payment and financial institutions are constantly inventing new ones. To complicate matters, preferences for financial instruments vary from country-to-country. Most nations include coins and bills that are legal tender in their money supply definitions but, from there, determining where to draw the line is problematic. Should checking accounts be included? How about savings accounts? Time deposits? Money market mutual funds? Frequent flyer miles? Groupons? Should virtual currencies, such as Bitcoins and Linden dollars, be included?

THE FUNCTIONS OF MONEY

We learned in Chapter 6, "Monetary Aggregates: Measuring Money" that money has four major functions. It is a medium of exchange, store of value, unit of account, and standard of deferred payment. As a unit-of-account, money is the base measure in terms of which items are valued. As a medium-of-exchange, it facilitates trade because most people accept it and want the things that money can buy. Finally, money's role as a store-of-value and standard-of-deferred-payment are functions over time. Money should retain its value so it can be saved and used later, and it should also be a means of valuing contracts that are negotiated today and executed in the future. Any virtual currency that fulfills all of these functions and has a significant economic or financial impact can unequivocally be called "money."[22]

> Any virtual currency that fulfills all of the functions of money and has a significant economic or financial impact can be called "money."

SHOULD VIRTUAL MONEY BE PART OF A NATION'S MONEY SUPPLY?

Even if virtual currencies have all the functions of money, it does not mean central banks would or should include them in their money supply figures. Only if they exist in *significant* quantities and only if they have meaningful effects on spending should they be included. By these criteria, VCU1, VCU2, and VCU3 should, likely, be excluded from any official money supply measures because they have immaterial effects on nations' purchasing power and major macro markets. As for VCU4, the diminutive size of these currencies means that, *currently*, they are not strong candidates for inclusion.

Just because the virtual currency market is relatively small and the flow of spending is mainly from the real world to the cyber-world does not mean the

---

[22] Bitcoins have fluctuated in value from fewer than five cents to $230. One could argue whether or not a currency with such drastic volatility should be called "money," but then "currencies" such as the Zimbabwean dollar, Argentine peso, Hungarian pengö, and German mark have also fluctuated dramatically in value. A major difference is the Bitcoin's value fluctuated mainly due to changes in demand; these other currencies' values fluctuated mainly due to oversupply.

potential is absent for virtual currencies to (one day) play a significant role. While this market is still in its infancy, some segments are growing at 30% to 40% per year.[23] At such rates, they could gain considerable financial clout in a relatively short period of time.

Millions of people acquire virtual currencies daily and spend them freely. If these currencies remain in their computer-generated worlds, rapid increases in quantities may cause the prices of virtual items to rise, but they should not affect significantly any nation's real GDP, and their price changes should not be part of a nation's GDP price index or consumer price index. Unless inflationary pressures in the virtual world spill over, somehow, into the real world, they should not affect the nominal or relative prices of real-world goods and services and hardly impact the *measured* quality of our lives—but they could affect the quality of our unmeasured lives.

> If virtual currencies remain in their computer-generated worlds, they should not have significant effects on any nation's financial or economic system.

TAXING AND REGULATING VIRTUAL CURRENCY TRANSACTIONS

Until tax authorities figure out how the revenues from virtual currency transactions differ from Groupons, OpenTable points, frequent flier miles, and the bonus points offered by credit card companies, hotels and car rentals, enforceable taxation of many virtual transactions will continue to be problematic. Companies, like Coca-Cola and Wells Fargo, are already exploring online advertising promotions that allow customers to pay for products with virtual currencies. If it continues, this trend will cause the line between virtual currency transactions and real-world transactions to blur and fade. If virtual currencies continue their firebrand growth, fiscal authorities throughout the world will surely become more vigilant in their efforts to tax online earnings, but taxing anonymous, untraceable currency transactions will be a bit like lassoing clouds with a rope.

> Taxing virtual currency transactions is problematic because they are anonymous and almost untraceable.

The increasing uses of virtual money for real and virtual transactions raise interesting questions about taxation. Clearly, if taxpayers are able to hide their transactions by using virtual currencies, the government's ability to collect taxes would be decimated.

How invisible are virtual transactions? In general, any transactions that are recorded and stored on the books of a central clearing house, such as a bank, mutual fund, or *Second Life*, are visible, or they can be forced by the government to be made visible. Governments and central banks can shut down centralized systems. When these regulators search for the individuals responsible for running a centralized operation, they can start by locating the company, its address, and, afterward, the names and addresses of the individuals who run them—bringing these individuals to justice, if necessary, is often considerably more difficult.

---

[23] Sean Takahashi, "U.S. Virtual Goods Revenue on Facebook to Grow 32 Percent to $1.65 B in 2012," *Gamesbeat,* September 20, 2011, http://venturebeat.com/2011/09/20/u-s-virtual-goods-revenue-on-face book-to-grow-30-percent-to-1-65b-in-2012/ (accessed June 22, 2013). Patricio Robles, "Mobile Virtual Currency Market to Hit $4.8 bn by 2016," *Juniper Research,* March 20, 2012, http://econsultancy.com/us /blog/8645-mobile-virtual-currency-market-to-hit-4-4-8bn-by-2016-report (accessed June 22, 2013).

With decentralized, peer-to-peer VCSs, such as Bitcoin, there is no central clearing house or central operation to shut down. Transactions are individual-to-individual, laptop-to-laptop, and in the privacy of users' homes around the world. Because there are no centralized clearing house records, no incorporated companies to search, and no corporate executives to question, justice may be thwarted because there is no "it" to find, no "where" to locate, and no "them" to question. The most well-known decentralized, peer-to-peer currency is Bitcoin, which is covered in "**The Rest of the Story**" section of this chapter.

Countries, like China, have already had to deal with virtual currency issues that increased the demand for domestic goods and services. In the mid-2000s, China's game developer, Tencent, introduced the *Q-coin*, which was a virtual currency that was quickly accepted for a wide variety of virtual games *and* real-world transactions. Chinese officials became concerned that Q-coins might challenge the Chinese yuan's legitimacy, and these concerns were fueled when Q-coins spread to the underground world of prostitution and pornography.[24] As a result, the Chinese government banned their use in 2009.

VIRTUAL MONEY AND COMMON CURRENCIES

Starting in the early post–World War II period, major European countries overcame repeated obstacles and formed, in 1999, a common currency called the euro. Despite this success and irrespective of the many benefits a common currency has bestowed upon many member nations, there have been tradeoffs, and one of the major ones is the loss of national monetary independence. Countries such as Greece, Portugal, Ireland, Spain, and Italy, which were ardent initial proponents of the common currency, began to question their decisions during the 2007–2009 recession, and this self-reflection continued, in earnest, during the debt crises that followed from 2010 to 2013+. For some nations, the European Monetary Union (EMU) had become like Hotel California, where "you can check out any time you like, but you can never leave." A 2011 UBS study estimated that the cost to leave the euro currency area for weak EMU countries, like Greece, was as high as 40% to 50% of its GDP during the first year, with significant additional costs for years thereafter.[25] Similarly, the estimated cost of departure for strong countries, like Germany, was estimated to be as high as 20% to 25% of GDP during the first year, with collateral damage for years to come.[26]

Concerns about whether to adopt a fixed-rate, floating-rate, or common currency have not been confined to European nations. Currency systems across

---

[24] Samuel Greengard, "Social Games, Virtual Goods," *Communication of the ACM*, Volume 54, Number 4, April 2011, pp. 20, 21.

[25] The UBS report estimated that Greece would lose between €9,500 and €11,500 per person during the first year and €3,000 to €4,000 per person in subsequent years. Stephane Deo, Paul Donovan, and Larry Hathaway, "Euro Break-Up–The Consequences," *UBS Investment Research: Global Economic Perspectives*, September 6, 2011, pp. 1–21.

[26] The same UBS report estimated that if Germany were to leave the EMU, it would lose between €6,000 and €8,000 per person during the first year and €3,500 to €4,500 per person in subsequent years. Stephane Deo, Paul Donovan, and Larry Hathaway, "Euro Break-Up–The Consequences," *UBS Investment Research: Global Economic Perspectives*, September 6, 2011, pp. 1–21.

the world run the full spectrum of possibilities,[27] and now these same concerns are confronting the issuers of virtual currencies. In many ways, the current-day development of virtual currencies has mirrored the historic development of real-world currencies. In particular, as we move through the twenty-first century, real and virtual currencies seem to behave like large planets with strong gravitational forces pulling smaller planets into their orbits. In some cases, the weakest planets (currencies) have self-destructed or been destroyed, but in others, even the seemingly large planets have not survived (e.g., Facebook [FB] credits).

> There are many similarities between the development of real currencies and virtual currencies.

Some economists see the day when the world will have just three dominant international currencies (perhaps the dollar, euro, and yen or yuan). Others feel the world may, someday, have just one. Will virtual currencies follow a similar pattern? Are there net economic advantages (e.g., significant economies of scale) that come from adopting a common virtual currency or from fixing all virtual currencies to a widely used one? In "**The Rest of the Story**" section of this chapter, the part entitled "Comparing Virtual and U.S. Currency Evolution" traces the development of the U.S. currency system to show how it parallels the development of virtual currencies. In the following section, entitled "Currency Evolution: Facebook versus Zynga," the development of two virtual currencies is followed to show how they face many of the same costs, benefits, and potential issues as the development of real-world currencies.

THE REST OF THE STORY

BITCOINS

A wave of enthusiasm has surrounded the development of peer-to-peer, virtual currencies, and one of the leading providers is Bitcoin, the supplier and creator of the *Bitcoin*, which is a completely distributed (i.e., noncentralized) and anonymous digital currency. Bitcoins were developed for real-world uses. Some businesses have already agreed to accept them, and, others, such as Wikileaks, Freenet, Pioneer One, and LulzSec (an admitted hacking organization), have received donations denominated in Bitcoins.[28]

> Bitcoin is a peer-to-peer, noncentralized virtual currency, which allows anonymous and almost untraceable digital currency transactions.

Bitcoin was the 2009 inspiration of *Satoshi Nakamoto*, which is, a pseudonym because no such person (connected to Bitcoin) exists.[29] Satoshi could be a man, woman, or group of individuals located anywhere in the world. No one knows. As of October 2013, the developer of both this currency and sophisticated computer program that runs it has not been discovered. Some may ascribe a sinister or unsavory purpose to any currency whose founder and developer is anonymous. While this may be the case, such an assumption

---

[27] Virtually all international exchange rate arrangements are reported annually by the International Monetary Fund. See IMF "Report on Exchange Rate Arrangements and Exchange Restrictions: 2012," Table 1: De Facto Classification of Exchange Rate Arrangements and Monetary Policy Frameworks, April 30, 2012, http://www.imf.org/external/pubs/nft/2012/eaer/ar2012.pdf (accessed June 21, 2013).

[28] A review of Bitcoin can be found at: Reuben Grinberg, "Bitcoin: An Innovative Alternative Digital Currency," *Hastings Science & Technology Law Journal*, Volume 4, December 21, 2011, http://papers.ssrn.com/sol3/papers.cfm?abstract_id=1817857 (accessed March 20, 2012).

[29] The first published description of a Bitcoin was in 1998 by Wei Dai on the Cypherpunks mailing list.

Bitcoins can be used for unsavory purposes, but they also have numerous potential good uses, such as breaking the chains of harmful monopoly currencies and providing an oasis of stability in turbulent financial times.

should be guarded because Bitcoins have numerous potential good uses and benefits for both individuals and nations. For one, they can free individuals from harmful monopoly currencies, such as the Zimbabwean dollar, and can be an oasis of financial stability, as they were during the 2013 financial crisis in Cyprus. If Bitcoins (or other private alternatives) prove to be highly successful, the day could come when they replace or reduce the demand for current safe-haven currencies, such as the U.S. dollar and Swiss franc.

The Bitcoin is a unit of account, medium of exchange, store of value, and standard of deferred payment. Transactions are anonymous, irreversible, and practically impossible to trace. Only the two parties involved in the transaction know who paid and who received the Bitcoins and how much was transferred. Bitcoin's computer algorithm is stored on personal computers, and it keeps track of who owns what and how much, but in this case, the "who" is simply a coded number. There is no clearing house and no way to determine if a transaction was to purchase a new bicycle or crack cocaine. As for taxes, payments using Bitcoins are taxable events, but, without any way to identify the payer and payee, efforts to tax these transactions are problematic, at best, and impossible, at worst.[30]

Bitcoin transactions are anonymous, irreversible, and practically impossible to trace.

To get Bitcoins, one can trade for them, purchase them with real-world money, or mine them by solving Bitcoin's time-consuming algorithm, which verifies block chains of Bitcoin transactions. Denominations are as low as the eighth decimal place, and the smallest unit (i.e., BTC 0.00000001) is often called a "satoshi," after the currency's purported inventor. Exchanging Bitcoins for other currencies can be accomplished via local payment networks, but the most common practice is to use online exchanges, such as Mt. Gox, Camp BX, Bitomat, Britcoin, and TradeHill. In 2013, Mt. Gox handled the overwhelming majority (80%+) of these trades.

Bitcoins are accepted by a growing number of legal establishments.

Bitcoins are accepted by a growing number of legal establishments, which includes online services, real estate, luxury automobiles, jewelry, watches, home goods, travel, consumer electronics, food beverages, movies, books, and much more.[31] In August 2013, the total value of Bitcoins in circulation was $1.5 billion, which was only 0.05% of the U.S. M1 money supply and 0.01% of M2.[32]

POTENTIAL BITCOIN MARKETS

Due to their scalability, Bitcoins have a natural affinity in the microfinance area, thereby putting them into direct competition with vendors, like PayPal and Venmo. The currency could also threaten well entrenched giants, like Visa, Mastercard, Google, and Apple. Bitcoins can also be used to support fledgling businesses in developing nations, just as M-PESA, a branchless, mobile-phone-based money transfer service for Safaricom, has done in Kenya, Tanzania, and Afghanistan. Small cross-border loans pose no difficulties for Bitcoin, as its trades can easily be made by third-party exchanges.

Bitcoin's continued growth may threaten entrenched companies such as PayPal, Visa, Mastercard, Google, and Apple.

---

[30] Satoshi Nakamoto, "Bitcoin: A Peer-to-Peer Electronic Cash System," http://bitcoin.org/bitcoin.pdf (accessed June 19, 2013).

[31] A list of these establishments can be found at Bitcoin, Trade, https://en.Bitcoin.it/wiki/Trade (accessed June 19, 2013).

[32] Bitcoin homepage, http://Bitcoin.org/en/about (accessed September 27, 2013).

To be sure, Bitcoins could make major inroads in Kenya during the coming years. Not only does a high percentage of Kenya's population have mobile phones, but Bitcoins offer low transaction costs compared to M-PESA, an ability to reduce losses caused by corruption and human error in the nation's financial system, and inflation protection compared to the Kenyan shilling. From 2004 to 2011, Kenyan inflation averaged 11.7% and exceeded 26% in 2008.

BITCOIN GROWTH AND MATERIALITY

Growth of Bitcoins is kept in check by a company-built algorithm that permits moderate growth at a continuously diminishing geometric rate, with the total quantity of Bitcoins programmed to reach a maximum of 21 million (i.e., BTC 21 million) by 2040.[33] This amount may seem small relative to other macroeconomic variables, such as the M1 or M2 money supplies, but be careful not to confuse quantity with value. The lowest denomination Bitcoin (i.e., a satoshi) equals BTC 0.00000001. Therefore, the potential supply of satoshis is 2.1 quadrillion (i.e., $2,100,000,000,000,000 \equiv 2.1E+15$).

Combine this with the fact that a Bitcoin's value changes. Like many major world currencies, it fluctuates with the forces of supply and demand. Exhibit 10-1 shows the Bitcoin's closing value against the dollar from July 17,

> Growth of Bitcoin's supply is regulated by a mathematical algorithm that permits moderate increases at a continuously diminishing geometric rate and reaches a maximum size of BTC 21 million by 2040.

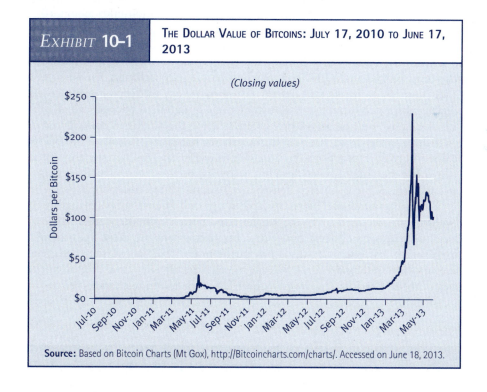

EXHIBIT 10-1	THE DOLLAR VALUE OF BITCOINS: JULY 17, 2010 TO JUNE 17, 2013

(Closing values)

Source: Based on Bitcoin Charts (Mt Gox), http://Bitcoincharts.com/charts/. Accessed on June 18, 2013.

[33] Bitcoin, Controlled Supply, https://en.Bitcoin.it/wiki/Controlled_supply (accessed June 19, 2013).

2010 to June 17, 2013. At its lowest, a Bitcoin was worth slightly under five cents (allegedly, due to a security leak). The currency rose to $29.60, presumably from favorable reaction to a Forbes Magazine article, and then soared to $230 in 2013 due to the currency crisis in Cyprus. Is it possible for a satoshi to equal $1? Yes, but the probability is very small (albeit positive).

Because they grow at a programmed rate that is not tied to any nation's business cycle, Bitcoins might be viewed as a twenty-first century embodiment of Milton Friedman's 1960 suggestion to abolish central banks and replace them with computers that increase the money supply at a constant (noninflationary) rate.[34] Friedman felt that central bankers' actions (inadvertently) exacerbated business cycles due to the time lag between when economic conditions change, central bankers act, and their policies take effect. The "k-percent rule" provides scheduled, yearly increases in liquidity by tying a nation's money supply growth rate to a fixed target, such as the rate of increase in real output. In this way, nations would not be penalized by well-meaning, but often misguided, central bankers, who have difficulties reading economic tealeaves and delivering monetary medicine when and where it is needed.

TRUST

For Bitcoin to succeed, trust in the currency is essential. Without it, the virtual currency will surely wither and die. Transaction verification takes about 10 minutes and is managed collectively by the network's users. A log of all Bitcoin transactions is made public, but identifying the counterparties to each transaction is virtually impossible, thereby assuring anonymity, for good reasons (e.g., purchasing a birthday gift) and bad (e.g., purchasing heroin).

In contrast to banks that defend customer privacy by keeping *transactions confidential*, Bitcoin publishes all transactions in database packets called "block-chains" and preserves privacy by keeping the *addresses confidential* for counterparties to each trade. In the privacy hierarchy, Bitcoins rank below real-world cash transactions, because details of Bitcoin transactions are posted online, but they rank above checking accounts, because it is virtually impossible to identify the counterparties to any Bitcoin-related transaction.

Bitcoin accounts can be compromised but only if customers' virtual "wallets" are accessed by hackers or infected with a computer virus.[35] Because there is no clearing house or centralized oversight, tracking, tracing, or retrieving lost Bitcoin funds is practically impossible. If lost, they are gone forever—like spilling a bag of 50-cent pieces over the edge of a ship on an ocean cruise. Already, malware has been developed, and hackers have

---

[34] Milton Friedman's idea is commonly known as the "k-percent rule." It spirited a lively debate, which continues to this day, on whether central bankers should use monetary rules or discretion. See Milton Friedman, "The Optimum Quantity of Money," in *The Optimum Quantity of Money and Other Essays* (Chicago: Aldine Publishing Company, 1969), pp. 1–50. Also see, Milton Friedman, "Monetary Policy: Theory and Practice," *Journal of Money, Credit, and Banking,* Volume 14, Number 3, August 1982, pp. 98–118.

[35] In 2011, the antivirus company Symantec warned Bitcoin about the possibility of illegal money creation.

targeted (and apparently succeeded in accessing) some Bitcoin wallets.[36] Clearly, the battle has just begun with new competitors to Bitcoin offering (presumably) better security. To protect against this possibility, some users have employed third-party storage providers, but such precautions run counter to the creator's goal of developing a fully anonymous, noncentralized, private currency.

VIRTUAL, PEER-TO-PEER CURRENCIES, AND CRIMINAL ACTIVITIES

Combining money and anonymity is a recipe for criminal activities, and virtual currencies open a Pandora's Box of possibilities. In South Korea, Mafia-like gangs have already been known to extort online users for "protection money." Crypto-cash has also led to the creation of cyber-brothels, illegal gaming sites, online scams, phishing, spyware, spam, hacking, keylogging,[37] and credit card thefts.

> Bitcoins have been and are being used for criminal activities, but the same is true of legal tender.

In 2011, U.S. Senators, Charles Schumer (D, NY) and Joe Manchin (D, WV), along with companies, such as Reuters, wrote formal letters to Attorney General, Eric Holder, and Drug Enforcement Agency head, Michelle Leonhart, expressing their concern about the potential black-market uses of Bitcoins. An online marketplace, called Silk Road, which is operated as a "Tor" hidden service[38] and has come to be known as the "Amazon of illegal drugs," relies heavily on Bitcoins for its anonymous transactions.[39]

Bitcoin will never become a bank because it is a totally distributed cryptocurrency system, but there is nothing preventing users from borrowing and lending it. Such transactions are totally anonymous, thereby evading the oversight of central bankers, state banking commissions, tax authorities, and consumer protection agencies. At the same time, if these transactions are done totally in the shadows, there may be no way to enforce virtual promissory notes in a court of law. Having no recourse for collections reduces the chances that a virtual credit market will grow to significant size.

COMPARING VIRTUAL AND U.S. CURRENCY EVOLUTION

The development of virtual currencies during the twenty-first century bears a striking resemblance to the evolution of real-world money during the

---

[36] Reports of a $8.75 million heist can be found at: Jason Mick, "Inside the Mega-Hack of Bitcoin: Full Story," *DailyTech*, June 24, 2011, http://www.dailytech.com/Inside+the+MegaHack+of+Bitcoin+the+Full+Story /article21942.htm (accessed October 28, 2013). See also James Ball, "LulzSec Rogue Suspected of Bitcoin Hack," *The Guardian*, June 22, 2011, http://www.guardian.co.uk/technology/2011/jun/22/lulzsec-rogue -suspected-of-bitcoin-hack (accessed June 22, 2013). Reports on a $450,000 heist can be found at: Helen A.S. Popkin, "Bitcoin: Virtual Monday Gets Hacked and Heisted," *Regator*, http://regator.com/p/252040141 /Bitcoin_virtual_money_gets_hacked_and_heisted/ (accessed June 22, 2013). Reports on a $200,000 heist can be found at: Morgen Peck, "Thousands of Bitcoins Stolen in a Hack in Linode," *IEEE Spectrum: Technology & Science News*, March 2, 2012, Blogs//Tech Talk http://spectrum.ieee.org/tech-talk/computing /networks/thousands-of-bitcoins-stolen-in-a-hack-on-linode (accessed July 30, 2013).

[37] Keylogging is the illicit capturing of personal information by attracting an unknowing party to an online link that installs and activates secret software, which records all the users' key strokes and mouse clicks (e.g., usernames, passwords, account numbers, and e-mail messages).

[38] A Tor hidden service allows users to conceal their locations while, at the same time, offering services.

[39] The Gizmodo website provides access to Silk Road. Its homepage is entitled "The Underground Website Where You Can Buy Any Drug Imaginable," http://gizmodo.com/5805928/the-underground-website-where- you-can-buy-any-drug-imaginable (accessed June 19, 2013).

eighteenth and nineteenth centuries in the United States. Understanding these similarities and differences might provide us with insights about the future.

EARLY MONEY

Money began as an assortment of physical objects with inherent value, such as yarn, bread, elephants, whales' teeth, coal, ivory, wine, cattle, gold, silver, beads, and stones. During World War II, cigarettes were used as money in German prison camps. These objects were far from homogeneous, many were inconvenient to transport, and they could be difficult to use. As a result, precious metals, like gold, silver, and copper, became objects-of-choice for currency because their malleability allowed for different sizes, weights, and degrees of standardization.

> **Early money had intrinsic value.**

Initially, paper money was just a handwritten claim (i.e., an IOU) on the gold, silver, or other precious metal that was deposited for safekeeping with the local goldsmith. Instead of withdrawing precious metals to purchase goods or services only to have the person paid redeposit the same precious metals with the same goldsmith, people began to exchange the goldsmith's IOUs. They were convenient, efficient, and trusted. Governments soon got involved in the creation of this "fiat" money, but, unfortunately, the history of government involvement has not been a flattering one. They have tended to debase "official" currencies and force their use by giving them legal tender status.[40]

> **Fiat money developed naturally for convenience and not from government orders.**

EARLY U.S. BANKING: 1836 TO 1879

Between 1836 and 1864, the United States had no federal bank regulations and no common currency. Banks were state-chartered and each one was free to print its own currency, which meant "trust" factored heavily into each currency's traded value. In general, the farther away from the bank-of-origin a note traveled, the lower its value due to the greater chances of counterfeiting and fraud. This laissez-faire system of banking may have been ideal for a young colonial nation that was growing in fits and starts because each bank's success was tied directly to the area in which it was located. If a settlement failed, its bank was sure to collapse, thereby highlighting the idea that *commerce follows community*—just as it does today with online currencies (more on this later).

> **Commerce follows community.**

With the onset of the Civil War in 1861, conditions changed, as the federal government's need for funds increased dramatically. Prior to the War, the U.S. federal government issued only gold and silver coins, but passage of the National Bank Act of 1863/1864 enabled it, for the first time, to issue paper currency to finance the Civil War. Lacking any precious metal backing, "greenbacks" (as they were called) were issued by Congress to finance the Civil War. The National Bank Act simultaneously established the U.S. national banking system and Comptroller of the Currency to regulate it.[41]

> **The United States issued its first common currency during the 1860s.**

---

[40] See footnote 34.
[41] The Comptroller of the Currency was made a part of the U.S. Treasury and charged with the responsibility of issuing national bank charters and regulating the activities of newly created national banks. To do so, the Comptroller was empowered to impose restrictions, such as minimum capitalization levels, reserve requirements against issued notes and deposits, loan limitations on collateral and amounts extended to any individual, and indemnity provisions.

The Act also required the U.S. government to deposit funds in national banks, thereby draining state banks of liquidity and providing national banks with immediate advantages over their state competitors. To ensure a steady flow of funding to federal coffers, national banks were required to purchase government bonds, and with the backing of these bonds, they were permitted to issue national bank notes equal to 90% of the bonds' value.[42] To ensure people would use the newly created federal currency, Congress declared it legal tender.[43]

Competition from state banks was clearly perceived as a problem because it interfered with a smooth financing of the Civil War. Congress preferred a uniform national banking system with a common currency and homogeneous national regulatory authority. Standing in the way of simply outlawing state banks was the U.S. Constitution, which gave the federal government the right to print and coin money but did not empower it to abolish state banks. Congress tried to resolve this inconvenience by taxing state banks out of existence. At the time, state-chartered banks earned substantial profits from their issuance of bank notes; so Congress imposed a 10% tax on any bank note that was issued after 1 July 1866. The tax seemed to guarantee the demise of state notes and state-chartered banks.

Initially, this tax caused a mass exodus from state charters to federal charters until the banks realized that they could survive and thrive by issuing a nonmaterial currency that could compete, head-on, with federal banks and U.S. notes. The electronic currency was called a demand deposit because banks had to honor depositor requests for currency "on demand." Today, we commonly refer to them as "checking accounts" or "checkable deposits." Checking accounts are intangible (i.e., digital or electronic), and their power to pay for goods and services made them "money."

> Federal taxes stopped state banks from issuing bank notes, which caused them to focus their attention on checking accounts, a type of nonmaterial money.

The U.S. government's actions during the Civil War are particularly relevant to the evolution of virtual currencies because they show how the power to tax holds the power to create and destroy—especially private commerce. The U.S. government did not and could not outlaw the issuance of paper currency issued by private, state-chartered banks; so it imposed an exorbitant tax on private currency issuance, drained state banks of liquidity, and topped it off by issuing its own currency (the greenback) and designating it legal tender.

> The power to tax is the power to create and destroy.

Gresham's law says that "bad money tends to drive out good money," which was exactly what happened during the Civil War. U.S. greenbacks quickly lost their value, while gold and silver circulated in tandem with this increasingly worthless fiat currency. As a result, people tried to pay their obligations with greenbacks and resisted using gold and silver. The good news

---

[42] This 90% rule was changed to 100% in 1900. The system of using government-issued bonds as collateral for newly issued federal notes lasted until 1935, when the U.S. government stopped issuing this type of note.

[43] U.S. Congress' bequeath of legal tender status on federal notes was angrily disputed, but in 1870, a 5-to-4 Supreme Court decision ruled it permissible. This decision reversed the Hepburn versus Griswold decision in December 1869. See *Legal Tender Cases*, 12 Wallace 457 (December 1870).

is that, by 1879, greenbacks had recovered their full gold backing, which demonstrates that not all experiments with paper money must end in failure.[44]

Virtual Currency Developments: 2009 to 2013

Game developers and social networking platforms might be viewed as the twenty-first-century equivalents of the eighteenth- and nineteenth-century U.S. state-chartered banks, with virtual currencies being the modern-day versions of these banks' notes. Online companies issue their own currencies in a relatively unregulated environment. Their success is not assured but rather based on a community of virtual-world users, which reinforces the notion that *commerce follows community*, just as it did 150 years ago. If a virtual community fails, its currency is sure to wither and die.

The rapid expansion of virtual currencies poses a threat to central bankers who wish to control inflation and also to governments that wish to fund their expenditures with broad and deep tax bases. One way to slow virtual currency growth is by attempting to outlaw it, which will just move these activities to other locations. The U.S. *Unlawful Internet Gambling Enforcement Act* of 2006 is a relatively recent example of how rules and regulations can be created and promulgated to address the spread of undesired Internet activities.[45] Another alternative is for a government to discourage virtual currency growth by imposing taxes on it, but, just as banks were able to evade bank-note taxes during the nineteenth century by issuing checking deposits, virtual currency issuers will likely find ways around future government controls. In short, whenever a money-related door closes, a window (albeit cybernetic in this case) seems to open.

CURRENCY EVOLUTION: FACEBOOK VERSUS ZYNGA

The interplay between FB, one of the dominant social networking platforms in the world, and Zynga, a leading developer of online games, offers insights into the evolution of virtual currencies.

Facebook

Virtual currencies populate the Internet, and one of the leading social networking platforms, FB, developed its own currency called Facebook credits (FBCs). FB's mission is "to make the world more open and connected,"[46] and, by any measure, the company is enormous, with 1.1 billion monthly active users (MAU) as of March 2013, an increase of 23% over March 2012. Daily active users (DAU) in March 2013 averaged 665 million, an increase of 26% over March 2012. Based on population/users alone, FB would be the third largest country in the world, behind only China and India.

---

[44] In 1862, $150 million of United States notes were issued. A second issue of $300 million followed in 1863. After the Civil War, the U.S. government reduced greenbacks in circulation by selling government bonds and lowering the outstanding amount to $347 million, an amount that still exists today. U.S. Congress declared, in 1878, that every greenback redeemed after that point would be reissued.

[45] H.R. 441 (109th): Internet Gambling Prohibition and Enforcement Act, http://www.govtrack.us/congress/bills/109/hr4411/text (accessed June 22, 2013).

[46] Facebook, Inc., *United States Securities and Exchange Commission, Form S-1: Registration Statement*, p. 1, http://www.sec.gov/Archives/edgar/data/1326801/000119312512034517/d287954ds1.htm (accessed June 22, 2013).

FB began developing its virtual currency in late 2007 and officially launched FBCs in 2009. At first, FBCs could be used only for virtual gifting and purchasing games, gaming items, and applications offered on FB's platform. At that time, independent developers had already built advanced and active VCSs, which funneled payments through credit cards, mobile payments, and online payment providers.

> FB's virtual currency was called the Facebook Credit.

The value of each FBC was set at 10 cents, making a convenient 10-to-1 fixed exchange rate to the dollar, but discounts were offered for bulk purchases. To accommodate foreign users, FB eventually expanded convertibility to 14 other currencies besides the dollar, but to exchange any one of these currencies for FBCs, one must first purchase dollars and then use the dollars to purchase FBCs.

For many, it was clear that FBCs were just a first shot over the bow of virtual currency development. FB continued its currency development during the next two years, giving developers on the FB platform time to use and develop their own currencies. By January 2011, FB had completed the beta stage of its development and announced that, as of 1 July 2011, all social gamers using FB's platform had to accept payment with FBCs. Developers were allowed to keep the name and appearance of their independent currencies, and they could also receive dollars via payment systems, such as PayPal and eBay, but FB insisted that they also accept FBCs. To sweeten the pot for potential and existing FBC users, FB offered incentives to use FBCs exclusively.[47]

As part of its new policy, FB also required developers to pay a 30% commission on their total FBC-denominated revenues. This rule had the potential benefit of introducing a degree of currency homogeneity to this online space. With more than 150 developers (e.g., Zynga, CrowdStar, PopCap Games, Playdom, Playfish, and RochYou) operating more than 650 games on FB's platform, the 30% commission provided FB with considerable profits.

> In 2011, FB forced all social gamers using its platform to accept payment with FBCs and to pay a 30% commission on currency sales.

Another benefit from FB's new policy was enhanced currency fungibility. Users could now move effortlessly from one currency to another on the FB platform, and they could do so for whatever reason they chose (e.g., boredom, curiosity, or lack of interest). Converting Virtual Currency A into Virtual Currency B was as easy as selling Virtual Currency A for FBCs and then buying Virtual Currency B with the FBCs.

Game developers were angered by FB's new policy, and Consumer Watchdog, a public advocacy group, filed a formal complaint with the U.S. Federal Trade Commission charging FB with abuse of power, just as Microsoft had been accused during the 1990s with antitrust violations for locking out competitor browser systems.[48]

---

[47] FB gave incentives in the form of preferred access to product features, premium advertising placement on FB's game dashboard, and co-promotion activities. See Alison Diana, "Facebook Makes Credits Sole Legal Currency," *Informationweek,* January 25, 2011, http://www.informationweek.com/news/software/soa_web-services/229100209 (accessed June 22, 2013).

[48] Jia Lynn Yang, "Facebook's Virtual Currency Draws Antitrust Complaints from Consumer Advocates," *The Washington Post,* June 28, 2011, http://www.washingtonpost.com/business/economy/facebooks-virtual-currency-draws-antitrust-complaints-from-consumer-advocates/2011/06/28/AG7cJypH_story.html (accessed June 22, 2013).

ZYNGA

Founded in 2004, San Francisco-based Zynga Inc. (hereafter, Zynga) is a world-class developer of online games that use FB's social networking platform. In general, this company's relationship with FB might have best been described as *strained symbiosis*. In 2010, Zynga's CEO, Mark Pincus, and his team were considering whether to strengthen the company's relationship with FB or develop independent distribution channels, either alone or with partners, such as Yahoo!, AOL, or MSN.[49] This issue came to a head in 2011, when FB demanded that all game developers using its platform accept FBCs and pay a 30% commission on gross revenues. Begrudgingly, Zynga agreed to FB's terms, but, in early March 2012, it counter-punched by launching "Project Z," which allowed users to play Zynga's most popular games (Cityville, Hidden Chronicles, Zynga Poker, and CastleVille) on its own company platform, Zynga.com. This gambit was a further attempt by Zynga to diversify its revenue platforms, having already begun to distribute directly to customers via mobile device apps (e.g., Apple's iPhone).[50] This move also allowed Zynga to differentiate its products in ways that, previously, it could not.

Zynga is a leading developer of online games that used FB's social networking platform.

For FB, the stakes were high because, in 2011, Zynga supplied 12% (excluding advertising on pages of Zynga's games) of its $3.71 billion of total revenues.[51] No other customer accounted for even 10% of FB's revenues in either 2010 or 2011. The stakes were equally high for Zynga because, in 2011, the company gained 93% of its revenues from the virtual items it sold on FB.[52]

This competition reached a new level in June 2012, when FB announced its intention to phase out FBCs by the end of the year and to return to using local currencies. Since then, users' accounts have been measured in dollars or the currency of their residence countries. By linking credit cards to FB accounts, users can purchase digital goods and services by drawing down existing account balances (e.g., from gift cards) or charging their credit cards.

In mid-2012, FB announced its intention to phase out FBCs by the end of the year and return to using local currencies.

This strategic move implied that FB was backing away from any intention to become a leader in the virtual currency environment, thereby sidestepping brewing discontent by game developers and also diffusing future government law suits and regulatory restrictions associated with virtual currencies. Nevertheless, there will be billions to earn from FB's decision to leverage existing real-world currencies.

FB's decision was strategic, which usually means the company felt its virtual currency was not a core competence that provided a competitive advantage and there were bigger opportunities to pursue elsewhere. For instance, FB's departure from the virtual currency space does not mean it will compete any less vigorously in the payment and credit card spaces, with the

---

[49] Mikolaj Jan Piskorski and David Chen, "Zynga," *Harvard Business School Publications*, Case: 9-710-464, January 6, 2011.

[50] Ian Sherr, "Game Changer for Zynga: No Facebook," *The Wall Street Journal*, March 2, 2012, p. B7.

[51] Ibid. Also see Facebook, Inc. *United States Securities and Exchange Commission, Form S-1: Registration Statement*, p. 50 and F-13, http://www.sec.gov/Archives/edgar/data/1326801/000119312512034517/d287954ds1.htm (accessed June 22, 2013).

[52] Shayndi Raice, "Facebook and Zynga: Sharing Riches Isn't Always Easy," *The Wall Street Journal*, February 3, 2012, p. B7.

likes of PayPal, Visa and MasterCard—especially when paid apps are introduced to FB's App Center. As one observer noted, "Facebook is PayPal on
steroids, with the strength of a billion members."[53]

> FB will likely turn its
> business focus to pay-
> ments and credit cards.

T-ACCOUNT APPROACH TO VIRTUAL CURRENCY SYSTEMS AND THEIR EFFECT ON NATIONAL MONEY SUPPLIES

In "The Basics" section of this chapter, four VCSs were defined by the extent
to which each intersected with the real-world economic and financial systems.
Let's take a closer look at each one, using T-accounts to determine their
influence on a nation's money supply and demand for real goods and services.

VIRTUAL CURRENCY SYSTEM #1 (VCS#1)

VCS#1 has no functional links to the real world in terms of its use as a unit of
account, medium of exchange, store of value, or standard of deferred payment. VCU1 cannot be purchased or sold and is acquired only by demonstrating online playing skills and/or accomplishing certain online tasks.
Because the use of VCU1 is sealed from the real world, its effects on the real
economy are negligible or nonexistent.

VIRTUAL CURRENCY SYSTEM #2 (VCS#2)

VCS#2 allows users to purchase a virtual currency (VCU2), but it does not
permit reverse flows from VCU2 back to a real-world currency. Let's investigate the effects of purchasing VCU2 with dollars and purchasing virtual items
with VCU2.

Economic Effects of Purchasing a Virtual Currency

Suppose Alice Arrowsmith (AA) purchases a virtual currency with dollars. At
an exchange rate of VCU 10 per dollar (i.e., VCU 10/$), AA would receive
VCU 10,000 for each $1,000 she spent. Exhibit 10-2 shows the balance sheet
changes for AA and the online company (OC) that result from this transaction
and why they have no net effect on the U.S. money supply.

- AA's checking account at Boston Bank falls by $1,000, and her
  VCU account at OC rises by VCU 10,000. While the composition
  of AA's assets changes, their total value remains the same.
- After the check is cleared, OC's checking account at San Francisco
  Bank rises by $1,000 and its VCU liability to AA rises by VCU
  10,000.[54]
- For the U.S. banking system, the transaction has no net effect on
  U.S. checking accounts or the monetary base because AA's account
  falls by $1,000 and OC's account rises by the same amount.

---

[53] Peter Vogel, "Why Facebook Is Folding on Credits and Doubling Down on Payments," *TechCrunch*, June 23, 2012, http://techcrunch.com/2012/06/23/why-facebook-is-folding-on-credits-and-doubling-down-on-payments/ (accessed June 22, 2013).

[54] These sales would be recorded as *deferred revenues*; so OC would increase both *cash* and *deferred revenues* in its balance sheet. There is no income statement effect—yet. As the virtual currency is spent, *deferred revenues* fall and *revenues* (in the income statement) rise. These revenues increase profits, which increase OC's *equity* (in the balance sheet).

EXHIBIT 10-2	EFFECTS OF PURCHASING A VIRTUAL CURRENCY WITH U.S. DOLLARS

AA's Balance Sheet

Assets		Liabilities & Equity
Checking Acct. at Boston Bank	−$1,000	
VCU Account with OC	+VCU 10,000	

OC's Balance Sheet

Assets		Liabilities & Equity	
Checking Account at San Francisco Bank	+$1,000	AA's VCU Account	+VCU 10,000

U.S. Banking System's Balance Sheet

Assets	Liabilities & Equity	
	AA's Checking Account at Boston Bank	−$1,000
	OC's Checking Account at San Francisco Bank	+$1,000

Economic Effects of Purchasing a Virtual Item from an Online Company with a Virtual Currency

Suppose AA uses her VCUs to purchase online real estate from OC. Exhibit 10-3 shows the effects this transaction has on AA's, OC's, and the U.S. banking system's balance sheets. Again, the U.S. money supply and monetary base are unaffected.

EXHIBIT 10-3	EFFECTS OF PURCHASING VIRTUAL REAL ESTATE FROM OC WITH VCU2

AA's Balance Sheet

Assets		Liabilities & Equity
VCU Account with OC	−VCU 10,000	
Virtual Real Estate	+VCU 10,000	

OC's Balance Sheet

Assets	Liabilities & Equity	
	AA's VCU Account	−VCU 10,000
	Equity	+$1,000

U.S. Banking System's Balance Sheet

Assets	Liabilities & Equity	
	AA's Checking Account at Boston Bank	No Change
	OC's Checking Account at San Francisco Bank	No Change

- AA loses her VCU 10,000 account with OC but gains virtual real estate of equal value. As a result, the value of her assets does not change.
- OC loses its VCU 10,000 liability to AA and recognizes revenues of $1,000, which increases the company's profits and equity.
- This transaction has no effect on the U.S. banking system because all the transactions take place in virtual space. There is no change in anyone's checking account in the U.S. banking system.

Economic Effects of Purchasing Virtual Items from Another Online Customer with a Virtual Currency

In the preceding example, OC sold virtual real estate to AA. Would it have made an economic difference if the virtual real estate had been sold to AA by Bjorn Bergstrom (BB), a creative OC customer? Exhibit 10-4 shows that the answer is "no"; it makes no net economic difference. AA's purchase of virtual real estate from BB reduces her account with OC by VCU 10,000, and increases her ownership of virtual real estate by the same amount. As a result, only the composition (not the total value) of her assets changes. Similarly, BB's account with OC rises by VCU 10,000, and his ownership of virtual real estate falls by the same amount. At OC, the VCU 10,000 account is simply

---

EXHIBIT 10–4	EFFECTS OF PURCHASING VIRTUAL REAL ESTATE FROM **BB** WITH **VCU2**

AA's Balance Sheet		OC's Balance Sheet	
Assets	**Liabilities & Equity**	**Assets**	**Liabilities & Equity**
VCU Account with OC −VCU 10,000			AA's VCU Account −VCU 10,000
Virtual Real Estate +VCU 10,000			BB's VCU Account +VCU 10,000

BB's Balance Sheet	
Assets	**Liabilities & Equity**
VCU Account with OC +VCU 10,000	
Virtual Real Estate −VCU 10,000	

U.S. Banking System's Balance Sheet	
Assets	**Liabilities & Equity**
	AA's Checking Account No Change
	OC's Checking Account No Change
	BB's Checking Account No Change

transferred from AA to BB. Finally, for the U.S. banking system, no changes occur because all these transactions are in the virtual world.

If the economic activity in this VCS continued to develop so that banks and/or other financial institutions began to lend and give interest on deposits, the effects would be the same. Because there is no seepage of purchasing power from the virtual world to the real world, macroeconomic demand would stay the same. Moreover, because the money supply and monetary base remain the same, the expansion of VCU2 creates no false signals that might confuse central bankers and other policymakers.

VIRTUAL CURRENCY SYSTEM #3 (VCS#3)

VCS#3 allows users to purchase a virtual currency (VCU3) with dollars and then freely convert it back into dollars later. Let's start by analyzing the effect of buying a virtual asset at a relatively low price, enhancing its value, selling it for a capital gain in virtual currency, and then cashing out by selling the virtual currency for dollars. Then, we will analyze the effects of loans made in a VCS#3 world.

Cashing Out Capital Gains Earned in a Virtual World

From our analysis of VCS#2, we know that AA's purchase of real estate from BB has no effect on the U.S. money supply or monetary base. Suppose she increases the value of her virtual property by 400%, sells it to Craig Coffee (CC) for VCU 50,000, and then cashes out the virtual currency gain by converting her VCU into dollars.

Exhibit 10-5 shows the effects on AA, CC, OC, and the U.S. banking system.

- AA loses a virtual real estate asset with a book value of VCU 10,000, but has VCU 50,000 deposited in her account with OC. The difference between the value of the virtual real estate she bought and sold increases AA's equity by VCU 40,000.
- CC gains virtual real estate worth VCU 50,000 and loses VCU 50,000 from his account with OC.
- OC increases AA's account by VCU 50,000 and reduces CC's account by the same amount.
- These transactions have no net effect on the U.S. banking system, money supply, monetary base, or demand for real-world goods and services.

Exhibit 10-6 shows the effects if AA cashes out her gain by converting VCU 50,000 into dollars at an exchange rate of VCU 10/$.

- AA loses her VCU 50,000 account with OC but gains a checking account at Boston Bank worth $5,000.
- OC loses its checking account at San Francisco Bank worth $5,000 and loses its VCU 50,000 liability to AA.
- In the U.S. banking system, AA's checking account at Boston Bank rises by $5,000, and OC's account at San Francisco Bank falls by $5,000. As a result, an existing checking account was simply transferred from OC to AA.

EXHIBIT 10–5 | SALES OF VIRTUAL ITEMS THAT HAVE APPRECIATED IN VALUE: VCU3

AA's Balance Sheet

Assets		Liabilities & Equity	
Virtual Real Estate	−VCU 10,000		
VCU Account with OC	+VCU 50,000	Equity VCU 40,000	

OC's Balance Sheet

Assets		Liabilities & Equity	
		AA's VCU Account	+VCU 50,000
		CC's VCU Account	−VCU 50,000

Craig Coffee's Balance Sheet

Assets		Liabilities & Equity
VCU Account with OC	−VCU 50,000	
Virtual Real Estate	+VCU 50,000	

U.S. Banking System's Balance Sheet

Assets	Liabilities & Equity	
	AA's Checking Account	No Change
	OC's Checking Account	No Change
	BB's Checking Account	No Change

© 2015 John E. Marthinsen

EXHIBIT 10–6 | CASHING OUT THE GAINS FROM A CAPITAL GAIN IN THE VIRTUAL WORLD: VCU3

AA's Balance Sheet

Assets		Liabilities & Equity
VCU Account with OC	−VCU 50,000	
Checking Acct. at Boston Bank	+$5,000	

OC's Balance Sheet

Assets		Liabilities & Equity	
Checking Account at San Francisco Bank	−$5,000	AA's VCU Account	−VCU 50,000

U.S. Banking System's Balance Sheet

Assets	Liabilities & Equity	
	AA's Checking Account at Boston Bank	+$5,000
	OC's Checking Account at San Francisco Bank	−$5,000

© 2015 John E. Marthinsen

These transactions cause no net changes in the U.S. money supply, monetary base, or demand for real goods and services. More generally, they have no effect on the real goods and services market, real loanable funds market, or foreign exchange market.

Borrowing and Lending VCU3

Suppose our virtual world developed banks with the ability to lend. What effect would such loans have on the money supply, monetary base, and demand for real goods and services? Using the same example in the last section, suppose that, this time, CC does not have VCU 50,000 to pay AA for the real estate, and he is able to secure a loan from OC. Exhibit 10-7 shows the effects of these transactions:

- CC gains a new asset in the form of his VCU 50,000 account with OC, and he also gains a new VCU 50,000 liability for the debt (borrowing) he owes to OC.
- OC gains a new asset in the form of the CC's VCU 50,000 loan and also a VCU 50,000 liability for the newly created deposit CC owns.
- There are no changes in the U.S. banking systems' balance sheet.

This loan increases the amount of virtual currency in circulation, but it has no effect on the U.S. money supply, monetary base, or net demand for goods and services.

If these newly created VCUs are spent on real-world goods and services, the effects would be the same as our previous example when CC purchased real estate from AA. There would be no net effect on the U.S. banking system checking account balances, money supply, monetary base, or demand for real

EXHIBIT 10-7	EFFECTS OF BORROWING: VCU3

OC's Balance Sheet

Assets		Liabilities & Equity	
Loan to CC	−VCU 50,000	CC's VCU Account	−VCU 50,000

Craig Coffee's Balance Sheet

Assets		Liabilities & Equity	
VCU Account with OC	+VCU 50,000	Borrowing from OC	+VCU 50,000

U.S. Banking System's Balance Sheet

Assets	Liabilities & Equity	
	OC's Checking Account at Boston Bank	No Change
	CC's Checking Account at San Francisco Bank	No Change

goods and services, and these results would be the same regardless of whether the exchange rate between VCUs and dollars was fixed or flexible.

VIRTUAL CURRENCY SYSTEM #4 (VCS#4)

VCS#4 creates an independent currency that can be bought and sold freely and is used in the real world as a medium of exchange for money transfers and outright purchases of goods and services.

Economic Effects of a Virtual Loan Spent on Real-World Goods with Payment in VCUs

Let's change the example slightly and consider what happens if CC borrows VCU 50,000 and uses it to purchase a real-world painting from Diane Duncan (DD). Exhibit 10-8 shows the net effects on CC's, DD's, OC's, and the U.S. banking systems balance sheets.

- In transaction (1) CC gains a VCU 50,000 account with OC and also gains a new liability from his borrowing liability to OC. In transaction (2), CC loses the VCU 50,000 account with OC and gains the $5,000 painting sold by DD. As a result, there is a change in the composition of his assets but not their total value.
- In transaction (1) OC gains a VCU 50,000 asset in the form of CC's loan, and it gains a VCU 50,000 liability in the account it creates for CC. In transaction (2), OC transfers CC's VCU 50,000 account to DD.
- DD is not a part of transaction (1). In transaction (2), DD gains a VCU 50,000 account with OC and loses a painting worth $5,000. As a result, there is a change in the composition of her assets but not their total value.
- In the U.S. banking system, there are no changes in any asset or liability. As a result, there is no change in the U.S. money supply or monetary base.

These transactions have no net effect on the U.S. money supply or monetary base, but should they? The demand for U.S. (real-world) goods and services increased. Not every increase in money supply increases the demand for real goods and services, but a nation's money supply should include those financial instruments that have a material impact on this demand. Therefore, it appears as if the unchanging U.S. money supply is not mirroring accurately changes in the demand for U.S. goods and services. If the volume of these transactions were substantial, it could threaten the nation's inflation targets and redistribute income in undesired ways. This conclusion is disconcerting because OC has (seemingly) unlimited power to create VCUs with no central bank restraints, reserve requirements, or system leakages that would weaken the deposit expansion multiplier.

VIRTUAL CURRENCIES AND SOCIAL MEDIA INTELLIGENCE

To date, the flow of transactions from the virtual world to the real world has been a more of a trickle than a flood. At the same time, platforms have been created and paths laid to increase this flow in the future. One attribute of the evolving integration between social and virtual networks is the ability to capture, store, retrieve, and use transaction data for marketing (and other)

EXHIBIT 10-8 EFFECT OF SPENDING A VIRTUAL LOAN ON A REAL-WORLD GOOD: VCU4

(When the Payment Is Made in VCUs)

Craig Coffee's Balance Sheet

Assets		Liabilities & Equity	
VCU Account with OC	+VCU 50,000 (1)	Borrowing from OC	+VCU 5,000 (1)
VCU Account with OC	−VCU 50,000 (2)		
Painting	+$5,000 (2)		

OC's Balance Sheet

Assets		Liabilities & Equity	
Loan to CC	+VCU 50,000 (1)	CC's VCU Account	+VCU 50,000 (1)
		CC's VCU Account	−VCU 50,000 (2)
		DD's VCU Account	+VCU 50,000 (2)

Diane Duncan's Balance Sheet

Assets		Liabilities & Equity
Painting	−$5,000 (2)	
VCU Account with OC	+VCU 50,000 (2)	

U.S. Banking System's Balance Sheet

Assets	Liabilities & Equity	
	CC's Checking Account	No Change
	OC's Checking Account	No Change
	DD's Checking Account	No Change

purposes. Social networking platforms, such as FB, MySpace, and Twitter, offer highly personalized contact grids, with a wealth of information on the particular habits and buying patterns of their customers. As a result, marketing strategies are creatively blending brand loyalty, identity, and reputation in ways that are both exhilarating and alarming but largely unknown.[55] Vendors now engage IT consulting firms, such as Accenture, Capgemini, IBM, and Deloitte, to help them sift, analyze, and more importantly, act on the semi-structured and unstructured customer-behavior data captured by social networking platforms. Industry users call it *mention analysis* or *sentiment analysis*, and, when combined with *social mobility analysis*,[56] the marketing implications are virtually limitless—some would say "mind-blowing."

Consider the implications. Individuals are using, with increasing frequency, location-based social networking programs on FB, like Foursquare,[57] to "check in" to places they visit, making customized marketing a reality. Even without such software, the vast majority of today's mobile phones are GPS-enabled, opening the possibility of location tracking regardless of whether or not users elect to share their information.

Picture yourself running an errand to the local pharmacy. Entering the store, your location-based program triggers an e-mail message from the pharmacy to your smartphone reminding you that it's been three months since you last purchased vitamins and offering you a coupon for your favorite brand. Immediately afterward, you receive a message from your dry cleaner, just a block away, saying your cleaning is done and ready to be picked up—and, by the way, while you're at it, would you like to take advantage of the attached coupon for a Venti-Nonfat-Latte (your coffee drink of choice) at Starbucks, just across the street?

What benefits do merchants gain from distributing these virtual coupons? To be sure, they may earn additional revenues and profits and also have an opportunity to strengthen brand loyalty and recognition. Equally important, they learn to better filter the white noise of massive behavioral databases into actionable insights, which raises the issue of privacy. As purchases of online goods and services become more widespread, vendors and social networking platforms will walk a razor's edge of (or delicately dance around) concerns about personal privacy. Ask yourself: at the online sites you frequent, who owns *your* behavioral data (hint: not you!), and what restrictions are there on how it is used or marketed? What limits, if any, should be put on vendors' access to, rights to know, and reaction to *your* buying habits and desires? Is *your* privacy sufficiently protected if this information is aggregated? Similarly, what limits, if any, should be put on social networking platforms' ability to sell customer-based information in an individual or aggregated form?

How do virtual currencies enter into this discussion? The increasing use of virtual currencies expands exponentially the horizon of marketing

> The evolving integration between growing social and virtual networks has enhanced the ability to capture, store, retrieve, and use transaction data for marketing (and other) purposes.

---

[55] Rodolfo Salazar, "The Bank of Facebook: Currency, Identity, Reputation," March 16, 2012, pp. 19–21, http://emergentbydesign.com/2011/04/04/the-bank-of-facebook-currency-identity-reputation/ (accessed June 22, 2013).

[56] In this context, *social mobility* is the art or science of analyzing the movement of individuals or groups.

[57] Foursquare uses GPS hardware to create a location-based social-networking website, on which members use their mobile devices (smartphones) to "check-in."

opportunities. As vendors allow, with increasingly regularity, purchases with virtual currencies, they are also likely to reward customers with these currencies, hoping to promote loyalty and strengthen their brands. Gamification[58] will be used for similar purposes, as vendors ask programmers to design gaming techniques and mechanics to solve problems, interest customers, and capture the attention of potential buyers. In short, the combination of virtual currencies, social media, sentiment analysis, social mobility analysis, and gamification are keys to customer-centric marketing strategies of the future, and we have only begun to tap or grasp the possibilities.

> The increasing use of virtual currencies expands the horizon of marketing opportunities.

CONCLUSION

Money exists to make transactions easier and was used long before governments became involved. Both virtual and real currencies are to economic systems as motor oil is to an automobile. With motor oil, cars run smoother and more efficiently than without it. While gas is the propellant, without oil, cars would seize up quickly. Money is a lubricant to economic activity. Societies have tried to exist without it, but they were far and few between and, ultimately, all unsuccessful.[59]

Central banks and governments are concerned about the creation of shadow currencies that might challenge the authority, validity, and acceptability of their official national money supplies. To the extent that virtual currencies can put significant demands on real-world goods and services and to the extent that they can be executed anonymously, serious questions arise about central banks' abilities to control inflation and governments' abilities to finance their activities from broad tax bases. Should decentralized peer-to-peer currencies grow considerably, they could pose additional problems for central banks and government tax authorities due to their stealth-like effects and anonymity.

Some observers herald the rise of virtual currencies for their potential to help oppressed individuals circumvent authoritarian governments and topple illicit regimes. Others cite their efficiency and also the capitalist, competitive, non-monopolistic, free-market nature as major advantages, but there are broader, disquieting implications for democratic governments with stable economies.

One thing is sure, because virtual currencies are internationally distributed, no country is totally free from their influence, but then the economic impacts of virtual currencies are also globally distributed rather than focused on any one nation. In the future, virtual currencies are bound to grow with increased Internet use. On December 31, 2000, there were an estimated

---

[58] Gamification uses game strategy, thinking, and mechanics in a nongame environment for purposes other than pure enjoyment. Among the possible objectives are to attract potential customers, increase brand recognition and loyalty, or solve complex problems.

[59] The Incas in South America during the sixteenth century had a system based on autocratic-theocratic socialism. Families were largely self-sufficient, ruled by very strong religious beliefs in an agriculturally-oriented society that was heavily tied to the State. The government cared for those who could not care for themselves. The Incan society was highly organized and disciplined. It combined strict dictatorial supervision and a general societal acceptance of the status quo, but Incan people sacrificed an enormous amount of individual freedom. See Walter W. Haines, *Money, Prices, and Policy* (McGraw-Hill Book Company: New York, 1961), pp. 7–8.

361 million Internet users, which was 5% of the world population.[60] By June 3, 2012, they had grown more than 566% to 2.5 billion users, which was more than 34% of the world population.

Virtual currencies have introduced a variety of perplexing issues which governments, courts, legal experts, and legislative bodies will have to resolve. Are virtual items private property? Is the exchange of virtual content a taxable event? What rights of transferability (e.g., inheritance) should exist with virtual content? These issues and many more have "real-world" counterparts, but the way we eventually resolve them could be quite different from the past.

We have come a long way from the days when nations relied exclusively on tangible currencies, but virtual currencies have brought a swarm of new challenges. One that is sure to stay with us is the concern about privacy. Virtual currencies permit computer networks to record, trace, and analyze every transaction we make. Personal privacy is further challenged by social networks, where individuals share confidential information with trusted friends, but this social intercourse also lends itself to recording, tracing, and evaluating. Every comment we make over the Internet, every photo we shoot or upload, and every mouse-click we make creates a potential information bonanza for someone with access to it and a product (or scam) to sell. In 2011, credit card companies alleged that, by analyzing the spending habits of their customers, they could predict divorces two years in advance and with a 98% accuracy rate.[61] Where will we be in 10 years?

In the future, trust and confidence are likely to be the driving forces behind the development of virtual currencies. Just as the value of bank notes during the nineteenth century was based on the trust individuals had in a particular state-chartered bank, the value of virtual currencies during the twenty-first century will be influenced increasingly by the trust we have in what our social networks do with our confidential information.

At present, virtual currencies do not appear to increase any nation's money supply or have significant effects on the financial and economic systems of any nation. In part, this is due to their relatively small size and lack of meaningful interaction with the three major macroeconomic markets. Substitution effects are possible but likely to be small.

As they mature, legal uncertainties surrounding virtual currencies will be clarified, but many threats and uncertainties will remain, such as cyber-attacks that could wipe out owners' wealth as well as the credit, liquidity, and operational risks that come with using private currencies. The road ahead is likely to be a rocky one. In 2012, a study by the European Central Bank concluded: "From the analysis of the existing information, it is already possible to draw an initial conclusion: it is very complicated to obtain a clear overview of the situation regarding virtual currency schemes at this stage."[62]

[60] "Internet World Stats: Usage and Population Statistics," http://www.internetworldstats.com/stats.htm (accessed June 21, 2013).

[61] Rodolfo Salazar, *The Bank of Facebook: Currency, Identity, and Reputation*, April 4, 2011, http://emergentbydesign.com/2011/04/04/the-bank-of-facebook-currency-identity-reputation/ (accessed June 22, 2013).

[62] See European Central Bank, *Virtual Currency Schemes: October 2012*, p. 33, http://www.ecb.europa.eu/pub/pdf/other/virtualcurrencyschemes201210en.pdf (accessed June 19, 2013).

REVIEW QUESTIONS

1. Are virtual currencies "money," and, if they are, should they be included in nations' money supplies? Should "trust" be one of the functions of money?

2. What effect does the purchase of virtual currencies have on a nation's monetary base, M2 money supply, and M2 money multiplier?

3. Under what conditions is the creation of virtual currencies inflationary?

4. What effect do purchases of virtual items with virtual currencies have on a nation's monetary base, M2 money supply, and M2 money multiplier?

5. How are Bitcoins different from VCU1, VCU2, and VCU3 currencies? How are they similar? What is the primary economic threat of Bitcoins?

6. Explain the costs and benefits of Bitcoins in terms of Milton Friedman's "k-percent rule."

7. Is it accurate to say that a major threat of virtual currencies is that all the transactions connected to them evade national income taxation?

8. How is the development of virtual currencies much like the development of the U.S. money and banking system prior to the U.S. Civil War?

9. Explain the phrase "commerce follows community." Do you agree?

10. As the volume use of virtual currencies rises, it is expected that one effect will be for people to hold less real-world cash, such as dollars, euros, and yen. If this is true for the United States, what should happen to the U.S. M2 money multiplier?

11. Explain how virtual currencies might be used for social media intelligence.

DISCUSSION QUESTIONS

12. Can social networking platforms, like FB, create money? If they can, should they be regulated? How can they be regulated?

13. Do virtual currencies affect economic activity, and if they do, should they be regulated?

14. How can central banks or governments regulate the spread of virtual currencies?

15. Explain the development of Zynga's and FB's relationship and the way it parallels and is different from the development of countries, such as Greece, in the EMU.

Chapter 11

Interest Rates and Why They Change

INTRODUCTION

Suppose you were the chief financial officer at a large U.S. company that wanted to expand operations in Japan. You knew that internal cash flows would not be sufficient to support the intended investments; so your company would have to borrow. Reasonable capital budgeting projections put the new financing needs at about $2 billion during the next five years. Therefore, in the coming weeks, you would be busy meeting with commercial and investment bankers to strike the best deal.

The specific financing details would come later, but for now there would be important, fundamental decisions for you to make. Should you borrow dollars or yen? Should your funding be short term or long term? Should it be on a floating-rate or fixed-rate basis? In large part, the answers to these questions depend on four major factors:

- the company's current position and net exposures created by the new investments,
- expectations about the future value of the yen relative to the dollar,
- expectations about future interest rate changes, and
- the company's tolerance for risk.

If you expected the dollar to depreciate against the yen, there would be a strong incentive to borrow dollars, convert them to yen, and invest in yen-generating assets. Similarly, if you expected interest rates to rise, you would be inclined to borrow now on a fixed-rate basis in order to beat the future rate increases. By contrast, if you expected interest rates to fall, you could profit from your expectations by borrowing long-term funds on a floating-rate basis or borrowing short-term funds and rolling them over (i.e., renewing them at prevailing interest rates) from year to year.

Correctly predicting what will happen to currency rates and interest rates could be crucial to the proposed investment's return, and the stakes are high. Shaving just a quarter percent off the interest cost of a $2 billion debt would save your company $5 million *a year*. Cutting a few cents off the currency cost could save millions more.

This chapter discusses interest rates and why they vary from nation to nation, industry to industry, and borrower to borrower. It builds on Chapter 5, "Inflation: Who Wins, and Who Loses?," where we learned that the nominal interest rate is composed of two main factors, the real interest rate and expected inflation rate (see the left side of Exhibit 11-1). Therefore, variations in

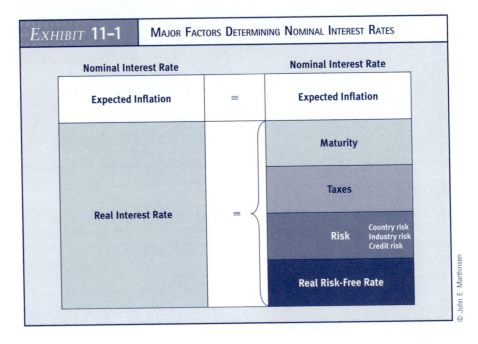

EXHIBIT 11-1 | **MAJOR FACTORS DETERMINING NOMINAL INTEREST RATES**

© John E. Marthinsen

national, industry, and company interest rates can be explained by the sources of differences in these two variables.

Chapters 12 and 15 will complement the discussion in this chapter by considering the causes of *short-term* movements of inflation and exchange rates—both actual and expected. Chapter 12, "Price and Output Fluctuations," focuses on the causes of price and real GDP movements, and Chapter 15, "Exchange Rates: Why Do They Change?" highlights the causes and effects of exchange rate fluctuations. *Long-term* interest rates are influenced by expectations about *long-term* inflation and exchange rate movements. Therefore, Chapter 21, "Causes of Long-Term Growth and Inflation," expands the discussion in this chapter to investigate the causes of long-term inflation, and Chapter 22, "Long-Term Exchange Rates Movements and Comparative Advantage," explains the major factors that influence long-term exchange rate movements and exchange rate expectations.

THE BASICS

WHY DO INTEREST RATES VARY?
The real interest rate is influenced by four major factors: the real risk-free interest rate, risk, taxes, and maturity. Imagine these four factors as stacked building blocks that, placed on top of each other, equal the real interest rate. An increase in any of them adds to the height of the stack, and discounts subtract from it (see the right side of Exhibit 11-1). Let's briefly discuss each of these major components.

REAL RISK-FREE INTEREST RATE

The real risk-free interest rate is the foundation of nominal interest rates because it is what a borrower would pay (and lenders/savers would earn) if there were no premiums for risk, taxes, maturity, or expected inflation. In a more technical sense, the real risk-free interest rate reflects society's time preference for money, which means it reflects the trade-off that society must make between consuming now and consuming later. The higher the real risk-free interest rate, the more a society is willing to save now and spend later.

The real risk-free interest rate is a reflection of a society's time preference for money.

In general, people who choose to save want to do so in ways that ensure they will be better off later than they are now. And why not? Lenders/savers enable borrowers to purchase goods and services immediately that might have required a considerable amount of time to finance. But the real risk-free interest rate is not determined solely by desires and preferences of lenders/savers. Rather, it is a function of the supply and demand forces created by lenders/savers *and* borrowers, who consider a broad spectrum of economic factors. Later in this chapter, we will discuss how the equilibrium real risk-free interest rate is determined and the factors that change it.

MACRO MEMO 11-1

Who Borrows at the Real Risk-Free Interest Rate?

The national governments of many countries are often considered to be risk-free borrowers because their securities are denominated in the domestic currency, and they have the power to repay or continue refinancing their debt obligations by taxing the public and/or creating money. If there is no country risk premium and expected inflation rate equals zero, a national government can borrow at the real risk-free interest rate.

This has raised an interesting question for countries that are now part of the European Monetary Union (EMU). By adopting a common currency (the euro) and establishing a supranational central bank (European Central Bank), these nations have relinquished their powers to conduct independent monetary policy. As a result, government borrowing in these nations is clearly not risk-free. Since 2007, debt problems in European nations, such as Greece, Ireland, Portugal, and Spain, have increased their risk premiums above those paid by healthy multinational companies.

RISK PREMIUM

To compensate investors for uncertainty in their returns, the market incorporates three risk premiums into the real interest rate: a country risk premium, industry risk premium, and credit risk premium. Let's briefly discuss each of them.

Country Risk Premium

Country risk premiums reflect the economic, political, and social conditions of the nation(s) in which a borrower operates. Small companies that rely solely on domestic capital markets have no option but to bear this premium. Therefore, it is possible for a small, first-class borrower in an unstable nation to pay a higher cost of capital than a lower-rated company in a stable nation. By contrast, large, multinational companies are able to choose from a variety of global markets, which reduces their vulnerability and exposures to the risks of any one nation.

Economic, political, and social conditions affect a nation's risk premium.

Country risk can be divided into two major components, market risk and political/social risk. These risks are interdependent, and many of the factors that influence them are subjective; so there is no clear way to separate and measure them. With this in mind, let's briefly discuss market risk and political/social risk and then investigate the qualitative ways in which they influence the real rate of interest.

Market Risk Premium: The market risk premium reflects the volatility of a borrower's cash flows due to unpredictable changes in key macroeconomic variables. Among the most important are changes in exchange rates, as well as changes in *relative* international interest rates, GDP growth rates, inflation rates, consumer preferences, expectations, credit availability, input prices, market structure, and productivity levels.

> A company's market risk premium is affected mainly by its cash flow volatility.

Volatility of Expected Inflation: Care should be taken when considering the effects that expected inflation has on a nation's interest rates because the *average* expected rate of inflation is not a part of the real interest rate. Rather, it enters as an independent factor into the nominal interest rate calculation because the market compensates lenders/savers for "expected" reductions in their purchasing power due to inflation (in Exhibit 11-1, see the top box labeled "Expected Inflation").

By contrast, the *volatility* of expected inflation is part of the real interest rate because it is a component of risk. Volatile markets are risky ones that increase the chances of borrowers and lenders suffering from unexpectedly high or low inflation rates. To compensate, the market incorporates a risk premium into the real interest rate to reflect expected inflation's unpredictability and instability.

As an example, from 1988 to 2001, Turkey's inflation rate averaged about 70%. Suppose 70% was Turkey's expected inflation rate for the coming year. The market would incorporate this 70% rate into the nominal interest rate to compensate lenders/savers for what they expected to lose in purchasing power.[1] If Turkey's inflation rate had been stable at 70% during the past few years, and the market expected it to remain at that level, then there would be no reason to incorporate a significant inflation risk premium into the nominal return.

But that was not the case. Even though Turkey's average inflation rate from 1988 to 2001 was 70%, it was far from stable. As Exhibit 11-2 shows, inflation varied from a high of 106% in 1994 to a low of 50% in 2000. With such wide fluctuations, the chances for borrowers or lenders/savers to be harmed by unanticipated inflation rate changes were rather high. To compensate for this risk, the financial markets incorporated an inflation risk premium into the real rate of interest. The greater the risk, the higher this premium.

---

[1] For a complete discussion of the relationship between expected inflation and the nominal interest rate, please see Chapter 5, "Inflation: Who Wins, and Who Loses?"

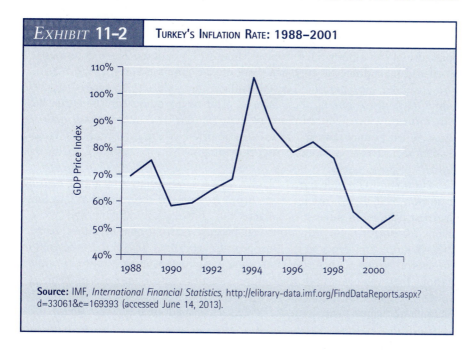

EXHIBIT 11-2 | **TURKEY'S INFLATION RATE: 1988–2001**

Source: IMF, *International Financial Statistics*, http://elibrary-data.imf.org/FindDataReports.aspx?d=33061&e=169393 (accessed June 14, 2013).

Political/Social Risk Premium: A nation's political/social risk premium reflects existing and expected changes in political and social conditions. Businesses look for fair and equal treatment under the law, and the market penalizes nations where such treatment is not present or when it is threatened. Political/social risk premiums also take into consideration the relative competence and stability of governments, frequency and evenhandedness of elections, fairness of the political process, and the government's willingness and ability to deal with social problems.

> The political/social risk premium is affected by a nation's political and social conditions relative to the rest of the world.

Perceived levels of corruption and bureaucracy in a nation are also important, as are fears of government intervention, confiscation, and/or expropriation. Finally, this premium is affected by ethnic, cultural, and religious turmoil, as well as the chances of social unrest or conflicts (e.g., riots, terrorism, strikes, and demonstrations).

MACRO MEMO   11-2

Where to Find a Country Risk Report

Detailed country risk analyses can take considerable time and effort. Fortunately, there are public and private institutions that provide country risk reports, thereby relieving companies from doing these analyses themselves. Examples are Business Environment Risk Intelligence (BERI) S.A., Control Risks Group, Coplin-O'Leary Rating System, Economist Intelligence Unit (EIU), Institutional Investor, Moody's Investor Service, Political Risk Services' *International Country Risk Guide* (*ICRG*), S. J. Rundt and Associates, Standard and Poor's Rating Group, and World Markets Research Centre.

Country risk can change quickly—sometimes for the better and sometimes for the worse. An example of a change for the better is the EMU, which was formed in 1999 among 11 European Union (EU) nations. These countries abolished their domestic currencies, adopted a common currency (the euro), and created a supranational central bank. As a result, any currency risk premium that existed *among these nations* prior to the union vanished after it was formed, which reduced many of these nations' real and nominal interest rates. When nominal interest rates fell, the prices of the EMU nations' fixed income securities (e.g., bonds) rose, providing substantial capital gains to the holders of these assets.

For some EU nations, the volatility of expected inflation also fell, causing a portion of their risk premiums to drop. Among the countries that had the sharpest declines in interest rates were Italy, Portugal, and Spain, and one major reason for these reductions was because international investors seemed to have more confidence in the European Central Bank (ECB) than they did in the central banks of these EMU nations. A similar scenario occurred in other nations that abolished both their currencies and central banks in order to adopt foreign currencies as their own. For example, Ecuador, El Salvador, and Panama abolished their domestic currencies and adopted the U.S. dollar.

Industry Risk

The cash flows in some industries are inherently riskier than they are in others. The market adjusts for these differences by incorporating an industry risk premium into the real interest rate. High-risk industries, such as nuclear power, volatile chemical production, aircraft building, biotechnology, offshore drilling, and shipping, are often associated with complex, hazardous, and/or highly interdependent activities. By contrast, examples of relatively low-risk industries are ones connected to personal consumption expenditures, such as food distribution, bulk chemicals production (e.g., vitamins and flavor ingredients), and consumer health care products.

> The industry risk premium increases with the volatility of an industry's cash flows.

Usually, industry risk premiums are slow to move, but occasionally, rapid change is possible. Quick and discrete adjustments can be caused by government legislation (e.g., local-content requirements, protectionist barriers to trade, sanctions, and costly regulations), turmoil in geographic areas of strategic importance (e.g., where vital inputs are sourced), changing consumer tastes, and government product warnings. For example, offshore oil drilling was made more risky due to British Petroleum's (BP's) oil spill on its Deepwater Horizon oil rig in the Gulf of Mexico in April 2010. The resulting deaths (11 in all), environmental destruction (estimated in the billions of dollars), and loss of tourism and livelihood (by commercial fisherman and shrimpers) created an outcry for greater regulations, control, and accountability. Similarly in March 2011, Japan's Fukushima nuclear accident ignited considerable pressure to impose greater controls on the expansion and distribution of nuclear power plants.

Credit Risk

Credit risk is the likelihood that a borrower will default on a loan or other debt obligation by failing to make the required principal and/or interest payments. Under such circumstances, the lender/saver suffers the loss of both principal and interest on the loan or security. A credit (i.e., default) risk premium reflects the ability and willingness of individual borrowers to repay their debts. This risk is composed of two major parts, solvency risk and liquidity risk.

Solvency Risk: A solvent company is one whose asset values are greater than its liability values, which means the company has a positive stockholders' equity. Therefore, the *solvency risk* premium is a reflection of the anticipated profitability and balance sheet health of a company. Expectations of weak operating results, rising exposures, underperforming assets, risky liabilities, and low capitalization rates (i.e., modest stockholders' equity relative to assets) increase the credit risk premium that a company must pay.

Liquidity Risk: Liquidity risk is the likelihood that borrowers will be unable to meet payment demands due to a lack of funds. This could be caused by unexpectedly low cash flows from operations, and incapacity to refinance, and/or an inability to sell financial (or other) assets quickly and without substantial loss of value. We discussed liquidity risk in Chapter 7, "Financial Intermediation, Markets, and Intermediaries," where we found that shortages of liquidity can lead to bankruptcy and default as quickly as insolvency.

It is important to separate solvency risk from liquidity risk. Many solvent and well-capitalized companies have failed because they did not have sufficient cash on hand to pay their obligations. The difference between these risks can be illustrated by considering banks. Most bank liabilities have short-term maturities (e.g., checking accounts and savings deposits), but banks invest these funds in assets with much longer-term maturities (e.g., mortgages). Even if a bank held only Triple A–rated securities and lent only to the highest-quality borrowers, it could still fail if depositors, en masse, tried to withdraw their deposits. No bank has sufficient cash (liquidity) on hand to meet such massive outflows.

TAXES

The level and breadth of tax rates can significantly affect supply and demand forces that determine the real interest rate.[2] On the supply side, taxes reduce the return earned by lenders/savers. In doing so, they reduce the attractiveness of these investments. On the demand side, changes in the level and breadth of taxes can lower after-tax investment returns and, therefore, reduce the demand for loanable funds that might be spent for real investments, such as greenfield construction sites and the expansion of current plant facilities.

Tax incentives have the opposite effect by encouraging the flow of real loanable funds to tax-supported areas. They also lower the cost of funds to borrowers that are considering direct investments in certain industrial sectors or geographic regions. Examples of tax incentives are investment tax credits for businesses and homeowner tax deductions for mortgage interest payments.

Sidebar notes:

Credit risk depends on a borrower's solvency and liquidity risks.

A solvent company's assets exceed its liabilities. Solvency risk increases when this relationship is threatened.

Liquidity risk is the likelihood that a company's cash flows will be insufficient to pay its debt obligations.

Solvent companies can fail due to a lack of liquidity.

Taxes reduce the returns to lenders/savers, which reduces the supply of real loanable funds. Business taxes reduce the after-tax profits of real business investments, which lower the demand for real loanable funds.

---

[2] Tax rate volatility also plays a role, but it is a part of the risk premium.

In the context of Exhibit 11-1, tax incentives should be viewed as reductions in the height of this risk building block.

MATURITY

A maturity premium is added to the real interest rate if lenders/savers require compensation for the length of time their funds are committed. Usually, the longer the interval, the higher the maturity premium, but this relationship can vary.

The relationship between an asset's *nominal* yield and its maturity is called the *term structure of interest rates*, and the graphical representation of this relationship is called the *yield curve*. A discussion of the yield curve and why it may be upward-sloping, downward-sloping, or horizontal would divert us from our current goal of determining how the real risk-free interest rate is determined. Therefore, this discussion is covered in the "**The Rest of the Story**" section of this chapter (see "Understanding the Yield Curve").

REAL LOANABLE FUNDS MARKET

Let's turn our attention to the forces that determine the *real risk-free interest rate* and cause it to change. For that, we will rely on the real loanable funds market (also called the *real credit market*), where the supply and demand for real credit meet. The sources of supply to the real loanable funds market are from domestic and foreign lenders/savers and from changes in the real money supply. The sources of demand are from domestic and foreign borrowers.

SOME BASICS

Before we begin our analysis, three important points should be highlighted. First, *real* loanable funds are inflation-adjusted quantities. Therefore, the amount of real loanable funds supplied or demanded increases only if the quantity of nominal loanable funds grows faster than prices. For example, if the amount of loanable funds supplied rose by 5% and prices also rose by 5%, the amount of real loanable funds supplied would not change.

Second, supply and demand forces in the real loanable funds market are flow variables—not stock variables. Therefore, our analysis will always be framed during a period of time—instead of a point in time. For this reason, we must be careful when graphing the real loanable funds supply and demand to put the real risk-free interest rate on the vertical axis and the quantity of real loanable funds *per time period* on the horizontal axis (see Exhibit 11-3).

The final point to remember is that only changes in the real risk-free interest rate and quantity of real loanable funds per period cause *movements along* the supply and demand curves in the real loanable funds market. These variables are called *endogenous* because they are determined within the real loanable funds market. A movement along the supply curve is called a *change in the quantity supplied* of real loanable funds per period, and a movement along the demand curve is called a *change in the quantity demanded* of real loanable funds per period.

Any other variables that affect the real loanable funds market are called *exogenous* and shift the entire supply or demand curves to the right or left. A shift of the entire supply curve is called a *change in supply*, and a shift of the entire demand curve is called a *change in demand*.

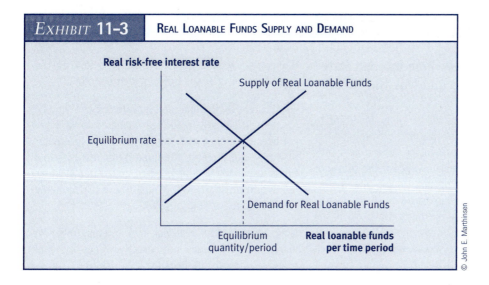

EXHIBIT 11-3   REAL LOANABLE FUNDS SUPPLY AND DEMAND

Real risk-free interest rate

Supply of Real Loanable Funds

Equilibrium rate

Demand for Real Loanable Funds

Equilibrium
quantity/period

**Real loanable funds
per time period**

© John E. Marthinsen

Distinguishing between exogenous and endogenous variables is important. Luckily, it is easy to do because endogenous variables are the only ones
visible on the axes of the supply and demand curves. Exogenous variables are
not visible on either axis, which means they are determined *outside* the real
loanable funds market.

MOVEMENTS ALONG THE SUPPLY AND DEMAND
CURVES FOR REAL LOANABLE FUNDS

Let's investigate the logic behind why the supply and demand curves in the
real loanable funds market are upward-sloping and downward-sloping,
respectively. Then, we will discuss equilibrium in the real loanable funds
market and finish by considering how equilibrium changes.

MOVEMENTS ALONG THE REAL LOANABLE FUNDS SUPPLY CURVE

Real loanable funds are supplied to the credit markets by domestic and foreign
households, businesses, financial institutions, governments, and central banks.
Like most supply curves, it is upward sloping, which means there is a positive
relationship between the real risk-free interest rate and the quantity of real
loanable funds supplied to the market per period (see Exhibit 11-4). Let's
see whether this upward slope is logical and consistent with our intuition.

**Domestic and foreign
individuals, businesses,
financial institutions,
governments, and central
banks are the sources of
real loanable funds
supply.**

Effects of the Real Risk-Free Interest Rate on
Household Sources of Supply

Changes in the real risk-free interest rate have two important effects on the
amount of credit supplied by households to the real loanable funds market.
They influence, first, the amount of saving and, second, the composition of
household portfolios.

MACRO MEMO   11-3

Why Is the "Real Risk-Free Interest Rate" on the Vertical Axis and Not the "Real Interest Rate"?

In the real loanable funds market, it is important to remember that the *real risk-free interest rate*—and not the *real interest rate*—is put on the vertical axis. Let's use the supply curve to explain why. For the supply of real loanable funds to be upward sloping, the interest rate on the vertical axis must cause direct changes in the quantity supplied on the horizontal axis. If the interest rate rises, more funds should be supplied, and if it falls, then less should be supplied. Such changes cause *movements along* the supply curve. If the *real interest* rate were put on the vertical axis, we might not get this effect. Here's why.

Suppose a nation was threatened by war. As a result, its risk premium would rise, causing the real interest rate to rise. This higher return would not provide an incentive for domestic and foreign savers, lenders, and financial institutions to increase the quantity of funds they supply to the real loanable funds market. As far as they are concerned, the real return might be higher, but the risk-adjusted return would be the same. The threat of war means they could lose dearly.

Higher risks require higher real returns to keep the same amount of funds flowing each period.

For this reason, the real interest rate is a poor choice for the vertical axis in the real loanable funds market because higher real interest rates due to greater risks may not increase the quantity of real loanable funds supplied. Similarly, when real interest rates fall due to sinking risks, the quantity of real loanable funds supplied should not fall.

Now, consider the real risk-free interest rate. An increase in risk does not directly affect the real risk-free interest rate because it is "risk free." Therefore, a higher *real risk-free* interest rate provides a clear incentive for domestic and international lenders/savers to increase the quantity of real loanable funds they supply to the credit market per period.

Summarizing, changes in the real risk-free interest rate (and not changes in the real interest rate) cause *movements along* the real loanable funds supply and demand curves. Only by putting the real risk-free interest rate on the vertical axis do we get the proper relationship with the quantity of real loanable funds supplied each period, which is put on the horizontal axis.

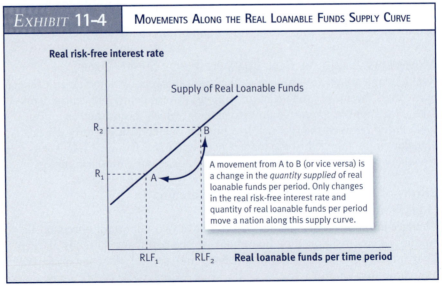

| EXHIBIT 11-4 | MOVEMENTS ALONG THE REAL LOANABLE FUNDS SUPPLY CURVE |

Real risk-free interest rate

Supply of Real Loanable Funds

R_2 ---------- B

R_1 ---- A

A movement from A to B (or vice versa) is a change in the *quantity supplied* of real loanable funds per period. Only changes in the real risk-free interest rate and quantity of real loanable funds per period move a nation along this supply curve.

RLF_1 RLF_2 **Real loanable funds per time period**

© John E. Marthinsen

Effects of the Real Risk-Free Interest Rate on the Quantity of Saving Supplied: When the real risk-free interest rate increases, it encourages saving because individuals have the opportunity to enjoy greater consumption opportunities in the future for the sacrifices made today. This is not to say that the real risk-free interest rate is the most important factor determining the average individual's saving rate. For many people, employment, income, and expected earnings may be more important than the real risk-free interest rate. Nevertheless, the point here is if the real risk-free interest rate rose, most of us would save more (not less) and, therefore, the amount supplied to the real loanable funds market would rise.[3]

> A rising real risk-free interest rate encourages households to save, which increases the quantity supplied of real loanable funds.

Effects of the Real Risk-Free Interest Rate on Portfolio Allocation: As the real risk-free interest rate increases, it encourages individuals to adjust their investment portfolios. Relatively lower-yielding assets, such as collectibles, precious metals, and real estate, are sold, and the proceeds are supplied to the real loanable funds market where relatively higher returns can be earned.

> A rising real risk-free interest rate encourages household portfolio adjustments, which increase the quantity of real loanable funds supplied.

Effect of Real Risk-Free Interest Rate on Businesses and Governments Sources of Supply

Changes in the real risk-free interest rate affect the cash management practices of businesses and governments (especially state and local governments). Like households, higher interest rates also encourage businesses to adjust the composition of their portfolios (i.e., nonoperating assets) in order to profit from the higher returns.

> A higher real risk-free interest rate encourages businesses and governments to increase the quantity of funds supplied to the real loanable funds market.

For businesses, designing and implementing national and international cash management systems can be expensive. Therefore, rising interest rates can be the incentive needed to upgrade cash management practices. For governments, rising interest rates can provide the incentive needed to improve tax collection and expenditure management systems. When private and government cash flows are more efficiently handled, the amount of credit supplied to the real loanable funds market increases. As a result, there is an increase in the quantity of credit supplied to the real loanable funds market when the real risk-free interest rate rises.

Effect of Real Risk-Free Interest Rate Changes on Foreign Sources of Supply

When a country's real risk-free interest rate rises and becomes more attractive relative to the rest of the world, foreign investors react to this stimulus by increasing their financial investments in the nation with the relatively higher real returns. Such financial investments increase the amount of credit supplied to that nation's real loanable funds market.

> Increases in a nation's real risk-free interest rate relative to other nations stimulate inflows of real loanable funds from foreigners.

---

[3] An increase in the real risk-free interest rate could cause some individuals, especially those with set retirement goals, to save less because the higher return would allow them to reach their financial goals with less saving. The number of individuals in this group is usually not large enough to offset those who save more as the real risk-free interest rate rises. Therefore, the net relationship between saving and the real risk-free interest rate is positive.

Diversification, Capital Market Imperfections, and the International Flow of Funds

If a nation's real risk-free interest rate rose relative to the rest of the world, why wouldn't it be swamped by foreign investors trying to take advantage of the relatively high returns? After all, these returns would be *risk-free*. Remember that investors seek diversified international portfolios. Also, imperfections (even small ones) in the international capital markets act to clog global financial arteries. The greater the blockage, the weaker the capital flows.

Among these imperfections are relative differences in central bank controls, access to information, and other impediments that prevent a nation's real interest rate from reflecting the pure risk-adjusted real returns on financial assets. The development level of a nation's stock and bond markets is a good example. Most developing nations' capital markets pale in comparison to the depth, breadth, sophistication, and freedom of developed nations, such as the United States and England. This unevenness impedes the flow of capital that might otherwise arbitrage away differentials in international interest rates.

For instance, between June 2004 and June 2006, the U.S. Federal Reserve raised short-term U.S. interest rates 16 consecutive times. These higher rates attracted international capital to the United States and helped fund consumer spending, business investments, and burgeoning government deficits.

Effect of Real Risk-Free Interest Rate on the Real Money Supply: Variations in the real risk-free interest rate cause banks and individuals to modify their behavior, and these behavioral changes affect the flow of funds to the real loanable funds market. We learned in Chapter 8, "The Power of Financial Institutions to Create Money," that a nation's M2 money supply is influenced by two major factors, the monetary base and the M2 money multiplier (see Exhibit 11-5). We also found that the M2 money multiplier is directly influenced by changes in a nation's real risk-free interest rate.

Three interest-sensitive factors were highlighted in our discussion of the M2 money multiplier—namely, the portion of loans that were diverted from checking accounts to currency in circulation (C_c), customary reserves of the banking system (U), and near-money deposits (N).[4] The M2 money multiplier is inversely related to the flow of funds into currency in circulation (C_c) and customary reserves (U), and it is directly related to funds flowing into near money accounts (N).[5]

If the real risk-free interest rate increases, the opportunity cost of holding currency in circulation rises, giving individuals an incentive to reduce it. Depositing these funds in financial intermediaries increases the banking system's ability to lend. Therefore, reductions in a nation's currency in

---

[4] More formally, these factors are captured by three preferred asset ratios, which are (1) the ratio of currency in circulation to checking accounts (C_c/D), (2) the ratio of banks' customary reserves to checking accounts (U/D), and (3) the ratio of near-money deposits to checking accounts (N/D).

[5] The M2 money multiplier is also affected by changes in reserve ratios (rr_D and rr_N), but they are controlled by the central bank and, therefore, are not interest sensitive.

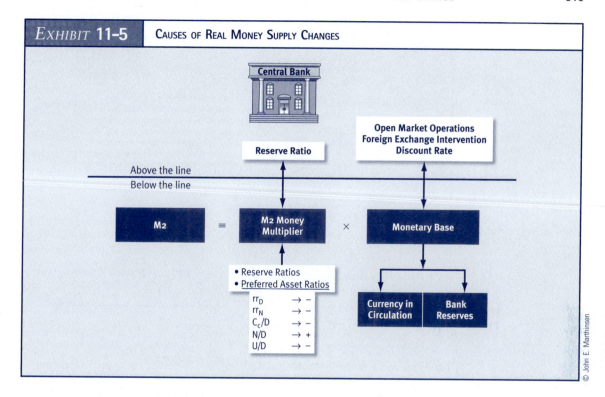

EXHIBIT **11-5**   CAUSES OF REAL MONEY SUPPLY CHANGES

circulation relative to checking deposits increase its M2 money multiplier, which increases the nation's M2 money supply.

Similarly, an increase in the real risk-free interest rate raises the opportunity cost for banks holding excess reserves, giving them an incentive to economize on their customary reserve holdings. Reductions in customary reserves relative to checking accounts increase the nation's M2 money multiplier, which increases the M2 money supply.

Finally, as the real risk-free interest rate increases, the public's demand for near money rises, due to its higher return relative to checking accounts. Because the reserve requirement on near money is lower than the reserve requirement on checking accounts, increasing the portion of near money deposits in household and business portfolios relative to checking accounts raises the M2 money multiplier.

MOVEMENTS ALONG THE REAL LOANABLE FUNDS DEMAND CURVE

Real loanable funds are demanded by domestic and foreign households, businesses, and governments. If the real risk-free interest rate falls, these participants have an incentive to borrow more; if it rises, they have an incentive to borrow less (see Exhibit 11-6). Therefore, the demand for real loanable funds is downward sloping.

As a nation's real risk-free interest rate falls, households borrow to purchase goods and services, such as appliances, vacations, automobiles, houses, and educational opportunities. Businesses approve more capital budgeting

Domestic and foreign individuals, businesses, and governments are the major borrowers of real loanable funds.

© John E. Marthinsen

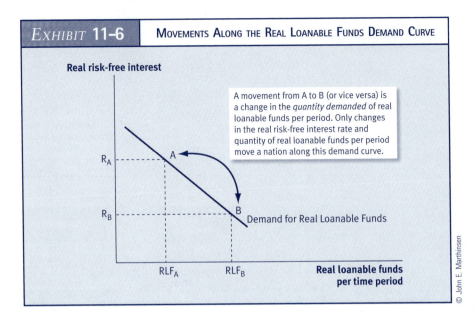

EXHIBIT 11-6   MOVEMENTS ALONG THE REAL LOANABLE FUNDS DEMAND CURVE

Real risk-free interest

A movement from A to B (or vice versa) is a change in the *quantity demanded* of real loanable funds per period. Only changes in the real risk-free interest rate and quantity of real loanable funds per period move a nation along this demand curve.

R_A

A

R_B

B   Demand for Real Loanable Funds

RLF$_A$ RLF$_B$ **Real loanable funds per time period**

© John E. Marthinsen

projects, carry larger inventories, and borrow to repair or improve existing plant and equipment. CFOs around the world act quickly to borrow at advantageous rates. Changes in relative international interest rates also provide opportunities (usually short-term ones) to arbitrage the markets by borrowing in a low-interest country, investing in countries with the higher real returns, and hedging their foreign exchange exposures.[6]

The same incentives apply to governments—especially state and local governments—that are sensitive to changes in the real risk-free interest rate. When interest rates fall, the cost of borrowing declines, which makes financing budget deficits less costly in terms of both interest costs and the repercussions of angry taxpayers.

EQUILIBRIUM REAL RISK-FREE INTEREST RATE

The equilibrium real risk-free interest rate is where the quantity of real loanable funds supplied and demanded per period are equal. In Exhibit 11-7, this occurs at Point E, where the equilibrium real risk-free interest rate is R_E, and the equilibrium quantity of real loanable funds per period is RLF$_E$. At R_A, the real risk-free interest rate is above equilibrium, causing a surplus of real loanable funds and generating natural market forces that drive down the rate toward R_E. At R_B, the real risk-free interest rate is below equilibrium, causing a shortage of funds and generating natural market forces that drive up the rate toward R_E.

The real risk-free interest rate is determined where the quantity of real loanable funds supplied and demanded per time period are equal.

[6]This set of transactions is called *covered interest arbitrage*. With the rapid increase in the global derivatives markets, firms can now borrow millions of euros, dollars, yen, or pounds and immediately hedge their foreign currency exposures.

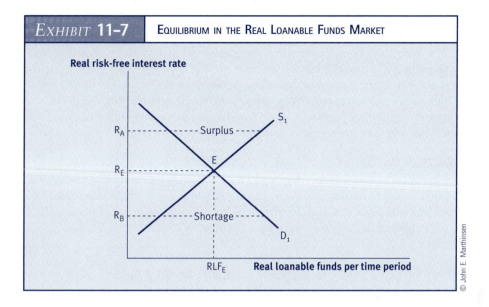

EXHIBIT **11-7**   EQUILIBRIUM IN THE REAL LOANABLE FUNDS MARKET

WHAT FORCES CHANGE THE EQUILIBRIUM REAL RISK-FREE RATE AND QUANTITY OF REAL LOANABLE FUNDS?

Simultaneous changes in both the real risk-free interest rate and quantity of real loanable funds per period move a nation along the supply and demand for real loanable funds curves. Changes in other relevant variables shift to the right or left the entire supply and/or demand curves.

A FRIENDLY "HEADS–UP"

Before we begin discussing the major exogenous factors that shift a nation's supply and/or demand for real loanable funds, a caveat is in order. The major participants in a nation's real loanable funds market are domestic and foreign households, businesses, governments, financial institutions, and central banks. Most of these same participants are also active in other macro markets, such as the real goods and foreign exchange markets. In each case, participants are affected by multiple overlapping economic, social, and political variables. The purpose of this section (and similar sections in later chapters) is not to introduce an exhaustive list of exogenous factors and relationships that should be memorized. Rather, it is to acquaint you with the most important and commonly recognized economic variables that affect supply and demand analyses and to explain their cause-and-effect relationships. In doing so, we can ensure that these relationships are logical and consistent with *your* common sense.

It is important for the economic relationships explained in this chapter (and book) to be consistent with your common sense and intuition because the economic analyses you perform in the future are likely to vary considerably. Most likely, they will involve changes in the variables highlighted in this and subsequent chapters, but your analyses could just as easily involve others. The point is that, in the business world, no one is going to ask you to list the variables that affect the supply and/or demand for real loanable funds, real GDP, or foreign exchange. Your job will be to identify the most important factors affecting an economy, determine the market(s) they influence, and establish whether their impact is direct, inverse, or uncertain.

SHIFTS IN THE SUPPLY OF REAL LOANABLE FUNDS

In this section, we will investigate the major factors that influence the supply of real loanable funds, and in the next one, we will investigate the major factors that influence demand. Remember that an increase in supply is a shift to the right of the entire curve, and a decrease is a shift to the left (see Exhibit 11-8).

Who Supplies Funds to the Real Loanable Funds Market?

There are five major participants on the supply side of the real loanable funds market: domestic and foreign households, businesses, governments, financial institutions, and central banks. Households supply funds to the real loanable funds market by saving, but the term "saving" may require further explanation because it is commonly misunderstood. When individuals earn incomes from the work they have done, there are only three uses to which these funds can be put: consumption, taxes, and saving. Therefore, real income (or real GDP) must equal the sum of consumption plus taxes plus saving. Because saving is what is left over after consumption expenditures and taxes have been deducted from a nation's income, anything that increases household consumption expenditures and tax payments relative to income reduces saving (and vice versa).

Real GDP ≡ Consumption + Saving + Taxes ≡ $C + S + T$

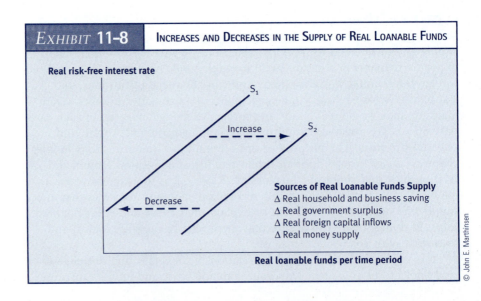

EXHIBIT 11-8   INCREASES AND DECREASES IN THE SUPPLY OF REAL LOANABLE FUNDS

Real risk-free interest rate

S_1

Increase →

S_2

← Decrease

Sources of Real Loanable Funds Supply
Δ Real household and business saving
Δ Real government surplus
Δ Real foreign capital inflows
Δ Real money supply

Real loanable funds per time period

© John E. Marthinsen

Businesses supply funds to the real loanable funds market from the excess cash flows they earn. The ultimate sources of these cash flows are (1) operating profits, (2) returns on nonoperating assets, and (3) asset disposals.[7] In general, positive cash flows can be used by businesses to make dividend payments to shareholders, invest in operating assets, and/or invest in nonoperating assets. By purchasing nonoperating assets (e.g., bills, bonds, and notes) with these financial resources, businesses increase the supply of real loanable funds.

Governments supply credit to the real loanable funds market when they run fiscal surpluses or have positive cash flows to invest for part of the fiscal year. What factors influence government surpluses? To answer this question, it is important to remember that changes in taxes and government spending can be nondiscretionary or discretionary. Nondiscretionary changes are automatic (i.e., passive) responses to fluctuations in real GDP as people gain and lose jobs with the ebb and flow of economic activity. Discretionary changes are due to the actions of the executive and legislative branches of government. We will have more to say about these later in the chapter and book.

Finally, the foreign supply of real loanable funds depends on a nation's balance of payments position. In Chapter 16, "Balance of Payments Fundamentals," we will discuss fully the concepts and relationships related to a nation's balance of payments. When we do, one of our main conclusions will be that a nation's net international borrowing or lending position is equal to and opposite from its net export position.[8] In short, if a country runs a net export deficit, it must finance the deficit by borrowing internationally, and if it runs a net export surplus, the nation must lend (invest) internationally.

Some of the key economic factors that influence a nation's net export position are changes in exchange rates and relative changes in GDP, prices, and trade restrictions, such as tariffs and quotas. Other factors relate to economic, political, and social conditions, such as fluctuations in *relative* resource costs and availability, political stability, the credibility and prudence of central bank policies, as well as tax rates, investment restrictions (e.g., currency controls, limits on profit repatriation, and local-content rules), bureaucratic red tape, civil unrest, chances of confiscation, corruption levels, government fractionalization, social conflicts, terrorism, and xenophobia.

With these participants in mind, let's discuss some of the key variables that affect their behavior and, in doing so, shift the supply of real loanable funds.

---

[7] *Operating profits* are the net returns on operating assets, such as plant, equipment, and working capital. *Nonoperating profits* are the net returns on net nonoperating assets, such as marketable securities. *Asset disposals* include the sale of physical capital, such as land and factories, as well as the divestment of entire divisions or departments.

[8] We will find that net international borrowing and lending are equal and opposite to a nation's *current international transactions*, which is a broader measure than *net exports*. Because *net exports* are the largest portion of most nations' current international transactions, there is little sacrifice to discuss international borrowing and lending in relation to a nation's net export position. Net international borrowing and lending also includes changes in a nation's international reserves.

Shifts in Supply Due to Changes in Real GDP

Changes in real GDP affect multiple sectors of the economy, all of which increase the supply of real loanable funds as real GDP rises. Let's take a closer look.

In the household sector, as a nation's real GDP increases, a portion of the newly generated income is consumed, a portion is paid in taxes, and the rest is saved. Therefore, increases in real GDP (i.e., real income) cause saving to rise, which increases the supply of real loanable funds. Increases in real GDP also tend to improve businesses' profitability and raise the return on their nonoperating assets. Therefore, there is a direct relationship between changes in real GDP and changes in real business saving, which increases the supply of real loanable funds.

As a nation's real GDP rises, the government benefits in two ways. First, it collects more taxes, and second, employment rates rise, causing government transfer payments for unemployment compensation and social welfare programs to fall. If these forces result in a government surplus, then the supply of real loanable funds increases.

Finally, as a nation's real GDP rises, residents import more goods and services, which causes net exports to fall. To pay for these net imported goods and services, foreign capital must flow to the deficit nation. As a result, there is a direct relationship between changes in a nation's real GDP and the supply of real loanable funds from foreign sources. As real GDP rises, foreign capital inflows rise.[9]

Increases in real GDP raise household and business saving, which increase the supply of real loanable funds.

An increase in real GDP that results in a government surplus raises the supply of real loanable funds.

Real GDP has a direct relationship with foreign funds supplied to the real loanable funds market.

Shifts in Supply Due to Changes in Real Household Wealth

Wealth is the market value of a household's net worth, which is the difference between the market values of its assets and liabilities. Increases in household wealth tend to reduce saving rates and decreases tend to increase it. To understand why, suppose you earned a yearly income of $100,000 and saved 10% of it. What would happen to your *saving rate* if the stock market crashed and housing prices plummeted, threatening your employment and causing the value of your financial assets and home equity to plunge by 60%? With such a dramatic reduction in wealth and job security, would you save more or less of your yearly income? Alternatively stated, would you consume more or less of your yearly income?

Such a decline in wealth would provide most people with an incentive to increase their saving rates (i.e., reduce their consumption rates) so they could retire as planned or have a buffer of precautionary savings. By increasing their saving rates, they could try to make up for losses in the financial and housing markets. Therefore, there is an inverse relationship between changes in wealth and changes in saving.

Does this relationship make sense in the other direction? In other words, what would happen to household saving if real wealth rose? Suppose you inherited $1 million or your portfolio increased in value by a large amount (e.g., by 60%) due to a stock market boom, like the one in the United States

---

[9] **"The Rest of the Story"** section of this chapter, entitled "Applications: Effects of Economic Shocks on the Real Risk-Free Interest Rate," covers an example that pulls together the effect that real GDP has on the supply *and* demand for real loanable funds.

during the 1990s. Would you save more or less of your current income? Many people would save less (i.e., consume more) of their current incomes because they would have sufficient funds set aside for retirement and also for precautionary purposes, like meeting unexpected expenses and emergencies. Greater wealth might encourage individuals to save only 5% of their incomes instead of 10%. It is for this reason that wealth and saving are inversely related.

For families whose incomes are so low that they can save nothing, the inverse relationship between wealth and saving may not seem intuitive and logical. If a family earns so little that nothing can be saved from current income, then an increase in wealth may actually raise that family's ability to save and not reduce it. As a result, increased real wealth would raise their saving rates.

Like most relationships in economics, the connection between wealth and saving can be tested for direction and strength. Does wealth affect saving? The answer is yes, and the net relationship between changes in wealth and changes in saving is inverse. As real wealth rises, the saving rate falls because the impact of the relatively few families that are exceptions to this relationship are dominated by the majority.

> Wealth has an inverse relationship with real household saving and the supply of real loanable funds.

Shifts in Supply Due to Changes in Expectations

Changing expectations can have significant effects on a nation's real risk-free interest rate. For example, favorable expectations about the economic, political, and/or social environment encourage individuals to consume more now because they feel assured that they will have jobs, be able to repay their debts, and, if necessary, make up in the future for lost saving now. Therefore, improved expectations cause a nation's real saving rate to fall, thereby reducing the supply of real loanable funds. The same is true for businesses. Expectations about favorable future conditions encourage businesses to invest funds in operating assets and new marketing strategies rather than supply these funds to the real loanable funds market.

> Favorable economic, political, and social expectations decrease real household and business saving.

Shifts in Supply Due to Changes in Real Indebtedness

Indebtedness levels are often measured relative to income, assets, and/or equity, and they can have a significant influence on the household and business saving rates. When real indebtedness rises relative to threshold levels of real income, credit availability diminishes due to lender concerns about debt repayments. As well, borrowers often react to rising indebtedness levels by curtailing their debt accumulation rates. For the household sector, this means reducing consumption and increasing saving. For businesses, it means cutting capital budgeting expenditures, and for governments, it means curtailing the rate of spending or raising taxes. As a result, there is a direct relationship between indebtedness levels and the supply of real loanable funds.

> Higher indebtedness levels increases saving rates.

Shifts in Supply Due to Changes in Discretionary Tax Rates

The effect that increased taxes have on the supply of real loanable funds from domestic and foreign households and businesses is diametrically opposite to the effect they have on governments. Because these forces are not offsetting, the real risk-free interest rate changes as discretionary taxes change. Here is why.

Earlier in this chapter, we learned that real GDP is equal to consumption plus taxes plus saving. Therefore, as taxes rise relative to real GDP, household consumption *and* saving must fall. Lower real saving reduces the supply of real loanable funds. Similarly, taxes reduce businesses' cash flows, diminishing their ability to supply credit to the real loanable funds market. As a result, there is an inverse relationship between taxes and both the household and business supply of real loanable funds.

Taxes paid by the household and business sectors flow to the government. When they do, they have another, more powerful, effect on the supply of real loanable funds. To understand the *net effect* of taxes, assume a government begins with a balanced budget (i.e., government spending equals tax revenues). Suppose further taxes increase by $100 billion, and the government uses these funds to repurchase outstanding debt. Under these circumstances, the government sector's supply of credit to the real loanable funds market rises by the full $100 billion (see Exhibit 11-9).

At the same time, if taxes rose by $100 billion, they would reduce the household sector's after-tax (i.e., disposable) income and/or the business sector's profits by a total of $100 billion. How would these sectors react to the higher taxes? Faced with a reduction in disposable income, individuals would cut both their consumption *and* saving. Faced with a reduction in profits, businesses would cut dividends, reduce investments in operating assets, *and/or* curtail their purchases of marketable securities.

Suppose the average consumer spent 90% of his or her disposable income and saved the remaining 10%. Suppose further that the business sector paid out 90% of its after-tax profits as dividends and investments; the remaining

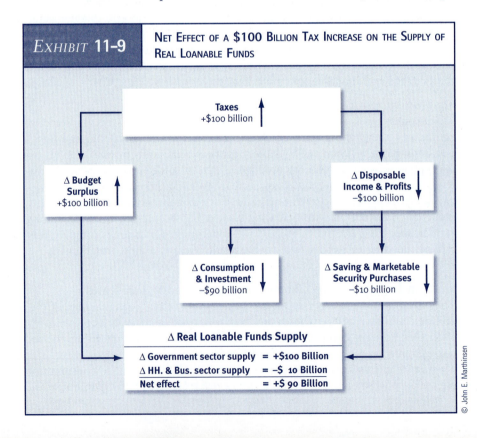

EXHIBIT 11-9 — NET EFFECT OF A $100 BILLION TAX INCREASE ON THE SUPPLY OF REAL LOANABLE FUNDS

Taxes
+$100 billion ↑

Δ Budget Surplus
+$100 billion ↑

Δ Disposable Income & Profits
−$100 billion ↓

Δ Consumption & Investment
−$90 billion ↓

Δ Saving & Marketable Security Purchases
−$10 billion ↓

Δ Real Loanable Funds Supply

Δ Government sector supply	= +$100 Billion
Δ HH. & Bus. sector supply	= −$ 10 Billion
Net effect	= +$ 90 Billion

© John E. Marthinsen

10% was used to fund additions to nonoperating assets. Under these circumstances, an increase in taxes by $100 billion would lower disposable incomes and profits by $100 billion. But this reduction would decrease household saving and business purchases of marketable securities by only $10 billion. Therefore, the $100 billion increase in government sector's supply of real loanable funds would be stronger than the $10 billion reduction in supply by the household and business sectors. The net effect would be an increase in the supply of real loanable funds by $90 billion (see Exhibit 11-9).[10]

Shifts in Supply Due to Changes in Country Risks

Changes in country risk have no direct effect on the real loanable funds market, but there could be a strong indirect one. This statement may seem paradoxical, but it is not because the real loanable funds market is where the real *risk-free* interest rate is determined. Risk is an additive component in our analysis, which increases the *real* interest rate and *nominal* interest rate. It does *not directly* increase the real *risk-free* interest rate.

If changing international risks and risk expectations do not have a direct effect on a nation's real risk-free interest rate, then what indirect effect might they have? This answer is best understood by putting the real loanable funds market into a broader context. Fluctuations in risks directly affect the economic markets in which important macroeconomic variables are determined. Real GDP, prices, and exchange rates are just a few of these variables. When they change, these macroeconomic variables go on to affect the supply of real loanable funds. Therefore, fluctuations in a nation's relative international risk level indirectly affect the supply of credit to its real loanable funds market. These indirect interconnections are thoroughly explored later in the book.

Shifts in Supply Due to Changes in Central Bank Monetary Policies[11]: The supply of real loanable funds changes with increases and decreases in the nation's real money supply. Recall from Chapter 8, "The Power of Financial Institutions to Create Money," that the M2 money supply changes with movements in a nation's monetary base and/or M2 money multiplier. Central banks change the monetary base by enacting open market operations, foreign exchange market intervention, and/or discount rate policies. The M2 money multiplier changes with the reserve ratios and/or household and business preferences for currency in circulation, customary reserves, and near money relative to checking deposits. If these relative preferences change, due to movements in factors other than the nation's real risk-free interest rate, then the M2 money multiplier, M2 money supply, and supply of real loanable funds change.

> Discretionary tax increases raise the supply of real loanable funds because the negative effects they have on households and businesses is offset by the positive effects they have on the government.

> Changes in country risks do not have direct effects on the supply of real loanable funds, but they can have strong, indirect effects.

> Changes in the supply of real loanable funds are influenced by fluctuations in the M2 money multiplier and monetary base.

---

[10] Note that an increase in taxes also would cause demand to fall, which would decrease real GDP. As a result, the reduction in real GDP would cause government tax revenues to passively decrease and offset part (but not all) of the surplus. Therefore, even if we considered the automatic stabilizers, our qualitative result would remain the same, which means higher taxes cause a net increase in the supply of credit to the real loanable funds market.

[11] "**The Rest of the Story**" section of this chapter, entitled "Applications: Effects of Economic Shocks on the Real Risk-Free Interest Rate," covers an example showing the effect expansionary monetary policy has on the real risk-free interest rate.

MACRO MEMO   11-5

Qualitative Changes: Some Helpful Abbreviations

Before we begin to summarize our analyses, let's review a few cause-and-effect abbreviations used in this and other chapters that will simplify our discussion of the key economic relationships. Exhibit 11-10 shows that any cause-and-effect relationship can be represented by a simple ratio. In the denominator is the change in a stimulus, and in the numerator is the corresponding change in a response.* If the stimulus and response move in the same direction, then the ratio is positive. If they move in opposite directions, the ratio is negative. Therefore, when a plus sign (+) is placed after a stimulus-response ratio, it implies a direct relationship: If the stimulus rises, the response rises, and if the stimulus falls, the response falls. When a negative sign (−) is placed after a stimulus-response ratio, it implies an inverse relationship: If the stimulus rises, the response falls, and if the stimulus falls, the response rises.

*Those with a background in calculus will recognize this ratio as the first derivative.

EXHIBIT **11-10**	CAUSE–AND–EFFECT RELATIONSHIPS

$$\text{Positive Qualitative Change} = \frac{\Delta \text{ Response}}{\Delta \text{ Stimulus}} = \frac{\text{Rises}}{\text{Rises}} \text{ or } \frac{\text{Falls}}{\text{Falls}} = +$$

$$\text{Negative Qualitative Change} = \frac{\Delta \text{ Response}}{\Delta \text{ Stimulus}} = \frac{\text{Rises}}{\text{Falls}} \text{ or } \frac{\text{Falls}}{\text{Rises}} = -$$

© John E. Marthinsen

Exhibit 11-11 summarizes the major factors that cause the real money supply to change.

Exhibit 11-12 lists all of the major sectors, exogenous factors, and cause-and-effect relationships on the supply side of the real loanable funds market.

SHIFTS IN THE DEMAND FOR REAL LOANABLE FUNDS

In this section, we will investigate the major factors that influence the demand for real loanable funds. Remember that an increase in demand is a movement to the right, and a decrease in demand is a movement to the left (see Exhibit 11-13).

Who Shifts the Demand for Real Loanable Funds?

There are four major participants on the demand side of the real loanable funds market: domestic and foreign households, businesses, governments, and financial institutions. Central banks are excluded from the demand side of this market because, typically, they are not borrowers. Rather, central banks are the ultimate sources of a nation's (or monetary union's) money supply. If they were net borrowers, then central banks would be included in demand.

Households borrow to finance a variety of durables and services, such as washers, dryers, automobiles, and vacations. Businesses borrow for other reasons, such as financing new construction, working capital, and existing

> Households, businesses, financial intermediaries, and governments are major borrowers in the real loanable funds market.

EXHIBIT 11–11 — MAJOR FACTORS AFFECTING THE REAL MONEY SUPPLY

	Cause(s) the Real Money Supply To:	Relationship
Factors affecting the monetary base		
Open market purchases	Rise	+
Foreign exchange purchases	Rise	+
Discount rate rises	Fall	−
Factors affecting the M2 money multiplier		
Reserve ratio rises	Fall	−
(C_c/D) rises	Fall	−
(U/D) rises	Fall	−
(N/D) rises	Rise	+

© John E. Marthinsen

EXHIBIT 11–12 — SUMMARY OF THE MAJOR SECTORS AND FACTORS INFLUENCING THE SUPPLY OF REAL LOANABLE FUNDS

	Household Supply	Business Supply	Government Supply	Foreign Supply	Real Money Supply	Net Supply Change	Qualitative Relationship
Real GDP ↑	Rises	Rises	Rises	Rises		Rises	+
Household wealth ↑	Falls					Falls	−
Expectations: economic, political, & social ↑	Falls	Falls		Rises		Uncertain	?
Indebtedness ↑	Rises	Rises				Rises	+
Discretionary government taxes ↑	Falls	Falls	Rises			Rises	+
Government budget surplus ↑			Rises			Rises	+
Country risk ↑				No direct effect		No direct effect	0
Monetary base ↑					Rises	Rises	+
M2 money multiplier ↑					Rises	Rises	+

© John E. Marthinsen

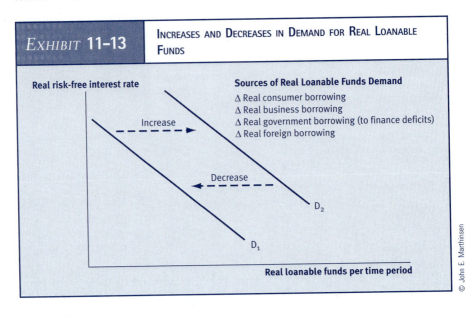

EXHIBIT 11–13   INCREASES AND DECREASES IN DEMAND FOR REAL LOANABLE FUNDS

Real risk-free interest rate

Sources of Real Loanable Funds Demand
Δ Real consumer borrowing
Δ Real business borrowing
Δ Real government borrowing (to finance deficits)
Δ Real foreign borrowing

Increase

Decrease

D_2

D_1

Real loanable funds per time period

© John E. Marthinsen

plant facilities. Government demand for real loanable funds is a reflection of its budget deficits.[12] Therefore, any factor or policy that increases a government's expenditures relative to tax revenues causes its budget deficits and demand for real credit to rise.[13]

Finally, the net demand for real loanable funds by foreigners depends on a nation's balance of payments position. If a country runs an export surplus, then it is a net lender to foreign nations, which means foreign nations are net borrowers from the surplus country.[14]

Let's discuss the exogenous factors that affect the demand for real loanable funds by domestic households, businesses, and governments, as well as the foreign sector.

> **Net foreign demand for real loanable funds depends on a nation's balance of payments position.**

Shifts in Demand Due to Changes in Real GDP

When a nation's real GDP (i.e., real income) increases, economic conditions improve, production increases, and businesses have incentives to expand capacity and ensure that their assets are well maintained. If internal cash flows are insufficient to support these investments, businesses borrow. Therefore, there is a direct relationship between the business sector's demand for real credit and the level of economic activity.

> **Business demand for real loanable funds tends to increase as real GDP rises.**

A rising real GDP has just the opposite effect on governments. As economic conditions improve and incomes (real GDP) rise, government tax revenues increase, and transfer payments for unemployment compensation and social welfare programs fall as people find jobs. Therefore, the government's

---

[12] In nations where it is allowed, governments could create the needed funds; so borrowing is not always the only alternative.

[13] "**The Rest of the Story**" section of this chapter, entitled "Applications: Effects of Economic Shocks on the Real Risk-Free Interest Rate," covers an example dealing with falling European deficits during the 1990s and the effect they had on the real risk-free interest rate.

[14] This relationship will be discussed, in depth, in Chapter 16, "Balance of Payments Fundamentals."

demand for real loanable funds tends to fall automatically during economic expansions and to rise during economic contractions.

Fluctuations in a nation's real GDP also affect the foreign demand for real loanable funds. A net export surplus means a nation is exporting more than it is importing and, to do so, it must be a net lender to the rest of the world. A net export deficit means just the opposite—a nation is buying more than it is selling to the rest of the world and financing the difference by borrowing internationally. For example, suppose a nation was a net international lender, which meant it had a net export surplus. As its real GDP rose, imports would rise causing net exports (i.e., exports minus imports) to fall and lowering the international demand for real loanable funds.

Notice that changes in real GDP have conflicting influences on the real risk-free interest rate. Rising real GDP increases demand by the business sector but decreases it for the government and foreign sectors. Changes in the household sector's demand for real loanable funds due to fluctuations in real GDP are uncertain. Rising real GDP alleviates the need for some families to borrow but gives a green light to others. Therefore, the net effect that changing real GDP rates have on the real risk-free interest rate is indeterminate until we know the relative strength of each force. "**The Rest of the Story**" section of this chapter, entitled "Applications: Effects of Economic Shocks on the Risk-Free Interest Rate" covers an example that pulls together all the supply and demand forces that real GDP has on the real loanable funds market.

Shifts in Demand Due to Changes in Expectations

Increases on expected interest rates cause domestic and foreign households and businesses to raise their current borrowing rates. Borrowing now rather than later allows them to lock in the relatively low current financing rates.

Similarly, expectations of higher incomes (i.e., real GDP) stimulate current household demand for credit because consumers feel more confident that they will have jobs and be able to repay their debts in the future. For businesses, expectations of higher real GDP imply healthier future sales revenues and greater profits, which stimulate current business demand for real loanable funds.

Notice that expected inflation was not mentioned in this section. The reason is expected inflation is not part of either the real risk-free interest rate or the real interest rate. Rather, it enters as a separate component in the nominal interest rate (see Exhibit 11-1).

Shifts in Demand Due to Changes in Tax Rates

Changes in taxes can strongly influence the demand for real credit. For example, if tax rules change so that households were allowed to deduct all interest expenses from the income taxes they pay, then the demand for real loanable funds would rise. Similarly, if the government provided tax incentives for particular types of consumer loans (e.g., as it does with educational loans), the household demand for credit would rise.

Governments give tax breaks, as well, to businesses (domestic and foreign) in order to stimulate economic activity and/or to encourage investments that will make their nations more competitive internationally. Therefore, lower taxes or greater tax incentives tend to increase business demand for real loanable funds.

As the rate of economic activity improves, government deficits and borrowing fall automatically.

As a nation's real GDP rises, its net exports fall causing the net international demand for real loanable funds in that nation to fall.

Changes in expected prices, income, and interest rates have a direct effect on real (domestic and foreign) household and business borrowing.

Lower taxes can increase real household borrowing.

Investment tax credits are perfect examples. An investment tax credit allows companies to claim as an expense a percentage of what they pay for new tangible assets, such as factories and machines. By claiming a greater portion of these expenditures as tax deductible expenses, businesses are able to lower their *reported* profits, which reduces their income tax payments and increases their cash flows.

By lowering tax rates, governments tend to increase their deficits. The only time this would not happen is when the *tax rate* reductions stimulated sufficient increases in GDP to cause *tax revenues* to rise. Suppose the average tax rate was 20% and GDP was $1,000 billion; tax revenues would equal $200 billion. If taxes were lowered to 15% and GDP increased above $1,333 billion, tax revenues would rise. For instance, if GDP rose to $1,500 billion, a 15% tax rate would generate tax revenues equal to $225 billion, which is greater than the original $200 billion in tax revenues.

In the absence of any new tax revenues, increased government spending causes budget deficits to rise. For example, when the United States invaded Iraq in 2003, it dramatically increased defense spending and caused U.S. budget deficits to rise. A similar result would have occurred if the spending had been on improvements to U.S. airports, highways, and bridges. If higher government spending increases a nation's demand for goods and services, and the greater demand increases real GDP, then part (but not all) of the spending-stimulated deficit will be offset by greater tax revenues.

Lower taxes can stimulate real business spending and borrowing.

Lower taxes usually increase government deficits and borrowing needs.

Shifts in Demand Due to Changes in Indebtedness

As household and business indebtedness levels rise, their willingness and ability to borrow decreases. For the household sector, indebtedness is usually measured relative to annual incomes and net equity values. For businesses it is often measured relative to the value of assets, equity, profits, and/or cash flows.[15] A borrower's ability to tap the real loanable funds market is monitored and restricted by banks and capital markets that set limits (or guidelines) on indebtedness. For example, if the debt-service-to-income limit was 40%, then a family earning $10,000 per month would have to keep its monthly interest and principal payments below $4,000. As its debt-service-to-income level approached this threshold level, the family's ability to borrow additional amounts would fall. The same is true for businesses as they approach threshold levels of indebtedness or suffer reductions in their credit ratings.

Increased indebtedness levels have an inverse relationship with real consumer and business borrowing.

Shifts in Demand Due to Changes in Regulations

Regulations can play important roles in determining businesses' demand for credit. Usually, government regulations that reduce business profitability cause reductions in investments, and, therefore, reductions in the demand for real credit, but there are some exceptions. For example, regulations that require businesses to invest in pollution abatement equipment may actually increase the demand for real loanable funds.

Regulations can raise or lower real business borrowing.

---

[15] Among the accounting measures of income used for this purpose are EBIT (i.e., earnings before interest and taxes), EBITA (i.e., earnings before interest, taxes, and amortization), and EBITDA (i.e., earnings before interest, taxes, depreciation, and amortization).

Shifts in Demand Due to Changes in Country Risks

As was the case with the supply of real loanable funds, risks do not have a direct effect on the demand for real loanable funds. Risk is an additive component in our analysis that increases the real interest rate and the nominal interest rate. Therefore, it does not *directly* change the real *risk-free* interest rate. At the same time, movements of relative international risks affect the real goods and foreign exchange markets. Through these markets, fluctuations in risk indirectly change the demand for real loanable funds and, thereby, the real risk-free interest rate. (More on this later in the chapter.)

Exhibit 11-14 summarizes the major sectors and factors that influence the demand for real loanable funds.

> Risk does not have a direct effect on the demand for real loanable funds, but it can have strong, indirect effects.

EXHIBIT **11–14**	SUMMARY OF THE MAJOR SECTORS AND FACTORS INFLUENCING THE DEMAND FOR REAL LOANABLE FUNDS					
	Household Demand	Business Demand	Government Demand	Foreign Demand	Net Demand Change	Qualitative Relationship
Real GDP ↑	Uncertain	Rises	Falls	Falls	Uncertain	?
Expectations						
• Interest expectations ↑	Rises	Rises		Rises	Rises	+
• Real GDP expectations ↑	Rises	Rises		Rises	Rises	+
• Profit expectations ↑		Rises		Rises	Rises	+
Indebtedness ↑	Falls	Falls			Falls	−
Discretionary government taxes ↑	Falls	Falls	Falls	Falls	Falls	−
Discretionary government spending ↑			Rises		Rises	+
Government budget deficit ↑				Rises	Rises	+
Regulations on business ↑		Uncertain		Uncertain	Uncertain	?
Country risk ↑				No direct effect	No direct effect	0

THE REST OF THE STORY

APPLICATIONS: EFFECTS OF ECONOMIC SHOCKS ON THE REAL RISK-FREE INTEREST RATE

Let's use what we have learned in this chapter to analyze five cases where external shocks to an economic system cause the real risk-free interest rate to change.

EFFECTS OF FALLING GOVERNMENT DEFICITS

In 1991, negotiations began in Maastricht, the Netherlands, to form a currency union among the 12 members of the EU. Agreement was reached in 1992; the treaty was ratified by all member nations by 1993, and the currency union was scheduled to begin on January 1, 1999.

Membership in the new currency union was not automatic. EU nations felt that the new currency union's chances of success would be greater if the members' economies converged prior to the union. Therefore, the Maastricht Treaty laid out five economic convergence criteria for nations to meet in order to qualify for membership in the EMU.[16]

To qualify, each EMU nation was required to meet the following criteria:
- Criterion 1: Control prices so its inflation rate was no more than 1.5% above the average of the three nations with the lowest inflation rates.
- Criterion 2: Restrict government budget deficits to no more than 3% of GDP.
- Criterion 3: Restrict the ratio of government debt to gross domestic product to no more than 60% of GDP.
- Criterion 4: Keep the nation's exchange rate relative to other EU nations within normal margins (i.e., a 30% band, which was 15% above and 15% below defined parity rates) for at least two years.
- Criterion 5: Control the nominal long-term interest rate so that it did not exceed by more than 2.0% the average of the three nations with the lowest inflation rates.

What does the real loanable funds framework predict should happen to real risk-free interest rates in the euro area if aspirant nations successfully fulfilled Criterion 2 and reduced their budget deficits? Exhibit 11-15 shows that a reduction in the demand for real loanable funds from D_1 to D_2 moves equilibrium from Point A to Point B. As a result, the real risk-free interest rate falls from R_1 to R_2, and the amount of real loanable funds supplied and demanded falls from RLF_1 to RLF_2.

Exhibit 11-16 shows that this is exactly what happened to the average real interest rate in the euro area between 1993 and the beginning of 1999, when the EMU began.[17]

---

[16] Nations were required to meet these conditions by July 1, 1998, but the evaluation of each country was based on its performance in 1997.

[17] The average real interest rate was calculated using the Eurozone's long-term convergence interest rates and the *actual* changes in the Consumer Price Index. Notice that the real interest rate, and not the real risk-free interest rate, is on the vertical axis. Therefore, other factors besides changes in the real risk-free interest rate could have been at work.

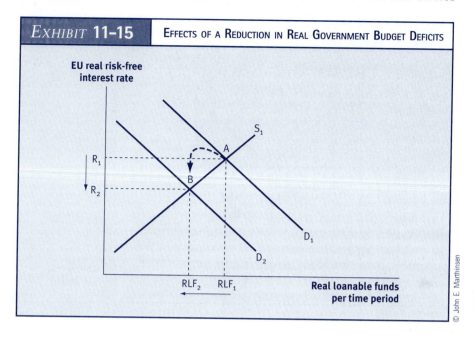

EXHIBIT **11-15**   EFFECTS OF A REDUCTION IN REAL GOVERNMENT BUDGET DEFICITS

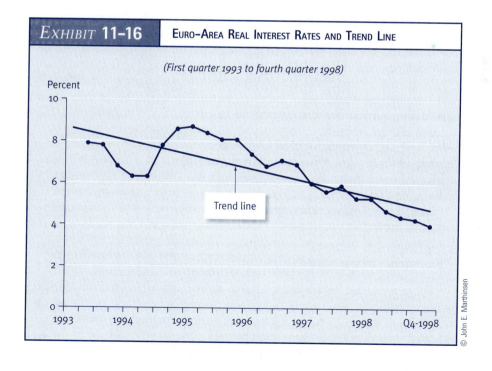

EXHIBIT **11-16**   EURO–AREA REAL INTEREST RATES AND TREND LINE

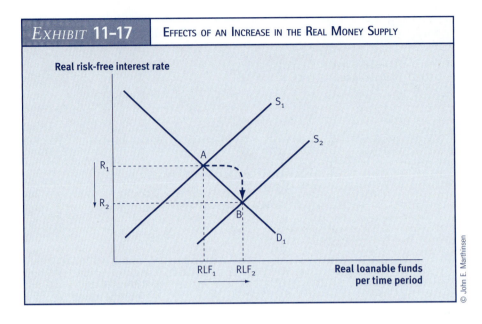

EXHIBIT 11-17 | EFFECTS OF AN INCREASE IN THE REAL MONEY SUPPLY

EFFECTS OF EXPANSIONARY MONETARY POLICY

What does the real loanable funds framework predict should happen if a central bank pursues expansionary monetary policy? An increase in a nation's real money supply causes the supply of real loanable funds to increase from S_1 to S_2 (see Exhibit 11-17), which lowers the real risk-free interest rate from R_1 to R_2, and increases the amount of real loanable funds supplied and demanded per period from RLF_1 to RLF_2.

From 2007 to 2013, the U.S. Federal Reserve and many other central banks around the world expanded their money supplies at historically rapid rates. The result was for interest rates to fall, as predicted in Exhibit 11-17.

EFFECTS OF SPECULATIVE CAPITAL OUTFLOWS

From 1984 to 1997, the Exchange Equalization Fund of Thailand tried to maintain a fixed exchange rate relative to the U.S. dollar of (approximately) 25 baht per dollar. In 1997, economic conditions began to deteriorate in Thailand, and many investors, speculators, and businesses, who expected the baht to depreciate, realized that this fixed rate would not last for long. If the fixed rate were abolished, anyone holding Thai baht would suffer capital losses, and anyone holding dollars would reap capital gains relative to the baht. Markets reacted swiftly and massively to these expectations.

The demand for baht loans soared as individuals arbitraged the markets by borrowing baht, converting them immediately into dollars, and investing the dollars in interest-earning assets. At the same time that borrowers increased their demand for real loanable funds, the supply of baht to the real loanable funds market fell as lenders/savers channeled their funds toward other investment assets.

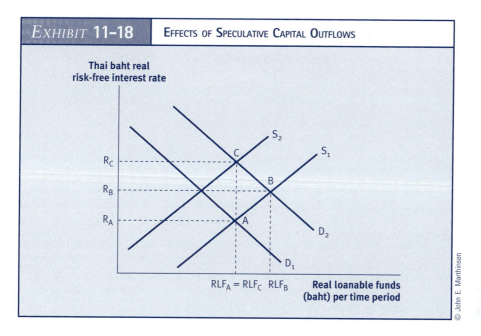

EXHIBIT 11–18   EFFECTS OF SPECULATIVE CAPITAL OUTFLOWS

As Exhibit 11-18 shows, if the demand for real baht loanable funds rises from D_1 to D_2 and the supply falls from S_1 to S_2, there is an unequivocal increase in Thailand's real risk-free interest rate from R_A to R_B to R_C. By contrast, the change in the quantity of real loanable funds per period is uncertain. Greater demand increases the equilibrium quantity per period, and the lower supply reduces it. Exhibit 11-18 shows no net change in the equilibrium quantity of real loanable funds per period, but this does not have to be the case. The net change depends on the relative strength of the supply and demand fluctuations.

EFFECTS OF BUSINESS CYCLES AND CHANGES IN REAL GDP

How does the real risk-free interest rate change during business cycles, as real GDP rises and falls? We will find that the answer is uncertain due to the multiple sectors that are influenced by real GDP and the conflicting effects it has on them.

> Changes in real GDP have conflicting effects on the real risk-free interest rate.

Suppose a nation is in the expansionary phase of its business cycle, which means real GDP is rising. The increase in real GDP (all other things remaining constant) increases household and business saving, thereby increasing the supply of real loanable funds and reducing the real risk-free interest rate. At the same time, increases in real GDP cause government budget deficits (i.e., national, state, and local) to fall because they collect more tax revenues, and their transfer payments for unemployment and social welfare programs are reduced. Due to declining budget deficits, the demand for real loanable funds falls, also causing the real risk-free interest rate to fall. Finally, rising real GDP increases imports and reduces net exports, thereby causing the foreign supply of real loanable funds to rise and the real risk-free interest rates to fall.

EXHIBIT 11-19	EFFECTS OF INCREASED REAL GDP ON THE REAL RISK-FREE INTEREST RATE	
If Real GDP Rises, Then	**Effect on Real Loanable Funds Market**	**Effect on Real Risk-Free Interest**
Saving increases	Increases supply	Falls
Government budget deficits fall	Decreases demand	Falls
Net exports fall	Increases supply	Falls
Borrowing by businesses increases	Increases demand	Rises
Net effect		**Uncertain**

So far, all the forces in an expansionary cycle have pushed down the real risk-free interest rate, but there are opposing forces that cause it to rise. For instance, rising real GDP stimulates business sector borrowing. Companies need borrowed funds to increase their capacity, raise inventory levels, and repair and/or improve existing plant and equipment. As the demand for real loanable funds increases, the real risk-free interest rate rises.

So what happens to the real risk-free interest rate as nations grow? Which forces are most powerful? The answer is "It depends." The qualitative change cannot be determined until more information is provided. All we can say now is, if the supply-side forces overpower the demand-side forces, the real risk-free interest rate will fall. If demand-side forces dominate, the real risk-free interest rate will rise. Exhibit 11-19 summarizes all of the effects changes in real GDP have on the real loanable funds market.

EFFECTS OF RISING INFLATIONARY EXPECTATIONS

On average, what effects do rising inflationary expectations have on a nation's real risk-free interest rate? The answer is "None," and Exhibit 11-20 shows why. The average expected inflation rate is a separate building block that contributes to the nominal interest rate, just as the premiums for risk, taxes, and maturity are added to the real risk-free interest rate. In the short term, changes in expected inflation depend on anticipated movements in a nation's demand and supply for goods and services. The factors that shift these supply and demand curves will be discussed in Chapter 12, "Price and Output Fluctuations." In the long run, expected inflation is determined mainly by expected changes in a nation's money supply. This relationship will be discussed fully in Chapter 21, "Causes of Long-Term Growth and Inflation."

> A nation's average inflationary expectation does not affect the real risk-free interest rate.

CAN CENTRAL BANKS SET INTEREST RATES?

Are central banks able to target interest rates? How much control do they actually have over them? The answers to these questions depend, in part, on what is meant by "control" and, in part, by what interest rate the central bank wants to target. Many central banks around the world use the nominal interbank interest rate (e.g., the federal funds rate in the United States) as an intermediate target for their monetary policies. Whether they succeed depends

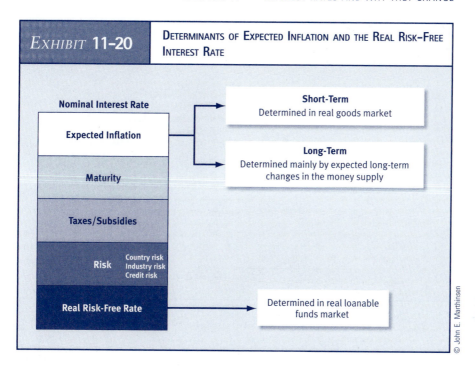

EXHIBIT 11-20   DETERMINANTS OF EXPECTED INFLATION AND THE REAL RISK–FREE INTEREST RATE

Nominal Interest Rate

Expected Inflation

Maturity

Taxes/Subsidies

Risk — Country risk / Industry risk / Credit risk

Real Risk-Free Rate

Short-Term
Determined in real goods market

Long-Term
Determined mainly by expected long-term changes in the money supply

Determined in real loanable funds market

© John E. Marthinsen

on three major factors: the competence and credibility of their monetary policies, financial artistry that often goes beyond what anyone can learn in a book, and a bit of luck.

Exhibit 11-20 shows that the nominal interest rate is composed of the real risk-free interest rate plus premiums for risk, taxes, maturity, and expected inflation. Central banks have a great deal of influence over the real risk-free interest rate and expected inflation, but they do not have complete control of them. Central banks have even less influence over a nation's country risk premium because economic, political, and social factors also influence it. Moreover, central banks do not influence the tax or maturity premiums on financial assets.

> Central banks do not control all the factors that affect nominal interest rates.

TARGETING THE REAL RISK-FREE INTEREST RATE

The real risk-free interest rate is determined by the forces of supply and demand in the real loanable funds market (see Exhibit 11-21). Central banks are just one source of supply, and they do not influence demand if they have no need to borrow. Therefore, the real risk-free interest rate changes with shifts in any important factor(s) influencing supply and/or demand. Nevertheless, if unwanted changes in the real risk-free interest rate occur, central banks have the power to change monetary policy and try to offset these undesired movements.

Therefore, central banks do not control the market-based, real risk-free interest rate in the same way they control, for example, the discount rate, which is set and not market-determined. They cannot just set the real risk-free interest rate and leave it. At the same time, if an unwanted change occurs,

> Central banks affect the real risk-free interest rate by changing the real money supply.

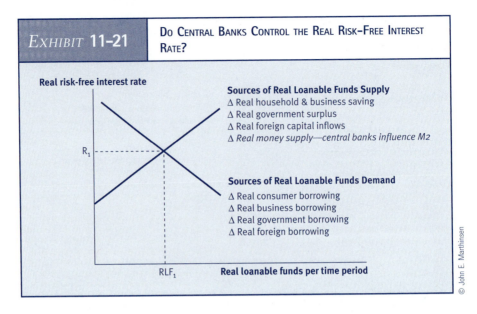

EXHIBIT 11-21   DO CENTRAL BANKS CONTROL THE REAL RISK-FREE INTEREST RATE?

Real risk-free interest rate

Sources of Real Loanable Funds Supply
Δ Real household & business saving
Δ Real government surplus
Δ Real foreign capital inflows
Δ *Real money supply—central banks influence M2*

R_1

Sources of Real Loanable Funds Demand
Δ Real consumer borrowing
Δ Real business borrowing
Δ Real government borrowing
Δ Real foreign borrowing

RLF_1 **Real loanable funds per time period**

© John E. Marthinsen

central banks can employ expansionary monetary policies to reduce the real risk-free interest rate, and they can use contractionary policies to increase it.

TARGETING NOMINAL INTEREST RATES

When central bank policies are effective, the real risk-free interest rate hovers around its target level. But this raises a new problem because any attempt by central banks to control the real risk-free interest rate could cause them to lose control of the nominal interest rate. Let's consider why this is the case.

Suppose a nation's expected inflation rate was 0%, and the central bank's target for the nominal and real risk-free interest rates was 3%. Suppose further that businesses increased their demand for real loanable funds and raised the real risk-free interest rate from 3% to 6%. As a result, the nominal risk-free interest rate would also rise from 3% to 6%.[18]

To reduce the real risk-free interest rate to its targeted level, the central bank might increase M2, which would increase the supply of real loanable funds and reduce the real risk-free interest rate. But the increased money supply would also stimulate spending, and the resulting expenditures could increase both inflation and inflationary expectations.

If expected inflation rose from 0% to 2% at the same time the real risk-free interest rate fell back to 3%, the nominal risk-free interest rate would equal 5% (i.e., 3% real risk-free interest rate plus 2% expected inflation). This figure would be above the central bank's target of 3%. Therefore, by reestablishing the central bank's 3% target for the real risk-free interest rate, it lost

By trying to control the real risk-free interest rate, a central bank can lose control over the nominal interest rate.

---

[18] Remember that the nominal interest rate is approximately equal to the real interest rate plus expected inflation.

the nominal risk-free interest rate target. As a result, the answer to the question "Can central banks effectively target nominal interest rates?" depends on whether they are able to keep the real risk-free interest rate under control without losing control of inflationary expectations.

UNDERSTANDING THE YIELD CURVE

The relationship between an asset's *nominal* yield and its maturity is called the *term structure of interest rates*, and the graphical representation of this relationship is called the *yield curve*. Why do nominal interest rates rise or fall with maturity? There are three major explanations for this relationship: the expectations theory, segmented markets theory, and preferred habitat theory.

> The term structure of interest rates shows the relationship between an investment asset's maturity and nominal yield.

EXPECTATIONS THEORY

The expectations theory views financial markets as perfectly integrated, and investors are considered to be indifferent to maturity risk. An indifference to maturity risk means that investors are both willing and able to arbitrage *any* exploitable differences in yields that vary with maturity. When capital markets are perfectly integrated and investors are indifferent to maturity risk, current nominal interest rates for different maturities can be viewed as weighted averages of expected future interest rates.

> In the expectations theory, nominal interest rates are weighted averages of expected future interest rates.

Consider how the market would react if interest rates during the next two years were expected to remain constant at 4%, but the one-year interest rate was 4% and the annual two-year rate was 6%.

- Investors could borrow $100 million for one year at 4% and invest the funds in securities with two-year maturities earning 6% per year.
- If their expectations were correct, then at the end of the first year, they could pay off their one-year loan by borrowing $104 million for an additional year at a 4% interest rate. They would need to borrow $104 million to repay the initial $100 million loan plus its 4% interest cost.
- At the end of the second year, their investment, which earned 6% each year, would mature, and the investors would receive $112.36 million.[19] In addition, the loan they took out at the end of Year 1 would mature, requiring investors to repay $108.16 million.[20] Therefore, investors' net return on this investment would be $4.20 million.

The take-away from this discussion is: If the market expected interest rates for the next two years to remain constant (say, at 4%), then the current one-year and two-year interest rates should also equal 4%, and the yield curve should be flat. If the market expected interest rates to rise from 4% this year to 6% next year, then the current one-year and two-year interest rates

---

[19] $100 million $\times$ $(1.06)^2$ = $112.36 million
[20] They borrowed $104 million at a 4% annual rate. Therefore, ($104 $\times$ 1.04) = $108.16 million

should equal 4% and 4.995%,[21] respectively. At this two-year interest rate arbitrageurs could not earn risk-free profits. To see why, suppose they borrowed $100 million for two years at 4.995% and invested them for one year at 4%. At the end of Year 1, the investment would mature, and the investor would receive $104 million. If expectations proved correct, these funds could be reinvested at 6%, and at the end of Year 2 the investor would receive $110.24 million.[22] At the end of Year 2, the principal and interest due on the $100 million loan would also equal $110.24 million.[23] Therefore, the investor would earn no net return.

SEGMENTED MARKETS THEORY

If the financial markets were perfectly integrated, then excessive maturity premiums or discounts would be arbitraged and eliminated. But if financial markets were segmented, these premiums or discounts could survive. *Segmented credit markets* are ones in which lenders/savers and/or borrowers are either unwilling or unable to switch freely from one maturity to another. For example, restrictions on the maturities of investments by insurance companies or pension funds and strong maturity preferences by lenders/savers could be the basis for segmented markets.

> Segmented capital markets are ones in which interest rate differentials based on maturity are not arbitraged.

The segmented markets theory explains the term structure of interest rates as a series of independent markets, based on maturity, in which interest rates are set by unique forces of supply and demand. As a result, interest differentials that appear to offer arbitrage opportunities, in fact, are illusions due to the market's inability and/or unwillingness to enter into such arbitrage transactions.

PREFERRED HABITAT THEORY

The preferred habitat theory is a combination of the expectations theory and the segmented markets theory. It views the financial markets as being imperfectly integrated but not completely segmented. As a result, current yields reflect expected future interest rates (like the expectations theory), but they also contain premiums that compensate investors for the risks and preferences associated with an investment's maturity (like the segmented markets theory). These risk premiums are not solely a function of maturity; rather, they reflect the returns that lenders must receive to supply credit to different maturity *habitats*. When the interest rate differentials between maturities become large enough, they can lure investors out of their *preferred habitats*. Therefore, the preferred habitat theory views current nominal interest rates as the average of expected future interest rates plus a risk premium or discount for each maturity that reflects a partially arbitraged and partially unique set of supply and demand conditions.

> The preferred habitat theory explains the term structure of interest rates as a combination of expected future interest rates and risk premiums.

---

[21] The no-arbitrage, two-year interest rate should equal 4.995% because only at this rate does $100 million × $(1.04995)^2$ = $100 million × (1.04) × (1.06).
[22] ($104 million × 1.06) = $110.24 million
[23] $100 million × $(1.04995)^2$ = $110.24 million

CONCLUSION

The nominal interest rate has two major components, the real interest rate and the expected inflation rate. Changes in the real interest rate are caused by movements in the real risk-free interest rate, plus premiums for risk, tax rates, and maturities.

The real risk-free interest rate is determined in the real loanable funds market by the forces of supply and demand. In this market, the major sources of supply are from domestic and foreign households, businesses, governments, financial intermediaries, and central banks. The demand for real loanable funds is determined by domestic and foreign households, businesses, financial intermediaries, and governments. Central banks are excluded from the demand side if they are not borrowers.

The risk premium paid by borrowers is related to relative levels of country risk, industry risk, and credit risk. Country risk depends on the relative volatility of a nation's economic, political, and social environment. Industry risk depends on the relative volatility of cash flows in a particular industry, and credit risk depends on the solvency and liquidity (i.e., access to cash) of the borrower.

Exhibit 11-22 shows the three major macroeconomic markets that are the focus of this book. At this point in our study of international macroeconomics, we have discussed only the real loanable funds market. In Chapter 12, "Price and Output Fluctuations," we will discuss the real goods market, and in Chapter 14 (i.e., "Basics of Foreign Exchange Markets") and Chapter 15 ("Exchange Rates: Why Do They Change?"), we will introduce the foreign exchange market, which will complete the building blocks needed for our macroeconomic analyses.

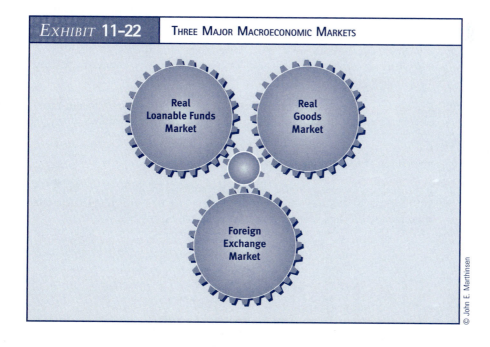

| EXHIBIT **11-22** | THREE MAJOR MACROECONOMIC MARKETS |

Real Loanable Funds Market

Real Goods Market

Foreign Exchange Market

© John E. Marthinsen

REVIEW QUESTIONS

1. What are the major components of the nominal interest rate?

2. What factors cause the real interest rate to change?

3. What factors cause the real *risk-free* interest rate to change?

4. Explain the difference between market risk and country risk.

5. Explain liquidity risk and default risk. Is it correct to say that if you have one type of risk, then you must have the other?

6. "If the supply of real loanable funds rises, the real money supply must rise." Explain whether you agree or disagree with this statement.

7. What effect, if any, does each of the following shocks (only consider the initial effect) have on Japan's real risk-free interest rate? Briefly explain and use supply and demand curves to support your conclusions. Make sure that you label all axes and curves.

   a. A decrease in the Japanese money supply with no change in prices
   b. A decrease in global lending to Japan
   c. An increase in real private saving in Japan
   d. An increase in the Japanese government's budget deficit
   e. Speculative short-term international capital inflows to Japan
   f. An increase in Japan's real GDP
   g. A rise in Japan's expected inflation rate

8. In commonsense terms (as if you were talking to a close relative), explain why the real interest rate is more important than the nominal interest rate. Use as the basis for your answer a nation that has a 20% nominal rate and a –5% real rate.

9. If Japanese interest rates are so much lower than Turkish interest rates, why don't Turkish corporations finance all or most of their expenditures by borrowing exclusively yen?

10. Explain how the preferred habitat theory of the term structure of interest rates combines elements of the expectations theory and segmented markets theory.

11. Is it accurate to say that central banks have complete control over nominal interest rates? Explain why or why not.

12. If the one-year interest rate was 6% and the annual rate for two-year funds was 10%, use the expectations theory of the interest rate term structure to determine what the market thinks one-year interest rates will be next year.

DISCUSSION QUESTIONS

13. Among developed nations of equal default risk and with highly developed capital markets (e.g., England and the United States), why do interest rates vary?

14. Suppose that you are in an employment interview with a company doing business in India. The interviewer says to you, "Economics is great in theory but lousy in practice. Here's an example. The central bank of India is increasing the money supply, yet interest rates are rising. That makes no economic sense. Right?" To reflect your understanding of macroeconomics, how should you respond? (Ignore the obvious answer, which is "You're completely right—please give me a job.")

15. Suppose the government of South Africa increased its budget deficit and financed the deficit by borrowing in the *domestic* private capital markets. Explain the effect this deficit financing would have on South Africa's real risk-free interest rate, monetary base, M2 money multiplier, and M2 money supply.

16. In 2013, President Cristina Fernández de Kirchner imposed exchange controls on the peso to slow the flight of capital from Argentina. What are the main causes of capital flight? What effect does it have on a nation's real risk-free interest rate?

Appendix 11–1

Perfectly Mobile and Perfectly Immobile International Capital Markets

International capital flows can respond weakly or powerfully to changes in relative international interest rates. The degree of international capital mobility can play a large role in the willingness and ability of nations to adopt fixed exchange rate systems, and for good reason. For nations with fixed or managed exchange rate systems, this mobility has important implications concerning changes in their international reserves and fluctuations in their money supplies. The two extreme cases are perfectly mobile and perfectly immobile international capital markets. This appendix explains the differences between these two extremes and their economic implications.

PERFECTLY MOBILE INTERNATIONAL CAPITAL MARKETS

As Exhibit A11-1 shows, perfectly mobile international capital markets are ones in which the supply of real loanable funds is horizontal (i.e., perfectly elastic) at a level equal to the international, real risk-free interest rate.

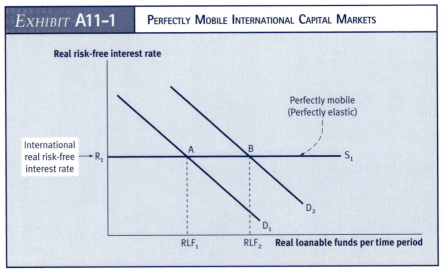

EXHIBIT A11-1 PERFECTLY MOBILE INTERNATIONAL CAPITAL MARKETS

If the real risk-free interest rate fell, capital outflows would create massive credit shortages that would raise the real risk-free interest rate back to the international level. Similarly, any slight increase in a nation's real risk-free interest rate would stimulate enormous capital inflows, which would cause credit surpluses that would reduce the real risk-free interest rate back to the international level. As a result, for any nation facing perfectly mobile international capital markets, the real risk-free interest rate is locked at the international level.

When this occurs, changes in the demand for real loanable funds have no effect on the real risk-free interest rate. For example, in Exhibit A11-1, the real risk-free interest rate remains at R_1 despite the increase in demand from D_1 to D_2. The increased demand changes only the amount of real loanable funds supplied and demanded per period from RLF_1 to RLF_2.

PERFECTLY IMMOBILE INTERNATIONAL CAPITAL MARKETS

Perfectly immobile international capital markets are ones in which foreign savers and investors are totally unresponsive to relative international changes in a nation's real *risk-free* interest rate. In other words, regardless of whether the nation's real risk-free interest rate rose or fell relative to the rest of the world, international savers and investors would be indifferent. The funds they supplied to the country's real loanable funds market would remain the same. To better understand this point, let's consider Zimbabwe.

Suppose Zimbabwe's real risk-free interest rate rose by 10% relative to the U.S. rate. If Zimbabwe faced perfectly immobile international capital markets, then despite the increase in Zimbabwe's relative return, U.S. savers and investors would not increase their financial investments in Zimbabwe.

But why would U.S. investors have any inhibitions about investing more in Zimbabwe if the return they earned was *risk-free*? For perfectly immobile international capital markets to exist, there must be major obstacles that block the flow of international capital to Zimbabwe. Among these barriers could be

- central bank or government currency controls that prevent the inflow of loanable funds to Zimbabwe,
- immature Zimbabwean stock and bond markets that are unable to handle the demands and needs of international investors,
- arbitrary taxes that expropriate the returns of foreign investors, or
- capital market imperfections and/or controls that distort Zimbabwe's real interest rates from their actual risk-adjusted returns.

Even if Zimbabwe's international capital markets were completely immobile, the nation's supply of real loanable funds would still be upward sloping (see Exhibit A11-2). But the upward slope would be the result of domestic savers (e.g., individuals and businesses) responding to the nation's changing

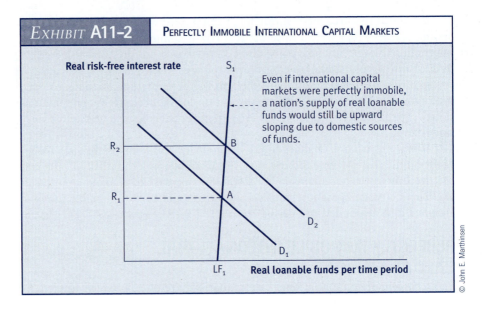

EXHIBIT A11-2   PERFECTLY IMMOBILE INTERNATIONAL CAPITAL MARKETS

Real risk-free interest rate

S_1

Even if international capital markets were perfectly immobile, a nation's supply of real loanable funds would still be upward sloping due to domestic sources of funds.

R_2 B

R_1 A

D_2

D_1

LF_1 Real loanable funds per time period

real risk-free interest rate. For example, a 10% increase in Zimbabwe's real risk-free interest rate would

- encourage domestic residents (individuals and businesses) to save more,
- increase the nation's money multiplier and therefore its real money supply, and
- persuade domestic residents with financial investments in the United States to reduce these holdings and invest more in Zimbabwe's real loanable funds market.

PART 3

THE REAL GOODS SECTOR

Chapter 12

Price and Output Fluctuations

INTRODUCTION

Vigorous sales growth is a manager's dream. Not only can it raise profits, stock prices, and salaries, but sales growth can boost morale and hide a multitude of management sins. Company sales revenues depend on two major factors: quantity sold and price. For most businesses, output growth is the primary focus because it is a sign of market acceptance and an indication that production, marketing, and distribution channels are working in harmony. It also enables companies to benefit from economies of scale and other production-related efficiencies.

Companies also try to increase their sales revenues (i.e., turnover) by raising prices, but competition often makes this route difficult or unreliable. In the absence of inflation, raising prices with any degree of certainty usually requires businesses to have at least a measure of market power, such as patents, trade secrets, product differentiation, or market niches.

Similarly, regardless of managers' capabilities and expertise, sales growth depends, in large part, on how rapidly economies are expanding. Operating in prosperous, swiftly moving nations is like swimming in a rapidly moving stream because it makes sales volume increases easier to achieve and price hikes easier to implement. When companies operate in nations with inflationary climates, price increases are necessary just to keep even in real terms.

What causes short-run changes in a nation's average price level (i.e., GDP Price Index) and output (i.e., real GDP)? What happens to the GDP Price Index and real GDP when oil prices rise due to an embargo, war in the Middle East, or increased demand by China and India? Are there economic differences when prices rise due to increasing costs as opposed to increasing demand? What is the relationship between a nation's unemployment rate and GDP Price Index? How can companies factor these changes into their financial planning? This chapter addresses these questions using the aggregate supply and aggregate demand framework.

THE BASICS

WHAT IS THE AGGREGATE SUPPLY CURVE?

The aggregate supply (AS) curve shows the quantity of domestically produced goods and services that firms are willing and able to produce and sell at various average national price levels during a given period of time. As Exhibit 12-1

> AS shows the quantity of domestically produced goods and services that firms are willing and able to produce and sell at various GDP Price Index levels during a given period of time.

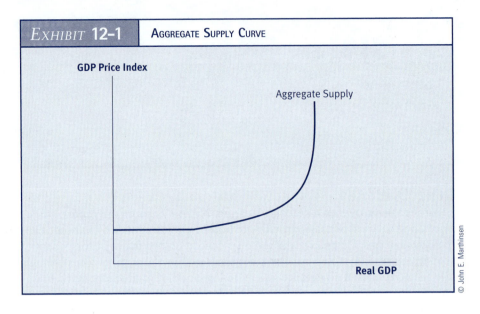

EXHIBIT **12-1** | AGGREGATE SUPPLY CURVE

GDP Price Index

Aggregate Supply

Real GDP

© John E. Marthinsen

shows, the nation's average price level, which is just another name for the GDP Price Index, is on the vertical axis of the AS graph, and real gross domestic product is on the horizontal axis.

The curvature of the AS curve is easiest to understand if we separate it into three major ranges, which are the: Keynesian range, classical range, and intermediate range (see Exhibit 12-2).

KEYNESIAN RANGE

The horizontal portion of AS is called the *Keynesian range*, where a nation's real GDP is extremely low (depression-like), unemployment is usually very high, and companies have plenty of excess capacity. In this segment of AS, businesses are much more interested in raising output levels, getting employees back to work, and reemploying machinery than they are about raising prices.

The Keynesian range was named in honor of John Maynard Keynes, a British economist whose thoughtful contributions to the science of economics were particularly applicable during the Great Depression, when AS was thought (by many) to be flat.[1]

The Keynesian range of AS is horizontal. It is associated with very low levels of real GDP and high excess capacity.

CLASSICAL RANGE

The vertical (far-right) portion of AS is called the *classical range* (see Exhibit 12-2). It is associated with a real GDP rate that fully employs

[1] Among Keynes's most famous works was a path-breaking book entitled *The General Theory of Employment, Interest, and Money* (1936). *The General Theory* was innovative, iconoclastic, and controversial because it focused on short-term, macroeconomic demand management. Keynes's book revolutionized the way the world looks at macroeconomics, and his theories opened the door to greater government intervention in the macroeconomy.

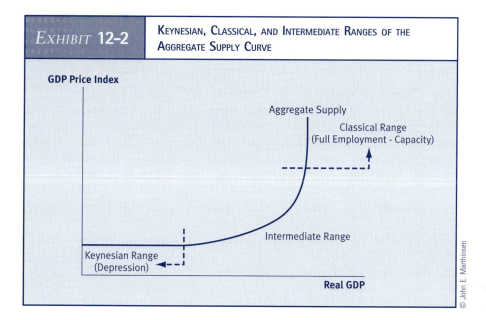

EXHIBIT **12-2**   KEYNESIAN, CLASSICAL, AND INTERMEDIATE RANGES OF THE AGGREGATE SUPPLY CURVE

© John E. Marthinsen

a nation's resources. At this rate of output, the nation has reached the limitations of its short-run capacity; so any attempt to increase employment or output beyond this rate would result only in higher average price levels.[2]

This range got its name from classical economic theory and its modern counterpart, neoclassical theory (also called monetarism), which are built on the logic that, in the long run, nations move gradually and automatically toward full employment. This inexorable-like movement toward full employment is the result of supply and demand forces that cause an array of important prices (e.g., wages, interest rates, and exchange rates) to adjust so that markets clear. Given enough time, fluctuating prices act to equilibrate the amounts supplied and demanded in all markets and, thereby, help to eliminate imbalances, such as unemployment.[3]

INTERMEDIATE RANGE

The upward-sloping portion of the AS curve lies between the Keynesian range and the classical range and is called the *intermediate range* (see Exhibit 12-2). In this AS segment, the GDP Price Index and real GDP rise (and fall) in

> The vertical portion of AS is called the classical range. It is associated with a real GDP rate that fully employs a nation's resources.

> The upward-sloping portion of the AS curve is the intermediate range. In this range, the average price level and real GDP rate increase (and decrease) together.

[2] Some prefer to view the "classical range" as the portion of the AS curve where a nation reaches some officially defined level of "full employment." If this interpretation is used, then it is possible for a nation to move beyond full employment for short periods of time. When this happens, inflationary pressures usually arise. For example in the United States, full employment is often associated with about 5% unemployment, but from 1997 to 2001 and from 2006 to 2007, the U.S. unemployment rate dropped below this level. Regardless of whether you interpret the classical range as an absolute output limit or an output threshold before rapidly rising prices begin, the basic point is the same: in the classical range, increases in demand are more likely to raise prices than they are to raise rates of output.
[3] To more fully understand the classical theory adjustment process, read "Classical Theory, The Forces of Supply and Demand, and Full Employment" in "The Rest of the Story" section of this chapter.

tandem. As most nations are somewhere in this range, it is the focus of the overwhelming majority of country analyses.

In general, the closer a nation is to the classical range, the steeper its AS curve. Likewise, the closer it is to the Keynesian range, the flatter its AS curve.

How Close Is a Nation to the Keynesian or Classical Range?

Among the initial decisions one makes when conducting a country analysis is where the nation lies on its AS curve. Because most countries are somewhere in the intermediate range, answering this question usually boils down to justifying whether the nation under scrutiny is in the relatively flat, middle, or relatively steep range. Support for this assumption comes from careful consideration of how fully employed the nation's labor force and capital resources are.

How fully employed is the nation's labor force? In general, the lower a nation's *unemployment rate* and the higher its *employment rate*, the closer that nation is to the classical range. For example, in the United States, full employment occurs when the unemployment rate is approximately 5% because it is thought that below this level, excessive inflationary pressures build. As the nation's unemployment rate falls below this 5% level, it draws nearer to the vertical portion of AS.

> The unemployment rate and employment rate are helpful indicators of where a nation is on its AS curve with respect to labor market capacity.

In the late 1990s and early 2000s, U.S. unemployment rates were below 5%; so, technically speaking, the United States was at full employment. Therefore, based on the unemployment yardstick, the nation should have been on or close to the vertical portion of its AS curve. By contrast, many European countries had unemployment rates considerably higher than that of the United States (almost double).

One interpretation of the relatively higher unemployment rates in European nations is that they were on relatively flatter portions of their AS curves. Another, and perhaps better, interpretation is that European labor laws, restrictions, and cultural norms created "full employment" rates (or natural unemployment rates) that were higher than in the United States. Therefore, even though some of these European nations had unemployment rates that were double the U.S. rate, attempts to reduce them might have resulted in constantly accelerating inflation. In short, the European nations' AS curves were more steeply sloped than they might have first appeared.

In addition to the unemployment rate, the employment rate can also provide helpful insights as to where a nation is on its AS curve. In fact, employment rates have proven to be better indicators of current economic conditions than unemployment rates, which are lagging economic indicators. Despite its superiority as a coincident economic indicator, the employment rate does not attract as much public attention as the unemployment rate, reflecting, perhaps, that people are less interested in the labor-force donut than they are the labor-force hole. Nevertheless, it is an important indicator for most country analyses.

Not many countries have targets for their employment rates like they have for their unemployment rates; so, at what level of employment do a nation's prices escalate? One way to answer this question is to compare the current level of employment with the nation's historic average or with various strong and weak levels of employment in the past. For example, a starting point could be to assume that the farther a nation is below its average historical employment rate, the flatter its AS curve. Likewise, the farther a nation's employment rate is above its historic average the steeper its AS curve.[4]

How fully employed are a nation's factories? The unemployment and employment rates provide insights into a nation's labor-force usage, but to determine the country's position on the AS curve, it is also important to know how fully employed its capital resources are. For this, a useful guide is the *capacity utilization index*[5] (CUI), which is a monthly indicator that measures how completely a nation is utilizing its capital base (e.g., machinery, equipment, tools, and factories). The higher the CUI, the closer a nation is to the vertical portion of its AS curve; the lower the CUI, the closer it is to the horizontal portion.

> The capacity utilization index is a helpful measure of where a nation is on its AS curve, with respect to the usage of capital resources.

Suppose a nation had 1 million machines, and all of them were being used. If purchases of goods and services rose, it would be difficult to increase production to meet the new desired demand. One option would be to run the machinery overtime (e.g., on double shifts or triple shifts), but there are only 24 hours in a day, and increased usage would cause more frequent breakdowns. Consequently, it would become challenging for efficient production to keep pace with demand. Therefore, prices would increase in the short run to ration the newly produced goods and services.[6]

By contrast, if only half of the nation's 1 million machines were fully employed, employers might be more interested in getting their idle machinery back to work than raising prices. Consequently, growing demand would be met by relatively large increases in output and relatively weak inflationary pressures.

Though 100% is the theoretical maximum for the CUI, it is unrealistic to expect any country to reach this level. A better approach is to look back at historical CUI rates and relate them to GDP Price Index changes. For instance, as the CUI approaches the 85% level in the United States, policymakers become concerned about the inflationary impacts of expansionary monetary and/or fiscal policies. Therefore, this 85% level can be viewed as a sort of tipping point for the U.S. inflation rate.

---

[4] An informative comparison of international employment rates can be found at ankei.com, Rankings and Records, http://www.aneki.com/highest_employment.html (accessed June 23, 2013).

[5] In the United States, the CUI is calculated monthly by the Federal Reserve and also by the Institute of Supply Management. The Fed's Web site is http://www.federalreserve.gov/releases/g17/current/ (accessed June 22, 2013) and the Institute of Supply Management's site is http://www.ism.ws/ (accessed June 23, 2013).

[6] Of course, it is possible to increase a nation's capacity by investing in new plant and equipment, but investments in plant and equipment need time to be built, brought on line, and made efficient. As a result, there is a gap between when investments are made and when output can be increased. In the short run, a nation's potential output should not increase substantially due to increased *current* investments. Remember that, in this section of the text, we are addressing short-run country analyses. Investment-related increases in a nation's long-term output potential will be addressed in Chapter 21, "Causes of Long-Term Growth and Inflation" and Chapter 22, "Long-Term Exchange Rate Movements & Comparative Advantage," where we discuss long-term economic analysis.

MACRO MEMO   12-1

Is the CUI Like a Canary in the (U.S. Economic) Coal Mine?

Some analysts view the U.S. CUI as a canary in the U.S. economic coal mine because sharp movements in its value have prefaced five of the past seven U.S. recessions. The only exceptions were in 1973, a recession precipitated by the Arab oil crisis, and the Great Recession of 2007–2009, which was precipitated by the U.S. housing market collapse.*

*See the "Capacity Utilization" Rate in March 2012: 78.7%, Bloomberg, http://www.bloomberg.com/portfolio-impact/2012-04-24/number-of-months-capacity-utilization-rose-since-june-2009.html#why_it_matters (accessed June 23, 2013).

MOVEMENTS ALONG THE AGGREGATE SUPPLY CURVE

A nation *moves along* its AS curve due to simultaneous changes in two endogenous variables, namely the GDP Price Index and real GDP. These variables are called endogenous because they are internal sources of change in the real goods market. The word "internal," in this context, means they are the only two variables that are visible on the vertical and horizontal axes of the AS curve. As they change, a nation moves along its AS curve. All other variables that have significant effects on supply are external (i.e., exogenous) and shift the entire curve.

Movements along the AS curve could be stimulated by either a change in the GDP Price Index, which would cause real GDP to change, or they could be stimulated by real GDP, which would cause the GDP Price Index to change. Let's consider these cause-and-effect relationships under the two possible stimulus scenarios. Suppose the GDP Price Index rose. Why would that ignite an increase in production and real GDP? One reason is during inflationary periods, if prices rise faster than wages, then business profits grow, thereby providing companies with incentives to hire and increase production. Similarly, rising real GDP often stimulates price increases because they force businesses to use less productive resources and push machinery beyond its most cost-efficient levels. In general, as productivity declines, costs per unit rise, causing prices to increase as companies try to pass these added costs on to consumers.

> The GDP Price Index and real GDP rate are endogenous variables that move a nation along its AS curve.

SHIFTS OF THE AGGREGATE SUPPLY CURVE

Simultaneous fluctuations in real GDP and the GDP Price index are the only variables that move a nation along its AS curve. Any other significant factors shift the entire AS curve. These "other factors" are called external or exogenous sources of change, and, as a result, they are not visible on the vertical or horizontal axes. What are the most important factors that shift a nation's AS curve? Among the key variables are changes in technology, productivity, input prices, exchange rates, climate, natural disasters, diseases, discoveries of new resources, immigration, regulations, and taxes.

> The entire AS curve shifts (to the right or left) due to changes in exogenous factors, such as technology, productivity, price of inputs, exchange rates, climate, natural disasters, diseases, new resource discoveries, immigration, regulations, and taxes.

CHANGES IN TECHNOLOGY AND PRODUCTIVITY

Among the major factors causing shifts in the AS curve are changing technology and productivity levels. Improvements in these factors cause output per

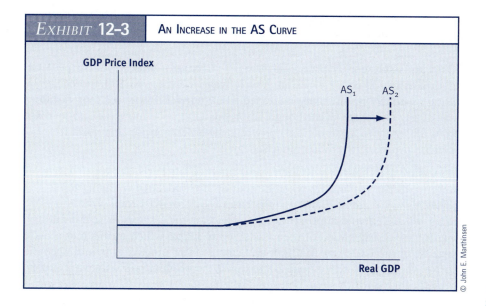

EXHIBIT **12-3** AN INCREASE IN THE AS CURVE

GDP Price Index

AS$_1$ AS$_2$

Real GDP

© John E. Marthinsen

unit of input to rise, which increases the AS curve (i.e., moves it to the right). Therefore, the relationship between the AS curve and productivity is positive (see Exhibit 12-3).[7]

Among the most important reasons for productivity improvements are expenditures for human capital development (i.e., education), the adoption of innovative and effective management practices, investments in physical assets (e.g., machinery, factories, roads, and dams),[8] invention of new technologies (e.g., computer software and biotech pharmaceuticals), and discovery of profitable ways to market and sell the new technologies.

CHANGE IN THE PRICE OF INPUTS

A second factor affecting the AS curve is a change in input costs. Declining input costs reduce business expenses, thereby increasing the AS curve. If input costs rise, the AS curve falls.

Oil provides a perfect example. Increases in oil prices raise the cost of production for a broad cross section of the economy. As a result, average output costs increase, causing the AS curve to fall.

Effects of Productivity Changes on Per Unit Input Costs

When analyzing the effect that changes in input prices have on AS, we must be sure to consider whether the resource's productivity level has changed as well. The reason for caution is because more productive resources should cost

---

[7] Remember that an increase in supply means that, at every price level, there is an increase in the quantity of goods and services that businesses are willing and able to produce and make available for sale each period.
[8] Usually, these productivity improvements are the result of investments made years before that are now fully integrated into company operations and contributing to profits.

more. Therefore, it is only when resource costs increase more rapidly than productivity that the nation's AS curve falls.

An example might help clarify this point. Suppose labor cost $50 per hour, and each worker produced 50 units per hour. On average, the per unit labor cost would equal $1. If the hourly wage increased to $60 and each worker's hourly productivity increased to 60 units, the cost per unit would stay at $1. Therefore, even though labor was paid 20% more (i.e., an increase from $50/hour to $60/hour), there would be no reason for unit costs to increase if productivity also increased by 20%.

Effects of a Resource's Relative Importance on Per Unit Input Costs

Another factor to consider when estimating the impact of changing input prices is the weight each input contributes to a product's total cost. Not all resources are equally important. For instance, some services (e.g., consulting) might have nearly 100% of their costs tied to labor, which means that a 20% increase in the wage rate (without any change in productivity) would raise the cost of these services by about 20%. But if the product had only 50% labor content, such as with some types of clothing, the same 20% wage increase would raise the cost by only 10% (i.e., 50% labor content times the 20% increase in wage).

Measuring Labor Productivity and Unit Labor Costs

Because labor is often the largest production cost, two important and helpful macroeconomic measures are labor productivity and unit labor costs. *Labor productivity* is the output produced per unit of labor input. When this figure rises, it means a nation's workforce is becoming more productive. If all else remains the same, improved productivity increases the size of the economic pie, enabling everyone to have more. It also makes the nation more competitive in the international marketplace.

For improved productivity to increase a nation's competitiveness, labor costs cannot rise faster than output. This is why unit labor costs are important. *Unit labor costs* are defined as total labor compensation divided by the value that labor adds to a nation's gross output. Total labor costs include wages, salaries, and benefits (e.g., social security and pension payments). Therefore, unit labor costs rise when total compensation rises faster than output. They fall when increases in labor compensation lag behind output growth.

> Unit labor costs equal total labor compensation divided by the value that labor adds to a nation's gross output.

If unit labor costs fall, a nation's AS curve rises, causing the GDP Price Index to fall, business profits to rise, and a nation's international competitiveness to improve. For these reasons, unit labor costs are closely monitored by both monetary and fiscal authorities, such as the U.S. Federal Reserve and U.S. Treasury Department. These statistics are also followed by many private analysts and think tanks.[9]

---

[9] The Organization for Economic Operation and Development is a rich source of information on unit labor costs among countries (see OECD, *OECD Economic Outlook*, www.oecd.org/economy/ [accessed January 27, 2013]).

Changes in International Currency Values—Exchange Rates

If a nation's currency appreciates (i.e., foreign currencies depreciate) and relative international prices remain the same, the country's global purchasing power increases. As a result, the cost of all imported inputs (i.e., inputs that are sourced abroad) falls. The reduction in this input price causes the nation's AS curve to increase. Of course, the extent to which it changes depends on how large imports are as a portion of total production costs.

Climate, Natural Disasters, and Diseases

Climate, natural disasters, and diseases are also key factors that affect the AS curve. Good weather conditions cause AS to increase, and poor conditions, natural disasters, and diseases cause it to decrease. Powerful freaks of nature, such as Hurricanes Sandy (October, 2012), Wilma (October, 2005), and Katrina (August, 2005), and tsunamis, such as the Indian Ocean tsunami (December, 2004), can cause massive destruction that decrease the AS curves of affected nations.[10] Earthquakes, storms, floods, and tsunamis are alike in their ability to destroy homes, disrupt normal living patterns, and incapacitate nations' transportation, communication, and production facilities, leaving hard-hit areas with years of work before they fully recover.

Discovery of New Resources and Immigration

The discovery of new resources and increased immigration are also important factors that can increase the AS curve. The more resources a nation has, the greater its potential output at every level of the GDP Price Index. Of course, some of the most resource-rich nations in the world, such as Brazil, Nigeria, and Venezuela, have living standards that are considerably below those of resource-poor nations, like Japan and Switzerland. Therefore, the availability of resources also must be combined with viable economic, political, and social systems for the AS curve to increase.

Changes in Regulations and Business Taxes

Businesses respond to after-tax cash flows and after-tax profits. Regulations often increase production costs, causing output rates to fall. Higher tax rates have the same effect, as they lower business cash flows and profits, making internal sources of investment funding scarcer, investor returns lower, and production rates slower. By contrast, less stringent regulations and lower tax rates tend to encourage business investments in plant and equipment.

---

[10] In October 2012, Hurricane Sandy caused more than $60 billion in damage as it worked its way from Jamaica to New England. Similarly, Hurricane Katrina destroyed major sections of New Orleans in August 2005, and Hurricane Wilma clocked the highest winds in recorded history while it inflicted substantial damage on the Yucatán Peninsula and Florida in October 2005. The Sumatra-Andaman earthquake in the Indian Ocean caused the deadliest natural disaster in modern history in late December 2004. The quake created 50-foot waves that demolished the shorelines of Indonesia, Sri Lanka, India, Thailand, and many other countries. Shocks were felt as far away as the east coast of Africa, which was over 2,800 miles from the earthquake's epicenter.

EXHIBIT 12-4	SUMMARY OF THE MAJOR EXOGENOUS FACTORS AFFECTING AGGREGATE SUPPLY	
Change In	**Δ Aggregate Supply**	**Relationship**
Technology (improves)	Increases	+
Productivity (improves)	Increases	+
Input price (rises)	Decreases	−
Exchange rate (rises) (i.e., value of the foreign currency)	Decreases	−
Climate (improves)	Increases	+
Natural disasters/diseases (increase)	Decreases	−
New resources (increase)	Increases	+
Immigration (increases)	Increases	+
Stricter regulations	Decreases	−
Business tax rate (increases)	Decreases	−

© John E. Marthinsen

SUMMARY AND OVERVIEW

Movements along a nation's AS curve are caused by simultaneous changes in the GDP Price Index and real GDP, which are the two endogenous variables in the real goods market.[11] But a nation's AS curve depends on many factors besides the GDP Price Index and real GDP. These other factors are called *exogenous variables*, and they include changes in worker productivity, technology, input prices, exchange rates, climate, natural disasters, diseases, new resource discoveries, immigration, regulations, and business tax rates. Exhibit 12-4 summarizes the qualitative effect that these exogenous variables have on a nation's AS.

WHAT IS THE AGGREGATE DEMAND CURVE?

The aggregate demand (AD) curve shows the inverse relationship between the quantity of domestically produced goods and services that individuals (both domestic and foreign) are willing and able to purchase at various levels of the GDP Price Index during a given time period (see Exhibit 12-5). The components of AD are consumption (C), gross private domestic investment (I), government spending for newly produced, final goods and services (G), and net exports (NE).

MOVEMENTS ALONG THE AGGREGATE DEMAND CURVE

The GDP Price Index and real GDP rate are endogenous variables that move a nation along its AD curve.

The endogenous variables affecting the AD curve are the same as for the AS curve—namely, the nation's GDP Price Index, which is on the vertical axis,

---

[11] The 'real goods market' is also called the "real goods and services market." These terms are used interchangeably in this text.

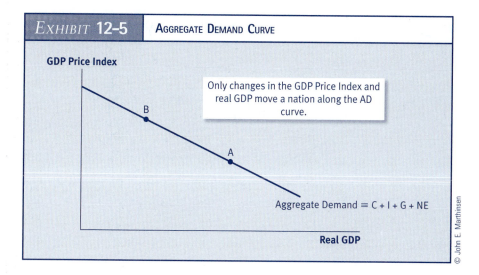

EXHIBIT **12-5** | AGGREGATE DEMAND CURVE

GDP Price Index

Only changes in the GDP Price Index and real GDP move a nation along the AD curve.

B

A

Aggregate Demand ≡ C + I + G + NE

Real GDP

© John E. Marthinsen

and real GDP, which is on the horizontal axis. When these endogenous variables change, a nation moves along its AD curve.

When a nation's GDP Price Index rises, the quantity of newly produced, final goods and services purchased by consumers, businesses, governments, and foreigners falls. For most people, this inverse relationship seems logical and consistent with intuition. It is used throughout this text and is the basis for virtually all macroeconomic analyses. Nevertheless, explaining the inverse macroeconomic relationship between a nation's GDP Price Index and real GDP is not as simple as explaining a downward-sloping demand for a company or industry. For this reason, a technical explanation is relegated to "**The Rest of the Story**" section of this chapter under the heading *Why Does a Nation's Aggregate Demand Slope Downward?*

SHIFTS OF THE AGGREGATE DEMAND CURVE

As was the case with the AS curve, shifts in the AD curve are caused by changes in exogenous economic variables. An increase in the AD curve is a shift of the entire curve to the right, which means that more quantity (real GDP) is demanded at every level of the GDP Price Index (see Exhibit 12-6), and a decrease in AD is a movement to the left.

> The AD curve shifts due to changes in exogenous (external) forces that affect C, I, G, and/or NE.

To explain the exogenous variables that shift a nation's AD, let's focus on each of the four principal components of AD, which are C, I, G, and NE.

EXOGENOUS FACTORS THAT AFFECT PERSONAL CONSUMPTION (C)

There is nothing esoteric about the major exogenous forces that affect a nation's personal consumption expenditures. In fact, they come quickly to mind because we deal with them every day of our lives. Among the most important are changes in real household wealth, indebtedness, real interest rates, personal income taxes, and expectations.

> Real personal consumption expenditures change due to fluctuations in wealth, indebtedness, real interest rates, taxes, and expectations.

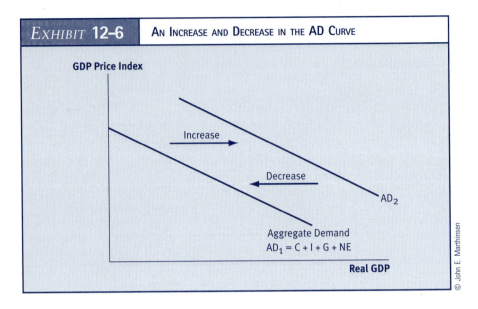

EXHIBIT 12-6   AN INCREASE AND DECREASE IN THE **AD** CURVE

© John E. Marthinsen

Changes in Real Wealth

Changes in an individual's personal wealth have a direct impact on C. For example, a rising stock market increases consumers' wealth, thereby raising their willingness and ability to spend more of their yearly incomes. We can conclude, therefore, as wealth rises, C rises, and AD shifts to the right. There is a positive relationship between changes in real wealth and C.

Changes in Consumer Indebtedness

The level of consumer indebtedness relative to household income has an inverse relationship to C. As indebtedness relative to income climbs, C falls because individuals are less willing to incur debt when substantial portions of their incomes are already being used to service existing loans. Moreover, increased levels of debt relative to income often increase borrowers' credit risk, which means banks are less willing to lend to them (i.e., individuals are less able to borrow). Therefore, there is a negative (inverse) relationship between consumer indebtedness and C.

Changes in Real Interest Rate

Changes in the real interest rate have an inverse relationship with C. If real interest rates rise, it is more expensive to borrow, and C falls. Therefore, there is an inverse relationship between real interest rate movements and C.

Changes in Personal Income Tax Rates

When tax rates increase, households' disposable incomes (i.e., after-tax incomes) fall, causing C to fall. Therefore, there is an inverse relationship between tax rates and C.

Changes in Consumer Expectations

Expectations are among the most mercurial of all factors influencing C. Though it is difficult to measure expectations, they can be estimated using surveys. For

---

EXHIBIT **12-7**	**EXOGENOUS FACTORS THAT INFLUENCE PERSONAL CONSUMPTION**

$$AD = \quad C \quad + I + G + (EX - IM)$$

W : Wealth $(+)$
ID : Indebtedness $(-)$
 R : Real risk-free interest rate $(-)$
Tx : Taxes $(-)$
Exp : Expectations $(?)$ → It depends on the expectation

- Expected prices $(+)$
- Expected real GDP $(+)$
- Expected real risk-free interest rate $(+)$

© John E. Marthinsen

---

example, in the United States, the Consumer Confidence Index (CCI), which is published monthly by the Conference Board,[12] and the Michigan Consumer Sentiment Index (MCSI), which is published monthly by the University of Michigan, try to measure consumer sentiment about future economic conditions.

Individuals have expectations about a variety of important economic variables, such as future incomes, interest rates, government regulations, and price changes. Because they are so varied and dissimilar in their effect on C, there is no single positive or negative relationship that can summarize all of them. Fortunately, the effects that changes in these expectations have on C are logical and not hard to discern. For instance, the expectation of rising inflation and higher interest rates encourages people to buy now in order to beat the more expensive future prices and greater financing costs.

Similarly, the expectation of rising incomes encourages people to consume now because they realize that they will be able to service and repay debts from their higher expected earnings. For example, many students enter the workplace with substantial debts and increase them when they finance homes, cars, and appliances. They do so realizing that their incomes will grow during the next 30–40 years of their working lives, making the repayment of these debts both realistic and possible.

Exhibit 12-7 summarizes the major factors that influence C.

EXOGENOUS FACTORS THAT AFFECT GROSS PRIVATE DOMESTIC INVESTMENT

Gross private domestic investment, which is a significant part of AD, is influenced by factors such as technology, the real interest rate, tax rates, and expectations.

Fluctuations in real gross private domestic investment are caused by changes in technology, real interest rates, tax rates, and expectations.

Changes in Technology

Changes in technology, both incremental and disruptive, can have substantial positive effects on I and therefore on AD. Examples of incremental technological developments are improvements in semiconductors, solar cells, and

---

[12] The Conference Board is a private, nonprofit research organization that focuses mainly on the creation and dissemination of business information.

batteries. Examples of disruptive technological changes are invention of the transistor, Internet, Google, and computers. In the past, Japan has made significant contributions to incremental technological advances, while the United States and Europe have been credited with the more disruptive ones. In both cases, advances have created enormous increases in I.

Changes in the Real Interest Rate

Changes in real interest rates have an inverse effect on I. If real interest rates rise, businesses' cost of capital increases, causing them to cut I.

Changes in Business Taxes

When business tax rates rise, profitability and cash flows fall, which cause I to fall (and vice versa). Therefore, the relationship between tax rates and I is inverse.

Changes in Business Expectations

Expectations are among the most volatile and most important factors influencing business investments. Because they are difficult to quantify, these expectations can be (mistakenly) trivialized or deemphasized. As is the case with consumption expenditures, expectations affect I in varied but intuitively straightforward and logical ways.

The expectation of rising prices or rising real interest rates encourages businesses to borrow, purchase investment assets at the relatively low current prices, and then sell the products later at the relatively higher prices. The housing bubble on the East and West Coasts of the United States as well as in Shanghai, China, during 2004 and 2005 are just two examples of how rising expected prices and higher expected interest rates can stimulate I. By contrast, the subprime crisis and Great Recession from 2007 to 2009 had just the opposite effect, as housing prices and price expectations tumbled in the United States.

Using similar reasoning, expectations of an economic expansion encourage businesses to invest more now so they can enjoy the fruits of rising future demand. By contrast, the expectation of rising taxes and greater regulations can have chilling effects on business investment.

Exhibit 12-8 summarizes the major factors that influence I.

EXHIBIT **12-8**	EXOGENOUS FACTORS THAT AFFECT GROSS PRIVATE DOMESTIC INVESTMENT

$$AD = C + \qquad I \qquad + G + (EX - IM)$$

Te : Technology changes (+)
R : Real risk-free interest rate (−)
Tx : Taxes (−)
Exp : Expectations (?) → It depends on the expectation

- Expected prices (+)
- Expected real GDP (+)
- Expected real risk-free interest rate (+)
- Expected regulations and taxes (−)

Exhibit **12-9**	**EXOGENOUS FACTORS THAT INFLUENCE GOVERNMENT SPENDING FOR NEWLY PRODUCED, FINAL GOODS AND SERVICES**

$$AD = C + I + \qquad G \qquad + (EX - IM)$$

DS : Discretionary spending

© John E. Marthinsen

EXOGENOUS FACTORS THAT AFFECT GOVERNMENT SPENDING FOR GOODS AND SERVICES

Government spending for newly produced, final goods and services is influenced by numerous economic, social, and political factors, which we combine under the heading "Discretionary Spending."

Changes in Discretionary Spending

Governments raise or lower AD for a wide variety of purposes, ranging from health care and defense to infrastructure and education. Much of this spending is financed by taxes, but excess spending is usually financed by borrowing. For as many government spending programs as there are, an even larger number of motivations exists behind them. Therefore, "discretionary spending" is listed in Exhibit 12-9 as a reminder that the government can increase or decrease AD for a variety of economic, social, or political reasons. It is not necessary for there to be a fluctuating economic variable—such as real GDP, interest rates, exchange rates, or wage rates—behind these decisions.

NET EXPORTS

The final component of AD is NE, which is equal to a nation's exports minus its imports. The major exogenous factors that influence NE are changes in exchange rates, foreign real GDP growth rates, and changes in *relative* international: price levels, real interest rates, and restrictions, like tariffs and quotas.

> Net exports are affected by changes in the exchange rate, foreign real GDP, relative international price levels, real interest rates, and restrictions, like tariffs and quotas.

Changes in Exchange Rates

A crucial factor influencing NE is the exchange rate, but this relationship is complicated because an exchange rate can be expressed as the amount of home currency per foreign currency unit, like 50 cents per euro ($0.50/€), or vice versa (i.e., 2 euros per dollar, or €2/$).

Suppose we were analyzing the United States, and the exchange rate was expressed as 50 cents per euro ($0.50/€). What would happen to NE if the exchange rate rose to 80 cents per euro ($0.80/€)? As the euro appreciated in value, goods and services produced in the euro area would become more expensive to U.S. residents, and U.S. goods and services would become more affordable to residents of the euro area. As a result, NE from the United States would rise as exports rose and imports fell. Therefore, there is a direct relationship between the exchange rate and U.S. NE when the exchange rate is expressed as the number of domestic currency units (dollars) per foreign currency unit (euro).

Changes in Foreign Real GDP Growth Rates

Changes in foreign income levels can have a significant influence on NE. If the income levels of Nation A's major trading partners rose, then residents of those nations could purchase more of Nation A's goods and services. As a result, Nation A's NE would rise, which means there is a direct relationship between changes in foreign incomes and Nation A's NE.

Changes in Relative International Prices

If a nation's GDP Price Index (P) rises relative to the rest of the world's average price level (P^*), that country's exports fall and imports rise, causing NE to fall. Therefore, there is an inverse relationship between changes in the domestic-price-to-foreign-price ratio and NE.

Changes in Relative International Real Interest Rates

A rising real interest rate relative to foreign nations has a negative effect on NE, but the relationship is not transparent. Here is one way to better understand it. Suppose the real interest rate rose in the United States relative to the rest of the world. As foreign demand for interest earning U.S. financial investments (e.g., bonds, notes, and bills) rose, so would the demand for U.S. dollars. As a result of these financial inflows to the United States, the value of the dollar would increase. Therefore, U.S. exports would fall because they would be more expensive for foreigners. Moreover, imports from other nations would increase because they would be less costly for U.S. residents. Therefore, as the real interest rate rises relative to foreign nations, NE falls, which means there is an inverse relationship between the real interest rate and NE. We will have more to say about this relationship in Chapter 15, "Exchange Rates: Why Do They Change?"

Changes in Relative International Tariffs and Quotas

Governments often impose tariffs and quotas to reduce imports. To the extent these restrictions are effective, they increase a nation's NE. Therefore, in the absence of any retaliatory measures by other nations or other offsetting effects, there is a direct relationship between changes in tariffs and quotas and changes in NE.

Exhibit 12-10 summarizes the major factors that influence a nation's NE.

EXHIBIT 12-10	EXOGENOUS FACTORS THAT INFLUENCE NET EXPORTS

$$AD = C + I \quad + \quad G \quad + \quad (EX - IM)$$

ER : Exchange rate (Foreign currency value) (+)
(P/P*) : Relative prices (−)
R : Real risk-free interest rate (−)
$RGDP_F$: Foreign Income (+)
TQ : Tariffs, Quotas, ... (+)
Exp : Expectations (?)

© John E. Marthinsen

EXHIBIT 12-11	MAJOR FACTORS CAUSING A CHANGE IN AGGREGATE DEMAND

AD = C + I + G + (EX – IM)

Move Along AD	RGDP & P	RGDP & P	RGDP & P		RGDP & P
Shift Entire AD	R (–)	R (–)			R (–)
	Tx (–)	Tx (–)	DS		TQ (+)
	Exp	Exp			RGDP$_F$ (+)
	ID (–)	Te (+)			ER (+) (Foreign currency value)
	W (+)				

© John E. Marthinsen

SUMMARY

Exhibit 12-11 summarizes the endogenous variables and major exogenous variables that influence the AD curve.

COMBINING AGGREGATE SUPPLY AND AGGREGATE DEMAND

Exhibit 12-12 combines a nation's AS and AD curves in the real goods market to determine the equilibrium GDP Price Index (P_E) and real GDP ($RGDP_E$). Any endogenous changes in price or real GDP that move a nation away from

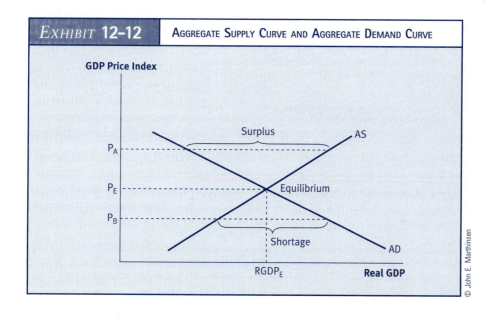

EXHIBIT 12-12	AGGREGATE SUPPLY CURVE AND AGGREGATE DEMAND CURVE

© John E. Marthinsen

the equilibrium point automatically set up forces that restore it to where the amount supplied equals the amount demanded. For instance, a GDP Price Index that is too high (e.g., P_A in Exhibit 12-12) creates a surplus that reduces prices, and a GDP Price Index that is too low (e.g., P_B in Exhibit 12-12) creates a shortage, causing prices to increase.

MACROECONOMIC EQUILIBRIUM: DESIRED AGGREGATE AMOUNT SUPPLIED = DESIRED AGGREGATE AMOUNT DEMANDED

Macroeconomic equilibrium occurs when the value of final goods and services that the business sector *desires* (or *expects or anticipates*) to produce and make available for sale is equal to the value of the final goods and services that the domestic and foreign buyers *desire* (or *expect or anticipate*) to purchase from these producers. More simply, one could say that equilibrium occurs when the *desired* quantity of goods and services demanded by consumers, businesses, governments, and foreigners equals the *desired* quantity supplied by the domestic business sector.

The adjectives *desired, expected*, and *anticipated* are synonymous and very important in macroeconomics because they refer to what suppliers and demanders intend to do and not what actually happens. An important takeaway is remembering that all supply and demand curves reflect relationships between desired (or expected or anticipated) amounts supplied and demanded because, after the fact, the actual amounts supplied and demanded always are the same. Here's why.

Suppose the desired amount supplied in Year 1 was 1 million units and the desired amount demanded was 1.5 million. This disequilibrium would cause the price index to rise as it adjusted back toward equilibrium. Nevertheless, at the end of Year 1, the actual amounts sold and bought (i.e., the actual amounts supplied and demanded) would equal 1 million units because that was all there was to buy. This distinction between the actual and desired quantities supplied and demanded is developed further in "**The Rest of the Story**" section of this chapter under the heading *Actual Quantity Supplied Always Equals Actual Quantity Demanded*.

If we use the mountain-of-goods-and-services analogy that was introduced in Chapter 2, "Taking an Economic Pulse: Measuring National Output and Income," then macroeconomic equilibrium means that the mountain of goods and services that the business sector desires to produce each period is completely and willingly swept off the market by domestic and foreign buyers, with no surplus or shortage remaining at the end (see Exhibit 12-13).

> Macroeconomic equilibrium occurs when the desired (or expected or anticipated) quantity supplied equals the desired (or expected or anticipated) quantity demanded for newly produced, final goods and services.

IS EQUILIBRIUM GOOD OR BAD FOR A NATION?

In the short term, macroeconomic equilibrium can occur at any level of real GDP, as long as desired quantity supplied equals desired quantity demanded. This means that, regardless of whether a nation's annual output is above or below its capacity, there could still be short-term macroeconomic equilibrium. Therefore, macroeconomic equilibrium is neither good nor bad. It is simply an economic condition where there is no tendency for businesses to hire or fire and no short-term propensity for the economy to change.

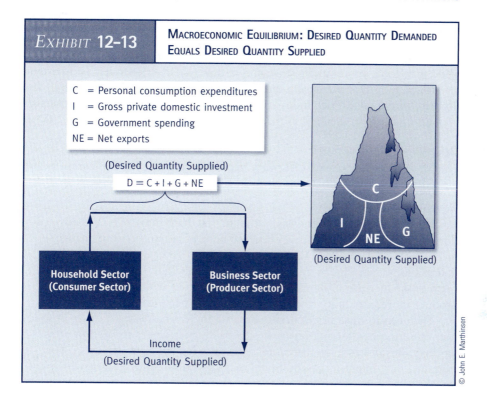

EXHIBIT 12-13 | MACROECONOMIC EQUILIBRIUM: DESIRED QUANTITY DEMANDED EQUALS DESIRED QUANTITY SUPPLIED

C = Personal consumption expenditures
I = Gross private domestic investment
G = Government spending
NE = Net exports

(Desired Quantity Supplied)

$$D \equiv C + I + G + NE$$

Household Sector (Consumer Sector)

Business Sector (Producer Sector)

Income

(Desired Quantity Supplied)

(Desired Quantity Supplied)

© John E. Marthinsen

DEMAND-PULL AND COST-PUSH INFLATION

With the basics of AS and AD in place, let's discuss demand-pull inflation and cost-push inflation. When inflation is caused by a change in AD, it is called *demand-pull inflation*. When the change is caused by a reduction in AS, it is called *cost-push inflation*. Finally, when inflation is due to reinforcing and self-perpetuating changes in AS and AD, it is called *spiral inflation*. As spiral inflation is a byproduct of demand-pull and cost-push inflation, it is dealt with in "**The Rest of the Story**" section of this chapter.

MACRO MEMO   12-2

Don't Confuse Increases in Prices with Increases in the Inflation Rate

Analyses using AS and AD are most useful for evaluating short-term changes in *prices* and not *inflation*. This distinction is important because increases in a nation's GDP Price Index do not necessarily mean increases in its inflation rate.

To better understand this point, suppose the initial GDP Price Index was 100, and it rose to 105. This would be an annual inflation rate equal to 5% (i.e., 5/100 = 5%). Next year, if the price index rose by 5 to 110, the nation would have higher prices than the year before, but its inflation rate would have fallen from 5% to 4.8% (i.e., 5/105 = 4.8%). Therefore, just because the price index rises does not mean the inflation rate must rise.

Despite the fact that AS and AD analysis is more useful for determining short-term price changes than short-term changes in inflation, it can still be a very insightful framework for evaluating the causes of inflation. All we have to do is to look upon any increase in a nation's GDP Price Index as inflationary in nature and/or increasing the likelihood of inflation. Similarly, any decrease in the GDP Price Index can be viewed as a reduction of inflationary pressures and/or an increase in the likelihood of deflation.

DEMAND–PULL INFLATION

The effects of an increase in AD vary depending on whether the nation is in the Keynesian, intermediate, or classical range.

Intermediate Range

It is easiest to begin our analysis in the intermediate range (i.e., the upward-sloping portion of the AS curve) because both prices and output change. In Exhibit 12-14, if the AD curve increases from AD^I_1 to AD^I_2, both the nation's GDP Price Index and real GDP rise. The GDP Price Index rises because the increase in demand provides businesses with an incentive to produce more, an ability to charge more, and a need to raise prices.

The need to raise prices occurs because increasing demand raises production rates, thereby forcing businesses to pay higher wages to keep or attract workers. Businesses may also be forced to use less efficient resources. For example, they might incur additional expenses to hire and train new employees. As costs rise, companies try to pass them on to consumers in order to maintain their margins.

If increasing resource costs lag behind these rising prices, as they often do, businesses have all the more reason to increase production rates. The incentive

> Demand-pull inflation is caused by an increase in aggregate demand.

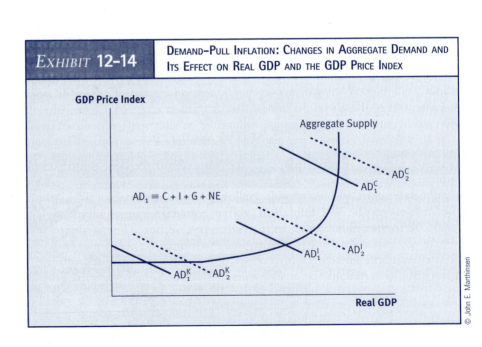

| E_{XHIBIT} **12-14** | **DEMAND–PULL INFLATION: CHANGES IN AGGREGATE DEMAND AND ITS EFFECT ON REAL GDP AND THE GDP PRICE INDEX** |

GDP Price Index

Aggregate Supply

AD^C_2

AD^C_1

$AD_1 \equiv C + I + G + NE$

AD^I_1 AD^I_2

AD^K_1 AD^K_2

Real GDP

© John E. Marthinsen

to raise prices and the ability to pass on price increases are created by the climate of growing demand. In such a favorable environment, price hikes can be more easily passed on to consumers.

Therefore, an increasing AD causes the GDP Price Index and real GDP to rise, which lowers the unemployment rate. Rising real GDP and falling unemployment rates can be viewed, then, as a silver lining to the otherwise dark cloud of rising prices caused by demand-pull inflation.

Classical Range

In the classical range (i.e., vertical portion of the AS curve), an increase in AD from AD^C_1 to AD^C_2 causes only the GDP Price Index to rise (see Exhibit 12-14). Because the nation is at (or near) full capacity, real GDP does not change. Therefore, in this range, changes in AD have their greatest impact on prices.

Keynesian Range

In the Keynesian range, if AD rises from AD^K_1 to AD^K_2, only real GDP changes (see Exhibit 12-14). The GDP Price Index remains the same because producers have neither the willingness nor the ability to raise them. As a result, demand-pull inflation does not occur in the Keynesian range.

More on Demand-Pull Inflation

In the short run, a change in any component of AD (i.e., C, I, G, or NE) could be the source of the demand-pull inflation. For example, excessive growth in a nation's money supply, falling personal income tax rates, a significant change in consumer expectations, an appreciation of foreign currencies (i.e., depreciation of the domestic currency's value), and/or a lower real interest rate are all possible sources.

An important take-away from this discussion is that, for any given increase in demand, the rate of change in the GDP Price Index relative to the rate of change in real GDP depends on how close the economy is to full employment. At capacity (i.e., the classical range in Exhibit 12-14), any increase in demand results purely in price increases because labor and capital are fully employed.

COST–PUSH INFLATION

Cost-push inflation is caused by a reduction in AS. Unlike demand-pull inflation, there is no silver lining to cost-push inflation. When the AS curve falls, the GDP Price Index rises and real GDP falls, which means the unemployment rate rises. This simultaneous increase of both inflation and unemployment is often called *stagflation*, which is simply a hybrid word that mergers *stagnation* and *inflation*.

> Cost-push inflation is caused by a reduction in aggregate supply.

The reduction in a nation's AS could be due to factors such as decreases in general levels of productivity, increases in resource costs (e.g., energy prices or wage hikes in excess of labor productivity growth), product markups, and/or natural disasters that physically reduce the availability and/or increase the prices of needed inputs for production. In Exhibit 12-15, when AS falls from AS_1 to AS_2, the GDP Price Index rises from P_1 to P_2, and real GDP falls from $RGDP_1$ to $RGDP_2$.

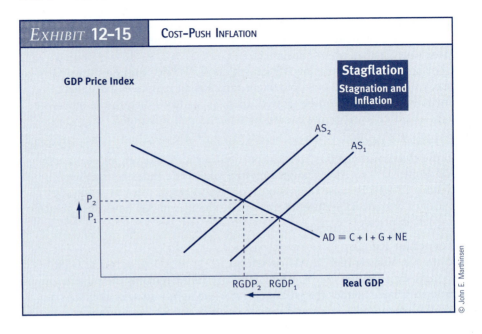

EXHIBIT **12-15**   COST–PUSH INFLATION

THE SPENDING MULTIPLIER

Any exogenous shock to a nation's AD has both initial (primary) and secondary effects. The primary change in spending directly affects real GDP (i.e., real income),[13] but this ignites recurring and self-perpetuating rounds of further spending and income changes that ripple through the economy and amplify the initial impact. The multiple by which these secondary effects change real GDP beyond the initial shock is called the *spending multiplier*. If it equals 2, then any initial (exogenous) increase in spending causes a total increase in real GDP by twice that amount. Therefore, with a spending multiplier equal to 2, exogenous spending increases of $50 billion cause real GDP to rise by $100 billion. When applied to central governments, the spending multiplier is called the *fiscal multiplier*, which we will explore in Chapter 13, "Fiscal Policy and Automatic Stabilizers: What Managers Need to Know."

Suppose that improved expectations (i.e., the exogenous shock) caused businesses to invest more in plant, equipment, tools, machinery, and inventories. This increased investment would provide new jobs to some workers and increased income to others as their hours of employment and/or wages rose. The nation's rising real income would stimulate follow-on changes in personal consumption expenditures (C), gross private domestic investment (I), government transfers (GT), taxes (Tx), and net exports (NE)—and these changes would then stimulate further adjustments. Let's investigate the secondary impacts that changes in real GDP have on C, I, GT, Tx, and NE.

---

[13] Remember from our investigation of the circular flow diagram that changes in real GDP are equivalent to changes in real income.

IMPACT OF REAL GDP ON C

As real GDP increases, household incomes rise, providing individuals with an ability to consume more. Therefore, the qualitative relationship between a change in real GDP and a change in C is positive. Beyond this initial adjustment, changes in C have spillover effects. As they rise, new rounds of incomes are earned, which stimulate fresh rounds of spending. As an aid to understanding, it is helpful to remember that income is earned from the expenditures of others, and when it changes, spillover adjustments in C, I, GT, Tx, and NE occur, which then feed back and affect income (see Exhibit 12-16).

IMPACT OF REAL GDP ON I

Increases in real GDP caused by the initial shock also affect the ability and willingness of companies to invest. As real GDP increases, business profitability improves, optimism rises, and new investments are encouraged. Therefore, the qualitative relationship between a change in real GDP and a change in I is positive (see Exhibit 12-16).

As was the case with C, this secondary increase in I sparks follow-on rounds of new income generation, which feed back into the economy and cause further changes in C, I, GT, Tx, and NE.

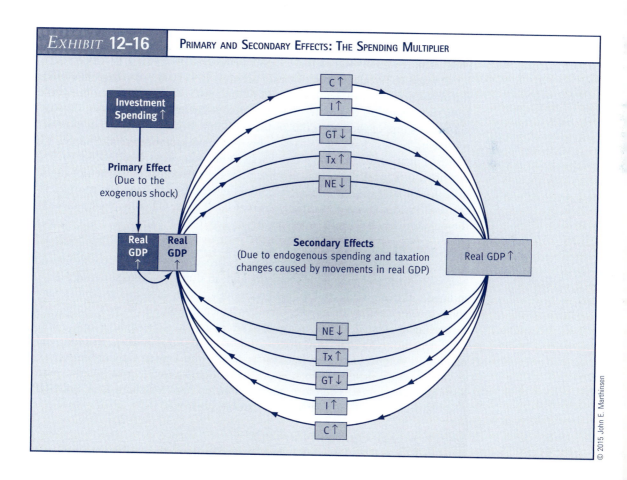

EXHIBIT 12-16   PRIMARY AND SECONDARY EFFECTS: THE SPENDING MULTIPLIER

© 2015 John E. Marthinsen

IMPACT OF REAL GDP ON GT AND TX

Government transfer payments and tax revenues are also affected by changes in real GDP. These changes are called nondiscretionary fiscal policies because, as real GDP rises and falls, G and Tx change automatically (i.e., passively).

Government Transfer Payments

Government transfer payments are for social welfare programs, such as social security, unemployment compensation, welfare, food stamps, housing allowances, and medical care. It is important to understand that these expenditures contribute significantly to AD, but they are not classified in the national income accounts as "government spending" (G) because they are purely financial transactions. No good or service is exchanged and nothing is directly produced by their expenditure. Rather, GT increase household incomes; when spent, they are included as part of C.

Due to their countercyclical nature, GT are often called *automatic stabilizers* because they help to reduce systemic fluctuations in national spending. For example, an initial increase in business investments causes real GDP to rise. As it does, the nation's unemployment rate falls, resulting in reductions in GT payments for social welfare programs. Reductions in these transfer payments are automatic, occurring without a need for the government to revise or pass new legislation. As entitlements, they are built into the economic system and activated by need and circumstance. Because transfer payments fall when economic activity improves and rise when it deteriorates, the relationship between changes in real GDP and changes in GT is inverse (see Exhibit 12-16).

As real GDP falls, the automatic increases in GT do not completely offset the initial decrease in spending. To do so, unemployment compensation would have to be equal to or greater than unemployed workers' lost wages. Higher GT takes some of the steam out of the economic downturn, but they do not reverse it. We will have more to say about automatic stabilizers in Chapter 13, "Fiscal Policy and Automatic Stabilizers: What Managers Need to Know." For now, it is most important to remember the relationship between changes in real GDP and changes in GT is unlike the relationship between changes in real GDP and changes in C and I. As real GDP rises, GT falls, which means the qualitative relationship is negative (see Exhibit 12-16).

Government Tax Revenues

Tax revenues are also automatic stabilizers because they change passively and positively with real income movements and, in doing so, take some of the momentum from rising and falling economies. As an economy expands, personal income tax payments rise, thereby reducing some of the new purchasing power being created. The increase in taxes helps reduce spending that might raise demand, real GDP, and prices (and/or inflation). Similarly, as economic conditions deteriorate, taxes fall automatically and lighten the burden on taxpayers. As a result, they help support demand and provide jobs when overall spending is declining. Therefore, the relationship between changes in real GDP and changes in taxes is positive (see Exhibit 12-16).

IMPACT OF REAL GDP ON NE

Just like C, I, GT, and Tx, NE expenditures are also influenced by changes in real income. Rising real GDP (real income) rates cause households and businesses to spend more, and some of these expenditures are on imported goods and ser-vices. Therefore, real imports increase with real GDP, causing NE (i.e., exports minus imports) to decrease. As a result, there is an inverse qualitative relationship between changes in real GDP and changes in NE (see Exhibit 12-16).

If increases in real GDP cause imports to rise, shouldn't they also affect exports? After all, if more is produced, some of it should end up being exported—right? In macroeconomics, the link between changes in real GDP and exports is deemphasized because it appears as if exports are not affected substantially by changes in a nation's real GDP. A much more important variable affecting a nation's exports is the change in *foreign nations'* incomes.

Net Impact of Real GDP on C, I, GT, Tx, and NE

When real GDP rises, the net effect on demand is positive even though it may appear to be indeterminate because expenditures on C and I rise, NE falls, and passive changes in GT and Tx cause C and I to fall. The possibility that the net effect of all these changes will be negative is an interesting theoretical possibility, but quite far removed from reality. We can conclude that the net qualitative relationship between changes in real GDP and changes in spending is positive, and this positive relationship is the basis for the spending multi-plier (see Exhibit 12-17).

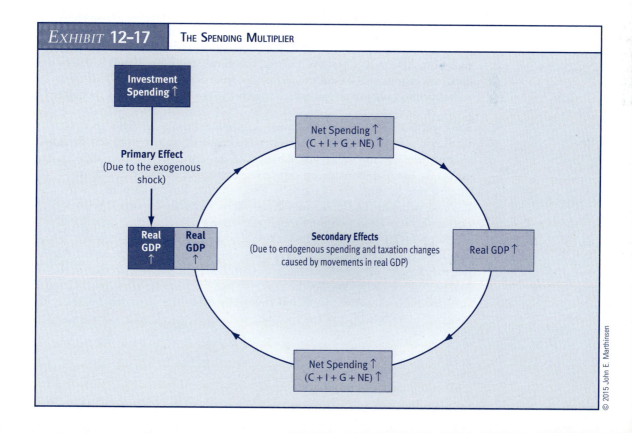

EXHIBIT 12-17   THE SPENDING MULTIPLIER

Investment Spending ↑

Primary Effect
(Due to the exogenous shock)

Net Spending ↑
(C + I + G + NE) ↑

Real GDP ↑ | Real GDP ↑

Secondary Effects
(Due to endogenous spending and taxation changes caused by movements in real GDP)

Real GDP ↑

Net Spending ↑
(C + I + G + NE) ↑

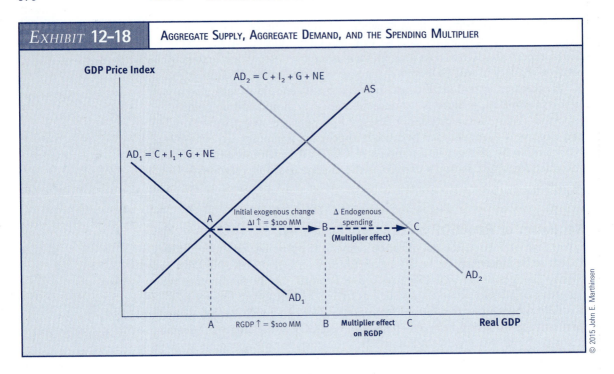

Exhibit 12-18   AGGREGATE SUPPLY, AGGREGATE DEMAND, AND THE SPENDING MULTIPLIER

AGGREGATE SUPPLY, AGGREGATE DEMAND, AND THE SPENDING MULTIPLIER

Exhibit 12-18 shows the primary and secondary effects initiated by an exogenous increase in spending. As a result of the initial stimulus and secondary effects, AD rises from AD_1 to AD_2. Of this change, the movement from A to B is due to the initial exogenous shock, and the movement from B to C is the result of the endogenous secondary effects, which together make up the spending multiplier.[14]

THE SPENDING MULTIPLIER AND REAL LOANABLE FUNDS MARKET

Until now, the real loanable funds market has been absent from our discussion of the spending multiplier. Changes in AD usually have simultaneous effects on the real loanable funds markets, which cause the real risk-free interest rate to change and partially offset the spending multiplier. Later in this text (Chapter 15, "Exchange Rates: Why Do They Change?"), we will find it also has effects on the foreign exchange market.

Suppose an exogenous shock caused business spending to increase. To finance these purchases, these companies might need to borrow, and if they do, the demand for real loanable funds would rise, causing increases in the real risk-free interest rate. As the real risk-free interest rate rises, both C and I fall, and these reductions in C and I partially offset the secondary increase in demand, thereby reducing the spending multiplier.

---

[14] It is possible for the spending multiplier to be less than one, in which case the shift from B to C in Exhibit 12-18 would be to the left.

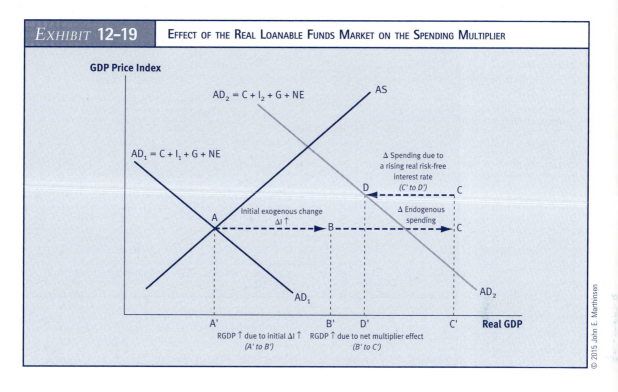

EXHIBIT 12-19   EFFECT OF THE REAL LOANABLE FUNDS MARKET ON THE SPENDING MULTIPLIER

If the businesses already had sufficient funds to invest, the net effect on the real risk-free interest rate would be the same because the supply of real loanable funds would fall, as businesses withdrew them from the real loanable funds market. This reduction in supply would increase the real risk-free interest rate, causing follow-on reductions in both C and I. In Chapter 13, "Fiscal Policy and Automatic Stabilizers: What Managers Need to Know," we will revisit this issue in the context of government spending and the effect it has on real GDP.

Using AS and AD curves, Exhibit 12-19 shows how feedback effects from the real loanable funds market reduce the spending multiplier. Notice how the initial exogenous shock increases AD from A to B, and the spending multiplier increases it once again from B to C. The movement from B to C is what occurs if there is no change in the real risk-free interest rate. As the real risk-free interest rate rises, AD falls from C to D and real GDP falls from C' to D'.

THE REST OF THE STORY

APPLICATIONS OF AGGREGATE SUPPLY AND AGGREGATE DEMAND ANALYSIS

Let's apply AS and AD analysis to see whether the results given by the model we have developed are consistent with common sense and intuition. In all our examples, the starting point will be at equilibrium, which is the point where the AS curve and AD curve intersect.

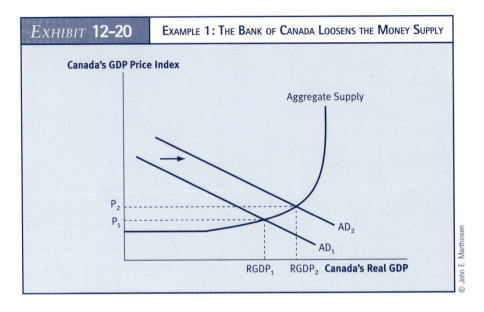

EXHIBIT 12-20   EXAMPLE 1: THE BANK OF CANADA LOOSENS THE MONEY SUPPLY

EXAMPLE 1: EXPANSIONARY MONETARY POLICY BY THE BANK OF CANADA

Suppose Canada's central bank, the Bank of Canada, increased the Canadian money supply. What effect would this expansionary monetary policy have on the nation's GDP Price Index and real GDP? Let's assume that Canada is on the intermediate range (as is normally the case).

An increase in the money supply would increase Canada's AD for two important reasons. First, more money would provide Canada with greater purchasing power, and greater purchasing power would increase Canada's AD. Second, an increased money supply would increase the supply of Canada's real loanable funds. As the supply of real loanable funds rose, the real risk-free interest rate would fall, causing C and I to rise. As a result, AD would shift from AD_1 to AD_2 (see Exhibit 12-20). Notice that our model predicts that expansionary monetary policy will cause Canada's GDP Price Index to rise and real GDP to rise.

EXAMPLE 2: DEPRECIATION OF THE THAI BAHT

Suppose the value of the Thai baht fell. How would this affect the Thai economy? A decrease in the baht's value makes Thailand's exports cheaper to foreigners and imports from other nations more expensive to Thai residents. Therefore, a depreciation of the baht causes Thailand's NE to rise, increasing the nation's AD curve from AD_1 to AD_2 and moving equilibrium from A to B (see Shift 1 in Exhibit 12-21). This increase in demand raises real GDP from $RGDP_1$ to $RGDP_2$ and raises the GDP Price Index from P_1 to P_2.

At the same time, a depreciation of the baht increases the cost of Thailand's imported inputs. As a result, the Thai AS curve falls from AS_1 to AS_2, and equilibrium moves from B to C. This decline in AS increases the GDP Price Index from P_2 to P_3 and reduces real GDP (see Shift 2 in Exhibit 12-21).

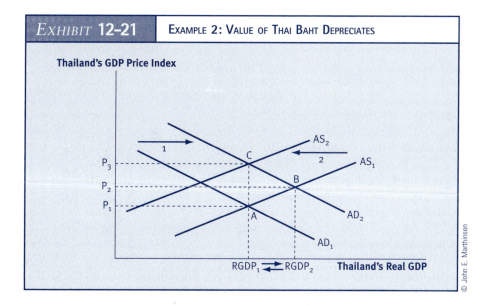

EXHIBIT 12-21 | **EXAMPLE 2: VALUE OF THAI BAHT DEPRECIATES**

Thailand's GDP Price Index

In Exhibit 12-21, there is no net change in real GDP, but that does not have to be the case. If Thailand were only marginally dependent on imports relative to exports, then the reduction in AS would be small relative to the increase in AD. In such a case, the net change in real GDP would be positive. Real GDP would fall from $RGDP_2$, but it would not fall back as far as $RGDP_1$.

In summary, our AS and AD analysis indicates that a depreciation of the baht should unambiguously increase Thailand's GDP Price Index. By contrast, the change in its real GDP is uncertain until we can determine the relative strength of shifts in AS and AD.

EXAMPLE 3: GERMANY REDUCES PERSONAL INCOME TAXES AND GOVERNMENT SPENDING ON GOODS AND SERVICES BY €50 BILLION

Suppose the German government reduced personal income taxes by €50 billion to stimulate the nation's economy. At the same time, suppose the government reduced its spending on goods and services by the same amount, hoping to prevent its budget deficit from rising. What effect would these changes have on the German economy?

A reduction in G by €50 billion would cause Germany's AD curve to fall by the same amount, but the reduction in taxes by €50 billion would not necessarily cause AD to rise by €50 billion. To see why, suppose you were given a tax rebate, causing your disposable income to rise by €50. You might spend a portion of that €50, but it is also likely that you would save a portion of it. The portion of any increase in a nation's disposable (i.e., after-tax) income that is consumed is called the *marginal propensity to consume* (MPC), and the portion saved is called the *marginal propensity to save* (MPS). Therefore, the MPC is the amount by which the household sector

> $MPC \equiv \Delta C/\Delta RGDP$ and
> $MPS \equiv \Delta S/\Delta RGDP$

changes its consumption per new euro (or dollar or yen) of disposable income earned.

If the MPC were 0.80, then consumers would spend only 80% of each additional euro (or dollar or yen) of disposable income. In Germany's case, if the MPC were 0.80, then only €40 billion (i.e., 0.80 × €50 billion) of the tax break would be consumed. Therefore, the policy of lowering spending and lowering taxes by the same amount would not be economically neutral, as you might first expect. Reducing G by €50 billion and reducing taxes by €50 billion would reduce (net) AD by €10 billion.[15]

Exhibit 12-22 shows graphically the changes in AD. Declining G causes the AD curve to shift to the left by €50 billion (i.e., from AD_1 to AD_2). As a result, the GDP Price Index falls from P_1 to P_2, and real GDP falls from $RGDP_1$ to $RGDP_2$.

At the same time, reducing taxes by €50 billion causes C to rise by €40 billion. As a result, the AD curve shifts from AD_2 to AD_3, causing real GDP to rise from $RGDP_2$ to $RGDP_3$ and the GDP Price Index to rise from P_2 to P_3. In short, real GDP does not go back to $RGDP_1$, where it started, and the GDP Price Index does not go back to P_1, where it started. The decrease in G, combined with the increase in C, causes a net decrease in AD by €10 billion.

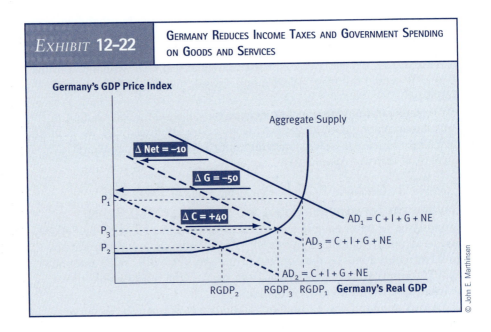

EXHIBIT 12-22   **GERMANY REDUCES INCOME TAXES AND GOVERNMENT SPENDING ON GOODS AND SERVICES**

Germany's GDP Price Index

Aggregate Supply

Δ Net = −10

Δ G = −50

Δ C = +40

P_1

P_3

P_2

$AD_1 = C + I + G + NE$

$AD_3 = C + I + G + NE$

$AD_2 = C + I + G + NE$

$RGDP_2$ $RGDP_3$ $RGDP_1$ **Germany's Real GDP**

© John E. Marthinsen

---

[15] This result assumes that the increased saving does not feedback positively into the economy. But it is highly likely that greater saving would lower the real risk-free interest rate, thereby, increasing C and I. The take-away from this example is that the qualitative change in aggregate demand will *usually* be in the direction of the change in G. Nevertheless, it should be kept in mind that feedback effects could reduce or offset this net change.

When we combine these two effects, the nation moves from AD_1 to AD_3, which means there is a net decrease in AD.

TYING UP LOOSE ENDS

Our analysis of the real goods market left us with some interesting questions to address. We will begin by exploring why classical economists took a laissez-faire attitude when it came to curing macroeconomic problems, such as unemployment, fully expecting market forces to self-correct the economy and restore full employment. From there, we move on to explore the reasons a nation's AD curve slopes downward. Because the inverse relationship between price and quantity demanded is so firmly ingrained in most of our minds, many would be willing to move forward without challenging the tenants of this relationship, but the explanation is important—if for no other reason than to dispel the notion that macroeconomics is simply a summation of microeconomic concepts.

Next, we deal with the concept of equilibrium, which is as misunderstood in macroeconomics as it is in microeconomics. From there, we focus next on two interesting offshoots from our discussion of demand-pull and cost-push inflation. We start with the *Short-Run Phillips Curve* to show how demand-pull inflation can be used to explain the frequently assumed inverse relationship between inflation and unemployment. Finally, we end with a section entitled "Spiral Inflation," which shows how demand-pull and cost-push inflation can cross-ignite causing one to feed off the other, thereby, accelerating unwanted inflation.

CLASSICAL THEORY, THE FORCES OF SUPPLY AND DEMAND, AND FULL EMPLOYMENT

Why do classical (and neoclassical) theorists feel that the forces of supply and demand will automatically move a nation toward full employment in the long run? Suppose a country has excessive unemployment. Classical economists would reason that one of the major causes of the unemployment is an average real wage rate that is above equilibrium.

In Exhibit 12-23, W_A represents this elevated real wage. At this wage rate, the amount of labor supplied exceeds the amount demanded, resulting in unemployment equal to the distance between L_S (people actively seeking work) and L_D (people employed).

The excess supply of labor (i.e., the unemployed) would put downward pressure on real wages. The reduction in real wage might be caused by nominal wages falling, but an easier (and more likely) road to the same result is for nominal wages to rise slower than prices. Falling real wages would then have two reinforcing effects that act simultaneously to bring the labor market back into equilibrium. First, lower real wages increase the incentive for businesses to hire workers, and, second, they reduce the number of individuals in the workforce. For instance, instead of looking for work, some individuals might stay in school or remain homemakers. If the real wage fell to W_E, the amount of labor supplied would equal the amount demanded (i.e., at L_E), and the unemployment problem would be solved.

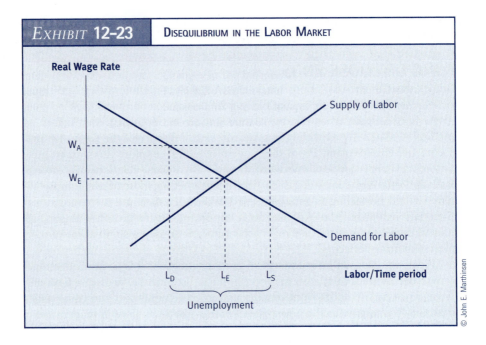

EXHIBIT 12-23 | **DISEQUILIBRIUM IN THE LABOR MARKET**

Real Wage Rate

Supply of Labor

W_A

W_E

Demand for Labor

L_D L_E L_S Labor/Time period

Unemployment

© John E. Marthinsen

WHY DOES A NATION'S AGGREGATE DEMAND SLOPE DOWNWARD?

The downward-sloping demand curve for an individual company's or industry's product can be explained by substitution and income effects. For example, as the price of Coke rises relative to Pepsi and other beverages, such as juices and bottled water, it becomes relatively less attractive, and consumers purchase less of it. This is the substitution effect. In addition, increases in the price of Coke reduce consumer real incomes, which decreases the amount bought. This is the income effect.

Explanations of why a nation's AD curve slopes downward are slightly different from the downward-sloping company or industry demand. One reason for the difference is because changes in the GDP Price Index imply that the average price level *for all products* has fluctuated. Therefore, substitution effects are of a different nature.

To start our analysis we need a stimulus, and the stimulus we choose is important. Remember that movements along the AD curve require simultaneous and inverse changes in a nation's GDP Price Index and real GDP (see Exhibit 12-24), but only one of them can be the initial stimulus; the other is the response. We start this section using the GDP Price Index as the initial stimulus. Afterwards, we will repeat the analysis using real GDP as the initial stimulus.

CAUSE–AND–EFFECT RELATIONSHIPS WHEN A CHANGE IN THE GDP PRICE INDEX IS THE STIMULUS

When a change in the GDP Price Index is the stimulus, three major cause-and-effect relationships account for the downward-sloping curvature of the AD curve: the real money supply effect, wealth effect, and net export effect.

> The AD curve is downward sloping due to the real money supply effect, wealth effect, and net export effect.

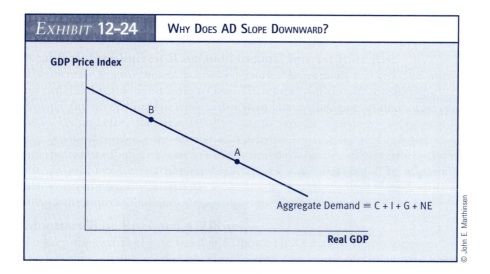

EXHIBIT **12-24**   WHY DOES AD SLOPE DOWNWARD?

GDP Price Index

B

A

Aggregate Demand ≡ C + I + G + NE

Real GDP

© John E. Marthinsen

Real Money Supply Effects: Interest-Induced C and I Movements

Increases in the GDP Price Index cause a nation's real (i.e., price-adjusted) money supply to fall,[16] which decreases the supply of real loanable funds and raises the real risk-free interest rate. As the real risk-free interest rate (R) rises, both C and I fall. These changes reduce real GDP and move the nation along AD from A to B in Exhibit 12-24. Exhibit 12-25 summarizes these the interest-induced C and I effects.

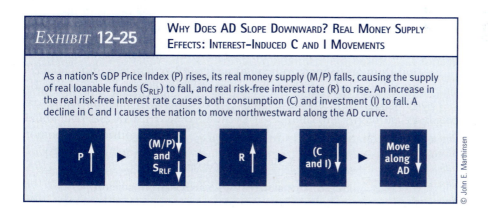

EXHIBIT **12-25**   WHY DOES AD SLOPE DOWNWARD? REAL MONEY SUPPLY EFFECTS: INTEREST-INDUCED C AND I MOVEMENTS

As a nation's GDP Price Index (P) rises, its real money supply (M/P) falls, causing the supply of real loanable funds (S_{RLF}) to fall, and real risk-free interest rate (R) to rise. An increase in the real risk-free interest rate causes both consumption (C) and investment (I) to fall. A decline in C and I causes the nation to move northwestward along the AD curve.

P ↑ ▶ (M/P)↓ and S_{RLF} ↓ ▶ R ↑ ▶ (C and I) ↓ ▶ Move along AD ↓

© John E. Marthinsen

[16] For example, if the money supply were equal to $100 billion and the price level were 1, the real money supply would be $100 billion (i.e., M/P = $100 billion/1 = $100 billion). If the money supply increased by 50% to $150 billion, but the price level doubled to 2, then the real money supply would fall to $75 billion (i.e., M/P = $150 billion/2 = $75 billion).

EXHIBIT 12-26 | **WHY DOES AD SLOPE DOWNWARD? WEALTH EFFECTS**

- As the GDP Price Index (P) rises, the real money supply (M/P) and supply of real loanable funds (S_{RLF}) fall, causing the real risk-free interest rate (R) to rise. An increase in R causes the value of fixed income securities and household wealth to fall. As real wealth falls, C falls, causing a reduction in real GDP (RGDP). Therefore, the increase in P and decrease in RGDP move the nation along its AD curve.
- As P increases, (M/P) falls, causing a reduction in household wealth. The decline in household wealth causes C and RGDP to fall. Therefore, the increase in P and decrease in RGDP move the nation along its AD curve.

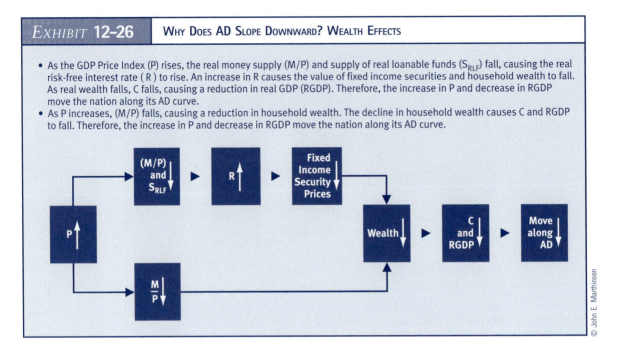

Price- and Interest-Induced Wealth Effect

A second reason for the inverse relationship between a nation's GDP Price Index and the amount demanded is the *wealth effect*, which has two causes First, if the average price level rises, the real value of a nation's money holdings falls with the decline in its purchasing power. This reduction in purchasing power decreases wealth, which reduces C. Second, we saw with the "interest-induced C and I Effects" that increases in a nation's GDP Price Index cause the real risk-free interest rate to rise. If a rising real risk-free interest rate causes nominal interest rates to rise, the value of fixed income securities (e.g., notes and bonds) held in financial investors' portfolios falls, which also reduces the wealth. As wealth falls, C falls, causing a decline in real GDP. These cause-and-effect linkages are shown in Exhibit 12-26.

Price- and Exchange Rate-Induced Net Export Effects

A final major reason for the inverse relationship between a nation's GDP Price Index and the amount demanded per period is the net export effect, which is closely aligned with the substitution effect in microeconomics. Again, there are two causes. First, as a nation's average price level increases, domestic exports become less competitive relative to foreign suppliers, causing export revenues to fall. At the same time, imported goods and services from foreign nations become more attractive, causing import expenditures to rise. The combination of falling export revenues and rising import costs causes NE to fall. Therefore, rising national prices lead to declining levels of spending on domestically produced goods and services, which causes a movement along the AD curve.

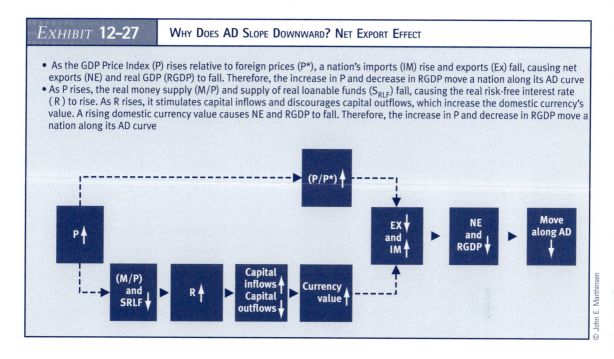

EXHIBIT 12-27   **WHY DOES AD SLOPE DOWNWARD? NET EXPORT EFFECT**

- As the GDP Price Index (P) rises relative to foreign prices (P*), a nation's imports (IM) rise and exports (Ex) fall, causing net exports (NE) and real GDP (RGDP) to fall. Therefore, the increase in P and decrease in RGDP move a nation along its AD curve
- As P rises, the real money supply (M/P) and supply of real loanable funds (S_{RLF}) fall, causing the real risk-free interest rate (R) to rise. As R rises, it stimulates capital inflows and discourages capital outflows, which increase the domestic currency's value. A rising domestic currency value causes NE and RGDP to fall. Therefore, the increase in P and decrease in RGDP move a nation along its AD curve

© John E. Marthinsen

Second, rising interest rates, caused by the rising GDP Price Index and falling supply of real loanable funds, attract international investors interested in earning the higher rates of return. To purchase these investments, they must first purchase the domestic currency, which makes it rise in value and causes exports to fall and imports to rise. As a result, NE falls, causing a reduction in real GDP, which moves the nation along AD. Exhibit 12-27 summarizes these net export effects.

Summary

A nation's AD curve is downward sloping because fluctuations in its GDP Price Index cause inverse changes in total spending via three major channels: the real money supply effect, wealth effect, and net export effect. Therefore, as a nation's GDP Price Index rises, C, I, and NE fall, moving a nation along its AD curve.

CAUSE-AND-EFFECT RELATIONSHIPS WHEN A CHANGE IN REAL GDP IS THE STIMULUS

In the previous section, we analyzed how changes in a nation's GDP Price Index (which is on the vertical axis of the AD curve) cause fluctuations in C, I, and NE. Now let's consider how changes in real GDP (on the horizontal axis of the AD curve) could cause fluctuations in the GDP Price Index. Our analysis uses reasoning that will be reinforced and expanded in Chapter 21, "Causes of Long-Term Growth and Inflation," where the equation of exchange is formally introduced. The equation of exchange shows the interconnections among nation's GDP Price Index (P), real GDP (Q), nominal money supply (M), and money velocity (V), where money velocity is the number of times a nation's money supply is spent for newly produced, final goods and services per period. We will find that the money supply times the velocity of money must equal the nation's GDP Price Index times real GDP (i.e., $M \times V \equiv P \times Q$).

If there is no change in a nation's money supply and no change in the number of times a nation's residents spend money each period (i.e., no change in the velocity of money), then increases in real GDP (i.e., output) must cause the average price level (i.e., GDP Price Index) to fall. The added workload put on the existing money supply to purchase the greater number of goods and services produced can only be accomplished if the GDP Price Index falls.

For example, if the money supply were $1,000 million, the quantity of goods and services produced were worth $1,000 million, and people spent each dollar in the money supply once per year, then the average price level would be 1.0 (i.e., $1,000 million of money supply/$1,000 million of goods and services). If output doubled to $2,000 million and the money supply and velocity remained constant, the added goods and services could be purchased only if the price level dropped to 0.50 (i.e., $1,000 million of money supply/ $2,000 million of goods and services).

ACTUAL QUANTITY SUPPLIED ALWAYS EQUALS ACTUAL QUANTITY DEMANDED

In the 1987 romantic comedy, *The Princess Bride*, swordsman Inigo Montoya turns to his Sicilian boss, Vizzini, and says: "You keep using that word. I do not think it means what you think it means." Montoya was referring to the word "inconceivable," but if we substitute the word "equilibrium," the link to macroeconomics is complete because both words are highly misunderstood.

Macroeconomic equilibrium occurs at a unique price where the *desired* (or *expected or anticipated*) quantity demanded equals the *desired* (or *expected or anticipated*) quantity supplied because the *actual* quantity demanded and *actual* quantity supplied are always equal.[17] To understand this statement, consider what would happen in an economy if prices were too low, causing the amount produced and supplied by the business sector to be less than the amount buyers desired to purchase. Exhibit 12-24 shows this situation at the price level P_B (i.e., a GDP Price Index *below* equilibrium).

At P_B, the amount buyers desire to purchase is greater than the amount suppliers desire to make available for sale. As a result, a shortage occurs, which means there is macroeconomic disequilibrium. Using the figures in Exhibit 12-28, the desired amount of goods and services demanded per year is $120 million, and the desired amount produced per year is $100 million, so a shortage of $20 million exists. As a result of this disequilibrium, many macroeconomic variables will adjust during the subsequent period(s) to

The *actual* amount supplied always equals the *actual* amount demanded, which is why "equilibrium" occurs where the *desired* amounts supplied and demanded are equal.

---

[17]To say that equilibrium occurs where expected aggregate supply equals expected aggregate demand is equivalent to saying the two curves completely overlap.

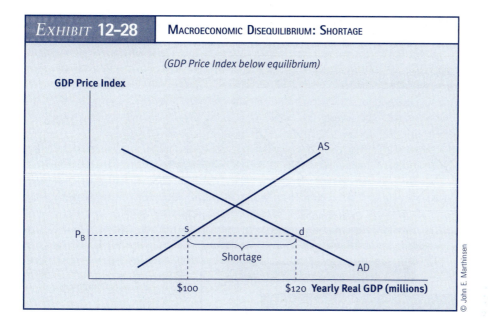

| EXHIBIT **12-28** | **MACROECONOMIC DISEQUILIBRIUM: SHORTAGE** |

(GDP Price Index below equilibrium)

eliminate the shortage. One of these major variables is the average national price level.

In Exhibit 12-28, P_B is not the equilibrium GDP Price Index, but this conclusion is clear only if we remember that the AS and AD curves represent *desired* supply and *desired* demand and not *actual* supply and *actual* demand. Making this distinction is important because at P_B (and at all other GDP Price Index levels), the business sector's *actual* quantity supplied is exactly equal to the *actual* quantity demanded. Here is why.

Consider P_B in Exhibit 12-28, which is a price level at which the business sector desires to supply only $100 million of final goods and services while the household sector desires to demand $120 million. If only $100 million are available, then only $100 million can be purchased, which means the actual amount supplied and actual amount demanded must be equal even though the desired amounts supplied and demanded are not. It is for this reason that macroeconomic equilibrium is defined as the position where *desired* quantity supplied equals *desired* quantity demanded per period and *not* the position where *actual* quantity supplied equals *actual* quantity demanded per period.

If the concept of desired quantity supplied and demanded versus actual quantity supplied and demanded still seems unclear, consider the opposite situation in which the GDP Price Index is at P_A (i.e., a price level *above* equilibrium). At P_A in Exhibit 12-29, the amount of goods and services that buyers desire to purchase ($100 million) is less than the amount suppliers desire to make available for sale ($130 million). As a result, producers are stuck with a surplus of goods and services (surplus = $30 million).

Despite the disequilibrium at P_A, the business sector's *actual* amount supplied ($130 million) is exactly equal to the *actual* amount demanded

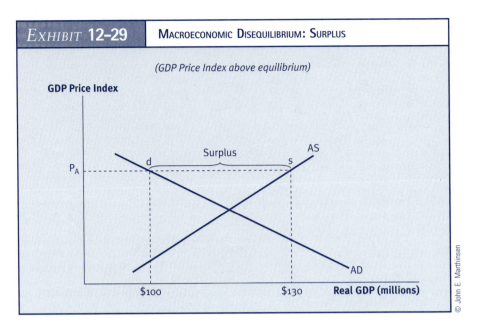

EXHIBIT **12–29**   MACROECONOMIC DISEQUILIBRIUM: SURPLUS

(GDP Price Index above equilibrium)

($130 million) because the unpurchased goods end up in business inventories ($30 million). An increase in inventories is counted as part of a nation's gross private domestic investment (I), which is part of actual business demand for GDP. In short, even though businesses did not want their inventories to increase by this amount ($30 million), they have no choice, and this increase is considered by the national income accounts as part of actual demand. Because everything produced has to be demanded (either willingly or unwillingly as unexpected changes in inventories), actual quantity supplied must equal actual quantity demand (i.e., C + I + G + NE).

THE SHORT-RUN PHILLIPS CURVE

Let's switch our attention now to the Phillips curve and its relationship to demand-pull inflation. The key to understanding this section is remembering that when a nation's AD rises, its GDP Price Index rises, real GDP rises, and, due to the greater output, unemployment falls. Increases in the GDP Price Index, in turn, put upward pressure on the inflation rate.

Originally, the Phillips curve was a statistical relationship that was spotted in 1957 by British economist A. W. Phillips, when he was analyzing the historic correlation between changes in British wage rates and British unemployment rates. His data showed there was an inverse relationship between these two economic variables, which meant that, in the past, as British unemployment rates fell, wage rates increased (and vice versa).

Today, most nations are more interested in prices (and inflation) than they are in wages (and wage rate changes). As a result, during the past half century, the Phillips curve has changed from its original focus on percentage changes in wages and unemployment rates to inflation and unemployment rates.

The Phillips curve is the inverse relationship between a nation's unemployment rate and inflation rate.

© John E. Marthinsen

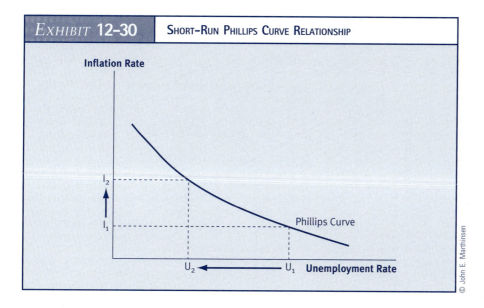

EXHIBIT 12-30   SHORT-RUN PHILLIPS CURVE RELATIONSHIP

Inflation Rate

Phillips Curve

I_2

I_1

U_2 U_1 Unemployment Rate

© John E. Marthinsen

Suppose a country's Phillips curve is the one shown in Exhibit 12-30. This downward-sloping curve indicates that the historic relationship between the nation's unemployment rate and inflation rate was inverse, which implies the predominant cause of the inflation was a rising AD (i.e., demand-pull inflation). For example, if the unemployment rate fell from U_1 to U_2, the inflation rate rose from I_1 to I_2 (and vice versa).

The Phillips curve became very popular in many nations (including the United States) during the 1960s. Some governments and central bankers felt they had found an economic Rosetta Stone, which could be used to translate macroeconomic policies into educated tradeoffs of one goal (e.g., inflation) for another (e.g., unemployment). Unfortunately, belief in this relationship faded as nations realized that this short-term trade-off did not stand the test of time. In other words, the inverse relationship between inflation and unemployment may hold in the short run but is more nebulous in the long run.

Exhibit 12-31 shows the inflation rates and unemployment rates in the United States from 1959 to 1968. If asked to draw just one line through these points that best represents them, most of us would choose a downward-sloping line like the one drawn.

Exhibit 12-32 shows U.S. inflation rates and unemployment rates from 1959 to 2012, which is a much longer period of time than the ten years covered in Exhibit 12-31. It provides a visual evidence for why the inverse relationship between unemployment and inflation is more ambiguous in the long run. If asked to draw just one line that best represents these inflation–unemployment rate combinations, would it be downward sloping like before, upward sloping, vertical, or horizontal? The answer is not clear.

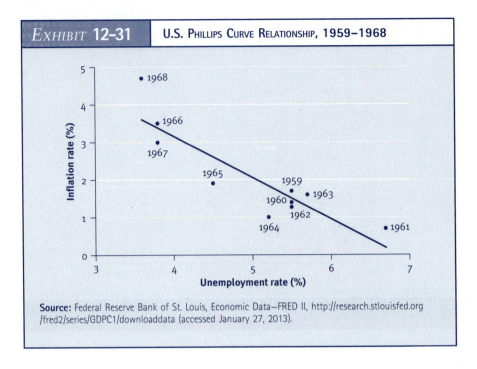

EXHIBIT 12-31   **U.S. PHILLIPS CURVE RELATIONSHIP, 1959–1968**

Source: Federal Reserve Bank of St. Louis, Economic Data—FRED II, http://research.stlouisfed.org /fred2/series/GDPC1/downloaddata (accessed January 27, 2013).

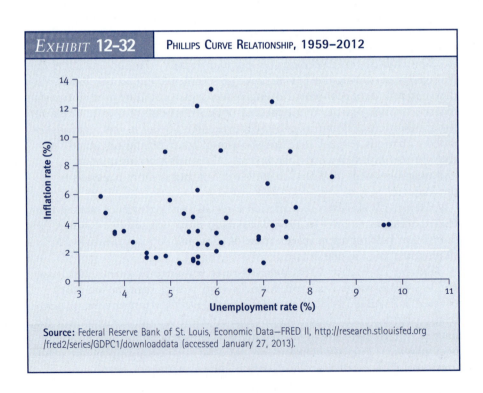

EXHIBIT 12-32   **PHILLIPS CURVE RELATIONSHIP, 1959–2012**

Source: Federal Reserve Bank of St. Louis, Economic Data—FRED II, http://research.stlouisfed.org /fred2/series/GDPC1/downloaddata (accessed January 27, 2013).

There is nothing theoretical about the Phillips curve relationship.[18] Rather, it is a statistical relationship in search of a theoretical explanation, and demand-pull inflation provides a possible one. Today, many believe that a *short-term* trade-off between inflation and unemployment still exists when these changes are stimulated by shifts in AD. Moreover, this inverse relationship is most likely to occur if the inflation is unexpected, causing unforeseen changes in business profitability. For example, if prices rise faster than resource costs, then profits rise and businesses have an incentive to hire more workers. As a result, the inflation rate rises and unemployment rate falls.

If the downward-sloping Phillips curve is due to unanticipated inflation that redistributes income from workers to businesses, then one can see why its effect may only be temporary. Given time, inflation and inflationary expectations tend to converge. When they do, business profitability and unemployment tend to settle back to their old rates. We will have more to say about the shapes of the short-term and long-term Phillips curves in Chapter 21, "Causes of Long-Term Growth and Inflation."

SPIRAL INFLATION

Demand-pull inflation and cost-push inflation are "pure models" of inflation because there is only one shift in supply or one shift in demand. By contrast, there are also "hybrid models" of inflation, which are caused by mutually reinforcing changes in AD and AS. These hybrid models are called *spiral inflation*.

> Spiral inflation is caused by mutually reinforcing changes in aggregate supply and aggregate demand.

PUSH–PULL INFLATION

Push-pull inflation occurs when cost-push inflation causes a subsequent round of demand-pull inflation. Suppose foreign oil prices increased substantially, causing the nation's AS curve to fall. Due to the effects of cost-push inflation, the nation's GDP Price Index would rise, and its real GDP would fall. The rising unemployment rate would provide an incentive for the government and/or central bank to stimulate demand. Fiscal authorities might respond by reducing Tx and/or raising G. The central bank might respond by increasing the real money supply. As the nation's AD rose, the GDP Price Index would rise, once again, due to demand-pull inflation.

> Push-pull inflation occurs when cost-push inflation causes demand-pull inflation.

PULL–PUSH INFLATION

Pull-push inflation is when demand-pull inflation causes a subsequent round of cost-push inflation. Suppose AD rose due to an increase in military spending. Demand-pull inflation would cause the nation's GDP Price Index and real GDP to rise. If the price increase were unexpected, it would likely be met with a negative reaction from wage earners and others who lost purchasing power. As a result, in subsequent rounds of wage and salary negotiations, workers would try to regain the inflationary tax on their incomes by bargaining for higher wages. If the escalation in wages were greater than the increase in worker productivity, per unit operating costs would rise, thereby causing the

> Pull-push inflation occurs when demand-pull inflation causes cost-push inflation.

---

[18] The Phillips curve is simply a regression line drawn through historic points that best represent the combination of all inflation rates and unemployment rates.

AS curve to fall. As it did, these added expenses would cause cost-push inflation, which would raise the GDP Price Index, once again.

PUSH–PUSH INFLATION

Push-push inflation (sometimes called *spillover inflation*) occurs when one
round of cost-push inflation causes another round of cost-push inflation. For
example, a significant increase in energy prices would shift the AS curve to
the left, causing the GDP Price Index to rise and real GDP to fall. A large
national labor union might negotiate an increase in wages to offset the
effects that inflation has on members' real wages. Again, the AS curve would
fall, causing the GDP Price Index to rise and real GDP to fall. Other unions
might then use this negotiated settlement as grounds for increasing their own
demands, thereby raising the GDP Price Index, once again. In this way, one
round of cost-push inflation could lead to recurring rounds of cost-push
inflation.

> Push-push inflation
> occurs when cost-push
> inflation causes another
> round of cost-push
> inflation.

PULL–PULL INFLATION

Finally, pull-pull inflation occurs when one round of demand-pull inflation
causes another round of demand-pull inflation. Suppose AD rose due to a
substantial increase in I. As a result, the nation's GDP Price Index would rise,
and real GDP would rise. If the increase in prices caused the expectation of
future price increases, it could set off new rounds of spending. As a result,
demand by consumers, businesses, governments, and foreigners could
increase, leading to further increases in the GDP Price Index.

> Pull-pull inflation occurs
> when demand-pull infla-
> tion causes another
> round of demand-pull
> inflation.

LAST WORD ON SPIRAL INFLATION

These cases of spiral inflation are only a few of many combinations and per-
mutations of hybrid inflation. The common denominator is that they all occur
for only short periods of time, *unless* they are fed by increases in the money
supply. For the GDP Price Index to rise when the money supply is constant,
the existing money supply would have to be spent more times each year (i.e.,
money velocity must rise). Huge increases in money velocity rarely occur
unless stimulated by excessive money supply growth.

CONCLUSION

It is a fair generalization to say that a keystone in the construction of most
companies' financial projections is sales growth. Changes in sales are hotwired
to some of the most important economic variables affecting business profits
and cash flows. Expenses, such as the cost of goods sold, marketing, and distribution, often change in tandem with sales.[19] Assets, such as accounts

---

[19] This relationship holds true even though many companies, especially technology services companies, place
an increasingly high priority on decoupling sales revenues and headcount growth, in an effort to become
leaner, more efficient, and more competitive.

receivable, and liabilities, such as accounts payable and debt, also change with sales.[20]

A company's revenues depend on the prices and quantities of the goods and services it sells. Raising sales volume and increasing prices are a lot easier to do when the economies in which a company operates are growing. Just as a rising tide lifts all ships, an expanding economy lifts the performance of all companies.

A useful framework for analyzing short-run changes in the GDP Price Index and real GDP is AS and AD analysis. The AS curve shows the quantity of domestically produced goods and services that businesses are willing and able to create and sell at various GDP Price Index levels during a given period of time. In general, there are three ranges on the AS curve, which are the: Keynesian (horizontal), intermediate (upward sloping), and classical (vertical) ranges.

AD shows the quantity of domestically produced goods and services that individuals (both domestic and foreign) are willing and able to purchase at various GDP Price Index levels during a given period of time. The AD curve is downward sloping, which means there is an inverse relationship between a nation's GDP Price Index and real GDP. This inverse relationship is caused by the real money supply effect, wealth effect, and net export effect.

For AD and AS analysis, it is important to distinguish between endogenous variables that move an economy along these curves and exogenous variables that shift them. The endogenous variables are the same for both the AS and AD—namely, the nation's GDP Price Index and real GDP. The exogenous variables affecting AS and AD may differ, but they conform closely to common sense and intuition.

Some of the major exogenous variables influencing AS are technology, productivity, price of inputs, climate, natural disasters, new resource discoveries, and immigration. The major exogenous variables affecting AD can be separated into the variables that affect C, I, G, and NE. C is affected mainly by real interest rates, taxes, indebtedness levels, wealth, and expectations. I is affected by real interest rates, regulations, taxes, technological changes, and expectations. G is affected by the discretionary decisions of politicians. Finally, NE is influenced by exchange rates, foreign real GDP growth rates, and relative international: prices, real risk-free interest rates, and restrictions, such as tariffs and quotas.

Any exogenous change in spending has primary and secondary effects. These secondary effects are the basis for the spending multiplier. The higher the spending multiplier, the greater the ultimate change in real GDP due to an exogenous, initial shock to AD. Feedback effects from the real loanable funds market can weaken the spending multiplier if changes in the real interest rate move C and I in directions counter to the initial shock.

Pure models of inflation are caused by either changes in AD *or* AS. Inflation that is caused by an increase in AD is called *demand-pull inflation*.

---

[20] Quality financial projections avoid tying all changes in a company's income statement, balance sheet, and cash flows to sales alone. While sales volume may influence many important business variables, the relationship to others (e.g., research, development, information technology, and maintenance) can be quite remote. Considerable care must be taken to determine key drivers of a business' revenues and expenses and to use them to predict earnings and cash flows.

Demand-pull inflation causes the GDP Price Index to rise and unemployment to fall, which is closely associated with the Phillips curve relationship. Inflation that is caused by a reduction in aggregate supply is called *cost-push inflation*. Cost-push inflation causes the GDP Price Index to rise and unemployment to rise. When inflation and unemployment rise, this condition is called *stagflation*. Spiral inflation occurs when one round of inflation causes another round of inflation (e.g., pull-push inflation, push-pull inflation, pull-pull, or push-push inflation).

Finally, the Phillips curve shows the historic inverse relationship between a nation's inflation and unemployment rates. It conforms to the results a nation should expect with demand-pull inflation, which suggests that most inflation has been caused by demand-pull (as opposed to cost-push) forces.

REVIEW QUESTIONS

1. What factors affect the steepness of the AS curve?

2. What factors cause a nation to move along its AS curve?

3. What factors cause a nation to move along its AD curve?

4. What economic factors cause the AD curve to shift?

5. What economic factors cause the AS curve to shift?

6. Suppose South Korea had a high GDP growth rate and little inflation. If the source of growth was from changes in AD, what would this imply about the shape of South Korea's AS curve?

7. Using AS and AD analysis, explain what effects, if any, the following changes have on each nation's GDP Price Index and real GDP. Explain your answer, and draw the appropriate supply and demand graphs (properly labeled).

    a. United States: A cold snap hits the southern part of the United States and destroys 25% of the crops.
    b. China: The People's Bank of China, which is China's central bank, tightens monetary policy.
    c. Japan: The yen appreciates relative to the British pound.
    d. Greece: The Greek government's budget deficit is reduced drastically in order to meet the bailout conditions of the European Monetary Union and International Monetary Fund.
    e. Japan: Japan's saving rate falls due to the nation's aging population.
    f. United States: Turmoil between Iraq and Iran causes a sharp increase in the price of oil.
    g. United States: The U.S. housing market crashes, causing wealth to fall for a large cross section of the United States.
    h. Mexico: The government increases its spending on goods and services and cuts taxes to stimulate the economy.
    i. China: China's government spending on goods and services increases significantly and state banks make loans to inefficient state enterprises rather than to more qualified borrowers.

8. If China allows its exchange rate to appreciate relative to the U.S. dollar, what should happen to its AD and AS? How will these changes affect China's GDP Price Index and real GDP?

9. Is the following statement true or false? "A nation's actual aggregate amount supplied *always equals* its actual aggregate amount demanded." Explain fully.

10. Under Indonesian law, the minimum wage is determined by local governments. In 2012, these local governments decided to increase the minimum wage by approximately 30%. Explain what effect this policy should have had on Indonesia's GDP Price Index, inflation rate, real GDP, and unemployment rate.

DISCUSSION QUESTIONS

11. Are the reasons for a nation's downward-sloping AD curve the same as for the downward-sloping demand facing a firm? Explain.

12. In the early 2000s, South Africa's gross saving rate was about 16%, but some economists felt that the country needed a saving rate of about 22% to make a dent in black poverty. Explain how an increase in saving might promote growth. How might it reduce economic growth?

13. Provide some examples of structural changes that you feel emerging nations, in general, could undertake to increase productivity. What effect do changes in productivity have on a nation's GDP Price Index and real GDP?

14. Mexico has been trying to make needed structural reforms that will improve overall labor productivity.

    a. Explain the likely effect that structural reforms will have on Mexico's real goods market. Be sure that, in your answer, you describe whether the changes are caused by shifts in aggregate supply or aggregate demand.
    b. Explain the spillover effects of these structural reforms from Mexico's real goods market to its real loanable funds market.

Chapter 13

Fiscal Policy and Automatic Stabilizers: What Managers Need to Know

INTRODUCTION

What is fiscal policy? How does it affect the key macroeconomic markets and, by way of them, a nation's economic well-being? When is fiscal policy successful? Should we evaluate the performance of government policymakers in the same way we evaluate business managers? Answering all but the last of these questions is relatively easy. Fiscal policy is the discretionary and non-discretionary use of government spending and taxation policies to achieve macroeconomic goals. Most fiscal policies affect aggregate demand in the real goods market, and success is measured by their ability to achieve macroeconomic objectives, such as increased growth, reduced unemployment, or lower inflation. The most elusive question to answer is the last because a country is not a company. Consider some of the differences.

Companies succeed or fail based on how well their customers' demands are met. If they produce goods or services that few people want, then sales and profits suffer. If they make frivolous expenditures, then costs rise, productivity wanes, share prices fall, and the likelihood of bankruptcies or takeovers increases. Finally, if companies take on too much debt, their debt-to-equity ratios rise, which increases borrowing costs to compensate for the greater levels of perceived risks. Capital markets understand very well that, unless borrowed funds are invested wisely, debt service demands can overwhelm a company's positive cash flows.

Governments are different in a number of ways. If a government offers services that few people want, it still has the power to finance them by taxing. In addition, a government does not have to worry about troublesome competitors or meddlesome shareholders. Of course, taxpayers could move to different countries in protest of a government's fiscal policies, but few do. Voters could try to fight fiscal imprudence by electing new representatives and leaders, but this process is slow. Furthermore, if a government spends indiscriminately, national productivity falls, but this injudicious spending is unlikely to spark foreign invasions (i.e., "takeovers") or force a nation to default on its financial obligations—at least not in the short run.

As for debt-to-equity ratios and their relationship to government risk, this financial measure is usually not available because very few governments publish national balance sheets.[1] As a result, there is almost no way to answer

> The art and skill of running and financing an efficient government are different from those required to run a successful business.

> Very few governments report national balance sheets; so there is no way to calculate if a nation's equity is changing.

---

[1] Australia, Canada, and New Zealand are among the few countries that publish annual balance sheets.

questions like, Does the nation have positive or negative equity (i.e., net worth)? Is national equity rising or falling?

Skeptics wonder why there is such widespread concern about government debts and deficits. After all, if a government borrows by selling securities that are denominated in the domestic currency, then why can't it just print the funds needed to pay off debts as they come due?

This chapter explores these questions and many more. It starts with a brief explanation of fiscal policy and then discusses the major funding sources available to governments, as well as the categories of uses to which these funds are put. Once the fundamentals are in place, this chapter goes on to addresses questions such as:

- What is the fiscal multiplier, and how does it influence the effectiveness of government policies?
- What are budget deficits, and how are active deficits different from passive ones?
- What effect, if any, do budget deficits or surpluses have on a nation's monetary base?
- Who owns the national debt, is it a burden on future generations, and can the debt grow so large that a government defaults on its obligations?

Fiscal policies are especially important to business managers due to the significant pressures they can put on key macroeconomic variables that affect business profitability and cash flows. Among these variables are interest rates, inflation, expectations, gross domestic product (GDP), exchange rates, wages, and expectations.

To better understand the focus of this chapter, suppose you worked for a U.S. company that was interested in building a Greenfield plant in Mexico. If you were responsible for preparing the capital budgeting analysis on this project, would you be optimistic or pessimistic about a projected increase in the Mexican government's budget deficit? Would you expect the deficit to be expansionary, contractionary, or neutral—or is it impossible to determine the effect? How about interest rates? Would you expect Mexican interest rates to rise and suggest borrowing now, or would you expect them to fall and suggest borrowing later? This chapter provides a framework for analyzing these and other questions related to the economic effects of fiscal policies.

THE BASICS

FISCAL VERSUS MONETARY POLICY

WHAT IS FISCAL POLICY?

Fiscal policy is the discretionary and nondiscretionary use of government spending and/or taxation to achieve macroeconomic goals, such as full employment and price stability. *Discretionary fiscal policies* require the government to pass new legislation or reform existing legislation before they can be implemented. Tax *rate* reductions, new spending on health and education,

Fiscal policy is the discretionary and nondiscretionary use of government spending and taxes to achieve macroeconomic goals.

cuts in military spending, and legislation to provide targeted assistance to families or small business are all examples of discretionary fiscal policies.

By contrast, *nondiscretionary fiscal policies* are changes in tax *revenues* and government *transfer payments* that are activated automatically by fluctuations in economic conditions. Governments determine the tax rates and prerequisites for receiving government transfers, but once established, the tax revenues and transfer payments change without any further need for legislation or action by the congress, parliament, president, or prime minister.

The payment of income taxes is a good example of a nondiscretionary fiscal policy. During recessions, tax revenues fall automatically with income even though legislated tax rates remain the same. Likewise, during expansions, tax revenues rise automatically with income.

Government transfer payments for social welfare programs are also examples of nondiscretionary fiscal policies. These payments rise automatically during recessions because the unemployment rate increases, causing the government to spend more on benefits, such as unemployment compensation, welfare, and aid to families with dependent children.

It is important to remember that government transfer payments are purely financial transactions for which no good or service is exchanged and for which nothing is directly produced. As a result, they are not part of government spending (G), but rather they increase household incomes, and, when spent, are included as part of personal consumption expenditures (C).

> Because they are purely financial transactions, government transfer payments are not part of government spending (G). Instead, they are classified as consumption (C), when they are spent by households.

Separating Fiscal Policy from Monetary Policy

Fiscal policies are different from monetary policies, and it is important to keep these differences in mind. Fiscal policies are enacted by the administrative and legislative branches of government. They do not require central bank approval or involvement. For instance, in the United States, fiscal policies are the responsibility of the President and Congress. The Federal Reserve may be asked to comment on proposed fiscal policies, but it does not have a vote in the final decision.

Monetary policies are determined and implemented by central banks, and the more independent central banks are from their governments, the better financial markets seem to like it. Borrowers and lenders pay close attention to a central bank's level of independence because the potential for inflation rises when big-spending governments have liberal access to central bank vaults and their ability to create new monetary base. As a result, the more independent a central bank is from the government, the lower the inflation risk premium that financial markets incorporate into a nation's nominal interest rate.

> Fiscal policy is the responsibility of the government, and monetary policy is the responsibility of the central bank.

TAXES AND OTHER SOURCES OF GOVERNMENT REVENUES

Technically speaking, government spending and taxation include *all* levels of government (e.g., national, state, provincial, cantonal, and local). Nevertheless, most macroeconomic discussions of fiscal policy focus only on national governments. For countries where state and local governments account for a large portion of total government spending and transfer payments, and/or a

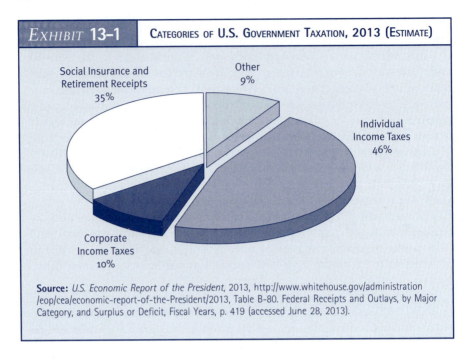

Exhibit **13-1**   CATEGORIES OF U.S. GOVERNMENT TAXATION, 2013 (ESTIMATE)

Source: *U.S. Economic Report of the President*, 2013, http://www.whitehouse.gov/administration/eop/cea/economic-report-of-the-President/2013, Table B-80. Federal Receipts and Outlays, by Major Category, and Surplus or Deficit, Fiscal Years, p. 419 (accessed June 28, 2013).

large portion of the nations' tax revenues (e.g., Argentina, Brazil, and Switzerland), this national focus could be misplaced.

National governments receive revenues from individual and company income taxes, as well as from tariffs and user fees. Exhibit 13-1 shows the principal wellsprings of the U.S. government's funding in 2013. Notice that 81% of them came from the combination of individual income taxes (46%) and social insurance and retirement (i.e., payroll) taxes (35%).[2]

> National government revenues come from income taxes, tariffs, and user fees.

GOVERNMENT SPENDING

The popular press is peppered with examples of wasteful government spending, such as $435 hammers, $640 toilet seats, $544 spark plug connectors, and multimillion-dollar bridges to nowhere. But actually, the majority of government expenditures is for rather mundane and less sensational items.[3]

> Most U.S. government spending is for health and Medicare, Social Security, and defense.

Exhibit 13-2 shows the major classifications of U.S. government expenditures for 2013. The largest portions of this spending were for health and Medicare, Social Security, and defense.

How much control do governments have over their expenditures? This question may seem rhetorical; after all, if governments don't control their expenditures, then who does? Actually, governments have far less control than

---

[2] In the United States, payroll taxes include Social Security, Medicare, and Medicaid tax payments. They are imposed on employees' compensation (e.g., salaries, wages, commissions, benefits, and employee stock options), withheld from employees' pay checks, and sent directly to the government by employers.

[3] See Citizens Against Government Waste, Homepage, http://cagw.org/ (accessed August 22, 2013).

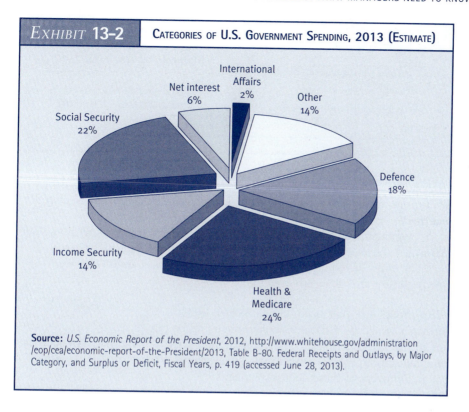

EXHIBIT 13-2 | CATEGORIES OF U.S. GOVERNMENT SPENDING, 2013 (ESTIMATE)

Source: *U.S. Economic Report of the President*, 2012, http://www.whitehouse.gov/administration /eop/cea/economic-report-of-the-President/2013, Table B-80. Federal Receipts and Outlays, by Major Category, and Surplus or Deficit, Fiscal Years, p. 419 (accessed June 28, 2013).

you might, at first, expect. In any year, the large majority of government expenditures is locked in by legislation that was passed in previous years. Therefore, only a relatively small portion is variable. This is significant because governments that want to stimulate their economies by increasing or redirecting spending or those that want to cool inflation by decreasing it may have significantly less discretion and influence than they are given credit for having.

> Governments have surprisingly little control over the bulk of their annual expenditures because much of it is committed from previous years.

BUDGET DEFICITS

Deficits occur when governments spend more than they earn in tax revenues and fees per period. These deficits have to be financed, and one way to do so is by borrowing. Even though many governments have the power to create the funds needed to finance their deficits, few do because it would increase the nation's money supply, and that is the responsibility of their central banks. Therefore, the primary focus of this chapter is on pure government borrowing and its effect on economic activity.

> Normally, governments finance their budget deficits by borrowing.

DIRECT FINANCING: ISSUING BILLS, NOTES, AND BONDS

Due to their taxing powers, most national governments have high credit ratings relative to other domestic borrowers. This power to tax provides assurance to investors, who are interested in whether the government securities they purchase will be serviced and eventually repaid. High credit ratings allow

EXHIBIT 13-3	TYPES AND MATURITIES OF GOVERNMENT SECURITIES
Security	**Maturity**
Treasury bills	Maturity ≤ 1 year
Treasury notes	1 year < Maturity ≤ 10 years
Treasury bonds	Maturity > 10 years

© John E. Marthinsen

governments to bypass financial intermediaries, such as banks and savings institutions, and borrow directly in the loanable funds market by issuing securities.

Governments tap the financial markets by issuing securities with varying maturities. *Treasury bills* have maturities less than or equal to 1 year; *Treasury notes* have maturities between 1 and 10 years, and *Treasury bonds* mature after 10 years (see Exhibit 13-3).

> **Governments borrow by issuing bills, notes, and bonds.**

WHO OWNS THE NATIONAL GOVERNMENT DEBT?

Securities issued by a national government can be purchased by virtually anyone in the world. Domestic and foreign: individuals, financial intermediaries, companies, nonprofit organizations, governments, and central banks are all potential buyers of these debt instruments.

Concerns are sometimes raised when an increasing portion of a nation's government debt is purchased by foreign residents, in general, and by foreign governments and central banks, in particular. Can large foreign creditors harm debtor countries by cutting off lending or dumping their security holdings? For example, what are the economic implications if China, a large international lender to the United States, refused to purchase more U.S. government securities, dumped the ones it held, and then sold all its dollar proceeds in the foreign exchange markets? What powers, if any, would China have over U.S. defense, foreign relations, and fiscal policies?

ACCOUNTING FOR GOVERNMENT DEFICITS

To better appreciate the meaning and implications of government deficits, it is helpful to understand the accounting logic behind government finances. What is included as a government expense and what is not? The answer to this question may be surprising because government budgets are measured on a cash basis, which means their accounting treatment is more like a business's cash flow statement than a profit-and-loss statement. Let's see why this is important.

Suppose a company earned $100 million in annual sales revenues, had operating expenses of $60 million, and therefore made operating profits equal to $40 million. What would happen if everything stayed the same, except the company purchased new machines worth $150 million? How would and should it account for the $150 million purchase? In a typical profit-and-loss statement, the company would depreciate the machines over their estimated life and count only the depreciation as an annual expense. If the life were 10 years, then $15 million (i.e., 10% of the $150 million) would count as an

MACRO MEMO   13-1

Who Owns the U.S. Government's Debt?

For the past decade, U.S. government debt has been increasingly purchased by foreign central banks, such as the People's Bank of China and Bank of Japan. Exhibit 13-4 shows how the owners of U.S. government debt have changed between 1981 and 2013. Notice that in 2013 about 34% of this debt was foreign-owned. The rest was held internally by U.S. residents, such as private investors, agencies, trusts, and the Federal Reserve.

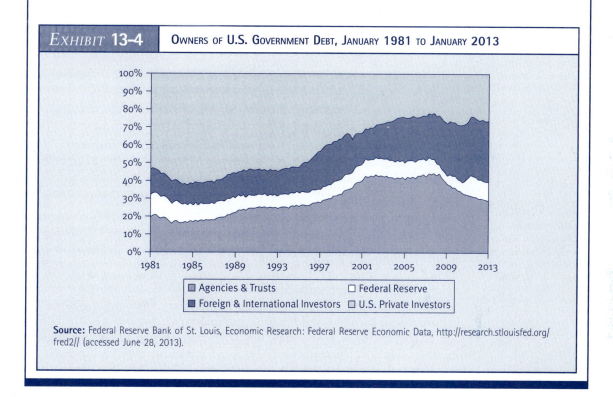

EXHIBIT **13-4**	OWNERS OF U.S. GOVERNMENT DEBT, JANUARY 1981 TO JANUARY 2013

■ Agencies & Trusts   □ Federal Reserve
■ Foreign & International Investors   □ U.S. Private Investors

Source: Federal Reserve Bank of St. Louis, Economic Research: Federal Reserve Economic Data, http://research.stlouisfed.org/fred2// (accessed June 28, 2013).

annual expense. Therefore, this year's profits would fall from $40 million to $25 million.[4]

By contrast, a cash flow statement would require the company to account for the entire $150 million investment during the year in which it was purchased. Consequently, the company's $40 million operating profit would turn into a $110 million net cash outflow.[5] Most national governments are required to report, as an expense, the full price of investment goods in the year they are purchased. Using this accounting practice, virtually any

> Government investment expenditures are not depreciated. They are accounted for as expenses when incurred.

[4] Operating revenues − Operating expenses − Depreciation expenses = $100 million − $60 million − $15 million = $25 million

[5] Operating revenues − Operating expenses − Cost of Investments = $100 million − $60 million − $150 million = −$110 million

profitable company in the world that invested heavily in plant and equipment would report losses.

THE FISCAL MULTIPLIER, CROWDING-OUT, AND CROWDING-IN

Prudent fiscal policies can have salutary effects on a nation's economy by keeping it on a steady, even, and upward course. Whether governments actually succeed in ironing out dramatic economic ups and downs is the subject of intense debate. This section explains how the economic effects of government spending and tax policies can be amplified by fiscal multipliers. It then goes on to explain how automatic adjustments in the three major macroeconomic markets (i.e., real goods, real loanable funds, and foreign exchange markets) directly affect the size of these fiscal multipliers.

THE FISCAL MULTIPLIER

Suppose the central government decided to stimulate economic growth and employment by spending $100 billion more on domestic infrastructure, such as bridges, roads, and tunnels. Assuming no offsetting effects from the real loanable funds or foreign exchange markets, GDP would rise by $100 billion, as new final goods and services were produced. Household incomes would increase hand-in-hand with greater production, causing consumer spending to rise. But the spending would not stop there. As we saw in Chapter 12, "Price and Output Fluctuations," this initial wave of spending would spur others, and the accumulation of these expenditure ripples would build to create the spending multiplier. When the source of an external shock is a discretionary change in government expenditures or taxation, the spending multiplier is usually called the *fiscal multiplier.*

> When an external shock is caused by a discretionary change in government spending or taxation, the spending multiplier is called the fiscal multiplier.

Exhibit 13-5 captures the combined impact that a discretionary increase in government spending and the fiscal multiplier have on a nation's real GDP and GDP Price Index. Notice how the initial change in government spending increases aggregate demand from AD_1 to AD_2, and the fiscal multiplier amplifies it by moving aggregate demand from AD_2 to AD_3. The net result of the increased aggregated demand from AD_1 to AD_3 is for real GDP to rise from $RGDP_1$ to $RGDP_3$ and the GDP Price Index to rise from PI_1 to PI_3.

If the fiscal multiplier were equal to 2.0, then an increase in real government spending by $100 billion would raise real GDP by $200 billion. A fiscal multiplier of 2.5 would increase real GDP by $250 billion.

FACTORS THAT WEAKEN THE FISCAL MULTIPLIER

There are forces built into macroeconomies that automatically weaken the fiscal multiplier and, therefore, limit the ultimate effect of fiscal policies and other exogenous shocks. These forces could lower the fiscal multiplier, for example, from 2.0 or 1.5. They could even reduce it to 0.5, which means an increase in government spending by $100 billion would raise real GDP only by $50 billion. These weakening forces are engaged automatically and occur in each of the three major macroeconomic markets (i.e., the real goods, real loanable funds, and foreign exchange markets). Let's review them market-by-market.

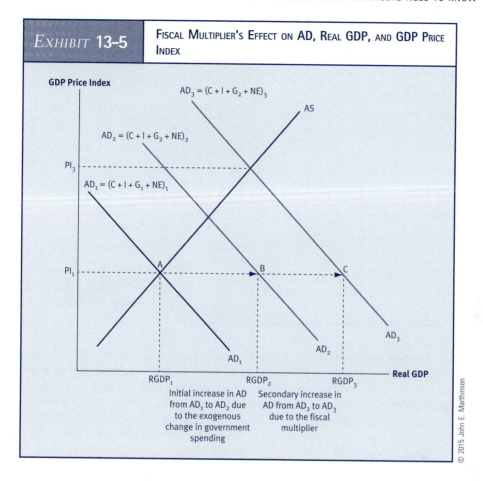

EXHIBIT 13-5   FISCAL MULTIPLIER'S EFFECT ON AD, REAL GDP, AND GDP PRICE INDEX

Forces in the Real Goods Market That Weaken the Fiscal Multiplier

Automatic changes in tax revenues, government transfers, and imports are among the major forces in the real goods market that weaken the fiscal multiplier. To see why, suppose real GDP increased. The rising real GDP rate would automatically increase tax revenues, thereby weakening the ability of households to consume. Increased real income would also cause automatic reductions in government transfer payments, as the unemployed found jobs and had less need for government support. Finally, as real GDP increased, imports would rise, strengthening the demand for foreign (not domestic) goods and services. Together, these automatic adjustments would weaken the fiscal multiplier and dampen (but not reverse) the ultimate effect of the external shock.

Automatic changes in tax revenues, government transfers, and imports are among the major forces in the real goods market that weaken the fiscal multiplier.

Forces in the Real Loanable Funds Market That Weaken the Fiscal Multiplier

To finance their deficit spending, most governments borrow in the domestic real loanable funds markets (i.e., capital and money markets). Their increased demand for funds raises the real risk-free interest rate, which has important effects on the quantity of real loanable funds supplied and demanded.

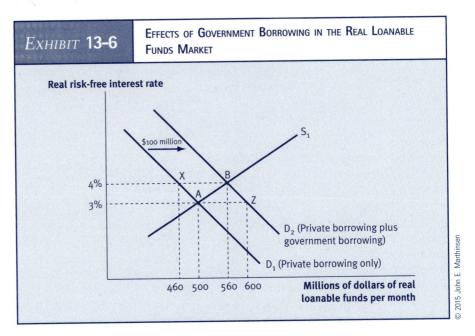

EXHIBIT **13-6**   EFFECTS OF GOVERNMENT BORROWING IN THE REAL LOANABLE FUNDS MARKET

Real risk-free interest rate

$100 million →

S_1

X   B
    A   Z
4% ------
3% ------

D_2 (Private borrowing plus government borrowing)

D_1 (Private borrowing only)

460 500 560 600

Millions of dollars of real loanable funds per month

© 2015 John E. Marthinsen

To more easily understand the effect such borrowing has on the economy, assume the government begins with a balanced budget (i.e., its initial demand for real loanable funds is equal to zero). In Exhibit 13-6, D_1 represents the private sector's demand for real loanable funds, and equilibrium is at Point A, where D_1 and S_1 intersect. The real risk-free interest rate equals 3%, and the equilibrium quantity of real loanable funds equals $500 million per month.

Now, suppose the government runs a $100 million budget deficit each month, which it finances by borrowing. This government borrowing increases the demand for real loanable funds by $100 million, which shifts demand from D_1 to D_2. The rightward shift in demand increases the real risk-free interest rate from 3% to 4% and the equilibrium quantity of real loanable funds from $500 million to $560 million per month (i.e., from Point A to B). How the nation moves from equilibrium at $500 million to equilibrium at $560 million is best understood if taken in steps. Let's start on the supply side.

Causes of the Increased Quantity of Real Loanable Funds Supplied The net increase of $60 billion in real loanable funds supplied to the market comes from a number of different sources, which were covered in Chapter 11, "Interest Rates and Why They Change." Let's review them. As the real risk-free interest rate increases, household saving rises, supplying fresh funds to the real loanable funds market. A higher real risk-free interest rate also increases the quantity of foreign funds supplied to the real loanable funds market, as global financial investors are attracted by the higher real returns.

The rising real risk-free interest rate also provides incentives for investors to adjust their portfolios to take advantage of changes in relative real returns. Individuals and businesses liquidate assets in their portfolios, such as precious metals, stocks, and real estate, and supply the liberated funds to the real loanable funds market.

Another way new funds are supplied to the real loanable funds market is by expanding the real money supply. As the real risk-free interest rate rises, the public sector's preferences for currency in circulation (C_c) and near money (N) and the banking sector's preferences for customary reserves (U) change relative to checking accounts, causing the nation's money multiplier to rise.[6] A rising money multiplier increases both the real money supply and quantity of real loanable funds supplied to the real credit market.

Causes of the Decreased Quantity of Real Loanable Funds Demanded: Crowding-out In Exhibit 13-6, the quantity of real loanable funds supplied and demanded increases by $60 billion (i.e., from $500 million to $560 million), which is $40 million less than the $100 million borrowed and spent by the government. What happened to the extra $40 million in stimulus spending? The answer is, it evaporated due to a reduction in private sector borrowing.

As government demand for real loanable funds rises from D_1 to D_2, the real risk-free interest rate increases from 3% to 4%, which causes private borrowing by the household, business, and foreign sectors to fall. Therefore, the movement from Z to B in Exhibit 13-6 is the due to private borrowers being crowded out of the real loanable funds market due to a rising real risk-free interest rate.

Normally, the household expenditures that are most affected by rising real interest rates are postponable, big-ticket items, such as appliances, automobiles, boats, houses, home improvements, and vacations. Businesses that are most likely to be affected by rising real rates are those that compete in capital-intensive industries or finance large inventories.

Crowding-out is the term used to describe the reduction in private borrowing due to the higher real risk-free interest rate from greater government borrowing. It is an appropriate term because individuals and businesses are accountable to budgets and bottom lines. Many governments are not. Therefore, a rising real risk-free interest rate crowds out individuals and businesses, rather than the government, from the real loanable funds market.

> **Crowding-out occurs when government borrowing raises the real risk-free interest rate and reduces private borrowing.**

It is important to remember that, as long as the supply of real loanable funds is upward sloping, crowding-out does not completely offset or reverse the fiscal multiplier. The government's increased demand for credit raises real interest rates and encourages new funds into the market, thereby easing, somewhat, the battle for funds between the government and private sectors. If the supply of real loanable funds were vertical (i.e., perfectly inelastic), the battle for funds would be a zero-sum game with the winners exactly offsetting losers in the competition for funds.

> **As long as the supply of real loanable funds is upward sloping, crowding-out will not completely erase the effects of expansionary fiscal policy.**

Forces in the Foreign Exchange Market That Weaken the Fiscal Multiplier

A higher real risk-free interest rate increases the quantity of foreign funds supplied to the domestic real loanable funds market, but these flows have a double-edged effect. To invest financially in a country with rising interest

---

[6] As the real risk-free interest rate rises, the nation's preferred asset ratios change. C_c/D, which is the currency-in-circulation-to-checking-deposit ratio, falls; N/D, which is the near-money-to-checking-deposit ratio, rises, and U/D, which is the customary-reserves-to-checking-deposit ratio, falls. All of these changes raise the M2 money multiplier.

rates, foreign investors must first purchase the nation's currency, which puts upward pressure on its international value. As the currency appreciates, imports become cheaper and exports more expensive, causing net exports to fall. As net exports fall, so does the quantity of real goods and services demanded, which weakens the fiscal multiplier.

A Factor That Strengthens the Fiscal Multiplier: Crowding-In

It is possible for government spending to encourage business investments if it enlarges markets, opens new business opportunities, and creates favorable expectations. For example, the construction of a new highway may increase service investments along the road, such as restaurants, and provide incentives for businesses to locate near communities that can now be accessed more easily. *Crowding-in* is the term used to describe the increase in private investments caused by greater government spending and its impact, which strengthens the fiscal multiplier.

Summary of the Fiscal Multiplier

Exhibit 13-7 captures the effect that government borrowing-and-spending have on a nation's real GDP and GDP Price Index. In the absence of any feedback or

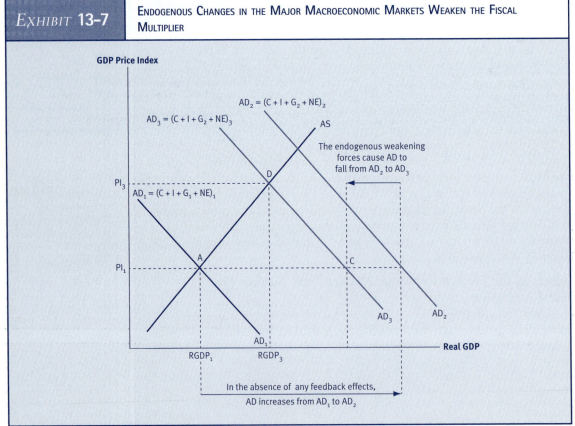

EXHIBIT 13-7   ENDOGENOUS CHANGES IN THE MAJOR MACROECONOMIC MARKETS WEAKEN THE FISCAL MULTIPLIER

What Happens When Fiscal Multipliers Are Misestimated? Is It Too Late to Say "I'm Sorry?"

What are the consequences when forecasters get it wrong and underestimate a nation's fiscal multiplier? The eyes of the world were opened to just such a mistake in January 2013, when Olivier Blanchard, chief economist at the International Monetary Fund (IMF), and Daniel Leigh, research economist at the IMF, concluded in a technical econometric paper that the fiscal multiplier applied by policymakers to Greece in 2010 (i.e., 0.5) may have been a third its actual size (i.e., 1.5).*

Why was this important? Between 2007 and 2010, Greece faced wide and growing fiscal deficits, which were caused by a severe domestic and worldwide economic downturn. The nation's reported deficits also increased when it was discovered that the Greek government had engaged in some creative accounting that resulted in grossly underreported expenditures. Shut out of the private international capital markets and strongly in need of bailout funds, Greece was forced to cut government spending and raise taxes. *Fiscal consolidation* was the term used to describe this dynamic-duo of contractionary policies, which was supposed to bring the nation's budget into closer balance. Unfortunately, fiscal consolidation caused reductions in Greece's real GDP and increases in its unemployment rate that were worse than expected.

Blanchard and Leigh conjecture that forecasters assumed Greece's fiscal multiplier was approximately 0.5, which means a €10 billion reduction in government spending should have reduced real GDP by about €5 billion during the subsequent two-to-three-year period. Such a reduction would have raised Greece's unemployment rate marginally but should not have sent it into stratosphere. By contrast, if the actual multiplier was between 1.0 and 1.5, then the same €10 billion reduction in government spending would have reduced real GDP by €10 billion to €15 billion, causing unemployment to increase considerably more than expected.

One of the most important take-aways from this IMF monograph is that fiscal multipliers vary with time and economic conditions. With respect to economic conditions, they rise when (1) interest rates are at near-zero levels, (2) a nation's economic and financial systems are malfunctioning, and (3) an economy has considerable excess capacity. All of these conditions were present in Greece, which is why its fiscal multiplier may have increased beyond forecasters' expectations.

Other European nations, such as Spain and Portugal, were also struggling with recession-induced budget deficits, but demands by private creditors, European Monetary Union (EMU) nations, and the IMF to employ contractionary fiscal policies were more moderate. Might the reason be traced to Greece's experience with fiscal consolidation and its misestimated fiscal multiplier?[†]

*Oliver Blanchard and Daniel Leigh, "Growth Forecast Errors and Fiscal Multipliers," *International Monetary Fund*, WP/13/1, January 2013, http://www.imf.org/external/pubs/cat/longres.aspx?sk=40200.0 (accessed June 23, 2013).

[†]Howard Schneider, "An Amazing Mea Culpa from the IMF's Chief Economist on Austerity," *The Washington Post*, January 3, 2013, http://www.washingtonpost.com/blogs/wonkblog/wp/2013/01/03/an-amazing-mea-culpa-from-the-imfs-chief-economist-on-austerity/ (accessed June 23, 2013).

spillover effects, aggregate demand would increase from AD_1 to AD_2, but when the endogenous weakening forces are added, AD falls from AD_2 to AD_3. The net effect is an increase in real GDP from $RGDP_1$ to $RGDP_3$, which decreases the unemployment rate. As well, the GDP Price Index rises from PI_1 to PI_3, which puts upward pressure on inflation.

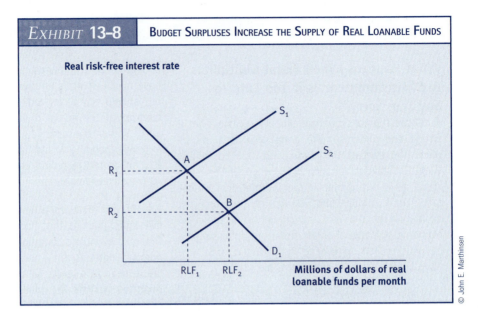

EXHIBIT 13-8   BUDGET SURPLUSES INCREASE THE SUPPLY OF REAL LOANABLE FUNDS

© John E. Marthinsen

GOVERNMENT SURPLUSES

Surpluses occur when governments spend less than they receive in tax revenues and fees. Normally, surpluses are thought to be contractionary because falling government expenditures and rising taxes reduce aggregate demand. Therefore, when taxes exceed spending, the government is often viewed as taking more away from aggregate demand than it contributes.

As was the case with government budget deficits, economic forces in the three principal macroeconomic markets react automatically and mitigate the contractionary impact of these surpluses. In the real goods market, as real GDP falls, tax revenues fall, government transfers rise, and imports fall. In the real loanable funds market, the surplus increases the supply of real loanable funds, thereby reducing the real risk-free interest rate and stimulating consumption and investment spending (see Exhibit 13-8). Finally, in the foreign exchange market, a lower real risk-free interest rate puts downward pressure on the exchange rate, which increases net exports. All of the factors help to reduce the contractionary effects of fiscal policy.

ACTIVE VERSUS PASSIVE DEFICITS AND SURPLUSES

Are government deficits expansionary, contractionary, or neutral, or is it impossible to determine their effects? Many people ask, "How can a budget deficit be anything but expansionary? If a government spends more than it earns in taxes, doesn't the net effect on aggregate demand have to be positive, which is expansionary?" Let's take a closer look and see why the answer is not obvious.

Determining whether a government budget deficit is expansionary, contractionary, or neutral is easy to do once the deficit is separated into its discretionary (i.e., active) and nondiscretionary (i.e., passive) components. *Active* deficits are expansionary; *active* surpluses are contractionary, and balanced

MACRO MEMO **13-3**

U.S. Deficits and Surpluses from 1970 to 2012

Exhibit 13-9 shows that government surpluses were not hallmarks of the U.S. economy during the 42-year period from 1970 to 2012. There were surpluses in only four years, and all others were deficits—many of them substantial.

EXHIBIT 13–9   U.S. GOVERNMENT DEFICITS AND SURPLUSES, 1970–2012

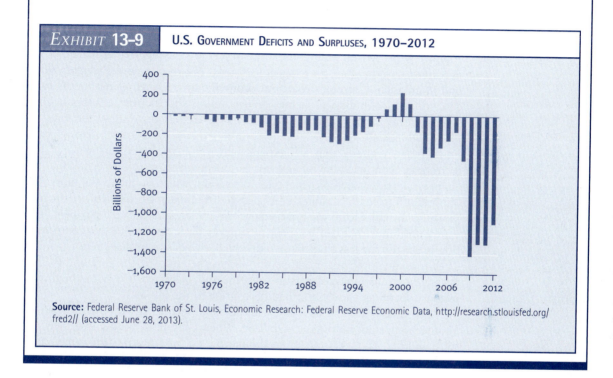

Source: Federal Reserve Bank of St. Louis, Economic Research: Federal Reserve Economic Data, http://research.stlouisfed.org/fred2// (accessed June 28, 2013).

active budgets are neutral. Let's focus first on passive deficits and nondiscretionary changes in government transfer payments and taxes. Afterwards, we will turn our attention to active deficits and discretionary fiscal policy.

> Active deficits are expansionary, active surpluses are contractionary, and balanced active budgets are neutral.

NONDISCRETIONARY GOVERNMENT TRANSFER PAYMENTS AND TAXATION: PASSIVE DEFICITS

Nondiscretionary changes in government expenditures are called *government transfers.*[7] Together with nondiscretionary changes in tax revenues, they make up a nation's automatic stabilizers. The term, *automatic stabilizers,* is descriptive because these expenditures and taxes respond passively

[7] Notice that these payments are called "government transfers (GT)" and not "government expenditures (G)" because they are payments for which no good or service is produced. Real GDP includes only expenditures for newly produced final goods and services.

(automatically) to the changing economic conditions and calm (stabilize) fluctuations in both real GDP and prices that would have occurred without them. An important take-away is that increases in passive deficits do not raise aggregate demand, which means they do nothing to move an underperforming nation closer to full employment. Similarly, decreases in passive deficits do not move a nation farther away from full employment. Rather, passive deficits restrain the movement of real GDP.

A helpful simile is to think of nondiscretionary changes in government transfers and taxes as if they were giant anchors attached to a seaworthy ship, except in this case, the ship is the nation's economy. Like a ship's anchor, the automatic stabilizers inhibit forward or backward movement, but they do not completely prevent it. Just as the force of a ship's engine, strong winds, or prevailing currents (i.e., all exogenous forces) can overcome the weight and pull of an anchor, strong exogenous economic forces, such as discretionary changes in fiscal policy, monetary policy, and/or shocks from changes in consumption, investment, and net exports, can overcome the drag of the automatic stabilizers.

A moment's reflection will explain why automatic stabilizers act only to restrain economic activity and not as independent sources of economic change. Consider unemployment compensation, which is one of the most important automatic stabilizers. As people lose their jobs, they collect unemployment benefits from the government. To the recipients, these payments are sources of funds that can be spent to support basic needs. But this compensation is usually far less than these individuals earned when they were working. Therefore, unemployment compensation has the effect of cushioning the decline in an unemployed person's income and spending. It is not enough to increase spending to where it had been prior to the job loss.

The same point can be made with personal income tax revenues, which is another important automatic stabilizer. When GDP falls, people lose their jobs, and tax payments fall. Even though the tax *rate* remains the same, tax revenues fall due to the declining income base. This reduction in tax revenues does not stimulate unemployed individuals' spending from where it would have been if they had jobs. It only reduces the tax burden to make it commensurate with their ability to pay. Imagine the unfairness, if the unemployed were required to pay the same taxes after they lost their jobs as they paid when they were fully employed.

Are the restraining influences of automatic stabilizers helpful to a nation? The answer is "It depends." Like an anchored ship, the automatic stabilizers are helpful if an economy is at or close to its destination or goal (e.g., full employment and price stability). In this case, the restraining influences of the automatic stabilizers help keep the nation close to where it wants to be. By contrast, they are not helpful (in fact, they are a hindrance) if a nation is far from its preferred position, such as in a deep recession or in the throes of rampant inflation.

DISCRETIONARY GOVERNMENT SPENDING AND TAXATION: ACTIVE DEFICITS

The deficits and surpluses that play important roles in stimulating or dampening economic conditions are called *active deficits* or *active surpluses*.

Passive deficits or surpluses are caused by the automatic stabilizers.

Automatic stabilizers only restrain movements of GDP. They are not sources of expansion or contraction.

Automatic stabilizers are helpful if a nation is at or near a desired economic position.

E_{XHIBIT} **13-10**	**Actual Deficit ≡ Active Deficit + Passive Deficit**		
Actual Deficit/Surplus	≡	**Passive Deficit/Surplus**	+	**Active Deficit/Surplus**
Current deficit/surplus	≡	Deficit/surplus due to the economy being below or above full employment	+	Deficit/surplus that occurs at full employment

© John E. Marthinsen

Increases or decreases in these deficits shift the nation's aggregate demand to the right or left. The way to determine whether the current (or projected) budget deficit/surplus is expansionary, contractionary, or neutral is to eliminate the passive component and to see what, if anything, is left. The remainder must be the active deficit or surplus.[8]

Suppose a government's actual budget deficit was $100 billion. If $60 billion of it was passive, then the rest ($40 billion) would be active, which would be expansionary. If the actual budget deficit were $100 billion and $110 billion of it were passive, then there would be an active surplus equal to $10 billion, which would be contractionary. In terms of fiscal policy, only active deficits and active surpluses provide independent power to change aggregate demand, thereby moving an economy forward or backward (see Exhibit 13-10). Increases in active deficits raise aggregate demand, and decreases reduce it.

The key to separating active deficits/surpluses from the passive deficits/surpluses is to remember that the automatic stabilizers are activated only when a nation is below or above full-employment GDP. Therefore, the deficits or surpluses that occur at full employment are active. For this reason, active deficits/surpluses are often called *full-employment deficits/surpluses*.

An example might help cement the differences among active, passive, and actual deficits and surpluses. In Exhibit 13-11, suppose the current level of GDP is $3,600 billion. At that level, the actual budget deficit is $72 billion because government spending plus transfer payments equal $792 billion and taxes equal $720 billion. Because the economy is below full employment, the government is running a passive deficit. To calculate the active part, we have to determine what the budget deficit (or surplus) would be if the economy were *at full employment*.

Suppose that full-employment real GDP was estimated to be $3,840 billion, which means at this level there would be no cyclical unemployment. At $3,840 billion, government taxes would be higher and government transfer payments would be lower than they are at $3,600. Assume that government economists estimate that taxes at full employment would be $48 billion higher than they are at present. Therefore, at full employment, total taxes would equal $768 billion. At the same time, suppose government economists

> Active deficits or surpluses are measured at full employment. They determine whether a government budget is expansionary or contractionary. Active deficits and surpluses are also called full-employment deficits and surpluses.

---

[8] "Separating Active and Passive Deficits and Surpluses," which is in "**The Rest of the Story**" section of this chapter, explains in greater detail an easy way to calculate active and passive deficits.

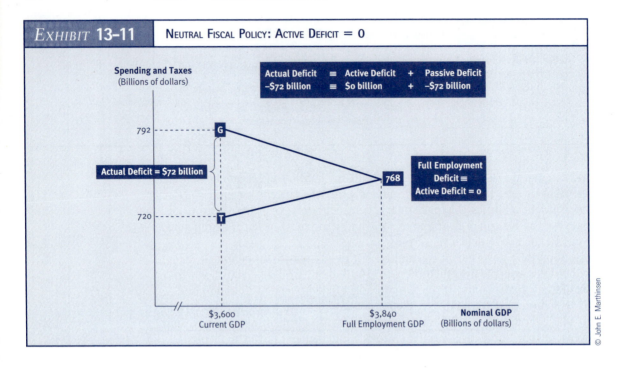

EXHIBIT **13-11**   NEUTRAL FISCAL POLICY: ACTIVE DEFICIT = 0

Spending and Taxes
(Billions of dollars)

Actual Deficit	≡	Active Deficit	+	Passive Deficit
–$72 billion	≡	$0 billion	+	–$72 billion

792 ---------- G

Actual Deficit = $72 billion

768   Full Employment
Deficit ≡
Active Deficit = 0

720 ---------- T

$3,600 $3,840   Nominal GDP
Current GDP   Full Employment GDP   (Billions of dollars)

© John E. Marthinsen

estimated that, due the reduced need for unemployment compensation and other social welfare benefits, government transfers at full employment would equal $768 billion, which is $24 billion lower than their current level.

In this example, both taxes and total government expenditures plus transfer payments at full employment would be $768 billion. Therefore, the *active* deficit/surplus would be equal to zero, which means that the entire current (i.e., actual) deficit at $3,600 billion is caused only by the automatic stabilizers. This finding is important because deficits caused by the automatic stabilizers do nothing to stimulate economic activity and, therefore, do not move a nation closer to full employment. They only restrain the economy, thereby preventing it from falling further into recession.

Only by discretionarily increasing government spending and/or reducing taxes could the government's budget become expansionary. Exhibit 13-12 shows the case where government spending is increased by $10 billion and taxes are reduced by $20 billion. As a result, the *active* deficit (i.e., the deficit at full employment) rises from $0 to $30 billion, indicating that fiscal policy is expansionary.

Example of an Active Surplus

From the previous example, it should be clear that a nation can have a budget deficit at the current level of GDP and a balanced budget, budget deficit, or budget surplus at the full-employment level of GDP. As a result, it is impossible to tell from the current deficit whether fiscal policy is expansionary, contractionary, or neutral. Exhibit 13-13 rounds out this discussion by showing the paradoxical case where a nation runs a budget deficit at the current level of GDP but would have a surplus at full employment.

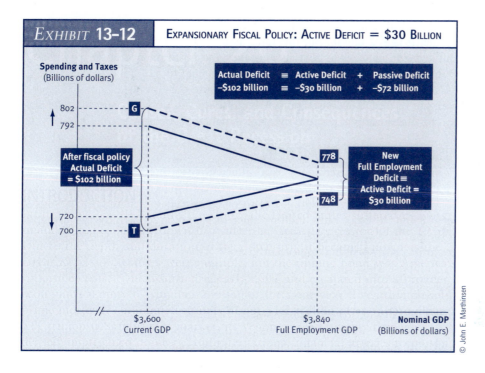

EXHIBIT 13-12 | **EXPANSIONARY FISCAL POLICY: ACTIVE DEFICIT = $30 BILLION**

Spending and Taxes
(Billions of dollars)

| Actual Deficit | ≡ | Active Deficit | + | Passive Deficit |
| –$102 billion | ≡ | –$30 billion | + | –$72 billion |

802   G

792

After fiscal policy
Actual Deficit
= $102 billion

778   New
Full Employment
Deficit ≡
Active Deficit =
$30 billion

748

720

700   T

$3,600
Current GDP

$3,840
Full Employment GDP

Nominal GDP
(Billions of dollars)

© John E. Marthinsen

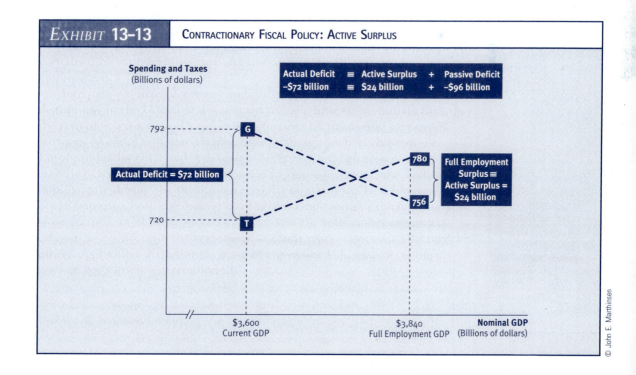

EXHIBIT 13-13 | **CONTRACTIONARY FISCAL POLICY: ACTIVE SURPLUS**

Spending and Taxes
(Billions of dollars)

| Actual Deficit | ≡ | Active Surplus | + | Passive Deficit |
| –$72 billion | ≡ | $24 billion | + | –$96 billion |

792   G

Actual Deficit = $72 billion

780   Full Employment
Surplus ≡
Active Surplus =
$24 billion

756

720   T

$3,600
Current GDP

$3,840
Full Employment GDP

Nominal GDP
(Billions of dollars)

© John E. Marthinsen

As before, suppose the current nominal GDP equals $3,600 billion and fiscal deficit is $72 billion. But this time, assume that, if the economy were at full employment, changes in government taxes and government transfer payments would be enough to create an active surplus equal to $24 billion. Therefore, fiscal policy appears to be expansionary because the current deficit is $72 billion, but in fact, it is contractionary because there is an active surplus. The reason for the illusion is because the passive deficit is equal to $96 billion.

FISCAL POLICY IN ACTION

In the short run, discretionary fiscal policies are most effective when they are used to solve demand-related problems. For example, if a nation was experiencing excessive inflation due to rising aggregate demand, the government could raise tax rates and/or reduce its spending to curb overall demand. If the problem was sluggish growth due to tepid demand, the government could increase spending and/or cut taxes.

Suppose a nation was faced with spiraling inflation. Let's see how fiscal policy tools could be used to reduce its inflation rate.

REDUCING DISCRETIONARY GOVERNMENT SPENDING

By reducing spending, governments can directly trim aggregate demand and a source of the inflation. These cuts in spending could be implemented across the board, or they could be targeted at specific sectors, such as defense, health, or social services.

Cutting government spending is usually controversial because people suffering the cuts take them personally, asking "Why gore my ox, when there are so many other oxen to gore?" A second problem with cutting government spending was mentioned earlier in the chapter, namely, that past legislation often locks in expenditures, thereby draining governments of the ability to make significant changes. Furthermore, these pieces of legislation are often difficult to change in the short term.

Government spending cuts are often very controversial, and a large portion of government spending is locked in by legislation.

INCREASING TAXES

Tax rate hikes are another way to reduce a nation's aggregate demand. If they are imposed on household incomes, then reduced disposable (i.e., after-tax) incomes cause personal consumption expenditures to fall. As consumption falls, so does aggregate demand. When higher tax rates are imposed on business profits, gross private domestic investment is cut as companies reduce their real investments. In addition, the reduction in after-tax profits cuts dividends and capital gains that otherwise would have flowed to the household sector, again, reducing demand.

Lower consumption and investment expenditures reduce demand, which lowers production and further reduces household income levels. As household earnings fall, so do their purchases of goods and services, which leads to subsequent rounds of spending cuts and slashed production (i.e., the fiscal multiplier effect). These cascading rounds of lower demand and income wind their way through the economy until equilibrium is (eventually) restored at a lower level of GDP. If successful, contractionary fiscal policies result in lower prices and/or lower inflation. At the same time, they may also reduce real GDP, causing unemployment to rise.

LAGS IN FISCAL POLICY

There is considerable controversy about the effectiveness of discretionary fiscal policies. Among the main reasons for concern and skepticism are its long and variable lags. Fiscal policies have the same three, generic lags as monetary policy—the recognition lag, implementation lag, and impact lag—but the lengths of these lags can vary substantially from period to period, and they can be quite different from their monetary counterparts. Let's take a closer look at the three fiscal policy lags.

Fiscal policies also have recognition, implementation, and impact lags.

Government officials have the same level of expertise and access to economic crystal balls as central bankers. They also observe and interpret the same data. Therefore, the time it takes to recognize that a fundamental change in the economy has occurred (i.e., the *recognition* lag) is the same for fiscal policy as it is for monetary policy, namely, three to six months (see Exhibit 13-14).

The *implementation lag* for fiscal policy can vary, depending on how controversial the issue is and the degree of urgency. Time is needed to propose, debate, and finally pass new legislation. Therefore, this lag can last anywhere from three months to two years, which is much longer than the implementation lag for monetary policy.

The *impact lag* for fiscal policy is usually shorter than its monetary counterpart. On average, it can take from three months to one year for new fiscal policies to take full effect.

As a result, the lag between a change in economic activity and when fiscal policies take full effect can vary between nine months and three-and-a-half years. By that time, the nation's economic environment could completely change. Therefore, it is quite possible for a fiscal policy cure to turn into a fiscal policy toxin by the time it is passed and takes effect.

As is the case with monetary policy lags, fiscal policy lags are long and variable.

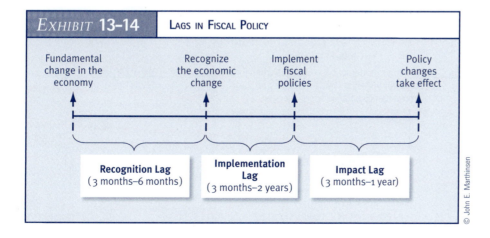

EXHIBIT 13-14   LAGS IN FISCAL POLICY

Fundamental change in the economy	Recognize the economic change	Implement fiscal policies	Policy changes take effect

Recognition Lag (3 months–6 months)   **Implementation Lag** (3 months–2 years)   **Impact Lag** (3 months–1 year)

© John E. Marthinsen

MONETARY EFFECTS OF FISCAL POLICY

Until now, we have discussed fiscal policy without regard to whether or not it affects a nation's monetary base. This section explains, in brief, why fiscal policies have no effect on a nation's monetary base. In the **"The Rest of the Story"** section of this chapter, a fuller explanation (using T-accounts) is provided.

In Chapter 9, "Who Controls the Money Supply and How?" we introduced a rule of thumb to help determine transactions that cause changes in a nation's monetary base. We found that changes occur only when a central bank crosses our imaginary horizontal line to increase or decrease the size of its balance sheet. Normally, it does this by purchasing or selling government securities and/or foreign exchange and, also, by making or withdrawing loans to financial intermediaries (see Exhibit 13-15). When a central bank's balance sheet rises, it is purchasing assets and pushing monetary base into the system. When a central bank's balance sheet falls, it is retiring monetary base by exchanging balance sheet assets (above the line) for monetary base (below the line).

Governments, individuals, financial intermediaries, and other businesses are all below the line. Therefore, when governments interact with these counterparties by taxing, spending, or borrowing, these transactions are entirely below the line and, therefore, do not affect the monetary base.

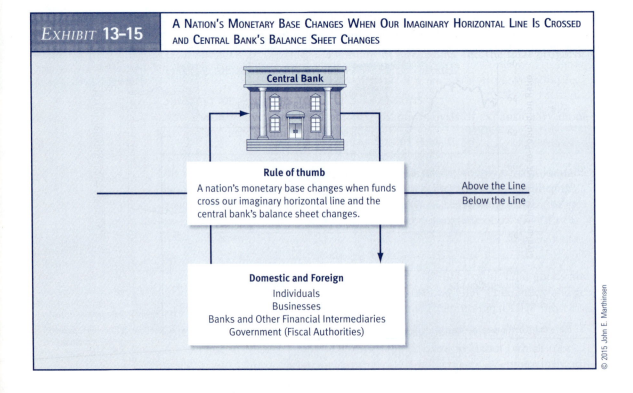

EXHIBIT 13-15   A NATION'S MONETARY BASE CHANGES WHEN OUR IMAGINARY HORIZONTAL LINE IS CROSSED AND CENTRAL BANK'S BALANCE SHEET CHANGES

Central Bank

Rule of thumb
A nation's monetary base changes when funds cross our imaginary horizontal line and the central bank's balance sheet changes.

Above the Line
Below the Line

Domestic and Foreign
Individuals
Businesses
Banks and Other Financial Intermediaries
Government (Fiscal Authorities)

THE REST OF THE STORY

WHEN ARE GOVERNMENT DEBTS AND DEFICITS PROBLEMS?

Deficits can accumulate into sizeable debts, so it is reasonable to ask, "When should we sound the warning bells? Do these debts eventually have to be repaid? Do they impose burdens on future generations? Can a nation's interest and principal payments become so large that the government is forced to default on its debts?" Let's address these issues by putting government debts and deficits into more familiar settings.

DEBT VERSUS DEFICITS

A good place to begin is by clarifying the differences between deficits and surpluses, which are flow variables, and debt, which is a stock variable. Deficits and surpluses measure the relationship between tax revenues and expenditures for a given period (e.g., a quarter or a year). Therefore, they are similar to cash flow statements that companies regularly report.

> **Deficits and surpluses are flow measures, and debt is a stock measure.**

By contrast, debt is the sum of all past deficits less what has been repaid. For this reason, government debt is similar to the debt obligations that companies report on the liability side of their balance sheets.

PUTTING GOVERNMENT DEBT INTO PERSPECTIVE

Exhibit 13-16 shows that between 1968 and 2013, U.S. government debt increased by more than 4,800% (i.e., more than 48 times) to about $16.8 trillion. Was (and is) this dramatic increase a reason for concern? Let's take a closer look.

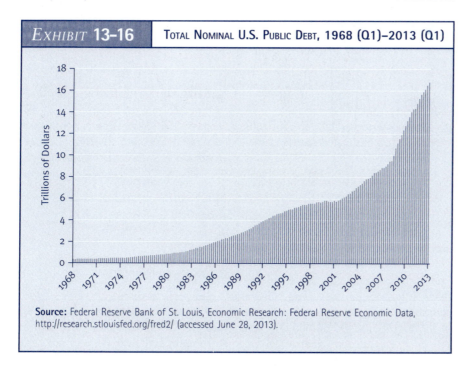

EXHIBIT **13-16**	TOTAL NOMINAL U.S. PUBLIC DEBT, 1968 (Q1)–2013 (Q1)

Source: Federal Reserve Bank of St. Louis, Economic Research: Federal Reserve Economic Data, http://research.stlouisfed.org/fred2/ (accessed June 28, 2013).

If you were asked whether a million-dollar debt was large or small, your answer would probably be "It depends." For someone earning $50,000 a year and possessing few assets, a million-dollar debt is relatively large, but for a company earning billions of dollars in annual sales and owning billions of dollars of financial and real assets, it is relatively small. The same is true for government debts. For this reason, it is helpful to adjust the nominal size of government debt so that it is put into better perspective.

Adjusting for Price Changes and Population Size

One way to adjust government debt figures so they convey more meaningful information is to remove the effects of inflation. If gross debt increases by 10%, but inflation also rises by 10%, then there is no change in the real value of the debt. Perspective can also be gained by adjusting the government debt for population size. A country with 100 million residents can support more debt than a nation with 5 million residents.

> Real per capita government debt is a better measure than nominal gross debt.

Exhibit 13-17 shows the real per capita debt of the U.S. government between 1968 and 2013. Notice that there was a dramatic increase during the 45-year period, but this increase was only by about 448% rather than the 4,800% increase in gross nominal debt, which is shown in Exhibit 13-16.

Debt, Assets, and Stockholders' Equity

Another way to put government debt into perspective is by remembering a familiar accounting tautology. The assets of any individual, company, or government *must equal* the sum of its liabilities plus (stockholders') equity.

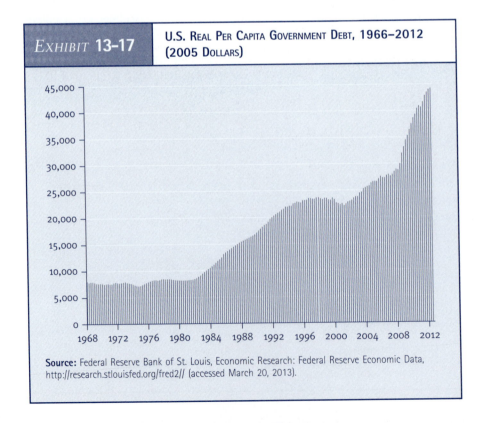

| EXHIBIT **13-17** | U.S. REAL PER CAPITA GOVERNMENT DEBT, 1966–2012 (2005 DOLLARS) |

Source: Federal Reserve Bank of St. Louis, Economic Research: Federal Reserve Economic Data, http://research.stlouisfed.org/fred2// (accessed March 20, 2013).

EXHIBIT 13-18	CHANGES IN A GOVERNMENT'S BALANCE SHEET: Δ ASSETS $\equiv$ Δ LIABILITIES + Δ STOCKHOLDER'S EQUITY	
Δ **Assets** $\equiv$	Δ **Liabilities** +	Δ **Stockholders' Equity**
Δ Roads	Δ Treasury bills	
Δ Dams	Δ Treasury notes	Δ **?**
Δ Schools $\equiv$	Δ Treasury bonds +	The main issue is whether the nation's equity level is growing.
Δ Parks	...	Because very few countries report national balance sheets
Δ Other assets	Δ Other liabilities	we often do not know.

© John E. Marthinsen

Businesses measure their success by how fast they increase stockholders' equity. Growing companies need to borrow to support investments in new physical assets, such as plant, equipment, and tools, as well as financial assets, such as accounts receivable. If they are successful, profits rise, assets appreciate, and stockholders' equity increases.

The same is true of governments in thriving nations. They also need to borrow in order to finance investments that will increase productive capacity. Expenditures for infrastructure (e.g., roads, bridges, tunnels, communication networks, and educational systems) are good examples of such investments. If governments are successful, the nation's well-being rises.

Therefore, the key issue is not whether a company's or government's debt is growing, but rather what is done with the borrowed funds. If governments borrow, invest in worthwhile projects, and create assets that will provide the means to service and repay these obligations, then large debts should not be worrisome. One problem is that few countries publish national balance sheets. Therefore, it is a challenge to determine whether a country's net worth (i.e., equity) is rising or falling (see Exhibit 13-18).

> Changes in a nation's equity are better measures of economic health than changes in the government's debt, but few nations report balance sheets that list assets, liabilities, and equity.

Debt-to-GDP Ratio

A final way to put government debt into perspective is by comparing it to nominal GDP. Of course, making such a comparison is mixing apples and oranges because debt is a stock concept, and GDP is a flow concept. Nevertheless, it's done all the time. For example, if you apply for a loan, the bank will surely want to know how much you earn and your level of existing debt.

> Debt-to-GDP ratios also help put government debt into perspective.

Exhibit 13-19 shows the federal debt-to-GDP ratios for the United States between 1966 and 2013. Notice how this ratio fell from approximately 40% in 1966 to about 32% in 1980.[9] Then, during the 1980s and 1990s, it gradually increased to about 66%, but since then it has exploded to more than 100% of GDP. This increase has shocked many who wonder if a tipping point

[9] The 40% debt-to-GDP level in 1968 was substantially below the 101% level just after World War II.

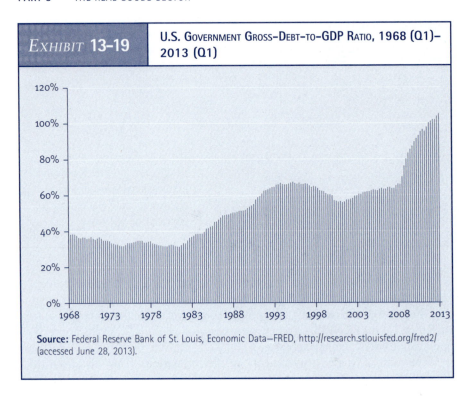

Exhibit 13-19

U.S. Government Gross-Debt-to-GDP Ratio, 1968 (Q1)–2013 (Q1)

Source: Federal Reserve Bank of St. Louis, Economic Data—FRED, http://research.stlouisfed.org/fred2/ (accessed June 28, 2013).

will be (or has been) reached that threatens the sustainability and long-term economic health of the United States.

Many countries report debt-to-GDP ratios. In fact, a 60% debt-to-GDP ratio was one of the Maastricht Treaty criteria for EMU membership in 1999.[10] Exhibit 13-20 shows the debt-to-GDP ratio in 2012 for the United States compared to other developed nations. It reinforces the view that U.S. debt is creeping to levels normally associated with European countries but is not nearly as high as in Japan.

Do Government Debts Have to Be Repaid?

Most people manage their financial affairs so that they repay all their debts before the end of their lives. Otherwise, they might burden relatives with debts. Do governments eventually have to repay all their liabilities and become debt-free? If not, why should governments be treated differently from the rest of us? The answers to these questions rest on a firm understanding of the difference between the debts of individuals and the debts of governments and companies.

---

[10] In fact, the debt-to-GDP criterion was *not* met by most of the countries that eventually joined the EMU. Violator countries were admitted anyway because the Maastricht Treaty criteria were divided into strong and weak standards. The 60% debt-to-GDP criterion was a weak standard, which meant that nations only had to show that they were making substantial progress toward meeting this goal. They did not have to actually achieve it by the time the EMU began in 1999.

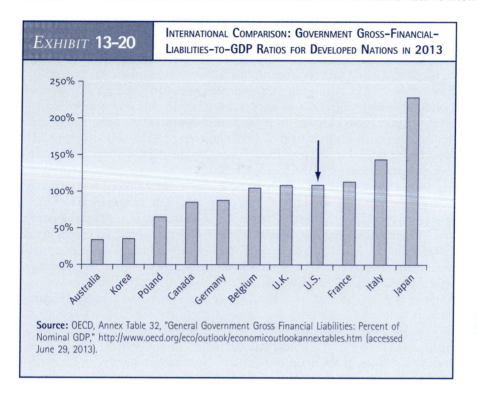

EXHIBIT 13-20   INTERNATIONAL COMPARISON: GOVERNMENT GROSS-FINANCIAL-LIABILITIES-TO-GDP RATIOS FOR DEVELOPED NATIONS IN 2013

Source: OECD, Annex Table 32, "General Government Gross Financial Liabilities: Percent of Nominal GDP," http://www.oecd.org/eco/outlook/economicoutlookannextables.htm (accessed June 29, 2013).

Governments and companies are different from you and me because, theoretically, they can live forever. With unlimited lifetimes, is there any reason to expect or want governments to reduce their debts to zero? The real issue is not whether governments should eventually become debt-free but whether they have the financial ability to service their debts and whether these expenditures are the best use of a nation's funds.

This conclusion may be easier to understand if we couch the same issue in terms of a profitable company. No one expects multinational companies, like Procter and Gamble, General Electric, Intel, Deutsche Bank, or Novartis, to reduce their debt levels to zero. Rather, it is taken for granted that these companies' debts will grow with sales and assets. In fact, it would be a fatal mistake for a company's management to have the strategic goal of periodically driving debt levels to zero (i.e., having 100% equity) because accomplishing this goal would mean passing up opportunities to increase shareholder value. Such a strategy would weaken the company and could cause unwelcome takeover bids. Successful companies are evaluated by how ably and safely they increase their stockholders' equity and not by how frequently they reduce their debt levels to zero.

Would we really want a debt-free government? Consider the implications and what might be lost. Treasury securities are owned by investors for their safety, reasonable return, and high liquidity. If governments paid off all their debts, security owners would have to find alternative, second-best investment

> Governments and companies are "going concerns" (i.e., currently operating, with the full intention of continuing indefinitely). Therefore, they do not have lifetimes at the end of which they have to repay all their debts.

assets for their portfolios. The notion of a *risk-free* interest rate would need reconsideration.

Moreover, if the government repaid its debts too quickly, the economic consequences could be very undesirable. To see why, suppose the U.S. government decided in 2013 to immediately repay the $16.8 trillion debt it owed. Cutting spending would not be enough; so it would either have to increase taxes or print enough money to repurchase the outstanding bills, notes, and bonds. If taxes were raised by $16.8 trillion, about 100% of U.S. annual GDP would have flowed to the government to repay the debt. On top of that, current expenditures would have needed funding.

Of the $16.8 billion in tax revenues, the 26% (see Exhibit 13-4) owned by U.S. private investors would flow directly back to U.S. taxpayers. The rest would flow to U.S. government agencies and trusts, the U.S. Federal Reserve, and foreign and international investors. Therefore, by taxing and repaying all government debts in 2013, the U.S. government would have caused one of the most massive redistributions of income in the history of world. The beneficial effects of this redistribution would have been highly questionable because funds would have flowed from the average taxpayer to the average Treasury security holder.

Another way a government (in conjunction with the central bank) could extinguish its debt is by creating enough money to buy it back. The problem with this solution is the nation's monetary base, money supply, and inflation rate would soar. For example, had the Federal Reserve created enough money in 2013 to repay the government's $16.8 trillion debt, the increase in U.S. monetary base would been by more than 500%, and the U.S. money supply would have grown by a multiple of that. Rampant inflation might have resulted, and, to the extent that it was unexpected, this inflation could have caused significant redistributions of income.

ARE GOVERNMENT DEBTS BURDENS ON FUTURE GENERATIONS?

One factor determining whether government debts are burdens on future generations is how the borrowed funds are spent. As long as the government uses them wisely to increase the nation's net worth, future living standards are improved by the sensible investments made now. While the current generation must sacrifice consumption for such investments, the hope is for significantly greater future rewards.

It is important to keep in mind that, just because government investments are beneficial to a nation does not mean that they should be made. Funds flowing to governments may crowd out private sector investments. As a result, government investments increase a nation's net well-being only if they produce goods and services with greater value than the private sector would have produced.

> Government debt is not a burden on future generations if the funds are spent more wisely than the private sector would have spent them.

Governments do not earn profits, so it is hard (if not impossible) to calculate investment returns on any particular budget item. Moreover, governments usually provide goods and services that the marketplace would not otherwise make available in sufficient quantities. Markets tend to underproduce these products because there are externalities that cannot be incorporated into their prices. As a result, it would be a challenge for a private company to earn a profit by producing them.

Positive externalities occur when part, or all, of the benefits that one individual enjoys from consuming a good or service spills over to others. Education, vaccines, national defense, law enforcement, pollution abatement, lighthouses, and street signs are just a few examples of products and services whose benefits spill over from those who finance them to those who do not. For instance, it would be impossible to charge some individuals for national defense but to prevent nonpayers from enjoying the benefits. Moreover, the benefits enjoyed by the nonpayers usually do not dilute the benefits or enjoyment of those who pay.

CAN GOVERNMENTS DEFAULT ON THEIR LOANS?

Governments can and have defaulted on their debts. In fact, there have been many occasions when heavily indebted countries defaulted, restructured, or required external assistance to avoid defaulting on their debt obligations. Since 1990, nations experiencing sovereign defaults and debt restructurings have included: Angola (1992–2002), Argentina (2002–2005), Brazil (1990), Cameroon (2004), Côte d'Ivoire (2000), Dominica (2003–2005), Dominican Republic (2005), Ecuador (2000 and 2008), Gabon (1999–2005), Greece (2012), Grenada (2004–2005), Indonesia (2000 and 2002), Iran (1992), Kenya (2000), Liberia (1989–2006), Madagascar (2002), Morocco (2000), Myanmar (2002), Nigeria (2001 and 2004), Paraguay (2003), Russia (1991 and 1998), Rwanda (1995), Sierra Leone (1997–1998), South Africa (1993), Sudan (1991), Surinam (2001–2002), Venezuela (2004), and Zimbabwe (2000 and 2006).[11]

Borrowing Foreign Currencies to Finance a Deficit

If governments borrow by issuing securities denominated in *foreign currencies*, then it is relatively easy to see how they could default. After all, these governments would have to pay back currencies they could not print or capture by taxing. The only way to repay these debts would be by earning the needed funds or borrowing them.

> Governments can default if they borrow with securities denominated in foreign currencies and cannot earn enough of it to service these debts.

Borrowing the Domestic Currency to Finance a Deficit

Even when a government's debt is denominated entirely in the domestic currency, default is still possible. Most nations give their central banks the power to control the nation's money supply. As a result, governments often do not have immediate authority to print or create the funds needed to repay outstanding debts. Surely, desperate governments could try (and have tried) to change their central banks' mandates, but this can be difficult and problematic to do quickly.[12]

---

[11] Carmen M. Reinhart and Kenneth S. Rogoff, "The Forgotten History of Domestic Debt," *NBER Working Paper Series,* Working Paper 13946, http://www.nber.org/papers/w13946.pdf (accessed February 23, 2013).
[12] In 2013, Japan, under the Shinzo Abe Administration, and Argentina, under the Cristina Fernández de Kirchner Administration, took steps that appeared to weaken the independence of their central banks.

Today, abrupt changes such as these are even less likely due to the international trend toward increasing central banks' independence. Therefore, it is unrealistic to believe that, just because governments have a constitutional right to coin money, they could or would wrestle monetary authority from their central banks and create enough money to avoid defaulting on their debt obligations.

Many people believe that it is nearly impossible for a government to default on its debts when most of this debt is internally held and all of it is denominated in the domestic currency, but consider the United States. Each week the U.S. Treasury Department borrows considerable amounts to finance new spending, repay maturing debt, and service outstanding debt. But the U.S. government's borrowing ability is limited by ceilings set by Congress, and once a ceiling is reached, renewed authority must be given. Hearings on whether or not to raise these ceilings have become punctuating events in the United States, embroiled in heated debates.[13]

What would happen if obstructive tactics in Congress, such as filibusters and rule-related delays, prevented the ceiling from being raised? Necessary payments might not be made. The government could try to cut expenditures and sell assets, but it is highly unlikely there would be sufficient time and adequate funds raised to repay all its obligations. Under these circumstances, a choice would have to be made concerning which bills to pay—or not. Many like to think that governments will always honor their debt obligations, but the truth is far less clear—especially if a large portion of this debt is owned by foreign investors.

> Governments can default if they lose the authority to borrow above a legal ceiling level and the ceiling is reached.

MACRO MEMO 13-4

Limits on U.S. Government Spending and U.S. Debt Limits: 1787–2013

The U.S. Constitution gives Congress the power to tax and initiate wars. Before World War I, it used this power in two major ways. First, it authorized funding for specific projects, such as construction of the Panama Canal (1904–1914), and military conflicts, such as the Spanish American War (1898). Congress also stipulated specific features or attributes of the U.S. Treasury's debt issues, such as the interest rates, maturities, redemption dates, and types of financial instruments that could be used. In 1917, during World War I, Congress introduced its first debt ceiling,

with the purpose of freeing the U.S. Treasury from the formal, administrative burden of constantly needing Congressional approval for every new debt issue. The initial ceiling was set equal to $7.5 billion (that's "billion" and not "trillion"). Since then, it has been raised numerous times. Between April 1993 and May 2013, the U.S. debt ceiling was raised or suspended 18 times, climbing from $4.37 trillion to $16.70 trillion.*

*D. Andrew Austin and Mindy R. Levit, "The Debt Limit: History and Recent Increases," *Congressional Research Service,* May 22, 2013, http://www.fas.org/sgp/crs/misc/RL31967.pdf (accessed June 29, 2013).

---

[13] D. Andrew Austin and Mindy R. Levit, "The Debt Limit: History and Recent Increases," *Congressional Research Service,* May 22, 2013, http://www.fas.org/sgp/crs/misc/RL31967.pdf (accessed June 29, 2013). Also see, Second Liberty Bond Act of 1917, Pub. L. No. 65–43, 40 Stat. 288 (codified as amended at 31 U.S.C. § 3101 (2000).

CROWDING-OUT: WHEN IS IT COMPLETE, NONEXISTENT, OR PARTIAL?

Exhibit 13-21 shows that, for any increase in government borrowing, the amount of crowding-out depends on the supply and demand elasticities in the real loanable funds market. Let's focus on supply. In Frame 1 (upper left corner), the supply of real loanable funds is perfectly elastic (i.e., supply is horizontal), which means any change in demand has no effect on the real risk-free interest rate but has a substantial effect on the equilibrium quantity.[14] In Frame 2 (upper right corner), the supply is perfectly inelastic (i.e., supply is vertical), which means any change in demand has no effect on the equilibrium

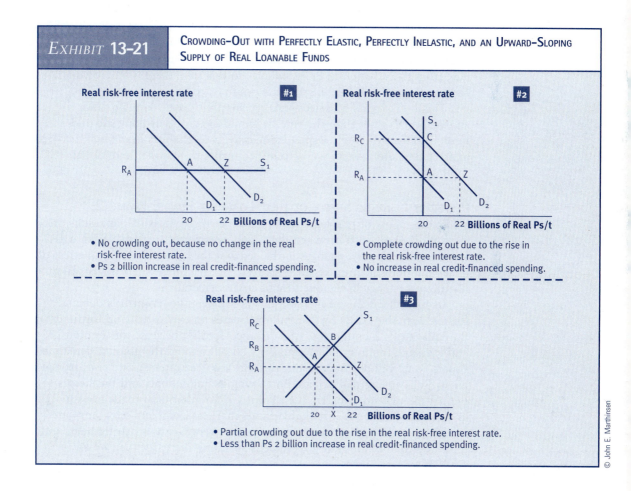

| EXHIBIT **13-21** | CROWDING-OUT WITH PERFECTLY ELASTIC, PERFECTLY INELASTIC, AND AN UPWARD-SLOPING SUPPLY OF REAL LOANABLE FUNDS |

© John E. Marthinsen

---

[14] The elasticity of supply for real loanable funds, ε, is defined as (%Δreal loanable funds/Δreal risk-free interest rate). If the supply is perfectly elastic, then the elasticity ratio equals infinity, which means any small change in the real risk-free interest rate causes an infinite change in the quantity of funds supplied. If supply is *perfectly* elastic, then we abbreviate this condition by $\varepsilon = \infty$. If supply is elastic (i.e., not perfectly elastic), then $\varepsilon > 1$.

quantity of funds supplied and demanded but has a substantial effect on the real risk-free interest rate.[15] Finally, in Frame 3 (bottom), the supply is upward sloping, which means the elasticity is somewhere between perfectly inelastic (i.e., zero) and perfectly elastic (i.e., infinity).

Let's assume the Mexican government increased its borrowing-and-spending by Ps 2 billion (i.e., two billion pesos). In Frames 1, 2, and 3, the increase in demand by Ps 2 billion is shown as a rightward shift from D_1 to D_2. Given this increase, let's analyze the crowding-out effect in each of the three cases.

PERFECTLY ELASTIC SUPPLY OF REAL LOANABLE FUNDS: FRAME 1

When the supply of real loanable funds is perfectly elastic, changes in the demand for real credit have no effect on the nation's real risk-free interest rate (see Exhibit 13-21). As a result, an increase in the government's demand for real loanable funds by Ps 2 billion (i.e., from D_1 to D_2) increases the equilibrium quantity of real pesos supplied and demanded by the full Ps 2 billion (i.e., from Ps 20 billion to Ps 22 billion). In this case, there is no crowding-out because the real risk-free interest rate does not rise.

This book treats a perfectly elastic supply of real loanable funds as an exception rather than the rule. It would exist only if domestic and foreign sources of credit responded massively to changes in the real risk-free interest rate and if there were no impediments to national and global capital flows.

PERFECTLY INELASTIC SUPPLY OF REAL LOANABLE FUNDS: FRAME 2

When the supply of real loanable funds is perfectly inelastic, our results are exactly the opposite from when the supply was perfectly elastic. With a perfectly inelastic supply, changes in the demand for real credit have no effect on the equilibrium quantity because the real risk-free interest rate adjusts to nullify any *net* change in the quantity of credit demanded.

In Exhibit 13-21, an increase in the Mexican government's demand for real loanable funds by Ps 2 billion creates an excess demand for funds at R_A equal to Ps 2 billion (i.e., the distance A to Z) because the amount of real loanable funds supplied equals Ps 20 billion and the amount demanded equals Ps 22 billion. As a result, the real risk-free interest rate rises from R_A to R_C, causing real private borrowing by individuals and businesses to fall. At the new equilibrium (i.e., Point C), no additional funds are supplied or demanded in the real loanable funds market. Complete crowding-out occurs because the rising real risk-free interest rate causes private borrowing to fall by the full amount government spending increases (i.e., by Ps 2 billion).

---

[15] If the supply is perfectly *in*elastic, then the elasticity ratio equals zero, which means that any change (large or small) in the real risk-free interest rate causes no change in the quantity of funds supplied. If supply is *perfectly* inelastic, then we abbreviate this condition by $\varepsilon = 0$. If supply is inelastic (i.e., not perfectly inelastic), then $\varepsilon < 1$.

This book treats a perfectly inelastic real loanable funds supply as an exception rather than the rule. Perfect inelasticity means that changes in the real risk-free interest rate provide no incentive for market participants to adjust the net quantity of real loanable funds they supply to the market.

UPWARD-SLOPING SUPPLY OF REAL LOANABLE FUNDS: FRAME 3

Frame 3 is the base case for all analyses in this text. When the real loanable funds supply curve is upward sloping, the supply elasticity is between zero and infinity. Therefore, changes in the demand for real loanable funds cause movements of both the real risk-free interest rate and equilibrium amount of real credit. In Frame 3, the increase in demand by Ps 2 billion (i.e., from D_1 to D_2) causes an excess demand for funds. At R_A, the new quantity demanded equals Ps 22 billion, but the quantity supplied equals only Ps 20 billion. This excess demand raises the real risk-free interest rate, which increases the quantity of real loanable funds supplied and reduces the quantity of real loanable funds demanded (i.e., crowding out private borrowers) until the equilibrium quantity is reached at the point labeled "X," which is somewhere between Ps 20 billion and Ps 22 billion.

The private sector bears the brunt of increases in a nation's real risk-free interest rate. As it rises, businesses' cost of capital increases and consumer budgets are pinched. Consequently, borderline business projects, such as purchases of new machinery and plant modernization, as well as nonessential consumer purchases, such as vacations, dishwashers, renovations, or new cars, are postponed or canceled.

The reason crowding-out is not complete is because new funds are supplied to the real loanable funds market as the real risk-free interest rate rises. Notice that an increase in the real risk-free interest rate from R_A to R_B causes the amount of real loanable funds supplied to rise from Ps 20 billion to Ps "X" billion. As a result, the government can borrow the Ps 2 billion it needs without taking them away, dollar-for-dollar, from the private sector. In the end, the real risk-free interest rate rises from R_A to R_B, but R_B is less than R_C (in Frame 2), where complete crowding-out would occur.

SEPARATING ACTIVE AND PASSIVE DEFICITS AND SURPLUSES

Suppose you wanted to estimate the size of the active deficit or surplus. How would you go about calculating it? This section shows that deriving a rough estimate is easier than you might, at first, expect.

Imagine the following scenario. Suppose a nation is in a recession. Unemployment is 10%, which is above the government's 4% goal, and GDP equals $3,600 billion. Due to sluggish economic activity, many people expect the government to stimulate the economy by either reducing taxes or increasing government spending. But conservatives in congress argue that the current deficit of $72 billion is already providing enough stimulus.

Suppose further that there are 100 million people in the labor force, which means 10 million people are unemployed[16]; the average tax rate is 20%, which means tax revenues equal $720 billion[17]; government spending for social welfare programs changes inversely by 10% for every dollar change in nominal GDP; and finally the current level of government spending plus transfer payments is $792 billion. (See Exhibit 13-22 for a summary of this information.) Due to the recession, the government's current deficit of $72 billion is a combination of an active deficit or surplus and a passive deficit.[18] But how much of it is active and how much is passive?

To determine whether fiscal policy is expansionary or contractionary, we must eliminate the passive part. This can be done by calculating what the government's budget would be if the nation were at full employment because at full employment, the passive deficit equals zero.

Our task can be accomplished in four easy steps.

Step 1: *Calculate how many more people would be employed if the nation were at full employment.*

If 10% of the labor force is currently unemployed, then there are 10 million unemployed individuals. At full employment, only 4% of the workforce (i.e., 4 million people) would be unemployed. Therefore, 6 million more people would be working at full employment.

EXHIBIT 13-22	ASSUMPTIONS FOR CALCULATING THE ACTIVE AND PASSIVE DEFICITS
Nominal GDP	$3,600 billion
Labor force	100 million
Unemployment rate	10%
Number unemployed (10% × 100 million labor force)	*10 million*
Full employment rate	4%
Average tax rate	20%
Tax revenues ($3,600 billion × 20%)	$720 billion
Government spending at $3,600 billion	$792 billion
Budget deficit (Government spending + transfers − taxes) at $3,600 billion	$72 billion
Δ Government spending/Δ Nominal GDP	−10%

[16] Number of unemployed = Unemployment rate × labor force = 10% × 100 million = 10 million
[17] Tax revenues = GDP × Tax rate = $3,600 billion × 20% = $720 billion
[18] Because the nation is in a recession, it could not have a passive surplus. A passive surplus occurs only if the economy is above full employment.

EXHIBIT 13-23	ACTUAL DEFICIT ≡ ACTIVE DEFICIT + PASSIVE DEFICIT			
Actual Deficit	≡	**Active Deficit**	+	**Passive Deficit**
−$72 billion	≡	$0 billion	+	−$72 billion

© John E. Marthinsen

Step 2: Calculate GDP per person and how much more GDP would be produced at full employment.

If nominal GDP is $3,600 billion, and 90 million people are working, then the average per capita GDP is equal to $40,000.[19] Employing 6 million more people, each producing $40,000 worth of goods and services, would increase GDP by $240 billion.[20]

Step 3: Calculate the automatic change in government transfer payments and taxation if the nation was at full employment.

An increase in nominal GDP by $240 billion would increase tax revenues by $48 billion[21] and reduce government transfers by $24 billion.[22] Together, these two automatic stabilizers sum to $72 billion, which is the entire deficit at the $3,600 billion GDP level.

In our example, the actual GDP of $3,600 billion is $240 billion below full-employment GDP. At this level, the government collects $48 billion less in taxes and transfers $24 billion more than it would have at full employment. Therefore, at $3,600, the passive deficit is equal to $72 billion, which is the sum of the $48 billion lost taxes and $24 billion additional expenditures.

Step 4: Calculate the active and passive deficit/ surplus, and draw your conclusions.

We know that the actual deficit is composed of an active part and a passive part. At a GDP of $3,600 billion, the actual deficit is $72 billion and the passive deficit is also equal to $72 billion. Therefore, the active part must be equal to zero (see Exhibit 13-23).

With an active deficit equal to zero, fiscal policy must be neutral. Therefore, it would be an illusion to believe that the current deficit of $72 billion is pushing the economy out of its recession.

Exhibit 13-24 is a graphic depiction of the scenario we just covered. At $3,600 billion, there is an actual budget deficit of $72 billion, but if the economy were at full employment, nominal GDP would be $240 billion higher (i.e., $3,840 billion). If GDP were $3,840 billion, taxes would equal $768 billion, which is $48 billion higher than before, and government spending plus transfer payments would equal $768, which is $24 billion lower than before. Therefore, at full employment, the deficit would be zero.

---

[19] $3,600 billion nominal GDP/90 million workers = $40,000/worker
[20] $40,000 per person × 6 million newly employed people = $240 billion
[21] ΔTaxes = 20% × $240 billion = $48 billion
[22] ΔGovernment transfers = −10% × $240 billion = −$24 billion

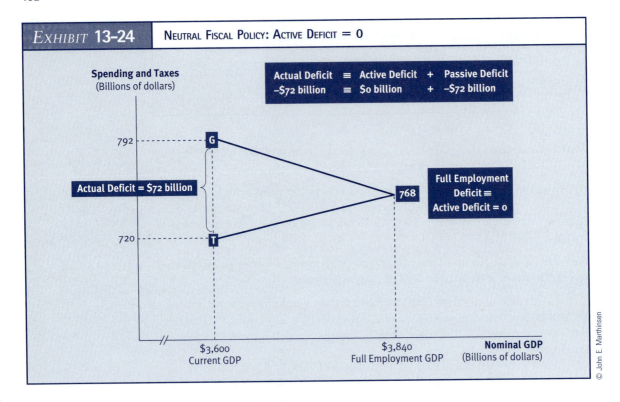

EXHIBIT 13-24	NEUTRAL FISCAL POLICY: ACTIVE DEFICIT = 0

Spending and Taxes
(Billions of dollars)

Actual Deficit	≡	Active Deficit	+	Passive Deficit
–$72 billion	≡	$0 billion	+	–$72 billion

792 — G

Actual Deficit = $72 billion

768

Full Employment Deficit ≡ Active Deficit = 0

720 — T

// $3,600
Current GDP

$3,840
Full Employment GDP

Nominal GDP
(Billions of dollars)

© John E. Marthinsen

A CLOSER LOOK AT THE MONETARY EFFECTS OF FISCAL POLICY

This section provides a more detailed explanation of why fiscal policies have no effect on a nation's monetary base. In each case, the answer is linked closely to our rule of thumb for when a nation's monetary base changes. In particular, the monetary base changes only when a central bank crosses our imaginary horizontal line and the size of its balance sheet changes. Let's consider the monetary effects of taxes, government spending, and deficit borrowing.

MONETARY EFFECTS OF TAXES

For most of us, taxes are automatically withdrawn from our paychecks and sent to the government each payday. We never see the funds. After we prepare our tax returns at the end of the year, any additional taxes owed are settled by writing checks or making direct transfers from our bank accounts to the Treasury. If we are fortunate enough to receive refunds, government checks or wire transfers arrive at our homes or banks a few weeks later.

Government Tax and Loan Accounts

After we pay our taxes, where do the funds go? Governments have the option of keeping their funds either in financial intermediaries (below the line) or in the central bank (above the line). In general, governments keep most of their funds in tax and loan accounts (T&L) at financial intermediaries, which are below the line. They do so to avoid large reductions in the monetary base when taxes are paid and to avoid large increases when government expenditures are made. Consider how chaotic changes in a nation's monetary base would be if it fell by billions of dollars, euros, or yen whenever the public paid taxes and then increased every time the national government spent these funds. By keeping their funds in financial intermediaries (below the line), a nation can avoid this problem.

Exhibit 13-25 shows an example in which U.S. taxpayers transfer $10 billion to the government. If the government holds these funds in T&L accounts at financial intermediaries (below the line), the government's T&L accounts rise by $10 billion. Simultaneously, the taxpayers' balances at these financial intermediaries decrease by the same amount. As a result, there is a change in the ownership of the deposit liabilities but not in the total amount. The government now owns $10 billion of deposits that were previously owned by taxpayers. Because the reserves of these financial intermediaries and currency in circulation remain the same, the monetary base does not change.[23]

> Tax payments have no effect on a nation's monetary base because all the transactions are below the line.

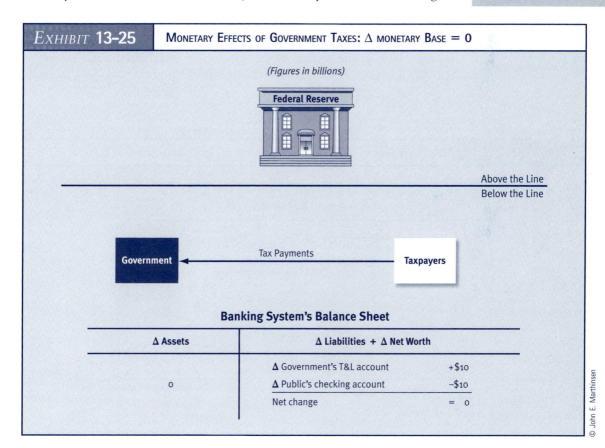

| EXHIBIT **13-25** | MONETARY EFFECTS OF GOVERNMENT TAXES: Δ MONETARY BASE = 0 |

(Figures in billions)

Federal Reserve

Above the Line
Below the Line

Government ← Tax Payments — **Taxpayers**

Banking System's Balance Sheet

Δ Assets	Δ Liabilities + Δ Net Worth	
	Δ Government's T&L account	+$10
0	Δ Public's checking account	−$10
	Net change	= 0

© John E. Marthinsen

---

[23] The transfer of funds could cause some specific financial intermediaries to lose reserves and others to gain them. This result occurs because the government may hold deposits in financial intermediaries that are different from the average taxpayer. Nevertheless, the banking system, as a whole, gains or loses nothing.

Government Deposits at the Central Bank

Even though governments keep the bulk of their deposits in financial intermediaries (below the line), they can (and do) write checks on and make wire transfers from their central banks. Remember that central banks are the financial agents of their governments. In this role, they perform financial services, such as tax collection, issuance of new debt, and administration of payments on outstanding debts. Therefore, governments need accounts at the central bank (above the line) for these fiscal services to be rendered.

To minimize the effects on the monetary base, governments usually transfer funds to the central bank only when they anticipate upcoming payments. These funds remain in the central bank (above the line) only for a short time. Transfers are done with full transparency to the central bank so that temporary changes in the monetary base can be offset, if desired. As a result, the discussions in this book will assume that government treasuries hold *all their deposits* in financial intermediaries (below the line).

> An increase in a government's deposits at the central bank reduces a nation's monetary base.

Exhibit 13-26 shows how the transfer of $10 billion of government funds to the central bank from financial intermediaries reduces the nation's monetary base by the amount of the transfer. Financial intermediaries lose $10 billion of deposit liabilities to the government, and they also lose an equal

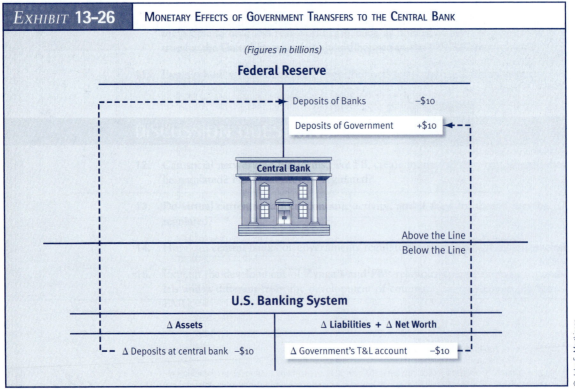

EXHIBIT 13-26   MONETARY EFFECTS OF GOVERNMENT TRANSFERS TO THE CENTRAL BANK

(Figures in billions)

Federal Reserve

Deposits of Banks	−$10
Deposits of Government	+$10

Central Bank

Above the Line
Below the Line

U.S. Banking System

Δ Assets	Δ Liabilities + Δ Net Worth
Δ Deposits at central bank −$10	Δ Government's T&L account −$10

© John E. Marthinsen

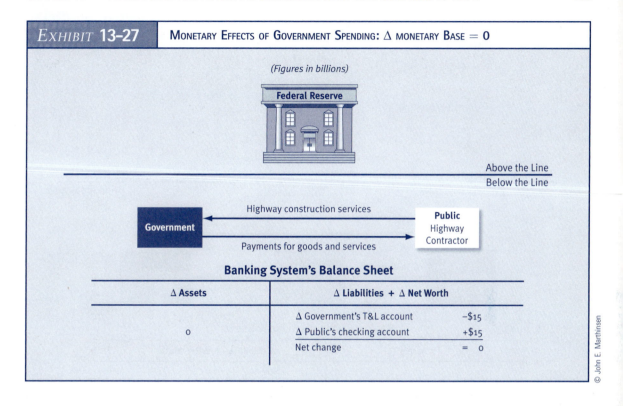

EXHIBIT 13-27   MONETARY EFFECTS OF GOVERNMENT SPENDING: Δ MONETARY BASE = 0

(Figures in billions)

Federal Reserve

Above the Line
Below the Line

Highway construction services

Government

Public
Highway
Contractor

Payments for goods and services

Banking System's Balance Sheet

Δ Assets	Δ Liabilities + Δ Net Worth	
	Δ Government's T&L account	−$15
0	Δ Public's checking account	+$15
	Net change	= 0

© John E. Marthinsen

amount of reserves in the form of deposits at the central bank.[24] Keep in mind that this transfer of funds is quite independent of the public's payment of taxes.

MONETARY EFFECTS OF GOVERNMENT SPENDING

As was the case with taxation, government spending has no effect on a nation's monetary base. To see why, suppose the government spent $15 billion on a new highway. Exhibit 13-27 shows that, after the payment cleared, the government's T&L account in the banking system would fall by the same amount that the highway contractor's account rose. As a result, the reserves of financial intermediaries and the monetary base would remain unchanged.

> Government spending has no effect on a nation's monetary base because all the transactions are below the line.

MONETARY EFFECTS OF GOVERNMENT BORROWING

Exhibit 13-28 shows why government borrowing has no effect on a nation's monetary base. Suppose the government borrowed $20 billion. As a result, the checking accounts of savers/lenders, which are below the line, would be transferred to the government's T&L accounts, which are also below the line. There would be no change in banking system reserves and, therefore, no change in the nation's monetary base.

> Government borrowing has no effect on a nation's monetary base because all the transactions are below the line.

---

[24] Notice that this example is one of the few exceptions to our *above-the-line/below-the-line* rule of thumb because there is no overall change in the central bank's balance sheet, but the monetary base falls.

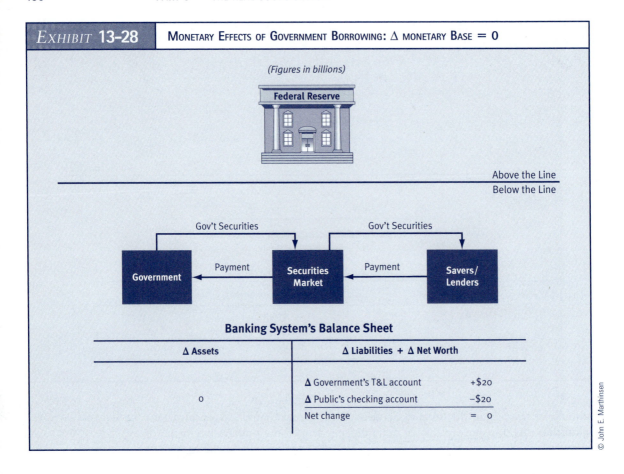

EXHIBIT 13-28   MONETARY EFFECTS OF GOVERNMENT BORROWING: Δ MONETARY BASE = 0

(Figures in billions)

Federal Reserve

Above the Line
Below the Line

Gov't Securities   Gov't Securities

Government ←Payment— Securities Market ←Payment— Savers/Lenders

Banking System's Balance Sheet

Δ Assets	Δ Liabilities + Δ Net Worth	
	Δ Government's T&L account	+$20
0	Δ Public's checking account	−$20
	Net change	= 0

CONCLUSION

This chapter discussed fiscal policies and the effects they have on economic activity. For managers, fiscal policies can have significant impacts on key economic variables that affect profitability and cash flows.

Discretionary fiscal policies require the government to pass or authorize new legislation or to change existing legislation. By contrast, nondiscretionary fiscal policies, which are also called *automatic stabilizers*, are activated passively as a nation's economic conditions change. Automatic stabilizers dampen fluctuations in GDP, and they are most helpful when nations are at or near full employment and price stability. The automatic stabilizers are not an independent source of economic expansion or contraction.

The economic effects of fiscal policies are amplified by the fiscal multiplier, but this multiplier is weakened by feedback and spillover effects from the real goods, real loanable funds, and foreign exchange markets. Therefore, changes in the automatic stabilizers, net exports, real risk-free interest rate, and exchange rate all work in concert to reduce the size of the fiscal (and spending) multipliers.

Government deficits can be divided into passive and active components. Passive deficits/surpluses are caused by the automatic stabilizers. Active deficits/surpluses are the difference between government spending and taxes that would occur if a nation were at full employment (i.e., without the influence of automatic stabilizers). It is for this reason that active deficits/surpluses are also called *full-employment deficits/surpluses*. If the active deficit rises, fiscal policy is expansionary, causing an increase in aggregate demand. If it falls (or creates an active surplus), then fiscal policy is contractionary, causing a decrease in aggregate demand.

In general, only if transactions between central banks (above the line) and noncentral bank counterparties (below the line) change the central bank's balance sheet size does a nation's monetary base rise or fall. Therefore, fiscal policies that are independent of the central bank have no effect on a nation's monetary base.

Perspective is needed to properly evaluate the size of a government's debt. This perspective can be gained by adjusting the debt for a nation's price changes, population size, and relationship to GDP. It is also useful to know whether national equity is growing, and how wisely the government is spending its tax revenues and borrowed funds. Identifying how much a government spends on investment goods is also important because investments should provide sources of funds to repay the debts. For this reason, government debts are not necessarily burdens on future generations. When these debts increase a nation's productive capability, then future generations can be the beneficiaries of past generations' debts.

REVIEW QUESTIONS

1. Suppose the Malaysian government's debt increased at a precipitous rate.
    a. Explain the effect these deficits would have on the nation's monetary base and M2 money supply.
    b. Explain these deficits' effects on the real risk-free interest rate and nominal interest rate.
    c. Suppose the Malaysian government wanted to pursue expansionary fiscal policy. Explain why separating the active and passive deficits would be important to policymakers.

2. In 2013, the U.S. federal government's total public debt reached $16.8 trillion, and it was expected to grow larger during the coming decade.
    a. Many people were (and are) concerned that the U.S. government could default on its loans, and the economy could face severe consequences. Under what conditions can a government default?
    b. Is the U.S. government's debt a burden on future generations?
    c. Does the U.S. government eventually have to pay off its debt?

3. What are "automatic stabilizers"? What effect do they have on the economy? What do they *automatically* stabilize, and how do they *automatically* do it?

4. During the administration of President Fernando Henrique Cardoso in the 1990s, the Brazilian budget deficit grew to become almost 8% of GDP. Explain how it was possible for Brazil's actual budget deficit to grow at the same time that President Cardoso was discretionarily cutting government spending and raising tax rates.

5. Suppose Colombia's fiscal deficit was 5% of GDP, and the Colombian economy was growing below capacity. Can we say that Colombia's entire 5% fiscal deficit was increasing aggregate demand and helping the economy grow? Explain.

6. In the section of this chapter entitled "**The Rest of the Story,**" use the figures in "Separating Active and Passive Deficits and Surpluses" to calculate the active and passive deficit or surplus if the marginal tax rate on nominal GDP above $3,600 billion is 25%, and government transfer payments change by −15% for any increase in nominal GDP above $3,600 billion.

7. Explain (using T-accounts) the effect that budget surpluses have on a nation's monetary base when they are used to retire a portion of the government's outstanding debt.

DISCUSSION QUESTIONS

8. Explain whether you agree or disagree with the following statements:
    a. "Ask any economist, and you will find that excessive government budget deficits are one of the principal causes of a nation's excessive money supply growth."
    b. "Ask any economist, and you will find that, for nations below full employment, budget deficits are sure signs that the government is increasing demand, stimulating economic activity, raising the inflation rate, and moving the economy closer to full employment."

9. Suppose India pursued a contractionary fiscal policy by raising taxes.
    a. Would this policy affect India's monetary base? Be sure to define the monetary base in your explanation.
    b. Will this policy crowd out private spending?
    c. How will this policy affect India's AS curve and/or AD curve?
    d. How, if at all, will the macroeconomic effects of this policy change the active and passive budget deficit/surplus of India? Explain.
    e. As a businessperson in India, suppose you anticipated this change in fiscal policy. Should you borrow before the policy was implemented or wait until after it changed? Consider only the direct effects on the real loanable funds market.
    f. Explain why the automatic stabilizers are important to countries like India.
    g. Explain the circumstances under which the Indian government might be forced or choose to default on its debts.

10. Suppose the Chinese government reduced substantially its budget deficit in order to slow the high rate of domestic growth and rising inflation rate. Would the government's policy be more effective if China's investment demand (i.e., demand for gross private domestic investment) was elastic or inelastic with respect to the real risk-free interest rate? In your answer, be sure to define what an "elastic" and "inelastic" investment demand means.

11. In 2006, Chile looked back on 18 years of consecutive fiscal surpluses. In part, the country was able to achieve this notable record because the government included privatization receipts as a part of current government revenues. What does this policy imply about crowding-out? Why might the International

Monetary Fund have been against Chile's policy of counting privatization receipts as current government revenues?

12. The strong Swiss franc has caused the Swiss economy to grow at a sluggish rate. Suppose the Swiss government decides to stimulate the domestic economy by spending SFr 50 billion on infrastructure projects, such as bridges, railroad tracks, and communications. To finance these expenditures, the Swiss government intends to borrow in the domestic capital markets. Use the real loanable funds market and real goods market to explain the effects this increase in government spending and borrowing is likely to have on the Swiss economy.

13. During 2010, Greece came under intense economic pressure as a result of its rising budget deficits and sizeable debt. In 2009, Greece's deficit exceeded 13% of GDP, and its debt level exceeded 125% of GDP. There was fear that Greece might default on its debts and could be the first nation to leave the EMU. Is it correct to say that deficits and debts as large as Greece's do irreparable damage to the nation and its future generations? Explain the costs and, if there are any, benefits of Greece's deficits and debts.

14. Suppose France increases personal income taxes on French residents. Use the real loanable funds market and real goods market to explain the effects this policy is likely to have on the French economy.

15. Read the following sentence and explain whether the economic logic is correct or incorrect: "If Iceland's government reduces its discretionary spending to balance the budget, then the nation's aggregate demand falls, causing the price index and real GDP to fall. But the reduction in prices causes the nation's aggregate supply to fall, thereby changing prices to a level that could be lower than, equal to, or higher than the original level."

PART 4

FOREIGN EXCHANGE MARKET

Chapter 14

Basics of Foreign Exchange Markets

INTRODUCTION

Imagine yourself on an international business trip. You have one hour before your next meeting, and you are hungry. With US$10 in your wallet, you walk by a fast-food restaurant and notice that it is offering a special promotion. The advertisement in the window says:

Special Offer!
Tasty Double Cheese Burger, Fries, & Soft Drink
Only $80 billion

© Dimitar Bosakov/Shutterstock.com; © Maria Komar/Shutterstock.com;
© Naypong./Shutterstock.com

Are you dreaming or is this someone's idea of a practical joke? Eighty billion dollars for a double cheeseburger, fries, and a soft drink? That's insane. As it turns out, it's no dream and no one's idea of a practical joke. This is what you would have paid had you been in Harare, Zimbabwe, in 2008, when inflation hit stratospheric levels. Had you exchanged US$1 for Zimbabwe dollars (Z$) at the end of December 2008, it would have brought you about Z$2 billion. Had you waited until mid-January 2009, you would have gotten Z$1trillion, and just few weeks later, one measly dollar would have gotten you Z$300 trillion. Before buying lunch, all you had to do was make a brief stop at a bank, exchange $1 for more than Z$100 billion, and

Exhibit 14-1	Currency Note Worth 100 Trillion Zimbabwe Dollars

spend only Z$80 billion of it on lunch.[1] In a matter of minutes, you would have satisfied your appetite and become a billionaire—all for the cost of $1. Any fears you might have had about carrying a heavy load of cash around the streets of Harare would have been extinguished when you learned that Zimbabwe's currency was issued in just two denominations, Z$25 billion bills and Z$50 billion bills. Later, denominations as high as Z$100 trillion were issued (see Exhibit 14-1).

This chapter discusses how currencies are traded in the foreign exchange markets. We will begin by covering the basics: What are exchange rates? What does it mean when a currency appreciates or depreciates? What effects, if any, do foreign exchange transactions have on a nation's monetary base and money supply? How can readers make sense of the foreign exchange quotations in business periodicals? In the next chapter (Chapter 15, "Exchange Rates: Why Do They Change?"), we will use these basics to discuss how exchange rates are determined and what causes them to change.

THE BASICS

EXCHANGE RATES

An *exchange rate* is the price of one currency in terms of another currency.

An exchange rate is the price of Currency A in terms of Currency B.

For example, if the British pound is worth $2, then $2/£ is the expression of this exchange rate.

---

[1] Chris V. Thangham, "50 Billion Zimbabwe Dollars for a Burger," *Politics*, July 2, 2008, http://digitaljournal .com/article/256844 (accessed March 20, 2013).

THE RECIPROCAL NATURE OF EXCHANGE RATES

The reciprocal of the dollar—pound ($/£) exchange rate is the pound—dollar (£/$) exchange rate, which means if £1 is worth $2, then $1 must be worth £0.50 (i.e., £1/$2 = £0.50/$). The expression for this exchange rate is £0.50/$ (which can be stated as "one-half pound per dollar"). It is important to remember that the currency being valued is always in the denominator. Therefore, $2/£ is the value (or price) of £1, and £0.50/$ is the value (or price) of $1.

> The currency being valued is always in the denominator.

WHAT IS AN APPRECIATION OR DEPRECIATION OF A CURRENCY?

An increase in the value of Currency A (e.g., the pound) relative to currency B (e.g., the dollar) is called an *appreciation* of Currency A. For example, the pound appreciates when it increases from $1/£ to $2/£. A decrease in value of Currency A (e.g., the pound) relative to Currency B (e.g., the dollar) is called a *depreciation* of Currency A. For example, the pound depreciates when its value falls from $2/£ to $1/£.

> Currency A appreciates when its value rises relative to Currency B. Currency A depreciates when its value falls relative to Currency B.

An Appreciation of One Currency Means a Depreciation of the Other

There is an unequivocal inverse relationship between the two currencies stated in an exchange rate. If Currency A appreciates in value relative to Currency B, then Currency B must depreciate in value relative to Currency A. This result is a mathematical necessity, caused by the reciprocal nature of exchange rates. An example shows why it is so.

Suppose the value of the pound was $2/£, which means the value of the dollar was £0.50/$. If the pound changed in value to $1/£, then its reciprocal must change to £1/$. Therefore, at the same time the value of the pound falls in value from $2 to $1 (i.e., the pound depreciates), the value of the dollar increases from £0.50 to £1 (i.e., the dollar appreciates). In short, an appreciation of the dollar relative to the pound carries exactly the same meaning as a depreciation of the pound relative to the dollar.

PAYING ATTENTION TO THE UNITS

Because exchange rates can be expressed in either of two ways (e.g., $2/£ or £0.50/$), we must pay particular attention to what is being valued. Accuracy at this fundamental level is crucial because foreign exchange transactions are often huge (in the millions), and small mistakes can result in large losses.

It is always a good idea to write down the exchange rate you are using alongside the foreign currency—denominated transactions you are conducting. Then, multiply the exchange rate times the foreign currency value of the investment or item being purchased or sold, making sure that the proper units cancel out. The cardinal rule is to be careful with the units.

> Using the correct exchange rate means making sure the proper units cancel out when multiplying the exchange rate times the transaction amount.

For example, suppose the exchange rate is €0.80/$ (which is equivalent to $1.25/€), and you want to buy a precision German machine costing €10 million. As Exhibit 14-2 shows, writing down the exchange rate next to the product price and then multiplying the two shows clearly that the dollars per euro (i.e., $1.25/€) exchange rate must be used because only with this rate will the common element, the euro, cancel in both the numerator and denominator of the equation terms. Exhibit 14-2 shows that the answer to the question "How many dollars are needed to purchase a machine costing €10 million?" is "$12.5 million."

EXHIBIT **14-2**	CORRECT ALIGNMENT OF EXCHANGE RATE AND PRICE

$$\frac{\$1.25}{€} \times \frac{€\,10\ \text{million}}{\text{Machine}} = \frac{\$12.5\ \text{million}}{\text{Machine}}$$

© 2015 John E. Marthinsen

EXHIBIT **14-3**	INCORRECT ALIGNMENT OF EXCHANGE RATE AND PRICE

$$\frac{€0.80}{\$} \times \frac{€\,10\ \text{million}}{\text{Machine}} = \frac{€^2\,8\ \text{million}}{(\$) \times (\text{Machine})}$$

$$\downarrow$$

Meaningless

© 2015 John E. Marthinsen

If embarrassing mistakes are made using foreign currencies, usually they are made at this level because of carelessness. Let's take the same example as before, but this time, suppose we use the wrong exchange rate (i.e., €0.80/$ instead of $1.25/€). As Exhibit 14-3 shows, multiplying the price of €10 million per machine times €0.80/$ gives us a nonsensical answer because nothing cancels. Using the incorrect exchange rate, the answer to the question "How many dollars are needed to purchase a machine costing €10 million?" would be €8 million squared per U.S. dollar machine—which is meaningless.

THE FOREIGN EXCHANGE MARKET

The foreign exchange market is a global network of dealers and financial institutions that connects buyers and sellers of international currencies. Participants in the foreign exchange markets are foreign exchange dealers (i.e., market-maker banks), other financial institutions (e.g., institutional investors, hedge funds, proprietary trading firms, small nondealer banks, and official sector financial institutions), and nonfinancial customers (e.g., individuals, corporations, and governments). Together, they use this worldwide network to communicate their supply and demand needs, transact deals, and settle trades by transferring funds. Payment for and delivery of currencies can occur immediately or in the future, but prices are set today.

> The foreign exchange market is a global network of dealers and financial institutions connecting the buyers and sellers of currencies.

BID AND ASK RATES

Foreign exchange is quoted in terms of bid and ask rates,[2] which are defined from the bank's point of view. The *bid rate* is the price at which a *bank is willing and able to buy* a currency from a customer, and the *ask rate* is the

---

[2] When to use bid and ask rates can be confusing. "The Rest of the Story" section of this chapter provides a fuller explanation of how and when to use them, along with two convenient rules of thumb, either of which will help prevent careless mistakes.

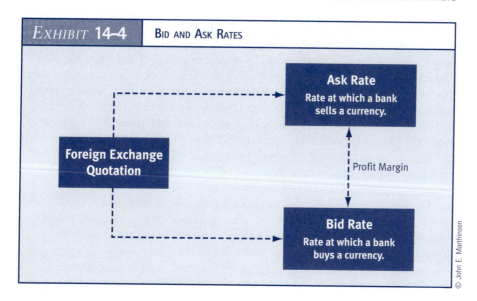

EXHIBIT 14-4 BID AND ASK RATES

Ask Rate
Rate at which a bank sells a currency.

Foreign Exchange Quotation

Profit Margin

Bid Rate
Rate at which a bank buys a currency.

© John E. Marthinsen

price at which a *bank is willing and able to sell* a currency to a customer. As Exhibit 14-4 shows, the bid (buy) rate is always lower than the ask (sell) rate because the bid-ask difference (i.e., spread) is a bank's gross margin. In effect, banks act like wholesalers or retailers by purchasing commodities (in this case, currencies) at lower prices than they sell them.

> The bid rate is the rate at which *banks buy* foreign exchange from customers, and the ask rate is the rate at which *banks sell* foreign exchange to customers.

RETAIL AND WHOLESALE MARKETS FOR FOREIGN EXCHANGE

There are two related, but differently priced, markets for foreign exchange: the retail market and the wholesale market. The retail market handles relatively small transactions that are conducted by low volume customers, such as small to moderate-sized companies, individual investors, and tourists. The wholesale market is for large customers with transactions of $1 million and more, such as bank dealers, hedge funds, institutional investors, proprietary trading firms, significant-sized corporations, supranational organizations, and central banks. About 99% of the total activity in the foreign exchange market is at the wholesale level.

> The retail market handles relatively small transactions, and the wholesale market handles large transactions (usually $1 million and more).

Retail customers pay bid-ask spreads that are much wider than the wholesale spreads. One reason for the difference is because retail trades have higher per unit transaction costs. Wholesale transactions allow dealers to spread their fixed costs over more units, thereby lowering the per-unit cost of the foreign exchange trade. After all, how much added time does it take a currency dealer to add a few extra zeros to a foreign exchange transaction slip? Another reason for the spread differential is because of the intense competition among banks in the wholesale market. Small spreads on transactions of immense size can provide banks with robust earnings, and foreign exchange transactions can be an entry point for doing other business with large customers.

TRADED OVER THE COUNTER AND ON EXCHANGES

Foreign currencies are traded over the counter and on exchanges. *Over the counter* means the transactions are handled using high-speed financial communication lines, such as dedicated computer information systems, telephone, Internet, fax, and telex connections. This market is electronic, without physical location, and without any distinct identity. By contrast, *exchange-traded* currencies are transacted on physical or electronic exchanges that have either a specific physical location or distinct electronic identity. The Chicago Board of Trade is an example of a physical exchange where currencies are still traded by human outcry, and Eurex is an electronic exchange with a distinct identity.[3]

> **Foreign exchange is traded over the counter and on exchanges.**

During the workweek, the foreign exchange market never sleeps. When currency traders in New York City wake each morning (normally around 5:00 A.M.), one of their first calls (often, before they get to work) is to London, where it is already 10:00 A.M. International foreign exchange markets overlap; therefore, quotes are transferred from market to market in a continual chain. From Wellington, New Zealand to Singapore and Hong Kong to Tokyo to Zurich to London to New York to Chicago to San Francisco, and finally back to New Zealand, trading activity passes smoothly from time zone to time zone—five days a week, 24 hours a day. In 2013, the largest foreign exchange markets were in the United Kingdom (40.9%), United States (18.9%), Singapore (5.7%), Japan (5.6%), Hong Kong (4.1%), Switzerland (3.2%), France (2.8%), and Australia (2.7%).[4]

> **The foreign exchange market is open for trading 24 hours a day, every working day of the year.**

GLOBALLY SOURCED SUPPLY AND DEMAND

Supply and demand in the foreign exchange markets are sourced globally, which means quoted prices do not depend on the inventories of any one participant. For instance, suppose a trader at Credit Suisse (CS) in Zurich received a huge order from the treasurer at Roche Holding Ltd., Basel to purchase 500 million U.S. dollars ($500 million) with Swiss francs. Without the international communication network provided by the over-the-counter, foreign exchange market, how would the trader price this transaction? Most likely, he would price it in the context of both the inventories of dollars owned by CS and the other dollar per Swiss franc transactions the trader expected the bank to conduct that day (or in the near future).

> **The supply of and demand for foreign exchange are globally sourced.**

Without the broader, worldwide perspective, this $500 million order could alter disadvantageously the price that Roche had to pay for dollars. A wider perspective is needed because it is likely that, at the same time Roche was demanding $500 million in Zurich, an equal amount of dollars (or more) was being supplied to the worldwide network by numerous individuals and businesses conducting a wide variety of relatively small and unrelated

---

[3] Eurex is one of the leading global derivative exchanges. It was formed in 1998 by merging the Swiss Options and Financial Futures Exchange (SOFFEX) with Germany's Deutsche Terminbörse (DTB). This exchange and its clearing operations are totally electronic.

[4] Bank for International Settlements, Monetary and Economic Department, "Triennial Central Bank Survey: Foreign Exchange Turnover in April 2013: Preliminary Global Results," Table 6, p. 14, http://www.bis.org/publ/rpfx13fx.pdf (accessed October 6, 2013).

transactions. Under these circumstances, the dollars demanded by Roche could be supplied through the network of dealers and financial institutions. It would not be important how many dollars CS owned or how much of the total dollar business was transacted through CS. It would only matter whether CS could buy these dollars from other financial institutions and then funnel a total of $500 million to Roche. This networking capability is a major function of the foreign exchange market.

Uniform Prices Worldwide

One of the key features of the foreign exchange market is that prices are identical across the globe. Exchange rates in Zurich, London, and Tokyo are identical to those quoted in New York City, and they should be. If they were not, savvy foreign exchange arbitrageurs,[5] with access to this information, would be able to buy in the cheap market and simultaneously sell in the expensive market, quickly earning millions of dollars in riskless profits. Think how easy life would be if riskless profit opportunities were available. We all could trade currencies for just a few days and then retire for life.

Competition and arbitrage ensure that foreign exchange rates are uniform worldwide.

If currency arbitrage sounds like fun and something you might like to try, be aware that it never happens on a grand scale in foreign exchange markets, and for a simple reason: everyone wants to make riskless profits. As a result, any slight differential in exchange rates across the globe triggers enormous flows of funds that quickly erase these discrepancies. Again, consider the magnitudes. A "small" transaction in the foreign exchange market is considered to be anything under $1 million, and the market's average *daily* volume in 2013 was $5.3 trillion. If there was a chance to earn riskless profits, the daily volume would rise dramatically to take advantage of the opportunity. Thousands of foreign exchange traders spend their entire workweek in front of computer screens looking for opportunities to earn just a few "pips"[6] in profits. Earning 10 risk-free pips on a billion British pound deal translates into a $1 million gain[7] for doing about 30 seconds of work!

The uniformity of foreign exchange rates across the globe requires virtually perfect information, but this does not mean that everyone who participates in the foreign exchange markets knows exactly what is happening all over the world at every minute of the day. What it means is that a core of marginal or peripheral traders buys and sells currencies based on the latest, most up-to-date information, and this information is available to anyone who has the technology, time, and motivation to acquire it.

The Size of the Foreign Exchange Market

The foreign exchange market is divided into six major segments: spot transactions, outright forwards, foreign exchange swaps, currency swaps, options and other products, and exchange-traded derivatives. As Exhibit 14-5 shows,

---

[5] Currency arbitragers simultaneously buy and sell currencies to earn riskless profits due to misaligned prices.

[6] One "pip" is worth one-hundredth of one cent, or $0.0001, per unit of foreign currency. Therefore, 100 pips equal 1%.

[7] £1,000,000,000 × $0.0001/£ × 10 pips = $1 million

EXHIBIT **14–5**	GLOBAL FOREIGN EXCHANGE MARKET TURNOVER[1]				

(Daily Averages in April, in Billions of U.S. Dollars)

COLUMN 1	COLUMN 2	COLUMN 3	COLUMN 4	COLUMN 5	COLUMN 6
	2001	**2004**	**2007**	**2010**	**2013**
Instruments	1,239	1,934	3,324	3,971	5,345
Spot transactions	386	631	1,005	1,488	2,046	←
Outright forwards	130	209	362	475	680	←
Foreign exchange swaps	656	954	1,714	1,759	2,228	←
Currency swaps	7	21	31	43	54	←
Options and other products[2]	60	119	212	207	337	←
			Memo		
Turnover at April 2010 exchange rates[3]	1,500	2,036	3,376	3,969	5,345
Exchange-traded derivatives[4]	12	26	80	155	160	←

[1]Adjusted for local and cross-border inter-dealer double-counting (i.e., "net-net" basis).

[2]The category "other FX products" covers highly leveraged transactions and/or trades whose notional amount is variable and where decomposition into individual plain vanilla components was impractical or impossible.

[3]Non-U.S. dollar legs of foreign currency transactions were converted into original currency amounts at average exchange rates for April of each survey year and then reconverted into U.S. dollar amounts at average April 2013 exchange rates.

[4]Sources: FOWTRADEdata; Futures Industry Association; various futures and options exchanges. Foreign exchange futures and options traded worldwide.

Source: Bank for International Settlements, Monetary and Economic Department, "Triennial Central Bank Survey: Report on Global Foreign Exchange Market Activity in 2010," December 2010, p. 7. See http://www.bis.org/publ/rpfxft10t.pdf (accessed July 11, 2013).

they are huge by any definition of the term. In 2013, daily turnover was more than $5.3 trillion, which means the annual turnover amounted to about $1,336 trillion.[8] To put these figures in perspective, in 2013 the *daily* turnover of the foreign exchange market was more than 83 times greater than the total number of seconds that had passed during the previous 2,013 years. Its *yearly* volume was about 82 times larger than the annual U.S. GDP ($16.24 trillion in 2012).

"The Basics" portion of this chapter focuses on the spot market, in which currency is purchased for immediate delivery. **"The Rest of the Story"** section discusses the forward exchange market. Macro Memo 14-1 The Major Segments of the Foreign Exchange Market explains the major segments of the foreign exchange market.

---

[8]This result is derived by multiplying 252 trading days per year times $5.3 trillion of foreign exchange turnover per day (252 working days/year × $5.3 trillion/day = $1,335.6 trillion/year).

The Major Segments of the Foreign Exchange Market

Spot Transactions

The spot market is for buying and selling currency "on the spot." Normally, the actual delivery of currencies occurs two business days after the transaction. Spot transactions are over-the-counter trades and done primarily by exchanging ownership of checking accounts between buyers and sellers.

Outright Forward Market

The outright forward market is for contractual obligations to deliver a specified amount of a currency on a predetermined future date in return for another currency of equivalent value. The price (or equivalency value) between the two currency units (e.g., U.S. dollars per Swiss franc) to be exchanged in the future is agreed on now, but delivery is delayed until a specified date in the future. Outright forward transactions are done primarily through banks. The contract terms (e.g., size and delivery date) are negotiable. This market exists mainly to handle nonspeculative trade and investment transactions.

Foreign Exchange Swap Market

The foreign exchange swap market involves two simultaneous transactions: the purchase (or sale) of a fixed amount of currency at one date (e.g., the spot purchase of yen or purchase of yen on the one-month forward market) and a transaction at a later date that reverses the first transaction (e.g., the sale of yen on the three-month forward market). Swap transactions are done primarily through banks, and their contract terms are negotiable. The swap market is large and liquid because it offers a convenient way for banks to hedge their foreign exchange exposures and for international investors and borrowers to reduce or eliminate their foreign exchange risks. Speculators also use the foreign exchange swap market when they want to bet on the exchange rate differential between two (value) dates. Swap participants are concerned only about the *differential* between the spot and forward rates and not the individual rates themselves.

Currency Swap Market

In the currency swap market, contracts commit two counterparties to exchange streams of interest payments in different currencies for an agreed period of time. At maturity, the principal amounts are exchanged at a currency rate determined when the deal was transacted.

Options and Other Product Markets

Options give *buyers* the *right, but not the obligation*, to buy or sell currency at a price (called the *strike price*) agreed upon now but with delivery delayed until or before a specified expiration date in the future. *Call* options give buyers the right, but not the obligation, *to purchase* a currency at a price agreed on now for future delivery, and *put* options give buyers the right, but not the obligation, *to sell* a currency at a price agreed on now for future delivery. By contrast, *sellers* of options *acquire obligations* and not rights. If buyers of currency options exercise their option rights, sellers have the obligation to buy or sell foreign exchange at the negotiated strike price. An exercised call option requires the option seller (writer) to sell currency at the agreed-on strike price. An exercised put option requires the option seller to buy currency at the agreed-on strike price.

Exchange-Traded Derivative Market

Futures, futures on options, and some options are traded on exchanges. Futures are similar in function to forward transactions because they are contractual obligations to deliver a specified amount of a currency on a predetermined future date in return for another currency of equivalent value. The principal differences are that futures contracts are exchange-traded, executed through brokers or electronically, and have terms (e.g., size and delivery dates) that are standardized. These differences give rise to dissimilar cash flow risks for users; so caution is advised for anyone contemplating using the futures markets. In general, the difference between a futures contract and a forward contract is like the difference between buying clothes

(CONTINUED)

off the rack and buying them custom-tailored. For a price, the forward market will tailor your contract to whatever terms you want. In the futures market, if the terms are not exactly to your liking, you can either accept them or not transact the deal. For instance, consider settlement dates and contract amounts. The Swiss franc contract traded on the Chicago Mercantile Exchange matures only four times per year (March, June, September, December cycle) and is SFr 125,000 in size. Forward contracts can have almost any maturity (e.g., 101 days in the future) and be almost any size (e.g., SFr 98,567). They are fit to meet an individual customer's specific needs. Most activity in the futures markets is speculative.

A Purely Competitive Market

The foreign exchange market ranks among the most competitive in the world; in fact, it comes as close as any market to the economic definition of *pure competition*. The number of buyers and sellers is so large that no one buyer or seller can influence the price.[9] There is virtually perfect information among a periphery of active traders. Entry into and exit from the market are impediment-free, and the markets trade homogeneous products. In fact, it is hard to imagine products more standardized than currencies because what could be more similar than a dollar (euro or yen) bill? Even better, what could be more homogeneous than a dollar (euro or yen) checking account?

> The foreign exchange market is close to perfectly competitive with many buyers and sellers, easy entry and exit from the market, near perfect information, and homogeneous products.

Total daily volume in the foreign exchange markets during 2013 amounted to more than $5.3 trillion (see Column 6 in Exhibit 14-5). The U.S. dollar was the dominant currency in the foreign exchange markets, with about 87% of all transactions having U.S. dollars as one of their counter currencies. Interestingly, there was a mild, but not substantial, change in the dollar's dominant position between 2001 and 2013, despite the introduction of the euro in 1999.[10] The U.S. dollar had a relative market share that was more than 2.5 times larger than the second-placed euro and almost 4 times larger than the third-placed Japanese yen (see Exhibit 14-6, Column 5).

> The U.S. dollar is the dominant currency in the foreign exchange market.

PARTICIPANTS IN THE FOREIGN EXCHANGE MARKET

The foreign exchange market is shaped like a pyramid with three major tiers (see Exhibit 14-7). At the base of the pyramid are nonfinancial customers, such as individuals, businesses, and governments. Foreign exchange dealers and other financial institutions, such as institutional investors, hedge funds, proprietary trading firms, and small nondealer banks, comprise the middle tier. The top tier is occupied by central banks.

> Dealers, institutional investors, hedge funds, proprietary trading firms, small nondealer banks, businesses, governments, and individuals are the major participants in the foreign exchange market.

NONFINANCIAL CUSTOMERS: INDIVIDUALS, BUSINESSES, AND GOVERNMENTS

Based on the sheer numbers of participants, the foundation of the foreign exchange market is the largest because it is comprised of hundreds of

---

[9] Perhaps one major exception is a central bank, which may have the power to move an exchange rate, but even this power is waning with the increasing size of international capital flows.

[10] The Bank for International Settlements explains the U.S. dollar's rapid market share expansion in 2001 as being caused, in part, by the decline in intra—European trading due to the introduction of the euro. Between 2010 and 2013, the euro's position deteriorated by nearly 15% due to the debt crises facing some of its member nations.

EXHIBIT 14-6	CURRENCY DISTRIBUTION OF REPORTED FOREIGN EXCHANGE MARKET TURNOVER[1]: 2001 – 2013				
CURRENCY	**2001**	**2004**	**2007**	**2010**	**2013**
US dollar	89.9	88.0	85.6	84.9	87.0
Euro	37.9	37.4	37.0	39.1	33.4
Japanese yen	23.5	20.8	17.2	19.0	23.0
Pound sterling	13.0	16.5	14.9	12.9	11.8
Australian dollar	4.3	6.0	6.6	7.6	8.6
Swiss franc	6.0	6.0	6.8	6.4	5.2
Canadian dollar	4.5	4.2	4.3	5.3	4.6
Hong Kong dollar	2.2	1.8	2.7	2.4	1.4
Mexican peso	0.8	1.1	1.3	1.3	2.5
Chinese yuan	0.0	0.1	0.5	0.9	2.2
New Zealand dollar	0.6	1.1	1.9	1.6	2.0
Other currencies	17.3	17.0	21.2	18.6	18.3
All Currencies	**200**	**200**	**200**	**200**	**200**

[1]Because two currencies are involved in each transaction, the sum of the percentage shares of individual currencies totals 200% instead of 100%. Adjusted for local and cross-border inter-dealer double-counting (i.e., "net-net" basis).

Source: "Triennial Central Bank Survey: Foreign Exchange Turnover in April 2013: Preliminary Global Results," Table 2, p.10, http://www.bis.org/publ/rpfx13fx.pdf (accessed October 6, 2013).

EXHIBIT 14-7	THE FOREIGN EXCHANGE MARKET

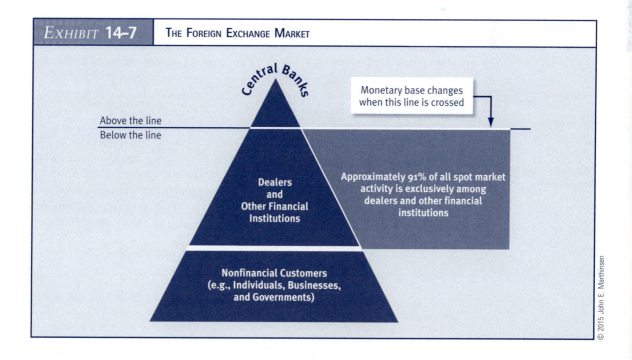

thousands of individuals, businesses, and governments who want to buy or sell foreign currency. Most people who have traveled to foreign countries are familiar with this tier because, as tourists, they have exchanged one currency (e.g., dollars) for another currency (e.g., euros, pesos, or yen). Unfortunately, our familiarity as tourists with exchange rates is not the most fruitful way to conceptualize the dynamics of the foreign exchange market because less than 1% of all the transactions in this market involve the physical exchange of one currency for another.

The study of international macroeconomics and finance makes a lot more sense if the foreign exchange market is pictured as an electronically linked, worldwide market, where transactions are settled only via bank accounts (i.e., checking accounts). Imagine a global Internet market for currencies that allows products (in this case currencies) to be bought, sold, and shipped to their destinations electronically (i.e., to the appropriate bank accounts). In short, erase from your mind the notion that the foreign exchange market is associated with individuals walking into banks and exchanging one physical currency (e.g., dollar bills and coins) for another physical currency.

DEALERS AND OTHER FINANCIAL INSTITUTIONS

As Exhibit 14-7 shows, approximately 91% of the foreign exchange activity is exclusively among dealers and other financial institutions.[11] A large portion of the remaining 9% is transacted between banks and large customers, such as large companies, governments, central banks, sovereign wealth funds, and other official institutions. Because these trades are relatively large, they also require funds to be transferred via bank accounts, rather than the physical exchange of currency.

> Approximately 91% of all foreign exchange transactions are among dealers and other financial intermediaries.

Interbank trading is a large part of daily foreign exchange volume, which is why banks employ numerous currency traders, who have little or no contact with business customers (e.g., importers, exporters, tourists, or investors). Rather, these traders try to make small speculative profits throughout the day by purchasing and selling foreign currencies within strict limits imposed by the bank. The life of a currency trader can be very stressful. Burnouts are frequent, and turnover rates are high.

Even though most foreign exchange trading is between dealers and other financial institutions and not done for the direct benefit of commercial (nonfinancial) customers, businesses still derive enormous indirect advantages from the large volume of daily trading generated by financial institutions. Trading among dealers and other financial institutions ensures that foreign exchange markets are liquid and efficient. It makes certain that large buy-or-sell orders by businesses and other customers will not move prices disadvantageously, and they can be executed in a cost-effective manner.

---

[11] The trend is clear. In 2007 and 2010, 82% and 87%, respectively, of all reported foreign exchange turnover was among dealers and other financial institutions. See Bank for International Settlements, Monetary and Economic Department, "Triennial Central Bank Survey: *Foreign Exchange Turnover in April 2013: Preliminary Global Results*," p. 6, http://www.bis.org/publ/rpfx13fx.pdf (accessed October 6, 2013).

Some financial institutions specialize in lightly traded currencies (e.g., the Thai baht or the Malta lira). Often, they become market makers in these shallow currency markets because there is not enough volume to support many dealers. *Market makers* are obliged to quote both bid (buy) *and* ask (sell) rates for currencies, thereby giving customers the right to be a buyer or a seller. For this reason, these financial institutions must be careful because, if their prices are not aligned with the competition or if they are misaligned with market fundamentals, they will create profitable arbitrage (i.e., no-risk) opportunities for customers.

Most foreign exchange transactions are done on a bid-ask basis, but some financial institutions act as brokers and offer foreign exchange services for a fee. An example helps to clarify how some financial institutions broker their services. Suppose Bank of America (BofA) in Boston, Massachusetts, received a large order to sell dollars and buy Norwegian krone. BofA would realize that any delay in executing the order could result in an unfavorable rate for the customer and damage this business relationship. To reduce the chances of a disadvantageous exchange rate movement, BofA might employ a broker, who would use its traders to hit the foreign exchange market all at once and purchase the needed krone. The hope would be that using such blitzkrieg tactics would move the price only after the deal was completed. For this service, the broker would charge a fee.

CENTRAL BANKS

At the peak of the foreign exchange market pyramid are central banks, which select certain banks as counterparties to their foreign exchange transactions. Often, the motivations behind central banks' buy and sell orders are to increase or decrease the value of the domestic currency relative to foreign currencies.[12]

For instance, if the U.S. Federal Reserve wanted to lower the value of the U.S. dollar relative to the euro, it would sell dollars (buy euros) in the foreign exchange market. If the dollar's value fell from €1/$ to €0.80/$ (i.e., which means the euro rose from $1/€ to $1.25/€), then U.S. goods and services would become less expensive relative to the euro area, and euro-area products would be more expensive relative to the United States. If U.S. and euro-area prices did not change to offset the dollar depreciation, U.S. exports to the euro area would rise, and imports would fall.

THE EFFECT OF FOREIGN EXCHANGE TRANSACTIONS ON A NATION'S MONETARY BASE

Any time a central bank buys or sells a foreign currency, its transactions affect the size of the nation's monetary base. This point is crucial in international economics and finance, and it is one we will stress in the remaining chapters of this book. To reinforce this relationship, a horizontal line has been drawn in Exhibit 14-7 separating central banks from the other tiers.[13] This line is used to remind us of this important relationship between central banks and

> Any time a central bank buys or sells foreign exchange and alters the size of its balance sheet, the nation's monetary base changes. Buying foreign exchange increases the nation's monetary base, and selling foreign exchange reduces it.

---

[12] In April 2013, central banks and other official financial institutions transacted less than one percent of the total foreign exchange volume.
[13] Chapter 9, "Who Controls the Money Supply and How?" explains fully the rule of thumb that relates central banks, the monetary base, and the use of this imaginary horizontal line.

the monetary base. Remember: *Whenever a central bank transaction crosses this imaginary horizontal line, the nation's monetary base changes if it alters the size of the central bank's balance sheet.*

CHECKING ACCOUNTS NEVER LEAVE THE COUNTRY

Earlier in the chapter we learned that large-denomination foreign exchange transactions are carried out by transferring funds from one checking account to another, rather than trading physical currencies (i.e., paper bills and coins). Of the $5.3 trillion worth of daily transactions in the foreign exchange market, the overwhelming majority of them are conducted in this manner. This fact is important because once it is clear that *checking accounts never leave their country of origin*, it is also clear that foreign exchange transactions do not affect the size of nations' monetary bases or their money supplies, unless a central bank is involved.

Using our above-the-line-below-the-line *rule of thumb*, foreign exchange transactions do not affect the monetary base because they are all conducted below the line.[14] They change only the ownership of domestic bank accounts; therefore, they remain fully accounted for in the balance sheets of domestic banks. As a result, foreign exchange transactions do not affect a central bank's ability to control its domestic monetary base or money supply. An example helps to clarify this important point.

> Checking accounts never leave the country of origin.

Suppose the dollar—pound exchange rate was $2/£, and Susan Berkley, a U.S. resident, wanted to exchange $20 million for the equivalent value in British pounds (i.e., £10 million). Susan would not care where her bank got the funds to fill this order, but suppose we were able to trace the transaction and found that the pounds came from Nigel Oxford, an English resident. In this transaction, Berkley is demanding pounds and supplying dollars, while Oxford is supplying pounds and demanding dollars.

Remember that a nation's monetary base includes currency in circulation (i.e., currency outside banks) plus the reserves of financial intermediaries, and the M2 money supply includes currency in circulation, checking accounts, and near money. As Exhibit 14-8 shows, this foreign exchange transaction simply transfers $20 million from Berkley's checking account at a U.S. bank (say, Citibank in New York City) to Oxford's checking account at a bank in the United States (say, at Wells Fargo in San Francisco). Berkley's U.S. checking account falls by $20 million, and Oxford's U.S. checking account rises by $20 million. Therefore, there is no change in the U.S. monetary base (because U.S. financial intermediaries' reserves stay the same) or M2 money supply (because total U.S. checking accounts stay the same).

> Foreign exchange transactions (by anyone other than central banks) have no effect on nations' money supplies or monetary bases.

Similar transfers occur in England. Oxford loses his £10 million checking account at an English bank (say, Barclays Bank in London), and Berkley receives a £10 million checking account in the bank of her choice in England (say, Lloyds Bank in London). As a result, there is no net change in the U.K. banking system's assets or liabilities and therefore no change in the U.K. monetary base or M2 money supply.

---

[14] The only exception is when central banks intervene in the foreign exchange markets. Central banks' foreign exchange transactions do change nations' monetary bases and money supplies. This exception to our rule of thumb was explained in Chapter 9, "Who Controls the Money Supply and How?"

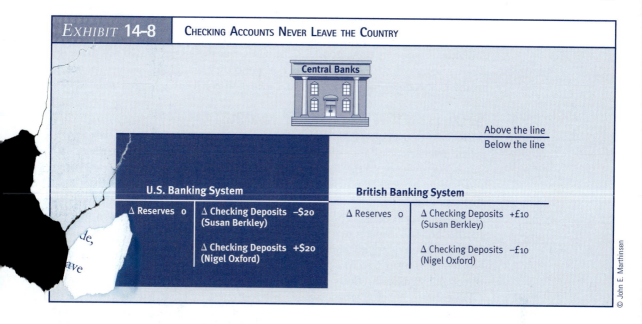

EXHIBIT 14-8 | **CHECKING ACCOUNTS NEVER LEAVE THE COUNTRY**

Central Banks

Above the line
Below the line

U.S. Banking System		**British Banking System**	
Δ Reserves 0	Δ Checking Deposits –$20 (Susan Berkley)	Δ Reserves 0	Δ Checking Deposits +£10 (Susan Berkley)
	Δ Checking Deposits +$20 (Nigel Oxford)		Δ Checking Deposits –£10 (Nigel Oxford)

INTERNATIONAL CHECK CLEARING

If you were wondering why U.S. dollar transactions are cleared through the U.S. banking system and pound transactions are cleared through the British banking system, the answer is related mainly to efficiency and cost. In this example, Berkley's and Oxfords' transactions had to be cleared, and the most efficient and cost-effective way to handle dollar transactions is to clear them through the U.S. banking system. The cost to clear U.S. dollar transactions through a British-built clearing system (or, more generally, any foreign clearing system) would be prohibitively high relative to the cost in the United States. Similarly, the cost for U.S. banks to clear pound-denominated transactions through a U.S.-built system would be prohibitively expensive relative to the British banking system. In general, foreign banks cannot compete with the more efficient, low-cost clearing systems that are already in place in a currency's country of origin. In part, the lower costs are driven by economies of scale, but there are also infrastructure and location factors that reduce costs for domestic clearing systems.

A foreign exchange transaction, like the one used in our example between Berkley and Oxford, has the effect of changing the ownership of the nations' checking deposits from domestic owners to foreign owners. You might be wondering whether nations, like the United States and England, should be concerned if too many foreigners own domestic checking accounts. For instance, could U.S. monetary authorities lose some control or could the United States be threatened in any way by these accumulations?

The answer depends on where your concerns lie. In general, there is no need for alarm because these checking accounts never leave the country. Should foreign holders of the dollar-denominated checking accounts suddenly want to get rid of them, they would have to find buyers (i.e., individuals with foreign currencies who wanted to buy dollars), and the dollar buyers would be the new owners of the deposits. Of course, massive sales could cause the value of the dollar to fall, which would affect import and export industries, along with many individuals who buy these goods and services, but these sales would not drain the United States of money or monetary base, and they would not change the ability of the U.S. central bank and fiscal authorities to enact discretionary policies.

SPOT FOREIGN EXCHANGE MARKET

Most media coverage of foreign exchange issues focuses on the *spot markets*, where the currencies are exchanged for immediate ("on the spot") or near-immediate delivery. The reason for this focus is because spot rates determine how much must be paid to purchase or sell currencies for *current delivery*. Importers, exporters, investors, tourists, speculators, politicians, the media, government officials, and central bankers around the world closely watch movements in the spot market because changes in exchange rates open and close opportunities for trade, investment, travel, political gain, and arbitrage. Political leaders and central bankers are sensitive to these changes because exchange rate movements can have direct and significant effects on important macroeconomic variables, such as GDP growth, unemployment, wages, interest rates, inflation, and wealth.

The spot foreign exchange market handles the day-to-day currency transactions for immediate or near-immediate delivery, but what does "immediate or near-immediate delivery" mean in this context? As tourists, we are familiar with making foreign exchange transactions by walking into a bank with one currency (e.g., U.S. dollars) and walking out with another currency (e.g., Japanese yen). Such transactions are made *on the spot*, so they are unquestionably a part of the spot market.

The problem is that exchanging physical currencies is a very small minority of the foreign exchange market's total daily volume. Most foreign exchange transactions are large and involve the transfer of deposits between banks; so settling and clearing them takes time. For this reason, the execution of most spot transactions takes (normally) two working days. Therefore, U.S. importers contracting on Monday to buy spot euros must wait until Wednesday, two working days later, for the funds they are buying to be deposited in their accounts (e.g., in a euro-area bank) and for the funds they are selling to be withdrawn from their accounts (e.g., in a U.S.-based bank). Transactions arranged on Thursday are settled and cleared on the following Monday. The two-day delivery time provides the back offices of banks, as well as the domestic and international clearing and communication systems, with the time needed to execute these transactions.

> Spot market transactions are for immediate or near-immediate delivery. Normally, there is a two-day settlement period.

UNDERSTANDING SPOT FOREIGN EXCHANGE QUOTATIONS

Exhibit 14-9 presents the foreign exchange quotations from *The Wall Street Journal* on Tuesday, July 9, 2013. Because *The Wall Street Journal* was available for sale early in the morning on July 9 (before the trading day began), the published rates were for the previous working day, which was Monday, July 8, 2013. These foreign exchange rates changed continuously throughout the day; so, there was no guarantee that the rates reported in *The Wall Street Journal* were a good reflection of the average rate for that day or held steady overnight.

Exhibit 14–9 | Foreign Exchange Quotes for Monday, July 8, 2013 from the July 9, 2013 Edition of the Wall Street Journal

Currencies

U.S.-dollar foreign exchange rates in late New York trading

COLUMN 1 COUNTRY/CURRENCY	COLUMN 2 IN US$	COLUMN 3 —MON— PER US$	COLUMN 4 US$ VS YTD CHG (%)
Americas			
Argentina peso	.1849	5.4080	10.0
Brazil real	.4420	2.2624	10.4
Canada dollar	.9470	1.0559	6.4
Chile peso	.001975	506.46	5.6
Colombia peso	.0005192	1926.23	9.0
Ecuador US$	1.0	1.0	unch
Mexico peso	.0776	12.8806	0.2
Peru new sol	.3584	2.790	9.6
Uruguay peso	.04819	20.7530	8.7
Venezuela b. fuerte	.157480	6.3500	46.0
Asia Pacific			
Australia dollar	.9132	1.0951	13.8
1-mo forward	.9110	1.0977	12.1
3-mos forward	.9071	1.1024	12.1
6-mos forward	.9016	1.1092	12.1
China yuan	.1630	6.1348	−1.6
Hong Kong dollar	.1289	7.7563	0.1
Europe			
Czech. Rep koruna	.04959	20.163	6.1
Denmark krone	.1725	5.7955	2.5
Euro area euro	1.2870	.7770	2.5
Hungary forint	.004365	229.07	3.7
Norway krone	.1628	6.1441	10.4
Poland zloty	.2982	3.3536	8.5
Russia ruble	.03012	33.200	8.9
Sweden krona	.1475	6.7789	4.3
Switzerland franc	1.0378	.9636	5.3
1-mo forward	1.0381	.9633	5.1
3-mos forward	1.0386	.9628	5.1
6-mos forward	1.0398	.9617	5.2
Turkey lira	.5138	1.9461	9.1
UK pound	1.4951	.6689	8.7
1-mo forward	1.4948	.6690	8.0
3-mos forward	1.4942	.6693	8.0
6-mos forward	1.4935	.6696	8.0

(Continued)

EXHIBIT 14-9   CONTINUED

Currencies

U.S.-dollar foreign exchange rates in late New York trading

COUNTRY/CURRENCY	COLUMN 2 — MON — IN US$	COLUMN 3 PER US$	COLUMN 4 US$ VS YTD CHG (%)
Americas			
India rupee	.01648	60.695	10.4
Indonesia rupiah	.0001005	9955.0	3.3
Japan yen	.009904	100.97	16.4
1-mo forward	.009905	100.96	14.1
3-mos forward	.009909	100.92	14.1
6-mos forward	.009917	100.83	14.1
Malaysia ringgit	.3116	3.2096	5.0
New Zealand dollar	.2700	1.2820	6.1
Pakistan rupee	.01000	100.030	2.9
Philippines peso	.0229	43.697	6.5
Singapore dollar	.7819	1.2789	4.7
South Korea won	.0008708	1148.40	7.9
Taiwan dollar	.03313	30.185	3.9
Thailand baht	.03176	31.484	3.0
Vietnam dong	.00004715	21210	2.0

COUNTRY/CURRENCY	COLUMN 2 — MON — IN US$	COLUMN 3 PER US$	COLUMN 4 US$ VS YTD CHG (%)
Europe			
Middle East/Africa			
Bahrain dinar	2.6528	.3770	unch
Egypt pound	.1425	7.0194	10.4
Israel shekel	.2733	3.6596	–1.9
Jordan dinar	1.4119	.7083	–0.2
Kuwait dinar	3.4910	.2865	1.8
Lebanon pound	.0006614	1512.05	0.7
Saudi Arabia riyal	.2667	3.7499	unch
South Africa rand	.0984	10.1587	20.1
UAE dirham	.2723	3.6730	unch

Source: International Monetary Fund.

The exchange rates printed on the same line as the country names are *spot exchange rates*, and the rates listed immediately under Australia, Japan, Switzerland, and the United Kingdom (U.K.) are the one-month, three-month, and six-month *forward exchange rates*. The forward exchange market will be discussed in "**The Rest of the Story**" section of this chapter.

Column 1 of Exhibit 14-9 identifies the major countries with currencies that are convertible on the foreign exchange market. Column 2 lists these currencies' late-day values in terms of how many dollars were needed to purchase one unit of foreign currency (i.e., dollars per foreign currency). For example, the closing price for U.K. pounds on Monday, July 8 was $1.4951 (i.e., $1.4951/£). Column 3 is also a spot exchange rate for July 8, but it is quoted in terms of the number of foreign currency units needed to purchase one U.S. dollar (i.e., foreign currency per dollar). Because the dollar per pound rate equaled $1.4951/£, it stands to reason that the pound per dollar rate would be the reciprocal, which equals £0.6689/$ (i.e., £1/$1.4951 = £0.6689/$). Finally, Column 4 shows the percentage yearly change in the dollar value of the foreign currencies listed. For example, the U.K. pound appreciated by 8.7%.

THE REST OF THE STORY

BUYING AND SELLING FOREIGN EXCHANGE: BID AND ASK RATES

In "The Basics," we learned that banks quote buy (bid) and sell (ask) rates, and these rates are defined from the perspective of the bank (see Exhibit 14-4). The *bid rate* is the price at which a *bank is willing and able to buy* a currency from a customer, and the *ask rate* is the price at which a *bank is willing and able to sell* a currency to a customer. The difference between these two rates is the bank's gross margin.

Anyone using foreign exchange markets must understand fully when to use the bid rate and when to use the ask rate. The choice may seem easy, but oftentimes it is not. Even though the difference between the bid and ask rates is slender for wholesale transactions (amounting to a small fraction of 1%), choosing the wrong rate can make a meaningful difference, given the massive size of foreign exchange transactions. This section explains the problem many people encounter with bid and ask rates, clarifies which rate should be used, and provides some tips on how to avoid making mistakes.

To understand why there is an issue, consider the foreign exchange market for dollars and Malaysian ringgits (MYR). Suppose a customer called his bank to purchase Malaysian ringgits. In terms of the Malaysian ringgit market, this customer would be demanding ringgits, and the bank would be supplying them. But looking at the same transaction in terms of the dollar market, the bank would be demanding dollars and the customer would be supplying them.

In other words, the role of supplier and demander is reversed by switching from the ringgit perspective to the dollar perspective. The customer, who demands ringgits in the ringgit market, becomes the supplier of dollars in the dollar market, and the bank that supplies ringgits in the ringgit market becomes the dollar demander in the dollar market. From these relationships, we can conclude that a bank's ask rate for ringgits must be exactly equal to the inverse of its bid rate for dollars (and vice versa). An example helps clarify this point.

Suppose the bid and ask rates for the Malaysian ringgit is $0.20/MYR and $0.25/MYR, respectively. A bid rate of $0.20/MYR means that banks are willing and able to *buy* ringgits from customers for $0.20 per ringgit. But if banks are willing and able to buy a ringgit for $0.20, then they must be willing and able to sell each U.S. dollar for MYR 5 (i.e., MYR 1/$0.20 = MYR 5/$). Therefore, if $0.20/MYR is the bid rate for a ringgit, then its reciprocal, MYR 5/$, is the ask rate for a dollar. These relationships are summarized in Exhibit 14-10. The take-away is that every foreign exchange transaction involves the purchase of one currency and the sale of another.

In a similar sense, an ask rate of $0.25/MYR means that banks are willing and able to sell a ringgit for $0.25, which means they are willing and able to buy $1 for MYR 4 (MYR 1/$0.25 = MYR 4/$). Therefore, the ask rate for a ringgit (i.e., $0.25/MYR) is exactly equal to the inverse of the bid rate for a dollar (i.e., MYR 4/$).

Understanding that the bid rate for ringgits is the inverse of the ask rate for dollars (and vice versa) still leaves us with the decision concerning which rate to use. To get a sense for the problem, let's use the bid and ask rates in Exhibit 14-10 and determine which rate should be used for each of the following transactions.

- **Transaction 1**: Microsoft, the U.S.-based software company, uses its Malaysian ringgit earnings to *purchase* $100 million.
- **Transaction 2**: International Malaysian Company (IMC), the Malaysian-based oil and gas company, uses its worldwide dollar earnings to *purchase* MYR 200 million.
- **Transaction 3**: IMC *sells* $100 million of its cash assets (i.e., portfolio investments) for ringgits in order to build a new factory in Malaysia.

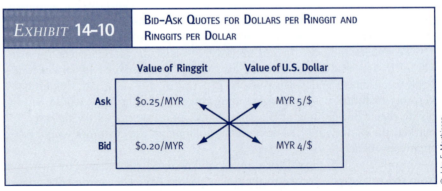

Exhibit **14-10**	Bid–Ask Quotes for Dollars per Ringgit and Ringgits per Dollar	
	Value of Ringgit	**Value of U.S. Dollar**
Ask	$0.25/MYR	MYR 5/$
Bid	$0.20/MYR	MYR 4/$

© John E. Marthinsen

- **Transaction 4**: Microsoft borrows MYR 200 million and then *sells* the ringgits in the foreign exchange market for dollars in order to acquire a medium-sized U.S. software company.

There are two separate and unrelated ways to understand whether the bid rate or ask rate should be used. The choice is left to the reader depending on your relative comfort level with the two methods.

Method 1: Always Put the Currency That You (the Customer) Want to Buy or Sell in the Denominator

One way to guard against using the wrong exchange rate is always to make sure the currency you want to buy or sell is in the denominator. Then, choose the bid rate if the bank is buying the currency in the denominator from you (i.e., you are selling the currency in the denominator to the bank), and choose the ask rate if the bank is selling the currency in the denominator to you (i.e., you are buying the currency in the denominator from the bank).

> One way to avoid calculations mistakes is to put the currency you want to purchase or sell in the denominator.

Transactions 1 and 3 are examples of deals in which customers want to buy or sell dollars. In Transaction 1, Microsoft is buying (demanding) dollars; in Transaction 3, IMC is selling (supplying) dollars. Therefore, the bid and ask exchange rates applicable to these transactions are ones that have the dollar in the denominator. In this form, it is easier to determine the proper exchange rate to use. In Transaction 1, Microsoft buys $100 million. Therefore, the company would use the ask rate (i.e., MYR 5/$) because it is the rate at which banks sell dollars to their customers. At the ask rate of MYR 5/$, Microsoft would spend MYR 500 million for the $100 million.[15]

In Transaction 3, IMC sells $100 million. Therefore, the correct exchange rate to use is the bid rate (MYR 4/$) because it is the rate at which banks buy dollars from their customers. At a rate of MYR 4/$, IMC would receive MYR 400 million for its $100 million.[16]

In Transactions 2 and 4, the bank customers buy or sell ringgits. In Transaction 2, IMC buys ringgits, and in Transaction 4, Microsoft sells ringgits. Therefore, the relevant bid and ask exchange rates are the ones that have the ringgit in the denominator. In Transaction 2, IMC buys MYR 200 million. Therefore, the appropriate exchange rate is the ask rate (i.e., $0.25/MYR) because this is the rate at which banks sell ringgits to their customers. To purchase MYR 200 million at $0.25/MYR means IMC spends $50 million.[17]

In Transaction 4, Microsoft's loan of MYR 200 million was outside the foreign exchange market because currencies were not exchanged, but the company's conversion afterward of ringgits to dollars was transacted in the foreign exchange market. For this transaction, Microsoft uses the bid rate ($0.20/MYR) because it is the rate at which banks buy ringgits from their customers. Therefore, the sale of MYR 200 million generates dollar proceeds equal to $40 million for Microsoft.[18]

---

[15] MYR 5/$ × $100 million = MYR 500 million
[16] MYR 4/$ × $100 million = MYR 400 million
[17] $0.25/MYR × MYR 200 million = $50 million
[18] $0.20/MYR × MYR 200 million = $40 million

Method 2: Always Remember That There Are Only Two Rates, and You Will Always Get the Disadvantageous One

Putting the currency you want to buy or sell into the denominator is a dependable way to always get the correct answer, but sometimes this method is problematic because it means dealing with some inconvenient fractions. For example on July 8, 2013 (see Exhibit 14-9), the U.S. dollar was worth about 1,926 Colombian pesos (Col$). Suppose the bid and ask rates for a dollar in terms of Colombian pesos were Col$ 1,923/$ and Col$ 1,929/$, respectively. That would mean that their reciprocals (i.e., the bid-ask rates for Colombian pesos in terms of dollars) would be $0.0005184/Col$ and $0.0005200/Col$— and that is after rounding.

To avoid using inconvenient fractions such as the ones for Colombian pesos and to provide another way of checking the soundness of your reasoning, a second way to determine which exchange rate to use is to forget about the terms *bid* and *ask* and simply to ask yourself one question: "Which of the two rates is to my disadvantage?" Once this question is answered, the choice of exchange rates is clear. You will always get the disadvantageous rate, and the bank will always get the advantageous one.

> There are only two rates (i.e., a bid rate and an ask rate); remember that you (the bank's customer) will always get the disadvantageous one.

Let's start by using the bid and ask rates for dollars (i.e., MYR 4/$ and MYR 5/$, respectively) to answer Transactions 1 to 4.

- In Transaction 1, Microsoft buys $100 million with ringgits. Which rate is more disadvantageous to Microsoft? At MYR 5/$, the company would pay MYR 500 million[19]; at MYR 4/$, it would pay only MYR 400 million.[20] Therefore, the rate Microsoft will get is MYR 5/$.
- In Transaction 2, IMC purchases MYR 200 million with dollars. Is the bid rate or the ask rate more disadvantageous to IMC? At MYR 4/$, the company would have to spend $50 million[21]; at MYR 5/$, it would have to spend $40 million.[22] Therefore, the rate IMC will get is MYR 4/$ because it is the disadvantageous one.
- In Transaction 3, IMC sells $100 million for ringgits. At the bid rate of MYR 4/$, IMC would receive MYR 400 million[23]; at the ask rate of MYR 5/$, it would receive MYR 500.[24] Therefore, IMC would get the bid rate because it is the disadvantageous one.
- In Transaction 4, Microsoft sells MYR 200 million for dollars. At the ask rate (MYR 5/$), Microsoft would receive $40 million[25]; at the bid rate (MYR 4/$), it would receive $50 million.[26] Therefore, Microsoft would get the ask rate because it is the disadvantageous one.

---

[19] $100 million × MYR 5/$ = MYR 500 million
[20] $100 million × MYR 4/$ = MYR 400 million
[21] MYR 200 million/MYR 4/$ = $50 million
[22] MYR 200 million/MYR 5/$ = $40 million
[23] $100 million × MYR 4/$ = MYR 400 million
[24] $100 million × MYR 5/$ = MYR 500 million
[25] MYR 200 million/MYR 5/$ = $40 million
[26] MYR 200 million/MYR 4/$ = $50 million

MACRO MEMO   14-2

Do Eurodollar Deposits Leave the Country?

In "The Basics" portion of this chapter, we learned that foreign exchange transactions have no effect on a nation's monetary base (i.e., "Checking accounts never leave the country"). Skeptics might ask if the same is true of eurodollar transactions. Even though currencies are not being traded in the eurodollar market, dollars are deposited in banks outside the United States. Wouldn't a eurodollar deposit be an example of a dollar-denominated checking account that leaves the country? The answer is no, and here is why.

Eurodollars are U.S. dollar deposits in banks outside the United States. They may appear to be unaccounted for in the U.S. banking system and beyond the control of U.S. banking authorities, but this loss of accountability and control are largely illusions. An example helps clarify why.

Suppose that attractive interest rates in the eurodollar market convince Mary Jones to withdraw $20 million from her Citibank account in New York and deposit them in a eurodollar account at Barclays Bank in London. To simplify the explanation, suppose Jones sends a $20 million check to Barclays Bank.

As Exhibit 14-11 shows, when the back office at Barclays receives Jones's check, it increases her eurodollar account by $20 million, but what does it do with the check for $20 million? Citibank does not know it was written and will not know until the check clears, which means Barclays has to send the check back to the United States for settlement.

To clear a U.S. dollar check, Barclays sends it to one of its many U.S. correspondent banks. Once in the United States, the check is then plugged into the normal clearing process. Citibank (Jones's bank) might be one of Barclays correspondents, but if

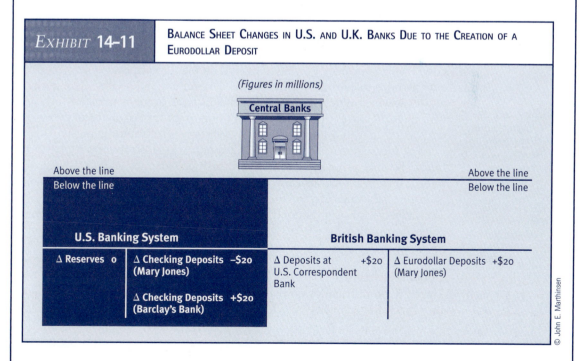

| Exhibit **14-11** | BALANCE SHEET CHANGES IN U.S. AND U.K. BANKS DUE TO THE CREATION OF A EURODOLLAR DEPOSIT |

(Figures in millions)

Central Banks

| Above the line | Above the line |
| Below the line | Below the line |

U.S. Banking System		**British Banking System**	
Δ Reserves 0	Δ Checking Deposits −$20 (Mary Jones)	Δ Deposits at +$20 U.S. Correspondent Bank	Δ Eurodollar Deposits +$20 (Mary Jones)
	Δ Checking Deposits +$20 (Barclay's Bank)		

© John E. Marthinsen

(CONTINUED)

another bank were chosen, the result would be the same. When the check clears through the U.S. banking system, Barclays Bank receives a U.S. dollar bank deposit for $20 million at its correspondent bank in the United States, and Jones's checking account at Citibank falls by $20 million.

Exhibit 14-11 summarizes the net effects of these transactions on the two nations' monetary aggregates. In the United States, Jones's checking account falls by $20 million, and Barclays account (at its U.S. correspondent bank) rises by $20 million. As a result, there is no net change in overall U.S. bank liabilities. All that changes is ownership of the dollar deposit. Therefore, the transaction is like transferring title to a piece of land located in the United States from a domestic

resident (Jones) to a foreign resident (Barclays Bank). The land never leaves the country. Similarly, there is no change in total U.S. bank reserves (in fact, there is no change in U.S. bank assets at all). As a result, there is no change in the U.S. monetary base.

In England, Barclays Bank increases its eurodollar liabilities by $20 million because it now owes this amount to Mary Jones. Because the English money supply includes only pounds, these eurodollar deposits are not included in England's money supply. Finally, the asset that Barclays now holds in the form of a $20 million deposit in its U.S. correspondent bank would not be counted as part of the British monetary base because it is denominated in dollars and not in pounds.

A good way to check your understanding of bid and ask rates is to go back through Transactions 1 to 4 and answer them using Method 2, but this time, instead of framing your answers in terms of the dollar bid and ask rates (i.e., MYR 4/$ and MYR 5/$, respectively), frame them in terms of the ringgit bid and ask rates (i.e., $0.20/MYR and $0.25/MYR, respectively).[27]

THE FORWARD EXCHANGE MARKET

The forward exchange market handles transactions for individuals who want to buy or sell currency in the future but want to lock in the exchange rate now. Foreign currency purchased or sold on the forward exchange market has only its price fixed today. Settlement is delayed until a specified date in the future, at which time it is done by means of bank account transfers (i.e., not with physical currencies). Therefore, an important take-away is that forward transactions have no (or virtually no) cash flow effects until maturity.

> The forward exchange market establishes prices today for the delivery of foreign exchange on a specified date in the future. Because only promises are traded today, there are no (or virtually no) cash flows effects with forward trades.

The forward market is really just a spot market for *promises to pay in the future*. Because promises, and not hard cash or bank accounts, are being traded, these transactions carry default risks. As a result, knowing the name and financial health of your forward counterparty are very important. Typically, a bank will reduce, by fractional amounts, the credit lines of companies transacting forward exchange contracts in order to properly account for these credit risks.[28]

LIQUID AND ILLIQUID FORWARD MARKETS

There are no restrictions on the size or maturity of forward contracts. They vary by customers' needs and banks' willingness and ability to accommodate

---

[27] This is also one of the end-of-chapter questions.
[28] This credit line haircut still has no negative cash flow implications.

these needs. As Exhibit 14-9 shows, the most frequently traded forward contracts have maturities of one month, three months, and six months, but other maturities are possible.[29]

Suppose that a U.S. customer called her bank wanting to lock in a forward rate for a SFr 23 million deal that would be executed in 101 days. The forward market could accommodate this deal, but filling this order could be difficult because there would be very few individuals in the market who wanted to transact forward deals with this exact size and maturity. The lack of an active market for this (or any) particular maturity and size is not an insurmountable problem for banks. They manage it by transacting deals at nearby maturities to ensure that the Swiss francs are available for customers when needed and then hedge their exposed positions in a variety of ways.

> The forward exchange market tailors contracts to customers' needs.

For instance, the bank might figure out the cost to buy Swiss francs for three-month (i.e., 90-day) delivery and then calculate the net amount that could be earned if these funds were invested for 11 days, so the funds would be available to the customer in 101 days. There are other ways a bank could service a 101-day deal, but the main point is that these transactions take time and could require the bank to take on added risks. Thus, customers should expect to pay a service charge and risk premium for their banks' efforts. By contrast, it is easy to find forward market counterparties for orders with one month, three-month, and six-month maturities. Therefore, there would be no need for a bank to charge an inconvenience fee or risk premium.

WHERE IS FORWARD EXCHANGE BOUGHT AND SOLD?

The global network of dealers and financial institutions that services spot transactions also services the forward market. Like the spot market, the forward market trades currencies over the counter rather than on exchanges. Bank customers, such as importers, exporters, borrowers, investors, arbitrageurs, governments, supranational institutions, and central banks, use the forward market just as they use the spot market. In addition, bid-ask spreads are quoted on all forward transactions, and they generate income for financial institutions. In fact, the forward market differs from the spot market mainly by the fact that the actual exchange of currencies is completed on a specific date in the future rather than currently.

> The forward exchange market is an over-the-counter market, using the same dealers and financial institutions as the spot market.

Forward currency markets are not the primary locus of speculative activities.[30] For that, speculators[31] have the futures market. Consequently, banks

---

[29] The forward rates quoted have maturities of one year or less. Therefore, they are *money market transactions*, and for purposes of calculating premiums, each month is assumed to have 30 days (regardless of how many days are in the month). As a result, one-month, three-month, and six-month transactions are calculated as if they had 30 days, 90 days, and 180 days, respectively.

[30] Banks are regulated entities with relatively low equity-to-asset ratios.

[31] Speculators buy or sell products (in this case, currencies) with the hopes of making a profit. Their willingness and ability to take on risk is a major defining characteristic of a speculator, and there is a very thin line between speculation and gambling. Gambling is a zero-sum game, in the sense that for each winner there must be a loser. Speculation is different. Futures markets allow participants in the market (e.g., importers, exporters, and investors) to transfer risks, which they are unable and/or unwilling to bear, to speculators, who are willing and able to bear them. Speculators also provide the market with liquidity, which allows all participants to enjoy firmer prices and lower transaction costs.

can (and do) refuse deals with individuals or companies whose sole purpose is to speculate in currencies.

In reality, speculation still takes place in the forward market, but it is opaque and rather hidden. Typically, banks give customers (mainly their commercial customers) lines of credit and allow them to conduct almost any business they want within these lines. It would be difficult for a bank to trace the motivations behind each of its customers' transactions; so, speculation can (and does) occur. Because commercial and investment customers are relatively unsupervised, banks regulate their speculative activities mainly by slicing off portions of existing credit lines with each transaction and by adjusting credit line limits when customers' credit ratings change.

Understanding Forward Foreign Exchange Quotations

Exhibit 14-9 presents the forward exchange quotes from *The Wall Street Journal* on Tuesday, July 9, 2013. Like the spot foreign exchange market, payment is due two days after the forward contract date.

It is worth noting that not every currency has an active forward exchange market. In *The Wall Street Journal*, only forward rates for the Australian dollar, Japanese yen, Swiss franc, and U.K. pound are quoted. Many lightly traded currencies have no forward markets, and if they do, these forward markets exist only through specialized financial institutions.

Column 2 in Exhibit 14-9 shows the one-month, three-month, and six-month forward currency values for Monday, July 8 in terms of how many dollars were needed to purchase one unit of foreign currency. Under the heading "U.K. pound," for example, the three-month forward price was $1.4942 per pound (i.e., $1.4942/£). As with the spot market, Column 3 shows the forward prices in terms of the number of units of foreign currency required to purchase one U.S. dollar.

Uses of the Forward Exchange Market

Individuals buying or selling currencies in the forward exchange market are able to lock in today the price of a currency that will be delivered on a specific date in the future. By dealing on this market, participants can eliminate (or substantially reduce) exchange rate risks, but keep in mind that, if this market is used to speculate, risks can be increased substantially. The difference in customers' risk levels depends on whether their forward transactions are undertaken to cover (offset) another open position or whether they are naked, which means transacted independently and therefore not offsetting another position.

Let's review a few examples of how the forward exchange market can be used to reduce or increase risk.

Example 1: A U.S. Importer Hedges the Purchase of Swiss Watches

Suppose on July 8, a U.S. importer was considering the purchase of Swiss watches worth SFr 10 million. These watches would be shipped immediately from Geneva, and payment in Swiss francs would be due in six months. By calling her bank, the importer could contract on the forward market to purchase these Swiss francs at a rate agreed upon now, but for delivery and payment in six months.

EXHIBIT 14-12	SWISS FRANC–U.S. DOLLAR SPOT AND FORWARD RATES	
	――――――――MON――――――――	
Country/Currency	In U.S.$	Per U.S.$
Switzerland franc	1.0378	.9636
1-mo forward	1.0381	.9633
3-mos forward	1.0386	.9628
6-mos forward	1.0398	.9617

© 2015 John E. Marthinsen

Looking at Exhibit 14-12 (which is reproduced from Exhibit 14-9), we see that each Swiss franc with a six-month forward delivery date cost $1.0398. At this rate, her payment would equal $10,398,000.[32] Whether this is a profitable exchange rate for the U.S. importer is something for her to decide. The important point is that she would know on the day she made the deal exactly what she would have to pay in the future. At the time the contract was being considered, if this forward rate were too expensive for her to make an adequate profit on the watches, then she might walk away from the deal or try to renegotiate it.

By contracting on the forward exchange market, she would be hedging her foreign exchange risks. On the positive side, this transaction insulates her from any losses connected to an unexpected rise in the Swiss franc's value. On the negative side, it prevents her from earning any gains if the price of the Swiss franc unexpectedly falls—but that is the price paid for hedging a bet.

Example 2: A U.S. Exporter Sells Computer Software to Japan

Suppose a U.S. software producer was considering the pros and cons of sales worth ¥150 million to a Japanese customer, with shipment to take place immediately (i.e., on July 8) and payment three months later. The U.S. exporter operates in dollars, so he would be planning to exchange the yen received in three months for dollars. By contracting on the forward exchange market, he could immediately lock in the value of these Japanese yen.

Exhibit 14-13 (which is reproduced from Exhibit 14-9), Column 2, shows that on July 8, the three-month forward yen rate equaled $0.009909/¥. By entering into this deal, the exporter guarantees his company revenues equal to $1,486,350.[33] As was the case in the previous example, if he found that this rate was too low for an adequate profit to be made, he could reject the deal, renegotiate it, or perhaps justify it on some other grounds besides visible profits (e.g., potential future business).

---

[32] $1.0398/SFr × SFr 10,000,000 = $10,398,000
[33] $0.009909/¥ × ¥150 million = $1,486,350

EXHIBIT **14-13**	JAPANESE YEN–U.S. DOLLAR SPOT AND FORWARD RATES	
	——————MON——————	
Country/Currency	**In U.S.$**	**Per U.S.$**
Japan yen	.009904	100.97
1-mo forward	.009905	100.96
3-mos forward	.009909	100.92
6-mos forward	.009917	100.83

Example 3: A U.S. Investor Hedges a Six-Month U.K. Bank Deposit

Investing in interest-earning foreign bank accounts or securities, like bonds and notes, means converting a principal amount of Currency A into Currency B now and then converting the principal and earnings, which are denominated in Currency B, back into Currency A later. Therefore from the outset, we know that three rates (or prices) influence this investment decision: the spot exchange rate (i.e., current price to convert Currency A into Currency B), the expected annualized rate of return on the foreign investment in Currency B (i.e., interest, dividends, and/or capital gains), and the cost of repurchasing Currency A when the investment matures. Without the forward market, conversion of Currency B back into Currency A would be done at whatever spot rate happened to materialize in three months.

If the investment were default-free (e.g., a one-year government treasury bill), then two of these factors (i.e., the spot rate and the return) would be known with certainty. The spot rate could be determined simply by calling a bank and getting the most recent quotes. Moreover, the annualized rate of return on a risk-free investment (assuming the investor intended to hold the security until maturity) would be known with certainty. By using the forward market, the last leg of the transaction (i.e., the value of the repatriated funds) could also be guaranteed. Therefore, any foreign exchange uncertainty could be eliminated, thereby neutralizing the foreign exchange risk.

Using the figures in Exhibit 14-14 (which is reproduced from Exhibit 14-9), suppose on July 8, a U.S. investor converted $10 million into U.K. pounds and invested them for six months in a Triple A—rated British bank account that earned 4% per year. Her major fear would be that the pound would fall in value during the coming half year. Therefore, to transact the deal and eliminate all foreign exchange exposure, she would take the following steps:

Now (July 8, 2013):

> **Step 1:** Convert $10 million into pounds on the spot market. The spot price of dollars in terms of pounds was £0.6689/$. Therefore, $10 million would have been worth £6,689,000.[34]
>
> **Step 2:** Deposit the £6,689,000 in the U.K. bank account earning a 4% annual rate of return (i.e., 2% per half year).

---

[34] $10,000,000 × £0.6689/$ = £6,689,000

EXHIBIT 14-14	U.K. POUND–U.S. DOLLAR SPOT AND FORWARD RATES	
	----------MON----------	
Country/Currency	In U.S.$	Per U.S.$
UK pound	1.4951	.6689
1-mo forward	1.4948	.6690
3-mos forward	1.4942	.6693
6-mos forward	1.4935	.6696

© 2015 John E. Marthinsen

Step 3: Sell forward the pounds (principal of the £6,689,000 plus 2% interest for the half year investment) that she will be receiving in six months. Therefore, she would sell forward £6,822,780.[35] Because the six-month forward rate on July 8 was $1.4935/£, she would expect to receive $10,189,821.93.[36]

In six months, she would complete the transactions as follows:

Step 4: Execute the forward deal that was transacted six months earlier and convert £6,822,780 into $10,189,821.93 (i.e., at the agreed forward rate of $1.4935/£). Her annualized return would be 3.80%[37] because she earned a 4% annualized rate on the U.K. deposit and lost 0.2% due to the pound's forward discount.

Example 4: Speculators Dump the U.S. Dollar

Suppose speculators were able to use the forward exchange market to place their bets. On July 8, the one-month forward price of a Swiss franc was $1.0381/SFr (see Exhibit 14-12). Suppose a speculator expected the Swiss franc to rise substantially in value during the next month (which means he expected the dollar to fall significantly during the next month), and wagered by purchasing SFr 10 million in the forward market (which means selling dollars in the forward market). Suppose he was correct, and the value of the Swiss franc rose above $1.0381/SFr during the month to $1.05/SFr. The speculator would earn $119,000[38] because he could purchase SFr 10 million at the agreed upon forward rate for $10,381,000 and sell them on the spot market in August for $10,500,000. (Keep in mind that all these earnings would be made without putting anything down.)

By contrast, if the speculator guessed wrong, the potential losses could be significant. For example, suppose our speculator purchased a one-month forward Swiss franc contract at $1.0381/SFr expecting the spot rate in one month to be $1.0500/SFr, but the exchange rate fell to $1.0200/SFr. As a

---

[35] £6,689,000 × (1 + 4%/2) = £6,822,780
[36] £6,822,780.00 × $1.4935/£ = $10,189,821.93
[37] $189,821.93/$10,000,000 = 0.01898 = 1.898% per half year or 3.796% per year
[38] SFr 10 million × ($1.0500/SFr − $1.0381/SFr) = $119,000

result, the speculator would lose $181,000[39] because he would have to purchase SFr 10 million for $10,381,000 and could sell them in the spot market for only $10,200,000.

WHY DO FORWARD RATES DIFFER FROM SPOT RATES?

Column 2 in Exhibits 14–9 and 14–12 show that, on July 8th, a Swiss franc cost $1.0378 in the spot market, and it cost $1.0381, $1.0386, and $1.0398 in the one-month, three-month, and six-month forward markets, respectively. A natural question is "Why would anyone buy the Swiss franc (or any currency) in the forward market when it is cheaper to purchase it in the spot market?"

One answer is that the forces of supply and demand determine both the spot and forward exchange rates. Therefore, the higher prices in the forward markets simply reflect the differing relative supplies and demands of importers, exporters, investors, speculators, governments, international institutions, and central banks. For example, U.S. importers may need to buy later because they do not have the credit capacity or financial resources to purchase Swiss francs in the spot market. Many businesses need time to sell the imported goods before they can pay their invoices. Similarly, exporters may need to sell in the forward market because they have extended trade credits to foreign customers that permit delayed payments.

A better explanation for why the spot and forward rates differ is related to investment incentives, interest differentials, and arbitrage. Suppose the annual U.S. and Swiss interest rates were 5% and 3%, respectively, and the one-year forward exchange rate was equal to the spot exchange rate. Under these circumstances, how would the international financial community respond?

There would be a huge incentive to borrow Swiss francs at 3%, convert them to dollars, invest in dollar-denominated assets earning 5%, and cover the forward dollar exposure by selling dollars for Swiss francs in the forward market. This investment would guarantee the investor a 2% annual return on every Swiss franc borrowed because dollars that were purchased on the spot market were simultaneously sold on the forward market at the same rate as the spot market price.

The incentive to borrow in Switzerland and invest in the United States would cause interest rates in the two countries to converge. In addition, changing supply and demand conditions for spot and forward dollars per Swiss franc would open a forward premium on the Swiss franc. The adjustments in exchange rates and interest rates would continue until riskless profits could no longer be earned by borrowing in Switzerland, investing in the United States, and covering the foreign exchange risk in the forward market. In other words, adjustments would end when the spot and forward exchange rates diverged enough to offset the interest advantage that dollar investments earned over Swiss franc investments. When this occurs, *interest parity* exists,

---

[39] SFr 10 million × ($1.0200/SFr − $1.0381/SFr) = −$181,000

and there is no way to arbitrage (i.e., earn riskless profits) by taking simultaneous positions on the credit and foreign exchange markets.

Assuming that Swiss interest rates and U.S. interest rates remain the same (i.e., at 3% and 5%, respectively), the incentive to arbitrage the markets disappears when the forward price of Swiss francs is (about) 2% more expensive than the spot price.[40] At this level, investors who borrow Swiss francs convert them to dollars, and invest on a covered basis in the dollar-denominated assets earn a zero *net* return. Their 3% Swiss franc borrowing cost exactly equals the 5% earned on the U.S. dollar investment minus the (approximate) 2% lost when the dollars are converted back into Swiss francs at the forward rate (i.e., in order to pay off the Swiss franc loan when the investment matures).

Similarly, investors—who borrow dollars, convert them to Swiss francs, and invest them on a covered basis in Swiss franc–denominated assets—also earn nothing. The 5% dollar borrowing cost is offset exactly by the 3% return on the Swiss franc–denominated investment plus the (approximate) 2% *gain* from converting Swiss francs into dollars at the forward rate when the investment matures.

We can summarize by saying that whenever two nations' interest rates differ, their spot and forward exchange rates should diverge by (approximately) an equal and opposite percentage. Otherwise, riskless profits could be earned by simultaneously borrowing in one market and lending in the other.

> Spot and forward exchange rates differ because different currencies have different interest rates.

An Example of Interest Parity

Exhibit 14-15 shows that the six-month forward discount on Australian dollars in terms of U.S. dollars was approximately 1.27%.[41] Because this divergence was for a three-month period, multiplying this figure by four gives us a non-compounded, annual rate of change equal to −5.08%.[42] Anyone entering into a simultaneous spot purchase and three-month forward sale of Australian dollars

EXHIBIT **14-15**	AUSTRALIAN DOLLAR–U.S. DOLLAR SPOT AND FORWARD RATES	
	----------MON----------	
Country/Currency	In U.S.$	Per U.S.$
Australia dollar	.9132	1.0951
1-mo forward	.9110	1.0977
3-mos forward	.9071	1.1024
6-mos forward	.9016	1.1092

© 2015 John E. Marthinsen

---

[40] The differential does not exactly equal 2% because the U.S. dollar–denominated investment earns interest, and these earnings are also translated into Swiss francs at the forward rate. Consequently, a forward premium of slightly less than 2% (closer to 1.94%) exactly offsets the 2% U.S. interest advantage.

[41] [(Forward rate/Spot rate) − 1] × 100% = [(0.9016/0.9132) − 1] × 100% = −0.0127 = −1.27% per three months

[42] On a compound annual basis, the rate would be −4.99% (i.e., $0.9873^4 − 1 = −0.0499 = −4.99\%$).

would be sure to suffer a 5.08% capital loss on the investment. Consequently, the annualized interest rate on an Australian dollar investment on July 8, 2013, should have been about 5.08% higher than the equivalent interest rate in dollars. Otherwise, arbitrageurs could borrow in one market, lend in the other market, and cover the foreign exchange risk to make arbitrage profits.[43]

CONCLUSION

The foreign exchange market is one of the largest and most competitive markets in the world. This global network of dealers and financial institutions connects buyers and sellers of international currencies. Trades are done either over the counter or on exchanges. Supply and demand are globally sourced, and prices are uniform worldwide. Business managers should have a firm understanding of how to use the spot markets in foreign exchange. Just as understanding a foreign language permits us to translate foreign words into more familiar native expressions, exchange rates permit foreign prices, rates, and returns to be translated into their domestic-currency counterparts.

Foreign exchange is traded using bid-ask rates. The bid rate is the price at which a bank will buy a currency from a customer, and the ask rate is the price at which a bank will sell a currency to a customer. Dealers, financial institutions, and exchanges are the veins and arteries through which foreign exchange trades travel to customers, such as institutional investors, hedge funds, proprietary trading firms, nondealer banks, central banks, sovereign wealth funds, corporations, and individuals. Because more than 99% of all foreign exchange transactions are large ($1 million and more), it is most helpful to think of the foreign exchange market as a global, electronic market where currency exchange only takes place by debiting and crediting checking accounts. This leads to the second rule of thumb in this text: *Rule of Thumb 2: Checking accounts never leave the country*. This rule of thumb is helpful because it fights against the belief that foreign exchange transactions change a nation's monetary base and/or money supply—they do not.

REVIEW QUESTIONS

1. In terms of the yen–peso exchange rate, is it *always true* that if the peso rises in value, the yen *must* fall in value?

2. Is the foreign exchange market a good example of pure competition, or is the market imperfectly competitive? Explain.

3. Suppose Sue Flay, a U.S. investor, purchases British pounds worth $1.5 million in the foreign exchange market. What effect does this transaction have on the U.S. and British monetary bases and M2 money supplies? Assume the spot exchange rate is $1.50/£, the pound floats against the dollar, and the transaction is sufficiently small so that the exchange rate does not change.

---

[43] Some of the arbitrage profits would be removed by transaction costs, such as bid-ask spreads and intermediary fees.

4. Due to the falling U.S. dollar, suppose Japanese investors have been purchasing U.S. real estate at bargain prices. Suppose further that Japanese banks lent yen and then borrowers converted them into U.S. dollars and paid for the real estate. Explain what effect these transactions would have, if any, on the Japanese and U.S. monetary bases.

5. Use Method 2 (i.e., *Always Remember That There Are Only Two Rates, and You Will Always Get the Disadvantageous One*) to explain whether the bid rate or ask rate should be used for each of the four transactions on pages 462 and 463. Assume the exchange rate is quoted in terms of dollars per Malaysian ringgit (i.e., $/MYR).

6. Given the information in the following table, what exchange rates would be used if you converted $1 million into euros, and then converted the euros into yuan, yuan into yen, and finally the yen into dollars?

Exchange Rate	Bid Rate	Ask Rate
Yuan—euro	10.60	10.65
Dollar—euro	1.29	1.31
Yen—dollar	104.60	104.90
Yen—yuan	12.60	12.80

7. Using the table that follows, calculate (showing all the exchange rates you used) how many dollars you would end with if you started with $1,000 and then converted the

    • $1,000 to Swiss francs,
    • Swiss francs to euros,
    • euros to pounds, and
    • pounds to U.S. dollars.

Exchange Rate	Bid	Ask
Dollars—pound	$1.50/£	$1.52/£
Swiss francs—euro	SFr 2.00/euro	SFr 2.03/euro
Swiss francs—dollar	SFr 1.30/$	SFr 1.32/$
Pounds—euro	£0.70/euro	£0.72/euro

8. Using the information in Question 7, calculate the bid and ask euro-per-dollar rates. Use the Swiss franc as the vehicle currency for these trades.

9. What is the forward exchange market? Explain how an Italian exporter, who is due to receive 30 million Japanese yen in 90 days, could use the forward market to reduce risk.

10. Why do forward rates differ from spot rates, and by how much should they differ? Explain.

11. What are eurodollars? Does an increase in eurodollar deposits change the U.S. monetary base?

12. Given the information in the following chart, determine whether there is interest parity between Switzerland and Mexico.

FINANCIAL INFORMATION ON SWITZERLAND AND MEXICO

	Bid	Ask
Swiss franc nominal interest rate (annual)	2.00%	2.5%
Mexican nominal interest rate (annual)	3.00%	3.5%
Spot exchange rate	Ps 4.00	Ps 4.04/SFr
One-year forward exchange rate	Ps 4.05	Ps 4.07/SFr
Expected Swiss inflation rate (annual)	4%	
Expected Mexican inflation rate (annual)	2%	

DISCUSSION QUESTION

13. Many people are very concerned about the rapid increase in worldwide use (and abuse) of financial derivatives. Meltdowns at companies like Long Term Capital Management, Barings Bank, and Amaranth Advisors LLC are evidence of the ways in which billions can be lost quickly in the derivatives market. At the same time, forward contracts are financial derivatives, and we know they have many good uses. Provide some balance to the discussion of derivatives by explaining some good business uses of forward contracts and some bad business uses.

Chapter 15

Exchange Rates: Why Do They Change?

INTRODUCTION

Effective business managers should be very familiar with foreign exchange markets and understand how to proactively adjust their positions and transactions to expected changes in international currency values. This chapter discusses combinations of four different types of exchange rates (i.e., bilateral, effective, nominal, and real) and the economic forces that cause them to fluctuate. Understanding these cause-and-effect relationships is important for making informed decisions about foreign trade and investment opportunities.

Attention is also paid in this chapter to the spectrum of different exchange rate regimes that countries adopt. Why do some nations allow their currencies to move freely, while others fix them to the currency of another nation or to a basket of foreign currencies? Put differently, what is it about foreign exchange markets that convinces some central banks to fix their exchange rates when they would not consider fixing the prices of commodities or financial assets? In short, what's so special about exchange rates?

THE BASICS

The value of a nation's currency can be measured relative to an individual foreign currency or relative to a basket of foreign currencies. Single currency measures are called *bilateral* exchange rates, and basket-based measures are called *effective* exchange rates.

A nation's currency can also be measured with or without taking into consideration differences in domestic and foreign price levels. Measures that ignore relative international prices are called *nominal* exchange rates and those that account for them are called *real* exchange rates.

Exhibit 15-1 shows the four alternative exchange rate measures that result from the bilateral-versus-effective and nominal-versus-real distinctions (i.e., the nominal bilateral, nominal effective, real bilateral, and real effective exchange rates). Let's review them to determine what they mean and when to use them.

BILATERAL VERSUS EFFECTIVE EXCHANGE RATES

A *bilateral exchange rate* is the value of one currency in terms of another currency. Therefore, dollars per euro ($/€), euros per pound (€/£), and yen per Swiss franc (¥/SFr) are all examples of bilateral exchange rates.

> A bilateral exchange rate is the value of one currency relative to a second currency.

EXHIBIT 15-1	FOUR PRIMARY EXCHANGE RATE MEASURES	
	Nominal Exchange Rate	**Real Exchange Rate**
Bilateral Exchange Rate	Nominal bilateral	Real bilateral
Effective Exchange Rate	Nominal effective	Real effective

© 2015 John E. Marthinsen

These rates are needed to translate prices, costs, and earnings denominated in one currency into their equivalents denominated in another currency. At the same time, they link only two currencies. Therefore, bilateral exchange rates are not useful tools for answering questions about whether the average value of a nation's currency has changed for better or worse. For this, we need effective exchange rates.

To better understand when effective exchange rates play a role, suppose a newspaper had the following headline: "U.S. Dollar Rises on International Markets," but after reading the accompanying article, you found that the dollar rose only against the Canadian dollar, euro, Mexican peso, and Japanese yen. At the same time, it fell against the Swiss franc, British pound, Thai baht, and Indian rupee. Before questioning the accuracy of the article's title, keep in mind that Canada, the euro area, Mexico, and Japan are the United States' major trading partners. Therefore, the headline was probably referring to the dollar's weighted-average value, which means it was referring to the dollar's effective exchange rate.

> An effective exchange rate is the price of one currency relative to a weighted basket of foreign currencies.

CHOOSING WEIGHTS FOR THE EFFECTIVE EXCHANGE RATE

Choosing the proper weight for each foreign currency in the effective exchange rate pool is important. The more significant the currency, the greater its weight, but here there is a decision to make. For example, when calculating the weights for the U.S. dollar's effective exchange rate, should the measures be based on trade the United States does with *all* its trading partners or just its *major* trading partners? Should trade flows be measured in terms of exports, imports, or the sum of both imports and exports? The answer is that each of these weighting methods can be and is used.

Instead of using trade volumes as the basis for the weights, the effective exchange rate could be based on other measures. For example, international capital flows or international supply and/or demand elasticities could be used. The variety of potential alternatives may seem bewildering, and a bit disconcerting, but the purpose for calculating a meaningful effective exchange rate is basically the same, namely, to provide information on the average value of a nation's currency. For the most part, reported effective exchange rates use trade flows as the basis for their weights.

> The weights of an effective exchange rate can be based on international trade flows, capital flows, or supply and demand elasticities.

NOMINAL VERSUS REAL EXCHANGE RATES

Newspapers, magazines, and television reports are filled with stories about exchange rates and the economic effects of exchange rate movements.

Most of these reports focus on *nominal exchange* rates because they are highly visible. Nominal exchange rates are the ones quoted to customers by bank tellers and foreign exchange dealers around the world and the ones we use to translate foreign prices into domestic prices.

A nominal exchange rate translates foreign prices into domestic currency units and domestic prices into foreign currency units.

The problem with nominal exchange rates is they do not convey enough meaningful information to determine whether nations' international competitive positions have changed because they ignore the effects of relative international price differences. For this reason, serious economic and financial analyses usually focus on real exchange rates rather than nominal ones.

The *real exchange rate* is calculated by adjusting the nominal exchange rate for relative international price differences. In generic terms, the real exchange rate is equal to the nominal exchange rate (units of Currency B per unit of Currency A) times the price (denominated in Currency A) of a tradable basket[1] of Country A's goods and services divided by the price (denominated in Currency B) of a tradable basket of Country B's goods and services (see Exhibit 15-2).

Real exchange rates are nominal exchange rates after they have been adjusted for both domestic and international price levels.

Care must be taken whenever real exchange rates are calculated because the currency units used to measure the nominal exchange rate and currency units used to measure the prices of tradable baskets must be aligned correctly for the real exchange rate to make sense. If the nominal exchange rate is expressed in units of Currency B per unit of Currency A, then the price of Country A's tradable basket, denominated in terms of Currency A, must be put in the numerator. An example helps clarify this point.

EXAMPLE 1

Suppose the nominal exchange rate equals \$1.25/€, the price of the euro area's tradable basket is €1,000, and the price of the United States' tradable basket is \$1,250. Under these circumstances, Currency B is the dollar, Country B is the United States, Currency A is the euro, and Country A is the euro area. Because the nominal exchange rate is expressed as dollars per euro (\$1.25/€), the euro

EXHIBIT 15-2	THE REAL EXCHANGE RATE

$$\text{Real exchange rate} \equiv \frac{\text{Nominal exchange rate}_{(B/A)} \times \text{Price}^A}{\text{Price}^B}$$

where

Nominal exchange rate$_{(B/A)}$ ≡ Units of Currency B per unit of Currency A,

Price^A ≡ Price of a tradable basket of Country A's goods and services denominated in terms of Currency A, and

Price^B ≡ Price of a tradable basket of Country B's goods and services denominated in terms of Currency B.

© John E. Marthinsen

[1] A *tradable basket* is a representative sample of a nation's exported goods and services.

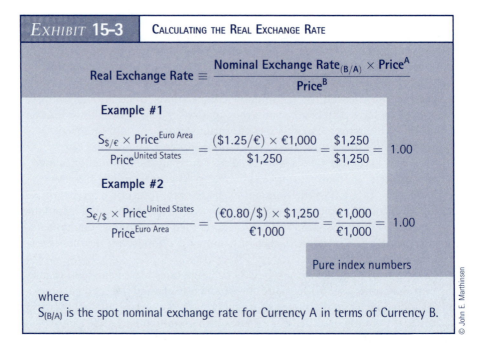

$$EXHIBIT\ \textbf{15-3} \quad \text{CALCULATING THE REAL EXCHANGE RATE}$$

$$\text{Real Exchange Rate} \equiv \frac{\text{Nominal Exchange Rate}_{(B/A)} \times \text{Price}^A}{\text{Price}^B}$$

Example #1

$$\frac{S_{\$/€} \times \text{Price}^{\text{Euro Area}}}{\text{Price}^{\text{United States}}} = \frac{(\$1.25/€) \times €1,000}{\$1,250} = \frac{\$1,250}{\$1,250} = 1.00$$

Example #2

$$\frac{S_{€/\$} \times \text{Price}^{\text{United States}}}{\text{Price}^{\text{Euro Area}}} = \frac{(€0.80/\$) \times \$1,250}{€1,000} = \frac{€1,000}{€1,000} = 1.00$$

Pure index numbers

where

$S_{(B/A)}$ is the spot nominal exchange rate for Currency A in terms of Currency B.

© John E. Marthinsen

When calculating real exchange rates, be careful to arrange the terms so the common currency element cancels.

price of the euro area's basket must be put in the numerator of the real exchange rate. In this way, the common (euro) term cancels, and the numerator becomes $\$1,250$.[2] Notice how the numerator and denominator both equal $\$1,250$, and the dollar signs cancel, which means the real exchange rate equals 1.0—which is a pure index number (see Exhibit 15-3).[3]

EXAMPLE 2

Alternatively, if the exchange rate is expressed as euros per dollar (i.e., €0.80/$),[4] then the dollar price of the U.S. tradable basket must be put in the numerator, so the common (dollar) element cancels.[5] Notice how the numerator and denominator both equal €1,000, the euro signs cancel, and the real exchange rate equals 1.0—again, a pure index number (see Exhibit 15-3).[6]

INTERPRETING REAL EXCHANGE RATES

Real exchange rates are pure index numbers (i.e., with no currency denomination).

Real exchange rates are pure index numbers, which means they have no currency denomination (i.e., they are not stated in terms of Currency A or Currency B). If a real exchange rate equals 1.0, then the average price of the tradable market basket is the same in both countries, and there should be no opportunities, on average, for international arbitrage.

---

[2] Notice how the common euro term cancels in the numerator and denominator. ($1.25/€ × €1,000) = $1,250
[3] ($1.25/€ × €1,000)/$1,250 = $1,250/$1,250 = 1.0
[4] €1/$1.25 = €0.80/$
[5] Notice how the common dollar term cancels in the numerator and denominator. (€0.80/$ × $1,250) = €1,000
[6] (€0.80/$ × $1,250)/€1,000 = (€1,000/€1,000) = 1.0

What does it mean when the real exchange rate is greater than or less than 1.0? If the real exchange rate is greater than 1.0, then the exchange-rate-adjusted price of the numerator country's tradable basket is higher than the price of the denominator country's basket. In our example, if the nominal exchange rate is expressed as dollars per euro ($/€) and the real exchange rate equals 1.15, then the dollar-denominated price of the euro area's basket is 15% higher than the dollar-denominated price of the U.S. basket.[7] As a result, there should be arbitrage opportunities to purchase goods in the United States and sell them in the euro area. Under these conditions, one would expect supply and demand pressures to depreciate the euro's value in the future.

An increase in the real exchange rate from 1.0 to 1.15 implies the euro area is pricing itself out of the international markets relative to the United States. This 15% loss of relative international competitiveness is the combined result of changes in the euro area's prices, U.S. prices, and the value of the euro. Again, one would expect the euro to depreciate and prices to adjust in both currency areas (i.e., the United States and euro area) for international competitiveness to be restored.

A real exchange rate less than 1.0 has the opposite meaning. If the nominal exchange rate is expressed as dollars per euro ($/€) and the real exchange rate equals 0.75, then the dollar-denominated price of the euro area's basket is 25% lower than the dollar-denominated price of the U.S. basket.[8] As a result, there should be arbitrage opportunities to purchase goods in the euro area and sell them in the United States. Under these circumstances, one would expect the dollar value of the euro to appreciate.

Purchasing power parity (PPP) exists when the real exchange rate equals 1.0. At that rate, the price of Country B's tradable basket equals the exchange rate–adjusted price of Country A's tradable basket.[9] Exchange rates tend to move toward their PPP levels because, if they did not, arbitrageurs could continue to make riskless profits by purchasing goods in the relatively cheap market and selling them in the relatively expensive one. Normally, convergence to PPP takes place over relatively long periods. Therefore, we will not deal with PPP in this chapter. Rather, we will save this discussion for Chapter 22, "Long-Term Exchange Rate Movements and Comparative Advantage," where long-term economic analysis (e.g., business scenario planning) is addressed.

> Purchasing power parity exists when the real exchange rate equals 1.0.

For now, we will focus our attention on developing a set of tools that can be used by business managers to conduct short-term country analyses that will improve analytical business reports, such as budgets and business plans. In the short run, real exchange rates can be quite different from 1.0. While they may approach PPP in the long run, a broad array of factors other than

---

[7] By contrast, if the nominal exchange rate is expressed as euros per dollar (€/$) and the real exchange rate equals 1.15, then the euro-denominated price of the U.S. basket is 15% higher than the euro-denominated price of the euro area's basket.

[8] By contrast, if the nominal exchange rate is expressed as euros per dollar (€/$) and the real exchange rate equals 0.75, then the euro-denominated price of the U.S. basket is 25% lower than the euro-denominated price of the euro area's basket.

[9] PPP exists when $P^B = S_{(B/A)} \times P^A$, where P^A and P^B are the average price levels in Country A and Country B, respectively, and $S_{(B/A)}$ is the value of Country A's currency in terms of Country B's currency.

international price differences, such as relative international incomes and interest rates, also plays a significant role.

NOMINAL VERSUS REAL EXCHANGE RATES: AN EXAMPLE

Given the choice between using real or nominal exchange rates in economic or financial analyses, it is usually wise to choose real exchange rates. An example helps clarify why this is the case.

Suppose the value of the Swiss franc rises from $1.00/SFr to $1.02/SFr, which is a 2% appreciation of the Swiss franc. What would you expect to happen to U.S. imports from Switzerland and U.S. exports to Switzerland? You might be tempted to say that U.S. imports from Switzerland should fall because Swiss goods and services, on average, are 2% more expensive to U.S. residents. Similarly, you might conclude that U.S. exports to Switzerland should rise because U.S. goods and services are now (about) 2% cheaper to Swiss residents. After all, Swiss franc holders would now receive 2% more dollars for each Swiss franc.

These answers would be correct if Swiss prices and U.S. prices remained the same, but that is not always the case. Changes in domestic and/or foreign prices can offset, reverse, or reinforce movements in nominal exchange rates. For this reason, real exchange rates, which consider nominal exchange rates *and* relative international prices, are used.

Exhibit 15-4 summarizes three cases in which relative international prices and the nominal exchange rate change by different amounts. Notice that the change in nominal exchange rate is the same, but incentives differ. For example, suppose the initial nominal exchange rate equals $1.00 per Swiss franc (see Column 2 in the row labeled "Base Case"), and the price of Switzerland's tradable basket equals SFr 1,000 (Column 3). As a result, the dollar price of Switzerland's basket equals $1,000 (Column 4),[10] which we assume is equal (in the Base Case) to the dollar price of the U.S. basket (Column 5).

From this initial position, let's assume that the nominal exchange rate changes from $1.00 to $1.02. In Cases 1 and 2, the real exchange rate (Column 6) does not change because fluctuations in U.S. or Swiss prices offset the nominal exchange rate movement. Only in Case 3 does the real exchange rate change. Let's look closer at the examples in Exhibit 15-4 to gain a better understanding of the real exchange rate and what it means when this rate changes.

Case 1: Swiss Franc Appreciates, and U.S. Prices Rise to Offset It

If the value of the Swiss franc rises from $1.00/SFr to $1.02/SFr (Column 2, "Case 1" row), and Swiss prices remain the same, then the dollar cost of the Swiss basket (Column 4) rises from $1,000 to $1,020.[11] If U.S. producers do not react to the higher Swiss prices and keep theirs the same, the United States gains a competitive advantage over Switzerland, but notice that in Case 1, this does not happen. The potential competitive advantage the United States might

---

[10] Column 4 = Column 2 × Column 3. Therefore, ($1.00/SFr) × SFr 1,000 = $1,000
[11] $1.02/SFr × SFr 1,000 = $1,020

EXHIBIT 15–4 REAL VERSUS NOMINAL EXCHANGE RATES

	COLUMN 2	COLUMN 3	COLUMN 4	COLUMN 5	COLUMN 6
COLUMN 1	Nominal exchange rate	Swiss franc price of Swiss basket	(Col. 2 × Col. 3) Dollar price of Swiss basket	Dollar price of U.S. basket	Real exchange rate*
					$\dfrac{\text{Col. 4}}{\text{Col. 5}}$
Base Case	$1.00/SFr	SFr 1,000	$1,000.0	$1,000	$\dfrac{\$1,000}{\$1,000} = 1.000$
Case 1	$1.02/SFr	SFr 1,000	$1,020.0	$1,020	$\dfrac{\$1,020}{\$1,020} = 1.000$
Case 2	$1.02/SFr	SFr 980.4	$1,000.0	$1,000	$\dfrac{\$1,000}{\$1,000} = 1.000$
Case 3	$1.02/SFr	SFr 995	$1,014.9	$1,010	$\dfrac{\$1,014.9}{\$1,010.0} = 1.005$

$$*\text{Real exchange rate} = \frac{(\text{Nominal exchange rate}_{(\$/\text{SFr})}) \times (\text{Swiss franc price of Swiss basket})}{(\text{U.S. dollar price of U.S. basket})} = \frac{\text{U.S. dollar price of Swiss basket}}{\text{U.S. dollar price of U.S. basket}}$$

have gained is erased by U.S. producers raising their prices by 2% from $1,000 to $1,020 (Column 5).

Despite the Swiss franc's appreciation (i.e., the dollar's depreciation), prices change to offset the exchange rate movement. The real exchange rate (Column 6) shows instantly that no competitive advantage has been gained or lost by either country because it starts at 1.0 (Base Case) and ends at 1.0.

Case 2: Swiss Franc Appreciates, and Swiss Prices Fall to Offset It

In Case 2 (see Exhibit 15-4, "Case 2" row), the value of the Swiss franc rises from $1.00/SFr to $1.02/SFr. This time, though, suppose that Swiss producers react to the appreciated Swiss franc (and the potential loss of U.S. business) by lowering the average price level of their tradable basket from SFr 1,000 to SFr 980.4. As a result, the dollar cost of Switzerland's basket (Column 4) remains the same, which means the Swiss franc's appreciation causes no net change in Switzerland's competitive advantage relative to the United States. Again, the real exchange rate communicates this conclusion immediately because it begins at 1.0 (Base Case) and ends at 1.0.

Case 3: A Change in the Real Exchange Rate

In Case 3 (see Exhibit 15-4, "Case 3" row), the value of the Swiss franc rises from $1.00/SFr to $1.02/SFr, but this time the price of Switzerland's basket of tradable products falls from SFr 1,000 to SFr 995 (Column 2), and U.S. prices rise from $1,000 to $1,010 (Column 5). As a result, the real exchange rate changes from 1.0 to 1.005, which means the competitive position of the United States relative to Switzerland improves as a net result of changes in relative prices and changes in the nominal exchange rate.

The combination of an appreciating Swiss franc and falling Swiss prices cause the dollar price of Switzerland's basket to rise from $1,000 to $1,014.9 (Column 4), which is about 0.5% higher than the price of the U.S. basket ($1,010). But we already knew this by looking at Column 6. An increase in the real exchange rate from 1.000 to 1.005 means that the dollar price of the Swiss tradable basket of goods and services is now 0.5% more expensive than the dollar price of the U.S. basket. In short, Swiss goods and services, on average, have become 0.5% more expensive than U.S. goods and services.

PERCENTAGE CHANGES IN REAL EXCHANGE RATES

Real exchange rates are frequently used in economic analyses; so it is important to understand them, but analysts are often more concerned about *changes* in real exchange rates than they are about real exchange rate *levels*. Exhibit 15-5 shows that the percentage change in the real exchange rate is (approximately) equal to the percentage change in the nominal value of Currency A (in terms of Currency B units) *plus* the percentage change in prices (i.e., inflation rate) of Country A's basket *minus* the percentage change in prices (i.e., inflation rate) of Country B's basket (i.e., %ΔReal exchange rate $\cong$ %ΔNominal exchange rate$_{(B/A)}$ + %ΔPrice in Country A − %ΔPrice in Country B).

This approximation is most accurate when the changes in prices and exchange rates are very small. Nevertheless, the elements in this equation and their relationship to each other are useful for conveying the key factors that

%ΔNominal exchange rate$_{(B/A)}$
+ %ΔPrice in Country A
− %ΔPrice in Country B
$\cong$ %ΔReal exchange rate

EXHIBIT 15-5	PERCENTAGE CHANGE IN THE REAL EXCHANGE RATE

Real exchange rate $\equiv \dfrac{S_{(B/A)} \times P^A}{P^B}$

$\%\Delta$ Real exchange rate $\cong \%\Delta S_{(B/A)} + \%\Delta P^A - \%\Delta P^B$

where

$\%\Delta S_{(B/A)} \equiv$ Percentage change in the spot nominal exchange rate stated in units of Currency B per unit of Currency A,

$\%\Delta P^A \equiv$ Inflation rate of Country A's basket of tradable products, and

$\%\Delta P^B \equiv$ Inflation rate of Country B's basket of tradable products.

© John E. Marthinsen

EXHIBIT 15-6	PERCENTAGE CHANGES: NOMINAL EXCHANGE RATES, INFLATION RATES, AND REAL EXCHANGE RATES

COLUMN 1	COLUMN 2	COLUMN 3	COLUMN 4	COLUMN 5	COLUMN 6
					(Col. 2 + Col. 3 − Col. 5)
	%Δ Nominal exchange Rate	%Δ SFr price of Swiss basket	%Δ $ price of Swiss basket	%Δ $ price of U.S. basket	%Δ Real exchange rate*
Case 1	+2%	0%	+2%	+2%	0%
Case 2	+2%	−2%	0%	0%	0%
Case 3	+2%	−0.5%	+1.5%	+1%	+0.5%

*%Δ Real ex. rate ≅ %Δ Nom. ($/SFr) ex. rate + %Δ SFr price of Swiss basket − %Δ $ price of U.S. basket

© John E. Marthinsen

cause real exchange rates to change, which are movements in the nominal exchange rate and relative in international inflation rates.

Exhibit 15-6 uses the same figures as Exhibit 15-4, but it restates them in terms of percentage changes. Notice how the real exchange rate does not change in Cases 1 and 2, but it rises by 0.5% in Case 3. As a result, the conclusions in Exhibit 15-6 are identical to the conclusions in Exhibit 15-4.

REVIEW OF EXCHANGE RATE MEASURES

Exhibit 15-7 distinguishes and defines the various combinations of bilateral, effective, nominal, and real exchange rates.

EXHIBIT 15-7	REVIEW OF EXCHANGE RATE MEASURES	
	NOMINAL	**REAL**
Bilateral	The **nominal, bilateral exchange rate** is the value of one currency in terms of another currency.	The **real, bilateral exchange rate** is the nominal, bilateral exchange rate adjusted for the international price levels of the two countries.
Effective	The **nominal, effective exchange rate** is the weighted-average value of a currency relative to many foreign currencies.	The **real, effective exchange rate** is the nominal, effective exchange rate adjusted for a nation's price level relative to many foreign countries' prices.

© John E. Marthinsen

Exhibit 15-8 profiles the nominal effective exchange rate and the real effective exchange rate for the United States during the 40-year period from January 1973 to July 2013.[12] Choosing 1973 as the starting point is intentional because it marks the end of an exchange-rate system that was established shortly after World War II.[13] Its collapse, during the period from 1971 to 1973, convinced many nations to float their currencies. In this exhibit, the weights for the effective exchange rates are based on a broad index of the currencies associated with the United States's major trading partners.

Notice that over this period, the real effective exchange rate for the dollar was relatively constant in comparison with the nominal effective exchange rate, which rose significantly (tripled). The reason for the discrepancy was the increase in the dollar's nominal effective rate during these years was largely offset by relative international inflation differences between the United States and its major trading partners.

HOW ARE EXCHANGE RATES DETERMINED?

In July 2013, the U.S. dollar was worth approximately 505 Chilean pesos, 1,510 Lebanese pounds, 1,150 South Korean wons, 9,960 Indonesian rupiahs, and 100 Japanese yen. At the same time, it was worth only about 0.80 euros, 0.30 Kuwaiti dinars, and 0.70 British pounds. Why do exchange rates differ so much? What determines a currency's international value? Is there any

---

[12] See Board of Governors of the U.S. Federal Reserve System, *Federal Reserve Statistical Release: Foreign Exchange Rates*, http://www.federalreserve.gov/releases/h10/summary/. The data are weighted average exchange rates for the U.S. dollar relative to a large group of major U.S. trading partners. The index weights reflect U.S. export shares relative to foreign import shares. For details on the construction of these weights, see Board of Governors of the U.S. Federal Reserve System, *Currency Weights*, http://www.federalreserve.gov/releases/h10/weights/default.htm (accessed July 14, 2013).

[13] The Bretton Woods system collapsed in December 1971, when President Richard Nixon broke the link between the U.S. dollar and gold. It was replaced shortly thereafter by the Smithsonian Agreement, which lasted until 1973.

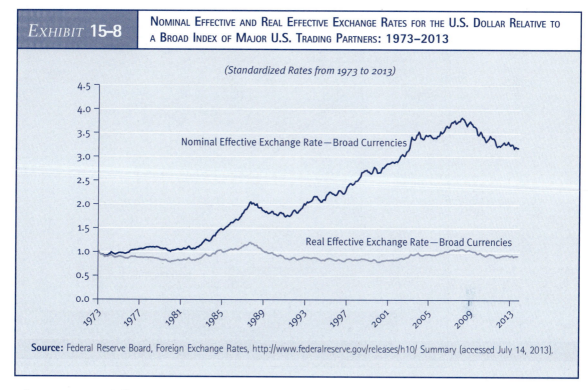

EXHIBIT 15-8   NOMINAL EFFECTIVE AND REAL EFFECTIVE EXCHANGE RATES FOR THE U.S. DOLLAR RELATIVE TO A BROAD INDEX OF MAJOR U.S. TRADING PARTNERS: 1973–2013

(Standardized Rates from 1973 to 2013)

Nominal Effective Exchange Rate—Broad Currencies

Real Effective Exchange Rate—Broad Currencies

Source: Federal Reserve Board, Foreign Exchange Rates, http://www.federalreserve.gov/releases/h10/ Summary (accessed July 14, 2013).

relevance to one dollar costing 0.30 currency units in one case and 9,960 units in another?

Exchange rates are determined by the forces of supply and demand, and they reflect the actions of all participants in the currency markets. The common element among these groups is that they are willing and able to exchange one currency for another currency.

> **Exchange rates are determined by the forces of supply and demand.**

SOME SUPPLY AND DEMAND BASICS

To understand how exchange rates are determined and why they change, it is important to have some supply and demand basics firmly in mind. Exhibit 15-9 shows supply and demand curves for a foreign exchange market. Prices (i.e., exchange rates) are on the vertical axis, and quantities per time period (i.e., the quantities of foreign exchange per time period) are on the horizontal axis. The supply curve is upward sloping, and the demand curve is downward sloping.

When first learning to analyze foreign exchange markets, many people have problems determining what currency belongs on the horizontal axis. For example, if the exchange rate is expressed as the number of dollars per Swiss francs ($/SFr), as it is in Exhibit 15-9, then should the quantity of dollars per time period or the quantity of Swiss francs per time period be put on the horizontal axis? To U.S. residents, a Swiss franc is the "foreign" currency; to Swiss residents, a dollar is the "foreign" currency, and to anyone else (e.g., European Union, Asian, and Middle Eastern residents), both currencies are "foreign." Correctly determining what to put on the horizontal axis is crucial because, if it is mislabeled, any investigation using graphical supply and

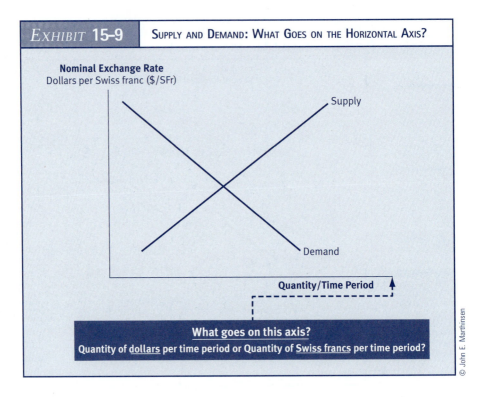

EXHIBIT 15-9 | **SUPPLY AND DEMAND: WHAT GOES ON THE HORIZONTAL AXIS?**

Nominal Exchange Rate
Dollars per Swiss franc ($/SFr)

Supply

Demand

Quantity/Time Period

What goes on this axis?
Quantity of <u>dollars</u> per time period or Quantity of <u>Swiss francs</u> per time period?

© John E. Marthinsen

demand analyses will produce answers that conflict with economic logic, common sense, and factual evidence.

One easy way to solve this labeling problem is to recast the question in a context that is familiar—a setting in which the answer is crystal clear. Once the transparent setting is in mind, it can be transferred to the foreign exchange market. For example, Exhibit 15-10 shows the market for apples. Notice that the vertical axis is stated in terms of dollars per pound of apples, and the equilibrium price is $1 per pound of apples. When the price (on the vertical axis) is stated in terms of dollars per pound of apples, then the market being analyzed is the apple market, and *pounds of apples per time period* belong on the horizontal axis.

Returning to Exhibit 15-9, if the exchange rate is stated in terms of dollars per Swiss franc, then the Swiss franc market is being analyzed. Therefore, *Swiss francs per time* period must be placed on the horizontal axis. By contrast, if the exchange rate is stated in terms of Swiss francs per dollar (as it is on the right side of Exhibit 15-11), then the market being analyzed is the dollar market. Therefore, *dollars per time period* (e.g., per week) should be placed on the horizontal axis.

The foreign exchange market can be analyzed using either the Swiss franc market (the left side of Exhibit 15-11) or the dollar market (the right side of Exhibit 15-11). It does not have to be analyzed both ways because these markets are mirror images of each other. We know this because, if the equilibrium value of the Swiss franc is $1.25/SFr, then the equilibrium value of the dollar must be SFr 0.80/$ because the reciprocal of $1.25/SFr is SFr 0.80/$. Similarly, if the equilibrium quantity of Swiss francs per week is SFr 500 billion,

> On the horizontal axis is the currency per time period that is being analyzed. On the vertical axis is the price of the currency being analyzed (i.e., the price of the currency on the horizontal axis).

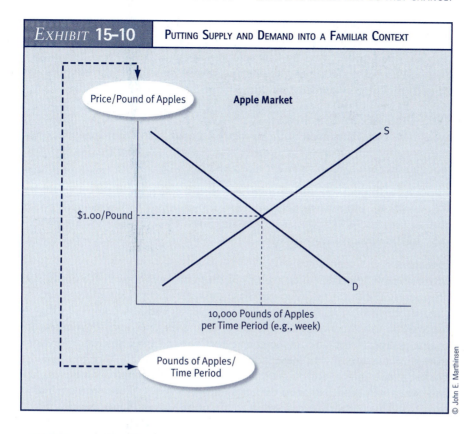

EXHIBIT 15-10   PUTTING SUPPLY AND DEMAND INTO A FAMILIAR CONTEXT

Price/Pound of Apples

Apple Market

S

$1.00/Pound

D

10,000 Pounds of Apples
per Time Period (e.g., week)

Pounds of Apples/
Time Period

© John E. Marthinsen

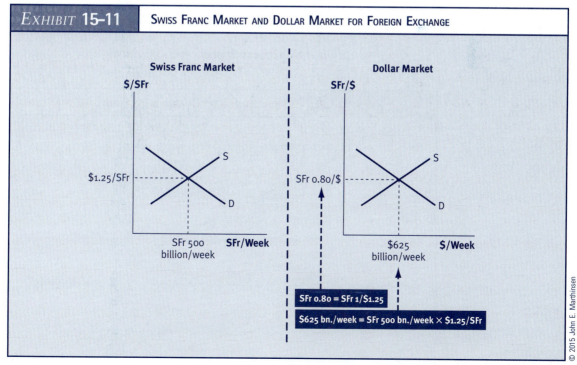

EXHIBIT 15-11   SWISS FRANC MARKET AND DOLLAR MARKET FOR FOREIGN EXCHANGE

Swiss Franc Market

$/SFr

S

$1.25/SFr

D

SFr 500
billion/week   **SFr/Week**

Dollar Market

SFr/$

S

SFr 0.80/$

D

$625
billion/week   **$/Week**

SFr 0.80 = SFr 1/$1.25

$625 bn./week = SFr 500 bn./week × $1.25/SFr

© 2015 John E. Marthinsen

then the equilibrium quantity of dollars per week must be $625 billion because SFr 500 billion × \$1.25/SFr = \$625 billion.

The value of the Swiss franc is determined by the supply and demand for Swiss francs per period, but who demands Swiss francs and who supplies them to the foreign exchange markets?

Who Demands Swiss Francs?

Swiss francs are demanded in the foreign exchange market for many reasons and by many participants. Let's briefly review the major participants and their motivations for using this market (see Exhibit 15-12).

Exporters, Importers, and Tourists

U.S. importers and tourists demand Swiss francs to pay for Swiss-made goods and services. Swiss exporters also demand Swiss francs when they are paid in U.S. dollars but wish to own Swiss francs.

Investors and Speculators

Investors include participants, such as institutional investors, hedge funds, and proprietary trading firms, who purchase foreign-currency-denominated financial instruments (i.e., debt and equity instruments) and also companies that make direct investments (e.g., build factories and make acquisitions) in foreign countries. Speculators are financial investors with a higher tolerance for risk than pure investors. All of these individuals participate in the foreign exchange market at two major levels: first, when they make their initial investments; second, when they repatriate their earnings and principal back into the original currency. This conversion can occur at maturity but could just as easily be done prior to maturity by selling their investments on the secondary markets. Therefore, examples of major demanders of Swiss francs are:

- U.S. financial investors who wish to purchase Swiss franc–denominated securities and U.S. companies that purchase Swiss francs to make direct investments in Switzerland,

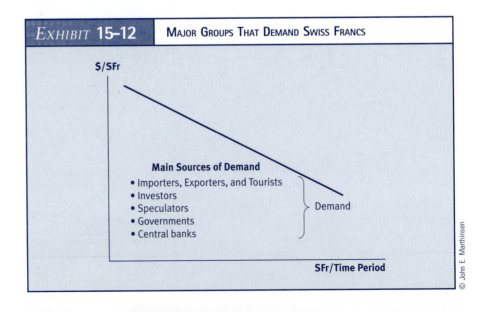

EXHIBIT 15-12   MAJOR GROUPS THAT DEMAND SWISS FRANCS

\$/SFr

Main Sources of Demand
- Importers, Exporters, and Tourists
- Investors
- Speculators
- Governments
- Central banks

Demand

SFr/Time Period

© John E. Marthinsen

- Institutional investors, companies, and private investors that convert their dollar-denominated principal and earnings (e.g., profits, interest, and/or dividends) into Swiss francs,
- Institutional investors, companies, and private investors that liquidate their U.S.-dollar assets and convert the proceeds into Swiss francs, and
- Speculators who purchase Swiss francs in anticipation of the currency's appreciation.

Governments and Central Banks

The U.S. government purchases Swiss francs with dollars in order to support activities such as those related to its embassies and consulates in Switzerland, as well as to make gifts, aid, and relief payments in Swiss francs. The U.S. and Swiss central banks (i.e., the Federal Reserve and Swiss National Bank) demand Swiss francs when they want to increase the Swiss franc's value relative to the dollar.

Others

There are other demand-side participants in the foreign exchange market who also purchase Swiss francs with dollars. Among them are U.S. residents who demand Swiss francs in order to make transfers, such as gifts and charitable contributions. Swiss individuals who receive dollar royalties and incomes, as well as Swiss companies that earn dollar license fees, also demand Swiss francs in the foreign exchange market.

> The main groups that demand foreign exchange are importers, exporters, tourists, investors, speculators, governments, and central banks.

Why Is the Demand for Foreign Exchange Downward Sloping?

As Exhibit 15-12 shows, there is an inverse relationship between the Swiss franc's value and the quantity of Swiss francs demanded each period. Because the exchange rate is expressed as dollars per Swiss franc, this relationship can be most easily understood by considering how a change in the exchange rate affects U.S. importers.

> There is an inverse relationship between exchange rates and the amount of foreign exchange demanded per period.

When U.S. importers purchase Swiss goods, they must consider two prices: the price to purchase a Swiss franc (i.e., the exchange rate) and the Swiss franc–denominated purchase price of Swiss products. If either price rises, the effective cost of Swiss products rises. As a result, an increase in the price of Swiss francs makes all Swiss goods and services more expensive to U.S. residents and therefore reduces the amount demanded per period.

WHO SUPPLIES SWISS FRANCS?

Swiss francs are supplied to the foreign exchange market by similar groups to those that demand them. As you read the list of Swiss franc suppliers, you will notice that anyone supplying Swiss francs to the (dollar-Swiss franc) foreign exchange market is simultaneously demanding dollars. We will discuss this point in more detail later in this chapter.

The major suppliers of Swiss francs in the foreign exchange market are presented in Exhibit 15-13 and described in the following sections.

Exporters, Importers, and Tourists

Swiss importers and tourists supply Swiss francs to the foreign exchange market in order to purchase dollars and, thereafter, U.S. goods and services. U.S. exporters supply Swiss francs to the foreign exchange market when they are paid in Swiss francs but want to own U.S. dollars.

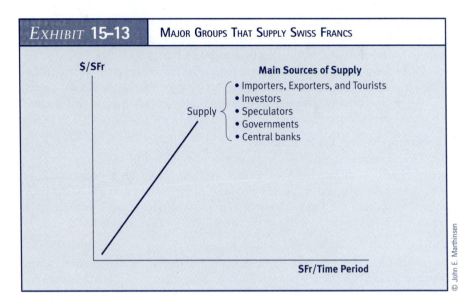

EXHIBIT **15-13**   MAJOR GROUPS THAT SUPPLY SWISS FRANCS

$/SFr

Main Sources of Supply
• Importers, Exporters, and Tourists
• Investors
Supply • Speculators
• Governments
• Central banks

SFr/Time Period

© John E. Marthinsen

Investors and Speculators

Swiss financial investors and Swiss companies supply Swiss francs to the for-eign exchange market in order to purchase dollars for financial investments and direct investments in the United States. U.S. individuals and companies supply Swiss francs to the foreign exchange market when they convert their Swiss franc principal and earnings (e.g., profits, interest, and/or dividends) into dollars. Finally, investors and speculators supply Swiss francs to the for-eign exchange market when they liquidate their Swiss franc–denominated assets and convert them into dollars.

Governments and Central Banks

The Swiss government supplies Swiss francs to the foreign exchange market (i.e., demands U.S. dollars) to support its embassies and consulates in the United States, as well as to make gifts, aid, and relief payments in U.S. dollars. The U.S. Federal Reserve and Swiss National Bank supply Swiss francs to the foreign exchange market when they want to decrease the value of the Swiss franc relative to the dollar.

The main groups that supply foreign exchange are importers, exporters, tourists, investors, spec-ulators, governments, and central banks. Sup-plying one currency means demanding another currency.

Others

Other suppliers of Swiss francs in the foreign exchange market include Swiss residents who supply Swiss francs in order to make dollar-denominated transfers, such as gifts and charitable contributions. U.S. individuals who receive Swiss franc royalties and incomes, as well as U.S. companies that earn Swiss franc license fees also supply Swiss francs to the foreign exchange market when they want these returns in U.S. dollars.

Why Is the Supply of Foreign Exchange Upward Sloping?

Exhibit 15-13 shows that there is a direct relationship between the exchange rate and the quantity of Swiss francs supplied to the market. As was the case with the downward-sloping demand curve, this relationship can be most easily understood by considering how exchange rates affect importers, but this time, we will focus on Swiss importers rather than on U.S. importers.

Swiss importers also consider two prices when they purchase U.S. goods and services: namely, the price to purchase a dollar and the dollar price of U.S. products. If either price changes, the effective cost of the U.S. goods and services changes. An increase in the value of the Swiss franc (which means a decrease in the value of the dollar) makes Swiss imports from the United States less expensive. Therefore, Swiss residents will have an incentive to purchase more U.S. products, which means they will demand a larger quantity of dollars per period.

When more dollars are demanded from the foreign exchange market, a larger quantity of Swiss francs is supplied to get them. Therefore, an increase in the value of the Swiss franc causes an increase in the quantity of Swiss francs supplied per period, which means the Swiss franc supply curve is upward sloping.[14]

Normally, there is a direct relationship between exchange rates and the amount of foreign exchange supplied per period.

EQUILIBRIUM BILATERAL NOMINAL EXCHANGE RATE

The equilibrium bilateral nominal exchange rate is the price at which the quantity of Swiss francs demanded per period equals the quantity of Swiss francs supplied per period. In Exhibit 15-14, this occurs at $1.00/SFr.

The equilibrium exchange rate is the price at which the quantity of foreign currency supplied equals the quantity demanded per period.

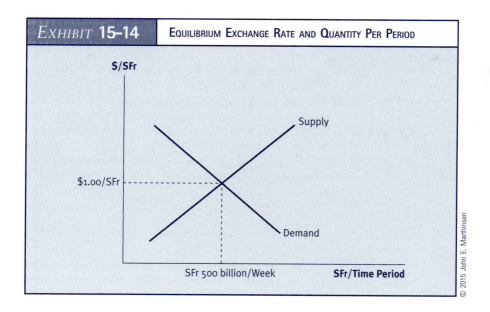

| EXHIBIT 15-14 | EQUILIBRIUM EXCHANGE RATE AND QUANTITY PER PERIOD |

$/SFr

Supply

$1.00/SFr

Demand

SFr 500 billion/Week   **SFr/Time Period**

© 2015 John E. Marthinsen

---

[14] In this book, the supply of foreign exchange will always slope upward, but under certain conditions, it is possible for it to slope downward. This anomaly is explained in Appendix 15-1, "Can the Supply of Foreign Exchange Slope Downward?"

The Demand for Swiss Francs Is the Mirror Image of the Supply of Dollars (and Vice Versa)

Consider the groups that demand Swiss francs (see Exhibit 15-12). Regardless of whether they are importers, exporters, tourists, investors, speculators, governments, or central bankers, to purchase Swiss francs, they perform their trades by contacting the foreign exchange desk of their banks, asking for exchange rate quotes, and if the price of Swiss francs is acceptable, purchasing them. After the funds clear (normally two days), Swiss francs are deposited in banks of the buyers' choice in Switzerland. At the same time these buyers gain Swiss franc deposits, they lose their dollar accounts in the United States because their dollars are transferred to whomever sold the Swiss francs. As a result, whenever Swiss francs are demanded in the foreign exchange market, dollars of equivalent value (i.e., the amount of Swiss francs demanded times the nominal exchange rate) must be supplied to the foreign exchange market.

Exhibit 15-15 shows that multiplying the quantity of Swiss francs demanded per period times the nominal ($/SFr) exchange rate converts it into the equivalent amount of U.S. dollars supplied. Graphically, they are mirror images of each other.

Similarly, Exhibit 15-16 shows that multiplying the quantity of Swiss francs supplied per period times the nominal ($/SFr) exchange rate converts it into the equivalent amount of U.S. dollars demanded. Graphically, they are mirror images of each other.

> At each exchange rate, the quantity of Currency A demanded is equal to the quantity of Currency B supplied after it has been adjusted for the nominal exchange rate (and vice versa).

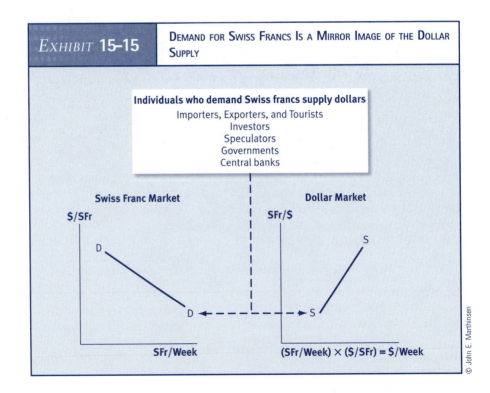

EXHIBIT 15-15   DEMAND FOR SWISS FRANCS IS A MIRROR IMAGE OF THE DOLLAR SUPPLY

Individuals who demand Swiss francs supply dollars
Importers, Exporters, and Tourists
Investors
Speculators
Governments
Central banks

Swiss Franc Market — $/SFr — D — D — SFr/Week

Dollar Market — SFr/$ — S — S — (SFr/Week) × ($/SFr) = $/Week

© John E. Marthinsen

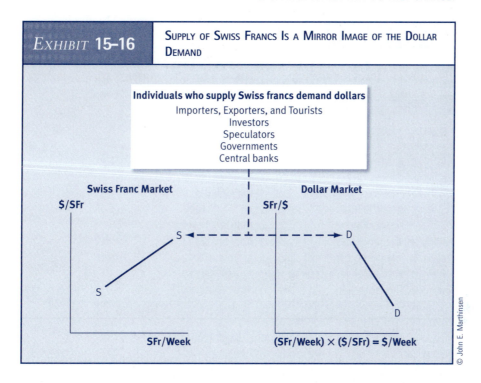

| EXHIBIT **15-16** | SUPPLY OF SWISS FRANCS IS A MIRROR IMAGE OF THE DOLLAR DEMAND |

Individuals who supply Swiss francs demand dollars
Importers, Exporters, and Tourists
Investors
Speculators
Governments
Central banks

Swiss Franc Market
$/SFr

Dollar Market
SFr/$

S ◄ ─ ─ ─ ─ ─ ─ ─ ─ ─ ─ ► D

S

D

SFr/Week

(SFr/Week) × ($/SFr) = $/Week

© John E. Marthinsen

A major takeaway from this discussion of bilateral exchange rates is that an increase in the demand for one currency automatically causes an increase in the supply of the other currency. Therefore, an increase in the demand for Swiss francs means an increase in the supply of dollars, and an increase in the supply of Swiss francs means an increase in the demand for dollars.

CHANGES IN FOREIGN CURRENCY SUPPLY ≠ CHANGES IN MONETARY BASE

It is crucial, when discussing the foreign exchange markets, not to confuse changes in the supply or amount of a currency supplied *to the foreign exchange market* with changes in a nation's monetary base or money supply. A nation's monetary base changes only if the central bank conducts open market operations, intervenes in the foreign exchange market, or changes its discount loans to banks. A nation's money supply varies only if the monetary base and/or money multiplier change. Unless a central bank is involved, foreign exchange operations have no effect on a nation's monetary base. All that changes are the owners of checking accounts, and (as we learned in the last chapter) these checking accounts never leave the country of issue.

> Unless a central bank intervenes, foreign exchange transactions do not change a nation's monetary base.

WHAT CAUSES EXCHANGE RATES TO CHANGE?

Exchange rates are not good reflections of nations' health, wealth, or productivity. For instance, one cannot say that because the Indonesian rupiah in July 2013 was worth only $0.0001005 and the Bahrain dinar was worth $2.6528, Bahrain was economically stronger than Indonesia—and clearly not 26,396 times stronger. At the same time, *changes* in the value of a currency are often used as barometers of relative economic conditions in and among nations.

EXHIBIT 15–17	MAJOR FACTORS THAT AFFECT NOMINAL EXCHANGE RATES

	A *RELATIVE* INCREASE IN DOMESTIC_____	... CAUSES THE SPOT MARKET VALUE OF THE DOMESTIC CURRENCY TO: *(QUALITATIVE CHANGE IN PARENTHESES)*
1	Prices	Depreciate (−)
2	Real GDP (i.e., real income)	Depreciate (−)
3	Real interest rates	Appreciate (+)
4	Risks	Depreciate (−)
5	Tax rates	Depreciate (−)
6	Expectations	
	• Asset returns	Appreciate (+)
	• Exchange rate (domestic currency value)	Appreciate (+)
7	Central bank purchases of the domestic currency	Appreciate (+)

© John E. Marthinsen

Exchange rates are determined by the supply and demand forces of individuals, businesses, governments, institutional investors, international institutions, and central banks. To understand why exchange rates change, it is important to identify and explain the factors that influence these participants' behavior.

Exhibit 15-17 lists seven major factors that are responsible for most international trade and investment decisions. Therefore, these factors are also responsible for most nominal exchange rate fluctuations. This section explains the qualitative influence these variables have on foreign exchange market behavior and, therefore, how they affect exchange rates. Before we begin, notice that the adjective *relative* precedes each of these seven factors. This qualification is important because exchange rates change only when relative incentives change. It is not enough for only the incentives in Nation A to change; they must change relative to other nations.

CHANGES IN RELATIVE INTERNATIONAL PRICE LEVELS

Movements in relative international prices are among the most important factors affecting nations' import and export activities. Suppose Mexico's prices rose faster than U.S. prices. Mexico's relatively higher prices would reduce the amount of Mexican goods and services demanded by the U.S. residents, thereby cutting the demand for pesos. Exhibit 15-18 shows that a reduction in the demand for pesos from D_1 to D_2 causes the value of the peso to fall from FX_1 to FX_2 (i.e., A − B).

At the same time, relatively higher Mexican prices provide incentives for Mexican consumers to increase their imports of U.S. goods and services, thereby increasing the demand for dollars. But keep in mind that Exhibit 15-18 shows the Mexican peso market and not the dollar market. Therefore, our analysis must be explained in terms of the supply and demand for Mexican pesos.

Relative increases in a nation's price level reduce the value of its currency.

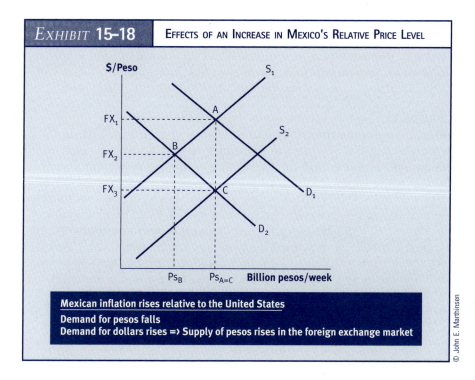

EXHIBIT 15-18   EFFECTS OF AN INCREASE IN MEXICO'S RELATIVE PRICE LEVEL

Mexican inflation rises relative to the United States

Demand for pesos falls

Demand for dollars rises ⇒ Supply of pesos rises in the foreign exchange market

© John E. Marthinsen

Fortunately this is easy to do because an increase in the demand for dollars is the same as an increase in the supply of pesos *offered to the foreign exchange market*.[15] Exhibit 15-18 shows that an increase in the supply of pesos from S_1 to S_2 further reduces the value of the peso from FX_2 to FX_3 (i.e., B − C).

The equilibrium quantity of pesos also changes with movements in Mexico's prices relative to the United States, but without further information, there is no way to determine the direction of change. When peso demand falls from D_1 to D_2, the equilibrium quantity of pesos per week falls from Ps_A to Ps_B. But when peso supply increases from S_1 to S_2, the equilibrium quantity per week rises. In Exhibit 15-18, these two changes have been drawn to offset one another so that there is no net change in quantity, but that does not have to be the case. The quantity could rise, fall, or stay the same. The net effect depends on the relative intensity of the supply and demand shifts.

Summary of Changes in Relative International Price Levels

We can make the following generalizations about changes in relative international prices: assuming all other variables remain constant, if Nation A's prices rise faster than Nation B's prices, then Nation A's currency should depreciate.

The depreciation occurs because the demand for Nation A's currency falls as residents of Nation B purchase fewer goods and services from Nation A.

---

[15] The phrase "offered to the foreign exchange market" is added to remind the reader that currency is being supplied to the foreign exchange market, but the nation's monetary base and money supply are not changing.

In addition, the supply of Nation A's currency offered to the foreign exchange market rises as residents of Nation A purchase more goods and services from Nation B. Without further information about the relative shifts of supply and demand, we have no way to determine whether the equilibrium quantity of Currency A rises, falls, or stays the same.

CHANGES IN RELATIVE INTERNATIONAL REAL GDP

When discussing the effects that relative international incomes have on exchange rates, it is important to distinguish between changes in nominal and real income. Nominal GDP can change as a result of price movements and/or fluctuations in output. In the last section, we analyzed the effects of changing relative price levels on exchange rates. Therefore, this section focuses solely on the relationship between relative changes in *real* GDP and exchange rates.

If Mexico's real GDP rose relative to the United States, the ability of Mexican consumers to purchase U.S. goods and services would rise.[16] As a result, their increased demand for dollars would increase the supply of pesos offered to the foreign exchange market, causing the peso to depreciate. In Exhibit 15-19, an increase in the supply of pesos in the foreign exchange market from S_1 to S_2 causes the equilibrium value of the peso to fall from FX_1 to FX_2 (i.e., A − B) and the quantity to rise from Ps_A to Ps_B billion pesos per week.

> Relative increases in a nation's real GDP (real income) reduce the value of its currency.

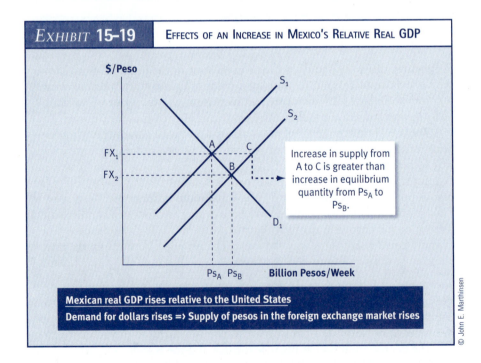

EXHIBIT 15-19 | EFFECTS OF AN INCREASE IN MEXICO'S RELATIVE REAL GDP

Increase in supply from A to C is greater than increase in equilibrium quantity from Ps_A to Ps_B.

Mexican real GDP rises relative to the United States
Demand for dollars rises ⇒ Supply of pesos in the foreign exchange market rises

© John E. Marthinsen

---

[16] The ability of Mexican consumers to buy all goods and services, including foreign- and Mexican-produced products, would rise, but we are discussing here only transactions that affect the dollar-per-peso exchange rate.

Notice in Exhibit 15-19 that the supply of pesos rose by an amount equal to A − C, but the equilibrium quantity rose by less than this amount (i.e., from Ps_A to Ps_B). The reason for this difference is because the falling peso changed incentives. As the peso depreciated, U.S. importers had more incentive to purchase Mexican products, causing an increase in the quantity of pesos demanded (i.e., A − B). Moreover, as the peso depreciated (i.e., the dollar appreciated), Mexican importers had less incentive to purchase U.S. products, causing the quantity of pesos supplied to the foreign exchange market to fall (i.e., C − B). Only if the demand for pesos was totally elastic (horizontal) would the change in equilibrium quantity be equal to the change in supply (i.e., A − C).

The Skeptics

Many people (let's call them skeptics) find it paradoxical and counterintuitive to conclude that there is an inverse relationship between the value of a country's currency and the nation's rate of economic growth. After all, higher economic growth is generally considered to be a good thing and currency depreciation is considered (perhaps unwisely) to be bad. They ask, "Shouldn't higher economic growth appreciate a nation's currency?" In general, the skeptics can be divided into two groups: the "growth-stimulates-exports" skeptics and "growth-stimulates-investment" skeptics. Let's look closer at their arguments.

Growth-stimulates-exports skeptics: These skeptics wonder why the connections between relative income movements and exchange rates focus solely on imports, with no consideration of exports. In particular, they ask: "If a nation produces more (i.e., if its real GDP rises), then additional goods and services are available for everyone—not just for domestic consumers, businesses, and governments but also for foreigners. Why doesn't some of this increased output find its way abroad, thereby increasing Nation A's exports, and increasing the international value of Nation A's currency?"

As tempting as this line of reasoning might be, it should be resisted in short-run analyses of exchange rates. It is true that increased production means that more is available for everyone, but having more to sell does not necessarily mean that foreigners will want to purchase it. To buy more, they need incentives. For example, if greater production in Nation A causes its price level to fall relative to foreign nations, then foreigners have a clear incentive to purchase more of Nation A's goods and services. But here, the incentive to purchase is triggered by a change in relative prices, and effects of changing relative prices were analyzed in the last section.

Growth-stimulates-investment skeptics: These skeptics feel there is an important missing link between changing relative income levels and exchange rates, which has to do with changing international investment incentives. They ask: "If Nation A's real GDP expands relative to Nation B, won't the profitability of Nation A's businesses increase relative to Nation B? As a result, won't these rising relative returns also raise (via arbitrage) the average return on other assets, like bonds and shares, in Nation A? And if Nation A's average investment return increases, won't the demand for Nation A's currency rise, thereby appreciating its value?"

This line of reasoning is very appealing, but it is deemphasized in discussions of the relationship between relative international real income changes and exchange rates because movements in relative international returns are important enough to be discussed separately. (We will handle them in the next section.) Furthermore, even though it is true that relative international investment returns may change directly with relative international real incomes, these relative returns can also increase for other reasons. In fact, investment returns can change with no movement in relative international real income levels.

A last word to the skeptics: The economic logic behind the inverse relationship between changes in relative international real GDP rates and exchange rates is sound, but if this conclusion is still unsettling, remember that many economic variables (not just relative incomes) change during economic expansions and contractions. It is possible for factors such as relative interest rates, price levels, and expectations, to outweigh the exchange-rate-related changes in relative international real incomes.

Summary of Changes in Relative International Real Incomes

We can make the following generalization about changes in relative international real income levels: assuming all other variables remain constant, if Nation A's (e.g., the United States') real GDP rises faster than Nation B's (e.g., Canada's) real GDP, then Nation A's currency (the U.S. dollar) should depreciate relative to Nation B's currency (the Canadian dollar).

The equilibrium value of Currency A falls because relatively higher incomes in Nation A cause its residents to purchase more goods and services from Nation B, and the resulting increase in the supply of Currency A in the foreign exchange markets causes its value to fall. The equilibrium quantity per period of Currency A rises as the supply of Currency A in the foreign exchange market increases.

CHANGES IN RELATIVE INTERNATIONAL INTEREST RATES/INVESTMENT RETURNS

Interest rates and investment returns affect both borrowers and lenders/investors. Actually, borrowers and lenders/investors are really just two sides of the same coin in the market for financial securities—one group is the payer, and the other is the payee (i.e., receiver). Suppose the Bank of Mexico feared a recession and wanted to stimulate the economy. As a result, it reduced Mexican real interest rates relative to the United States. The relative decrease in Mexican real interest rates would change borrowing and investment incentives between Mexico and the United States. Let's analyze the effect these new incentives would have on the dollar-per-peso exchange market.

The Effect of Lower Mexican Interest and Investment Returns on Lenders/Investors

The reduction in Mexican interest rates makes financial investments in Mexico less attractive, causing the U.S. investors' demand for Mexican pesos to fall. A decrease in the demand for pesos causes the value of the peso to fall. Exhibit 15-20 shows a decreased demand for pesos from D_1 to D_2, which causes the value of the peso to drop from FX_1 to FX_2 (i.e., A − B).

Relative increases in a nation's average real interest rates or real investment returns increase the value of its currency.

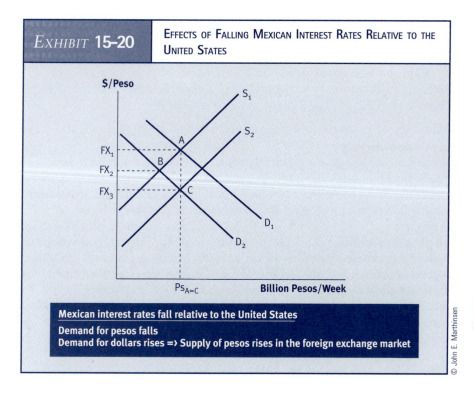

EXHIBIT 15-20   EFFECTS OF FALLING MEXICAN INTEREST RATES RELATIVE TO THE UNITED STATES

$/Peso

S_1

S_2

A

FX_1

B

FX_2

FX_3

C

D_1

D_2

$Ps_{A=C}$ Billion Pesos/Week

Mexican interest rates fall relative to the United States
Demand for pesos falls
Demand for dollars rises => Supply of pesos rises in the foreign exchange market

© John E. Marthinsen

The Effect of Lower Mexican Interest and Investment Returns on Borrowers

If Mexican interest rates fall relative to the United States, there is an incentive to borrow more pesos and fewer dollars. But the resulting increase in peso loans does not directly affect the foreign exchange market because it does not involve the exchange of pesos for dollars (or vice versa). The supply and demand for pesos in the credit market (real loanable funds market) is different from the supply and demand for pesos in the foreign exchange market. The real loanable funds market is where the real risk-free interest rate is determined, and the foreign exchange market is where the nominal exchange rate is determined.

The foreign exchange market would be affected *after* the pesos were borrowed because investors would want to invest the borrowed funds in a currency with relatively higher real returns. As U.S. interest rates are relatively higher than Mexican interest rates, the demand for dollar-denominated financial assets would rise. Therefore, the supply of pesos to the foreign exchange market would increase as borrowers purchased dollars. The increased peso supply would depreciate the dollar value of the peso.

Let's start from the beginning and trace the cause-and-effect interactions due to changing relative interest/investment return levels. The reduction in Mexico's interest rates relative to the United States creates incentives to borrow Mexican pesos, convert the pesos to dollars in the spot market, and invest in dollar-denominated financial assets, which carry relatively higher interest rates than in Mexico. Due to these transactions, the supply of pesos in the spot market rises as investors demand dollars, and the value of the peso falls (i.e., the value of the dollar rises).

Exhibit 15-20 shows that an increased supply of pesos in the foreign exchange market from S_1 to S_2 causes the value of the peso to fall from FX_2 to FX_3 (i.e., B − C).

Summary of Changes in Relative International Interest Rates and Investment Returns

We can make the following generalization about changes in relative real international interest rates and real investment returns. Assuming all other variables remain constant, if Nation A's real interest rate (or real investment return) falls relative to Nation B's, then Nation A's currency should depreciate.

The depreciation occurs because the demand for Currency A decreases as Nation B purchases fewer investment assets in Nation A, and the supply of Nation A's currency in the foreign exchange market rises (i.e., the demand for Currency B rises), as Nation A invests more in Nation B. Without further information about the relative shifts of supply and demand, there is no way to determine whether the equilibrium quantity per period of Currency A rises, falls, or stays the same.

EFFECTS OF CHANGING RISKS, TAXES, AND EXPECTATIONS ABOUT RELATIVE INTERNATIONAL INVESTMENT RETURNS

What effect do changes in relative international risks, taxes, and expectations have on a nation's exchange rate?

Suppose there was an increase in Mexico's taxes or country risks relative to the United States. What would happen to the value of the peso?

U.S. investors would reduce their demand for peso-denominated financial investments (e.g., stocks and bonds) and direct investments (e.g., factories and acquisitions). As a result, the demand for pesos would fall, causing the value of the peso to fall. In Exhibit 15-21, a decline in peso demand from D_1 to D_2 causes the value of the peso to fall from FX_1 to FX_2 (i.e., A − B).

Similarly, these changes in Mexico's relative international risks, taxes, or return expectations cause Mexicans to increase their demand for dollar-denominated investments, which are now relatively more attractive. As a result of the increased supply of pesos in the foreign exchange market, the dollar value of the peso falls. Exhibit 15-21 shows that an increased supply of pesos from S_1 to S_2 causes the exchange rate to fall from FX_2 to FX_3 (i.e., B − C).

Changing expectations about currency values can also have a significant impact on exchange rates. Speculators are influenced greatly by the changing tides of exchange rate expectations, and they can wager their bets with huge financial resources at their disposal.

Suppose speculators expected the Mexican peso to rise in value during the next six months. To take advantage of this expectation, they could acquire pesos in the spot market, but, if they did, it would be foolish to leave these

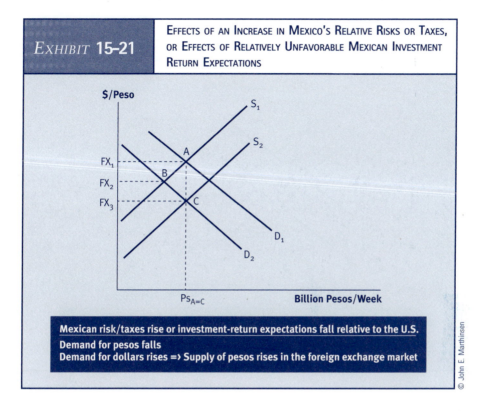

| EXHIBIT **15-21** | EFFECTS OF AN INCREASE IN MEXICO'S RELATIVE RISKS OR TAXES, OR EFFECTS OF RELATIVELY UNFAVORABLE MEXICAN INVESTMENT RETURN EXPECTATIONS |

Mexican risk/taxes rise or investment-return expectations fall relative to the U.S.

Demand for pesos falls

Demand for dollars rises => Supply of pesos rises in the foreign exchange market

© John E. Marthinsen

pesos in noninterest-earning accounts. Therefore, speculators would look for investment opportunities with the highest rate of return commensurate with the risks they wanted to bear. If they were averse to taking on substantial credit (i.e., default) risks, they could purchase Mexican government securities, or they could invest in safe Mexican bank deposits.

Speculation of this sort is called *spot market speculation* because the spot market is used to obtain foreign currency (pesos, in this case), and the spot market is used again at the end of the investment period, when the funds are repatriated (i.e., converted back into the original currency at whatever spot rate exists when the investments mature).

For example, an expected increase in the peso's value during the next six months encourages U.S. speculators to purchase pesos in the spot market, invest them in peso-denominated financial assets, and then wait six months to repatriate the funds. In Exhibit 15-22, an increased spot demand for pesos from D_1 to D_2 raises the value of the peso from FX_1 to FX_2 (i.e., A − B).

At the same time, Mexican speculators would reduce their demand for dollar-denominated assets, which would cause the supply of pesos in the spot foreign exchange market to fall. Exhibit 15-22 shows that a decline in the supply of pesos from S_1 to S_2 causes the exchange rate (i.e., the dollar value of the peso) to rise from FX_2 to FX_3 (i.e., B − C).

In six months, when the pesos are repatriated, they will be sold for dollars on the spot market at that time. As a result, these speculators bear

> The expectation that a currency will appreciate in the future causes its current price to rise.

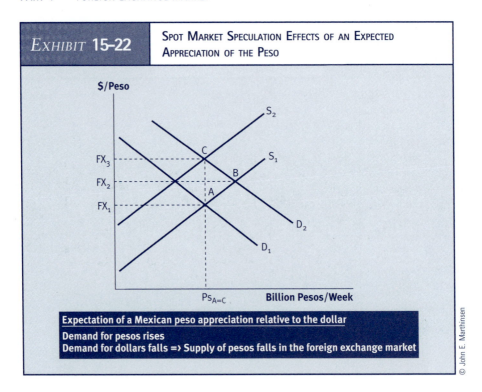

EXHIBIT 15–22   SPOT MARKET SPECULATION EFFECTS OF AN EXPECTED APPRECIATION OF THE PESO

Expectation of a Mexican peso appreciation relative to the dollar

Demand for pesos rises

Demand for dollars falls => Supply of pesos falls in the foreign exchange market

© John E. Marthinsen

considerable risks during the six months that their funds are invested and unhedged because, over such an extended period of time, the exchange rate could change considerably.

For *pure* speculators (i.e., those who finance their investments with borrowed funds), another way to profit from the expectation of an appreciating peso is to borrow dollars, convert them to pesos in the spot market, and invest in peso-denominated financial investments for six months. Again, the increased demand for pesos in the spot market would increase the value of the peso.

Summary of Changes in Relative International Risks, Taxes, and Expectations

We can make the following generalization about changes in relative international risks, taxes, and expectations. Assuming all other variables remain constant, there is an inverse relationship between the value of Nation A's currency and its relative international risks, taxes, and pessimistic expectations. As these variables rise, Nation A's currency value falls (and vice versa). This depreciation occurs because the demand for Currency A falls as Nation B invests less in Nation A, and the supply of Currency A rises in the foreign exchange market (i.e., the demand for Nation B's currency rises) as Nation A invests more in Nation B. Without further information about the relative shifts of supply and demand, there is no way to determine whether the equilibrium quantity per period of Currency A rises, falls, or stays the same.

A currency value falls if the nation's relative risks increase, taxes rise, or if there is deterioration in expectations about investment returns.

CHANGES IN RELATIVE CENTRAL BANK INTERVENTION

Central banks can have significant influences on exchange rates. One of the main reasons for them to intervene in foreign exchange markets is to discretionarily change the international value of their currencies.[17] To raise the value of the domestic currency, a central bank would purchase it from banks and brokers in the foreign exchange markets (i.e., below our imaginary horizontal line). And to do this, the central bank would need international currency reserves with which to make the purchases.

For example, if the Bank of Mexico wanted to raise the value of the peso in terms of the dollar, it would need to own or have access to dollars in order to purchase the pesos. If it did not own dollars, the central bank could purchase them with its holdings of other convertible foreign currencies, like euros, pounds, yen, or Swiss francs, and then use the newly acquired dollars to purchase the pesos. Alternatively, it could try to borrow dollars from an international institution, like the International Monetary Fund (IMF), or it might try to arrange a currency swap with the U.S. Federal Reserve. If it was the case that the Bank of Mexico neither owned dollars nor had access to them, then it could not intervene directly in the foreign exchange markets.

Exhibit 15-23 shows the effect of intervention by the Bank of Mexico to raise the value of the peso. An increase in demand from D_1 to D_2 raises the value of the peso from FX_1 to FX_2 (i.e., A − B), and the equilibrium quantity of foreign exchange rises from Ps_A to Ps_B.

> Central bank purchases raise a currency's value and raise the equilibrium quantity per period. Sales lower the value and raise the quantity per period.

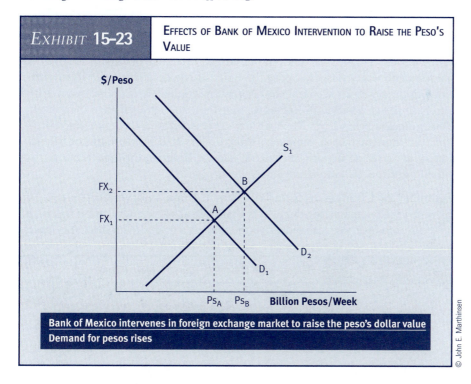

| EXHIBIT **15-23** | EFFECTS OF BANK OF MEXICO INTERVENTION TO RAISE THE PESO'S VALUE |

Bank of Mexico intervenes in foreign exchange market to raise the peso's dollar value
Demand for pesos rises

© John E. Marthinsen

---

[17] For nations with relatively undeveloped capital markets, another reason to use the foreign exchange markets is to change their domestic monetary bases.

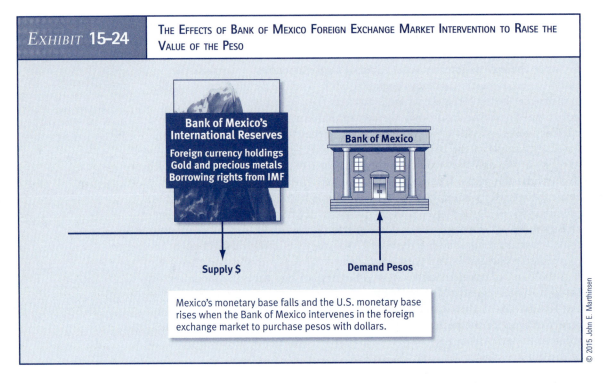

The Effect of Foreign Exchange Intervention on a Nation's Monetary Base

When a central bank intervenes in the foreign exchange market, it changes the domestic monetary base. Suppose the Bank of Mexico intervened to raise the value of the peso. To accomplish this goal, it would sell its dollar reserves and purchase pesos. Exhibit 15-24 shows that these foreign exchange market purchases remove pesos from Mexican banks' reserves and thereby reduce the Mexican monetary base. Similarly, if the dollars sold by the Bank of Mexico were previously on deposit at the U.S. Federal Reserve, this intervention would raise the U.S. monetary base.

When a central bank purchases its own currency, the domestic monetary base falls. Sales of the domestic currency in the foreign exchange market increase the domestic monetary base.

Summary of Changes in Relative Central Bank Intervention

Exhibit 15-25 summarizes the effects that central bank intervention has on a nation's exchange rate, as well as on the domestic and foreign monetary bases.

EXHIBIT 15-25	SUMMARY OF EFFECTS OF CENTRAL BANK INTERVENTION		
	VALUE OF CURRENCY A IN TERMS OF CURRENCY B	CHANGE IN THE MONETARY BASE OF COUNTRY A	CHANGE IN THE MONETARY BASE OF COUNTRY B
A central bank buys Currency A with Currency B	Rises	Falls	Rises

THE REST OF THE STORY

INTERNATIONAL EXCHANGE RATE SYSTEMS

Exhibit 15-26 shows that fixed and flexible exchange are two extremes of the currency regime spectrum, just as black and white are two extremes of the light gradient scale. Between these two extremes are shades of gray, where countries differentiate themselves by the degree of central bank intervention in the foreign exchange markets.

TO FIX OR NOT TO FIX, THAT IS THE QUESTION

Why do nations choose different currency regimes? Is there an optimal exchange rate system for all countries, or does the ideal system vary from country to country and from period to period?[18] What guidelines do nations use in choosing their exchange rate regimes?

Exchange rates are important economic shock absorbers because they reduce the impact that foreign economic jolts might have on domestic markets. For instance, if the U.S. dollar was fixed to the euro, and the euro area experienced excessive inflation, demand for lower-priced U.S. goods and services would rise, causing the U.S. inflation rate to rise. A flexible exchange rate system would diffuse the full force of this demand by raising the dollar's value with the increased foreign demand, thereby reducing the incentive for euro-area residents to purchase U.S. goods and services. Flexible exchange rates have the added benefit of empowering central banks with an ability to

> Exchange rates are like economic shock absorbers.

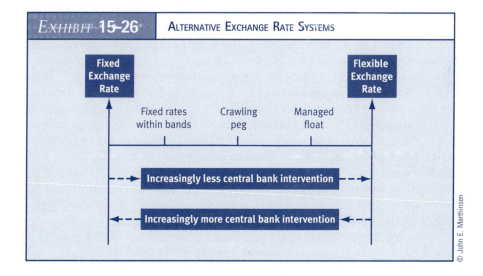

EXHIBIT 15-26   ALTERNATIVE EXCHANGE RATE SYSTEMS

Fixed Exchange Rate — Flexible Exchange Rate

Fixed rates within bands   Crawling peg   Managed float

Increasingly less central bank intervention

Increasingly more central bank intervention

© John E. Marthinsen

---

[18] See Hélène Poirson, "How Do Countries Choose Their Exchange Rate Regime?" *International Monetary Fund*, IMF Working Paper WP/01/46, 2001, http://www.imf.org/external/pubs/ft/wp/2001/wp0146.pdf (accessed July 14, 2013).

pursue independent monetary policies without the need to intervene in the foreign exchange markets each time their currency values change.

Despite these advantages, many nations chose to fix their exchange rates relative to a foreign currency or to a basket of foreign currencies, and they do so fully convinced that the benefits outweigh the costs. Let's consider some of the major advantages of a fixed exchange rate system. First and foremost, it emasculates the inflationary tendencies of domestic central bankers and government representatives. Inflation causes the value of a nation's currency to fall, which forces its central bank to intervene in the foreign exchange market and reduce the domestic monetary base. A declining monetary base decreases the M2 money supply, which raises domestic real interest rates and reduces aggregate demand. In effect, a fixed exchange rate system replaces the lax monetary standards of domestic central bankers with (hopefully) more rigorous foreign ones.

Fixed exchange rates emasculate the inflationary tendencies of domestic central bankers and government officials.

Fixed exchange rates can also enhance the economic impact of government fiscal policies. For example, expansionary fiscal policies (i.e., increases in government spending or reductions in taxes) that are financed by borrowing can raise domestic real interest rates. Rising real interest rates appreciate the domestic currency's value, which reduces net exports and weakens the expansionary fiscal policies. If the exchange rate is fixed by the central bank, then this contractionary feedback effect is eliminated.

Fixed exchange rates can enhance the effectiveness of fiscal policies.

By anchoring the value of the domestic currency to a particular foreign currency or mooring it to a basket of foreign currencies, nations can reduce costs by eliminating the bid-ask spread on foreign currency transactions and removing the need to hedge. It also promotes international price transparency, and, thereby, fosters international trade, investment, and business expansion. This can be especially important for countries that have dominant foreign trading partners.

Fixed exchange rates can reduce international transaction costs and risks. They can also make global prices more transparent.

If a central bank offers credible guarantees, then fixed exchange rates can reduce a major source of market risk. In effect, a fixed exchange rate system between Mexico and the United States would treat exporters, importers, borrowers, and lenders on both sides of the Rio Grande the same as U.S. residents on opposite sides of the Rocky Mountains.

Fixed exchange rates can reduce some risks associated with international transactions.

Fortunately, the currency system a nation chooses is reversible, and during the past 20 years, many nations have taken advantage of this two-way street. More often than not, those countries switching from a fixed- to a flexible-rate system were forced to change. One problem with fixed exchange rate systems is they seem to work best in tranquil economic, political, and social settings but become problematic and unsustainable when markets are turbulent and remain that way for extended periods of time.

If conditions are severe enough, a fixed exchange rate system can eventually collapse, causing systemic changes in prices as the markets disappear and prices spiral with abandon. In these circumstances, exchange rates can easily overshoot their equilibrium levels, causing greater economic damage than if they were free to fluctuate from the beginning. This happened in nations such as Mexico (1994), Thailand (1997), Russia (1998), and Argentina (2002) that began defending their exchange rate systems, only to fail due to the magnitude of international supply and demand forces.

Turbulent economic, political, and social conditions can render a fixed exchange rate system problematic and unsustainable.

As financial markets become larger, more global, and more tightly inter-connected, international capital flows can quickly overwhelm the resources of small and even large countries. These flows may be triggered by real, funda-mental economic forces, but they can just as easily be set off by imagined ones, such as a misinterpreted remark by a central banker or government official.

Even under tranquil conditions, flexible-exchange-rate proponents find serious flaws in the case for fixed exchange rates. First, they point out that exchange rate movements are just one of many risks business managers must consider. Why is exchange rate risk more important than price, interest, income, wage, or default risks? Moreover, they argue that reducing exchange rate volatility often serves to increase the volatility of other economic vari-ables, causing no overall reduction in risk. If they are correct, then nations are only trading one type of risk (exchange rate volatility) for another (e.g., interest and price volatility) when they choose to fix their currency values. More troublesome, if fixed exchange rates only mask fundamental economic problems by giving the illusion of stability when none exists, then they may cause more harm than good.

> Flexible exchange rate advocates feel that fixed exchange rates do not reduce overall interna-tional risks and may mask instability in the market.

FIXED BAND EXCHANGE RATE SYSTEM

A nation that wishes to enjoy some of the benefits of both a fixed and floating exchange rate system may choose a *fixed band system*, which allows a cur-rency's value to fluctuate within a predetermined range. As long as the exchange rate remains within this band, the system performs as if the rate was flexible. But once either limit is reached, central bank intervention is needed to keep the exchange rate in place. At this point, the system functions as if the exchange rate was fixed. The Bretton Woods system, which lasted from the end of World War II until 1971, is an example of a fixed-band system. Similarly, the exchange rate system used by the European Union (EU), as a precursor to the EMU, from the early 1970s to the late 1990s was a fixed band system.[19]

> A fixed band system permits exchange rates to vary freely within a pre-determined range, but once either range limit is reached, it becomes a fixed exchange rate regime.

CRAWLING PEG

An alternative exchange rate system that allows nations to enjoy some of the benefits of both fixed and floating rates is the *crawling peg* system, which requires central banks to lock-in their exchange rates for short periods of time (e.g., a year) and then to adjust them according to some predetermined formula. This formula is normally based on important economic variables that have changed since the exchange rate was fixed, such as inflation differentials. In gen-eral, this formula is nothing more than an economic reality check to make sure the exchange rate stays aligned with economic fundamentals. During the 1990s, Brazil fixed its exchange rate relative to the U.S. dollar and then adjusted this rate annually based on the differential between Brazilian and U.S. inflation rates. Today, nations such as Nicaragua, Bolivia, and Botswana have chosen crawling peg systems.

> A crawling peg exchange rate system requires central banks to fix their exchange rates for short periods of time and then to adjust them according to a predetermined formula.

---

[19]Today, members of the European Monetary Union (EMU) have a common currency, the euro. One of the criteria for members of the EU and nonmembers that wish to join the EMU is following a fixed-band sys-tem linked to the euro.

MANAGED FLOAT

Under a managed float, a central bank allows the exchange rate to fluctuate with the forces of supply and demand, but it intervenes when unwanted volatility occurs or there is a perceived need to achieve some macroeconomic goal.

Nations that choose a *managed float system* allow their exchange rates to change with the forces of supply and demand, but their central banks intervene when there is a perceived need, such as reducing exchange rate volatility, controlling excessive currency appreciation or depreciation, thwarting the efforts of speculators, or achieving other macroeconomic goals (e.g., export-led growth).

If the purpose of a managed float is to smooth the peaks and valleys of exchange rate movements, then it is helpful to keep in mind that the central bank is presuming that it knows better than the markets what the nation's long-term equilibrium exchange rate should be. If central banks do not possess superior knowledge about this rate, then intervention might actually destabilize exchange rates. An example shows how the success or failure of central bank intervention might be evaluated.

In Exhibit 15-27, suppose that England's long-term equilibrium (euro per pound) exchange rate is FX_1, and the normal fluctuation around this equilibrium rate (i.e., the fluctuations that would take place if there were no central bank intervention) is represented by the solid line AA. If the Bank of England is successful at stabilizing the value of the pound, then the range of exchange rate fluctuations after its intervention should follow a dotted line like BB, which is less volatile than AA.

One way to test the Bank of England's success at stabilizing the exchange rate is to calculate its profits at the end of each period. If the Bank of England is truly stabilizing the domestic currency's value, then it should have sold

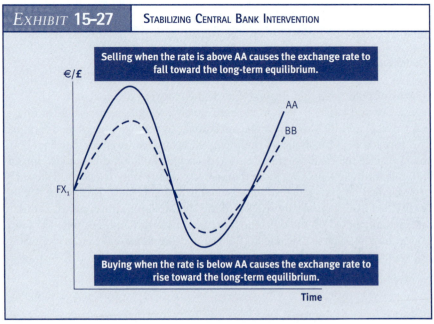

| EXHIBIT 15-27 | STABILIZING CENTRAL BANK INTERVENTION |

Selling when the rate is above AA causes the exchange rate to fall toward the long-term equilibrium.

€/£

AA

BB

FX_1

Buying when the rate is below AA causes the exchange rate to rise toward the long-term equilibrium.

Time

© John E. Marthinsen

pounds when they were overvalued (i.e., above AA) and bought them when they were undervalued (i.e., below AA). In doing so, its actions would have raised rates that were too low and lowered those that were too high. If there were no profits at the end of each accounting period, then serious questions might be raised regarding whether this central bank possessed superior knowledge about the equilibrium exchange rate and whether its actions stabilized or destabilized exchange rates.

> One test for whether central bank intervention is stabilizing or destabilizing is to measure its profits on these transactions. Positive earnings imply that stabilization efforts were successful.

INTERNATIONAL EXCHANGE RATE SYSTEMS AROUND THE WORLD

What type of exchange rate system does your home country use? Exhibit 15-28 lists the de facto currency regimes for all the nations belonging to the IMF, as of April 30, 2013. It is evident from the diversity that there are considerable differences of opinion about the virtues and vices of fixed versus flexible exchange rates.

The IMF's classification system shown in Exhibit 15-28 is based on the member nations' actual, de facto arrangements, which may differ from their officially announced, de jure arrangements. Nations are classified primarily by the extent to which their exchange rates are determined by the market forces of supply and demand as opposed to official (i.e., central bank or government) intervention or decree. The four major categories are: (1) hard pegs (e.g., arrangements in which a nation has no separate legal tender and also currency board arrangements), (2) soft pegs (e.g., pegged rates within predefined bands, crawling pegs, stabilized arrangements, and crawl-like arrangements), (3) floating regimes (e.g., floating and free floating systems), and (4) a residual category that catches all remaining exchange rate regimes.

Exhibit 15-28 also includes these nations' monetary policy frameworks in order to reinforce the symmetry needed between a chosen exchange rate system and the monetary framework to support it. Along with the different exchange rate systems, the IMF also identifies four monetary policy frameworks, which are: exchange rate anchor, monetary aggregate target, inflation-targeting, and other.

EXCHANGE RATE ANCHOR

In an *exchange rate anchor* framework, the central bank buys or sells foreign exchange to fix the exchange rate at a predetermined level or to ensure that it does not vary outside the preset range. Fixing the exchange rate in this way allows the currency value to serve as an anchor on domestic inflationary and deflationary monetary and fiscal policies. The exchange rate anchor framework is used by nations with no separate legal tender, currency board arrangements, banded and nonbanded pegs (or stabilized arrangements), crawling pegs, and crawl-like arrangements.

MONETARY AGGREGATE TARGET

In the *monetary aggregate target* framework, central banks use their policy instruments to attain a defined target, such as growth in the monetary base, M1, or M2.

EXHIBIT 15-28   DE FACTO EXCHANGE RATE ARRANGEMENTS AND MONETARY POLICY FRAMEWORKS, APRIL 30, 2012

EXCHANGE RATE ARRANGEMENT (NUMBER OF COUNTRIES)	Monetary Policy Framework						
	EXCHANGE RATE ANCHOR				MONETARY AGGREGATE TARGET (29)	INFLATION TARGETING FRAMEWORK (32)	OTHER[1] (38)
	U.S. DOLLAR (43)	EURO (27)	COMPOSITE (13)	OTHER (8)			
No separate legal tender (13)	Ecuador El Salvador Marshall Islands Micronesia Palau Panama Timor-Leste Zimbabwe	Kosovo Montenegro San Marino		Kiribati Tuvalu			
Currency board (12)	**ECCU** Antigua and Barbuda Dominica Grenada St. Kitts and Nevis St. Lucia St. Vincent and the Grenadines Djibouti Hong Kong SAR	Bosnia and Herzegovina Bulgaria Lithuania[2]		Brunei Darussalam			
Conventional peg (43)	Aruba The Bahamas Bahrain Barbados Belize Curacao and Sint Maarten Eritrea Jordan Oman Qatar Saudi Arabia Turkmenistan United Arab Emirates Venezuela	Cape Verde Comoros Denmark[2] Latvia[2] Sao Tome and Principe **WAEMU** Benin Burkina Faso Cote d'Ivoire Guinea-Bissau Mali Niger Senegal Togo **CAEMC** Cameroon Central African Rep. Chad Congo, Rep. of Equatorial[1] Guinea Gabon	Fiji Kuwait Libya Morocco[3] Samoa	Bhutan Lesotho Namibia Nepal Swaziland			

EXHIBIT 15-28 | CONTINUED

EXCHANGE RATE ARRANGEMENT (NUMBER OF COUNTRIES)	Monetary Policy Framework						
	EXCHANGE RATE ANCHOR				MONETARY AGGREGATE TARGET (29)	INFLATION TARGETING FRAMEWORK (32)	OTHER[1] (38)
	U.S. DOLLAR (43)	EURO (27)	COMPOSITE (13)	OTHER (8)			
Stabilized arrangement (16)	Cambodia Guyana Iraq Lebanon Maldives (04/11) Suriname Trinidad and Tobago	FYR Macedonia	Vietnam[5]		Tajikistan[4,5] (09/11) Ukraine[5]	Guatemala[5] (06/11)	Angola[4,5] (11/10) Azerbaijan[5] Egypt[4,6] (04/11) Lao P.D.R.[5]
Crawling peg (3)	Nicaragua		Botswana				Bolivia[4,5] (11/10)
Crawl-like arrangement (12)	Ethiopia Honduras (07/11) Jamaica (06/11) Kazakhstan	Croatia			Argentina[5] China[5] Rwanda[5] Uzbekistan[5,7] (04/08)	Dominican Republic[5]	Haiti[5] Tunisia[6] (09/11)
Pegged exchange rate within horizontal bands (1)			Tonga				
Other managed arrangement (24)	Liberia[4] (11/11)		Algeria Iran (05/11) Singapore[4] (09/11) Syria[4] (04/11) Vanuatu		Bangladesh (12/11) Burundi (07/11) Congo, Dem. Rep. of the (11/11) Guinea Kyrgyz Rep. Malawi (08/11) Nigeria Paraguay Yemen		Belarus (05/11) Costa Rica Malaysia Mauritania Myanmar Russia Solomon Islands (02/11) Sudan Switzerland (09/11)

(Continued)

EXHIBIT 15-28   CONTINUED

Monetary Policy Framework

EXCHANGE RATE ARRANGEMENT (NUMBER OF COUNTRIES)	EXCHANGE RATE ANCHOR				MONETARY AGGREGATE TARGET (29)	INFLATION TARGETING FRAMEWORK (32)	OTHER[1] (38)
	U.S. DOLLAR (43)	EURO (27)	COMPOSITE (13)	OTHER (8)			
Floating (35)					Afghanistan (04/11)	Albania	India
					The Gambia	Armenia[8]	Mauritius
					Kenya	Brazil	
					Madagascar	Colombia	
					Mongolia	Georgia[8]	
					Mozambique	Ghana	
					Pakistan[4] (04/11)	Hungary	
					Papua New Guinea	Iceland	
					Seychelles	Indonesia (02/11)	
					Sierra Leone	Korea	
					Sri Lanka (02/12)	Moldova	
					Tanzania	Peru (04/11)	
					Uganda	Philippines	
					Zambia	Romania	
						Serbia	
						South Africa	
						Thailand	
						Turkey	
						Uruguay	

EXHIBIT 15-28   CONTINUED

EXCHANGE RATE ARRANGEMENT (NUMBER OF COUNTRIES)	Monetary Policy Framework						
	EXCHANGE RATE ANCHOR				MONETARY AGGREGATE TARGET (29)	INFLATION TARGETING FRAMEWORK (32)	OTHER[1] (38)
	U.S. DOLLAR (43)	EURO (27)	COMPOSITE (13)	OTHER (8)			
Free floating (31)						Australia Canada Chile Czech Rep. Israel (08/11) Mexico (11/11) New Zealand Norway Poland (12/11) Sweden United Kingdom	Japan Somalia United States EMU Austria Belgium Cyprus Estonia (01/11) Finland France Germany Greece Ireland Italy Luxembourg Malta Netherlands Portugal Slovak Republic Slovenia Spain

Note: If the member country's de facto exchange rate arrangement has been reclassified during the reporting period, the date of change is indicated in parentheses.

[1] Includes countries that have no explicitly stated nominal anchor, but rather monitor various indicators in conducting monetary policy.

[2] The member participates in the European Exchange Rate Mechanism (ERM II).

[3] Within the framework of an exchange rate fixed to a currency composite, the Bank Al-Maghrib (BAM) adopted a monetary policy framework in 2006 based on various inflation indicators with the overnight interest rate as its operational target to pursue its main objective of price stability. Since March 2009, the BAM reference interest rate has been set at 3.25%.

[4] The exchange rate arrangement was reclassified retroactively, overriding a previously published classification.

[5] The de facto monetary policy framework is an exchange rate anchor to the U.S. dollar.

[6] The de facto monetary policy framework is an exchange rate anchor to a composite.

[7] This reclassification reflects a methodological correction and does not imply a judgment that there was an alteration in the exchange arrangement or other policies. The change is applied retroactively to April 30, 2008, the date on which the Revised System for the Classification of Exchange Rate Arrangements became effective.

[8] The central bank has taken preliminary steps toward inflation targeting and is preparing for the transition to full-fledged inflation targeting.

Source: International Monetary Fund, *Annual Report on Exchange Rate Arrangements and Monetary Policy Frameworks,* April 30, 2012. Classification of Exchange Rate Arrangements and Monetary Policy Frameworks, De Facto Exchange Rate Arrangements and Anchors of Monetary Policy as of April 30, 2012, http://www.imf.org/external/pubs/nft/2012/eaer/ar2012.pdf (accessed July 14, 2013).

INFLATION-TARGETING

In the *inflation-targeting* framework, an official inflation target is announced, along with a time horizon and commitment to achieve it. Thereafter, monetary policies are adjusted by the extent to which actual and forecasted inflation rates deviate from the announced targets.

OTHERS

In the *Other* framework, nations rely on numerous economic indicators to conduct their monetary policies. The IMF also uses this category when it has insufficient information about a nation to classify its monetary policy into one of the other categories.

    The countries and exchange rate classifications listed in Exhibit 15-28 are not etched in stone. Rather, they are snapshot pictures of exchange rate arrangements that are constantly in motion. During the past two decades (even as recently as the past few years), many of the countries listed in Exhibit 15-28 have changed their exchange rate systems.

MACRO MEMO   15-1

What Is the European Monetary Union?

In 1999, 11 of the 15 countries belonging to the European Union (EU) became members of the European Monetary Union (EMU). EMU members relinquished independent control over their money supplies to the European Central Bank (ECB), a supranational monetary authority located in Frankfurt, Germany. They also adopted the euro as their common currency.

Their hope was to create a currency of sufficient stature, size, and financial strength to compete with the U.S. dollar. EMU members also expected to benefit from more transparent prices, lower trade costs (e.g., no currency bid-ask spreads or hedging costs), economies of scale, and the development of mutual economic interests that might diffuse the potential for future wars. For economically weaker nations (e.g., Portugal, Spain, Italy, and Greece), the hope was for lower interest rates as a result of reduced inflationary risks and diminished inflationary expectations. Of course, there was a significant price to pay for these potential benefits, and this price was the loss of monetary autonomy and the ability to stimulate growth via monetary expansion.

From 1999 to 2002, the euro existed only in checking account form, rather than as a physical currency, like a bill or a coin. As a result, during this three-year transition period, the national currencies of member nations (e.g., the French franc, German mark, Italian lira, and Spanish peseta) continued to circulate, but they did so at absolutely fixed exchange rates—much like the exchange rates in the United States between pennies, nickels, dimes, quarters, half dollars, and dollars. In 2002, the EMU member currencies were abolished and completely replaced by the euro, which made its first appearance that year in physical form.

In 2013, there were 28 members of the EMU. Of them, 17 were euro-area members, and 11 were from outside the euro area. With more nations waiting in line to join, the big question in 2013 was whether any existing members (e.g., Greece) might leave. After years of grappling with economic recessions and popular unrest, a significant number of individuals in struggling nations longed for the days when they had their own currencies and independent central banks that might try to stimulate economic activity.

For example, members of the EMU have moved from the fixed band system, which existed before 1999, to a common currency (the euro), which fluctuates freely against foreign currencies. Other countries have moved from fixed (or relatively fixed) systems to floating exchange rate regimes.[20] Some have moved in the opposite direction, from managed currencies with no predetermined path to conventional fixed peg systems.[21] And, finally, still other countries have won their independence or ended military conflicts and therefore created new currencies.[22]

Exhibit 15-28 is helpful for matching specific countries with particular exchange rate arrangements, but one important piece of information that it does not show is when the exchange rate system chosen by a nation is (or was) a mistake. The choice of exchange rate regimes matters because selecting the wrong one, sticking with it for too long, and defending it with scarce resources (e.g., international reserves) can have a significant negative impact on a nation's economic health. By contrast, choosing the right exchange rate system is like putting wind in the sails of a clipper ship.

Exchange rate crises have occurred for centuries, and they are likely to reappear for years to come. Spectacular currency collapses occurred immediately following World War I, during the Great Depression, and just after World War II. The collapse of the Bretton Woods System in the early 1970s was just another example of an exchange rate system that eventually fizzled out.

Our search for failed exchange rate systems does not have to go back very far to capture the intrigue of rampant speculation, the frustration of bewildered central bankers, and the collapse of economic systems. During the past 20 years, there have been exchange rate disasters of considerable magnitude. For instance in 1992–1993, speculative attacks against European currencies caused the United Kingdom and Italy to leave the fixed band system. It also forced the Spanish peseta, Irish punt, Portuguese escudo, Swedish krona, and Finnish markka to devalue, pushed Sweden and Ireland to raise overnight interest rates above 500% and 300%, respectively, and led to the temporary imposition of exchange controls in Ireland, Spain, and Portugal.

In 1994, an overvalued Mexican peso led to international reserve losses amounting to billions of dollars, followed by a large depreciation of the peso, skyrocketing peso interest rates, and plummeting Mexican economic growth. The "tequila crisis," as it was called, spilled over, spreading contagion to other Latin American nations, as well. The collateral damage caused to other nations was (and is) often referred to as the "tequila effect."

About two-and-a-half years after the Mexican peso crisis (1997–1998), the "Asian Tiger" crisis broke out, with similar economic effects in nations

---

[20] Examples are Brazil, Liberia, Mexico, Norway, Papua New Guinea, Somalia, and Tanzania.

[21] Examples are Mauritania, Pakistan, Trinidad and Tobago, and Vietnam.

[22] Examples are the former Soviet Union satellites (e.g., Latvia, Azerbaijan, Belarus, Estonia, Moldova, Georgia, Armenia, Kazakhstan, Kyrgyz Republic, Lithuania, Slovak Republic, Ukraine, Uzbekistan, Mongolia, Tajikistan, and Turkmenistan), regions of former Yugoslavia (e.g., Bosnia and Herzegovina, Croatia, Macedonia, and Slovenia), African nations (e.g., Namibia, Mozambique, Democratic Republic of Congo, and Eritrea), and nations of Asia/Oceania (e.g., Palau and Myanmar).

such as Thailand, Korea, and the Philippines. In 1998, the Russian ruble depreciated, causing shockwaves that were felt worldwide. Indeed, it is likely that the 1999 depreciation of the Brazilian real was accelerated by the economic events in Russia. Finally, in early 2002, the Argentine debt crisis caused an overvalued peso, which had been fixed to the U.S. dollar on a one-to-one basis since 1991, to depreciate substantially.

SHOULD THERE BE ONE GLOBAL CURRENCY?

As previously mentioned, choosing and defending the wrong exchange rate system can cost a nation dearly in terms of lost income, diminished wealth, and sacrificed opportunities. The sources of these losses are often from the imprudent decisions of central bankers. As a result, some analysts and policymakers have begun to reconsider the need for each country to have its own domestic currency and central bank. Indeed, there are countries that have already decided to abolish their currencies, eliminate their central banks, and adopt foreign currencies as their own. Ecuador, El Salvador, and Panama are three examples of nations that have adopted the U.S. dollar as their domestic currency. *Dollarization* is the generic name given to the debate that surrounds this issue—a debate that focuses on the advantages and disadvantages countries derive from abolishing their currencies in favor of foreign ones or using a foreign currency (or currencies) in parallel with their own.

Dollarization is the term given to nations that abolish their domestic currencies and adopt a foreign currency or use a foreign currency in parallel with their own.

Some economists have argued that the process of unifying and globalizing currencies should not stop with just a few countries, but rather should be extended to the world. As you might imagine, adopting a global currency would have many advantages and disadvantages. So, the real issue is not whether negatives or positives exist but whether the world would derive *net* benefits from such a move.

On the positive side, a global currency would make international prices more transparent, thereby increasing competition. Travel would be easier, and international transactions would be less risky. Foreign exchange dealers and analysts, as well as the battery of experts in corporate treasuries who deal on a daily basis with exchange rate risk, would be freed by the thousands to pursue other, more productive careers. The bid-ask spreads on foreign exchange transactions would be eliminated, making international transactions cheaper.

Some of the advantages of a global currency are greater transparency, ease of use, better utilization of resources, and reduced costs.

Consider the magnitudes involved. Daily turnover on the foreign exchange markets is approximately $5.3 trillion, which means that yearly turnover is about $1,336 trillion.[23] Assuming an average bid-ask spread of only 5 basis points (i.e., 0.05% or 5/100th of 1%), the *annual* saving from a global currency would be worth approximately $668 billion.[24]

On the negative side, countries would lose the ability to respond to changing economic conditions by varying their exchange rates and/or money supplies. Both of these key economic variables would be controlled by a global central bank. Assuming that discretionary exchange rate adjustments

---

[23] (252 working days per year) × ($5.3 trillion per day) = $1,335.6 trillion per year
[24] $1,336 trillion/year × 0.0005 = $668 billion/year

and money supply changes can have positive effects on a nation's economic growth and stability (the verdict is still out on this issue), the loss of a central bank and monetary independence could be a huge sacrifice.

There are also political apprehensions about a global currency. For example, who would run the central bank, and how would it be run? Would its top priority be stable prices or low unemployment? Without the power to create money, the credit ratings of economically weak central governments could fall below the level of many large companies.

A human, emotional factor must also be considered in the debate over a global currency. Many people have the same feelings about their home currencies as they do about their flags, languages, cultures, and systems of measurement. These emotional ties could be huge barriers preventing the adoption of a common global currency.

> Some of the disadvantages of a global currency are the loss of discretionary monetary policy, increased credit risks for some national governments, political uneasiness, and barriers due to emotional ties to the domestic currencies.

The world is still quite a distance from adopting a single global currency, but there are signs that it is moving slowly toward three dominant currency areas (e.g., the dollar, euro, and yen or yuan areas). Clearly, the precedent for currency unification was set when 11 of the countries belonging to the EU established the EMU in 1999, by abolishing their currencies, creating the euro, and founding the European Central Bank.

CONCLUSION

There are different types of exchange rates; so it is important to choose the right one for the purpose at hand. This chapter discussed bilateral, effective, nominal, and real exchange rates. A bilateral exchange rate is the price of one currency in terms of another currency. An effective exchange rate is the price of one currency in terms of a weighted-average of foreign currencies. A nominal exchange rate is one that has not been adjusted for relative international prices, and a real exchange rate is a nominal exchange rate that has been adjusted for relative international prices. In most macroeconomic analyses, changes in real exchange rates are more important than changes in nominal rates because they show more accurately if and when consumer and business incentives should change.

Exchange rates are determined by the forces of supply and demand. When analyzing exchange rates, it is important to remember that the currency being valued is always placed on the horizontal axis of the supply and demand curves, and its price is always placed on the vertical axis. It is also vital to keep in mind that exchange rates are reciprocals of each other, and that the supply of Currency A in the (A-B) foreign exchange market is the mirror image of the demand for Currency B.

The major participants in the foreign exchange markets are importers, exporters, tourists, investors, speculators, governments, and central banks. The primary factors that affect their behaviors are relative changes in international prices, real GDP, interest rates/investment returns, tax rates, risks, expectations, and central bank intervention.

In general, the international value of Nation A's currency is inversely related to relative (i.e., domestic versus foreign) prices, real GDP, risks, and taxes. Central bank intervention and worsening expectations could also be the causes of declining currency values. By contrast, Nation A's currency value is directly related to relative international interest rates/investment returns, favorable expectations, and central bank intervention that push up the rate.

Exchange rate systems are categorized into four basic types: fixed, fixed band, managed (including the crawling peg), and flexible, which vary by the degree of central bank intervention. We will find in subsequent chapters that the choice of exchange rate system has large implications for a nation's ability to manage its own money supply. In particular, we will find that a flexible exchange rate regime permits a nation to pursue independent monetary policies; a fixed exchange rate system takes away this independence, and a hybrid system has some of the advantages and disadvantages of both.

REVIEW QUESTIONS

1. Is the following statement true, false, or uncertain? Briefly explain. "In the yen–peso foreign exchange market, an increase in the demand for pesos causes an increase in the supply of yen."

2. What is the "real" exchange rate, and why are changes in it usually more important in macroeconomic analyses than changes in the nominal exchange rate?

3. Suppose England's real exchange rate relative to the United States was 1.32. What does this mean? Is there an opportunity to arbitrage the markets? If so, explain how, and if not, explain why not.

4. Suppose England decided to fix its exchange rate relative to the euro as a precursor to joining the EMU. Under these circumstances, is it possible for England's real exchange rate relative to the euro to change?

5. If China's nominal exchange rate was fixed at 6.1 yuan per U.S. dollar, then the *real* exchange rate will depreciate if _____.

6. Suppose the Bank of Canada intervened in the foreign exchange market to lower the value of the Canadian dollar relative to the yen. What effect, if any, would this intervention have on Canada's monetary base?

7. Explain whether you agree or disagree with the following statement: "Foreign capital inflows cause the receiving country's monetary base to rise."

8. Using supply and demand analysis, explain the effect each of the following economic changes has on the Swedish krone value of the Argentine peso. Also, explain the effect each transaction has on the respective countries' monetary bases.

    a. A decline in the real risk-free interest rate on krone securities relative to peso securities
    b. An increase in Argentina's real GDP relative to Sweden
    c. A decline in Sweden's inflation rate relative to Argentina
    d. Intervention by the Banco Central de la República Argentina (the central bank of Argentina) to raise the value of the peso
    e. A growing expectation that Argentina will impose exchange controls on the peso

9. What are the major advantages and disadvantages of having a global currency? What name would you give the single currency (your own name or the name of a favored pet is not allowed)?

10. Based on the graph below, explain what happened to the value of the Indian rupee relative to the U.S. dollar between 1973 and 2013.

Source: Federal Reserve Bank of St. Louis, *Economic Research: Federal Reserve Economic Data,* http://research.stlouisfed.org/fred2// (accessed July 25, 2013).

DISCUSSION QUESTIONS

11. Suppose you read the following quote in the financial press: "Japanese capital that was flowing to the United States has now begun to return home." What are the implications of these inflows for Japan's M2 money supply, monetary base, real risk-free interest rate, value of the yen in terms of the dollar, and economic health?

12. Suppose there were strong speculative capital flows into the euro from the Nigerian naira due to political turmoil in Nigeria. Explain what would happen to the EMU's money supply, monetary base, and spot exchange rate. (Assume that interest rates did not change.)

13. Suppose the Moroccan dirham was tightly managed relative to a euro-dominated basket of currencies. Many business analysts felt the peg was useful for anchoring Morocco's inflation rate. Explain how a fixed exchange rate can anchor a country's inflation rate.

14. Why are fixed exchange rates a problem for any nation coming under intense speculative international pressure?

15. Explain whether the following statement makes economic sense: "A fixed exchange rate can cause an emerging country's real exchange rate to increase sharply when the emerging country's inflation rate does not fall to the level of industrialized nations."

16. Suppose you were an investment portfolio manager located in New York City and were satisfied with the composition of your internationally diversified portfolio until you read that the U.S. money supply was expected to grow rapidly during the next year relative to the euro money supply. What changes would you make to the portfolio? Explain.

17. Does the real exchange rate have meaning only for a country, or can a company derive meaningful benefits from constructing its own real exchange rate? Explain.

18. Suppose you read the following quote in a business magazine. Fully explain whether you agree with the author's logic and conclusions. "For some years now, the dirham, Morocco's currency, has been pegged to the euro. As a result, Morocco's money market (i.e., real loanable funds market) has been swamped due to remittances of Moroccan citizens who are living in Europe and sending weekly earnings home. Luckily, the nation's fixed exchange rate has acted as an anchor, allowing Morocco to ease the money supply without serious inflationary consequences."

19. Suppose Turkey was in the grip of a crisis that threatened the nation's chances of entering the EU. Explain why many analysts might feel that, if Turkey wanted to end decades of high inflation, it had to fix its exchange rate to the euro.

    a. Suppose that other analysts recommended a crawling peg exchange rate system. Explain a crawling peg system, and then explain its advantages and disadvantages relative to a fixed exchange rate regime.

20. From 2006 to 2013, the IMF wanted China to allow much more exchange rate flexibility between the yuan and the U.S. dollar. What reasons can you provide for why the Chinese government was reluctant to follow the IMF's advice?

21. Suppose the yuan floated relative to the U.S. dollar, and foreign investors became optimistic about financial investments in China. How would the capital flows resulting from this optimism affect the dollar value of the yuan? How would it affect China's real risk-free interest rate, monetary base, and money supply? Explain.

Appendix 15-1

Can the Supply of Foreign Exchange Slope Downward?

Normally, the supply of foreign exchange is upward sloping, but it is possible for it to slope downward, which means the relationship between the nominal exchange rate and the amount of foreign exchange supplied per period is inverse. This possibility is easiest to understand if we use an example and keep in mind that the supply of Swiss francs, in the dollar-Swiss franc foreign exchange market, is the mirror image of the demand for dollars. The results are summarized in Exhibit A15-1.

EXHIBIT A15-1	DOWNWARD-SLOPING SUPPLY OF SWISS FRANCS		
	Column 1	Column 2	Column 3	Column 4 (1/Col. 1)
Row 1	$/SFr exchange rate	Quantity of Swiss francs supplied per period (Figures in billions)	Quantity of dollars demanded per period (Figures in billions)	SFr/$ exchange rate
Row 2	$1.00/SFr	SFr 500	$500 (SFr 500 × $1.00/SFr = $500)	SFr 1.00/$
Row 3	$1.60/SFr	SFr 375 (SFr 0.625/$ × $600 = SFr 375)	$600 (20% increase in quantity of dollars demanded)	SFr 0.625/$

© 2015 John E. Marthinsen

Suppose the initial exchange rate is $1.00/SFr (Column 1, Row 2) and the amount of Swiss francs supplied per week is SFr 500 billion (Column 2, Row 2). This exchange rate can be restated as SFr 1.00/$ (Column 4, Row 2), which means the quantity of dollars demanded per week equals $500 billion (Column 3, Row 2).[25] Suppose the value of the Swiss franc rises by 60% from $1.00 to $1.60 (Column 1, Row 3). What will happen to the amount of Swiss francs supplied? To answer this question, let's look at it from Swiss importers' viewpoint.

When the Swiss franc appreciates from $1.00/SFr to $1.60/SFr, the value of the dollar depreciates from SFr 1/$ to SFr 0.625/$ (Column 4, Row 3). As a result, U.S. goods and services become cheaper to the Swiss. Suppose Swiss residents increase the amount of dollars they demand per period by 20%. Notice that this 20% increase in the amount demanded is smaller than the 60% reduction in the Swiss franc value of the dollar. As a result, the elasticity of demand for dollars is less than one, which means it is inelastic.

A 20% increase in the amount of dollars demanded per period raises Switzerland's weekly purchases from $500 billion (its original value, Column 3, Row 2) to $600 billion (Column 3, Row 3).[26] But demanding $600 billion per week at an exchange rate of SFr 0.625/$ means the Swiss are supplying only SFr 375 billion per week[27] (Column 2, Row 3) after the exchange rate changed, as compared to SFr 500 billion per week (Column 2, Row 2) prior to the change. As a result, the amount of Swiss francs supplied per week falls from SFr 500 billion to SFr 375 billion as the value of the Swiss franc rises from $1.00/SFr to $1.60/SFr. The consequence of these changes is the downward-sloping supply curve shown in Exhibit A15-1.

> If a nation's elasticity of demand for foreign goods and services is low, there can be an inverse relationship between exchange rates and the amount of domestic currency supplied to the foreign exchange market.

[25] SFr 500 billion × $1.00/SFr = $500 billion
[26] $500 billion/week ×1.2 = $600/week
[27] SFr 0.625/$ × $600 billion/week = $375 billion per week

Chapter 16

Balance of Payments Fundamentals

INTRODUCTION

Since World War II, international trade and investment flows have grown at much faster rates than world gross domestic product. Some nations,[1] such as the United States, that once thought they were relatively self-sufficient and therefore immune from foreign economic influences have learned quickly that the benefits of internationalization accrue only to those willing to pay the price of greater economic vulnerability. Other countries, such as Belgium, Germany, and France, have long known the benefits and exposures created by increased international trade and investment flows. Still others, such as Japan and China, have built economic development strategies based on export-led growth.

The purpose of this chapter is to provide a systematic way to analyze and understand the incentives behind international trade and investment flows, as well as their economic effects. It begins by describing the balance of payments, a statement that catalogues international transactions between residents of one nation and the rest of the world.

The chapter goes on to explain some fundamental economic concepts, such as the effect balance of payments transactions have on a nation's monetary base, the relationship between a country's balance of payments and foreign exchange markets, and the tautological (i.e., true by definition) relationship among a nation's current account, net domestic saving rate, and government budget surplus/deficit. Finally, the chapter ends by (1) taking a close look at the balance of payments as a sources and uses of funds statement, (2) defining and explaining the importance of frequently cited balance of payments measures, and (3) using the 1994 Mexican peso crisis as a macroeconomic case study.

Balance of payments reports are compiled by different domestic and international agencies, each using its own (slightly different) definitions, terminology, and reporting format. For instance, U.S. balance of payments statistics are reported not only by the Bureau of Economic Analysis of the Department of Commerce but also by the International Monetary Fund (IMF) and United Nations (UN). Due to the variety of reporting sources, cross-country comparisons can be problematic.

---

[1] Throughout this chapter, the words "nation" and "country" are used interchangeably with "union" and "area" so that currency areas, such as the European Monetary Union, are also covered.

This text focuses on the IMF's terminology, statistics, and reports because, unlike other sources, they are standardized, allow for cross-country comparisons, and cover most nations.[2] For business managers, who might be located anywhere in the world, understanding the IMF's approach to the balance of payments offers the greatest return for the time invested. Even though the terminology and format for reporting balance of payments (transactions) may vary, the analytical tools and framework explained in this chapter are applicable to any nation, regardless of location and time.

THE BASICS

WHAT IS THE BALANCE OF PAYMENTS?

The balance of payments is a summary of all *transactions* between the *residents* of one nation and the *residents* of the rest of the world during a given *time period*.

The balance of payments summarizes the transactions between the residents of one country and the rest of the world over a period of time.

To better understand the balance of payments, let's take a closer look at the italicized words and phrases in its definition.

TRANSACTIONS—NOT PAYMENTS

All transactions (monetary and nonmonetary) between residents and nonresidents should be included in a nation's balance of payments.[3] Therefore, this macroeconomic measure includes a wide variety of transnational interactions, such as imports and exports of goods and services, purchases and sales of natural resources, derivative deals, interest and dividend earnings, in-kind[4] gifts, monetary aid, remittances, loans, direct and financial investments, as well as central bank intervention in the foreign exchange markets.

The balance of payments includes all international transactions and not just bank-settled ones.

The term *balance of payments* can be misleading because there are many international transactions for which no immediate monetary "payment" is made. Barter exchanges, credit agreements, and real investments (e.g., shipping a machine abroad for use in a foreign factory) are just a few examples of the international transactions that enter into the balance of payments but for which no bank-settled payment is made.

BETWEEN RESIDENTS

Balance of payments transactions are between domestic and foreign residents and not between domestic and foreign citizens.

Balance of payments transactions are between *residents* and nonresidents and not between the *citizens* and noncitizens (i.e., citizens of foreign nations). Citizenship is a narrower concept than residency because it requires a legalized status (e.g., citizenship by birth or naturalization). Residency implies only

---

[2] *International Financial Statistics* is a monthly report published by the IMF. It contains balance of payments figures and other vital macroeconomic information on more than 200 countries and areas since 1948. The IMF database has approximately 32,000 time series and accounts for the vast majority of world trade. See http://www.imf.org/external/data.htm (accessed August 9, 2013).

[3] The verb "should be" is used because some international transactions evade detection, such as black market activities and tax evasion.

[4] "In kind" means that payment is in terms of goods, services, sacrificed debt, or sacrificed interest.

MACRO MEMO   16-1

Who Is a Resident?

For individuals and households, residency status can depend on a number of factors. Among them are a person's intention to remain in a country for one year or longer, the location of his/her personal dwellings, employment locus, migration and income tax status, asset holdings, citizenship, and portion of income received in a nation. As might be expected, the wide variety of individuals and personal circumstances requires nations to adjust and nuance their rules for diverse groups, such as foreign students, medical patients, ship crews, diplomats, military personnel, the staff of scientific stations, and civil servants employed in foreign nations. In general, residing in a country for one year or more or intending to do so qualifies most individuals as residents.

Students who travel abroad for full-time study might be interested to know that they are considered by the IMF to be residents of their home countries, even if their foreign studies are expected to continue for more than one year. This status changes if and when they intend to remain after graduation. Until such time, the tuition they pay is counted in the balance of payments as a service under the heading "travel."

that an individual's *primary center of predominant economic interest* is tied to a particular country.

For companies, residency depends on having a substantial connection to a country. Among the criteria are significant production capabilities, incorporation, income tax status, legal domicile, and compliance with certain national regulations.

> To be considered a resident (for balance of payments purposes), a person must remain in a nation for one year or more or intend to do so.

DURING A GIVEN TIME PERIOD

The term *balance of payments* can also be misleading because the word *balance* implies a stock concept, which means it is measured at a point in time. By contrast, the balance of payments is a flow concept that measures international transactions during a period of time.

By analogy, a bank statement is a stock measure because it shows an individual's *balance* at the end of an accounting period, like a month. The balance of payments does not show the balance at the end of the month but rather the net flows of funds into and out of the account during the course of that month.[5] Therefore, it shows both the flow of international transactions during a month (e.g., exports and imports) and changes in month-end balances (e.g., bank accounts).

> The balance of payments is a flow measure that always covers a period of time, rather than a point in time.

BALANCE OF PAYMENTS AND THE FOREIGN EXCHANGE MARKET

Balance of payments transactions are not the same as the supply and demand forces that enter into the foreign exchange market. The balance of payments is a much broader measure because it includes *all transactions* between domestic and foreign residents and not just those transactions for which there is an exchange of currencies.

The following example may help explain why a strict one-to-one relationship does not exist. Suppose a Japanese auto manufacturer sold cars on a

> Balance of payments transactions are broader than the supply and demand forces in the foreign exchange markets.

[5] Pity the term *balance of payments*. The word *balance* is incorrect, and the word *payments* is too narrow, which means the only descriptively accurate word in the phrase is *of*.

quarterly basis to an Australian auto dealership. These transactions would be counted in both Japan's and Australia's balance of payments because they are between domestic and foreign residents. If the Japanese manufacturer was willing to accept Australian dollars, rather than Japanese yen, then no foreign exchange transaction would take place. The Australian importer's bank account would fall and the Japanese exporter's bank account would rise by the same amount. In a similar way, if the Japanese manufacturer extended the Australian dealership a 90-day trade credit denominated in yen (or Australian dollars), then no foreign exchange transaction would occur. The Japanese manufacturer would simply increase its accounts receivable rather than its yen (or Australian dollar) bank account.

BALANCE OF PAYMENTS IN A NUTSHELL

A SIMPLE WAY TO VIEW THE BALANCE OF PAYMENTS

A simple and useful way to understand the balance of payments is by dividing it into two parts: current international transactions and net international borrowing/ lending transactions. If current international transactions are in deficit, then the nation's international expenditures exceed its earnings, and the country must be a net international borrower. By contrast, if current international transactions are in surplus, just the opposite occurs. International earnings exceed expenditures, and the nation must be a net international lender (investor). Finally, if the nation's current international transactions are in balance, then it has no need to be (and will not be) a net international borrower or lender (see Exhibit 16-1).

> In the balance of payments, current international transaction deficits equal net international borrowing, and current international transaction surpluses equal net international lending.

It is important to notice in Exhibit 16-1 that the equal sign separating current international transactions and net international borrowing/lending has three lines, which means this relationship is a tautology and also the basis for why the balance of payments, as a whole, must sum to zero.

BALANCE OF PAYMENTS ALWAYS SUMS TO ZERO

When taken as a whole, the balance of payments must sum to zero. We know this for a fact because the balance of payments is a sources and uses of funds statement.[6] For every use of funds, there must be a source. Because sources of

$Exhibit$ **16–1**	A SIMPLE WAY TO VIEW THE BALANCE OF PAYMENTS	
Current International Transactions	$\equiv$	**Net International Borrowing/Lending**
Deficit	Implies	Net International borrowing
Surplus	Implies	Net International lending
Balance	Implies	Net International borrowing/lending = 0

© 2015 John E. Marthinsen

---

[6] A full explanation of the balance of payments as a sources and uses of funds statement is provided in "**The Rest of the Story**" section of this chapter.

EXHIBIT 16-2	BALANCE OF PAYMENTS ≡ SOURCES & USES OF FUNDS STATEMENT

Balance of Payments Is a Sources and Uses of Funds Statement

Uses of Funds	Must equal	Sources of Funds
Negative values	Must equal	Positive values

The sum of uses (negative values) and sources (positive values) must equal zero

© 2015 John E. Marthinsen

funds are positive values in the balance of payments, and uses are negative values, their sum must equal zero. This important identity is summarized in Exhibit 16-2.

> The entire balance of payments always sums to zero.

WHAT ARE BALANCE OF PAYMENTS SURPLUSES AND DEFICITS?

If the positives always equal the negatives, then how can a nation have a balance of payments deficit or surplus? The answer is that surplus and deficit measures are found by considering only segments of the balance of payments. Deficits occur when the sum of the minus transactions for a particular account or combination of accounts is greater than the sum of the plus transactions. Surpluses occur when just the opposite happens. Therefore, any subsegment of the balance of payments can be in deficit or surplus if the rest is in surplus or deficit.

> Surpluses and deficits measure only parts of the total balance of payments.

"**The Rest of the Story**" section of this chapter defines and explains the most frequently used balance of payments measures. Two of them are of particular interest in macroeconomics, namely, the reserves account, because it reflects net central bank intervention in the foreign exchange markets, and the current account, because it is frequently misunderstood and can become the focal point of misdirected discussions and policy decisions, especially concerning unemployment problems. In "**The Rest of the Story**" section of this chapter, we explore in greater detail the meaning and implications of various balance of payments measures. For now, let's investigate the three major parts of the balance of payments.

THREE MAJOR PARTS OF THE BALANCE OF PAYMENTS

Exhibit 16-3 shows the three major accounts in a nation's balance of payments: the current account (CA), capital account (KA),[7] and financial account (FA). Relating the items in Exhibit 16-3 to the ones in Exhibit 16-1, current international transactions are equivalent to the sum of the CA plus KA, and net international borrowing/lending is equivalent to FA.

> The three major parts of the balance of payments are the CA, KA, and FA.

If (CA + KA) is negative, then the nation is spending internationally more than it earns, and if it is positive, the reverse is true. Similarly, FA is positive when a nation is a net international borrower and negative when it is a net international lender. Therefore, (CA + KA + FA) must equal zero. See Exhibit 16-4.

Let's briefly explain each of these three accounts and their components.

> CA + KA ≡ Current International Transactions
> FA ≡ Net International Borrowing/Lending Transactions
> CA + KA + FA ≡ 0

---

[7] The abbreviation for capital account is KA and not CA because the letter *C* has already been taken by the word "current" in *current account*.

EXHIBIT 16-3 PRINCIPAL PARTS OF THE BALANCE OF PAYMENTS

Current International Transactions		Net International Borrowing/Lending
Current Account (CA)		**Financial Account (FA)**
Exports/imports (goods and services)		Direct Investments
Net International Income		Portfolio Investments
Remittances/Transfers	≡	Financial Derivatives
Capital Account (KA)		Other Investments
Tangible asset transactions		Reserve Assets (RA)
Intangible asset transactions		Net Errors and Omissions
Capital transfers (debt forgiveness)		
Deficits/Surplus: CA & KA	≡	**Net Borrowing/Lending: FA**

© 2015 John E. Marthinsen

EXHIBIT 16-4 $CA + KA + FA \equiv 0$

Current International Transactions	≡	Net International Borrowing/Lending
Deficit $(CA + KA) < 0$	Implies	Net International borrowing $FA > 0$
Surplus $(CA + KA) > 0$	Implies	Net International lending $FA < 0$
In balance $(CA + KA) = 0$	Implies	Net International borrowing/lending $= 0$ $FA = 0$
	Therefore, $CA + KA + FA \equiv 0$	

© 2015 John E. Marthinsen

The current account includes international exports and imports of goods and services, as well as net international income, remittances, and transfers.

CURRENT ACCOUNT (CA)

The CA includes international exports and imports of goods and services, as well as net international income payments/receipts, remittances, and transfers.

Exports and Imports of Goods and Services

Goods are the result of a production process and include internationally traded products over which ownership rights can be both established and transferred to others. In general, purchases and sales of consumer merchandise, as well as products used in manufacturing processes and nonmonetary gold fit these criteria.[8] By contrast, the sale of labor services, natural resources, and financial assets are included in other accounts.

[8] *Nonmonetary gold* is gold that is not part of the official reserves owned by a nation's central bank or government. It is used for private purposes, such as jewelry manufacturing.

Services are internationally traded intangibles for which ownership and transfer rights may be problematic because the acts of producing, selling, and consuming them are often difficult (or impossible) to separate. Examples of internationally traded services are communications, computer software, information services, consulting, financial services, franchises, insurance policies, leasing, licenses, maintenance, postal deliveries, recreation, royalties, technical support, transportation, and travel (tourist and business). Payments for the use of intellectual property are also included, such as for research and development, patents, trademarks, copyrights, industrial processes and designs, and trade secrets.

Net International Income

Net international income is earned (or paid) as compensation for the *temporary* use of labor (wages), financial resources (interest), business enterprises (profits), and natural resources (rent).[9] Net wages equal the sum of compensation received by domestic residents from foreign companies minus the compensation paid to foreign residents by domestic companies. Similarly, net interest, profits, and rent are the difference between the international returns received from and paid to foreign residents.

Profits enter prominently into the net international income account and can be either distributed as dividends or reinvested. Portfolio returns are mainly in the form of interest, dividends, and capital gains. Rent is compensation for right to use an asset on a temporary basis. Examples are payments for subsoil, fishing, forestry, and grazing rights. Therefore, if China Forestry Inc. purchased timber rights in Alberta, Canada, its periodic payments would be counted as rent.

> Net international income reflects compensation for the *temporary* use of nations' labor (wages), financial resources (interest), business enterprises (profits), and natural resources (rent).

Remittances/Transfers

Remittances and transfers are one-sided transactions for which nothing of value is given in return. Most remittances are funds sent home by migrant (emigrant) workers. Examples of international transfers are government aid, charitable contributions, social contributions, social benefits, pensions, expenditures that promote international cooperation, and insurance claims. These outlays may be paid in cash or in-kind, and payments also include taxes on income and wealth. The IMF refers to "remittances and transfers" as "secondary income" because it represents redistributive payments, as opposed to expenditures for productive assets. By contrast, the financial press often refers to "remittances and transfers" as "unilateral transfers" or "unrequited transfers."

> Remittances and transfers are one-sided transactions.

Capital Account (KA)

The KA includes both tangible and intangible asset transactions, as well as transfers, that are not included in the CA.[10] Therefore, the CA and KA are two parts of a whole, which is financed by the FA. In general, the KA

---

[9] The IMF uses the term "primary income" to describe net income flows from wages, interest, profits, and rent.
[10] IMF uses the term "nonproduced nonfinancial assets" for natural resources and related assets.

tends to play a minor role in the balance of payments of most developed nations.

The transactions included in the KA are for the *acquisition and disposal of ownership rights* to (as opposed to the temporary use of) (1) natural resources,[11] (2) legal and accounting creations, and (3) marketing assets. To be included as a KA transaction, there must be clear ownership rights. Examples of natural resource transactions are sales of land (e.g., for foreign embassies), reservoirs, and lakes, as well as fishing, mineral, forestry, and air space rights.

Under a broad umbrella called "legal and accounting creations," the KA includes internationally traded contracts, leases, licenses, and goodwill. Similarly, under the category called "marketing assets," the KA includes brand names, mastheads, trademarks, logos, and domain names, but only when they are sold separately from the company that owns them. Therefore, the independent sale of PepsiCo's domain name to a French beverage company would be included in the KA.

> **The capital account includes capital transfers (mainly debt forgiveness), as well as the acquisition and disposal of nonproduced nonfinancial assets, which include natural resources, contracts, leases, licenses, and marketing assets (including goodwill).**

Capital transfers are mainly for international liability forgiveness and the transfer of assets other than cash or inventories.[12] For example, the *Haiti Debt Relief and Earthquake Recovery Act*, which was passed by the U.S. Congress in 2010, is an example of a capital transfer. Capital transfers also include debt forgiveness, which is a narrower concept than you might first expect because it includes only voluntary cancellations of all or part of outstanding debts (i.e., principal, interest arrears, and accrued interest), as opposed to the cancellation of future obligations.[13] Capital transfers are often large but also relatively infrequent.

FINANCIAL ACCOUNT

The *financial account* reflects a nation's net international borrowing or lending transactions. When the sum of a country's CA plus KA is negative (i.e., in deficit), then the FA must be positive, which means the country is a net international borrower. Similarly, when the sum of a nation's CA plus KA is positive (i.e., in surplus), then the FA must be negative, which means the country is a net international lender (investor).[14] Included in the FA is a wide assortment of real and financial cross-border investments, which will be explained in detail, later.

> **The financial account is the financing or lending counterbalance to the current plus capital accounts.**

In balance of payments discussions, we must be careful to treat the word *investments* very broadly because it includes changes in bonds, loans, bank deposits, ownership of company shares, and direct investments. Six functional categories of FA transactions are used to differentiate these investments: direct

---

[11] A helpful way to distinguish the natural resource transactions included in the capital account from those in the current account is to remember that capital account natural resources (e.g., land) remain in the nation after they are sold. By contrast, oil is also a natural resource, but sales to nonresidents cause it to leave the country, which means they are included as merchandise exports in the current account.

[12] By contrast, transfers in the current account affect after-tax income, which influences the consumption of goods and services. Other capital transfers are inheritances, taxes on asset values, as well as investment grants by governments for fixed assets and capital formation.

[13] Debt forgiveness is not the same as debt write-offs or debt repudiations.

[14] Notice that international investments are recorded in a nation's financial account, and the returns on these investments are recorded in the current account, under net international income.

investments, portfolio investments, financial derivatives, other investments, reserve assets, and net errors and omissions.

Direct Investments

Direct investments include the purchase and sale of international assets that have lasting interests, such as the construction of foreign production facilities, reinvested earnings, intercompany capital transactions, and changes in equipment. Direct investments also occur with purchases of substantial equity interests in foreign companies, where "substantial equity interests" means ownership of 10% or more of the voting shares. Direct investments can be monetary or in kind (e.g., a company supplying a machine to its foreign affiliate), as well as mergers, acquisitions, corporate restructurings, and borrowing to support government-owned or controlled enterprises.

To qualify as a direct investment, owners must have significant control or influence over the foreign company.

Portfolio Investments

Portfolio investments are mainly for cross-border exchanges of debt and equity[15] instruments that are not otherwise counted as direct investments or reserve assets.

Financial Derivatives

Changes in the market value of *financial derivatives* are included in the balance of payments, rather than changes in their notional values. This is important because the initial market value of most derivatives is zero, while at the same time their notional values can be many million (or even hundreds of million) dollars. For example, a forward currency contract with a notional value of $100 million (normally) has asset and liability values of equal size, causing its initial market value to equal zero. Only with changes in the currency's value (i.e., underlier's value) would the market value of this forward contract vary. Financial derivatives are off-balance sheet transactions that have become very popular throughout the world due to their ability to efficiently transform risks faced by the private and public users.

Changes in the market value of financial derivatives are part of the balance of payments.

Other Investments

Other Investments is a residual account that measures transactions and changes in positions that are not included in direct investments, portfolio investments, financial derivatives, or reserve assets. At first glance, *Other Investments* may appear to be a relatively unimportant account, but this is hardly the case. In fact, this account is among the most active and important in the balance of payments because it includes changes in bank deposits, trade credits, advances, and loans. These transactions are crucial because the balance of payments is a double-entry bookkeeping system that requires two accounting entries for each transaction. Because at least one side of most transactions is a payment or receipt, the *Other Investments* account is quite active.

The *Other Investments* account includes changes in bank deposits, which makes it one of the most active balance of payments components.

[15]The equity holdings included in portfolio investments have ownership rights less than 10% of the voting shares.

MACRO MEMO   16-2

Be Careful of the Terms "Capital Account" and "Capital Flows"

The term "capital account" is often used in the financial press and also in many academic articles when referring to real and financial cross-border investments, but the IMF uses this term to describe the purchase and sale of natural resources and capital transfers. Confusion can result when news articles or technical reports refer to international "capital flows" or "capital flight." Usually, in the context of the article or report, it is easy to understand what the author means. For example, if the focus is on international currency speculation or cross-border investments in factories, mergers, or acquisitions, then the word "capital" is referring to the IMF's FA and not its KA.

Reserves Account (RA)

The *reserves account* (RA) is a summary of the *changes in* a nation's official international reserves, which a central bank and/or government authority can use to intervene in the foreign exchange markets. These assets must be highly liquid and unconditionally available to a central bank for immediate use. Among the most important reserve assets are holdings of convertible foreign currencies (cash and deposits), securities denominated in foreign currencies, monetary gold, other precious metals, special drawing rights (SDRs), a nation's reserve position at the IMF, and borrowing rights from other central banks (see Exhibit 16-5). It is important to remember that the balance of payments is a flow measure. Therefore, the value of a nation's reserve assets is not recorded in the balance of payments but rather *changes in the value* of these official reserves.

> The reserves account shows net changes in the assets a central bank can use to intervene in the foreign exchange markets.

Net Errors and Omissions

The *net errors and omissions* account is an accounting necessity because, taken as a whole, the balance of payments must always sum to zero. At the same time, individual accounts in the balance of payments are subject to estimation mistakes, inaccuracies due to poor data quality, measurement errors, and incomplete data, which may cause the sum of all balance of payments accounts to be greater or less than zero. When this happens, the net errors and

EXHIBIT 16-5   COMPONENTS OF THE RESERVES ACCOUNT

The Reserves Account includes changes in a central bank's holdings of:

- Foreign currencies and deposits
- Foreign currency-denominated securities (debt and equity)
- Monetary gold and other precious metals
- Special drawing rights
- Reserve position in the IMF
- Net borrowing rights from foreign central banks (swap arrangements)
- Financial derivative values

MACRO MEMO   16-3

Why Are Monetary Gold and Precious Metals a Part of Reserves Account?

Monetary gold and other precious metals cannot be used directly to raise the value of a nation's currency, but they can be used indirectly. To understand why, suppose the U.S. Federal Reserve wanted to raise the dollar's value relative to the euro but did not have sufficient euro reserves to purchase the required amount of dollars. The central bank could sell some of its monetary gold holdings, purchase euros, and then use the euros to purchase dollars, thereby raising the dollar's value. For this reason, monetary gold and other precious metals are part of a nation's RA.

MACRO MEMO   16-4

What Are Special Drawing Rights?

Special drawing rights (SDRs) were created by the IMF in 1969 as a means of providing needed liquidity for the world's rapidly expanding international trade and investment flows. An SDR is not a physical currency. Rather, it is a monetary account (like a checking account) that central banks and/or governments hold in the IMF. An SDR represents an unconditional right to obtain foreign exchange or other reserve assets from other IMF members. Originally, it had a value of $1, but in 1974, the SDR's value was changed to a weighted basket of 16 currencies. In 1981, the basket was changed to five currencies. Since the euro's creation in 1999, the SDR has been valued as a weighted average of four currencies: the U.S. dollar, euro-area euro, Japanese yen, and British pound.

MACRO MEMO   16-5

Are Sovereign Wealth Funds a Part of Reserve Assets?

Sovereign wealth funds (SWFs) hold, manage, and/or administer large pools of financial assets to achieve certain macroeconomic objectives. They are often byproducts of massive cash inflows from privatization programs or the result of balance of payments surpluses created by a dominant export (e.g., oil) or central bank intervention in the foreign exchange markets to reduce the domestic currency's value. If a SWF is on the books of a central bank (or an agency of the central government) and the central bank has substantial control over its assets, then changes in the SWF's net assets are included in the RA. By contrast, if the funds are invested in long-term assets and managed independently from the central bank, they do not qualify as reserve assets.

---

omissions account is adjusted to make sure the sum of the entire balance of payments equals zero. Therefore, if all the other accounts in a nation's balance of payments sum to −$100 billion, the net errors and omissions account would be set to +$100 billion so the total of all the accounts equals zero. While the net errors and omissions account may seem trivial, it is not. Wild fluctuations in errors and omissions can hamper balance of payments interpretations and act as bellwethers of more serious economic issues (e.g., burgeoning black market activity).

> The net errors and omissions account is adjusted to ensure that the sum of reported balance of payments figures equals zero.

RESERVES ACCOUNT AND CURRENT ACCOUNT IMBALANCES

Because the RA and CA hold special meanings in macroeconomics, this section explains the truths, fallacies, and consequences of deficits and surpluses in these balance of payments measures.

RESERVES ACCOUNT

Changes in the RA are important because they reflect active central bank intervention in the foreign exchange markets, which alters the nation's monetary base. If these transactions are not offset, they may simultaneously affect the monetary bases of foreign nations. In general, most RA transactions are intended to alter exchange rate levels or moderate their speed of adjustment. Some central banks also use this account as a normal part of their monetary operations to expand or contract their nations' money supplies.

Changes in the Reserves Account and the Monetary Base

In Chapter 9, "Who Controls the Money Supply and How?" we learned how central banks control and adjust their domestic money supplies. To simplify our analysis, we drew a hypothetical horizontal line across the page, with central banks above the line and everything else below it (see Exhibit 16-6).

We found that a central bank can increase its international reserves by crossing this imaginary horizontal line to purchase foreign currencies, thereby sending domestic monetary base below the line and taking foreign currencies above it. As a result, purchases of foreign exchange by a central bank increase the nation's monetary base, and sales cause it to fall. In effect, central bank intervention in the foreign exchange markets has monetary effects that are almost identical to open market operations (i.e., the buying and selling of government securities).

> Central bank intervention in the foreign exchange markets changes a nation's monetary base and money supply.

EXHIBIT 16-6	EFFECT OF INCREASING INTERNATIONAL RESERVE ASSETS ON THE MONETARY BASE

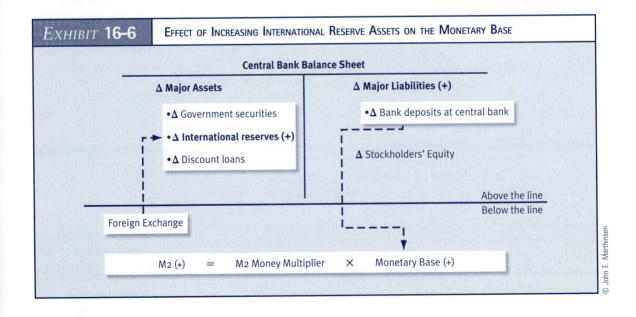

© John E. Marthinsen

Suppose the U.S. Federal Reserve held $150 billion of official reserve assets and wanted to increase the international value of the dollar relative to the euro. If the exchange rate were €1/$ and the Fed purchased $20 billion in the foreign exchange market, it would need to use reserves worth €20 billion. By supplying €20 billion to the foreign exchange market, the Fed would demand $20 billion, thereby increasing the dollar's value relative to the euro (e.g., say, to €1.05/$).[16] At the same time, by purchasing these dollars, the Fed would also remove them from the market (from below the line), thereby reducing the U.S. monetary base (see Exhibit 16-7).

Our example of Federal Reserve intervention in the foreign exchange market highlights four important points. First, a nation's ability *to raise* the international value of its currency by intervening directly in the foreign exchange market is limited by the amount of reserve assets it holds or can access by borrowing. Second, the domestic currency is not included in a nation's official reserves. This is logical because the domestic currency cannot be used in the foreign exchange markets to raise its own value. Take, for example, the Fed, which has unlimited access to dollars. If it were to demand dollars in the foreign exchange market with newly created dollars, the transaction would be self-canceling.

> Central banks can intervene in the foreign exchange markets only if they have sufficient international reserves. The domestic currency is not part of a nation's international reserves.

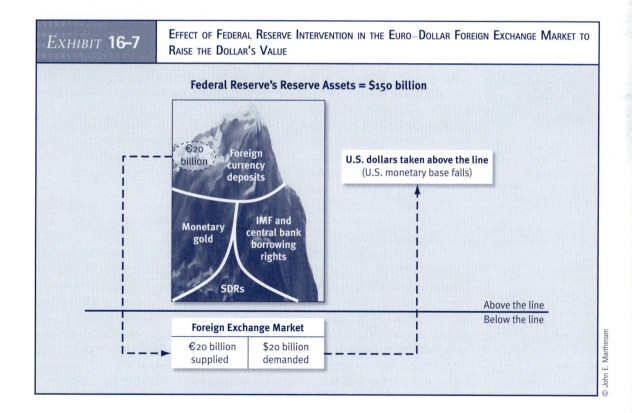

| EXHIBIT 16-7 | EFFECT OF FEDERAL RESERVE INTERVENTION IN THE EURO–DOLLAR FOREIGN EXCHANGE MARKET TO RAISE THE DOLLAR'S VALUE |

Federal Reserve's Reserve Assets = $150 billion

€20 billion — Foreign currency deposits

Monetary gold

IMF and central bank borrowing rights

SDRs

U.S. dollars taken above the line
(U.S. monetary base falls)

Above the line
Below the line

Foreign Exchange Market

| €20 billion supplied | $20 billion demanded |

© John E. Marthinsen

---

[16] This is the same as saying that an increased supply of euros would lower the euro's value relative to the U.S. dollar from $1.00/€ to $0.952/€ (i.e., $1.00/€1.05 = $0.952/€).

The third lesson to be drawn from Exhibit 16-7 is that a central bank can lose a large portion, and perhaps all, of its reserve assets by supporting for too long an overvalued exchange rate. It is for this reason that reserve assets are represented in the exhibit as a mountain of limited size. Every time a central bank intervenes in the foreign exchange market to raise the value of the domestic currency, a portion of its mountain of reserve assets is eroded.

Finally, Exhibit 16-7 shows foreign exchange market intervention by a central bank affects both the domestic and foreign monetary bases. For example, if the Federal Reserve held its reserves as deposits in foreign central banks (i.e., above the line), then these funds would not have been part of the foreign nations' monetary bases. As a result, their injection into the world economy (below the line) would increase the monetary base and money supply of the foreign nation(s) that issued these currencies. In an ironic twist of roles, the U.S. central bank, in its attempt to change the value of the dollar, would affect both its own monetary base and also the monetary bases of foreign nations.

CURRENT ACCOUNT

Besides the RA, the CA attracts considerable attention in international macroeconomic discussions and analyses. A nation's CA includes its imports and exports of goods and services, international flows of income, remittances, and transfers. As one of the most popular and frequently reported balance of payments measures, it is often used for international comparisons in a wide variety of debates and studies related to employment, growth, and development. Important to remember is that CA deficits must be financed by surpluses in the combined KA and FA, just as CA surpluses must be complemented by combined KA and FA deficits.

For example, if Peru ran CA deficits, it would likely finance them by borrowing internationally, liquidating international investments, and/or selling official reserves.[17] By contrast, if Peru ran CA surpluses, it would most likely use the funds to purchase foreign investments, repay private or government foreign debts, and/or increase official reserve assets.

For these reasons, CA deficits imply rising net international debt levels for nations and/or the depletion of their reserve assets. Both of these effects *could have* disquieting economic consequences.

For example, debt could reach levels where international creditors become concerned about a nation's ability to repay its obligations. To acquire further loans, the borrowing nation might have to pay hefty interest premiums to cover the added country risk. New financing could also be sharply curtailed or eliminated. Similarly, if the country continually uses its reserve assets to finance CA deficits, at some point, these reserves could be exhausted, thereby extinguishing the nation's ability to finance future deficits in this way.

The international debt crisis of the 1980s is a good example of the difficulties nations can face when they borrow too much. Fear that some heavily indebted, developing nations, like Argentina, Bolivia, Mexico, and Peru, might

---

[17] KA is excluded from this discussion because it is not a financing item and is usually small/immaterial.

default on loans worth hundreds of billions of dollars created panic and caused sharp reductions in loans to these countries.[18] Net capital inflows to these developing nations turned into net capital outflows, and much-needed funding ended up carrying higher interest costs, reflecting growing risk premiums.

For countries like Peru, not only was the flow of international capital dramatically curtailed, but the nation also used up virtually all of its international reserves. The situation in Mexico, Brazil, and other Latin American nations was similar. Without access to international capital markets, they could not fund CA deficits or roll over existing debts. As a result, some of them declared debt moratoriums.[19]

Ultimate Causes of Current Account Surpluses and Deficits

Between 2000 and the end of 2012, the United States had a continuous stream of CA deficits. During the same period, Japan and China had uninterrupted surpluses in their CAs (see Exhibit 16-8). What causes these deficits and surpluses? For nations that wish to reduce such imbalances, what needs to be done?

Extensive political and economic attention has focused on protectionism (e.g., tariffs, quotas, subsidies, and exchange rate controls) as a means of solving CA problems. Behind many of these arguments has been the persistent notion that, to cure CA deficits, a "level international playing field" is needed and, for that to happen, foreign nations must reduce their trade restrictions. In the absence of such changes, large nations often threaten to impose their own penalties.

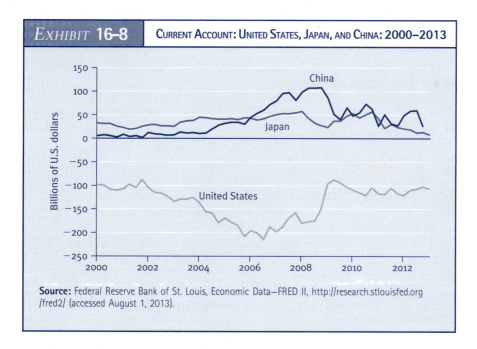

EXHIBIT 16–8   **CURRENT ACCOUNT: UNITED STATES, JAPAN, AND CHINA: 2000–2013**

Source: Federal Reserve Bank of St. Louis, Economic Data—FRED II, http://research.stlouisfed.org/fred2/ (accessed August 1, 2013).

---

[18] The countries that were generally associated with the 1980s' debt crisis were Argentina, Bolivia, Brazil, Chile, Colombia, Côte D'Ivoire, Ecuador, Mexico, Morocco, Nigeria, Peru, the Philippines, Uruguay, Venezuela, and Yugoslavia.

[19] A moratorium is a temporary suspension of debt payments.

Exhibit 16–9	COMPONENTS OF GDP: AGGREGATE DEMAND PERSPECTIVE
	$$GDP \equiv C + I + G + NE$$
	Condition 1

© John E. Marthinsen

Can protectionist measures play important roles in correcting CA deficits? Let's put this question into a broader perspective that draws on some basic economic principles of national income accounting. Recall that gross domestic product (GDP) is the market value of all final goods and services produced by a nation during a given time period. There are two equally valid and fruitful ways to define GDP. One way is by using the four components of aggregate demand, which are personal consumption expenditures (C), gross private domestic investment (I), government expenditures on final goods and services (G), and the balance on goods and services (NE). Let's call this relationship Condition 1 (see Exhibit 16-9).

Notice that Condition 1 has an equal sign with three bars, which (as pointed out previously) means the relationship is a definitional identity—there is no disagreement about its validity.

Another way to define GDP is by the uses to which the household sector puts its income. We know from our circular-flow discussion in Chapter 2, "Taking an Economic Pulse: Measuring National Output and Income" that income paid to the household sector can be used for personal consumption expenditures (C), personal saving (S), and taxes (T). Let's call this relationship Condition 2 (see Exhibit 16-10).

Notice that Condition 2 also has an equal sign with three bars, which means the relationship is definitional.

By combining Conditions 1 and 2, canceling like terms, and rearranging elements, we arrive at our goal, $NE \equiv (S - I) + (T - G)$, which says that a nation's balance on goods and services (NE) must equal the sum of its net private saving/investment $(S - I)$ plus the net government surplus/deficit $(T - G)$.[20] Let's call this relationship Condition 3 (see Exhibit 16-11).

> The current account is approximately equal to net private saving/investment plus the net government surplus/deficit. $CA \cong (S - I) + (T - G)$.

Because the balance on goods and services is nearly the same as the CA, we will substitute "current account" for "balance on goods and services" in Exhibit 16-12 and call this useful relationship Condition 4, which is: $CA \cong (S - I) + (T - G)$. See Exhibit 16-12.

Condition 4 is an important relationship in international macroeconomics on a number of levels but mainly because it shows what a nation has to change in order to correct a CA deficit or surplus. To make the CA more

Exhibit 16-10	COMPONENTS OF GDP: INCOME PERSPECTIVE
	$$GDP \equiv C + S + T$$
	Condition 2

© John E. Marthinsen

[20] Remember that government surpluses/deficits include national, state, and local surpluses/deficits.

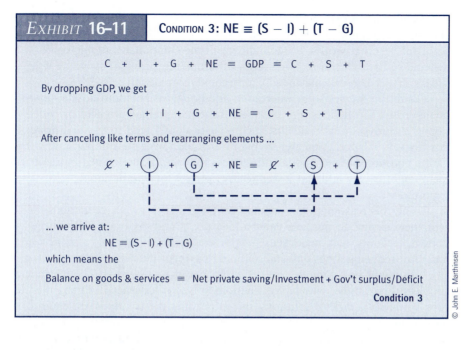

EXHIBIT 16-11 | **CONDITION 3: NE ≡ (S − I) + (T − G)**

$$C + I + G + NE \equiv GDP \equiv C + S + T$$

By dropping GDP, we get

$$C + I + G + NE \equiv C + S + T$$

After canceling like terms and rearranging elements ...

$$\cancel{C} + I + G + NE \equiv \cancel{C} + S + T$$

... we arrive at:

$$NE \equiv (S − I) + (T − G)$$

which means the

Balance on goods & services ≡ Net private saving/Investment + Gov't surplus/Deficit

Condition 3

© John E. Marthinsen

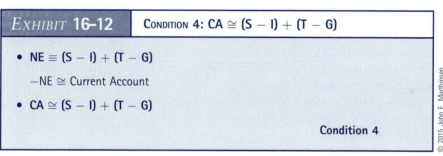

EXHIBIT 16-12 | **CONDITION 4: CA ≅ (S − I) + (T − G)**

- **NE ≡ (S − I) + (T − G)**

  −NE ≅ Current Account

- **CA ≅ (S − I) + (T − G)**

Condition 4

© 2015 John E. Marthinsen

positive or less negative, the sum of net private saving/investment plus the net government surplus/deficit must increase. To make it more negative or less positive, the opposite must occur.

Condition 4 also shows that, if a nation's private sector invests more than it saves and the government sector runs a budget deficit, the CA must be negative. No amount of political or economic rhetoric can change this basic fact, and no solution offered can correct this imbalance without making the sum of net private saving/investment plus the net government surplus/deficit more positive.

In the absence of economic growth, reducing a deficit or creating a surplus in the CA means finding ways to increase saving (i.e., reduce consumption expenditures), restrain investment, raise tax revenues, and/or reduce government spending. All of these policies are problematic because they are contractionary and could drive the nation into a recession. If they do, then one might question the government's motivation for prioritizing the reduction of CA deficits over increasing real GDP growth and creating jobs.

In the absence of economic growth, enacting policies to make CA more positive can be economically painful.

Turning a CA deficit into a surplus (or lowering a CA deficit) is easier in a climate of economic growth because a nation does not have to rob Peter to pay Paul. In other words, growth allows all the components of aggregate demand to rise. The correction comes from making sure that spending rises slower than GDP, causing the CA to become more positive.

Condition 4 gives some interesting additional insights into how a nation might reduce CA deficits. For instance, if the national government provided saving incentives to its residents, such policies would tend to create a more positive CA balance. A greater saving rate would lower consumption, and if a nation consumed fewer goods and services than it produced, then more of them might be available (at lower relative prices) for international exportation.

Using this reasoning, government proposals, such as tax deductions on retirement saving accounts, a value-added tax,[21] and tax breaks on college savings accounts, may make sense—both in their own right and also as a means of reducing a nation's international payment deficits.

You might be asking yourself, "If the answer to a current account deficit problem is so simple, why haven't nations solved it long ago?" Often, the problem is not a lack of solutions, but rather that the solutions are painful and/or involve difficult tradeoffs. Moreover, with every solution comes new problems, and sometimes unknown problems are perceived as worse than the familiar old ones. Finally, superimposed on all these decisions is the web of vested interest groups (e.g., unions and lobbies) and political logrolling deals that can play significant parts in our political process. This added political dimension complicates already difficult economic decisions.

Solutions to economic problems cannot ignore political and social issues.

For instance, consider the suggestion that the United States introduce a value-added tax. Such a tax would encourage saving by discouraging consumption, and if it raised government revenues, the tax might reduce U.S. budget deficits. Therefore, a value-added tax could have a double-barreled positive effect on the U.S. CA.

But what impact would such taxes have on public incentives to work? Might workers be discouraged? How would you answer critics who argued that government spending should be cut before a single penny more was paid in taxes? How could you ensure that the value-added tax was fair and did not raise the cost of living disproportionately for low-income earners (i.e., make sure it was not regressive)? Any reasoned change in policy needs to address a multitude of economic questions before it can be passed, but it also has to overcome the multitude of vested interest groups that are gored by any changes in legislation.

Nations with budget deficits may have current account surpluses.

What the International Condition Does Not Say: Condition 4 does not say that any country with a budget surplus will necessarily have a surplus in its CA. From 1989 to 1996 (just before the Asian Tiger crisis), Thailand

---

[21] A *value-added tax* is a tax imposed on a product whenever its value increases at each stage between production, distribution, and sale. For individuals, it is a consumption tax rather than a tax on earned income.

Can Protectionism Cure Current Account Deficits?

Let's return to the discussion at the beginning of this section and explore the possible effects of protectionist policies on a nation's CA. It is important to notice that tariffs, quotas, subsidies, and other forms of international protectionism are not mentioned in Condition 4. Their absence is striking only because protectionism is often the first solution offered by many people when CA deficits are discussed. Condition 4 implies that the CA will become positive only if protectionist measures, in some way, cause the sum of net private saving/investment plus the net government surplus/deficit to become more positive.

A simple example can illustrate how powerful an understanding of Condition 4 can be. Suppose you were working in Brazil at a time when the nation was experiencing large and growing CA deficits. Suppose further that politicians blamed Brazil's burgeoning deficits on Argentina's practice of selling exported goods at prices below their costs of production (i.e., dumping). Backed by the media, politicians argued that tariffs were the answer because they would make Argentine goods and services more expensive relative to Brazilian products. As a result, Brazilian imports would fall, more would be produced domestically, and the nation's CA would improve.

This line of reasoning is appealing because it tastes so good going down, but when it is served in the context of Condition 4, the conclusion is difficult to digest. For instance, if tariffs caused Brazil to purchase fewer goods and services from Argentina, then the demand for the Argentine peso would fall, thereby lowering the peso's value in terms of Brazil's currency (i.e., the real).

A lower-valued peso would stimulate (not reduce) Brazil's purchases of Argentine products. As a result, it is possible for the reduction in Brazil's imports due to higher tariffs to be offset (partially or fully) by an increase in Brazilian imports due to the lower-valued peso.

Moreover, if Argentina's exports to Brazil fell, Argentina's GDP might fall, causing the Argentine demand for Brazilian exports to decline. Again, the benefits that Brazil expected to derive from imposing tariffs could be offset by lower exports due to falling Argentine incomes.

The problem with protectionist arguments is not that they are totally wrong, but rather that they are myopic. What seems so simple in isolation (e.g., "tariffs reduce imports and help a nation") turns out to be rather nebulous in a broader context. For this major reason, Condition 4 is one of the fundamental pillars of international trade theory and describes a key international macroeconomic relationship. The condition is important because it provides the broader framework needed to conceptualize issues dealing with a nation's CA.

Condition 4 tells us that no protectionist policies will change a country's CA, unless they change the sum of net private saving/investment plus the net government surplus/deficit. Tariffs *may* have this effect. For instance, they might discourage some forms of consumption and thereby encourage saving. In addition, tariff revenues might reduce a government budget deficit or add to a government budget surplus, but note how different this line of reasoning is from the normal line used by tariff advocates, and notice how it relies on the assumption of non-retaliation by foreign nations.

ran persistent government budget surpluses at the same time that it had deficits in its CA. Similarly, between 1998 and 2001, the United States had budget surpluses but deficits in its CA. By contrast, countries such as Japan, Germany, and Switzerland have often had budget deficits but surpluses in their CAs.

No protectionist (or other) policy will increase a nation's current account balance unless it increases the sum of net private saving/investment plus the net government surplus/deficit.

The cause of these different international positions can be traced to disparities in these nations' rates of net private saving/investment and net government surplus/deficit. Japan, Germany, and Switzerland had surpluses in their CAs *because* their net private saving exceeded government budget deficits. Similarly, the United States and Thailand had deficits in their CAs *because* their negative net private saving more than offset government budget surpluses or was reinforced by budget deficits.

The Source of Current Account Deficits May Be Financial Account Surpluses

Among the economic variables that are often suggested as the causes of CA deficits are relatively high inflation rates, weak labor productivity, lack of meaningful research and development, and deteriorating educational systems. These factors seem logical and may bear direct influences on nations' CA deficits, but in many cases, the actual cause could be due to economic shocks in a nation's FA (i.e., changes caused by cross-border investment flows and/or transactions by central banks in their RAs).

Movements in relative real interest rates and expectations affect cross-border investment flows, which change the FA. In the absence of central bank intervention in the foreign exchange markets, as the FA increases the CA must fall (and vice versa).[22] Let's use the United States as an example and consider how relative movements of interest rates can set off a chain reaction of economic events that ultimately affects the CA.

Suppose the return on U.S. investments rose relative to foreign investments, and as a result, foreign demand for dollar-denominated investments rose. To acquire these assets, two separate transactions would normally occur. First, foreign investors would purchase U.S. dollars with their own currencies, and the increased demand would raise the dollar's international value. Once purchased, these dollars would then be used to buy high-yielding U.S. investments.

Similarly, as the relative return on U.S. investments increased, U.S. demand for foreign investments would fall, causing the U.S. demand for foreign currencies to fall. The reduced demand for foreign currencies would lower their value relative to the dollar (i.e., increase the dollar's international value).

A more valuable dollar would cause the all-in price of U.S. exports to rise relative to imports. As a result, demand would shift away from U.S.-produced goods and services and toward foreign-produced products. This shift would cause U.S. exports to fall and U.S. imports to rise, which would reduce the U.S. CA surplus (or increase the size of the deficit).

> Because of their effect on FA, rising interest rates tend to reduce CA surpluses or increase CA deficits.

Do Current Account Deficits Mean a Nation Is Living Beyond Its Means?

Nations with CA deficits are often said to be "living beyond their means." What potential problems, if any, are connected to persistent CA deficits?

[22] Relative to the other accounts in the balance of payments, the capital account is very small and, therefore, it is removed from this analysis. It is also removed because natural resource transactions that enter into the capital account are not for newly produced goods or services and, therefore, are excluded from GDP.

Did Financial Account Surpluses Cause U.S. Current Account Deficits During the 1980s?

Consider the U.S. balance of payments situation during the early 1980s. In those years, the U.S. CA turned dramatically negative, and analysts searched for identifiable causes. Much of their focus centered on factors that directly affected components of the U.S. CA. High oil prices, lagging productivity, stifled innovation, and a poorly educated workforce were all offered as possible explanations, but the major cause of these CA deficits might have had little to do with them. Rather, they may have been caused by factors that directly influenced the FA, such as lower taxes, higher real interest rates, and fewer investment restrictions.

During the 1980s, both tax reform and high real (i.e., inflation-adjusted) U.S. interest rates attracted significant flows of investment capital to the United States. Exhibit 16-13 shows the correlated movements between the U.S. CA and non-central-bank-related movements in the FA.* At that time, the Reagan Administration and Federal Reserve advertised a hands-off policy, which meant foreign exchange market intervention was intended to be kept to a minimum. Notice in Exhibit 16-13 that, between 1983 and 1990, there was a surge of investment inflows to the United States that was unrelated to central bank intervention. At the same time, U.S. CA deficits also increased sharply. Of course, changes in other macroeconomic variables, such as exchange rates, real GDP, and productivity, also had effects on the U.S. CA, but the major cause of these deficits can likely be traced to factors that directly affected the private investment flows that were reflected in the FA.

*Removing the effects of reserve account changes was done to eliminate the impact of central bank intervention in all dollar-related foreign exchange markets.

Exhibit **16–13**	**U.S. Current Account and Financial Account Without Reserves Account Effects, 1975–1991**

Source: Federal Reserve Bank of St. Louis, Economic Data—FRED II, "U.S. Trade and International Transactions," http://research .stlouisfed.org/fred2/categories/13 (accessed January 27, 2006).

To better understand the key issues, think of your own balance of payments. If you spent more than you earned in combined wages, net investment income, and gifts received, you would be living beyond your means, but would this be a problem? To finance this deficit, you would have three basic choices: (1) borrow, (2) liquidate some of your investments, and/or (3) sell or pawn[23] some of your household possessions to make up the difference.

On the flip side, if you earned more than you spent and gave away as gifts, then you would be living within your means. The surplus could be used to (1) invest in financial or real assets (e.g., stocks, bonds, and income-generating businesses), (2) repay old debts, and/or (3) repurchase the assets that you sold or pawned when you were living beyond your means. Countries are similar to individuals in this regard because, when their spending exceeds the combined value of earnings and net transfers, they have the same three options: (1) borrow from international sources, (2) liquidate international investment assets, and/or (3) sell reserve assets.

There is a natural tendency to assume that surpluses are desirable and deficits are undesirable. After all, given the choice between wealth and a pile of debts, almost everyone would choose the former. Nevertheless, one of the first rules of balance of payments analysis is *never assume that a positive current account is good or a negative current account is bad for a nation*. Here's why.

A CA deficit means a nation's international debt level is rising and/or its international reserves are falling. But rising debts and falling reserves are not necessarily bad things. The real issue is how the newly acquired funds are spent. In short, a CA deficit only hurts a nation if the funds are used unwisely.

Suppose a family borrowed $50,000 to purchase a deluxe around-the-world vacation. A lifetime of fond memories could come from such vacations, but the expenditures would be for consumption and not investment. Without assets that could generate positive cash flows, the entire burden of this debt would fall directly on the family's future income.

Contrast the previous situation with one where the family borrows $50,000 to finance a new line of business. Assuming the venture is profitable, the family would have invested in assets that generated both a means of repaying the loan and earning a positive rate of return. In this case, the debt would not be burdensome because it was self-liquidating and improved the family's living standards.

The same is true for a nation. A CA deficit implies that a country is spending more than it earns. Is that good or bad? The answer is "It depends on what assets are purchased with the expenditures." If the internationally borrowed funds are used to support current consumption, then the loans are not self-liquidating, and the burden of repayment will fall on future generations. By contrast, if the borrowed funds are used to finance new factories or improve a nation's infrastructure (e.g., roads, bridges, sanitation, and communications), then these investments would be self-liquidating or increase the nation's productivity, and, therefore, not be a burden on future generations.

Living beyond their means is not a bad thing for all nations. It depends on how the funds are spent.

---

[23] To *pawn* something means to borrow by giving the lender personal property, such as a watch or painting, as collateral for the loan.

THE REST OF THE STORY

BALANCE OF PAYMENTS: SOURCES AND USES OF FUNDS STATEMENT

What determines whether a balance of payments transaction should be recorded as a plus or a minus? The key to unlocking the accounting logic is to remember that a balance of payments is just like a company's sources and uses of funds statement. Transactions are recorded with positive signs if they are sources of funds (i.e., inflows) and negative signs if they are uses of funds (i.e., outflows). Due to double-entry bookkeeping, every transaction must have two sides, with one showing the use of funds (a minus) and the other showing the source of funds (a plus). As a result, every balance of payments transaction must net to zero. Therefore, it stands to reason that if every balance of payments transaction must net to zero, the sum of all transactions in the balance of payments must also net to zero.

> The balance of payments is a "sources and uses of funds" statement that always sums to zero.

SOURCES OF FUNDS (INFLOWS)

Transactions that either reduce domestic residents' assets or increase their liabilities relative to foreign residents are sources of funds (see Exhibit 16-14). Examples of transactions that reduce a nation's assets relative to foreigners are exports of goods and services, earnings received on foreign investments,[24] gifts and aid from foreign residents,[25] and reductions in central bank reserves.[26] Transactions that increase a nation's liabilities to foreigners are borrowings from foreign financial institutions, sales of domestic debt and equity instruments to foreign residents, and foreign direct investments in the domestic economy.

> Sources of funds either reduce domestic residents' assets or increase their liabilities relative to foreign residents.

EXHIBIT **16–14**	SOURCES AND USES OF FUNDS IN THE BALANCE OF PAYMENTS
Sources of Funds (Inflows)	**All transactions that either:** • Decrease domestic residents' assets relative to foreigners • Increase domestic residents' liabilities relative to foreigners
Uses of Funds (Outflows)	**All transactions that either:** • Increase domestic residents' assets relative to foreigners • Decrease domestic residents' liabilities relative to foreigners

© John E. Marthinsen

---

[24] One way to understand why earnings received from foreign investments (e.g., dividends and interest) are treated as reductions in foreign assets is to think of them, prior to payment, as receivables that foreigners owe to domestic residents. Payment of these earnings means domestic residents are losing (reducing) these receivable assets and gaining cash.

[25] It may be helpful to think of these gifts and aid as if the domestic nation was selling an asset called goodwill to foreigners.

[26] Central bank reserves are treated like any good. For example, by selling gold or its holdings of foreign currencies, a nation loses an asset relative to foreign residents. Therefore, the sale of reserves is a source of funds to the nation.

USES OF FUNDS (OUTFLOWS)

On the flip side, transactions that either increase domestic residents' assets or reduce their liabilities relative to foreign residents are uses (outflows) of funds (see Exhibit 16-14). Examples of international transactions that increase a nation's assets relative to foreigners are imports of foreign goods and services, dividend and interest payments to foreign residents,[27] foreign security purchases by domestic residents, direct investments by domestic residents in foreign countries, gifts and aid given to foreigners,[28] and increases in a nation's official reserve assets.[29] Transactions that decrease a nation's liabilities relative to foreigners are, for example, payments to foreign residents for the retirement of domestic debt (e.g., bills, notes, and bonds) and payables.

Exhibit 16-15 puts together the chief components of the balance of payments and summarizes the transactions that give rise to sources and uses of funds. Next to each entry is a short explanation of why the account is recorded as a source or use of funds.

Uses of funds either increase domestic residents' assets or decrease their liabilities relative to foreign residents.

EXHIBIT **16–15**	SOURCES AND USES OF FUNDS IN THE BALANCE OF PAYMENTS			
	SOURCES OF FUNDS (+) (INFLOWS)		**USES OF FUNDS (−) (OUTFLOWS)**	
CURRENT ACCOUNT	Transaction	Explanation	Transaction	Explanation
• Goods and services	Exports	Decrease assets	Imports	Increase assets
• Net international income	Income earned	Decrease assets	Income paid	Reduce liabilities
• Remittances/Transfers	Transfers received	Decrease assets	Transfers given	Increase assets
CAPITAL ACCOUNT				
• Natural resources	Sales	Decrease assets	Purchases	Increase assets
• Legal & accounting creations	Exports	Decrease assets	Imports	Increase assets
• Capital transfers	Transfers received	Decrease assets	Transfers paid	Increase assets
FINANCIAL ACCOUNT				
• Direct investments	Investment Inflows	Increase liabilities	Investment Outflows	Increase assets
• Portfolio investments	Investment Inflows	Increase liabilities	Investment Outflows	Increase assets
• Financial derivatives	Investment Inflows	Increase liabilities	Investment Outflows	Increase assets
• Other investments	Investment Inflows	Increase liabilities	Investment Outflows	Increase assets
• Reserve account	Loss of reserves	Decrease assets	Gain of reserves	Increase assets
• Net errors and omissions	Positive accounting entry when minuses exceed pluses		Negative accounting entry when pluses exceed minuses	

© 2015 John E. Marthinsen

[27] Prior to the payment of the dividends or interest, the domestic country would have a type of accounts payable to foreigners, which is a liability. By making dividend and interest payments, the country would be losing (reducing) this liability.
[28] It may be helpful to think of gifts and aid to foreigners as if the domestic economy was buying an asset called goodwill from foreigners.
[29] Central banks usually purchase reserve assets when they want to lower the international value of their domestic currencies.

MACRO MEMO   16-8

Another Way to Understand Sources and Uses of Funds

Basic accounting teaches us that assets must equal the sum of liabilities plus equity (see Equation 1).

- Assets $\equiv$ Liabilities + Equity   **Equation 1**

As a result, changes in assets must equal changes in the sum of liabilities plus equity (see Equation 2).

- Δ Assets $\equiv$ Δ Liabilities + Δ Equity **Equation 2**

We can divide assets into two parts, Cash Assets and Noncash Assets, which turns Equation 2 into Equation 3.

- Δ Cash Assets + Δ Noncash Assets $\equiv$ Δ Liabilities + Δ Equity   **Equation 3**

By rearranging terms, Equation 3 becomes Equation 4, which is the basis for all entries in a cash flow statement and the balance of payments.

- Δ Cash Assets $\equiv$ Δ Liabilities + Δ Equity − Δ Noncash Assets   **Equation 4**

In Equation 4, changes that cause the right side of the equation to rise are sources of funds, and changes that cause the right side of the equation to fall are uses of funds.

MACRO MEMO   16-9

Every Use of Funds Must Have a Source: Examples to Prove the Point

A few examples help to convince even the most ardent skeptics that a nation's balance of payments must balance every second of the day, day of the week, and week of the year because every transaction nets to zero. Suppose a U.S. company sells $10 million in telecommunications (telecom) equipment to a Swiss manufacturer in Zurich, and the exchange rate is $1/SFr. Let's trace the effects if:

Example #1: The Swiss importer pays with Swiss francs (SFr 10 million);

Example #2: The Swiss importer pays with U.S. dollars ($10 million);

Example #3: The Swiss importer pays with chocolate worth $10 million;

Example #4: The Swiss importer pays nothing because the telecom equipment is a gift; or

Example #5: The Swiss importer pays with cocaine, an illegal drug.

Example #1: Payment in Swiss Francs (SFr 10 million)

One side of this double-entry transaction is the telecom equipment, which is recorded as an export in the U.S. CA. Because the United States is losing assets (telecom equipment) relative to foreign residents, these exports are recorded as positive values. On the other side is the clearing of Swiss francs from the Zurich importer's bank account to the U.S. manufacturer's account in Switzerland. These transactions are captured in the FA. Because the Swiss bank account is an asset to the U.S. exporter and because any increase in U.S. assets relative to foreign nations is recorded as a negative value in the balance of payments, the U.S. FA falls by $10 million, which exactly offsets the increase of $10 million in the CA (see Exhibit 16-16).

(CONTINUED)

EXHIBIT 16-16	EXAMPLE #1: PAYMENT IN SWISS FRANCS (SFR 10 MILLION)	
Accounts	**Dollar Value**	**Explanation**
Current Account	+$10 million	Telecom equipment exports • A reduction in U.S. assets relative to foreign residents
Capital Account		No change
Financial Account	−$10 million	Δ U.S. bank account in Switzerland worth SFr 10 million • An increase in U.S. assets in foreign nations
Net	0	The balance of payments always sums to zero

© 2015 John E. Marthinsen

Example #2: Payment in U.S. Dollars ($10 Million)

The export of telecom equipment is recorded the same as in Example #1 (i.e., the U.S. CA rises by $10 million). On the other side is the clearing of dollars from the Zurich importer's bank account in the United States to the U.S. manufacturer's account in the United States. These transactions are also captured in the FA. Because the United States loses a liability (i.e., the bank account) to a foreign resident, the U.S. FA falls by $10 million. See Exhibit 16-17.

EXHIBIT 16-17	EXAMPLE #2: PAYMENT IN U.S. DOLLARS ($10 MILLION)	
Accounts	**Dollar Value**	**Explanation**
Current Account	+$10 million	Telecom equipment exports • A reduction in U.S. assets relative to foreign residents
Capital Account		No change
Financial Account	−$10 million	Δ U.S. Swiss company's U.S. bank account by $10 million • A reduction in U.S. liabilities to foreigners
Net	0	The balance of payments always sums to zero

© 2015 John E. Marthinsen

Example #3: Payment in Swiss Chocolate Worth $10 Million

The export of telecom equipment is recorded the same as it was for the previous two examples (i.e., the U.S. CA rises by $10 million). On the other side is the imported chocolate, which carries a negative value because the U.S. gains assets relative to foreign residents. Therefore, telecom equipment exports and chocolate imports are both included in the current account (under merchandise/goods exports and imports) and offset each other in the CA. See Exhibit 16-18.

(CONTINUED)

EXHIBIT 16–18	EXAMPLE #3: PAYMENT IN SWISS CHOCOLATE WORTH $10 MILLION	
Accounts	**Dollar Value**	**Explanation**
Current Account	+$10 million	Telecom equipment exports
		• A reduction in U.S. assets relative to foreign residents
	−$10 million	Chocolate imports
		• An increase in U.S. assets relative to foreign residents
Capital Account	0	No change
Financial Account	0	No change
Net	0	The balance of payments always sums to zero

Example #4: Telecom Equipment Is a $10 Million Gift

The export of telecom equipment is recorded the same as in the previous examples (i.e., the U.S. CA rises by $10 million). As nothing is given in return, the "remittances and transfers" account is debited to capture the other side of this transaction. It might be easiest to think of such transfers as purchases of goodwill, which are intangible assets and, therefore, recorded in the U.S. CA with negative values. See Exhibit 16-19.

EXHIBIT 16–19	EXAMPLE #4: TELECOM EQUIPMENT IS A $10 MILLION GIFT	
Accounts	**Dollar Value**	**Explanation**
Current Account	+$10 million	Telecom equipment exports
		• A reduction in U.S. assets relative to foreign residents
	−$10 million	Remittances and Transfers
		• This account captures the other side of a one-sided transaction.
Capital Account	0	No change
Financial Account	0	No change
Net	0	The balance of payments always sums to zero

Example #5: Payment in Cocaine Worth $10 Million

The export of telecom equipment is recorded the same as in the previous examples (i.e., the U.S. CA rises by $10 million). If cocaine were a legal import, it would have the same balance of payments effect as the imported chocolate in Example #3. But as an illegal import, the cocaine would not be reported to U.S. customs agents, which means the U.S. balance of payments would reflect only one side of the transaction (i.e., the export of telecom equipment) and, therefore, not sum to zero. In such cases, the net errors and omission account would be set equal to −$10 million to correct the imbalance. See Exhibit 16-20.

(CONTINUED)

EXHIBIT 16-20	EXAMPLE #5: PAYMENT IN COCAINE WORTH $10 MILLION	
Accounts	**Dollar Value**	**Explanation**
Current Account	+$10 million	Telecom equipment • Reduction in U.S. assets relative to foreign residents
	~~−$10 million~~	~~Cocaine imports~~ • ~~Increase in U.S. assets relative to foreign residents~~
Capital Account	0	No change
Financial Account	−$10 million	Net errors and omissions • Changes to make the balance of payments equal zero
Net	0	The balance of payments always sums to zero

© 2015 John E. Marthinsen

BALANCE OF PAYMENTS MEASURES

As mentioned in "The Basics" portion of this chapter, balance of payments deficits and surpluses refer to segments of balance of payments because the entire balance of payments must sum to zero. Deficits occur when the sum of the minus transactions for a particular account or combination of accounts is greater than the sum of the plus transactions. Surpluses occur when just the opposite occurs.

The five most frequently used balance of payments measures are the: (1) trade balance; (2) balance on goods and services; (3) balance on goods, services, and income; (4) CA; and (5) overall balance (see Exhibit 16-21). Business managers and policymakers who are concerned about how to

EXHIBIT 16-21	MAJOR BALANCE OF PAYMENTS MEASURES

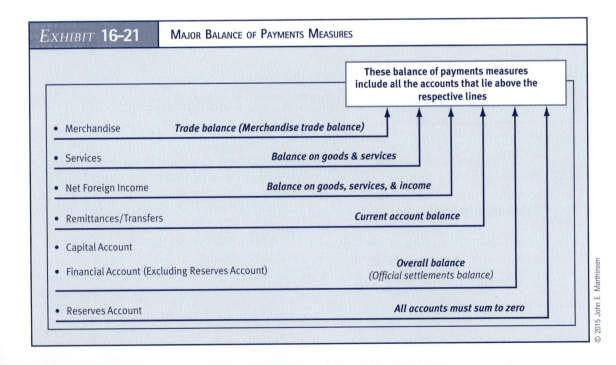

These balance of payments measures include all the accounts that lie above the respective lines

• Merchandise — *Trade balance (Merchandise trade balance)*

• Services — *Balance on goods & services*

• Net Foreign Income — *Balance on goods, services, & income*

• Remittances/Transfers — *Current account balance*

• Capital Account

• Financial Account (Excluding Reserves Account) — *Overall balance (Official settlements balance)*

• Reserves Account — *All accounts must sum to zero*

© 2015 John E. Marthinsen

interpret significant shifts in balance of payments statistics should understand these measures and be able to put them into perspective.

TRADE BALANCE

The narrowest of all the balance of payments measures is the trade balance, which is often called the merchandise trade balance because it includes *only* a nation's imports and exports of merchandise. The trade balance is a highly visible statistic in the media and also the focus of many heated (often misdirected) debates about whether imports take jobs away from the domestic workforce. The main problem with the trade balance is its limited range. As nations have become more service-oriented, the trade balance has become increasingly less relevant because jobs, productivity, and foreign exchange transactions are just as closely tied to international service flows as they are to merchandise transactions.

> The balance of trade measures only imports and exports of merchandise.

BALANCE ON GOODS AND SERVICES

A broader (and better) measure of a nation's international economic position is the balance on goods and services because it includes a nation's imports and exports of both goods and services. Recall from the Chapter 2, "Taking an Economic Pulse: Measuring National Output and Income," that the balance on goods *and* services (i.e., net exports [NE]) is one of the four components of a nation's GDP and aggregate demand (AD). The other three components of GDP and AD are personal consumption expenditures (C), gross private domestic investment (I), and government spending for final goods and services (G)—see Exhibit 16-22. As a result, the balance on goods and services is closely watched by most nations and useful for making international comparisons in discussions related to GDP.

> The balance on goods and services includes everything in the trade balance plus net changes in international services.

BALANCE ON GOODS, SERVICES, AND INCOME

As its name indicates, the balance on goods, services, and income includes everything in the balance on goods and services account plus net income earned from (or paid to) foreign residents. A deficit in a nation's balance on goods, services, and income is often interpreted as a sign that the nation is living beyond its means, which invites critical scrutiny. Whether such criticisms are warranted usually depends on whether the funds are being spent on self-liquidating investments and/or productivity-increasing infrastructure. If they are, then the debts incurred to finance these deficits are not burdens on future generations.

> The balance on goods, services, and income includes everything in the balance on goods and services, plus net international income earned/paid. It is a way of showing if a nation is living beyond its means.

We learned in the Chapter 2, "Taking an Economic Pulse: Measuring National Output and Income" that the sum of a nation's gross *domestic* product (GDP) plus net international income equals its gross *national* product (GNP). Therefore, GNP is equal to personal consumption expenditures, gross

EXHIBIT **16-22**	**COMPONENTS OF GROSS DOMESTIC PRODUCT**

Personal consumption expenditures
+ Gross private domestic investment
+ Government spending
+ Balance on goods and services
= GDP

© John E. Marthinsen

EXHIBIT 16-23	COMPONENTS OF GROSS NATIONAL PRODUCT

Personal consumption expenditures
+ Gross private domestic investment
+ Government spending
+ Balance on goods, services, and income
≡ **GNP**
GNP ≡ GDP + Net foreign income

© John E. Marthinsen

private domestic investment, government spending, and the balance on goods, services, and income (see Exhibit 16-23).

CURRENT ACCOUNT

The CA includes international exports and imports of goods and services, as well as net international income payments/receipts, remittances, and transfers. This highly visible balance of payments measure was covered in considerable depth on pages 530–531 and 538–546.

> The current account includes everything in the balance on goods, services, and income plus net international remittances and transfers.

OVERALL BALANCE (OFFICIAL SETTLEMENTS BALANCE)

The final balance of payments measure is the overall balance, which is also known as the official settlements balance. Despite its name, the overall balance does not include all the accounts in the balance of payments. Rather, it includes everything except the RA, which means it includes the CA, KA, and FA minus the RA. In short, the overall balance is equal to and opposite from the RA. If the overall balance equals zero, then RA must equal zero, which means the central bank is not intervening (net) in the foreign exchange markets. If the overall balance equals +\$100 billion, then RA must equal −\$100 billion, which means the central bank is buying (increasing its) reserve assets. Finally, if the overall balance equals −\$100 billion, then RA must equal +\$100 billion, which means the central bank is selling (reducing its) reserve assets.

> The overall balance is equal to and opposite from the reserves account. It reflects central bank intervention in the foreign exchange markets.

MEXICAN PESO CRISIS, 1994: A BALANCE OF PAYMENTS CASE STUDY

With the basics of the balance of payments now behind us, let's investigate the years 1992–1996 in order to understand the 1994 Mexican peso crisis.[30] What economic information did Mexico's balance of payments reveal about the domestic economy? Exhibit 16-24 shows the balance of payments figures for Mexico between 1992 and 1996. A casual glance at these statistics is enough to convince us that something major happened between 1994 and 1995, causing huge changes in Mexico's balance of payments situation.

Trade deficits that varied between \$13,481 million and \$18,464 million in 1993 and 1994 changed in 1995 by more than \$25,500 million and became surpluses of \$7,089 million in 1995 and \$6,533 million in 1996. Similarly,

[30] The Mexican peso crisis peaked in December 1994.

| EXHIBIT 16-24 | MEXICAN BALANCE OF PAYMENTS 1992–1996 |

(Figures in millions of dollars)

ACCOUNTS	1992	1993	1994	1995	1996
Current account	−24,442	−23,400	−29,662	−1,576	−2,529
Goods: exports f.o.b.*	46,196	51,885	60,882	79,542	96,002
Goods: imports f.o.b.*	−62,130	−65,366	−79,346	−72,453	−89,469
Trade balance	*−15,934*	*−13,481*	*−18,464*	*7,089*	*6,533*
Net services	−2,684	−2,529	−2,722	64	−94
Balance on goods and services	*−18,618*	*−16,010*	*−21,186*	*7,153*	*6,439*
Net income	−9,209	−11,030	−12,258	−12,689	−13,473
Balance on goods, services, and income	*−27,827*	*−27,040*	*−33,444*	*−5,536*	*−7,034*
Net current transfers	3,385	3,640	3,782	3,960	4,505
Capital Account	0	0	0	0	0
Financial account	*24,442*	*23,400*	*29,662*	*1,576*	*2,529*
Net direct investment	4,393	4,389	10,973	9,526	9,186
Net portfolio investments	19,206	28,355	7,415	−10,377	4,081
Other investment	3,440	1,016	−2,601	−9,636	−9,019
Financial derivatives	0	0	0	0	0
Net errors and omissions	−852	−3,128	−3,324	−4,249	229
Reserves account	−1,745	−7,232	17,199	16,312	−1,948

*f.o.b. means "free on board." It is the value of the exported goods at the border of the exporting country. It excludes freight costs and insurance beyond the border of the exporting country.

Source: IMF, *International Financial Statistics Yearbook 2003*, (Washington D.C.: 2003).

deficits in Mexico's net services account changed from $2,529 million in 1993 and $2,722 million in 1994 to a small surplus in 1995 and a small deficit in 1996. Finally, Mexico's CA deficit fell from $23,400 million in 1993 and $29,662 million in 1994 to levels under $3,000 million in 1995 and 1996.

During the 1992–1993 period, Mexico was a darling of the international investment community. International investors poured billions of dollars into Mexico with the expectation of earning attractive returns. So much was invested that Mexico was able to finance its large CA deficits and still have enough to fund healthy annual increases in its reserve account.[31] For instance

---

[31] Remember that when a nation acquires assets, the transactions are recorded in its balance of payments with negative signs because they are classified as uses of funds. Therefore, the negative entries in Mexico's reserves account during 1992 and 1993 were consistent with the nation gaining reserve assets.

in 1992, net capital flows to Mexico amounted to $26,187 million.[32] Of this amount, $24,442 million financed the nation's CA deficit, and the extra $1,745 million funded an increase in Mexico's reserves. Similarly in 1993, Mexico's international reserves grew by $7,232.

Positive net investment flows to Mexico slowed considerably in 1994, dropping more than 59% to $12,463 million from $30,632 million in 1993.[33] The following year, these positive net investment flows reversed themselves, resulting in net outflows (i.e., capital flight) amounting to $14,736 million—a decline of $27,199 million in one year!

What happened? From a trade perspective, it appears as if Mexico's international competitive position improved. Why else would there have been such a huge positive shift in Mexico's (1) trade balance, (2) balance on goods and services, (3) balance on goods, services, and income, and (4) current account? Were 1994 and 1995 years of significant improvements in Mexican productivity? Did rising oil prices cause a colossal increase in Mexican export revenues? Unfortunately, the answer to both of these questions is no.

By focusing on Mexico's FA, the changes that took place in its CA during 1994 and 1995 can be more clearly explained. Between 1992 and 1993, Mexico was able to run large CA deficits because it was perceived as offering acceptable risk-adjusted returns. This optimism diminished and then collapsed in 1994, when a series of economic, business, financial, political, and social problems surfaced.

International investors became increasingly concerned about the safety and economic viability of their Mexican investments. They responded by sharply curtailing new investments in Mexico and liquidating some of their existing investments there. Mexican residents also responded to the domestic turbulence and uncertainty by investing funds outside Mexico. As a result, Mexico's CA deficit fell sharply because net international loans vanished, and without such loans, the nation could no longer live beyond its means.

What conditions in 1994 caused Mexico's world to implode? Looking at the economic fundamentals in Exhibit 16-25, it is not at all clear. There were positive and negative changes in key macroeconomic indicators; but even the negatives were not that bad. On the positive side, Mexico's inflation had fallen from 26% in 1990 to a mere 7% in 1994. During the same period, exports grew considerably in excess of real GDP, spurred in part by trade liberalization provisions of the recently negotiated North American Free Trade Agreement (NAFTA).[34]

The philosophy of liberalization inherent in NAFTA also spilled over to domestic economic policies. In 1994, Mexico continued to promote competition and aggressively moved to privatize domestic industries.[35]

---

[32] This figure was calculated by taking the financial account minus reserves account = $24,442 million − (−$1,745) = $26,187 million.

[33] This figure was calculated by taking the financial account minus reserves account = $29,662 million − $17,199 = $12,463 million.

[34] NAFTA was passed in 1992 by the United States, Canada, and Mexico to eliminate tariffs on most traded products during the 10-year period from 1994 to 2004. The agreement also addressed the liberalization of financial investments and services, as well as the protection of intellectual property.

[35] Liberalization was not new to Mexico. During the administration of President Miguel De la Madrid Hurtado (1982–1988), Mexico adopted many market-based policies. This trend toward liberalization continued and gained momentum during the administration of President Carlos Salinas de Gortari (1988–1994).

EXHIBIT 16-25	MEXICAN ECONOMIC CONDITIONS, 1989–1995						
	1989	**1990**	**1991**	**1992**	**1993**	**1994**	**1995**
Inflation (CPI)	20%	26%	23%	16%	10%	7%	35%
Export growth	26%	32%	13%	10%	12%	25%	134%
Government budget/GDP	−4.9%	−2.7%	3.2%	4.5%	0.5%	−0.03%	−0.5%
Money market rates	47%	37%	24%	19%	17%	16%	53%
Real interest rate*	NA	NA	NA	NA	7%	10%	16%
Real GDP growth	4.2%	5.1%	4.2%	3.6%	1.9%	4.5%	−6.2%

*World Bank, "World Development Indicators," http://data.worldbank.org/data-catalog/world-development-indicators (accessed August 25, 2013).

Source: IMF, *International Financial Statistics Yearbook 2003*, (Washington D.C.: 2003).

On the fiscal side, government budget deficits showed considerable improvement. Deficits, which had reached more than 9% of GDP in 1988,[36] fell to 4.9% in 1989, continued to improve, and turned into surpluses in 1991, 1992, and 1993. Though a budget deficit did recur in 1994, it was small in relation to Mexico's GDP (i.e., less than 0.3% of GDP). To put this deficit into some perspective, it was far lower than the average for all member nations of the Organization of Economic Cooperation and Development (OECD) and well below the 3.0% Maastricht criterion for nations that wished to join the European Monetary Union (EMU) in 1999.

One of the perceived negative aspects of Mexico's 1994 economic position was the nation's anemic real GDP growth, which was out of line with solid performances in other developing economies (e.g., the Asian Tiger nations). Slow growth was especially problematic in light of Mexico's skewed income distribution that left nearly 50 million Mexicans below the poverty line.[37] This meant real suffering and left little hope for a significant segment of the population. The result was heightened social unrest.

Political turmoil and social disorder added to Mexico's problems. In 1994, two political luminaries (Mexican presidential candidate Luis Donaldo Colosio and Institutional Revolutionary Party official Jose Francisco Ruiz Massieu) were assassinated. Formal allegations of political corruption were leveled against high-ranking officials of the ruling party, and two highly visible government officials (Special Investigator and Deputy Attorney General Mario Ruiz Massieu and Interior Secretary Jorge Carpizo McGregor) resigned their posts. In addition, armed uprisings by Chiapas rebels added a new dimension to the real and perceived economic risks associated with Mexican investments.

[36] Exhibit 16-25 does not show 1988 figures.
[37] Compared to the United States in 1995, Mexico's per capita GDP was one-eighth as large, life expectancy was five years shorter, and infant mortality was four times higher. World Bank, *World Development Report 1997* (New York: Oxford University Press, 1997).

These economic, political, and social problems did not escape the attention of international investors, and the opinions of these investors were crucial if Mexico wanted to continue financing its growing CA deficits. Mexico was vulnerable because it was highly dependent on international capital flows and this vulnerability was intensified because the clear majority of these flows were in the form of portfolio investments rather than direct investments. As a result, changes in investor sentiment, for real or imagined reasons, could activate the sale of investment assets in massive amounts and put considerable downward pressure on the value of the peso.

Exhibit 16-24 shows the composition of foreign investments in Mexico during the 1992 to 1994 period. Only 17% of the net international investment flows to Mexico in 1992, and 14% of them in 1993, were in the form of direct investments. The composition of Mexico's FA changed dramatically in 1994. Investors expected trade flows between Mexico and the United States to grow rapidly due to NAFTA's enactment in 1994. As a result, net direct investments rose by $6,584 million to $10,973 million in 1994. At the same time, Mexico's seeming economic weakness and international vulnerability caused portfolio investments to fall by $20,940 million—a precipitous drop of nearly 74%.

Direct investments are reassuring to nations because they signal a general degree of confidence and permanence on the part of international investors. They are also comforting because investments in plant and equipment aren't going anywhere, and they usually cannot be sold quickly. Throughout history, only in the most extreme cases (like the Soviet Union after World War II) have foreign residents dismantled and physically taken investments with them when they left.

In light of all the uncertainties surrounding the Mexican economy in 1994 and the increasing likelihood that the peso might be allowed to depreciate, investors (both domestic and foreign) began to shun the Mexican capital markets. Capital flight from Mexico was exacerbated by U.S. interest rates, which rose during most of 1994 in an effort to reduce rising U.S. inflation. Attempts by the Bank of Mexico to support the peso in the foreign exchange markets depleted the nation's official reserve assets from approximately $25 billion at the end of 1993 to about $13 billion on December 1, 1994.[38] During December, the Bank of Mexico lost an additional $7 billion of its official reserves and was forced to depreciate the peso.[39]

The peso's devaluation was controversial, and clearly not Mexico's only alternative. There were vocal critics who felt that, despite some obvious short-term problems, the Mexican economy was relatively healthy, and devaluation was the wrong course of action.[40] Some suggested that a better policy would have been to employ restrictive monetary policies. By substantially raising Mexican real interest rates, they felt the peso could have been defended.

During the year after the peso's devaluation (1995), Mexico's economy seemed to go from bad to worse. Real GDP fell by more than 6%, causing unemployment to rise. Consumer prices soared by 35%. Real interest rates climbed steadily from 7.5% in 1993 to 16% in 1995. The combined pressures

---

[38] December 1, 1994 was the day Ernesto Zedillo was inaugurated as president of Mexico.
[39] International Monetary Fund, *International Financial Statistics Yearbook 2003*, (Washington D.C.: 2003).
[40] Robert L. Bartley, "Mexico: Suffering the Conventional Wisdom," *The Wall Street Journal*, February 8, 1995, A14.

of rising real interest rates, higher inflationary expectations, and greater risk premiums forced Mexico's nominal (money market) interest rates to 53%.

Fortunately by 1996, Mexico was on the path to recovery. Despite its relatively short duration, the *peso crisis* was a punctuating event in the 1990s because of its severity and because of the lasting scars it left on the Mexican economy. As well, the crisis had negative spillover effects (i.e., called the "tequila effect") on the economies of other Latin American nations.

CONCLUSION

The balance of payments is a summary of all transactions between the residents of one nation and the residents of the rest of the world during a given time period. Because it includes all transactions, and not just those for which currency is exchanged, the balance of payments is much broader than the supply and demand forces that enter into the foreign exchange market.

The balance of payments is like a company's sources and uses of funds statement, with sources entering as positive values and uses entering as negative values. Because every use of funds must have a source, the sum of the entire balance of payments must equal zero. Therefore, balance of payments deficits or surpluses refer to only a portion of the entire statement.

The principal parts of the balance of payments are the current account (CA), capital account (KA), and financial account (FA), which implies $CA + KA + FA \equiv 0$. Deficits in the CA and KA are financed by the FA, and surpluses in these accounts are invested via the FA. Five widely cited balance of payments measures are the (1) trade balance; (2) balance on goods and services; (3) balance on goods, services, and income; (4) current account; and (5) overall balance. As is the case with any economic measures, what these balances reveal is important but what they conceal is crucial.

For the study of macroeconomics, the RA is important because it reflects central bank intervention in the foreign exchange markets. Such intervention directly affects the nation's monetary base and indirectly affects its money supply.

At this point in the text, we have investigated the real loanable funds market, real goods and services market, and foreign exchange market (including the balance of payments). Starting in the next chapter, we will bring together these three sectors to decipher the effects of significant economic shocks to national economies.

REVIEW QUESTIONS

1. Does the entire balance of payments *always* have to sum to zero? Explain. If the sum must equal zero, what economic forces cause this result? If not, is the imbalance because market forces are not functioning properly? If not, does the RA adjust to make it equal zero? Explain.

2. Suppose Japan's RA equaled −¥400 billion (i.e., negative 400 billion yen).
    a. Is the Bank of Japan (BoJ) intervening in the foreign exchange markets? If it is intervening, is the central bank buying or selling yen? Explain.
    b. Is Japan's monetary base rising or falling by an amount greater than, less than, or equal to ¥400 billion, or does the monetary base remain unchanged? Explain.

c. Is the BoJ raising the value of the yen, lowering it, or is the change impossible to determine? Explain.

3. Suppose the treasurer of your company stops by your office and asks you to make a brief report in 30 minutes about the likelihood of Croatia devaluing its currency, the kuna. Currently, the kuna is managed by the central bank, but it is not fixed. Your company's treasurer is worried about a depreciation of the kuna and the negative effect it might have on the company's profitability. You send your assistant to get the balance of payments figures online from the IMF's *International Financial Statistics*, and he returns in 10 minutes with the following unorganized and noninterpreted figures:

BALANCE OF PAYMENTS, CROATIA

(Figures in millions)	
Transfers	−90
Imports of goods and services	−510
Investment income	−30
Reserves account	−45
Exports of goods and services	+324
Long-term investments	+300
Short-term investments	+55
Net errors and omissions	0
Capital account	−4

a. Arrange the balance of payments figures in their proper order.
b. Explain whether Croatia is "living within its means." Which account best shows this?
c. Comment on whether the Croatian central bank is intervening in the foreign exchange market. If it is intervening, explain whether it is buying or selling foreign exchange.
d. Explain how likely it is that the kuna will depreciate in the near future. Is it more likely that the kuna will appreciate? Explain.
e. What actions, if any, could your company take to profit from the economic changes implied by these balance of payments figures?

4. Is it correct to say that a CA deficit is bad for a nation? If so, explain why. If not, give an example of how it might be good for a nation to have a CA deficit.

5. *Must* a country with a deficit in its CA also have a government budget deficit? Under what conditions, if any, could the nation with a government budget surplus have deficit in its CA? Fully explain.

6. Suppose a nation had a large budget deficit. What economic market forces would be set in motion to cause a deficit in the nation's CA?

7. Suppose Mexico had sizable capital inflows in 1996 (i.e., a little more than a year after its currency crisis in December 1994), and its currency fluctuated freely.
a. What effect should these flows have had on the three major accounts (i.e., CA, KA, and FA) of Mexico's balance of payments? Indicate the accounts that would change.

b. What effect should these flows have had on the international value of the Mexican peso?

c. What effect should these flows have had, if any, on Mexico's monetary base?

8. Suppose that you had business holdings in a small country that had borrowed from the IMF because of serious debt problems. The IMF recommended that the small country peg its exchange rate at the equilibrium level. You observed that the country's foreign exchange reserves were falling very rapidly. Do you think the country's exchange rate was undervalued or overvalued? Why? As a business manager, what actions might you take, if any, to increase your profits or to protect your business interests?

9. If a Japanese bank lent ¥100 million to finance a U.S. takeover, where payment was to be made in dollars for the acquired company, what effect would this transaction have on Japan's monetary base, the value of the yen, and the RA? Explain.

10. Suppose you were in a conversation with colleagues who were discussing the economic positions of two U.S. presidential candidates. How would you respond if one of your colleagues said: "Ask any economist, and you will find that if the government's budget deficit rises, the nation always ends up importing more than it exports. The U.S. is no different. If fiscal policies cause the U.S. government budget deficits to rise, you can be sure that U.S. foreign debts will also rise. It's almost a one-to-one relationship."

11. Assume Bolivia's fiscal deficit is 3% of GDP. If the nation had a CA surplus equal to 2% of GDP, what could be said, if anything, about the relationship between Bolivia's gross private domestic investment and saving rate relative to GDP?

12. Thailand's CA went into deficit for the first time in 7 years in 2005. If the government wanted to correct this, what *must* it do?

13. In 1982, Mexico precipitated an international debt crisis when it defaulted on billions of dollars of international loans. As a result, the international financial community virtually stopped all loans to Mexico. Suppose it was 1981 (one year before the crisis); you knew the crisis would occur and net lending to Mexico next year would fall to zero. Explain what *must* have happened to Mexico's CA balance if the peso fluctuated freely in the international markets.

14. Explain the economic meaning and usefulness of the following balance of payments measures: (1) trade balance; (2) balance on goods and services; (3) balance on goods, services, and income; (4) CA; and (5) overall balance. What information do they convey to a business manager?

15. From the following data, fill in the missing information:

BALANCE OF PAYMENTS ACCOUNTS	2012	2013	2014
International income receipts	500	700	850
International income payments	400	300	450
Merchandise imports	24,300	23,500	24,900
Merchandise exports	20,700	20,900	23,200
Financial account: inflows	100	50	900

BALANCE OF PAYMENTS ACCOUNTS	2012	2013	2014
Financial account: outflows	2,800	1,200	1,300
Remittances and transfers paid	1,000	1,100	900
Remittances and transfers received	1,500	1,600	1,600
Service imports	8,100	8,000	7,700
Service exports	6,600	7,500	7,200
Statistical discrepancy	0	0	0
Capital account: inflows	5	10	20
Capital account: outflows	8	14	12
Trade balance	____	____	____
Balance on goods and services	____	____	____
Balance on goods, services, and income	____	____	____
Current account	____	____	____
Reserves account	____	____	____

DISCUSSION QUESTIONS

16. Many observers have blamed large U.S. CA deficits on China's artificially low exchange rate. At the same time, China has blamed these deficits on the U.S. government's large government budget deficits. Explain both sides of this argument.

17. In the past, U.S. government debt was owned mainly by countries that were considered friendly toward the United States (like Japan), but now there is concern that the situation has changed as countries such as China and many oil-producing countries (e.g., Saudi Arabia) have acquired an increasingly large share of the U.S. government debt. Explain whether it matters how friendly the owners of this debt are to the United States. Could an unfriendly nation punish the United States—if so, how and if not, why not?

18. Suppose France decided to provide debt forgiveness equal to €25 billion to Cameroon, one of the African CFA-zone countries. What effect would this debt relief have on France's CA, KA, and FA?

19. Fully explain the following statement. "A spokesman for the People's Bank of China announced recently that the central bank was trying to reduce the nation's foreign exchange reserves, which had increased to nearly $4 trillion, mainly due to China's fixed-exchange-rate policy. The central bank spokesman indicated that this policy had pumped excess cash into the economy and now threatened to increase domestic inflation."

20. Suppose China decides to keep its current level of foreign exchange reserves but to change their composition from mainly U.S. dollars to euros.
    a. Explain the effect this policy will have on the Chinese, U.S., and euro-area monetary bases.
    b. Explain the effect it will have on Chinese, U.S., and euro-area interest rates.
    c. Explain the effect it will have on the dollar per yuan, euro per yuan, and dollar per euro exchange rates.

PART 5

SHORT-TERM ECONOMIC CHANGES: PUTTING IT ALL TOGETHER

Chapter 17

Putting It All Together

INTRODUCTION

The goal of this chapter and the subsequent three is to explain the interconnections among the three major macroeconomic markets. Until this point, our focus has been on explaining how equilibrium prices, rates, and quantities per period are established in each *individual* market, and what causes them to change. We learned how a nation's gross domestic product (GDP) Price Index and real GDP are determined in the real goods market, how a nation's real risk-free interest rate and the quantity of real credit per time period are determined in the real loanable funds market, and, finally, how the international value and quantity of a nation's currency per time period are determined in each foreign exchange market.

In Exhibit 17-1, the markets of our Three-Sector Model are represented by the familiar image of three interconnected spinning gears. The focus until now has been on factors that change the speed and/or direction of only one gear. We have not considered systematically how the movement of one affects the other two. With this in mind, it is time to take a broader view and fully explore how the three gears are interconnected. From Exhibit 17-1, it is evident that the three gears move synchronously, and if one of them moves in a certain direction and at a particular speed, the other two will also move in predictable directions and at particular speeds.

THE BASICS

DOES THE THREE-SECTOR MODEL MEET THE TEST OF COMMON SENSE?

Before we begin to integrate the macroeconomic markets, let's reflect on what we have done. If the previous chapters in this text were successful, the economic relationships in each of the markets of our Three-Sector Model should reflect the way *you* think people behave and markets work. At this point, the main question to answer is "Do these economic relationships reflect *your common sense*, or are they pure memorization?" If they seem logical and sound, then a significant step has been taken. If not, now is the time to identify and dispel misunderstandings.

The reason it is so important for these economic relationships to be consistent with *your* common sense is the Three-Sector Model should be treated as the first significant step toward the goal of building a solid understanding

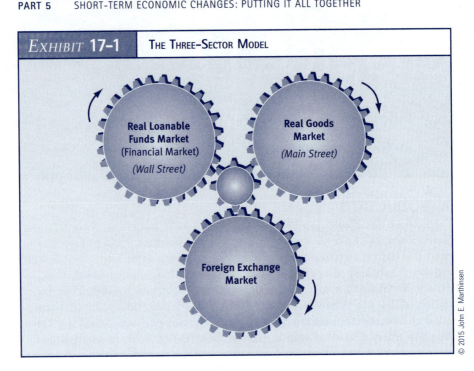

EXHIBIT 17-1   THE THREE-SECTOR MODEL

Real Loanable Funds Market (Financial Market) (Wall Street)

Real Goods Market (Main Street)

Foreign Exchange Market

© 2015 John E. Marthinsen

of international macroeconomics. Refining and improving this skill is a life-time job, but if the logic on which the Three-Sector Model is built seems rational, it will provide a foundation and framework on which to organize and interpret new experiences, information, and insights.[1]

Let's do a quick reality check to see if some of the most important pillars on which the Three-Sector Model has been built reflect your common sense. Each of the following statements is consistent with the logic that we have developed. If the reasoning is inconsistent with the way you feel the world works, then it is worth pausing to understand why there is a difference.

According to the Three-Sector Model, *if all other things remain constant,* then the following are true:

- A higher national price level (i.e., GDP Price Index) increases the ability and willingness of domestic businesses to supply goods and services, but it decreases consumers' willingness and ability to buy them. (*These adjustments are in the real goods market.*)
- An increase in demand for a nation's goods and services (aggregate demand) normally causes an increase in the amount produced

---

[1] If you feel that the Three-Sector Model developed in this book is logical and reflects common sense, but it is not a reflection of how the economy actually works (i.e., the model is logical but invalid), then it is worth pursuing alternative economic paradigms, such as monetarist models, Marxist models, or heterodox models, which might be more in line with your views. The key is to begin building a solid macroeconomic structure that is durable, defendable, expandable, and useful as a decision-making tool. For further information, see Bennett T. McCallum, "Monetarism," *Library of Economics and Liberty: The Concise Encyclopedia of Economics,* http://www.econlib.org/library/Enc/Monetarism.html; David L. L. Prychitko, "Marxism," http://www.econlib.org/library/Enc/Marxism.html; and "Heterodox Economics: Marginal Revolutionaries," *The Economist Magazine,* December 31, 2011, http://www.economist.com/node/21542174, and Homepage, "Association of Heterodox, Economics," http://www.hetecon.net/ (accessed August 7, 2013).

(i.e., real GDP) and a higher average price level (i.e., GDP Price Index). Usually, if output increases, it creates more jobs, which reduces the nation's unemployment rate and raises its employment rate. (*These adjustments are in the real goods market.*)

- An increase in a nation's supply of goods and services (aggregate supply) tends to raise the amount sold per time period and lowers the nation's average price level. Greater output creates more jobs, which reduces the nation's unemployment rate and raises its employment rate. (*These adjustments are in the real goods market.*)
- A higher inflation-adjusted (i.e., real) risk-free interest rate increases the willingness and ability of lenders/savers to supply real loanable funds (i.e., real credit), and it decreases the willingness and ability of individuals and companies to borrow. (*These adjustments are in the real loanable funds market.*)
- An increase in borrowing demand causes the real risk-free interest rate and the equilibrium quantity of real credit per period to rise. (*These adjustments are in the real loanable funds market.*)
- An increase in the supply of a nation's real credit reduces the inflation-adjusted risk-free interest rate and increases the equilibrium quantity of real credit per period. (*These adjustments are in the real loanable funds market.*)
- An increase in the value of a nation's currency encourages imports and discourages exports. (*These adjustments are in the foreign exchange market.*)
- An increase in the demand for a nation's currency raises both its international value and equilibrium quantity per period. (*These adjustments are in the foreign exchange market.*)
- An increase in the supply of a nation's currency lowers its international value and raises the equilibrium quantity per period. (*These adjustments are in the foreign exchange market.*)

INTEGRATING MACROECONOMIC MARKETS IN THE THREE-SECTOR MODEL

As previously mentioned, it is helpful to view national and international macroeconomic markets as spinning, interconnected gears that continue to turn at the same rate until they are disturbed by an external force. After an initial shock hits one (or more) of the gears (markets), it adjusts and the changes simultaneously affect the other gears (markets).

> Macroeconomic changes are due to external shocks that directly affect one market (or more) and then spread to the others.

We will use a three-step process to analyze the economic consequences of these external shocks. Step 1 describes the initial economic setting or landscape of the nation being analyzed. Once the economic landscape has been defined, Step 2 identifies the initial shock or the expected initial shock that causes the economic changes. This disturbance might be the result of economic, political, and/or social changes, such as newly implemented fiscal or monetary policies, revised expectations, greater risks, war, or the threat of economic sanctions. Our last step (Step 3) analyzes the economic chain of events that results from the initial external shock. Exhibit 17-2 summarizes these three steps.

EXHIBIT 17-2	THREE-STEP ANALYSIS OF OUR THREE-SECTOR MODEL

Step 1	Describe the initial economic setting of the three major macroeconomic markets (i.e., the real goods market, real loanable funds market, and foreign exchange market) for the nation being analyzed.
Step 2	Identify the economic shock (or expected shock) to the nation.*
Step 3	Analyze the chain reaction of economic interactions.

*For now, we will analyze only one external shock at a time.

© John E. Marthinsen

STEP 1: DESCRIBE THE INITIAL ECONOMIC SETTING OF THE THREE MAJOR MARKETS BEING ANALYZED

Having a view of a nation's economic landscape is important because the consequences of any shock can be highly sensitive to economic conditions. For example, a rising real risk-free interest rate could have a much different impact on developed nations—such as England, Germany, Japan, Switzerland, and the United States—than they have on developing nations—such as Argentina, Brazil, Egypt, Malaysia, and Mexico. These asymmetries could be caused by factors, such as relative differences in capital market sophistication, risk, investment alternatives, unemployment rates, levels of unused capital, natural resource availability, exchange rate regime, and degree of international capital mobility.

An important step toward identifying a nation's economic landscape is to clarify or define the slope and/or elasticity[2] of the supply and demand curves in each of the three principal macroeconomic markets. The greater the elasticity, the larger the percentage change in quantity per time period for any percentage change in stimulus (e.g., price or rate).

Real Goods Market: Describe the Initial Economic Setting

Exhibit 17-3 shows the general shape of the aggregate supply (AS) curve. Among the most important factors influencing its shape are the nation's rate of resource utilization, efficiency, and degree of resource mobility. Over a short-term horizon, the AS curve becomes steeper as a nation approaches full employment, which means it becomes increasingly more difficult to increase output by raising demand. Fewer resources (i.e., labor, capital, land, and entrepreneurs) are available, bottlenecks often occur, and the productivity of newly hired resources tends to be relatively low. Therefore, any increase in demand tends to raise prices more than it raises output.

The shape of the AS curve is affected by the level of resource utilization, efficiency, and resource mobility.

---

[2] Elasticity is the percentage change in a response divided by the percentage change in a stimulus. Three examples of macroeconomic-relevant elasticities are: (%ΔReal GDP per period/%ΔGDP Price Index), (%ΔQuantity of real loanable funds per period/%ΔReal risk-free interest rate), and (%ΔQuantity of foreign exchange per period/%ΔNominal exchange rate). These relationships are elastic, inelastic, or unit elastic depending on whether their absolute values are greater than, less than, or equal to one, respectively. Slope is not the same as the elasticity, but for our analyses, a steeply sloped supply or demand curve will indicate that the relevant portion of the curve is relatively inelastic. A relatively flat-sloped supply or demand curve will indicate an elastic relationship.

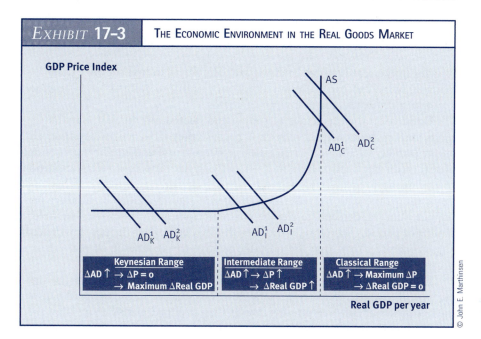

EXHIBIT **17-3**   THE ECONOMIC ENVIRONMENT IN THE REAL GOODS MARKET

GDP Price Index

AS

AD_C^1 AD_C^2

AD_K^1 AD_K^2

AD_I^1 AD_I^2

Keynesian Range	Intermediate Range	Classical Range
$\Delta AD \uparrow \rightarrow \Delta P = 0$ $\rightarrow$ Maximum ΔReal GDP	$\Delta AD \uparrow \rightarrow \Delta P \uparrow$ $\rightarrow \Delta$Real GDP $\uparrow$	$\Delta AD \uparrow \rightarrow$ Maximum ΔP $\rightarrow \Delta$Real GDP = 0

Real GDP per year

© John E. Marthinsen

Among the key economic indicators that provide clues about where a nation is on its AS curve are the unemployment rate, employment rate, and capacity utilization rate, as well as estimates of labor and capital mobility. In general, a nation's AS curve is more elastic the higher its rate of unemployment, the larger its degree of resource mobility, and the lower its rates of capacity utilization and employment. All of these characteristics imply a greater capacity to increase production with any increase in aggregate demand (AD).

Exhibit 17-3 illustrates how identical shifts in AD produce different results depending on where a nation is on its AS curve. In the Keynesian range (i.e., the horizontal region where a nation has very low levels of resource utilization), when demand rises from AD_K^1 to AD_K^2, it causes no price change and only an increase in real GDP.

By contrast, in the classical range (i.e., where the AS curve is vertical because resources are fully employed), an increase in AD from AD_C^1 to AD_C^2 causes no change in real GDP and only an increase in prices. Finally, increasing AD from AD_I^1 to AD_I^2 in the intermediate range causes both prices and real GDP to rise.

Real Loanable Funds Market: Describe the Initial Economic Setting

The effects of economic, political, and social shocks to a nation's economy are influenced greatly by how sensitive borrowers and lenders/savers are to changes in the real risk-free interest rate. A highly elastic demand for real loanable funds means that any movement in the real risk-free interest rate causes significant changes in borrowers' willingness and ability to tap the domestic credit markets. In such cases, there are numerous investment projects that have their net profitability tied closely to the real cost of capital and many consumer expenditures that rely heavily on the real cost of credit.

The unemployment rate, employment rate, and capacity utilization rate provide clues as to where a nation is on its AS curve.

In the Keynesian range, the AS curve is horizontal. Changes in real GDP are greatest and changes in the GDP Price Index are smallest for any shift in AD.

In the classical range, the AS curve is vertical. Changes in real GDP are smallest and changes in the GDP Price Index are largest for any shift in AD. Most nations are in the intermediate range.

On the supply side, the more elastic a nation's supply of real loanable funds, the more sensitive domestic savers, banks, institutional investors, hedge funds, foreign investors, and government suppliers of real credit are to changes in the real risk-free interest rate. The international supply of real loanable funds can vary substantially from country to country, and therefore it can be a critical factor in country analyses.

One reason the elasticities of supply and demand in the real loanable funds market are of central interest is because they have a sizeable influence on the stability of a nation's real risk-free interest rate and equilibrium volume of real credit per period. Exhibit 17-4 shows a nation on the inelastic portion of its demand for real loanable funds.[3] Any shift in the supply of real loanable funds causes the nation's real risk-free interest rate to change by a larger percentage than the percentage change in equilibrium quantity of real loanable funds per period. Therefore, nations with low demand elasticities have real risk-free interest rates that are unstable relative to the amount of real credit supplied and demanded per period.

Exhibit 17-5 arrives at similar conclusions on the supply side. If the supply of real loanable funds is inelastic, then any change in the demand causes the nation's real risk-free interest rate to vary proportionately more than the change in equilibrium quantity of real credit per period.[4] Therefore, in nations

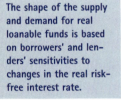

The shape of the supply and demand for real loanable funds is based on borrowers' and lenders' sensitivities to changes in the real risk-free interest rate.

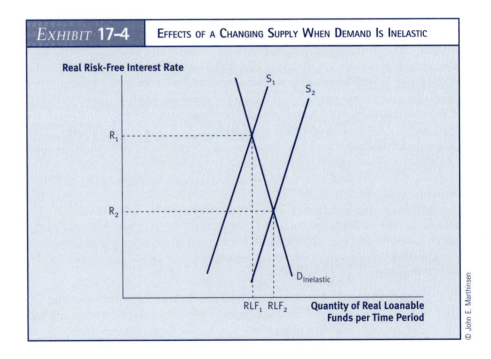

| EXHIBIT 17-4 | EFFECTS OF A CHANGING SUPPLY WHEN DEMAND IS INELASTIC |

Real Risk-Free Interest Rate

S_1 S_2

R_1

R_2

$D_{Inelastic}$

RLF_1 RLF_2 Quantity of Real Loanable Funds per Time Period

© John E. Marthinsen

---

[3] In Exhibit 17-4, demand is steeply sloped to simulate inelasticity. All straight-line, downward-sloping demand curves have inelastic, elastic, and unit elastic portions. The use of a steep slope is to trigger an intuitive feeling for the inelastic relationship.
[4] In Exhibit 17-5, supply is steeply sloped to motivate an intuitive feeling for the inelastic relationship.

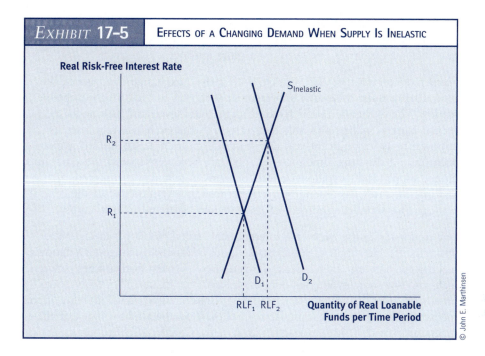

EXHIBIT 17-5   EFFECTS OF A CHANGING DEMAND WHEN SUPPLY IS INELASTIC

Real Risk-Free Interest Rate

$S_{Inelastic}$

R_2

R_1

D_1 D_2

RLF_1 RLF_2 Quantity of Real Loanable
Funds per Time Period

© John E. Marthinsen

with low supply elasticities, the real risk-free interest rate is unstable relative to the amount of real credit supplied and demanded.

"**The Rest of the Story**" section of this chapter expands on our discussion of elasticities in the real loanable funds market by relating them to the effectiveness of monetary and fiscal policies.

Foreign Exchange Market: Describe the Initial Economic Setting

The exchange rate system adopted by a nation is a key factor in virtually all macroeconomic analysis. Exchange rate movements can have significant effects on economic behavior, and when they are held steady by central banks, intervention can have powerful spillover effects on the real loanable funds market. In Chapter 15, "Exchange Rates: Why Do They Change?" we learned that exchange rate regimes vary from freely flexible, at one extreme, to absolutely fixed, at the other extreme. If a nation chooses a fixed exchange rate system, then its central bank must intervene to offset any shortage or surplus of the domestic currency in the foreign exchange market.

As was the case when we discussed the real loanable funds market, the less elastic a nation's supply or demand for foreign exchange, the more unstable its nominal exchange rate relative to its equilibrium quantity of foreign exchange per period.

Flexible Exchange Rates: If a nation chooses a flexible exchange rate system, then the currency value is free to move with the forces of supply and demand. With a flexible exchange rate system, currency values can be major risk factors in international trade and investment decisions. At the same time, a flexible exchange rate system empowers a nation's central bank with significant control over the domestic monetary base and money supply. Consequently, changes in

> The economic setting in the foreign exchange market depends on the exchange rate regime a nation chooses (e.g., fixed, flexible, or something in between).

> Flexible exchange rates reduce business risks associated with changes in a nation's money supply but increase business risks associated with currency value movements.

the monetary base and money supply (along with subsequent causes-and-effects, such as inflation) become less significant risk factors at the same time that the exchange rate becomes a more important risk factor.

Fixed Exchange Rates: By contrast, with a fixed exchange rate system, the central bank must offset any shortages or surpluses in the foreign exchange market. The exchange rate is fixed at its targeted level, and as long as the central bank is willing and able to maintain it, the exchange rate loses its importance as a significant risk factor in international trade and investment decisions. At the same time the exchange rate becomes less risky, the nation's money supply and its spillover effects in terms of actual and expected inflation and interest rates, become more risky because intervention causes the central bank to lose significant control of its monetary base and money supply.

> A fixed exchange rate may reduce business risks associated with changes in a nation's international currency value, but it increases risks associated with changes in a nation's money supply.

International Capital Mobility: International capital mobility is the extent to which the foreign supply of real loanable funds responds to changes in a nation's real risk-free interest rate relative to foreign rates. This text distinguishes between high- and low-mobility international capital markets. Exhibit 17-6 shows four broad categories of exchange rate regimes and international capital mobility. In the following three chapters, the implications of these combinations will be explained for countries with flexible exchange rate systems (Chapter 18, "Economic Shocks to Nations with Flexible Exchange Rates") and fixed exchange rate systems (Chapter 19, "Economic Shocks to Nations with Fixed Exchange Rates").

STEP 2: IDENTIFY THE ECONOMIC (OR EXPECTED) SHOCK TO THE NATION

The second step of our analysis is to identify the economic shock that jolts the economy and disrupts existing economic conditions. For this, it is important to make the distinction between *endogenous* and *exogenous* economic variables because changes in exogenous variables are always the sources of the

EXHIBIT 17-6	FOREIGN EXCHANGE MARKET SETTING	
International Capital Mobility / Exchange Rate System	**High Mobility**	**Low Mobility**
Flexible	Chapter 18, "Economic Shocks to Nations with Flexible Exchange Rates" addresses this scenario.	Chapter 18, "Economic Shocks to Nations with Flexible Exchange Rates" addresses this scenario.
Fixed	Chapter 19, "Economic Shocks to Nations with Fixed Exchange Rates" addresses this scenario.	Chapter 19, "Economic Shocks to Nations with Fixed Exchange Rates" addresses this scenario.

© John E. Marthinsen

initial changes in an economic system. Endogenous variables react to changes triggered by exogenous forces.

The key to understanding the difference between endogenous and exogenous variables is to remember that our Three-Sector Model was built to determine six endogenous economic variables: the real risk-free interest rate and quantity of real loanable funds per period in the real loanable funds market, GDP Price Index and real GDP in the real goods market, and nominal exchange rate and quantity of currency per period in the foreign exchange market. These variables remain in equilibrium (i.e., where the quantity supplied equals the quantity demanded per period) until a shift in supply and/or demand occurs.

By contrast, exogenous variables are determined outside the three macroeconomic markets of the country being analyzed. They are the sources of supply-side or demand-side changes in one or more of our three macroeconomic markets. For this reason, all of our analyses begin with an exogenous shock to the existing macroeconomic system.

An example helps explain the difference between exogenous and endogenous variables as well as the reason care should be taken when using them. Suppose you were working as finance manager for the Russian affiliate of a large multinational company headquartered in the United States. Anticipating a management committee review of the company's Eastern European strategy, suppose the chief financial officer (CFO) asked you to develop an analysis that explained the effects a higher real risk-free interest rate might have on the Russian economy.

Russia's real risk-free interest rate is determined in its real loanable funds market; therefore, it cannot change by itself. A higher real risk-free interest rate could be caused either by a reduction in the supply of real credit (perhaps due to contractionary monetary policies) or by an increase in the demand for real credit (perhaps due to increased government budget deficits). For this reason, you would need further clarification because the source of change could make a big difference to your conclusions.

By contrast, suppose your assignment was to present an analysis of the likely economic effects of a legislated change in Russia's tax rate. The tax rate is not an endogenous variable that is determined by the forces of supply and demand in any of the three principal macroeconomic markets. Rather, it is an exogenous variable that is determined solely by the government. In this case, no further clarification would be needed to conduct your analysis.

STEP 3: ANALYZE THE CHAIN REACTION OF ECONOMIC INTERACTIONS

Once the economic setting has been described (Step 1) and the exogenous source of change has been identified (Step 2), we can start our analysis. But where do we begin? There are three markets to consider, and the choice of where to start is important. The answer is to begin your analysis in the market that is most directly affected by the initial economic shock.

For example, if the shock is caused by a change in monetary policy, the analysis should begin in the real loanable funds market because changes in a nation's monetary base and/or money multiplier affect the real supply of money, which affects the supply of real loanable funds. By contrast, if we are analyzing the effects of tariffs or quotas, the analysis should start in the foreign exchange market because changes in imports and exports affect the international demand for and supply of a nation's currency.

> An exogenous variable is always the source of an initial economic change. Movements in endogenous variables are induced by these exogenous forces.

> Endogenous macroeconomic variables are determined by the forces of supply and demand within the Three-Sector Model.

> Exogenous variables are determined outside the analyzed nation's Three-Sector Model. Remember that all of our macroeconomic analyses begin with an exogenous shock.

In most cases, deciding where to begin the analysis is obvious, but there are cases where caution is advised. For instance, where would you begin your analysis if the government pursued expansionary fiscal policy by increasing government spending? You might be quick to start the analysis in the real goods market because government spending is a part of AD, but consider this: before the government can purchase anything, it needs funding.

If it funded the spending by borrowing, then the initial effect would be an increase in demand in the real loanable funds market. Spending would follow only after the funds were borrowed. Alternatively, if the government funded its spending by borrowing directly from the central bank,[5] the initial effect would increase the nation's monetary base, real money supply, and supply of real loanable funds. Again, the analysis would begin in the real loanable funds market. Finally, if the government imposed higher income taxes to fund its spending, the increased taxes would cut the budget deficit (or increase the budget surplus) as well as reduce disposable income and saving. Once again, the analysis would begin in the real loanable funds market. The important take-away from this discussion is that an exogenous shock usually impacts one market first and then spreads to the others. The point of impact is normally easy to identify and the subsequent spillover effects logical to follow.

Primary and Secondary Effects

In preparing for our macroeconomic analyses in the next three chapters, it is also helpful to distinguish between *primary* and *secondary* effects. The former are always stronger than the latter; they are also relatively simple to identify because primary effects shift the entire supply or demand curves. By contrast, secondary effects move a nation along these curves (see Exhibit 17-7).

It is important to understand that an exogenous shock can have a primary effect on more than one market. For example, capital flight from a nation has a primary effect on the foreign exchange market and the real loanable funds market. If the difference between primary and secondary effects seems nebulous, it will become clearer as we work our way through different economic scenarios in the following three chapters.

> An exogenous shock has primary and secondary effects as it spreads through the three macroeconomic markets. The primary effects are stronger than the secondary effects.

> An exogenous shock can have primary effects on more than one market.

Exhibit 17-7	Primary and Secondary Effects	
Effect	**Description**	**Supply or Demand Effect**
Primary	Initial exogenous shock	Shifts the entire demand and/or supply curve(s)
Secondary	Endogenous changes triggered by the exogenous shock	Movements along supply and/or demand curves
Notice	An exogenous shock can have two primary effects.	Shifts supply and/or demand in two macromarkets

© 2015 John E. Marthinsen

[5] The ability of governments to borrow directly from their central banks is restricted in most developed countries.

Where to Begin?

A useful rule of thumb to use when making your decision about where to begin an analysis is "Show me the money!" This expression is helpful because it reminds us to *follow the money* when it comes to matters of economics and finance.

Exhibit 17-8 provides some suggestions for where to begin your macroeconomic analysis due to changes in various exogenous variables.

A useful rule of thumb for determining where to begin your analysis is "Show me the money!"

EXHIBIT **17-8**	WHERE TO BEGIN YOUR ANALYSIS

Begin your analysis in the real goods market if there is a shift in:

GDP Price Index

Aggregate Supply

Aggregate Demand

Real GDP/time period

aggregate supply due to a change in:

- input prices,
- productivity,
- resource availability,
- supply-related government regulations that change business costs, and/or
- expectations.

Begin your analysis in the real loanable funds market if there is a shift in the:

Real risk-free interest rate

S Real loanable funds

D Real loanable funds

Real loanable funds/
time period

supply of real loanable funds due to changes in the:

- real money supply,
- real saving rate,
- speculative supply of funds,
- real government budget surplus, and/or
- supply of foreign credit to the domestic real loanable funds market.

demand for loanable funds due to changes in:

- real consumer credit demand,
- real speculative demand for funds,
- real business credit demand,
- real government credit demand (i.e., budget deficits), and/or
- real foreign credit demand.

(Continued)

EXHIBIT **17-8**	CONTINUED

Begin your analysis in foreign exchange market if there is a shift in the:

Nominal exchange rate
(Foreign currency/Domestic currency)

S Domestic currency

D Domestic currency

Domestic currency/
time period

supply of domestic currency in the foreign exchange market due to changes in *relative:*
- international capital flows (e.g., due to changed expectations and risks),
- international levels of protectionism (e.g., tariffs, quotas, and exchange controls),
- *foreign* real risk-free interest rate and *foreign* real incomes,
- international capital controls, and/or
- speculative supply.

demand for domestic currency in the foreign exchange market due to changes in *relative:*
- international capital flows (e.g., due to changed expectations and risks),
- international levels of protectionism (e.g., tariffs, quotas, and exchange controls),
- *foreign* real risk-free interest rate and *foreign* real incomes,
- international capital controls, and/or
- speculative demand.

Your analysis *never* begins with a:
- movement of any endogenous variable in the analyzed country (i.e., GDP Price Index, real GDP, real risk-free interest rate, quantity of real credit per period, nominal exchange rate, or quantity of currency (domestic or foreign) per period).*

*Keep in mind that, for any nation, changes in *foreign* real GDP, GDP Price Index, and/or real risk-free interest rate are treated as exogenous variables.

© John E. Marthinsen

THE REST OF THE STORY

Supply and demand elasticities in the real loanable funds market have significant impacts on the effectiveness of fiscal and monetary policies. **"The Rest of the Story"** section of this chapter is devoted to understanding the role that demand elasticities play.

CREDIT MARKET ELASTICITIES AND THE EFFECTIVENESS OF FISCAL AND MONETARY POLICIES

Is it better for a nation to have a high or low demand elasticity for real loanable funds? How do these elasticities affect fiscal and monetary policies? Do they act as unwanted anchors or as stimulants that improve fiscal and monetary policy effectiveness?

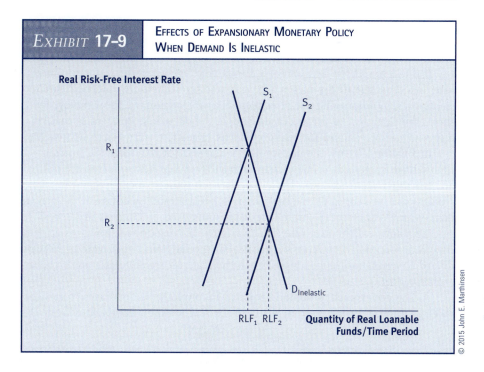

| EXHIBIT 17-9 | EFFECTS OF EXPANSIONARY MONETARY POLICY WHEN DEMAND IS INELASTIC |

EFFECTIVENESS OF MONETARY POLICY WHEN THE DEMAND FOR REAL LOANABLE FUNDS IS INELASTIC

For nations with inelastic demands for real loanable funds, monetary policy is weaker than in nations where demand is elastic. To understand why, suppose a nation was in a recession, and the central bank used expansionary monetary policy to stimulate spending. Exhibit 17-9 shows that increasing the supply of real loanable funds on an inelastic portion of a demand curve reduces significantly the real risk-free interest rate, but it does not stimulate much new borrowing. As a result, the central bank's efforts to encourage growth would be hindered by this lethargic reaction.

In the same sense, suppose the nation was overheating, and the central bank contracted the money supply (or its growth rate) to slow spending. The reduction in the real money supply would lower the nation's supply of real loanable funds and raise the real risk-free interest rate, but it would not reduce substantially the amount of borrowing. Therefore, with an inelastic demand for real loanable funds, monetary policy tends to be weak during recessions, when the central bank is trying to stimulate demand, and also weak during periods of rapid expansion, when the central bank is trying to cool the economy.

> Monetary policy becomes less effective as the elasticity of demand for real loanable funds falls.

EFFECTIVENESS OF FISCAL POLICY WHEN THE PRIVATE DEMAND FOR REAL LOANABLE FUNDS IS INELASTIC

Fiscal policies tend to be more effective the lower a nation's elasticity of demand for real loanable funds. To see why, consider what would happen if a government tried to stimulate the economy by increasing its active budget deficit (i.e., spending more and/or reducing taxes). The budget deficit would increase the demand for real loanable funds, thereby raising the real risk-free interest rate. As a result, the higher real risk-free interest rate would reduce private borrowing and spending.

If the demand for real loanable funds were inelastic, the reduction in private spending due to the higher real risk-free interest rate would be relatively small, thereby improving the effectiveness of expansionary fiscal policy. In short, the net effect of an increased budget deficit would be to raise the AD more when the demand for real credit was inelastic than when it was elastic.

In Exhibit 17-10A, the government's demand for real loanable funds is represented by a vertical line to reinforce the fact that governments are not accountable to bottom lines. Under such circumstances, their demand for real credit is not influenced by the real risk-free interest rate. By contrast, the private demand for real credit (Exhibit 17-10B) is influenced by changes in the real risk-free (and real) interest rate, which is why this demand is shown as a downward-sloping line. You will recall that the reduction in private borrowing due to government-induced increases in the real risk-free interest rate is called *crowding out*.

As the government's demand for real loanable funds increases from D_{G1} to D_{G2} (Exhibit 17-10A), total demand for real loanable funds rises from D_1

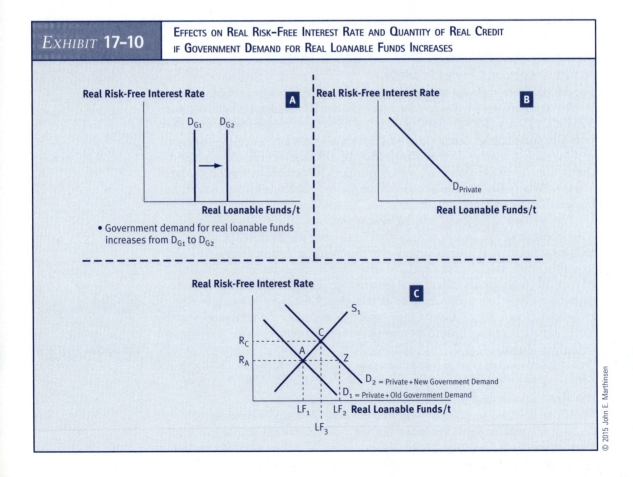

| EXHIBIT **17-10** | EFFECTS ON REAL RISK-FREE INTEREST RATE AND QUANTITY OF REAL CREDIT IF GOVERNMENT DEMAND FOR REAL LOANABLE FUNDS INCREASES |

to D_2 (Exhibit 17-10C), which creates an excess demand for funds equal to $LF_2 - LF_1$ (i.e., $Z - A$) at real risk-free interest rate R_A. Therefore, the real risk-free interest rate rises from R_A to R_C, causing the quantity of private funds demanded to fall from LF_2 to LF_3. If the private demand for real loanable funds (over this range) had a low elasticity, the amount of crowding out would be small. As a result, the net increase in the equilibrium quantity of real credit (i.e., the movement from LF_1 to LF_3) would be relatively large. By contrast, if the elasticity of demand for real loanable funds were high, a considerable amount of crowding out would result.

Similarly, if the economy were overheating, contractionary fiscal policy (i.e., lowering government spending and/or raising taxes) would cause the federal deficit to fall, thereby reducing the nation's demand for real loanable funds and real risk-free interest rate. A falling real risk-free interest rate would increase the amount of private borrowing and increase spending. But if the demand for real loanable funds were inelastic, the increase in private borrowing would be relatively small; so, again, the effectiveness of fiscal policy would be improved.

> Fiscal policy becomes more effective as the elasticity of demand for real loanable funds falls.

CONCLUSION

This chapter sets the stage for the country analyses discussed in the following three chapters. In our Three-Sector Model, the GDP Price Index and real GDP rate are determined in the real goods market; the real risk-free interest rate and the quantity of real credit per period are determined in the real loanable funds market, and the nominal exchange rate and quantity of currency per period are determined in the foreign exchange market. At this point, it is important that the economic relationships in each of these markets are logical and consistent with your common sense about how people react to economic incentives, such as changing prices, interest rates, and real income.

This chapter also laid out the methodology we will follow in our macroeconomic analyses. In Step 1, we describe the initial economic environment of the economy being analyzed. This step consists mainly of determining the economic factors that influence the slope or elasticity of supply and demand in each of the three principal macroeconomic markets. In Step 2, we identify the exogenous shock to the nation's economy. Finally, in Step 3, we analyze the chain of economic reactions that result from an initial shock. For each analysis, we must make sure to begin in the market that is most directly affected by the exogenous economic shock and clearly distinguish primary from secondary effects. As for where to start our analyses, when in doubt, remember the simple rule of thumb "Show me the money!"

REVIEW QUESTIONS

1. Explain the three-step process used to analyze the effects that external shocks have on a nation's economy.

2. Give three examples of external shocks that could cause major changes in our Three-Sector Model.

3. What economic indicators provide evidence that a nation is on the inelastic portion of its AS curve?

4. If a nation were near the classical range of its AS curve, what should be assumed about the relative change in prices, as opposed to the relative change in real GDP, for any increase in AD?

5. In the context of the Three-Sector Model, what is wrong with the following statement? "Let's begin our analysis of the United States with a depreciation of the U.S. dollar in terms of the euro."

6. What rule of thumb should be followed to determine in which of the three markets to begin your macroeconomic analysis?

7. Name two exogenous shocks that would begin your Three-Sector-Model analysis in the foreign exchange market. Name two exogenous shocks that would begin it in the real goods market. Finally, name two exogenous shocks that would begin your analysis in the real loanable funds market.

8. Why should a change in an endogenous variable never be the starting point of a macroeconomic analysis?

9. Explain the four broad combinations of exchange rate regimes and international capital mobility.

10. Is the following statement true or false? "In nations with high demand elasticities for real loanable funds, any shift of supply causes the real risk-free interest rate to fluctuate wildly relative to the equilibrium quantity of real credit per period." Explain.

11. Is the following statement true or false? "The higher the elasticity of demand for real loanable funds, the more this demand acts like a stimulus to economic activity when the real risk-free interest rate falls." Explain.

12. Is the following statement true or false? "In nations with elastic demands for real loanable funds, monetary policy should be relatively more powerful than in nations where demand is inelastic." Explain.

13. Is the following statement true or false? "Fiscal policies tend to be less effective the higher a nation's elasticity of demand for real loanable funds."

14. If a nation's supply of real loanable funds were perfectly elastic, how effective would monetary policy be at changing the real risk-free interest rate? Explain.

Chapter 18

Economic Shocks to Nations with Flexible Exchange Rates

INTRODUCTION

This chapter uses the Three-Sector Model to analyze the economic effects of shocks to nations with flexible exchange rates. Our methodology will follow the three-step process that involves describing the initial economic setting of the nation being analyzed, identifying the economic, political, or social shock, and, finally, analyzing the macroeconomic implications of the shock (see Exhibit 18-1).

We begin by analyzing the economic effects of expansionary fiscal policy and then go on to explain the effects of expansionary monetary policy. Our analysis will show that differences in the degree of international capital mobility can have a significant (sometimes unexpected) impact on the effectiveness of monetary and fiscal policies. The analytical techniques developed in this chapter will also be helpful in the next chapter (Chapter 19, "Economic Shocks to Nations with Fixed Exchange Rates"), where we will extend our analysis to nations with fixed exchange rates.

THE BASICS

EFFECTS OF EXPANSIONARY FISCAL POLICY

Picture yourself working as the new finance manager in Mexico City, Mexico for Fenway, Inc., a large, multinational health care company based in Boston, Massachusetts. You just got off the phone with the CFO in

What are the effects of expansionary fiscal policy for nations with flexible exchange rates?

EXHIBIT 18-1	ANALYSIS METHODOLOGY: THREE ANALYTICAL STEPS
Step 1	Describe the initial economic setting of the three key macroeconomic markets (i.e., the real goods market, real loanable funds market, and foreign exchange market) for the country being analyzed.
Step 2	Identify the shock (or expected shock) to the nation.
Step 3	Analyze the chain reaction of economic causes and effects.

© John E. Marthinsen

Boston, who is concerned about an article in a well-respected business publication that mentions the populist Mexican government's desire to reduce its high unemployment rate by dramatically increasing government spending. He promises to e-mail the article to you shortly.

The reason for the CFO's concern is that potential investments in Mexico play a significant role in Fenway's current five-year business plan, and, therefore, a careful review of expected future cash flows from these investments is being made. Your job, as spelled out by the CFO, is to analyze the likely economic effects of Mexico's expansionary fiscal policy and to lead a conference-call discussion the next morning at 11:00. Because the corporate treasurer and three members of a divisional task force have been working on this portion of the business plan, the CFO has also invited them to participate in tomorrow's conference call with you.

During the phone conversation, you learned that the CFO is especially interested in the likely effects that Mexico's expansionary fiscal policy will have on the most important business plan variables. In particular, he is concerned about changes in Mexico's:

- GDP Price Index and real GDP,
- nominal GDP,
- unemployment and employment rates,
- real and nominal wages,
- real and nominal interest rates,
- monetary base,
- money supply,
- gross private domestic investment,
- real and nominal exchange rate (i.e., dollars per peso), and
- significant balance of payments components.

Some of these variables are key factors built into Fenway's spreadsheet analyses to project the company's business plan cash flows.

After hanging up the phone, you realize the CFO is looking not only for your answers and insights but also for a logical and fruitful framework that will allow everyone to participate in the conversation tomorrow. A consensus viewpoint is needed so that analytical work on the business plan can proceed. You also know that your analysis will be carefully and critically scrutinized by everyone in the group—especially in light of the strong and varied vested interest groups taking part in the meeting. One thing is clear: Your reasoning must be logical and consistent because any unsupported claims or errors in reasoning will cast doubts on the objectivity and depth of your analysis.

Within a few minutes of your phone call with the CFO, you receive the e-mailed article shown on the next page. Given the information in the article, how will you go about preparing your remarks for tomorrow's meeting and organizing your thoughts for the possible questions and comments of others?

Mexican President Seeks to Reduce Unemployment

By J. E. Marthinsen

MEXICO CITY, Mexico—For the past two years, high unemployment, low plant utilization, and sluggish growth have plagued Mexico. Unfortunately, the nation has also been suffering from large and rising current account deficits, which it has managed to finance by borrowing in the international capital markets. Due to fears of speculative international investment flows and concerns over foreign hegemony, the government has placed restrictions on foreign nations' investments in Mexico and on domestic citizens' investments abroad. As a result, financing these current account deficits has been expensive.

On the bright side, the value of Mexico's currency, the peso, has held steady during the past few months, but the nation's commitment to flexible exchange rates could come under pressure with the president's recent proposal to reduce the unemployment rate to single-digit levels by dramatically increasing government spending. Despite a budget deficit that is already approaching 4% of GDP, the president indicated that any increase in the deficit resulting from his expansionary policies would be financed by borrowing in the domestic capital markets.

Step 1: Describe The Initial Economic Setting of the Three Major Markets in Mexico

Let's begin by making reasonable assumptions about the shape (slope or elasticity) of the supply and demand curves in Mexico's real goods market, real loanable funds market, and foreign exchange market.

> Mexico is on the intermediate range of the AS curve but closer to the Keynesian range than the classical range.

Real Goods Market: Economic Setting

Due to the high level of unemployment, low plant utilization, and sluggish GDP growth, there should be ample resources available to expand output. As a result, let's assume that Mexico is on a relatively flat portion of its AS curve (see the circled region shown in Exhibit 18-2). It is important to remember that our assumption of a relatively flat aggregate supply means that we are expecting any increase in aggregate demand to cause Mexico's real GDP to change by a larger percent than its GDP Price Index.

Real Loanable Funds Market: Economic Setting

At a minimum, Mexico's supply of real loanable funds is upward sloping because the real risk-free interest rate affects the behavior of domestic and foreign credit sources, such as households, businesses, banks, and governments. At the same time, being a developing nation with a relatively low per

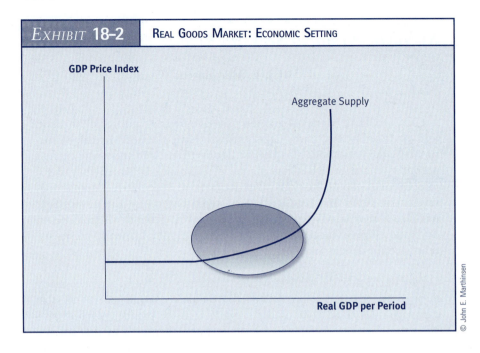

EXHIBIT 18-2   REAL GOODS MARKET: ECONOMIC SETTING

capita GDP, it is unlikely that changes in the real risk-free interest rate will significantly affect the nation's saving rate. Other variables, such as income levels and expectations, are likely to be much more important.

While foreign investments in Mexico and Mexican investments abroad are affected by changes in a nation's real risk-free interest rate relative to foreign nations, due to the nation's investment restrictions and relatively unsophisticated domestic financial market, these flows will be hindered. Therefore, in our analysis, let's assume that the supply of real loanable funds is upward sloping but inelastic, which means that the percentage change in the amount of funds supplied to the real loanable funds market is less than the percentage change in Mexico's real risk-free interest rate (see Exhibit 18-3).

As for demand, we will assume, for now, that Mexico's demand for real loanable funds is also rather inelastic. Given the current state of the economy, the private sector is not anxious to borrow if the real risk-free interest rate falls, and, likewise, a higher real risk-free interest rate does not significantly discourage borrowing (see Exhibit 18-3).

Foreign Exchange Market: Economic Setting

Exhibit 18-4 shows the dollar–peso foreign exchange market. We have no information on whether the international market responds forcefully or weakly to changes in the nominal dollar–peso exchange rate. Therefore, we cannot make any initial assumptions about whether Mexico's foreign exchange supply

Mexico's supply and demand for real loanable funds are relatively inelastic.

The peso floats freely in the foreign exchange market.

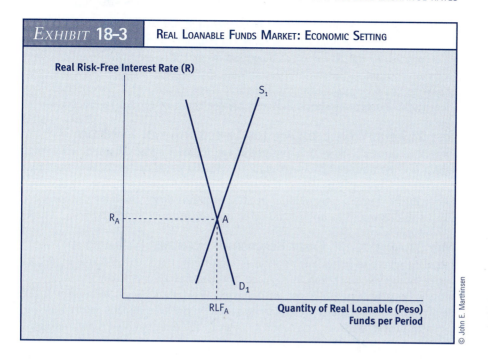

EXHIBIT 18-3	REAL LOANABLE FUNDS MARKET: ECONOMIC SETTING

Real Risk-Free Interest Rate (R)

S_1

R_A

A

D_1

RLF_A

Quantity of Real Loanable (Peso) Funds per Period

© John E. Marthinsen

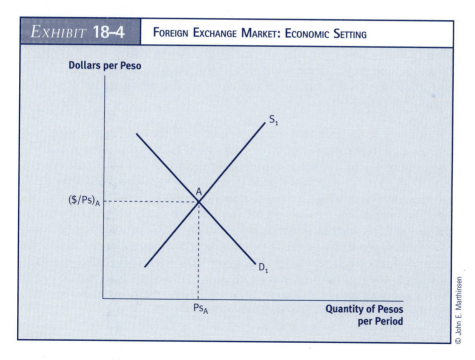

EXHIBIT 18-4	FOREIGN EXCHANGE MARKET: ECONOMIC SETTING

Dollars per Peso

S_1

A

$(\$/Ps)_A$

D_1

Ps_A

Quantity of Pesos per Period

© John E. Marthinsen

and demand curves are elastic or inelastic. Nevertheless, we do know that Mexico has a freely fluctuating exchange rate system, which means the nation's central bank (Bank of Mexico) has made a policy decision not to intervene in the foreign exchange market—even if there are significant exchange rate fluctuations. As a result, the Bank of Mexico will not try to maintain any particular exchange rate goal or to stabilize fluctuations in the peso's international value relative to the dollar. Let's also assume that foreign central banks refrain from intervening in the dollar–peso foreign exchange market.[1]

With the economic setting in the three markets tentatively established, let's identify the exogenous shock that sets off the chain of economic reactions.

STEP 2: IDENTIFY THE ECONOMIC (OR EXPECTED) SHOCK TO MEXICO

The exogenous shock in this analysis is the increase in government spending, which will be financed by borrowing in Mexico's real credit market (i.e., real loanable funds market). The change in government spending is an exogenous factor in the Three-Sector Model because it is not determined by the forces of supply and demand in any of the three macroeconomic markets.

The shock to the Three-Sector Model is expansionary fiscal policy.

STEP 3: ANALYZE THE CHAIN REACTION OF ECONOMIC INTERACTIONS

Deciding where to begin our analysis is important, but the decision is made easier by the rule of thumb introduced in the last chapter. "Show me the money!" is a helpful guidepost for determining where to begin because it emphasizes the fact that funds must be raised by the government before they can be spent. Therefore, let's begin our analysis in the real loanable funds market.

Where to begin? Show me the money!

Economic Effects in the Real Loanable Funds Market

The increase in government borrowing is an exogenous factor in the real loanable funds market that raises demand. In Exhibit 18-5, the increase in government borrowing causes the total demand for real loanable funds to rise from D_1 to D_2, thereby raising Mexico's real risk-free interest rate from R_A to R_B and raising the equilibrium quantity of real loanable funds per period from RLF_A to RLF_B. Notice that the change in demand is a primary effect because it shifts the entire demand for loanable funds curve.

Increased government borrowing raises the real risk-free interest rate and quantity of real loanable funds per period.

Crowding Out: Exhibit 18-5 shows an increase in the equilibrium quantity of real loanable funds per period from RLF_A to RLF_B, but the increase in government borrowing and spending is equal to $RLF_Z - RLF_A$ (i.e., the distance A to Z). The reason the net increase in real credit spending is less than the government's demand for funds is because of *crowding out*.[2] As the government borrowing and the demand for real loanable funds rise from D_1 to D_2, the real risk-free interest rate increases from R_A to R_B, causing private borrowing (e.g., gross private domestic investment and consumption) to fall. The amount of real credit that would have been demanded at R_A falls from RLF_Z to RLF_B as the real risk-free interest rate rises to R_B. This reduction in private borrowing (and spending), due to government-induced increases in the real risk-free interest rate, is called *crowding out*.

Crowding out occurs when government borrowing raises the real risk-free interest rate and reduces private borrowing.

---

[1] For the dollar–peso exchange rate to fluctuate freely and for Mexico to maintain maximum control over its monetary base, foreign central banks (e.g., the U.S. Federal Reserve) and the Bank of Mexico cannot intervene (net) in the dollar–peso foreign exchange market, which means during each period, there has to be either no intervention or self-cancelling intervention.

[2] For an extended discussion of crowding out see Chapter 13, "Fiscal Policy and Automatic Stabilizers: What Managers Need to Know" in "**The Rest of the Story**" section entitled "Crowding-Out: When Is It Complete, Nonexistent, or Partial?"

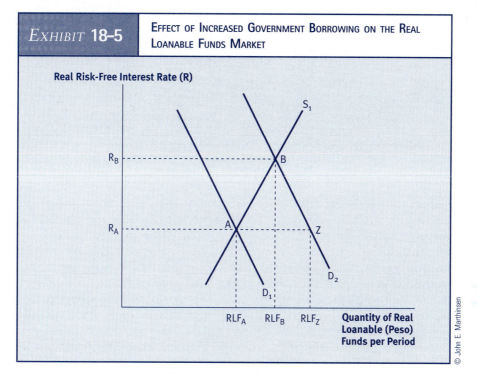

EXHIBIT 18-5   EFFECT OF INCREASED GOVERNMENT BORROWING ON THE REAL LOANABLE FUNDS MARKET

Economic Effects in the Real Goods Market

Exhibit 18-6 builds on this conclusion. An increase in net borrowing causes Mexico's aggregate demand (i.e., the sum of consumption [C], gross private domestic investment [I], government spending on final goods and services [G],

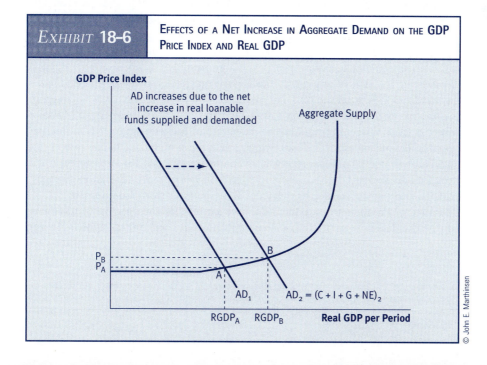

EXHIBIT 18-6   EFFECTS OF A NET INCREASE IN AGGREGATE DEMAND ON THE GDP PRICE INDEX AND REAL GDP

E_{XHIBIT} **18-7**	**PRIMARY AND SECONDARY EFFECTS**			
Expansionary fiscal policy	$G \uparrow$ = Borrowing $\uparrow$	$AD \uparrow$	Primary effect	
Real risk-free interest rate $\uparrow$	$C \downarrow$ & $I \downarrow$	$AD \downarrow$	Secondary effects coming from the real loanable funds market	
Net effect	$(C + I + G)\uparrow$	$AD \uparrow$	**Primary > secondary effects**	

and net exports [NE]) to rise. In the real goods market, an increase in aggregate demand from AD_1 to AD_2 causes prices to rise from P_A to P_B and real GDP to rise from $RGDP_A$ to $RGDP_B$.

This change in aggregate demand deserves a bit more attention because it involves a primary and secondary effect. The primary effect is the initial increase in government spending (i.e., the fiscal stimulus that is financed by borrowing), which increases AD by the full rise in government spending. At the same time, there are secondary effects at work here. Because the real risk-free interest rate increases, both C and I fall (i.e., they are crowded out). Nevertheless, the primary effect is stronger than the secondary effects. But we already knew this because, looking at the real loanable funds market, we see that net borrowing rises when the government enters the market. These primary and secondary effects are summarized in Exhibit 18-7.[3]

Economic Effects in the Foreign Exchange Market

Let's turn our attention to the last macroeconomic market in the Three-Sector Model and determine what happens to Mexico's nominal exchange rate. The foreign exchange market is affected only when individuals exchange one currency for another currency. Therefore, the Mexican government's demand for credit in the real loanable funds market and its subsequent expenditures have no *direct* effect on the dollar–peso exchange rate.

Despite the lack of any direct effect, government borrowing and spending have indirect effects on the nominal exchange rate because they cause changes in the nation's real risk-free interest rate, GDP Price Index, and real GDP. Movements in these three important economic variables trigger adjustments in international trade and investment flows, which affect the nominal exchange rate.

The balance of payments is a convenient framework for organizing our thoughts on the supply and demand forces at work in the foreign exchange market, but before we do, let's review some basics. From Chapter 16, "Balance of Payments Fundamentals," we know that the balance of payments can be divided into two parts: (1) current international transactions (CT) and

---

[3] For a more complete explanation of why the primary increase in government spending is greater than all the secondary reductions in spending, read in "The Basics" of Chapter 13, "Fiscal Policy and Automatic Stabilizers: What Managers Need to Know" the section entitled "Forces in the Real Loanable Funds Market That Weaken the Fiscal Multiplier."

(2) net international borrowing/lending (NIB/L). We also know that the entire balance of payments must sum to zero; therefore, CT + NIB/L ≡ 0.

$$CT + NIB/L \equiv 0.$$

CT includes both current account (CA) and capital account (KA) transactions, which means it comprises a nation's imports and exports of goods and services, net international income flows from wages, interest, rent, and profits, transfers (both current account and capital account), and other capital account transactions (e.g., exchanges of natural resources, legal and accounting creations, as well as marketing assets).

$$CT \equiv CA + KA$$

Net international borrowing/lending includes: (1) net nonreserve-related international borrowing and lending transactions (NI), such as foreign portfolio and direct investments by private individuals and businesses, and also (2) reserve-related transactions by the central bank (RA). Therefore, NIB/L equals NI and RA.

$$NIB/L \equiv NI + RA$$

If CT plus NIB/L must equal zero, then CT plus NI plus RA must also equal zero.

$$CT + NI + RA \equiv 0.$$

Changes in a nation's nominal exchange rate are not determined by all balance of payments transactions but rather only by those transactions that enter into the foreign exchange market. For this reason, we will make the following distinctions and abbreviations.

- CTX: Current international transactions that affect the foreign exchange market will be abbreviated as CTX,
- NIX: Net nonreserve-related international borrowing/lending transactions that affect the foreign exchange market will be abbreviated as NIX, and
- RAX: Reserve-related (central bank) transactions that influence the foreign exchange markets will be abbreviated as RAX.

Therefore, the supply and demand forces in the foreign exchange market can be separated into three major parts: CTX forces, NIX forces and RAX forces.

Exhibit 18-8 summarizes the major macroeconomic variables that cause supply and demand changes via CTX, NIX, and RAX. Normally, imports and exports are the most important transactions behind the CTX forces, and the key macroeconomic variables causing them to change are relative movements of international prices and real income. By contrast, NIX forces are influenced mainly by changes in relative real international interest rates. Finally, RAX forces are determined by central bank intervention in the foreign exchange markets. With this in mind, let's take a closer look at our analysis of expansionary fiscal policy in Mexico.

> Supply and demand forces in the foreign exchange market can be separated into three major parts: CTX, NIX, and RAX forces.

| EXHIBIT **18-8** | MACROECONOMIC VARIABLES THAT INFLUENCE **CTX, NIX,** AND **RAX** |

Balance of Payments Components Affected	Abb.	Macroeconomic Variables That Influence Supply and/or Demand
Current international Transactions	CTX	• Changes in relative international prices • Changes in relative international incomes
Net Nonreserve-Related International Borrowing/Lending Transactions	NIX	• Changes in relative international (real) interest rates
Reserve-Related (Central Bank) Transactions	RAX	• Central bank intervention

© 2015 John E. Marthinsen

CTX-related supply and demand forces in the foreign exchange market: So far, we have found that expansionary fiscal policy increases Mexico's real risk-free interest rate, GDP Price Index, and real GDP. We also know that movements in Mexico's GDP Price Index and real GDP have the most significant effects on the nation's imports and exports.

Real GDP Effects on CTX—Growth of real GDP increases the purchasing power of Mexico's household sector. While many of the goods and services that Mexicans consume are produced domestically, others are imported. Exhibit 18-9 shows that, as Mexicans purchase U.S. goods and services, they supply pesos to the foreign exchange market in order to purchase dollars. Therefore, this increase in Mexico's imports raises the supply of pesos to the foreign exchange market, which depreciates the peso's value.

Higher Mexican real GDP depreciates the peso.

| EXHIBIT **18-9** | EFFECTS OF RISING REAL GDP ON THE PESO'S VALUE |

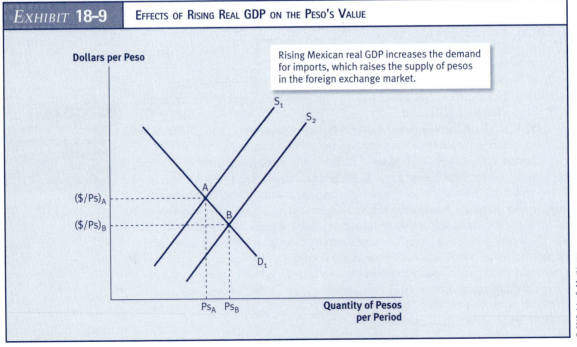

Rising Mexican real GDP increases the demand for imports, which raises the supply of pesos in the foreign exchange market.

© 2015 John E. Marthinsen

Relative Price Level Effects on CTX—Higher Mexican prices relative to the United States provide incentives to increase Mexico's imports from the United States and decrease its exports to the United States. As Mexico's imports rise, the demand for dollars increases, which raises (once again) the supply of pesos in the foreign exchange market. Exhibit 18-10 shows that, as the supply of pesos to the foreign exchange market increases, the peso depreciates from ($/Ps)$_A$ to ($/Ps)$_B$. Similarly, falling Mexican exports reduces the U.S. demand for Mexican goods and services, and, therefore, decreases the demand for pesos. As the demand for pesos falls, the peso depreciates from ($/Ps)$_B$ to ($/Ps)$_C$.

> CTX-related supply and demand forces decrease the value of the peso due to the higher real GDP and higher prices.

The quantity of pesos traded in the foreign exchange market per period is not an important decision variable for Fenway's business plan analysis. Nevertheless, let's determine if the volume of activity in the dollar–peso market rises or falls.

When more pesos are supplied to the foreign exchange market, the equilibrium quantity of pesos increases; but when the demand for pesos falls, the equilibrium quantity falls. Therefore, without further information, there is no way to determine the *net* change in quantity of pesos supplied and demanded. Exhibit 18-10 shows no net change in the equilibrium quantity of pesos per period, but this result would vary depending on the relative magnitudes by which supply and demand shift.

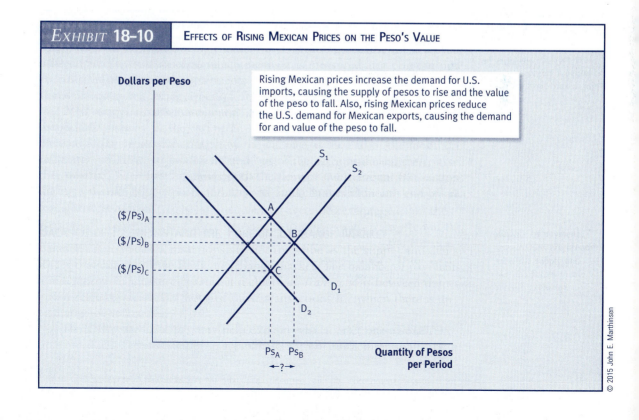

EXHIBIT 18-10	EFFECTS OF RISING MEXICAN PRICES ON THE PESO'S VALUE

Rising Mexican prices increase the demand for U.S. imports, causing the supply of pesos to rise and the value of the peso to fall. Also, rising Mexican prices reduce the U.S. demand for Mexican exports, causing the demand for and value of the peso to fall.

NIX-related supply and demand forces in the foreign exchange market:
Mexico's NIX-related transactions include short- and long-term international
investment outflows and inflows. Of the four economic variables that changed
in the real loanable funds market and real goods market, movements in
Mexico's real risk-free interest rate relative to the United States have the
most significant effect on these investment flows.

The increased demand for real loanable funds by Mexico's government
increases the nation's real risk-free interest rate. This makes peso-denominated
interest-earning assets, such as bills, notes, and bonds, more attractive relative
to dollar-denominated securities. In Exhibit 18-11, as dollar holders purchase
pesos to invest in peso-denominated assets, the demand for pesos in the foreign exchange market increases from D_1 to D_2. This increased demand causes
the peso to appreciate relative to the dollar from $(\$/Ps)_A$ to $(\$/Ps)_B$.

Similarly, the change in Mexico's relative real interest yield provides an
incentive for Mexican investors to adjust the composition of their investment portfolios toward peso-denominated assets. At the same time, to
keep diversified portfolios, they are unlikely to invest everything in peso-
denominated assets. Exhibit 18-11 shows that a decrease in the supply of
pesos to the foreign exchange market (i.e., which is the same as a decrease
in the demand for dollars in the foreign exchange market) causes the peso to
appreciate relative to the dollar (i.e., from $(\$/Ps)_B$ to $(\$/Ps)_C$).

> NIX-related supply and
> demand forces increase
> the value of the peso due
> to the higher real risk-
> free interest rate.

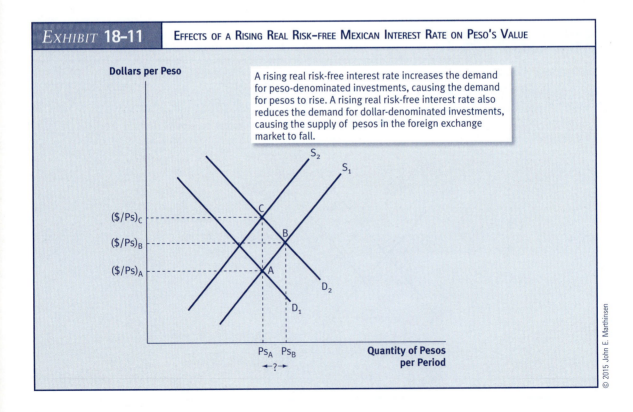

EXHIBIT **18-11**   EFFECTS OF A RISING REAL RISK-FREE MEXICAN INTEREST RATE ON PESO'S VALUE

Dollars per Peso

A rising real risk-free interest rate increases the demand
for peso-denominated investments, causing the demand
for pesos to rise. A rising real risk-free interest rate also
reduces the demand for dollar-denominated investments,
causing the supply of pesos in the foreign exchange
market to fall.

As was the case when we analyzed CTX's supply and demand forces, the quantity of pesos traded per period in the foreign exchange market is not an important decision variable for Fenway's business plan analysis. Nevertheless, notice that the increase in Mexico's real risk-free interest rate stimulates supply and demand responses due to NIX transactions. The rising demand for pesos causes the equilibrium quantity per period to increase, but the declining supply causes it to fall. Exhibit 18-11 shows the two effects canceling each other so there is no net change in quantity, but this does not have to be the case. An increase in demand that is relatively stronger than the reduction in supply would raise the equilibrium quantity per period, and a relatively strong reduction in supply would reduce it. Without further information, there is no way to determine the net change in quantity.

RAX-related supply and demand forces in the foreign exchange market: RAX-related transactions occur only when central banks intervene in the peso-related foreign exchange markets (i.e., in this case, the dollar–peso market). Because Mexico has a flexible exchange rate system, we have assumed that neither the Bank of Mexico nor any foreign central bank (e.g., the U.S. Federal Reserve) intervenes in this foreign exchange market. As a result, there are no RAX-related supply and/or demand forces at work in the foreign exchange market.

> There is no central bank intervention in the foreign exchange market and, therefore, no RAX-related changes in supply or demand.

Summary of supply and demand forces in the foreign exchange market: Exhibit 18-12 summarizes the supply and demand shifts in the foreign exchange market due to the spillover effects from the real loanable funds market and real goods market.

EXHIBIT **18-12**	SUMMARY OF CHANGES IN THE VALUE OF THE PESO	
Sources of Supply and Demand Changes	**Changes in the Supply and/or Demand for Pesos**	**Change in the Peso's Value**
CTX–Related Forces		
Prices ↑	Exports ↓ → D $_{pesos}$ ↓ Imports ↑ → S $_{pesos}$ ↑	Peso depreciates
Real GDP ↑	Imports ↑ → S $_{pesos}$ ↑	
NIX–Related Forces		
Real risk-free interest rate ↑	Financial capital inflows ↑ → D $_{pesos}$ ↑ Financial capital outflows ↓ → S $_{pesos}$ ↓	Peso appreciates
RAX–Related Forces		
No central bank intervention (flexible exchange rates)	No change	No change
Net change		**Depends on degree of international capital mobility**

International capital mobility: It appears as if the change in the peso's value is uncertain, due to conflicting CTX and NIX forces. CTX's supply and demand forces cause the peso to depreciate, but NIX's forces cause it to appreciate. To determine which one dominates, we need to introduce the distinction between *high-mobility* and *low-mobility* international capital markets.

High-mobility international capital markets exist when NIX forces in our Three-Sector Model outweigh CTX forces. In other words, high-mobility international capital markets exist when changes in a nation's real risk-free interest rate relative to other nations stimulate international investment flows that are *greater than* the trade flows stimulated by changes in a nation's relative GDP Price Index and relative real GDP.

By contrast, *low-mobility* international capital markets are just the opposite. Low mobility exists when NIX-related investment flows, which are stimulated by movements in the real risk-free interest rate relative to the rest of the world, are *less than* CTX-related forces, which are stimulated by changes in a nation's relative GDP Price Index and relative real GDP. In general, the greater the international capital market impediments and imperfections facing a nation (e.g., central bank controls and taxes), the more immobile the international capital markets it faces. Exhibit 18-13 summarizes the two different levels of international capital mobility.

Notice that high and low international capital mobility are relative concepts, which are connected to relative international incomes, prices, and interest rate elasticities. In the short run, most countries face high-mobility international capital markets because global investments (especially financial investments) can be executed in a matter of seconds, but changes in trade flows usually react with a considerable lag. After all, it takes time for businesses and consumers to notice that relative prices have changed and then act on them by changing suppliers, developing new purchasing and marketing strategies, adjusting selling channels, entering into new contracts, and canceling existing contracts.

Because the Mexican government imposes restrictions on international investment flows, you could start your analysis by assuming low-mobility international capital markets. But keep in mind that it would take very severe restrictions, indeed, to reduce investment flows to this level. Therefore, to cover yourself for tomorrow's meeting, it would be a good idea to analyze the effects of both high- and low-mobility international capital markets. Perhaps one or more of the conference-call participants will have strong beliefs one way or the other.

High-mobility international capital markets exist when NIX forces on the nominal exchange rate are greater than the CTX forces.

Low-mobility international capital markets exist when NIX forces on the nominal exchange rate are less than CTX forces.

EXHIBIT 18-13	HIGH-MOBILITY AND LOW-MOBILITY INTERNATIONAL CAPITAL MARKETS	
Mobility	**Description**	
High international capital mobility	NIX-Related Forces > CTX-Related Forces	
Low international capital mobility	NIX-Related Forces < CTX-Related Forces	

In any case, this is not going to be the last time you are asked to make an analysis like this. As Fenway's finance manager in Mexico City, you should expect to be called on regularly for market feedback and advice. Therefore, your analysis for tomorrow's meeting is just the beginning of a self-education process and not an end in itself.

How would the results of high international capital mobility differ from low international capital mobility? If Mexico faced high-mobility international capital markets, the forces of international investment flows would overpower the trade flows, causing the peso to appreciate. By contrast, if the nation faced low-mobility international capital markets, then the peso would depreciate because the CTX-related trade flows would overpower the NIX-related investment flows.

> With high international capital mobility, the peso's value rises in our example. With low mobility, it falls.

Summary of Answers to the CFO's Questions

Fenway's CFO was looking for feedback, and so far, our Three-Sector Model has produced some interesting results. Let's review the conclusions we have derived.

GDP Price Index and Real GDP Rise

From our analysis of the real goods market, we found that Mexico's GDP Price Index and real GDP should rise due to the net increase in aggregate demand, caused by increased government spending.

Nominal GDP Rises

Nominal GDP is equal to the prices times the quantities of all final goods and services produced each period. If Mexico's GDP Price Index and real GDP rise with the increase in aggregate demand, then nominal GDP must rise.

Unemployment Rate Falls and Employment Rate Rises

If Mexico's real GDP increases, more workers will be needed to produce these new goods and services. Therefore, the increase in real GDP should cause the nation's unemployment rate to fall and its employment rate to rise as the demand for labor increases.

Real and Nominal Wages Rise

Rising rates of output in Mexico cause an increase in the demand for labor. As a result, there should be upward pressure on real wages. Because the percentage change in nominal wage is (approximately) equal to the percentage change in real wage plus the expected inflation rate, an increase in both the real wage and expected price level implies that Mexico's nominal wage rate should rise.

Real and Nominal Interest Rates Rise

Our analysis of the real loanable funds market shows that an increase in government demand for real credit causes the real risk-free interest rate to rise. It also shows that the increased AD raises prices, which means the anticipated expansionary fiscal policy is likely to increase expected inflation. Because the nominal interest rate is (approximately) equal to the real interest rate plus expected inflation, increases in both the real risk-free interest rate and inflationary expectations (due to the prospect of expansionary fiscal policy) should increase Mexico's nominal interest rate.

Monetary Base Does Not Change

Mexico's monetary base remains the same because there is no change in the central bank's open market operations or discount loans. Notice, as well, that RA does not change. Therefore, there is no central bank intervention in the foreign exchange market that changes the monetary base.

Money Supply (M2) Rises

M2 equals the monetary base times the M2 money multiplier. We know already from our previous answer that Mexico's monetary base does not change. Therefore, M2 can change only if Mexico's M2 money multiplier varies.

Fluctuations in the M2 money multiplier are caused by movements in a nation's reserve requirement ratio(s) and preferred asset ratios (i.e., C_c/D, N/D, and U/D). The Mexican central bank has not changed the reserve ratio(s), and we have no reason to believe Mexico's preferred asset ratios will be affected *directly* by expansionary fiscal policy.

As the same time, there is an *indirect* stimulus that will cause adjustments in Mexico's preferred asset ratios. As the nation's real risk-free interest rate rises, the preferred asset ratios for currency in circulation (C_c/D) and customary reserves (U/D) fall, and the preferred asset ratio for near money (N/D) rises. All three of these movements increase the ability of banks to lend and, therefore, cause the M2 money multiplier to rise, which increases the M2 money supply.

Gross Private Domestic Investment Change is Uncertain

The increase in Mexico's real risk-free interest rate raises companies' cost of capital, thereby causing marginal business investments to be postponed or abandoned. At the same time, Mexico's growing GDP is likely to stimulate new investments. Therefore, the net change in real gross private domestic investment is uncertain until we know more about the relative magnitudes of interest-induced movements and real income-induced movements in real investment spending.

Fenway's CFO may not be happy to hear that you have come back with an ambiguous answer, but ambiguity with an explanation is worth much more than an unqualified answer that cannot be supported. Everyone (CFOs included) understands and appreciates that some questions have equivocal answers.

If the change in Mexico's gross private domestic investment is ambiguous, then the next step should be to see how important it is to our business plan analysis. If it is relatively unimportant, then perhaps further analysis is not needed. But if it is a key factor, then statistical analysis should be used to determine the change. In cases where statistical analysis is too costly, the results ambiguous, or the task impossible to complete, then gross private domestic investment might be entered as one of the sensitivity variables in our "what if" scenarios.

The major point here is that equivocal answers have the effect of setting some variables apart from the others. Under closer scrutiny, they may be consciously dropped from the analysis. But if they are important, then the highlighted ambiguity increases their visibility.

Nominal Exchange Rate Change Is Uncertain

We saw in our analysis of the foreign exchange market that changes in the value of the peso depend on the degree of international capital mobility. If Mexico faces high-mobility international capital markets, then the nominal value of the peso rises. If it faces low-mobility international capital markets, the peso's value falls.

Real Exchange Rate Change is Uncertain

The Mexican real exchange rate is equal to:

$$\frac{\text{Nominal Exchange Rate}_{(\$/Ps)} \times \text{Average Price Level}_{Mexico}}{\text{Average Price Level}_{United\ States}}$$

To unravel the change in Mexico's real exchange rate, let's review the effects of changes in the nation's price level and nominal exchange rate.

Price-level change: From our analysis of the real goods market, we learned that an increase in government spending raises Mexico's aggregate demand, thereby increasing its GDP Price Index. This price-level change causes the real exchange rate to rise.

Nominal exchange-rate change: If Mexico faces high-mobility international capital markets, then the nominal exchange rate appreciates. Therefore, assuming U.S. prices remain relatively constant, Mexico's real exchange rate must rise if it faces high-mobility international capital markets because prices *and* the nominal exchange rate increase. An increase in the real exchange rate causes Mexico to lose international competitiveness, which causes CTX to fall. If Mexico faces low-mobility international capital markets, the change in real exchange rate is ambiguous because the nominal exchange rate falls at the same time Mexican prices are rising.

Changes in Mexico's Balance of Payments

The balance of payments is an accounting tautology that measures a nation's international sources and uses of funds. In total, it always sums to zero, and this relationship holds true for every country in the world, every second of the day, week, month, or year. There is no need for macroeconomic variables, such as relative real risk-free interest rates, real GDPs, exchange rates, or relative prices, to adjust in order for the sources of funds in the balance of payments to equal the uses of funds. At the same time, macroeconomic equilibrium requires this accounting tautology, over time, to co-exist with international forces because imbalances cause economic variables to fluctuate until they do.

The balance of payments identity tells us that: $CT + NI + RA \equiv 0$. Because it is an identity, any change in one part must have an equal-and-opposite effect on the other two. Let's take a look at the expected changes in the Mexican economy as a result of expansionary fiscal policy and see if we can draw any conclusions about adjustments in the nation's balance of payments.

Changes in RA: Because Mexico has a flexible exchange rate system (relative to the dollar), there are no changes in the nation's RA. This result is summarized in Row 3 of Exhibit 18-14.

Changes in NI: Mexico's NI is affected by changes in the real risk-free interest rate relative to other nations. A rising real risk-free interest rate in Mexico causes *net* investment inflows, which are recorded as positive values in the balance of payments. Therefore, Mexico's NI becomes more positive as its real risk-free interest rate rises. These flows tend to raise the value of the Mexican peso. These results are summarized in Row 2 of Exhibit 18-14.

Changes in CT: If RA is zero and NI is positive, then CT must be negative. Let's see if this conclusion is consistent with the economic forces we have laid out. We will start with Mexico facing high mobility international capital markets and then deal with low mobility capital markets.

EXHIBIT 18-14	CHANGES IN MEXICO'S BALANCE OF PAYMENTS ASSUMING *HIGH-MOBILITY* INTERNATIONAL CAPITAL MARKETS			
	Balance of Payments Accounts and Changes in the Economic Variables Affecting these Accounts	Causes	Changes in the Balance of Payments Accounts and Subaccounts due to Changes in Economic Variables	Net Change in Balance of Payments Account
1	**CT: Current International Transactions**	→	**Net exports ↓**	
	Real exchange rate ↑	→	Δ Net exports ↓	CT becomes more negative
	Prices ↑	→	Exports ↓ and imports ↑	
	Nominal peso value ↑	→	Exports ↓ and imports ↑	
	Real GDP ↑	→	Imports ↑ → Δ Net exports ↓	
2	**NI: Net Nonreserve-related International Borrowing/Lending**	→	**Net financial capital inflows ↑**	NI becomes more positive
	Real risk-free interest rate ↑	→	Financial capital inflows ↑ and outflows ↓	
3	**RA: Reserve-Related (Central Bank) Transactions**	→	No change	No change
	No central bank intervention			
Net change				0

Changes in CT when Mexico Faces High-Mobility International Capital Markets—CT is affected by changes in real GDP, the GDP Price Index, and the nominal exchange rate. As real GDP increases, Mexico's imports rise, thereby causing CT to fall. As Mexican prices rise, the nation's imports rise and exports fall, causing CT to fall even further. Finally, with high-mobility international capital markets, the peso would appreciate, and this appreciation combined with higher domestic prices raises the real exchange rate, causing CT to fall even deeper into deficit. Therefore, when Mexico faces high-mobility international capital markets, economic incentives drive the nation's CT toward a deficit position (see Row 1 in Exhibit 18-14). These results are consistent with our conclusion that, if RA equals 0 and NI is positive, then CT must be negative.

Changes in CT when Mexico Faces Low-Mobility International Capital Markets—How are things different with low mobility international capital markets? Exhibit 18-15 is similar to Exhibit 18-14, except that it shows the balance of payments effects if Mexico faces low-mobility international capital markets. As in Exhibit 18-14, the increase in real GDP and GDP Price Index cause Mexico's CT to fall. But with low-mobility international capital markets, the change in real exchange rate seems uncertain

EXHIBIT **18-15**	CHANGES IN MEXICO'S BALANCE OF PAYMENTS ASSUMING *LOW-MOBILITY* INTERNATIONAL CAPITAL MARKETS			
	Balance of Payments Accounts and Changes in the Economic Variables Affecting these Accounts	**Causes**	**Changes in the Balance of Payments Accounts and Subaccounts due to Changes in Economic Variables**	**Net Change in Balance of Payments Account**
1	**CT: Current International Transactions**	→	**Net exports ↓**	CT becomes more negative
	Real exchange rate ?	→	Net exports (?)	*(Real GDP and price effects overpower nominal exchange rate effects.)*
	Prices ↑	→	Exports ↓ and imports ↑	
	Nominal peso value ↓	→	Exports ↑ and imports ↓	
	Real GDP ↑	→	Imports ↑ → Δ Net exports ↓	
2	**NI: Net Nonreserve International Borrowing/Lending**	→	**Net financial capital inflows ↑**	NI becomes more positive
	Real risk-free interest rate ↑	→	Financial capital inflows ↑ and outflows ↓	
3	**RA: Reserve-Related (Central Bank) Transactions**	→	No change	No change
	No central bank intervention			
Net change				**0**

MACRO MEMO   18-1

A Second Way to Understand Why Mexico's CT Must Fall

This Macro Memo presents another way to understand why Mexico's CT must fall when expansionary fiscal policy is pursued under a flexible exchange rate regime with low-mobility international capital markets. We will find by the end of this Macro Memo that a decrease in net exports due to the combined forces of rising prices and rising real GDP must be greater than the increase in net exports due to the *nominal* depreciation of the peso. This conclusion is clearer after we separate the primary and secondary effects.

Low international capital mobility exists when CTX forces in the foreign exchange market overpower NIX forces. Therefore, with low-mobility international capital markets, expansionary fiscal policy

lowers the nominal value of the peso because the real income and price effects, which reduce the value of the peso (i.e., CTX forces), are greater than the real risk-free interest rate effects, which raise the exchange rate (i.e., NIX forces).

In Exhibit 18-16, what would happen if the net change in demand for pesos from the CTX forces were equal to negative Ps 20 billion (see the movement from D_1 to D_{CTX}), and the change in the demand for pesos from the NIX forces was equal to positive Ps 15 billion (see the movement from D_{CTX} to $D_{(CTX+NIX)}$)? At exchange rate $(\$/Ps)_A$, the net change in demand from D_1 to $D_{(CTX+NIX)}$ would cause the quantity of pesos demanded per period to equal Ps_Z and the quantity supplied per period to equal Ps_A. As a result, the surplus of pesos in the foreign exchange market would cause the currency

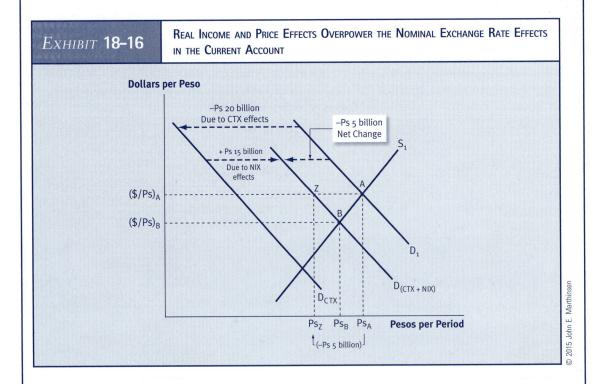

| EXHIBIT 18-16 | REAL INCOME AND PRICE EFFECTS OVERPOWER THE NOMINAL EXCHANGE RATE EFFECTS IN THE CURRENT ACCOUNT |

© 2015 John E. Marthinsen

(CONTINUED)

to depreciate from $(\$/Ps)_A$ to $(\$/Ps)_B$—that is, from Point A to Point B.

When it does, the quantity of pesos demanded per period rises from Ps_Z to Ps_B, as foreigners increase their purchases of relatively cheap Mexican exports (e.g., agricultural products, petroleum, and metals). Similarly, the quantity of pesos supplied falls from Ps_A to Ps_B, as the depreciating peso makes U.S. products more expensive to Mexicans (e.g., electronics and pharmaceuticals). The new equilibrium quantity per period, Ps_B, is located between the original quantity per period, Ps_A, and Ps_Z. This means that Ps_B is above Ps_Z by less than Ps 5 billion.

Therefore, the nominal depreciation of the peso causes net exports (and CT) to rise by an amount less than Ps 5 billion, but the real income and price effects cause

them to fall by Ps 20 billion. Therefore, the nominal exchange rate effects on CT must be weaker than the real income and price effects.* In short, CT falls.

Similar conclusions result when analyzed from the supply side. Increasing real income and prices raise imports and the supply of pesos in the foreign exchange market, which lowers the peso's value. As a result, the primary (i.e., exogenous) income-related and price-related effects on the balance of payments exceed the secondary (i.e., endogenous) exchange-rate-related effects.

*Even if we made the extreme assumption that the supply of foreign exchange (i.e., pesos) was perfectly inelastic, net exports could rise, at most, by Ps 5 billion, which would still be insufficient to offset the Ps 20 billion decrease in net exports from the real income and price effects.

because rising prices and the depreciating peso work in opposite directions.

Nevertheless, we can make inferences about changes in CT because Mexico's increased real risk-free interest rate causes net investment inflows, and the lack of central bank intervention means there is no change in RA. If Mexico's NI is more positive and RA stays unchanged, then its CT must become more negative because the balance of payments must sum to zero. Therefore, relative price and real income effects must offset the nominal exchange rate effects.

Conclusions: Economic Effects of Expansionary Fiscal Policy

The methodology we have used to analyze the effects of expansionary fiscal policy on a nation with a flexible exchange rate system will be reinforced in the next section of this chapter, when we investigate the economic effects of expansionary monetary policy. This methodology will also be useful in the next chapter, when our focus shifts to nations with fixed exchange rates.

Exhibits 18-17 and 18-18 summarize all the cause-and-effect relationships that occur when a government pursues expansionary fiscal policy under a flexible exchange rate regime. Exhibit 18-17 summarizes these effects when the nation faces high-mobility international capital markets, and Exhibit 18-18 summarizes them when it faces low-mobility international capital markets.

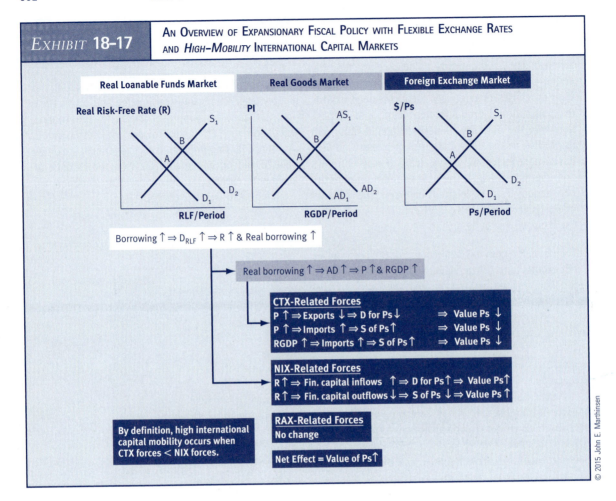

EXHIBIT 18-17 AN OVERVIEW OF EXPANSIONARY FISCAL POLICY WITH FLEXIBLE EXCHANGE RATES AND *HIGH-MOBILITY* INTERNATIONAL CAPITAL MARKETS

© 2015 John E. Marthinsen

EFFECTS OF EXPANSIONARY MONETARY POLICY

Let's employ the methodology and tools of the Three-Sector Model to analyze the economic effects of expansionary monetary policy. Again, picture yourself working as the new finance manager in Mexico City, Mexico, for Fenway, Inc. Suppose you just got off the phone with the CFO, who is concerned about an article that indicates Mexico's central bank will pursue expansionary monetary policy to reduce the nation's unemployment rate. The article (which follows) was just e-mailed to you, and you have until 11:00 tomorrow morning to analyze the likely economic effects.

STEP 1: DESCRIBE THE INITIAL ECONOMIC SETTING OF THE THREE MAJOR MARKETS IN MEXICO

Mexico's economic setting is the same as in our analysis of expansionary fiscal policy. Therefore, we will assume, the country is on the relatively flat portion of its AS curve (see Exhibit 18-2); its supply of and demand for real loanable

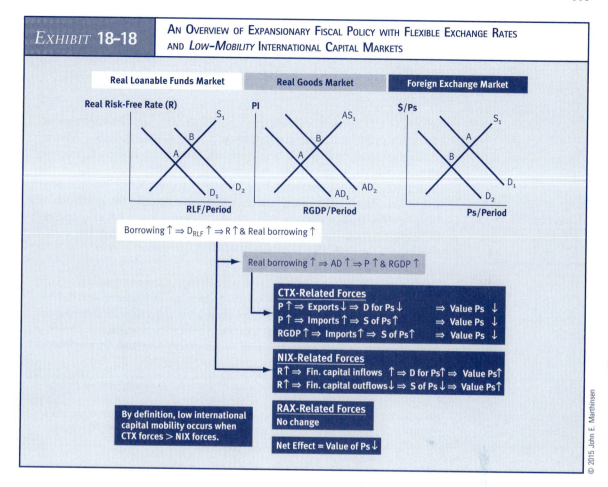

EXHIBIT **18-18**   AN OVERVIEW OF EXPANSIONARY FISCAL POLICY WITH FLEXIBLE EXCHANGE RATES AND *LOW-MOBILITY* INTERNATIONAL CAPITAL MARKETS

funds are inelastic (see Exhibit 18-3); and the nominal exchange rate fluctuates freely against the dollar (Exhibit 18-4). Thus, there is no central bank intervention in the dollar–peso foreign exchange market.

STEP 2: IDENTIFY THE ECONOMIC (OR EXPECTED) SHOCK TO MEXICO

The exogenous shock that sets off the chain of economic reactions is the increase in Mexico's real money supply due to the changed reserve ratio. We know from our discussion of monetary policy and bank regulation that central banks have four major monetary tools.[4] They can alter the nation's monetary base via open market operations, foreign exchange market intervention,[5] or changing the discount rate (thereby affecting the amount of discount loans to financial intermediaries), or they can change the money multiplier by adjusting financial intermediaries' reserve requirements. Therefore, we will start our analysis with a change in the M2 money multiplier.

> The shock to the Three-Sector Model is expansionary monetary policy, caused by a lower reserve ratio requirement.

[4] See Chapter 9, "Who Controls the Money Supply and How?"
[5] Because Mexico's exchange rate is flexible, changes in the monetary base due to central bank intervention in the foreign exchange market are ruled out.

Bank of Mexico Seeks to Reduce Unemployment

By J. E. Marthinsen

MEXICO CITY, Mexico— For the past two years, high unemployment, low plant utilization, and sluggish growth have plagued Mexico. Unfortunately, the nation has also been suffering from large and rising current account deficits, which it has managed to finance by borrowing in the international capital markets. Due to fears of speculative international investment flows and concerns over foreign hegemony, the government has placed restrictions on foreign nations' investments in Mexico and on domestic citizens' investments abroad. As a result, financing these current account deficits has been expensive.

On the bright side, the value of Mexico's currency, the peso, has held steady during the past few months, but the nation's commitment to flexible exchange rates could come under pressure with the *central bank's recent decision to pursue expansionary monetary policy by lowering the reserve ratio on bank deposits until the level of unemployment falls to single-digit levels.*

*The article title and italicized phrase are the only differences between this e-mail and the one presented earlier in this chapter, when we analyzed the economic effects of expansionary fiscal policy.

STEP 3: ANALYZE THE CHAIN REACTION OF ECONOMIC INTERACTIONS

Where to begin? Show me the money!

Deciding in which market to begin our analysis is, again, made easier if we use our rule of thumb—Show me the money! Changes in the M2 money multiplier directly affect the real M2 money supply and the supply of real loanable funds. Therefore, let's begin our analysis in the real loanable funds market.

Economic Effects in the Real Loanable Funds Market

An increase in the real money supply lowers the real risk-free interest rate and increases the equilibrium quantity of real loanable funds per period.

If the Bank of Mexico increases the nation's real money supply, then the supply of real loanable funds rises. Exhibit 18-19 shows that an increase in the supply of real loanable funds from S_1 to S_2 creates a surplus of funds at R_A (the original real risk-free interest rate) equal to $RLF_Z - RLF_A$ (i.e., the distance A to Z). As a result, the real risk-free interest rate falls from R_A to R_B, causing the amount of real credit borrowed per period (e.g., gross private domestic investment and consumption) to rise from RLF_A to RLF_B, and causing the amount of real loanable funds supplied per period to fall from RLF_Z to RLF_B.

A lower real risk-free interest rate increases personal consumption and gross private domestic investment expenditures.

Exhibit 18-20 provides a summary of the results and a progress report on our Three-Sector Model. We have now completed our analysis of the real loanable funds market and are ready to analyze the spillover effects in the real goods market.

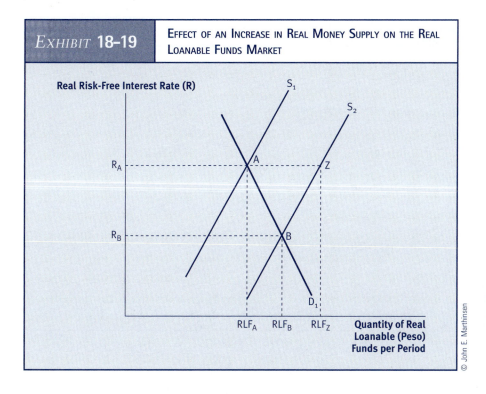

EXHIBIT 18-19   EFFECT OF AN INCREASE IN REAL MONEY SUPPLY ON THE REAL
LOANABLE FUNDS MARKET

Real Risk-Free Interest Rate (R)

S_1

S_2

R_A ········· A ········· Z

R_B ········· B

D_1

RLF$_A$ RLF$_B$ RLF$_Z$ **Quantity of Real
Loanable (Peso)
Funds per Period**

© John E. Marthinsen

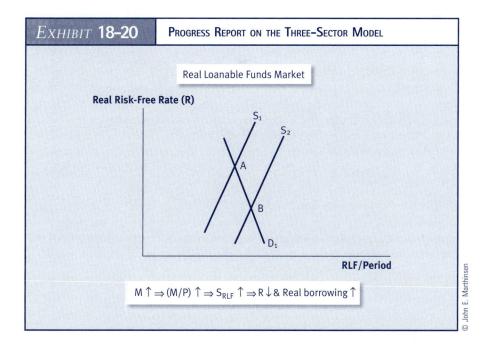

EXHIBIT 18-20   PROGRESS REPORT ON THE THREE-SECTOR MODEL

Real Loanable Funds Market

Real Risk-Free Rate (R)

S_1

S_2

A

B

D_1

RLF/Period

$$M \uparrow \Rightarrow (M/P) \uparrow \Rightarrow S_{RLF} \uparrow \Rightarrow R \downarrow \ \& \ \text{Real borrowing} \uparrow$$

© John E. Marthinsen

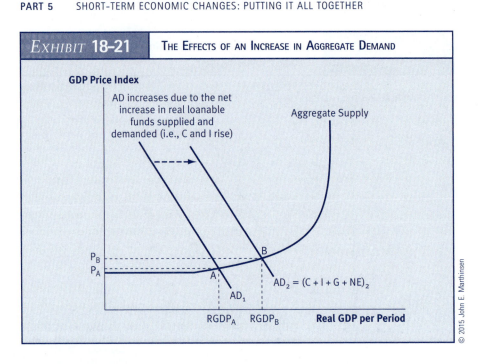

EXHIBIT 18-21	THE EFFECTS OF AN INCREASE IN AGGREGATE DEMAND

GDP Price Index

AD increases due to the net increase in real loanable funds supplied and demanded (i.e., C and I rise)

Aggregate Supply

P_B
P_A

A

B

AD_1

$AD_2 = (C + I + G + NE)_2$

$RGDP_A$ $RGDP_B$ **Real GDP per Period**

© 2015 John E. Marthinsen

Economic Effects in the Real Goods Market

The net increase in borrowing causes aggregate demand in the real goods market to increase. Exhibit 18-21 shows that an increase in aggregate demand from AD_1 to AD_2 causes Mexico's GDP Price Index to rise from P_A to P_B and real GDP to rise from $RGDP_A$ to $RGDP_B$.

Exhibit 18-22 provides another summary of results and a progress report on our Three-Sector Model analysis. Now we are ready to analyze the spill-over effects in the foreign exchange market.

Economic Effects in the Foreign Exchange Market

To determine the change in Mexico's nominal exchange rate, we must analyze the spillover effects from the real loanable funds market to the foreign exchange market and also from the real goods market to the foreign exchange market. As we did when we analyzed the effects of expansionary fiscal policy, we will use the balance of payments format to organize the supply and demand forces at work. In particular, we will address the CIX-related, NIX-related, and RAX-related forces affecting the peso-dollar foreign exchange market.

CTX-related supply and demand forces in the foreign exchange market: An increase in real GDP raises Mexico's ability and willingness to purchase imports, which increases the supply of pesos in the foreign exchange market.[6] Exhibit 18-23 shows that an increase in the supply of pesos in the foreign

---

[6] Remember that an increase in the supply of pesos in the dollar–peso foreign exchange market is the same as an increase in the demand for dollars.

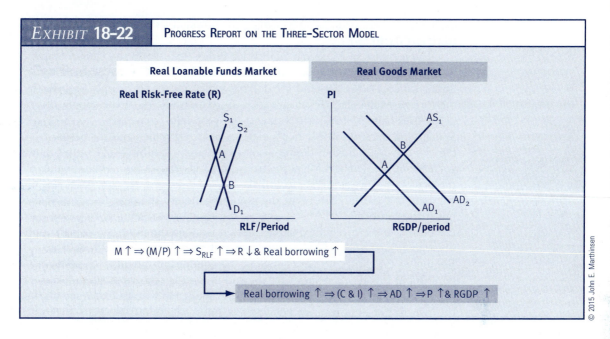

EXHIBIT **18–22**   PROGRESS REPORT ON THE THREE–SECTOR MODEL

$M \uparrow \Rightarrow (M/P) \uparrow \Rightarrow S_{RLF} \uparrow \Rightarrow R \downarrow$ & Real borrowing $\uparrow$

Real borrowing $\uparrow \Rightarrow (C \& I) \uparrow \Rightarrow AD \uparrow \Rightarrow P \uparrow$ & RGDP $\uparrow$

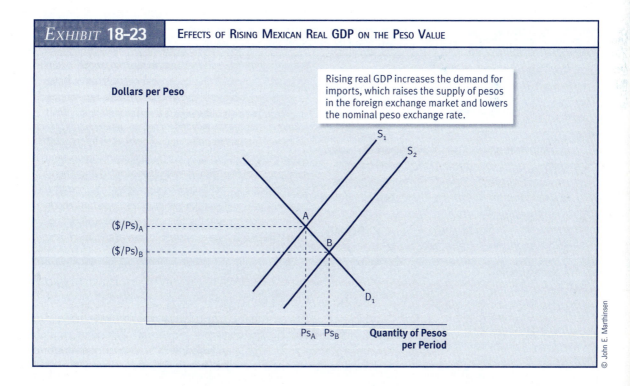

EXHIBIT **18–23**   EFFECTS OF RISING MEXICAN REAL GDP ON THE PESO VALUE

Rising real GDP increases the demand for imports, which raises the supply of pesos in the foreign exchange market and lowers the nominal peso exchange rate.

© 2015 John E. Marthinsen

© John E. Marthinsen

exchange market from S_1 to S_2 causes the nominal value of the peso to fall from $(\$/Ps)_A$ to $(\$/Ps)_B$.

The increase in Mexico's GDP Price Index (relative to the United States) increases the nation's imports and reduces its exports. Greater Mexican imports increase the demand for dollars, which means the supply of pesos in the foreign exchange market increases. In Exhibit 18-24, as the supply of pesos rises from S_1 to S_2, the value of the peso falls from $(\$/Ps)_A$ to $(\$/Ps)_B$. Similarly, a decrease in Mexico's exports reduces the demand for pesos, thereby causing a further depreciation of the peso. Exhibit 18-24 shows that a decrease in the demand for pesos from D_1 to D_2 causes the nominal value of the peso to fall from $(\$/Ps)_B$ to $(\$/Ps)_C$.

Our analysis indicates that the nominal value of the peso falls, but without further information, the change in the equilibrium quantity of pesos per period in the foreign exchange market is indeterminate. The rising supply of pesos raises the equilibrium quantity and the falling demand lowers it. Exhibit 18-24 shows no net change in the equilibrium quantity of pesos per period, but this result would vary depending on the relative magnitudes of the supply and demand shifts. Fortunately, the change in foreign exchange market turnover is not important to Fenway's business plan analysis.

NIX-related supply and demand forces in the foreign exchange market: As Mexico's real risk-free interest rate falls (due to the increased supply of real loanable funds), peso-denominated securities become less attractive relative to dollar-denominated securities. This causes the demand for pesos in the foreign

Rising Mexican prices cause the value of the peso to fall.

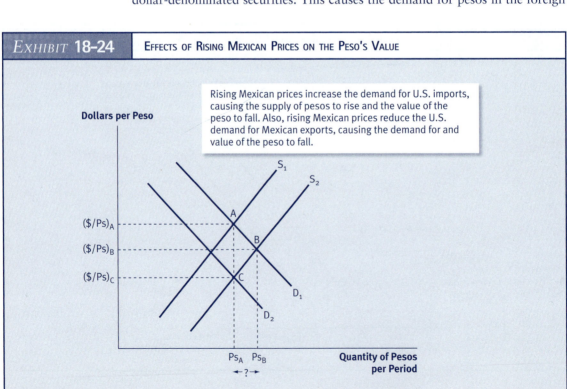

| EXHIBIT **18-24** | EFFECTS OF RISING MEXICAN PRICES ON THE PESO'S VALUE |

Rising Mexican prices increase the demand for U.S. imports, causing the supply of pesos to rise and the value of the peso to fall. Also, rising Mexican prices reduce the U.S. demand for Mexican exports, causing the demand for and value of the peso to fall.

Dollars per Peso

© John E. Marthinsen

exchange market to fall, as foreign investors adjust their portfolios away from the less attractive peso-denominated investments and toward dollar-denominated securities. Similarly, the supply of pesos in the foreign exchange market rises as Mexican investors respond to the relatively more attractive dollar-denominated investments.

> **Lower Mexican interest rates cause the value of the peso to fall.**

Exhibit 18-25 shows that an increase in the supply of pesos causes the peso to fall in value from $(\$/Ps)_A$ to $(\$/Ps)_B$. The decrease in the demand causes the peso's value to fall even further from $(\$/Ps)_B$ to $(\$/Ps)_C$. The change in equilibrium quantity per period is indeterminate.

RAX-related supply and demand forces in the foreign exchange market: Mexico's flexible exchange rate system implies that neither the Bank of Mexico nor any foreign central bank intervenes in the dollar–peso foreign exchange market. Therefore, there are no RAX-related forces in the foreign exchange market.

> **There are no RAX-related forces in the foreign exchange market.**

Exhibit 18-26 summarizes the supply and demand changes in the foreign exchange market due to the spillover effects from the real loanable funds market and real goods market.

With expansionary monetary policy, the degree of international capital mobility does not influence the *qualitative* change in the peso's value. We know this because international trade flows, which are connected to CTX forces, *and* investment flows, which are connected to NIX forces, both lower the peso's value. Therefore, the peso depreciates whether Mexico faces

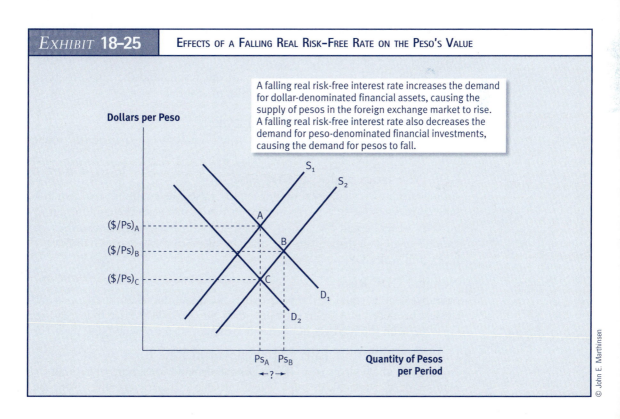

EXHIBIT 18-25   EFFECTS OF A FALLING REAL RISK-FREE RATE ON THE PESO'S VALUE

A falling real risk-free interest rate increases the demand for dollar-denominated financial assets, causing the supply of pesos in the foreign exchange market to rise. A falling real risk-free interest rate also decreases the demand for peso-denominated financial investments, causing the demand for pesos to fall.

Dollars per Peso

© John E. Marthinsen

Exhibit **18–26**	Summary of Changes in the Value of the Peso	
Source of Supply and Demand Changes	**Change in Supply of and/or Demand for Pesos**	**Change in the Value of the Peso**
CTX-Related Forces		
Prices ↑	Exports ↓ → D_{pesos} ↓ Imports ↑ → S_{pesos} ↑	Peso depreciates
Real GDP ↑	Imports ↑ → S_{pesos} ↑	
NIX-Related Forces		
Real risk-free interest rate ↓	Capital inflows ↓ → D_{pesos} ↓ Capital outflows ↑ → S_{pesos} ↑	Peso depreciates
RAX-Related Forces		
No central bank intervention (flexible exchange rates)	No change	No change
Net change		**Peso depreciates**

© 2015 John E. Marthinsen

high-mobility or low-mobility international capital markets. Of course, the higher the degree of capital mobility, the lower the peso will fall in value. Notice how this result is different from expansionary fiscal policy, where the degree of international capital mobility determines whether the nominal exchange rate appreciated or depreciated.

Exhibit 18-27 provides a summary of our results and the final progress report of the adjustments in our Three-Sector Model.

SUMMARY OF ANSWERS TO CFO'S QUESTIONS

Now that we have completed our first-round analysis of expansionary monetary policy, let's summarize the results.

GDP Price Index and Real GDP Rise

An increase in Mexico's real money supply raises the supply of real loanable funds, lowers the real risk-free interest rate, and increases the equilibrium quantity of real credit per period. This increase in borrowing causes the nation's aggregate demand to rise, thereby increasing Mexico's GDP Price Index and real GDP.

Nominal GDP Rises

Nominal GDP is equal to the prices times the quantities of all final goods and services produced in Mexico each period. If Mexico's GDP Price Index and real GDP rise with the increase in aggregate demand, then nominal GDP must rise.

Unemployment Rate Falls and Employment Rate Rises

An increase in Mexico's real GDP raises the demand for labor, which (normally) reduces Mexico's unemployment rate and increases its employment rate.

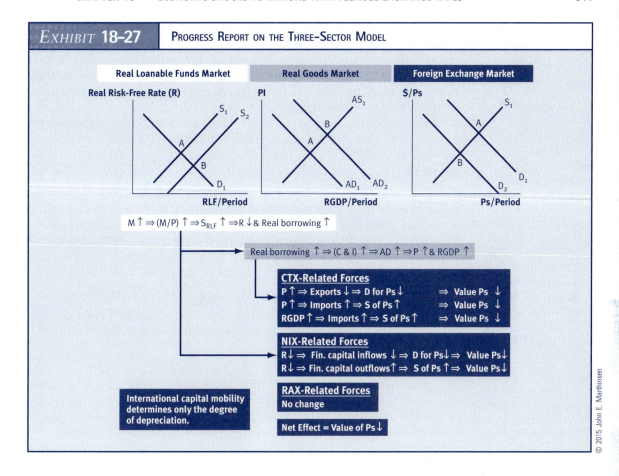

Exhibit **18-27** | PROGRESS REPORT ON THE THREE-SECTOR MODEL

Real and Nominal Wages Rise

The percentage change in nominal wage rate is (approximately) equal to the percentage change in the real wage rate plus inflationary expectations. An increase in the demand for labor puts upward pressure on real wages, therefore nominal wages should rise because both the real wage and expected inflation rate rise.

Real Risk-Free Interest Rate Falls and Nominal Interest Rate Change Is Uncertain

The nominal interest rate is (approximately) equal to the real interest rate plus expected inflation rate. Therefore, the change in Mexico's nominal interest rate is ambiguous. An increase in the supply of real loanable funds reduces Mexico's real risk-free interest rate, but the anticipated increased aggregate demand raises inflationary expectations. Therefore, the net change in nominal interest depends on the relative movements of these two variables. Nevertheless, it is important to remember that changes in the real interest rate should be more important to your business plan analysis than changes in the nominal interest rate.

Monetary Base Does Not Change, M2 Multiplier rises, and M2 Rises

Because the central bank lowered the reserve ratio on bank deposits, the nation's M2 money multiplier and, therefore, M2 money supply rise. At the same time, the central bank did not conduct open market operations, change its discount loans, or intervene in the foreign exchange market. Therefore, Mexico's monetary base remains constant.

There are secondary effects, due to changes in Mexico's preferred asset ratios, that weaken (but do not reverse) the increased M2 money multiplier. For instance, as Mexico's real risk-free interest rate falls, (C_c/D) and (U/D) rise and (N/D) falls, causing the lending potential of the banking system to fall and with it, the M2 money multiplier.

Gross Private Domestic Investment Rises

A decrease in Mexico's real risk-free interest rate stimulates gross private domestic investment. In addition, a rising real GDP spurs new investments. Therefore, the net change in gross private domestic investment is positive from both of these forces.

Nominal Exchange Rate (Peso Value) Falls

The increase in Mexico's GDP Price Index, growth in real GDP, and decrease in real risk-free interest rate (all) cause the nominal value of the peso to fall.

Real Exchange Rate Falls

Mexico's real exchange rate equals:

$$\frac{\text{Nominal Exchange Rate}_{(\$/Ps)} \times \text{Average Price Level}_{\text{Mexico}}}{\text{Average Price Level}_{\text{United States}}}$$

It looks as if the change in real exchange rate is ambiguous because the nominal exchange rate falls and Mexico's GDP Price Index rises, which means they move in opposite directions. We will find in the next section how to clarify this ambiguity and understand why Mexico's real exchange rate must fall.

CT Rises, NI Falls, and RA Does Not Change

We know that Mexico's entire balance of payments must sum to zero. Therefore, if we can determine the direction in which the sum of NI and the RA change, then we can infer the direction in which CT must move.

A falling real risk-free interest rate increases investment outflows from Mexico and decreases inflows, thereby reducing NI. Because Mexico has a flexible exchange system, RA does not change. Therefore, we can infer that, the sum of CT + NI + RA can equal zero only if CT rises in value.

Mexico's CT is affected by changes in real GDP and the real exchange rate. The increase in real GDP raises the nation's imports and thereby causes CT to become more negative. Higher Mexican prices increase imports and reduce exports, thereby further lowering the nation's CT. Both of these effects move CT in the opposite direction from what we know must happen.

By contrast, a depreciation of the nominal peso exchange rate causes CT to become more positive. Therefore, nominal exchange rate forces must

EXHIBIT 18-28	CHANGES IN MEXICO'S BALANCE OF PAYMENTS		
Balance of Payments Accounts and Changes in Economic Variables Affecting these Accounts	**Causes**	**Changes in Balance of Payments Accounts and Subaccounts due to Changes in Economic Variables**	**Net Change in Balance of Payments Accounts**
1 **CT: Current International Transactions**	→	**Net exports ↑**	CT becomes less negative
Real exchange rate ↓	→	Net exports ↑	*(Nominal exchange rate effects offset the price and real GDP effects.)*
Prices ↑	→	Exports ↓ and imports ↑	
Nominal peso value ↓	→	Exports ↑ and imports ↓	
Real GDP ↑	→	Imports ↑ → Net exports ↓	
2 **NI: Net Nonreserve International Borrowing/Lending**	→	**Net financial capital outflows ↑**	NI becomes less positive
Real risk-free interest rate ↓	→	Financial capital inflows ↓ and outflows ↑	
3 **RA: Reserve-Related (Central Bank) Transactions**	→	No change	No change
No central bank intervention			
Net change			**0**

© 2015 John E. Marthinsen

overpower the income and price forces in CT. Another way to state this conclusion is to say that the real exchange rate must fall enough to make CT more positive. These results are summarized in Exhibit 18-28.

THE REST OF THE STORY

FEEDBACK EFFECTS IN THE THREE-SECTOR MODEL
At this point in our analysis, we have linked Mexico's three most important macroeconomic markets and shown how they function like interdependent gears (see Exhibit 18-29). But our analysis has only considered the first iteration of cause-and-effect relationships (i.e., the first turn of each gear). Feedback effects occur after the initial round, which cause recurring rounds of changes as adjustments in each market spill over and affect the other two markets.

Feedback Effects with Expansionary Fiscal Policy
Recall that we started our analysis of expansionary fiscal policy in the real loanable funds market with the government increasing its demand for real

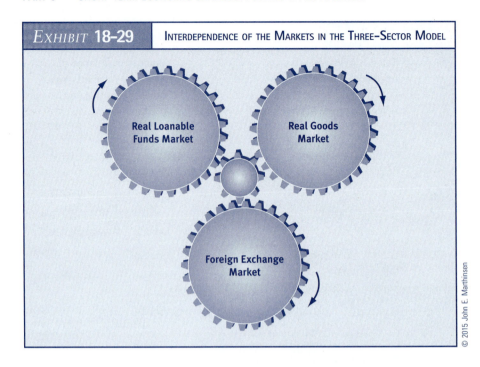

credit. Then, we analyzed the spillover effects that changes in the real loanable funds market have on the real goods market. We ended by examining the spillover effects that changes in the real loanable funds market *and* the real goods market have on the foreign exchange market. The problem is these changes set off new rounds of spillover effects.

Exhibit 18-30 summarizes only the second round of feedback effects from expansionary fiscal policy. Changes in the price level and real GDP in the real goods market feed back into the real loanable funds market (see Feedback 1 in Exhibit 18-30). In addition, changes in the nominal currency value, which is determined in the foreign exchange market, feed back into the real loanable funds market (see Feedback 2), and they also affect the real goods market (see Feedback 3).

Feedback Effects with Expansionary Monetary Policy
Similarly, Exhibit 18-31 shows the second round of feedback effects from expansionary monetary policies. Notice that the forces move from the real goods market to the real loanable funds market (Feedback 1), from the foreign exchange market to the real loanable funds market (Feedback 2), and from the foreign exchange market to the real goods market (Feedback 3).

General Comments on Feedback Effects
As explained in the previous section, feedback effects do not stop after one round. Rather, they are the beginning of seemingly endless and recurring rounds of adjustments. Fortunately, these continuous rounds of changes do not prevent us from drawing definitive conclusions because the qualitative

Feedback effects occur in the Three-Sector Model, but they are weaker than the first-round effects.

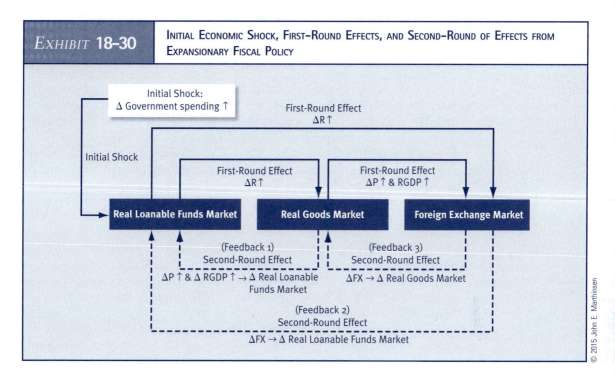

EXHIBIT 18–30   INITIAL ECONOMIC SHOCK, FIRST-ROUND EFFECTS, AND SECOND-ROUND OF EFFECTS FROM EXPANSIONARY FISCAL POLICY

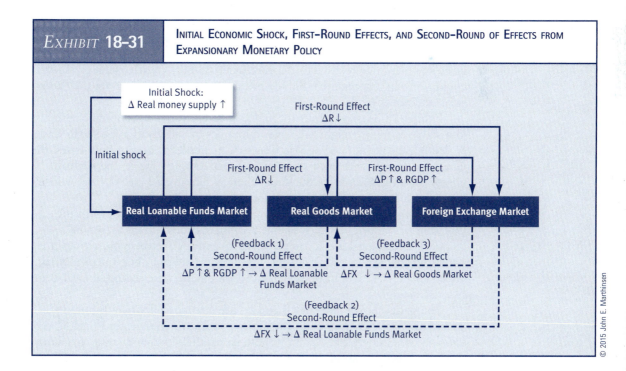

EXHIBIT 18–31   INITIAL ECONOMIC SHOCK, FIRST-ROUND EFFECTS, AND SECOND-ROUND OF EFFECTS FROM EXPANSIONARY MONETARY POLICY

© 2015 John E. Marthinsen

change of each variable in our Three-Sector analysis is ultimately in the direction of the first-round change. In other words, all the subsequent rounds of adjustments do not offset (and may even reinforce) the initial change.

It is important to remember that the Three-Sector Model is a powerful framework for determining *qualitative* changes in six key macroeconomic variables (i.e., the GDP Price Index, real GDP, real risk-free interest rate, quantity of real credit per period, nominal exchange rate, and quantity of foreign exchange per period). It is also a useful framework for drawing inferences about many other macroeconomic variables (e.g., the real wage and unemployment rate). But the Three-Sector Model does not provide insights about the magnitude of these changes (e.g., whether a variable will change from 3% to 3.5% or from 3% to 5%). Answers to questions such as these need healthy doses of econometrics and model estimation.

The reason we can stop our analysis after the first round of cause-and-effect interactions is because most economies are *stable*. Therefore, macroeconomic models are based on the assumption that economic changes grow smaller with each iterative round of interaction. Is this assumption reasonable? To answer this question, consider the consequences of a world in which economies were unstable. Under such circumstances, any small change in economic activity would produce spillover effects that grew progressively larger as they worked their way through the economy. Generally speaking, most nations do not face such volatile and unstable economic environments.

Exhibit 18-32 shows the path an economic variable might take in an unstable economy, such as Mexico, when the peso was forced to fluctuate in 1994, Brazil in 1999, when the real came under considerable speculative pressure, or Switzerland in 2012, when the central bank fixed the Swiss franc's upper value relative to the euro at €0.83/SFr. Clearly, such changes could occur in a speculative bubble or market mania, but they are the exceptions and not the rules.

Exhibit 18-33 shows four (of many) possible paths an economic variable in a stable economy might take over a number of rounds of analysis. In Cases A and A^1, the economic variable rises to a higher level, and in both cases, the changes diminish with each subsequent round. Along Line A, the feedback effects constantly reinforce the initial change, but along Line A^1, the feedback effects oscillate, *partially* offsetting the initial round.

Nevertheless, in both cases, the ultimate qualitative change is in the direction of the primary movement. For fluctuations in real GDP, the feedback effects on Line A are preferred to Line A^1 because more output is produced. But if the variable were Mexico's price level, then the oscillating effects of Line A^1 would be preferred to Line A because the price level does not rise as high.

The paths shown by Lines B and B^1 are also possible. Line B follows a path that constantly reinforces the initial downward change, and Line B^1 follows an oscillating path. Again, in both cases, the ultimate qualitative change is in the direction caused by the initial shock.

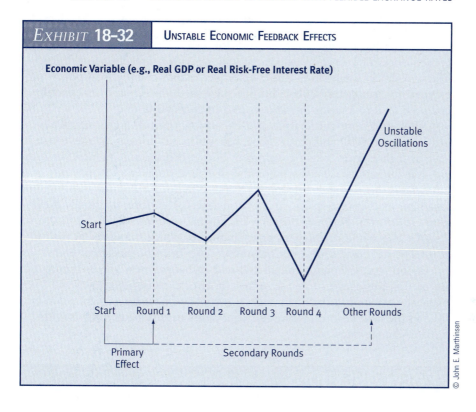

EXHIBIT 18-32   UNSTABLE ECONOMIC FEEDBACK EFFECTS

© John E. Marthinsen

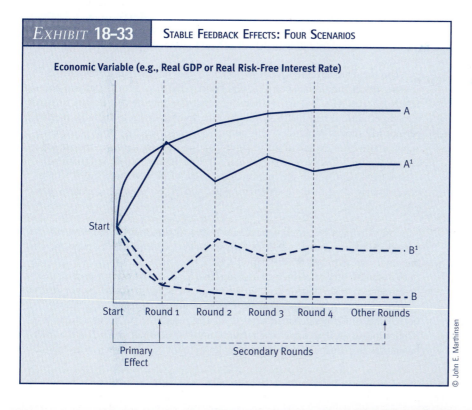

EXHIBIT 18-33   STABLE FEEDBACK EFFECTS: FOUR SCENARIOS

© John E. Marthinsen

CONCLUSION

This chapter has provided a framework for analyzing the short-term economic consequences of exogenous shocks to nations with flexible exchange rates. The two shocks analyzed in this chapter were expansionary fiscal policy and expansionary monetary policy, but the same methodology and set of tools could be used to analyze any shocks to a nation's economy.

We found from our analysis that expansionary fiscal policy stimulates growth in real GDP and creates jobs, but it also has unpleasant side effects, such as higher prices, rising government budget deficits, and an increasing real risk-free interest rate. Furthermore, the change in nominal exchange rate is ambiguous due to the conflicting CTX and NIX forces. Because most nations face high mobility international capital markets, NIX forces normally dominate CTX forces, but our approach left this an open question.

We also found that expansionary monetary policy stimulates growth in real GDP and creates jobs, but the nation must bear the burden of higher prices and face declining nominal and real exchange rates. The methodology we used in this chapter to analyze the effects of expansionary fiscal and expansionary monetary policy under a flexible exchange rate regime will be used in the next chapter, when our focus shifts to shocks on nations with fixed exchange rates.

REVIEW QUESTIONS

1. In 2013, the U.S. housing market appeared to be improving, and many analysts began to wonder what effects, if any, the recovery might have on U.S. economic activity during the rest of the year. The prevailing sentiment was that rising home prices would increase homeowner wealth and stimulate a surge in consumer spending.

   Use the Three-Sector Model to determine the effects that increased U.S. housing prices should have on U.S. real GDP, GDP Price Index, real and nominal exchange rates (U.S. dollars relative to euros), quantity of U.S. dollars or euros traded per period, real risk-free interest rate, quantity of real loanable funds per period, M2 money multiplier, and nominal interest rate. Use both graphical analysis and brief explanations to support your answers. Assume the United States: (1) has a flexible exchange rate, (2) faces highly mobile international capital markets, (3) is in the intermediate range of its aggregate supply curve but relatively close to the Keynesian range, and (4) government currently has a budget deficit.

2. Suppose Australia's unemployment rate began to rise, and the government passed an investment tax credit to help stimulate the economy. Explain the effect this policy would have on the nation's GDP Price Index, real risk-free interest rate, nominal interest rates, real and nominal GDP, gross private domestic investment, unemployment rate, inflation rate, real and nominal exchange rate, current international transactions (CT), net nonreserve-related international borrowing and lending transactions (NI), and reserve-related transactions (RA). (Definition of an *investment tax credit*: An investment tax credit (ITC) allows businesses to reduce taxable income by an amount equal to their new capital

costs times the percentage ITC. Unlike depreciation, an ITC is offered when an investment asset is purchased.)

3. How would your answer to Question 2 change if a politically unstable country (e.g., Syria or Egypt in 2013) and not Australia passed an investment tax credit? Think in terms of how capital mobility facing Syria or Egypt is different from Australia and the effect it would have.

4. How would your answers to Question 2 change if Australia pursued a contractionary monetary policy?

5. On August 8, 2013, the Federal Reserve Bank of New York issued the following announcement.
   • All else remaining the same, was RA greater than, less than, or equal to zero for the quarter from April to June 2013? Fully explain.

NEW YORK—The U.S. monetary authorities did not intervene in the foreign exchange markets during the April–June quarter, the Federal Reserve Bank of New York said today in its quarterly report to the U.S. Congress.

During the three months that ended June 30, 2013, the dollar appreciated 5.2 percent against the Japanese yen and depreciated 1.5 percent against the euro. In this period, the dollar's nominal trade-weighted exchange value increased 1.7 percent, as measured by the Federal Reserve Board's major currencies index.

The report was presented by Simon Potter, executive vice president of the Federal Reserve Bank of New York and the Federal Open Market Committee's manager for the System Open Market Account, on behalf of the Treasury and the Federal Reserve System.

---

6. Suppose the current dollar–peso spot exchange rate equals \$0.08/Ps, but it fluctuates with the forces of supply and demand. Due to domestic turmoil, assume that Mexican peso holders suddenly demand the U.S. dollar.
   a. Draw the supply and demand curves in the Mexican peso real loanable funds market. Make sure you correctly label both axes. Show the effect that capital flight from Mexico should have, if any, on the peso real risk-free interest rate. Provide a reason for why supply and/or demand will change. If there are no changes in either supply or demand, explain why.
   b. To provide jobs for the poor, suppose that Mexico's president increases government spending. Explain what effect, if any, this spending should have on Mexico's monetary base.
   c. Draw the supply and demand curves for the dollar–peso foreign exchange market. Make sure you correctly label both axes. Show the effect capital flight from Mexico should have, if any, on the value of the peso.
   d. Is it correct to say that, if the Mexican central bank does not intervene in the foreign exchange market, capital flight will cause the nation's CT to go into surplus? Explain.

DISCUSSION QUESTIONS

7. What factors will increase or decrease the degree of international capital mobility between one nation and the rest of the world?

8. Assume Japan has a flexible exchange rate relative to China and pursues expansionary fiscal policy to lower the Japanese unemployment rate. Would the expansionary fiscal policy be more effective if Japan had high or low international capital mobility with respect to China?

Chapter 19

Economic Shocks to Nations with Fixed Exchange Rates

INTRODUCTION

In Chapter 18, "Economic Shocks to Nations with Flexible Exchange Rates," currency values were free to fluctuate with the forces of supply and demand when an exogenous shock (economic, political, or social) disrupted equilibrium in our Three-Sector Model. This chapter investigates how things change when a nation adopts a fixed exchange rate regime. We will see that this decision is a serious one because choosing a fixed exchange rate means either losing monetary autonomy or depriving residents of economic freedoms to transact international trade and/or investment activities.

The chapter begins with an explanation of fixed exchange rates, why nations adopt them, and two ways in which central banks can keep them fixed. It goes on to discuss the economic effects and business implications of expansionary fiscal policy and expansionary monetary policy for nations with fixed exchange rates. In doing so, the effectiveness of these policies in a fixed-rate regime can be compared to a flexible-rate regime, which was our focus in the last chapter.

"The Basics" section of this chapter also covers an important macroeconomic take-away, called the "impossible trinity." One reason for its importance is because the impossible trinity is an economic law, rather than a rule of thumb, which means no country, rich or poor, large or small, can escape its binding constraints.

"**The Rest of the Story**" section of this chapter provides a case study of the Asian Tiger[1] crisis. It traces the economic rise of these developing nations between 1985 and 1996 and then their collapse in 1997. This crisis was a punctuating economic event during the late twentieth century and is noteworthy on a number of levels. For those interested in international macroeconomics, it provides an insightful example of the impact that *capital flight* can have on nations with fixed exchange rates.

---

[1] Asian Tiger countries that are the focus of this chapter are Hong Kong, Indonesia, Malaysia, the Philippines, Singapore, South Korea, Taiwan, and Thailand.

THE BASICS

WHY DO NATIONS CHOOSE FIXED EXCHANGE RATES?

Exchange rates are important economic shock absorbers.[2] Just as shock absorbers in an automobile protect passengers from unexpected bumps and changes in driving conditions, flexible exchange rates protect nations from unexpected changes in foreign economic conditions. For example, they can protect a nation from high rates of foreign inflation.

To understand why, suppose the U.S. inflation rate was low relative to the high and rising rates of its major trading partners. Foreign residents would turn their demands toward lower-priced U.S. products, and U.S. residents would do the same. As the demand for U.S. goods and services increased, upward pressure would be put on the nation's prices and inflation rate. Flexible exchange rates would absorb (all or a portion of) the increase in foreign demand by allowing the value of the dollar to rise, rather than stoke U.S. inflation.

Flexible exchange rates are also important because they give nations the ability to determine their own monetary policies, a power that is essential for stabilizing and reducing inflation, as well as creating an environment for healthy growth and development. This important characteristic of flexible exchange rate systems will be fully explained later in this chapter.

You might be asking yourself, "If exchange rates are really like economic shock absorbers and if the ability to conduct independent monetary policy has a significant positive value, then why would any nation voluntarily give up a flexible exchange rate regime for a fixed one?" The answer to this question is multifaceted and controversial.

Some nations choose fixed exchange rates because they have lost confidence in the willingness and/or ability of their own central banks to control inflation. By choosing fixed exchange rates, governments can emasculate the independent decision-making powers of their central banks and place these powers in the hands of a foreign nation's central bank. This is another topic that will be discussed later in this chapter.

Other nations choose fixed exchange rates to promote trade and investment relations with their major trading partner(s). For example, a Latin American nation might fix its currency value relative to the U.S. dollar because the vast majority of its trade and investment flows are with the United States. By fixing the exchange rate, traders and investors no longer have to worry that the value of their foreign-currency payments or receipts will change with adverse exchange rate movements.

This is not to say that traders and investors who operate in countries with flexible exchange rates are always victimized by adverse exchange rate movements. On the contrary, these exposures can be hedged, but hedging is always done at a cost. For instance, the purchase or sale of forward currency

Sidebar notes:

Fluctuating exchange rates are like economic shock absorbers.

Flexible exchange rates can absorb part or all of the impact of rising foreign prices.

Flexible exchange rates give nations the ability to pursue independent monetary policies. Fixed exchange rates take away this power.

One reason nations choose fixed exchange rate regimes is because they have lost confidence in their own central banks.

Another reason nations choose fixed exchange rate regimes is to reduce exchange rate-related risks associated with international trade and investment transactions.

---

[2]To reinforce your understanding of the fixed-versus-flexible exchange rate decision, see "To Fix or Not to Fix, That Is the Question" in "The Basics" section of Chapter 15, "Exchange Rates: Why Do They Change?"

contracts requires the payment of bid-ask spreads, and hedging with options requires the payment of premiums. These costs would not be present if exchange rates were credibly fixed.

No exchange rate system is appropriate for all nations at all times. To understand why flexible exchange rates are not always appropriate, consider this: If flexible exchange rates were always better than fixed exchange rates, then every nation would be better off if it had a currency that was free to fluctuate. But if this is true for every nation, then it should also be true for every state, province, or canton within a nation. After all, many states in the United States, provinces in Canada, and some cantons in Switzerland are as large as countries.

> No exchange rate system is appropriate for all nations at all times.

Would the United States be better off if every state had its own freely fluctuating currency? If this idea seems plausible, then why stop there? Should every city and town within each state have its own currency? And if having a freely fluctuating currency is beneficial for every city and town, then shouldn't it also be beneficial for every individual? Clearly at some point, the costs of having a freely fluctuating, independent currency outweigh the benefits. A currency for each person would be economic lunacy because it would make even the simplest purchase a complicated mess. For example, it would require businesses to deal with a different currency for each employee, supplier, and customer.[3]

HOW DO NATIONS FIX THEIR EXCHANGE RATES?

A nation can fix the value of its currency to another in two major ways. The first is to impose strict exchange controls that require all foreign-currency purchases and sales to be transacted through the central bank. The second way is for the central bank to intervene in the foreign exchange market to offset any upward or downward pressure on the exchange rate. Let's see how these two systems work.

FIXING CURRENCY RATES BY EXCHANGE CONTROL

Suppose the People's Bank of China (PBoC), China's central bank, decided to fix the value of the yuan relative to the U.S. dollar at 20 cents per yuan (i.e., $0.20/¥). If by chance, $0.20/¥ were also the free-market equilibrium rate, there would be nothing for the central bank to do. The market would supply exactly the amount of yuan demanded per period. In Exhibit 19–1, $0.20/¥ is the equilibrium exchange rate, and at that rate, the quantity supplied and quantity demanded are equal to ¥1,000 million per day (Point A).

Fixing an Exchange Rate below Equilibrium

Exhibit 19-2 shows the case where PBoC fixes the value of the yuan below the free-market equilibrium, where the amount of yuan demanded per day exceeds the amount supplied per day. Suppose at $0.20/¥, the quantity demanded was equal to ¥1,100 million per day (Point B), but only ¥900 million

---

[3] The classic paper written on this topic is Robert Mundell, "A Theory of Optimum Currency Areas," *American Economic Review*, Volume 51, Number 4, 1961, pp. 657–665.

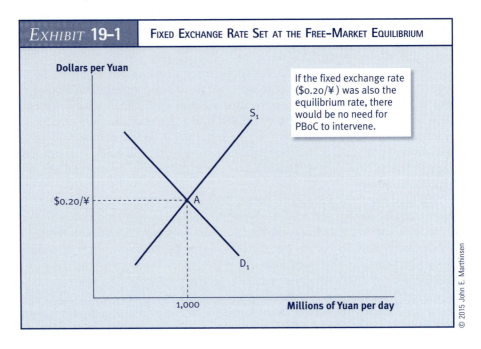

EXHIBIT 19-1 | FIXED EXCHANGE RATE SET AT THE FREE-MARKET EQUILIBRIUM

Dollars per Yuan

If the fixed exchange rate ($0.20/¥) was also the equilibrium rate, there would be no need for PBoC to intervene.

S_1

$0.20/¥

A

D_1

1,000

Millions of Yuan per day

© 2015 John E. Marthinsen

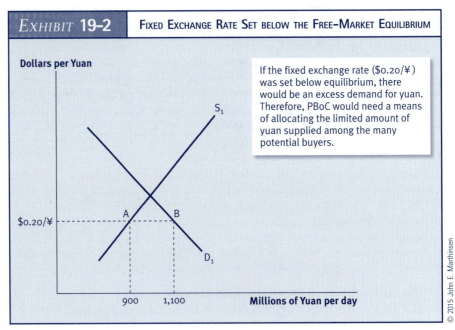

EXHIBIT 19-2 | FIXED EXCHANGE RATE SET BELOW THE FREE-MARKET EQUILIBRIUM

Dollars per Yuan

If the fixed exchange rate ($0.20/¥) was set below equilibrium, there would be an excess demand for yuan. Therefore, PBoC would need a means of allocating the limited amount of yuan supplied among the many potential buyers.

S_1

$0.20/¥

A   B

D_1

900   1,100

Millions of Yuan per day

© 2015 John E. Marthinsen

per day were supplied (Point A). PBoC would need a practical way to allocate the limited quantity of yuan supplied among the many willing buyers.

One way to allocate these yuan is to discriminate among buyers based on their needs. For example, priority could be given to foreign companies that want to purchase yuan to buy targeted Chinese exports or bring high-tech operations

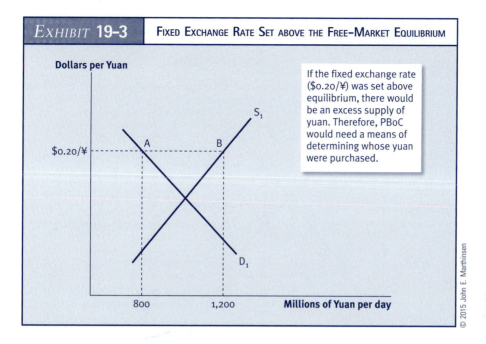

EXHIBIT 19-3 | **FIXED EXCHANGE RATE SET ABOVE THE FREE-MARKET EQUILIBRIUM**

Dollars per Yuan

If the fixed exchange rate ($0.20/¥) was set above equilibrium, there would be an excess supply of yuan. Therefore, PBoC would need a means of determining whose yuan were purchased.

S_1

A   B

$0.20/¥

D_1

800   1,200   Millions of Yuan per day

© 2015 John E. Marthinsen

to China. The limited supply of yuan might also be allocated on a "first come, first served" basis or by political favoritism. The only thing we know for certain is that allocating yuan at $0.20/¥ cannot be based solely on price.

Fixing an Exchange Rate above Equilibrium

Exhibit 19-3 shows what happens if PBoC sets the exchange rate above the free-market equilibrium. Suppose at $0.20/¥, only ¥800 million per day are demanded (Point A), but ¥1,200 million per day are supplied (Point B). Therefore, the central bank needs a practical way to determine whose yuan can be purchased because only ¥800 million of the ¥1,200 million offered are bought. Preference might be given to those who are supplying yuan (i.e., demanding dollars) to import necessities, rather than luxury goods, or to those who wish acquire, invest in, and/or develop foreign resources for Chinese use, rather than speculative financial investments. The limited selling rights could also be allocated by nonmarket alternatives, such as political or economic favoritism or first come, first served.

FIXING CURRENCY VALUES BY FOREIGN EXCHANGE MARKET INTERVENTION

A more familiar, market-oriented way for central banks to fix exchange rates is by intervening in the foreign exchange market.

Intervention to Keep the Yuan Undervalued

Suppose PBoC fixed the yuan's value below the free-market equilibrium (i.e., it overvalued the U.S. dollar).[4] In Exhibit 19-4, if supply and demand were

---

[4] Through most of the first decade of the twenty-first century, China was accused of manipulating its currency in this way. These accusations have continued in the second decade, as well.

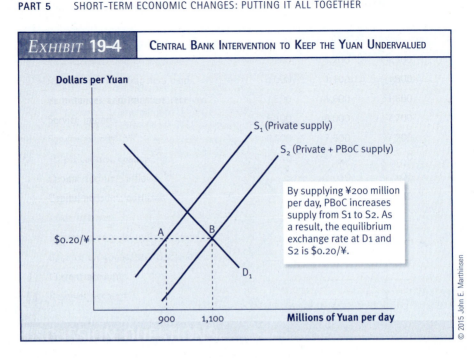

EXHIBIT 19-4   CENTRAL BANK INTERVENTION TO KEEP THE YUAN UNDERVALUED

Dollars per Yuan

S_1 (Private supply)

S_2 (Private + PBoC supply)

By supplying ¥200 million per day, PBoC increases supply from S1 to S2. As a result, the equilibrium exchange rate at D1 and S2 is $0.20/¥.

$0.20/¥

A   B

D_1

900   1,100

Millions of Yuan per day

S_1 and D_1, respectively, and the central bank fixed the exchange rate at $0.20/¥, the resulting shortage would be equal to ¥200 million per day (i.e., the distance B − A = ¥200 million/day). To keep the exchange rate fixed at $0.20/¥, the central bank would have to act as the *seller of last resort*, and supply ¥200 million per day to the foreign exchange market. These transactions would increase the supply of yuan from S_1 to S_2. Therefore at $0.20/¥, the quantity demanded per day (¥1,100 million) would equal the amount supplied per day by the market (¥900 million) and central bank (¥200 million).

It is important to remember that central bank intervention in the foreign exchange market changes the domestic and foreign monetary bases. Exhibit 19-5 shows that, to keep the $0.20/¥ exchange rate, $40 million per day[5] must cross above our imaginary horizontal line in exchange for ¥200 million, which flow below the line. As a result, China's monetary base rises by ¥200 million, the U.S. monetary base falls by $40 million, and China's international reserves rise by $40 million (see Exhibit 19-5).

Intervention to Keep the Yuan Overvalued

If PBoC tried to fix the dollar price of a yuan above the free-market equilibrium (i.e., it undervalued the U.S. dollar), there would be an excess supply of yuan in the foreign exchange market. In Exhibit 19-6, if private demand and supply were D_1 and S_1, respectively, then an exchange rate of $0.20/¥ would create an excess supply of yuan equal to ¥400 million per day (i.e., the distance B − A = ¥400 million). To keep the exchange rate fixed at $0.20/¥, PBoC would need to intervene by acting as the *buyer of last resort*

[5] $40 million = ¥200 million × $0.20/¥

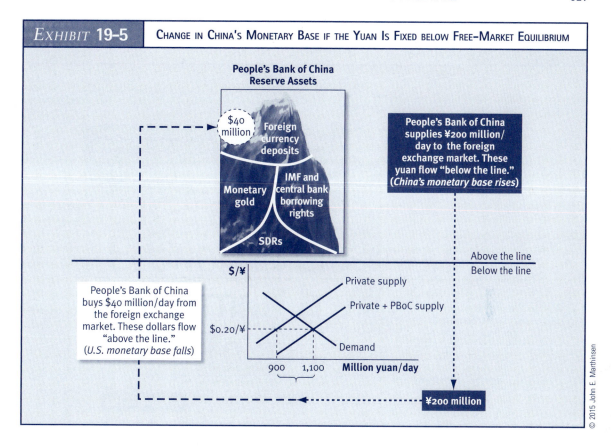

EXHIBIT 19-5 | CHANGE IN CHINA'S MONETARY BASE IF THE YUAN IS FIXED BELOW FREE-MARKET EQUILIBRIUM

People's Bank of China Reserve Assets

$40 million — Foreign currency deposits

Monetary gold

IMF and central bank borrowing rights

SDRs

People's Bank of China supplies ¥200 million/day to the foreign exchange market. These yuan flow "below the line." (*China's monetary base rises*)

People's Bank of China buys $40 million/day from the foreign exchange market. These dollars flow "above the line." (*U.S. monetary base falls*)

Above the line
Below the line

$/¥

Private supply

Private + PBoC supply

$0.20/¥

Demand

900   1,100   **Million yuan/day**

¥200 million

© 2015 John E. Marthinsen

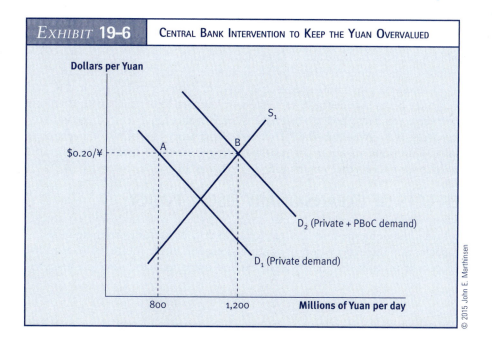

EXHIBIT 19-6 | CENTRAL BANK INTERVENTION TO KEEP THE YUAN OVERVALUED

Dollars per Yuan

S_1

$0.20/¥ - - - - A   B

D_2 (Private + PBoC demand)

D_1 (Private demand)

800   1,200   **Millions of Yuan per day**

© 2015 John E. Marthinsen

EXHIBIT 19-7	CHANGE IN THE MONETARY BASE IF THE EXCHANGE RATE IS SET ABOVE THE FREE-MARKET EQUILIBRIUM

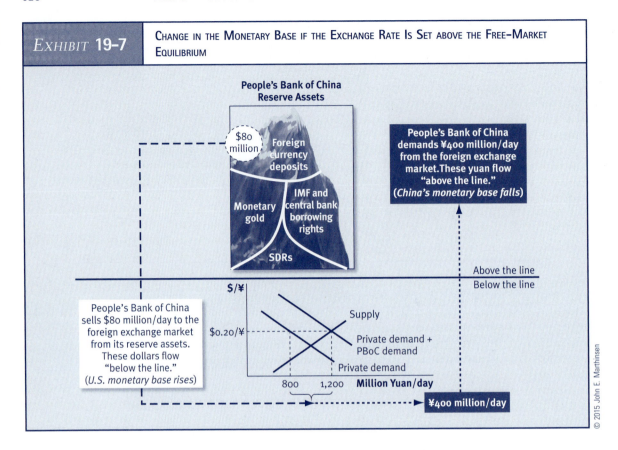

(i.e., purchasing the excess yuan with dollars), thereby increasing demand from D_1 to D_2.

Such purchases would decrease China's international reserves by $80 million per day, increase the U.S. monetary base by $80 million per day, and reduce China's monetary base by ¥400 million per day[6] (see Exhibit 19-7).

The effects that PBoC intervention have on China's and the United States' monetary bases are identical, regardless of whether PBoC deals with domestic or foreign residents. Because further coverage of this topic is more specialized in nature, it is covered in the "The Rest of the Story" section of this chapter; so, let's turn our attention now to the economic effects of fiscal and monetary policies for nations that maintain fixed exchange rates.

EFFECTS OF EXPANSIONARY FISCAL POLICY

Suppose you own a growing business in Argentina, with sales split evenly between the domestic and U.S. markets. With your factories running near capacity and the expectation of continued growth in the future, you are in the process of planning the best way to expand operations and renovate existing

---

[6] $80 million/day = ¥400 million/day × $0.20/¥

production facilities. If all goes well, construction could start within the next year.

Your concern centers on a recent announcement that the Argentine government intends to raise government spending in an effort to reduce the nation's growing unemployment rate and to stimulate economic growth. You realize that increased government spending will probably boost your domestic sales, but what effect, if any, might it have on your export sales to the United States?

Suppose the Argentine peso is fixed to the U.S. dollar at $1/peso, and you are fairly certain it will stay pegged at this rate during the capital-budgeting period. Therefore, you are not apprehensive about adverse exchange rate movements reducing your exports sales. At the same time, you realize that Argentina's central bank, Banco Central de la República Argentina (BCRA), will have to intervene in the foreign exchange market to keep the peso fixed. Your concerns center on the economic effects of this intervention.

Financing is also an issue. Argentina has been liberalizing its capital markets, and you are confident that the government will not retreat from the progress it has made. In fact, there is a good chance that liberalization could move forward. Therefore, the likelihood is remote that your access to future credit will be restricted by government controls. Nevertheless, there is a timing issue. If government spending is going to increase, should you borrow now in anticipation of rising real interest rates or wait until later, expecting them to fall?

Let's analyze the effects of expansionary fiscal policy (with fixed exchange rates) in the context of the Three-Sector Model and see what answers we uncover. Once we understand how increased government spending affects the major economic variables, your investment decisions may be easier to make.

STEP 1: DESCRIBE THE ECONOMIC SETTING OF ARGENTINA'S THREE MAJOR MARKETS

As usual, we will begin our analysis by characterizing Argentina's economic setting in the real goods, real loanable funds, and foreign exchange markets.

Argentina's Real Goods Market: Economic Setting

The Argentine government is concerned about the nation's high unemployment rate and slow gross domestic product (GDP) growth. Let's assume the nation is on the relatively elastic portion of its AS curve (i.e., relatively close to the Keynesian range) (see Exhibit 19-8).

> Argentina is near the Keynesian range of its AS curve.

Argentina's Real Loanable Funds Market: Economic Setting

Because Argentina has liberalized its capital markets and is likely to continue in this direction, let's assume that the nation's supply and demand for real loanable funds are relatively elastic and normally sloped[7] (see Exhibit 19-9).

> Argentina's supply and demand for real loanable funds are elastic.

---

[7] *Normally sloped* means that the supply of real loanable funds is directly related to the real risk-free interest rate (i.e., it is upward-sloping), and demand is inversely related to the real risk-free interest rate (i.e., it is downward-sloping).

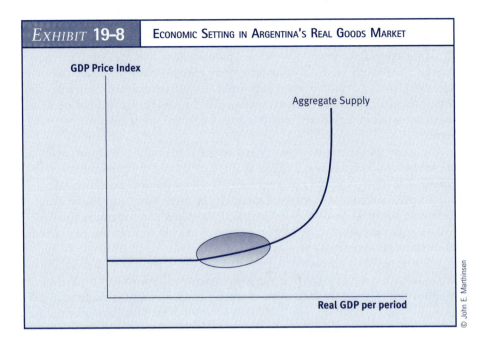

EXHIBIT 19-8   ECONOMIC SETTING IN ARGENTINA'S REAL GOODS MARKET

GDP Price Index

Aggregate Supply

Real GDP per period

© John E. Marthinsen

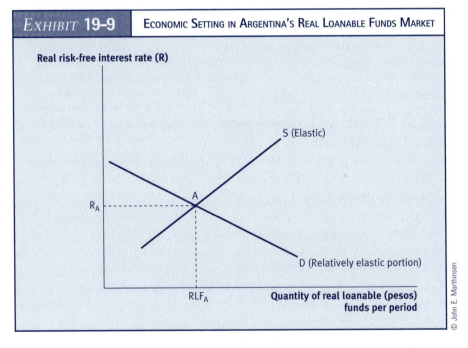

EXHIBIT 19-9   ECONOMIC SETTING IN ARGENTINA'S REAL LOANABLE FUNDS MARKET

Real risk-free interest rate (R)

S (Elastic)

R_A ---- A

D (Relatively elastic portion)

RLF_A

Quantity of real loanable (pesos)
funds per period

© John E. Marthinsen

Argentina's Foreign Exchange Market: Economic Setting

Argentina's central bank fixes the value of the peso.

Exhibit 19-10 shows the dollar–peso foreign exchange market. To fix the exchange rate at $1/peso, BCRA must intervene whenever there is pressure on the peso. Therefore, a dashed, horizontal line is drawn across Exhibit 19-10 at $1/peso as a reminder of this fixed-rate commitment. We assume the foreign exchange market starts in equilibrium at $1/Ps.

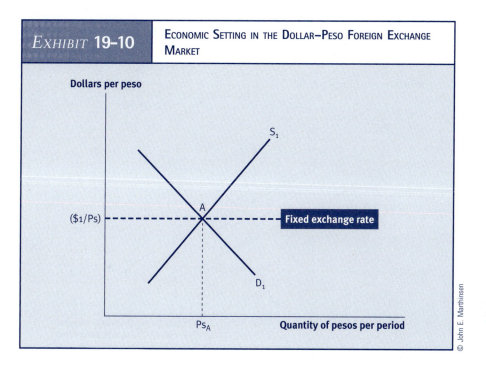

EXHIBIT 19–10   ECONOMIC SETTING IN THE DOLLAR–PESO FOREIGN EXCHANGE MARKET

With Argentina's economic setting in mind, let's identify the exogenous shock that sets off the chain of economic reactions and then analyze the economic effects of the shock.

STEP 2: IDENTIFY THE ECONOMIC (OR EXPECTED) SHOCK

The exogenous shock in this analysis is the expected increase in government spending, but this spending raises a financing issue. From where will the Argentine government get its funding?

Where to begin? Show me the money!

STEP 3: ANALYZE THE CHAIN REACTION OF ECONOMIC INTERACTIONS

Using our rule of thumb ("Show me the money!"), we will begin our analysis in the real loanable funds market because the Argentine government must first borrow before it can spend.

Economic Effects in the Real Loanable Funds Market

The increase in government borrowing raises the demand for real loanable (peso) funds. In Exhibit 19-11, when demand increases from D_1 to D_2, Argentina's real risk-free interest rate rises from R_A to R_B, and the equilibrium quantity of real loanable funds (i.e., the amount borrowed and lent) per period rises from RLF_A to RLF_B. Notice that the increase in demand from D_1 to D_2 is a primary change because it shifts the entire curve.

As the real risk-free interest rate rises, part of the increased government demand is offset by reductions in household consumption and business investment expenditures. Nevertheless, *net* borrowing increases, which means that crowding out does not completely offset the increase in government spending. Remember that the fluctuations in consumption and investment, which are due to the rise in the real risk-free interest rate, are secondary changes because they are movements along the demand for real loanable funds curve.

Increased government borrowing raises Argentina's real risk-free interest rate and quantity of real loanable funds per period.

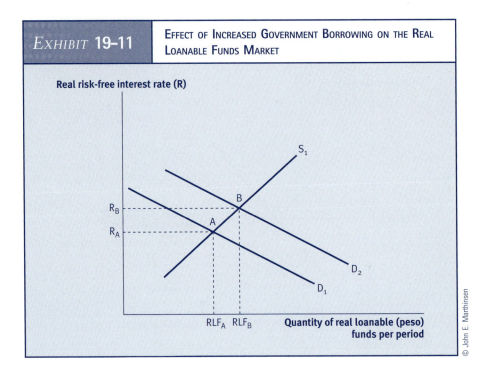

EXHIBIT 19-11   EFFECT OF INCREASED GOVERNMENT BORROWING ON THE REAL LOANABLE FUNDS MARKET

© John E. Marthinsen

Economic Effects in the Real Goods Market

In Argentina's real loanable funds market, there is a net increase in borrowing, which causes aggregate demand to rise in the real goods market. Exhibit 19-12 shows that the net increase in Argentina's aggregate demand from AD_1 to AD_2 causes the nation's prices to rise from P_A to P_B and real GDP to rise from $RGDP_A$ to $RGDP_B$ (Point A to Point B).

The primary effect is the initial increase in government spending (i.e., the fiscal stimulus), which raises AD from AD_1 to AD_2 (i.e., by the full rise in government spending). But from the loanable funds market, we also know that the rising real risk-free interest rate causes both C and I fall (i.e., they are crowded out), partially offsetting the increase in government spending/borrowing. Because the primary effect is greater than the secondary effect, AD rises in the real goods market. These primary and secondary effects are summarized in Exhibit 19-13.

> The primary effects of fiscal policy outweigh the secondary effects; therefore, net expenditures increase when the government borrows to spend.

Economic Effects in the Foreign Exchange Market

Let's complete our analysis of expansionary fiscal policy by determining what BCRA has to do to keep the exchange rate fixed at $1/peso. To analyze these effects, we will organize our thoughts, as we did in the last chapter, around the supply and demand forces that occur in Argentina's three major balance of payments components, which are current international transactions that affect the foreign exchange market (CTX), net nonreserve-related international borrowing/lending transactions that affect the foreign exchange market (NIX), and reserve-related (central bank) transactions that affect the foreign exchange market (RAX). Changes in Argentina's price level and real GDP affect CTX, and changes in Argentina's real risk-free interest rate relative to other countries affect NIX. Finally, central bank intervention affects RAX.

> The peso's value is fixed by the central bank at $1/peso, which means it must offset the net CTX-related and NIX-related forces.

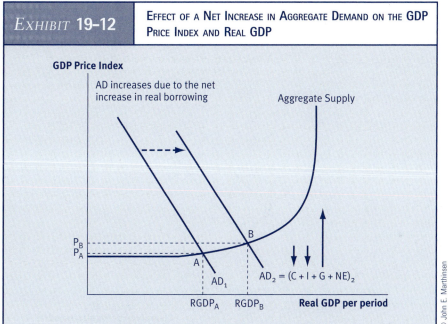

EXHIBIT **19-12**   **EFFECT OF A NET INCREASE IN AGGREGATE DEMAND ON THE GDP PRICE INDEX AND REAL GDP**

GDP Price Index

AD increases due to the net increase in real borrowing

Aggregate Supply

P_B
P_A

B

A

AD_1

$AD_2 = (C + I + G + NE)_2$

$RGDP_A$ $RGDP_B$ **Real GDP per period**

EXHIBIT **19-13**   **PRIMARY AND SECONDARY EFFECTS**

Expansionary fiscal policy	G ↑ = Borrowing ↑	AD ↑	Primary effect
Real risk-free interest rate ↑	C ↓ & I ↓	AD ↓	Secondary effects in the real loanable funds market
Net effect	**(C + I + G) ↑**	**AD ↑**	**Primary > secondary effects**

If the CTX and NIX forces put upward pressure on the peso, BCRA will have to intervene to lower the exchange rate back to the fixed rate. Conversely, if the net pressure from CTX and NIX forces puts downward pressure on the peso, the central bank will have to use its reserves to lift the exchange rate back to the fixed level.

CTX-Related Supply and Demand Forces in the Foreign Exchange Market: CTX-related forces cause the peso to depreciate. As Argentina's real GDP increases, imports rise, which increase the supply of pesos in the foreign exchange market and cause the peso to depreciate. In Exhibit 19-14, this increased supply is shown as a shift from S_1 to S_2, which causes the exchange rate to fall from Point A to Point B.

At the same time, higher Argentine prices relative to U.S. prices increase the nation's imports and decrease its exports. As Exhibit 19-15 shows, the increased imports raise the supply of pesos from S_1 to S_2, which puts downward pressure on the peso (Point A to Point B). Similarly, falling Argentine

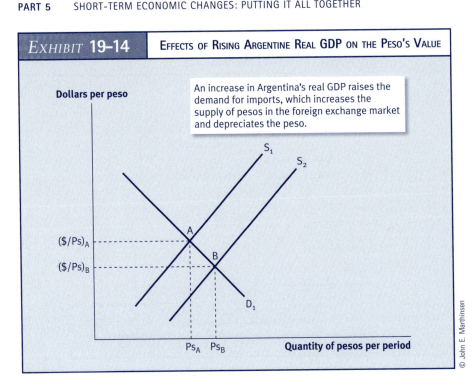

EXHIBIT 19–14 EFFECTS OF RISING ARGENTINE REAL GDP ON THE PESO'S VALUE

An increase in Argentina's real GDP raises the demand for imports, which increases the supply of pesos in the foreign exchange market and depreciates the peso.

© John E. Marthinsen

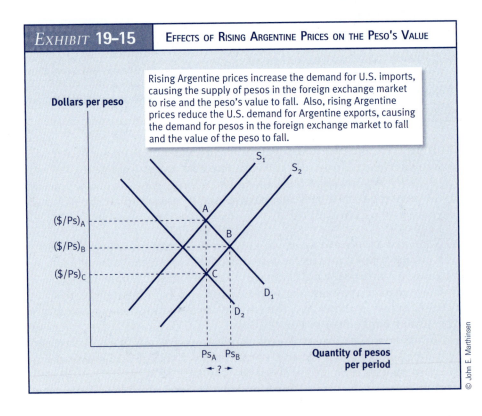

EXHIBIT 19–15 EFFECTS OF RISING ARGENTINE PRICES ON THE PESO'S VALUE

Rising Argentine prices increase the demand for U.S. imports, causing the supply of pesos in the foreign exchange market to rise and the peso's value to fall. Also, rising Argentine prices reduce the U.S. demand for Argentine exports, causing the demand for pesos in the foreign exchange market to fall and the value of the peso to fall.

© John E. Marthinsen

exports reduce the demand for pesos, which also puts downward pressure on the peso (Point B to Point C).

Even though the qualitative change in Argentina's exchange rate is certain, the net change in the quantity of pesos traded per period is ambiguous. An increase in supply raises the equilibrium quantity per period, and a decrease in demand reduces the equilibrium quantity per period. Exhibit 19-15 shows the two forces canceling each other, but there is no reason for this to be true in all cases.

CTX-related forces in the foreign exchange market reduce the value of the peso.

NIX-Related Supply and Demand Forces in the Foreign Exchange Market: As Argentina's real risk-free rate increases, foreign investors are attracted to the relatively high investment returns on peso-denominated investments and, therefore, they increase their demand for pesos. In Exhibit 19-16, this is shown as a shift in demand from D_1 to D_2.

At the same time, Argentine investors adjust the composition of their investment portfolios away from dollar-denominated assets and toward peso-denominated investments. Therefore, the supply of pesos in the foreign exchange market falls from S_1 to S_2. The increased demand and reduced supply cause the peso to appreciate from $(\$/Ps)_A$ to $(\$/Ps)_B$ to $(\$/Ps)_C$.

Again, the *net* change in equilibrium quantity per period is uncertain. A greater demand raises the quantity, and a reduced supply lowers it. Exhibit 19-16 shows the two forces canceling each other, but this is not always the case.

NIX-related forces cause the value of the peso to rise.

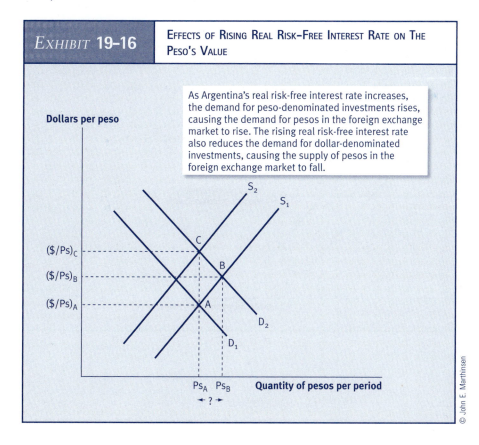

EXHIBIT **19-16**	EFFECTS OF RISING REAL RISK-FREE INTEREST RATE ON THE PESO'S VALUE

As Argentina's real risk-free interest rate increases, the demand for peso-denominated investments rises, causing the demand for pesos in the foreign exchange market to rise. The rising real risk-free interest rate also reduces the demand for dollar-denominated investments, causing the supply of pesos in the foreign exchange market to fall.

© John E. Marthinsen

RAX-Related Supply and Demand Forces in the Foreign Exchange Market:
Determining whether and how BCRA has to intervene in the foreign exchange
market depends on whether the combined CTX and NIX forces put upward
or downward pressure on the peso. The CTX forces cause the value of the
peso to fall, but the NIX forces cause it to rise.

At the beginning of this analysis, the Argentine capital markets were
described as liberalized, and there was optimism that even more progress
on this front might be made. Therefore, let's assume Argentina faces high-
mobility international capital markets. As a result, the NIX forces dominate
the CTX forces, putting net upward pressure on the peso. To offset these
pressures, BCRA is forced to supply pesos to the foreign exchange market.

Exhibit 19-17 summarizes the supply and demand shifts in the foreign
exchange market.[8] Because the NIX forces dominate, there is a net increase in
the demand for pesos from D_1 to D_2, which puts upward pressure on the peso
(Point A to Point B). To relieve this pressure, BCRA must intervene by supplying pesos to the foreign exchange market. When it does, supply increases
from S_1 to S_2, and the peso's equilibrium value falls from $(\$/Ps)_B$ back to
$(\$/Ps)_A$, which is equal to \$1/peso (Point B to Point C).

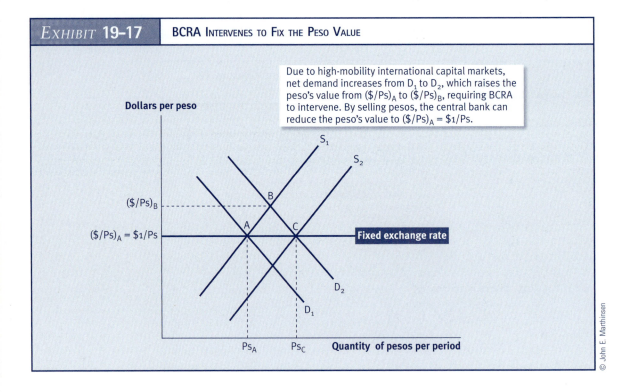

EXHIBIT **19-17**	BCRA INTERVENES TO FIX THE PESO VALUE

Due to high-mobility international capital markets, net demand increases from D_1 to D_2, which raises the peso's value from $(\$/Ps)_A$ to $(\$/Ps)_B$, requiring BCRA to intervene. By selling pesos, the central bank can reduce the peso's value to $(\$/Ps)_A = \$1/Ps$.

Dollars per peso

S_1

S_2

$(\$/Ps)_B$

B

$(\$/Ps)_A = \$1/Ps$

A   C   Fixed exchange rate

D_2

D_1

Ps_A Ps_C Quantity of pesos per period

© John E. Marthinsen

[8] Exhibit 19-17 shows only the increase in demand for pesos per period and not the reduction in supply,
which would also raise the peso's value. Including the supply change is more accurate but would complicate the graph and not change the conclusion (i.e., what the central bank must do to fix the exchange
rate).

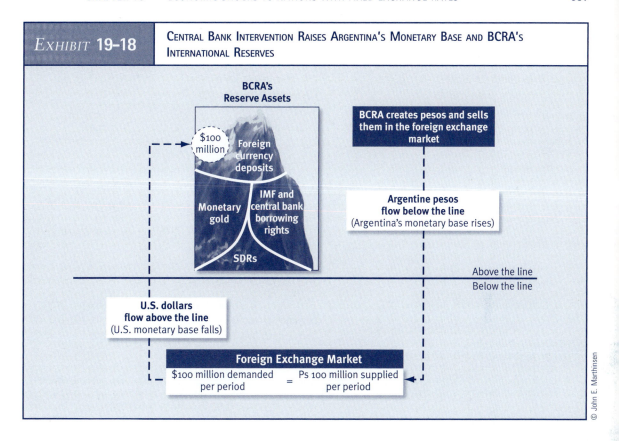

EXHIBIT 19-18   CENTRAL BANK INTERVENTION RAISES ARGENTINA'S MONETARY BASE AND BCRA'S INTERNATIONAL RESERVES

BCRA's Reserve Assets

$100 million · Foreign currency deposits

BCRA creates pesos and sells them in the foreign exchange market

Monetary gold

IMF and central bank borrowing rights

SDRs

Argentine pesos flow below the line (Argentina's monetary base rises)

Above the line
Below the line

U.S. dollars flow above the line (U.S. monetary base falls)

Foreign Exchange Market

$100 million demanded per period = Ps 100 million supplied per period

© John E. Marthinsen

By supplying pesos to the foreign exchange market, BCRA increases its mountain of reserve assets and Argentina's monetary base. As Exhibit 19-18 shows, pesos flow below our imaginary horizontal line, and dollars flow above it.

> Intervention by BCRA to reduce the peso's value causes the nation's monetary base to rise.

Changes in Argentina's Balance of Payments

What happens to Argentina's balance of payments? An increase in Argentine prices and real GDP causes CT to become more negative (or less positive). The increase in the real risk-free interest rate causes NI to become more positive (or less negative). Finally, central bank intervention causes Argentina to gain reserve assets. Because increases in a nation's assets relative to the rest of the world are recorded in the balance of payments as negative values, RA is negative. All of these effects are summarized in Exhibit 19-19.

SUMMARY OF ECONOMIC EFFECTS

Now that we have completed our analysis, let's summarize the results and see how they might affect your business decisions during the upcoming capital-budgeting period.

GDP Price Index Rises, Real GDP Rises, and Nominal GDP Rises

The increased government spending raises Argentina's aggregate demand, causing the nation's GDP Price Index and real GDP to rise. Because nominal

EXHIBIT **19-19**	CHANGES IN ARGENTINA'S BALANCE OF PAYMENTS ASSUMING *HIGH-MOBILITY* INTERNATIONAL CAPITAL MARKETS

Balance of Payments Accounts and Changes in Economic Variables Affecting them	Causes	Changes in the Balance of Payments Accounts and Subaccounts due to Changes in Economic Variables	Net Effect on the Balance of Payments Accounts
1 **CT: Current International Transactions**	→	**Δ Net exports ↓**	
Δ Real exchange rate ↑	→	Δ Net exports ↓	CT becomes more negative (Use of funds)
Δ Prices ↑	→	Δ Exports ↓ and Δ imports ↑	
Δ Nominal exchange rate = 0	→	No change in exports or imports	
Δ Real GDP ↑	→	Δ Imports ↑ → Δ Net exports ↓	
2 **NI: Net Nonreserve-related International Borrowing/Lending**	→	**Δ Net financial capital inflows ↑**	NI becomes more positive (Source of funds)
Δ Real risk-free interest rate ↑	→	Δ Financial capital inflows ↑ and Δ outflows ↓	
Due to *high-mobility* international capital markets, NIX forces dominate CTX forces.			
3 **RA: Reserve-Related (Central Bank) Transactions**	→	**Δ International reserves ↑**	RA becomes more negative (Use of funds)
Central bank intervention	→	Buy dollars and sell pesos	
Sum of all accounts			**0**

GDP is the sum of all newly produced, final goods and services per period times their prices, Argentina's nominal GDP also increases. This means that the average business will be able to raise its prices by the rate of inflation. Because your business is growing, you should expect the same. Moreover, when real GDP rises, the domestic demand for your products should also rise.

Unemployment Rate Falls, Employment Rate Rises, Real Wages Rise, and Nominal Wages Rise

The increase in Argentina's real GDP should create more jobs, thereby decreasing the unemployment rate and increasing the employment rate. As labor markets become tighter, competition for workers should increase. Therefore, staffing should become more challenging. There will be a greater need for human resource departments, executive boards, and the boards of directors to make sure that succession planning has been carefully considered—especially for skilled workers, R&D staff, and managers.

Rising stars (especially those in vital positions) should be identified, and care should be taken to ensure that their salaries and benefits are competitive. As the economy improves, individuals will have greater opportunities to switch jobs. Companies should expect increased turnover, and they should expect to pay higher real wages to attract and retain competent workers.

Real Risk-Free Interest Rate and Nominal Interest Rate Rise

The increase in government borrowing causes Argentina's real risk-free interest rate (and real interest rate) to rise. Therefore, you should consider borrowing any needed funds earlier rather than later or hedging so that a rate can be locked in before they rise.

Nominal interest rates should also increase because the real risk-free interest rate and inflation rate are both expected to increase. Nevertheless, it is the real risk-free interest rate (and real interest rate) that should be of particular concern because, on average, you should be able to offset the added burden of the expected inflation by raising your product prices.

Monetary Base Rises and M2 Rises

To keep the exchange rate fixed at $1/peso, BCRA has to supply pesos to the foreign exchange market. As these pesos cross below our imaginary line, Argentina's monetary base increases, thereby enlarging the domestic money supply by a multiplier effect.[9]

Argentina's money supply will also change as a result of fluctuations in the money multiplier because the higher real risk-free interest rate will alter the nation's preferred asset ratios. A higher real risk-free interest rate will reduce two preferred asset ratios, namely, currency-in-circulation-to-checking deposits (C_c/D) and customary-reserves-to-checking deposits (U/D). As a result, the M2 money multiplier will rise. It will also increase the preferred asset ratio of near-money-to-checking deposits (N/D), thereby reinforcing the increase in Argentina's M2 money multiplier.[10]

The Nominal Value of the Peso Does Not Change but the Real Value of the Peso Changes, Making Argentina Less Competitive

Due to central bank intervention, the nominal value of the peso remains unchanged. By contrast, Argentina's real exchange rate *does* change. Argentina's real exchange rate can be expressed in two ways. If the nominal exchange rate is stated as $/Ps, then the real exchange rate must be constructed as shown by *Real Exchange Rate #1* (see below). Because Argentina's nominal exchange rate remains constant and its GDP Price Index increases *Real Exchange Rate #1* rises, reflecting Argentina's reduced competitive position.

Real Exchange Rate #1

$$\frac{\text{Nominal Exchange Rate}_{(\$/P_S)} \times \text{Average Price Level}_{\text{Argentina}}}{\text{Average Price Level}_{\text{United States}}}$$

By contrast, if Argentina's nominal exchange rate is expressed as Ps/$, then the real exchange must be constructed as shown by *Real Exchange*

---

[9] Remember that $\Delta M2 \equiv \Delta$ (M2 Money Multiplier $\times$ Monetary Base).

[10] The actual change in the M2 money multiplier is likely to be very small because Argentina's rising real money supply will subsequently put downward pressure on the real risk-free interest rate.

Rate 2 (see below). In these circumstances, the nominal exchange rate (i.e., peso value of the dollar) remains the same and Argentina's average price level rises, causing the *Real Exchange Rate #2* to fall. The drop in this real exchange rate also means that Argentina's competitive position has deteriorated.

Real Exchange Rate #2

$$\frac{\text{Nominal Exchange Rate}_{(P_S/\$)} \times \text{Average Price Level}_{\text{United States}}}{\text{Average Price Level}_{\text{Argentina}}}$$

Whichever way the real exchange rate is stated, the interpretation is the same. Argentina will become less competitive internationally. Therefore, you should expect shrinking sales in your export markets and increased competition from foreign companies selling in Argentina.

CT Falls, NI Rises, and RA Falls

Argentina's CT becomes more negative as rising real GDP and rising prices increase imports and reduce exports. Governments often link CT deficits (or reduced CT surpluses) with the loss of jobs.[11] In this environment, protectionist legislation is easier to pass. Therefore, you should be sensitive to political pressures that could increase tariffs and quotas because such measures can be met with severe international retaliation.

Argentina's NI rises due to the higher real risk-free interest rate relative to the United States. As international capital flows toward Argentina to purchase peso-denominated investment assets, the nation's liabilities to foreigners increase, and these flows are recorded in the balance of payments as positive values.

NI surpluses are not usually the focus of front-page news stories, but they can be when foreign investments are made for the purchase of natural resources, strategic (e.g., defense-related) companies, landmarks (e.g., Rockefeller Center), and other sensitive direct investments. Some critics associate foreign ownership of domestic properties and companies with the potential for exploitative colonialism. This perception can become a political lightening rod, resulting in unfortunate legislation that puts restrictions on international capital flows.

Finally, the increase in Argentina's international reserves, due to central bank intervention, is recorded in the nation's RA as a negative balance. If it is overdone, the addition of international reserves could create an inflation problem as the central bank increases the nation's monetary base and money supply.

Effects of Low-Mobility International Capital Markets

How would our results change if Argentina faced low-mobility international capital markets? Exhibit 19-20 shows that the qualitative changes in CT and NI are the same, but with low international capital mobility, the CTX-related forces in the foreign exchange market are now stronger than the NIX-related forces. As a result, BCRA would have to intervene to *raise* the value of the peso.

Central bank sales of its dollar reserves reduce the nation's monetary base and supply of real loanable funds. As the supply of real loanable funds falls,

---

[11] Normally, these arguments are couched in terms of the current account (CA), which is part of CT.

Exhibit **19-20**	Changes in Argentina's Balance of Payments Assuming *Low-Mobility* International Capital Markets		
Balance of Payments Accounts and Changes in Economic Variables Affecting them	**Causes**	**Changes in the Balance of Payments Accounts and Subaccounts due to Changes in Economic Variables**	**Net Effect on the Balance of Payments Accounts**
1 CT: Current International Transactions	→	Δ **Net exports** ↓	
Δ Real exchange rate ↑	→	Δ Net exports ↓	CT becomes more
Δ Prices ↑	→	Δ Exports ↓ and Δ imports ↑	negative (Use of funds)
Δ Nominal peso value = 0	→	No change in exports or imports	
Δ Real GDP ↑	→	Δ Imports ↑ → Δ Net exports ↓	
2 NI: Net Nonreserve-related International Borrowing/Lending	→	Δ **Net financial capital inflows** ↑	
Δ Real risk-free interest rate ↑	→	Δ Financial capital inflows ↑ and Δ outflows ↓	NI becomes more positive (Source of funds)
Due to *low-mobility* international capital markets, CTX forces dominate NIX forces.			
3 RA: Reserve-Related (Central Bank) Transactions	→	Δ **International reserves** ↓	RA becomes more positive (Source of
Central bank intervention	→	Sell dollars and buy pesos	funds)
Net change			**0**

© 2015 John E. Marthinsen

the real risk-free interest rate rises and amplifies the increase in real risk-free interest rate that was caused by greater government borrowing. As a result, there is even more incentive to lock in current interest rates.

GRAPHICAL SUMMARY OF EXPANSIONARY FISCAL POLICY EFFECTS

Exhibit 19-21 and Exhibit 19-22 summarize all the major economic effects of expansionary fiscal policy. Exhibit 19-21 shows the effects when a nation faces high-mobility international capital markets. The analysis reveals that, in the short term, expansionary fiscal policy can be an effective tool for increasing aggregate demand. Moreover, with high-mobility international capital markets, expansionary fiscal policy causes the central bank to intervene in the foreign exchange market to lower the value of the domestic currency. This intervention raises the nation's monetary base and money supply, which reinforces the effects of expansionary fiscal policy.

Exhibit 19-22 shows the effects when a nation confronts low-mobility international capital markets. In this case, central bank intervention in the foreign exchange market lowers the nation's supply of real loanable funds and, therefore, reinforces the upward climb in the real risk-free interest rate. As the real risk-free interest rate rises, private borrowing falls, thereby weakening some, but not all, of the stimulus from expansionary fiscal policy.

> Fiscal policy is more effective when a nation faces highly mobile international capital markets.

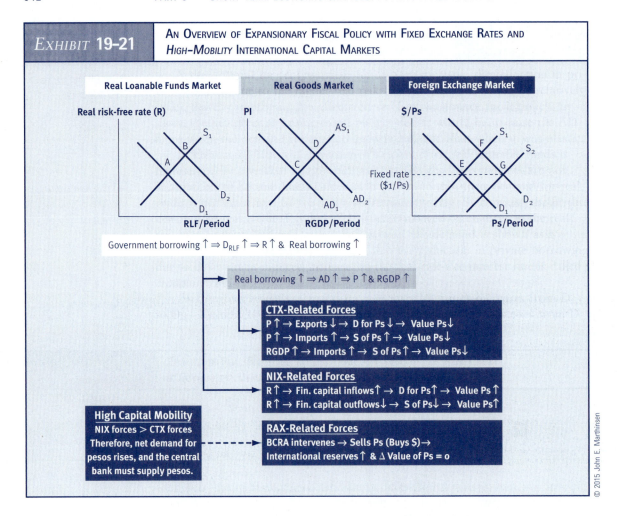

EXHIBIT **19-21**   AN OVERVIEW OF EXPANSIONARY FISCAL POLICY WITH FIXED EXCHANGE RATES AND HIGH-MOBILITY INTERNATIONAL CAPITAL MARKETS

EFFECTS OF EXPANSIONARY MONETARY POLICY

Assume that you own the same growing business in Argentina as in the last section, but this time your concern is over the possible economic effects of expansionary monetary policy. Suppose you just finished listening to an interview with the chairman of BCRA in which he indicated the central bank's intention to increase Argentina's money supply by lowering the reserve ratio. Realizing that the effects of expansionary monetary policy will be different from expansionary fiscal policy, you conduct a Three-Sector Model analysis to help build a strategy for dealing with the possible future changes.

STEP 1: DESCRIBE THE ECONOMIC SETTING OF ARGENTINA'S THREE MAJOR MARKETS

The economic environment in Argentina is the same as before.

Argentina's economic setting is the same in this analysis as it was for expansionary fiscal policy. Therefore, the country is on the relatively flat portion of its AS curve (see Exhibit 19-8). Its supply of and demand for real loanable funds are relatively (but not perfectly) elastic (see Exhibit 19-9), and the nominal exchange rate is pegged at $1/peso (see Exhibit 19-10).

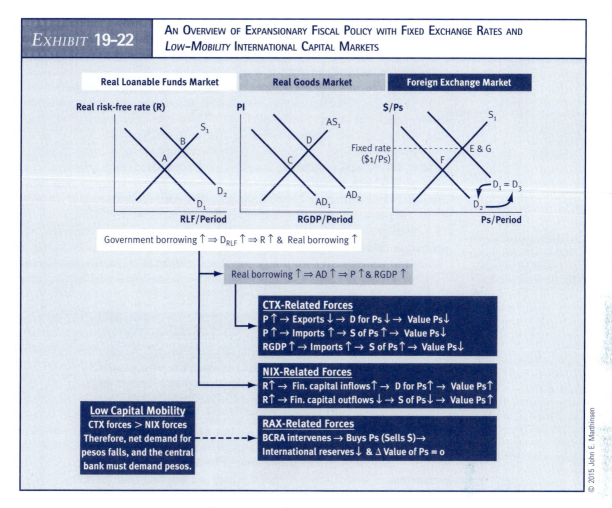

EXHIBIT 19-22   AN OVERVIEW OF EXPANSIONARY FISCAL POLICY WITH FIXED EXCHANGE RATES AND LOW-MOBILITY INTERNATIONAL CAPITAL MARKETS

STEP 2: IDENTIFY THE ECONOMIC (OR EXPECTED) SHOCK

The exogenous shock in this analysis is the discretionary increase in Argentina's money supply, which will be implemented by reducing the required reserve ratio.

STEP 3: ANALYZE THE CHAIN REACTION OF ECONOMIC INTERACTIONS

An increase in Argentina's money supply will have its most immediate impact on the nation's real loanable funds market, so let's begin our analysis there.

Economic Effects in the Real Loanable Funds Market

By increasing the real money supply, BCRA expands the peso supply of real loanable funds. In Exhibit 19-23, an increase in the supply of real loanable funds from S_1 to S_2 causes Argentina's real risk-free interest rate to fall (Point A to Point B). As the real risk-free interest rate declines, gross private domestic investment (I) and personal consumption expenditures (C) rise, thereby increasing the amount of real credit borrowed.

Economic Effects in the Real Goods Market

The net increase in borrowing causes Argentina's aggregate demand to rise. In Exhibit 19-23, an increase in aggregate demand from AD_1 to AD_2 causes Argentina's GDP Price Index and real GDP to rise (Point C to Point D).

Where to begin? Show me the money!

An increase in the supply of real loanable funds lowers the real risk-free interest rate, which increases C and I.

Increases in C and I cause AD to rise.

EXHIBIT **19-23**   ECONOMIC EFFECTS OF EXPANSIONARY MONETARY POLICY FOR A NATION WITH A FIXED EXCHANGE RATE

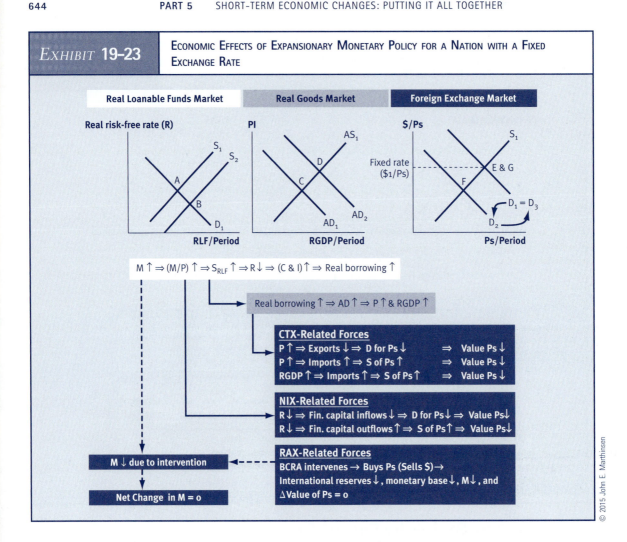

Economic Effects in the Foreign Exchange Market

To analyze the exchange rate effects of expansionary monetary policy, let's consider the CTX-, NIX-, and RAX-related supply and demand forces. Exhibit 19-24 summarizes these cause and effect relationships.

CTX-Related Supply and Demand Forces in the Foreign Exchange Market: Rising real GDP increases Argentina's imports from the United States, which increases the supply of pesos in the foreign exchange market and puts downward pressure on the peso's value. Moreover, an increase in Argentina's GDP Price Index (relative to the United States') boosts imports and reduces exports. As imports rise, the supply of pesos in the foreign exchange market increases, putting downward pressure on the peso. Similarly, lower Argentine exports reduce the demand for pesos, thereby exerting even greater downward pressure on the value of the peso. In summary, the CTX forces put downward pressure on the value of the peso by increasing the supply of pesos and decreasing the demand.

> CTX forces put downward pressure on the peso.

EXHIBIT 19-24	CHANGES IN THE PESO'S VALUE DUE TO EXPANSIONARY MONETARY POLICY	
Sources of Supply and Demand Changes	**Changes in the Supply and/or Demand for Pesos**	**Net Change in the Peso's Value**
1 **CTX-Related Forces**	**Net exports ↓**	
Δ Prices ↑	Δ Exports ↓ → D $_{Pesos}$ ↓	
	Δ Imports ↑ → S $_{Pesos}$ ↑	**Peso depreciates**
Δ Real GDP ↑	Δ Imports ↑ → S $_{Pesos}$ ↑	
2 **NIX-Related Forces**	**Net financial capital inflows ↑**	
Δ Real risk-free interest rate ↓	Δ Financial capital inflows ↓ → D $_{Pesos}$ ↓	**Peso depreciates**
	Δ Financial capital outflows ↑ → S $_{Pesos}$ ↑	
3 **RAX-Related Forces**	**Δ International reserves ↓**	
Central bank intervention (flexible exchange rate = $1/peso)	Purchase Pesos with dollars	**Peso appreciates**
Net change		**0**

© 2015 John E. Marthinsen

NIX-Related Supply and Demand Forces in the Foreign Exchange Market: Argentina's real risk-free interest rate falls as a result of the increased supply of real loanable funds. Therefore, the demand for pesos in the foreign exchange market falls, as foreign investors reduce their demand for relatively low-yielding peso-denominated assets. In addition, the supply of pesos in the foreign exchange market rises as Argentine investors purchase relatively more attractive dollar-denominated investments. These factors cause the peso to depreciate.

> NIX forces put downward pressure on the peso.

RAX-Related Supply and Demand Forces in the Foreign Exchange Market: The CTX-induced and NIX-induced changes in supply and demand put downward pressure on the value of the peso. As a result, Argentina's fixed exchange rate system obligates BCRA to offset this downward pressure. To accomplish this, BCRA must purchase pesos with its dollar reserves. Therefore, intervention causes a reduction in BCRA's mountain of international reserves.

> BCRA must intervene to purchase pesos in order to raise its value back to the fixed rate.

To simplify the graphical analysis (but not our qualitative conclusions), Exhibit 19-23 shows only the reduction in demand for pesos and not the increase in supply, which is caused by the CTX forces and NIX forces. As non-central bank demand falls from D_1 to D_2, BCRA must intervene by increasing the demand for pesos from D_2 to D_3.[12]

Unlike expansionary fiscal policy, the CT forces and the NI forces associated with expansionary monetary policy are reinforcing and not offsetting. Therefore, the actions of the central bank do not depend on the degree of international capital mobility. High international capital mobility only causes

[12] Note that $D_1 = D_3$.

Exhibit 19-25	Effects of Intervention by BCRA to Raise the Peso's Value

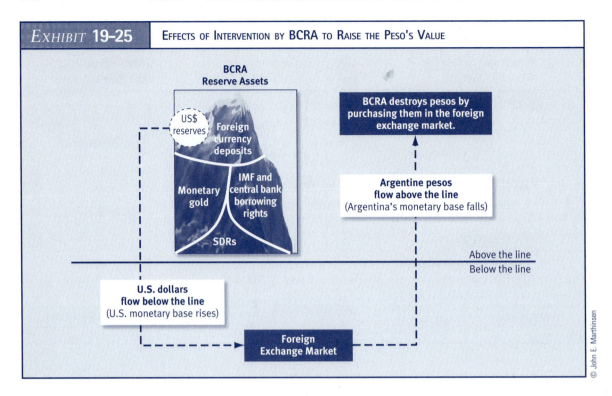

the peso's nominal value to depreciate further than it would with low-mobility international capital markets. This means that more central bank intervention would be required and a larger portion of its mountain of international reserves would be used.

As Exhibit 19-25 shows, the required central bank intervention reduces Argentina's monetary base and M2 money supply. An interesting conclusion from our analysis is that, over all, Argentina's M2 money supply does not change because the effect of an increased M2 money multiplier, due to the reduction the reserve ratio change, is exactly offset by the reduction in monetary base. The next section discusses this point in greater detail.

EFFECTIVENESS OF MONETARY POLICY FOR NATIONS WITH FIXED EXCHANGE RATES

Let's pause here to consider the effectiveness of monetary policy for countries with fixed exchange rates. More specifically, the issue is whether expansionary monetary policy can be effective at all. Clearly, if a central bank tries to increase the nation's money supply but is unable to do so because required foreign exchange market intervention interferes, then monetary policy is ineffective, and another policy tool, such as fiscal policy, should be considered.

It is tempting to think that the initial increase in Argentina's money supply, which is caused by the reduction in the reserve ratio, is the primary effect, and therefore the one that dominates any and all secondary effects. But there is a problem with this conclusion. An increase in Argentina's real money supply causes changes in the nation's price level, real GDP, and real risk-free interest rate. And fluctuations in these economic variables affect the value of the peso, which forces BCRA to intervene.

Central bank intervention is also a primary effect (i.e., a shift factor), which stops only when there is no longer any pressure on the exchange rate to change. In our case, downward pressure on the peso ends only when Argentina's prices, real GDP, and the real risk-free interest rate return to their original levels or rates. But this happens only when the initial increase in the nation's money supply is completely offset by central bank intervention. In short, a new equilibrium is established only when the *net* change in the money supply is equal to zero.[13]

If the Argentine markets were completely frictionless, the offsetting effects of central bank intervention would occur immediately. Under these circumstances, there would not be even a brief interval when monetary policy was effective.

Of course, economic frictions could delay, for a brief period, the offsetting effects of central bank intervention. But this lag is not likely to be long, and its duration would dwindle as the public became more familiar with the effects of monetary policy. For this reason, most macroeconomic analyses evaluate the effects of monetary policy after considering the offsetting effects of central bank intervention.

> With a fixed exchange rate, expansionary monetary policy is ineffective because any reduction in the reserve ratio, which increases the M2 money multiplier, is offset by central bank intervention, which decreases the monetary base.

IMPOSSIBLE TRINITY

Our conclusions lead us to an important macroeconomic law, called the "impossible trinity,"which is easiest to understand in the context of national economic goals. Suppose a nation had the following three macroeconomic goals:

1. a fixed exchange rate,
2. free and open international trade and capital markets, and
3. monetary independence.

The impossible trinity tells us that it is possible for a nation to achieve any two of these goals, but it is impossible to simultaneously achieve all three.

Argentina is a perfect illustration of the impossible trinity. The country adopted fixed exchange rates (Goal 1) and had reasonably free international trade and capital flows (Goal 2). But as a result, the central bank lost independent control of the nation's money supply (Goal 3). We know this because BCRA tried to increase the money supply by lowering the reserve ratio, but this policy was unsuccessful. Money that was created when the money

> Impossible Trinity: A nation can simultaneously achieve two, but never all three, of the following goals: (1) a fixed exchange rate, (2) free and open international trade and capital markets, and (3) monetary independence.

---

[13] In the context of the Three-Sector Model, an alternative (perhaps, easier) way to understand this conclusion is by putting the foreign exchange market analysis directly after (to the right of) the real loanable funds market analysis in Exhibit 19-23 and then putting the real goods market directly after (to the right of) the foreign exchange market. The economic analysis reveals that intervention sterilizes changes in the real money supply, which means there are no economic spillover effects to the real goods market.

multiplier rose was destroyed by a reduction in the monetary base due to central bank intervention in the foreign exchange market.

The impossible trinity tells us that, if Argentina wanted to regain independent control of its money supply, it could do so only by adopting a flexible exchange rate or imposing heavy restrictions on international trade and capital flows.

SUMMARY OF ECONOMIC EFFECTS

If the net change in Argentina's money supply is zero, then the nation's most important macroeconomic variables remain constant. The only significant changes are in the nation's monetary base, money multiplier, and balance of payments.

No Change in the Real Risk-Free Interest Rate, Real GDP, Nominal GDP, GDP Price Index, Unemployment Rate, Employment Rate, Real Wages, Nominal Wages, Nominal Peso Value, and Real Peso Value

With no net change in Argentina's money supply, there would be no change in the supply of real loanable funds and, therefore, no change in the real risk-free interest rate or net borrowing. As a result, aggregate demand would remain constant, and there would be no change in Argentina's GDP Price Index or real GDP.

With no change in real GDP, there would be no change in Argentina's unemployment rate or employment rate. As a result, the demand for labor would remain constant, and there would be no pressure for Argentina's real and/or nominal wage rates to change.

Due to central bank intervention, Argentina's nominal exchange rate would remain constant. Finally, the nation's real exchange rate would remain constant because neither the nominal exchange rate nor the domestic price level would change.

M2 Multiplier Rises, Monetary Base Falls, and M2 Money Supply Does Not Change

The reduction in the nation's reserve ratio increases the nation's money multiplier, but central bank intervention reduces the monetary base. In the end, these two (primary) effects are self-canceling. Therefore, Argentina's money supply remains constant.

CT Does Not Change, NI Falls, and RA Rises

Expansionary monetary policy causes BCRA to lose international reserves due to its intervention in the foreign exchange market. The loss of international reserves is a source of funds, which is recorded in Argentina's balance of payments as a positive value. Therefore, RA rises.

Argentina's relative prices have not changed, and neither has its real GDP or exchange rate. Therefore, there is no economic reason for Argentina's CT to change. Similarly, Argentina's relative real risk-free interest rate has not changed; so there is no economic reason for NI to change. But if this is the case, where is the negative entry that offsets the positive balance in the reserve assets?

The easiest way to answer this question is to rely on our knowledge of balance of payments accounting. When BCRA intervenes in the foreign exchange market, the transactions *below the line* involve changes in bank checking accounts, which are recorded in NI. As a result, Argentina's positive RA would be counterbalanced by a negative value in NI.

Exhibit 19-26 summarizes the effects of expansionary monetary policy on Argentina's balance of payments, and Macro Memo 19-1, "Balance of Payments Accounting and Central Bank Intervention," explains in greater detail why central bank intervention is counterbalanced by changes in NI.

Exhibit **19-26**	**EFFECT OF THE EXPANSIONARY MONETARY POLICY ON ARGENTINA'S BALANCE OF PAYMENTS**		
Balance of Payments Accounts and Changes in Economic Variables Affecting them	**Changes in the Balance of Payments Accounts and Subaccounts due to Changes in Economic Variables**		**Net Effect on the Balance of Payments Accounts**
1 **CT: Current International Transactions**	→	**Δ Net exports = 0**	
Δ Real exchange rate = 0	→	Δ Net exports = 0	*No change in the CA*
Δ Prices = 0	→	Δ Exports = Δ imports = 0	
Δ Nominal peso value = 0	→	Δ Exports = Δ imports = 0	
Δ Real GDP = 0	→	Δ Imports = Δ Net exports = 0	
2 **NI: Net Nonreserve-related International Borrowing/Lending**	→	**Δ Net financial capital inflows ↑**	
Δ Real risk-free interest rate = 0	→	No change	
		Due to intervention, Argentina's financial assets abroad rise or its financial liabilities to foreigners fall.	NI becomes more negative
3 **RA: Reserve-Related (Central Bank) Transactions**	→	**Δ International reserves ↓**	RA becomes more positive because reserve assets fall (Source of funds)
Central bank intervenes	→	Sell dollars and buy pesos	
Net change			**0**

MACRO MEMO   19-1

Balance of Payments Accounting and Central Bank Intervention

This Macro Memo considers two examples of foreign exchange market intervention. In the first example, BCRA's counterparty is a foreign resident, and, in the second example, the counterparty is an Argentine resident. We will find that the effects on the nation's balance of payments and monetary base are the same in both cases.

Effects of Intervention When Central Bank's Counterparty Is Not an Argentine Resident

Suppose BCRA sold $10 million of its U.S. dollar reserve assets in the foreign exchange market and Hercules, Inc., a U.S. resident company, was the counterparty. Because the exchange rate is fixed at $1/peso, the peso value of the $10 million deal would be Ps10 million. Exhibit 19-27 shows the accounting entries connected to these transactions.

EXHIBIT 19-27	ACCOUNTING ENTRIES WHEN BCRA SELLS DOLLARS IN THE FOREIGN EXCHANGE MARKET TO A FOREIGN RESIDENT

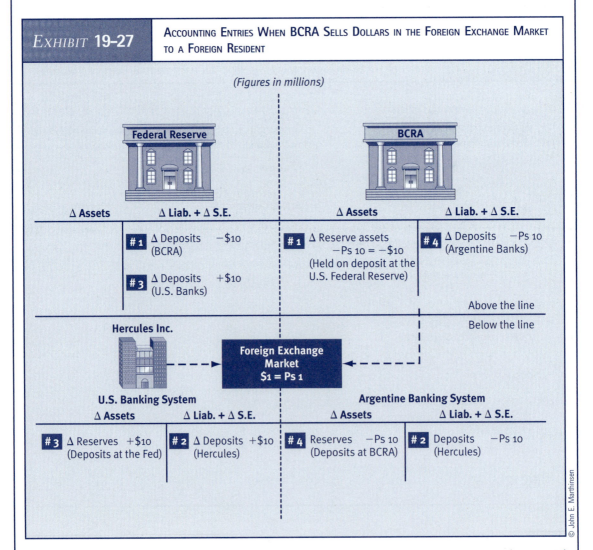

(Figures in millions)

Federal Reserve

Δ Assets	Δ Liab. + Δ S.E.
	#1 Δ Deposits −$10 (BCRA)
	#3 Δ Deposits +$10 (U.S. Banks)

BCRA

Δ Assets	Δ Liab. + Δ S.E.
#1 Δ Reserve assets −Ps 10 = −$10 (Held on deposit at the U.S. Federal Reserve)	#4 Δ Deposits −Ps 10 (Argentine Banks)

Above the line

Below the line

Hercules Inc.

Foreign Exchange Market $1 = Ps 1

U.S. Banking System

Δ Assets	Δ Liab. + Δ S.E.
#3 Δ Reserves +$10 (Deposits at the Fed)	#2 Δ Deposits +$10 (Hercules)

Argentine Banking System

Δ Assets	Δ Liab. + Δ S.E.
#4 Reserves −Ps 10 (Deposits at BCRA)	#2 Deposits −Ps 10 (Hercules)

© John E. Marthinsen

(CONTINUED)

1. BCRA's reserve assets, which are held on deposit at the U.S. Federal Reserve, fall by $10 million. Therefore, the Federal Reserve reduces its deposit liabilities to BCRA by $10 million. See the two entries marked #1 in Exhibit 19-27.

2. Because Hercules purchases $10 million with Ps 10 million, its account at a U.S. bank rises by $10 million, and its deposit at an Argentine bank falls by Ps 10 million. See the two entries marked #2 in Exhibit 19-27.

3. When the dollar side of the transaction clears, the deposits at the Fed for Hercules' U.S. bank increase by $10 million, and therefore, the liabilities of the Fed to Hercules' U.S. bank increase by $10 million. Notice that the increase in U.S. bank reserves causes the U.S. monetary base to rise. See the two entries marked #3 in Exhibit 19-27.

4. Finally, when the peso transaction clears, the Argentine banking system loses Ps 10 million of deposits at BCRA, and BCRA reduces the Argentine banking system's deposits by Ps 10 million. Notice that the reduction in Argentine bank reserves causes Argentina's monetary base to fall. See the two entries marked #4 in Exhibit 19-27.

The $10 million reduction in BCRA's reserve assets in the U.S. Fed would be recorded in Argentina's RA as a positive Ps 10 million figure because it represents a loss of assets relative to foreign nations. The reduction in Argentina's bank liabilities to Hercules (a foreign resident) would be recorded as negative Ps 10 million in Argentina's NI because it represents a reduction in liabilities to foreigners, which is a use of funds. Exhibit 19-28 summarizes these results.

EXHIBIT 19-28	EFFECT OF CENTRAL BANK INTERVENTION ON ARGENTINA'S BALANCE OF PAYMENTS WHEN THE COUNTERPARTY IS A FOREIGN RESIDENT	
Δ Current International Transactions	=	0
Δ Net Nonreserve-Related international Borrowing/Lending	=	−Ps 10 million
Δ Reserve-Related (Central Bank) Transcations	=	+Ps 10 million

Effects of Intervention When Central Bank's Counterparty Is an Argentine Resident

Let's take the same example as before, but this time, we will assume that Rincon, Inc., an Argentine resident company, is the counterparty to the central bank transaction. Exhibit 19-29 shows the accounting entries connected to these transactions. Notice that all the entries are the same as in our previous example, except the deposits of Rincon rather than Hercules change.

1. As was the case in the previous example, BCRA's reserve assets, which are held on deposit at the U.S. Federal Reserve, fall by $10 million. Therefore, the Federal Reserve reduces its deposit liabilities to BCRA by $10 million. See the two entries marked #1 in Exhibit 19-29.

2. Because Rincon purchases $10 million with Ps 10 million, its account at a U.S. bank rises by $10 million, and its deposit at an Argentine bank falls by Ps 10 million. See the two entries marked #2 in Exhibit 19-29.

3. When the dollar side of the transaction clears, the deposits at the Fed for Rincon's U.S. bank increase by $10 million, and therefore, the liabilities of the Fed to Rincon's U.S. bank increase by $10 million. Notice that these transactions increase the U.S. monetary base. See the two entries marked #3 in Exhibit 19-29.

(CONTINUED)

EXHIBIT 19–29   ACCOUNTING ENTRIES WHEN BCRA SELLS DOLLARS IN THE FOREIGN EXCHANGE MARKET TO AN ARGENTINE RESIDENT

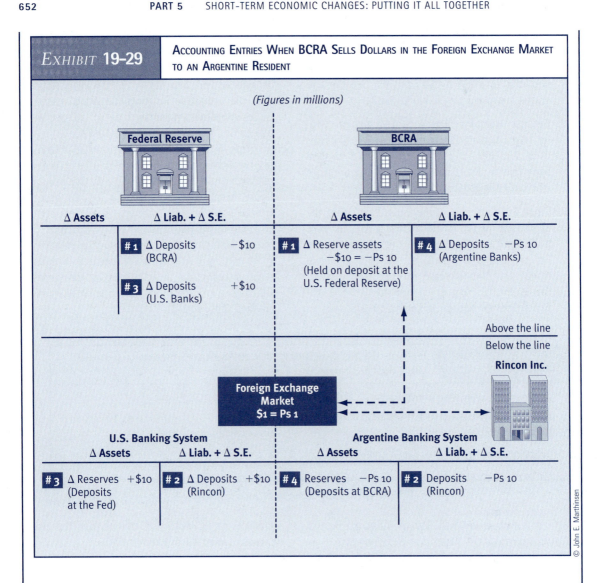

(Figures in millions)

© John E. Marthinsen

4. Finally, when the peso transaction clears, the Argentine banking system loses Ps 10 million of deposits at BCRA, and BCRA reduces the Argentine banking system's deposits by Ps 10 million. Notice that the reduction in Argentine bank reserves causes Argentina's monetary base to fall. See the two entries marked #4 in Exhibit 19-29.

The $10 million reduction in Argentina's reserves assets is recorded in RA as a positive Ps 10 million figure because it represents a loss of assets relative to foreign nations. At the same time, the $10 million increase in Argentine investment assets abroad (i.e., the U.S. bank account of Rincon) is recorded as a negative in NI because it represents an increase in Argentina's assets abroad, which is a use of funds. These effects are summarized in Exhibit 19-30.

(CONTINUED)

EXHIBIT 19-30	EFFECT OF CENTRAL BANK INTERVENTION ON ARGENTINA'S BALANCE OF PAYMENTS WHEN THE COUNTERPARTY IS AN ARGENTINE RESIDENT		
Δ Current International Transactions		=	0
Δ Net Nonreserve-Related international Borrowing/Lending		=	−Ps 10 million
Δ Reserve-Related (Central Bank) Transcations		=	+Ps 10 million
Net change		=	0

© 2015 John E. Marthinsen

THE REST OF THE STORY

RISE AND FALL OF THE ASIAN TIGERS: 1985–1997

Let's use what we have learned about fixed exchange rates to analyze the rise and fall of the Asian Tiger countries from 1985 to 1997. For more than a decade prior to 1997, GDPs in these developing nations grew at blistering paces. Their economic performance was even more remarkable because it was achieved in an environment of relatively low and stable inflation, guarded fiscal policies, and increasingly liberalized capital markets.

Favorable economic conditions attracted numerous international investors, but what clinched the deal for many of them was the fixed link these nations maintained between their currencies and the U.S. dollar. As long as exchange rates were convincingly fixed, international investors did not have to worry about currency fluctuations depreciating their asset values and reducing their investment returns. Consequently, foreign investments streamed into these Asian countries, lured by the expectation of high real rates of return.

In 1997, economic conditions changed, and these high-flying economies came crashing to the ground. Many of them were forced to abandon their fixed exchange rates and depreciate their currencies. Asset values plunged, and investment returns turned horribly negative, causing investors to seek more stable markets with safer currencies, such as in Germany, Switzerland, and the United States.

THE RISE OF THAILAND

Because the crisis began in Thailand, we will use Thailand to represent the average Asian Tiger country during this period. Let's begin with the good times. From 1985 to 1996, Thailand's real GDP grew by about 9% per year, and during this period, the Thai baht was fixed to the U.S. dollar at $0.04/฿ (i.e., ฿25/$).[14] Strong capital inflows put upward pressure on the baht, requiring steady central bank intervention to keep the exchange rate constant.

Step 1: Describe the Economic Setting of Thailand's Three Major Markets

What was the economic setting in Thailand's real goods, real loanable funds, and foreign exchange markets between 1985 and 1996?

[14] See Bank of Thailand, Homepage, http://www.bot.or.th/English/Pages/BOTDefault.aspx (accessed August 20, 2013).

Thailand's Real Goods Market: Economic Setting: Exhibit 19-31 shows that, during this period, Thailand's unemployment rate varied between 1.1% and 5.9%. Because Thailand was close to full employment for most of these years, we will assume in our analysis that the nation was on the relatively steep portion of its AS curve, close to the classical range (see the circled region shown in Exhibit 19-32).

Thailand's Real Loanable Funds Market: Economic Setting: Thailand's supply of real loanable funds was upward sloping, and the demand for real

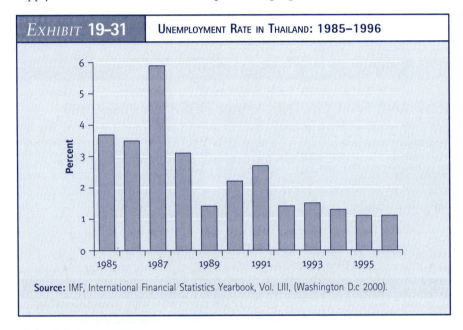

EXHIBIT 19-31   UNEMPLOYMENT RATE IN THAILAND: 1985–1996

Source: IMF, International Financial Statistics Yearbook, Vol. LIII, (Washington D.c 2000).

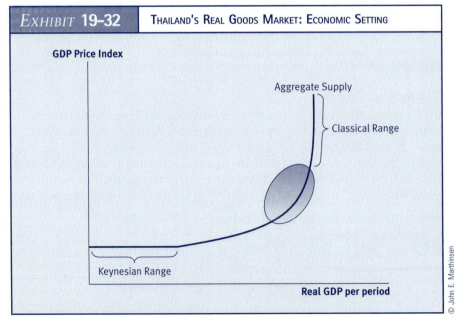

EXHIBIT 19-32   THAILAND'S REAL GOODS MARKET: ECONOMIC SETTING

© John E. Marthinsen

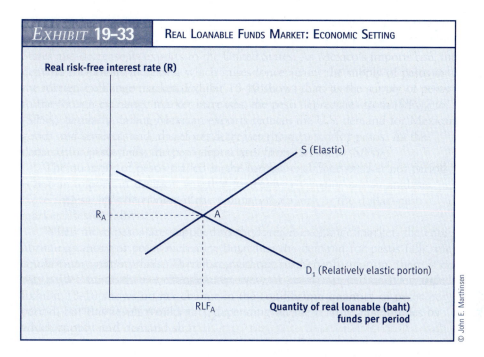

EXHIBIT 19-33 | REAL LOANABLE FUNDS MARKET: ECONOMIC SETTING

Real risk-free interest rate (R)

S (Elastic)

R_A A

D_1 (Relatively elastic portion)

RLF_A Quantity of real loanable (baht) funds per period

© John E. Marthinsen

loanable funds was downward sloping. Higher real interest rates discouraged borrowing and encouraged lending. Because Thailand was liberalizing its capital markets the supply and demand for real loanable funds were becoming more elastic (see Exhibit 19-33).

Thailand's Foreign Exchange Market: Economic Setting: By fixing the exchange rate at $0.04/฿ (i.e., ฿25/$), the Bank of Thailand (Thailand's central bank) was committed to offset any pressure on the baht's international value. In Exhibit 19-34, a horizontal line runs across the graph at $0.04/฿ to reinforce the point that central bank intervention was required to keep the exchange rate fixed at this level.

Step 2: Identify the Economic (or Expected) Shock
Between 1985 and 1996, heavy capital flows to Thailand set off a cascade of economic changes. Then in 1997, they massively reversed themselves. Let's use these capital flows (first inflows and then outflows) as the exogenous shocks for our analysis and trace their effects in the Three-Sector Model.

Step 3: Analyze the Chain Reaction of Economic Interactions
Where should we begin our analysis? To invest in Thailand, foreigners needed first to purchase bahts. Therefore, we will start our analysis in the foreign exchange market. In Exhibit 19-35, purchases of bahts by investors and speculators shifted demand from D_1 to D_2.

   If the baht were free to fluctuate, the increased demand from D_1 to D_2 would have raised its value from A to B. But Thailand's fixed exchange rate system obligated the central bank to offset any and all changes in supply or demand. With demand at D_2 and supply at S_1, there would be an excess demand of ฿100 million per period at the fixed rate of $0.04/฿ (i.e., C − A = ฿100 million). Therefore, the Bank of Thailand would need to supply ฿100 million each period

Thailand's supply and demand for real loanable funds were normally shaped and relatively elastic.

The Bank of Thailand fixed the value of the baht at $0.04/฿

Where to begin? Show me the money!

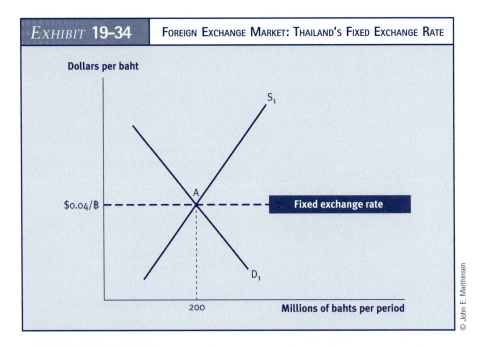

EXHIBIT 19-34   **FOREIGN EXCHANGE MARKET: THAILAND'S FIXED EXCHANGE RATE**

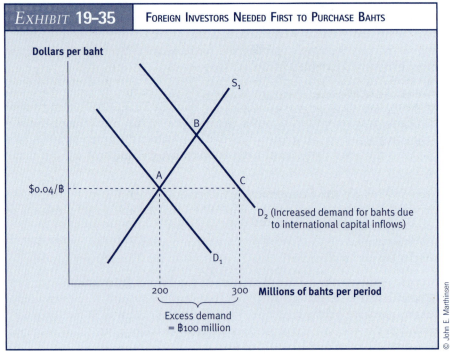

EXHIBIT 19-35   **FOREIGN INVESTORS NEEDED FIRST TO PURCHASE BAHTS**

to bring the exchange rate back to the fixed level. In Exhibit 19-36, if the supply of bahts increased from S_1 to S_2 (i.e., by ฿100 million per day), the exchange rate would stabilize at $0.04/฿ (Point C).

Intervention that decreased the value of the baht also raised the Bank of Thailand's international reserve assets. In our example, the Bank of Thailand's

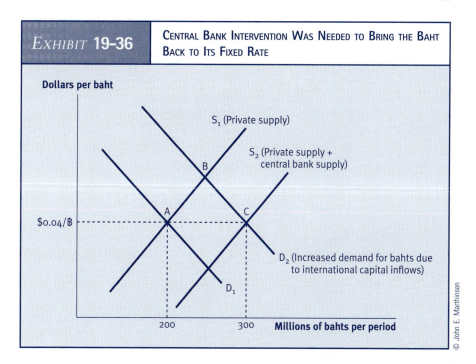

EXHIBIT 19-36

CENTRAL BANK INTERVENTION WAS NEEDED TO BRING THE BAHT BACK TO ITS FIXED RATE

Dollars per baht

S_1 (Private supply)

S_2 (Private supply + central bank supply)

B

A   C

$0.04/฿

D_2 (Increased demand for bahts due to international capital inflows)

D_1

200   300   **Millions of bahts per period**

© John E. Marthinsen

reserves would grow by $4 million per period,[15] and this increase in reserves would cause Thailand's monetary base to grow by ฿100 million per period (see Exhibit 19-37). Central bank intervention to hold down the baht's value caused a rapid increase in Thailand's monetary base, and once in the public domain, these funds were lent and re-lent by Thai banks. As a result, Thailand's rapidly rising money supply created inflationary fears.

> Central bank intervention to reduce the value of the baht raised Thailand's monetary base, money supply, and international reserves.

To counter the inflationary effects of intervention, the Bank of Thailand tried to use *sterilization* tactics to mop up some of the excess liquidity. Sterilization occurs when a central bank uses open market operations, the discount rate, and/or the reserve ratio to offset part or all of the monetary effects of foreign exchange market intervention. For Thailand, this meant selling government securities, raising the discount rate, and/or increasing the reserve ratio.

Despite the central bank's sterilization efforts, they were not enough. As a result, Thailand's bank reserves rose dramatically between 1985 and 1996, as did its money supply (see Exhibit 19-38).

During this period, Thai banks earned easy and ample profits. Not only did they have plenty of liquid assets to lend, but they (and also their customers) also were able to enhance profits by taking large currency risks. Between 1985 and 1996, the difference between money market rates in Thailand and the United States averaged about 3.1% (see Exhibit 19-39). Therefore, banks were able to borrow dollars, invest in baht-denominated assets, and earn healthy returns.[16]

---

[15] Remember that the exchange rate is $0.04/฿. Therefore, (฿100 million per period × $0.04/฿) = $4 million per period.

[16] Macro Memo 19-2, "The Carry Trade: Earning Profits by Taking Currency Exposures," explains how Thai banks and other investors earned these profits.

EXHIBIT 19–37	EFFECT OF THE BANK OF THAILAND'S PURCHASES OF U.S. DOLLARS

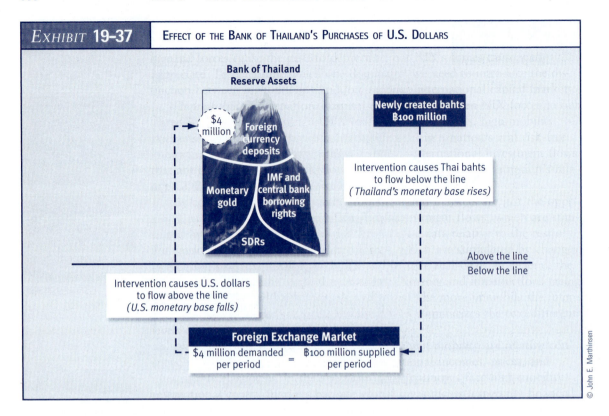

Bank of Thailand Reserve Assets

$4 million

Foreign currency deposits

Monetary gold

IMF and central bank borrowing rights

SDRs

Newly created bahts ฿100 million

Intervention causes Thai bahts to flow below the line (*Thailand's monetary base rises*)

Above the line
Below the line

Intervention causes U.S. dollars to flow above the line (*U.S. monetary base falls*)

Foreign Exchange Market

$4 million demanded per period = ฿100 million supplied per period

© John E. Marthinsen

EXHIBIT 19–38	THAILAND'S MONEY SUPPLY AND BANK RESERVES: 1985–1996

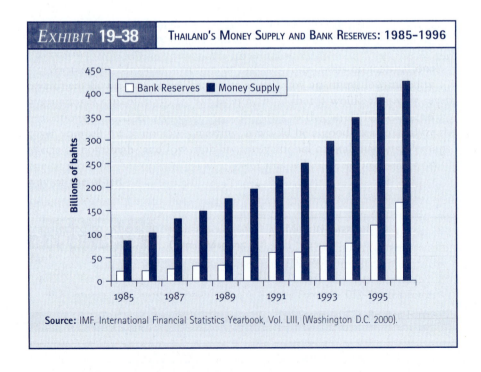

□ Bank Reserves ■ Money Supply

Billions of bahts

Source: IMF, International Financial Statistics Yearbook, Vol. LIII, (Washington D.C. 2000).

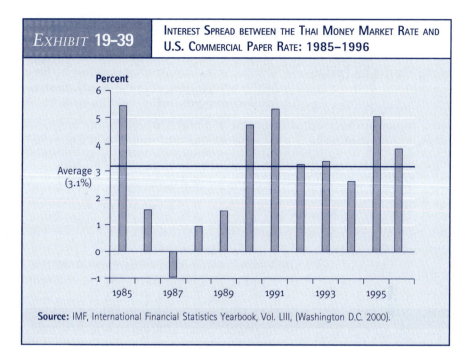

EXHIBIT **19-39**   INTEREST SPREAD BETWEEN THE THAI MONEY MARKET RATE AND U.S. COMMERCIAL PAPER RATE: 1985–1996

Source: IMF, International Financial Statistics Yearbook, Vol. LIII, (Washington D.C. 2000).

The problem was that these profits depended on the exchange rate remaining fixed. A collapse of the baht could wipe out or reverse these profits.

Thailand's money supply rose because central bank sterilization policies did not completely offset the rise in monetary base caused by foreign exchange intervention. As Exhibit 19-40 shows, the increase in Thailand's monetary

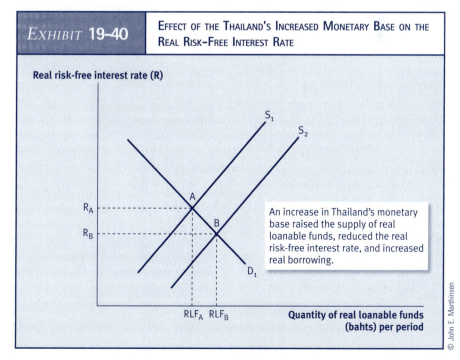

EXHIBIT **19-40**   EFFECT OF THE THAILAND'S INCREASED MONETARY BASE ON THE REAL RISK-FREE INTEREST RATE

An increase in Thailand's monetary base raised the supply of real loanable funds, reduced the real risk-free interest rate, and increased real borrowing.

© John E. Marthinsen

MACRO MEMO   19-2

The Carry Trade: Earning Profits by Taking Currency Exposures

This Macro Memo explains how Thailand's banks and other investors took currency risks to increase their profits during the period when the baht was fixed to the U.S. dollar. Let's assume that one-year money market interest rates in Thailand and the United States were 9% and 6%, respectively, and the exchange rate was fixed at $0.04/฿ (i.e., ฿25/$).

Exhibit 19-41 summarizes the way profits were earned. Thai banks and investors could:

1. borrow $10 million at 6% per annum;

2. convert the dollars to bahts at the fixed exchange rate of ฿25/$ and receive ฿250 million;*

3. use the ฿250 million to purchase Thai investment assets earning 9% per annum;

4. wait until the assets matured (one year later);

5. at maturity, receive the principal (฿250 million) and a 9% return (฿22.5 million) for a total of ฿272.5 million;

6. convert the ฿272.5 million into dollars at the fixed exchange rate of $0.04/฿ and receive $10.9 million; and, finally,

7. repay the $10 million, 6% dollar loan and harvest a profit. The loan repayment would equal $10.6 million. Therefore, the banks would earn $0.3 million, which is a 3% net return on this $10 million investment. As long as the exchange rate remained constant at $0.04/฿ (฿25/$) and the investments were risk-free, banks were assured of earning this 3% net return.

These transactions are called the *carry trade*, which can be viewed as three interconnected acts: (1) borrowing in a relatively low-interest currency, (2) investing in a relatively high-interest currency, and, (3) waiting until the investment matures—all the time worrying that currency fluctuations might wipe out all profits or cause losses.

*$10 million × ฿25/$ = ฿250 million

Exhibit **19-41**	THE CARRY TRADE: EARNING PROFITS BY BORROWING DOLLARS AND INVESTING IN BAHT ASSETS

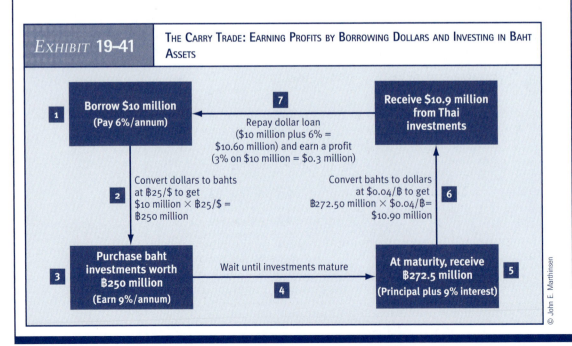

© John E. Marthinsen

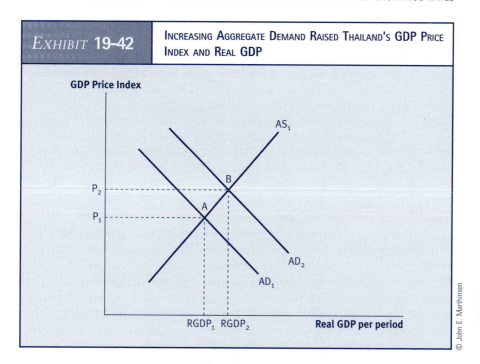

EXHIBIT 19–42 | **INCREASING AGGREGATE DEMAND RAISED THAILAND'S GDP PRICE INDEX AND REAL GDP**

base raised the nation's supply of real loanable funds and reduced the real risk-free interest rate. As the real risk-free rate fell from R_A to R_B, borrowing increased from RLF_A to RLF_B. Even though a portion of this borrowing was for productive purposes, a large part was speculative.

The increase in borrowing raised Thailand's aggregate demand. In terms of Exhibit 19–42, increased aggregate demand from AD_1 to AD_2 caused Thailand's real GDP to rise from $RGDP_1$ to $RGDP_2$ and its GDP Price Index to rise from P_1 to P_2. As a result, inflationary pressures rose.

THAILAND'S FINANCIAL CRISIS AND ECONOMIC DECLINE

Despite more than a decade of rapid growth, Thailand was forced to abandon its fixed exchange rate system on July 2, 1997. By October 31, the baht had already depreciated by nearly 40% against the U.S. dollar, and by mid-January 1998, it had fallen by 55%. The collapse of the baht set off a wave of speculation against other Southeast Asian currencies, such as the Indonesian rupiah, Malaysian ringgit, and the Philippine peso. Let's see what went wrong.

Thailand's remarkable decade of growth began to show signs of fading in the mid-1990s. In part, slower growth was demand-related and outside the control of either Thailand's government or central bank. But there were also problems on the domestic supply side, and many of these problems could be traced to overindulgences during Thailand's decade of rapid growth.

On the demand side, Thailand was victimized by falling sales in its leading export markets. During the early 1990s, Japan slid into recession and stagnated there. Starting in 1993, growth rates for most European Union (EU) members also slowed as they cut government spending, raised taxes, and reduced money supply growth in an effort to meet the Maastricht Treaty criteria for 1999 entry in the European Monetary Union (EMU).[17] With its major export markets becalmed, Thailand's economic growth began to slow.

The demand for Thailand's exports also fell due to the 1994 depreciation of the real effective exchange rate for both the Chinese yuan and Japanese yen. Immediately, export prices in these nations fell and posed a greater competitive threat to Thailand. Finally, Thailand's exports suffered when Taiwan entered the computer chip market and took away significant market share.

On the supply side, Thailand faced equally serious problems because domestic industries were losing their international competitiveness. With the baht fixed against the dollar, the only ways Thai industries could compete internationally were to keep their prices low by improving productivity and/or cutting profit margins. The problem was the nation's productivity levels were waning, and cutting profit margins had its limits.

A large part of Thailand's declining productivity was caused by excessive bank lending. Central bank supervision of the banking system was lax. The average Thai bank was inadequately capitalized and poorly managed. During the years of rapid growth, intervention by the Bank of Thailand provided Thai banks with plenty of funds to lend. Therefore, loans and profits grew quickly, masking flagrant bank mismanagement. Thai businesses found that the nation's rising tide of economic activity lifted all ships, even those guided by incompetent captains and loaded with worthless cargoes.

The problem was that it became increasingly difficult to find quality customers. As a result, Thailand's already-low borrowing standards dropped even lower. The situation was made even worse by *crony capitalism*. In banking, crony capitalism occurs when banks lend to favored friends, relatives, and politically connected individuals rather than to the best-qualified customers.

As a result of mismanagement, crony capitalism, and poor investment choices, Thailand's banking system began to accumulate a mountain of non-performing loans. Bad loans were especially problematic for weakly capitalized banks. If they cut off loans to struggling and/or delinquent debtors, these banks could force customers to default and discontinue business operations. As a result, the banks would immediately have to report losses on these delinquent loans.

When a bank writes off bad loans, its assets and shareholderes' equity fall by the full amount of the unrecoverable loans. Because Thailand's banking system had paper-thin stockholders' equity levels, even moderate losses would have caused massive bank failures. Moreover, there were concerns that the failure of enough banks might trigger the collapse of the entire banking system.

> **Thailand lost international competitiveness due to inflation, depreciation of the yuan and yen, low productivity, and a developing banking crisis.**

> **Crony capitalism added to Thailand's problems.**

> **Thailand's banks were poorly capitalized and weakly managed.**

---

[17] The Maastricht Treaty established five convergence criteria, which nations were expected to meet, in order to qualify for EMU membership in 1999. These criteria were: (1) an inflation rate not more than 1.5% above the average of the three nations with the lowest inflation rates, (2) government deficits of not more than 3% of GDP, (3) a ratio of government debt-to-GDP no higher than 60%, (4) currency fluctuations relative to other EU nations within a 30% band, which was 15% above and 15% below defined parity rates, and (5) a long-term nominal interest rate not more than 2% above the average of the three nations with the lowest inflation rates. Fulfillment of these conditions was determined on July 1, 1998, based on each country's performance in 1997. See Europa, "Summaries of EU Legislation," http://europa.eu /legislation_summaries/other/l25014_en.htm (accessed August 14, 2013).

For example, take a Thai bank with stockholders' equity equal to only 3% of its assets. With this degree of leverage, all it would take for the bank to become insolvent is a reduction in the value of its assets, an increase in the value of its liabilities, and/or losses totaling 3% of assets.

During the years of rapid GDP growth, Thailand's excessive money creation raised the prices of all goods and services in the country. The prices of investment assets (e.g., buildings) rose especially quickly due to the actions of speculators. By 1997, it was clear Thailand had created an asset bubble. There were too many overpriced and empty buildings, too many idle factories, and too many banks with nonperforming loans. The writing was on the wall for all to see. Thailand was going down. The only question was when.

As borrowers began to default on their loans, banks became the owners of assets with plunging market values. Nonperforming loans had to be written off, and when they were, the stockholders' equity of banks was too thin to cushion the losses. As a result, a widespread banking crisis developed in Thailand.

Compounding the problem of nonperforming loans were the mismatched currency positions in the balance sheets of Thai banks and their customers. The baht's depreciation in 1997 caused the value of Thailand's dollar liabilities to rise by about 55% within a half year. As a result, even if Thailand's asset prices had remained constant (and they did not), Thai banks would have faced significant problems.

Exhibit 19-43 summarizes the sequence of events that caused Thailand's dramatic and rapid downward spiral. Massive capital outflows caused the supply of bahts in the foreign exchange market to rise from S_1 to S_2, putting downward pressure on the dollar value of the baht (Point A to Point B). Due to its fixed exchange rate regime, the Bank of Thailand had to offset the downward pressure. Therefore, it was forced to intervene by purchasing bahts with dollars, which caused demand for bahts to rise from D_1 to D_2 and equilibrium to move from Point B to Point C.

Intervention caused Thailand's monetary base and the central bank's mountain of international reserves to fall. As Thailand's monetary base fell, the nation's supply of real loanable funds decreased from S_1 to S_2, and the real risk-free interest rate rose (Point D to Point E).

A rising real risk-free interest rate reduced both C and I, which caused a decline in aggregate demand from AD_1 to AD_2. Due to the lower demand, Thailand's price level and real GDP fell (Point F to Point G), which plunged the nation into a recession that increased the unemployment rate.

Thailand's financial crisis spread swiftly to South Korea, Indonesia, Malaysia, the Philippines, Hong Kong, and Singapore. In fact, its *contagion effects* (also called *spillover effects*) stretched as far away as Latin America (e.g., Argentina). International investors responded massively to the perception that worldwide risks had increased by purchasing secure assets denominated in safe currencies, such as U.S. treasury bills and Swiss bank deposits. In the end, most Asian Tiger countries (e.g., Thailand, Indoensia, Malaysia, the Philippines, and Taiwan) were forced to abandon their fixed or managed exchange rates, and their currencies depreciated by amounts ranging from 40% and 70%.

> The contagion effects from Thailand's crisis spread to many other countries.

EXHIBIT 19–43	ECONOMIC EFFECTS OF FINANCIAL CAPITAL OUTFLOWS FROM THAILAND

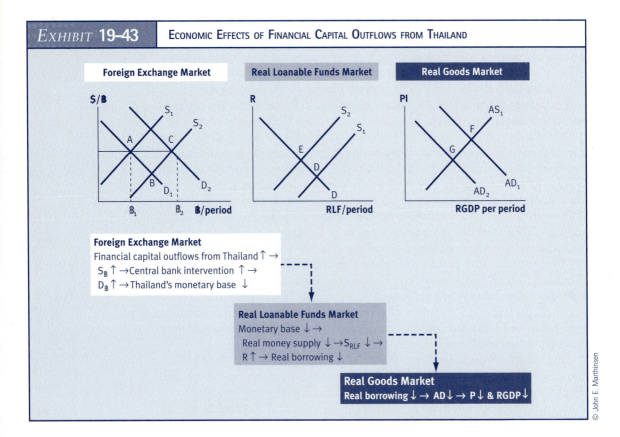

The Asian Tiger crisis is an excellent case study for understanding the costs and benefits of fixed exchange rates. It also shows clearly how a nation's independent power to determine monetary policy is compromised by a fixed exchange rate system. When capital flowed toward Thailand, the central bank was forced to buy dollars and sell bahts, which increased the domestic monetary base. When capital flowed out, the central bank was forced to reduce the monetary base.

CONCLUSION

This chapter provided a framework for analyzing short-term changes in economic conditions for nations with fixed exchange rates. Three exogenous shocks were analyzed in this chapter: expansionary fiscal and monetary policies in "The Basics" and international capital flows in "The Rest of the Story." Our analysis provided strong support for the conclusion that, for nations with fixed exchange rates, fiscal policies can be effective economic tools, while monetary policies are ineffective.

From our investigation, we learned that it is impossible for a nation to simultaneously have a fixed exchange rate, free and open international trade and capital markets, and independent control of its money supply. This conclusion, called the *impossible trinity*, is an important take-away from any study of international macroeconomics.

Our analysis also showed that a nation choosing a fixed (or managed) exchange rate during turbulent times may force its central bank to intervene constantly in the foreign exchange market. This intervention can cause major changes in the nation's monetary base, money supply, and international reserves. If intervention requires a central bank to sell its reserves, then this support can continue only as long as the nation has reserves available or has access to them.

REVIEW QUESTIONS

1. Use the Three-Sector Model to determine the effects that higher Chinese housing prices, which increase household wealth, have on China's real GDP, GDP Price Index, real exchange rate (yuan relative to U.S. dollars), quantity of yuan or dollars traded per period, real risk-free interest rate, real and nominal interest rate, quantity of real loanable funds per period, reserve assets and M2 money multiplier. Use both graphical analysis and brief explanations to support your answer. Assume the Chinese: (1) exchange rate is fixed relative to the dollar, (2) international capital markets are highly mobile, (3) aggregate supply curve is in the intermediate range, relatively close to the Keynesian range, and (4) government currently has a budget deficit.

2. Suppose the Swiss federal government in Bern proposed building a high-speed train line from Zurich to Geneva. Instead to taking the normal 2.5 hours to get from one city to the other, the new line would reduce the travel time to only 55 minutes. In doing so, Zurich residents could commute and work in Geneva and vice versa. Similarly, tourists would have much quicker access to cities in the nation's northeast and southwest regions. The estimated cost of the project is SFr 5 billion, which the government intends to finance from domestic capital markets.
   a. Is this policy an example of fiscal policy, monetary policy, or is it a combination of policies?
   b. Use the Three-Sector Model to determine the effects this government spending will have on Switzerland's real and nominal GDP, GDP Price Index, real exchange rate, quantity of Swiss francs traded per period, real risk-free interest rate, real and nominal interest rates, and quantity of real loanable funds per period. Use both graphical analysis and brief explanations to support your answers. Assume: (1) the Swiss National Bank commits itself to fix the exchange rate at 1.20 Swiss francs per euro (i.e., SFr1.2/€, which is €0.833/SFr); (2) Switzerland's international capital markets are highly mobile; (3) Switzerland is in the intermediate range of its aggregate supply curve; and (4) the Swiss national government has a budget deficit before the policy change.

3. Suppose the value of India's international reserves rose from $287 billion to $300 billion.
   a. Can we conclude that the Indian central bank was intervening in the foreign exchange market, not intervening, or it is impossible to tell? Explain why.
   b. Explain whether the Indian exchange rate was higher or lower than it would have been under a flexible exchange rate regime.
   c. Explain whether the Indian monetary base was rising, falling, or impossible to determine.

4. In 2011, an array of factors, including the conflict in Libya, contributed to soaring oil prices. One of the beneficiaries of the situation was Venezuela, whose main export was (and is) oil. Venezuela had a fixed exchange rate (the Bolivar was pegged to the U.S. dollar) and low international capital mobility. How would the increased value of Venezuelan oil exports affect:

    a. Venezuela's nominal, bilateral (Bolivars per U.S. dollar) exchange rate (i.e., $/VEF or VEF/$)? (Show graphically and briefly explain)

    b. Venezuela's real risk-free interest rate? (Show graphically and briefly explain)

    c. Venezuela's reserve assets?

5. On June 11, 2010, the FIFA Soccer World Cup started in Ellis Park Stadium, Johannesburg, South Africa with the opening match played between host country South Africa and Mexico. This was the first soccer World Cup event ever hosted by an African nation, and to ensure its success, the South African government spent billions of rands (the local currency) on sports-related infrastructure, such as stadiums.

    a. Use the Three-Sector Model to explain the effects this increased government spending had on the South African economy. Use both graphical analysis and brief explanations to support your answer. Assume that South Africa's: (1) international capital markets were highly mobile; (2) economy was in the intermediate range of AS; (3) real loanable funds market had the normal supply and demand shapes and elasticities; (4) national government had a budget deficit; and (5) exchange rate was fixed against the U.S. dollar.

6. A 1991 front-page article in *The Wall Street Journal* entitled "Foreign Rate Increases May Worsen Slump" explained how the German central bank (the Bundesbank) raised the domestic real risk-free interest rate in order to reduce inflation below a 3% level.

    a. Explain the pressures that a rising German real risk-free interest rate put on the other EU countries' currencies. Specifically, assume exchange rates within the EU were absolutely fixed. Explain the economic effects a rise in Germany's real risk-free interest rate put on the German mark (i.e., deutsche Mark) per French franc exchange rate (i.e., DM/FF) and what the French central bank (i.e., the Bank of France) had to do to keep the exchange rate fixed. Then, explain the resulting changes in France's real and nominal GDP, monetary base, M2 money supply, real risk-free interest rate, nominal interest rate, balance of payments accounts (i.e., CT, NI, and RA), real investment spending, unemployment rate, GDP Price Index, and real exchange rate.

    b. Explain what the German central bank (i.e., the Bundesbank) had to do to keep the exchange rate fixed. How would the economic results have differed if the Bundesbank intervened rather than the Bank of France?

7. Suppose the U.S. Treasury Secretary made a trip to China to discuss currency manipulation charges against the People's Bank of China. Suppose further that China refused to bend on its fixed exchange rate policy relative to the dollar, but it agreed to begin liberalizing controls on its current international transactions, as well as international borrowing and lending. Explain the effect this agreement should have, if any, on China's ability to control its M2 money supply.

8. Suppose that turmoil in Turkey caused nervous investors to sell $3.5 billion worth of Turkish-lira bonds and invest the proceeds in euro-denominated securities. Assume that at the time, Turkey's central bank maintained a fixed exchange rate between the lira and euro. Explain the effect these transactions

would have on the three components of Turkey's balance of payments. What effect, if any, would these transactions have on Turkey's monetary base, money supply, and M2 money multiplier?

9. Suppose Korea's industrial policies focus on modernizing plant and equipment, promoting innovation, and enhancing labor productivity. As a result, these policies cause an increase in the nation's AS but not in AD. Assuming Korea has a fixed exchange rate with the U.S. dollar, use the Three-Sector Model to determine the effect Korea's policies should have on the nation's GDP Price Index, real risk-free interest rate, nominal interest rates, real and nominal GDP, balance of payments accounts (i.e., CT, NI, and RA), real exchange rate relative to the dollar, gross private domestic investment, unemployment rate, and level of international reserves.

10. Suppose a bipartisan bill is introduced in the U.S. Congress that proposes a 27.5% tariff on all U.S. imports from China, unless the Chinese national government revalues the yuan within six months. Use the Three-Sector Model to explain the effect such a tariff would have on the following Chinese macroeconomic variables: GDP Price Index, real and nominal GDP, real exchange rate, real risk-free interest rate, nominal interest rate, and real interest rate. Assume the dollar-yuan exchange rate is fixed.

11. Suppose you were working as an Asian investment analyst and were asked to provide a brief report on the Japanese economy during the coming two years. Use the Three-Sector Model to explain the effects an increase in China's real GDP should have on the Japanese economy. Remember that if China's real GDP rises, the nation will import more from Japan. Assume that Japan and China have high-mobility international capital markets and that Japan wants to keep the yen tied to the yuan so the exchange rate between the yuan and yen is fixed.

12. Rösti Technologies AG is a Zurich-based company with affiliates around the world. Suppose you were working as Rösti's finance manager in Khartoum, Sudan. A recent business report explained that the Sudanese government was planning on raising personal income taxes to help reduce inflation and correct the nation's large government budget deficit. Using the Three-Sector Model, explain how an increase in personal income taxes would affect Sudan's economy. Assume the Sudanese pound (SDD) was fixed against the dollar at SDD4.4 per U.S. dollar, and Sudan faced relatively low-mobility international capital markets.

13. For more than a half century, a dozen African countries pegged their currency, the CFA franc, to the French franc. Many analysts felt that central bank intervention caused the CFA franc to become overvalued by approximately 50%.
    a. Exchange rates are set by the forces of supply and demand. What did the analysts mean when they said that the CFA franc was "overvalued"?
    b. What impact did intervention by the CFA central bank have on the CFA zone's monetary base, real risk-free interest rate, nominal interest rates, GDP Price Index, nominal and real GDP, current international transactions balance, and reserve assets?

14. Using the impossible trinity, explain whether you agree or disagree with the following statement. "If a central bank sets an exchange rate target, it abandons control of the domestic money supply and nominal interest rate."

15. Suppose the Bank of Thailand fixes the value of the baht to the U.S. dollar, but the dollar can float freely relative to other nations. If the U.S. dollar increases in value, what will happen to Thailand's exports to other Asian countries?

16. If there are capital inflows into a country with a fixed exchange rate, should fiscal policy be contractionary or expansionary to offset the effects of exchange rate intervention? Show graphically and briefly explain.

17. Suppose that from the beginning to the end of 2014, central bank reserve assets in Venezuela increased from $29.5 billion to $35 billion. Given this information, answer the following questions.
    a. Was Venezuela's central bank intervening in the foreign exchange market?
    b. If the central bank was intervening, was it trying to raise or lower the Bolivar's value?
    c. Did Venezuela's central bank intervention raise, lower, not affect the nation's monetary base, or is it impossible to determine?

DISCUSSION QUESTIONS

18. Chile has been very successful at liberalizing its international capital markets. Suppose you worked for a New York–based company that was considering a large investment in Chile. Explain whether capital market liberalization would be a positive or negative factor in your investment decision, assuming Chile had a fixed exchange rate relative to the U.S. dollar.

19. Suppose Malaysian authorities implemented economic policies designed to insulate the nation's monetary policy from external volatility. The measures included pegging the ringgit to the U.S. dollar, imposing selected exchange rate and capital controls, and pursuing expansionary fiscal policies. Suppose the controls caused Malaysia to face low-mobility international capital markets.
    a. Using the Three-Sector Model, explain the effect Malaysia's expansionary fiscal policy (assume it was an increase in government spending) should have on the Malaysian economy.
    b. Explain whether the government's fiscal policy would be more effective at increasing GDP if Malaysia allowed the ringgit to float against the dollar.

20. Suppose the *Financial Times* reported that Japan intended to promote inflows of foreign direct investments by reducing or eliminating bureaucratic restrictions that discouraged foreign investors (specifically, foreign companies) from entering Japan. Assume the Japanese yen was fixed relative to the U.S. dollar, the current exchange rate was ¥100/$, and foreign investors borrowed outside Japan and converted their funds to yen. Assume further that international capital markets between the United States and Japan were highly mobile. Explain the effect (if any) these inflows should have on Japan's real exchange rate, monetary base, M2 money multiplier, real risk-free interest rate, and reserve assets in the balance of payments.
    a. Would these international capital flows be more or less stimulatory/contractionary if Japan's consumption (C) and gross private domestic investment (I) had very low interest-rate elasticities? Explain.

21. From 2012 to 2014, political, military, and social unrest in Syria sparked many individuals to flee the Syrian pound (SYP) in favor of other, more stable, currencies and currency systems.

a. In preparation for their flight to other currencies, individuals and families moved funds from time deposits to checking accounts. From there, they intended to purchase other currencies. Explain the effect (if any) the movement of funds from Syrian time deposits to checking deposits had on Syria's monetary base, M2 money multiplier, and real risk-free interest rate.

b. If the Syrian central bank decided to intervene in the foreign exchange market as this capital flight took place, explain the effect (if any) these massive capital outflows should have had on Syria's monetary base, real risk-free interest rate, and reserve assets.

c. If the Syrian central bank decided *not to intervene* in the foreign exchange market as this capital flight took place, explain the effect (if any) these massive capital outflows should have had on Syria's monetary base, real risk-free interest rate, and reserve assets.

d. Due to the significant social unrest in Syria, suppose the president was reluctant to impose any major restrictions on the importation and exportation of goods and services or to interfere in the movement of financial capital across Syria's borders. At the same time, suppose he expressed a strong preference for maintaining a fixed exchange rate in order to provide, at least, a small oasis of stability in the economy. Fearing that rising unemployment would add to the political turmoil, suppose the president decided to pressure the central bank to increase the nation's monetary base in the hopes that it would stimulate the economy and provide jobs. Explain how likely the chances were for this policy to succeed.

Chapter 20

Causes, Cures, and Consequences of the Great Recession

INTRODUCTION

From December 2007 until June 2009, the United States suffered its worst financial and economic downturn since the Great Depression of the 1930s. Due to the depth and duration of the downturn, it became known as the *Great Recession*. Causes were multiple, but the tipping point was America's subprime crisis,[1] which started in early 2007 and escalated into a broader economic calamity by summer and fall of the same year. Even though subprime mortgages amounted to only about $1.2 trillion of an (approximate) $11 trillion U.S. mortgage market, its venom spread quickly through densely intertwined domestic and international financial arteries to poison overleveraged and overexposed financial institutions and homeowners.

At the beginning of the recession, signals were mixed. The United States was clearly embroiled in a financial crisis because well-established financial institutions, like Bear Stearns, Lehman Brothers, and Merrill Lynch, were fighting for their lives. Nevertheless, the nation's unemployment rate and real gross domestic product (GDP) appeared to be holding steady. It was reasonable to ask if the United States had reached a stage in its economic growth and development where financial disruptions could be contained or cauterized so they did not affect overall real production or employment.

International macroeconomic indicators told a similar story. Financial disruptions in the United States seemed to have little or no initial effect on the economic growth and prosperity of major U.S. trade and investment partners. Skeptics wondered if developed nations, such as those in the European Union (EU) and Asia, might be strong enough to withstand the cratering U.S. financial markets. Answers to these queries came swiftly and unpleasantly during the third quarter of 2008, when the U.S. financial crisis began battering both the domestic real goods and foreign exchange markets. If we learned anything from this crisis, it was the folly of believing that calamities can occur in the real loanable funds market without affecting the others. As Exhibit 20-1 shows, gears of the major U.S. macroeconomic markets are closely interconnected.

> If we learned anything from this crisis, it was the folly of believing that calamities can occur in financial markets without affecting the real goods and foreign exchange markets.

---

[1] Subprime mortgages are real estate loans to borrowers with relatively low creditworthiness, as measured by their credit ratings and other indicators of borrowing capacity. To compensate for this added risk, lending institutions typically charge higher rates on subprime mortgages than on prime mortgages.

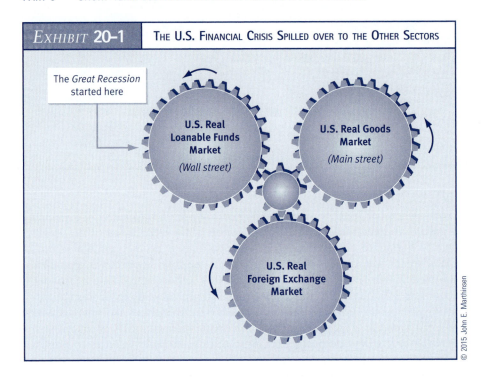

EXHIBIT 20–1   THE U.S. FINANCIAL CRISIS SPILLED OVER TO THE OTHER SECTORS

The *Great Recession* started here

U.S. Real Loanable Funds Market *(Wall street)*

U.S. Real Goods Market *(Main street)*

U.S. Real Foreign Exchange Market

© 2015 John E. Marthinsen

This chapter begins by reviewing the macroeconomic measures of devastation from 2007 to 2009. It goes on to explain the incentives that caused this financial and economic calamity. After the Great Recession struck, two problems needed to be solved. One was figuring out how to stop the hemorrhaging by rebuilding trust in the U.S. financial system. The other was how to kick-start the faltering U.S. economy. This chapter moves on to discuss how the U.S. government and Federal Reserve diagnosed these problems and tried to solve them. "**The Rest of the Story**" section discusses the process of mortgage securitization and, in doing so, exposes the multiple levels of dysfunctional economic incentives that contributed to the crisis.

THE BASICS

MEASURES OF ECONOMIC DEVASTATION

The Great Recession began on Wall Street (in the financial sector) but soon spilled over to Main Street (the real goods sector) and foreign economies. Traditional macroeconomic measures of performance showed clearly that a significant illness, with staying power, had struck. Hidden beneath these deteriorating indicators were millions of real-life stories about individuals who had lost their jobs and homes and were waging fierce battles to maintain living standards that they and their families once enjoyed.

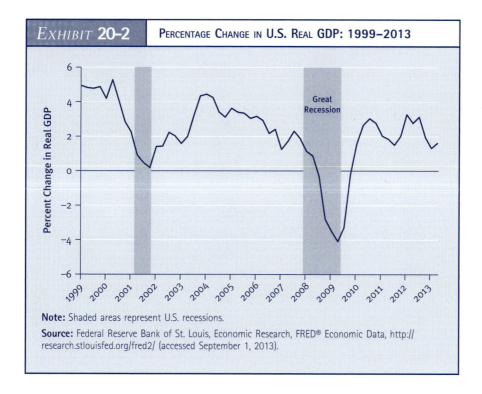

EXHIBIT 20-2 | **PERCENTAGE CHANGE IN U.S. REAL GDP: 1999–2013**

Note: Shaded areas represent U.S. recessions.

Source: Federal Reserve Bank of St. Louis, Economic Research, FRED® Economic Data, http://research.stlouisfed.org/fred2/ (accessed September 1, 2013).

DECLINING REAL GDP

Between October 2007 and April 2009, real GDP in the United States plunged by more than 4% (see Exhibit 20-2), wiping out approximately $640 billion of annual production. Based on the percentage decline in real GDP, it was the deepest recession since the Great Depression of the 1930s. What made this recession even worse was the slow recovery afterward, with the nation's real GDP growth rate falling below 2.5% for most quarters between June 2009 and September 2013 (when this chapter was written).

RISING UNEMPLOYMENT

The U.S. unemployment rate rose from the near-full-employment level of 5% in December 2007 to 9.5% in June 2009, resulting in the loss of more than 7 million jobs. As Exhibit 20-3 shows, even after the Great Recession officially ended in June 2009, the U.S. unemployment rate continued rising to 10%, providing circumstantial evidence for why it is considered to be a lagging indicator of a nation's economic activity.

Other measures of unemployment were equally, if not more, dispiriting. As Exhibit 20-4 shows, the U.S. employment-to-population ratio fell from 63% to 59%, its lowest level since May 1984. At the same time, the mean unemployment duration (i.e., the average number of weeks an unemployed individual is out of work) rose to its highest levels in more than 60 years.

Not all sectors suffered the same burdens because job losses were unevenly spread. For example, the construction, leisure, hospitality, and manufacturing

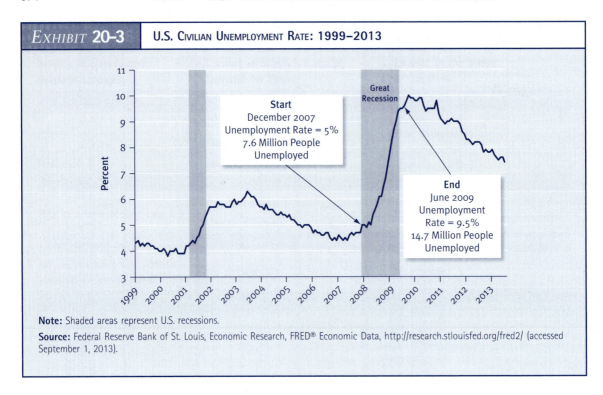

EXHIBIT 20-3   U.S. CIVILIAN UNEMPLOYMENT RATE: 1999–2013

Note: Shaded areas represent U.S. recessions.

Source: Federal Reserve Bank of St. Louis, Economic Research, FRED® Economic Data, http://research.stlouisfed.org/fred2/ (accessed September 1, 2013).

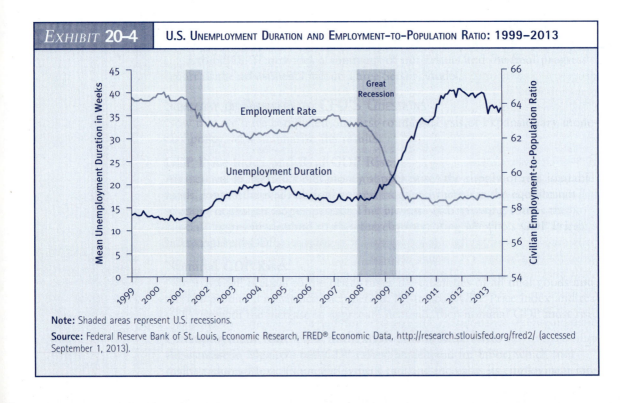

EXHIBIT 20-4   U.S. UNEMPLOYMENT DURATION AND EMPLOYMENT-TO-POPULATION RATIO: 1999–2013

Note: Shaded areas represent U.S. recessions.

Source: Federal Reserve Bank of St. Louis, Economic Research, FRED® Economic Data, http://research.stlouisfed.org/fred2/ (accessed September 1, 2013).

sectors were especially hard hit, while employment remained relatively healthy in the government, health services, and educational services sectors.

FALLING INFLATION RATES

The combination of ever-increasing job losses and falling incomes caused household demand and consumer prices to fall. In fact, they ushered in a period of deflation, with threats of more to come (see Exhibit 20-5). In the past, the United States had experienced and learned to adjust to moderate-to-high inflation rates, but it had no recent experience dealing with deflation. There were concerns among U.S. Federal Reserve officials and other experts that deflation could pose serious problems—problems that have plagued nations, such as Japan, for decades.

DECLINING WEALTH

The Great Recession wiped out years of accumulated wealth and savings, forcing baby boomers and many others to seriously reconsider important decisions, such as retirement. Between 2006 and 2009, nominal and real (inflation-adjusted) home prices fell in the United States by approximately 30% and 35%, respectively.[2] Stock market prices fared no better. Between the beginning of

> The Great Recession was marked by declining real GDP, deflation, wealth erosion, and rising unemployment.

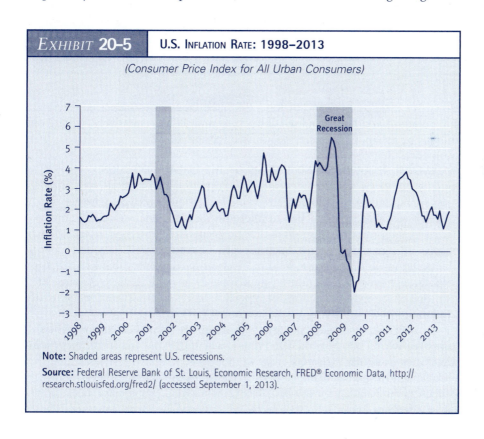

| EXHIBIT **20-5** | U.S. INFLATION RATE: 1998–2013 |

(Consumer Price Index for All Urban Consumers)

Note: Shaded areas represent U.S. recessions.

Source: Federal Reserve Bank of St. Louis, Economic Research, FRED® Economic Data, http://research.stlouisfed.org/fred2/ (accessed September 1, 2013).

[2] Exhibit 20-8 provides evidence of this price compression and puts it into a broader perspective.

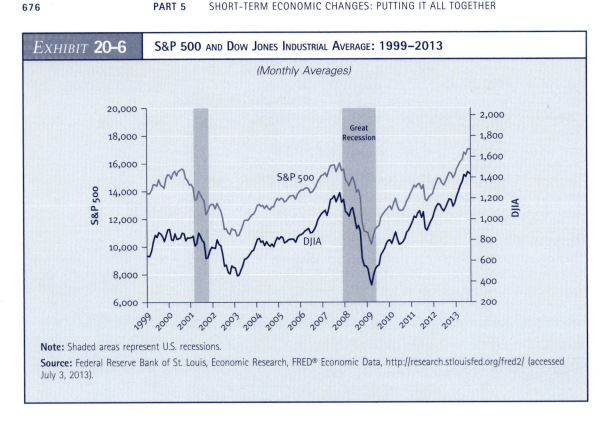

EXHIBIT 20-6   **S&P 500 AND DOW JONES INDUSTRIAL AVERAGE: 1999–2013**

(Monthly Averages)

Note: Shaded areas represent U.S. recessions.

Source: Federal Reserve Bank of St. Louis, Economic Research, FRED® Economic Data, http://research.stlouisfed.org/fred2/ (accessed July 3, 2013).

December 2007 and the end of June 2009, the Dow Jones Industrial Average and Standard and Poor's Index fell by 37% and 38%, respectively, wiping out trillions of dollars of financial wealth (see Exhibit 20-6).

INSOLVENCY, ILLIQUIDITY, AND VICTIMS OF THE GREAT RECESSION

Initially, the crisis was confined to a few large financial institutions, but it soon spread industry-wide and beyond. The key question was whether the United States was experiencing an illiquidity or insolvency crisis. The difference was important because illiquidity problems are caused by a lack of cash to meet current expenditures. Such problems have relatively easy and identifiable solutions and, therefore, tend to be short-lived. Central banks normally help nations over these liquidity rough spots by providing needed funds. In fact, one of the major functions of central banks is to adjust nations' liquidity availability to their varying levels of economic need.

By contrast, insolvency is a much thornier problem because companies' assets are worth less than their liabilities, which calls for major business solutions, such as equity infusions, asset liquidations, financial restructuring, replacement of management, new strategies, and the elimination of redundancies (a euphemism for layoffs). Insolvency is also problematic because it raises questions about who will be the most seriously affected victims. The battle lines are between shareholders, creditors, workers, and taxpayers. Without recovery, every victory is sure to be Pyrrhic, in the sense that there is a loser for every winner and a bunch of losers without any winners.

Insolvency problems are more difficult to solve than illiquidity problems.

MACRO MEMO   20-1

Paradox of Leverage

One problem that contributed to the Great Recession was the excessively leveraged investment positions of many large financial institutions and households, which amplified gains and losses. Leverage occurs when individuals borrow to finance the purchase of new assets. A common measure of leverage is the assets-to-equity ratio. As this ratio rises, financial risks rise.

To reduce their balance sheet risks during the Great Recession, financial institutions tried to sell assets and repay loans (i.e., de-lever their balance sheets), which is a technique that works so long as an insignificant portion of the industry is doing so, but it has less (or no) success when there is a mass exodus from the same financial markets.

Massive asset sales cause their prices to fall. As a result, attempts to reduce leverage can be thwarted by these shrinking market values, resulting in no change, an increase, or just a slight decrease in leverage. This cause-and-effect relationship is called the Paradox of Leverage.* An example helps clarify the enigma.

Suppose XYZ Inc. owned $1,000 million of financial assets (e.g., bonds) and financed them with $100 million of equity and $900 million of debt. (See Exhibit 20-7, Base Case.) With an assets-to-equity ratio of 10-to-1, the company's return on equity would be 10 times larger than its return on assets.

In other words, for every 1% gain or loss on the company's assets, the return on equity would be plus or minus 10%. If the company had 100% equity, the same 1% gain or loss on assets would cause only a 1% gain or loss on equity.

If XYZ successfully reduced its balance sheet risk by selling $100 million of financial assets and retiring $100 million of debt, its leverage would look like Case #1 in Exhibit 20-7. After the sale and debt repayment, its assets, debt, and equity would be worth $900 million, $800 million, and $100 million, respectively. Therefore, XYZ's leverage would have fallen from 10-to-1 to 9-to-1, which is a less risky financial position.

Case #2 in Exhibit 20-7 shows the Paradox of Leverage. Suppose XYZ and many other investors tried to de-lever their balance sheets at the same time, causing asset prices to fall. Suppose further that, when XYZ sold $100 million of its assets into this declining market, it received only $50 million in return, and used the proceeds to retire outstanding debt. These security sales and debt repayment transactions would cause XYZ's assets to fall by $100 million, and cause its liabilities and equity each to fall by $50 million. As a result, XYZ's revalued assets, liabilities, and net worth would equal $900 million, $850 million, and $50 million, respectively. Instead of falling, the company's leverage ratio rose from 10-to-1 to 18-to-1, and this calculation is before revaluing the assets that still remain on XYZ's balance sheet.

| EXHIBIT 20-7 | PARADOX OF LEVERAGE | | | | | |

(Figures in Millions of Dollars)

Case	Assets	≡	Debt	+	Equity	Leverage (Assets-to-Equity Ratio)
Base	$1,000	≡	900	+	100	$1,000/$100 = 10-to-1
1	900	≡	800	+	100	$900/$100 = 9-to-1
2	900	≡	850	+	50	$900/$50 = 18-to-1
3	450	≡	850	+	−400	Insolvent

(CONTINUED)

The increase in XYZ's leverage is due to the 50% reduction in the company's equity (the denominator of the leverage ratio) but only a 10% reduction in assets. As a result of plummeting stock market and housing prices during the Great Recession, U.S. households and financial institutions found themselves in a similar predicament. Attempts to escape from their leverage prisons only served to incarcerate them in even harsher, less forgiving ones.[†]

You may be asking yourself: If sales of this sort end up increasing companies' (or individuals') leverage ratios (rather than lowering them), why would they do it? The answer has two parts. First, in declining markets, asset sales may be forced upon companies because they need liquidity to meet customer and/or collateral demands. Second, these results are supercharged, if companies are required to calculate their balance sheets at market values, which is a process called *marking to market*.

Consider the effects in Case 2 (Exhibit 20-7), if asset values fell by 50%, XYZ was forced to sell $100 million of them, and accounting rules compelled the company to revalue the remaining assets (i.e., $900 million) at market prices. After the sale and revaluation, XYZ's remaining assets would be worth $450 million (not $900 million), liabilities would be worth $850 million, and, therefore, equity would equal minus $400 million (i.e., $450 million − $850 million = −$400 million). XYZ would be technically insolvent! See Case 3, in Exhibit 20-7.

*John E. Marthinsen, Chapter 9, "Four Paradoxes of the 2008–2009 Economic and Financial Crisis," in Robert W. Kolb (ed.), *Lessons from the Financial Crisis: Causes, Consequences, and Our Economic Future* (Hoboken, NJ: John Wiley & Sons, 2010).

[†]See Hyman Minsky, "The Financial Instability Hypothesis: Capitalist Processes and the Behavior of the Economy," in Charles Kindleberger and J. Laffargue (eds.), *Financial Crisis: Theory, History, and Policy* (New York: Cambridge University Press: 1982), pp. 13–38.

When a company fails and is liquidated, shareholders stand last in line, recovering only what is left after creditors have been paid. Liquidated companies also affect debt holders, who are paid before shareholders but may receive little (or nothing) of what they are owed.

Liquidations also affect workers due to the layoffs, renegotiated contracts, and reductions in benefits that typically accompany significant asset sales and business disruptions. Workers are especially vulnerable due to the financial, social, economic, and psychological ties they have to the companies for which they work. Job losses threaten these workers' economic livelihoods by reducing income, pensions, and other benefits, and they also take a social and emotional toll. This hierarchy of claimants changes if governments rescue failing companies (or industries) because taxpayers or interest-sensitive borrowers pick up the check for firm-specific errors, misjudgments, and excesses.

CAUSES OF THE GREAT RECESSION

Many factors aided and abetted the economic meltdown that is now known as the Great Recession. Each had its own special influence, but the tipping point was clearly the collapse of the U.S. financial market due to the housing/subprime market's implosion. Understanding why housing prices collapsed and why they threatened the solvency of America's most revered and (formerly) most successful financial institutions helps demystify the economic upheaval. Once recognized, reasons for the dramatic decline in U.S. aggregate demand (AD) become evident.

CAUSES OF THE U.S. HOUSING MARKET COLLAPSE

Exhibit 20-8 shows the U.S. housing market's price profile between 1980 and 2013, rising in a spectacular fashion from 2000 to 2006 and soon reaching unsustainable heights. Whether the increase is measured in nominal or real terms, it is clear from Exhibit 20-8 that home prices became grossly out of line with historical trends.

What caused the bubble, and why did it burst after 2006? The answers to these questions lie in the particular set of incentives that coalesced in the early part of the twenty-first century and caused financial institutions and individuals to take excessive bets that risked their financial solvency. It was not the case that players in this financial tragedy acted irrationally. On the contrary, their actions were rational and totally consistent with the incentives they faced. Unfortunately, these incentives created economic excesses, and the whistles that normally warn of impending dangers were silenced by the pandemonium of illusory wealth creation.

Four major factors caused the U.S. housing market to collapse. They were:

1. Moral hazard,
2. U.S. regulatory changes and government incentives to homeowners,
3. Lack of financial transparency connected to counterparty risk, and
4. Monetary policy initiatives.

Understanding each of them in isolation (i.e., as individual tiles) is insightful, but appreciating them together as a broader mosaic helps provide true insight into the misguided incentives that created this crisis.

> The four major causes of the U.S. housing market collapse were moral hazard, U.S. regulatory changes and government incentives to homeowners, lack of counterparty transparency, and monetary policy initiatives.

EXHIBIT **20–8**	NOMINAL AND REAL MEDIAN U.S. HOUSING PRICES: 1980–2013

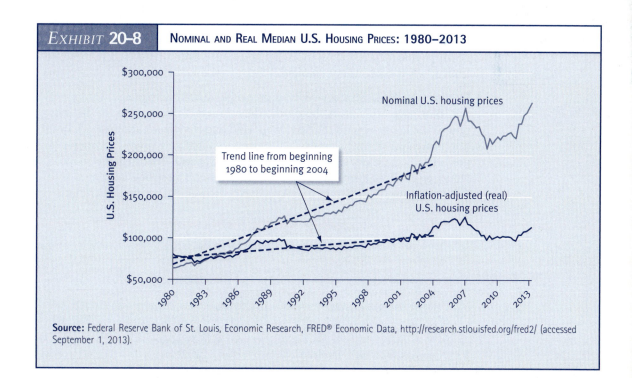

Source: Federal Reserve Bank of St. Louis, Economic Research, FRED® Economic Data, http://research.stlouisfed.org/fred2/ (accessed September 1, 2013).

Moral Hazard

Moral hazard occurs when individuals or institutions do not bear the full cost of their own mistakes, which provides incentives to take excessive risks. Two major forces created an environment for moral hazard during the Great Recession. The first was a change in bank strategy from *originate-to-hold* to *originate-to-distribute*, and the second was mortgage securitization, which is the process of originating, bundling, packaging, and selling mortgage-backed securities to investors. Let's discuss each of these forces.

Change in Bank Strategy: From "Originate-to-Hold" to "Originate-to-Distribute": From the end of World War II until the late twentieth century, U.S. mortgages were financed mainly by savings and loan associations (S&Ls). These mortgages were secured by the real estate they financed; so in cases of default,[3] lenders foreclosed borrowers' ownership rights and sold the properties, usually at auction, for what they were worth. If a property was sold at a loss, the bank suffered losses, which weakened its equity position. Large losses threatened the bank's solvency. In cases of default, U.S. states have different rules regarding the rights of banks to recover losses from borrowers. *Nonrecourse* states prohibit banks from going after other assets or the income of defaulting borrowers. *Recourse* states permit it.

> For decades, U.S. mortgages have had features that have made them both appealing and affordable to homeowners.

Since the early 1930s, U.S. mortgages have had features that have made them both appealing and affordable to homeowners. Among these features are 30-year maturities, self-amortizing payment schedules,[4] fixed interest rates, and constant monthly payments (e.g., 360 equal payments on a 30-year loan). To reduce the likelihood of losses due to default, lenders required borrowers to have skin-in-the-game by making substantial down payments (often 20%). Banks required borrowers without sufficient funds to meet the minimum down payment to purchase mortgage guaranty insurance, which reimbursed lenders when borrowers defaulted.[5]

Originate-to-Hold Strategy—Under an originate-to-hold strategy, banks (i.e., mortgage originators) hold onto the mortgages they extend for the duration of the loans or until the homes are sold and the debts extinguished. Profits are earned only if the monthly cash flows (principal and interest payments) are greater than the bank's financing and servicing costs.[6] Because a mortgage lender might hold a loan for as long as 30 years, it has strong incentives to scrutinize carefully whether a prospective borrower can repay his/her loan.

---

[3] A default occurs when a borrower fails to meet his/her contractual responsibilities to make timely principal and interest payments.

[4] Self-amortizing means the monthly payment includes both principal and interest so that, at the end of the 30-year period, the debt is extinguished. During the early part of the twentieth century, mortgage loans had much shorter maturities, carried variable rates, and required total repayment of the loan at maturity (i.e., borrowers paid only interest until maturity). This mortgage structure led to defaults and a lack of liquidity during the Great Depression. See Robert Kolb, *The Financial Crisis of Our Time* (Oxford: Oxford University Press, 2011).

[5] Private mortgage insurance is typically limited to 20% to 25% of the outstanding mortgage value.

[6] Servicing will be discussed in "The Rest of the Story" section of this chapter in the context of the securitization process.

For this reason, lenders try to develop high-quality underwriting procedures to determine an individual's capacity to borrow and willingness to repay a loan. Done right, top-notch underwriting also protects homeowners from themselves by denying loans when there is no clear capacity to repay.

> With the originate-to-hold strategy, banks hold onto the mortgages they create.

Because the financed property serves as collateral for the mortgage loan, having an underwriting system with qualified appraisers narrows the potential gaps between a property's market value and asking price. Evaluating an individual's borrowing capacity usually involves (1) verifying the status of employment, income, and net worth, (2) checking personal credit ratings,[7] and (3) ensuring principal, interest, property taxes, and insurance payments (i.e., PITI payments) do not exceed reasonable limits relative to the individual's before-tax income.

The originate-to-hold strategy makes lenders the victims of their own mistakes, and, therefore, creates incentives that promote a healthy and sound financial system. This situation changes with the introduction of the originate-to-distribute strategy and securitization.

Originate-to-Distribute Strategy—Under an originate-to-distribute strategy, originators do not hold onto their mortgages until they mature or until the properties are sold. Rather, these mortgages (and the cash flows connected to them) are sold to investors, and funds flowing to lenders from the sales are used to make new loans. The problem with the originate-to-hold strategy is it becomes a financial straightjacket that limits the number and amount of new loans mortgage lenders can make. Once a loan is made, it depletes funds, ties up equity, and curtails the lender's ability to make new mortgages.

The change in bank strategy from originate-to-hold to originate-to-distribute created a moral hazard problem. With the ill effects of bad mortgage decisions shifted to investors, banks became mortgage mills with clear incentives to increase quantity at the expense of quality. Credit checks were often ignored, and the due diligence that one would expect from reputable (formerly conservative) financial institutions became a sham. *NINJA loan* was the expression coined to describe mortgages that banks made to borrowers with <u>n</u>o <u>i</u>ncomes, <u>n</u>o <u>j</u>obs, and no <u>a</u>ssets. In their anxious efforts to increase volume, some banks made loans on properties that did not exist because no one took the time to check. Maturities were lengthened, and innovative ways were found to reduce homeowners' monthly bills (e.g., interest-only mortgages)—all in an effort to make homes more affordable to a wider distribution of individuals.

> With the originate-to-distribute strategy, banks sell the mortgages they create, which causes a moral hazard problem.

Securitization To facilitate the sale of these mortgages, large financial institutions bundled them into pools, created investor-friendly securities based on the underlying cash flows, and sold the securities to domestic and international investors—a process called securitization. Securitization was an important piece of the housing crisis puzzle because it enabled the originate-to-distribute strategy.

> The process of purchasing, bundling, creating, and selling mortgage-backed securities is called securitization.

---

[7] The most often used credit rating measure is the FICO score. FICO is an abbreviation for the Fair Isaac Corporation, a public U.S. company that was founded in 1956 and uses analytical methods to determine an individual's credit history. FICO scores are used by financial institutions (and many others) as an important piece of information when evaluating an individual's willingness and ability to pay past debts.

Mortgage-backed securities (MBS) were ideal for anyone wishing to invest in the rapidly rising U.S. real estate market. Foreign financial institutions without licenses or other footholds in the United States were especially interested because these securities allowed them to take U.S. real estate positions without having a physical presence in the country and without having to make messy decisions about any particular homeowner's ability to repay.

Mortgage originators who lacked the expertise, volume, and/or willingness to create their own MBS could participate in the securitization process by selling their mortgages to securitizers, such as large investment banks or government-sponsored entities (i.e., Fannie Mae and Freddie Mac) that specialized in purchasing, bundling, creating, selling, and insuring MBS to investors. From 2000 to 2006, these securitizers found an almost insatiable global appetite for U.S. mortgage-backed investments.[8]

Once purchased and bundled, the securities could be packaged in different ways. When the risk-return profile of bundled mortgages is the same as the underlying mortgages, the securities are called mortgage-backed obligations (MBO), mortgage-backed securities (MBS), or pass-through securities.

Clever investment bankers soon realized that the cash flows from underlying mortgages could be sliced and diced to create securities with risks, returns, maturities, and payments that were quite different from the underlying mortgages. These new mortgage-backed securities came to be known as collateralized mortgage obligations (CMOs). The basic idea behind CMOs is to separate the cash flows from a pooled collection of mortgages into different tranches, with each tranche having its own risk-return profile. Disassociating a newly created security from the underlying cash flows opened new doors to financial creativity, but it also enabled the invention and construction of complex financial instruments for which few understood the true risks.

Tranches are like pools of multi-plateaued waterfalls. As cash flows over the falls, the debt tranche with the lowest risk is satisfied first. Flows to all the remaining tranches are subsequently satisfied in their order of riskiness. For this reason, the least risky tranche often has a Triple-A rating. By contrast, the most risky one corresponds to the lowest plateau of the waterfall, and for this reason might have junk-bond status. If everything goes well, returns to these lowest-rated securities are high, but the risk of earning substantially less or nothing is also relatively high.

A major problem with securitization is it creates the potential for moral hazard by shifting the consequences of mistakes from mortgage originators to investors. It was for this reason that investors also bear part of the blame for the "securitization problem." For a while, continuously high profits lulled them into believing MBS were risk free. Many relied too heavily on credit rating agencies and too lightly on self-analysis. As for the companies that insured MBOs and CMOs, investors erred in believing these companies could not fail—but they did.

---

[8] "The Rest of the Story" section of this chapter explains the housing industry securitization process from beginning (mortgage origination) to end (the purchase of MBS).

Government-Sponsored Enterprises: Fannie Mae and Freddie Mac

The Federal National Mortgage Association (commonly known as Fannie Mae) was created by Congress in 1938, near the end of the Great Depression. In 1968, its charter was changed to a GSE. The Federal Home Loan Mortgage Corporation (commonly known as Freddie Mac) was created by Congress in 1970 to assist in the development of secondary markets for U.S. mortgages.

Fannie Mae and Freddie Mac are called *government-sponsored enterprises* (GSEs) or *quasi-government* enterprises because they were created for a public purpose but were to be run as private companies. Their social goal is to foster secondary markets in U.S. real estate mortgages. With implicit guarantees that the U.S. government would step in if anything threatened their solvency or liquidity, Fannie and Freddie were able to borrow at lower interest rates than purely private institutions.

Both institutions participate in the U.S. mortgage markets by borrowing, purchasing mortgages with the acquired funds, securitizing their mortgages, and selling them to investors. For a fee, they also sell credit risk insurance on the securities they package. GSEs purchase only "conforming loans," which are mortgages meeting certain requirements, such as maximum size, maximum loan-to-value ratios, maximum total indebtedness relative to income, acceptable credit scores, as well as sufficient funds for the down payment, closing costs, and two months of mortgage payments.

Between 1970 and 2000, Fannie and Freddie's share of the market for residential single-family mortgages rose from 5% to nearly 40%. And from 1980 to 2003, these sister GSEs went from holding no MBS to holding more than $2 trillion of them. Based on total assets, Fannie and Freddie were once the second and third largest companies in the United States.*

Fannie's and Freddie's services are (and have been) valuable because they enable financial institutions and investors to more easily adjust their real estate returns and exposures. Even though these GSEs seemed to function well for most of their pre-Great-Recession histories, a haunting question has always been whether private entities could have done the job better.

Controversy Surrounding Fannie and Freddie

For years, critics complained about the special treatment these GSEs got from borrowing at reduced government-supported rates. Opponents advocated Fannie's and Freddie's abolition and their replacement with private sector counterparts. The push for reform got a boost during the first few years of the twenty-first century, when these GSEs came under scrutiny for accounting scandals that rocked their reputations. Freddie Mac was forced to pay a $50 million fine in 2003 for understating its profits for two of three years between 2000 and 2002. By contrast, Fannie was found to have overstated its 2006 earnings, allegedly to pay its executives larger salary bonuses. During the proceedings, evidence showed that these GSEs spent approximately $175 million between 1998 and 2008 on lobbying activities, which only served to fuel flames of public resentment.

For many critics, Fannie and Freddie exemplified the problems that occur when governments become too tightly connected to politicians and too loosely connected to free-market competition. When their losses soared to critical levels during September 2008, Fannie and Freddie were placed into conservatorship, which meant they were supervised by the Federal Housing Finance Agency (FHFA).

*See W. Scott Frame and Lawrence J. White, "Fussing and Fuming over Fannie and Freddie: How Much Smoke, How Much Fire?" *Journal of Economic Perspectives,* Volume 19, Number 2, Spring 2005, pp. 161–162.

(CONTINUED)

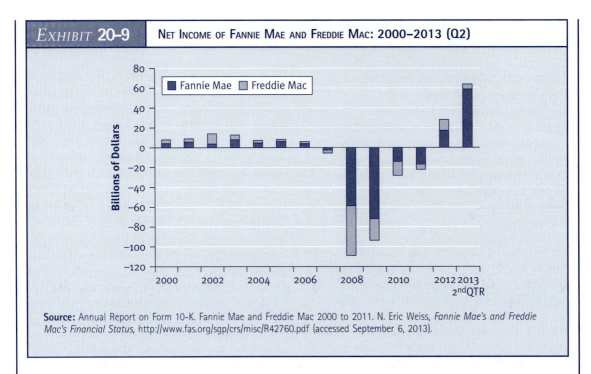

EXHIBIT 20-9 | NET INCOME OF FANNIE MAE AND FREDDIE MAC: 2000–2013 (Q2)

Source: Annual Report on Form 10-K. Fannie Mae and Freddie Mac 2000 to 2011. N. Eric Weiss, *Fannie Mae's and Freddie Mac's Financial Status*, http://www.fas.org/sgp/crs/misc/R42760.pdf (accessed September 6, 2013).

How Did Fannie Mae and Freddie Mac Fare during the Great Recession?

A quick look at Exhibit 20-9 is all that is needed to understand how severely these GSEs hemorrhaged cash, as their combined net incomes sunk from relatively healthy levels to losses in excess of $100 billion. In 2008, the combined real estate positions of Fannie Mae and Freddie Mac totaled approximately $5.4 trillion, which was about half of the U.S. mortgage market. As real estate prices fell, the portfolio values of these GSEs dropped and their insurance liabilities on MBS rose. Losses soon exceeded these institutions' equity positions, making them technically insolvent.

In November 2008, the U.S. government committed $600 billion to purchase assets from Fannie and Freddie. Both GSEs tried, but failed, to raise sufficient equity, and when they were finally taken over, each had been given $100 billion credit lines from the government. Soon thereafter, the government expanded these lines to $400 billion. In 2011, these GSEs were still not out of trouble. Losses had moderated but remained strongly negative. By 2012, profits had returned, and during the second quarter of 2013, Fannie Mae reported record gains of $59 billion, while Freddie recorded healthy profits of $5 billion.[†]

[†]N. Eric Weiss, *Fannie Mae's and Freddie Mac's Financial Status: Frequently Asked Questions*, Congressional Research Service, 7-5700, August 13, 2013, http://www.fas.org/sgp/crs/misc/R42760.pdf (accessed September 6, 2013).

Change in Bank Strategy + Securitization = Subprime Mortgage Crisis: The change in U.S. bank strategy from originate-to-hold to originate-to-distribute, together with the reckless growth of securitization primed the pump for the subprime crisis. Underwriting standards had sunk to all-time lows, and investors, worldwide, were seeking exposures to the U.S. real estate market.

MACRO MEMO   20-3

Paradox of Financial Innovation

Financial products, such as bonds, can be combined with derivatives in many different ways to create hybrids with risk-return profiles that are difficult to understand, track, and hedge. In some cases, these financial hybrid products are specifically engineered to moderate the risk-return concerns of buyers and sellers, but things do not always work out as planned. When these products become popular enough to establish significant financial positions, they can threaten a nation's entire financial community.

The *Paradox of Financial Innovation* states: If not fully understood by users and regulators, financial products designed to optimize and moderate risk/return trade-offs, can unravel, spill over, and threaten the stability of the financial system as a whole.* It is a classic example of what happens when already-complex

corporate risk-management systems are made even more opaque by adding additional layers of financial uncertainty due to the use of novel financial instruments, such as credit default swaps and CMOs. Without detailed price histories to guide current and future risk-return decisions, corporate finance departments become rudderless, and the probability of systemic macroeconomic calamities increase.[†]

*John E. Marthinsen, Chapter 9, "Four Paradoxes of the 2008–2009 Economic and Financial Crisis," in Robert W. Kolb (ed.), *Lessons from the Financial Crisis: Causes, Consequences, and Our Economic Future* (Hoboken, NJ: John Wiley & Sons, 2010).

[†]See Richard Bookstaber, "Risk Management in Complex Organizations," *Financial Analysts Journal*, Volume 55, Number 2, March–April, 1999, pp. 18–20. Richard Bookstaber, *A Demon of Our Own Design: Markets, Hedge Funds, and the Perils of Financial Innovation* (Hoboken, NJ: Wiley, 2007).

Rising real estate prices created a frenzied demand for mortgages to back these assets. The supply of securitized mortgages met only part of this demand.

Subprime mortgages are loans made to customers with lower credit ratings than would normally be approved for such debt. The above-average risk of default makes these loans nonconventional, inducing lenders to charge higher rates of interest on them. Immediately before the Great Recession, approximately 80% of all subprime mortgages had adjustable rates, which made their owners vulnerable to rising interest rates.[9]

> Subprime mortgages are loans made to customers with lower credit ratings than would normally be approved for such debts.

When the U.S. interest rates began to rise in 2004 (more about this later), the cost burden was initially absorbed by borrowers because they expected steady home price appreciation. In short, many homeowners trivialized the interest rate increases because they felt assured of capital gains when they sold their homes. The rapid decline in U.S. housing prices after mid-2006 poured icy water on these hopes. As adjustable-rate mortgages reset at constantly higher rates and housing prices fell, mortgage delinquencies skyrocketed.

Exhibit 20-10 shows the meteoric rise in subprime mortgages between 2000 and 2005/2006 and then their swift retreat once the crisis struck in 2007. Many subprime loans were securitized and sold to investors, leaving investors with substantial losses as these investments eroded in value, thereby, providing little or no incentive to purchase new ones. Among these investors

---

[9]Geetesh Bhardwaj and Rajdeep Sengupta, "Where's the Smoking Gun: A Study of Underwriting Standards for U.S. Subprime Mortgages," *Federal Reserve Bank of St. Louis*, Working Paper Series, October 2008.

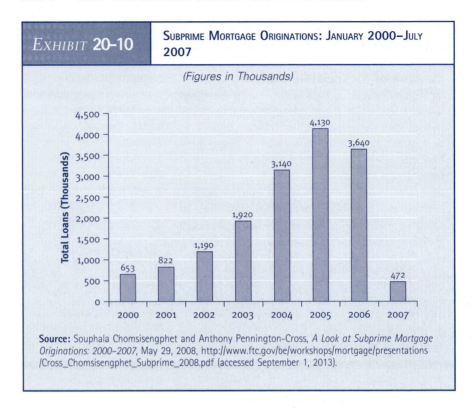

| EXHIBIT 20-10 | SUBPRIME MORTGAGE ORIGINATIONS: JANUARY 2000–JULY 2007 |

(Figures in Thousands)

Source: Souphala Chomsisengphet and Anthony Pennington-Cross, *A Look at Subprime Mortgage Originations: 2000–2007*, May 29, 2008, http://www.ftc.gov/be/workshops/mortgage/presentations/Cross_Chomsisengphet_Subprime_2008.pdf (accessed September 1, 2013).

were financial institutions working on wafer-thin equity-to-asset levels. Losses severely reduced their willingness and ability to extend new subprime loans and to purchase securities backed by the cash flows of subprime loans. As credit tightened around the world, borrowing fell, causing reductions in AD and real GDP. As a result, unemployment rates rose.

The subprime crisis began in January 2007 and by August had turned into a full blown bank panic, as the undercapitalized U.S. banking system strained under the weight of losses, borrower bankruptcies, foreclosures, and falling asset values. Unhealthy banks were threatened with seizure by the Federal Deposit Insurance Corporation (FDIC). As conditions worsened, the Federal Reserve shifted its focus from fighting inflation to stabilizing the financial system, and finally to rescuing it. Due to uncertainties caused by the crisis, lenders began making collateral calls, which led to the sale of financial assets at drastically reduced prices to meet these demands.

The United States was hit by the lethal combination of declining home prices and plummeting stock markets. In 2008, alone, U.S. households lost more than $11 trillion in net worth, an 18% drop, bringing their total net worth to $51.5 trillion. The decline wiped out the previous five years of wealth expansion.[10] After five years of double-digit growth in debt, falling

---

[10] Rex Nutting, "Household Net Worth Plunges 18% in 2008," *The Wall Street Journal*, Market Watch, March 12, 2012.

MACRO MEMO   20-4

Paradox of Thrift

Benjamin Franklin once said "a penny saved is a penny earned," implying that saving is an admirable personal quality. At the macroeconomic level, the verdict is still out concerning the wholesomeness of saving. It is true that saving is necessary for nations to grow because it frees resources to move from the production of consumption-oriented products to investment-oriented ones. At the same time, higher saving means lower spending, and lower spending reduces AD, which causes both real GDP and the GDP price index to fall.

Thrift is problematic because, by trying to save more, a nation may reduce its GDP, which means households may end up saving a larger portion of a shrinking pie. In the end, the actual amount saved may remain the same, rise slightly, or fall. An example helps clarify the point.

Suppose a nation's real GDP equals $1,000 billion, with consumption, saving, and taxes equaling $650 billion, $100 billion, and $250 billion, respectively. If saving increases from 10% of GDP to 25%, but due to spending reductions, real GDP falls from $1,000 billion to $400 billion, then total saving remains the same because 10% of $1,000 billion equals 25% of $400 billion. This logical, albeit disturbing, result is called the *Paradox of Thrift*.

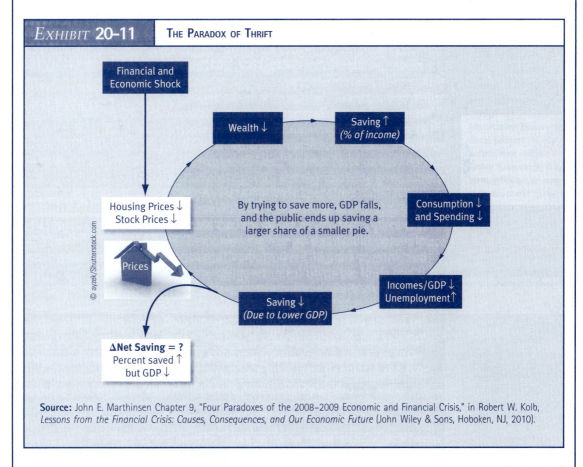

EXHIBIT **20-11**   THE PARADOX OF THRIFT

Source: John E. Marthinsen Chapter 9, "Four Paradoxes of the 2008–2009 Economic and Financial Crisis," in Robert W. Kolb, *Lessons from the Financial Crisis: Causes, Consequences, and Our Economic Future* (John Wiley & Sons, Hoboken, NJ, 2010).

(CONTINUED)

EXHIBIT 20-12 | U.S. SAVING AS A PERCENT OF PERSONAL INCOME: 1999–2009

Exhibit 20-11 shows the Paradox of Thrift and the role it played during the Great Recession. Declining U.S. housing and stock market prices pummeled household wealth, causing families to cut spending and increase saving rates to restore their retirement nest eggs and precautionary savings balances. By saving larger portions of their incomes, consumption and AD fell, causing a multiplied reduction in real GDP via the spending multiplier. As a result, the saving rate increased on a shrinking American pie, causing net saving to languish.

Between 1999 and 2007, U.S. personal saving as a percent of after-tax income fell dramatically, reflecting the wealth created by rising real estate prices and home-heavy U.S. portfolios. From nearly 6% at the beginning of 1999, the saving rate fell to a paltry 2.6% in November 2007—just before the Great Recession began (see Exhibit 20-12). The housing crisis and declining demand reversed the saving trend, causing it to rise to 8% by May 2008 and 8.1% in May 2009. To understand just how significant such a change could be, consider that personal consumption expenditures in the United States were about $10 trillion, which was approximately 70% of the nation's $14 trillion GDP. Assuming no secondary (e.g., spending multiplier or credit market) effects, for every 1% increase in the annual U.S. saving rate, household incomes fall by about $100 billion. Therefore, an increase in the U.S. personal saving rate by 4.3% (i.e., from 2.6% to 6.9%) implies annual income reductions of about $430 billion.

asset values encouraged households to deleverage their balance sheets. In the fourth quarter of 2008, households paid off more debt than they acquired—for the first time since 1952.

Falling housing and stock market prices decimated U.S. wealth, causing consumption, investment, and, therefore, AD to fall.

Homes represent about one-third of the average American family's net worth, and many baby boomers and their elders were counting on selling their homes at profits and retiring on the capital gains. These plans had to be revised. Declining wealth provided new incentives to save and few incentives to spend, which depressed AD and increased unemployment rates. Between January 2008 and July 2009, real personal consumption expenditures fell by more than $191 billion (−1.9%), and real gross private domestic investment fell by nearly $713 billion (−28.3%). Personal consumption comprises more than 70% of U.S. GDP; when it fell significantly, a recession was virtually inevitable.

U.S. Regulatory Changes and Government Incentives to Homeowners

The clear and identifiable fingerprints of the U.S. government were all over the scene of the financial crisis. For many families, the *American Dream* has been to own their homes. Since the Great Depression, it has also been a goal of many U.S. politicians, such as Presidents Herbert Hoover, Franklin Roosevelt, and William (Bill) Clinton, to enable families to own them. Results of these efforts were impressive, as the percent of families owning homes rose from approximately 45% at the end of World War II to 64% in 1980 (see Exhibit 20-13).

In 1994, President Clinton reinvigorated this national campaign by initiating a program called the *National Home Ownership Strategy: Partners in the American Dream*, which was a public-private initiative that directed the Department of Housing and Urban Development (HUD) to increase U.S. homeownership to 67.5% by the end of 2000.[11] Evidence indicated that U.S. ownership rates were low and falling—especially among low-income, young,

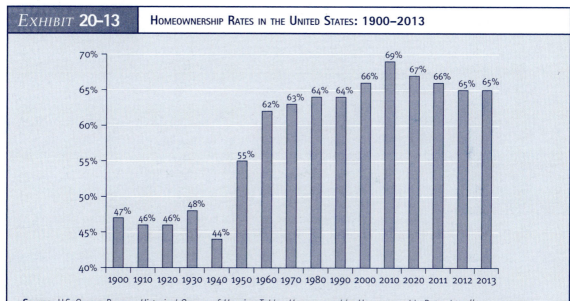

EXHIBIT 20-13	HOMEOWNERSHIP RATES IN THE UNITED STATES: 1900–2013

Source: U.S. Census Bureau, *Historical Census of Housing Tables, Homeownership: Homeownership Rates,* http://www.census.gov /hhes/www/housing/census/historic/owner.html. U.S. Census Bureau, Housing Vacancies and Homeownership (CPS/HVs). *Table 14: Homeownership Rates for the U.S. and Regions: 1965 to Present,* http://www.census.gov/housing/hvs/data/histtabs.html (accessed September 1, 2013).

[11] United States, Department of Housing and Urban Development, The National Homeownership Strategy: Partners in the American Dream, May 1995 http://confoundedinterest.files.wordpress.com/2013/01 /nhsdream2.pdf (accessed October 8, 2013).

and minority households. Consequently, President Clinton's strategy focused there. This initiative centered on removing mortgage financing barriers for starter homes, rewarding creative alternative home-buying techniques, providing housing subsidies, relaxing unnecessary underwriting standards (e.g., loan-to-value and down payment restrictions), and leveraging partnerships between public and private institutions. This initiative together with other Congressional Acts, such as the Community Reinvestment Act, are often cited as reasons individuals with low incomes and relatively poor credit histories were able to qualify for so many mortgage loans.

A carrot-and-stick strategy was used on banks to increase homeownership. The carrot was to give them easy access Fannie Mae and Freddie Mac, who were under mandate to purchase and securitize increasingly more low-quality mortgages. Fannie and Freddie became regulated in 1992 by Federal Housing Enterprise Financial Safety and Soundness Act, which established the Office of Federal Housing Enterprise Oversight (OFHEO) within HUD. OFHEO eventually became responsible for setting the goals defining the degree of help Fannie Mae and Freddie Mac could provide to low-income families and also to families in relatively neglected geographic areas of the country.

OFHEO's rules began in earnest in 1995, when purchases of securities backed by subprime mortgages were counted toward the GSEs' homeownership goals. By the early 2000s, regulators required the GSEs to devote more than 50% of their mortgage purchases to affordable housing. As a result, their acquisitions of subprime mortgages, between 2000 and 2004, rose 10-fold. Accounting scandals during the early-to-mid-2000s weakened the ability of GSEs to defend themselves against political pressures and ushered in relaxed underwriting standards.

The stick applied to banks by the politicians and regulators was through the passage of legislation, such as the Community Reinvestment Act (CRA), which set up rules and measures for licensing and relicensing banks. In 1999, the Gramm-Leach-Bliley Act reinforced this incentive structure by prohibiting bank mergers if the financial intermediaries had unsatisfactory CRA compliance reports, thereby incentivizing banks to lend to individuals with relatively weak credit histories and questionable prospects to repay.

Government incentives for homeownership added to the real estate demand frenzy.

U.S. financial regulations, or the lack thereof, may have also played a role in causing the Great Recession. During the 77-year period between 1930 and 2007, when the Great Recession began, U.S. financial regulations changed dramatically. Exhibit 20-14 shows the pendulum of financial regulation clearly on the side of strict government supervision from the early 1930s to 1980 and then decidedly on the side of deregulation from 1980 to 2009. Since the end of the Great Recession in 2009, the nation has entered a third period, but the direction in which the United States will move is uncertain. Passage of the Dodd-Frank Bill in August 2010 was intended to increase government regulations that rein in the actions of U.S. financial institutions, but Congressional staffs and government regulators had difficulties implementing rules to enforce it.

Exhibit 20-15 lists in chronological order the major pieces of U.S. legislation between 1980 and 1999 that relaxed financial market supervision. The election of Ronald Regan in 1980 set a new regulatory tone in Washington D.C.

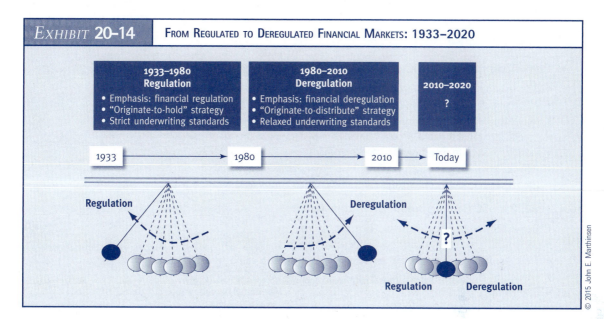

EXHIBIT 20-14 | FROM REGULATED TO DEREGULATED FINANCIAL MARKETS: 1933–2020

Starting with the Depository Institutions Deregulation and Monetary Control Act (1980) and continuing until the Gramm-Leach-Bliley Act (1999), U.S. financial markets became progressively less regulated—able to engage in new (riskier) activities, as well as merge and form alliances that were once forbidden.

President Reagan was a catalyst for change, but financial deregulation was fundamentally a reaction to unsustainable economic conditions for mortgage lenders in the United States. For years, these financial institutions had made 30-year, fixed-rate mortgages at low, single-digit rates. During the James (Jimmy) Carter Administration (1977–1981), U.S. interest rates increased with rising inflation and mounting inflationary expectations. When credit was restricted by the Fed (starting in 1979), real interest rates rose, inflationary expectations remained high, and U.S. financial institutions found themselves financing low-earning mortgages with double-digit, short-term interest rates.

Additional suffering was caused by restrictions on the interest rates banks could pay for customers' deposits. As rates rose, customers withdrew funds from these financial institutions to earn higher interest rates elsewhere, such as in the U.S. government securities and Eurodollar markets—an effect called *financial disintermediation*. Funding was expensive, liquidity was shallow, and something had to be done.

If properly implemented, financial deregulation would not have been a major cause of the Great Recession, but proper implementation required market and government systems to discipline the actions of financial institutions—systems that normally operate with careful regulatory oversight. If something was lost in translation during the deregulation process, it was the belief that deregulation meant the absence of both regulations and self-disciplining systems to punish offenders.

Exhibit **20–15**	Major Acts That Deregulated the U.S. Financial Industry

- **1980: Depository Institutions Deregulation and Monetary Control Act**
  - First major act to reduce regulations on U.S. banks and S&Ls
  - Abolished usury laws
  - Abolished Regulation Q (i.e., interest ceilings on customer deposits)
  - Federally chartered banks & credit unions allowed to make mortgage loans
  - Permitted S&Ls to diversify into consumer loans
  - Allowed credit unions and S&Ls to offer checking accounts
  - Gave the Federal Reserve greater control over nonmember banks

- **1982: Garn–St. Germain Depository Institutions Act**
  - Banks allowed to offer adjustable-rate mortgages
  - S&Ls allowed to offer money market deposit accounts
  - Liberalized the commercial and consumer loans that S&Ls could make
  - Liberalized the assets S&Ls could hold
  - Evened the playing field with commercial banks by allowing S&Ls to pay higher interest rates, borrow from the Fed, and issue credit cards

- **1982: Alternative Mortgage Transaction Parity Act**
  - Encouraged mortgage flexibility (e.g., adjustable-rate and interest-only loans)

- **1989: Financial Institutions Reform, Recovery, and Enforcement Act**
  - Abolished the Federal Home Loan Bank Board
    - Created the Office of Thrift Supervision
  - Abolished the Federal Savings and Loan Insurance Corporation (FSLIC)
    - Created the Savings Association Insurance Fund (SAIF)
    - In 2005, the FDIC's Bank Insurance Fund (BIF) and SAIF were merged to create the Deposit Insurance Fund (DIF).
  - Created the Federal Housing Finance Board to oversee the 12 federal home loan banks
  - Created Resolution Trust Corporation to oversee the closure and resale of bankrupt S&Ls
  - Gave GSEs the responsibility to support mortgages for low- and moderate-income families

- **1994: Riegle–Neal Interstate Banking & Branching Efficiency Act**
  - Permitted nationwide branch banking, regardless of state law
  - Allowed affiliate banks within bank holding companies to act as branches for each other (e.g. deposit acceptance, payment collection, and other customer services)
  - Required a review of federally chartered banks wanting to expand in order to determine if they were in compliance with the Community Reinvestment Act

- **1999: Gramm–Leach–Bliley Act**
  - Repealed the Glass-Steagall Act (1933) provision that separated commercial and investment banks

Source: Information on these acts can be found at: FDIC Federal Deposit Insurance Corporation, *Regulations & Examinations*, http://www.fdic.gov/regulations/laws/rules/8000-4100.html (accessed September 6, 2013).

Lack of Financial Transparency Connected to Counterparty Risk

Another important cause of the Great Recession was the lack of transparency among financial institutions. The problem was that perceived (unhealthy) positions of many financial institutions were quite different from their actual positions. To reduce risks, financial institutions can offset long positions by taking short positions and can offset short positions with long ones. As a result, when their net positions are evaluated, actual exposures can be much less risky than gross positions might appear.

When the Great Recession struck, numerous derivative and other financial transactions were over-the-counter, which meant there were no central clearing houses that could verify the net position of financial institutions. As a result, it was easy for each to assume the worst about the other, which resulted in curtailed credit lines and restricted business with companies (even healthy ones) that needed financing. Overreaction caused a credit crunch at the same time security prices were tanking. For many borrowers, credit availability became disconnected from market fundamentals.

> Due to a lack of financial transparency, a mismatch between actual risks and perceived risks added to the financial crisis by contracting credit.

The lack of transparency about counterparty positions also led to funding difficulties in the repurchase agreement (commonly called the "repo") and commercial paper markets. Repos and commercial paper are the means by which businesses finance assets and short-term mismatches between their daily inflows and outflows of cash. Without these multi-trillion-dollar markets, financial and nonfinancial businesses would shrivel up for lack of liquidity needed to fund their daily operations.[12] These markets nearly came to a standstill during the financial crisis because security prices fell so rapidly that no one knew exactly how to value them and worries about default led to distrust. Without firm values and counterparty trust, credit risks increased, causing numerous prudent lenders to withdraw from the markets. Many companies were left facing serious concerns, such as how to make payroll at the end of the week, which left numerous equally desperate households with the task of managing the trickle-down effects from employers in the throes of a liquidity panic.

Declining economic conditions and undercapitalized U.S. financial institutions caused countless households and businesses to withdraw their funds from troubled banks, mutual funds, and hedge funds. These "runs" on the U.S. financial system were the result of investors seeking safe havens in government securities. To meet the rising tide of withdrawals, financial institutions had to sell their investment assets in markets unwilling and unable to buy them. This set off an international search for value in complex financial assets having almost no historic record of performance and risk.

Liquidity also contracted as many financial institutions curtailed lending due to the losses they incurred and as they de-levered their balance sheets. As financial asset prices fell, so did the collateral backing existing loans. Due to the decrease, lines of credit were cut and new lines, at lower levels, were imposed. The desperate need for cash prompted fire sales as companies and

---

[12] They are called "repurchase agreements" because each deal involves the simultaneous sale and repurchase of a security. Because the sales price is lower than the repurchase price, the difference is the effective interest earned (paid) on this collateralized loan.

individuals tried to salvage whatever value they could under the circumstances. Those willing to accept collateral for repurchase agreements did so at significantly discounted prices (i.e., collateral was given a haircut).

Monetary Policy Initiatives

U.S. interest rates during the first part of the twenty-first century were low for a combination of reasons. Massive capital flows from around the world poured into the United States due to high global saving rates—especially in developing nations, such as China. Furthermore, foreign exchange market intervention by central banks in nations, such as China and Japan, increased their international reserves leaving trillions of dollars to invest in safe financial assets. The currency of choice was the dollar, and the financial instruments of choice were U.S. government securities. Nominal U.S. interest rates were also kept low by muted inflationary expectations, due to cheap imports from developing nations in Asia, mainly China and India.

Low U.S. interest rates during the first few years of the twenty-first century were also the result of declining economic conditions (a recession) and the Fed's efforts to restore economic growth. The financial panic that arose as a result of the September 11, 2001 terrorist attacks on New York City and Washington D.C. was also soothed by (accommodating) expansionary monetary policies.

Exhibit 20-16 shows the profile of short-term and long-term U.S. interest rates between 1999 and 2013. Notice the grayed-out section, which corresponds to the U.S. recession in 2001. The U.S. Federal Reserve reacted to

Expansionary monetary policies combined with low expected inflation, steep international capital inflows, the 9/11 aftermath, and declining economic activity to keep U.S. interest rates low during the first part of the twenty-first century.

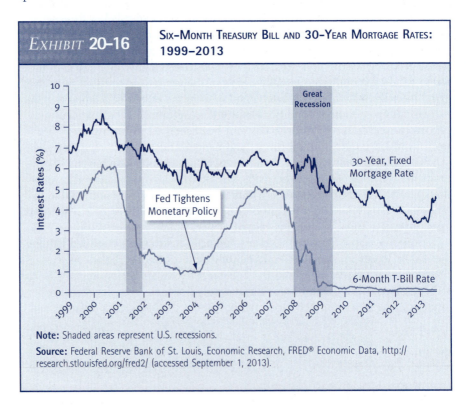

EXHIBIT 20-16   SIX-MONTH TREASURY BILL AND 30-YEAR MORTGAGE RATES: 1999–2013

Note: Shaded areas represent U.S. recessions.

Source: Federal Reserve Bank of St. Louis, Economic Research, FRED® Economic Data, http://research.stlouisfed.org/fred2/ (accessed September 1, 2013).

the decline in economic activity and 9/11 attacks by expanding the U.S. money supply and reducing interest rates in the hopes of spurring consumption and investment spending. Interest rates also sank as the demand for loanable funds fell during the recession.

The problem was not what happened to interest rates during the recession and 9/11 panic but rather afterward. During expansions, interest rates should rise with demand and contractionary monetary policies of the central bank. U.S. rates fell during the 2000–2001 recession (as they should have) but afterward remained low, thereby fueling demand. At times, nominal U.S. interest rates were below expected inflation levels, causing real U.S. interest rates to dip below zero. Borrowers went on real estate spending sprees and were encouraged to finance their purchases with adjustable-rate mortgages, which shadowed movements in falling short-term rates.

Low and declining interest rates increased the competition among banks for sources of profits. One of the most promising areas of growth was in the real estate markets because rising housing prices were earning homeowners substantial capital gains. To participate in the action, banks competed in many areas such as lowering mortgage rates, down payments, and qualifications for loan approval. They also battled in areas such as approval speed, the terms on variable-rate versus fixed-rate loans, and a host of other conditions that affect marginal borrowers. In general, the philosophy was to "lend freely because the risks are low." Many banks felt that, even if a borrower was unable to repay a mortgage, rising real estate prices would enable them to recover the outstanding debt on a foreclosed home.

During the second quarter of 2004 (see Exhibit 20-16), the Fed began to tighten monetary policy, causing interest rates to rise. As it did, the interest burden on holders of variable-rate mortgages rose, encouraging some homeowners to default on their loans. Rising mortgage rates also reduced the demand for houses, causing their prices to fall, and as they fell, new rounds of defaults and foreclosures occurred. Houses that were purchased on the thinnest of down payments were soon underwater (i.e., their mortgage values exceeded their market values), prompting many homeowners to walk away from their loans, leaving banks to sell a rapidly increasing inventory of homes with depreciating values.

> Contractionary monetary policy, starting in 2004, had strong negative effects on households with variable-rate mortgages.

AD plunged as a result of the U.S. housing market bust. Falling home prices and tumbling stock markets caused wealth to evaporate quickly, which reduced consumption and AD. The seizing up of U.S. money markets, in general, and the repo and commercial paper markets, in particular, led to a credit crunch that cut off corporate and household access to the money markets. As a result, households cut consumption further, and businesses reacted by slashing investment spending and laying off workers. The combination of spending disincentives and declining expectations caused AD to plummet, and with it U.S. real GDP and prices fell (see Exhibit 20-17).

FIXING THE FINANCIAL AND ECONOMIC SECTORS

The Great Recession started in the financial sector; so it made sense for the government and central bank to focus their initial recovery efforts there. But addressing the major issues in the financial (loanable funds) market was not enough. The real goods market also needed substantial relief.

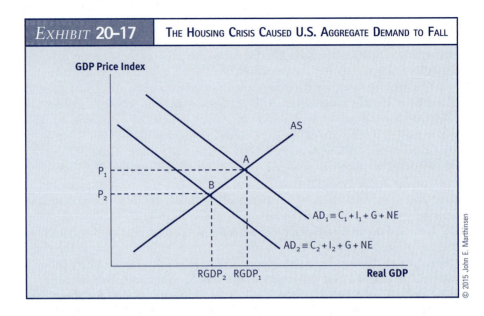

EXHIBIT 20-17   THE HOUSING CRISIS CAUSED U.S. AGGREGATE DEMAND TO FALL

GDP Price Index

AS

P_1

A

B

P_2

$AD_1 \equiv C_1 + I_1 + G + NE$

$AD_2 \equiv C_2 + I_2 + G + NE$

$RGDP_2$ $RGDP_1$ **Real GDP**

Exhibit 20-18 shows, in chronological order, the trail of financial destruction caused by a collapsing U.S. housing market and the financial institutions that were overexposed to the U.S. real estate market. September 2008 was the most brutal month of all.

FIXING THE U.S. FINANCIAL SECTOR

Two problems were standing in the way of any meaningful U.S. recovery. The first was insolvency. Had their balance sheets been valued at market prices, some of the largest and most influential U.S. commercial and investment banks would have been insolvent, with liability values exceeding asset values. Economically speaking, they were zombie banks—members of the living dead. Not only had the asset values of their mortgage and nonmortgage assets fallen, but they were continuing to fall in what seemed to be an endless spiral.

The second problem was liquidity—or more specifically the lack of it. Sharp contractions in lending among financial institutions forced many of them to sell financial assets, which compressed asset prices. For businesses, access to short-term credit (e.g., bank loans) and commercial paper issues was insufficient to finance their basic working capital needs. As a result, many financial and commercial businesses were like healthy fish gasping for air in shallow puddles of water.

> Fixing the U.S. financial problem meant solving both insolvency and illiquidity problems.

Curing the Insolvency Problem

To cure the insolvency problem, commercial and investment banks had to be relieved of the toxic assets on their balance sheets and/or infused with new equity (see Exhibit 20-19). Private solutions to the problem seemed unpromising. Had the struggling banks sold their toxic assets for what they were worth, losses would have triggered numerous bankruptcies. Similarly on the equity side, private infusions of new capital into these financial institutions were unlikely given their precarious and ever-worsening performance and the fear of more to come.

EXHIBIT 20-18	CHRONOLOGY OF MAJOR EVENTS DURING THE U.S. FINANCIAL MELTDOWN: 2007–2009

Event	Date
2007	
Freddie Mac backs out of purchasing subprime mortgages	February–April 2007
Subprime mortgage lenders begin to file for bankruptcy	February–April 2007
American Home Mortgage Company files for bankruptcy	August 6, 2007
Great Recession begins	December
2008	
Carlyle Capital Corporation defaults	March 5
JPMorgan Chase acquires Bear Stearns & Co.	March 24
Bank of American takes over Countrywide Financial Corp.	June 5
Office of Thrift Supervision closes IndyMac	July 11
Fannie Mae and Freddie Mac forced into conservatorship	September 7
Lehman Brothers files for bankruptcy and is sold to Barclays	September 15
American International Group (AIG) rescued by Federal Reserve	September 16
Reserve Primary's net asset value falls below $1	September 16
U.S. Securities and Exchange Commission (SEC) temporarily bans short sales of financial companies	September 17
Morgan Stanley and Goldman Sachs become commercial banks	September 21
Office of Thrift Supervision closes Washington Mutual Bank (WAMU), and WAMU is acquired by JPMorgan Chase.	September 25
FDIC increases insurance limits from $100,000 to $250,000 per depositor	October 7
Wells Fargo acquires Wachovia Corporation	October 12
PNC Financial Services Group, Inc. purchases National City Corp.	October 24
American Express and American Express Travel Related Services become bank holding companies	November 10
Lincoln National, Hartford Financial Services Group, and Genworth Financial become savings & loan associations	November 17
Bank of America acquires Merrill Lynch	November 26
CIT Group Inc. becomes a bank holding company	December 22
GMAC LLC and IB Finance become bank holding companies	December 24
2009	
Stress testing of large bank holding companies announced by the Federal Reserve, FDIC, Comptroller of the Currency, and Office of Thrift Supervision	February 25
OneWest acquires IndyMac	March 19
General Motors files for bankruptcy	June 1
CIT Group Inc. files for bankruptcy	November 1

Source: Federal Reserve Bank of St. Louis, *The Financial Crisis: A Timeline of Events and Policy Actions*, http://timeline.stlouisfed.org/ (accessed September 6, 2013).

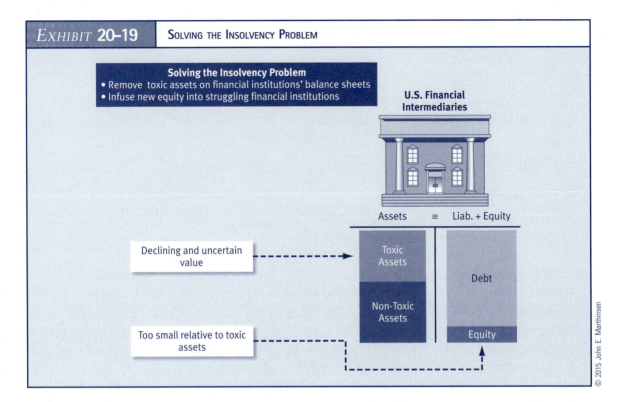

EXHIBIT 20-19 | SOLVING THE INSOLVENCY PROBLEM

Solving the Insolvency Problem
- Remove toxic assets on financial institutions' balance sheets
- Infuse new equity into struggling financial institutions

U.S. Financial Intermediaries

Assets ≡ Liab. + Equity

Declining and uncertain value → Toxic Assets

Non-Toxic Assets

Debt

Too small relative to toxic assets → Equity

© 2015 John E. Marthinsen

That left the government and central bank as the likely sources of financing for any financial system bailout. Governments have the power to tax, borrow, and spend; so the potential existed for the U.S. government to purchase the toxic assets of banks and/or to infuse them with equity. By contrast, central banks have the power to ease liquidity problems by lending to financial institutions or by purchasing the assets that these financial institutions need to sell. The solutions may seem obvious, but there were four troublesome problems.

Problem #1: Transferring the Problem is Not Solving It: By purchasing toxic bank assets, the problem would have only been transferred from the nation's financial institutions to the federal government and central bank. As a result, the U.S. government and Fed were threatened with owning the same worthless stock and mortgage-backed assets that were formerly owned by private financial institutions. The situation for the Fed was both ironic and problematic because the central bank was threatened with transforming its conservative balance sheet into one looking more like a hedge fund and paying for it with newly created monetary base (see Exhibit 20-20).

Problem #2: Nationalization, Favoritism, and Nonconventional Policy: If the government ended up taking equity positions in financial institutions, cries of nationalization would have been raised (see Exhibit 20-21). Many would object to such actions on grounds that the government was playing a greater, different, and unwanted role in the economy than needed, warranted, or

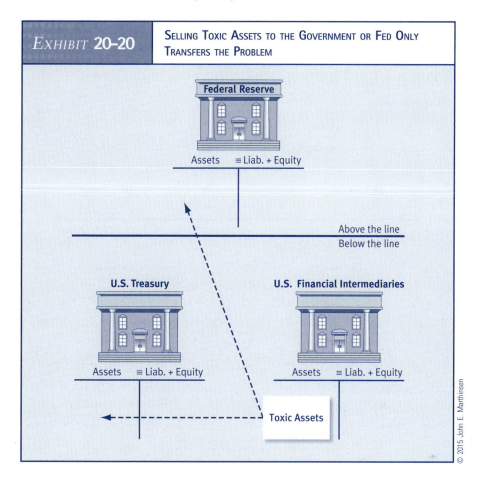

EXHIBIT 20-20 | SELLING TOXIC ASSETS TO THE GOVERNMENT OR FED ONLY TRANSFERS THE PROBLEM

Federal Reserve

Assets   ≡ Liab. + Equity

Above the line
Below the line

U.S. Treasury

Assets   ≡ Liab. + Equity

U.S. Financial Intermediaries

Assets   ≡ Liab. + Equity

Toxic Assets

© 2015 John E. Marthinsen

desired. When the U.S. government intervened in precisely these ways (i.e., purchasing shares of nine large U.S. banks), the conservative public's outcry was loud and expected.[13]

Fear of political fallout was one of the strong reasons government officials, such as Henry Merritt "Hank" Paulson, Jr., Treasury Secretary under George W. Bush, resisted purchasing bank equity. It smacked of industrial policy with the government choosing winners and losers, which the Republican Administration wanted to avoid. Another concern was that needy banks might not participate due to the stigma attached to any form of government nationalization and because they feared government meddling after the funds were distributed.

Problem #3: Government Funding Increases Debt and Can Put Upward Pressure on Interest Rates: To purchase toxic bank assets or bank shares, the

---

[13] The banks were Bank of America (including Merrill Lynch), Bank of New York, Citigroup, Goldman Sachs, JP Morgan Chase, Mellon, Morgan Stanley, State Street Bank, and Wells Fargo.

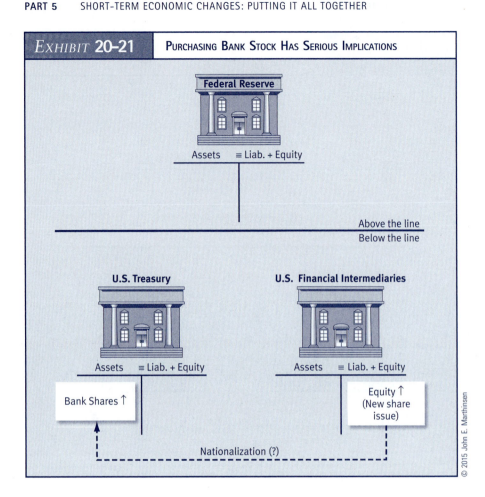

EXHIBIT **20-21** | PURCHASING BANK STOCK HAS SERIOUS IMPLICATIONS

© 2015 John E. Marthinsen

government needed funds, and two major sources were through taxation and borrowing (see Exhibit 20-22). Increasing taxes in the middle of the Great Recession would have been political suicide and economically unwise for the effect it could have on AD. The major problem with government borrowing was it could have put upward pressure on real U.S. interest rates. Fortunately, the tumbling U.S. economy took pressure off the real loanable funds market; so government borrowing did not dramatically increase real interest rates, but the size of the government debt exploded due to the numerous spending programs passed to restore economic growth.

Problem #4: Central Bank Funding Increases the Monetary Base: Central bank purchases of banks' toxic assets carried a different set of financial risks because these actions create new monetary base, which has the potential to increase the money supply, AD, and inflation (see Exhibit 20-23). In the end, the Fed acquired MBS worth billions of dollars. In June 2008, the U.S.

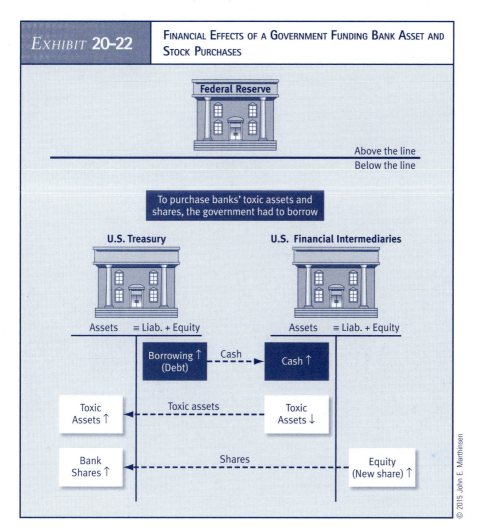

EXHIBIT 20-22   **FINANCIAL EFFECTS OF A GOVERNMENT FUNDING BANK ASSET AND STOCK PURCHASES**

Federal Reserve

Above the line
Below the line

To purchase banks' toxic assets and shares, the government had to borrow

U.S. Treasury   **U.S. Financial Intermediaries**

Assets ≡ Liab. + Equity   Assets ≡ Liab. + Equity

Borrowing ↑   Cash   Cash ↑
(Debt)

Toxic   Toxic assets   Toxic
Assets ↑   Assets ↓

Bank   Shares   Equity
Shares ↑   (New share) ↑

© 2015 John E. Marthinsen

monetary base equaled $864 billion. One year later, the Fed's expansionary policies had already increased it by 107% to $1,792 billion, and, at the end June 2010 (i.e., the end of the Great Recession), the monetary base stood at $2,012 billion—a cumulative increase since June 2008 of 133%.[14]

Curing the Illiquidity Problem

The illiquidity problem was quickly brought under control when the Fed began conducting aggressive expansionary monetary policies. Nevertheless, pumping monetary base into any economy is a bit like pushing on a string. Just because there are more funds available in the system does not mean they will be lent or demanded.

[14] Exhibit 20-28 shows this increase and puts it into a broader historic perspective.

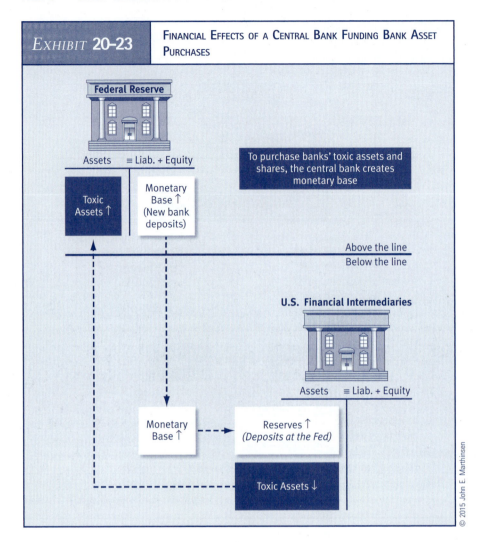

EXHIBIT 20-23   **FINANCIAL EFFECTS OF A CENTRAL BANK FUNDING BANK ASSET PURCHASES**

Preventing Runs on Banks: The financial crisis put extreme pressures on weak banks and financial institutions, as depositors withdrew funds, en masse. Despite the $100,000 guarantee the FDIC put on these customer deposits, withdrawals were rampant—especially by individuals with deposits that exceeded this limit and those who did not want to deal with the administrative delays and problems that might accompany gaining access to their insured funds. Even those fully insured panicked as trust in the U.S. financial system evaporated. To reduce fears and, thereby, the risk of bank runs, the FDIC, in 2008, increased (until December 31, 2010) the maximum FDIC-insured deposits from $100,000 to $250,000. Congress extended this coverage in 2010 until year-end 2013.[15]

---

[15] The Dodd-Frank Wall Street Reform and Consumer Protection Act extended this coverage.

Reinvigorating the Repo and Commercial Paper Market: Because the repo and commercial paper markets had seized up and interrupted the flow of short-term funds to healthy financial and commercial business organizations, counterparty trust and confidence had to be restored. It was an enormous task and one that could not be accomplished quickly.

FIXING THE ECONOMIC SYSTEM

Fixing the U.S. economic system went hand-in-hand with fixing its financial system, and to a large extent, the solutions to both problems were mutually reinforcing. When a nation is in the throes of a recession, the usual economic prescription is for the government to pursue expansionary fiscal policies by increasing spending and/or reducing taxes. The monetary prescription is to purchase government securities, lower reserve requirement ratios, and lower the discount rate, thereby increasing the money supply.

> Fixing the U.S. economic problem meant repairing the U.S. financial system and increasing aggregate demand.

Expansionary Fiscal Policies

Expansionary fiscal policies have a direct effect on spending. By lowering personal income taxes, the government can try to stimulate household consumption. By lowering business income taxes, it can try to stimulate business investments (see Exhibit 20-24). Standing in the way of successful taxation policies were pessimistic expectations about the future, which threatened to offset government tax incentives.

The other alternative is for the government to directly spend to increase AD. As Exhibit 20-24 shows, government spending is one of the major

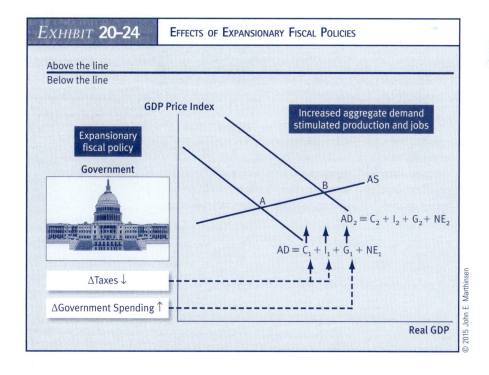

EXHIBIT 20-24	EFFECTS OF EXPANSIONARY FISCAL POLICIES

Above the line
Below the line

GDP Price Index

Increased aggregate demand stimulated production and jobs

Expansionary fiscal policy

Government

AS

B

A

$AD_2 \equiv C_2 + I_2 + G_2 + NE_2$

$AD \equiv C_1 + I_1 + G_1 + NE_1$

ΔTaxes ↓

ΔGovernment Spending ↑

Real GDP

© 2015 John E. Marthinsen

components of a nation's AD. Increasing it, without offsetting reductions among the other sources of demand, can stimulate economic activity and kick-start the nation back toward economic health.

Problems with Fiscal Stimuli: One of the major issues with fiscal stimuli—especially when the expenditures are desired as quickly as possible—is what to purchase. The Obama Administration thought it had a good idea in asking town and city officials for suggestions of shovel-ready projects. Its thinking was that mayors, town councils, and selectmen were closest to the true needs of communities and would recommend productivity-enhancing projects with long-term benefits, such as infrastructure spending for roads, bridges, and communications.[16] It was disappointing (but not surprising) when the list of suggested projects included tennis facilities, music halls, museums, antiprostitution programs, waterpark rides, swimming pools, elevated catwalks, and fitness centers.

> How government funds should be spent became a major issue connected to expansionary fiscal policy.

Congress passed and the President signed numerous pieces of legislation to get the U.S. economy moving. Exhibit 20-25 lists the

EXHIBIT **20-25**	MAJOR EXPANSIONARY FISCAL POLICY MEASURES: 2008–2009
2008	
Economic Stimulus Act	February 13
Housing & Economic Recovery Act	July 30
Emergency Economic Stabilization Program (TARP)	October 3
Treasury and FDIC acquire shares of Citicorp	November 23
Treasury lends to General Motors and Chrysler	December 19
2009	
Treasury, FDIC, & Fed give guarantees, liquidity access, & capital to Bank of America	January 16
Treasury, FDIC, & Fed give loans to Chrysler America	January 16
American Recovery and Reinvestment Act	February 17
Homeowner Affordability and Stability Plan	February 18
Auto Supplier Support Program	March 19
Public-Private Investment Program (Fed, Treasury, & FDIC)	March 23
Helping Families Save Their Homes Act	May 20
Treasury acquires shares of CIT Group Inc.	November 1

Source: Federal Reserve Bank of St. Louis, *The Financial Crisis: A Timeline of Events and Policy Actions*, http://timeline.stlouisfed.org/ (accessed September 6, 2013).

[16] There are more than 600,000 bridges in United States, most built in 1950s and 1960s, and their approximate lifespan is 50 years. In 2005, the American Society of Civil Engineers estimated that 160,000 bridges were structurally deficient. In 2007, the I-35W Mississippi River Bridge (Bridge 9340) in Minneapolis collapsed, killing 13 people and injuring 145.

major stimulatory programs. They included government spending
increases, subsidies, tax breaks, import duties, and the expansion of
unemployment compensation from 20 weeks to 79 weeks to 2 years.
Legislation also included novelty programs that targeted certain industries and particular individuals. Among them were an $8,000 tax break
for first-time homeowners, a "cash for clunkers" program, and an initiative that allowed businesses to claim back taxes by means of a carry
forward provision.

Expansionary Monetary Policies and Quantitative Easing

Stimulating spending at a time when unemployment was rising and
future prospects looked dim was a daunting task for the Federal Reserve;
so the Fed used its monetary tools to flood the market with liquidity (see
Exhibit 20-26).

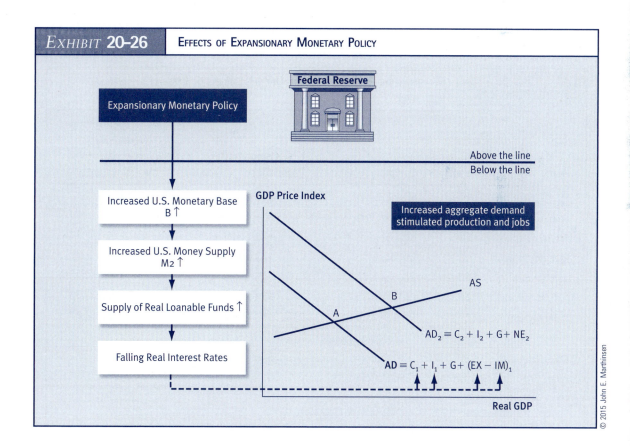

EXHIBIT 20-26   EFFECTS OF EXPANSIONARY MONETARY POLICY

Federal Reserve

Expansionary Monetary Policy

Above the line
Below the line

Increased U.S. Monetary Base
B ↑

Increased U.S. Money Supply
M2 ↑

Supply of Real Loanable Funds ↑

Falling Real Interest Rates

GDP Price Index

Increased aggregate demand
stimulated production and jobs

AS

B

A

$AD_2 \equiv C_2 + I_2 + G + NE_2$

$AD \equiv C_1 + I_1 + G + (EX - IM)_1$

Real GDP

© 2015 John E. Marthinsen

MACRO MEMO   20-5

A Problem with Bailing Out the Financial Sector

One of the problems with using taxpayer dollars to bail out an insolvent financial sector is the disproportionate difference in compensation between the kingpins of giant financial institutions and the average taxpayer. Exhibit 20-27 shows why public dander was raised when it seemed these high-flying denizens of corporate leadership would escape the mess they created without any meaningful personal financial sacrifices. While it is true that most of them lost their positions, it is also a fact that compensation clawbacks were few and far between. Exhibit 20-27 shows how many years the average U.S. taxpayer

would have had to work to earn just one year's salary of the listed financial leaders.

Public concern was also raised when the Obama Administration brought no financial big-wheels to justice and found no one guilty of any crimes. The Administration explained the absence of prosecutions as the result of Wall Street barons having engaged in greedy, stupid, and immoral conduct, without breaking any laws.*

*Peter Schweizer, Why Can't Obama Bring Wall Street to Justice? May 6, 2012, http://mag.newsweek.com/2012/05/06/why-can-t-obama-bring-wall-street-to-justice.html (accessed October 8, 2013).

Exhibit 20-27	MEASURING THE BURDEN OF BAILING OUT THE LEADERS OF LARGE U.S. FINANCIAL INSTITUTIONS			
Name	Position	Company	Compensation (Most Recent ≈ 2008)	Years Needed for the Average U.S. Worker to Earn the Equivalent*
Stan O'Neal	CEO	Merrill Lynch	$162 million	2,613
Richard Fuld	CEO	Lehman Bros.	$34.4 million	555
Jimmy Cayne	CEO	Bear Stearns	$32.1 million	518
Richard Syron	CEO	Freddie Mac	$19 million	306
Ken Thomson	CEO	Wachovia	$15 million	242
Martin Sullivan	CEO	AIG	$14.3 million	231
Daniel Mudd	CEO	Fannie Mae	$13.4 million	216
Angelo Mozilo	CEO	Countrywide Financial	$10.8 million	174
Kerry Killinger	CEO	Washington Mutual	$4.5 million	73
Allan Greenspan	Chairman	Federal Reserve	$180,100	3

*In 2008, the average yearly U.S. wage was approximately $62,000.

Source: Joanna Chung, Greg Farrell, Francesco Guerrera, and Saskia Scholtes, "The Fallen Giants of Finance," *Financial Times*, December 23, 2008, p. 12.

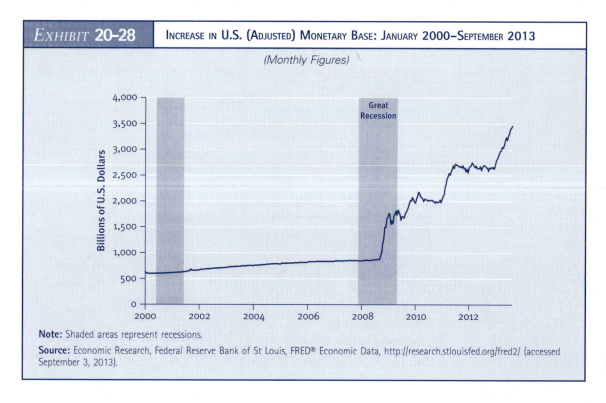

EXHIBIT 20-28 | **INCREASE IN U.S. (ADJUSTED) MONETARY BASE: JANUARY 2000–SEPTEMBER 2013**

(Monthly Figures)

Note: Shaded areas represent recessions.

Source: Economic Research, Federal Reserve Bank of St Louis, FRED® Economic Data, http://research.stlouisfed.org/fred2/ (accessed September 3, 2013).

As a result of the Fed's policies, the U.S. monetary base exploded (see Exhibit 20-28) and short-term U.S. interest rates tumbled close to zero (see Exhibit 20-16), which created a dilemma.[17] If monetary policy affects the economy by reducing real interest rates, thereby, increasing consumption and investment, what happens to its effectiveness when interest rates hit 0%? The answer to this question led to a policy called "quantitative easing," which means flooding the market with money in the hopes that households and businesses will eventually spend it regardless of whether interest rates fall or remain constant.

Of course, central banks have other means of stimulating their economies, such as trying to reduce long-term interest rates and lending directly to private companies, but there are risks with each of these solutions. Exhibit 20-29 lists the major Federal Reserve policies that were initiated to jump-start the U.S. economy between 2007 and 2009.

> "Quantitative easing" is the term applied to expansionary monetary policies when nominal interest rates approach zero.

HOW EFFECTIVE WERE U.S. MONETARY AND FISCAL POLICIES?

"V-U-L-W" is not an eye examination chart but rather the possible paths a nation might take when recovering (or not) from a recession. "V" means a quick, steep recovery; "U" stands for a slow, prolonged one; "L" means no recovery at all, and "W" means a double-dip recession. Of these four possibilities, the United States came closest to the "U."

> The U.S. recovery was U-shaped.

---

[17] The Fed targeted the federal funds rate between 0% and 0.25%.

EXHIBIT 20-29	MAJOR EXPANSIONARY MONETARY ACTIONS: 2007–2009

2007	
Central bank swaps: dollar liquidity lines and foreign-currency liquidity lines	December
Term Auction Facility	December 17
2008	
Primary Dealer Credit Facility	March 17
Maiden Lane LLC formed to facilitate merger of JPMorgan Chase & Bear Stearns	March 14
Fed rescues AIG	September 16
Asset-Backed Commercial Paper Money Market Mutual Fund Liquidity Facility	September 19
Money Market Investor Funding Facility	October 21
Commercial Paper Funding Facility	October 27
Maiden Lane II created to restructure AIG support (to purchase residential MBS from AIG)	November 10
Maiden Lane II created to restructure AIG support (to purchase collateralized debt obligations from AIG)	November 10
Fed joins with Treasury and FDIC to rescue Citicorp	November 23
Term Asset Backed Securities Lending Facility (TALF)	November 25
Fed announces intention to purchase housing obligations of GSEs	November 25
Maiden Lane III created	November 25
2009	
New York Fed begins buying MBS	January 5
Treasury, FDIC, & Fed extend loans to Chrysler America	January 16
Public- Private Investment Program (Fed, Treasury, & FDIC)	March 23

Source: Federal Reserve Bank of St. Louis, "The Financial Crisis: A Timeline of Events and Policy Actions," http://timeline.stlouisfed.org/ (accessed September 6, 2013).

Despite precedent-breaking fiscal and monetary stimuli, the U.S. economy did not recover quickly. In fact, as of September 2013, when this chapter was finalized, the unemployment rate was still at a troublesome 7.3%, and real GDP growth was languishing at less than 2%. In fact, the average rate of growth since the official end of the recession was a paltry 2.2%.

Monetary policy had reduced interest rates so far that it was difficult to comprehend how increased stimuli could bring about recovery. It was much easier to understand how contractionary central bank policies could throw the nation back into in to a tailspin.

Expansionary fiscal policy had almost reached its limits, not only because the U.S. Congress and President appeared to be in a dysfunctional deadlock but also because the central government's deficit had grown to alarming heights. Further tax cuts and/or spending hikes would be difficult to pass. Exhibit 20-30 shows how, as percent of GDP, the central government's budget deficit moved from slight surpluses near the turn of the twenty-first century to large deficits.

Large fiscal deficits and a rapidly growing government debt became major issues connected to expansionary fiscal policy.

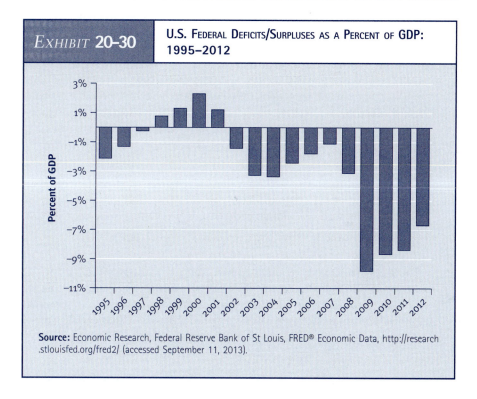

EXHIBIT 20-30 | U.S. FEDERAL DEFICITS/SURPLUSES AS A PERCENT OF GDP: 1995–2012

Source: Economic Research, Federal Reserve Bank of St Louis, FRED® Economic Data, http://research.stlouisfed.org/fred2/ (accessed September 11, 2013).

By fall 2013, progress had been made, but for every two steps forward it seemed as if there was at least one step back. For instance, the Dodd-Frank (Wall Street Reform and Consumer Protection) Act was signed into law in 2010 to address many of the perceived flaws in U.S. financial regulation. This 2,223-page document contained many industry-reforming measures, but even after three years of work, regulations had still not been drafted for many parts of the Act.

> The Dodd-Frank Act addressed many of the perceived deficiencies in the U.S. financial system, but enactment was slow.

Among the most important areas addressed by the Dodd-Frank Bill were:

SYSTEMIC THREATS TO THE U.S. FINANCIAL SYSTEM

- U.S. Congress created the Financial Services Oversight Council (FSOC) to monitor the U.S. financial system, as a whole, so that significant risks could be identified, market discipline promoted, and timely reactions to threatening conditions enacted. The Council consists of 10 voting members and 5 nonvoting members, among whom are top federal and state financial regulators. Both FSOC and the Fed were given authority to impose regulations on nonbank financial institutions.

Too Big to Fail

- Both FSOC and the Fed were given authority to break up financial institutions that had grown so large that their failure or imminent failure might touch off a negative systemic reaction. Such decisions could be based on absolute or relative size, systemic importance (i.e., interconnections), and/or role in key markets.
- The FDIC was also given power to take over or close failing nonbank financial institutions but only if they are large enough or in strategic positions that could threaten systemic disruptions to the U.S. financial

system. Again, such determinations could be based on absolute or relative size, systemic importance, and/or role in key markets.

Credit Rating Agency Supervision

- The Office of Credit Ratings (OCR) was created as a part of the Securities and Exchange Commission (SEC) to protect investors, promote capital formation, and maintain fair, orderly, and efficient markets by monitoring and examining U.S. credit rating agencies that have registered with the SEC as "nationally recognized statistical rating organizations."

Preventing Spillovers

- Financial holding companies that own banks were prohibited from investing in hedge funds. This rule tries to reduce the possibility of losses at large speculative hedge funds weakening an affiliated bank or rendering it insolvent.

Skin in the Game

- Securitizers were required to hold onto a portion of their securitized portfolios to ensure they suffer losses if their underwriting is lax. Exceptions to these skin-in-the-game provisions were permitted only if the underlying assets in the security issue met certain standards (e.g., qualified residential mortgages in the housing industry).

THE REST OF THE STORY

SECURITIZATION: FROM MORTGAGE ORIGINATION TO SECURITY SALES

Exhibit 20-31 shows that securitization is a process of many steps, and it is probably fair to say that, leading up to the financial crisis, elements of moral hazard and market failure occurred at each one. Let's review each stage of the process.

Mortgage Origination (Columns A and B)

On the far left side of Exhibit 20-31 (in Column A) are mortgage originators, such as thrift institutions (e.g., S&Ls and mutual savings banks), commercial banks, and mortgage brokers, whose job is to extend mortgages (Column B) to borrowers. Under the originate-to-hold strategy, these mortgages are held on the balance sheets of banks and thrift institutions, but under the originate-to-distribute strategy, they are pooled and securitized.

Due Diligence and Mortgage Servicing (Column C)

An important part of the securitization process is due diligence, much of which is conducted by companies that are hired specifically by securitizers to determine the quality of mortgages offered for bundling into securitized issues.[18] The due diligence process vets mortgages and prunes ones that do not

---

[18] At the time, among the most well-known due-diligence companies were American Mortgage Consultants, Bohan Group, Clayton Holdings, Fidelity Information Services, Opus Capital Markets Consultants, RR Donnelly, Watterson Prime, and 406 Partners.

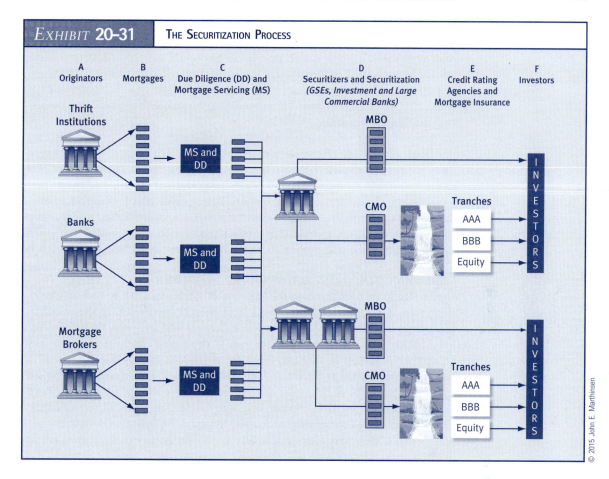

EXHIBIT **20-31** | THE SECURITIZATION PROCESS

meet certain quality standards. Mortgage originators that securitize their own issues have greater familiarity with the borrowers behind the loans; so they typically have less need for external due diligence services. By contrast, financial institutions that purchase mortgages from others rely on this (often outsourced) function to protect them against credit risk.

Mortgages need to be serviced until they mature, and many mortgage originators earn attractive profits from servicing activities, even if the loans they originate have been sold to others and securitized. Mortgage servicing involves all the administrative responsibilities involved with collecting monthly principal and interest payments, collecting and paying property taxes, holding funds in escrow, collecting mortgage insurance payments, notifying borrowers of delinquencies, assessing penalties for late payments, tracking outstanding principal balances, foreclosures, and (sometimes) negotiating debt modifications (i.e., workouts) in cases of threatened default. Mortgages that are securitized and sold in secondary markets (i.e., as MBS) may continue to be serviced by the financing bank for a fee.

SECURITIZERS AND SECURITIZATION (COLUMNS D)
Securitizers fund their mortgage purchases in three ways: borrowing, issuing equity to investors seeking real estate exposures, and generating positive cash

flows from operations. Once purchased, these mortgages are bundled in ways that make their risks and cash flows most appealing to likely investors. Securities with the same risk-return profiles as the underlying mortgages are called mortgage-backed-obligations (MBO), mortgage-backed securities (MBS), or pass-through securities. Securities with risks, returns, maturities, and payments that are different from the underlying mortgages are called collateralized mortgage obligations (CMOs).

Exhibit 20-31 shows images of plateaued waterfalls to represent the various levels of risk associated with different CMOs. The least risky CMO securities are first to receive a return and principal repayment. The riskiest CMO securities receive their returns and repayments last—if anything is left.

The largest mortgage securitizers are Fannie Mae and Freddie Mac, but during the subprime frenzy, investment banks took over an increasingly large share of the market. Unfortunately, their participation also ushered in a severe deterioration in the quality and increase in the quantity of MBOs and CMOs.

CREDIT RATING AGENCIES AND INSURANCE (COLUMN F)

Credit rating agencies evaluate the riskiness of MBS and CMOs. One might think that, if the individual mortgages have already been vetted at the due diligence stage (Column C), why is there a need here? The answer is that securitizers are a bit like financial magicians, but instead of turning canes into scarves, they create CMOs with risks that can range from Triple-A to junk-bond status. Prior to and during the Great Recession, Standard & Poor's and Moody's accounted for more than 90% of the credit risk-evaluation business, but Fitch, A.M. Best, and Egan-Jones Ratings Company were also active. The financial role of credit rating companies is to act as guardians-at-the-gates for investors, by evaluating MBOs and CMOs and providing feedback on their levels of risk. If they fail to do an adequate job (which was the case), the consequences can be dire.

To further reduce default risks, many securitized issues were insured. Fannie Mae and Freddie Mac earn handsome fees from insuring their securitized issues, but there are (and have been) large private insurance companies that do the same. AMBAC Financial Group and MBIA Inc. were among the largest, but between 2008 and 2010, MBIA's credit rating fell from Triple-A to speculative grade. Similarly, AMBAC's credit rating in 2008 was Triple-A, but in 2010, the company was forced to file for bankruptcy.

CONCLUSION

Financial crises are not new to the world, and they will surely be infrequent and unwanted visitors in the future.[19] The *Great Recession* was the result of a confluence of economic forces connected to problems of moral hazard, U.S. regulatory changes and government incentives to homeowners, lack of counterparty transparency, and monetary policy changes. Underlying all of these causes were incentives that coalesced to create one of the largest U.S. economic calamities in the past century. In the end, the problem was one of

---

[19] See Charles P. Kindleberger and Robert Z. Aliber, *Manias, Panics and Crashes: A History of Financial Crises,* Sixth Edition, (New York, NY: Palgrave Macmillan, 2011). Also see, Charles Mackay, *Extraordinary Popular Delusions, and the Madness of Crowds* (New York: Three Rivers Press, 1980).

mispriced risks, which encouraged excessive borrowing and speculation. Leverage ratios became so extreme that any economic or financial downturn was bound to have major negative consequences; and when problems did arise, they were concentrated in the largest and most sophisticated financial institutions, which contributed to a systemic decline in real estate prices, securitized financial asset values, and wealth.

From its start in 2007, the world witnessed the massive destruction of wealth as financial malaise spread from IndyMac to Bear Stearns to Lehman Brothers to financial institutions, industries, governments, and countries around the world. Governments and central banks responded to the *financial* crisis by recapitalizing financial institutions and providing them with easy access to liquidity. Similarly, governments and central banks responded to the *economic* crisis by reducing taxes, increasing government spending, and pursuing expansionary monetary policies that reduced interest rates, in some countries, nearly to zero.

As with long-term inflation, the burst in business and consumer demand for real estate would have been much more difficult without sufficient liquidity to support it. For this reason, the U.S. Federal Reserve was the focus of critical scrutiny during and after the financial crisis. To revive the U.S. economy, the Fed made unprecedented increases in the U.S. monetary base, which continued well after the recession ended. The long-term effects of having so much monetary base in the banking system may haunt the United States for years. Missing from the financial news was any clear indication of an exit strategy, which caused the potential consequences to be both uncertain and disconcerting.

REVIEW QUESTIONS

1. The values of existing homes are not included in a nation's AD, yet their compression in 2008 caused a decline in AD during the Great Recession. Explain the cause and effect relationship.

2. Explain the Paradox of Leverage, how it contributed to the Great Recession, and how it made recovery more difficult.

3. Distinguish between a liquidity problem and a solvency problem. What are the major solutions to these problems?

4. What is moral hazard? Explain why it was one of the main causes of the Great Recession.

5. Explain the difference between the originate-to-hold and the originate-to-distribute strategies. What is the connection between these strategies, moral hazard, and the Great Recession?

6. Explain NINJA loans and their relationship to the Great Recession.

7. Define "securitization" and the "originate-to-distribute" strategy. How did they combine to help create the Great Recession?

8. Explain the role of Fannie Mae and Freddie Mac in the U.S. housing market.

9. What role, if any, did Fannie Mae and Freddie Mac play in the Great Recession?

10. Explain the Paradox of Financial Innovation and the role it played in the Great Recession.

11. Explain the Paradox of Thrift and the role it played in the Great Recession.

12. Explain how U.S. regulatory changes helped create conditions that led to the Great Recession.

13. Explain financial disintermediation.

14. Explain how a lack of financial transparency helped create the Great Recession.

15. What are repurchase agreements (repos)? Are they sources of funds or uses of funds? How did the collapse of the repo market contribute to the Great Recession?

16. What is the commercial paper market? Is it a source of funds or a use of funds? How did the collapse of the commercial paper market contribute to the Great Recession?

17. Explain how expansionary *and* contractionary monetary policies contributed to the Great Recession.

18. In the context of the Great Recession, explain "quantitative easing" and the economic problems it poses.

19. What was the relevance of the Dodd-Frank (Wall Street Reform and Consumer Protection) Act in the aftermath of the Great Recession?

20. Explain the role that credit rating agencies were supposed to play in the mortgage securitization process and how failures at that level contributed to the housing crash.

DISCUSSION QUESTIONS

21. How effective were U.S. fiscal and monetary policies at curing the Great Recession?

22. Use the Three-Sector Model to explain the effects monetary policy had on the U.S. economy while the Fed was trying to fix the U.S. economy and financial system. Assume the United States had highly mobile international capital markets and a flexible exchange rate. What problems connected with Fed policies are likely to be with the United States for years?

23. Use the Three-Sector Model to explain the effects fiscal policy had on the U.S. economy. Assume the United States had highly mobile international capital markets and a flexible exchange rate.

24. Why did the U.S. government have a greater motivation to supply equity to troubled U.S. banks than to purchase their troubled assets?

25. Looking back at the Great Recession, was it an illiquidity problem or an insolvency problem?

PART 6

LONG-TERM ECONOMIC CHANGES

Chapter 21

Causes of Long-Term Growth and Inflation

INTRODUCTION

Until now, we have focused on building a framework for analyzing short-term changes in economic activity. The Three-Sector Model provided us with an integrated and systematic way to evaluate the economic consequences of financial, real, political, and social shocks to a nation. The results from these analyses could then be used to strengthen annual budgets, country studies, business plans, capital budgets, and strategic decisions.

This chapter and the next focus on the long run. Rather than examine changes in economic activity for one- to five-year periods, we will concentrate on changes that span a decade or more. We start by discussing the role played by scenario analyses in a company's strategic planning process. Then, our attention will turn to issues of economic growth and development and the ways in which governments and natural resource endowments affect them. In the process, we will learn about the power of compounding and why annual growth rates, even at seemingly low levels, can have significant effects on long-term living standards.

Monetarism,[1] which is based on the quantity theory of money (QTM), will serve as the springboard for our discussion of long-term price movements and the major cause(s) of long-term inflation. Monetarism will also play a valuable role in explaining the long-term effects of fiscal policies.

Theories are controversial, and monetarism is no different. So before discussing monetarism, we will first introduce the equation of exchange (EOE), which is the foundation on which QTM and monetarism are built. EOE is an economic relationship on which we all can agree because it expresses an economic tautology.

The chapter moves on to discuss the long-term Phillips curve and focuses on whether nations face long-term trade-offs between inflation and unemployment. Our discussion will center on the *natural-rate hypothesis*, which considers how short-term and long-term unemployment rates are affected by differences between a nation's actual and expected inflation rates.

"The Rest of the Story" section of this chapter considers embellishments connected to monetarist theory. It begins by discussing the costs and benefits of central banks obeying strict long-term monetary rules instead of using short-term discretionary policies to solve ever-changing economic problems.

> This chapter focuses on the causes of long-term growth, inflation, and unemployment.

---

[1] Monetarism is also called monetarist theory or neoclassical economic theory.

Finally, the chapter ends with a monetarist theory reality check, which is simply an evaluation of whether the theory's conclusions seem consistent with common sense and intuition.

THE BASICS

SCENARIO PLANNING

Scenario plans have 10- to 20-year time horizons.

Having a framework for evaluating long-term economic changes is important because it complements the strategic planning needs of businesses and governments. Yearly or biannual scenario plans are created and actively discussed by many well-organized companies. These plans typically have 10- to 20-year time horizons and concentrate on structural issues, such as the future composition of a company's product portfolio and centers of business interests.

Companies use scenario analyses to address issues such as:

- What will our industry look like in a decade or more, and how can we be a major part of it?
- Given our current strengths and the direction of world trends, what acquisitions and/or alliances will provide us with the greatest synergies?
- What existing products or lines of business should we shed because they no longer make strategic sense?

Long-run economic analyses focus more on supply-side factors than demand-side factors.

As we change our perspective to the long run, our focus will shift from factors that mainly affect demand to those that affect supply. These supply-side factors usually move at a glacial pace, but over time, their cumulative effects tend to overwhelm other forces standing in their way. Among these supply-side forces are broad-based demographic, technological, business, and government trends, such as aging populations, immigration and emigration, informatics, automation, miniaturization, robotics, research (e.g., genetic engineering), corporate governance practices, labor–management relations, government intervention and regulations, infrastructure, fiscal and monetary priorities, international protectionism, property rights, tax policies, and risks (e.g., political, terrorist, social, and economic).

MEASURING GROWTH AND DEVELOPMENT

Just as businesses create, execute, and assess their performances using balanced scorecards, countries can do the same.[2] Two of the most frequently used measures to gauge a nation's level of economic development are real per capita gross domestic product (GDP), which is a flow concept, and wealth, which is a stock concept. But these statistics are only road signs that indicate whether nations are moving in the right direction.

---

[2] See Robert S. Kaplan, Conceptual Foundations of the Balanced Scorecard," *Harvard Business School Working Paper 10-0734, 2010*, http://www.hbs.edu/faculty/Publication%20Files/10-074.pdf (accessed October 1, 2013). Robert S. Kaplan and David P. Norton, *The Strategy-Focused Organization: How Balanced Scorecard Companies Thrive in the New Business Environment* (Boston: Harvard Business Review Press, 2001).

More important to nations than the goods and services they produce each year or the wealth they accumulate over time are visible signs that every citizen has (1) widespread access to basic life-sustaining amenities, (2) freedom to pick from a wide range of social and economic choices, and (3) better self-esteem through higher standards of living.[3] Viewing economic growth in terms of sustenance, freedom, and self-esteem helps us focus on the mountains in the horizon rather than landmarks along the way.

> A balanced set of long-term goals for many nations could include freedom, sustenance, and self-esteem. Growth of real GDP is simply a means to these ends.

INCREASING REAL GDP AND REAL PER CAPITA GDP

A nation can increase real GDP in two basic ways. One of them is to augment and/or improve the resources used in the production process. The other is to increase the efficiency of the production process. Exhibit 21-1 shows three stages of production. Stage 1 is the *input stage*, Stage 2 is the *production process stage*, and Stage 3 is the *output stage*.

Stage 1: Growth Caused by More and/or Better Inputs

Whenever a nation employs more labor, land, capital, and/or entrepreneurship, its real GDP should rise. But to increase living standards, nations not

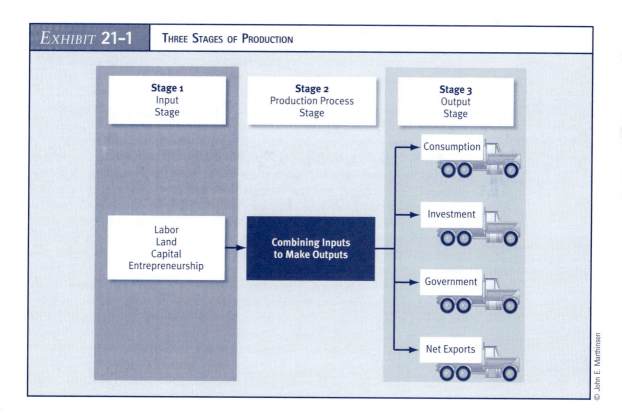

EXHIBIT 21-1   THREE STAGES OF PRODUCTION

Stage 1
Input Stage

Stage 2
Production Process Stage

Stage 3
Output Stage

Labor
Land
Capital
Entrepreneurship

Combining Inputs to Make Outputs

Consumption

Investment

Government

Net Exports

© John E. Marthinsen

---

[3] For more information on this way of viewing economic growth and development, see Amartya Sen, *Development as Freedom* (Oxford: Oxford University Press, 1999). Also see Paul Collier, *The Bottom Billion: Why the Poorest Countries Are Failing and What Can Be Done* (Oxford: Oxford University Press, 2007) and Jeffrey D. Sacks, *The End of Poverty: Economic Possibilities for Our Time* (New York: Penguin Group, 2005).

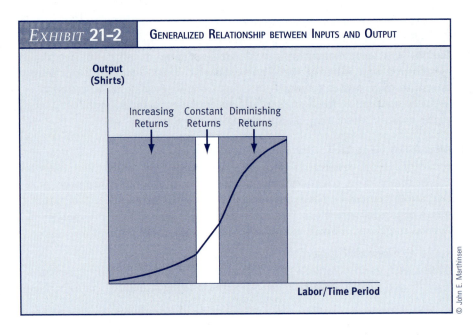

EXHIBIT 21-2   GENERALIZED RELATIONSHIP BETWEEN INPUTS AND OUTPUT

only have to increase real GDP; they also must increase real per capita GDP. Because of *diminishing returns*, this is often hard to do.

Exhibit 21-2 shows the generalized relationship between inputs and outputs, when a variable resource is added to one or more fixed resources. Suppose Exhibit 21-2 represents the output of shirts at a garment factory as labor is added to fixed amounts of land, capital, and entrepreneurship.

In the beginning, the number of shirts produced may rise at an increasing rate because machinery and work space are abundant. Qualified workers are relatively easy to find, and any increase in output is relatively large because it is measured against a low base. Therefore, increasing production at a growing rate is possible for a short period of time. But this production stage of *increasing returns* is not sustainable. If it were, a nation could clothe itself and the rest of the world simply by increasing the amount of labor it employed in this single factory.

Increasing returns occur when output grows at a rate greater than inputs.

As more labor is hired, the factory's machinery is increasingly stretched. Average and marginal worker productivities decline as more frequent bottlenecks occur, logistical complexity increases, and the normal wear and tear on machinery takes its toll. These productivity measures also decline when new workers with below-average ability are hired and have to be trained.

As a company moves out of the increasing returns stage, it encounters *constant returns*, where output grows proportionately with labor inputs. Eventually, it reaches the stage of *diminishing returns*. At this point, output continues to rise, but at an ever-decreasing rate. Diminishing returns is not a theory but rather an economic fact of life, which means every company and nation should expect to experience it.

Eventually, nations encounter diminishing returns, and output increases at rates that are slower than inputs.

Understanding the generalized relationship between inputs and outputs helps explain why differences in nations' growth rates may have nothing to do with one country doing something right (well) and the other doing something wrong (poorly). Rather, it could be due to the disparity in their stages of production and relative usage of resources.

For example, developing nations often grow more rapidly than developed countries when they have a plentiful supply of labor relative to capital, and they are deriving relatively high returns from their investments in plant, equipment, and education. Furthermore, they are comparatively undercapitalized and enjoy access to technological advances that can be imported at relatively low costs.

By contrast, developed countries are already operating at relatively high levels of capacity and efficiency. Their capital-to-labor ratios are already high in comparison with those of developing nations. Moreover, huge majorities of their workforces are already educated, and they must invent new technologies to gain competitive advantages.

Stage 2: Growth Caused by Changes in the Production Process

There are only two ways to postpone diminishing returns. One of them is to find ways to increase all resources together; another is to improve the efficiency of the production process (Stage 2 in Exhibit 21-1). By increasing all resources together or improving productivity, the entire production function shifts upward (see Exhibit 21-3).

> To postpone the effects of diminishing returns, nations can try to increase all resources simultaneously or improve the production process.

Economic growth that cannot be explained by increases in the quantity or quality of inputs must be due to something happening within the production process stage. This unexplained residual could be caused by discovery, invention, or innovation, but it could just as easily be the result of a novel management style, cultural differences, or political ideology. Identifying the exact cause(s) of this output residual is problematic because the inner workings of the production process stage are not always visible and well understood.

> Growth that cannot be explained by changes in resource quantity or quality must be due to the production process.

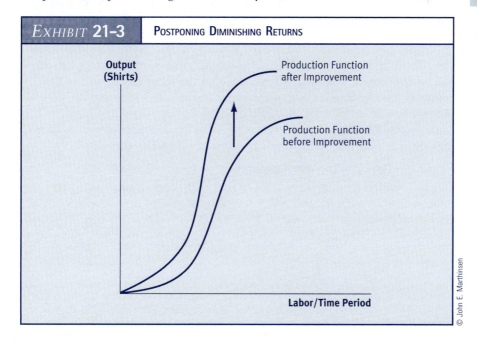

EXHIBIT 21-3   POSTPONING DIMINISHING RETURNS

Output (Shirts)

Production Function after Improvement

Production Function before Improvement

Labor/Time Period

© John E. Marthinsen

An example helps explain why identifying the source of a nation's growth can become a politically sensitive issue. During the 1950s and 1960s, member nations of the Soviet Union grew at much faster rates than the United States or Western Europe. Many analysts attributed the difference to the Communistic ideology. Some even suggested that higher growth rates and better living standards might be worth the cost of a few sacrificed freedoms in Western nations.

In the end, the notion was discredited that Communism was the cause of rapid *and* sustained economic growth. Today, Communism is seen by many to be more of an anchor to growth than an economic sail. But it did not take the dissolution of the Soviet Union or the crumbling of the Berlin Wall to prove this point. Analysts knew for years that virtually all of the Soviet Union's growth could be explained by the relationship between inputs (Stage 1 in Exhibit 21-1) and outputs (Stage 3 in Exhibit 21-1). They knew because there was no residual in the production process (Stage 2 in Exhibit 21-1) to explain.

Soviet output grew mainly as a result of substantial, and often compulsory, increases in the quantity and quality of inputs. The Soviet government forced thousands of people from their farms to work in cities. Men and women (but especially women) were compelled to enter the labor force and required to work overtime. Expenditures for education increased dramatically, which substantially increased the nation's literacy rates and productivity.[4]

With such radical changes in the quantity and quality of inputs, one would expect Soviet output to rise—and it did. But therein was the problem. A nation can double its literacy rate once, but if more than half of the population can already read and write, then it is impossible to double the percentage again. Similarly, a government can force people from farms to cities, but when more than half the people are already in cities, it cannot double the percentage again. In short, the Soviet Union eventually encountered diminishing returns. Its growth rate slowed, and finally, the ceiling caved in. Public unrest caused remarkable political and economic changes that led to the dissolution of the Soviet Union.

Soviet Communism is rarely cited today as a cure-all for economic malaise. Nevertheless, ideological questions about growth and development are still hotly debated. The only difference is that the focus has shifted as new countries have sprinted ahead of the pack. During the 1960s and 1970s, Japan was seen as the economic role model for growth and development. Then, in the 1980s and early 1990s, the Asian Tiger countries were held in high esteem. Now, in the 2000s, it is China's and India's turn.

ECONOMIC GROWTH AND THE IMPORTANCE OF COMPOUNDING

Due to compounding, positive rates of real growth, even small ones, are important to living standards when they are considered over long periods of time. Compounding is a powerful force because each year the base on which growth is calculated gets larger. Due to compounding, a nation growing at a

---

[4]See Paul Krugman, "The Myth of Asia's Miracle," *Foreign Affairs*, Volume 73, Number 6, November/December 1994, pp. 62–78. George F. Gilboy, "The Myth Behind China's Miracle, *Foreign Affairs*, Volume 83, Number 4, July–August 2004, pp. 33–48. Joe Studwell, *How Asia Works: Success and Failure in the World's Most Dynamic Region* (New York: Grove Press, 2013).

4% annual rate needs fewer than 18 years to double its annual GDP. Without compounding, it would take 25 years.

To see the power of compounding in a different light, suppose we considered the period from 1947 (just after World War II) to 2014 and compared the per capita incomes of two nations that started at the same level but grew at different rates. If per capita income in 1947 for both countries were $1,000, and Country A grew at an average annual rate of 1%, while Country B grew at an average annual rate of 3%, how large would the difference in their living standards be at the end of the 67-year period?

Clearly, growth would make both countries better off. Slow-growing Country A's per capita GDP would be $1,948, which is more almost 95% higher than in 1947, but Country B's results would be much more impressive. At the end of the period, Country B's per capita income would be $7,246, which is almost 625% higher than in 1947 and more than 370% higher than the 2014 level of Country A.

The take-away is that nations need forward-looking government officials and central bankers who are willing and able to keep the ball of economic progress rolling forward. They can do this by enacting policies that contribute to sustainable economic growth rates because each year new gains are compounded on the shoulders of all previous years' gains. If public officials keep this vision, they will end up providing better standards of living for their children and grandchildren, as well as for their current constituents.

WHAT ROLE SHOULD GOVERNMENTS PLAY IN ECONOMIC DEVELOPMENT?

What does history tell us about the role governments should play, if any, in the promotion of economic growth and development? Do government policies matter in the long run? Can they make a difference?

HOW CAN GOVERNMENTS PROMOTE ECONOMIC GROWTH?

The government's role in promoting long-term economic growth is still being sorted out. Exhibit 21-4 summarizes some of the policies that have been successful for many developed nations, like the United States, England, and Switzerland. These governments have established fair rules of behavior and provided the means to enforce them.[5] They have also done a good job creating stable and predictable political environments, encouraged competitive markets, and promoted national and international flows of financial capital, labor, goods, and services. In addition, they have pursued sensible fiscal policies, appointed prudent central bankers, and imposed reasonable marginal tax rates.

Governments seem to function best when they provide needed goods and services that otherwise would not be provided effectively and/or efficiently by the private sector (e.g., defense against foreign invasion). Of course, a large part of delivering on this responsibility is knowing when they have crossed the line and started to provide goods and services that would or could be supplied

> Compound changes in GDP can make a large difference in living standards—especially over long periods.

> Nations need forward-thinking public officials who are willing and able to keep the ball of economic progress rolling forward.

> Governments play an important role supplying needed goods and services that otherwise would not be provided, in sufficient quantity and/or quality, by the private sector.

---

[5] For example, they defined individual property rights, followed the "rule of law," and enacted antitrust legislation.

EXHIBIT 21-4	HOW GOVERNMENTS CAN PROMOTE ECONOMIC GROWTH

- Legislate and enforce fair rules of behavior
  - Individual property rights
  - Rule of law
  - Antitrust legislation
- Reduce risks
  - Stable and predictable political environment
- Encourage competitive markets
- Promote national and international flows of financial capital, labor, and traded products
- Pursue sensible fiscal policies
- Appoint prudent central bankers, and provide them with the independence to do their jobs
- Impose reasonable marginal tax rates

© John E. Marthinsen

more efficiently and effectively by the private sector. Historically, governments have not been especially successful at choosing industry winners, and after nationalizing industries, their record has been relatively poor at developing new technologies and staying at the forefront of technological efficiency.

How Can Governments Impede Economic Growth?

There are six primary ways by which governments can impede economic growth (see Exhibit 21-5). First, to fund their expenditures, governments must either borrow or tax. If borrowing raises the real interest rate, it can crowd out private investment (and also consumption) expenditures. Taxes lower profits (and/or disposable incomes), which also reduces investment (and/or consumption). This reduction in private spending can lower economic growth.

> **Government spending can crowd out private spending.**

Taxes may also diminish work incentives by lowering the opportunity cost of leisure. For example, someone who works eight hours a day, earns $20 an hour, and pays a 10% tax rate sacrifices $144 for each day off.[6] If taxes were raised to 40%, the same day off would cost the worker only $96.[7] Therefore, higher taxes make leisure cheaper.

> **Government taxes may diminish work incentives.**

EXHIBIT 21-5	HOW GOVERNMENTS CAN IMPEDE ECONOMIC GROWTH

- Government borrowing can crowd out private investment
- High taxes may reduce investment, consumption, and work incentives
- Government projects may have relatively low marginal returns
- Lack of accountability to a bottom line allows wasteful spending
- Regulation may redistribute income and wealth rather than create them
- Protectionist policies may interfere with international labor, capital, and trade flows

© John E. Marthinsen

---

[6] Disposable income = Income − Taxes = ($20/hr × 8 hr/day) − (10% × $20/hr × 8 hr/day) = $144/day
[7] Disposable income = Income Taxes = ($20/hr × 8 hr/day) − (40% × $20/hr × 8 hr/day) = $96/day

Third, at some point, government spending begins to encounter diminishing returns, but this is no surprise. Why should governments be any different from private companies? The marginal returns on government projects, such as educational programs, roads, tunnels, and bridges, follow the same inevitable pattern of diminishing returns as private investments in buildings, factories, machinery, and tools. As more projects are undertaken, the return on government projects, at some point, is bound to sink below the return on private projects.

Fourth, governments are accountable to voters and constituents, but they are not accountable to bottom lines or to shareholders. As a result, they are more likely to spend too much and unwisely. Government accountability is also diminished because there is often no way to measure the economic return on nonprofit government projects.

Another way governments can impede growth is by focusing more on the redistribution of assets and annual production than they do on increasing growth, wealth, and national equity. Often, issues of *fairness* and *creating a level playing field* become major considerations in many government debates, when increasing the size of the economic pie should be the focus.

Even though income redistribution and economic growth do not have to be at odds with each other, they often are. Similarly, there seems to be an inverse relationship between the extent of government regulations and the rate of economic growth. Therefore, balance and care are needed when changing or imposing rules, guidelines, and procedures.

Finally, markets have the remarkable power to increase a nation's wealth and well-being. This is not to say that the markets are always right, but as Winston Churchill said about democracy, they are better than the alternatives. For this reason, governments that interfere with the national and international flow of financial capital, labor, goods, and services can cause more harm than good to their domestic economies.

> Government spending eventually encounters diminishing returns.

> Governments are not accountable to bottom lines in the way business are.

> Government redistribution efforts can come at the expense of economic growth.

> Misguided government regulations can impede economic growth.

> Government restrictions on trade and capital flows often create economic results that are inferior to market-created outcomes.

THE ROLE OF NATURAL RESOURCES IN ECONOMIC GROWTH

It is no accident that nations' natural resource endowments are deemphasized as major sources of economic growth. Clearly, if all other things were equal, then nations with abundant resources would have advantages over nations with fewer resources. But "other things" are rarely equal, and there is ample empirical evidence that natural resource endowments are not prerequisites to high living standards or rapid economic growth. If they were, nations like Argentina, Brazil, and Venezuela, which have some of the most abundant natural resources in the world, would have higher living standards than Japan and Switzerland, where natural resources are relatively scarce. To grow, nations need *access* to resources, which means they need open trade and investment channels; they do not need to own the resources.

> Access to natural resources (not necessarily ownership) is a prerequisite for economic growth.

With the sources of long-term economic growth behind us, let's now turn our attention to the causes of long-term inflation. A convenient framework for integrating economic growth with inflation is EOE. Gaining a firm understanding of EOE is an entrée to the QTM and monetarism, which put the causes of long-term inflation into better perspective.

EQUATION OF EXCHANGE

EOE is a particularly useful and appealing way to frame long-term economic issues. This intuitive tautology isolates four important macroeconomic variables: GDP Price Index (P), Real GDP (Q), Money supply (M), and Velocity of money (V).

For macroeconomic analyses using EOE, the best price index to use is a nation's GDP Price Index (P). Because the M2 money supply has been the focus of this book, we will use M2 as the money supply definition in our discussion of EOE. As a result, we will abbreviate the velocity of money as V_2, to indicate that it is the average number of times financial assets in the M2 money supply need to be spent per period to purchase newly produced final goods and services.

How are P, Q, M2, and V_2 related? To answer this question, let's rely on two standard ways to calculate GDP. Remember that nominal GDP is defined as *the market value of all final goods and services produced in a nation during a given period*. Therefore, one way to calculate nominal GDP is by multiplying the price and quantity of every end product made during a given time period and then summing together the results. This gives the same result as multiplying a nation's GDP Price Index by its real GDP (see Exhibit 21-6).

Nominal GDP can also be calculated by multiplying a nation's money supply (M2) times the velocity of money (V_2). To understand why this is true, let's use the United States as an example. In 2012, the M2 money supply in the United States averaged about $10,000 billion, and the nation's nominal GDP was about $16,000 billion. How is it possible for a nation to have such a large GDP with such a small money supply? The answer is that each dollar was spent approximately 1.6 times in 2012 to purchase the newly produced, final goods and services. Therefore, it must be the case that nominal GDP is equal to the product of the M2 money supply and the velocity of money (V_2) (see Exhibit 21-7).

It is helpful to remember that V_2 is not determined by surveying companies and/or consumers. Rather, it is a derived figure that is calculated by

---

E_{XHIBIT} **21–6**	**GDP Relationship 1: Nominal GDP $\equiv$ P $\times$ Q**

Nominal GDP $\equiv (P_1 \times Q_1) + (P_2 \times Q_2) + (P_3 \times Q_3) + \cdots + (P_n \times Q_n)$

Therefore, Nominal GDP $\equiv$ Sum of all (P $\times$ Q),
which we can abbreviate as

$$\text{Nominal GDP} \equiv P \times Q$$

where
  $P_i \equiv$ prices of individual goods and services,
  $Q_i \equiv$ quantity of individual final goods and services produced per period,
  $P \equiv$ GDP Price Index, and
  $Q \equiv$ real GDP.

© John E. Marthinsen

EXHIBIT 21-7   GDP RELATIONSHIP 2: NOMINAL GDP $\equiv$ M2 $\times$ V$_2$

$$\text{Nominal GDP} \equiv M2 \times V_2$$

where
  M2 $\equiv$ M2 money supply, and
  V$_2$ $\equiv$ M2 velocity to purchase final goods and services produced per period.

© John E. Marthinsen

---

dividing the nominal GDP by the M2 money supply (see Exhibit 21-8). After a nation has estimated both its nominal GDP and M2 money supply, V$_2$ can be calculated. By studying how the velocity of money has changed in the past, economists can determine how stable it has been and the factors primarily responsible for changing it.

Merging *GDP Relationship 1* in Exhibit 21-6 and *GDP Relationship 2* in Exhibit 21-7 gives us EOE. From Relationship 1, we know that a nation's nominal GDP equals P $\times$ Q, and from Relationship 2, we know that nominal GDP equals M2 $\times$ V$_2$. Therefore, (P $\times$ Q) must equal (M2 $\times$ V$_2$). This identity is known as the *equation of exchange* (see Exhibit 21-9).[8]

M2 $\times$ V$_2$ $\equiv$ P $\times$ Q

EXHIBIT 21-8   V$_2$ IS A DERIVED VALUE

$$V_2 \equiv \frac{\text{Nominal GDP}}{M2}$$

© John E. Marthinsen

EXHIBIT 21-9   EQUATION OF EXCHANGE

Because
  Nominal GDP $\equiv$ P $\times$ Q
and
  Nominal GDP $\equiv$ M2 $\times$ V$_2$
then it must be that
  P $\times$ Q $\equiv$ GDP $\equiv$ M2 $\times$ V$_2$
Therefore,

$$P \times Q \equiv M2 \times V_2$$

© John E. Marthinsen

---

[8] The equation (P $\times$ Q $\equiv$ M $\times$ V) is often called the *Fisher equation* in honor of Irving Fisher (1867–1947), a Yale economist who developed this line of thought.

CONVERTING EOE TO PERCENTAGE TERMS

A nation's GDP Price Index, real GDP, money supply, and money velocity are all important macroeconomic variables, but most policy discussions are couched in terms of the rates of change and expected rates of change. Rather than discuss price indices, most people are concerned with inflation or deflation rates. Rather than discuss real GDP, people are more interested in whether a nation's real economic growth is positive, negative, high, low, rising, or falling. Similarly, instead of focusing on the absolute level of a nation's money supply or velocity, people focus on rates of change.

To make EOE more useful and relevant, let's convert it into percentage-change terms. There are two ways to accomplish this task: the rigorous mathematical way and the commonsense way. Let's take the commonsense route.

How would you answer the following question? If a nation's GDP Price Index (P) increased by 10% and real GDP (Q) increased by 10%, by how much would nominal GDP (which is $P \times Q$) rise? To answer this question, let's use a simple example. Suppose that the original average price index was 1.00, and real GDP (e.g., stated in 2009 dollars) was $1,000. By multiplying them together, we see that nominal GDP would equal $1,000.

MACRO MEMO 21-1

Income Velocity versus Transactions Velocity

Picture yourself in the following situation. You're arguing with a friend about why some nations have excessive long-term inflation rates and others don't, and you're doing your best to work EOE into the conversation. After a heated exchange, your friend suddenly asks, "How large is this velocity of money that you keep mentioning? Do you have any idea?"

Proud to know the answer, you authoritatively state that the U.S. velocity for M2 is about 2.0. At that point, your friend turns to you and says, "Do you mean to tell me that the dollar I spend today for a cup of coffee will only (on average) be spent one more time this entire year? If 'velocity' is a serious part of your argument, then you'd better get straight what it is because the way you're explaining it cannot be right."

How should you respond? Clearly, she's right. A dollar spent today will be spent many more times than once during the next year. But if that is true, why

does EOE tells us that it will be spent only about twice per year?

A good place to begin your answer is by pointing out the difference between a nation's *income velocity* and its *transactions velocity*. Income velocity is the number of times money (M2) is exchanged each year to purchase *newly produced* final goods and services. Because EOE focuses on the variables in GDP, income velocity is its focal point.

By contrast, the transactions velocity is the average number of times money is exchanged each year for *any* good, service, donation, or financial asset. People spend money on a wide variety of products. Some of these transactions are for newly produced final goods and services, but many more are for transactions that are not included in GDP. For example, purchases and sales of foreign exchange, financial securities (e.g., stocks, bonds, and notes) and used goods are included in the transactions velocity but not the income velocity. Therefore, the transactions velocity is always larger (usually much larger) than income velocity.

EXHIBIT 21-10	GDP COMPONENTS IN PERCENTAGE TERMS: AN APPROXIMATION

$$\%\Delta GDP \cong \%\Delta P + \%\Delta Q$$

$$\%\Delta GDP \cong \%\Delta M2 + \%\Delta V_2$$

Note: "%Δ" means a percentage change.

© John E. Marthinsen

If prices rose by 10% to 1.10, and real GDP rose by 10% to $1,100, then nominal GDP would rise to $1,210, which is a 21% increase.[9] This 21% increase in nominal GDP is *approximately equal* to the sum of the percentage change in the price index *plus* the percentage change in real GDP (i.e., 10% + 10% = 20% ≅ 21%).

Therefore, we will use the following generalization: For small movements, when two variables are multiplied together, the percentage change in the product of those two variables changes by approximately the sum of each variable's growth rate.[10] Therefore, $\%\Delta GDP \cong \%\Delta P + \%\Delta Q$, and $\%\Delta GDP \cong \%\Delta M2 + \%\Delta V_2$ (see Exhibit 21-10).

By combining terms in Exhibit 21-10, we see that the percentage change in GDP Price Index ($\%\Delta P$) plus the percentage change in real GDP ($\%\Delta Q$) must approximately equal the percentage change in money supply ($\%\Delta M2$), plus the percentage change in velocity of money ($\%\Delta V_2$) (see Exhibit 21-11).

Once EOE has been transformed into percentage terms, its variables take on new meaning. A nation's GDP Price Index (P), real GDP (Q), money supply (M2), and money velocity (V_2) are replaced by the nation's inflation rate ($\%\Delta P$), growth rate of real GDP ($\%\Delta Q$), M2 money supply growth rate ($\%\Delta M2$), and percentage change in the velocity of money ($\%\Delta V_2$). With the EOE in mind, let's turn our attention to monetarism and QTM.

Rule of Thumb
For small changes, when two variables are multiplied, the percentage change in their product is approximately equal to the sum of each variable's growth rate.

EXHIBIT 21-11	EQUATION OF EXCHANGE IN PERCENTAGE TERMS

Because

$$\%\Delta P + \%\Delta Q \cong \%\Delta GDP \cong \%\Delta M2 + \%\Delta V_2,$$

it must be the case that

$$\%\Delta P + \%\Delta Q \cong \%\Delta M2 + \%\Delta V_2,$$

where

$\%\Delta P \equiv$ percentage inflation or deflation rate,
$\%\Delta Q \equiv$ percentage real GDP growth rate,
$\%\Delta M2 \equiv$ percentage M2 growth rate, and
$\%\Delta V_2 \equiv$ percentage V_2 growth rate.

© John E. Marthinsen

[9] 1.10 × $1,100 = $1,210/year
[10] This approximation is less accurate as the percentage changes become larger.

MONETARISM AND THE QUANTITY THEORY OF MONEY

EOE draws our attention to four key macroeconomic variables, namely, P, Q, M2, and V_2. It also defines a relationship among these variables that is true by definition. Because EOE is a tautology and makes no assumptions about the behavior of these macroeconomic variables, it cannot be used to predict or to explain how economies function as they do. This is where QTM and monetarism[11] make significant contributions to macroeconomic analysis because they breathe life into EOE by making behavioral assumptions about what causes P, Q, M2, and V_2 to change.[12]

We know from EOE that $\%\Delta M2 + \%\Delta V_2 \cong \%\Delta P + \%\Delta Q$, which means $\%\Delta P \cong \%\Delta M2 + \%\Delta V_2 - \%\Delta Q$. Therefore, inflation must be caused by a combination of rising money supply, rising money velocity, and/or falling real GDP (see Exhibit 21-12). But which of these variables is the main long-term source of inflation, and what causes it to change?

Let's take a closer look at what causes each of the variables in EOE to change. In the case of the M2 money supply and real GDP, you will be glad to learn that we already know the answer. As for the causes of long-term velocity changes, the answer will be new—but not surprising.

QTM breathes life into the variables included in EOE.

WHAT CAUSES LONG-TERM CHANGES IN M2 (%ΔM2)?

Answering the question "What causes long-term changes in M2?" is relatively easy because we have already addressed this issue in Chapter 8, "The Power of Financial Institutions to Create Money" and Chapter 9, "Who Controls the Money Supply and How?" In these chapters, the money creation process and central bank controls were discussed. Remember that M2 is equal to the M2 money multiplier times the monetary base. Central banks have a large degree of influence over the money multiplier because they determine the reserve

E_{XHIBIT} **21-12**	**EOE: CAUSES OF INFLATION**

If

$$\%\Delta M2 + \%\Delta V_2 \cong \%\Delta P + \%\Delta Q,$$

then

$$\%\Delta P \cong \%\Delta M2 + \%\Delta V_2 - \%\Delta Q.$$

Therefore,

Inflation (%ΔP) is caused by

%ΔM2 rising,
%ΔV_2 rising, and/or
%ΔQ falling.

© John E. Marthinsen

---

[11] Monetarism is built on QTM. In this discussion, they are referred to interchangeably.

[12] The classic article that set the stage for a modern investigation of QTM was published by Milton Friedman in 1956. See Milton Friedman, "The Quantity Theory of Money: A Restatement," in *Studies in the Quantity Theory of Money* (Chicago: University of Chicago Press, 1956).

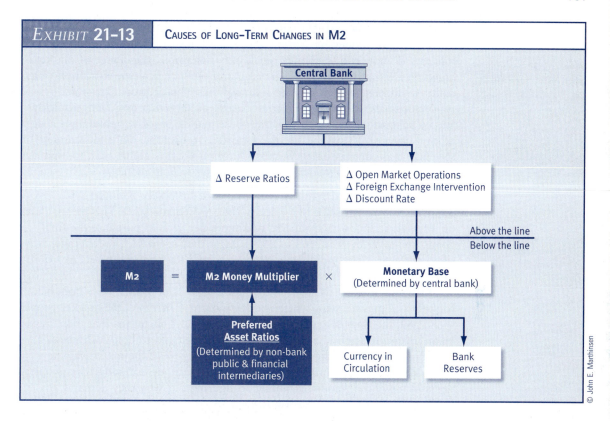

EXHIBIT 21-13 | **CAUSES OF LONG-TERM CHANGES IN M2**

Central Bank

Δ Reserve Ratios

Δ Open Market Operations
Δ Foreign Exchange Intervention
Δ Discount Rate

Above the line
Below the line

M2 = M2 Money Multiplier × Monetary Base (Determined by central bank)

Preferred Asset Ratios (Determined by non-bank public & financial intermediaries)

Currency in Circulation

Bank Reserves

© John E. Marthinsen

ratio(s) on financial intermediaries' deposit liabilities. But they lack complete control over it because central banks do not determine the preferred asset ratios of households[13] and the preferred asset ratios of financial intermediaries[14] (see Exhibit 21-13).

By contrast, central banks have complete control over the monetary base. Therefore, if a nation's monetary base changes, it is due to voluntary central bank action(s), such as open market operations, foreign exchange market intervention, and/or discount rate changes.

> A nation's money supply changes with movement in the money multiplier and monetary base.

WHAT CAUSES LONG-TERM CHANGES IN REAL GDP (%ΔQ)?

Monetarists agree with the conclusions we drew at the beginning of this chapter. In particular, they believe that a nation's long-term economic growth is based mainly on its ability to increase the quantity and quality of resources, improve production processes, and enact sensible public policies. Simply put, to consume more, nations have to produce more. To produce more, they need well-educated workforces, efficient machinery, reasonable governments and central banks, as well as freedom to pursue economic opportunities.

> Long-run economic growth depends on fundamental economic, social, and political factors.

---

[13] The preferred asset ratios of households are C_c/D, which is (Currency in circulation/Checking accounts), and N/D, which is (Near money/Checking accounts).
[14] The preferred asset ratio of financial intermediaries is U/D, which is (Customary reserves/Checking accounts).

What Causes Long-Term Changes in M2 Velocity (%ΔV_2)?

The velocity of money has strong and direct links to broad institutional factors that do not tend to change quickly. For example, the degree of market liquidity, fluctuations in payment risks, and the technical sophistication of a nation's payment system are just a few of these "institutional" factors.

Velocity also depends on market-based variables that can change quickly and by substantial amounts. Whether these market-based variables have a significant effect on V_2 will be discussed shortly. To facilitate our understanding of the effect these market-based variables have on V_2, it is useful, first, to establish a link between money velocity and the demand *to hold* money.

Money Velocity and Money Demand Are Inversely Related

Suppose that in 2014 the M2 velocity (i.e., V_2) equaled 2.0. This means that, on average, individuals spent M2 two times per year to purchase the final goods and services produced in 2014. But if they spent M2, on average, two times per year, these individuals must have held the financial assets in M2 for one-half year, which is six months.

Likewise, if M2 was spent four times a year, then it must have been held for only one-quarter year, which is three months. Therefore, the quicker people spend M2, the shorter period of time they hold it. This means that there must be an inverse relationship between V_2 and the demand to hold M2 assets.

Monetarists view the assets in M2 as just a few of the many ways in which individuals can hold their wealth. Therefore, determining why people demand (i.e., hold) money is similar to figuring out why they demand any investment asset in their portfolios. Demand is influenced mainly by factors such as the returns on substitutes and expectations.

Substitutes for the financial assets in M2 are investments, such as interest-earning securities (e.g., bills, notes, and bonds), equities, and real assets (e.g., collectibles, precious metals, antiques, business inventories, and real estate). As the returns on these substitute assets rise relative to the return on M2, the demand to hold money falls, which means the velocity of money rises.

Expectations also affect the demand to hold money. For example, an increase in expected inflation reduces the demand for money. Money demand falls because the assets in M2 lose purchasing power as inflation rises. To protect their wealth, people try to replace their M2 assets with real and financial investments that will rise in value with inflation. As the demand to hold money falls, M2's velocity rises. Similarly, when the expected returns on investment assets, such as fixed income securities, equities, and/or real assets, rise relative to the expected returns on M2 assets, money demand falls, which means the velocity of money increases.

Exhibit 21-14 summarizes the variables we have discussed that affect velocity and shows the qualitative effect they have on V_2 and the demand to hold M2.

The Cause of Long-Term Inflation in the Monetarist Model

Monetarism is based on two major pillars. If you accept these assumptions, then the conclusions are logical and consistent. In particular, it assumes that:

1. A nation's long-term growth rate depends on its ability to increase the quantity and quality of resources, improve production processes, and enact sensible public policies; and

(margin notes)

V_2 is affected by broad-based institutional factors that change slowly.

V_2 is also affected by market-based variables.

V_2 and the demand to hold money are inversely related.

The demand to hold money is inversely related to changes in the relative return on substitute investments.

The demand to hold money is inversely related to the expected inflation rate and expected relative returns on substitute investments.

EXHIBIT 21-14	FACTORS THAT AFFECT THE PORTFOLIO DEMAND TO HOLD M2 AND THE M2 VELOCITY	
MARKET-BASED VARIABLES	**DEMAND FOR M2**	**VELOCITY OF M2**
If the returns relative to M2 rise for:		
Fixed-income securities	Falls	Rises
Equities	Falls	Rises
Real assets	Falls	Rises
If expected inflation rises	Falls	Rises
If expected returns relative to M2 rise for:		
Fixed income securities	Falls	Rises
Equities	Falls	Rises
Real assets	Falls	Rises

© John E. Marthinsen

MACRO MEMO   21-2

Income Velocity, Money Demand, and "Hot Potatoes"

In many ways, the characteristics of money demand and money velocity are captured by a hikers' game called "hot potato." Hungry after a long day of hiking and possessing little or no cooking skills, hikers often put potatoes wrapped in aluminum foil on the hot coals of a fire. When the potatoes are fully cooked (i.e., burning hot!) and ready to eat, a decision has to be made about who eats first. That's where the game of "hot potato" comes in. A potato is removed carefully with tongs or sticks from the coals and passed quickly from person to person. The first person able to hold the potato gets to eat it, and it is breach of honor to let a potato fall to the ground.

M2 is like the number of potatoes passed from hiker to hiker, and the velocity of money is the speed at which potatoes are exchanged. With M2, instead of a few hot potatoes being passed, billions of dollars, euros, pesos, or yen are used. Like in the game of hot potato, one person can get rid of his/her money, but the group, as a whole, cannot. When one person gets out of money by purchasing something or investing, someone else gets in. Finally, just as heat from the fire determines how fast potatoes are exchanged, the market-based variables listed in Exhibit 21-14 determine how fast money is spent (and, therefore, how long it is held).

2. V_2 is stable and predictable around its long-run trend.

Based on these assumptions and empirical evidence to support them, monetarists conclude that long-term inflation is a monetary phenomenon. For example, if the long-term growth rate of real GDP in the United States had been 3.5% per year and long-term V_2 increased annually by 0.5%, then the United States would have zero long-term inflation if the Federal Reserve increased the money supply annually by 3.0%. By contrast, if M2 grew annually by 5.0%, V_2 rose by 0.5%, and real GDP grew by 3.5%, then long-term inflation would be 2% (see Exhibit 21-15).

EXHIBIT 21-15	DISCRETIONARY CHANGE IN M2 TO ACHIEVE 0% OR 2% LONG-TERM INFLATION						
INFLATION %ΔP	≅	DISCRETIONARY CHANGE %ΔM2	+	LONG-TERM CHANGE %V2	−	LONG-TERM CHANGE %ΔQ	
0%	=	3.0%	+	0.5%	−	3.5%	
2%	=	5.0%	+	0.5%	−	3.5%	

© John E. Marthinsen

Knowing this, we can go one step further: If the central bank's goal were to achieve 0% inflation, then its long-term monetary target should be to increase M2 by 3.0%. If the goal were a 2% inflation rate, then M2 should rise by 5.0%. A 2% goal might be chosen instead of a 0% goal if the central bank believed that the nation's GDP Price Index overstated the actual inflation rate. This would occur if the price index did not reflect factors such as annual quality changes, the introduction of new products, and the substitution of relatively cheap products for relatively expensive ones.[15]

The main conclusion from monetarist theory is that, if the long-run growth of real GDP is determined by fundamental economic, social, and political factors that are not connected to monetary policy, and if V_2 is stable and predictable, then a nation's long-term inflation rate will change passively with fluctuations in the money supply. Therefore, if a nation has excessive long-term inflation, the source of the inflation must be from the excessive growth of a nation's money supply, which was induced or enabled by its central bank (see Exhibit 21-16).[16]

> Monetarists assert that long-term inflation is caused by excessive money creation, which means long-term inflation is a monetary phenomenon.

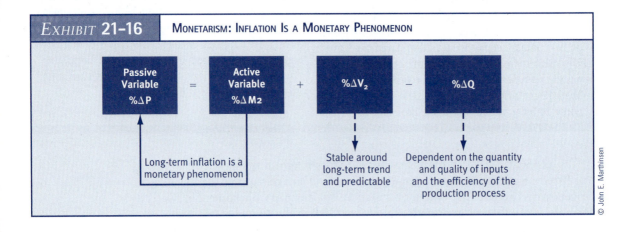

| EXHIBIT 21-16 | MONETARISM: INFLATION IS A MONETARY PHENOMENON |

Passive Variable %ΔP = Active Variable %ΔM2 + %ΔV2 − %ΔQ

Long-term inflation is a monetary phenomenon

Stable around long-term trend and predictable

Dependent on the quantity and quality of inputs and the efficiency of the production process

© John E. Marthinsen

[15] See Chapter 4, "Inflation, Real GDP, and Business Cycles," for a full discussion of these effects.
[16] "The Rest of the Story" section of this chapter provides another way to arrive at the monetarist conclusion that excessive money growth is the fundamental cause of long-term inflation.

LONG-RUN EFFECTS OF FISCAL POLICY: A MONETARIST VIEW

What are the long-term effects of expansionary fiscal policy? To answer this question, it is important to remember the two major assumptions on which monetarism is built—namely:

1. A nation's long-term growth depends on its ability to increase the quantity and quality of resources, improve production processes, and enact sensible public policies; and
2. V_2 is stable and predictable around its long-run trend.

Monetarists argue that increased government spending does not guarantee that a nation's business sector will be more profitable, domestic financial assets will earn higher real returns, or natural resources will be more productive. If expansionary fiscal policy could accomplish all these feats, it would be the universal remedy for global poverty and slow economic growth. We know this is not the case.

We also know that fiscal policies that do not involve the central bank have no effect on a nation's monetary base. Therefore, only if they affect the nation's money multiplier do fiscal policies change the money supply. Let's assume that any unwanted changes in a nation's money supply caused by fiscal policies can be offset by central banks—especially in the long run.[17] Therefore, expansionary fiscal policy should have no long-term effect on a nation's growth of real GDP ($\%\Delta Q$), velocity ($\%\Delta V_2$), or money supply ($\%\Delta M2$), which means it should not affect the long-term inflation rate.

If this is true, then what effect, if any, does expansionary fiscal policy have on economic activity? The monetarist answer is that fiscal policy mainly redistributes GDP. To spend, governments need funding. For that, they either tax or borrow. If they tax, household consumption and/or business investments fall. Therefore, governments are able to purchase goods and services only to the extent that taxpayers are forced to reduce their demands. By contrast, if governments borrow, they cause the real interest rates to rise. As real yields rise, private borrowing and spending fall, thereby allowing governments to purchase goods and services by reducing private spending.

> Monetarists believe that fiscal policies mainly redistribute income rather than cause long-term inflation or long-term economic growth.

To monetarists, whether to tax or borrow is a bit like the choosing which part of a pie the government should cut. By taxing, it chooses a piece that would have gone to taxpayers. By borrowing, the government chooses a piece that would have gone to interest-sensitive borrowers, like the construction industry. One thing is sure: because the government owns the knife and is responsible for cutting, it usually ends up with the slice of pie it wants.

To summarize our conclusions about the effects of monetary and fiscal policies, monetarists assert that long-term inflation can be (and should be) blamed directly on central banks because, if central banks do not support inflation, it dies out eventually. By contrast, the long-term effects of fiscal policy are mainly redistributive. Fiscal policy does little to enlarge the economic pie but rather divides it by taxing and/or borrowing.

---

[17] If the increase in government spending causes the nation's real risk-free interest rate to rise, the M2 money multiplier rises (due to changes in the preferred assets ratios), which increases M2. This effect is likely to be small and easily reversible; therefore, it is ignored in this analysis.

The final section of "The Basics" deals with the long-run Phillips curve controversy. The long-run Phillips curve debate is about whether nations can trade off inflation and unemployment for extended periods of time. Does a long-run Phillips curve exist? If it does, then what policies should nations pursue to permanently lower their unemployment rates? Will these policies cause inflation to rise rapidly, or will inflation remain at reasonable levels?

LONG-RUN PHILLIPS CURVE AND THE NATURAL-RATE HYPOTHESIS

Our Three-Sector Model showed how an inverse relationship could exist between inflation and unemployment in the short term. For this trade-off to occur, aggregate demand had to increase along the intermediate range of a nation's aggregate supply (AS) curve. In other words, there had to be demand-pull inflation.

The Phillips curve trade-off confronts nations with a bitter choice. Either they can reduce their unemployment rates by tolerating more inflation, or they can reduce their inflation rates at the cost of higher unemployment. For example, in Exhibit 21-17, a decrease in the unemployment rate from 7% to 5% is at the expense of an increase in inflation from 4% to 6% (and vice versa).

During the 1960s, many economists and politicians believed that nations could fine-tune their economies by estimating the Phillips curve trade-off and then using monetary and fiscal policies to move their economies along the predicted curve. Exhibit 21-18 shows why their belief was so strong. From 1959 to 1968, the correlation between U.S. inflation and U.S. unemployment was obviously inverse.

Time has not been kind to advocates of the Phillips curve—especially those who felt that a discernible, long-term trade-off existed. During the years since 1968, the inverse relationship between inflation and unemployment has become unhinged. Exhibit 21-19 shows the inflation–unemployment relationship in the

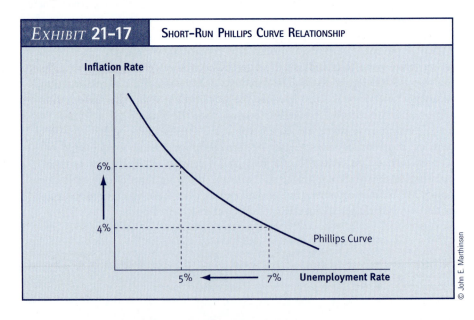

EXHIBIT 21-17   SHORT-RUN PHILLIPS CURVE RELATIONSHIP

Inflation Rate

6%

4%

Phillips Curve

5%   7%   Unemployment Rate

© John E. Marthinsen

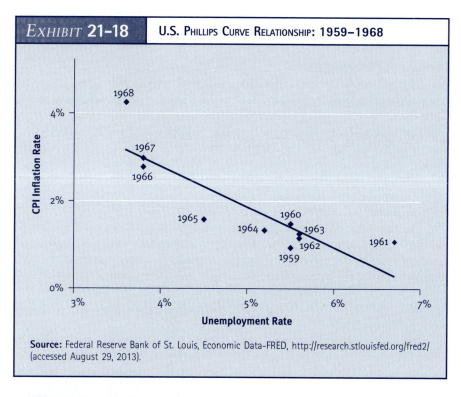

EXHIBIT 21-18 | **U.S. PHILLIPS CURVE RELATIONSHIP: 1959–1968**

Source: Federal Reserve Bank of St. Louis, Economic Data-FRED, http://research.stlouisfed.org/fred2/ (accessed August 29, 2013).

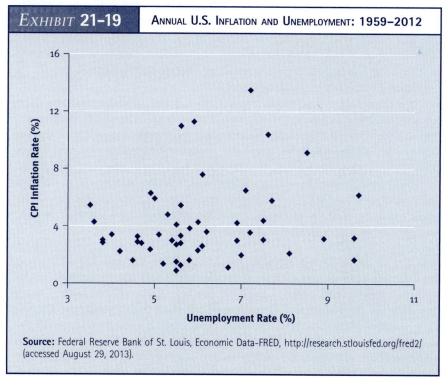

EXHIBIT 21-19 | **ANNUAL U.S. INFLATION AND UNEMPLOYMENT: 1959–2012**

Source: Federal Reserve Bank of St. Louis, Economic Data-FRED, http://research.stlouisfed.org/fred2/ (accessed August 29, 2013).

United States from 1959 to 2012. It would be a challenge, indeed, to find one, single Phillips curve that fairly represents all of these points.

Natural Rate Hypothesis

The natural-rate hypothesis asserts that nations have a vertical, long-run Phillips curve at the natural rate of unemployment and a family of downward-sloping, short-term Phillips curves that shift due to changes in expected inflation.

A thoughtful explanation for the shotgun-like pattern of inflation–unemployment points in Exhibit 21-19 is the *natural-rate hypothesis*, which is often included as a part of monetarism. The natural-rate hypothesis asserts that nations confront a dominant long-run Phillips curve and a family of short-run Phillips curves. The dominant long-run Phillips curve is vertical at the nation's natural rate of unemployment. The family of short-run Phillips curves is downward sloping and shifts with changes in the expected inflation rate. As expected inflation rises, the short-term Phillips curve shifts rightward; when expected inflation falls, it shifts leftward.

The natural rate of unemployment is a level that allows a nation to sustain its current inflation rate. Therefore, if a nation were at its natural unemployment rate, economic conditions would be aligned so that no pressure existed for inflation to rise or fall. For this reason, another name for the natural rate of unemployment is *nonaccelerating inflation rate of unemployment* (NAIRU) or the *nonincreasing inflation rate of unemployment* (NIIRU)

The natural rate of unemployment is also called the nonaccelerating inflation rate of unemployment (NAIRU) or nonincreasing inflation rate of unemployment (NIIRU).

The natural rate of unemployment varies from country to country and is based on socioeconomic and institutional differences. Many factors, such as the labor market structure, worker mobility, levels of unemployment benefits, social welfare programs, ability of workers to respond to market incentives, male and female participation rates, minimum wage levels, labor union strength, and real wage flexibility, enter into determining a nation's natural rate of unemployment (see Macro Memo 21-3: "What Is the Natural Rate of Unemployment?"). At any point in time, these factors vary widely from nation to nation, and they also change over time. Therefore, the natural rate of unemployment is not a standing target.

It is important to recognize that the natural rate of unemployment is not the level of unemployment that is consistent with the maximum amount a nation is capable of producing. In other words, it does not represent the vertical portion of the AS curve where the productive potential of a nation has been totally exploited. Rather, the natural rate of unemployment represents a threshold level of unemployment, below which persistent and rising inflation rates occur and above which persistent reductions in inflation (or deflation) occur. As a result, it is possible for a nation to operate, for short periods of time, below or above the natural unemployment rate.

Short-Run Movements around the Long-Term Phillips Curve

Let's use the natural-rate hypothesis to explain the scatter of inflation and unemployment points in Exhibit 21-19. We will start our analysis at Point A in Exhibit 21-20. Notice that Point A is on the short-term Phillips curve labeled $PC_{2\%}$. At this point, the actual inflation rate, which is shown on the vertical axis, and expected inflation rate, which is attached to the short-run Phillips curve, are both equal to 2%, and the nation's unemployment rate equals 5.5%,

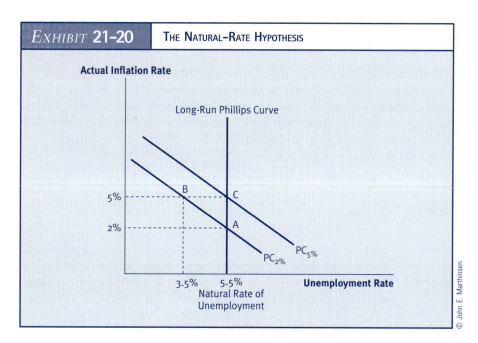

EXHIBIT 21-20 | **THE NATURAL-RATE HYPOTHESIS**

which is the natural rate of unemployment. If actual inflation equals expected inflation, the nation is considered to be at an equilibrium point because individuals and companies can confidently incorporate expected inflation rates into their contracts and not have unexpected surprises (positive or negative) at the end of the contract period.

Suppose the central bank pursued expansionary monetary policies that caused inflation to rise from the expected 2% rate to an unexpected 5% rate. Real wages would fall by 3%. As real wages fell, businesses would have more incentive to hire, which would reduce the unemployment rate. In addition, individuals would have less incentive to stay in or to enter the workforce. For example, some individuals might leave work and go back to school (e.g., enter graduate programs or finish high school), and current students might stay in school. Therefore, the higher-than-expected inflation would reduce the unemployment rate and move the nation northwestward along PC$_{2\%}$ from Point A to Point B. At Point B, the actual inflation rate (5%) would be higher than the expected inflation rate (2%), and the unemployment rate would be lower (3.5%) than the natural rate (5.5%) at Point A.

The level of unemployment at Point B can be maintained only if the actual and expected inflation rates continue to be 5% and 2%, respectively. This is highly unlikely to occur because labor will adjust its inflation expectations and also try to regain its lost real wage by negotiating new contracts with the higher inflation rate in mind. As these contracts are renegotiated, the real wage rate rises back toward its initial level, business incentives to hire fall, and labor incentives to seek work rise. Consequently, the unemployment rate gradually creeps, horizontally, from 3.5% back toward 5.5% (B to C).

> The natural rate of unemployment is like a nation's economic center of gravity. The nation returns to this level in the long run.

> Short-term Phillips curves are downward sloping because unexpected changes in inflation affect hiring and job-seeking incentives.

MACRO MEMO   21-3

What Is the Natural Rate of Unemployment?

The *natural rate of unemployment* is the rate to which a nation gradually moves if the real wage rate is free to fluctuate and the nation's actual inflation rate equals its expected inflation rate. If these two conditions are met, the forces of supply and demand act to gradually move the economy back to equilibrium (see Exhibit 21-21).

When the unemployment rate is above the natural rate, rising unemployment causes the real wage to fall. As the real wage falls, businesses have more incentive to hire workers, and individuals have less incentive to remain in or to enter the workforce. Therefore, the unemployment rate falls. By contrast, when there is an excess demand for labor, the real wage rises, which reduces businesses' incentive to hire and encourages individuals to remain in and to enter the labor force.

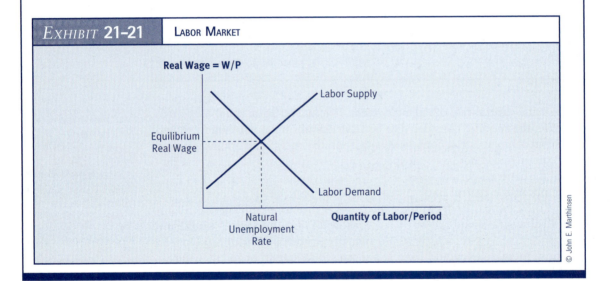

EXHIBIT **21-21**   LABOR MARKET

© John E. Marthinsen

If inflationary expectations remain at 5%, the economy will return to equilibrium at Point C, where expected inflation and actual inflation are equal at 5%. At Point C, the nation's unemployment rate, again, would equal 5.5%, and the inflation rate (both actual and expected) would be 5%.

Exhibit 21-22 shows that if there is a family of short-term Phillips curves, then almost all of the U.S. inflation–unemployment points between 1959 and 2012 can be explained. The long-term Phillips curve divides the mass of points at the natural rate of unemployment.

POLICY RECOMMENDATIONS

What policy prescriptions emerge from our discussion of the long-run Phillips curve? If the long-run Phillips curve is vertical, as the natural-rate hypothesis asserts, then governments and central banks should focus on keeping inflation as low, stable, *and* predictable as possible.

EXHIBIT **21-22**	LONG–TERM AND SHORT–TERM PHILLIPS CURVES: 1959–2012

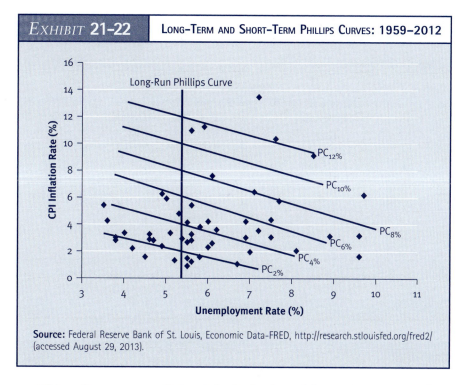

Source: Federal Reserve Bank of St. Louis, Economic Data-FRED, http://research.stlouisfed.org/fred2/ (accessed August 29, 2013).

This policy recommendation is both simple and frustrating. It is simple because governments and central banks have only one goal, namely, to focus on controlling inflation. It is frustrating because it seems to imply that governments and central banks have no direct control over the nation's ultimate long-term unemployment rates.

This latter conclusion is not necessarily true because the natural rate of unemployment can change. As Exhibit 21-23 shows, if the natural rate of unemployment falls, then the entire long-run Phillips curve shifts to the left; if it rises, the long-run Phillips curve shifts right.

Shifts of the long-run Phillips curve occur when there are changes in supply-side factors that affect labor market conditions, productivity, and/or per unit costs. Among the most important factors that shift the long-run Phillips curve leftward (in a favorable direction) are:

- reductions of input prices due to the greater availability of resources (e.g., increased worker participation rates, greater numbers of talented immigrants, and reductions in imported oil costs);
- improvements in productivity brought on by invention and innovation;
- reductions of unnecessary and costly government regulations; and
- exchange rate appreciation (especially for countries that are relatively dependent on foreign-sourced inputs).

In short, many of the same supply-side factors that we discussed in the beginning of this chapter as being the essential ingredients for real economic growth and national well-being are also the factors that improve a nation's natural unemployment rate.

> The long-run Phillips curve shifts with changes in supply-side factors that affect labor market conditions, productivity, and/or per unit costs.

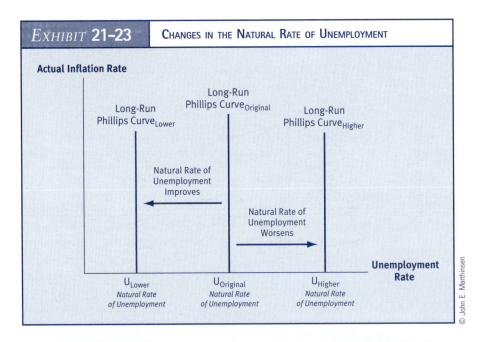

EXHIBIT 21-23   **CHANGES IN THE NATURAL RATE OF UNEMPLOYMENT**

© John E. Marthinsen

THE REST OF THE STORY

MONEY "RULES"

Discretionary monetary and fiscal policies may have destabilizing effects on domestic and international economies. As Exhibit 21-24 shows, the time lag between a fundamental change in economic activity and when monetary policy finally takes effect can vary between approximately 6 months and 2.7 years. For

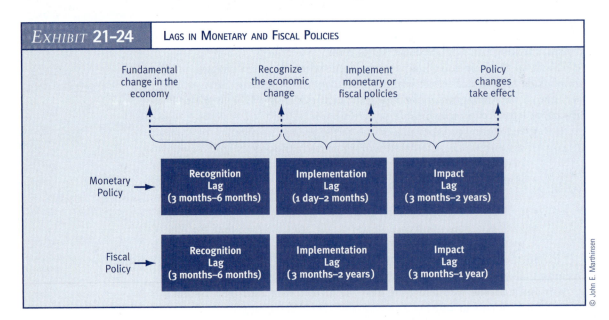

EXHIBIT 21-24   **LAGS IN MONETARY AND FISCAL POLICIES**

© John E. Marthinsen

EXHIBIT 21-25	MONETARY RULE: TARGET INFLATION RATE = 0%					
GOAL %ΔP	≅	MONETARY RULE %ΔM2	+	LONG-TERM AVERAGE %ΔV₂	−	LONG-TERM AVERAGE %ΔQ
0%	=	3.0%	+	0.5%	−	3.5%

© John E. Marthinsen

fiscal policy, the lag is between 9 months and 3.5 years. As a result, many economists, especially monetarists, believe that nations would be better off with central banks and governments that had little or no discretionary powers. Rather than change the money supply according to current or expected economic conditions, central banks would be required to follow a *monetary rule*, which means changing the money supply at a fixed rate (e.g., 3% per year).[18] Similarly, instead of encouraging or allowing governments to change spending and/or taxation to balance current or expected economic activity, discretionary fiscal policies would be discouraged or severely restricted.

DETERMINING THE MONETARY RULE

If central banks were forced to follow a monetary rule, then what rule should they follow? Exactly how fast should a nation's money supply grow? Let's address these questions by looking at the United States.

Earlier in this chapter, we learned that a nation's inflation rate is determined by changes in money supply, velocity, and real GDP. Specifically, we discovered that $\%\Delta P \cong \%\Delta M2 + \%\Delta V_2 - \%\Delta Q$. Therefore, if the long-term rate of change in U.S. velocity and real GDP have been 0.5% and 3.5%, respectively, and the United States had the long-term goal of 0% inflation, then the annual growth of its money supply ($\%\Delta M2$) should be 3.0% (see Exhibit 21-25).

HOW STABLE IS THE VELOCITY OF MONEY?

Whether or not V_2 has a significant or immaterial effect on the economy is an empirical question. As you might expect, V_2's level and volatility vary from nation to nation. Therefore, we cannot analyze just one country and assume the same is true everywhere. Nevertheless, by considering the United States, we can, at least, get a feeling for how stable V_2 is in a large, developed nation. Understanding V_2 in the United States can provide us with insights about how monetarists view velocity and its effect on inflation.

HOW STABLE IS V_2 IN THE UNITED STATES?

Exhibit 21-26A is based on quarterly data from 1959 to 2013. During this 54-year period, V_2 varied within the relatively narrow range of approximately

> If the goal is 0% inflation, then the long-run growth of money should be just enough to offset the net percentage growth in money velocity minus the percentage growth in output.

[18] This monetary rule is also known as the "k-percent rule". See, Milton Friedman, "The Optimum Quantity of Money," in The Optimum Quantity of Money and Other Essays (Chicago: Aldine Publishing Company, 1969), pp. 1–50. Milton Friedman, "Monetary Policy: Theory and Practice," Journal of Money, Credit, and Banking, Volume 14, Number 3, August 1982, pp. 98–118. Also see, Chapter 10, "The Economics of Virtual Currencies".

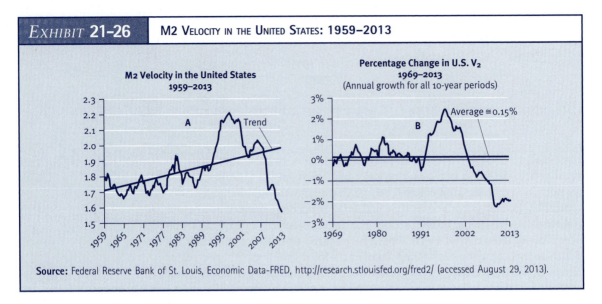

EXHIBIT 21-26 | M2 VELOCITY IN THE UNITED STATES: 1959–2013

Source: Federal Reserve Bank of St. Louis, Economic Data-FRED, http://research.stlouisfed.org/fred2/ (accessed August 29, 2013).

1.6 to 2.2. As for the stability of V_2, Exhibit 21-26B shows that, for the sample period of more than a half century, the yearly percentage change in V_2 for all the intervening 10-year periods was about +0.15%.

Of course, there were fluctuations around this long-term average. From 1991 to 1997, the volatility of V_2 increased considerably above the trend, then fell back from 1997 to 2004, and plunged during the Great Recession (December 2007–June 2009) and remained considerably below the trend as of 2013. Nevertheless, the volatility throughout this extended period remained within about a 4.5% band. Therefore, if the past is any indication of the future, we can say V_2 has not been (and should not be) a major source of demand fluctuation in the United States.

> V_2 appears to be rather stable in the United States.

HOW CLOSELY CORRELATED ARE CHANGES IN V_2 AND INFLATION IN THE UNITED STATES?

Exhibit 21-27 shows average annual inflation rates and average annual percentage changes in V_2 for each of the 10-year periods between 1959 and 2013. It is clear from the exhibit that the linear correlation between inflation and changes in V_2 was very weak.

> Long-term changes in V_2 do not appear to have a close linear correlation with long-term inflation.

Therefore, the take-aways from Exhibits 21-26 and 21-27 are that, in the United States, long-term fluctuations in the M2 velocity appear to be rather stable, and there is no apparent linear relationship between M2 velocity and inflation. Even though there are market-based variables that affect V_2, their impact appears to be relatively weak. Either the influences are offsetting so that the net change is small, or their independent effects are immaterial.

MONETARISM: AN INTUITIVE REALITY CHECK

INTRODUCTION

In economic discussions, it is all too easy to lose sight of the forest for the trees, so let's step back and see if monetarism makes sense without any of its assumptions. Suppose a shirt company (e.g., the one mentioned at the

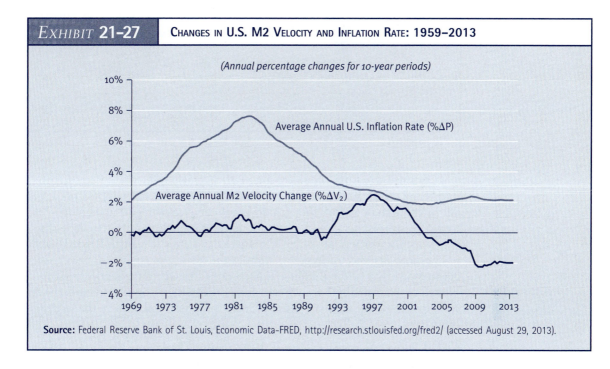

EXHIBIT **21-27**   CHANGES IN U.S. M2 VELOCITY AND INFLATION RATE: 1959–2013

(Annual percentage changes for 10-year periods)

Source: Federal Reserve Bank of St. Louis, Economic Data-FRED, http://research.stlouisfed.org/fred2/ (accessed August 29, 2013).

beginning of this chapter) was considering a large investment in a Latin American country. Due to the competitive market structure of the target country's industry and because of government regulations, suppose it would be extremely difficult for this company to raise prices. Therefore, a high inflation rate during the investment payback period could seriously erode the company's return.

To stimulate discussion on the merits of the investment project, suppose the CFO of the shirt company asked you to make a presentation on the likely causes of future inflation in the target country. As a scenario for your presentation, the CFO requested that you use a 10-year time horizon and explore the possibility of a 30% annual inflation rate. How could you frame this scenario and at the same time open the discussion to a broader audience?

DETERMINING THE CAUSES OF AN ANNUAL 30% INFLATION RATE

EOE tells us that price changes are due to the effects of three macroeconomic variables—namely, the percentage change in money supply (i.e., $\%\Delta M2$), velocity of money ($\%\Delta V_2$), and/or real GDP growth rate ($\%\Delta Q$). Let's apply a bit of common sense to see which of these three variables—$\%\Delta Q$, $\Delta\%V_2$, or $\%\Delta M2$—could be the cause of a decade-long inflation rate of 30% per year.

Could Falling Real GDP Cause a 30% Annual Inflation Rate?

Suppose that during the 10-year period, there was no change in the target country's money supply and velocity of money. Under these circumstances, EOE indicates that the quantity of final goods and services produced would have to fall by 30% each year to fuel the 30% decade-long inflation rate (see Exhibit 21-28).

EXHIBIT **21-28**	CAN FALLING REAL GDP CAUSE LONG-TERM (30%) INFLATION?

(Annual changes)

%ΔP	≅	%ΔM2	+	%ΔV$_2$	−	%ΔQ
+30%/year	=	0%/year	+	0%/year	−	(−30%/year)

© John E. Marthinsen

Consider what this would mean. A 30% yearly reduction in real GDP that began today and ended 10 years later would cause the nation's output to fall by more than 97%.[19] In such an economic environment, unemployment would be stratospheric, and living conditions would be at intolerable levels.

Is such a scenario possible? The answer is yes. Is it realistic? No. There has been no instance of hyperinflation in the history of the world that has been caused by real GDP falling at such rates for such an extended period. Therefore, your analysis would earn little credibility if you identified declining real GDP to be the primary cause of high, long-term inflation in the target country.

High long-term inflation is not caused by falling real GDP.

Could Rising Velocity Cause a 30% Annual Inflation Rate?

For changes in velocity (V$_2$) to be the sole, long-term cause of a 30% annual increase in prices, it would have to explode. Suppose the nation's velocity was equal to 1.0 this year. To fuel a 30% annual inflation during the next 10 years, it would have to rise from 1.0 to 13.8, which is an increase of almost 1,280%.[20] Is such a dramatic increase possible? Yes. Is it likely? No. Normally, velocity adjusts sluggishly to changes in expected inflation and expected real returns. It also responds to slow-moving changes in other institutional factors, such as spending habits, market liquidity, payment risks, and the development of financial institutions. Without some enormous external shock, it is implausible that rising velocity could be the cause of persistent inflation (see Exhibit 21-29).

High long-term inflation is not caused by rising velocity.

EXHIBIT **21-29**	CAN RISING VELOCITY CAUSE LONG-TERM (30%) INFLATION?

(Annual changes)

%ΔP	≅	%ΔM2	+	%ΔV$_2$	−	%ΔQ
+30%/year	=	0%/year	+	30%/year	−	0%/year

© John E. Marthinsen

---

[19] $(1 - 0.30)^{10} = 0.028$: therefore, if output fell by 30% per year for 10 years, it would reduce the base from 1.00 to 0.028, which is a decrease of 97.2%.
[20] $(1 + 0.30)^{10} - 1 = 12.79 = 1,279\%$

EXHIBIT **21-30**	CAN RISING VELOCITY AND FALLING REAL GDP CAUSE LONG-TERM (30%) INFLATION?

(Annual changes)						
%ΔP	$\cong$	%ΔM2	+	%ΔV$_2$	−	%ΔQ
+30%/year	=	0%/year	+	15%/year	−	(−15%/year)

© John E. Marthinsen

Could Rising Velocity and Falling Real GDP Cause a 30% Annual Inflation Rate?

Could the combination of rising velocity *and* falling real GDP cause a 10-year annual inflation rate equal to 30%? For instance, is it possible for velocity to rise by 15% and real GDP to fall by 15% each year to cause the 30% annual inflation? If they did, the nation's real GDP would have to fall by more than 80% by the end of the 10 years,[21] and the velocity of money would have to rise by more than 300%.[22] Again, these magnitudes seem out of line with any realistic historic touchstones (see Exhibit 21-30).

High long-term inflation is not caused by falling output and rising velocity.

Could a Rising Money Supply Cause a 30% Annual Inflation Rate?

In contrast to the unlikely cases where falling real GDP and/or increasing velocity were the primary causes of a decade-long inflation of 30% per year, consider the possibility of a rising money supply being the culprit (see Exhibit 21-31).

Is it possible for a nation's money supply to rise by 30% in any one year? Yes. Is it possible for a central bank to continue this rate of growth for a decade? The answer, again, is yes.

Exhibit 21-32 shows two examples of countries that experienced high inflation rates for more than a decade. Between 1975 and 1992, Argentina's annual inflation rate averaged 517%, and its money supply increased at an average annual rate of 400%. Between 1978 and 2003, Turkey's average yearly inflation rate was 60%, and its money supply grew by an average annual rate of 74%. Without dramatic increases in these nations' money supplies, inflation at these high rates could not have survived.

EXHIBIT **21-31**	CAN RISING MONEY SUPPLY CAUSE LONG-TERM (30%) INFLATION?

(Annual changes)						
%ΔP	$\cong$	%ΔM	+	%ΔV	−	%ΔQ
+30%/year	=	30%/year	+	0%/year	−	0%/year

© John E. Marthinsen

[21] $(1 - 0.15)^{10} = 0.197$, which means the output fell by 80.3% to 19.7%.
[22] $(1 + 0.15)^{10} - 1 = 3.05 = 305\%$

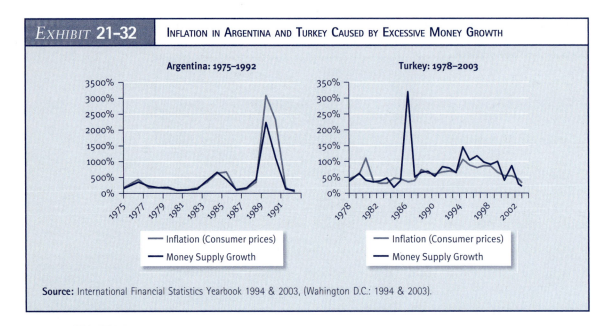

EXHIBIT 21-32   INFLATION IN ARGENTINA AND TURKEY CAUSED BY EXCESSIVE MONEY GROWTH

Source: International Financial Statistics Yearbook 1994 & 2003, (Wahington D.C.: 1994 & 2003).

> Intuition leads us to conclude that long-term inflation is a monetary phenomenon.

Our intuition leads us to the conclusion that a rapidly expanding money supply is the primary cause of a nation's high and persistent inflation. Therefore, companies that are interested in the prospects of high, long-term inflation would be well advised to focus on expected central bank policies in the target nation. This conclusion is exactly in line with monetarism.

CONCLUSION

In the long run, growth and development depend on supply-side factors, such as the quantity and quality of inputs and the efficiency of production processes. The most common measures of economic development are real per capita GDP and wealth. But these output-related indicators are only means to an end because the ultimate goals of nations are to provide their citizens with widespread access to basic life-sustaining amenities, freedom to pick from a wide range of social and economic choices, and better self-esteem through higher standards of living. In the end, if goods and services are not produced, they cannot be consumed. Therefore, long-run economic policy should be concerned more with the creation of income and wealth than with their redistribution.

Increasing real GDP is one way to improve a nation's living standards. But eventually, economic growth encounters diminishing returns. To fight diminishing returns, nations must find ways to expand and improve their resource bases, as well as make their production processes more efficient.

Governments with the best records for promoting long-term growth are those that restrict their activities to defining and enforcing property rights, setting basic rules of human behavior, and encouraging competitive markets. They also play significant roles by creating stable and predictable economic and political environments.

Without resources of sufficient quantity and quality, growth could not occur. Nevertheless, for a nation to grow, access to natural resources is more important than ownership. Some of world's most developed nations have natural resource endowments that rank among the scarcest in the world, and among the world's poorest countries are ones with relatively abundant natural resources.

EOE shows the tautological economic relationship between $(M \times V)$ and $(P \times Q)$. Monetarism, which is based on QTM, breathes life into EOE by making behavioral assumptions about what causes these variables to change. Monetarists believe that long-run growth is determined by a nation's ability to increase the quantity and quality of resources, improve production processes, and enact sensible government policies. They also assert that V_2 is stable and predictable along a long-term trend.

Therefore, monetarists conclude that long-run inflation is caused by excessive increases in the money supply. By contrast, expansionary fiscal policy merely redistributes real GDP. It does little or nothing to increase a nation's economic growth rate or to stimulate long-term inflation.

The natural-rate hypothesis asserts that, if there is a short-run trade-off between unemployment and inflation, then this inverse relationship is strongest when price changes are unexpected. But over time, if the price changes become easier to predict, the Phillips curve trade-off is substantially weakened or eliminated.

The reason for the trade-off's disappearance is because individuals and businesses revise their contacts and portfolios to reflect new inflationary conditions and expectations. As they do, temporary changes in unemployment, caused by fluctuations in the real wage, are eliminated and the economy moves back to the natural rate of unemployment.

If the long-run Phillips curve is vertical, as the natural-rate hypothesis indicates, then governments and central banks should focus on reducing the rate and volatility of inflation. To accomplish this goal, they must control their money supply growth rates, which is usually the responsibility of central banks. To improve the natural rate of unemployment, governments need to focus on supply-side factors, such as quantity and quality of the labor force, labor mobility, invention, innovation, and the level of competitiveness.

REVIEW QUESTIONS

1. What causes some nations to grow faster than others? Are there identifiable engines or commonalities? Are there identifiable anchors (i.e., hindrances) to growth?

2. Is the velocity of money (V_2) just another name for the M2 money multiplier? Explain.

3. How is EOE similar to and different from monetarism?

4. Explain the major assumptions and conclusions of monetarism.

5. Suppose the Swiss National Bank (SNB) wished to have inflation grow at a 2% rate during the coming year. Swiss nominal GDP is expected to grow during the period from SFr 8,000 million to SFr 8,080 million. The M2 velocity is

expected to grow from 4.00 to 4.24. Calculate the percentage change in the money supply needed for the SNB to accomplish its goal. Given your answer, list the tools that the SNB could use to change the money supply and how they would have to change.

6. Suppose you are in a meeting with the CFO, treasurer, and treasury staff at corporate headquarters. The discussion suddenly focuses on expanding operations in Latin America, in general, and Brazil, in particular. A colleague at the table mentions that Brazil is probably not a good prospect for investment because she fears that the nation may return to the 7,000% inflation rate it once experienced. When asked for the cause of the hyperinflation, your colleague says that most of her fears are centered on the potential for the Brazilian government to pursue highly expansionary fiscal policies. All eyes turn toward you for a comment on the validity of your colleague's statement. The question boils down to this: Can expansionary fiscal policy without an accommodating increase in money supply cause extended periods of hyperinflation? Using QTM (i.e., monetarism) as the basis for your reply, explain whether a 7,000% inflation rate is possible under these conditions. If it is possible, what would have to occur to make it happen? Otherwise, explain why it is impossible or improbable.

7. Determine whether the following statements are true, false, or uncertain according to monetarist theory. If any one is false or uncertain, change it so that the statement is correct.
   a. A decrease in the real rate of return on bonds increases the velocity of money.
   b. An increase in the real return on equity increases the velocity of money.
   c. An expected decline in the rate of inflation increases the velocity of money.

8. Use the natural-rate hypothesis to explain the economic adjustments that would occur if a nation's inflation rate fell from its expected level of 6% to an unexpected 2% rate.

9. Explain the natural-rate hypothesis and how it arrives at the conclusion that the long-run Phillips curve is vertical.

DISCUSSION QUESTIONS

10. Mexico has made structural reforms that should help increase the nation's labor force productivity in the twenty-first century. According to monetarism, explain the effect these reforms should have, in the long run, on Mexico's inflation rate.

11. Suppose Turkey's inflation rate was 55%, and its real GDP growth rate was 7.3%. The country's exchange rate fell by 54% against the U.S. dollar, its velocity of money was unchanged, and government spending rose by 45%. Use the QTM (i.e., monetarist theory) to explain whether Turkey's inflation was due to fiscal policy, monetary policy, or the exchange rate.

12. Suppose Belgium's natural rate of unemployment increased from 5% to 6%, and the current rate of unemployment was 4.5%. What economic adjustments would the increased natural rate cause?

Chapter 22

Long-Term Exchange Rate Movements and Comparative Advantage

INTRODUCTION

The potential gains from buying, selling, and investing abroad can be wiped out by unexpected changes in exchange rates. This is especially true in the long run, when hedging alternatives are scarce and hedging markets are shallow. Because foreign exchange rate movements can cause significant gains and losses, managing currency exposures should be an important part of every company's long-term planning process—even firms that might consider themselves immune from exchange rate fluctuations.

Consider a U.S. company (let's call it Boston Company) that has only domestic customers and sources all its inputs from U.S. producers. If the dollar appreciates relative to the United States' major trading partners, how would Boston Company be affected? First, foreign-made products would now be cheaper for U.S. consumers to buy. As a result, U.S. demand would turn toward foreign-made products, thereby eroding Boston Company's customer base. Second, to the extent that Boston Company's domestic competitors sourced their ingredients internationally, the dollar appreciation would lower these companies' costs of production, thereby increasing their profits relative to Boston Company and/or allowing them to lower prices. Finally, the dollar appreciation might provide Boston Company's competitors with an incentive to relocate production facilities to take advantage of shifting incentives. As a result, fluctuating exchange rates could cause the competitive structure of the U.S. marketplace to adapt.

This chapter focuses on why exchange rates change during long periods of time. It begins by looking at the Law of One Price (LOOP), which explains how prices and nominal exchange rates should adjust to equate the prices of *identical products* in two different nations. The chapter then considers absolute purchasing power parity (APPP), which explains how nominal exchange rates should adjust to equate the prices of *identical product baskets* in two different nations.

LOOP and APPP consider exchange rates at a point in time. Therefore, relative purchasing power parity (RPPP) is introduced to explain how nominal exchange rates should vary, over time, due to differing international inflation rates. Finally, our discussion of long-term exchange rates ends by linking RPPP and the quantity theory of money (QTM), thereby providing even more insight into why exchange rates change over long periods of time.

We move on to address comparative advantage, which is clearly a major take-away from any course in international economics. Understanding comparative advantage is important to economists and policymakers because it shows how free international trade can provide net benefits to all trading partners—regardless of a nation's absolute level of international competitiveness. For business leaders, comparative advantage is an insightful tool for long-term planning.

The chapter ends by discussing why the reasoning that goes into making sound macroeconomic (economy-wide) decisions is often different from the reasoning that goes into making sound business decisions. It provides insights into why successful business leaders are not always the most effective central bankers or finance ministers, and successful central bankers and finance ministers may be ineffective business leaders. In short, the chapter ends by highlighting why *countries are not companies* and should not be treated as such.

THE BASICS

LONG–TERM CHANGES IN EXCHANGE RATES

What causes long-term movements in nominal exchange rates? This is the question to keep in mind as we turn our attention to a concept called purchasing power parity (PPP), which focuses on the relationship between the prices of internationally traded products and nominal exchange rates. PPP requires an understanding of three core economic concepts—namely, LOOP, APPP, and RPPP.

LAW OF ONE PRICE (LOOP)

> According to LOOP, arbitrage should equate the exchange rate–adjusted prices of identical (and tradable) goods and services among nations.

According to LOOP, the price of a product in one country should equal the exchange rate–adjusted price of the same product in another country. If this were not the case, there would be opportunities to make riskless profits by purchasing the product in the lower-priced country and selling it in the higher-priced country.

More formally, LOOP states that P_1^B, the price of Product 1 in Country B, should equal P_1^A, the price of the same product in Country A, times the spot exchange rate, $S_{B/A}$. Notice that the spot exchange rate is the value of Country A's currency in terms of Country B's currency (see Exhibit 22-1).

Consider a car sold in both the United States and England. LOOP states that the dollar price of that car in the United States should equal the pound price in England times the exchange rate. If the price in the United States were $40,000 and the price in England were £20,000, then the spot exchange rate

$EXHIBIT$ **22–1**	THE LAW OF ONE PRICE

$$\text{Price}_{\text{(Product 1 in Country B)}} = \text{Price}_{\text{(Product 1 in Country A)}} \times \text{Spot exchange rate}_{\text{(B/A)}}$$

$$P_1^B = P_1^A \times S_{B/A},$$

where $S_{B/A} \equiv$ Country B's currency/Country A's currency.

© John E. Marthinsen

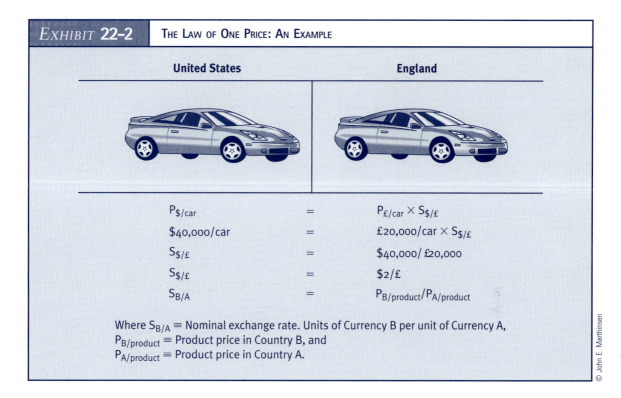

EXHIBIT 22-2   THE LAW OF ONE PRICE: AN EXAMPLE

United States   **England**

$P_{\$/car}$	=	$P_{£/car} \times S_{\$/£}$
$\$40,000/car$	=	$£20,000/car \times S_{\$/£}$
$S_{\$/£}$	=	$\$40,000/£20,000$
$S_{\$/£}$	=	$\$2/£$
$S_{B/A}$	=	$P_{B/product}/P_{A/product}$

Where $S_{B/A} \equiv$ Nominal exchange rate. Units of Currency B per unit of Currency A,
$P_{B/product} \equiv$ Product price in Country B, and
$P_{A/product} \equiv$ Product price in Country A.

© John E. Marthinsen

that equates $40,000 and £20,000 would be $2/£. If the exchange rate were different from $2/£, arbitrage could occur (see Exhibit 22-2).

One problem with LOOP is that the equilibrium exchange rate for Product 1 (e.g., automobiles) may be different from the equilibrium exchange rate for Product 2 (e.g., bracelets). In such cases, which is the equilibrium exchange rate for the nation? We will address this question in the next section where APPP is discussed.

ABSOLUTE PURCHASING POWER PARITY (APPP)

LOOP considers exchange rates on a product-by-product basis. But we know that exchange rates are affected by all traded goods and services. APPP calculates the equilibrium (no-arbitrage) exchange rate based on the price difference between identical baskets of tradable goods and services in two nations. The equilibrium exchange rate is the one that equates the price of these two baskets.

If the basket prices were different, there would be an opportunity to earn riskless profits by purchasing the basket in the lower-priced country and selling it in the higher-priced country.

Consider identical baskets of American and English goods and services. If the U.S. basket cost $6,000 and the English basket cost £3,000, then the exchange rate determined by APPP would be $2/£. The APPP exchange rate would be equal to the price of the U.S. basket divided by the price of the English basket (see Exhibit 22-3).

> According to APPP, arbitrage should equate the exchange rate–adjusted prices of identical baskets of goods and services (both in quantity and kind) among nations.

EXHIBIT 22-3   **ABSOLUTE PURCHASING POWER PARITY**

United States	England
Average U.S. Price Level	Average English Price Level

$$P_{\$/basket} = P_{£/basket} \times S_{\$/£}$$

$$\$6{,}000/basket = £3{,}000/basket \times S_{\$/£}$$

$$S_{\$/£} = \$6{,}000/£3{,}000$$

$$S_{\$/£} = \$2/£$$

$$S_{\$/£} = P_{\$/basket}/P_{£/basket}$$

$$S_{B/A} = P_{B/basket}/P_{A/basket}$$

where $S_{B/A} \equiv$ Nominal exchange rate. Units of Currency B per unit of Currency A,
$P_{B/basket} \equiv$ Price of Country B's tradable market basket, and
$P_{A/product} \equiv$ Price of Country A's tradable market basket.

© John E. Marthinsen

Is there a theoretical or practical reason why the LOOP exchange rate and APPP exchange rate should be the same? In fact, there is no reason for them to be equal, and furthermore there is every reason to believe they will be different because the APPP rate is a weighted average of the individual LOOP exchange rates.

RELATIVE PURCHASING POWER PARITY (RPPP)

APPP is the exchange rate that eliminates arbitrage incentives for identical baskets of goods and services *at a point in time*. RPPP is the *percentage change* in an exchange rate that is needed to offset international inflation differentials. It is important to remember that RPPP does not show the absolute exchange rate that is needed to equate the prices of identical market baskets in two nations. This point will be made clearer shortly.

> RPPP estimates the change in exchange rates based on relative inflation rates.

Suppose the current spot exchange rate is $2/£, and during the upcoming year, the inflation rate is expected to be 15% in the United States and 10% in England (see Exhibit 22-4). Therefore, a U.S. basket of goods and services with a normalized price of $2.00 this year is expected to cost 15% more next year; the same basket in England with a normalized price of £1 this year is expected to cost 10% more next year. Given this information, what exchange rate next year would offset the inflation differential?

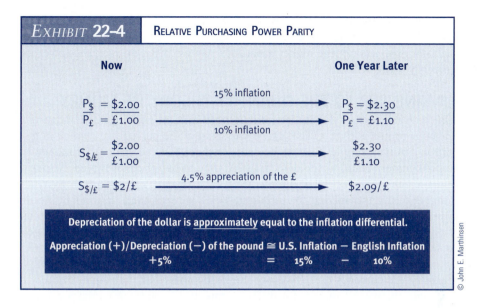

EXHIBIT 22-4   **RELATIVE PURCHASING POWER PARITY**

Now

One Year Later

15% inflation

$P_\$ = \$2.00$ ⟶ $P_\$ = \$2.30$
$P_£ = £1.00$ ⟶ $P_£ = £1.10$

10% inflation

$S_{\$/£} = \dfrac{\$2.00}{£1.00}$ ⟶ $\dfrac{\$2.30}{£1.10}$

4.5% appreciation of the £

$S_{\$/£} = \$2/£$ ⟶ $\$2.09/£$

Depreciation of the dollar is **approximately** equal to the inflation differential.

Appreciation (+)/Depreciation (−) of the pound ≅ U.S. Inflation − English Inflation
+5%   =   15%   −   10%

© John E. Marthinsen

With a 15% inflation rate, U.S. products worth $2.00 today would cost $2.30 next year ($2.00 × 1.15 = $2.30). And with a 10% inflation rate, English products worth £1 today would cost £1.10 next year (£1.00 × 1.1 = £1.10). To offset the inflation differential, the exchange rate next year has to equate the U.S. basket costing $2.30 and the English basket costing £1.10. To calculate this rate, we divide the expected U.S. price next year by the counterpart English price level to get $2.09/£, which is a 4.5% appreciation of the pound (see Exhibit 22-4).[1]

Notice that England's inflation rate is 5% lower than the U.S. inflation rate, and this inflation differential causes the pound to appreciate by 4.5%, which is *approximately* 5%. As a general rule, RPPP tells us that, when inflation rate changes are small, the percentage change in the value of two countries' currencies should be *approximately equal* to the difference in their inflation rates (see Exhibit 22-5).

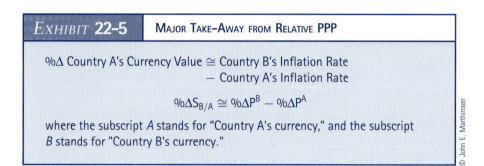

EXHIBIT 22-5   **MAJOR TAKE-AWAY FROM RELATIVE PPP**

%Δ Country A's Currency Value ≅ Country B's Inflation Rate
                                    − Country A's Inflation Rate

$$\%\Delta S_{B/A} \cong \%\Delta P^B - \%\Delta P^A$$

where the subscript *A* stands for "Country A's currency," and the subscript *B* stands for "Country B's currency."

© John E. Marthinsen

[1] $2.30/£1.10 = $2.09/£, which is a 4.5% appreciation of the pound from $2/£. At the same time, this is equivalent to a 4.3% depreciation of the U.S. dollar because the dollar would change in value from £0.50/$ to £0.478/$.

There are two major take-aways from RPPP. First, long-run changes in a nation's currency value depend on the country's inflation rate relative to foreign nations. Second, the higher a nation's relative inflation rate, the lower its currency value will fall.

LINKING PPP TO THE QUANTITY THEORY OF MONEY

One way to improve our understanding of long-term exchange rate movements is to link PPP to QTM. QTM shows how the percentage change in a nation's money supply plus the percentage change in the velocity of money is approximately equal to the percentage change in the price level plus the percentage change in real GDP (i.e., $\%\Delta M2 + \%\Delta V_2 \cong \%\Delta P + \%\Delta Q$). By rearranging terms and solving for inflation, $\%\Delta P$, we see that a nation's inflation rate is approximately equal to the percentage change in its money supply plus the percentage change in the velocity of money *minus* the percentage change in real GDP ($\%\Delta P \cong \%\Delta M2 + \%\Delta V_2 - \%\Delta Q$) (see Line 1 in Exhibit 22-6).

RPPP states that, in the long run, the percentage change in the value of Country A's currency (i.e., $\%\Delta S_{B/A}$) should be approximately equal to the difference between Country B's inflation rate and Country A's inflation rate (i.e., $\%\Delta S_{B/A} \cong \%\Delta P^B - \%\Delta P^A$) (see Line 2 in Exhibit 22-6).

If Country A's inflation rate, $\%\Delta P^A$, is equal to $\%\Delta M2^A + \%\Delta V_2^A - \%\Delta Q^A$, and Country B's inflation rate, $\%\Delta P^B$, is equal to $\%\Delta M2^B + \%\Delta V_2^B - \%\Delta Q^B$, then

$$\%\Delta S_{B/A} \cong (\%\Delta M2^B + \%\Delta V_2^B - \%\Delta Q^B) - (\%\Delta M2^A + \%\Delta V_2^A - \%\Delta Q^A).$$

Rearranging terms, we can conclude that

$$\%\Delta S_{B/A} \cong (\%\Delta M2^B - \%\Delta M2^A) + (\%\Delta V_2^B - \%\Delta V_2^A) - (\%\Delta Q^B - \%\Delta Q^A):$$

Therefore, the percentage change in Country A's currency value should equal the percentage difference between Country B's and Country A's money supply growth rate, plus the percentage difference between their velocity growth rates, *minus* the percentage difference between their real GDP growth rates (see Exhibit 22-6).

$E\textsc{xhibit}$ **22-6**	**LINKING PPP TO QTM**

QTM: $\%\Delta P \cong \%\Delta M2 + \%\Delta V_2 - \%\Delta Q$

Relative PPP: $\%\Delta S_{B/A} \cong \%\Delta P^B - \%\Delta P^A$

Linking Relative PPP and QTM:

$\%\Delta S_{B/A} \cong \%\Delta P^B - \%\Delta P^A$

$\%\Delta S_{B/A} \cong (\%\Delta M2^B + \%\Delta V_2^B - \%\Delta Q^B) - (\%\Delta M2^A + \%\Delta V_2^A - \%\Delta Q^A)$

$\%\Delta S_{B/A} = (\%\Delta M2^B - \%\Delta M2^A) + (\%\Delta V_2^B - \%\Delta V_2^A) - (\%\Delta Q^B - \%\Delta Q^A)$

An example helps cement this relationship. Suppose that, during 2014, the Mexican and U.S. M2 money supplies grew at 4% and 2%, respectively; their M2 velocities changed by +1.5% and −0.5%, respectively, and their real GDPs grew by 1% and 3%, respectively. Even though PPP is not a particularly good short-term predictor of exchange rates,[2] let's see what estimate it gives us for the peso per dollar exchange rate.

$$\%\Delta S_{peso/dollar} \cong (\%\Delta M2^{MEX} - \%\Delta M2^{USA}) + (\%\Delta V_2^{MEX} - \%\Delta V_2^{USA}) - (\%\Delta Q^{USA} - \%\Delta Q^{MEX})$$

$$= (4\% - 2\%) + [1.5\% - (-0.5\%)] - (1\% - 3\%) = 6\%.$$

Therefore, if the dollar was worth Ps 12.5 at the beginning of 2014, LOOP-QTM forecasts a rate, at year's end, of (approximately) Ps 13.25/$.

Using the United States and Mexico as examples, the value of the U.S. dollar, $S_{Ps/\$}$, should appreciate whenever Mexico's money supply and/or money velocity grows relatively faster than in the United States and/or whenever Mexico's real GDP grows relatively slower than U.S. real GDP. Of course, any time the dollar appreciates in terms of the peso, the peso must depreciate in terms of the U.S. dollar.

COMPARATIVE ADVANTAGE

Why do countries trade the goods and services they do? For nations that can produce anything, why do they tend to specialize in only certain products? Do the gains that one country derives from international trade come at the expense of other nations? One of the most insightful economic concepts to help answer such questions is *comparative advantage*, which convincingly shows us how free trade can create net gains for participants, regardless of their absolute levels of productivity.

For business managers, understanding the concept of comparative advantage is essential for two reasons. First, it is a helpful framework for analyzing changes in long-term international trade and production patterns. Therefore, comparative advantage should be a part of every business manager's scenario-planning toolkit. Second, comparative advantage highlights an important way in which countries differ from companies. In particular, the reaction of a company to improvements in competitors' productivity levels should be quite different from a country's reaction to improvements in its major trading partners' productivity gains.

Let's begin this section by taking a closer look at the concept of comparative advantage and, afterwards, explain the major ways in which countries are different from companies.

WHAT IS COMPARATIVE ADVANTAGE?

The U.S. Bureau of Census uses the North American Industrial Classification (NAICS, pronounced "Nakes") to categorize exports and imports. There are thousands of codes for imports and exports, and for each particular industry,

---

[2] This issue is discussed in "The Rest of the Story" section of this chapter.

there are likely as many different reasons for why trade takes place. For instance, trade relationships could be based on factors such as cost, quality, productivity, personal friendships, patents, chance meetings, language preferences, cultural similarities, or climate. Comparative advantage focuses on one major reason for trade and trade patterns, namely relative differences in international productivity.

Let's use two hypothetical countries, Inland and Outland, to understand how relative productivity differences influence international trade. Suppose Inland is a highly developed nation with the latest technologies and highest worldwide living standards. By contrast, Outland is among the least developed nations in the world, using primitive technologies and having extremely low living standards. A constant lament among Inland businesses is that they cannot compete against Outland's extremely low resource costs (e.g., wages). At the same time, businesses in Outland complain that they cannot compete against Inland's advanced technologies.

ABSOLUTE ADVANTAGE

Suppose the average worker in Inland could produce 1,000 high-tech products per day *or* 200 units of clothing. In Outland, the average worker could produce 100 high-tech products per day or 100 units of clothing (see Exhibit 22-7). Given these conditions, which country should produce and export high-tech products and which one should produce and export clothing? On the surface, it appears as if Outland has no chance competing against Inland in either product because Inland has an *absolute advantage* (i.e., absolute productivity advantage) in both products. An absolute advantage exists when the resources in one country can produce absolutely more products per time period than the resources in another country.

Is absolute advantage the basis for international trade? If it is, then Outland is in real trouble. Under these circumstances, what alternatives would Outland have? Countries don't go out of business: so does this mean that Outland should close its borders and protect domestic industries by imposing tariffs and quotas on foreign imports? Let's take a closer look at the causes of trade, but this time, we will use comparative advantage (not absolute advantage) as our guide.

OPPORTUNITY COSTS AND COMPARATIVE ADVANTAGE

For Inland, employing a worker in the high-tech industry means that he or she is not working in the clothing industry. Therefore, the *opportunity cost* of producing 1,000 high-tech products per day is the sacrifice of 200 units of

> **Absolute advantage exists when the resources in one country can produce absolutely more products per time period than the resources in another country.**

> **Absolute advantage is not a good explanation for why trade between nations occurs. Comparative advantage offers a better explanation.**

EXHIBIT 22-7	OUTPUT PER WORKER PER DAY IN INLAND AND OUTLAND	
	HIGH-TECH PRODUCTS PER DAY	**CLOTHING PER DAY**
Inland	1,000	200
Outland	100	100

© John E. Marthinsen

EXHIBIT 22-8	OPPORTUNITY COSTS FOR INLAND AND OUTLAND	
	1 HIGH–TECH PRODUCT COSTS	**1 UNIT OF CLOTHING COSTS**
Inland	0.20 units of clothing	5 high-tech products
Outland	1 unit of clothing	1 high-tech product

© John E. Marthinsen

clothing. On a standardized basis, this means that one high-tech product in Inland costs 0.20 clothing units (i.e., 200 clothing units/1,000 high-tech goods = 0.20 clothing units/high-tech good). Alternatively, expressing costs in terms of high-tech products, it means that the cost of producing one clothing unit is the sacrifice of five high-tech products (i.e., 1,000 high-tech goods/200 clothing units = 5 high-tech goods/clothing unit). See Exhibit 22-8.

In Outland, the cost of producing 100 units of high-tech products is the sacrifice of 100 units of clothing. Therefore, on a standardized basis, one high-tech product costs one clothing unit, and one unit of clothing costs one high-tech product (see Exhibit 22-8).

Based on opportunity costs, Inland is the low-cost producer of high-tech products because it gives up only 0.20 clothing units to produce one high-tech product, as compared with Outland, which sacrifices one clothing unit. At the same time, Outland is the low-cost producer of clothing because it sacrifices only one high-tech product to produce a unit of clothing. It costs Inland five high-tech products to get the same clothing unit. Because Inland's opportunity cost for producing high-tech products is lower than Outland's, Inland is said to have a *comparative advantage* in high-tech products. Similarly, Outland has a comparative advantage in clothing because its opportunity cost is lower than Inland's opportunity cost.

Exhibit 22-9 shows the range of opportunity costs between Inland's and Outland's domestic trade-offs. Notice in Column 2 how Inland's opportunity cost for high-tech products (0.20-to-1) is lower than Outland's cost (1-to-1), and notice in Column 4 how Outland's opportunity cost for clothing (1-to-1) is lower than Inland's cost (5-to-1). For trade to benefit both nations, Inland should produce high-tech products and trade them for clothing with Outland. At the same time, Outland should produce clothing and trade it with Inland for high-tech products.

MUTUALLY ADVANTAGEOUS TRADE BETWEEN INLAND AND OUTLAND

Mutually advantageous trade between Inland and Outland occurs at *any trading ratio* between the two extremes (i.e., anywhere between the two domestic opportunity costs in Exhibit 22-9). At the same time, the closer this *trading ratio* is to Inland's domestic trading ratio, the less Inland benefits and the more Outland benefits. The closer the trading ratio is to Outland's domestic trading ratio, the less Outland benefits and the more Inland benefits. Let's use an example to show why both countries gain at a trading ratio between the two extremes.

> Opportunity cost is the amount of Product A sacrificed to produce Product B.

> A country has a comparative advantage in the production of a good or service if its opportunity cost to produce that product is lower than in another country.

> Mutually advantageous trade takes place at any trading ratio between two nations' domestic opportunity costs.

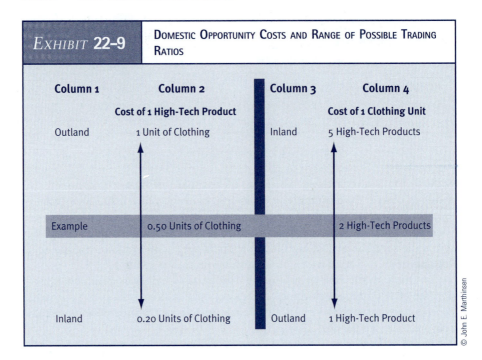

	Column 1	Column 2	Column 3	Column 4
		Cost of 1 High-Tech Product		**Cost of 1 Clothing Unit**
	Outland	1 Unit of Clothing	Inland	5 High-Tech Products
Example		0.50 Units of Clothing		2 High-Tech Products
	Inland	0.20 Units of Clothing	Outland	1 High-Tech Product

EXHIBIT **22-9**   DOMESTIC OPPORTUNITY COSTS AND RANGE OF POSSIBLE TRADING RATIOS

© John E. Marthinsen

Suppose the trading ratio was two high-tech products for one unit of clothing, which also means that 0.50 units of clothing can be exchanged for each high-tech product. First, let's focus on the 2-to-1 trading ratio to see why both countries benefit. At the 2-to-1 trading ratio, Inland benefits because it gets one unit of clothing by trading two high-tech products instead of it costing five high-tech units at home. Outland also benefits because it gets two high-tech products for each clothing unit it trades with Inland. At home, Outland would get only one high-tech product for each unit of clothing.

The same point can be made by focusing on the trading ratio of 0.50 clothing units per high-tech product. Inland benefits because it gets 0.50 clothing units for each high-tech product it trades, instead of getting only 0.20 clothing units at home. Outland also benefits from this trading ratio because it gets one high-tech product by trading only 0.50 units of clothing, instead of it costing one unit of clothing at home.

TRADING RATIOS OUTSIDE THE EXTREMES

Trade between Inland and Outland will not take place at a trading ratio that is outside the range of domestic opportunity costs because, at this rate, both countries would want to produce and export the same product. For example, at a trading ratio of 10 high-tech products per clothing unit, both countries would want to produce and export clothing. Inland would want to do so because it would get 10 high-tech products for each clothing unit traded instead of the 5 high-tech products it would get at home. Similarly, Outland would want to produce clothing because it would get 10 high-tech products for each unit of clothing traded instead of the one unit it would get by producing high-tech products domestically.

If the trading ratio were outside the extremes set by nations' domestic opportunity costs, both countries would want to produce and export the same product.

But if both countries wanted to produce and export clothing, what would happen? With two sellers and no buyers at the 10-to-1 ratio, clothing would flood the market, thereby lowering the trading ratio to within the 5-to-1 and 1-to-1 range.

Similar reasoning can be used if the trading ratio was below the range of opportunity costs. For example, suppose the trading ratio was 0.5 high-tech products per unit of clothing. Under these circumstances, both countries would want to produce and export high-tech products. Inland would want to do so because it could get one unit of clothing by trading only 0.5 high-tech products. Producing them at home would cost five high-tech products. At the same time, Outland would want to produce and export high-tech products because it could get one clothing unit for only 0.5 high-tech products traded instead of costing one high-tech product at home.

MUTUALLY ADVANTAGEOUS TRADE AND RESOURCE COSTS

For mutually advantageous trade to take place, Inland and Outland must also have relative resource costs that are within certain bounds, and these bounds are determined by the two nations' *relative* production levels. Inland's high-tech productivity per worker is 10 times higher than Outland's (i.e., 1,000 vs. 100 high-tech products), and its clothing productivity is two times higher than Outland's (i.e., 200 vs. 100 clothing units). Therefore, resource costs in Inland must be no less than 2 times higher than in Outland and no more than 10 times higher than in Outland.

Suppose Inland's resource costs were five times higher than in Outland, with Inland's resources earning $100 per day and Outland's resources earning $20 per day. Exhibit 22-10 shows that, at these relative resource costs, high-tech products would be cheaper in Inland ($0.10/unit) than in Outland ($0.20/unit), and clothing would be cheaper in Outland ($0.20/unit) than in Inland ($0.50/unit).

If the costs of these nations' resources were anywhere outside the limits of 2-to-1 and 10-to-1, they would trump comparative advantage and prevent trade from taking place. Exhibit 22-11 shows what would happen if resource costs in Inland equaled Outland's resource costs, causing the ratio of labor costs to be 1-to-1, which is outside the mutually advantageous trading limits. If resource costs in both countries were $100 per day, Inland could produce and sell both products cheaper than Outland. High-tech products would cost $0.10 per unit in Inland compared with $1 in Outland, and clothing would cost $0.50 per unit in Inland compared with $1 in Outland.

> Mutually advantageous trade requires relative international resource costs that do not offset relative international productivity differences.

*E*XHIBIT **22-10**	DOLLAR COST OF HIGH-TECH PRODUCTS AND CLOTHING

(Inland's resources earn $100/day, and Outland's resources earn $20 per day)

	COST OF HIGH-TECH PRODUCTS	COST OF CLOTHING
Inland	$100 per 1,000 units → $0.10/unit	$100 per 200 units → $0.50/unit
Outland	$20 per 100 units → $0.20/unit	$20 per 100 units → $0.20/unit

© John E. Marthinsen

EXHIBIT 22-11	DOLLAR COST OF HIGH-TECH PRODUCTS AND CLOTHING	
(Inland's resources earn $100/day, and Outland's resources earn $100 per day)		
	COST OF HIGH-TECH PRODUCTS	COST OF CLOTHING
Inland	$100 per 1,000 units → $0.10/unit	$100 per 200 units → $0.50/unit
Outland	$100 per 100 units → $1.00/unit	$100 per 100 units → $1.00/unit

© John E. Marthinsen

What would happen if, by chance, relative resource costs were equal (as in Exhibit 22-11 at $100 per day) and both products were cheaper in Inland? Market forces should take over and solve the problem. As unemployment in Outland rose, its resource costs would fall, thereby making it more competitive with Inland. As the demand for Inland's products rose, so would the demand for resources, causing resource costs to rise and making Inland less competitive relative to Outland. Finally, the increased demand for Inland's currency would appreciate its value, thereby making Inland's products relatively more expensive.

> **If a nation's relative resource costs were so high that they nullified international trade, automatic adjustments in resources costs and exchange rates should remedy the imbalance.**

COMPARATIVE ADVANTAGE: KEY TAKE-AWAYS

Our examples explained comparative advantage using only two countries producing two products at constant costs. The real world is much more complex, with many countries producing many products—some at increasing costs, others at constant costs, and still others at decreasing costs. Nevertheless, the conclusions regarding comparative advantage are essentially the same:

- First, international trade does not depend on nations' absolute levels of productivity. Rather, it depends on relative international opportunity costs. As a result, a nation should be able to compete internationally even if it has an absolute productivity disadvantage relative to every other country in the world and for every possible product sold. And the likelihood of two countries having exactly the same opportunity costs for all products is miniscule (i.e., nearly impossible).
- Second, insisting that the resources (e.g., workers) earn the same level of compensation (e.g., wages) in all nations is counterproductive because it negates nations' comparative advantages and takes away the mutual benefits that come from trade.
- Finally, international trade provides net benefits to all nations, but within each country, some groups are hurt while others are helped. For example, export industries benefit at the expense of the import-competing industries because demand for exports rises, but demand for import-competing products falls. Similarly, the relatively abundant resources in each country benefit at the expense of the relatively scarce resources because the net demand for the abundant resource rises and the net demand for the scarce resource falls. Nevertheless, the net effect on each nation is still positive.

THE REST OF THE STORY

HOW WELL DOES PPP PREDICT EXCHANGE RATES?

There is an old aphorism that says, "If you want to make a small fortune in the currency markets, use PPP to forecast your exchange rates. But to make this small fortune, you have to start with a large one." Like many old sayings, this one provides a valuable lesson.

CRITERIA FOR EVALUATING PPP'S EFFECTIVENESS

There are three standard ways to measure the accuracy of PPP exchange rate predictions. One is to compare how close the PPP-estimated exchange rates were to the actual spot exchange rates. Another is to determine how often actual exchange rates moved in the direction of PPP-predicted rates, and finally, accuracy can be evaluated by how often actual exchange rates were within a narrow band of the PPP-predicted values (e.g., two standard deviations).

How Close Were PPP Rates to Actual Exchange Rates?

In the short term, there are large and persistent deviations between the exchange rates predicted by PPP and the rates that eventually occur. Nevertheless, the predictive abilities of PPP improve dramatically in the long run. Therefore, PPP can be a useful tool for anyone preparing 10- to 20-year scenario plans.

    The short-term predictive abilities of PPP also improve dramatically when the two nations under consideration have high inflation rates. In these situations, changes in relative prices overwhelm the other forces that affect nominal exchange rates. Therefore when inflation is high, PPP can provide useful inputs for short-term budgets and business plans.

> High inflation rates and long periods of time improve the predictive powers of PPP.

Did Actual Exchange Rates Move in the Direction of PPP Rates?

In the short run, exchange rates do not converge quickly to the rates predicted by PPP, but they do converge in the long run. PPP rates are like huge economic magnets that attract exchange rates with a subtle but steady force. Over time, this force of attraction exerts its influence. Therefore, the farther away an exchange rate is from its parity rate, the more likely it is that the next currency movement will be in the direction of the PPP-predicted rate. Similarly, the more times an exchange rate moves away from PPP, the more likely it is that the next change will be closer to parity. For these reasons, PPP is much better at predicting the direction in which exchange rates move than predicting actual exchange rate levels.

> With time, exchange rates converge toward PPP rates.

How Often Were Exchange Rates within a Narrow Band of PPP?

Maybe we are requiring too much from PPP. No estimate is expected to be exact. Statisticians realize this and often put two standard deviations of variation around their estimates for 95% accuracy. If we put a two-standard-deviation band around the PPP forecasts, their predictive powers would look relatively good. More concisely stated, parity rates with some room for random fluctuations tend to predict a relatively large number of actual exchange rate observations. As you might expect, the wider the band, the more accurate the PPP forecasts appear. Exhibit 22-12 provides a

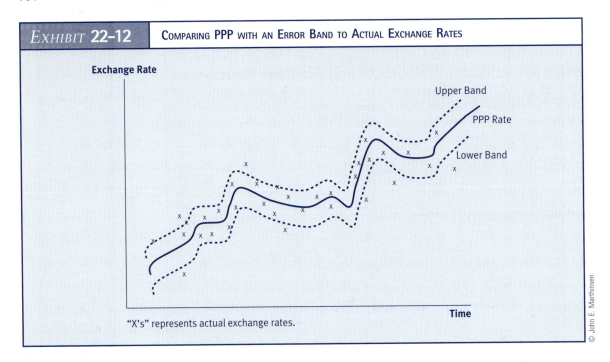

EXHIBIT 22-12   COMPARING PPP WITH AN ERROR BAND TO ACTUAL EXCHANGE RATES

Exchange Rate

Upper Band

PPP Rate

Lower Band

"X's" represents actual exchange rates.

Time

© John E. Marthinsen

hypothetical example of how a small band of tolerated errors can improve the appearance of PPP's results.

PREDICTIVE POWERS OF RPPP VERSUS APPP

The predictive powers of PPP improve if it is judged based on a confidence interval around the estimated values.

In general, the predictive abilities of RPPP tend to be better than APPP. One of the major reasons for the difference is because APPP calculates the exchange rate that exactly matches the prices of identical product baskets in two countries. RPPP shows only the change in exchange rate that is necessary to offset two nations' relative inflation differences. To calculate meaningful results using RPPP, exchange rates do not have to start or end with APPP. By contrast, meaningful APPP results require exchange rates to equate the prices of international market baskets both at the beginning *and* the end of the period.

RPPP is better at predicting exchange rates than APPP.

WHY ARE PPP-FORECASTED RATES OFTEN INACCURATE?

"How can something so logical be so wrong? If exchange rates are out of line with PPP levels, then why don't arbitrageurs earn riskless profits and bring them back into alignment?" These are the questions that many people ask when they learn about the lackluster predictive powers of PPP.

Different Market Baskets, Different Proportions, and Nontraded Goods and Services

PPP rates can be inaccurate if the international product baskets are not identical or consumption patterns differ.

One reason arbitrage may not occur is because PPP rates are estimated using representative market baskets of goods and services for two nations. The contents of the market baskets may be the same, but the basket values may differ because the residents of each country have different consumption preferences and patterns. For example, the average U.S. resident drinks more dairy products, uses more fragrances, and eats more meat than the average Japanese resident.

Furthermore, even if the market baskets were the same and the proportions were equal, only a portion of the goods and services in each nation's market basket is actually traded. Therefore, the Consumer Price Index, Producer Price Index, and GDP Price Index are too broad for an accurate PPP forecast. What PPP needs is a pure basket of internationally traded products that remains the same during long periods of time. Unfortunately, such a basket does not exist.

PPP rates can be inaccurate because there are products in the market basket that are not traded.

Government Restrictions and Transport Costs

Another reason PPP rates are often inaccurate is because government restrictions, such as tariffs and quotas, prevent or constrain arbitrageurs. In addition, transportation costs cut potential profits on many arbitrage transactions and open unarbitrageable price gaps.[3]

PPP rates can be inaccurate when there are trade restrictions or transport costs.

Capital Flows and Central Bank Intervention

A final reason PPP rates are inaccurate is because exchange rates are set by more than just trade flows. We know from our discussion about exchange rate determination that international capital flows and central bank intervention can have significant effects on exchange rates (see Chapter 15, "Exchange Rates: Why Do They Change?"). It is rather presumptuous to expect trade flows alone to account for every exchange rate movement. This is especially true when there are significant international capital flows or when central banks manage their exchange rates. In these situations, it may be difficult or impossible for exchange rates to mirror relative price changes.

PPP rates can be inaccurate due to significant capital flows and central bank intervention(s).

All the aforementioned reasons for why PPP might provide inaccurate estimates of equilibrium exchange rates are summarized in Exhibit 22-13.

Exhibit **22-13**	**Why PPP-Predicated Rates May Be Inaccurate**

1. Market basket and price index problems
   a.   Different market baskets in two countries
   b.   Different consumption patterns in two countries
   c.   What index? CPI? PPI? GDP Price Index?
   d.   Nontraded goods and services
2. Government restrictions and transportation costs
   a.   Tariffs and quotas
   b.   Transportation costs reduce arbitrage profits
3. Exchange rates are not set by trade flows alone
   a.   Capital flows must be considered
   b.   Central bank intervention must be considered

© John E. Marthinsen

---

[3] Transportation costs may not drive a significant wedge between the exchange rate–adjusted prices of Country A and Country B. Here's why. Consider a third country—call it Country C—that is equal distance from Country A and Country B. Country C would have to pay transportation costs regardless of whether it bought from Country A or Country B. Therefore, Country C would buy from the country that had the lower price, and it would be indifferent only when the prices (before transportation costs) in Country A and Country B were equal. Such purchases help to equate Country A's and Country B's prices.

SUMMARY OF PPP

Let's summarize some of the most important lessons from our discussion about PPP. First, APPP is used to predict the nominal exchange rate that equates the prices of identical baskets of goods and services in two nations. RPPP is used to measure percentage changes in exchange rates for these baskets. Second, the longer the period of time and the higher the inflation rate, the more accurate PPP is at predicting future exchange rates. Similarly, the longer the period analyzed, the more likely it is that exchange rates will converge toward the predicted PPP levels. Finally, PPP is much better at predicting the direction of exchange rate changes than it is at predicting their exact levels.

A COUNTRY IS NOT A COMPANY

Transparency, fairness, stability, and predictability are a few of the common characteristics shared by successful companies and countries, but the principles that make companies efficient and profitable are not always the same as those that make healthy and prosperous countries. CEOs, division heads, and company directors do not (and should not) use the same rules of thumb and economic logic as public officials. Central bankers and finance ministers do not (and should not) think in the same ways as CFOs. Appreciating the differences between the economic reasoning applied to companies and the reasoning applied to countries is an important part of economic literacy. Let's look at a few of the most important dissimilarities between companies and countries.[4]

DIFFERENCES IN CUSTOMERS AND SUPPLIERS

Most companies sell only a tiny fraction (if any) of the products they make to their own employees, and they also produce only a small fraction of their own ingredient needs. By contrast, countries sell the vast majority of what they produce to domestic residents, and they source huge amounts internally. For example in 2012, 86% of all U.S. production was sold to domestic residents, and 83% of the nation's production needs were produced internally.[5] Few, if any, important U.S. companies came anywhere close to these national levels. Clearly, the external world is important to the United States, but domestic demand and supply are far more crucial. For most companies, just the opposite is true (i.e., external sales and sourcing are more important than internal sales and sourcing).

> Countries consume most of what they produce and source mainly from internal suppliers. Companies do exactly the opposite.

EFFECTS OF INCREASED PRODUCTIVITY

Companies in the same industry, like Ford and General Motors, are competitors, which means the success of one often comes at the expense of the other. If

---

[4] See Paul Krugman, "A Country Is Not a Company," *Harvard Business Review*, January February 1996, product number 96108; Paul Krugman, *Pop Internationalism* (Cambridge, MA: MIT Press, 1996).

[5] In 2012, U.S. exports were about 14% of GDP, and U.S. imports were about 17% of GDP. Euromonitor International from International Monetary Fund (IMF), *International Financial Statistics*, http://www.euromonitor.com/ (accessed August 27, 2013).

Ford's productivity increases, it expects to be rewarded in the marketplace by earning higher profits. But these rewards usually materialize only if Ford's productivity is greater than General Motors'. For example, if Ford's productivity grew by 2% but General Motor's productivity grew by 8%, then Ford would be at a competitive disadvantage. The company's profitability could suffer, layoffs could result, its stock price could fall, and acquisition vultures would soon begin to circle Ford's corporate headquarters in Dearborn, Michigan.

By contrast, increased productivity at the country level is beneficial, regardless of whether it is greater than, less than, or equal to other nations. Greater productivity means there is more for everyone to share. Unlike Ford and GM, which compete vigorously with each other and sell most of what they produce to third parties, countries are each other's major suppliers and major customers. When countries on Earth produce more, then the people on Earth have more to consume. To date, Earth has not had to compete with any foreign planets.

> A country benefits with any foreign nation's productivity gains. Companies benefit mainly when their productivity improves relative to competitors'.

If U.S. productivity grew by 2% and China's productivity grew by 8%, both nations and the world would benefit. China would gain because rising real output would improve its living standards. The United States would also benefit from its own 2% growth because most of the newly produced goods and services would be consumed by U.S. residents. But the United States would also benefit from China's growth. U.S. consumers would gain because the increased availability of Chinese products should reduce their prices. U.S. producers would gain because rising Chinese GDP would increase the nation's income, making China a better customer for U.S. products.

EFFECTS OF SALES GROWTH ON EMPLOYMENT

When companies increase top-line sales revenues, they normally employ more labor. Therefore, growth in companies' sales volume usually means growth in head count. This relationship is much weaker at the country level and even weaker at the global level. At the global level, the main effect of free trade is to redistribute production from where it is currently located to the most efficient locations. It does not necessarily increase worldwide employment because many of the jobs created in net export nations are lost in net import nations. For world employment to grow, trade would have to increase worldwide demand.

> The major effect of free international trade is to increase global output rather than increase worldwide employment. By contrast, when a company increases third-party sales, it usually increases employment.

One avenue through which trade could stimulate demand and increase employment is via its effect on world income. As free trade increases global production, it increases world income, and rising world income stimulates demand. Clearly, if the world were at full employment prior to trade liberalization, this increased demand would not (and could not) increase employment.

At the country level, free trade boosts demand in net export nations, but these increases are likely to be small. Empirical evidence supports this conclusion. Exhibit 22-14 shows the relationship between the net-export-to-GDP ratios and unemployment rates of more than 52 countries. The randomly scattered points indicate that no strong linear relationship exists between net exports and unemployment.

One reason for the loose relationship between net exports and unemployment is because nations employ monetary and fiscal policies to offset undesired changes in demand. For example, if global demand for U.S. goods

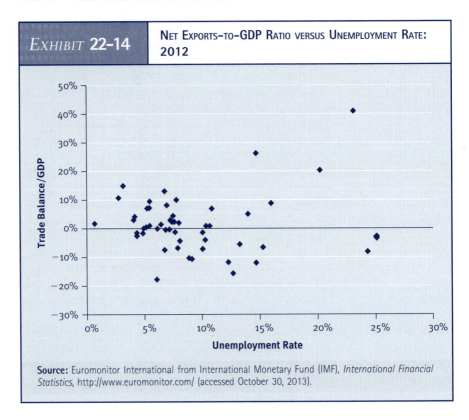

| EXHIBIT 22-14 | NET EXPORTS–TO–GDP RATIO VERSUS UNEMPLOYMENT RATE: 2012 |

Source: Euromonitor International from International Monetary Fund (IMF), *International Financial Statistics*, http://www.euromonitor.com/ (accessed October 30, 2013).

and services plunged, causing net exports to fall and unemployment to rise, both monetary and fiscal authorities would respond with expansionary policies. Similarly, if foreign demand for U.S. products rose, causing inflation to rise too rapidly, monetary and fiscal authorities would respond by tightening their policies.

DIFFERENCES IN PRICE AND EMPLOYMENT GOALS

Companies tightly monitor their employee head counts in order to control costs, and they hire and fire based on profitability considerations. No company has the goal of providing employment to anyone who is unemployed and actively seeking work. Moreover, just because a company increases employment does not mean that it can raise prices. Nor does it mean that just because a company releases workers that it has to lower prices. Prices are set by market forces and not by company head count changes.

Things are different at the national level. Many countries have full-employment targets and try to provide meaningful employment to anyone who is unemployed and actively seeking work. In fact, they adjust their monetary and fiscal policies to achieve these employment goals.

At the national level, there is often a short-term inverse relationship between inflation and unemployment. We know this inverse relationship as the *Phillips curve* trade-off. Nothing comparable to this exists at the company level.

Countries face short-term Phillips curve trade-offs between inflation and unemployment. Companies do not.

Employment in Open versus Closed Systems

Companies are open systems, and countries are closed systems. Open systems place no binding constraints on the ability of companies to grow. They can hire workers to expand old lines of business and/or develop new ones, without worrying about the new lines encroaching on the old ones. Closed systems are different because they face binding constraints, such as fixed amounts of arable land and limited workforce populations. Once a country reaches full employment, it is impossible to expand all existing lines of business, and new lines of business can be pursued only by reducing old lines.

Suppose a company produced a very popular product, borrowed liberally to finance expansion by investing in new plant and equipment, and increased its capacity by 20%. What should happen to the company's top-line sales volume, employment, and profits? The answer (in all likelihood) is sales volume, employment, and profits would grow. If this is true, then is the same true for a country? What should happen to the net exports of a nation that borrows liberally from foreign nations and invests the funds in new plant and equipment? We know from our balance of payments discussion that new exports (a country's equivalent of top sales volume) *must fall* because current international transactions plus net international borrowing/lending must equal zero.[6] In this case, net international borrowing/lending is a plus item in the balance of payments, which means current international transactions (mainly net exports) must be minus. Therefore, countries that are net international borrowers are not the ones with current account surpluses. By contrast, companies that are net borrowers can simultaneously increase third-party sales.

> Companies are open systems, and countries are closed systems.

Countries Have Currencies

Even though there are nations that have given up their domestic currencies for a common currency (e.g., EMU) or that of another country (Panama), most countries still have their own currencies. When global demand for a nation's products drops, so does the demand for its currency, causing the currency to depreciate. Such depreciations reduce the effective price of a nation's goods and services and increases demand for them. Countries have currencies that can depreciate (or appreciate); there is no equivalent among companies.

> Most countries have their own currencies; companies do not.

Making Economic Policies

The level of diversification a company pursues is a strategic decision made by top management. A company's chief executive officer, management team, and board of directors can choose to engage in numerous activities, streamline multiple lines into one, or select an intermediate structure. In contrast, countries have thousands of business lines and far more subactivities. Imagine how difficult it would be to make strategic and operating decisions for a company with thousands of divisions, each having thousands of business units. For this

> Companies have relatively narrow strategic interests compared with countries because countries must consider the well-being of widely diverse industries and well-being and demands of a much larger and more diverse group of "customers."

---

[6] Chapter 16, "Balance of Payments Fundamentals," explains, in detail, how the balance of payments is like a sources and uses of funds statement and the necessitous relationship between current international transactions and net international borrowing/lending.

reason, strategic planning at the national level has an entirely different meaning from strategic planning at the company level.

Hands-On versus Hands-Off Strategies

Businesses function best when important operating and strategic decisions are closely managed, directed, and monitored by top management (i.e., the CEO, executive committee, and board of directors). It is for this reason that annual budgets, business plans, and capital budgeting analyses are used for making short-term decisions, and scenario plans are used for making long-term decisions.

By contrast, economies seem to function best when their markets are free to operate without burdensome central government (i.e., top management, so to speak) supervision, control, and intervention. During the twentieth century and now into the twenty-first century, many countries have tried to use *industrial policies*[7] for purposes such as promoting research and development, improving economic conditions, enhancing company performance, and helping industries adapt to changing economic conditions.

The final verdict is still out, but in general, industrial policy disappointments have far outnumbered successes. For example, import substitution experiments in Latin America during the 1950s and 1960s were mainly futile. U.S. and European subsidies to industries, such as agriculture, semiconductors, shipbuilding, steel, and textiles, were generally a waste of taxpayers' money. The Soviet Union's industrial planning fiascos during the period from 1947 to the late 1980s were legendary for their ineffectiveness. And, finally, Japan's industrial planning policies since the 1960s (e.g., mainly in the aircraft, aerospace, aluminum, biotechnology, computer, HDTV, nonferrous metal, and steel industries) were largely fruitless.[8]

It is not that government planning is always wrong and business planning is always right. The issue is often what is at stake. When businesses make decisions (right or wrong), the changes they make are usually marginal rather than discrete, and the results provide vital feedback to others. In other words, business decisions are typically small compared with government decisions, and regardless of whether they succeed or fail, these decisions provide critical information to the rest of the market about what to pursue and what to avoid. By contrast, government decisions are usually large and discrete, which means successes and failures are massive and do not provide quality, incremental feedback to market participants.

> Well-managed companies tend to have considerable direction from top management. Countries tend to function best when markets can operate without significant central government involvement.

CONCLUSION

LOOP asserts that the price of a product in one country should equal the exchange rate–adjusted price of the same product in a foreign country;

---

[7] Industrial policies are government actions that influence industry supply and/or demand. The term *industrial policy* derives from early cases where governments tried to promote their *industrial* sectors. Since then, governments have branched into many other areas, such as agriculture, but the term *industrial policy* remains.

[8] Japan's Ministry of International Trade and Industry (MITI) targeted more than 60 industries to support, but very few of these efforts succeeded.

otherwise riskless arbitrage profits could be earned. APPP is similar to LOOP, except that APPP equates the exchange rate–adjusted prices for the same *basket* of goods and services in two nations. RPPP is different from LOOP and APPP because it calculates a percentage change in the exchange rate, rather than the absolute exchange rate level. More specifically, RPPP measures the percentage by which an exchange rate must vary to offset the difference between two nations' inflation rates.

In the short term, PPP forecasts are normally inaccurate, due to factors such as differences in nations' market baskets, consumption patterns, government regulations, transportation costs, and nontrade transactions, such as international capital flows and central bank intervention in the foreign exchange markets. These forecasts improve as the period of time grows longer and as inflation rates in the considered nations increase. PPP accuracy also improves if the results are evaluated on the basis of how often actual rates converge toward PPP-predicted levels and whether the actual rates fall within reasonable confidence intervals of the predicted PPP rates. Of the two PPP approaches, RPPP tends to be more accurate at predicting exchange rates than APPP.

Merging PPP and QTM shows us that six major variables (i.e., $M2^B$, V_2^B, Q^B, $M2^A$, V_2^A, and Q^A) affect nominal exchange rates.[9] Changes in the long-run value of Country A's currency are determined by relative differences in: the growth of the Country B's and Country A's money supplies ($\%\Delta M2^B - \%\Delta M2^A$), velocity of money ($\%\Delta V_2^B - \%\Delta V_2^A$), and real GDP ($\%\Delta Q^B - \%\Delta Q^A$). Country A's currency depreciates if, relative to Country B, its money supply and/or velocity grow more quickly and/or if its real GDP grows more slowly.

Comparative advantage exists when a nation can produce a good or service at a lower opportunity cost than another country. As long as markets are free to adjust, a nation should have a comparative advantage in at least one product, which it should be able to export. Similarly, in spite of how productive a nation is, free markets guarantee that it should have a comparative disadvantage in at least one product, which it should import.

To ensure mutually advantageous trade, a nation's resource costs must be within bounds set by relative international productivity levels. Therefore, international pressure to equalize resource compensation levels among nations could seriously erode or totally offset the reason for and advantages of free trade.

Unlike the game of poker, international trade is not a zero-sum game, where one player's gains equal other players' losses. Rather, it is a positive-sum game played by teams, with all teams leaving the table as net winners. But remember that within each team certain individuals will be victims of trade. It is the team, not each member, that leaves as a net winner.

A country is not a company, which means good business decisions are often different from decisions that are good for the nation as a whole. Some of

---

[9] The superscript *A* stands for "Country A"; and the superscript *B* stands for "Country B."

the most important differences between countries and companies are as follows:

- Each country will always have a comparative advantage in at least one product. A company may not.
- Countries consume internally most of what they produce and source internally the large majority of their needed inputs. Companies do not.
- Countries benefit regardless of how fast they grow, which is one of the major reasons economists are generally in favor of unrestricted international trade. Companies benefit mainly when they grow faster than their competitors.
- Often, when companies increase third-party sales, they also increase head count (i.e., employment). By contrast, there is not a strong correlation (or cause-and-effect relationship) between a nation's export sales and overall employment.
- Countries often face short-term Phillips curve trade-offs between inflation and unemployment. Companies do not.
- Countries have full-employment targets and use monetary and fiscal policies to reach these goals. Nothing comparable exists at the company level.
- Most counties have their own currencies. Companies do not.
- Countries have thousands of business lines, and companies have relatively few. Therefore, strategic planning at the country level is different from strategic planning at the company level.
- Finally, well-managed companies usually exercise a considerable degree of top-down management, supervision, direction, and control. Countries seem to perform best when individuals and markets are relatively free from central government intervention.

REVIEW QUESTIONS

1. What is LOOP, and how is it different from APPP?

2. How is APPP different from RPPP?

3. Given the information below, use RPPP to determine what the Swiss franc per U.S. dollar exchange rate should be in 2014. Which currency should have appreciated, and which currency should have depreciated?

Information	2000	2014
Exchange Rate	SFr 1.5/$	SFr/$ = ?
U.S. Price Index	105	115.5
Swiss Price Index	102	106.1

4. What are the main problems with PPP as a tool for forecasting exchange rates?

5. Link the variables in the EOE to RPPP, and then use QTM to explain why exchange rates change.

6. Suppose the M2 money supply grows by 3% in England and 10% in Mexico. At the same time, England's real GDP grows by 2% and Mexico's grows by 5%. Finally, assume that the velocity of money in England remains the same but falls by 1% in Mexico. RPPP and QTM imply that the value of the pound should _____ (*appreciate or depreciate—choose one*) by approximately _____. If the original value of the pound was Ps 20/£, the new value would be _____.

7. Suppose that from 2009 to 2014 (i.e., five years), Japan's yearly average inflation rate was −2%, and the U.S. yearly inflation rate averaged +2.5%. If the spot exchange rate was ¥100/$ in 2009, use RPPP to determine the equilibrium exchange rate at the end of 2014.

8. Suppose that each worker in Belgium can produce either 20 units of food per hour or 80 units of machinery per hour. At the same time, workers in France can produce either 15 units of food per hour or 30 units of machinery per hour.
    a. Explain which country has an absolute advantage in the production of food. Explain which country has an absolute advantage in the production of machinery.
    b. Calculate the opportunity costs for food and machinery in France and Belgium.
    c. Which country, if any, has a comparative advantage in the production of food? Explain why.
    d. Which country, if any, has a comparative advantage in the production of machines? Explain why.
    e. Choose a mutually advantageous trading ratio, if any exists, and explain why it improves the well-being of both trading parties. If none exists, explain why.
    f. Explain the consequences if France's and Belgium's trading ratio is five machines per unit of food.
    g. Suppose workers in France and Belgium earned €20 per hour. Calculate the cost per unit of food and cost per unit of machinery in both countries. Will trade take place at these compensation levels?
    h. Suppose that Belgium increases its worker productivity in both food and machinery by 300% (i.e., three times). How (if at all) would this increased productivity change your answers to Questions 8a, 8b, 8c, and 8d?

9. Suppose that each worker in Argentina can produce either 20 units of food per hour or 80 units of machinery per hour. At the same time, workers in Ecuador can produce either 80 units of food per hour or 320 units of machinery per hour.
    a. Explain which country has an absolute advantage in the production of food. Which country has an absolute advantage in the production of machinery?
    b. Calculate the opportunity costs for food and machinery in Argentina and Ecuador.
    c. Which country, if any, has a comparative advantage in the production of food? Explain why.

10. In what major ways are companies economically unlike countries?

11. Why do changes in relative productivity levels have a different meaning for companies than they do for countries?

12. How does the relationship between price movements and employment at the country level differ from the relationship between price movements and employment at the firm level?

13. Why does free trade have only a minimal impact on the total number of jobs worldwide?

14. Nations often face a short-run Phillips curve trade-off between unemployment and inflation. What is its counterpart, if any, at the firm level?

DISCUSSION QUESTIONS

15. Explain the relationship between APPP and the real exchange rate.

16. Companies often create long-term planning documents that focus on improving their core competencies. If the government wanted to create a similar document for the nation, what problems would it have composing the first draft?

17. In 2014, suppose Brazil had 7.4% inflation and the nominal value of Brazil's currency (the real) fell 14% against the Argentine peso. Argentina had 1.1% deflation over the same period.
    a. Calculate the percentage change in Argentina's real exchange rate compared with Brazil's. Did Brazil gain or lose competitive advantage?
    b. Based on this information, use RPPP to predict the value of the real (or the value of the peso) for the year ending December 2014. Assume that the exchange rate in December 2013 was R2/peso (i.e., two reals per peso).
    c. Using your answer in Question 17b, explain whether the Argentine peso was overvalued or undervalued according to RPPP.

Index

Note: "f" following a page number indicates a figure, and "n" following a page number indicates a footnote.

Abbreviations

Managing in a Global Economy: Demystifying International Macroeconomics (2nd Edition)	
ABBREVIATIONS OF MAJOR VARIABLES, CONCEPTS, AND THEORIES	
AD	Aggregate demand
APPP	Absolute purchasing power parity
AS	Aggregate supply
B	Monetary base
C	Personal consumption expenditures
CA	Current account in the balance of payments
C_c	Currency in circulation
C_c/D	Preferred asset ratio for currency in circulation (i.e. C_c)
CT	Current international transactions
CTX	Current international transactions affecting the FX market
D	Demand deposits, checking accounts, and checkable deposits
DS	Discretionary spending
EOE	Equation of exchange
ER	Exchange rate
EX	Exports
Ex	Expectations
FA	Financial account in the balance of payments
FX	Foreign exchange or foreign exchange rate
G	Government spending for final goods & services
GDP	Gross domestic product
GNP	Gross national product
HH	Household
I	Gross private domestic investment
ID	Indebtedness
IM	Imports

(Continued)

KA	Capital Account in the balance of payments
LOOP	Law of one price
M/P	Real money supply
M1	M1 money supply
M2	M2 money supply
mm2	M2 money multiplier
N	Near money
N/D	Preferred asset ratio for near money
NE	Net exports
NI	Net nonreserve-related international borrowing/lending transactions
NI_f	Net foreign income
NIB/L	Net international borrowing/lending NI + RA
NIX	Net nonreserve-related borrowing/lending transactions affecting the FX market
P	Domestic price level
P*	Foreign price level
P^e	Expected inflation rate
PI	Price index
$Price^A$	Price of a tradable basket in Country and Currency A
$Price^B$	Price of a tradable basket in Country and Currency B
Q/t	Quantity per period
R	Real risk-free interest rate
RA	Reserves account in the balance of payments
RAX	Reserve-related central bank transactions affecting the FX market
R^E	Excess reserves
RGDP	Real gross domestic product
RLF/t	Real loanable funds quantity per period
RPPP	Relative purchasing power parity
R^R	Required reserves
rr_D	Reserve ratio for checking deposits
rr_N	Reserve ratio for near money
R^T	Total reserves
S	Saving
$S_{B/A}$	Spot price of currency A in terms of B
Tx	Taxes
Te	Technology
TQ	Tariffs and quotas

U/D	Preferred asset ratio for customary reserves
V_2	Velocity of M2 money supply
W	Wealth
Symbols	
Δ	Change in
≡	Is defined as being equal to
Currency Symbols	
€	Euro
Ps	Pesos
SFr	Swiss franc
฿	Thai Baht
¥	Yen and Yuan
John E. Marthinsen	